CAMBRIDGE
PAPERBACK GUIDE TO
LITERATURE IN ENGLISH

Ian Ousby

From reviews of
The Cambridge Guide to Literature in English

——

'the most authoritative survey of English literature in one volume'
SUNDAY INDEPENDENT

*

'an indispensable and indeed path-breaking guide'
LOS ANGELES TIMES

*

'immense browsability'
ANTHONY BURGESS

*

'conceptually generous... on overall points Cambridge wins.
Its breadth of vision is the chief reason'
THE GUARDIAN

*

'an unparalleled overview of the vast complex of writing in English'
THE WEEKLY MAIL & GUARDIAN

CAMBRIDGE
PAPERBACK GUIDE TO
LITERATURE IN ENGLISH
Ian Ousby

CAMBRIDGE
UNIVERSITY PRESS

Published by the Press Syndicate of the University of Cambridge
The Pitt Building, Trumpington Street, Cambridge CB2 1RP
40 West 20th Street, New York, NY 10011–4211, USA
10 Stamford Road, Oakleigh, Melbourne 3166, Australia

First published 1996

Printed in Great Britain at The Bath Press, Avon

A catalogue record for this book is available from the British Library

Library of Congress cataloguing in publication data
Ousby, Ian 1947–
Cambridge paperback guide to literature in English / Ian Ousby.
442 p. 234 cm.
ISBN 0 521 43627 3 (pbk).
1. English Literature – Dictionaries.
2. Commonwealth literature (English) – Bio-bibliography.
3. Commonwealth Literature (English) – Dictionaries.
4. Authors, Commonwealth – Biography – Dictionaries.
5. Authors, American – Biography – Dictionaries.
6. Authors, English – Biography – Dictionaries.
7. American literature – Bio-bibliography.
8. English literature – Bio-bibliography.
9. American literature – Dictionaries.
I. Title
PR85.097   1996   820.9'0003–dc 20   95–38664 CIP

ISBN 0 521 43627 3 paperback

Editor's Note

This concise version of *The Cambridge Guide to Literature in English* aims to provide a handier (and hence cheaper!) reference aid than its parent volume, originally published in 1988 and revised in 1993. Not all students or general readers of literature necessarily want the 'full story' and can appreciate a shorter account which quickly introduces them to, or reminds them of, some central fact they are seeking about a particular topic.

Yet such users can still have wide-ranging needs and any volume, even a compact one, must seek to meet them. So conciseness has largely been achieved by abbreviating the text of the 1993 volume entry by entry rather than by radical omission. This version retains the original purpose of representing all the literatures in English produced by all the various English-speaking cultures throughout the world and hence a scope extending beyond the United Kingdom and Ireland to include the USA, Canada, the Caribbean, Africa, India, Australia and New Zealand as well. There is no cut-off-date for writers and works noticed either in passing or in detail. Users will find a broad coverage of 'living literature' in these pages, profiting at every point from the major revisions made for the 1993 complete version of the *Guide*. No major category of entry has been excluded. As well as entries on writers and major works, this version contains entries on movements, groups or schools in literature and criticism; literary magazines; theatres; genres and sub-genres; critical concepts; and rhetorical terms. Only a small number of entries which appeared in the complete version of the *Guide* have been left out, largely longer essay-length entries whose original purpose does not easily survive abbreviation and entries on minor writers and lesser works.

Entries are listed in alphabetical word-by-word order. Headings for writers, movements, literary terms and so forth appear in bold face and headings for titles of books and magazines in bold face italics. The appearance of small capitals or small italic capitals in the course of an entry indicates that the topic receives an entry of its own elsewhere in the *Guide*.

In the case of writers who published under an abbreviated version of their full name, the heading supplies the unused part in brackets; thus T. S. Eliot appears as Eliot, T(homas) S(tearns). Writers such as George Eliot and Mark Twain, who are remembered by the pseudonyms under which they commonly wrote, are listed under their pseudonyms with their real names given in square brackets afterwards. People who published under their real names as well, or used more than one pseudonym, or adopted an obviously fanciful pseudonym ('Q' or 'Phiz'), appear under their real names. Names beginning 'Mc' have been put with those beginning 'Mac'. Medieval writers who take their last name from a place are listed under their first name: Geoffrey of Monmouth rather than Monmouth, Geoffrey of.

Works commonly known by the name of the protagonist which appears in their title are listed under that name: *Huckleberry Finn, The Adventures of* not *Adventures of Huckleberry Finn, The*. Works like *Comus* and *Gulliver's Travels*, which have been retitled by posterity, appear under the names by which they are popularly known. Archaic spelling has in general been modernized but phrases and titles still universally known and recognized in their original form – *The Compleat Angler, The Faerie Queene* – have not been tampered with.

IAN OUSBY
Cambridge, 1995

Acknowledgements

Abbreviating and updating this guide has expanded the list both of contributors and of those who helped with advice in addition to or instead of contributions. They are: Martin Banham, Andrew Brown, Elinor Cole, Graham Coster, Geoffrey Day, Christopher Dobson, Stephen Fender, R. J. Gray, Andrew Gurr, Paul Hartle, Mark Hendy, Ann Hill, John N. Marsh, Ann Mason, Valerie Mattar, Patrick Spedding, Don B. Wilmeth and Robert Wyke. Sarah Stanton and Ann Stonehouse, my editors at Cambridge University Press for the first edition, proved invaluable. Their successors, Adrian du Plessis, Anna Hodson and Caroline Bundy, have been equally long-suffering, as have the copyeditor, Stephen Adamson, and the proofreader, Michael Coultas. Those readers of earlier editions who took the trouble to contact me with encouragement or chastisement also deserve my thanks. I can only hope this edition will find so helpful an audience.

Contributors

Michael Abbott
Robert Ackerman
James Aikens
Stephen M. Archer
Christopher Baldick
Cameron Bardrick
Gillian Beer
Alan Bell
Jeremy Black
M. H. Black
Alison Blair-Underwood
Paul Bongiorno
John L. Bradley
Andrew Brown
Frances Bzowski
Jo-Anne Carty
Paul Chipchase
Jean Chothia
David Christie
Henry Claridge
Alan Clark
Michael Collie
Graham Coster
David Daniell
Geoffrey Day
Seamus Deane
Nicholas Drake
Rod Edmond
Colin Edwards
John Elsom
Geraint Evans
Mark Fisher
Michael Freeman
Helen Fulton
Robin Gilmour
Jon Glover
Michael Grosvenor Myer
Valerie Grosvenor Myer

Andrew Gurr
Paul Hartle
Laura Henigman
Ann Hill
Meridel Holland
Richard Hollick
Coral Ann Howells
Robin Howells
Jane Hughes
C. L. Innes
Russell Jackson
Elizabeth Jay
David Johnston-Jones
Philip Kolin
Grevel Lindop
Tony Lopez
Eric Lott
James Lynn
James Malpas
Robyn Marsack
Desmond Maxwell
David McKitterick
Paul McNeil
Isobel Murray
Alastair Niven
Christopher Norris
Nancy Nystul
Ian Ousby
W. R. Owens
Geoffrey Parrinder
Graham Parry
Neil Powell
David Profumo
Richard Proudfoot
Gay Raines
Arthur Ravenscroft
Bronwen Rees
Jane Remus
Peggy Reynolds

Lucy Rinehart
Gareth Roberts
Jane Roberts
Allan Rodway
Anne Rooney
Clare Rossini
George Rowell
Frank Salmon
Jack Salzman
Andrew Sanders
Christopher Scarles
Raman Selden
Robert Sheppard
Mark Sherman
C. H. Sisson
Iain Crichton Smith
Brian Stableford
David Staines
Sarah Stanton
Simon Stevens
Margarita Stocker
Ann Stonehouse
Bernard Stonehouse
Sally Stonehouse
Barbara Strang
Jordan Sullivan
John Thieme
Peter Thomson
Nicholas Tredell
Nicholas Tucker
Ann Turner
Norman Vance
Lindeth Vasey
Judy Weiss
Don B. Wilmeth
Barry Wood
Robert Wyke
Alan Young

À Beckett, Gilbert (Abbott) 1811–56 Humorist. He combined a distinguished legal career with comic writing, particularly for *Punch*, of which he was a founding member. *The Comic History of England* (1847) and *The Comic History of Rome* (1852), both illustrated by John Leech, were his most successful works. He also wrote over 50 plays.

À Wood, Anthony See Wood, Anthony à.

Abbey Theatre A Dublin theatre, named after the street in which it stood and opened in 1904 as headquarters of the Irish National Theatre Society, originally founded as the Irish Literary Theatre by Yeats, George Moore and Edward Martyn in 1899. Productions of work by the Abbey's directors, Yeats, Lady Gregory and Synge, quickly made it the focus of the new Irish drama. A second phase, dominated by the work of O'Casey, began with *The Shadow of a Gunman* (1923) and ended with the rejection of *The Silver Tassie* in 1928. The theatre was sustained by the work of lesser dramatists, like Lennox Robinson and George Shiels, until its destruction by fire in 1951. A second Abbey opened in 1966.

Abbot, The See Scott, Sir Walter.

Abercrombie, Lascelles 1881–1938 Poet and critic. His poetry, which belongs to the Georgian period before the revolution brought about by Pound and Eliot, was collected in 1930; the posthumous *Lyrics and Unfinished Poems* appeared in 1940. His criticism includes an important study of Hardy (1912), *The Idea of Great Poetry* (1925) and *Principles of Literary Criticism* (1932). Abercrombie was appointed professor of English literature at Leeds University in 1922 and Goldsmith's Reader in English at Oxford in 1935.

Abrahams, Peter 1919– South African novelist. He has settled in Jamaica. Black deprivations under apartheid are vividly detailed in *Mine Boy* (1946) as well as in his account of a return visit to South Africa, *Return to Goli* (1953), and an autobiography, *Tell Freedom* (1954). His understanding of Third World politics informs: *Wild Conquest* (1950), a historical novel; *A Wreath for Udomo* (1956), *A Night of Their Own* (1965) and *This Island Now* (1966), three remarkably prescient works; and *The View from Coyaba* (1985).

Absalom, Absalom! A novel by William Faulkner, published in 1936. From their room at Harvard, Quentin Compson (see *The Sound and the Fury*) and Shreve McCannon reconstruct the story of Thomas Sutpen's failed attempt to found a dynasty in Jefferson, Mississippi. Sutpen manages to build a mansion but is finally defeated by the complex pattern of miscegenation embodied in his sons, Henry and Charles. Dividing its attention between Sutpen and Quentin's attempt to understand him, the novel is about the decay of the old South.

Absalom and Achitophel A poem by Dryden, published in 1681. It adapts characters and story from the Old Testament (2 Kings) to create an allegory satirizing contemporary politics. Dryden's main target is the efforts of Lord Shaftesbury and his party to exclude the future James II, a Catholic, from the succession in favour of Charles II's bastard son, the Duke of Monmouth. The poem is famous for its verse portraits of Monmouth (Absalom), Shaftesbury (Achitophel),

Buckingham (Zimri) and Charles II (David). A second part (1682) was written chiefly by Tate and revised by Dryden, who contributed 200 savage lines about two of his rivals, Shadwell (Og) and Settle (Doeg).

Abse, Dannie (Daniel) 1923– Poet. His anthology *Mavericks* (with Howard Sergeant; 1957) was designed to advocate 'the image and Dionysian excitement' and expose the Movement as limited. His own work, from *After Every Green Thing* (1949) to *White Coat, Purple Coat: Collected Poems 1948–88* (1989) and *Remembrance of Crimes Past: Poems 1986–89* (1990), remains within the English tradition of intimate address but seeks to include his wider range of experience as a doctor and Jewish cultural outsider. *A Poet in the Family* (1974) and *There was a Young Man from Cardiff* (1991) are autobiographical.

Absentee, The A novel by Maria Edgeworth, published in the second series of *Tales of Fashionable Life* in 1812. It is set on a large landholding in Ireland, whose absentee landlord, Lord Clonbrony, is finally persuaded to return to his responsibilities by his son.

Absurd, Theatre of the Literally meaning 'out of harmony', absurd was Albert Camus's designation for the dilemma of modern man, a stranger in an inhuman universe. Martin Esslin's influential *Theatre of the Absurd* (1961) applied the term to contemporary playwrights who presented man's metaphysical absurdity in an aberrant dramatic style mirroring the situation. His main examples were Adamov, Ionesco, Genet and Beckett, whose *Waiting for Godot* brought international acclaim to the Theatre of the Absurd. Albee and Pinter received less attention. Journalists soon seized upon the term, confusing it with the everyday meaning of absurd as outrageously comic and applying it to almost every non-realistic modern dramatist.

Abt Vogler A dramatic monologue by Robert Browning, published in *Dramatis Personae* (1864). The speaker is the Abbé Georg Josef Vogler (1749–1814), advocate of a new system of harmony based on mathematics and precursor of the musical theories of Liszt and Wagner.

Academy, The A periodical founded by Charles Edward Cutts Birch Appleton in 1869. Covering a wide range of topics in art, literature and the sciences, it included Mark Pattison, Matthew Arnold and Thomas Henry Huxley among its contributors and Lord Alfred Douglas among its editors.

accentual metre See metre.

Achebe, Chinua 1930– Nigerian novelist, short-story writer, essayist, editor and writer of children's literature. His first novel, *Things Fall Apart* (1958), has been recognized as an African classic. It was followed by *No Longer at Ease* (1960), *Arrow of God* (1964, revised 1974), *A Man of the People* (1966), and *Anthills of the Savannah* (1987), about the failures of African politicians and intellectuals. He has also published *The Sacrificial Egg and Other Stories* (1962), *Girls at War and Other Stories* (1972) and children's books: *Chike and the River* (1966), *How the Leopard Got His Claws* (1972), *The Flute* and *The Drum* (1977). His many other works, expressing his commitment to African literature and society, include: editions and co-editions of contemporary writing; *Morning Yet on Creation Day: Essays* (1975) and *Hopes and Impediments:*

Selected Essays, 1965–87 (1988); and *The Trouble with Nigeria*, a political statement written during the 1983 elections.

Ackerley, J(oseph) R(andolph) 1896–1967 Literary editor. As literary editor of THE LISTENER from 1932 to 1959 he published work by many distinguished writers, including FORSTER and ISHERWOOD. *Hindoo Holiday* (1932) records his experiences in India. *My Dog Tulip* (1956) and the novel *We Think the World of You* (1960) are about his relationship with a pet Alsatian. *My Father and Myself* (1968) gives a fascinating account of his father, who managed to live a secret life behind the trappings of respectability.

Ackroyd, Peter 1949– Novelist and biographer. His lives of POUND (1980), T. S. ELIOT (1984) and DICKENS (1990) have been acclaimed. Literary and biographical criticism also informs much of his fiction: *The Great Fire of London* (1982), about the filming of *LITTLE DORRIT*; *The Last Days of Oscar Wilde* (1983), a pastiche of WILDE's final diary; *Hawksmoor* (1985), about the architect; and *Chatterton* (1987), about THOMAS CHATTERTON. Subsequent novels are *First Light* (1989), *English Music* (1992), *The House of Doctor Dee* (1993) and *Dan Leno and the Limehouse Golem* (1994).

acrostic A poem in which letters in successive lines make a word or pattern. A true acrostic, like the 'Argument' at the beginning of JONSON's *VOLPONE*, forms the word from the first letter of each line. Variants are the mesostich, using the middle letters, and the telestich, using the final letters. See also PALINDROME.

Acton, Sir Harold (Mario Mitchell) 1904–94 Poet, novelist and 'aesthete'. He accepted the label in two volumes of autobiography, *Memoirs of an Aesthete* (1948) and *More Memoirs of an Aesthete* (1970), while stressing that he meant by it a 'citizen of the world' with a duty to 'remind ... fellow creatures of what they are fast forgetting, that true culture is universal'. Of his early volumes of poetry, *Aquarium* (1923) and *This Chaos* (1930), the first appeared while he was still an Oxford undergraduate. A special affinity with China, which he visited in the 1930s, resulted in a novel, *Peonies and Ponies* (1941), translations of Chinese poetry and writings on Chinese art and culture. His connection with Italy – Acton was born and later settled at the family villa near Florence – is expressed in *The Last Medici* (1932) and *The Bourbons of Naples* (1957), historical studies. He also published short stories and a 'memoir' of NANCY MITFORD.

Acton, Sir John (Emerich Edward Dalberg), 1st Baron Acton 1834–1902 Historian. From the 1860s he acquired a reputation as a writer and teacher of liberal Catholic ideas, many of which brought him into conflict with the ecclesiastical authorities, notably his rejection of Papal infallibility in *Letters from Rome on the Council* (1870). In 1886 he was instrumental in founding the *English Historical Review*, to which he contributed the article 'German Schools of History'. He was appointed Regius Professor of Modern History at Cambridge in 1895, and became first editor of the *Cambridge Modern History* (1899–1900). His influential lectures on modern history and the French Revolution were published posthumously in 1906 and 1910.

Acts and Monuments A work of Protestant history and propaganda by FOXE, formally entitled *Acts and Monuments of These Latter and Perilous Days, Touching Matters of the Church* in its first English edition (1563), but soon popularly known as 'Foxe's Book of Martyrs'. It had been published in Latin at Strasburg and Basle while Foxe was in exile during Queen Mary's reign, a period which supplied part of its subject and fuelled its fervent tone. Expanded in 1570 and many times reprinted, *Acts and Monuments* proved enormously popular, especially in Puritan households. Its account of Roman Catholic persecution and Protestant martyrdom, illustrated with graphic woodcuts, helped to shape anti-Catholic – particularly anti-Spanish – sentiment in the 16th century and afterwards.

Adam Bede GEORGE ELIOT's first full-length novel, published in 1859. Adam Bede, a carpenter in the Midland village of Hayslope, is in love with Hetty Sorrel, niece of the farmer Martin Poyser. The squire, Arthur Donnithorne, is attracted to Hetty and she is vain enough to dream of becoming his wife. Adam watches the flirtation with growing anxiety and tries unsuccessfully to intervene. Arthur abandons Hetty after seducing her. Adam earns the reward of his loyalty to Hetty when, heartbroken at Arthur's desertion, she agrees to marry him. But she finds herself pregnant and flies from home in a desperate search for her lover. Adam is supported in his grief by Dinah Morris, a young Methodist preacher, with whom his brother Seth is hopelessly in love. Unable to find Arthur, Hetty is arrested, charged with the murder of her child and convicted. Dinah becomes her comforter and the close of the novel describes how Hetty, with Dinah's help, faces her final ordeal. But she is reprieved and her sentence commuted to transportation. Adam later marries Dinah. The novel was exceptionally well received by contemporary reviewers, who praised its evocation of English rural life and its character studies, particularly Martin's wife, Mrs Poyser.

Adams, Andy 1859–1935 American novelist. He spent much of his life in the Texas cattle country and the mining centres of Colorado. He is best known for *The Log of a Cowboy* (1903), an authentic, unsentimental depiction of life on the open range. Other works include *The Outlet* (1905), *Cattle Brands* (1906), *Reed Anthony, Cowman* (1907), *Wells Brothers* (1911) and *The Ranch on the Beaver* (1927).

Adams, Arthur Henry 1872–1936 Novelist and poet. Novels and stories with an Australasian background include *Tussock Land* (1904), *The New Chum and Other Stories* (1909), *Galahad Jones* (1910), *The Australians* (1920) and *A Man's Life* (1929). His verse included a war poem, *My Friend, Remember* (1914). He also wrote *Three Plays for the Australian Stage* (1914) and light fiction under the pseudonyms of Henry James James and James James.

Adams, Douglas (Noël) 1952– Script-writer and novelist. *The Hitch-Hiker's Guide to the Galaxy* began as a BBC radio serial in 1978 before becoming a best-selling novel (1979). It was followed by *The Restaurant at the End of the Universe* (1980), *Life, the Universe and Everything* (1982), *So Long, and Thanks for All the Fish* (1984) and *Mostly Harmless* (1992). The series uses SCIENCE FICTION to satirize human delusions of significance. *Dirk Gently's Holistic Detective Agency* (1987) and *The Long Dark Tea-Time of the Soul* (1988) are absurdist DETECTIVE FICTION.

Adams, Francis William Lauderdale 1862–93 Australian poet. Educated in England, he went to Australia in 1884. *Henry and Other Tales* (1884), *Poetical Works* (1887) and *Songs of the Army of the Night* (1888) were admired by WILLIAM MICHAEL ROSSETTI for their 'intensity and fierceness of tone'. Adams also wrote novels, including *John Webb's End: Australian Bush Life* (1891), and two volumes of essays, *Australian Essays* (1886) and *The Australians* (1893).

Adams, Henry (Brooks) 1838–1918 American historian and man of letters. He was born in Boston, the grandson of John Quincy Adams, the sixth President of the United States, and the great-grandson of John Adams, the second President. He studied and taught history at Harvard (1870–7), edited the *The North American Review*, observed the political scene at first hand in Washington and, partly out of discontent with life in America, travelled widely in Europe, the Orient and the Sierras. His nine-volume *History of the United States of America during the Administrations of Thomas Jefferson and James Madison* (1889–91) was the most ambitious of his many studies of history and politics. He is chiefly remembered, however, for *Mont-Saint-Michel and Chartres* (privately printed 1904, published 1913), a study of 13th-century culture, and *The Education of Henry Adams* (privately printed 1907, published 1918), an autobiographical exploration of his heritage and a critical examination of the age in which he lived. In *The Education* he self-consciously presents himself as representative of the American mind at a particular historical moment; he has taken his place as such in the literary and critical tradition.

Adams, Richard (George) 1920– Novelist and writer of CHILDREN'S LITERATURE. *Watership Down* (1972) – his first and most famous book, about the wanderings of a group of rabbits – was rejected by many publishers before appearing to acclaim from both children and adults. *Shardik* (1974), about a humanized bear, reflects his preoccupation with man's cruelty to beasts. He has also written humorous ballads for children but otherwise moved towards adult fiction with *The Plague Dogs* (1977) and *The Girl in a Swing* (1980), his first exclusively adult book. *Day Gone By* (1990) is his autobiography.

Adcock, Fleur 1934– New Zealand/English poet. She has lived in Britain since 1963. Her poetry is notable for its unsentimental treatment of personal and family relationships, its psychological insights and its interest in classical themes. Volumes include *The Eye of the Hurricane* (1964), *Tigers* (1967), *High Tide in the Garden* (1971), *The Scenic Route* (1974), *The Inner Harbour* (1979), *Selected Poems* (1983), *The Incident Book* (1986), *Hotspur* (1986), *Meeting the Comet* (1988), *Time Zones* (1991) and several translations. She has edited *The Oxford Book of New Zealand Verse* (1982) and *The Faber Book of Twentieth Century Women's Poetry* (1987).

Adding Machine, The A play by ELMER RICE, first produced in 1923. Among the earliest and most successful American experiments with EXPRESSIONISM, it depicts the over-mechanized, joyless existence of Mr Zero. He murders his boss when the department store where he works replaces him by an adding machine. Condemned to death and executed, he goes to a pastoral heaven but is unable to adjust until he is set to work on a giant adding machine. Finally the authorities send him back to earth, to operate an even more efficient machine.

Addison, Joseph 1672–1719 Essayist, poet and playwright. Son of the Dean of Lichfield, he was educated at Charterhouse (where he first met STEELE) and at Magdalen College, Oxford, of which he became a fellow. *The Campaign* (1704) is a poem in HEROIC COUPLETS celebrating the English victory at Blenheim. Whig friends in London, where he joined Steele as a member of the KIT-KAT CLUB, secured him a succession of public appointments, as Commissioner of Excise (1705), MP (from 1708 until his death), secretary to Lord Wharton, the Lord Lieutenant of Ireland (1709), Chief Secretary for Ireland (1715) and a Lord Commissioner of Trade (1716). He married the Countess of Warwick in 1716. One of the leading editorial journalists of his age, Addison wrote urbane and familiar prose, a model of the 'middle style' so admired in the period. He contributed papers to Steele's *The Tatler* between 1709 and 1711, when he joined his friend in founding *The Spectator*. He also contributed to Steele's *The Guardian* in 1713 and founded his own political newspaper, *The Freeholder* (1715–16). His last journalistic venture, *The Old Whig*, showed a growing estrangement from Steele. His BLANK-VERSE tragedy, *Cato* (1713), scored a great success at DRURY LANE but his later prose-comedy, *The Drummer* (1715), failed.

Ade, George 1866–1944 American humorist, short-story writer and playwright. He made his mark with *Fables in Slang* (1899), *Forty Modern Fables* (1901), *People You Know* (1903), and *Hand-Made Fables* (1920). His musical and dramatic comedies include *The Sultan of Sulu* (1903) and *The College Widow* (1904).

Adelphi, The A journal founded by JOHN MIDDLETON MURRY in 1923 and edited by him until 1930, chiefly as a forum for his ideas and those of D. H. LAWRENCE. It appeared monthly until 1927 and quarterly thereafter, being known as *The New Adelphi* from 1927 until Murry handed over the editorship to Max Plowman and Richard Rees in 1930. Before it ceased publication in 1955 it had counted AUDEN, T. S. ELIOT, ORWELL and YEATS among its contributors.

Admirable Crichton, The A comedy by BARRIE, first produced in 1902. A model butler in the household of Lord Loam, Crichton becomes lord of the island when the family is shipwrecked. After supervising the rescue in the last act, he reverts to his subservient role.

Adonais: An Elegy on the Death of John Keats SHELLEY's lament for his fellow poet, published in 1821. Written in SPENSERIAN STANZAS, the ELEGY moves from an account of the mourning at KEATS's bier to a triumphant affirmation of his immortality.

Advancement of Learning, The A treatise (1605) by FRANCIS BACON, constituting the preliminary section of his great scheme for intellectual and scientific reform, the *Instauratio magna* ('Great Instauration'), continued in *Novum Organum* (1620). *The Advancement of Learning* itself was extended in the Latin version, *De augmentis scientiarum* (1623). It begins by disposing of objections to the idea of learning and championing its advantages. Bacon goes on to attack the various methods of education currently in practice, based on the Aristotelian structures of knowledge, and to suggest the student work from experiment and observation rather than theory. The principal subdivisions of knowledge (history, poetry and philosophy) are then considered.

AE [A. E.] See RUSSELL, GEORGE WILLIAM.

Aelfric *fl. c.* 955–*c.* 1010 Aelfric *Grammaticus*, 'the grammarian', studied with the Benedictines at Winchester under St Aethelwold, whom he followed in promoting monastic reform. His best-known works were written while he was teaching at Cerne Abbey: a Latin *Grammar* and *Glossary*, and the *Colloquy*, a primer with a parallel Old English/Latin text which gives a vivid picture of everyday life. Other writings included: two sets of homilies in English, largely based on the works of BEDE, Augustine, Jerome and Gregory; a translation of Bede's *De temporibus*; a collection of SAINTS' LIVES; and translations from the Old and New Testaments (see BIBLE IN ENGLISH). As abbot of Eynsham, he wrote a life of

Aethelwold and several minor treatises. His lucid style and wide interests ensured Aelfric's lasting popularity: copied throughout the Middle Ages, his writings became the first in Old English to be printed.

Aelred [Ailred] of Rievaulx 1110-67 Abbot of Rievaulx from 1147. Born of a long line of married Benedictine priests from Northumbria, he spent his boyhood in Hexham, went to school in Durham, and entered the household of David I of Scotland, whose steward he became. At Rievaulx, which he entered as a novice in 1134, he wrote: *Speculum caritatis*, inspired by two friends, with an introductory letter by Bernard of Clairvaux; *Genealogia regum anglorum* (1152-3), containing a eulogy of King David; an account of the saints of Hexham (1155), to celebrate their translation; sermons on Isaiah and *De spirituali amicitia*, about monastic friendships (1158-63); *De institutione inclusarum*, for his sister; and a life of Edward the Confessor (1163). *De anima* was apparently unfinished at his death. Walter Daniel, who entered Rievaulx in 1150, wrote Aelred's biography.

Aesthetic Movement A movement of mind, or shift in sensibility, arising in the 1880s. Its credo of 'Art for Art's sake' ran counter to high-Victorian optimism, UTILITARIANISM and the belief that art should be moral. Touched with melancholy and pessimism, and stirred by exotic art forms, novel precepts and remote cultures, it was shaped by the work of PATER as well as by contemporary activities in France. OSCAR WILDE, LIONEL JOHNSON, ERNEST DOWSON, MAX BEERBOHM, ARTHUR SYMONS, AUBREY BEARDSLEY, RICHARD LE GALLIENNE and the young YEATS were attracted to various phases of the movement. THE YELLOW BOOK and The Savoy were important outlets and the RHYMERS' CLUB was an important nucleus.

Agate, James (Evershed) 1877-1947 Drama critic. His reviews for The Sunday Times from 1923 until his death established him as the most feared and most courted of theatrical judges. The very title of Ego (1938-47), his nine-volume selection from his diary, confesses that he became too conscious of his own personality. Volumes of selected criticism include Brief Chronicles (1943), Red-Letter Nights (1944) and Immoment Toys (1945).

Age of Innocence, The A novel by EDITH WHARTON, published in 1920 and awarded a PULITZER PRIZE. It is mainly set in New York during the 1870s. Newland Archer, a lawyer, falls in love with Ellen Olenska, the wife of a Polish count, but marries her cousin, May Welland. His continuing interest in Ellen prompts May to tell her that she is pregnant. Ellen leaves New York for Paris. Visiting the city 30 years later, the widowed Newland decides to preserve his idealized memories rather than call on her.

Age of Reason, The A tract by THOMAS PAINE, published in 1794-6. Showing his inclination towards DEISM, it makes a stark critique of accepted religious belief and practices. The first part argues that a rational knowledge of God does not accord with traditional conceptions of the Deity; the second illuminates inconsistencies in the Bible in order to invalidate both literal and figurative readings of the text. The book estranged Paine from many of his more orthodox American friends.

Agee, James 1909-55 American journalist, social critic, poet and novelist. He is perhaps best known for Let Us Now Praise Famous Men (with photographs by Walker Evans, 1941), describing the plight of three rural Alabama families during the Depression. His novels, The Morning Watch (1951) and A Death in the Family (1957; PULITZER PRIZE), are partly autobiographical, the first dealing with religious piety and the second with the effects on a family of a father's early death. He also wrote filmscripts, including The African Queen (with John Huston, 1951), The Bride Comes to Yellow Sky (based on STEPHEN CRANE's short story, 1953) and The Night of the Hunter (1955). Agee's poems and short stories were collected and edited by Robert Fitzgerald (1968).

Agnes Grey A novel by ANNE BRONTË, published in 1847. It is based on her experiences as a governess. Agnes Grey, a rector's daughter employed by the Murray family, is badly treated and her loneliness is relieved only by the kindness of the curate, Weston, whom she eventually marries.

Ahlberg, Alan 1938- Writer of CHILDREN'S LITERATURE. With his illustrator-wife Janet, he has produced many successful picture-books for small children. They include: Each Peach Pear Plum (1978); the Happy Families series stretching from Mr Biff the Boxer (1980) to Mr Creep the Crook (1988); the inventive Peepo! (1981); and most successfully of all, The Jolly Postman (1987).

Aidoo, Ama Ata 1942- Ghanaian playwright, novelist, short-story writer and poet. Her first play and still her best-known work, The Dilemma of a Ghost (1965), is a serious comedy about a black American girl who marries into a Ghanaian family. She has also written: Anowa (1969), a play based on a traditional legend; No Sweetness Here (1970), short stories; Our Sister Killjoy (1977) and Changes (1991), novels; Someone Talking to Sometime (1985), poems; and CHILDREN'S LITERATURE. She is one of the leading writers to be concerned about the position of women in modern Africa.

Aiken, Conrad (Potter) 1889-1973 American poet, short-story writer and novelist. His fiction and poetry both reflect his interest in psychology, and his reading of Freud, WILLIAM JAMES and French SYMBOLISM, as well as of POE, his most obvious American antecedent. Volumes of poetry include Earth Triumphant, and Other Tales in Verse (1914), Turns and Movies (1916), The Jig of Forslin; A Symphony (1916), Selected Poems (1929), And in the Human Heart (a SONNET sequence, 1940), Collected Poems (1929) and Thee (1967), a book-length poem. His short stories include Bring! Bring! (1925), Costumes by Eros (1928) and Among the Lost People (1934); his five novels were gathered in The Collected Novels (1964).

Aiken, Joan (Delano) 1924- Novelist and writer of CHILDREN'S LITERATURE. The daughter of CONRAD AIKEN, she began with a collection of stories, All You've Ever Wanted (1953). A series of vividly imaginative children's novels, beginning with The Wolves of Willoughby Chase (1962) and including Black Hearts in Battersea (1964) and The Cuckoo Tree (1981), invent whole new periods of history. Other children's novels include Midnight is a Place (1974), an evocation of Victorian industrialism, and supernatural tales such as The Shadow Guests (1980), A Goose on Your Grave (1987) and A Foot on the Grave (1989). Her writing for younger children includes A Necklace of Raindrops (1968). She has also written many adult novels.

Aikin, John 1747-1822 Essayist and physician. He collaborated with his sister, ANNA LAETITIA BARBAULD, on Miscellaneous Pieces (1773) and the six-volume Evenings at Home (1792-6), and wrote several reports on prisons for the reformer John Howard, whose literary executor he became.

Ailred See AELRED.

Ainger, Alfred 1837–1904 Essayist, editor and critic. He was particularly drawn to the work of CHARLES LAMB, contributing a *Life* to the English Men of Letters series (1882) and editing the *Essays* (1883), the *Poems and Plays* (1884) and the *Letters* (1888, 1904). He also wrote a life of CRABBE for the English Men of Letters series (1903). His collected *Lectures and Essays* were published in two volumes in 1905.

Ainsworth, William Harrison 1805–82 Novelist. *Rookwood* (1834), a romanticized account of the highwayman Dick Turpin, was a great commercial and popular success. *Jack Sheppard* (1839) features another notorious criminal and so helped to fuel the controversy about the NEWGATE NOVEL. Other historical romances included: *The Tower of London* (1840), about the short reign of Lady Jane Grey; *Old St Paul's* (1841), which uses the Plague and Great Fire of London; *Windsor Castle* (1843), set in the reign of Henry VIII; and *The Lancashire Witches* (1849), set in Pendle Forest.

Akenside, Mark 1721–70 Poet. Most of his work is minor, but *The Pleasures of Imagination* (1744) – revised as *The Pleasures of the Imagination* in 1757 – is remembered for anticipating the concerns of later Romantic poets.

Alabaster, William 1567–1640 Divine, scholar, mystical exegete and poet. His life saw extraordinary religious vacillations, conversions, reconversions and recantations, beginning with his conversion to Roman Catholicism in 1597 and ending with his appointment as Anglican chaplain to JAMES I in 1618.

JOHNSON praised his Senecan tragedy *Roxana* (performed *c.* 1592, printed 1632) as the only Latin work by an Englishman worthy of note before MILTON's elegies, and SPENSER praised *Elisaeis*, his unfinished Latin epic glorifying Elizabeth I. Alabaster's interest in mystical theology, particularly eschatology and the Apocalypse, was expressed in *Apparatus in revelationem Jesu Christi* (1607), *De bestia Apocalypsis* (1621) and *Ecce sponsus venit* (1633). His devotional poems, unpublished in his lifetime, are METAPHYSICAL in their tone and use of paradox and typology; many resemble DONNE's religious poems.

Alastor: or, The Spirit of Solitude A poem by SHELLEY, published in 1816. It reflects his interest in the figure of the contemplative idealist, condemning his attitude as self-centred while at the same time lamenting the condition of the real world.

Albee, Edward (Franklin) 1928– American playwright. He rose to prominence with *The Zoo Story* (1959), *The Death of Bessie Smith* (1960), *The Sandbox* (1960) and *The American Dream* (1961), angrily disenchanted with American middle-class values and influenced by the THEATRE OF THE ABSURD. His reputation was confirmed by *WHO'S AFRAID OF VIRGINIA WOOLF?* (1962), about marital conflict and reconciliation, and the enigmatic *Tiny Alice* (1964). Later work, aiming at formal elegance rather than emotional intensity, has not always been so highly acclaimed. It includes experimental chamber pieces and more substantial work, notably *A Delicate Balance* (1966; PULITZER PRIZE), *Seascape* (1975; Pulitzer Prize), *The Lady from Dubuque* (1980) and *Three Tall Women* (1990), which won him a third Pulitzer Prize. Albee has also dramatized CARSON MCCULLERS's *Ballad of the Sad Café* (1963), JAMES PURDY's *Malcolm* (1966) and NABOKOV's *LOLITA* (1981).

Alchemist, The A comedy by JONSON, first produced in 1610 and published in 1612. Lovewit leaves his servant Face in charge of his London house during an outbreak of plague. A confidence trickster, Face introduces Subtle and Doll Common to make the house a centre for frauds. Trading on Subtle's alleged powers as an alchemist, the trio dupes a succession of victims: Sir Epicure Mammon, a greedy voluptuary; Abel Drugger, a meek tobacconist; Dapper, a lawyer's clerk; Ananias and Tribulation Wholesome, hypocritical Puritans; and young Kastril, newly rich and quarrelsome, looking for a suitable match for his sister, Dame Pliant. Surly, a gambler, sees through their imposture and the villains are finally confounded by Lovewit's unexpected return. Subtle and Doll take to their heels, but Face cleverly makes peace with his master by arranging his marriage to Dame Pliant, comely as well as rich.

Alcott, (Amos) Bronson 1799–1888 American educationalist and father of LOUISA MAY ALCOTT. Founder of the Concord School of Philosophy (1879–88), he applied the doctrines of TRANSCENDENTALISM to education, rejecting mechanical discipline and attempting to instil the joy of learning in his students. His ideas have had a lasting influence, though his books are no longer widely read. They include *Observations on the Principles and Methods of Infant Instruction* (1830), *Record of a School* (with ELIZABETH PEABODY, 1835), *The Doctrine and Discipline of Human Culture* (1836) and *Tablets* (1868). *Sonnets and Canzonets* (1882) was written in memory of his wife.

Alcott, Louisa May 1832–88 American novelist and writer of CHILDREN'S LITERATURE. Although she was only 16 when she finished her first book (later published as *Flower Fables*, 1855) and went on to produce nearly 300 titles in a variety of genres, she is best known for *LITTLE WOMEN*. It originally appeared in two parts, as *Little Women: or, Meg, Jo, Beth, and Amy* (1868) and *Good Wives* (1869), though both are now generally published together under the same title. The story follows the fortunes of the March sisters, who live in a small New England town and struggle to increase the family's small income. In womanhood Meg and Mary marry, Beth dies, Jo becomes a successful novelist and marries a professor, Dr Bhaer. *Little Men: Life at Plumfield with Jo's Boys* (1871) and *Jo's Boys and How They Turned Out* (1886), about the school founded by Jo and Dr Bhaer, are among Alcott's other wholesome domestic tales. *Work: A Study of Experience* (1873) is a feminist and autobiographical novel. When she became 'tired of providing moral pap for the young', Alcott wrote *A Modern Mephistopheles* (1877), in which an innocent young woman resists seduction by the diabolic genius with whom her poet-husband has made a Faustian pact; *Whisper in the Dark* (1889) has a similar theme. She died on the day her father, BRONSON ALCOTT, was buried.

Alcuin [Albinus] *c.* 735–804 Theologian and educationalist. His Anglo-Saxon name was Ealhwine. In 781 he went from the episcopal school in York to head Charlemagne's palace school at Aachen, where he supervised educational reforms which quickly spread throughout France and Europe. His *quadrivium* and *trivium* shaped the pattern of education throughout the Middle Ages. Study centred on religious texts and Latin – the remnants of classical culture preserved by Boethius, St Augustine, Isidore, Capella and Cassiodorus, and the grammar of Priscian and Donatus. By revising the liturgy, introducing the sung Creed, re-editing the Vulgate Bible and arranging votive masses for days of the week, Alcuin played an influential part in the development of Catholicism. His writing includes handbooks for teaching Latin, religion, arithmetic and computation; dialogues on rhetoric and dialectic; studies in theology and philosophy; biblical commentaries; several SAINTS' LIVES; and some mediocre Latin verses. Over 300 of his letters survive, a valuable source. Alcuin retired to be abbot of Tours in 796 and built up the reputation of the school there, remaining its head until his death.

Aldhelm, St d. 709 or 710 Writer of Latin prose and verse. As abbot of Malmesbury (from 675) and then bishop of Sherborne, he was an enthusiastic and sympathetic churchman as well as a famous scholar partly responsible for the resurgence of learning in England. He wrote Latin treatises, letters and verse, and probably some verses in English which no longer survive. The treatises include *De laude virginitate*, about virginity; a version of it in verse; a work about writing verse which includes a collection of riddles in Latin; and an examination of the Pentateuch. Though Aldhelm's language is repetitious, bombastic and difficult, showing frequent evidence of his Celtic knowledge and training, it set the style for the Anglo-Latin poets who came after him.

Aldington, Richard 1892–1962 Poet, novelist and biographer. A member of the group which pioneered IMAGISM, he published *Images 1910–1915* (1915) and *Collected Poems* (1928). He was married to the imagist poet HILDA DOOLITTLE (H. D.) from 1913 to 1937. His novels include the savage *Death of a Hero* (1929), deriving from his experience of World War I, *The Colonel's Daughter* (1931), satirizing English village life, and *All Men are Enemies* (1933). He also wrote controversial biographies of D. H. LAWRENCE (*Portrait of a Genius, But ...*, 1950) and T. E. LAWRENCE (1955). *Life for Life's Sake* (1941) is an autobiography. His correspondence with LAWRENCE DURRELL, *Literary Lifelines*, was published in 1981.

Aldiss, Brian W(ilson) 1925– Writer of SCIENCE FICTION. Novels like *Non-Stop* (1958) and *Greybeard* (1964) develop stock themes. Other work pushes the conventions of the genre to new limits: *Hothouse* (1962) is a fantasia of the far future; *The Primal Urge* (1961) and *The Dark Light-Years* (1964) are satires; *Report on Probability A* (1968) is an anti-novel; and *Barefoot in the Head* (1969) is an extravaganza influenced by JOYCE. His most sustained exercise in invention is a trilogy, *Helliconia Spring* (1982), *Helliconia Summer* (1983) and *Helliconia Winter* (1985). Several short-story collections confirm his versatility. Non-fantastic fiction includes *The Hand-Reared Boy* (1970), *Life in the West* (1980) and *Forgotten Life* (1989). He has also written a history of science fiction, *Billion-Year Spree* (1973; revised with David Wingrove as *Trillion-Year Spree*, 1986).

Aldrich, Thomas Bailey 1836–1907 American novelist and journalist. His best-known work is *The Story of a Bad Boy* (1870), a novel based on his childhood. Other notable works are *Marjorie Daw and Other People* (1873), a collection of short stories, and *The Stillwater Tragedy* (1880), a detective novel. He was editor of THE ATLANTIC MONTHLY in 1881–90.

Alexander, Sir **William,** Earl of Stirling c. 1567–1640 Poet and playwright. Courtier to JAMES I and Charles I, he became Secretary of State in 1626 and Earl of Stirling in 1633, but died in poverty. *Aurora* (1604), his best-known work, is a book of songs and SONNETS. Other works include *The Monarchick Tragedies* (1603–7), four plays on the theme of destructive ambition, and a long poem, *Doomsday* (1614); these have been described as 'unactable plays' and 'an unreadable poem'.

Alexander of Hales c. 1170 or 1180–1245 Philosopher and theologian. Born at Hales in Gloucestershire, he held various church offices before joining the Franciscan order and founding the Schola Fratrum Minorum in Paris. Occupying the first Franciscan chair in the university, he was largely responsible for establishing the order as a teaching body. Although his name was traditionally attached to the *Summa theologica*, ROGER BACON denies his authorship; it is a composite work of which Alexander wrote some sections. His works include a commentary on the *Sententiae*, part of an *Expositio regulae*, and sermons. His work influenced St Bonaventure among others, and earned him the title *doctor irrefragibilis*.

alexandrine See METRE.

Alfred, King c. 848–99 King of Wessex (871–99), largely responsible for the restoration of learning in England after the decay which the Norse raids had accelerated. From his work as translator, the following texts survive: Gregory the Great's *Cura pastoralis*, a manual of instruction for the clergy, with a preface outlining his own educational plans; the *Historia adversus paganos* of Paulus Orosius, a textbook of universal history, to which he added accounts of the experiences of contemporary travellers; a version of Boethius' *De consolatione philosophiae*, originally in prose but with verse renderings of Boethius' metrical passages added later; Augustine's *Soliloquia*, probably Alfred's final work. The last two include a good deal of extra material. He probably had a hand in translating a shortened version of BEDE's *Historia ecclesiastica gentis Anglorum*, once attributed wholly to him, and may have been instrumental in planning the ANGLO-SAXON CHRONICLE, begun during his reign, though there is nothing to suggest he was involved in writing it. His friend and teacher ASSER left a personal account of the king in *De rebus gestis Aelfredi Magni*, sometimes naive, subjective and fulsome in its praise, but nevertheless an invaluable source.

Alger, Horatio 1832–99 American novelist and writer of CHILDREN'S LITERATURE. His adult novels were largely unsuccessful, in striking contrast to more than 100 novels he wrote for boys, most of them based on a rags-to-riches theme and the moral that a boy can rise from poverty to wealth if he has a good character. The most popular were *Ragged Dick* (1867), *Luck and Pluck* (1869) and *Tattered Tom* (1871). In the same vein as his fiction he wrote several biographies of famous self-made men, under such titles as *From Canal Boy to President* (about Abraham Lincoln; 1881) and *From Farm Boy to Senator* (about James Garfield; 1882).

Algerine Captive, The A novel by TYLER, published in 1797. It makes a satiric commentary on American pretension and quackery through Underhill's narrative of his adventures. His experience of the South and of work as a doctor on board a slave ship prompts a sharp condemnation of slavery. Abandoned in Africa, he is himself made a slave by the Algerians but finally gains his freedom and returns to America.

Algren, Nelson 1909–81 American novelist. He is best known for his novel about drug addiction, *The Man with the Golden Arm* (1949). Other books are *The Neon Wilderness* (1947), *Chicago: City on the Make* (1951), *A Walk on the Wild Side* (1956), *Who Lost an American?* (1963), *Notes from a Sea Diary: Hemingway All the Way* (1965), *The Last Carousel* (1973) and *The Devil's Stocking* (1983).

Ali, Ahmed 1912– Indian/Pakistani novelist. Born in India, he moved to Pakistan after Partition. *Twilight in*

Delhi (1940), written while he was still an Indian, is a magnificent historical novel about Muslim life in Delhi. *Ocean of Night* (1964), less well received, is set in Lucknow and depicts the decline of an aristocratic way of life. *Rats and Diplomats* (1985) is a novella, while *The Prison House* (1985) translates a selection of his Urdu stories.

Alice's Adventures in Wonderland A fantasy by LEWIS CARROLL, originally published as *Alice's Adventures Under Ground* (1865), with illustrations by TENNIEL. Beginning famously as a story told to children on a boating picnic in 1862, it is half dream, half nightmare and always diverting. Plunging down a rabbit hole the seven-year-old Alice grows first too large and then too small. The Cheshire Cat, the Mad Hatter, the March Hare, the King and Queen of Hearts and other strange characters she meets involve her in logic-chopping, PARODY and pun. Favourite moments include the parodies 'You are Old, Father William' and 'Twinkle Twinkle Little Bat', the Lobster Quadrille, the Hatter's Tea Party and Alice's own understandable comment, 'Curiouser and curiouser'. An immediate best-seller, the book had a lasting and revolutionary effect on CHILDREN'S LITERATURE by abandoning didacticism for good-humoured iconoclasm.

alienation A theatrical intention, or technique, derived from the plays and critical writings of Bertolt Brecht. He used alienation effects to bring home to audiences the strangeness of social and economic conditions they took for granted, drawing attention to social structures, ideas, principles, motives or conflicts that would normally be ignored in such a way as to prove them alterable. Brecht coined the word *Verfremdung* to carry his meaning. Marx had already used a kindred word, *Entfremdung*, for the condition of the proletariat in a capitalist economy. For Brecht, *Entfremdung* was a condition and *Verfremdung* a method of making that condition clear to audiences. His use of alienation effects influenced all the major political writers of the post-war English theatre from ARDEN and McGRATH to EDGAR and BRENTON.

All for Love: *or, The World Well Lost* A tragedy in blank verse by DRYDEN, performed in 1677 and published in 1678. He borrowed freely from SHAKESPEARE'S *ANTONY AND CLEOPATRA* to create a very different play which emulates the form of tragedy advocated by French neoclassical theory. Dryden confines the action to the period following the battle of Actium and concentrates on Cleopatra's struggle for possession of Antony with his general Ventidius, his friend Dolabella and his wife Octavia before their final reunion and death.

All the Year Round A weekly magazine edited by DICKENS from 1859, when it took over from *HOUSEHOLD WORDS*, until his death in 1870. Like its predecessor, it offered a blend of fiction (including some of Dickens's own later novels) and journalism.

All's Well That Ends Well A comedy by SHAKESPEARE, probably written or revised in 1602–4. It was not published until the First Folio of 1623. The source is a story from Boccaccio's *Decameron*, probably read in English in PAINTER's *The Palace of Pleasure*. Never a favourite among Shakespeare's plays, *All's Well* is often grouped with *MEASURE FOR MEASURE* and *TROILUS AND CRESSIDA* as one of the PROBLEM PLAYS.

Helena, ward of the Countess of Rousillon, vainly loves the young count Bertram. She succeeds in marrying him only when she follows him to the French court and cures the sick with a remedy inherited from her father. Invited to choose a husband from among the courtiers, she selects Bertram. He grudgingly complies but escapes immediately afterwards with the help of the cowardly braggart Parolles. He promises to accept her fully as his wife only if she can get a treasured ring from his finger and bear him a child. She succeeds by taking the place in his bed of Diana, a widow's daughter whom he has been courting; she persuades him to exchange rings with her. Unaware of the trick and believing Helena dead, Bertram plans to remarry, but his possession of Helena's ring arouses suspicions of foul play. Matters are resolved when the pregnant Helena appears, with his ring. Confronted by the evidence of his wife's persistence, Bertram accepts her with good grace.

Allan Quatermain A novel by HAGGARD, published in 1887. A sequel to *KING SOLOMON'S MINES*, it is more sombre in tone and more scholarly in its portrait of a 'primitive' people. Curtis and Good return to Africa because they are disillusioned with 'civilization'; Quatermain joins their expedition because his life has become meaningless since the death of his only son. After various preliminary adventures, they reach the lost land of Zu-Vendis by a journey along an underground river. Zu-Vendis is ruled by two queens, the dark Sorais and her fair sister Nylephta. Both fall in love with Curtis, who chooses Nylephta. Sorais declares war but is defeated and kills herself. Curtis becomes king, but the price to be paid is the death of both Quatermain and the heroic 'primitive' Umslopogaas.

allegory Description or narrative – in verse, prose or drama – presenting literal characters and events which contain sustained reference to a simultaneous structure of other ideas or events. The intention may be didactic, political or humorous, and the subject of the secondary level(s) may be philosophical, historical, theological or moral. In figural allegory the form and structure of what is described correspond to the features and structure of what is intended: the goddess Fortune is blind to indicate the arbitrary nature of luck. In narrative allegory the literal sequence of events corresponds to a psychological, spiritual, moral or historic progression.

All religions have a large allegorical content. Medieval exegesis, the explication of biblical passages to develop theological and spiritual significances, detected a fourfold scheme of allegory in the Bible. The levels of meaning are (1) the literal, (2) the allegorical, (3) the tropological or moral and (4) the anagogical. These correspond to (1) the historical account, (2) the life of Christ and the Church Militant, (3) the individual soul and moral virtue, (4) the divine schema and the Church Triumphant. Another common method of reading the Bible allegorically was typology, in which the Old Testament stories were seen both as historical fact and as foreshadowing events of the New Testament. Such habits of reading encouraged the development of allegory in literary texts. It is found at its simplest in medieval EXEMPLA and FABLES, where the relationship between the literal narrative (usually fictional) and a spiritual or moral lesson is indicated or explained by the author. In other cases (e.g. *PIERS PLOWMAN*), the relation of literal to other levels is complex and shifting, as the author searches for appropriate ways of exploring difficult concepts. Although it is predominantly associated with the Middle Ages, allegory has persisted in conventional and original forms, which have included the deliberately unfathomable allegories of the 16th century and the allegories of later poets such as BLAKE which depend on the poet's own private mythological system. Notable post-medieval examples include *THE FAERIE QUEENE*, *PILGRIM'S PROGRESS*, *THE SCARLET LETTER*, *MOBY-DICK* and *ANIMAL FARM*.

Allen, (Charles) Grant (Blairfindie) 1848–99 Novelist and popularizer of science. His scientific books, influenced by HERBERT SPENCER, include *Physiological Aesthetics* (1877), *The Colour Sense* (1879), which won him high praise from the scientific community, *The Evolutionist at Large* (1881) and *The Evolution of the Idea of God* (1897). *The Woman Who Did* (1895) is the best-remembered of his nearly 30 novels. Its sensational story of a women who lived unmarried with her lover but suffers the miseries of the outcast when he dies earned it a brief *succès de scandale*, though not the approval of feminists.

Allen, James Lane 1849–1925 American novelist and short-story writer. His article, 'Realism and Romance' (1886), attacked claims for the primacy of REALISM as practised by WILLIAM DEAN HOWELLS and others, defending the merits of the older tradition of romance associated with HAWTHORNE. Allen himself is best known for his romances set in the South, especially *A Kentucky Cardinal* (1894), about the reclusive nature-lover Adam Moss and his courtship of Georgiana Cobb. In the sequel, *Aftermath* (1895), Adam returns to his interest in nature, repelled by the tensions of pre-Civil War politics and saddened by Georgiana's death. Other works include *Summer in Arcady* (1896), *The Choir Invisible* (1897), *The Mettle of the Pasture* (1903), *The Bride of the Mistletoe* (1909), *The Kentucky Warbler* (1918) and a last collection of short stories, *The Landmark* (1925).

Allen, Paula Gunn 1939– American poet. Of Laguna Pueblo, Sioux and Chicano ancestry, she is preoccupied with her people's mythic heritage and present dilemmas and, in particular, with the dual role of Native American women as victims and reformers of their culture. Her collections of poetry are *The Blind Lion* (1974), *Coyote's Daylight Trip* (1978), *Starchild* (1981), *A Cannon between My Knees* (1981), *Shadow Country* (1982), *Skins and Bones* (1988) and *Grandmothers of the Light: A Medicine Woman's Sourcebook* (1991). *The Woman Who Owned the Shadows: The Autobiography of Ephanie Atencio* (1983) is a novel. Allen has also written a scholarly study, *The Sacred Hoop: Recovering the Feminine in American Indian Traditions* (1987).

Allen, Walter (Ernest) 1911–95 Critic and novelist. He is best known for two popular studies, *The English Novel: A Short Critical History* (1954) and *Tradition and Dream* (1964; called *The Modern Novel in Britain and the United States* in USA). Other critical works include *Writers on Writing* (1948; *The Writer on His Art* in USA), *Reading a Novel* (1949), *The Novel Today* (1955) and studies of ARNOLD BENNETT (1948), JOYCE CARY (1953), DEFOE, FIELDING, SCOTT, DICKENS, STEVENSON and CONRAD (jointly in *Six Great Novelists*, 1955) and GEORGE ELIOT (1964). His early novels, *Innocence is Drowned* (1938), *Blind Man's Ditch* (1939) and *Living Space* (1940), are pictures of working-class life on the eve of World War II. Later fiction includes *The Black Country* (1946), *Rogue Elephant* (1946), *Dead Man Over All* (1950; *The Square Peg* in USA) and *All in a Lifetime* (1959; *Threescore and Ten* in USA).

Alleyn, Edward 1566–1626 Actor. He was best known for creating the towering heroes of MARLOWE's tragedies in the 1580s and early 1590s, first with

Worcester's Men and then with the Admiral's Men at the Rose (see PUBLIC THEATRES). When he returned to the stage with the opening of the Fortune in 1600, his highly rhetorical style may have seemed old-fashioned, particularly by comparison with his rival, RICHARD BURBAGE. He had probably retired finally from acting by 1604. Alleyn's friendship with Henslowe, the Rose's manager, and his marriage to Henslowe's stepdaughter forged a business partnership that made him a rich man. His second marriage, to DONNE's daughter, confirms the social status he had achieved.

Allingham, Margery (Louise) 1904–66 Writer of DETECTIVE FICTION. She made her reputation with Albert Campion, a light-hearted amateur modelled on SAYERS's Lord Peter Wimsey, who appeared in *The Crime at Black Dudley* (1929), *Mystery Mile* (1930), *Look to the Lady* (1931), *Police at the Funeral* (1931), *Sweet Danger* (1933), *Death of a Ghost* (1934), *Flowers for the Judge* (1936), *Dancers in Mourning* (1937), *The Case of the Late Pig* (1937) and *The Fashion in Shrouds* (1938). Her grasp of character and Dickensian eye for the oddities of London life are more strongly developed in post-war novels, particularly *The Tiger in the Smoke* (1952).

Allingham, William 1824–89 Poet. His work (collected 1888–93), some of it illustrated by his close friend DANTE GABRIEL ROSSETTI, Arthur Hughes and Millais, is graceful and charged with lyric simplicity; it can also become national in spirit and touched by local colour. Through LEIGH HUNT, he came to know CARLYLE, TENNYSON and other literary lions so that, not surprisingly, his *Diary* (first published in 1907) is a mine of information about Victorian aesthetic life. In 1874 he married the water-colourist and illustrator Helen Paterson.

alliteration The repetition of a sound in two or more words. In its commonest form, initial consonants are repeated: 'Peter Piper picked a peck of pickled peppers'. Though it is no less alliterative, the repetition of initial vowels is less common and usually makes less impact: 'An Austrian army awfully arrayed'. Such repetition of initial sounds is sometimes styled initial-rhyme (or head-rhyme).

Consonance (apart from its unspecialized sense of agreement or harmony) consists in the repetition of similar consonants along with different vowels ('pipe/pep' or 'rife/reef'), assonance being the reverse ('grope/throne'). Since both by definition avoid rhyme, consonance and assonance are the main forms of that near rhyme (or para-rhyme or half-rhyme) which features so prominently in modernist poetry and old-fashioned nursery rhymes alike.

Initial, internal, and final repetitions are often so intertwined (as in 'life's fitful fever') or similar in effect (as with the internal alliteration of 'Peter Piper') that it seems sensible, where it is critically convenient, to speak of alliteration for all cases.

alliterative verse Originally Old English, alliterative verse survived – perhaps through an oral tradition – to enjoy a revival in the Middle Ages with works such as *SIR GAWAIN AND THE GREEN KNIGHT* and *PIERS PLOWMAN*. It continued to be written until the end of the 15th century in England and the early 16th century in Scotland. Initially the unrhymed alliterative line had four major stresses, two in each half-line; any number of minor stresses could be included. Usually the two major stresses of the first half-line and the first of the second half-line alliterate, though variations were common. Consonants alliterate with the same consonant but all vowels (and some words beginning with 'h') were deemed to alliterate with each other. A special poetic vocabulary, marked by a wide range of synonyms for common nouns, developed to allow the poet greater flexibility; many of these words are unknown outside alliterative poetry.

Alton Locke: *Tailor and Poet* A novel by CHARLES KINGSLEY, published in 1850. It reflects the turbulence of the 1840s, expressing Kingsley's CHRISTIAN SOCIALISM and making a significant contribution to the CONDITION OF ENGLAND NOVEL. As a tailor's apprentice, Alton Locke experiences the squalid conditions of sweated labour and takes readily to Chartism. His poetry brings him into contact with Eleanor Staunton, her cousin Lillian, and Saunders Mackaye, a Scottish bookseller loosely modelled on THOMAS CARLYLE. The Mackayes urge him to tone down his verse for publication, earning him the contempt of his Chartist comrades. Their taunts lead him to provoke a riot, and he is sentenced to three years' imprisonment. Lillian, with whom he has fallen in love, deserts him and it is Eleanor who nurses him when he catches typhus and helps convert him to Christian Socialism. He dies on his way to the USA.

Aluko, T(imothy) M(ofolorunso) 1918– Nigerian novelist. His satirical fiction, in which the clash between old and new values generates comedy, includes *One Man, One Wife* (1959), the first full-length novel in English to be published by a Nigerian publisher, *One Man, One Matchet* (1964), *Kinsman and Foreman* (1966), *Chief the Honourable Minister* (1970), *His Worshipful Majesty* (1973) and *Wrong Ones in the Park* (1982).

Alvarez, A(lfred) 1929– Critic, anthologist and poet. He acknowledged his debt to DONNE in a critical study (1961) and rejected the MOVEMENT in an anthology, *The New Poetry* (1962). *The Savage God: A Study of Suicide* (1971), about SYLVIA PLATH among others, and *Beyond All This Fiddle: Essays 1955–1967* (1968) define his taste for art expressing psychic disorder. In *Fantasy Poets 15* (1952), *Apparition* (1971) and *Autumn to Autumn, and Selected Poems 1953–76* (1978) he uses dark IRONY and mordant WIT to treat the ebb and flow of human relationships. He has also published several novels and *Off-Shore: A North Sea Journey* (1987).

Amadi, Elechi 1934– Nigerian novelist and playwright. Although he is regarded as a leading African novelist, his reputation has tended to languish in the shade of CHINUA ACHEBE. His fiction includes a trilogy, *The Concubine* (1966), *The Great Ponds* (1969) and *The Slave* (1978), drawing on the traditional spiritual and mythic life of Eastern Nigeria, and *Estrangement* (1986), about the desolation and confusion following the Nigerian Civil War. *Sunset in Biafra* (1973) is an account of his own war experiences. His plays, which include *Isiburu* (1973), *The Road to Ibadan* (1977) and *Dancer of Johannesburg* (1978), are slight in scale.

Ambassadors, The A novel by HENRY JAMES, published in 1903. Lambert Strether, a middle-aged widower, is sent to Paris by Mrs Newsome, a wealthy widow, to persuade her son Chad to return to his responsibilities as head of the family business in Massachusetts. His success as an ambassador will ensure his marriage to Mrs Newsome. He finds Chad sophisticated and refined by the influence of Madame de Vionnet. His letters to Mrs Newsome reveal declining enthusiasm for his embassy and she sends her daughter Sarah, with Sarah's husband and sister-in-law. They receive little help from Strether and their lack of success further estranges him from Mrs Newsome. In the ensuing action Strether makes two discoveries: that Chad's liaison with Madame de Vionnet is an intimate one, and that his sympathies rest with Chad. Content to observe life rather than participate in it, he eventually returns to Massachusetts.

Ambler, Eric 1909– Novelist. Their fast-moving plots, carefully controlled suspense and skilful use of foreign locations have made his many thrillers admired models for later writers. The best-known include *Epitaph for a Spy* (1938), *The Mask of Dimitrios* (1939; called *A Coffin for Dimitrios* in USA), *Journey into Fear* (1940), *Judgment on Deltchev* (1951), *The Night-Comers* (1956), *Passage of Arms* (1959) and *Dirty Story* (1967). He has also written many screenplays, beginning with *The Way Ahead* (with Peter Ustinov; 1944).

Amelia The last novel by HENRY FIELDING, published in 1751. Its intense depiction of evil and injustice has always made it less popular than his other work. William Booth, an attractive but impetuous young army officer, runs away with the virtuous and beautiful Amelia against her mother's wishes. The couple fall foul of the predatory world of London. Unjustly imprisoned in Newgate, William is seduced by Miss Matthews. Amelia meanwhile resists the attentions of several men. She forgives William, but his gambling gets him imprisoned again. Their desperate suffering is ended by the discovery that Amelia, not her sister, is the rightful heiress to her family's property.

American, The A novel by HENRY JAMES, serialized in 1876–7 and published in volume form in 1877. Christopher Newman, a wealthy American businessman, travels to Paris to find a wife. Mrs Tristram, an expatriate American, serves as his guide and confidante. His engagement to Claire de Cintré is ended by her aristocratic family, the Bellegardes. Newman introduces Valentin Bellegarde, Claire's brother, to Noémie Nioche, a copyist of paintings. Valentin fights a duel on her behalf and is killed. Before dying he sends Newman to Mrs Bread, the Dowager Marquise's maid, who reveals that the Marquise had caused her husband's death by withholding his medicine. Newman decides not to use this information to force the marriage. Claire becomes a nun.

American Crisis, The A series of 16 pamphlets by THOMAS PAINE, published between 1776 and 1783. Written during the War of Independence, they discuss human nature and the individual's proper relationship to the state, tyranny, the spirit of liberty and the future of colonialism. The pamphlets made an important contribution to the American Revolutionary cause and influenced the young nation's ideology.

American Mercury, The A magazine founded by H. L. MENCKEN and GEORGE JEAN NATHAN in 1924 and edited by Mencken in 1925–33. It survived until 1975, publishing fiction, literary criticism, and social and political commentary by a wide range of distinguished contemporaries.

American Notes DICKENS's account of his first visit to America in 1842, published later the same year. Although mainly a casual travel journal, it includes serious consideration of the treatment of the blind at the Perkins Institute in Boston, the prison system in Philadelphia and slavery in the southern states. Its hostile view of America is echoed in Dickens's next novel, *MARTIN CHUZZLEWIT*.

American Tragedy, An A novel by THEODORE DREISER, published in 1925. It is based on the Chester Gillette–Grace Brown murder case of 1906. Anxious to escape his family's dreary life, Clyde Griffiths gets a job in a factory belonging to his wealthy uncle, Samuel Griffiths. He falls in love with a rich girl, Sondra Finchley, but also seduces Roberta, a young factory worker. When she becomes pregnant and demands that he marry her, Clyde takes her to a lake resort and murders her. The rest of the novel traces the investigation of the case, describing Clyde's indictment, trial, conviction and execution in relentless detail.

Amis, Sir Kingsley 1922– Novelist and poet. During the 1940s and 1950s he was associated with the ANGRY YOUNG MEN generation and the poets of the MOVEMENT. His own poetry appeared in *Bright November* (1947), *A Frame of Mind* (1953), *A Case of Samples* (1956) and *Collected Poems 1944–1979* (1979). He achieved popular recognition with his first novel, *LUCKY JIM* (1954), showing a gift for comedy and mild SATIRE continued in *That Uncertain Feeling* (1955), *I Like It Here* (1958), and *Take a Girl Like You* (1960) and, with increasing vehemence, in *One Fat Englishman* (1963), *Ending Up* (1974) and *Jake's Thing* (1978). Other novels experiment with specific genres: the spy story in *The Anti-Death League* (1966) and *Colonel Sun* (1968); the ghost story in *The Green Man* (1969); DETECTIVE FICTION in *The Riverside Villas Murder* (1973); and SCIENCE FICTION and fantasy in *The Alteration* (1976). Later novels, such as *Stanley and the Women* (1984), *The Old Devils* (BOOKER PRIZE; 1986), *The Folks That Live on the Hill* (1990) and *The Russian Girl* (1992), turn to gloomy FARCE. Nonfiction includes his vitriolic *Memoirs* (1991).

Amis, Martin 1949– Novelist. He is the son of KINGSLEY AMIS. *The Rachel Papers* (1973), *Dead Babies* (1975) and *Success* (1978) are ferociously witty, baleful SATIRES of metropolitan torpor and cultural trendiness. His fiction has steadily grown more menacing and more experimental in: *Other People* (1981), a psychological thriller; *Money* (1984), a comedy set in high-life America; *London Fields* (1989), a Gothic exploration of London low life; *Time's Arrow* (1991), about the Nazi death camps; and *The Information* (1995). *Einstein's Monsters* (1986) is a collection of short stories on the theme of nuclear destruction. *The Moronic Inferno* (1986) gathers nonfictional pieces about America.

Amis and Amiloun A late 13th-century VERSE ROMANCE, adapted from a 12th-century French romance, *Amis et Amile*. Amiloun impersonates his foster-brother Amis in combat and is afflicted with leprosy as a result. Years later, in obedience to the bidding of an archangel, Amis sheds the blood of his own children to cure Amiloun. Not only is Amiloun restored to health but the children are returned to life.

Ammons, A(rchie) R(andolph) 1926– American poet. His first book of poetry, *Ommateum with Doxology* (the title refers to the compound eye of an insect), appeared in 1955 but it was his second, *Expressions of Sea Level* (1964), which established him as a major poet. His prolific output since then, notable for its precise descriptions of the natural world, has been summarized in *Collected Poems: 1951–1971* (1972), *The Selected Poems 1951–1977* (1977) and *Selected Longer Poems* (1980), and continued in *Worldly Hopes* (1982), *Lake Effect Country* (1983) and *Sumerian Vistas* (1987).

Amoretti SPENSER's contribution to the Elizabethan SONNET vogue, published together with *EPITHALAMION* in 1595. *Amoretti* ('little loves'), consisting of 89 sonnets (83 repeating 35) followed by four short lyrics, is a record of a courtship which reflects Spenser's wooing of Elizabeth Boyle. The sequence covers a period of just over two years, beginning in a New Year (4) and punctuated by another New Year (62) and two Easters (22 and 68). It is remarkable among English Renaissance sonnet cycles for this chronological narrative, its comparatively unconventional and characterized mistress and its innovative rhyme scheme of linked quatrains (abab bcbc cdcd ee). The courtship and the time scheme may well be intended to culminate in the wedding celebrated in *Epithalamion*.

Amory, Thomas *c.* 1691–1788 Irish novelist. An acquaintance of SWIFT, he wrote *The Memoirs of Several Ladies of Great Britain* (1755) and *The Life and Opinions of John Buncle, Esquire* (1756 and 1766). The first describes the adventures of Mrs Marinda Benlow, a BLUESTOCKING. The second, practically a sequel but purporting to be an autobiography, describes the travels and matrimonial adventures of its narrator.

Amours de Voyage A verse novel in five CANTOS by CLOUGH, published in 1858. It is narrated chiefly by Claude, a doubting intellectual, in letters from Rome, Florence, Bagni di Lucca and other towns visited by the middle-class English in the last century. The plot, which concerns Claude's tepid affair with Mary Trevellyn, is slight and the interest lies in Claude's reflections on art, ancient and modern Rome, patriotism, love, politics and Christian belief.

amphibrach See METRE.

amphimacer See METRE.

anacreontic A poem celebrating wine, love and song, after the example of the Greek lyric writer Anacreon of Teos (6th century BC) and his subsequent classical imitators. COWLEY first used the English term in his *Anacreontiques* (1656), though JONSON and HERRICK had already been notable practitioners of the form. THOMAS MOORE published a famous verse translation, the *Odes of Anacreon* (1800), for which BYRON dubbed him 'Anacreon Moore'.

anagnorisis The term used by Aristotle for the moment in TRAGEDY when a character moves from ignorance to knowledge, particularly knowledge of his or her tragic error (HAMARTIA). More loosely, it refers to the DÉNOUEMENT of a drama.

Anand, Mulk Raj 1905– Indian novelist. His realistic novels, angry, satirical and generous, include *Untouchable* (1935), the trilogy headed by *The Village* (1939), *Across the Black Waters* (1940), *The Sword and the Sickle* (1942), *The Big Heart* (1945), *Private Life of an Indian Prince* (1953) and *The Woman and the Cow* (1960; reissued as *Gauri*, 1976). A projected series of autobiographical novels, *The Seven Ages of Man*, has so far included *Seven Summers* (1951), *Morning Face* (1968), *Confessions of a Lover* (1976), *The Bubble* (1984) and the first section of a fifth, *Little Plays of Mahatma Gandhi* (1990). Anand has also published short stories and *Conversations in Bloomsbury* (1981), containing his recollections of T. S. ELIOT, D. H. LAWRENCE and VIRGINIA WOOLF.

anapaest See METRE.

anaphora The repetition of the first word or words in successive sentences or clauses. Famous examples are John of Gaunt's eulogy on England in SHAKESPEARE's *RICHARD II* ('This royal throne of kings, this scept'red isle,/ This earth of majesty ...') and the opening paragraphs of DICKENS's *BLEAK HOUSE* ('Fog everywhere. Fog up the river ...').

Anatomy of Melancholy, The A paramedical treatise by ROBERT BURTON, published in 1621. This curious and colourful work is elaborately subdivided but comprises three main parts: the first deals with the causes and symptoms of melancholy, the second with its cures and the third with specific melancholies attaching to love and religion. Physical and mental health are only the starting point of Burton's study, which digresses continually to encompass topics such as politics and religion, its pages abounding in quotations from wide-ranging sources including the Bible, the classics and learned contemporary works. The style is both comic and serious, lively and informed.

Ancients and Moderns, The A literary and cultural debate of the AUGUSTAN AGE. See SIR WILLIAM TEMPLE, RICHARD BENTLEY and THE BATTLE OF THE BOOKS.

Ancrene Riwle [*Ancrene Wisse*] A devotional manual (*c.* 1200) in Middle English, also surviving in French and Latin versions. It was written for a small group of anchoresses – women who passed their lives confined to the isolation of an eremitical cell. Despite the austere subject matter, it is a work of considerable charm, enlivened with graphic details of everyday life.

It deals with the 'inner' and 'outer' rules of the anchorite life, i.e. both the psychological and physical aspects of devotion and conduct. The approach reflects the change which took place in the 12th century, subordinating formal prayer to private meditation.

Anderson, Jessica 1925– Australian novelist and short-story writer. She has published *An Ordinary Lunacy* (1963), *The Last Man's Head* (1970), *The Commandant* (1975), *Stories from the Warm Zone and Sydney Stories* (1987) and *Taking Shelter* (1990), but is best known for two novels: *Tirra Lirra by the River* (1978), an elderly woman's account of her constricting life, and *The Impersonators* (1980; called *The Only Daughter* in the USA), about a woman rediscovering her native Sydney. Her writing has a flair for the poetic and a laconic IRONY, reflecting her admiration for HENRY GREEN, EVELYN WAUGH and MURIEL SPARK. CHRISTINA STEAD is the most significant Australian influence on her work.

Anderson, Maxwell 1888–1959 American playwright. His most successful plays were staged in the 1930s and 1940s: *Elizabeth the Queen* (1930), a blank-verse tragedy; *Night over Taos* (1932); *Both Your Houses* (1932; PULITZER PRIZE); *Mary of Scotland* (1933); *Valley Forge* (1934); *Winterset* (1935), a verse tragedy based on the Sacco and Vanzetti case; *Wingless Victory* (1937); *High Tor* (1937), a comedy about a struggle over land rights; *The Masque of Kings* (1937); *The Star Wagon* (1937); *Knickerbocker Holiday* (1938), a musical comedy with Kurt Weill; *Key Largo* (1939), another tragedy; *Journey to Jerusalem* (1940), about Christ's childhood; *The Miracle of the Danube* (1941) and *Candle in the Wind* (1941), two anti-Nazi plays; *The Eve of St Mark* (1942) and *Storm Operation* (1944), about the lives of soldiers; *Truckline Café* (1946); *Joan of Lorraine* (1946); and *Anne of the Thousand Days* (1948), completing his Elizabethan trilogy. *Lost in the Stars* (1950), another collaboration with Weill, was an adaptation of ALAN PATON's *Cry the Beloved Country*.

Anderson, Sherwood 1876–1941 American novelist and short-story writer. *Windy McPherson's Son* (1916) was followed by *Marching Men* (1917), a novel about coal miners in Pennsylvania, and *Mid-American Chants* (1918), a volume of unrhymed verse. He achieved recognition with *WINESBURG, OHIO* (1919), interrelated stories of small-town life, and *POOR WHITE* (1920), a novel exploring the effects of technological change on American culture. Later work includes short stories – *The Triumph of the Egg* (1921), *Horses and Men* (1923) and *Death in the Woods* (1933) – and the novels *Many Marriages* (1923), *Dark Laughter* (1925), *Tar: A Midwest Childhood* (1926) and *Beyond Desire* (1932). His autobiography, *A Story Teller's Story*, was published in 1924. A volume of *Letters* was issued in 1953, and a critical edition of his *Memoirs* in 1973. His minimalist prose style and bleak vision of life influenced such writers as HEMINGWAY and FAULKNER.

Andrea del Sarto A DRAMATIC MONOLOGUE by ROBERT BROWNING, published in *Men and Women* (1855). Andrea del Sarto (1486–1531), a contemporary of Michelangelo and Raphael known as 'The Faultless Painter' (Browning's sub-title), talks to his wife Lucrezia with sad resignation about his enslavement to her.

Andreas An Old English poem preserved in the VERCELLI BOOK, relating the deeds of Sts Andrew and Matthew. God sends Andrew to free Matthew, imprisoned and condemned by the cannibal Mermedonians, and protects him when he is himself threatened by a demon. A flood which destroys the city recedes only when Andrew requires it; the cannibals are converted and the dead resurrected. The poet takes every opportunity to expand the narrative with description and dialogue, and pays great attention to atmosphere, setting and sentiment. The style shows the influence of CYNEWULF, to whom the poem has sometimes been attributed.

Andrew of Wyntoun *c.* 1355–1422 Scots chronicler. Little is known of his life but he was a canon regular at St Andrews and prior of St Serfs Inch, Lochleven, in 1395–1413. His single surviving work, the *Orygynale Cronykil*, belongs to the late 14th century and is probably the earliest surviving example of Scots verse. A CHRONICLE in nine books, it narrates the history of Scotland from the Creation to the reign of Robert I.

Andrewes, Lancelot 1555–1626 Churchman and translator of the Bible. A moderate who exercised a lasting influence on Anglican theology, Andrewes became Dean of Westminster in 1601 and ended his career as Bishop of Winchester (from 1619). His scholarship, and his mastery of 15 languages, made him foremost among the translators selected to work on the Authorized Version of the Bible in 1604 (see BIBLE IN ENGLISH). His sermons are classics of Anglican homiletic, though their appeal has been limited by a taste for exhaustive textual analysis. *Ninety-Six Sermons* was published in 1629, *A Pattern of Catechistical Doctrine* in 1630, and *Preces privatae* (*Private Devotions*) in 1648. T. S. ELIOT's essay (1928) is an important reappraisal.

Angel in the House, The A sequence of poems in praise of married love by COVENTRY PATMORE, published at intervals between 1854 and 1863. *The Betrothal* (1854) and *The Espousals* (1856) follow the courtship and marriage of Felix Vaughan and Honoria, with preludes and epigrams proclaiming Patmore's philosophy of love and the beneficent power of women. *Faithful for Ever* (1860) and *The Victories of Love* (1863) continue the story in letters by Felix, Honoria, her former suitor Frederick Graham, and his wife Jane. *The Angel in the House* was among the most popular poems of its day.

Angelou, Maya 1928– Black American actress, director, playwright and autobiographer, born Marguerita Johnson. She is best known for her autobiographies dramatizing the challenges confronting black women: *I Know Why the Caged Bird Sings* (1969), *Gather Together in My Name* (1974), *Singin' and Swingin' and Gettin' Merry Like*

Christmas (1976), *The Heart of a Woman* (1981) and *All God's Children Need Travelling Shoes* (1986). Her long and varied career in the performing arts has included a film (*All Day Long*, 1974), television documentaries and plays, including *Cabaret for Freedom* (with Godfrey Cambridge; 1960), an adaptation of Sophocles' *Ajax* (1974), *And Still I Rise* (1976) and *King* (1990).

Anglo-Saxon Chronicle The main literary source for Anglo-Saxon history, a prose CHRONICLE begun in the reign of ALFRED (871–99) and contined, in the Peterborough version, until 1134. Manuscripts of the first section were circulating in the early 890s, and some were continued in various religious houses throughout the country. Seven versions and a fragment survive, containing matters of local interest as well as common material. The early 9th and mid 10th centuries are least well represented, while the reign of Aethelred II and the years from Edward Confessor's reign onwards are treated most fully.

Angry Young Men A group of writers of the late 1950s, characterized by what Kenneth Allsop defined in *The Angry Decade* (1958) as 'irreverence, stridency, impatience with tradition, vigour, vulgarity, sulky resentment against the cultivated'. Their stance arose from the sense of betrayal and futility which succeeded the exalted aspirations generated by post-war reforms. COLIN WILSON's study of alienation, *The Outsider* (1956), was judged by many an important manifesto. The classic dramatic embodiment is OSBORNE's *LOOK BACK IN ANGER* (1956), with a definitive anti-hero in Jimmy Porter. The seminal novels are WAIN's *Hurry on Down* (1953), KINGSLEY AMIS's *LUCKY JIM* (1954), BRAINE's *Room at the Top* (1957) and SILLITOE's *Saturday Night and Sunday Morning* (1958).

Animal Farm A novel by GEORGE ORWELL, published in 1945. This satirical ALLEGORY or FABLE is directed primarily against Stalin's Russia. Led by the pigs, the animals on Mr Jones's farm expel their human masters and decide to run the farm on egalitarian principles. However, the pigs are corrupted by power and, under Napoleon (Stalin), a new tyranny is established. Snowball (Trotsky), an idealist, is driven out and Boxer, the noble carthorse, is sent to the knacker's yard. The final betrayal occurs when the pigs engineer a *rapprochement* with Mr Jones. Originally rejected for publication by T. S. ELIOT, the book has remained very popular, especially with younger readers.

Anna of the Five Towns A novel by ARNOLD BENNETT, published in 1902. The harsh codes of her father, Ephraim Tellwright, and the economic realities of Bursley, a Potteries town, weigh heavily on the heroine. The news that she will inherit a fortune makes her attractive to a successful businessman, Henry Mynors, whom she eventually marries. In the process she is estranged from another suitor, Willie Price, an industrial tenant of her father, though she saves him from public disgrace when he and his father try to pay her father with a forged bill of credit. Ephraim disinherits her. Willie, learning that his father has embezzled £50 from the chapel building fund before committing suicide, commits suicide himself.

Annals of the Parish, The See GALT, JOHN.

Anne of Geierstein See SCOTT, SIR WALTER.

Anne of Green Gables See MONTGOMERY, L. M.

Annual Register, The An annual review of the year's events founded in 1758 by DODSLEY and EDMUND BURKE, who edited it for the first eight years of its life.

Anson, George, Baron 1697–1762 Sailor and travelwriter. His journal of an eventful and hazardous expedition in 1740–4 was edited as *Voyage round the World* (1748) by his chaplain, Richard Walter. It includes accounts of the storms at Cape Horn which wrecked four of the seven ships in the squadron, and of the capture in the Pacific of a Spanish galleon with a million and a half dollars.

Anstey, Christopher 1724–1805 Poet. He made his reputation with *The New Bath Guide* (1766), a series of verse letters describing the comic adventures of the Blunderhead family at the fashionable spa town.

Anstey, F. [Guthrie, Thomas Anstey] 1856–1934 Humorist. He was diverted from the law by the success of *Vice Versa: or A Lesson to Fathers* (1882), the story of a father and son who exchange ages and personalities. He contributed regularly to *PUNCH* and joined the staff of the magazine in 1887. His large output included *The Brass Bottle* (1900), a comedy about an inefficient jinnee.

Anthony, Michael 1932– Trinidadian novelist. His gentle but shrewdly observant talent is perhaps more recognized outside the Caribbean than within it. Four novels are concerned with childhood or adolescence: *The Games were Coming* (1963), *The Year in San Fernando* (1965), *Green Days by the River* (1967) and *All That Glitters* (1981). *Streets of Conflict* (1976) is set in Rio de Janeiro in the late 1960s. He has also published a collection of short stories, *Cricket in the Road and Other Stories* (1973), and *The Bright Road to Eldorado* (1982).

Anti-Jacobin, The A weekly journal published in 1797–8 to oppose the radical politics and philosophy encouraged by the French Revolution. It was founded by GEORGE CANNING and edited by WILLIAM GIFFORD, who, with JOHN HOOKHAM FRERE and George Ellis, were responsible for its lively blend of news and satirical verse, which included Canning's anti-French *The New Morality* and Canning and Frere's *The Loves of the Triangles*, a PARODY of ERASMUS DARWIN.

Antiquary, The A novel by SIR WALTER SCOTT, published in 1816. When Isabella Wardour obeys her father, Sir Arthur, and rejects his suit, Major Neville calls himself William Lovel and follows her to Scotland. There he meets Jonathan Oldbuck, the eccentric antiquary of the title, and the king's bedesman, Edie Ochiltree. He saves Sir Arthur and Isabella from drowning and with Ochiltree's help exposes Dousterswivel, a German scoundrel who has deceived Sir Arthur. Lovel proves to be the heir of Glenallan and all ends happily.

antithesis A rhetorical device which uses opposites balanced and contrasted to create sharpness of effect. Antithetical expression is common in neoclassical poetry and an important element of the 'closed couplet' (see HEROIC COUPLET): 'Tis the first Virtue, Vices to abhor/ And the first Wisdom, to be Fool no more' (POPE, *Imitations of Horace*). See also CHIASMUS.

Antonio and Mellida and **Antonio's Revenge** A play in two distinct but related parts by MARSTON, first performed in 1599 or 1600 and published in 1602. *Antonio and Mellida* is a love-story, though with dark aspects. Genoa and Venice are at war but Antonio, son of Andrugio, Duke of Genoa, loves Mellida, daughter of Piero, Duke of Venice. He persuades Mellida to run away with him. When they are captured, Andrugio offers himself to the enemy. Piero relents and allows Antonio and Mellida to marry. This happy ending is overthrown in *Antonio's Revenge*, a REVENGE TRAGEDY closely related to *HAMLET* and KYD's *SPANISH TRAGEDY*. Piero kills

Andrugio, marries his widow, and contrives to dishonour Mellida, who dies of grief. Andrugio's ghost prompts Antonio to kill Piero.

Antony and Cleopatra A tragedy by SHAKESPEARE, first performed c. 1607 and published in the First Folio of 1623. Its source is NORTH's Plutarch. Richer in language and imagery than *JULIUS CAESAR* and *CORIOLANUS*, with which it is inevitably associated, it is more appropriately viewed as one of the group of great tragedies Shakespeare wrote c. 1603–7 than as part of a scattered group of Roman plays.

Infatuated with Cleopatra, Antony neglects his duties as a Roman triumvir and lingers in Alexandria. Only when news of Pompey's rebellion is added to news of the death of his own wife, Fulvia, does he leave for Rome with his loyal general, Enobarbus. He patches up relations with his fellow triumvirs, the scheming Octavius Caesar and the foolish Lepidus, and agrees to marry Octavius' sister, Octavia. Even Pompey accepts peace terms. But Antony and Octavius soon begin to disagree. Octavia returns to Rome on a peace mission, and Antony goes back to Egypt and Cleopatra. Octavius embarks his army and, against Enobarbus' advice, Antony combines with the Egyptian fleet to fight at sea. The battle at Actium becomes a fiasco when Cleopatra's ships turn tail. In despair, Enobarbus deserts his leader and dies soon afterwards. Antony recovers his firmness of purpose but, after an initial victory, is again drawn into defeat by the Egyptian army's defection. The fearful Cleopatra hides in her monument and sends Antony a message that she is dead. Defeated and despairing, he falls on his sword, and is carried to the monument, where he dies in Cleopatra's arms. Octavius visits Cleopatra and leaves confident that she will return as his prisoner to Rome. But Cleopatra robs him of his triumph, preferring to join Antony by committing suicide.

Apologia pro Vita Sua The spiritual autobiography of NEWMAN, serialized in 1864 (when it was sub-titled *Being a Reply to a Pamphlet Entitled: 'What, Then, Does Dr Newman Mean?'*) and published in book form in 1865 (when it was sub-titled *Being a History of his Religious Opinions*). The first sub-title reflects its origin in a pamphlet war with the militantly Protestant CHARLES KINGSLEY, which Kingsley had begun with this allegation: 'Truth for its own sake has never been a virtue of the Roman clergy. Father Newman informs us that it need not and on the whole ought not to be.' The second sub-title reflects the extent to which the jibe, a clear statement of the distrust with which the English public had long regarded him, prompted Newman into describing his first career as an Anglican clergyman, his conversion to Roman Catholicism and his subsequent career as a Catholic priest. The account asserts the sincerity and consistency of his spiritual development. In addition to its value as a record of personal faith, the *Apologia* is also a primary historical source for the OXFORD MOVEMENT.

Apology for Poetry, An A critical treatise by SIR PHILIP SIDNEY, published in 1595 in two separate editions, one bearing the title *The Defence of Poesy*. Few of the ideas it presents are original, being Renaissance critical commonplaces. However, the work is a masterpiece of elegant persuasion, and its easy and engaging style conceals a careful rhetorical structure. Sidney claims that imaginative literature is a better teacher than philosophy or history. He defends it against the charges of timewasting, lying and allurement to vice, and deals also with Plato's famous decision to ban poets from the state

in his *Republic*. In Sidney's view, literature has the power to reproduce an ideal golden world, not just the brazen one we know, and so to offer 'a speaking picture – with this end, to teach and delight'. A digression looks at the state of English literature and finds it sadly wanting, but makes honourable exceptions of CHAUCER's *TROILUS AND CRISEYDE*, SURREY's poems, *THE MIRROR FOR MAGISTRATES*, SPENSER's *SHEPHEARDES CALENDER* and the play *GORBODUC*.

Apostles, The Officially 'The Cambridge Conversazione Society', formed at Cambridge in 1820 to promote formal discussion between friends. Early members included TENNYSON and ARTHUR HENRY HALLAM. G. E. MOORE's influence made the turn of the century a period of particular brilliance. Among the BLOOMSBURY GROUP, members included Roger Fry, DESMOND MACCARTHY, E. M. FORSTER, LEONARD WOOLF, Saxon Sydney-Turner, LYTTON STRACHEY and JOHN MAYNARD KEYNES.

Apperley, C(harles) J(ames) 1779–1843 Writer on sport and rural life, under the pseudonym Nimrod. His first book, *Memoirs of the Life of John Mytton* (1837), was about a Shropshire neighbour. *The Life of a Sportsman* (1842) contains a vivid picture of country life. His friend and rival R. S. SURTEES lampooned Apperley in *JORROCKS'S JAUNTS AND JOLLITIES* and *HANDLEY CROSS*.

Arbuthnot, John 1667–1735 Physician and creator of 'John Bull', the archetypal Englishman. He became a convivial member of the SCRIBLERUS CLUB and a valued friend of SWIFT and POPE, whose *Epistle from Mr Pope to Dr Arbuthnot* (1735) is a magnificent final testimony to their intimacy. Arbuthnot himself was a leading contributor to the *Memoirs of Martinus Scriblerus* and *THREE HOURS AFTER MARRIAGE* (1717). He is best known for *THE HISTORY OF JOHN BULL* (1712), five satirical pamphlets designed to end Marlborough's European campaign and bring about a return to peace and common sense. His 'A Sermon Preached to the People at Mercat Cross, Edinburgh' (1706) supported the union of Scotland with England. His scientific works include *An Essay concerning the Nature* of Ailments (1731), which stressed the value of proper diet in the treatment of patients, *An Essay concerning the Effects of Air on Human Bodies* (1733), and *An Essay on the Usefulness of Mathematical Learning* (1701). He published a single poem, 'Know Thyself', in 1734.

Arcadia, The A prose romance, interspersed with poems, by SIR PHILIP SIDNEY. Enormously popular in its age, it appealed to the Renaissance love of PASTORAL but was also read as COURTESY BOOK, moral treatise, discussion of love and philosophy, and even rhetorical handbook. Sidney wrote the bulk of it in 1580 while staying at Wilton House with his sister, the Countess of Pembroke, to whom it is dedicated; a later revision was never finished. As a result, the work exists in three different forms.

The unrevised *Old Arcadia*, never printed in the 16th century but circulated in manuscript, was devised as a tragicomedy in five acts. Warned by an oracle of enigmatic disasters, Duke Basilius retires to Arcadia with his wife, Gynecia, and daughters, Philoclea and Pamela. Two princes, Pyrocles and Musidorus, arrive and fall in love with Philoclea and Pamela. Pyrocles disguises himself as an Amazon to be near Philoclea. Basilius falls in love with the disguise, but Gynecia and Philoclea fall in love with Pyrocles. Musidorus decides to elope with Pamela and tries to rape her. Pyrocles arranges to meet both Basilius and Gynecia in a cave. There, as the oracle predicted, the Duke commits adultery with his own wife. Pyrocles seduces Philoclea, Basilius apparently dies from a love philtre, and Pamela and Musidorus are carried off by rebels. At the end all the major characters are arraigned before Euarchus. Gynecia is condemned to be buried alive for killing her husband; Pyrocles and Musidorus will die; and Philoclea is to go to a nunnery. Euarchus will not alter his verdict even when he realizes that he has condemned his son Pyrocles and nephew Musidorus. Tragedy is averted when Basilius revives, and a general pardon is extended.

The second version, known as the *New Arcadia*, was published in 1590, perhaps under the supervision of SIR FULKE GREVILLE. It presented the revised and greatly expanded text of the first three books, without the attempted rape of Pamela. New subsidiary stories include that of the blind Paphlagonian king which SHAKESPEARE borrowed for the Gloucester sub-plot in *KING LEAR*. In 1593 *The Countess of Pembroke's Arcadia* was published, perhaps under the supervision of the Countess herself. It brought together the first three revised books of the *New Arcadia* and the last two books of the unrevised *Old Arcadia*, thus making a hybrid version of the text.

Archer, William 1856–1924 Scottish journalist and dramatic critic. His alliance with SHAW in championing Ibsen helped to raise the literary standards of British drama in the late 19th century. His translation of Ibsen, *Quicksands: or, The Pillars of Society*, was performed in London in 1880, and a collected edition in 11 volumes was published in 1906–8. *The Old Drama and the New* (1923) argues vigorously that the English drama since THOMAS WILLIAM ROBERTSON had a greater claim for stage performance than all but a tiny minority of earlier plays.

archetypal criticism See FRYE, NORTHROP.

Arden, John 1930– Playwright and novelist. *Live Like Pigs* (1958) and *SERJEANT MUSGRAVE'S DANCE* (1959), early work for the ROYAL COURT THEATRE, established him as the most original, allusive and socially conscious playwright of the post-war generation. *The Workhouse Donkey* (1963), about local government, explored a recurrent concern: the conflict between rigid values and anarchic subversion. As in *Armstrong's Last Goodnight* (1964) and a play about King John and the barons, *Left-Handed Liberty* (1965), it expressed his preference for 'curvilinear' Celtic disorder without discrediting 'rectilinear' Roman order. In *The Hero Rises Up* (1968) and overtly political plays about Ireland – *The Ballygombeen Bequest* (1972), the six-part *The Non-Stop Connolly Show* (1975) and *Vandaleur's Folly* (1978) – Roman rigidity receives short shrift. Arden's progress from liberal socialism to the politics of revolution, particularly with regard to the British 'occupation' of Northern Ireland, is recorded in the essays of *To Present the Pretence* (1978). Ventures into fiction, notably *Silence among the Weapons* (1982) and *Books of Bale* (1988), show the same combination of topical commitment with sense of history that informs his plays.

Arden of Feversham, The Tragedy of Mr An anonymous play, published in 1592 and once attributed to Shakespeare (see SHAKESPEARE APOCRYPHA). An early domestic tragedy, based on an actual murder which took place at Faversham in Kent, it follows the initially frustrated but eventually successful attempts of Mistress Arden to rid herself of an unloved husband.

The murder is discovered and she is executed for the crime, with her lover and fellow conspirator.

Ardizzone, Edward 1900–79 Writer and illustrator of CHILDREN'S LITERATURE. Born in China of an Italian father and Scots mother, Ardizzone settled in England at the age of five. His first children's book, *Little Tim and the Brave Sea Captain* (1936), established him as a leading author-illustrator with a good eye for adventure and a brilliant, elusive drawing style concentrating on the essentials of line and form. He went on to illustrate over 100 books by other writers, but remained best loved for his children's work.

Areopagitica: *A Speech of Mr John Milton for the Liberty of Unlicensed Printing to the Parliament of England* MILTON's celebrated plea for a free press and free discussion (1644). It takes its title from the Greek *Areopagus*, the hill of Ares in Athens where the highest judicial tribunal used to meet. Milton attacks the Parliamentarians' reimposition of censorship in 1643 by accusing them of borrowing the methods of the Papal regimes. He argues that freedom to pursue learning is essential to the Christian 'ethos' and the development of virtue.

Areopagus A group of Renaissance courtiers and poets, whose best-known members were SIR EDWARD DYER, SIR FULKE GREVILLE and SIR PHILIP SIDNEY, with SPENSER apparently on the fringe. It took its name from the hill in Athens where the earliest aristocratic council met. The group's exact nature and constitution is unclear, though it was certainly concerned with prosody and classical metres, perhaps in imitation of the French 16th-century academies. Its members may also have discussed political and religious matters.

Argument Against Abolishing Christianity, An A satirical pamphlet by SWIFT, written in 1708 and published in 1711. Pretending to be a mild objection to an imaginary campaign to remove Christianity altogether, this ironical performance points out that such a move might be 'attended with some Inconveniences'. Concerned at the extremes of religious thinking then current, Swift attacks both the 'low' churchmen (freethinkers and Deists: see DEISM) and the high Tories (nonjurors and Jacobites) who in their different ways threaten the strength of the established Anglican church.

Arlen, Michael [Kouyoumdjian, Dikran] 1895–1956 Novelist and short-story writer. Born in Bulgaria of Armenian parents, he was educated in Britain but lived in the South of France after his marriage in 1928 and in New York after World War II. He achieved a brief popularity with his acerbic but stylish portrait of London life in collections of short stories such as *The Romantic Lady* (1921) and *These Charming People* (1923), and particularly in his best-selling novel *The Green Hat* (1924).

Armah, Ayi Kwei 1939– Ghanaian novelist. His vivid, eloquent novels lament centuries of African suffering and cultural obliteration. *The Beautyful Ones Are Not Yet Born* (1969), *Fragments* (1970) and *Why are We So Blest?* (1972) suggest almost total disillusionment with independent Africa. The need for a truly African cultural integrity is implicit in *Two Thousand Seasons* (1973), which rewrites the history of both Islamic and Christian assaults as simple epic, and *The Healers* (1975), about the crumbling 19th-century Ashanti empire.

Armstrong, John *c.* 1709–79 Poet and physician. *The Oeconomy of Love* (1736) is a blank-verse sex manual for the newly married and *The Art of Preserving Health* (1744) a didactic work pleasantly done in the manner of his friend THOMSON, who included a portrait of Armstrong in *THE CASTLE OF INDOLENCE*.

Arnold, Sir Edwin 1823–1904 Poet and translator. A student of Eastern languages, he published his first translation, from Sanskrit, in 1861: *Hitopadésa* (*The Book of Good Counsels*). His BLANK-VERSE epic on the life and teachings of the Buddha, *The Light of Asia* (1879), was enormously popular. He did not repeat his success with *The Light of the World* (1891).

Arnold, Matthew 1822–88 Poet, critic and educational administrator. The son of THOMAS ARNOLD of Rugby, he was educated at Winchester, Rugby and Balliol College, Oxford. He became a fellow of Oriel College in 1845 but left shortly afterwards to work as private secretary to Lord Lansdowne, travel on the Continent and eventually to take up the post of inspector of schools which brought him financial security.

Arnold's poetic career began with *The Strayed Reveller, and Other Poems* by 'A' (1849) and ended with *New Poems* (1867). Between these dates, however, he published *Empedocles on Etna, and Other Poems* (1852), *Poems* (1853), *Poems Second Series* (1855) and *Merope* (1858). The variety of poetic expression in these volumes is apparent: lyrics (the 'Marguerite' poems, *THE FORSAKEN MERMAN*, *DOVER BEACH*, 'Philomela'); poetic drama (*EMPEDOCLES ON ETNA* and *Merope*); narrative poems (*TRISTRAM AND ISEULT* and *SOHRAB AND RUSTUM*); elegies (*THYRSIS*, *THE SCHOLAR-GIPSY* and 'Memorial Verses'). Often deriving from classical subjects, Arnold's poetry is frequently informed by alienation, stoicism, despair and spiritual emptiness.

In 1858 Arnold became professor of poetry at Oxford, perhaps savouring the mild irony that, save for the 1867 volume, he wrote prose for the rest of his life. Like other Victorian polymaths sensitive to the stresses of the age, he addressed these problems in literary, political, religious and educational writings. Holding an inspectorate in education until his retirement in 1886 and possessed of European rather than insular vision, Arnold contemplated the British and Continental pedagogical scenes through a series of reports on differing educational problems, marked by clear writing, advocacy of the humane disciplines and emphasis on the Bible as a moral and a literary strength. He was also a trenchant critic of elementary and secondary education, of teacher training, and an advocate of state instruction at home and abroad. Above all, his educational writings put the case for a national instruction rising above local and political interests. The first series of his *ESSAYS IN CRITICISM* (1865; the second appeared posthumously in 1888), and particularly his essay 'The Function of Criticism at the Present Time', advocates criticism as a disinterested and flexible mode of thought whose application extends far beyond literature. Such a view leads naturally to the broad consideration of the dilemmas of English society in his great prose work, *CULTURE AND ANARCHY* (1869), where culture is recommended as 'the great help out of our present difficulties'. By the 1870s Arnold had joined the long list of Victorian thinkers to consider the theological controversies of the age, with *Saint Paul and Protestantism* (1870), *Literature and Dogma* (1873), *God and the Bible* (1875) and *Last Essays on Church and Religion* (1877).

Of the major Victorian poets Arnold is perhaps the least generous, but what he lacks in abundance he compensates for in subtlety and variety. His melancholy,

delicately moving stanzas are an exquisite register of the feelings of those intellectuals 'wandering between two worlds,/ One dead, the other powerless to be born'. The despairing gentleness of Arnold's poetry renders it unique in the Victorian canon. And as a prose writer tackling insuperable problems – in language often sardonic and invariably articulate – he is forthright, courageous and impervious to hostility. In their advocacy of culture, his appeals are as applicable in our own day as a century ago.

Arnold, Thomas 1795–1842 Educator, historian and father of MATTHEW ARNOLD. Appointed headmaster of Rugby School in 1828, he established a regime stressing classical education and religious training, intended to develop the boys' character and sense of duty. His success made Rugby the model for the English public-school system in the 19th century. Arnold returned to Oxford as Regius Professor of Modern History in 1841. He published an edition of Thucydides (1830–5) but left his *History of Rome* (1838–42) unfinished. Admiringly described by THOMAS HUGHES in *TOM BROWN'S SCHOOLDAYS* and made the subject of a respectful biography by ARTHUR PENRHYN STANLEY, Arnold was later caricatured by LYTTON STRACHEY in *Eminent Victorians* (1918).

Arthur Mervyn A GOTHIC NOVEL by CHARLES BROCKDEN BROWN, published in two volumes in 1799 and 1800. Dr Stevens, the narrator, cares for Arthur Mervyn, a farmboy who has come to Philadelphia and fallen ill during the plague year of 1793. Mervyn tells his story when suspicion arises that he is not the country innocent he appears. On first arriving in Philadelphia he had worked for Thomas Welbeck but discovered him to be a seducer, thief, forger and murderer. After Welbeck apparently died while trying to escape, Mervyn went to live on Mr Hadwin's farm, where he fell in love with his daughter Eliza. Later he discovered $20,000 of stolen money in a manuscript by Welbeck he had brought with him. When he encountered Welbeck, still alive, in Philadelphia, he burned the money before falling ill. Having dispelled the suspicions about his character, Mervyn returns to Eliza and finds that she has inherited the farm. He has a final confrontation with the now dying and repentant Welbeck. Meanwhile, new suspicions arise and his explanations prove less satisfactory; indeed, the second part of the book casts doubt on the story he had originally told. At the end, when Eliza turns out not to have inherited the farm, he marries Mrs Fielding, a widow of means.

Arthurian literature Our fairly unified picture of Arthurian legend derives from MALORY's 15th-century *LE MORTE DARTHUR*. Before Malory this unity does not exist; there is only a great mass of fable, legend and pseudo-history.

Arthur's first 'biography' in GEOFFREY OF MONMOUTH's *Historia regum Britanniae* (*c.* 1135) drew together scattered references preserved in folk-tales, the Welsh triads and CHRONICLES by writers such as Gildas, BEDE, Nennius, the author of the 10th-century *Annales Cambriae* and William of Malmesbury. The British commander of Roman descent, or the Christian *dux bellorum*, who fought the Saxon invaders at Mons Badonicus (or Badonis or Badon) became, in Geoffrey's account, a king in the Norman mould: a descendant of Constantine who conquered the French and the Romans, and made his court a hub of civilization. Geoffrey kept the story of the Saxon wars, identifying

Badon with Bath. Arthur is the son of Uter Pendragon and Ygraine, with a capital at Caerleon; he possesses the sword Caliburn (Excalibur), the shield Pridwen and the lance Ron; he is married to Guanhumara and his principal warriors are the Normanized Kai and Bedivere, while Gualguanus (Gawain) and Mordred are his sister Morgan's sons by King Lot. Merlin Ambrosius reappears from Nennius as a prophet aiding Uter but never meeting Arthur. After a battle with Mordred, who has attempted to usurp his kingdom and marry his queen, Arthur is wounded and translated to Avalon; he is succeeded by Constantine of Cornwall.

The 12th century sees the flowering of the pseudohistorical Arthur. The Jersey writer Wace translated Geoffrey's *History* into French in his *Roman de Brut* (1155), greatly enlarging it by adding more marvels to the story, especially the Round Table, and making Arthur's court a centre of *courtoisie*. His Arthur is still in Avalon, his return awaited by the Bretons: references to this belief appear from 1113 onwards. In 1191 fraudulent 'discoveries' of Arthur and Guinevere's tombs at Glastonbury sought both to identify it with Avalon and to quash the idea of Arthur's survival. LAYAMON, a priest in the Severn valley, is the first to put the legend of Arthur into English in his late 12th-century *Brut*, a free and expanded adaptation of Wace.

The pseudo-historical Arthur of chronicle now begins to wane, surfacing only briefly in the Saxon wars of *Arthour and Merlin* (English, 13th–14th century) before re-emerging in splendour in the epic alliterative *MORTE ARTHURE* (early 15th century). He is replaced by the Arthur of romance: the head of a brilliant chivalric court from which individual knights leave on adventures. Much of the material derives ultimately from Celtic tradition, which offered the Welsh prophet Myrddin as a powerful source for Merlin; other elements were noticed fleetingly by the Troubadour poets of Southern France and treated briefly in MARIE DE FRANCE's *Lanval*. But the earliest writer of Arthurian romance – as well as one of the greatest – was Chrétien de Troyes, working in northern France during the last quarter of the 12th century. Chrétien's five verse romances – *Erec et Enide, Yvain, Lancelot, Le Conte du Graal* and *Cligés* – introduce many permanent features of the legend: Lancelot and his love for Guinevere; Gawain as a model of prowess and courtesy, often however surpassed by the eponymous heroes; Kay as a churlish boaster; Perceval and the quest for the mysterious *graal*; and a king subordinated to his knights, inactive and increasingly ignoble. The degradation of Arthur, and of some of his best warriors, has begun. Guinevere has already appeared in an ambiguous light through her forcible annexation by Mordred in Geoffrey's *History*, which Layamon interprets as willing treachery to Arthur; the *Lai du cor* (1150–75) shows her failing a chastity test.

Chrétien's influence is huge, not least perhaps on a group of Welsh stories, *c.* 1200, about Owain, Peredur and Geraint, part of the so-called *MABINOGION*, which may however derive from his sources, not him. There are many continuations of his unfinished Grail story and several romances inspired by the theme, notably Wolfram von Eschenbach's *Parzival* (1200–12), *Perlesvaus* (1225–50), the *Didot Perceval* (c. 1202), and Robert de Boron's *Joseph d'Arimathie* (c. 1200). This last interprets the *graal* as the vessel used at the Last Supper and also to catch Christ's last drops of blood at the Crucifixion, and

which is brought to England by Bron, the Rich Fisher, Joseph's brother-in-law. Boron's *Merlin* introduced yet more elements to the legend, such as Arthur's fostering by Antor (Ector) and the sword in the stone which designates his kingship.

A version of it forms part of the so-called Vulgate Cycle, a huge 13th-century collection of prose romances by various authors, in five parts: *Estoire del Saint Graal*, prose *Merlin, Lancelot, Queste del Saint Graal* and *Mort Artu*. These portray Arthur and his court as embodying a worldly chivalry doomed to be surpassed by the spiritual chivalry of the Grail knights, and flawed from the start, when Arthur unwittingly and incestuously begets Mordred on his sister Morgause. The quest for the Grail by most of Arthur's hitherto praiseworthy knights, above all Gawain, is barren; Lancelot is displaced as the greatest knight by his son Galaad, and his adulterous love for Guinevere leads to the collapse of the Round Table. Only Galaad, Perceval and Bors achieve the Grail, and only Bors returns to the secular life of Camalot.

The Vulgate and its successors, such as the *Roman du Graal*, are attempts to combine some of the branches of the Arthurian legend, but there are also vast numbers of miscellaneous romances. In French these range from *Le Bel Inconnu* (1185–90) to Froissart's *Meliador* (1388); there are four in Latin, from the 12th to the 14th century, and many in other languages such as Spanish, Portuguese, Dutch, Norwegian and Icelandic. Though Italy provides us with evidence of early diffusion of the legend in the form of the baptismal names of Artusius and Walwanus, from 1100 on, and in the Modena archivolt (1099–1120), there is no accompanying literary record until the 13th-century prose romances. Arthur's popularity is then plain in literature and art (witness the Pisanello frescoes in Mantua) and leads to his later celebration by Boiardo. German versions of the legend appear from the end of the 12th century, at first influenced by Chrétien, and include, in addition to the *Parzival*, Hartmann von Aue's *Erek* and *Iwein* (c. 1190, c. 1202); Ulrik von Zatzikhoven's *Lanzelet* (from 1194); *Wigalois* and *Diu Krône* (13th century). English romances, in verse and prose, featuring Arthur and his knights range from the second half of the 13th century (*Arthur and Merlin*) to the 16th century. The most notable are Thomas Chestre's *SIR LAUNFAL* (c. 1350), *YWAIN AND GAWAIN* (c. 1350), the stanzaic *MORTE ARTHUR* (c. 1400), *SIR GAWAIN AND THE GREEN KNIGHT* (late 14th century), and *THE AWNTYRS OF ARTHURE* (late 14th century) with its reproach of the 'covetous' Arthur and its hint of an adulterous Guinevere. Many of the English romances use French originals but compress and adjust their material to give a clear and action-packed storyline.

Sir Thomas Malory's *Le Morte Darthur*, completed in 1469 or 1470, distils these sources, drawing on both French texts (the Vulgate Cycle, the *Roman du Graal* and the prose *Tristan*) and English ones (the alliterative *Morte Arthure* and the stanzaic *Morte Arthur*). It is the culmination of the tradition, the last and greatest attempt to consolidate all the Arthurian material into a unified cycle. In CAXTON's printed text of 1485 it achieves a wider circulation than any of its predecessors, and later reworkings of the legend – such as TENNYSON's *IDYLLS OF THE KING* and T. H. WHITE's *The Once and Future King* – take it as their model.

As I Lay Dying A novel by WILLIAM FAULKNER, published in 1930. It treats the events surrounding the illness, death and burial of Addie Bundren, wife of Anse and mother of Cash, Darl, Jewel, Dewey Dell, and Vardaman. Anse is stubbornly insistent that her wish to be buried in her home town of Jefferson, Mississippi, should be respected, despite the accidents and setbacks which the family encounters on its 10-day journey with the coffin. Experimental in both subject and narrative structure, the novel is divided into 59 short interior monologues (see STREAM OF CONSCIOUSNESS) from the characters.

As You Like It A comedy by SHAKESPEARE, first performed *c*. 1599 and published in the First Folio of 1623. The source is LODGE'S *ROSALYNDE*. Frederick usurps the dukedom from his brother but his daughter Celia remains friendly with Rosalind, the deposed duke's daughter. Rosalind falls in love with Orlando, already deprived of his birthright by his older brother Oliver de Boys, when he wins a wrestling match with the court champion. Orlando flees to the Forest of Arden and Rosalind, banished in her turn, disguises herself as a boy (Ganymede) and follows, with Celia and the court fool, Touchstone. In the forest Orlando is welcomed by the banished duke, whose exiled court includes the wryly speculative Jaques. Orlando posts love poems to Rosalind on trees; she finds them and uses her male disguise to test his love. She is disturbed to find herself loved by the pastoral Phebe. Duke Frederick sends Oliver to find his brother, but he undergoes a change of heart and falls in love with Celia. Rosalind oversees the matching of Celia and Oliver, Phebe and Silvius, Touchstone and his wench Audrey, and Orlando and herself. Suddenly repentant, Duke Frederick restores his banished brother to the dukedom and, with Jaques, takes refuge from the world. However improbable the incidents, the harmony of their outcome is satisfying, making *As You Like It* the most charitable of Shakespeare's mature comedies.

Ascham, Roger 1515–68 Scholar and teacher. As well as being an authority on Greek, which he taught at Cambridge, Ascham was a Latin scholar, an accomplished musician and a fine calligrapher. In 1548 he became tutor to Princess Elizabeth, a position to which he was reappointed on her accession, reading Cicero, Livy and the Greek New Testament with her. He was also Latin secretary to Queen Mary, with the extraordinary dispensation that he was permitted to continue in the reformed religion. Of his two important works in English, *Toxophilus* (1545) is a dialogue on archery, stressing the importance of physical exercise in education and pleading for the use of English. *The Schoolmaster* (posthumously printed in 1570) argues against excessive discipline in education, warns against idleness and Italian travel, and recommends a method of teaching Latin grammar. Latin writings include translations of commentaries on the epistles to Titus and Philemon (1542) and a treatise against the Mass (1577).

Ash, John 1948– Poet. Born in Britain, he now lives in New York. *Casino* (1978), *The Bed* (1981), *The Goodbyes* (1982), *The Branching Stairs* (1984), *Disbelief* (1987) and *The Burnt Pages* (1991) have shown him digesting various influences: French SYMBOLISM, European MODERNISM and the work of ROY FISHER, LEE HARWOOD and JOHN ASHBERY. His own style emerges as committed to innovation, eclectically knowledgeable and intellectually challenging.

Ashbery, John (Lawrence) 1927– American poet. The best-known member of the NEW YORK SCHOOL, he presents an essentially sceptical view of the world in verse that is generally self-referential and self-enclosed

but still capable of humour and dazzling playfulness. *Turandot and Other Poems* (1953) has been followed by *Some Trees* (1956), *The Poems* (1960), *The Tennis Court Oath* (1962), *Rivers and Mountains* (1966), *Sunrise in Suburbia* (1966), *Three Madrigals* (1966), *Fragment* (1969), *The Double Dream of Spring* (1970), *The New Spirit* (1970), *Three Poems* (1972), *The Vermont Notebook* (with Joe Brainard; 1975), *Self-Portrait in a Convex Mirror* (1975; PULITZER PRIZE), *The Serious Doll* (1975), *Houseboat Days* (1977), *As We Know* (1979), *Shadow Train* (1981), *A Wave* (1984), *Selected Poems* (1985), *The Ice Storm* (1987), *April Galleons* (1987) and *Hotel Lautreamont* (1992). He has also published a novel, *Nest of Ninnies* (with James Schuyler; 1969), and drama, collected as *Three Plays* (1978). *Repeated Sightings: Art Chronicles, 1957–1987* (1989) testifies to the strong interest in the visual arts which marks his work and to his long career as an art critic.

Ashford, Daisy 1881–1972 Juvenile novelist. She dictated her first story at the age of four and gave up writing when she was 13. *The Young Visiters*, a long-forgotten, imperfectly spelled manuscript written when she was nine, was rediscovered and published with an introduction by BARRIE in 1919. A lively eye for detail and occasional understandable confusions combine to make the story – how Ethel Monticue is courted both by Bernard Clark, her favourite, and Mr Salteena – a classic of unconscious humour, never out of print since its first appearance. Other manuscripts written when Ashford was a child and since published are *Love and Marriage* (1965) and *The Hangman's Daughter* (1982).

Ashmole, Elias 1617–92 Antiquary and virtuoso. His wide interests embraced astrology, alchemy, Freemasonry, Hebrew, engraving and heraldry, the last subject prompting his major work, *The Institution, Laws and Ceremonies of the Order of the Garter* (1672). Ashmole inherited the collections of the naturalist John Tradescant and gave them, with additions of his own, to the University of Oxford on condition a suitable building was made available. The Ashmolean Museum opened in 1683, with Dr Robert Plot as its first curator.

Ashton-Warner, Sylvia 1908–84 New Zealand novelist. She spent most of her career as a schoolteacher and did not publish her first novel, *Spinster* (1958), until she was nearly 50. It immediately made an impact in New Zealand as a ROMAN À CLEF and internationally for its STREAM OF CONSCIOUSNESS presentation of the teacher-protagonist's turbulent inner life. *Incense to Idols* (1960) and *Bell Call* (1965) use Romantic narrative modes which complement the challenge offered to conventional society and its notions of communication and education. *Teacher* (1963) and *Myself* (1967), supposedly the author's diary from the early 1940s, are presented in a documentary mode. *Greenstone* (1966), moving between fantasy and realism, draws heavily on Maori myth to make a plea for racial and cultural harmony. Ashton-Warner's other works include *Three* (1970) and *I Passed This Way* (1979).

Asimov, Isaac 1920–92 American writer of SCIENCE FICTION. His pulp stories are among the most popular ever produced, especially those collected in the three-volume Foundation series (1942–50; in book form 1951–3) and the classic collection *I, Robot* (1950), which made famous the 'three laws of robotics'. This programmed ethical system was elaborated in *The Caves of Steel* (1954), *The Naked Sun* (1956) and *The Bicentennial Man and Other Stories* (1976). His other science fiction novels include *The Currents of Space* (1952), *The End of Eternity* (1955), *The Gods Themselves* (1972) and *Nemesis* (1989). In the years before his death he attempted to bind his two most famous series together into a single pattern of future history, as *Foundation's Edge* (1982), *The Robots of Dawn* (1983), *Robots and Empire* (1985), *Foundation and Earth* (1986) and *Prelude to Foundation* (1988).

Aspern Papers, The A story by HENRY JAMES, published in 1888. The narrator, an American editor, travels to Venice to recover letters written by Jeffrey Aspern, a Romantic poet of the early 19th century, to his mistress, 'Juliana'. He rents rooms from Juliana, now the aged Miss Bordereau, who lives with her niece, Tina, an unattractive spinster. After Miss Bordereau dies Tina says that she could give the letters only to 'a relative' of the family. The editor balks at the veiled proposal and when they next meet Tina reveals that she has burned them.

Assembly of Ladies, The A poem of unknown authorship once attributed to CHAUCER (see CHAUCERIAN APOCRYPHA), probably written *c.* 1450–75 in the London area. A DREAM-VISION presented as the work of a woman, it describes an assembly held by Lady Loyalty where women air their grievances.

Asser d. 908 or 910 Reputed author of a Latin biography of ALFRED, *De rebus gestis Aelfredi Magni*. A monk of St David's, Asser joined the royal household in 887, becoming the king's teacher, friend and adviser. At his death he held the bishopric of Sherborne. *De rebus gestis Aelfredi Magni* culls the ANGLO-SAXON CHRONICLE for a history of events in England between 849 and 887, but adds an account of Alfred's life until 887 based on admiring personal observation. It is thus an important historical source, as well as the earliest biography of a secular figure written in England.

The only known manuscript was destroyed in the Cotton library fire of 1731 (see COTTON, SIR ROBERT). Of the two editions based on it, that of 1574 is full of arbitrary alterations while that of 1722, though more reliable, preserves many errors from the earlier edition.

assonance See ALLITERATION.

Astley, Thea 1925– Australian novelist and short-story writer. Her work frequently concentrates on outsiders and misfits, attacking the philistinism and hypocrisy of middle-class, small-town life. Novels include *Girl with a Monkey* (1958), *A Descant for Gossips* (1960), *The Well-dressed Explorer* (1962), *The Slow Natives* (1965), *A Boat Load of Home Folk* (1968), *The Acolyte* (1972), *A Kindness Cup* (1974), *An Item from the Late News* (1982), *Beach-masters* (1985), *Reaching Tin River* (1989) and *Slow Nature* (1990). *Hunting the Wild Pineapple* (1979) and *It's Raining for Mango* (1987) are collections of related short stories.

Astrophil and Stella A SONNET sequence by SIR PHILIP SIDNEY, the first in English, probably written in 1582 but not printed until 1591. Astrophil ('star-lover') unsuccessfully courts Stella ('star'). Punning use of the word 'rich' in sonnets 24, 35 and 37 invites the reader to identify her with Penelope Devereux, Lady Rich after her marriage in 1581. Astrophil's preoccupation with poetry makes the sequence a critical account of attitudes to love poetry as well as love: he makes a concise list of 16th-century poetic conventions and styles (6) and proclaims independence of PETRARCHAN predecessors (15).

Atalanta in Calydon A verse drama by SWINBURNE, published in 1865. He intended to re-create 'the likeness of a Greek tragedy with something of the true poetic life and charm'. The subject is the myth of Meleager, in love with the virgin huntress Atalanta, and the hunt for the

Calydonian boar sent by the goddess Artemis to punish King Oeneus for neglecting to honour her. Several lyrics achieved a fame beyond their original context: the chief huntsman's address to Artemis and Apollo ('Maiden, and mistress of the months and stars'); the choric hymn to the goddess that follows ('When the hounds of spring are on winter's traces'); and the chorus's comment when Althaea goes to prepare her son for the hunt ('Before the beginning of years / There came to the making of man').

Atheist's Tragedy, The: *or, The Honest Man's Fortune* A REVENGE TRAGEDY by TOURNEUR, published in 1611. Scholars have found it so inferior to THE REVENGER'S TRAGEDY as to cast doubt on Tourneur's authorship. The 'atheist' D'Amville murders his brother and marries his own sickly son to the wealthy Castabella. The son's impotence thwarts D'Amville's plans, and there follows an extraordinary graveyard scene in which his attempt on Castabella is prevented by Charlemont, her original betrothed. D'Amville offers to serve as executioner when Charlemont is condemned to death for killing D'Amville's servant, but 'As he raises up the axe strikes out his own brains'. Charlemont concludes that 'patience is the honest man's revenge'.

Athelston A mid-14th-century VERSE ROMANCE based on an Old English story. When Athelston becomes King of England he rewards his sworn companions with high office. One, the Earl of Stane, marries his sister but another, the Earl of Dover, lays false accusations against the couple. Athelston is deceived until a popular rising forces him to give way and a trial by ordeal proves Stane innocent. Stane's son is made Athelston's heir; the poem makes a romantic connection with history by identifying him with St Edmund.

Athenaeum, The A weekly review founded in 1828 and shaped by CHARLES WENTWORTH DILKE, editor 1830–46. ROBERT BROWNING, CARLYLE, LAMB and PATER were among 19th-century contributors. Probably its finest hour came with the brief editorship of JOHN MIDDLETON MURRY (1919–21), who published work by BERTRAND RUSSELL, T. S. ELIOT, ALDOUS HUXLEY and KATHERINE MANSFIELD. In 1921 it merged with *Nation*, appearing as the *Nation and Athenaeum* until it was absorbed by *The New Statesman* in 1931.

Atlantic Monthly, The A magazine devoted to literature and current affairs, founded in Boston in 1857 by OLIVER WENDELL HOLMES and JAMES RUSSELL LOWELL. Its editors have included WILLIAM DEAN HOWELLS and THOMAS BAILEY ALDRICH.

Atterbury, Francis 1662–1732 Churchman and theologian. Appointed Dean of Westminster in 1713, he was imprisoned for alleged complicity in a plot to restore the Stuarts in 1720 and deprived of his offices and banished in 1723, to die in exile. He was a notable contributor to the Phalaris controversy (see SIR WILLIAM TEMPLE) and a preacher of renown. His chief published works were concerned with church dogma and include *Sermons* (1740) and *Miscellaneous Works* (1789–98).

Atwood, Margaret (Eleanor) 1939– Canadian novelist, poet, short-story writer and critic. She first attracted attention as a poet with volumes such as *The Circle Game* (1966), *The Animals in that Country* (1968) and *The Journals of Susanna Moodie* (1970), belonging to the mythopoeic tradition of JAY MACPHERSON. Her best-known novel, *SURFACING* (1972), traverses similar terrain in relating its narrator-protagonist's quest for personal truth to a journey into the national past and ultimately prehistory, also a concern in a later novel, *Life before Man* (1979). *Lady Oracle* (1976) is a social comedy in which the heroine once again 'escapes' from contemporary consumer society. *The Handmaid's Tale* (1986) is a SCIENCE-FICTION ALLEGORY which comments on the rise of right-wing fundamentalism and new forms of patriarchy in North America in the 1980s. *Cat's Eye* (1989) is based on flashback, as the narrator, like earlier Atwood protagonists, reviews and reassesses her past. Atwood's other works include: novels, *The Edible Woman* (1969) and *Bodily Harm* (1981); volumes of verse, *Procedures for Underground* (1970), *Power Politics* (1971), *Two-Headed Poems* (1978), *True Stories* (1981), *Interlunar* (1984) and *Selected Poems: 1966–1984* (1990); and the short-story collections *Dancing Girls* (1977) and *Bluebeard's Egg* (1983). *Survival: A Thematic Guide to Canadian Literature* (1972) is a work of archetypal criticism which shows the influence of NORTHROP FRYE's *The Bush Garden*. Atwood edited *The New Oxford Book of Canadian Verse in English* (1982). *Second Words* (1982) is a collection of her shorter critical pieces.

Aubrey, John 1626–97 Biographer and antiquary. An active Fellow of the Royal Society (from 1663) and an associate of the intellectual *avant-garde* of his day, Aubrey pursued scientific interests in natural history and comparative religion. His sense of history led him to make topographical and archaeological collections in the tradition of CAMDEN, largely about Wiltshire, his native county. His discovery and survey of Avebury give him some claim to be among the first field archaeologists in Britain. But he is best known for the so-called *Brief Lives*. What began in 1667 as compilations of notes for ANTHONY À WOOD's *Historia et antiquitates universitatis oxoniensis* (1674) and *Athenae oxonienses* (1691–2) survived to occupy a far more interesting place in the history of biography. Although he took account of figures from the previous age (SHAKESPEARE and SIR WALTER RALEIGH, for example), Aubrey's principal aim was to set down accurate records of contemporaries. The *Lives* are a serious exercise in biographical truth-telling (perhaps the first in English), packed with detail, mostly observed at first hand and conveyed in an inimitable style. Aubrey's sense of the force of individual personality, to which the *Lives* are a monument, also informs another of his pioneering works, *An Idea of Education of Young Gentlemen* (completed 1684).

It is to be regretted that Aubrey published only one book in his lifetime: *Miscellanies* (1696). His *Lives, Idea of Education* and other work remained in manuscript for a variety of later editors, not all of them equal to the task; some remain unedited to this day. The standard, though somewhat bowdlerized, edition of the *Brief Lives* is by Andrew Clark (1898). *A Perambulation of the County of Surrey*, edited and enlarged by Richard Rawlinson, appeared in 1719. The work on Wiltshire has appeared as *The Natural History of Wiltshire* (1847) and *Wiltshire: The Topographical Collections* (1862). *Aubrey on Education* appeared, poorly edited, in 1972. *Miscellanies, Remaines of Gentilisme and Judaisme* and *Observations* are printed as *Three Prose Works*, edited by John Buchanan-Brown (1972). Aubrey is the subject of a biography, *John Aubrey and his Friends* (1948; revised 1963), by ANTHONY POWELL, who has also edited the best selection from the *Lives* and other works (1949).

Audelay, John Early 15th-century poet. The unique manuscript of Audelay's poems comprises 55 religious pieces – didactic, narrative and descriptive, plus 25 poems labelled Christmas carols. Most are penitential,

inspired by a fear of damnation. The theology is orthodox and the poetry unoriginal except in its fondess for metrical experiment. Nothing is known of Audelay's life beyond the information in the manuscript. He apparently lived at Haughmond Abbey near Shrewsbury. He was blind, deaf and, at least towards the end of his poetic career, ill. The collection bears a colophon dated 1426, and Audelay was at some time first priest to Lord Strange (who held the title 1397–1449).

Auden, W(ystan) H(ugh) 1907–73 Poet, playwright and critic. He began to make a name for himself while still an undergraduate at Oxford, where his contemporaries included WARNER, BETJEMAN, SPENDER, DAY-LEWIS and MACNEICE. *Poems* (1930), *The Orators* (1932), *The Dance of Death* (1933) and *Look Stranger!* (1936) established him as the leading poet of his generation, bringing a reading of Freud and Marx and a strong left-wing commitment to the forms suggested by ELIOT's THE WASTE LAND. He wrote three plays in collaboration with ISHERWOOD: *The Dog beneath the Skin* (1935), *The Ascent of F6* (1936) and *On the Frontier* (1939). His brief service as an ambulance driver for the Republicans in the Spanish Civil War resulted in *Spain* (1937). Other travels produced *Letters from Iceland* (with MacNeice, 1937) and *Journey to a War* (with Isherwood, 1939), about China. He emigrated to the United States with Isherwood in 1939, becoming an American citizen in 1946. While sometimes adopting American verse forms, he remained unmistakably a British poet. *New Year Letter* (1941; as *The Double Man* in USA), the first of his American books, was followed by *For the Time Being: A Christmas Oratorio* (1944), *The Age of Anxiety: A Baroque Eclogue* (1947; PULITZER PRIZE), *Nones* (1951), *The Shield of Achilles* (1955), *The Old Man's Road* (1956) and *Homage to Clio* (1960).

He was professor of poetry at Oxford in 1956–60, becoming a Student (i.e. fellow) of Christ Church, his old college, in 1962 and returning to live in his old college in 1972. His life in Kirchstetten, Austria, is celebrated in *About the House* (1967). Final volumes were *City Walls and Other Poems* (1969), *Academic Graffiti* (1971) and *Epistle to a Godson* (1972). He also revised his early work from his later viewpoint as a Christian, presenting his personal canon in *Collected Shorter Poems* (1966), *Collected Longer Poems* (1968) and *Collected Poems* (1976). *The English Auden* (1977) reissued his early poetry and some prose in the original versions. His critical writing includes *The Enchafèd Flood* (1951), *The Dyer's Hand* (1963) and *Secondary Worlds* (1968). He also collaborated with his lifelong companion Chester Kallman on the libretto for Stravinsky's *The Rake's Progress* (1951).

Audubon, John James 1785–1851 American naturalist and artist. Born in Haiti, he was educated in the USA and later in France, where he studied with Jacques-Louis David. *The Birds of America* (1827–38) is famous for its accurately detailed, delicately coloured illustrations. Sections of his journals also have been published as *Delineations of American Scenery and Character* (1926), *Journal of John James Audubon, Made during His Trip to New Orleans in 1820–21* (1929) and *Audubon's America* (1940).

Augie March, The Adventures of A novel by BELLOW, published in 1953. One of three sons born to a feeble-minded Jewish woman on Chicago's West Side, Augie does not finish college, becomes involved briefly in union organizing, travels to Mexico, returns to the USA and joins the navy, marries and, after leaving the service, goes to Europe to write his 'memoir'. In it he records his encounters with the people who have shaped (or tried to shape) his life: his Grandma Lausch; his employer William Einhorn; the wealthy Renlings, who want to adopt him; the tough waitress Mini Villar; the rich Thea Fenchel, who takes him to Mexico; the millionaire Robey, who hires him to help write a masterwork; Stella Chesney, the showgirl he marries; and the lunatic scientist Bateshaw, with whom he shares a lifeboat after their ship has been torpedoed.

Augustan Age, The A term applied loosely to the literature and art of the Restoration and early 18th century. It refers back to the heyday of classical writing during the reign of the Roman emperor Augustus (27 BC–AD 14) and the stylistic achievements of the Latin poets of the golden age, Virgil, Horace and Ovid, whose writings were much admired and imitated by the authors of this later period of NEOCLASSICISM. Although imprecise, it is convenient for bracketing together the writings and styles of many authors from DRYDEN and SAMUEL BUTLER to SAMUEL JOHNSON, and is most frequently applied to the work of POPE and JONATHAN SWIFT. Common literary concerns, especially among the poets, included: the development of an elegant, well-turned style; the pursuit of fluency, precision of expression and a dislike of cant or slang; the observation of decorum; and the cultivation of good taste and the refinement of manner. More generally, the period is characterized by a desire for common sense and compromise in the face of the wilder extremes of contemporary fashion and thought. This moderation is sometimes called the *via media* or golden mean, its artistic manifestation being a delight in proportion, poise and WIT.

Auld Lang Syne See AYTON, SIR ROBERT and BURNS, ROBERT.

Aurora Leigh A novel in verse by ELIZABETH BARRETT BROWNING, published in 1856 (postdated 1857). Her most sustained piece of work, it confronts many contemporary issues (the role of women, the plight of the poor and the efficacy of Utopian socialism) and embodies her 'highest convictions upon Life and Art'. The story traces Aurora's development as an artist in opposition to the active philanthropy of her cousin Romney. The resolution lies in the recognition by both cousins that each has placed too great an emphasis on limited aspects of man's character.

Austen, Jane 1775–1817 Novelist. She was born at Steventon in Hampshire where her father, who was also her tutor, was rector. On his retirement in 1801 the family moved to Bath, a city that frequently appears in her fiction, but returned to Hampshire after his death in 1805. With her mother and sister, she lived first in Southampton and then in Chawton, near Alton, remaining there until she died. Her life was conspicuous for its lack of event – allowing biographers to make it a study in quiet contemplation or quiet frustration – and for the strength of her family ties, most importantly with her sister Cassandra. She died in Winchester at the age of 41 and is buried in the cathedral.

She began her literary career at the age of 15 with *Love and Friendship*, a BURLESQUE of SAMUEL RICHARDSON; other pieces belonging to the 1790s caricature the excessive 'sensibility' fashionable in the 18th-century SENTIMENTAL NOVEL. Her eye for the ridiculous in contemporary taste also inspired *NORTHANGER ABBEY* (published posthumously in 1818 but probably her earliest extended work of fiction), which satirizes her heroine's penchant for GOTHIC FICTION, and *SENSE AND SENSIBILITY* (begun in 1797 but not published until 1811).

Begun in 1796 or 1797 and published after revision in 1813, *PRIDE AND PREJUDICE* has the same high spirits as its predecessors but, more clearly than they, marks out the territory, the subject and the mode of her mature work. It looks forward to her later novels: *MANSFIELD PARK* (begun 1811, published 1814), *EMMA* (begun 1814, published 1816) and *PERSUASION* (begun 1815, published posthumously in 1818). In these works she chose deliberately to portray small groups of people in a limited, perhaps confining, environment, and to mould the apparently trivial incidents of their lives into a poised comedy of manners. Her characters are middle-class and provincial; their most urgent preoccupation is with courtship and their largest ambition is marriage. The task she set herself required careful shaping of her material, delicate economy and precise deployment of IRONY to point the underlying moral commentary. She developed not by obvious enlargement of her powers but by the deepening subtlety and seriousness with which she worked inside the formal boundaries she had established.

Although her novels did not prove especially popular in her own day, *Emma* was reviewed favourably by SIR WALTER SCOTT and was dedicated to another admirer of her work, the Prince Regent. *Lady Susan*, an EPISTOLARY NOVEL, and *The Watsons* were not published until they appeared in the second edition of J. E. Austen Leigh's *Memoir of Jane Austen* (1871). The fragment of *SANDITON*, on which she was working in the last months of her life, was first published in 1925.

Austin, Alfred 1835–1913 Poet. An Imperialist and supporter of DISRAELI, he was joint editor of *The National Review* from 1883 and sole editor from 1887 to 1895. He published 20 volumes of poetry between 1871 and 1908, and was appointed POET LAUREATE in 1896, to general mockery. He was especially parodied for his ode on the Jameson Raid. His autobiography appeared in 1911.

Authorized Version, The See BIBLE IN ENGLISH.

Autocrat of the Breakfast Table, The A collection of essays, poems, and occasional pieces by OLIVER WENDELL HOLMES, first published in *THE ATLANTIC MONTHLY* in 1857–8 and in volume form in 1858. It takes the form of table talk in a Boston boarding house. Besides the autocrat (mouthpiece for Holmes's own wit and social commentary), those present at the breakfast table include the landlady, her daughter, a poor relation, a schoolmistress, a divinity student and an old gentleman.

Ave atque Vale An ELEGY by SWINBURNE to Baudelaire, based on a false report of the French poet's death. First published in *THE FORTNIGHTLY REVIEW* (1868), it was reprinted in the second series of *Poems and Ballads* (1878).

Avison, Margaret (Kirkland) 1918– Canadian poet. Her output has been small, consisting of contributions to magazines and the volumes *Winter Sun* (1960), *The Dumbfounding* (1966), *Sunblue* (1978) and *No Time* (1990). Nevertheless, she is recognized as one of Canada's finest poets, concentrating with delicate precision on imaginative perception in the bleak landscapes of the 20th century.

Avowynge of King Arthur, Sir Gawan, Sir Kaye, and Sir Bawdewyn of Bretan, The An anonymous poem in TAIL-RHYME stanzas, probably written *c.* 1425 in the North of England. No single source has been discovered. It describes the adventures of Arthur and his companions after they each make vows while hunting near Carlisle. The central figure is Bawdewyn, who undertakes never to be jealous of his wife, never to deny food to any man and not to fear death. See also ARTHURIAN LITERATURE.

Awakening, The A novel by KATE CHOPIN, published in 1899. Edna Pontellier, wife of a Creole speculator in Louisiana, is awakened by her flirtation with Robert Lebrun while spending the summer at Grand Isle. Questioning the roles of wife and mother she had previously fulfilled, she takes up painting, gains some financial independence and leaves the family home. After having an affair she again sees Lebrun, but the summons to help her friend Adele Ratignolle in childbirth provokes a crisis. In a last, desperate assertion of independence, she returns to Grand Isle and drowns herself.

Awdry, Rev. **W(ilbert) V(ere)** 1911– Writer of CHILDREN'S LITERATURE. The success of *The Three Railway Engines* (1945) spawned a series, including *Gordon, the Big Engine* (1953) and *Edward, the Blue Engine* (1954), in which the Fat Controller repeatedly tries to supervise the characters. Succeeding illustrators have maintained the idyllic tradition laid down by C. Reginald Dalby. *Starlight Express* (by Andrew Lloyd Webber and Richard Stilgoe; 1984) is a stage musical loosely based on Awdry's train characters.

Awkward Age, The A novel by HENRY JAMES, serialized in 1898–9 and published in volume form in 1899. It is written almost entirely in dialogue. Its heroine, Nanda Brookenham, is a 'knowing' young woman while her friend, Aggie, is a 'pure' young lady who has been strictly raised by her aunt, the Duchess. The action revolves around their relations with Mr Vanderbank and Mr Mitchett. Nanda loves Mr Vanderbank but, realizing that he does not return her feeling, graciously gives him up. Meanwhile, Mr Mitchett, who had hoped to marry Nanda, instead marries Aggie with the Duchess's encouragement. Nanda retires from the marriage market.

Awntyrs of Arthure at the Terne Wathelyne, The An alliterative late 14th-century poem written in Northern England or Scotland. Some have identified it with the *Awntyre of Gawayn* mentioned in ANDREW OF WYNTOUN's *Cronykil* (*c.* 1420) as the work of HUCHOWN OF THE AWLE RYALE. The Terne Wathelyne is Wadling Tarn near Hesket, Cumbria. Arthur appears only in the second of the two *awntyrs* (adventures), and Gawain is the central figure in each. In the first, Gawain and Dame Gaynoure (Guinevere) are confronted by the tormented spirit of Gaynoure's mother, who rises from the tarn to warn against the Queen's sins and prophesy the downfall of the court. The second adventure concerns Gawain's combat with Galleron of Galway, finally resolved by Arthur. Though some critics have seen the poem as two separate works brought together, the two adventures illuminate each other and share a moral criticism of Arthur's court. See also ARTHURIAN LITERATURE.

Awoonor, Kofi 1935– Ghanaian poet and novelist, formerly known as George Awoonor Williams. He writes in both English and Ewe. The poetry in *Rediscovery*

(1964), *Night of My Blood* (1971), *Ride Me Memory* (1973) and *The House by the Sea* (1978) tries to bridge modern and pre-colonial culture by combining the oral poetry of the Ewes with the influence of POUND and DYLAN THOMAS. He has also written *Guardians of the Sacred Word* (1974), about traditional Ewe poetry, and *The Breast of the Earth: A Survey of the History, Culture, and Literature of Africa* (1975). *This Earth, My Brother ...* (1972) is a novel about Ghana before and after independence.

Ayckbourn, Alan 1939– Playwright. Since *Relatively Speaking* (1967), his sharp-witted increasingly sour FARCES about middle-class anxiety and neurosis have transferred from Scarborough, where he directs the Stephen Joseph Theatre, to London with extraordinary critical acclaim. Outstanding among them are *How the Other Half Loves* (1969), *Absurd Person Singular* (1972), the trilogy grouped under the title *The Norman Conquests* (1973), *Bedroom Farce* (1975), *Joking Apart* (1978), *A Chorus of Disapproval* (1985), *A Small Family Business* (1987), *Henceforward ...* (1988) and *Man of the Moment* (1990).

Ayenbite of Inwyt A religious tract completed by Dan Michel of Northgate, Kent, in 1340, freely translated from *Le Somme des vices et des vertues* by Frère Lorens (1279). Its title means the 'again-biting' (remorse) of the 'inner wit' (conscience). It teaches good Christian living by discourses on the Ten Commandments, the 12 articles of the Creed, the seven deadly sins, the virtues, the art of death and the knowledge of good and evil. Unlike similar works, *Ayenbite* explains the vices and virtues by analysis rather than anecdote and EXEMPLUM.

Ayer, Sir **A(lfred) J(ules)** 1910–89 Philosopher. His professorial career was spent mainly at London and Oxford. His first book, *Language, Truth and Logic* (1936, revised 1946), provided a link between the logical positivism of the Vienna Circle and nascent English linguistic analysis. *The Problem of Knowledge* (1956) deals with questions of scepticism in philosophy. His autobiographies (1977, 1984) cover his varied social life as well as his intellectual career.

Ayrshire Legatees, The See GALT, JOHN.

Ayton [Aytoun], Sir **Robert** 1570–1638 Scottish poet. A friend of JONSON and HOBBES, Ayton was secretary to Anne of Denmark, JAMES I's queen, and then to Henrietta Maria. Fluent in several languages, he was probably the first Scot to write in the English of the south. His verses are popular with anthologists; best known is the song 'Should Old Acquaintance be Forgot', credited to him by James Watson in 1711. 'Auld Lang Syne', the melody to which BURNS's more famous version is sung, is an old Scots air and would have been known to Ayton.

Aytoun, William Edmonstoune 1818–65 Scottish poet and critic. He coined the term 'SPASMODIC' (see SPASMODIC SCHOOL OF POETRY) in unflattering description of the febrile Romantic verse of SYDNEY DOBELL, PHILIP JAMES BAILEY and ALEXANDER SMITH, whom he satirized in *Firmilian: or, The Student of Badajoz: A Spasmodic Tragedy* (1854). With Theodore Martin, he was author of the *Bon Gaultier Ballads* (1855), which contain parodies of TENNYSON and ELIZABETH BARRETT BROWNING. *Lays of the Scottish Cavaliers* (1849) and *The Ballads of Scotland* (1858) were extremely popular in their day.

B

Bab Ballads, The A series of humorous verses by W. S. GILBERT, originally contributed to *Fun* and other periodicals between 1862 and 1871, many with illustrations by the author. A first collected edition was published in 1868, *More Bab Ballads* in 1872, and a comprehensive edition in 1882. The ironic tone and many of the themes helped to form the characteristic style and content of Gilbert's lyrics for the SAVOY OPERAS.

Babbitt A novel by SINCLAIR LEWIS, published in 1922. It depicts the complacency and materialism of George F. Babbitt, a real-estate agent and representative middle-class family man from the city of Zenith in the American Midwest. Babbitt briefly rebels but soon finds the price of nonconformity too great and once again resigns himself to the superficial values of his business culture.

Babbitt, Irving 1865–1933 American scholar and critic. With Paul Elmer More he was a leading figure among the New Humanists, emphasizing the ethical component of art and rejecting more romantic ideals. His major works are *Literature and the American College* (1908), *The New Laokoön* (1910), *Masters of Modern French Criticism* (1912), *Rousseau and Romanticism* (1919), *Democracy and Leadership* (1924), *On Being Creative* (1932) and *The Spanish Character and Other Essays* (1940). His ideas influenced T. S. ELIOT, who was his student at Harvard.

Back to Methuselah: *A Metabiological Pentateuch* A play by SHAW, published in 1921 and produced in New York in 1922 and in Birmingham in 1923. Its five parts, each separately titled, stretch from the Garden of Eden to the year 21,920, allowing Shaw ample space to dramatize the essential opposition, in the development of human society, between stagnation and creative evolution. His aim was to demonstrate the capacity of humankind to will its own betterment.

Bacon, Sir Francis, 1st Viscount St Albans 1561–1626 Philosopher and essayist. A practising lawyer and MP, Bacon had to wait until the death of Elizabeth I before his ambition was rewarded. JAMES I appointed him Solicitor-General, Attorney-General, Lord Keeper of the Seal and, finally, Lord Chancellor in 1618. He was created Baron Verulam in the same year and Viscount St Albans in 1621. SIR EDWARD COKE, Bacon's fiercest opponent, successfully instigated a charge of corruption against him in 1621 and forced him into retirement, which he largely devoted to writing. His first works had been political: the *Temporis pastus masculus* (1584) outlined a policy of tolerance and moderation, but a *Letter of Advice to Queen Elizabeth* later advocated tough anti-Catholic measures. His *ESSAYS* grew from a volume of 10 in 1597 to 58 by 1625. After THE ADVANCEMENT OF LEARNING (1605) Bacon turned to Latin for *De sapientia veterum* (1609; translated by GORGES as *The Wisdom of the Ancients*, 1619), which sought to decipher the scientific, political and moral knowledge embodied in Greek myths and fables, and for the celebrated NOVUM ORGANUM (1620). He returned to English in *The History of the Reign of King Henry the Seventh* (1622) and *Apophthegms New and Old* (1624). Bacon's unpublished writings included *Sylva sylvarum: or, A Natural History* and an unfinished Utopian fiction, THE NEW ATLANTIS, both

published in 1627, the year after he died from a chill contracted while studying the properties of snow.

His works are suffused with the curiosity of a scientific mind and written in a concise, epigrammatic style. Bacon's greatest achievement is the programme of intellectual and scientific reform proposed under the title *Instauratio magna* ('Great Instauration'), begun in *The Advancement of Learning* and continued in *Novum organum* and *Sylva sylvarum*, as well as informing *The New Atlantis*. These works reject the older, Aristotelian structures of knowledge and seek to discover a new system of philosophic instruction based upon a clearer, empirical perception of nature. Ironically, it was Bacon's reputation for polymathic intelligence that gave rise to the so-called BACONIAN HERESY.

Bacon, Roger *c*. 1220–*c*. 1292 Philosopher and scientist. Born at either Ilchester in Somerset or Bisley in Gloucestershire, he worked in Paris and Oxford studying mathematics, optics, alchemy and astronomy as well as languages. As part of a projected encyclopaedia of all known science he produced the *Opus majus*, together with the *Opus minus* and *Opus tertium*, for Clement IV but the Pope's death in 1268 frustrated the project as well as Bacon's desire to see the sciences fully recognized by the university curriculum. He was imprisoned at some time between 1277 and 1279 on account of his unorthodox teaching, probably his attacks on scholasticism and his interest in alchemy and astrology. He acquired the title *doctor admirabilis* after his death, though exaggerated accounts of his experiments also made him a figure in popular literature (like FRIAR BACON AND FRIAR BUNGAY).

Baconian Heresy The theory that FRANCIS BACON wrote the works of SHAKESPEARE. Though derided by most professional Shakespearean scholars, it has enjoyed a considerable vogue with amateur investigators, particularly in the closing years of the 19th and the early years of the 20th century. Their case rests on a variety of arguments. As a rustic from Stratford, Shakespeare is seen as too boorishly illiterate to make a poet; Francis Bacon, on the other hand, was a man of admittedly wide learning with reason to conceal any involvement in the contemporary theatre. Linguistic similarities between Bacon and Shakespeare's work are enumerated, and cryptogrammatic references to Bacon's name discovered in the text of the plays. The attack on Shakespeare the man has also been used to serve rival theories attributing authorship to the Earls of Derby and Oxford, to a committee including either or both of these peers, and even to MARLOWE.

Bage, Robert 1728–1801 Novelist. As well as running a paper-mill at Elford, near Tamworth, he produced six novels expressing radical views of politics and society: *Mount Henneth* (1781), *Barham Downs* (1784), *The Fair Syrian* (1787), *James Wallace* (1788), *Man As He Is* (1792) and *Hermsprong: or, Man As He is Not* (1796). In the last, Bage's most important work, Hermsprong claims to be an American Indian, and has fixed views on the importance of physical fitness, the corruption of the rich, and the necessity of female education and of equality. At the end he proves to be acceptable in polite society. SIR WALTER SCOTT deplored Bage's political and atheistic tendencies but commended his humour, very much in the vein of STERNE, and his command of dialogue. In his private life he was, according to Scott, an impeccable exemplar of his beliefs.

Bagehot, Walter 1826–77 Political thinker, economist and literary critic. *The English Constitution* (1867) is a classic appraisal of the workings of government. *Physics or Politics* (1872) attempts to relate contemporary theories of natural selection and inheritance to the workings of the state. *Lombard Street* (1873) and *Economic Studies* (edited by R. H. HUTTON, 1880) examine the money market and commerce. Bagehot's literary criticism, in *Estimates of Some Englishmen and Scotchmen* (1858) and *Literary Studies* (edited by Hutton, 1879), adopts the same stance of the worldly, moderate man which marks his approach to economic and political affairs.

Bagnold, Enid 1889–1981 Playwright and novelist. Her first success was with a novel, *Serena Blandish* (1925), later dramatized by S. N. BEHRMAN. She herself dramatized a more famous novel, *National Velvet* (1935), about a girl who wins the Grand National; it also became a popular film. *Lottie Dundas* was both a novel (1941) and a play (1943). *The Chalk Garden* (1955), a social comedy, was her last success in the theatre.

Bail, Murray 1941– Australian short-story writer and novelist. Widely regarded as one of the most cosmopolitan of contemporary Australian writers, he frequently adopts a playful, Borgesian stance to take issue with the tradition of REALISM in the Australian short story. The title-piece of *The Drover's Wife and Other Stories* (1986) is ostensibly a response to Russell Drysdale's painting but implicitly an ironic rebuttal of the classic HENRY LAWSON story with the same title. His novels include *Homesickness* (1980), about tourism, and *Holden's Performance* (1987), a comic epic about the passage of an innocent through Australian society. Non-fictional works are *Longhand* (1989), a diary of his years in London, and a study of the artist Ian Fairweather (1981).

Bailey, Philip James 1816–1902 Poet. 'Festus' Bailey gained his nickname and brief reputation with *Festus* (1839; grossly enlarged until 1889), an overheated blank-verse epic based on the Faust legend. Originally praised by the reviewers, it was effectively ridiculed by WILLIAM AYTOUN, who identified Bailey as father of the SPASMODIC SCHOOL OF POETRY.

Baillie, Joanna 1762–1851 Poet and playwright. The first volume of her *Plays on the Passions* (1798–1812) included *De Montfort*, in which Mrs Siddons enjoyed considerable success in 1800. Her most notable collections of verse appeared as *Fugitive Verses* (1790) and *Metrical Legends* (1821). She was a close friend of SIR WALTER SCOTT.

Bain, Alexander 1818–1903 Philosopher. Professor of Logic at Aberdeen from 1860, as well as a friend of JOHN STUART MILL and biographer of JAMES MILL (1882), he developed the ideas of UTILITARIANISM in his own writings. They include *The Senses and the Intellect* (1855), *The Emotions and the Will* (1859), *Mental and Moral Science* (1868) and *Logic* (1870).

Bainbridge, Beryl 1934– Novelist. Works such as *The Dressmaker* (1973), *The Bottle Factory Outing* (1974), *Injury Time* (1977), *Mum and Mrs Armitage* (1985), *Filthy Lucre* (1986) and *An Awfully Big Adventure* (1989) are terse black comedies dealing in menace and grotesque violence. Several novels tackle historical subjects: Hitler's possible stay in Liverpool in *Young Adolf* (1978); a Victorian murder case in *Watson's Apology* (1984); and Captain Scott's expedition in *The Birthday Boys* (1991).

Baker, Father Augustine 1571–1641 Catholic mystic and author of more than 40 treatises, or 'Directions for the Prayer of Contemplation'. His work was published posthumously as the *Sancta Sophia* (1657), a kind of Catholic parallel to TRAHERNE's *Centuries of Meditations*.

Baker, Nicholson 1957– American novelist. *The Mezzanine* (1988), *Room Temperature* (1990) and *U and I* (1991), in which the 'U' is JOHN UPDIKE, are less conventional novels than fantastic speculations on reality and, especially, its minute interstices. *Vox* (1992) and *The Fermata* (1993) abandon delightful, if self-obsessed, whimsy for controversial sexual explicitness.

Baldwin, James (Arthur) 1924–87 Black American novelist, playwright and essayist.

The promise of his first novel, *Go Tell It on the Mountain* (1953), reflecting his relations with his father, a Harlem preacher, was fulfilled in later work showing him to be a powerful enemy of racism. After *Giovanni's Room* (1956), set in Paris, where he lived, he returned to black America as a setting. *Another Country* (1962) takes place in Harlem. Other fiction includes *Going to Meet the Man* (1965), *Tell Me How Long the Train's Been Gone* (1968), *If Beale Street Could Talk* (1974) and *Just above My Head* (1979). His essays appeared in *Notes of a Native Son* (1955), *Nobody Knows My Name: More Notes of a Native Son* (1961; as *No Name in the Streets* in Britain, 1972), *The Fire Next Time* (1963), *The Devil Finds Work* (1976), *The Evidence of Things Not Seen: An Essay* (1985) and *The Price of the Ticket: Collected Nonfiction, 1948–1985* (1986). His plays are: *Blues for Mr Charlie* (1964), *The Amen Corner* (1965), *One Day, When I was Lost* (1972) and *A Deed from the King of Spain* (produced 1974). *Jimmy's Blues* (1986) is a volume of poetry.

Baldwin, Joseph G(lover) 1815–64 American jurist. *The Flush Times of Alabama and Mississippi* (1853) is a collection of anecdotes about frontier law, combining serious portraits with comic tales. The latter pieces, which remain better-known, include 'Ovid Bolus, Esq.', about a chronic liar, and 'Simon Suggs, Jr, Esq.: A Legal Biography', about a dishonest lawyer. Baldwin also published *Party Leaders* (1855), containing studies of JEFFERSON, Alexander Hamilton and Andrew Jackson.

Bale, John 1495–1563 Playwright. His Protestant polemics earned him the patronage of Thomas Cromwell, for whose troupe of itinerant players Bale wrote several anti-Catholic plays between 1537 and Cromwell's fall in 1540. Of the five surviving ones, four are MORALITY PLAYS in an already well-established style but the fifth, *King John*, despite using abstract characters as Dissimulation, Private Wealth and Sedition, looks forward to the English history plays of MARLOWE and SHAKESPEARE in its portraits of the King, Stephen Langton and Cardinal Pandulphus. Unlike Shakespeare's, Bale's King John is an idealized Christian hero battling with the Pope. Bale's historical researches brought him in contact with the antiquary LELAND, whom he mentions in *King John*.

Balfour, Arthur James, 1st Earl of Balfour 1848–1930 Politician and philosopher. He was leader of the Conservative Party (1902–11), Prime Minister (1902–5) and Foreign Secretary (1916–19). *A Defence of Philosophic Doubt* (1879), *The Foundation of Belief* (1895) and his two series of Gifford Lectures, *Theism and Humanism* (1915) and *Theism and Thought* (1923), rest on his belief that the ultimate convictions of mankind depend on religious faith and are not susceptible to the probing of logic and science. He became President of the Society for Psychical Research in 1893.

ballad Two main types are to be distinguished, the least unsatisfactory names perhaps being 'traditional' and 'street'. There is no proof that the first is earlier than the second, though internal evidence points that way. Both have been transmitted mainly through printed BROADSIDES (the earliest known example dating from 1513), both have influenced major poets and been imitated by them, but as a popular creative form the traditional ballad seems unlikely to have been composed after the 16th century, while street ballads are still being composed today. The difference may be summed up as follows: the former, deriving from a pre-literate rural community, tended to be tragic, romantic and heroic, telling a story in arbitrary fragments, whereas the latter, developing with the growth of towns and the printing press, tended to be comic, realistic and unheroic, telling a more leisurely and circumstantial story. All ballads, of whatever type, must not only tell a story in verse but also lend themselves to being sung. These two conditions imply a third: the narrative and style must be simple enough to be followed at a hearing. So most, but by no means all, ballads use a simple metre: QUATRAINS of alternating lines of iambic tetrameter and iambic trimeter.

Ballad of Reading Gaol, The A poem by OSCAR WILDE, published in 1898, about the hanging of a murderer, Charles Thomas Wooldridge, while Wilde was himself a convict. Its harsh eloquence is in contrast to the aestheticism of Wilde's earlier poems, but shows the same technical control. It concludes with a plea for Christ's forgiveness and a protest against prison conditions.

ballad opera A dramatic form pioneered by GAY, whose *BEGGAR'S OPERA* (1728) was the most popular play of the 18th century. Designed to counteract imported Italian opera, it presented a combination of FARCE, PANTOMIME, street literature, lyrics and musical comedy, salted with topical SATIRE.

ballade An Old French verse form, consisting of three eight-line STANZAS, rhyming ababbcbC, and a four-line envoy, rhyming bcbC (the capital letter indicating that the line is used as a refrain). They are not common in English, and even the best examples – by CHAUCER and SWINBURNE – fall far short of François Villon.

Ballantyne, R(obert) M(ichael) 1825–94 Scottish writer of CHILDREN'S LITERATURE. His first adventure story for boys, *The Young Fur-Traders* (1856), was based on his experiences working for the Hudson's Bay Company. Many of the more than 80 books he went on to publish draw on first-hand knowledge in the same fashion: three weeks on Bell Rock led to *The Lighthouse* (1865) and a short spell as a London fireman to *Fighting the Flames* (1867). His most famous title, *The Coral Island* (1858), describes how three young friends – Ralph, Jack and Peterkin – survive after being shipwrecked. A sequel, *The Gorilla Hunters* (1861), is disturbing in its enthusiasm for slaughtering wild animals. Such elements in Ballantyne's work, and his obtrusive piety, have guaranteed that his immense contemporary popularity should have faded. Yet his influence is still obliquely acknowledged, most memorably by WILLIAM GOLDING in his pessimistic reworking of *Coral Island* in LORD OF THE FLIES.

Ballard, J(ames) G(raham) 1930– Novelist and short-story writer. Novels such as *The Drowned World* (1962), *The Drought* (1965) and *The Crystal World* (1966), and the short stories in *The Four-Dimensional Nightmare* (1963) and *The Terminal Beach* (1964), are *avant-garde* SCIENCE FICTION, anticipating the more extreme experimentalism of *The Atrocity Exhibition* (1970), a collection of 'fragmented novels', and *Crash* (1973). However, Ballard is now best known for the semi-autobiographical realism of *Empire of the Sun* (1984), drawing on his boyhood experience of a Japanese internment camp in Shanghai during World War II, and its sequel, *The Kindness of Women* (1991), set in post-war Britain.

Bancroft, George 1800–91 American historian. A Jacksonian Democrat, he held a variety of government positions: Secretary of the Navy (1845–6), Minister to England (1846–9) and Minister to Germany (1867–74). His life's work, the 10-volume *History of the United States* (1834–75), tells the story of the progressive tendency towards liberty exemplified by American history, culminating in the American Revolution. Highly nationalistic in viewpoint and resoundingly rhetorical in style, it was popular in its day.

Banim, John 1798–1842 Irish playwright and novelist. He collaborated with his elder brother MICHAEL BANIM on *Tales by the O'Hara Family* (1825–7). His tragedy *Damon and Pythias* was produced at COVENT GARDEN in 1821, and his satirical essays, *Revelations of the Dead Alive*, appeared in 1824.

Banim, Michael 1796–1874 Irish novelist. He collaborated with his younger brother JOHN BANIM in *Tales by the O'Hara Family* (1825–7). *The Croppy* (1828) is a novel set in the Irish rebellion of 1798. Other fiction includes *Father Connell* (1842) and *The Town of the Cascades* (1864).

Bannatyne, George 1545–?1608 Anthologist. The 'Bannatyne Manuscript', his anthology of 15th- and 16th-century Scottish poetry, contains work by DUNBAR, HENRYSON and SIR DAVID LINDSAY, as well as minor poets (like Alexander Scot) who would otherwise be unknown, and anonymous writers. It influenced the 18th-century revival of interest in Scottish poetry. The Bannatyne Club was founded in Edinburgh in 1823, under the presidency of SIR WALTER SCOTT, to encourage the study of Scottish history and literature.

Bannerman, Helen (Brodie Cowan) 1862–1946 Writer and illustrator of CHILDREN'S LITERATURE. Her first and most famous book, *The Story of Little Black Sambo* (1890), was followed by titles such as *Little Black Mingo* (1902), *Little Black Quibba* (1902) and *Little Black Quasha* (1908). Earlier arguments over their relish for violent incident has been overshadowed by the charge of racism. Little Black Sambo has been particularly criticized for his name and his guileless enjoyment of bright new clothes.

Baraka, (Imamu) Amiri 1934– Black American playwright, poet, novelist and essayist. Born LeRoi Jones, he changed his name on converting to Islam in 1965. A prominent voice in the black movement since the mid-1950s, he established his reputation with plays – *A Good Girl is Hard to Find* (1958), *Dante* (1961; adapted as a novel, *The System of Dante's Hell*, 1965), *DUTCHMAN* (1964), *The Slave* (1964) and *Slave Ship: A Historical Pageant* (1967) – dealing with black–white relations and using drama as a weapon against racism. *The Baptism* (1964) and *The Toilet* (1964) explore personal identity. After 1974 his separatist fervour gave way to a commitment to the overthrow, by blacks and whites alike, of an oppressive capitalist system. Plays like *S-1* (1976), *The Motion of History* (1977) and *What was the Relationship of the Lone Ranger to the Means of Production?* (1979) exemplify this stage of his career. *Selected Poems* (1979) reprints most of his best verse.

Barbauld, Anna Laetitia 1743–1825 Editor, poet and anthologist. She collaborated with her brother, JOHN

AIKIN, on two collections of essays, mainly on literary topics, *Miscellaneous Pieces* (1773) and the six-volume *Evenings at Home* (1792–6); published a collection of poems (1773) and produced the didactic, highly successful *Hymns in Prose for Children* (1781). Her 50-volume anthology, *The British Novelists* (1810), is introduced by a lengthy and intelligently argued essay 'On the Origin and Progress of Novel-writing' and includes important biographical and critical notices. Possibly her most important contribution to literature was her six-volume edition of SAMUEL RICHARDSON's correspondence (1804), never superseded. Her own slightly less voluminous correspondence throws interesting light on contemporary literary and moral concerns.

Barbellion, W. N. P. [Bruce Frederick Cummings] 1889–1919 Diarist. *The Journal of a Disappointed Man*, covering the years 1903–17, was published a few months before his death as extracts from the diaries of Wilhelm Nero Pilate Barbellion. It reveals a brave, intelligent personality whose ambitions and aspirations are bedevilled by lack of opportunity and disseminated sclerosis. *A Last Diary* (1920) gives additional information.

Barbour, John *c.* 1320–95 Scottish poet. Barbour spent most of his life in his native Aberdeen, becoming Clerk of Audit and Auditor of the Exchequer to Robert II in 1372. *THE BRUCE* gives a patriotic account of Robert the Bruce (Robert I). *The Brut* (about the mythical history of Britain from its foundation by Brutus) and *The Stewartis Original* (tracing the pedigree of the Stewarts from Banquo) are lost, though a record of them survives in ANDREW OF WYNTOUN's *Orygynale Cronykil*.

Barchester Towers The second of TROLLOPE's BARSETSHIRE NOVELS, published in 1857. When the Bishop of Barchester dies the fall of the Conservative ministry means that he is succeeded not by his son, Archdeacon Grantly, but by the timeserving Dr Proudie, who arrives with his Low Church wife and evangelical chaplain Obadiah Slope. Battle is joined between them and Grantly's traditionalists. Mrs Proudie wants to appoint Quiverful to the wardenship of Hiram's Hospital but Slope, attracted to the newly widowed Eleanor Bold, supports the reappointment of her father Mr Harding. However, Slope becomes infatuated with the crippled Signora Neroni, daughter of Dr Vesey Stanhope, falls out with Mrs Proudie and is dismissed by the Bishop. Quiverful is appointed to the wardenship. Eleanor rejects both Slope and the charming wastrel Bertie Stanhope for the shy Francis Arabin, Dr Grantly's High Church champion, who becomes Dean of Barchester.

Barclay, Alexander ?1475–1552 Poet and translator. Originally a priest and monk, Barclay survived the Reformation to hold Protestant livings. A prolific translator, his most important works were his translation of Sebastian Brant's *Das Narrenschiff* as *The Ship of Fools* (1509) and his *Egloges*, from the work of Aeneas Piccolomini (Pope Pius II) and the pastorals of Mantuan. *The Ship of Fools* is ESTATES SATIRE, containing an attack on SKELTON. The *Egloges* are important as early English attempts at the PASTORAL form used by SPENSER in *THE SHEPHEARDES CALENDER*.

Barclay, John 1582–1621 Miscellaneous writer in Latin. His *Euphormionis Satyricon* (1603–7) is an episodic collection of satire, adventures and discourses modelled on Petronius. *Icon Animorum* (1614), translated by MAY as *The Mirror of Minds* (1631), is a book of essays on national and temperamental types. *Argenis* (1621) is an allegorical

romance with a contemporary setting, many times translated.

Barclay, Robert 1648–90 Quaker apologist. He joined the movement in 1667 and became its leading theologian. His Latin apologia was translated as *Apology for the True Christian Religion, as the Same is Set Forth and Preached by the People Called in Scorn 'Quakers'* (1678). Barclay was held in favour by James II, and assisted PENN in founding Pennsylvania; he was appointed governor of East New Jersey in 1683.

Barfoot, Joan 1946– Canadian novelist. *Abra* (1978; reissued in Britain as *Gaining Ground*, 1980), *Dancing in the Dark* (1982), *Duet for Three* (1985) and *Family News* (1990) are women-centred fictions which present female protagonists isolated by choice, insanity or old age from defining social contexts.

Barham, Rev. R(ichard) H(arris) 1788–1845 Poet and novelist. A friend of THACKERAY, DICKENS, SAMUEL ROGERS and SYDNEY SMITH, he achieved fame only with *The Ingoldsby Legends*, appearing in *BENTLEY'S MISCELLANY* and *The New Monthly Magazine* from 1837 onwards and in various collections from 1840. These humorous mock-medieval BALLADS are interesting mainly as a repository of early 19th-century slang and as precursors of the work of W. S. GILBERT in their outrageous rhymes and lively anapaestic rhythms.

Baring, Maurice 1874–1945 Novelist and playwright. Closely associated with BELLOC and CHESTERTON, he produced several novels, *Passing By* (1921), *C* (1924) and *Cat's Cradle* (1925), and a novella, *The Lonely Lady of Dulwich* (1934), often cited as his best work. His plays include *The Black Prince* (1902) and *Diminutive Dramas* (1911). Two historical tales, *Robert Peckham* (1930) and *In My End is My Beginning* (1931), show the influence of Roman Catholicism, to which he became a convert. His experience as a diplomat and journalist in Moscow is reflected in several works on Russian literature, which helped to introduce the works of Chekhov. *The Puppet Show of Memory* (1922) is an autobiography.

Baring-Gould, Sabine 1834–1924 Novelist, amateur antiquary and writer of hymns. He was rector of Lewtrenchard in Devon for the last 40 years of his life. His first novel, *Through Fire and Flame* (1868), describing his marriage to a mill girl in 1867, was followed by over 30 others, of which *Mehalan* (1880) is often considered most noteworthy. Among his non-fictional works were several volumes of *The Lives of the Saints* (1872–7), a biography of R. S. HAWKER, *The Vicar of Morwenstow* (1876), and numerous works of travel, folklore and local legend (see FOLK REVIVAL). His many hymns included 'Onward Christian Soldiers'.

Barker, George (Granville) 1913–91 Poet. The facile rhetoric of *Thirty Preliminary Poems* (1933), *Poems* (1935) and *Calamiterror* (1937) prompted a comparison with DYLAN THOMAS and the NEW APOCALYPSE movement which dogged him throughout his career. His language became progressively limpid in *Lament and Triumph* (1940), *Eros in Dogma* (1944), *News of the World* (1950) and his first masterpiece, the notorious *True Confession of George Barker* (1950), omitted from *Collected Poems 1930–1955* (1957). Later volumes, which include another masterpiece, *Anno Domini* (1983), and frequently show his mastery of the ELEGY as well as autobiographical forms, were gathered in *Collected Poems* (1987). *Street Ballads* appeared posthumously in 1992. He also published *Essays* (1970) and novels, including *The Dead Seagull* (1950).

Barker, Harley Granville See GRANVILLE-BARKER, HARLEY.

Barker, Howard 1946– Playwright. His first plays looked at British society from the stance of the underworld as well as the underdog: twin gangsters in *Alpha Alpha* (1972), pimps in *Claw* (1975) and a criminal who invades the house of his judge in *Stripwell* (1975). Barker is adept at reversing moral expectations: the prison governor in *The Hang of the Gaol* (1978) becomes an arsonist, while an entrepreneur of graveyard mementoes is the hero of *The Love of a Good Man*. *No End of Blame* (1981) debates censorship, East and West. Work for other media includes *Scenes from an Execution* (radio, 1984; staged 1988).

Barker, James Nelson 1784–1858 American playwright. Only five of his 10 plays have survived: *Tears and Smiles* (1807), a comedy of manners; *The Indian Princess: or, La Belle Sauvage* (1808; produced in London as *Pocahontas: or, The Indian Princess*, 1820), the first extant play to deal with American-Indian life; *Marmion: or, The Battle of Flodden Field* (1812), an adaptation of SIR WALTER SCOTT, made successful by its implicit criticism of the British stance towards the United States during the war of 1812; *How to Try a Lover* (published 1817; produced as *The Court of Love*, 1836), a romantic comedy adapted from a French novel; and *Superstition: or, The Fanatic Father* (1824), a verse tragedy about Puritan intolerance.

Barlaam and Josaphat A 14th-century SAINT'S LIFE written in Middle English and based on a story which appears in the *Legenda aurea* (later translated by CAXTON as *The Golden Legend*). Barlaam fulfils a prophecy by converting Josaphat, son of a heathen king, who then converts his dying father, gives up his kingdom and ends his life as a hermit.

Barlow, Joel 1754–1812 American poet. He is best remembered as one of the CONNECTICUT WITS and a contributor to their most notable production, *The Anarchiad* (1786–7), a satire in MOCK-HEROIC verse attacking democratic liberalism in favour of federalist conservatism. His 17 years in France estranged him from the group and turned him into a champion of democracy. The change is evident in three political pamphlets of the 1790s – *Advice to the Privileged Orders*, *The Conspiracy of Kings* and *A Letter to the National Convention of France* – and the transformation of his youthful EPIC poem in HEROIC COUPLETS, *The Vision of Columbus*, into *The Columbiad* (1807). The first version affirms America's manifest destiny by offering an essentially conservative vision congenial to Federalists of the new republic. The second, expanded and copiously annotated, is the work of a liberal democrat. His *Hasty Pudding* (1796) is a mock epic celebrating the native American dish and 'simplicity of diet'.

Barnaby Rudge A novel by DICKENS, published in MASTER HUMPHREY'S CLOCK in 1841. It is set during the Gordon or 'No Popery' riots (1780), which provide the most vivid episodes in what is otherwise one of Dickens's least successful works. Part of the plot derives from the unsolved murder of Reuben Haredale 20 years earlier. The villain is finally identified as his former steward, Mr Rudge. He is hanged and his son Barnaby, a half-crazed youth unwittingly drawn into the riots, only narrowly escapes the gallows. Another strand of the action concerns the hostility between Reuben's brother Geoffrey and the villainous Mr (later Sir John) Chester, who are nevertheless agreed in opposing a match between Chester's son Edward and Geoffrey's niece, Emma. Chester dies in a duel with Geoffrey. A rich cast of characters also includes: the beguiling Dolly Varden, her father Gabriel and suitor Joe Willet, and Joe's obstinate old father John; the ludicrous Simon Tappertit; and Dennis, the despicable hangman.

Barnes, Barnabe ?1569–1609 Poet and playwright. Son of the Bishop of Durham, he had an eventful life, travelling with Essex to Normandy (1591) and being arraigned before the Star Chamber for poisoning (1598). His poetic works are his SONNET sequence *Parthenophil and Parthenope* (?1594) and *A Divine Century of Spiritual Sonnets* (1595). He wrote one prose work, *Four Books of Offices* (1606). One play, *The Battle of Hexham*, is lost but *The Devil's Charter* (1607), an anti-Catholic portrayal of Pope Alexander VI, survives.

Barnes, Djuna 1892–1982 American novelist, playwright and poet. Her best-known work is the novel *Nightwood* (1936), about the relationships of a group of expatriates in Paris and Berlin. Other works include: *The Book of Repulsive Women* (1915), a collection of poems; *A Book* (1923), stories and plays, the stories revised and reissued as *A Night among the Horses* (1929) and later still as *Spillway* (1972); *Ryder* (1929), a satiric chronicle of family history; *Ladies' Almanack* (1929), a celebration of lesbian life and love; and *The Antiphon* (1958), a blank-verse tragedy about family history.

Barnes, Julian 1946– Novelist. *Metroland* (1981) and *Before She Met Me* (1982) combine flamboyant WIT with a psychological sensitivity recalling Flaubert, the oblique subject of *Flaubert's Parrot* (1984), a highly original mixture of biography, speculation and fantasy. *Staring at the Sun* (1986) and the more elegantly accomplished *A History of the World in 10½ Chapters* (1989) are comparably heterogeneous, ranging through history and diverse literary modes. *Talking It Over* (1991) returns to a realistic idiom, and *The Porcupine* (1992) is a novella about a political trial in a former Soviet satellite country.

Barnes, Juliana See THE BOOK OF ST ALBANS.

Barnes, Peter 1931– Playwright. *Sclerosis* (1965), an attack on British colonialism, was followed by *The Ruling Class* (1968), which contained many distinguishing features of his style: fierce PARODY of the upper classes, rapid changes of mood and a delight in rhetoric. Subsequent plays have made moral and historical themes the subjects for black comedy: the Spanish Succession in *The Bewitched* (1974), the Holocaust in *Laughter!* (1978) and the Black Death in *Red Noses* (1985). *Barnes' People* (1981, 1983, 1986) is a series of radio monologues. Despising NATURALISM, he looks back to JONSON, the Jacobeans and Wedekind, all of whom he has adapted for the modern stage.

Barnes, William 1801–86 Dialect poet and philologist. He was a schoolteacher and, from 1862 until his death, rector of Winterbourne Came, near Dorchester. His philological writings, notably *Tiw: or A View of the Roots and Stems of English as a Teutonic Tongue* (1861), reject imported foreign words and advocate a return to pure Anglo-Saxon English. Barnes turned to the speech of his native county in his three collections of *Poems in the Dorset Dialect* (1844, 1859, 1862). His command of folk idiom and lyric form gave his poetry more than a philological value, and helped attract a distinguished, if small, circle of admirers which included THOMAS HARDY.

Barnfield, Richard 1574–1627 Poet. A friend of DRAYTON and THOMAS WATSON, he was the author of *The Affectionate Shepherd* (1594), a series of homoerotic

ECLOGUES; *Cynthia*, published together with 20 sonnets in 1595; and a satire, *The Encomion of Lady Pecunia* (1598), in mock-praise of money. Two of his poems appeared in *THE PASSIONATE PILGRIM* (1599).

Barrack-Room Ballads and Other Verses A collection of poems by KIPLING, published in 1892. It contains some of Kipling's most popular verse, as do later collections which also deal with the life of the British soldier overseas: *The Seven Seas* (1896), *The Five Nations* (1903) and *The Years Between* (1919). Looking beneath the patriotic surface of poems like 'The Widow at Windsor', recent criticism has begun to acknowledge the satirical force and originality of Kipling's depiction of the harsh life of the ill-paid common soldier. He gives the DRAMATIC MONOLOGUE popular force with Irish, Scottish and Cockney accents, invoking the traditions of the BALLAD and street-song, the hymn tune and (in 'Mandalay') its music-hall song. *The Complete Barrack-Room Ballads of Rudyard Kipling*, collected by Charles Carrington, was published in 1973.

Barrett, Elizabeth See BROWNING, ELIZABETH BARRETT.

Barrie, Sir **J(ames) M(atthew)** 1860–1937 Scottish playwright and novelist. He described the early encouragement he received from his mother in his admiring biography of her, *Margaret Ogilvy* (1896). He called his native Kirriemuir 'Thrums' in a series of homely stories and novels which identified him as a member of the KAILYARD SCHOOL: *Auld Licht Idylls* (1888), *A Window in Thrums* (1889) and *The Little Minister* (1891). Subsequent work included *Sentimental Tommy* (1896) and *Tommy and Grizel* (1900). Theatrical recognition came with a dramatization of *The Little Minister* in 1897, *QUALITY STREET* and *THE ADMIRABLE CRICHTON* in 1902, and his overwhelming triumph, *PETER PAN*, in 1904. A story, *Peter Pan in Kensington*, appeared in 1906. It is unfortunate that Barrie has become so identified with Peter Pan. He was too ready to resort to cloying fantasy, as he did again in *Dear Brutus* (1917) and *Mary Rose* (1920), but although his solutions were characteristically sentimental, the problems he investigated were real enough. There is a shrewd feeling for the theatre in *WHAT EVERY WOMAN KNOWS* (1908), the single completed act of *Shall We Join the Ladies?* (1921) and the excellent one-act comedy *The Twelve-Pound Look* (1910).

Barrow, Isaac 1630–77 Divine. First fellow and then Master of Trinity College, Cambridge, he resigned the Lucasian Professorship of Mathematics to his pupil, NEWTON, in 1669, preferring to concentrate on theological studies. His sermons were famous for their reasonable views in an age of pious recrimination. *Exposition of the Creed, Decalogue and Sacraments* (1669) was published during his lifetime; theological works edited after his death include *A Treatise on the Pope's Supremacy* (1680). COLERIDGE praised his prose syle.

Barry, Philip 1896–1949 American playwright. Several of his plays – such as *Holiday* (1929), *Tomorrow and Tomorrow* (1931), and *The Animal Kingdom* (1932) – are comedies puncturing the snobbish pretensions of wealthy society. His other works include *Here Come the Clowns* (1938), *The Philadelphia Story* (1939), *Liberty Jones* (1941) and *The Foolish Notion* (1945). *Second Threshold*, another comedy, unfinished at his death, was completed in 1951 by ROBERT SHERWOOD.

Barry Lyndon A novel by THACKERAY, serialized as *The Luck of Barry Lyndon* in 1844 and revised and reprinted as *The Memoirs of Barry Lyndon* in 1852. A notable contribution to rogue literature, and a sustained exercise in the use of the unreliable narrator, it is the boastful autobiography of an 18th-century Irish adventurer. Born Redmond Barry, he fights a duel, escapes to Dublin and changes his name to Barry Redmond. He serves as a soldier on both sides in the Seven Years War, eventually meeting his uncle, Cornelius Barry, who as the Chevalier de Balibari joins him in cardsharping. He marries the wealthy Countess of Lyndon, changes his name to Barry Lyndon and embarks on a career of cruelty and extravagance. With the death of his son Bryan in a riding accident, Barry's luck starts to run out, and after Lady Lyndon's death he ends his life in the Fleet prison, tended by his faithful old mother.

Barsetshire Novels, The A sequence of novels by ANTHONY TROLLOPE, set in the fictional West Country county of Barsetshire, or Barset, and particularly the cathedral city of Barchester, whose clergy are the main characters. It consists of *THE WARDEN* (1855), *BARCHESTER TOWERS* (1857), *DOCTOR THORNE* (1858), *FRAMLEY PARSONAGE* (1860–1), *THE SMALL HOUSE AT ALLINGTON* (1862–4) and *THE LAST CHRONICLE OF BARSET* (1866–7).

Barstow, Stan(ley) 1928– Novelist. Although he has written many novels about Yorkshire life, he remains best known for his first, *A Kind of Loving* (1960), an example of the working-class realist fiction developed by JOHN BRAINE and ALAN SILLITOE.

Barth, John (Simmons) 1930– American novelist and short-story writer. *The Floating Opera* (1956), about a nihilist contemplating suicide, is informed by the sense of the absurd which has coloured all his work. Other fiction, fluent in pastiche and helping to establish POSTMODERNISM by its narrative contingency, includes *The End of the Road* (1958), *The Sot-Weed Factor* (1960), *Giles Goat-Boy: or, The Revised New Syllabus* (1966), *Lost in the Fun-house* (1968), *Chimera* (1972), *Letters* (1979), *Sabbatical* (1982), *The Tidewater Tales* (1987) and *The Last Voyage of Somebody the Sailor* (1991).

Barthelme, Donald 1931–89 American short-story writer and novelist. His novels, notably *Snow White* (1967) and *The Dead Father* (1975), are deliberately fragmented narratives made up of word games and allusions to literature and popular culture. His collections of stories – *Come Back, Dr Caligari* (1964), *Unspeakable Practices, Unnatural Acts* (1968), *City Life* (1970), *Guilty Pleasures* (1974) and *Amateurs* (1976) – also pursued a satiric commentary on contemporary American life and language.

Bartholomew Fair A comedy by JONSON, first performed in 1614 but not published until 1631. Jonson makes the annual fair held at Smithfield on St Bartholomew's Day (24 August) the setting for one of his most adventurous and original plays, less intent on correcting than simply observing the folly and villainy of his contemporaries. Adam Overdo, a justice, comes to spy out the fair's iniquities and is engulfed by them. The country squire, Bartholomew Cokes, brings his lively betrothed, Grace Wellborn, but is easily outwitted by her rival suitors, Winwife and Quarlus, and robbed of everything. His servant, the satirical Waspe, ends up in the stocks. So does the hypocritical Puritan Zeal-of-the-Land Busy, drawn like all the other characters, but more greedily, to the stall of the foul-mouthed pig-woman, Ursula, whose roast pork and small beer attract the crowds.

Bartleby the Scrivener See *PIAZZA TALES, THE*.

Barton, Bernard 1784–1849 Poet. Although collections

such as *Metrical Effusions* (1812), *Poems* (1820) and *Devotional Verses* (1826) secured him a steady following as a writer of homely and unaffected religious verse, he is now hardly read and is chiefly remembered for his friendship with SOUTHEY and LAMB, who was intrigued by his staunch Quakerism. EDWARD FITZGERALD wrote Barton's biography (1849) and made an unhappy marriage with his daughter.

Bartram, John (1699–1777) and **Bartram, William** (1729–1823) American naturalists and travellers. A Philadelphia Quaker, John Bartram went on various expeditions in his official capacity as botanist for the American colonies, publishing *Observations on the Inhabitants, Climate, Soil ... Made by John Bartram in his Travels from Pensilvania to Lake Ontario* (1751). On later trips he was accompanied by his son William, who made ornithological and anthropological as well as botanical contributions, and painted some of the flora and fauna he observed. William is best remembered, though, for his descriptions of the American landscape and imaginative, romantic reflections on the wilderness and natural man in *Travels through North and South Carolina, Georgia, East and West Florida, the Cherokee Country, the Extensive Territories of the Muscogulges, or Creek Confederacy, and the Country of the Chactaws* (1791).

Bates, H(erbert) E(rnest) 1905–74 Novelist and short-story writer. His work is often set in the countryside of his native Midlands. *The Woman Who Had Imagination* (1934), *My Uncle Silas* (1939), *Colonel Julian* (1951), *The Daffodil Sky* (1955) and *The Enchantress* (1961) are among his outstanding collections of stories. Wartime experience in the RAF prompted his best-known novel, *Fair Stood the Wind for France* (1944). *The Darling Buds of May* (1958), *A Breath of French Air* (1959), *Hark, Hark, the Lark* (originally called *When the Green Woods Laugh*; 1960), *Oh! To Be in England* (1963) and *A Little of What You Fancy* (1970) are a popular series of novels about the hedonistic Larkin family.

Bateson, F(rederick) (Noel) W(ilse) 1901–78 Critic. For most of his career he was a fellow of Corpus Christi College, Oxford. As the title of his book *The Scholar-Critic* (1972) suggests, he aimed to inform literary-critical judgements with higher standards of historical and linguistic scholarship. He edited *The Cambridge Bibliography of English Literature* (1940) and founded the periodical *ESSAYS IN CRITICISM* in 1951.

bathos An unwitting drop from elevation into triteness or triviality, or pathos so overdone that it tumbles into the ludicrous. Many enjoyable excruciating examples are to be found in *The Stuffed Owl* (1930), an anthology of bad verse, edited by D. B. Wyndham Lewis and C. Lee.

Battle Hymn of the Republic, The An American patriotic song by JULIA WARD HOWE, written after a visit to a Union army camp near Washington and published in 1862. The melody was provided by *John Brown's Body*.

Battle of Brunanburh, The An Old English poem giving a vivid, perhaps eye-witness, account of a battle between an army of Norsemen and Scots and another of West Saxons and Mercians, which took place in 937. The location of Brunanburh is unknown, but it was apparently near the sea. TENNYSON wrote a version of it.

Battle of Life, The A Christmas story by DICKENS, published in 1846 and collected in *CHRISTMAS BOOKS* (1852). It follows the fortunes of Dr Anthony Jeddler, who regards the world as 'a gigantic practical joke', and his daughters, Grace and Marion. Into the girls' lives come Alfred Heathfield, an honest young medical student,

and Michael Warden, a wastrel who reforms. Lesser figures – the lawyer Snitchey, the sour Benjamin Britain ('Little Britain') and the worthy Clemency Newcombe – round off a brisk, expressive tale.

Battle of Maldon, The A fragment of an Old English poem, probably written at the end of the 10th century, describing a battle (991) which also appears in the *ANGLO-SAXON CHRONICLE*. The beginning and end are lost. The surviving part tells how the Saxon leader Byrhtnoth contemptuously rejects the Vikings' demand for tribute when they land near Maldon in Essex and over-confidently allows them to cross the causeway before joining battle. The Saxons flee when he is killed and, though rallied by Aelfwin, continue to fall in the fight. Despite its late date, the work is heroic, recalling the values of *BEOWULF* and Germanic epics. Unlike *THE BATTLE OF BRUNANBURH*, it describes the actions of individuals, giving their speeches and boasts.

Battle of the Books, The A prose SATIRE by SWIFT, written in 1697 and published in 1704. It remains the classic, humorous treatment of the debate between Ancients and Moderns. In his *Essay upon the Ancient and Modern Learning* (1690) SIR WILLIAM TEMPLE, Swift's patron, had opposed the New Learning and unfavourably compared contemporary writers and philosophers with their classical counterparts. Temple exposed himself to attack, from RICHARD BENTLEY and William Wotton, by singling out the spurious epistles of Phalaris for special praise.

Swift's reply on his patron's behalf takes the form of a MOCK-HEROIC drama in the Royal Library, where books championing the ancient and modern causes prepare to fight over the right to occupy the higher peak of Parnassus. A dispute meanwhile arises between a spider and a bee; Aesop's intervention identifies the spider with the Moderns, who spin out empty pedantry, while the bee, like the Ancients, goes directly to Nature and produces honey and wax, 'sweetness and light'. The verdict goads the Moderns into attack, and battle commences. Under the protection of Pallas, Homer leads the Ancients against the Moderns under MILTON's leadership. Individual duels are nicely matched, as when Virgil takes on his translator DRYDEN and Aristotle shoots Descartes while aiming at FRANCIS BACON. The book ends in mid-battle, supposedly because of a defective manuscript.

Baughan, Blanche 1870–1958 New Zealand poet. Her best poetry belongs to the years immediately after she emigrated to New Zealand from England, and appeared in *Reuben and Other Poems* (1903) and *Shingle-Short and Other Verses* (1908). The latter contains colloquial DRAMATIC MONOLOGUES and penetrating studies of society's pariahs and misfits. In subsequent years she mainly devoted herself to social work and became an important figure in the movement for prison reform. She also wrote many works on New Zealand rural life and topography, of which *Brown Bread from a Colonial Oven* (1912) is the best known.

Baum, L(yman) Frank 1856–1919 American writer of CHILDREN'S LITERATURE. His first book, *Mother Goose in Prose* (1897), was based on stories told to his children. Its last chapter introduced Dorothy, the farm-girl who reappeared in *The Wonderful Wizard of Oz* (1900), an immediate success leading to 14 more titles in the same vein. Baum wrote the lyrics for a musical version in 1902. Three different film versions followed, the most famous starring Judy Garland in 1939. After Baum's death 26 more adventures of Oz appeared, written by diverse authors including Baum's own son. The series had sold over seven million copies when it finished in 1951.

Bawden, Nina 1925– Novelist and writer of CHILDREN'S LITERATURE. Children's novels such as *The Witch's Daughter* (1966), the highly successful *Carrie's War* (1973) and *Keeping Henry* (1988) show good-humoured understanding of the child's point of view. Her adult fiction provides a consistently incisive analysis of life among the upper middle classes. *The Birds in the Trees* (1969) is about a tormented adolescent; *Anna Apparent* (1972) and *Familiar Passions* (1979) explore illegitimacy and adoption. *Circles of Deceit* (1987) was shortlisted for the BOOKER PRIZE.

Baxter, James K(eir) 1926–72 New Zealand poet, playwright and critic. He achieved early recognition with *Beyond the Palisade* (1944), the first of more than 30 books of poetry which appeared before his death at the age of 46. His early verse is notable for its lyrical rendition of the New Zealand rural world and the effect of this landscape on its inhabitants. Baxter then concentrated on narrative verse, BALLADS and other poems about local figures. The poetry he wrote before his conversion to Roman Catholicism is collected in *In Fires of No Return* (1958). *Pig Island Letters* (1966) and *Jerusalem Sonnets* (1970), appearing after a relatively unproductive period, are outstanding later works, the latter volume using a fluid version of the SONNET to express his highly personal sense of religious conviction. *Howrah Bridge* (1961) and *Autumn Testament* (1972) are among his other notable volumes of verse. Baxter began to write for the stage in the late 1950s, achieving recognition as a playwright with works such as *The Band Rotunda* (1967), *The Sore-Footed Man* (1967), *The Devil and Mr Mulcahy* (1967) and *The Temptations of Oedipus* (1970). His criticism includes *Recent Trends in New Zealand Poetry* (1951) and *Aspects of Poetry in New Zealand* (1967).

Baxter, Richard 1615–91 Presbyterian divine. A clergyman of uncompromising conscience and a prolific writer of devotional literature, Baxter is best known for *The Saint's Everlasting Rest* (1651), *A Call to the Unconverted* (1658) and his moving, intimate tribute to his beloved wife who died in 1681, *A Breviate of the Life of Margaret Baxter* (1681). His own account of his turbulent life, *Reliquiae Baxterianae*, was published in 1696.

Bay Psalm Book, The: *or, The Whole Book of Psalms Faithfully Translated into English Meter* The authoritative hymnal of the Massachusetts Bay Colony and the first book published in America (Cambridge, Massachusetts, 1640). The translation, by RICHARD MATHER, JOHN ELIOT and Thomas Weld, replaced the Sternhold and Hopkins version, which the Bay Puritans rejected because it sacrificed the literal rendering of the Hebrew text to poetic effect. Following a second printing in 1647, it was revised by Henry Dunster (the president of Harvard) and Richard Lyon, and reprinted in 1651 as *The Psalms, Hymns and Scriptural Songs of the Old and New Testament*, an edition which was reissued several times over a period of almost a century. See also PSALTERS.

Bayly, (Nathaniel) Thomas Haynes 1797–1839 Poet, playwright and novelist. He was famous in his time for sentimental songs and BALLADS, most notably 'I'd be a Butterfly', 'She Wore a Wreath of Roses', and 'Oh No, We Never Mention Her'. Among his 36 plays *Perfection: or, the Lady of Munster*, a FARCE, enjoyed considerable commercial success. His novels include *The Aylmers* (1827).

Baynton, Barbara 1857–1929 Australian short-story writer. Although she also published a novel, *Human Toll* (1907), her reputation rests on the stories in *Bush Studies* (1902). While not without humour, they present the bush as a harsh, inimical environment, in contrast to the robust nationalism of A. B. PATERSON and even equivocal attitudes which characterize many of HENRY LAWSON's stories. Classic stories such as 'Squeaker's Mate' and 'The Chosen Vessel' vividly dramatize the plight of bush women, frequently regarding them as victims of both malevolent nature and male brutality.

Be Domes Daege ('Of Doomsday') An Old English poem eloquently translating the *De die judicii* once attributed to both ALCUIN and BEDE. It urges men to contemplate Doomsday and to shun luxury in favour of the hardships which promise salvation.

Beaman, S(ydney) G(eorge) Hulme 1886–1932 Writer and illustrator of CHILDREN'S LITERATURE. *Tales of Toytown* (1928) is a picture-book about a small town where a stuffy mayor and slow-witted policeman try to govern a cast of eccentrics. It became famous through adaptations on BBC radio's *Children's Hour* from 1929 to 1963, with Beaman himself writing over 30 episodes.

Beardsley, Aubrey (Vincent) 1872–98 Illustrator and writer. His sensuous black-and-white drawings created a visual style for the 1890s. Art editor of THE YELLOW BOOK in 1894–5, he illustrated WILDE's *SALOME*, POPE's THE RAPE OF THE LOCK and JONSON's *VOLPONE*. A censored version of his erotic novel, *The Story of Venus and Tannhauser*, originally appeared in *The Yellow Book* as *Under the Hill*; it was privately printed without expurgation in 1907.

Beats, The A group of writers centred in San Francisco and New York City in the latter half of the 1950s. The term 'beat', first used in JOHN CLELLON HOLMES's novel, *Go* (1952), has been variously interpreted as meaning 'beaten down' and 'beatific'. The group despised middle-class values, commercialism and conformity, and sought visionary states through religious meditation, sex, jazz and drugs. Prominent members included GINSBERG, KEROUAC, WILLIAM S. BURROUGHS, CORSO, SNYDER, and FERLINGHETTI.

Beattie, James 1735–1803 Philosopher and poet. His *Essay on the Nature and Immutability of Truth* (1770) attacked the philosophy of DAVID HUME. *The Minstrel* (1771–4), a poem in SPENSERIAN STANZAS on the development of an imaginary poet in past times, won praise from SAMUEL JOHNSON among others.

Beaumont, Francis 1584–1616 Playwright. After publishing *Salmacis and Hermaphroditus* (1602), a poem in the sub-erotic Ovidian manner then fashionable, he turned to the stage with *The Woman Hater* (1605), a prose comedy in servile imitation of his friend JONSON. THE KNIGHT OF THE BURNING PESTLE (1607), the other piece of which Beaumont is now believed to have been sole author, is altogether finer: a witty outcome of avid theatre-going in which the dramatic taste of unsophisticated audiences is mocked without much malice.

Beaumont's collaboration with JOHN FLETCHER marks a separate and substantial stage in his dramatic career. They seem to have replaced SHAKESPEARE in about 1609 as chief dramatists of the KING'S MEN, for whom they probably wrote PHILASTER (c. 1609), THE MAID'S TRAGEDY (c. 1610), *A KING AND NO KING* (1611), *Cupid's Revenge* (c. 1611), *The Coxcomb* (1612), *The Scornful Lady* (c. 1613) and *The Captain* (1613). The collaborators were sufficiently sensitive to the shifts in public taste to become leaders of it. Their plays exploited the scenic scope of the

PRIVATE THEATRE at the Blackfriars Theatre, sacrificing Shakespearean profundity to the less durable appeal of the decorated stage, ambiguity to intrigue, and the complexity of metaphor to the easy flow of language. The popularity of the Beaumont and Fletcher plays tempted contemporary publicists and publishers, and scholars following in their wake, to ascribe to the partnership far more work than belonged to it: a total of over 50 plays, in which *The Knight of the Burning Pestle* stubbornly featured. Beaumont probably abandoned the theatre soon after his marriage to an heiress in 1613, while Fletcher continued to write, either singly or with other collaborators, for over 10 years.

Beaux' Stratagem, The A comedy by FARQUHAR, first performed two months before his death in 1707. Down on their luck at a Lichfield inn, Aimwell and Archer decide that Aimwell shall pose as his titled brother and Archer as his servant. Dorinda, daughter of the local Lady Bountiful, falls in love with Aimwell, and the wife of her oafish brother Sullen is attracted to Archer. When Lady Bountiful's house is attacked by highwaymen, Aimwell and Archer rescue the ladies. Struck by love and remorse, Aimwell confesses the deception to Dorinda, whose love survives the revelation. Mrs Sullen's brother, Sir Charles Freeman, arrives with the news that Aimwell's brother is dead and Aimwell's title therefore real. He also persuades Sullen to consent to the dissolution of his marriage, thus leaving the way clear for Archer to ask for Mrs Sullen's hand.

Beaver, Bruce 1928– Australian poet. *Letters to Live Poets* (1969) broadens the range of his rough-hewn early verse to a consideration of the conflicts involved in artistic perception. *Lauds and Plaints* (1974), marked by his reading of WILLIAM CARLOS WILLIAMS, is formally innovative. Other books include *Odes and Days* (1975), *Death's Directive* (1978), the autobiographical *As It Was* (1979), *Charmed Lives* (1988), *New and Selected Poems: 1960–1990* (1991) and the novels *The Hot Spring* (1965) and *You Can't Come Back* (1966). He has been an important influence on younger Australian poets.

Beckett, Samuel (Barclay) 1906–89 Irish-born playwright and novelist. As a young man he left Dublin for Paris, where he became JOYCE's associate and assistant. He usually wrote in French and translated himself into English. Early work, including the novel *Murphy* (1938), made little impact on its first publication and his fame (which won him the Nobel Prize for Literature in 1969) rests almost entirely on his writings after 1950.

Beckett's major novels, the French 'trilogy' *Molloy* (1951; translated 1955), *Malone meurt* (1951; *Malone Dies*, 1956) and *L'Innommable* (1953; *The Unnameable*, 1958) and the English *Watt* (1953), exist in and through their narrators: social misfits, old and ill, embarked on a quest for the explanation of 'I'. The difficult *Comment c'est* (*How It Is*, 1961) is insistently aural, while the short prose fictions that followed replace the puzzled subjectivity of the novels with a bleak objectivity which still finds room for unexpectedly spry humour. They include: *Stories and Texts for Nothing* (1967); *Mercier and Camier* (1974); the trilogy (later published as *Nohow On*, 1989) formed by *Company* (1980), *Ill Seen Ill Said* (1981) and *Worstward Ho* (1983); and *Stirrings Still* (1988), a meditation on ageing.

Beckett is probably more widely known for his plays, above all for *WAITING FOR GODOT* (produced in French in 1953, in English in 1955), which identified him as a leading exponent of the THEATRE OF THE ABSURD. The three full-length works, *Godot*, *ENDGAME* (produced in French in 1957, in English in 1958) and *HAPPY DAYS* (1961) are all concerned with human suffering, survival and immobility. The shorter, but still substantial, *Krapp's Last Tape* (1958) and *Play* (1963) seek to identify moments in the characters' past when something actually happened, as does the radio play *All That Fall* (1957). In the fragmentary *Breath* (1970) the image is all we have. The mysterious *Come and Go* (1966), a 'dramaticule', does not allow the audience to hear the whispers that may explain the patterned movements of its three female characters. In *Not I* (1972) and *Footfalls* (1976) the detailed direction of stage lighting dictates what the audience sees (a mouth and feet respectively) as the spoken words reverberate.

Beckford, William 1759–1844 Connoisseur and man of letters. A compulsive builder and collector, he reconstructed his Wiltshire mansion as an elaborate Gothic fantasy, Fonthill Abbey, substantially complete in 1809 but abandoned after the fall of its immense tower in 1825. His travel book *Dreams, Waking Thoughts and Incidents* (1783) was revised and reissued as the first volume of *Italy, with Sketches of Spain and Portugal* (1834). Beckford's fantastic story *VATHEK* was written in French and published in an English translation in 1786. Two pseudonymous BURLESQUES, *Modern Novel Writing: or, the Elegant Enthusiast* (1796) and *Azemia* (1797), were followed by another travel book, *Recollections of an Excursion to the Monasteries of Alcobaça and Batalha* (1835).

Beddoes, Thomas Lovell 1803–49 Poet. A nephew of MARIA EDGEWORTH and a solitary, anomalous, even bizarre figure, he studied medicine in several European cities and practised in Zurich. He published *The Improvisatore* (1821) and *The Bride's Tragedy* (1822) but is best known for *DEATH'S JEST-BOOK*, a REVENGE TRAGEDY in the Jacobean manner which he began in 1825, repeatedly revised and left unpublished when he committed suicide. It appeared in 1850.

Bede [Baeda] *c*. 673–735 Historian, known as 'The Venerable Bede'. Probably born at Monkton, Durham, he went to the monastery at Wearmouth at the age of seven and the monastery at Jarrow in 682, remaining there for the rest of his life. His Latin *Historia ecclesiastica gentis Anglorum*, finished in 731, was a pioneering work which earned him the title of 'The Father of English History'. It traces the development of Christianity in Britain from the disparate Christian and heathen groups left after Roman withdrawal to the evangelizing work of saints such as Patrick, David, Augustine, Ninian, Aidan and Columba, and the establishment of a stable Roman church. A thorough historian, Bede collated evidence and verified facts wherever possible. He treated his material sympathetically, to produce a lively account full of insights into daily life in the 7th century. Although his predominant concerns were theological, Bede's other writings reflect wide-ranging interests. They include: *De orthographia*, perhaps his earliest work, about spelling; *De natura rerum*, about natural science; a hagiographic account of the early Northumbrian abbots; biblical commentaries and translations; homilies; and hymns.

Bede, Cuthbert [Bradley, Edward] 1827–89 Humorist. His comic account of undergraduate life, *The Adventures of Mr Verdant Green, an Oxford Freshman* (1853–6), enjoyed great popularity in its day.

Beecher, Henry Ward 1813–87 American preacher and brother of HARRIET BEECHER STOWE. As minister of the Plymouth Church in Brooklyn, New York, he preached a theology of love rather than fear and addressed current social issues. The published texts of his sermons, lecture tours, weekly newspaper columns and his journal, *Christian Union*, made him a prominent spokesman on secular issues. He was associated in the popular mind with the radical Abolitionists in the 1850s; later he was known for his support of female suffrage. *Norwood: or, Village Life in New England* (1867) is a novel whose characters have long conversations about religious values. In the 1870s Beecher incorporated many of CHARLES DARWIN's ideas to support his old teachings of evangelical liberalism, the community benefits of virtuous self-improvement, and the moral value of material success.

Beer, Patricia 1924– Poet. Her verse, from *Loss of the Magyar* (1959) to *Collected Poems* (1988), is precise and economical in its observation of everyday matters and West Country scenes. She has also published *Mrs Beer's House* (1969), a memoir of her childhood, and *Reader, I Married Him* (1974), an influential study of Jane Austen, CHARLOTTE BRONTË, ELIZABETH GASKELL and GEORGE ELIOT.

Beerbohm, Sir (Henry) Max(imilian) 1872–1956 Humorist, essayist and cartoonist. A precociously poised figure in the decadent literary world of the 1890s, he began by publishing caricatures in THE STRAND MAGAZINE and essays in THE YELLOW BOOK, the latter facetiously gathered as *The Works of Max Beerbohm* (1896). He succeeded SHAW as dramatic critic of THE SATURDAY REVIEW in 1898. Three works best epitomize his sunny and gentle wit: *ZULEIKA DOBSON* (1911); *A Christmas Garland* (1912), containing PARODIES of JAMES, CONRAD, WELLS and BENNETT, among others; and *Seven Men* (1919), which includes 'Enoch Soames' and a spoof of portentous historical drama in 'Savonarola Brown'. *The Poets' Corner* (1904), a collection of cartoons, wryly comments on major writers. In later years Beerbohm became a noted broadcaster.

Beeton, Mrs (Isabella Mary) 1836–65 Author of *Household Management*. It was first published in *The Englishwoman's Domestic Magazine* in 1859–61 and as a separate volume in 1861. Usually remembered for its sections on cookery, which have been reprinted many times, it gives a full picture of the duties of the Victorian middle-class housewife.

Beggar's Opera, The A BALLAD OPERA by GAY, with songs arranged by John Christopher Pepusch, who also composed an overture. It was first staged by John Rich at Lincoln's Inn Fields in 1728 to such success that it made 'Rich gay and Gay rich'. Apparently responding to SWIFT's idea for a 'Newgate pastoral', Gay produced a fresh and original work combining a riposte to the fashionable Italian opera with satire of corrupt government. Frequently revived, *The Beggar's Opera* provided the inspiration for Bertolt Brecht's *The Threepenny Opera* (1928), with original music by Kurt Weill.

Peachum, a receiver of stolen goods, is mortified when his daughter Polly marries the highwayman Macheath, whom he then informs against. Sentenced to death and imprisoned in Newgate, Macheath is rescued by the warder's pretty daughter, Lucy Lockit. The rivalry between Polly and Lucy maintains the piece's characteristic balance of romance and cynicism. Recaptured in a brothel, Macheath is saved again from the gallows by the improbable intervention of a compulsory happy ending, demanded on behalf of the audience by one of the players.

Behan, Brendan 1923–64 Irish playwright. He joined the IRA at the age of 14, spending two years in an English Borstal (described in *Borstal Boy*, 1958) and five years in prison for shooting at a policeman. He achieved fame with two works which continued the tradition of O'CASEY's urban drama: *The Quare Fellow* (1954), a grimly comic account of the hours preceding a prison hanging, and *The Hostage* (1958), about an English soldier held hostage in an Irish brothel, derived from his one-act Gaelic play *An Giall*. A clamorous Dublin presence, belligerent or convivial, Behan illuminated the theatrical drabness of the 1950s.

Behn, Aphra 1640–89 Playwright, novelist and translator. Probably the first Englishwoman to see herself as a professional writer, she led an adventurous life, although our knowledge of its details is unreliable. A childhood in the West Indies apparently suggested the setting for her best prose romance, *OROONOKO*. The date of her marriage is uncertain, as is the exact nature of her spying mission in Antwerp in 1666. Imprisoned for debt in the late 1660s, she turned to writing plays after her release. Her early work was in what contemporaries took to be the style of BEAUMONT and FLETCHER. Even the more distinguished comedies – *The Town Fop* (1676), *The Rover* (1677), *Sir Patient Fancy* (1678), *The Second Part of the Rover* (1681) and *The Lucky Chance* (1686) – are derivative, while a political piece *The City Heiress* (1682) borrows from THOMAS MIDDLETON's *A Mad World, My Masters*. The farce *The Emperor of the Moon* (1687), based on the Italian *COMMEDIA DELL'ARTE*, helped make popular the harlequinade, forerunner of the English PANTOMIME. Successful in their time, her plays still deserve revival, not least because of their advocacy of mature relationships between the sexes. Her translations from French and Latin were money-making ventures.

Behrman, S(amuel) N(athaniel) 1893–1973 American playwright. His plays are mostly sophisticated social comedies dealing with success, wealth, love and marriage. They include *Bedside Manners* (with J. Kenyon Nicholson, 1923), *A Night's Work* (1924), *The Man Who Forgot* (with Owen Davis, 1926), *Serena Blandish: or, The Difficulty of Getting Married* (adapted from ENID BAGNOLD's novel, 1929), *Meteor* (1929), *Love Story* (1933), *End of Summer* (1936), *Wine of Choice* (1938), *No Time for Comedy* (1939), *Jacobowsky and the Colonel* (1944), *Jane* (adapted from a SOMERSET MAUGHAM short story, 1952), *Fanny* (with Joshua Logan, 1954) and *But for Whom Charlie* (1964). Behrman also wrote more than 25 screenplays, as well as essays and short stories.

Bekederemo, J. P. Clark See CLARK BEKEDEREMO, J. P.

Belasco, David 1853–1931 American playwright, theatrical impresario, director and actor. He enjoyed a successful career in San Francisco and then New York, where he owned and managed his own Broadway theatre. He wrote or co-wrote more than 50 plays, including *Chums* (1879; retitled *Hearts of Oak*, 1880) with JAMES A. HERNE and various works with Henry C. De Mille. Popular in their day, they are now largely forgotten, though *Madame Butterfly* (with John L. Long, 1900) and *The Girl of the Golden West* (1905) were given enduring life in Puccini's operatic versions.

Bell, (Arthur) Clive (Howard) 1881–1964 Critic of art and literature. At Cambridge he was influenced by the philosopher G. E. MOORE and in London he became a central figure in the BLOOMSBURY GROUP. He married VIRGINIA WOOLF's sister Vanessa Stephen in 1907. With Roger Fry, he was one of the first critics to recognize the achievements of the Post-Impressionists. *Art* (1914) introduced his concept of 'Significant Form', which separated and elevated the element of form above content in works of art. Other works include *Since Cézanne* (1922), *Civilization* (1928), *Proust* (1929), *Account of French Painting* (1931) and *Old Friends: Personal Recollections* (1956).

Bell, Currer, Ellis and **Acton** Pseudonyms of CHARLOTTE, EMILY and ANNE BRONTË.

Bell, Gertrude (Margaret Lowthian) 1868–1926 Travel-writer. Among the books describing her travels as a field archaeologist in the Middle East are *Safar Nameh: Persian Pictures* (1894), *The Desert and the Sown* (1907) and *Amurath to Amurath* (1911). She died in Baghdad. Her vivid personality is well conveyed in her posthumously published letters (1927).

Bell, Martin 1918–78 Poet. He was a leading member of the GROUP. Though his work was frequently anthologized his only major book was *Collected Poems 1938–67* (1967). Deliberately populist, he wrote many poems about his peers, including a satire on the Group's meetings called 'Mr Hobsbaum's Monday Evening Meeting'. His most famous poem is the corruscating attack, 'Headmaster: Modern Style'.

Bellamy, Edward 1850–98 American novelist. He was working as a journalist when he wrote *LOOKING BACKWARD: 2000–1887* (1888), an immensely popular Utopian romance. In *The New Nation*, a journal he founded in 1891, and in *Equality* (1897), a sequel to *Looking Backward*, he developed and disseminated his political ideas – notably a government programme of strict state capitalism, resulting in non-revolutionary socialist reform. Bellamy clubs and a Nationalist party were founded in support. Earlier, less political writings include *The Duke of Stockbridge* (1879), about Shay's Rebellion, and *Dr Heidenhoff's Process* (1880) and *Miss Ludington's Sister* (1884), novels dealing with psychic phenomena in the tradition of HAWTHORNE. *The Blind Man's World and Other Stories* (1898) was published just before his death.

Belloc, (Joseph) Hilaire (Pierre René) 1870–1953 Poet, novelist, biographer, historian and travel-writer. Born of half-French parentage in France, he became a British citizen in 1902. His close friendship with CHESTERTON was based on common beliefs and interests; their anti-Imperial, pro-Boer contributions to *The Speaker* made SHAW nickname them the 'Chesterbelloc'. After serving as a Liberal MP Belloc recorded his disillusionment with party politics in *The Party System* (with Cecil Chesterton, 1911) and *The Servile State* (1912). His other writings cover many genres. His robust, often comic poetry includes *Verses and Sonnets* (1896), *The Bad Child's Book of Beasts* (1896), *Cautionary Tales* (1907) and *Sonnets and Verses* (1923). His lively and partisan biographies and histories include *Danton* (1899), *Robespierre* (1901), *Marie Antoinette* (1909), *The French Revolution* (1911), *History of England* (1915) and *Cromwell* (1927). Books of travel include *The Path to Rome* (1902), *The Pyrenees* (1909), *The Cruise of the Nona* (1925) and *Return to the Baltic* (1938). *Hills and the Sea* (1906), *First and Last* (1911), *Short Talks with the Dead* (1926) and *The Silence of the Sea* (1940) are among his collections of essays. He also wrote novels, sometimes illustrated by Chesterton, among them *Mr Clutterbuck's Election* (1908), *The Girondin* (1911), *The Green Overcoat* (1912) and *Belinda* (1928).

Bellow, Saul 1915– American novelist. *Dangling Man* (1944) and *The Victim* (1947) were followed by the exuberant PICARESQUE of *THE ADVENTURES OF AUGIE MARCH* (1953), *Seize the Day* (1956) and *Henderson the Rain King* (1959), about a middle-aged American's travails in Africa. *HERZOG* (1964) and *Humboldt's Gift* (1975; PULITZER PRIZE), his most widely admired novels, best exemplify his reputation for interpreting the struggles of modern city dwellers to define their roles and responsibilities in the modern world. His other fiction includes the novels *Mr Sammler's Planet* (1970), *The Dean's December* (1982) and *More Die of Heartbreak* (1987), and several collections of shorter work: *Mosby's Memoirs and Other Stories* (1968), *Him with His Foot in His Mouth and Other Short Stories* (1984) and *Something to Remember Me By* (1993). He has also written plays, a travel book about modern Israel and academic studies which include *Recent American Fiction: A Lecture* (1963), *The Future of the Moor* (1970) and *Technology and the Frontiers of Knowledge* (1975). He received the Nobel Prize for Literature in 1976.

Bells, The A MELODRAMA adapted by LEOPOLD LEWIS from *Le Juif polonais* by Erckmann and Chatrian, first staged in 1871. Sir Henry Irving's success as the guilt-ridden Mathias established him as a leading actor.

Belton Estate, The A novel by TROLLOPE, serialized in 1865–6 and published in volume form in 1866. Although not rated highly by Trollope himself, it is of some interest for its characteristically sympathetic exploration of the plight of the single, dependent woman. Clara Amedroz, daughter of the squire of Belton Castle, at first refuses her cousin Will Belton, heir to the estate, but eventually accepts him after becoming disillusioned with the lukewarm Captain Aylmer.

Ben-Hur: A Tale of the Christ A historical novel by LEW WALLACE, published in 1880. After years of unmerited suffering as a galley slave, Judah Ben-Hur returns to Judaea, a free man and Roman officer. At the chariot races in Caesarea he defeats Messala, who had made false accusations against him. He rescues his mother and sister, now lepers, and with them witnesses the Crucifixion. Ben-Hur recognizes Christ as a man who had shown him compassion while he was a slave. Christ's passing cures the lepers. Ben-Hur and his family become Christians.

Benchley, Robert (Charles) 1889–1945 American humorist. Theatre critic for *THE NEW YORKER* in 1929–40, he also wrote humorous sketches about the daily lives of ordinary people. They were collected in *Of All Things* (1921), *Love Conquers All* (1922), *Pluck and Luck* (1925), *The Early Worm* (1927), *20,000 Leagues Under The Sea: or, David Copperfield* (1928), *The Treasurer's Report* (1930), *My Ten Years in a Quandary* (1936), *After 1903 What?* (1938), *Inside Benchley* (1942) and *Benchley Beside Himself* (1943). He made frequent appearances in films and on the radio.

Benét, Stephen Vincent 1898–1943 American poet, short-story writer and novelist. He is best known for *John Brown's Body* (1928), a PULITZER PRIZE-winning collection of verse about the Civil War. *Western Star* (1943) deals with American roots in 17th-century European migrations. A collection of short stories, *Thirteen O'Clock* (1937), includes the popular 'The Devil and Daniel Webster', which has been made into an opera and a film. Other volumes of his stories are *Tales Before Midnight* (1939) and *The Last Cycle* (1946). He also wrote five novels, and a number of radio scripts collected in *We Stand United* (1945).

Benét, William Rose 1886–1950 American poet, founder of the *SATURDAY REVIEW* (1924) and elder brother of STEPHEN VINCENT BENÉT. His verse includes

Merchants from Cathay (1913), *Moons of Grandeur* (1920), *Days of Deliverance* (1944) and *The Stairway of Surprise* (1947). *Rip Tide* (1932) is an experimental verse novel. He won a PULITZER PRIZE for his verse autobiography, *The Dust Which is God* (1941).

Benito Cereno See *PIAZZA TALES, THE*.

Benlowes, Edward 1602–76 Religious poet. The heir of a rich Roman Catholic family, he changed his faith. Staunch support of the Royalist cause in the Civil War reduced him to poverty. His long religious poem, *Theophilia: or, Love's Sacrifice* (1652), is a rambling theological romance containing many curious expressions and the occasional fine line.

Bennett, Alan 1934– Playwright and actor. He has remained in the public eye ever since *Beyond the Fringe* (1960). *Forty Years On* (1968) and *Getting On* (1971) are political comedies, *Habeas Corpus* (1973) a FARCE. Their half-ironic, half-sentimental preoccupation with British institutions has an obvious counterpart in plays about post-war treason: *The Old Country* (1977), *An Englishman Abroad* (TV, 1983; stage, 1988) and *A Question of Attribution* (stage, 1988 ; TV, 1991). The appearance of the Queen in the last led the way to an ambitious treatment of monarchy, *The Madnesss of George III* (1992), in which sentiment predominates. More promising are works derived from his northern roots, examined in *Talking Heads* (TV, 1988; stage, 1992), which, like so much of his best work, establishes a two-way communication between TV and the stage. Other work includes: the screenplay for *Prick Up Your Ears* (1987), based on John Lahr's biography of JOE ORTON; an acclaimed stage adaptation of *WIND IN THE WILLOWS* (1991); and *Writing Home* (1994), a collection of diaries and prose pieces.

Bennett, (Enoch) Arnold 1867–1931 Novelist, short-story writer, playwright and journalist. Deeply influenced by French REALISM, he found his most congenial subject in his native Potteries (or Five Towns), in novels such as *ANNA OF THE FIVE TOWNS* (1902) and the two works widely regarded as his greatest achievement, *THE OLD WIVES' TALE* (1908) and *CLAYHANGER* (1910), as well as the stories in *Tales of the Five Towns* (1905) and *The Grim Smile of the Five Towns* (1907). The fortunes of the Clayhanger family are followed further in *Hilda Lessways* (1911), *These Twain* (1916) and *The Roll Call* (1918). His preoccupation with the rich and the worldly is apparent in lesser novels such as *The Grand Babylon Hotel* (1902), *The Card* (1911), *Mr Prohack* (1922), *Lord Raingo* (1926) and *Imperial Palace* (1930). *RICEYMAN STEPS* (1923), in which he again considered the lives of ordinary and undistinguished people, greatly enhanced his reputation.

Milestones (with Edward Knoblock, 1912) was the most successful of his plays. Also a busy working journalist for much of his career, he contributed an influential series on 'Books and Persons' to Lord Beaverbrook's *Evening Standard* from 1926 until his death. His three-volume *Journal* (1932-3), inspired by the example of the Goncourt brothers, was begun in 1896.

Benson, A(rthur) C(hristopher) 1862–1925 Man of letters. The elder brother of E. F. BENSON, he was Master of Magdalene College, Cambridge, from 1915 until his death. A prolific but minor writer, he is best remembered for his poems and hymns, and particularly for his words to Elgar's first 'Pomp and Circumstance' march, 'Land of Hope and Glory' (1902), part of the Coronation Ode for Edward VII.

Benson, E(dward) F(rederic) 1867–1940 Novelist and younger brother of A. C. BENSON. He wrote some 93 books, the most popular being his comic novels about Dodo (*Dodo*, *Dodo the Second* and *Dodo Wonder*, 1914–21) and Lucia, starting with *Queen Lucia* (1920) and *Lucia in London* (1927). He also published five volumes of personal and family reminiscences (1911–40).

Bentham, Jeremy 1748–1832 Philosopher. *A Fragment on Government: Being an Examination of What is Delivered in William Blackstone's Commentaries* (1776) outlined his theory of government and a programme of future reform. *Introduction to the Principles of Morals and Legislation* (1789) expanded its arguments, while *The Panopticon: or, Inspection House* (1791) put forward a plan for prison reform. The lack of official interest in his schemes gradually dislodged Bentham's early faith in enlightened monarchic reform and stimulated him to develop the 'philosophical radicalism' known as UTILITARIANISM. This system was based on the dual ideas that all reform should be dictated by the greatest happiness of the greatest number as a measure of right and wrong, and that human motivation was founded on self-interest. The coincidence of interest and duty became an ideal of social and moral reform. Bentham's *Poor Laws and Pauper Management* (in *Annals of Agriculture*, 1797) provided the principles for the New Poor Law of 1834. Other influential tracts included *Chrestomathia* (1816), which discussed education, *A Catechism of Parliamentary Reform* (1817), *A Radical Reform Bill, with Explanations* (1819) and *A Constitutional Code for the Use of All Nations* (1830). His *Rationale of Evidence* (1825) was edited by JOHN STUART MILL, the son of Bentham's closest Utilitarian colleague, JAMES MILL. Bentham founded *THE WESTMINSTER REVIEW* in 1824 as the organ of the Philosophical Radicals and was a guiding force behind the establishment of the University of London.

Bentley, E(dmund) C(lerihew) 1875–1956 Journalist, writer of light verse and DETECTIVE FICTION. He earned a minor place in literary history by inventing the comic verse form known as the CLERIHEW, after the middle name he used as pseudonym for his first collection, *Biography for Beginners* (1905). *Trent's Last Case* (1903) was meant as an exposure of detective stories but was quickly hailed as a classic of the genre. Bentley revived his artist-detective in *Trent's Own Case* (with H. Warner Allen; 1936) and a collection of short stories, *Trent Intervenes* (1938). *Elephant's Work: An Enigma* (1950) is a thriller. More enduring than these works is 'Greedy Night' (1939), a wickedly accurate PARODY of SAYERS.

Bentley, Phyllis 1894–1977 Novelist. Born and brought up in the West Riding of Yorkshire, she drew on her mother's family recollections for her best-known novel, *Inheritance* (1932), which chronicles the lives of families involved in the textile industry. Her other work includes *The World's Bane* (1918), a volume of four allegorical stories influenced by OLIVE SCHREINER, *Cat-in-the-Manger* (1918), *The Spinner of the Years* (1928), *The Partnership* (1928) and several studies of the BRONTËS.

Bentley, Richard 1662–1742 Scholar. He made his reputation with the *Epistola ad Millium* (1691), a learned appendix on the Greek dramatists contributed to John Mill's edition of the Byzantine chronicler John Malalas. In 1697-9 he was embroiled in the dispute provoked by TEMPLE's *Essay upon the Ancient and Modern Learning*, showing that the Phalaris epistles Sir William had praised as examples of classical excellence were spurious. (See *THE BATTLE OF THE BOOKS*.) In 1700 Bentley was appointed Master of Trinity College, Cambridge, a post he despotically enjoyed for some 40 years despite repeated controversy. As an editor Bentley was renowned for diligent work on Horace and Manilius, though his arbitrary treatment of MILTON's PARADISE LOST (1732) discredited him. POPE caricatured him in THE DUNCIAD as a 'mighty scholiast, whose unwearied pains/ Made Horace dull, and humbled Milton's strains'.

Bentley's Miscellany A monthly magazine issued by the publisher Richard Bentley from 1837 to 1869. DICKENS, its first editor, was succeeded by AINSWORTH. Contributors included FRANCIS SYLVESTER MAHONY (Father Prout) and R. H. BARHAM, many of whose *Ingoldsby Legends* first appeared in its pages.

Beowulf The most famous and the longest surviving poem in Old English, written c. 1000 in the West Saxon dialect. The story probably developed orally, achieving its present form during the 8th century in Mercia or Northumberland. The poem makes no reference to Britain, but is set in southern Scandinavia during the migrations of the 5th and 6th centuries. It is an EPIC recording the deeds of the Geatish warrior Beowulf. In youth he defeats the monster Grendel, who has been terrorizing Hrothgar's Danish kingdom; when Grendel's mother comes for revenge, he kills her and the wounded Grendel in their underwater lair. On returning to his native Geat-land, Beowulf is given land and eventually becomes Lord of the Geats. He is fatally wounded fighting a dragon enraged by the theft of a goblet from its treasure hoard. The poem ends with Beowulf's magnificent funeral and a prophesy of disaster for the Geats.

The second half (after Beowulf's return to the Geats) is often considered inferior, but it is generally accepted that *Beowulf* was originally the work of a single poet. The action is slowed by elaboration of other episodes, inset stories and the rhetorical development of laments and speeches. The names of characters in peripheral episodes link the central story to a network of other legends and epics; some names are historical, firmly attaching the poem to the history of Germanic Europe. Its central preoccupations are with the prowess of Beowulf, and the feasting and fighting which characterize masculine feudal society. Yet the hero's supernatural powers (he can fight underwater for days) and the larger reflections the poem incorporates (on life and death, war and peace, society and the individual, good and evil) have encouraged Christian, mythic and allegorical interpretations.

Beppo: A Venetian Story A poem by BYRON in OTTAVA RIMA, published in 1818. It satirizes both English and Italian life, telling of the return during a carnival of a long-lost soldier, Beppo (Giuseppe). Disguised as a Turkish merchant, he finds that his wife has consoled herself with a *cavaliere servente*. The scene is set for a violent confrontation but the dilemma is resolved over a cup of coffee. MOCK-HEROIC in manner and pervaded by gentle IRONY, the poem marks an important change from Byron's early work and introduces the style (and verse form) he refined in DON JUAN and THE VISION OF JUDGEMENT.

Berenson, Bernard 1865–1959 American art historian. Born Bernhard Valvrojenski in Lithuania, he was a student of CHARLES ELIOT NORTON at Harvard. He quickly established a reputation as a connoisseur, particularly of Italian Renaissance art, and attracted wealthy buyers and dealers as clients by his expertise in attributing and authenticating paintings. His scholarly works include *Venetian Painters of the Renaissance* (1894), *Florentine Painters of the Renaissance* (1896), *Central Italian Painters of*

the Renaissance (1897), *The Study and Criticism of Italian Art* (1902) and *Drawings of the Florentine Painters* (1903). *Sketch for a Self-Portrait* (1949) is autobiographical.

Berger, John 1926– Novelist and art critic. His preoccupation with the nature and possibilities of individual freedom is expressed in several novels: *A Painter of Our Time* (1958), about an artist's career; *Corker's Freedom* (1964), about the hero's attempt to break free of suburbia; and *G* (1972), awarded the BOOKER PRIZE, which mixes narrative, reflection, political treatise and historical reconstruction in pursuing the fortunes of its ambiguous central figure. *Into Their Labours*, a trilogy about modern peasant life in the French Jura, combines fiction, poetry and reportage. The constituent volumes are *Pig Earth* (1979), *Once in Europa* (1989) and *Lilac and Flag* (1991). His interest in photography has led to collaborations with Jean Mohr in *A Fortunate Man* (1967) and *Another Way of Telling* (1982). His art criticism, influenced by Marxism and sometimes combative, includes *Permanent Red* (1960), *Ways of Seeing* (1972), *The White Bird* (1985) and *Keeping a Rendezvous* (1991).

Berkeley, George 1685–1753 Philosopher. The son of an English family settled in Ireland, he studied at Trinity College, Dublin, where he was ordained and became a junior fellow in 1707. He was appointed Dean of Derry in 1724 and Bishop of Cloyne in 1734. *An Essay towards a New Theory of Vision* (1709) advanced a psychological theory of perception based on two propositions: that the objects and ideas of sight have nothing in common with the objects and ideas of touch; and that the connection between them comes only from experience, there being no abstract element common to both. The first part of *The Treatise Concerning the Principles of Human Knowledge* followed in 1710; a draft of the second part was lost and Berkeley could never bring himself to rewrite it. In essence, the treatise insists that mind is the creative force: rather than being representations of reality, ideas are reality. This theory of immaterialism is based on the principle *esse est percipi* (to be is to be perceived), which holds that there is no external reality independent of mental perception. Concerned to oppose philosophical theories that might nurture atheism or scepticism, Berkeley ranged himself against HOBBES and LOCKE, especially the latter's concept of the dualism of spirit and matter. His argument for belief in the existence of God rests on the notion that Nature is a regular series of material objects existing continuously in God's own perception, which lends them uniformity. Berkeley further defended the theory in *Three Dialogues between Hylas and Philonus* (1713).

Subsequent work, reflecting the diversity of his interests and activities, included: contributions to STEELE's THE GUARDIAN; *Proposal for the Better Supplying of Churches in our Foreign Plantations* (1725), describing his scheme to found a missionary college in Bermuda; *Alciphron: or, the Minute Philosopher* (1732), Platonic dialogues about religion, written during a three-year stay in the USA; *Theory of Vision: or, Visual Language Vindicated and Explained* (1733); *The Analyst* (1734), on mathematics; *The Querist* (1735), on Ireland; and *Siris: A Chain of Philosophical Reflexions* (1744), examining both physical and metaphysical questions chiefly concerning the virtues of tar-water. Berkeley retired to Oxford, where he died. His notes, *The Commonplace Book*, were first published in 1871.

Berkoff, Steve(n) 1937– Playwright, actor and director. His tightly choreographed productions for the London Theatre Group have featured his adaptations of works by Kafka, SHAKESPEARE, Aeschylus and POE. Berkoff himself often plays the leading role. His own plays, which often use a mannered PARODY of other styles, include: *East* (1975), about his East End boyhood, written in a BLANK VERSE which simultaneously echoes Shakespeare and the football terraces; *Greek* (1979); *Decadence* (1981); *Kvetch* (1987); and *Acapulco* (1992).

Berners, 2nd Baron See BOURCHIER, JOHN.

Berners, Juliana See *THE BOOK OF ST ALBANS*.

Berry, James 1924– Poet. Born in Jamaica, he was among the first immigrants to arrive in Britain after World War II. His collections of poetry include *Fractured Circles* (1979), *Lucy's Letters and Loving* (1982; an enlarged version of *Lucy's Letter*, 1975), *Chain of Days* (1985), *When I Dance* (1988) and *Future-Telling Lady* (1991). He is also a prolific editor of poetry, his anthologies including *News for Babylon* (1984), a selection of West Indian–British poetry. Berry is often humorous, particularly in his ability to capture Caribbean speech, but there is also a plangent aspect to some of his poems. *A Thief in the Village* (1987) is a collection of short stories.

Berryman, John 1914–72 American poet. *Poems* (1942) was followed by *The Dispossessed* (1948), the acclaimed *Homage to Mistress Bradstreet* (1956) and *77 Dream Songs* (1964). The poems in the latter volume became the first section of a sequence, *The Dream Songs*, continued in *His Toy, His Dream, His Rest* (1968) and published in its entirety in 1969. It presents a meditation on American literary and cultural history through the dreams of Henry, a character partly modelled on the poet himself. *Delusions* (1972) and a novel, *Recovery* (1973), both published after his suicide, show Berryman looking towards the end of his life. He also wrote a notable biography of STEPHEN CRANE (1950; revised and reissued, 1962) and *The Freedom of the Poet* (1976), a collection of essays on poets and poetry.

Bertrams, The A novel by TROLLOPE, published in 1859. Although Trollope considered the plot 'more than ordinarily bad', the novel is redeemed by his unconventional handling of the hero and heroine, George Bertram and Caroline Waddington, as disenchantment overtakes their initial high hopes. They meet and fall in love in the Holy Land but break off their engagement after it has dragged on for three years. Her marriage to Sir Henry Harcourt, the Solicitor-General, fails and he commits suicide. In due course Caroline and George are reconciled and marry.

Besant, Sir Walter 1836–1901 Novelist and historian. His early novels, of which *Ready Money Mortiboy* (1872) and *The Golden Butterfly* (1876) were the most popular, were collaborations with James Rice. His own later historical fiction was less widely read than two realistic works, *All Sorts and Conditions of Men* (1882) and *Children of Gibeon* (1886), which exposed conditions in the East End of London. His Royal Institution lecture of 1884 on the status of the novel provoked HENRY JAMES's famous reply, 'The Art of Fiction'. He planned and inaugurated a great 10-volume topographical survey of London, which appeared after his death under other editors (1902–12).

Bestall, Alfred (Edmeades) 1892–1986 Writer and illustrator of CHILDREN'S LITERATURE. In 1935 he took over the *Rupert Bear* comic strip from MARY TOURTEL, who had been producing it since 1920. The popularity of the series stayed high, and by the time he retired in 1965 over 34 million *Rupert Bear* annuals had been sold.

Bestiary, The A Middle English poem of the late 12th or early 13th century, the only English example surviving from the many medieval European works which describe animals, real or mythical, and explain their allegorical significance. The form may date from the 4th century, though it derived more immediately from the 7th-century *Etymologiae* of Isidore of Seville and the 11th-century *Physiologus* of Thetbaldus. Fictitious beasts included the unicorn, phoenix, cockatrice and the bizarre manticora, with scorpion's tail, lion's body, man's head, red eyes, triple row of teeth and taste for human flesh. Such descriptions result not just from invention but also from misinterpretation of accounts of real animals and from the belief that the etymology of an animal's name reflected its real character (thus barnacle geese were supposed to hatch from barnacles, and the crocodile was thought to be so called because it was saffron-, or crocus-, coloured).

Bethell, Ursula 1874–1945 New Zealand poet. Born in England, she spent most of her life in a family of farmers in the South Island and established a community of Church of England women in Christchurch in the 1930s. Known as the poet of the Cashmere Hills, near Christchurch, she produced domestic, unassertive, openly meditative verse in *From a Garden in the Antipodes* (published under the pseudonym of Evelyn Hayes in London, 1929) and two later volumes published by the Caxton Press in Christchurch. *Collected Poems* appeared posthumously in 1950.

Betjeman, Sir John 1906–84 Poet, critic of architecture, journalist and broadcaster. Although he published many volumes of verse from *Mount Zion* (1931) onwards, he was probably best known for the autobiographical *Summoned by Bells* (1960) and the Earl of Birkenhead's edition of his *Collected Poems* (1958; revised 1962), which was reprinted many times and sold close to a million copies. Particularly after his success as a television personality, Betjeman's very popularity often stood in the way of serious recognition, though this came from fellow poets like AUDEN and LARKIN. Technically conservative and deceptively simple, his poetry creates a wry comedy of middle-class life that is shot through with sadness. His sense of the superficiality of contemporary life, his melancholy Christianity and, above all, the abiding sustenance he took from English landscape and architecture also found a voice in his large output of prose from *Ghastly Good Taste* (1933) onwards. The introduction to *Collins Guide to English Parish Churches* (1958) is outstanding among his architectural writings. He succeeded DAY-LEWIS as POET LAUREATE in 1972.

Betrothed, The See SCOTT, SIR WALTER.

Between the Acts VIRGINIA WOOLF's last novel, published posthumously in 1941. Pointz Hall, an English country house owned by the ageing Bartholomew Oliver and his widowed sister, Lucy Swithin, is also home to their nephew, Giles Oliver, a stockbroker, and his wife, Isa, whose poetic inner thoughts are rendered in STREAM OF CONSCIOUSNESS and correspond to the metaphorical impulse which underlies the main action. This centres on the performance of a village pageant during a June afternoon in 1939 in the grounds of Pointz Hall. It is directed by Miss La Trobe, a lesbian artist whose creative aspirations are continually thwarted by reality. The pageant itself, a fragmentary re-enactment of English history, occupies the bulk of the novel. The intention is apparently to celebrate the lasting values in English country life and to indict the present for its shallow pretensions. The imminent threat of annihilation in World War II is a recurrent background theme.

Bevis of Hampton [*Beves of Hamtoun*] A VERSE ROMANCE in TAIL-RHYME stanzas and octosyllabic couplets, probably written in Southampton *c.* 1300. In the course of many adventures Bevis is captured by pirates and sold as a slave, marries Josian, daughter of the Saracen King of Armenia, avenges the murder of his father by his mother's lover, becomes Earl of Southampton and subdues the giant Ascopart. Touches of humour and sympathetic portraits of the hero and heroine enliven the lengthy narrative. The story exists in several European languages; an Anglo-Norman version provided the source for this romance.

Bewick, Thomas 1753–1828 Engraver. He is credited with having revived the neglected art of wood engraving. Although his early work is based on previous illustrators, he swiftly developed into a remarkable interpreter of animal life and a humorist in the tradition of HOGARTH. His most original and characteristic work is to be found in the lovingly executed wild-life illustrations and vignettes of country life in *A General History of Quadrupeds* (1790), and *A History of British Birds* (1797–1804). He also cut blocks for poems by GOLDSMITH and PARNELL (1795), THOMSON's *THE SEASONS* (1805) and Aesop's fables (1818). His admirers included WORDSWORTH, CARLYLE, RUSKIN and AUDUBON. His *Memoir* (1862) contains absorbing descriptions of his Northumberland childhood and the development of the techniques of his craft.

Bhattacharya, Bhabani 1906–88 Indian novelist. His fiction, which confronts many Indian social problems, includes *So Many Hungers* (1947), about the Bengal famine of 1942–3, *Music for Mohini* (1952), *A Goddess Named Gold* (1960), *He Who Rides a Tiger* (1954), *Shadow from Ladakh* (1967) and *A Dream in Hawaii* (1978). *Steel Hawk* (1968) is a volume of short stories. Bhattacharya also published non-fiction and translated RABINDRANATH TAGORE.

Bible in English, The For over 1000 years before the Reformation, the Bible existed primarily in Latin, descended from Jerome's 4th-century versions, known as the Vulgate. Parts were paraphrased or translated into Anglo-Saxon (by AELFRIC, for example) and Middle English; in the late 14th century WYCLIF and his LOLLARD followers translated the entire Vulgate into English for the first time. The pastoral aim of the two Lollard Bibles (*c.*1375–96) was not far from the spirit of the Protestant Reformation and, in particular, the work of TYNDALE. His urgent need to enable 'the boy that driveth the plough' to know Scripture impelled him to give his life to the work, in two senses. His translations of the New Testament, between 1525 and 1534, were from the original Greek (ERASMUS had just established a good text), and his translations of the Old Testament books of the Pentateuch (1530 and 1534), Jonah (1531) and Judges to 2 Chronicles from the original Hebrew. This work set a norm.

It is remarkable that the very first printed translations into English remain in many ways the best. Tyndale produced phrases often so clear and arresting that all but the most bizarre of later attempts, even down to our own day, stand in some relation to his work. Yet there have been enough later changes to make his translations still have extraordinary freshness. His serpent says to Eve not 'Ye shall not surely die' as in the Authorized Version (Genesis 3.4) but 'Tush ye shall not die'; and the sixth chapter of Matthew, part of the Sermon on the Mount, does not end 'Sufficient unto the day is the evil thereof', as in the Authorized Version, but 'For each day hath enough of his owne trouble.'

Only one copy of Tyndale's first complete New Testament of 1526 survives, so ruthless were the authorities; readers in England were persecuted, and there was a public burning of books at St Paul's Cross in London. Tyndale worked in permanent exile, often in hiding and even on the run, until his execution at Vilvorde, near Brussels, in 1536. His fellow worker COVERDALE, whose Englishing of the Psalms is cherished to this day in the BOOK OF COMMON PRAYER, used his work, some then unpublished, to produce a complete Bible – the first to be printed in English – at Cologne in 1535. A year later Henry VIII gave royal licence for an English Bible. Known as Matthew's Bible, it was said to have been edited by John Rogers, but these names were devices to conceal the work of Tyndale. A revised version by Richard Taverner followed in 1539. Later in the same year the first Great Bible, the only 'official' Bible in English, was ordered to be set up in churches. It was prepared by Coverdale as another revision of Matthew's Bible (and thus again of Tyndale) and carried a prologue by CRANMER, Archbishop of Canterbury.

Two decades later the most international of all English Bibles appeared, a remarkable result of humanist and Reformation scholarship. English Protestants escaping from Mary had arrived in Geneva, then a powerhouse of textual research and translation into European vernaculars, of secular classics as well as Scripture. The English exiles, including Coverdale, worked on a new translation into English which they were able to present to Queen Elizabeth soon after her accession, in 1560. This, the Geneva Bible, had indexes, copious explanatory notes on every page, maps and elucidatory pictures, in a tradition going back to Tyndale: illumination, as a preface frankly said, 'of all the hard places'. It set a new standard in Greek and Hebrew scholarship, while at the same time being a Bible for readers at all levels. For nearly a century it remained the Bible of the English people, influencing SHAKESPEARE, MILTON and many others. In 1576 the New Testament was revised, with only slight changes to the text but complete reworking of the notes, now full and often surprisingly engaging, by Laurence Tomson of Magdalen College, Oxford. In 1599 the Book of Revelation was given vast new notes by the European theologian 'Junius'. In the hundred years of its life, the Geneva Bible came in many forms, large and small, black-letter and Roman, but – especially when it had Tomson's New Testament – it was encyclopaedic. A whole world of learning, often including concordances, the Book of Common Prayer, Sternhold and Hopkins's metrical psalms (see PSALTERS) and changing but usually impressive preliminary matter, it made a *locus* of Reformation and Renaissance scholarship. Even the two Roman Catholic, Vulgate-based retorts to Geneva, a New Testament from Rheims in 1582 and an Old Testament from Douai in 1609, make use of it, for all their huffing against Protestants. Yet the Geneva Bible has been quite forgotten. Worse, it was replaced for political reasons, being dismissed as bitterly Calvinistic, which it is not. Worst of all, it has been shrivelled to a vulgar nickname and called the Breeches

Bible because in Genesis 2.7 it says (as did the Lollard Bibles, incidentally) that Adam and Eve 'made themselves breeches'.

The Bishops' Bible, an attempt led by Archbishop PARKER to rival Geneva with a more Latinate, Vulgate-based translation, with few notes, appeared in 1568 but did not establish itself. JAMES I, however, decided that he found the Geneva Bible objectionable and at the Hampton Court Conference of 1604 he initiated a new translation. A panel of 54 scholars was appointed, divided into six groups. ANDREWES was head of one of the groups at Westminster. The Authorized Version (so called, although it was never authorized) or King James Bible appeared in 1611, incidentally to broadside attacks on its accuracy. It carried an obsequious dedication to James which contrasts with the urgent religious concern of the dedication of the Geneva Bible to Elizabeth. This translation was in fact largely a revision heavily dependent on the scholarship of the Geneva Bible and the phrasing of Tyndale but taking from the Bishops' Bible and Rheims New Testament a more lofty, Latinate orotundity. The translators' declared aim, 'to make a good one better', was often doubtfully achieved. The Authorized Version certainly contains many famous beauties, such as 'And the glory of the Lord shall be revealed, and all flesh shall see it together: for the mouth of the Lord hath spoken it' (Isaiah 40.5), or Jesus's 'Father, forgive them, for they know not what they do' (Luke 23.34) or 'In my Father's house are many mansions' (John 14.2). But the phrase from Isaiah comes from the Geneva Bible, and the two New Testament phrases come from Tyndale. The much-loved Christmas stories in Matthew 2 and Luke 3 are virtually unchanged from Tyndale and Geneva. Where the Authorized Version differs, whether or not from the Bishops' Bible, it can in fact be very unlovely: 'Nevertheless the dimness shall not be such as was in her vexation' (Isaiah 9.1); 'The treacherous dealers have dealt treacherously; yea, the treacherous dealers have dealt very treacherously' (Isaiah 24.16); 'I long after you all in the bowels of Jesus Christ' (Philippians 1.8). Though King James had set his translators specifically to avoid marginal notes, the Authorized Version was later printed eight times with Geneva's notes.

The Authorized Version gradually ousted the Geneva Bible. Its overwhelming impact on English literature since its first appearance, though commonly asserted, is in fact quite hard to substantiate. Certainly a reader who does not know an earlier Bible in English will miss much of the meaning of religious writing like the poems of GEORGE HERBERT or the poetry and much of the prose of HENRY VAUGHAN, or of a satire like DRYDEN's *ABSALOM AND ACHITOPHEL*. In spite of what is sometimes said, BUNYAN's English comes from common speech rather than the Authorized Version. SWIFT, however, in *A Proposal for Correcting the English Tongue* (1712), wrote that 'the translators of the Bible were masters of an English stile much fitter for the work, than we see in any of our present writings' and praised 'the simplicity of the whole'; COLERIDGE believed that 'without this holdfast, our vitiated imaginations would refine away language to mere abstractions'. By the time of its first official revision in the Revised Version of 1881–5, the Authorized Version had become a hallowed classic of English literature, and the revisers could state, wrongly, that it had been revered from its first appearance.

Between the Authorized Version of 1611 and the Revised Version of 1881–5 there were some 150 published translations of all or parts of the Bible, some admirable and some odd. Some, like Dr Challoner's revisions of Douai and Rheims, were influential in their time. Between the 1880s and 1939 at least seven 'one-man' translations of the whole Bible into English were printed. Two dozen 'one-man' New Testaments have appeared in the last hundred years, not to mention a host of parts of the Bible. In the last 25 years, for example, over 150 translations of sections of the Bible into English have been published. Modern printing techniques can conceal the sheer size of the undertaking, to say nothing of the necessity of professional expertise in textual scholarship and so many different kinds of Hebrew and Greek. In this century, translations by Moffatt, by Weymouth, by Ferrar Fenton, by Goodspeed, by Knox and by Barclay have been influential and are still well regarded. Just after World War II, the English editions of the (American) Revised Standard Version were widely used; the translations of Paul's letters by J. B. Phillips alerted a generation to the fact that Paul made vivid modern sense. As the Bible in local vernaculars spreads now across the world – the Bible, or part of it, is to date in over 1700 languages – so more is learned about how the special revelations of the Old and New Testaments might best come across to late 20th-century English-reading people. There are now many different versions of the Bible in English in print, including several attempts to modernize the Authorized Version. Those with greatest impact have been: The New English Bible (1970), which is lucid but sometimes disliked; The Living Bible (1971), a paraphrase; Today's English Version (1976), popularly known by its American title, the Good News Bible, which combines accuracy with a relaxed readability that is a long way from the Authorized Version; The Jerusalem Bible (1966), an often ponderous antidote to raciness; and the rather patchwork New International Version (1979). New Testament scholars often use the excellent Translator's New Testament (1973), which hits the theological nail on the head every time; it is designed to help those who translate the New Testament into remoter languages. More Bibles in English are now sold than ever before: the number of English readers has risen from six million under Elizabeth I to 600 million.

Bible in Spain, The GEORGE BORROW's colourful narrative of his travels through Portugal and Spain, published in 1843. Ostensibly an account of his five years' service (1835–40) as an agent of the British and Foreign Bible Society, it describes adventures in remote regions, encounters with gypsies and bandits and frequent confrontations with authority. The reader has no means of distinguishing between fact and fiction. The book was a best-seller on both sides of the Atlantic and was never out of print during the 19th century.

Bickerstaff, Isaac A character invented by JONATHAN SWIFT, and supposedly the author of *Predictions for the Ensuing Year* (1708), a collection of spoof prophecies at the expense of John Partridge, an astrologer who published a fashionable almanac. Swift's version foretold Partridge's death and, despite the hapless quack's protestations, claimed the prediction had been fulfilled. STEELE adopted the nickname of Bickerstaff when he started THE TATLER in 1709.

Bickerstaffe, Isaac 1733–c. 1808 Playwright. He was largely responsible for the emergence and fashionable acceptance of English comic opera. *Thomas and Sally*

(1760) and the excellent *Love in a Village* (1762) had accompanying music by Thomas Arne. *The Maid of the Mill* (1765) and *The Royal Garland* (1768) were provided with music by Samuel Arnold. *Lionel and Clarissa* (1768) was the best fruit of Bickerstaffe's collaboration with DIBDIN. His career was brought to a sudden end in 1772, when he was threatened with arrest as a homosexual. He fled to the Continent, where he lived in obscurity for a further 40 years.

Bierce, Ambrose (Gwinnett) 1842–c. 1914 American journalist and short-story writer. As a journalist in San Francisco he contributed to the OVERLAND MONTHLY and became an influential member of the Western literary circle which originally included BRET HARTE, MARK TWAIN and JOAQUIN MILLER. A prolific writer, he is chiefly remembered for *Tales of Soldiers and Civilians* (1891; entitled *In the Midst of Life* in Britain and in the 1898 US edition), a volume of short stories drawn largely from his own disillusioning experiences during the Civil War. The best known include: 'The Middle Toe of the Right Foot', about a murderer haunted to death by his victim; 'A Horseman in the Sky', about a young Union soldier forced by circumstances to kill his own father; and 'An Occurrence at Owl Creek Bridge', presenting the fantasy which a man who is being hanged experiences in the last seconds of his life. *The Cynic's Word Book* (1906) is a volume of ironic definitions. A solitary and discontented man, Bierce disappeared in Mexico during its Civil War. It is not known exactly when or how he died.

Big Money, The See *USA*.

Bigg, John Stanyon 1828–65 Journalist and poet of the SPASMODIC SCHOOL OF POETRY. He published *The Sea King*, a metrical romance in six CANTOS; *Night and Soul* (1854); a novel, *Alfred Staunton* (1860); and a final volume of poetry, *Shifting Scenes and Other Poems* (1862).

Bildungsroman A 'novel of development', tracing the protagonist's growth, usually from birth or early childhood, into adulthood and maturity. The prototype is Goethe's *Wilhelm Meister's Apprenticeship* (1795–6), translated into English by THOMAS CARLYLE in 1824. Even an incomplete list of major examples suggests how important a part the form has played in English fiction since then: DICKENS's *DAVID COPPERFIELD* and *GREAT EXPECTATIONS*, BUTLER's *THE WAY OF ALL FLESH*, LAWRENCE's *SONS AND LOVERS*, JOYCE's *PORTRAIT OF THE ARTIST AS A YOUNG MAN* and FORSTER's *THE LONGEST JOURNEY*.

Billings, Josh [Shaw, Henry Wheeler] 1818–85 American comic writer. ARTEMUS WARD helped him publish his first collection, *Josh Billings: Hiz Sayings* (1865). Thereafter he became a favourite exponent of agrarian folk wisdom and reached an immense public with his comments on government, fashionable pretension and political corruption in *Josh Billings on Ice, and Other Things* (1868), *Everybody's Friend* (1874), *Josh Billings' Trump Kards* (1877) and *Josh Billings' Spice Box* (1881), as well as his PARODY annual, *Farmer's Allminax* (1869–80). He lectured widely in his Josh Billings persona and commanded a large popular audience.

Billy Budd, Sailor A short novel by HERMAN MELVILLE, begun in 1886 and left in a semi-final draft at his death in 1891. It was first published in 1924. It is set aboard HMS *Bellipotent* in 1797, following the naval mutinies during the war between England and France. Billy Budd, the 'Handsome Sailor', is impressed from a merchantman and quickly becomes a favourite of the crew.

But he also arouses the hostility of the brutal master-at-arms, John Claggart, who falsely accuses him of being involved in a mutinous plot. Unable to answer the charge because of a chronic stammer, Billy strikes Claggart and kills him. Captain Vere, though sympathizing with the agonized Billy, calls a drumhead court and in effect instructs it to find him guilty of a capital crime. Billy is hanged from the yard-arm after crying out, 'God bless Captain Vere!'

Bingham, Joseph 1668–1723 Church historian. He is remembered for his exhaustive ten-volume *Origines Ecclesiasticae: or, The Antiquities of the Christian Church* (1708–22), a 20-year labour.

Binyon, (Robert) Laurence 1869–1943 Poet, playwright and art historian. The subject of his poetry is frequently classical and its theme is often mutability and decay. Volumes include: *Winnowing Fan* (1914), which contains 'For the Fallen', a famous ELEGY for the dead of World War I; two collections of ODES, *The Sirens* (1924) and *The Idols* (1928); and *The Burning of the Leaves and Other Poems* (1944). In addition to works of art history, he also wrote several verse dramas, including *Arthur* (1923) with music by Elgar, *Brief Candles* (1938) and the unfinished *Madness of Merlin* (1947).

Biographia Literaria A philosophical and autobiographical work by SAMUEL TAYLOR COLERIDGE, published in 1817. Originally conceived in 1814 as a preface to *Sibylline Leaves*, it rapidly grew into a two-volume *causerie* on his 'literary life and opinions'. Unsystematic, inexhaustibly communicative, and untied to a single literary register, it is entirely lacking in the aesthetic and recapitulatory 'finish' of conventional autobiography. As in the lectures and *Table Talk*, his method is excitingly oblique and inspirational, the moment of insight sudden and often wonderfully incandescent.

The underlying philosophical concern of the *Biographia* is the process, as opposed to the fact, of human creativity. The predominantly empirical English tradition of literary and philosophical thought bequeathed by the 18th to the early 19th century had tended, for Coleridge, to view culture and creativity as simple givens rather than as the products of a specifically constituted intelligence. His famous definition of the creative intelligence, or the 'Imagination', issues from an exploration (which takes him through pioneering readings of Kant, Fichte, Schelling and the brothers Schlegel) of the structure of the relations between subjectivity and objectivity, self and world, speculative reason and rational understanding (chapters IX, XII, XIII). As the universal human faculty through which these antinomies are reconciled, or rendered merely apparent, the Imagination is by no means the monopoly of a particular group or a specific practice, though Coleridge is in no doubt that it finds its greatest adepts among poets, and its highest form of expression in poetry and aesthetic culture. Before SHELLEY's unpublished *Philosophical View of Reform* of 1820, Coleridge's theory of the imagination and the commitments it enjoined was English ROMANTICISM's most carefully articulated response to the multiple contradictions of early industrial society. Its influence upon later 19th- and 20th-century cultural theory has been, to say the least, pervasive, and its model of the creative process is the one with which students of poetry and literature are still most readily familiar.

Bird, Robert (Montgomery) 1806–54 American novelist and playwright. *Nick of the Woods: or, The*

Jibbenainosay (1837) is a novel about a bloodthirsty Quaker and ignoble Indians, set at the end of the American Revolution. Other novels include *Calavar: or, the Knight of the Conquest* (1834) and its sequel, *The Infidel: or, The Fall of Mexico* (1835), *The Hawks of Hawk-Hollow* (1835), about a well-to-do Pennsylvania family's fatal lack of patriotism, and *Sheppard Lee* (1836), a satire on contemporary society informed by Bird's Whig politics. His work for the stage includes romantic plays about Philadelphia life and historical dramas.

Birmingham, George A. [Hannay, James Owen] 1865–1950 Irish novelist and playwright. Originally a Church of Ireland clergyman, he settled in England in 1924. Early novels such as *Hyacinth* (1906) and *The Bad Times* (1908) are serious, compassionate explorations of recent Irish history. The more light-hearted *Spanish Gold* (1908) won him a large popular audience, but he unintentionally offended Roman Catholic and extreme nationalist sensibilities with *The Seething Pot* (1905), *Red Hand of Ulster* (1912) and a stage comedy, *General John Regan* (1913). His later books are chiefly well-observed light comedies of Irish (and English) life.

Birney, (Alfred) Earle 1904– Canadian poet. Although did not begin writing verse until the late 1930s, he has come to be regarded as one of Canada's most important poets. He deals with an encyclopaedic range of Canadian subjects, but has also written poems about virtually every part of the globe. His early writing is characterized by a belief that art can change the course of experience. More recently these attitudes have been replaced by an absurdist view of the human experience, and from *Ice Cod Bell and Stone* (1962) onwards he has written in a more colloquial North American voice. His best work includes a verse drama, *Trial of a City* (1952; reissued as *The Damnation of Vancouver*), in which the 'trial' debates whether Vancouver, representing modern urban civilization, ought to be destroyed, and a comic 'military picaresque', *Turvey* (1977). His other volumes of poetry include *David and Other Poems* (1942), *Near False Mouth* (1964) and *Collected Poems* (1975).

Birrell, Augustine 1850–1933 Politician and essayist. He served as President of the Board of Education (1905) and Chief Secretary for Ireland (1907–16). His collections of literary essays, *Obiter Dicta* (1884, 1887 and 1924), were popular. Other writings include a biography of CHARLOTTE BRONTË (1887) and studies of HAZLITT (1902) and MARVELL (1905) for the English Men of Letters series.

Birthday Party, The A play (1957) by PINTER, his first work to attract attention. Stanley lives in a seaside boarding-house belonging to a deck-chair attendant and his eccentric wife, Meg. Already suffering from persecution mania, he is terrified at the arrival of a Jew called Goldberg and an Irishman called McCann. At his birthday party a game of blind man's buff drives him to hysteria. The next day Goldberg and McCann remove him to an unknown destination.

Bishop, Elizabeth 1911–79 American poet. Her volumes include: *Poems: North and South a Cold Spring* (1955); *The Diary of 'Helena Morley'* (1957), a translation from the Portuguese; *Questions of Travel* (1965), which contains poems about her experiences in Brazil, where she spent 16 years; *Complete Poems* (1969); and *Geography III* (1976). *Collected Prose* (1984) includes autobiographical sketches, travel accounts, a memoir of MARIANNE MOORE and several short stories.

Bishop Blougram's Apology A DRAMATIC MONOLOGUE by ROBERT BROWNING, published in *Men and Women* (1855). The worldly but highly intelligent Bishop treats his listener, the journalist Gigadibs, to a virtuoso performance that leaves him and the reader still uncertain of the extent or nature of his religious faith. In the process, the poem offers a minute and skilful examination of the various grounds for faith and doubt in the 19th century.

Bishop Orders His Tomb at Saint Praxed's Church, The A DRAMATIC MONOLOGUE by ROBERT BROWNING, included in *Dramatic Romances and Lyrics* (1845). Even as he is dying, the Renaissance bishop still clings desperately to the world of the senses. RUSKIN praised it as 'nearly all that I have said of the central Renaissance in thirty pages, of THE STONES OF VENICE, put into as many lines.'

Black, William 1841–98 Scottish novelist. He is best remembered for his novels with a Scottish setting, most notably *A Daughter of Heth* (1871), *A Princess of Thule* (1874) and *Macleod of Dare* (1878). *The Strange Adventures of a Phaeton* (1872) combines elements of fiction, romance, guidebook and natural description. Black contributed a study of GOLDSMITH (1878) to the English Men of Letters series. See also CELTIC REVIVAL.

Black Arrow, The A novel by ROBERT LOUIS STEVENSON, serialized in 1883 and published in book form in 1888. Stevenson himself ridiculed it as a pseudohistoric potboiler. It is set in late 15th-century England, during the final stages of the Wars of the Roses. The diffuse plot has three main strands: the first concerns the conflict between Yorkists and Lancastrians, the second the Brotherhood of the Black Arrow, an outlaw band led by 'John Amend-All' (Ellis Duckworth), and the third Richard Shelton, Joanna Sedley, and their relations with his deceitful uncle and guardian, Sir Daniel Brackley. The book ends with Dick and Joanna's marriage and his retreat into private life, abandoning the 'heroism' which the novel has exposed as self-seeking and treacherous.

Black Beauty A novel for children by ANNA SEWELL, published in 1877. It charts the decline and fall of a well-bred horse brought low by neglectful grooms and overwork in the cab trade. He also suffers sadly from the hated 'bearing rein', a harness designed to keep a horse's head up; the novel's protest helped to end this practice. Black Beauty himself is finally saved from the knacker's yard to enjoy an honourable retirement. Less fortunate is his high-spirited friend in harness Ginger, who dies ignobly in the streets of London.

Black Dwarf, The See SCOTT, SIR WALTER.

Black Elk 1863–1950 Sioux warrior and priest. His oral autobiography, *Black Elk Speaks* (recorded and edited by John Neihardt; 1932), is a moving account of his life and mission. He also delivered an account of the religious rites of the Oglala Sioux, *The Sacred Pipe* (recorded and edited by John Epes Brown; 1953).

Black Mask, The A magazine of DETECTIVE FICTION, founded by H. L. MENCKEN and GEORGE JEAN NATHAN in 1920. It began by publishing stories in the traditional English mould but introduced 'hard-boiled' fiction and private-eye heroes in the work of HAMMETT and CHANDLER, as well as Erle Stanley Gardner, George Harmon Coxe, Frederick Nebel, Lester Dent and Horace McCoy.

Black Mountain school A group of American poets attracted to Black Mountain College, North Carolina, in the early 1950s to study with CHARLES OLSON. His theory of 'projective verse' advocated 'open forms' and 'composition by field' which abandoned conventional METRE. The group included CREELEY, ROBERT DUNCAN and LEVERTOV. Its work appeared in the *Black Mountain Review*, published from 1954 to 1957.

Blackburn, Paul 1926–71 American poet. His prolific output included the early poems in *The Dissolving Fabric* (1955), *Brooklyn–Manhattan Transit* (1960) and *The Nets* (1961), the middle-period poems in *The Cities* (1967) and *In. On. Or about the Premises* (1968), and the late poems in *Halfway down the Coast* and *The Journals* (both 1975). The *Collected Poems of Paul Blackburn* appeared in 1985. He also established a reputation as a translator of the Provençal troubadours and the works of Julio Cortázar and Antonio Jiménez-Landi.

Blackmore, Sir Richard *c.* 1655–1729 Poet. The physician to Queen Anne, he published a *Satyr against Wit* (1700), admired by his friend, Samuel Wesley. Blackmore's uncontrolled EPIC verses, pious and patriotic, include *The Creation* (1712) and *Redemption* (1722), which attempt to promote adherence to religion on the basis of natural reason.

Blackmore, R(ichard) D(oddridge) 1825–1900 Novelist. Called to the Bar in 1852, Blackmore preferred instead to divide his time between writing and market gardening. His earliest published works were poems and translations but he gained his first real success, and lasting fame, with LORNA DOONE (1869), a historical novel set on Exmoor. Other books, all overshadowed by the popularity of *Lorna Doone*, include *Clara Vaughan* (1864), *Alice Lorraine* (1875), *Cripps the Carrier* (1877), *Christowell: A Dartmoor Tale* (1881) and *Springhaven: A Tale of the Great War* (1887), set in southern England during the Napoleonic era.

Blackstone, Sir William 1723–80 Jurist. His four-volume *Commentaries on the Laws of England* (1765–9), derived from his annual lectures as the first Vinerian Professor of English Law at Oxford, was admired for its lucid exposition and regarded for many years as a definitive historical account. Blackstone proceeds from the law of nature (the revealed or the inferred will of God) to municipal law, which he defines as a rule of civil conduct prescribed by the supreme power in the state. Yet Blackstone was by no means a scientific jurist. His attempt to find a basis in history and reason for all the most characteristic English institutions was attacked by BENTHAM in *A Fragment on Government* (1776).

Blackwood's (Edinburgh) Magazine A monthly periodical started in 1817. JOHN GIBSON LOCKHART, JOHN WILSON ('Christopher North') and JAMES HOGG gave it a reputation for bitter attacks on those of whom it disapproved, most famously the so-called COCKNEY SCHOOL of writers. They were joined by WILLIAM MAGINN in writing *Noctes Ambrosianae*, a series of lively imaginary conversations whose appearance between 1822 and 1835 greatly contributed to the magazine's success. Known familiarly as the 'Maga', *Blackwood's* dropped the 'Edinburgh' from its title in 1906 and survived, though without its former influence, until 1980.

Blair, Robert 1699–1746 Poet. *The Grave* (1743) owed much to EDWARD YOUNG'S *NIGHT THOUGHTS* and identified him with the GRAVEYARD POETS. Its morbid meditation was popular with middle-class Dissenters for many years, and one edition (1808) was illustrated by WILLIAM BLAKE.

Blaise, Clark 1940– Canadian novelist and short-story writer. His short-story collections, *A North*

American Education (1973) and *Tribal Justice* (1974), and his novels, *Lunar Attractions* (1979) and *Lusts* (1983), focus on the often victimized outsider, the isolated individual struggling to find a place in an increasingly bizarre contemporary society. *Resident Alien* (1986) combines autobiographical essays and autobiographical fiction. He collaborated with his wife, the novelist Bharati Mukherjee, on *Days and Nights in Calcutta* (1977), an account of a stay in India.

Blake, Nicholas See DAY-LEWIS, C.

Blake, William 1757–1827 Poet and painter. The son of a London hosier, he was educated at home, reading widely in the Bible and the English poets and somehow picking up a knowledge of French, Italian, Latin, Greek and Hebrew. At the age of 14 he was apprenticed to the engraver James Basire, making drawings of Westminster Abbey and other old churches and studying Henry Fuseli's *Reflections on the Painting and Sculpture of the Greeks*. When he was 21 he entered the recently founded Royal Academy, though he soon became restless with its traditional approach.

In 1782 he married Catherine Boucher and in 1783 two friends issued his *Poetical Sketches*, a collection which includes 'To the Muses' and 'My Silks and Fine Array'. In 1789 he published *Songs of Innocence*, the first of his engraved or illuminated books, and *The Book of Thel*, which illustrates his early mysticism. *Tiriel*, written in 1788–9, is the first of his elaborately symbolic writings. In 1794 Blake added *Songs of Experience* to an edition of *Songs of Innocence*, now retitled *SONGS OF INNOCENCE AND OF EXPERIENCE Shewing the Two Contrary States of the Human Soul*. His dislike of human authority and his radical sympathies, which made him a friend of GODWIN and PAINE, were expressed in the two sets of prose aphorisms called *There is No Natural Religion* and the third called *All Religions are One* (all *c.* 1788), as well as *The French Revolution: A Poem in Seven Books* (*c.* 1791). His most important prose work, THE MARRIAGE OF HEAVEN AND HELL, was engraved in 1790.

In the years that followed Blake executed some of his most famous engravings, including those for *The Book of Job* and for YOUNG'S *NIGHT THOUGHTS*, and began work on his 'prophetic books', the visionary poems partly modelled on MILTON'S *PARADISE LOST*, which elaborate his own mythology and philosophy. *The Visions of the Daughters of Albion* (1793) introduced Urizen, the symbol of restrictive morality, and Orc, the arch-rebel, whose opposition fuels the evolving drama of *America: A Prophecy* (1793), *Europe* and *The Book of Urizen* (1794), *The Book of Ahania*, *The Book of Los* and *The Song of Los* (1795). *Vala*, probably begun in 1795, was rewritten as *The Four Zoas: The Torments of Love and Jealousy in the Death and Judgement of Albion the Ancient Man* (1797), in which Urizen's oppressive moral code is condemned, Orc and liberty triumph, and the figure of Jesus as Redeemer is introduced.

In 1800–3 the Blakes went to live with WILLIAM HAYLEY, a bad poet but a patron of good ones, at Felpham in Sussex. The association was not a success, and Blake's time at Felpham was soured by his arrest on trumped-up charges of sedition. On his return to London he finished and engraved *Milton: A Poem in Two Books, To Justify the Ways of God to Men* (1803–8). The most famous part, when Milton returns to earth and in the person of the living poet corrects the spiritual error glorified in *Paradise Lost*, appears at the conclusion of the preface in the lines beginning 'And did those feet in ancient time'. *Jerusalem: The Emanation of the Giant Albion*, written between 1804 and 1820, is a complex account of Albion (Man) torn between the forces of imagination and of natural religion. *The Ghost of Abel* (1822) challenges BYRON's *CAIN* in a minute poetic drama of 70 lines.

Other notable poems are difficult to date. *Auguries of Innocence* probably dates from 1802, for example, and *The Everlasting Gospel* perhaps from 1810. Some works were unknown until his papers were examined after his death, while many were not issued in the conventional way. Defying the usual methods of publication, Blake became a one-man industry, designing, engraving and producing his own works like the medieval craftsmen who so intrigued him. His books did not reach more than a small circle of readers, and to fellow writers he remained an eccentric and a curiosity, known more through rumour and report than directly through his writings. He never shook off poverty. The publisher Cromek cheated him over the commission of 'The Canterbury Pilgrims', while an exhibition of his work in 1809 was a commercial fiasco, though the *Descriptive Catalogue* is a prized addition to his output.

A peculiarly difficult artist to assess, Blake was a mixture of extremes, by turns profound and naive. Though the mythology he evolved was highly complex, it was never meant to be private and impenetrable, and the image of Blake as a totally isolated figure is no longer acceptable. His vision of the contradictory forces beneath human civilization mirrors the intense political turmoil of his age. His interest in legend and antiquity anticipated the Romantics' rediscovery of the past, while his insistence on the need to remake those legends pointed the way to the poetry of later generations. But it was left to later generations to recognize his importance.

blank verse Verse in unrhymed iambic pentameters (see METRE). A flexible form able to accommodate a variety of English speech rhythms, it is used in most Elizabethan drama (including the plays of SHAKESPEARE) and many long narrative poems (MILTON's *PARADISE LOST*, WORDSWORTH's *THE PRELUDE* and TENNYSON's *IDYLLS OF THE KING*).

Blast: The Review of the Great English Vortex A periodical of art and literature, intended as the mouthpiece of VORTICISM but published only twice (July 1914 and July 1915). The guiding figures were WYNDHAM LEWIS and POUND. The first issue attacked Victorianism and the BLOOMSBURY GROUP. The second, a 'War Number', was mostly written by Lewis, though it contained some poems by T. S. ELIOT.

Bleak House A novel by DICKENS, published in monthly parts in 1852-3 and in volume form in 1853.

An indictment of the Court of Chancery and its endless bungling of the case of Jarndyce v. Jarndyce gives the novel its scope and meaning. In one main plot Esther Summerson (who narrates much of the story) becomes protégée of John Jarndyce, also guardian of two wards of Chancery, Ada Clare and Richard Carstone. Ada and Richard marry but he dies worn out after enmeshing himself in the Jarndyce lawsuit. Another plot concerns Sir Leicester Dedlock and his proud wife, whose guilty past – an affair with Captain Hawdon which produced Esther – is unravelled by the calculating lawyer Tulkinghorn. Before he can expose her, Tulkinghorn is murdered by her waiting woman Mademoiselle Hortense, who is brought to book by

Inspector Bucket. Lady Dedlock dies at the graveyard where the Captain lies. Esther eventually marries the surgeon Allan Woodcourt.

Other characters who contribute to the complex portrait of society include: the selfish Harold Skimpole (modelled on LEIGH HUNT) and the boisterous Boythorn (modelled on LANDOR); Krook, who dies by 'Spontaneous Combustion'; Gridley and Miss Flite, ruined by Chancery; Mrs Jellyby, exponent of 'Telescopic Philanthropy'; the greasy Mr Chadband; the grasping Smallweeds; and the lawyers Conversation Kenge and Mr Vholes. The brutish life and death of Jo the crossing-sweeper is central to the moral design of the novel.

Bleasdale, Alan 1946- Playwright. Often set in Liverpool, his work shows a gift for comedy veering towards FARCE and for lively rather than subtle characterization. Despite the popularity of *Having a Ball* (1981), a stage play about vasectomy, his greatest success came with two television drama series: *Boys from the Blackstuff* (1983), about the unemployed, and *GBH* (1991), about the rise and fall of the leader of a far-left faction. *Are You Lonesome Tonight?* (1985) is a musical about the last days of Elvis Presley.

Blessed Damozel, The A poem by DANTE GABRIEL ROSSETTI, first published in 1850 in the short-lived literary magazine *THE GERM*. The Damozel leans out 'from the gold bar of Heaven' yearning for her earthly lover, whose reflections are expressed parenthetically throughout. The embodiment of PRE-RAPHAELITE verse, it is complemented by a Rossetti painting of the same name.

Blessington, Marguerite, Countess of 1789-1849 Woman of letters. One of the most colourful Regency figures, she was a literary hostess, the companion of Count d'Orsay and the friend of BYRON, whom she remembered in her *Journal of Conversations with Lord Byron* (1832). After the Earl of Blessington's death in 1829, she maintained herself by writing countless pieces for periodicals, annuals and magazines, editing *The Book of Beauty* and *The Keepsake*; and publishing highly successful travel books such as *The Idler in Italy* (1839) and *The Idler in France* (1841) as well as many three-volume novels.

Blickling Homilies, The Nineteen Old English HOMILIES, or sermons; the date of composition is unknown, though they appear in a manuscript of 971. They deal largely with biblical stories and religious festivals, but one takes as its theme the imminent end of the world and another the futility of worldly pleasures.

Blind Harry See WALLACE.

Blithedale Romance, The A novel by HAWTHORNE, published in 1852. The narrator, Miles Coverdale, goes to the Utopian community of Blithedale (based on BROOK FARM), where he meets Zenobia (based on MARGARET FULLER), Hollingsworth and Priscilla. Zenobia, an exotic feminist, loves the egotistic Hollingsworth, who wants to make Blithedale an institution for criminal reform. Priscilla has escaped from the control of the evil Westervelt. Fearing competition for Hollingsworth from Priscilla, Zenobia delivers her back to Westervelt, but Hollingsworth intervenes to save the girl. It emerges that she is Zenobia's half-sister and will receive the inheritance Zenobia thought was hers. Hollingsworth has chosen her because he needs the money to realize his plans. Zenobia drowns herself. Hollingsworth and Priscilla marry but he is a broken man. Coverdale lapses back into a lonely bachelor's life, explaining that all along he has been in love with Priscilla.

Blitzstein, Marc 1905–64 American composer, librettist and lyricist. He is best remembered for his works of social protest in the 1930s: an oratorio, *The Condemned* (1932), about the martyrdom of Sacco and Vanzetti; a radio play, *I've Got the Tune* (1937); and a musical play, *THE CRADLE WILL ROCK* (1937). After World War II he completed a ballet, *The Guests* (1949), a musical, *Regina* (1949), based on LILLIAN HELLMAN's *The Little Foxes*, and an adaptation of Brecht's *The Threepenny Opera* (1954).

Blixen, Karen See DINESEN, ISAK.

Bloomfield, Robert 1766–1832 Poet. He briefly attracted attention with *The Farmer's Boy* (1800), an imitation of THOMSON's *THE SEASONS* describing the life of an orphan ploughboy, Giles, published with wood engravings by BEWICK. Later works, which did not repeat his success, included *Rural Tales* (1802), *Good Tidings or News from the Farm* (1804) and *The Banks of the Wye* (1811). His last years were dogged by illness and partial blindness, and he died in extreme poverty.

Bloomsbury Group, The The name given to a group of writers, artists and intellectuals who began meeting in about 1905 at the Bloomsbury house of the Stephen sisters, Vanessa Bell and VIRGINIA WOOLF. It grew to include CLIVE BELL, DAVID GARNETT, Duncan Grant, MAYNARD KEYNES, DESMOND MACCARTHY, Adrian and Thoby Stephen, LYTTON STRACHEY, Saxon Sydney-Turner, LEONARD WOOLF and, peripherally, E. M. FORSTER. Strachey's death in 1932 and Virginia Woolf's suicide in 1941 can both be seen as ends of an era. Although its members denied being a group in any formal sense, they were united in an abiding belief in the importance of the arts. Their philosophy can perhaps best be summarized in G. E. MOORE's statement that 'one's prime objects in life were love, the creation and enjoyment of aesthetic experience and the pursuit of knowledge'. They were sceptical and tolerant, reacting against the artistic and social restraints of Victorian society. Through writing (biography, novels, art criticism, economics, political theory), painting (in the works of Vanessa Bell and Duncan Grant), publishing (the Hogarth Press started in 1917 and in 1923 published ELIOT's *THE WASTE LAND*) and support of new developments in the arts, they exercised a considerable influence on the *avant-garde* of the early 20th century.

bluestocking A term for a woman of pronounced literary or intellectual interests, later coming to mean a female pedant. It derives from 'The Blue Stocking Society', the circle who attended ELIZABETH MONTAGU's assemblies; the nickname probably derives from the costume of one of its male members. It included BURNEY, CHAPONE, HANNAH MORE and HORACE WALPOLE.

Blume, Judy 1938– American writer of CHILDREN'S LITERATURE. Her novels have provoked controversy by their comparative outspokenness: *Are You There, God? It's Me, Margaret* (1970) is about an 11-year-old girl who longs to reach puberty so that she can wear a bra, while *Forever* (1975) describes an adolescent girl's first sexual experience.

Blunden, Edmund (Charles) 1896–1974 Poet and critic. His early verse appeared in *GEORGIAN POETRY*. Volumes include *The Waggoner and Other Poems* (1920), *The Shepherd and Other Poems of Peace and War* (1922), *English Poems* (1929), *Collected Poems* (1930), *After the Bombing and Other Short Poems* (1950) and *A Hong Kong*

House Poem (1962). His autobiographical account of the World War I, *Undertones of War*, appeared in 1928. He published biographies of LEIGH HUNT (1930) and SHELLEY (1943), a study of HARDY (1941) and pioneering editions of CLARE (1920), WILFRED OWEN (1931) and IVOR GURNEY (1954).

Blunt, Wilfrid Scawen 1840–1922 Poet, diplomat and Arabist. His first collection, *Sonnets and Songs by Proteus* (1875), contained addresses to women, poems on the Sussex countryside, and adaptations from the Arabic. He wrote and worked in support of Egyptian, Indian and Irish independence, publishing *The Future of Islam* (1882), *Ideas about India* (1885) and *The Secret History of the English Occupation of Egypt* (1907). During a spell in an Irish prison he wrote the SONNET sequence *In Vinculis* (1899). *My Diaries* (1919–20) refer to his friendships with Lord Lytton (EDWARD ROBERT LYTTON), Curzon, WILLIAM MORRIS, LADY GREGORY, ALICE MEYNELL and OSCAR WILDE.

Bly, Robert 1926– American poet. His verse is filled with images of rural Minnesota, which often become figures for his unconscious. Since *Silence in the Snowy Fields* (1962), he has published many volumes together with a distinguished body of translations from Swedish, German (Rilke), Spanish (Neruda and Machado) and Russian.

Blythe, Ronald (George) 1922– Miscellaneous writer. He has written a novel (*A Treasonable Growth*, 1960), short stories (collected in 1985) and essays on literature, but is principally known for *Akenfield: Portrait of an English Village* (1969). Blythe used its technique of transcribed interviews with linking commentary again in *The View in Winter: Reflections on Old Age* (1979).

Blyton, Enid (Mary) 1897–1968 Writer of CHILDREN'S LITERATURE. She was prodigiously energetic in organizing competitions and charitable appeals as well as producing poems, stories, journalism and full-length books. Her 'Famous Five' adventures, appearing from 1942, feature a gang of well-born, privately educated children who solve various mysteries during their largely unsupervised vacations. Little Noddy and Big Ears, introduced after the war, are humanized toys enjoying mild adventures in a bland, domestic setting. Critics have questioned the effect of Blyton's limited literary style on young children and pointed to her racist and snobbish attitudes, but without destroying her popularity, which continues even today.

bob and wheel A wheel is a group of short lines at the end of a longer stanza of longer lines. If its first line is even shorter than the others, it is known as a bob and the whole group is then styled a 'bob and wheel'. The medieval romance *SIR GAWAIN AND THE GREEN KNIGHT* provides the best-known example.

Bodkin, (Amy) Maud 1875–1967 Critic. She is remembered for *Archetypal Patterns in Poetry* (1934), the first work in English to apply Jung's theories to literature. It argued that poetry, as the objectification of 'universal forces of our nature', allows special access to the collective unconscious of the race. A sequel, *Studies of Type-Images in Poetry, Religion, and Philosophy* (1951), used Jungian ideas in an attempt to synthesize poetry and religion.

Bodley, Sir Thomas 1545–1613 Scholar and diplomat. Brought up in Geneva and educated at Oxford, he became a fine Hebrew scholar, also instrumental in encouraging the study of Greek. Having served as Elizabeth I's permanent resident at The Hague, he withdrew from active political service in 1596 and channelled his energies into establishing the great library opened at Oxford in 1603 and given his name in 1604. SIR HENRY SAVILE assisted him in the project.

Boece [Boethius]**, Hector** ?1465–1536 Scottish historian. A native of Dundee, he helped Bishop Elphinstone in plans to establish a university in Aberdeen. His *Historia Scotorum* (1527) prefers narrative and rhetoric to accuracy: LELAND thought Boece wrote as many lies as there are waves or stars. The *Historia* gave HOLINSHED the story of Macbeth, thus transmitting it to SHAKESPEARE.

Bogan, Louise 1897–1970 American poet. She was poetry reviewer for THE NEW YORKER from 1931 to 1968 and published the highly regarded *Achievement in American Poetry 1900–1950* (1951). Her own poetry, strongly influenced by 16th- and 17th-century English verse, appeared in *Body of This Death* (1923), *Dark Summer* (1929), *The Sleeping Fury* (1937), *Poems and New Poems* (1941), *Collected Poems 1923–1953* (1954) and *The Blue Estuaries: Poems 1923–1968* (1968). *A Poet's Alphabet* (1970) is a prose collection.

Boker, George Henry 1823–90 American playwright and poet. Only six of his 11 plays were produced professionally. The most successful were the historical verse tragedies *Leonor de Guzman* (1853), about the rivalry between the mistress of King Alfonso of Spain and his wife Maria, and *Francesca da Rimini* (1855), based on Dante's story of the lovers Paolo and Francesca. The latter won great critical acclaim on its revival in 1882. *Nydia* (1885) and *Glaucus* (1886), both unproduced, were based on BULWER LYTTON's novel *The Last Days of Pompeii* (1834). His patriotism during the Civil War was rewarded by his appointment as Ambassador to Turkey (1871–5) and Russia (1875–8).

Boland, Eavan (Aisling) 1944– Irish poet. Recognized as one of her country's leading writers, she has embraced themes ranging from Irish myth and legend to suburbia and the intimacies of love and motherhood in her volumes *New Territory* (1967), *The War Horse* (1975), *In Her Own Image* (1980), *Night Feed* (1982), *The Journey and Other Poems* (1987; her first book published in Britain), *Selected Poems* (1989) and *Outside History* (1990). She returned to national concerns in *A Kind of Scar: Woman Poet in a National Tradition* (1989).

Boldrewood, Rolf [Browne, Thomas Alexander] 1826–1915 Australian novelist. His family emigrated from London to Sydney in 1830. His best-known novel, *Robbery under Arms* (serial, 1881; volume, 1888), is a racy tale, with authentic scenes and dialogue, about an infamous bush-ranger, Captain Starlight. It soon established itself as a classic adventure story. Of some 17 other novels the most popular were *The Miner's Right* (1890), *A Colonial Reformer* (1890) and *The Squatter's Dream* (1890), first published in 1878 as *Ups and Downs of Australian Life*.

Bolingbroke, 1st Viscount [St John, Henry] 1678–1751 Statesman and historian. He entered Parliament in 1701, supporting ROBERT HARLEY's Tory party with his powerful oratory and becoming Secretary of State in 1710. He was created 1st Viscount Bolingbroke in 1712. Already a friend and patron of writers, he founded the Brothers Club, which included SWIFT, ARBUTHNOT, PRIOR and other Tory adherents.

An opponent of the Hanoverian succession, he fled to France when George I came to the throne in 1714 and briefly served as Secretary of State to Prince James Stuart (the Old Pretender). *Reflections in Exile*, written in 1716, was followed by the self-justifying *Letter to Sir William Wyndham*, written and privately circulated in 1717 but not published until 1753. After friends had secured his pardon, Bolingbroke returned to England in 1725 and was soon in active opposition to the Whigs, then securely in power under Robert Walpole. His attacks on the administration for Nicholas Amherst's periodical, *The Craftsman*, were collected in *A Dissertation upon Parties* (1735) and *Remarks upon the History of England* (1743).

Disillusioned with party politics, Bolingbroke retired to France again in 1735. *Letters on the Study and Use of History* (published in 1752) argued that, since history teaches philosophy by example, England should follow the example of her European neighbours and produce written histories. The book was widely read, and not only in England, for Bolingbroke's friend and protégé Voltaire acknowledged its influence. *A Letter on the True Use of Retirement and Study* and *A Letter on the Spirit of Patriotism* were both written in 1736. The latter (published in 1749) looks hopefully to a future Tory Party inspired by patriotism, an influential argument developed in *The Idea of a Patriot King* (1738, published in 1749). *Some Reflections on the Present State of the Nation* (1749) examines the question of the public debt.

The collection of Bolingbroke's writings edited by DAVID MALLET in 1754 included *Philosophical Works*, the occasional writings believed to have influenced POPE in his ESSAY ON MAN.

Bolt, Robert (Oxton) 1924–95 Playwright. His early successes include *Flowering Cherry* (1957), a domestic play, and *The Tiger and the Horse* (1960), reflecting his concern for nuclear disarmament. Bolt's best work consists of large-scale historical plays distinguished by their immediately effective stagecraft: *A Man for All Seasons* (1960), about THOMAS MORE, *Vivat! Vivat! Regina* (1970), about Elizabeth I and Mary Queen of Scots, and *State of Revolution* (1977), about Lenin, Trotsky and the Russian Revolution. His screenplays, which involved him in collaborations with the director Sir David Lean, include *Lawrence of Arabia* (1962), *Dr Zhivago* (1965), *Ryan's Daughter* (1970) and *The Mission* (1986).

Bond, Edward 1934– Playwright. *Saved* (1965), a bleak presentation of cultural deprivation in which a group of bored youths stone a baby, and *Early Morning* (1968), a surreal historical fantasy, were both banned by the Lord Chamberlain. *Narrow Road to the Deep North* (1968; revised as *The Bundle*, 1978), impartially compares fascism and imperialism. *Lear* (1971) is a startlingly cruel reappraisal of SHAKESPEARE's KING LEAR, and *Bingo* (1973) takes Shakespeare himself as its central character, speculating on his complicity in the agricultural enclosures that disinherited the rural population. The relationship between artist and society is also central to *The Fool* (1975), a disturbing dramatization of scenes in the life of CLARE. Other plays in which Bond uses historical settings to expose modern injustices include *The Woman* (1978) and *Restoration* (1981). Bond has also written the libretti for two operas by Hans Werner Henze, *We Come to the River* (1976) and *The English Cat* (1983), as well as adapting work by Chekhov and Wedekind.

Bond, (Thomas) Michael 1926– Writer of CHILDREN'S LITERATURE. *A Bear Called Paddington* (1958) created a favourite character later to appear in numerous sequels popular both in Britain and abroad. Other successful characters include an orphan mouse, first appearing in *Here Comes Thursday* (1966), and a guinea-pig named Olga da Polga.

Bontemps, Arna (Wendell) 1902–73 Black American novelist. *Black Thunder* (1936) and *Drums at Dusk* (1939) are novels about slave revolts in Virginia and in Haiti. *God Sends Sunday* (1931) was dramatized by COUNTEE CULLEN as *St Louis Woman* (1946). The CHILDREN'S LITERATURE he wrote with JACK CONROY includes *Sam Patch* (1951). His non-fiction includes *They Seek a City* (with Conroy; 1945), *The Story of the Negro* (1948) and *100 Years of Negro Freedom* (1961).

Book of Common Prayer, The The name for the service-book used by the Church of England from 1549 until the mid 1970s, when it was largely replaced by Alternative Services, and in particular one called Series 3.

Christian service-books can be traced from the earliest times. The first chapters of Luke's gospel contain four great hymns, later called the Magnificat (1.46–55), the Benedictus (1.66–79), the Gloria (2.14) and the Nunc Dimittis (2.29–32), and there are many evidences of Christian worship in the New Testament: fragments of hymns throughout Revelation, corporate prayer in Acts 4.23–30. Examination of the service-books of the Fathers, for example in 6th-century Rome, reveals eight daily services, mostly of Scripture reading. Complication, accretion and local variation followed over the centuries; scripture was often replaced by legends. Additional services, for the Virgin Mary, or for the dead, or of other kinds, multiplied so much in number and length as to demand at least four different service-books; all were in Latin.

At the English Reformation, there was great need for simplification and standardization: an agreed order in one book in English. The large number of daily Latin 'uses' was clarified into Matins and Evensong (Morning and Evening Prayer after 1552), Holy Communion and Baptism (two, not seven, sacraments) and five other services, all in English. The first Book of Common Prayer of 1549, under the young Edward VI, was the work of committees, based on the best 'use', that of Sarum (Salisbury), and influenced by several Continental service-books. Like all Prayer Books that follow, it put daily Bible reading first in importance: all the Psalms to be read through once a month, the whole New Testament three times a year, and most of the Old Testament once a year. The Bible was to be read from the Great Bible of 1540, COVERDALE's printing and continuation of the work of TYNDALE (see BIBLE IN ENGLISH). The Psalms, though based on Coverdale, made use of earlier Middle English Psalters and carried forward a more ancient tradition (see PSALTERS). The special gifts of CRANMER, the Archbishop of Canterbury, especially in the brief, beautiful daily prayers known as 'collects', link his name for ever with the Prayer Book. His prose – lively, supple, quiet in manner and simple in effect – remained a living English inheritance until the 1960s.

John Merbecke's music for the Prayer Book was printed in 1550. Composed on the sound principle of 'one syllable, one note', it was used whenever the services were sung for over 400 years. The 1549 Prayer Book was revised in 1552 and, though hardly used, this Second Prayer Book influenced later revisions. After the savagery of Queen Mary's five years, during which Cranmer, among hundreds of others, was martyred, the Third Prayer Book of 1559 was instituted on the accession of Elizabeth. It made some revision, and bound in additional services and other matter: the 39 Articles (setting out Anglican belief), some hymns, and sometimes metrical Psalms. The same Hampton Court Conference of 1604 which initiated the Authorized Version under King James produced also the Fourth Prayer Book, with some fresh variations. In 1637 the Scottish Prayer Book was printed in Edinburgh, to local hostility; it later influenced Scottish, English and American liturgies. From 1645 to 1660 the use of the Book of Common Prayer was forbidden by law. Its place was taken by the Directory for Public Worship, which gave only general directions to the minister.

At the Restoration the old Book of Common Prayer was instantly in demand, quickly revised and lavishly reissued. The Fifth Prayer Book was completed in 1661, but as it became attached to the Act of Uniformity of 1662, it has been known ever since as '1662'. This Prayer Book – and Parliament – went a little way towards incorporating the professions of opponents, but then threw tolerance away and hardened the divisions in the nation, making non-adherence to the Prayer Book a most serious handicap for nearly two centuries. Its several hundred alterations changed obsolete phrases, transferred the source for all the Bible except the Psalms to the Authorized Version, and gave new directions to the minister. State services, particularly those for remembering 'King Charles the Martyr' and the Restoration, joined the revised older service commemorating the Gunpowder Treason of 1605. New collects were introduced. Richly and frequently issued, '1662' represented Anglicanism for three centuries, transmitting Cranmer's prose and the Prayer Book Psalms across the world. It was the basis of the service-books for what were to become nearly 20 independent Anglican churches around the globe.

Proposals for further revision and reform continued, particularly in the 18th century. A new Scottish liturgy was accepted in 1764, an American Prayer Book in 1789, an Irish Prayer Book in 1877, and the Scottish Prayer Book in 1912. In 1859 the Gunpowder Treason and Stuart services were dropped. Later proposals were in the direction of more universally Protestant evangelicalism, and more powerfully in the opposite direction. The wholesale revision proposed in the 1920s was twice rejected by the House of Commons in 1928. The arguments continued, notwithstanding, and some of the 1928 proposals resurfaced in the 1960s, when moves towards alternative services produced three sets. One from the Bishops was called the First Series, and another from the Liturgical Commission was called the Second Series. International religious commissions, dominated by the United States, made proposals which the Church of England largely incorporated in what it called Series 3. This has become standard in many Anglican churches, which now use '1662' for perhaps one early Holy Communion a month. Cranmer and the Reformers (and Merbecke) have been replaced. So, often, have Morning and Evening Prayer. The emphasis is frequently on one weekly 'Parish' or 'Family Eucharist'. The supposed 'popularizing' of the words and order of the services has been in line with the Englishing of the Roman Catholic Mass. But the Church of England must be held responsible for the ugliness of Series 3 – in, for example, replacing Cranmer's 'The Lord be with you: and with thy spirit' with 'The Lord be with you: and also with you', which is tautological, vacuous, and the result, apparently, of an international commission's insistence that 'spirit' would be misunderstood in English (it remains in European revisions).

Book of Martyrs, Foxe's See ACTS AND MONUMENTS.

Book of St Albans, The Four verse treatises, which had existed separately since c. 1400, published together at St Albans in 1486. They deal with hawking, hunting, coat-armour and blazoning of arms; WYNKYN DE WORDE's 1496 edition added a treatise on fishing. The collection proved enduringly popular, appearing only slightly altered under various titles in the 16th and 17th centuries. Juliana Berners (or Barnes), whose name appears at the end of the miscellanea following the hunting treatise in the 1486 edition, was once claimed as author of the whole collection, but it is unlikely she contributed more than the 'company terms' and other terminology. The details usually offered about her life are fabrications by early editors.

Book of the Duchess, The A poem by CHAUCER on the death of John of Gaunt's first wife Blanche, Duchess of Lancaster, in 1368. It was written within a few years of the event and so is one of Chaucer's earliest works. In a DREAM-VISION the narrator sees the hunt of the Emperor Octavian and comes upon a knight in black (probably representing John of Gaunt) who describes his love for the lady White and tells of her death. At this point the dream ends and the narrator awakes determined to write the poem.

Booker Prize An annual award open to new novels by British and Commonwealth writers, inaugurated in 1969 and now the most widely known literary prize in Britain. It is administered by the Book Trust (formerly the National Book League) and sponsored by the multinational conglomerate Booker McConnell. Winners have been: P. H. Newby, *Something to Answer For* (1969); Bernice Rubens, *The Elected Member* (1970); V. S. NAIPAUL, *In a Free State* (1971); JOHN BERGER, *G* (1972); J. G. FARRELL, *The Siege of Krishnapur* (1973); NADINE GORDIMER, *THE CONSERVATIONIST* with STANLEY MIDDLETON, *Holiday* (1974); RUTH PRAWER JHABVALA, *Heat and Dust* (1975); DAVID STOREY, *Saville* (1976); PAUL SCOTT, *Staying On* (1977); IRIS MURDOCH, *The Sea, The Sea* (1978); Penelope Fitzgerald, *Offshore* (1979); WILLIAM GOLDING, *Rites of Passage* (1980); SALMAN RUSHDIE, *Midnight's Children* (1981); THOMAS KENEALLY, *Schindler's Ark* (1982); J. M. COETZEE, *The Life and Times of Michael K* (1983); ANITA BROOKNER, *Hôtel du Lac* (1984); KERI HULME, *The Bone People* (1985); KINGSLEY AMIS, *The Old Devils* (1986); PENELOPE LIVELY, *Moon Tiger* (1987); PETER CAREY, *Oscar and Lucinda* (1988); KAZUO ISHIGURO, *The Remains of the Day* (1989); A. S. BYATT, *Possession* (1990); BEN OKRI, *The Famished Road* (1991); Barry Unsworth, *Sacred Hunger* with MICHAEL ONDAATJE, *The English Patient* (1992); RODDY DOYLE, *Paddy Clarke Ha Ha Ha* (1993); and JAMES KELMAN, *How Late It Was, How Late* (1994).

Boorde, Andrew ?1490–1549 Writer on medicine and travel. A Carthusian released from his vows in 1529, he practised medicine in Glasgow and travelled throughout Europe. His works include the popular *A Dietary of Health* (1542), *The Breviary of Health* (1547) and *The First Book of the Introduction of Knowledge* (?1548), the earliest Continental guidebook in English. He is sometimes identified with the 'A. B.' who wrote *The Merry Tales of the Mad Men of Gotham*, a collection of popular jests first printed in 1630.

Booth, Charles 1840–1916 Social critic and reformer. *Life and Labour of the People in London* (1902–3), taking 17 years and running to 17 volumes, is a monumental survey in the tradition of HENRY MAYHEW. BEATRICE WEBB, his wife's cousin, was one of his researchers for the early volumes. Enough of a Manchester liberal to dislike state intervention in business and trade, Booth nevertheless welcomed measures to regulate incomes (he coined the term 'poverty line') and advocated old-age pensions.

Borough, The A poem by CRABBE, published in 1810. It takes the form of 24 letters describing life in a town which is clearly based on Crabbe's native Aldeburgh. Particularly important are the seven letters which each describe the life of a single person, one of the 'Inhabitants of the Alms-House' or one of 'The Poor of the Borough'. These include *Clelia*, about an irredeemably trivial flirt, *Ellen Orford* and *Peter Grimes* (Letter XXII). Grimes is a fisherman driven by the desire to inflict pain and hurt. The apprentices he buys from the London workhouses perish under his brutal treatment. Eventually forced to live and work in solitude, he is visited by the ghosts of his father and the tormented boys. He goes insane with guilt and remorse, and dies in mental agony. The story was made into an opera by Benjamin Britten (1945).

Borrow, George (Henry) 1803–81 Autobiographer, translator, linguist and traveller. The son of a recruiting officer in the militia, he spent most of his childhood moving around Britain and had only three or four years of formal schooling. Nevertheless, he acquired an intimate knowledge of gypsy life and fluency in at least 12 languages, including Latin, Greek, French, Welsh, Irish, Italian, German, Danish and Dutch; he later added Portuguese, Russian, Arabic and Spanish. In 1824–32 he divided his life between Norwich and London, where he tried to establish himself as a writer with a translation of *Faustus: His Life, Death, and Descent into Hell* (1825), hackwork which included a six-volume edition of THE NEWGATE CALENDAR (1826), and *Romantic Ballads, Translated from the Danish* (1826). His linguistic proficiency commended him to the British and Foreign Bible Society, for which he worked in St Petersburg (1833–5), where he produced two volumes of verse translations, *Targum* and *The Talisman* (both 1835), and then in Portugal and Spain (1835–40), where he supervised the printing and distribution of the New Testament in Spanish and Basque. His experiences gave imaginative substance to the two books which made him famous: *The Zincali* (1841) and THE BIBLE IN SPAIN (1843).

After his marriage in 1840 Borrow lived on his wife's estate at Oulton, Norfolk, albeit with long periods in Yarmouth (1853–60) and London (1860–?70). During this period he wrote the three works on which his reputation chiefly depends: LAVENGRO (1851), THE ROMANY RYE (1857) and WILD WALES (1857). Though he declined to provide the literal autobiography he at one time promised, these works, especially the first two, for many years enjoyed the status of established classics, simultaneously delighting and puzzling the reader with a racy, convincing, but impenetrable amalgam of fact and fiction. He spent his later years in further forays into translation (a second edition of his *Gypsy Luke*) and philology (*Romano Lavo-Lil*), at the same time consolidating his reputation as a traveller by walking tours through Norfolk, Wales, Ireland and Scotland.

Bosman, Herman Charles 1905–51 South African short-story writer, essayist and novelist. His reputation rests especially on *Mafeking Road* (1947), *Unto Dust* (1963), *Jurie Steyn's Post Office* (1971) and *A Bekkersdal Marathon* (1971), collections of stories about rural Afrikaner life, told with sardonic detachment, shrewd observation and folk comedy. Bosman spent several years in prison for killing his stepbrother; *Cold Stone Jug* (1949) recounts his experience with humour and pathos. *A Cask of Jerepigo* (1957) gathers essays and sketches. *Jacaranda in the Night* (1947) and *Willemsdorp* (1977) are novels. *Collected Works* (2 vols) appeared in 1981.

Boston, Lucy (Maria) 1892–1990 Writer of CHILDREN'S LITERATURE. She began, when she was over 60, with a series about her 12th-century manor house near Cambridge: *The Children of Green Knowe* (1954), *The River at Green Knowe* (1959), *A Stranger at Green Knowe* (1961), *An Enemy at Green Knowe* (1964) and *The Stones of Green Knowe* (1976). *The Sea Egg* (1967), more strikingly original, tells of a greenish stone that hatches a small triton.

Bostonians, The A novel by Henry James, serialized in 1885–6 and published in volume form in 1886. A satirical study of the movement for female emancipation in New England, it recounts the story of Basil Ransom, a young Southern lawyer who comes to Boston on business. He meets his cousins, the widowed Mrs Luna, who falls in love with him, and the feminist Olive Chancellor. At a suffragette meeting both Olive and Basil are struck by a beautiful young speaker, Verena Tarrant. Olive sets out to make her a leader of the feminist cause, pleading with her to forswear the thought of marriage, but Basil falls in love with her. Forced to choose between Olive and Basil, Verena finally accepts Basil's proposal.

Boswell, James 1740–95 Journal writer and biographer of SAMUEL JOHNSON. Born in Edinburgh, the son of Alexander Boswell (later Lord Auchinleck), judge of the Court of Session, he studied law with little enthusiasm at the Universities of Edinburgh and Glasgow. In 1760 he left for London, where his colourful life – by turns libertine and puritanical – involved him in a protracted battle of wills with his formidable father.

Ambitious for literary and political reputation, he became friendly with GARRICK and, in 1763, Samuel Johnson. Almost at once began the records of Johnson's activities and conversation which eventually resulted (with encouragement from MALONE) in his two major works: THE JOURNAL OF A TOUR TO THE HEBRIDES (1785), about their travels together in 1773, and the magnificent LIFE OF SAMUEL JOHNSON LL.D. (1791). Although these books are ample testimony to his intimacy with Johnson and his circle, the common impression that he had little literary or even social life independent of his friend is wrong. Boswell recorded his elaborate view of contemporary London life, published in 1950 as *Boswell's London Journal 1762–3*. His Continental travels in 1763–6 made him an admirer of the redoubtable General Paoli and champion of the Corsican cause in *Account of Corsica* (1768) and *Essays in Favour of the Brave Corsicans* (1769). *Dorando* (1767) is an allegorical romance set in Spain, concerning the Douglas inheritance case.

He eventually overcame his reluctance to embark on a legal career, completing his studies at Utrecht and being admitted to the Scottish Bar in 1766 and the English Bar in 1786. After many well-documented philanderings he married his cousin, Margaret Montgomerie, in 1769.

He was renowned as good company, with his lively mind and formidable memory, a man exuberant and melancholy by turns. His several journals and private papers, many discovered at Malahide Castle, have been collected and edited by Frederick A. Pottle; they con-

firm Boswell as a talented writer and a man worth remembering in his own right.

Bottomley, Gordon 1874–1948 Playwright and poet. His interest in Celtic folklore was already evident in his first collection of poetry, *The Mickle Drede and Other Verses* (1896). His plays, notably *The Crier by Night* (published 1902; performed 1916), *King Lear's Wife* (published 1920; performed 1915) and *Gruach* (published 1921; performed 1923), are always historically and geographically distanced. *Lyric Plays* (1932) collects his later work, influenced by YEATS.

Boucicault, Dion(ysius) (Lardner) 1820–90 Irish playwright, actor and theatre manager. Success came early with his comedies LONDON ASSURANCE (1841) and *Old Heads and Young Hearts* (1844). Hastily written but clever versions of French plays, including *The Corsican Brothers* (1852) and *The Vampire* (1852), established him as a leading playwright in England. In 1853 he emigrated to the United States, where he enjoyed an equally successful career, particularly with the MELODRAMAS *The Poor of New York* (1857), *Jessie Brown: or, The Relief of Lucknow* (1858) and THE OCTOROON (1859). Three outstanding Irish melodramas, the COLLEEN BAWN (1860), *Arrah-na-Pogue* (1864) and THE SHAUGHRAUN (1874), confirmed his position. Nearly 200 plays have been ascribed to Boucicault.

Bourchier, John, 2nd Baron Berners ?1469–1533 Translator and statesman. A faithful servant of Henry VII and Henry VIII, he became Chancellor of the Exchequer in 1516.

As a translator he favoured medieval chivalry and romance, COURTESY BOOKS and CHRONICLES. His translation of Froissart (1523–25) influenced the later chronicles of EDWARD HALL and HOLINSHED. HUON OF BORDEAUX, a romance which introduced the fairy prince Oberon to English readers, was printed after Berners's death, probably by WYNKYN DE WORDE in 1534. His most popular work was *The Golden Book of Marcus Aurelius* (first printed 1535), a translation from the French version of Antonio de Guevara's original Spanish.

Bourne, George See STURT, GEORGE.

Bourne, Randolph 1886–1918 American essayist and social critic. His writings reflected broad interests, notably education (*The Gary Schools*, 1916, and *Education and Living*, 1917), the development of socially responsible fiction, and the depreciation of an ethnically diverse American culture ('Trans-National America', 1916). A fervent pacifist, he became an eloquent and increasingly isolated advocate of American non-intervention in World War I (in, for example, *Untimely Papers*, 1919). His prowess as a conversationalist also impressed a generation of writers and critics.

Bowdler, Thomas 1754–1825 Editor. His version of SHAKESPEARE, *The Family Shakespeare* (1818), cut the text by omitting 'whatever is unfit to be read aloud by a gentleman to a company of ladies' and so gave rise to the term 'to bowdlerize'. He also prepared an edition of GIBBON's DECLINE AND FALL OF THE ROMAN EMPIRE on the same principles.

Bowen, Elizabeth (Dorothea Cole) 1899–1973 Novelist and short-story writer. Born in Dublin, she lived in Ireland, France, Italy and London. Volumes of stories, notable for their subtle use of language, include *Encounters* (1923), *Ann Lee's* (1926), *Joining Charles* (1929), *The Cat Jumps* (1934), *Look at All Those Roses* (1941) and *The Demon Lover* (1945). Her *Collected Stories*, introduced by

ANGUS WILSON, appeared in 1980. Early novels included *The Hotel* (1927), *The Last September* (1929), *Friends and Relations* (1931) and *The House in Paris* (1935). Best known, however, are *The Death of the Heart* (1938), a sensitive study of the adolescent Portia Quayne, and *The Heat of the Day* (1949), a tragic love-story set in war-time London. Later novels were *A World of Love* (1955) and *Eva Trout* (1969). Her writing follows HENRY JAMES in its attention to style and its subtle delineation of character (especially female character) and setting. Her impressionistic descriptions of the landscape, both urban and rural, and its seasonal changes add a highly effective dimension to her work. She also wrote *Seven Winters* (1942), a partial autobiography, and *Bowen's Court* (1942), a history of the family seat in Dublin which she inherited.

Bowering, George 1935– Canadian poet, novelist and critic. His early poetry, strongly influenced by the BLACK MOUNTAIN SCHOOL, includes *Points on the Grid* (1964), *Baseball* (1967), *Rocky Mountain Foot* (1968) and *The Gangs of Kosmos* (1969). Later works include *In the Flesh* (1974) and *Another Mount* (1979) and several book-length poems: *George Vancouver* (1970) and *Autobiology* (1972), collected in *The Catch* (1976) and *West Window* (1982). His most acclaimed novel, *Burning Water* (1980), is a deconstructionist account of Vancouver's search for the Northwest Passage. Other novels – *A Short Sad Book* (1977), *A Place to Die* (1983) and *Harry's Fragments* (1990) – adopt a playful stance towards narrative conventions. His critical books include *A Way with Words* (1982) and *Imaginary Hand* (1988).

Bowles, Paul 1910– American novelist and short-story writer. While living in Paris he wrote music and music criticism before publishing his first novel, *The Sheltering Sky* (1949). *The Delicate Prey* (1950; as *A Little Stone in Britain*), *Let It Come Down* (1952) and *The Spider's House* (1955) further explore the lives of spiritually weary Westerners in the Orient. Resident in Tangier since 1952, he has tape-recorded and translated several original accounts of indigenous life. Other work includes: short stories in *Pages from Cold Point and Other Stories* (1968), *Collected Stories* (1979), *Midnight Mass* (1985), *Call at Corazón* (1988) and *A Thousand Days for Mokhtar* (1989); travel sketches; poetry; and autobiography in *Without Stopping* (1972) and *Two Years beside the Strait* (1990), a journal.

Bowles, William Lisle 1762-1850 Poet. *Fourteen Sonnets, Elegiac and Descriptive, Written during a Tour* (1789) revived the neglected SONNET and influenced both COLERIDGE and SOUTHEY. An edition of POPE (1806) brought Bowles into conflict with THOMAS CAMPBELL, to whom he replied in *The Invariable Principles of Poetry* (1819), and BYRON.

Bowra, Sir (Cecil) Maurice 1898-1971 Scholar and critic. The warden of Wadham College, Oxford, from 1938 to 1970, he was a celebrated host, raconteur and wit. His many works on classical literature include *Tradition and Design in the Iliad* (1930), *Ancient Greek Literature* (1933), *The Greek Experience* (1957); his more modern interests appear in *The Heritage of Symbolism* (1943) and *The Romantic Imagination* (1949). Bowra also published translations of Greek and Russian poetry, and edited *The Oxford Book of Greek Verse in Translation* (1938).

Boyd, Martin (A'Beckett) 1893-1969 Australian novelist. Born in Lucerne and brought up in Melbourne, Boyd divided his time between Australia and Europe.

The Montforts (1928), one of the early novels published under the pseudonym of Martin Mills, is a dense but elegant and ironic family chronicle of Anglo-Australian life. Its preoccupations recur in much of his best work, which includes *Lucinda Brayford* (1946), *Such Pleasure* (1949), *The Cardboard Crown* (1952), *A Difficult Young Man* (1955), *Outbreak of Love* (1957) and *When Blackbirds Sing* (1962).

Boyd, William 1952– Novelist. A fluent and good-humoured writer, he has used Africa, his childhood home, as the setting for several works: *A Good Man in Africa* (1981), chronicling the misadventures of the lecherous Morgan Leafy; *An Ice-Cream War* (1982), about an obscure African interstice of World War I; and *Brazzaville Beach* (1990), a sober tale of a female animal behaviourist observing chimpanzees. Leafy reappears in a collection of short stories, *On the Yankee Station* (1981). *Stars and Bars* (1984) is a more predictable Englishman-abroad comedy set in the USA. *The New Confessions* (1987), his most substantial book, is an energetic fictive history of the 20th century.

Boyer, Abel 1667-1729 Historian. A Huguenot who came to England in 1689, he published an annual calendar of events from 1703 until 1713. His chief works were *The History of King William III* (1702), *The History of the Life and Reign of Queen Anne* (1722) and a translation of the *Mémoires de la vie du Comte de Gramont* (1714), revised and annotated by SIR WALTER SCOTT (1811).

Boyle, Kay 1903-93 American novelist and short-story writer. Resident in Europe for many years, she was a foreign correspondent for THE NEW YORKER in 1946-54. Her fiction often deals with a young and unworldly American who travels to Europe. Among her novels are *Year before Last* (1932), *My Next Bride* (1934), *Monday Night* (1938), *The Crazy Hunter: Three Short Novels* (1940), *Avalanche* (1944) and *A Frenchman Must Die* (1946). Collections of short stories include *Short Stories* (1929), *Wedding Day and Other Stories* (1930), *The First Lover and Other Stories* (1936), *The White Horse of Vienna and Other Stories* (1936) and *Thirty Stories* (1946).

Boyle, Robert 1627-91 Chemist and philosopher. His early interest was in alchemy but, following the lead of Descartes and Gassendi, he became convinced that the structure of matter was corpuscular and its operations open to rational investigation. His work proved instrumental in turning chemistry from an occult science to a recognizably modern discipline. His method of experiment, observation and hypothesis owed much to FRANCIS BACON. Boyle's law established the relationship between the pressure and the volume of a gas at a constant temperature. As a founder-member of the Royal Society in 1660, he was associated with all the leaders of the early scientific movement in England. Later in life his religious concerns merged with his scientific interests, and he was anxious to refute the suspicion that atomism led to atheism. The desire to demonstrate the intellectual compatibility between scientific enquiry and revealed Christianity led him to endow the Boyle Lectures, which became a vehicle for those who strove to maintain a consensus between science and religion in the early 18th century.

Boyle was a prolific writer, his most enduring works being *The Sceptical Chymist* (1661), a dialogue attacking the theories of matter based on elements and qualities that derived from Aristotle and Paracelsus. *The Origin of Forms and Qualities* (1666) defended the corpuscular theory of matter. His *Occasional Reflections on Several Subjects*

(1665) provided material for SWIFT's satire in *GULLIVER'S TRAVELS* and *Meditations on a Broomstick*. His sentimental religious romance, *The Martyrdom of Theodora and Didymus* (1687), was adapted to provide a libretto for Handel's opera *Theodora*.

boys' companies Companies of choristers, long known for staging occasional plays at court, who also performed in public during the late 16th and early 17th century. Notable were the boys of the Chapel Royal at the Blackfriars theatre (see PRIVATE THEATRES) and the St Paul's Boys, who staged the work of LYLY. They fell seriously out of favour and did not act in public *c.* 1590–8 but returned to popularity in the next decade, when many leading dramatists wrote for them.

Boz The early pseudonym of DICKENS.

Bracebridge Hall*: or, *The Humorists: A Medley A book of 49 tales and sketches by WASHINGTON IRVING, published in 1822 under the pseudonym, Geoffrey Crayon, Gent., that he had used for its predecessor, *THE SKETCH BOOK*. Though the collection uses English, French and Spanish settings, the best-remembered tales, 'Dolph Heylinger' and 'The Storm-Ship', are set in America.

Brackenbury, Alison 1953– Poet. She has established herself as one of the leading poets of her generation with several volumes of deft, precise verse: *Dreams of Power and Other Poems* (1981), in which the title-poem is a DRAMATIC MONOLOGUE by one of history's victims; *Breaking Ground and Other Poems* (1984), in which the title-poem evokes episodes from the life of JOHN CLARE; and *Christmas Roses and Other Poems* (1988), dealing confidently with urban and rural themes. *Selected Poems* appeared in 1991.

Brackenridge, Hugh Henry 1748–1816 American novelist and poet. Born in Scotland, he was taken to Pennsylvania by his family when he was five. At Princeton University he collaborated with FRENEAU on *Father Bembo's Pilgrimage to Mecca* (1770), a prose SATIRE on American manners, and a patriotic poem, *The Rising Glory of America* (1772), which he followed with several patriotic works during the Revolutionary War. A distinguished lawyer who ended his career on the Pennsylvania Supreme Court, he acted as a mediator during the Whiskey Rebellion provoked by Alexander Hamilton's excise tax on liquor, describing it in *Incidents of the Insurrection in the Western Parts of Pennsylvania, in the Year 1794* (1795). As founder of *The Pittsburgh Gazette* (1786), the first Western newspaper, he frequently contributed satires on Eastern and Western manners and of Federalist and Republican politics. His literary reputation rests on *MODERN CHIVALRY*, a seven-volume satirical novel he published in instalments between 1792 and 1815.

Bradbrook, M(uriel) C(lara) 1909– Critic. Long associated with Cambridge, she became professor of English (1965–76) and Mistress of Girton College (1968–76). Although her many critical studies include books on Ibsen (1946), T. S. ELIOT (1950), MALORY (1957), LOWRY (1974) and WEBSTER (1980), she is best known as an authority on SHAKESPEARE and the Elizabethan theatre. *Themes and Conventions of Elizabethan Tragedy* (1934), *The Growth and Structure of Elizabethan Comedy* (1955) and *The Rise of the Common Player* (1962) have been reprinted with other works as the six-volume *History of Elizabethan Drama* (1979).

Bradbury, Malcolm (Stanley) 1932– Novelist and critic. *Eating People is Wrong* (1959) and *Stepping Westward* (1965) are PICARESQUE novels of academic life in the manner of *LUCKY JIM*. *The History Man* (1975), with its bitter portrait of a sociology lecturer, was hailed as the definitive fictional response to 1960s culture. *Rates of Exchange* (1982) continues the preoccupation with academic life but its whimsical self-consciousness anticipates subsequent work, which includes *Cuts* (1987), a novella, and *Dr Criminale* (1992), a novel. From 1970 to 1995 Bradbury was professor of American Studies at the University of East Anglia, where with ANGUS WILSON he presided over Britain's only notable university course in creative writing. His academic publications include *Possibilities* (1973), a collection of essays on contemporary fiction, and *The Modern American Novel* (1983).

Bradbury, Ray (Douglas) 1920– American writer of SCIENCE FICTION. He made his reputation with *The Martian Chronicles* (1950; called *The Silver Locusts* in Britain), about the conquest and colonization of Mars. *Fahrenheit 451* (1953) is set in a future when the written word is forbidden. Among his other works are *Something Wicked This Way Comes* (1962), a novel, and many short-story collections: *The Illustrated Man* (1951), *The Golden Apples of the Sun* (1953), *The October Sky* (1955), *A Medicine for Melancholy* (1959; called *The Day It Rained Forever* in Britain), *The Machineries of Joy* (1964), *I Sing The Body Electric!* (1969), *The Last Circus and the Electrocution* (1980) and *A Memory of Murder* (1984). His poetry is collected in *The Complete Poems of Ray Bradbury* (1982). *Death is a Lonely Business* (1985) is a Californian murder mystery.

Braddon, Mary Elizabeth 1835–1915 Novelist. She lived with John Maxwell, a publisher of journals, for 14 years before the death of his wife allowed them to marry. *LADY AUDLEY'S SECRET* (1862), her first published work, became the most popular SENSATION NOVEL of the day. Its success overshadowed the rest of a long and hard-working career in which she produced some 80 novels. Some were in the same vein as *Lady Audley's Secret*: *Aurora Floyd* (1863), *John Marchmont's Legacy* (1863), *Henry Dunbar: The Story of an Outcast* (1864), *Sir Jasper's Tenant* (1865), *Birds of Prey* (1867) and *Charlotte's Inheritance* (1868). Others demonstrate a greater range and seriousness: *The Doctor's Wife* (1864) adapts Flaubert's *Madame Bovary*; *The Lady's Mile* (1866) and *The Lovels of Arden* (1871) are novels of society; *Vixen* (1871) is a SATIRE; *Ishmael* (1884) is a historical romance; and *Dead Love Has Chains* (1907) is a tragedy.

Bradford, William 1590–1657 Governor and historian of Plymouth Colony. Born in Yorkshire, he sailed to America on the *Mayflower* in 1620. At Plymouth he served as governor for all but five years of the period 1621–56. His *History of Plymouth Plantation* describes the origins of the Separatist movement in England, the settlement in Leyden, the plans to emigrate, the voyage of the *Mayflower*, and the sacred and secular affairs of the colony from 1620 to 1646. Written between 1630 and 1651, it remained unpublished until 1856, though his nephew, NATHANIEL MORTON, consulted it for *New England's Memorial* (1669). Bradford's incomplete *Letter Book* (1624–30) and his letters to John Winthrop show a leader working out the colony's internal problems as well as negotiating with England, the neighbouring Massachusetts Bay Colony and the Indians.

Bradley, A(ndrew) C(ecil) 1851–1935 Critic. The younger brother of F. H. BRADLEY and professor at, successively, Liverpool, Glasgow and Oxford, he is best known for his *Oxford Lectures on Poetry* (1909) and especially for *Shakespearean Tragedy* (1904), a series of lectures in which he approached the major tragedies of

SHAKESPEARE through an extended study of the characters. This approach has often been challenged since the 1930s, but Bradley's book is still read.

Bradley, F(rancis) H(erbert) 1846–1924 Philosopher. He was elected a fellow of Merton College, Oxford, in 1870. His most important philosophical works were *Ethical Studies* (1876), *The Principles of Logic* (1883), *Appearance and Reality* (1893) and *Essays on Truth and Reality* (1914), the last two being a discussion of the state of contemporary metaphysical speculation. Bradley's thought was the subject of T. S. ELIOT's Harvard PhD thesis, eventually published as *Knowledge and Experience in the Philosophy of F. H. Bradley* (1964).

Bradshaigh, Lady c. 1706–85 Letter-writer. Beginning under the pseudonym of Mrs Belfour, she enjoyed a lengthy correspondence with SAMUEL RICHARDSON about the progress of *CLARISSA* and *THE HISTORY OF SIR CHARLES GRANDISON*, which prompted him to some remarkable pieces of self-analysis. Recognizing the commercial and literary value of the letters, he persuaded her to edit them for publication. They were eventually incorporated in BARBAULD's edition (1804).

Bradstreet, Anne 1612–72 America's first published poet. The daughter of Thomas Dudley, who had been steward to the Earl of Lincoln, she sailed for America at the age of 18 with her husband and father, both of whom eventually became governors of Massachusetts. Her collection, *The Tenth Muse Lately Sprung Up in America*, was published without her knowledge by her brother-in-law in London in 1650. A second edition, corrected and expanded, appeared in Boston as *Several Poems Compiled with a Great Variety of Wit* six years after her death. Her work generally follows Elizabethan models, and shows the influence of SPENSER, SIR PHILIP SIDNEY, Du Bartas and SIR WALTER RALEIGH. Later poems are more personal in subject and less conventional in form, often meditating on domestic topics from a religious point of view; this group includes poems to her husband and ELEGIES on her dead children.

Bragg, Melvyn 1939– Novelist and broadcaster. The principal achievement of his broadcasting career has been the creation of a distinguished television arts programme, *The South Bank Show*. As a novelist, he is unashamedly provincial, usually returning to his native Cumbria for the settings of works which range from *The Hired Man* (1969), sober and emotionally exact, to the breathless *A Time to Dance* (1990). *The Silken Net* (1974) is a sensitive study of a woman's inter-war life and *The Maid of Buttermere* (1987) an ingenious treatment of an episode from Lake District history.

Braine, John 1922–86 Novelist. He is best known for his first novel, *Room at the Top* (1957), a classic product of the ANGRY YOUNG MEN generation. Set against a sharp picture of Northern life, the unscrupulous and opportunistic hero, Joe Lampton, chooses wealth and success rather than true love. A sequel, *Life at the Top*, appeared in 1962. None of Braine's other novels attracted comparable attention.

Braithwaite, William Stanley (Beaumont) 1879–1962 Black American poet, novelist, short-story writer and editor. He played an influential role in the renewal of creative activity later termed the HARLEM RENAISSANCE, partly through his annual *Anthology of Magazine Verse and Year Book of American Poetry* (1913–29), which served as a major outlet for black writers. His own work included: volumes of poetry such as *Lyrics of Life and Love* (1904), *The House of Falling Leaves* (1908) and

Selected Poems (1948); two novels, *The Canadian* (1901) and *Going over Tindel* (1924); a volume of short stories, *Frost on the Green Tree* (1928); and an autobiography, *The House under Arcturus* (1941).

Brathwaite, Edward Kamau [Brathwaite, Edward Lawson] 1930– Caribbean poet and historian. One of the Caribbean's most important poets, he attempts to establish a Caribbean aesthetic by retrieving and re-orchestrating surviving and submerged echoes of African culture. His shorter poems appear in *Other Exiles* (1975), *Days and Nights* (1975), *Black and Blues* (1976) and *Third World Poems* (1983), but his excellence was established by three long poems: *Rights of Passage* (1967), *Masks* (1968) and *Islands* (1969), reprinted together as *The Arrivants: A New World Trilogy* (1973). *Mother Poem* (1977), *Sun Poem* (1982) and *X-Self* (1987) make up a second trilogy. He is also a prolific literary critic, concerned with the oral aspects of Caribbean discourse, notably in *History of the Voice: The Development of Nation Language in Anglophone Caribbean Poetry* (1984). Historical writings include *The Development of Creole Society in Jamaica, 1770–1820* (1970), from which *The Folk Culture of the Slaves of Jamaica* (1970) is extracted.

Brautigan, Richard 1935–84 American novelist and poet. A leading exponent of radical values in the 1960s, he is usually remembered for *Trout Fishing in America* (1967), a best-selling novel about an unfulfilled search for a morning of good fishing in a crystal-clear stream. His many other novels include *A Confederate General from Big Sur* (1964) and *In Watermelon Sugar* (1968), about a commune. His best-known collection of poetry is *The Pill versus the Springhill Mine Disaster* (1968).

Brave New World A novel by ALDOUS HUXLEY, published in 1932. The title is taken from Miranda's words in *THE TEMPEST*: 'O brave new world/ That has such people in't!' The story presents a scathing criticism of the myth of social salvation through technological expertise. In the year 632 After Ford (i.e. the 26th century) the world has attained a kind of scientific Utopia in which biological engineering fits different categories of workers – Alphas, Betas, Gammas, etc. – to their stations in life, and universal happiness is preserved by psychotropic drugs. The Savage, raised in a reservation of American Indian primitives, comes into this world as a stranger, takes up the arguments introduced by the disaffected intellectuals Bernard Marx and Helmholtz Watson, and finally kills himself in disgust.

Brazil, Angela 1868–1947 Writer of CHILDREN'S LITERATURE. In more than 50 novels, from *The Fortunes of Philippa* (1906) to *The School on the Loch* (1946), she made the girls' boarding-school into an idealized world, emphasizing hearty games-playing and the strong emotions that often spring up between pupils, and sometimes earning the disapproval of teachers and parents for her use of schoolgirl slang.

Brennan, Christopher John 1870–1932 Australian poet. Strongly influenced by the German Romantics and Mallarmé, with whom he corresponded, he wrote erudite and crafted verse which still possesses considerable lyricism, as his sequence 'The Wanderer' shows. He published little in his lifetime, *Poems 1913* (1914) being the most important collection.

Brent-Dyer, Elinor M. [Dyer, Gladys Eleanor May] 1894–1969 Writer of CHILDREN'S LITERATURE. She was known for girls' school stories with breezy titles, such as *The Feud in the Fifth Remove* (1931) or *Monica Turns up Trumps* (1936), which give a fair idea of their uncomplicated content. The first of 58 stories about Chalet School, an international girls' school romantically situated in the Austrian Alps, appeared in 1925.

Brenton, Howard 1942– Playwright. A leading spokesman for the political drama that flourished after 1968, he came to prominence with *Christie in Love* (1969) and *Revenge* (1969). *Magnificence* (1973) explored urban terrorism, *The Churchill Play* (1974) and *The Weapons of Happiness* (1976) the structures of political power, while *Epsom Downs* (1977) took a broader sweep. *The Romans in Britain* (1980) pursued an elaborate analogy between the Roman invasion and the British 'occupation' of Northern Ireland. The sexual explicitness of one scene gave rise to a private prosecution, eventually dropped, when it was produced at the ROYAL NATIONAL THEATRE. After *The Genius* (1983), Brenton collaborated with HARE in *Pravda* (1985), about the corruptions of newspaper ownership. Its success was not repeated by *Moscow Gold* (with Tariq Ali; 1990), an ambitious study of political change in the Soviet Union

Breton, Nicholas ?1555–1626 Poet and miscellaneous writer. He produced over 60 works of pastoral and religious poetry, pamphlets, satires, dialogues and letters. His prose works are moral and pious; the poverty of poets is a constant theme in his poetry. Early work, like *A Small Handful of Fragrant Flowers* (1575), is influenced by GASCOIGNE, his stepfather. Its laboured diction and excessive alliteration improves by the 1590s so that MERES can rank him (undeservedly) with SHAKESPEARE, SPENSER and DRAYTON as a lyricist. Some of Breton's best poems appeared in ENGLAND'S HELICON (1600).

Breton lay Although no original Breton lays survive, they were apparently narratives accompanied by music. The name became attached to later poems claiming to be adapted from earlier lays or Breton in origin. MARIE DE FRANCE's *Lais*, written in the late 12th century, are simple, short narrative poems, usually treating love and often involving magic. Other surviving English lays belong to the 14th century: SIR LAUNFAL and LAI LE FREINE (both translated from Marie's *Lais*), SIR ORFEO, EMARE, SIR DEGARE, SIR GOWTHER and THE EARL OF TOULOUS. Though claiming to be a Breton lay, CHAUCER's *Franklin's Tale* (in THE CANTERBURY TALES) has an Italian source and a complex narrative structure.

Brewer's Dictionary of Phrase and Fable A reference book or 'Treasury of Literary bric-à-brac' compiled by the educational writer Ebenezer Cobham Brewer (1810–97), published in 1870 and revised by Brewer in 1881 and 1895. It forms a unique, delightfully odd, compendium of folklore, mythology, superstition, slang, etymology, adages, catchphrases and 'words with a tale to tell', as Brewer put it. Since a major revision in 1952, the much-expanded modern editions (notably Ifor H. Evans's Centenary Edition of 1970) have added new curiosities from Australia and America, while some of Brewer's original entries have been omitted.

Bridal of Triermain, The A poem by SIR WALTER SCOTT, published in 1813. Framed by the bland courtship of Lucy by Arthur (the poor man and the lady), the central narrative describes Sir Roland de Vaux of Triermain's quest for Gyneth, daughter of King Arthur and the enchantress Guendolen, who lies sleeping in the Valley of St John as the result of a spell by Merlin.

Bride of Abydos, The: *A 'Turkish Tale'* A poem by BYRON, published in 1813. It describes the tragic love affair of Selim and his supposed half-sister Zuleika, daughter of the Pasha Giaffir and intended bride of the elderly Bey of Carasman. The poem contributed to the late 18th-century and Romantic cult of Orientalism, while also encouraging the fascination with piracy that runs through the work of Byron and his fellow Romantics.

Bride of Lammermoor, The A novel by SIR WALTER SCOTT, published in 1818 in the third series of *Tales of My Landlord*. It tells the story of the Master of Ravenswood's unhappy and eventually tragic love for Lucy Ashton, opposed by her mother, the imperious and deceitful Lady Ashton. Donizetti used the story as the basis for his opera, *Lucia di Lammermoor* (1835).

Brideshead Revisited: *The Sacred and Profane Memories of Captain Charles Ryder* A novel by EVELYN WAUGH, published in 1945. It broke with the satirical mode of his earlier works. Billeted at Brideshead during the war, Ryder recalls his past experiences there as a guest of the Marchmains, a great Roman Catholic family, whom he met through his dazzling young Oxford friend, Sebastian Flyte. Sebastian sinks into alcoholism, and after the death of his mother, Lady Marchmain, becomes a menial in an African monastery. Ryder's feelings centre on Julia but she marries a non-Catholic, a vulgar politician, and then after her divorce is prompted to return to the faith by her father's deathbed reconciliation with Catholicism. Ryder's doubts about his own faith are resolved by her renunciation of him, and his agnosticism withers.

Bridge, The A long poem by HART CRANE, published in 1930. New York's Brooklyn Bridge, both 'harp and altar', is the central image of a work whose nine sections explore the negative as well as the positive aspects of the American experience while seeking to present an affirmative, epic vision of America.

Bridges, Robert (Seymour) 1844–1930 Poet and critic. He published his first volume in 1873 but it was the successful one-volume edition of his *Collected Poems* (1912) which introduced him to a wider audience. He became POET LAUREATE the following year. The most ambitious – and popular – of his later works was *The Testament of Beauty* (1929), on spiritual and artistic wisdom. Its use of 'loose alexandrines' was typical of a poet whose work is distinguished by a subtle and experimental approach to METRE which always stops short of the radical experimentalism of his friend GERARD MANLEY HOPKINS, whose work he edited in 1918. His own widely anthologized pieces include 'London Snow', 'Awake My Heart' and 'The Storm is Over'. Bridges also wrote eight plays and influential studies of MILTON's prosody (1893) and KEATS (1895).

Bridges, Roy(al) 1885–1952 Australian novelist. *The Barb of an Arrow* (1909), dealing with the convict days of Tasmania, was the first of more than 30 novels, which often returned to the period of the early settlement. They include *By His Excellency's Command* (1909), *Mr Barrington* (1911), *Rat's Castle* (1924) and *The League of the Lord* (1950).

Bridie, James [Mavor, Osborne Henry] 1888–1951 Scottish playwright. A doctor, Mavor wrote over 50 plays, first achieving success with *The Anatomist* (1930), a witty scrutiny of medical ethics in the light of Dr Knox and the bodysnatchers Burke and Hare. *A Sleeping Clergyman* (1933) also directs its iconoclasm against the medical profession. In *Tobias and the Angel* (1930) and *Jonah and the Whale* (1932) Bridie's target is humourless fundamentalism; he calls on the Devil to do some of his work for him in *Mr Bolfry* (1943). Other plays include

Colonel Wotherspoon (1934), *Susannah and the Elders* (1937), *Daphne Laureola* (1949) and *Mr Gillie* (1950). Bridie's genial humour is an easily penetrated disguise for his IRONY, which allies him with SHAW rather than BARRIE, to whom he has sometimes been compared.

Briggs, Raymond (Redvers) 1934– Writer and illustrator of CHILDREN'S LITERATURE. He was first noticed for a series of taboo-breaking books, often with proletarian heroes: *Jim and the Beanstalk* (1970), *Father Christmas* (1973), *Father Christmas Goes on Holiday* (1975), the immensely sucessful *Fungus the Bogeyman* (1977) and *The Snowman* (1979). Later books, notably *When the Wind Blows* (1982), a bitter SATIRE on government advice about surviving nuclear war, and *The Tin Pot Foreign General and the Old Iron Woman* (1984), about the politics of the Falklands War, make no pretence of being written for children.

Brighouse, Harold 1882–1958 Playwright. Of the 70 or so plays he produced between 1909 and 1952, the majority are one-act comedies. The best known of his full-length works is *HOBSON'S CHOICE* (1915). Its durable popularity has eclipsed the almost equally accomplished *Lonesome-Like* (1911), *The Odd Man Out* (1912) and *Sack* (1916).

Brighton Rock A novel by GRAHAM GREENE, published in 1938. Pinkie ('The Boy'), a 17-year-old Brighton gang leader hell-bent on establishing himself, kills Fred Hale, a journalist who indirectly caused the death of the gang's former leader. Realizing that Rose, an innocent young waitress, unknowingly holds evidence against him, Pinkie dates her and then reluctantly agrees to marriage, to prevent her testifying against him. The middle-aged Ida Arnold, a brief but loyal acquaintance of Hale's, fails to persuade Rose to abandon Pinkie. He panics and arranges a fake suicide pact. Rose's conscience stops her going through with it, and Ida arrives with a policeman; blinded by the vitriol he always carries, Pinkie falls to his death over a cliff. Though Greene called the novel an 'entertainment' (in the US edition), it is profoundly influenced by his Catholicism. The tensions between Pinkie (a nominal Catholic, still superstitious), the saintly Rose and the fun-loving, secular Ida Arnold create an ambiguous moral drama foreshadowing his later novels.

Brink, André 1935– South African novelist. An Afrikaans writer concerned with Afrikaner history and morality, he has also written in English, especially after *Kennis van die aand* (1973) was banned. He translated it as *Looking on Darkness* (1974) and has since published his novels in both languages: *'n Oomblik in die wind* as *Rumours of Rain* (1978), *'n Droë wit seisoen* as *A DRY WHITE SEASON* (1979), *Houd-den-bek* as *A Chain of Voices* (1982) and *Die muur van die pes* as *The Wall of the Plague* (1984). He has also written short stories and plays in Afrikaans, CHILDREN'S LITERATURE, travel books, academic criticism and many translations into Afrikaans. A selection of his essays appeared as *Mapmakers: Writing in a State of Siege* (1983).

Brinkelow, Henry d. 1546 Satirist. A Protestant reformer, he attacked clerical abuses and land enclosures, adopting the pseudonym Roderigo Mors in *The Lamentation of a Christian* (1542) and *The Complaint of Roderick Mors* (?1542).

Brittain, Vera (Mary) 1893–1970 Author of autobiography, poetry and fiction. Although she wrote many volumes of poetry and fiction, she is best known for three autobiographical works. *Testament of Youth* (1933) deals with her girlhood (during which she was strongly influenced by OLIVE SCHREINER), early struggles to get an education and work as a VAD (Voluntary Aid Detachment) nurse in World War I. It was immediately acclaimed and has become an important feminist text. *Testament of Friendship* (1940) is a memorial to her close friend WINIFRED HOLTBY. *Testament of Experience* (1957) is a sequel to the early autobiography, covering the years 1925–50.

broadside A song or poem printed on one side of a large single sheet of paper, offered for sale on the streets by ballad sellers and hawkers from the Renaissance onwards. Generally doggerel verse or BALLADS to popular airs, broadsides particularly enjoyed a great circulation during the second part of the 17th century when the production of street literature was at a peak.

Brodsky, Joseph (Iosif Alexandrovich) 1940– Russian-born American poet. Convicted in 1962 of dissident activities, he was forced to leave the USSR in 1972. He received the Nobel Prize for Literature in 1987 and was US POET LAUREATE in 1991–2. His work, which frequently treats the themes of exile and loss, is distinguished by its IRONY and WIT. Collections of his verse in English include *A Halt in the Wilderness* (1970), *Brodsky: Selected Poems* (1974), *A Part of Speech* (1977) and *To Urania* (1984). He has also written: a play, *Marbles* (1989); the prose writings collected in *Less Than One: Selected Essays* (1986); and a book-length essay, *Watermark* (1992).

Broken Heart, The A tragedy by JOHN FORD, first performed c. 1629 and published in 1633. A bleak drama of suppressed feeling, it is fittingly set in Laconia (Sparta). Penthea has been forced by her brother Ithocles to marry the brutal and jealous Bassanes, though she loves Orgilus. The King gives Ithocles his daughter Calantha as a bride. Orgilus watches Penthea die of self-starvation and determines to take revenge on Ithocles. At a feast, Calantha hears of the deaths of Penthea and her father, then of Orgilus' murder of Ithocles.

She waits, feelings under control, until the feast is over before ordering Orgilus' execution. Then she dies of a broken heart.

Brome, Richard c. 1590–1652 Playwright. One of the many efficient professionals who continued to write for the Caroline stage until the closing of the theatres in 1642, Brome is said to have begun his career as JONSON's servant. A Jonsonian influence is certainly detectable in much of his work, though the geniality is Brome's own. The best of his surviving plays are *The Northern Lass* (1629), *The City Wit* (c. 1630), *The Late Lancashire Witches* (with THOMAS HEYWOOD; 1634), *The Antipodes* (1638) and *A Jovial Crew* (1641).

Bromfield, Louis 1896–1956 American novelist and short-story writer. His work often reflects a profound distrust of industrialism and materialism, which he saw as dehumanizing factors in 20th-century American life. His novels include *The Green Bay Tree* (1924), *Possession* (1925), *Early Autumn* (1926), *The Farm* (1933), *The Rains Came* (1937), *Night in Bombay* (1940), *Wild is the River* (1941), *Mrs Parkinson* (1943) and *Pleasant Valley* (1945). He also published collections of short stories, including *Awake and Rehearse* (1929), *It Takes All Kinds* (1939) and *The World We Live In* (1944), and such plays as *The House of Women* (1927) and *De Luxe* (1935).

Brontë, Charlotte 1816–55; **Brontë, Emily (Jane)** 1818–48; **Brontë, Anne** 1820–49 Novelists and poets. They were daughters of Patrick Brontë, a Church of England clergyman born in Ireland, and his Cornish wife, Maria Branwell. The couple's other children were Maria (1813–25), Elizabeth (1815–25), born at Hartshead near Dewsbury in Yorkshire, and Patrick Branwell (1817–48), born, like the novelists, at Thornton near Bradford. In 1820, the year before his wife's death, Mr Brontë took up the living of Haworth, a weaving village a few miles north-west of Thornton. The Haworth parsonage and its surrounding moorland became, as it always remained, the centre of his children's lives. All the girls save Anne attended the Clergy Daughters' School run by the Reverend William Carus Wilson at Cowan Bridge. Its harsh regime contributed to the early deaths of Maria and Elizabeth. In 1831–2 Charlotte was sent to Miss Wooler's school at Roe Head, near Dewsbury, where she met her lifelong friends Mary Taylor and Ellen Nussey. During her subsequent time as governess there (1835–8), Emily and Anne were also pupils.

Their real education, however, was at the Haworth parsonage, where they read the Bible, Homer, Virgil, SHAKESPEARE, MILTON, BYRON, SIR WALTER SCOTT, Aesop and *The Arabian Nights' Entertainments*, as well as illustrated keepsakes and periodicals. Around a set of wooden soldiers they wove tales and legends associated with remote Africa, where they situated an imaginary Glass Town. Later came narratives about the kingdom of Angria recorded by Charlotte and Branwell in minute notebooks; Emily and Anne created the Gondal saga. The strength of the children's attachment to each other and to the Haworth parsonage is shown by the desultory and usually unhappy nature of their forays into the world beyond. Branwell's plan to study painting at the Royal Academy lasted only a few days, and he went on to fail both as a portrait painter and as a railway clerk. His sisters worked as governesses. Anne's longest stint (1840–5) was with the Robinson family at Thorp Green Hall, near York; she left when Branwell, who held a tutorial post in the same household, became involved with its mistress. The most important sojourn away from home for any of the family was Charlotte's time at the *pensionnat* run by M. Constantin Heger and his wife in Brussels (1840–4). For much of her stay she was anxious, melancholy and hostile to the atmosphere around her, and her position was not improved by her growing attachment to M. Heger, who broke off the correspondence she attempted after her return to England.

A joint publication, *Poems by Currer, Ellis and Acton Bell* (1846), passed unnoticed by the reading public. Charlotte's first novel, *THE PROFESSOR*, which drew heavily on her experiences in Brussels, was rejected and did not appear until in 1857. But the encouragement she received from GEORGE SMITH emboldened her to complete and submit *JANE EYRE*. It appeared in 1847, two months before Emily Brontë's *WUTHERING HEIGHTS* and Anne Brontë's *AGNES GREY*. Anne's second novel, *THE TENANT OF WILDFELL HALL*, appeared in 1848. The public interest aroused by these works, particularly *Jane Eyre*, was made the more piquant by the sisters' continued use of their apparently male pseudonyms, Currer, Ellis and Acton Bell. By this time, however, the family was involved in private sorrow. Branwell's alcoholism contributed to his early death in September 1848. He was followed by Emily, who died of tuberculosis in December, and by Anne, who died calmly and resignedly at Scarborough in July 1849.

Charlotte survived to cope with a father now sorely tried and going blind. She published *SHIRLEY* (1849) and

VILLETTE (1853), again drawing on her life in Brussels. She began to move in literary society, meeting THACKERAY, G. H. LEWES, and becoming friendly with HARRIET MARTINEAU and, particularly, ELIZABETH GASKELL, her future biographer. In June 1854 she married her father's curate, Arthur Bell Nicholls; the couple lived together with Mr Brontë at the parsonage. She died the following March, apparently from the complications of a chill caught during early pregnancy. Her father survived until 1861 and her husband until 1906.

Brook Farm A co-operative reform community, founded in 1841 by GEORGE RIPLEY and other followers of TRANSCENDENTALISM in West Roxbury, Massachusetts. It survived until 1847. Its aim was to simplify and purify economic relations. Visitors and residents included MARGARET FULLER, EMERSON, WILLIAM ELLERY CHANNING, THEODORE PARKER, ORESTES BROWNSON and HAWTHORNE, who based *THE BLITHEDALE ROMANCE* on his Brook Farm experience.

Brooke, Charlotte 1740–93 Irish translator and poet. The youngest daughter of HENRY BROOKE and the only one of his 22 children to survive him, she caught his enthusiasm for Irish antiquities, further stimulated by the controversies surrounding JAMES MACPHERSON's alleged *Poems of Ossian* (1765). Her *Reliques of Ancient Irish Poetry* (1789), modelled on her friend THOMAS PERCY's *Reliques of Ancient English Poetry* (1765), contains not merely some of the earliest verse translations of traditional Irish poems about the Red Branch Knights and the Fenians but also an original composition, *Maön, an Irish Tale*, coloured by this material. Though censured for slack paraphrase and conventionally elegant English metres, her polished translations were often reprinted and did much to stimulate an emerging Irish literature in English.

Brooke, Henry 1703–83 Irish poet, playwright and novelist. He is remembered today for his popular SENTIMENTAL NOVEL, *THE FOOL OF QUALITY* (1766–72). A second novel, *Juliet Grenville* (1774), was soon forgotten. His poetry includes: *Design and Beauty: An Epistle* (1734); the ambitious *Universal Beauty* (1734–6), on the perfection of design in the universe; and a translation of Books I and II of Tasso's *Gerusalemme Liberata* (1738). His tragedy, *Gustavus Vasa* (1739; called *The Patriot* for its Dublin production, 1744) was banned because Sir Robert Walpole fancied a likeness to himself in the villain of the piece.

Brooke, Rupert (Chawner) 1887–1915 Poet. His verse is characteristically Georgian, colloquial and nostalgic. Well-known anthology poems include 'The Old Vicarage, Grantchester' (1912), 'Clouds' (1913) and 'The Dead' (1914), though to contemporaries he became best known for his five 'war sonnets' (1915), particularly the one entitled 'The Soldier' ('If I should die, think only this of me'). His good looks and early death in World War I, *en route* to the Dardanelles, ensured his transformation into a symbol of romantic patriotism – a process encouraged by the posthumous appearance of *1914 and Other Poems* (1915), *Letters from America* (1916), with a preface by HENRY JAMES, and *Collected Poems* (1918), edited with a memoir by his friend SIR EDWARD MARSH, with whom he had been associated in the anthologies of *GEORGIAN POETRY*. A *Complete Poems* edited by Geoffrey Keynes appeared in 1946. Other posthumous publications are *John Webster and the Elizabethan Drama* (1916) and *Lithuania* (1935), a one-act play.

Brooke-Rose, Christine 1926– Novelist and critic. A European intellectual influenced by the French *avant-*

garde of the 1950s, she moved from the SATIRE of early work such as *The Languages of Love* (1957) to a concern with the nature of words and their meanings in *Such* (1966), *Between* (1968), *Thru* (1975), *Amalgamemnon* (1984), *Xorander* (1986) and *Verbivore* (1990). Her criticism includes *A Grammar of Metaphor* (1958), *A ZBC of Ezra Pound* (1971) and *A Rhetoric of the Unreal: Studies in Narrative and Structure, Especially the Fantastic* (1981).

Brookner, Anita 1928– Novelist. Her wry, delicate stories of single women and their failure to secure lasting relationships have been compared to the novels of BARBARA PYM and ELIZABETH TAYLOR. *Hôtel du Lac* (1984), which won the BOOKER PRIZE, remains the best known; others are *A Start in Life* (1981), *Providence* (1982), *Look at Me* (1983), *A Misalliance* (1986) and *A Friend from England* (1987). *Family and Friends* (1985) differs in attempting a concentrated family saga.

Brooks, Cleanth 1906–94 American critic. A leader of the NEW CRITICISM, he elaborated the critical principles of T. S. ELIOT in *Modern Poetry and the Tradition* (1939). *The Well-Wrought Urn* (1947) offers close readings of poems from DONNE to Yeats. With ROBERT PENN WARREN, he wrote *Understanding Poetry* (1938) and *Modern Rhetoric* (1949), two college textbooks which helped to entrench the New Criticism as an academic orthodoxy. *Literary Criticism: A Short History* (with W. K. Wimsatt; 1957) still commands wide respect. Other works include *The Hidden God* (1963), *A Shaping Joy* (1971), *The Language of the American South* (1985) and *Historical Evidence and the Reading of Seventeenth-Century Poetry* (1991).

Brooks, Gwendolyn 1917– Black American poet. Her first volume, *A Street in Bronzeville* (1945), was followed by *Annie Allen* (1949; PULITZER PRIZE). *Bronxville Girls and Boys* (1956) and *The Bean Eaters* (1960) were written for children. Subsequent volumes, showing her command of direct, colloquial language inside complex formal structures, are *Riot* (1970), *Family Pictures* (1970), *Aloneness* (1971), *Aurora* (1972), *Beckonings* (1975), *To Disembark* (1981) and *Blacks* (1991). An updated edition of her *Selected Poems* appeared in 1982. She has also published *Maud Martha* (1953), an early work of fiction, and *Report from Part One: An Autobiography* (1972).

Brophy, Brigid (Antonia) 1929– Novelist and critic. A lively writer with the disciplined mind of a classical scholar, she uses the term 'baroque' for her technique of presenting contrasted forces and unexpected views. Her novels include *Hackenfeller's Ape* (1954), *Flesh* (1963), *The Snowball* (1964), *In Transit* (1970) and *Palace without Chairs* (1978). Her criticism includes studies of Mozart (1964), AUBREY BEARDSLEY (1969) and RONALD FIRBANK (1973), and *Baroque 'n' Roll* (1987).

Brougham, Henry Peter, Baron Brougham and Vaux 1778–1868 Lawyer, politician and journalist. With FRANCIS JEFFREY, SYDNEY SMITH and FRANCIS HORNER he founded THE EDINBURGH REVIEW in 1802. His own contributions included the notorious review of BYRON's *Hours of Idleness* which prompted the poet to respond with *English Bards and Scotch Reviewers*. In the course of his long and distinguished career as lawyer and Whig politician, which he ended as Lord Chancellor, Brougham defended Queen Caroline in her divorce case, worked for the abolition of slavery and for Parliamentary reform, and played an important role in founding the University of London. His books include *The Colonial Policy of European Nations* (1803), *Practical Observations on the Education of the People* (1825), *Historical Sketches of Statesmen* (1839), *Political Philosophy and Other*

Essays (1832), *Albert Lunel: or, the Chateau of Languedoc* (a novel, 1844), *Lives of Men of Letters and Science* (1845; second series 1846) and *Contributions to the Edinburgh Review* (1856). His memoirs, *Life and Times of Henry, Lord Brougham*, appeared posthumously in 1871.

Brougham, John 1810–80 American playwright. He wrote or adapted at least 125 plays. He is best known for his two-act musical BURLESQUE, *Po-ca-hon-tas! or, Ye Gentle Savage* (1855). Also notable are *A Row at the Lyceum: or, Green Room Secrets* (1851), an innovative one-act skit, and the *Game of Love* (1855). Other burlesques include *Metamora: or, The Last of the Pollywoags* (1847), *Columbus* (1857) and *Much Ado about the Merchant of Venice* (1869).

Broughton, Rhoda 1840–1920 Novelist. *Not Wisely But Too Well* and *Cometh Up As a Flower* (both 1867) were considered audacious in their time and offended Victorian propriety. She said of her own writing that she began as Zola and finished as CHARLOTTE YONGE.

Brown, Charles Brockden 1771–1810 Novelist, often considered America's first professional author. He briefly practised law in his native Philadelphia before moving to New York in 1796 and devoting himself to writing. *Alcuin: A Dialogue* (1798) was a treatise on the rights of women, influenced by GODWIN. Brown went on to produce four novels which translate the GOTHIC NOVEL into an American idiom: *WIELAND* (1798), *ARTHUR MERVYN* (1799–1800), *Ormond* (1799) and *Edgar Huntly* (1799). Although widely read in America and England, they were not commercially successful. Two more novels sold well, while lacking the artistic innovation of their predecessors: *Clara Howard* (1801; called *Philip Stanley* in England) and *Jane Talbot* (1801). *Memoirs of Carwin*, a sequel to *Wieland*, was serialized in Brown's newly founded and highly successful *The Literary Magazine and American Register* in 1803–5, but remained unfinished at his death in 1810.

Brown, E(dward) K(illoran) 1905–51 Canadian critic. He is best remembered for his work on Canadian literature at a time before the discipline had become fashionable. From 1932 to 1942 he was editor of the *University of Toronto Quarterly*. As well as helping to construct a canon and revaluating earlier poets' work, *On Canadian Poetry* (1943) did much to establish parameters for Canadian criticism. Brown particularly stressed the problems that faced the writer in a materialistic society.

Brown, George Mackay 1921– Scottish poet and novelist. Growing out of his life in the Orkney Islands, his poems are influenced by the 13th-century Icelandic *Orkneyinga Saga*, the work of GERARD MANLEY HOPKINS and EDWIN MUIR, and the symbolic structures of his Roman Catholicism. Early volumes, such as *The Storm* (1954), *Loaves and Fishes* (1959) and *The Year of the Whale* (1965), have been followed by *Fishermen with Ploughs* (1971), *Winterfold* (1976), *Voyages* (1983), *Andrina* (1983) and several limited editions. His novels include *Greenvoe* (1972), *Magnus* (1973), a lyrical account of the Orkney saint's martyrdom, and *Time in a Red Coat* (1984). Short stories include *A Calendar of Love* (1967), *The Golden Bird: Two Orkney Stories* (1987) and *The Masked Fisherman and Other Stories* (1989).

Brown, Dr John 1810–82 Scottish essayist. His three-volume collection of essays, *Horae Subsecivae* ('Hours of Leisure', 1858–62), was particularly admired by contemporaries for two items, *Marjorie Fleming* and a story of a dog, *Rab and His Friends*.

Brown, Rita Mae 1944– American novelist and poet. *Rubyfruit Jungle* (1973) put her at the forefront of the feminist and gay rights movements. Other novels include: *In Her Day* (1976); *Six of One* (1978); *Southern Discomfort* (1982); *Sudden Death* (1983), about the world of professional tennis; *High Hearts* (1986); *Bingo* (1988); and *Wish You were Here* (1990). Her poetry has appeared in *The Hand That Cradles the Rock* (1971) and *Songs to a Handsome Woman* (1973). *A Plain Brown Rapper* (1976) gathers her essays.

Brown, Sterling A(llen) 1901–89 Black American poet and critic. His first volume, *Southern Road* (1932), with its direct style and use of folk material, shows the influence of CARL SANDBURG. A leading characteristic of Brown's poetry is the appropriation of folk idioms, such as work-songs and BALLADS, which he transforms into contemporary statements of social protest. Most of his work appeared in magazines, though it was anthologized in JAMES WELDON JOHNSON's *The Book of American Negro Poetry* (1922). *The Last Ride of Wild Bill, and Eleven Narrative Poems* appeared in 1975 and *The Collected Poems*, edited by Michael S. Harper, in 1980. An active and prolific critic of black literature in the 1930s, he also wrote *The Negro in American Fiction* (1937) and *Negro Poetry and Drama* (1939), and co-edited the influential anthology of HARLEM RENAISSANCE writers, *The Negro Caravan* (1941).

Brown, Thomas 1663–1704 Translator and satirist. When Dr John Fell, the Dean of Christ Church, Oxford, threatened to expel him, Brown adapted one of Martial's EPIGRAMS to make a famous jingle: 'I do not love you, Dr Fell'. He collaborated in the English version of Paul Scarron's *Le Roman comique* and translations from Petronius and Lucian. Brown's sketches of London life were published as *Amusements Serious and Comical* (1700).

Brown, William Hill 1765–93 American novelist, poet, essayist and great-great-grandson of INCREASE MATHER. His first book, *THE POWER OF SYMPATHY* (1789), is generally considered to be the first American novel. Before his early death at the age of 28, he contributed poetry and literary and political essays to Boston magazines. Posthumously published works include a tragedy, *West Point Preserved: or, the Treason of Arnold* (1797), and a second novel, *Ira and Isabella: or, The Natural Children* (1807), with a plot similar to that of *The Power of Sympathy* except for its happy ending.

Brown, William Wells *c.* 1816–84 Black American writer. Born into slavery in Kentucky and raised in St Louis, he helped runaway slaves in Ohio and became a leading black advocate of Abolition. His *Narrative of William W. Brown, a Fugitive Slave* (1847) was followed by a collection of poems, *The Anti-Slavery Harp* (1848), and *Three Years in Europe: or, Places I Have Seen and People I Have Met* (1852). *Clotel: or, The President's Daughter* (1853; issued in USA, 1864), the story of the mulatta daughter of JEFFERSON's black slave, is thought to be the first novel published by a black American.

Browne, Hablot K(night) 1815–80 Illustrator. Under the pseudonym of Phiz he took over the illustrations for *PICKWICK PAPERS* after the suicide of Robert Seymour in 1836, and went on to provide the plates for many other novels by DICKENS: *NICHOLAS NICKLEBY, MARTIN CHUZZLEWIT, DOMBEY AND SON, DAVID COPPERFIELD, BLEAK HOUSE, LITTLE DORRIT* and *A TALE OF TWO CITIES*. He also illustrated works by AINSWORTH, LEVER and SURTEES.

Browne, Sir Thomas 1605–82 Scientific and religious writer. Born in London and educated at Winchester and Oxford, he studied medicine at Montpellier, Padua and Leyden, qualified as a doctor and practised first in Oxford, then in Norwich, where he settled in 1637. A fervent Royalist and anti-Puritan, Browne remained in Norwich through the Civil War, and eventually became a celebrated local figure, knighted by Charles II during the royal visit of 1671. His prose tracts demonstrate a widely enquiring intelligence and an inimitable liveliness of expression. *RELIGIO MEDICI*, an examination of his religious beliefs, was published in 1642 but written several years earlier. It was followed by *PSEUDODOXIA EPIDEMICA*, or *Vulgar Errors* (1646). *HYDRIOTAPHIA* or *Urn Burial*, a reflection on burial ceremonies, and *The Garden of Cyrus*, a treatise on the application of the quincunx, appeared in 1658. The latter was the last of the author's works to be published during his lifetime; posthumous publications included *Certain Miscellany Tracts* (1684) and *Christian Morals* (1716; later edited by JOHNSON in 1756). Browne also conducted an extensive and interesting correspondence with such distinguished contemporaries as AUBREY, EVELYN and ASHMOLE.

Browne, William 1591–*c.* 1643 Poet. A scholarly admirer of SPENSER, SIR PHILIP SIDNEY and DRAYTON, he wrote PASTORAL verse which influenced MILTON and KEATS. *Britannia's Pastoral*, a long poem in three books (the first published in 1613, the next in 1616, but the third not until 1852), combined stock motifs of the rural tradition with occasional descriptive freshness. He collaborated with WITHER and others on *The Shepherd's Pipe* (1614).

Browning, Elizabeth Barrett 1806–61 Poet. The eldest of the 12 children of Edward Moulton-Barrett and his wife Mary, she was born at Coxhoe Hall, near Durham, and brought up mainly at Hope End, near Malvern. The decline in Mr Barrett's fortunes forced a move to Sidmouth and, in 1835, to London. Childhood illness, followed by a lung haemorrhage which necessitated a three years' convalescence at Torquay (1838–41), rendered her an invalid in the family's London home at 50 Wimpole Street and thus tied her to the household of a tyrannical father reluctant to grant any of his children independence. A precocious and ardent student, she had issued several youthful volumes, beginning with *The Battle of Marathon* (privately printed, 1820) and including a translation of Aeschylus' *Prometheus Bound* (1833), which she later repudiated and substantially revised. *Seraphim and Other Poems* (1838) was favourably received by the reviewers. In London she contributed a series of notable essays on English literature and the Greek Christian poets to *THE ATHENAEUM* (1842) and corresponded with MARY RUSSELL MITFORD and R. H. HORNE, collaborating with Horne in the *New Spirit of the Age* (1843). *Poems* (1844), which included 'A Drama of Exile' and 'Lady Geraldine's Courtship', and *Poems* (1850), which included *SONNETS FROM THE PORTUGUESE*, attracted considerable acclaim and made her a serious candidate to succeed WORDSWORTH as POET LAUREATE in 1850, though in the event the honour was bestowed on TENNYSON.

Her work had also attracted the admiration of ROBERT BROWNING, whose poetry she complimented in 'Lady Geraldine'. Their correspondence quickly grew into friendship and romance, followed by their secret marriage in September 1846 and departure for Italy almost immediately afterwards. After staying in Pisa they moved to Florence and settled at Casa Guidi, where their son was born in 1849. *Casa Guidi Windows* (1851) was followed by *AURORA LEIGH* (1856), a novel in verse which secured her position as the foremost woman poet in English. *Poems before Congress* (1860), reflecting her ardent political interests, was received by the critics with dismay as hysterical and unwomanly. Saddened by the deaths of her sister Henrietta and the Italian leader, Cavour, she fell ill and died at Casa Guidi. She was buried in the Protestant Cemetery. Robert Browning prepared her *Last Poems* (1861) for publication.

Browning, Oscar 1837–1923 Historian and teacher. He was an assistant master at Eton and then a history lecturer at King's College, Cambridge, where he became notorious for his snobbery and argumentativeness. Among his works were a biography of GEORGE ELIOT (1890) and various historical studies. He is frequently mentioned in memoirs by former students, such as A. C. BENSON and E. F. BENSON.

Browning, Robert 1812–89 Poet. He was born in Camberwell and educated at home by his father. SHELLEY, his first literary hero, was a major influence on his first published work, *Pauline: A Fragment of a Confession* (1833), in which JOHN STUART MILL found 'a more intense and morbid self-consciousness than I ever knew in any sane human being'. Such censure may have encouraged Browning to turn to the dramatic creation of character and the use of the DRAMATIC MONOLOGUE, which characterizes his best work. *PARACELSUS* (1835) dealt with the life of the Swiss alchemist. A play, *Strafford* (1837), was not a popular success despite the efforts of the actor William Macready and JOHN FORSTER in revising it for the stage. *SORDELLO* (1840), written after a visit to Italy in 1838, concentrated on 'the incidents in the development of a soul' as evinced in the life of Dante's contemporary. From 1841 to 1846 Browning published a series of pamphlets under the general title of *Bells and Pomegranates*. These included *PIPPA PASSES* (1841), *Dramatic Lyrics* (1842), *Dramatic Romances and Lyrics* (1845), *Luria and A Soul's Tragedy* (1846) and the plays *King Victor and King Charles* (1842), *The Return of the Druses* (1843), *A Blot on the 'Scutcheon* (1843) and *Colombe's Birthday* (1844). Many of Browning's best-known poems date from this period. *Dramatic Lyrics* included 'Porphyria's Lover' and 'Johannes Agricola' along with *MY LAST DUCHESS*, *SOLILOQUY OF THE SPANISH CLOISTER* and *THE PIED PIPER OF HAMELIN*. *Dramatic Romances and Lyrics* included *HOW THEY BROUGHT THE GOOD NEWS FROM GHENT TO AIX*, 'Home Thoughts from Abroad', *THE BISHOP ORDERS HIS TOMB IN ST PRAXED'S CHURCH* and 'The Flight of the Duchess'.

Browning returned from Italy in 1844 to take part in the chorus of admiration greeting *Poems* by Elizabeth Barrett (see ELIZABETH BARRETT BROWNING). Their correspondence led to friendship and, in 1846, a secret marriage designed to frustrate the opposition of her tyrannical father. Leaving England for Italy immediately afterwards, they eventually settled in Florence, where their son was born in 1849. *Christmas-Eve and Easter-Day* (1850) attracted little attention. *Men and Women* (1855), though it included *FRA LIPPO LIPPI*, *A TOCCATA OF GALUPPI'S*, '*CHILDE ROLAND TO THE DARK TOWER CAME*', *BISHOP BLOUGRAM'S APOLOGY*, *ANDREA DEL SARTO*, 'Love among the Ruins', 'Saul', 'Cleon' and the eloquent dedication 'One Word More: To E.B.B.', received grudging reviews. RUSKIN made the familiar complaint of obscurity that dogged Browning throughout his career.

After his wife's death in 1861, he returned to England

with his son. *Dramatis Personae* (1864) included 'James Lee's Wife', *ABT VOGLER*, 'Prospice', 'Rabbi Ben Ezra', 'A Death in the Desert', 'Mr Sludge, 'The Medium' and *CALIBAN UPON SETEBOS*. *THE RING AND THE BOOK*, the 'Roman murder-story' on which he had been working for some years, was serialized in 1868–9 and received complimentary reviews which at last made Browning, 'king of the mystics', popular with the reading public. The foundation of the Browning Society (1881) is an indication of the status he had achieved in old age. Nevertheless his remarkable later works have been too frequently undervalued: *Balaustion's Adventure* (1871), *Prince Hohenstiel-Schwangau* (1871), *Fifine at the Fair* (1872), *Red Cotton Night-Cap Country* (1873), *Aristophanes' Apology* (1875), *THE INN ALBUM* (1875), *Pacchiarotto and How He Worked in Distemper* (1876), an idiosyncratic translation of Aeschylus' *Agamemnon* (1877), *La Saisiaz* and *The Two Poets of Croisic* (1878), *Dramatic Idyls* (1879 and 1880), *Jocoseria* (1883), *Ferishtah's Fancies* (1884), *Parleyings with Certain People of Importance in Their Day* (1887) and *Asolando: Fancies and Facts* (1889). He died while visiting his son in Venice.

Brownjohn, Alan 1931– Poet. His volumes since *The Railings* (1961) include *Collected Poems* (1988). Associated with the GROUP and influenced principally by HARDY and LARKIN, he writes scrupulous, controlled verse which often satirizes contemporary British life.

Brownson, Orestes (Augustus) 1803–76 American novelist and social critic. Although associated with TRANSCENDENTALISM and the BROOK FARM experiment, his own activities were often more radical. *New Views of Christianity, Society and the Church* (1836) attacked organized Christianity; *Charles Elwood: or, The Infidel Converted* (1840) is a semi-autobiographical novel about a man's conversion to Unitarianism; *The Meditational Life of Jesus* (1842) outlines his Roman Catholic tendencies; *The Spirit Rapper: An Autobiography* (1854) is less an autobiography than a novel about the Satanic influences evident in contemporary spiritualism; *The Convert: or, Leaves from My Experiences* (1857) is an account of his religious growth.

Bruce, The A poem by JOHN BARBOUR, giving a patriotic account of the struggle of Robert the Bruce (Robert I) and Sir James Douglas against English domination of Scotland. Barbour's concern for historical accuracy prevents the figure of Robert being elevated to mythic status. Battles – notably Bannockburn – are vigorously treated, and the tone combines chivalric elements from VERSE ROMANCE with touches of humour.

Bruce, James 1730–94 Explorer. *Travels to Discover the Source of the Nile* (1790), his account of a two-year expedition to Abyssinia which succeeded in tracing the source of the Blue Nile, was considered fanciful until verified by RICHARD BURTON and J. H. SPEKE.

Bruce, Mary Grant 1878–1958 Australian writer of CHILDREN'S LITERATURE. *A Little Bush Maid* (1910), originally serialized in the Melbourne *Leader*, depicted an idealized rural existence in the story of Jim and Norah Linton, who live with their father at Billabong, a fictional station in Victoria. Independent, hard-working and adventurous, the Lintons soon became firm favourites with readers, the last of their 15 stories appearing in 1942. Mary Grant Bruce also wrote *The Stone Age of Burkamukk* (1922), a book of Aboriginal legends, and *The Happy Traveller* (1929), the story of a resourceful boy escaping from his orphanage.

Brutus, Dennis 1924– South African poet. Banned, arrested and imprisoned for his resistance to apartheid, he went into exile in 1966. His works include: *Sirens, Knuckles, Boots* (1962), combining vatic, sometimes bitter utterance on public themes with tender love poetry; the spare, disturbing *Letters to Martha and Other Poems from a South African Prison* (1968); *Poems from Algiers* (1970), *China Poems* (1970) and *Thoughts Abroad* (1970), poems of exile; *A Simple Lust* (1973), gathering previous volumes with new poems; and *Stubborn Hope* (1979) and *Strains* (1981), reiterating the concerns of the exile but also dramatizing the private conflict between sensual indulgence and spiritual discipline.

Bryant, William Cullen 1794–1878 American poet and editor. He made his reputation with *Thanatopsis* (1817) and two collections of *Poems* (1821 and 1832), strongly influenced by European ROMANTICISM, and WORDSWORTH in particular, but showing a concern with distinctively American political and philosophical issues. A vigorous opponent of slavery and an advocate of the new Republican party, he became an editor of the *New York Review* and *Athenaeum Magazine* in 1825, and chief editor of the *New York Evening Post* in 1829, a position he held for nearly 50 years.

Bryce, James, 1st Viscount 1838–1922 Historian. He was Chief Secretary for Ireland (1905–6) and ambassador to Washington (1907–13). He is remembered for *The Holy Roman Empire* (1864) and *The American Commonwealth* (1888, revised 1920). Other works include *Studies in History and Jurisprudence* (1901) and *Impressions of South Africa* (1897), a sharply observed picture of the country on the eve of the Boer War.

Bryden, Bill (Campbell Rough) 1942– Playwright. He has worked widely as a director for both TV and the stage. His own plays, distinguished by naturalistic detail, clear handling of complex historical material and a socialist fervour which never becomes blindly polemical, include *Willie Rough* (1972), about the Greenock shop steward who led a shipyard strike during World War I, *Benny Lynch* (1974) and *Old Movies* (1977).

Buchan, John 1875–1940 Scottish novelist, biographer, historian, essayist, journalist, editor, poet and publisher. He is famous for his five Richard Hannay thrillers, particularly the first, *The Thirty-Nine Steps* (1915). His 100 books include nearly 30 novels and seven collections of short stories. Many are still widely praised and read, both historical fiction such as *Salute to Adventurers* (1915), *Midwinter* (1923), *Witch Wood* (1927) and *The Blanket of the Dark* (1931), and contemporary tales such as the charming *Huntingtower* (1922) or *Castle Gay* (1930) and the profounder Sir Edward Leithen novels, especially Buchan's last, *Sick Heart River* (1941). His 24-volume *Nelson's History of the War* (1915–19) has a global view free from jingoism. He wrote biographies of Montrose (1913, 1928), SIR WALTER SCOTT (1932), Oliver Cromwell (1934) and Augustus (1937). As Lord Tweedsmuir he became Governor-General of Canada.

Buchanan, George 1506–82 Historian and scholar. The most important of the 16th-century Scottish humanists, he tutored the sons of noble families (including the future JAMES I) and corresponded with the leading scholars of the day, ASCHAM, Languet and Tycho Brahe among them. His attack on the Franciscans prompted a period of Continental exile in the 1540s, during which he produced four tragedies – two on biblical subjects and two translated from Euripides – and a Latin paraphrase of the Psalms. He returned to Scotland in 1562. After celebrating Mary Queen of Scots' marriage to Darnley in an epithalamion, he became her

enemy, authenticating her handwriting in the incriminating 'Casket Letters' and writing *De Maria Scotorum Regina ... Conjuratione*, which appeared simultaneously in Scottish as *Ane Detection of the Duinges of Marie Queene of Scottes* in 1571. Later years saw the publication of *De Jure Regni*, a defence of limited monarchy, and his major work, *Rerum Scotiarum Historia* (1582).

Buchanan, Robert (Williams) 1841–1901 Poet, novelist and playwright. Several strands are detectable in his varied output of verse. *London Poems* (1866) shows an attraction to mean streets and squalid city lives. *Idyls and Legends of Inverburn* (1865), *Ballad Stories of the Affections* (1866) and *North Coast and Other Poems* (1867) deal with the Scottish peasantry and the exacting northern life. *The Book of Orm* (1870), *Balder the Beautiful* (1877) and *The City of Dream* (1888), betray an affinity with the SPASMODIC SCHOOL OF POETRY in their penchant for epic verse. More down-to-earth, *Saint Abe and His Seven Wives* (1872) and *White Rose and the Red* (1873), deal with life in the New World. Buchanan also wrote plays, including *Sophia* (an adaptation of TOM JONES; 1886), and a good many novels, including *The Shadow of the Sword* (1876), *God and the Man* (1881), *Foxglove Manor* (1885) and *Effie Hetherington* (1886). The literary histories usually remember him for 'The Fleshly School of Poetry', a scurrilous attack on the PRE-RAPHAELITES which developed from a magazine article into a pseudonymous pamphlet (1872). DANTE GABRIEL ROSSETTI, the chief target, replied in 'The Stealthy School of Criticism' and SWINBURNE in *Under the Microscope* (1872).

Buck, Pearl S(ydenstricker) 1892–1973 American novelist. A prolific writer who produced over 100 titles – novels, collections of stories, plays, screenplays, verse, CHILDREN'S LITERATURE and non-fiction – she won the Nobel Prize for Literature in 1938. Many of her novels are set in China, where she spent much of her life. *The Good Earth* (1931), probably her best-known novel, is the story of a peasant's relationship with the soil. It opens a trilogy continued in *Sons* (1932) and *A House Divided* (1935), and collectively called *The House of Earth*. Other novels about China include *East Wind, West Wind* (1930), *The Mother* (1934), *This Proud Heart* (1938), *Dragon Seed* (1941) and *Kinfolk* (1949). Her biographies of her parents, *The Exile* (1936) and *Fighting Angel: Portrait of a Soul* (1936), are considered classics.

Buckeridge, Anthony 1912– Writer of CHILDREN'S LITERATURE. He is famous for creating the innocent but disaster-prone schoolboy Jennings, his friend Darbyshire, and Mr Carter and Mr Wilkins, their masters at Linbury Court School. They appeared in comedies broadcast on BBC radio's *Children's Hour* from 1948 to 1964 and in books published from 1950.

Buckingham, 2nd Duke of [Villiers, George] 1628–87 Playwright. Son of James I's favourite, he was brought up in the royal household of Charles I and was constantly involved in intrigue, both before and after the Restoration. He wrote an adaptation of JOHN FLETCHER's *The Chances* (1667) and, perhaps in collaboration with SAMUEL BUTLER and others, *THE REHEARSAL* (1671), a BURLESQUE of heroic tragedy which long outlived the taste it satirized. DRYDEN, mocked in the person of Bayes, took his revenge by portraying Buckingham as Zimri in *ABSALOM AND ACHITOPHEL*.

Buckle, Henry Thomas 1821–62 Historian. A solitary man, largely without formal education, he used a small inherited fortune to devote himself to studying history from a scientific standpoint influenced by JOHN STUART

MILL. The first volume of his ambitious and briefly popular *History of Civilization* appeared in 1857 and the second in 1861, but he died in Damascus with the work unfinished.

Buckler, Ernest (Redmond) 1908–84 Canadian novelist. His best-known work, *The Mountain and the Valley* (1952), is a classic novel of life in maritime Canada. Other works include *The Cruelest Month* (1963), *Ox Bells and Fireflies: A Memoir* (1968) and *Whirligig: Selected Prose and Verse* (1977). Some of his engaging short stories were collected in *The Rebellion of Young David and Other Stories* (1975).

Buckley, Vincent 1925–88 Australian poet and critic. *The World's Flesh* (1954), *Masters in Israel* (1961) and *Arcady and Other Poems* (1966) are concerned with contemporary culture, particularly religion and politics. After *Golden Builders and Other Poems* (1975) he dealt more directly with the process of perception and the way art constructs and enacts meanings. Volumes include *Late Winter Child* (1979), *The Pattern* (1979) and the posthumous *Last Poems* (1991). As a critic, he wrote the influential *Essays in Poetry* (1957), and, as poetry editor of the *Bulletin* in 1961–3, he published poets who questioned the prevailing orthodoxies.

Buckstone, John Baldwin 1802–79 Playwright, actor and theatre manager. Of the 100 or so pieces he wrote between 1825 and 1850, most were short FARCES, operettas or burlettas, but one of the earliest, *Luke the Labourer* (1826), helped set the fashion for domestic MELODRAMA. *The Wreck Ashore* (1830) is an adventure story; *The Irish Lion* (1838) and *Single Life* (1839) are comedies; and *The Green Bushes* (1845) is a tear-jerker. As manager of the HAYMARKET THEATRE in 1853–76 he staged work by TOM TAYLOR, WESTLAND MARSTON and W. S. GILBERT.

Buke of the Howlat, The An alliterative poem in Middle Scots, written *c.* 1450 by SIR RICHARD HOLLAND. A moral ALLEGORY, it describes how Dame Nature and a parliament of birds donate feathers to the owl, who has complained of his dull plumage; the owl then becomes too proud and Nature revokes the favour.

Bukowski, Charles 1920– American poet, novelist and screenwriter. His screenplay for the film *Barfly* (1987) introduced a wider audience to a writer descended from the BEATS, whose life has been that of an angry, irreverent outsider. Collections have included *Drowning in Flame: Selected Poems 1955–1973* (1974), *Love is a Dog from Hell: Poems 1974–1977* (1977), *War All the Time: Poems 1981–1984* (1984), *Roominghouse Madrigals: Early Selected Poems 1946–1966* (1988) and *Septuagenarian Stew: Stories and Poems* (1990). Novels include *Post Office* (1971), *Factotum* (1975), *Women* (1978) and *Ham on Rye* (1982).

Bullins, Ed 1935– Black American playwright. Originally inspired to turn to the theatre by the example of AMIRI BARAKA, he showed his sensitivity to life in the ghetto in his first piece, *Clara's Ole Man* (1965), and has since become one of the most prolific and internationally known American playwrights. Among his best-known works are *Goin' a Buffalo* (1966), *In the Wine Time* (1968), *The Duplex* (1970), *In New England Winter* (1971), *The Fabulous Miss Marie* (1971) and *The Taking of Miss Janie* (1975). They combine formal discipline with an improvisatory energy which embraces black ritual, jazz and blues.

Bulwer Lytton, Edward (George Earle Lytton), 1st Baron Lytton 1803–73 Novelist, playwright and poet. Few English writers are known by such a variety of names. He began as plain Edward Bulwer, though often calling himself Edward Lytton Bulwer. After being knighted in 1837 he expanded his name to Sir Edward (Lytton) Bulwer Lytton. Raised to the peerage in 1866, he was known thereafter as Lord Lytton. He is sometimes confused with his son, EDWARD ROBERT BULWER LYTTON.

One of the most accomplished authors of his day, he is marked above all by the versatility of his talents. His two dozen novels, written over an active career of 45 years, tackle almost every genre popular with contemporaries. They include: historical romances, notably *THE LAST DAYS OF POMPEII* (1834), *RIENZI* (1835), *THE LAST OF THE BARONS* (1843) and *Harold* (1848); tales of magic, spiritualism and SCIENCE FICTION such as *Zanoni* (1842), *A Strange Story* (1862) and *The Coming Race* (1871); SILVER-FORK NOVELS of high society such as *PELHAM* (1828); light novels of middle-class domestic life such as *The Caxtons* (1849), *My Novel* (1853) and *What Will He Do with It?* (1858); NEWGATE NOVELS such as *Paul Clifford* (1830) and *EUGENE ARAM* (1832); and philosophical novels about gifted young men seeking the meaning of life, such as *Godolphin* (1833), *Ernest Maltravers* (1837) and *Alice* (1838). He also published 10 plays, including *The Lady of Lyons* (1838), *Richelieu* (1839) and *MONEY* (1840), as well as short stories, poetry, translations and a pioneering study, *England and the English* (1833). That he is now forgotten would have surprised contemporaries, many of whom regarded him as England's leading man of letters.

Bulwer Lytton, Edward Robert, 1st Earl of Lytton 1831–91 Diplomat and poet. The son of EDWARD BULWER LYTTON, he eventually became Viceroy of India (1876–80). ROBERT BROWNING and ELIZABETH BARRETT BROWNING influenced his poetry, which included *Wanderer* (1857), *Lucile* (1860), *Glenaveril* (1885) and *King Poppy* (1892). His early work was published under the pseudonym of Owen Meredith.

Bunting, Basil 1900–85 Poet. His reputation was well established abroad before he became widely known in Britain for his long autobiographical poem *Briggflatts* (1966), celebrating and seeking to define a distinct Northumbrian community with its own language and history. *Collected Poems* appeared in 1968 and Richard Caddel's edition of his *Uncollected Poems*, which includes some fine translations, in 1991. Influenced both by POUND and LOUIS ZUKOFSKY, Bunting also took many of his poetic concerns from the tradition of WORDSWORTH.

Bunting, Edward 1773–1843 Irish musicologist. His three volumes, *A General Collection of the Ancient Irish Music* (1796), *A General Collection of the Ancient Music of Ireland* (1809) and *The Ancient Music of Ireland, Arranged for the Piano Forte* (1840), form the basis for the attempt to preserve Irish traditional music. His work, continued by GEORGE PETRIE, is an integral part of the CELTIC REVIVAL.

Bunyan, John 1628–88 Nonconformist preacher and writer. The son of a tinker, he was born and brought up to his father's trade at Elstow, near Bedford, to which he returned after serving in the Parliamentarian army in 1644–7. He married for the first time in 1648, when he was already undergoing the prolonged crisis described in his spiritual autobiography, *Grace Abounding to the Chief of Sinners* (1666). Convinced that he was sinful and destined for hell, he tried repeatedly to reform his life (by giving up his favourite pastimes, dancing and bell-ringing) and made intensive study of the Bible. His search for spiritual enlightenment and fellowship brought him into contact with several of the religious sects which had emerged in the 1650s, including the Ranters and Quakers, though he later rejected their doctrines. About 1653 he joined an Independent (or Congregational) church which had been established in Bedford since 1650, but it took several more years of struggle before he felt assured that his sins were forgiven and that he was an elect child of God.

Two or three years later Bunyan began to preach in public, drawing on his own experience of spiritual conflict, and so came repeatedly into conflict with the regular clergy. He also engaged in doctrinal disputes with other sectarian preachers, and his earliest published works, *Some Gospel-Truths Opened* (1656) and *A Vindication of Some Gospel-Truths* (1657), were written against the Quakers. These provoked replies from Edward Burrough, a young Quaker polemicist, and from GEORGE FOX. Bunyan's first non-controversial work, *A Few Sighs from Hell: or, The Groans of a Damned Soul* (1658), took as its text the parable of Dives and Lazarus, castigating the rich for their pride, covetousness and oppression of the poor. *The Doctrine of the Law and Grace Unfolded* (1659), his most important theological statement, gave a lengthy exposition of the Calvinist doctrine of the two covenants of works and grace. He married his second wife, Elizabeth, in 1659, following the death of his first wife the previous year.

Bunyan was one of the first Nonconformist preachers to suffer after the Restoration. He was arrested in November 1660 and remanded in custody to appear at the quarter sessions in Bedford in January 1661, on charges of failing to attend the established church and preaching without licence to unlawful assemblies, or 'conventicles'. Bunyan's own account of his arrest and trial is to be found in the penultimate section of *Grace Abounding*, and in *A Relation of My Imprisonment*, a series of verbatim reports of his trial and subsequent interviews with officials of the court, written for his friends in the Bedford congregation and not published until the middle of the 18th century. Bunyan stubbornly refused to give an undertaking to cease preaching and spent most of the next 12 years in Bedford jail in consequence. He occupied himself making shoe laces to help support his family, preaching to his fellow prisoners, and writing. His first prison book, *Profitable Meditations* (1661), put doctrine into popular verse. *I Will Pray with the Spirit* (c. 1662) defended extempore prayer, while *Christian Behaviour* (1663) was a conduct manual. Two more volumes of poetry followed in 1665, as well as *The Holy City*, a millenarian vision of the approaching establishment of the true church on earth, when the saints would no longer suffer persecution. The last and most important prison work was *Grace Abounding*, though it is likely that he also embarked on his masterpiece of religious ALLEGORY, *THE PILGRIM'S PROGRESS*, during these years.

He was released in 1672 as a result of a royal pardon following Charles II's first Declaration of Indulgence. As pastor of the Bedford congregation, he obtained a licence to preach, and for the remainder of his life he was an active Nonconformist organizer, travelling throughout Cambridgeshire, Hertfordshire and Bedfordshire, and to London, earning for himself the nickname 'Bishop Bunyan'. The threat of further imprisonment was always present, though the warrant issued for his arrest in 1675 seems not to have been executed. He was jailed again for six months in 1677, and it was during this second imprisonment that he put the finishing touches to *The Pilgrim's Progress*. Such was its success when it appeared in 1678 that its publisher,

Nathaniel Ponder, became known in the trade as 'Bunyan Ponder'. In the 10 years before Bunyan's death more than 11 authorized editions had appeared, the book had been published in New England, and it had been translated into French, Dutch and Welsh. Following its success, he turned his attention to the ungodly in a realistic tale, *THE LIFE AND DEATH OF MR BADMAN* (1680). *THE HOLY WAR* (1682) is in many ways Bunyan's most ambitious work. In 1684, following the appearance of spurious 'continuations' to *The Pilgrim's Progress*, Bunyan published his own Second Part.

As well as these works for which he is remembered, Bunyan continued to publish theological treatises, sermons, verse and controversial works. His bibliography runs to nearly 60 titles, 14 of which were published posthumously. In addition to writing and preaching, he devoted much energy to the pastoral care of his group of congregations. Shortly after coldshouldering James II's attempt to woo his support for a policy of toleration towards Catholic and Protestant Dissenters, he died from a fever caught by riding from Reading to London in heavy rain. He was buried in the Dissenting burial ground at Bunhill Fields, Finsbury.

Burbage, Richard c. 1569–1619 Actor. A founder, shareholder and leading member of the KING'S MEN, the company to which SHAKESPEARE belonged, he is known to have played the title roles in *HAMLET*, *OTHELLO*, *KING LEAR* and *RICHARD III*, Ferdinand in WEBSTER'S *THE DUCHESS OF MALFI*, and Malevole in MARSTON'S *THE MALCONTENT*. Contemporaries found his style more lifelike than that of his chief rival, ALLEYN. A skilful business man, Burbage helped supervise the move from the Theatre, which his father had built, and guided the company at the GLOBE and the Blackfriars Theatre to considerable fame and financial stability. He was also a painter of reputation and it is probably a self-portrait which can now be seen in the Dulwich picture gallery.

Burgess, Anthony [Wilson, John Anthony Burgess] 1917–93 Novelist and critic. His experience as an educational officer in the Colonial Service is reflected in *Time for a Tiger* (1956), *The Enemy in the Blanket* (1958) and *Beds in the East* (1959), published together as *The Malayan Trilogy* (1972; reissued as *The Long Day Wanes*, 1982). *A Clockwork Orange* (1962), a dystopian novel, achieved cult popularity after the controversial film version by Stanley Kubrick (1972). Its verbal inventiveness and social SATIRE, though not its bleakness, are typical of the many works which followed. They include *The Wanting Seed* (1962), *Nothing Like the Sun* (about SHAKESPEARE, 1964), *Napoleon Symphony* (1974), *ABBA ABBA* (1977) and a comic sequence, *Inside Mr Enderby* (1963), *Enderby Outside* (1968), *The Clockwork Testament* (1974) and *Enderby's Dark Lady* (1984). Notably ambitious are *Earthly Powers* (1980) and *The Kingdom of the Wicked* (1985), about early Christianity. His many other writings include: *Here Comes Everybody* (1965) and *Joysprick* (1973), studies of JOYCE; *Urgent Copy* (1968) and *Homage to Qwertyuiop* (1987), culled from reviews and essays; screenplays; and translations of foreign drama. *Little Wilson and Big God* (1987) and *You've Had Your Time* (1990), are teeming volumes of autobiography.

Burgoyne, John 1722–92 Soldier and playwright. As commander of the British forces at Saratoga in 1777 he lost both an army and a well-earned reputation as a soldier. His literary reputation rests on his witty comedy, *THE HEIRESS* (1786). Other work includes: *The Maid of the Oaks* (1774), staged before the American debacle; *The Lord* *of the Manor* (1780), virtually a libretto for the music of William Jackson of Exeter; and *Richard Coeur de Lion* (1786), a more ambitious but undistinguished musical piece. SHAW made Burgoyne a character in *The Devil's Disciple*.

Burke, Edmund 1729–97 Political philosopher. Born in Dublin, he went to Trinity College and then studied law in London at the Middle Temple. His first published works were *A Vindication of Natural Society* (1756), an ironical treatise examining the divisions in society, and *A Philosophical Enquiry into the Origin of Our Ideas of the Sublime and the Beautiful* (1757). Friends in literary circles included SAMUEL JOHNSON and JOSHUA REYNOLDS, whom he joined in 'the Club'.

A Whig, Burke entered Parliament in 1765 and, with only one short interruption, served successively as MP for Wendover, Bristol and Malton until his retirement in 1794. He rose no higher in public office than the post of Paymaster of the Forces (1782), his influence always residing in his powerful oratory and the pamphlets and treatises which echoed it. He supported the American colonies in their conflict with Britain in *Observations on 'The Present State of the Nation'* (1769), *On American Taxation* (1774) and *On Conciliation with the Colonies* (1775). *Thoughts on the Cause of the Present Discontents* (1770) voiced concern at the control exercised over the House by George III's friends. *Two Letters ... to Gentlemen in the City of Bristol* (1778) and the *Speech at the Guildhall* (1780) defended his belief in free trade with Ireland, a cause unpopular with his Bristol constituents. He also championed the Irish Catholics in *To a Peer of Ireland on the Penal Laws* (1782) and *To Sir Hercules Langrishe* (1792). He supported Fox's Bill for reforming the administration in India, delivering a celebrated speech 'On the Nabob of Arcot's Private Debts' (1785) and leading the unsuccessful prosecution of Warren Hastings, first Governor-General of India, for corruption in 1788. Always an eloquent defender of the oppressed, Burke then supported Wilberforce's campaign against the slave trade.

His opposition to the French Revolution prompted his most famous treatise, *REFLECTIONS ON THE REVOLUTION IN FRANCE* (1790). *A Letter ... to a Member of the National Assembly* and an *Appeal from the New to the Old Whigs* (1791) rejected the charge that his attitudes towards the French and the American Revolutions were inconsistent, while *Thoughts on French Affairs* (1791), *Remarks on the Policy of the Allies* (1793) and *Letters on a Regicide Peace* (1795–7) returned to the discussion of French revolutionary politics. *A Letter to a Noble Lord* (1796) defended his acceptance of a public pension on his retirement.

Burke is remembered for the spirited manner in which he consistently defended the cause of civil justice, for his intellectual integrity and for the magnificent power of his rhetoric; he was a master of persuasive prose.

Burke, Kenneth 1897–1986 American critic, short-story writer, novelist and poet. He is best known as a theorist of literary forms, whose studies also encompass history, rhetoric and philosophy. *A Grammar of Motives* (1945) and *A Rhetoric of Motives* (1950), his most famous books, examine the ways in which all human activity is ordered in language. Other works are *Counter-Statement* (1931), *Permanence and Change* (1935), *Attitudes toward History* (1937), *The Philosophy of Literary Form* (1941), *The Rhetoric of Religion* (1961), *Perspective by Incongruity* (1964), *Terms for Order* (1964) and *Language as Symbolic Action*

(1966). His stories and poetry are collected in *The Complete White Oxen* (1968) and *Collected Poems, 1915–1967* (1968). *Towards a Better Life* (1932) is his only novel.

burlesque A kind of mockery found in all the arts; in literature, a mocking, but not contemptuous, imitation of a genre or work or author. In its widest sense, it covers MOCK-HEROIC, travesty, and PARODY. A narrower definition would distinguish between high-burlesque (otherwise mock-heroic) and low-burlesque (otherwise burlesque or travesty), the former treating a low theme or subject in a high style and the latter travestying a high theme in a low style (as in the 'Pyramus and Thisbe' episode in *A MIDSUMMER NIGHT'S DREAM*). Parody, then, is the mockery of specific works or authors.

Burnet, Gilbert 1643–1715 Historian and divine. A notable moderate, he ended his career in the Church as Bishop of Salisbury. His chief works are *The History of the Reformation of the Church of England* (three parts, 1679, 1681 and 1714) and the conversational and anecdotal *History of My Own Times* (published posthumously, 1724–34). *The Memoires of the Lives and Actions of James and William Dukes of Hamilton and Castleherald* (1677) undertakes biography in the French manner, presenting documents held together by his own narrative links. The results of his conversations with the dying ROCHESTER appeared in 1680 and his biography of SIR MATTHEW HALE in 1682. His admired translation of MORE'S *UTOPIA* was published in 1684. Burnet's *Exposition of the Thirty-Nine Articles* (1699) became a standard work in English divinity studies.

Burnet, Thomas ?1635–1715 Theologian. *Telluris Theoria Sacra*, which he published in Latin in 1681–9 and translated as *The Sacred Theory of the Earth* in 1684–90, argued that the world was smooth and egg-shaped at the Creation but given its present form when waters burst out of its interior during the biblical Flood. Though Burnet intended to reconcile religion and science, the book confirmed his reputation for freethinking. Its sombrely magnificent evocation of mountains and rivers as 'Ruins of a Broken World' remained influential for well over a century.

Burnett, Frances (Eliza) Hodgson 1849–1924 American novelist and writer of CHILDREN'S LITERATURE. She was born in Manchester and moved to Tennessee in 1865. Although she became popular with her first book, a sentimental novel entitled *That Lass o'Lowrie's* (1877), she is remembered for her children's books: *Little Lord Fauntleroy* (1886), *The Little Princess* (1905) and *The Secret Garden* (1911). In *Little Lord Fauntleroy* the title character is Cedric Erroll, curly-haired and velvet-suited, affectionate and loved by all, who comes to England from New York to win the heart of his estranged grandfather, the Earl of Dorincourt. In *The Secret Garden* the orphaned Mary and her cousin Colin achieve happiness reviving an abandoned garden. Other works include *Editha's Burglar* (1888), *The White People* (1917), a novel about the supernatural, and *The One I Knew Best of All* (1893), an autobiography. Burnett was also instrumental in establishing the legal precedent which gave American authors control over the English publication of their work.

Burney, Fanny [Frances] 1752–1840 Novelist and woman of letters. The daughter of the musician Dr Charles Burney, she enjoyed from early youth the entrée to literary society, notably SAMUEL JOHNSON's circle. After uncongenial service as Second Keeper of the

Robes to Queen Charlotte in 1786–91, she married a French refugee officer, General Alexandre Gabriel Jean-Baptiste d'Arblay, in 1793 and lived in France with him in 1802–12. She spent her time in Bath and, after her husband's death, in London, devoted much of her later life to editing *The Memoirs of Dr Burney* (1832).

As a novelist, she inherited the form from SAMUEL RICHARDSON and HENRY FIELDING and handled it in a way that would prove useful to AUSTEN. Her strength lay in comedy, particularly the comedy of domestic life, developed around innocent heroines as they enter a sophisticated social world. Her first novel, *EVELINA: or, The History of a Young Lady's Entrance into the World* (1778), made her famous while her second, *CECILIA: or, Memoirs of an Heiress* (1782), and third, *CAMILLA: or, A Picture of Youth* (1796), confirmed her reputation. *The Wanderer* (1814) proved unsuccessful. Of her eight plays only one, *Edwy and Elgiva*, was produced during her lifetime. Her diaries are not the least of her literary achievements. The *Early Diary 1768–78* (1889) gives firsthand accounts of Johnson and GARRICK, and the *Diary and Letters 1778–1840* (1842–6) includes the years at court.

Burns, Robert 1759–96 Scottish poet. The son of a small farmer from Alloway in Ayrshire, he turned to farming with his brother at Mossgiel after their father's death in 1784. Here he produced some of his first verse, including 'The Twa Dogs' and a striking cantata, THE JOLLY BEGGARS. Many pieces from his Mossgiel period, such as 'The Cotter's Saturday Night' and 'Halloween', appeared in the 'Kilmarnock' edition of *Poems Chiefly in the Scottish Dialect* (1786). The volume brought him fame and he went to Edinburgh, where a new edition was published in 1787. He immortalized himself as a songwriter by contributing some hundreds of songs, new and reworked, to James Johnson's *The Scots Musical Museum* (1787–1803), including 'Auld Lang Syne' and 'A Red, Red Rose'.

Though lionized as an untutored rustic genius (HENRY MACKENZIE hailed him as 'a heaven-taught ploughman'), Burns was too sensible to trust in his brief fame. In 1788 he bought a small farm at Ellisland, where he settled with his wife, Jean Armour. Poverty soon forced him to take on additional work as an exciseman, though his radical sympathies and support for the French Revolution made him ill-suited to the work and caused him to be regarded with suspicion. He abandoned the farm in 1791 and moved to Dumfries, where he wrote little of importance except for TAM O'SHANTER, 'Captain Matthew Henderson' and the 100 or so lyrics he contributed to George Thomson's *A Select Collection of Original Scottish Airs* (1793–1811). He died at the age of 37, his health undermined by rheumatic fever.

Although he became a cult figure as a ploughman poet, Burns had taught himself to read widely in English and French poetry. In the tradition of ALLAN RAMSAY and ROBERT FERGUSSON, he also worked skilfully in the Scots vernacular, drawing on Scottish folklore and daily life in many of his lyrics. His poems about animals are famous, and often anthropomorphic ('To a Mouse'). He also penned some vigorous SATIRES on religion ('The Ordination' and HOLY WILLIE'S PRAYER) and at least one narrative masterpiece, *Tam O'Shanter*. His rural poems dating from the late 1780s are consistently the best, with a blend of humour and sadness that have made him accepted as the Scottish national poet.

Burroughs, Edgar Rice 1875–1950 American novelist. He began writing for pulp magazines in 1912, when he published the first of many SCIENCE-FICTION fantasies (reprinted as *A Princess of Mars*, 1917) and the first of many novels about Tarzan, an English aristocrat raised by apes in the African jungle. His extravagant and exotic adventure stories deteriorated after 1925, but his early books have an escapist verve which overrides their essential silliness.

Burroughs, William S(eward) 1914– American novelist. Associated with the circle of writers later known as the BEATS, he spent much of his life in Paris and Tangier. He remains most famous for two books drawing on his experience of heroin addiction: *Junkie* (published under the pseudonym of William Lee; 1953) and the notorious *Naked Lunch* (1959), banned for obscenity. His many later books, progressively less noticed as his cult reputation waned, have included *The Soft Machine* (1961), *The Ticket That Exploded* (1962), *Nova Express* (1964), two collections of correspondence with ALLEN GINSBERG (1963 and 1982) and *Queer* (1984).

Burton, Sir Richard (Francis) 1821–90 Orientalist, traveller, diplomat and eccentric. He began to study Arabic privately while at Oxford, which he left without taking a degree, and went on to master 35 languages (or 25 with their various dialects) in the course of his wayward and adventurous life. In the 1850s he was the first Englishman to explore Somaliland, the first (with SPEKE) to discover Lake Tanganyika and among the first to make the pilgrimage to Mecca in disguise. His work as consul for the Foreign Office (from 1861) provided experiences for many further books of travel, but his most famous works, deriving from his interest in erotica, were his translations of *The Kama Sutra* (1883), *The Arabian Nights* (1885–8) and *The Perfumed Garden* (from the French; 1886). For the last 14 years of his life he worked on a translation of *The Perfumed Garden* from the Arabic but his widow, who had suffered from his drunkenness and frequent absences, chose to burn it after his death. As a memorial, she built an Arab tent in stone and marble at Mortlake crematorium, and set up the 'Burton Memorial Lecture Fund', inaugurated in 1921.

Burton, Robert 1577–1640 Author of THE ANATOMY OF MELANCHOLY (1621). He spent most of his life in Oxford, as an undergraduate at Brasenose and then a student (i.e. fellow) of Christ Church, as well as vicar of St Thomas's. Little more is known of him beyond the occasional facts he let drop in the splendidly digressive course of his *Anatomy*.

Bussy D'Ambois A tragedy by CHAPMAN, first performed in 1604 and published in 1607. Its hero (played in the first production by the actor and playwright NATHAN FIELD) has earned comparison with the hero of MARLOWE's TAMBURLAINE. He is based on the historical figure of Louis de Clermont Bussy-d'Amboise, favourite of the Duc d'Alençon, brother of the French king Henri III. Bussy is introduced to the court as the protégé of Monsieur (Alençon) and proves himself courageous but insolent. Forced to defend himself against three courtiers, he kills them. He also quarrels with the Duc de Guise. Monsieur is in love with the Countess of Montsurry (Monsoreau) but she favours Bussy. Out of jealousy, Monsieur tells Montsurry of his wife's infidelity and the Count tortures her into sending a letter summoning her lover. Bussy is overpowered and murdered on his arrival.

Butler, Joseph 1692–1752 Divine. *Fifteen Sermons* (1726) gained him a reputation as an exponent of natural theology and ethics. His most famous work, *The Analogy of Religion, Natural and Revealed, to the Constitution and Course* *of Nature* (1736), is a defence of Christianity against the 'natural' religion of DEISM. He became Bishop of Bristol in 1738 and of Durham in 1750.

Butler, Samuel 1612–80 Satirist. He served as secretary to various gentlemen, including the DUKE OF BUCKINGHAM, whom he may have helped with *THE REHEARSAL*. His fame rests on the long BURLESQUE poem *HUDIBRAS* (1663–78). Charles II liked it and granted him a pension, though he is reputed to have died penniless. Butler's other works include numerous prose 'characters', epigrammatic 'thoughts' and various verses, the most accomplished of which is his poem *The Elephant in the Moon*, a satire on Sir Paul Neale (of the Royal Society) about a mouse that gets into a telescope. It was printed, along with other writings unpublished during Butler's lifetime, in Robert Thyer's collected edition of 1759.

Butler, Samuel 1835–1902 Novelist, satirical poet, painter, art critic, amateur scientist and philosopher. His unhappy childhood in a strictly religious household is described in his semi-autobiographical novel *THE WAY OF ALL FLESH* (1903). He rejected his father's wish that he take holy orders and emigrated to New Zealand, where he became a successful sheep-farmer. His first publications were *A First Year in Canterbury Settlement* (1863) and an anonymous pamphlet, *The Evidence for the Resurrection of Jesus Christ as Given by the Four Evangelists Critically Examined* (1865), which became the core of *Fair Haven* (1873), a SATIRE so veiled that some orthodox readers missed the joke. Returning home in 1865, he embarked on a career as a painter, exhibiting at the Royal Academy. *EREWHON* (1872) is a satirical novel, to which he later added a sequel, *Erewhon Revisited* (1901). On a visit to Canada in 1874–5 he found the material for the satirical poem 'A Psalm of Montreal' (1878) and started *Life and Habit* (1877), the first of a series of works, which included *Evolution Old and New* (1879), *Unconscious Memory* (1880) and *Luck or Cunning* (1886), pursuing his critical debate with DARWIN's theory of evolution.

Butler's eclectic interests and unfocused talent, best displayed in the *Notebooks* (1912), later surfaced in art criticism, to which he contributed *Alps and Sanctuaries* (1881) and *Ex Voto* (1888), and music. In collaboration with H. Festing Jones, he composed Handelian pieces and a comic oratorio, *Narcissus* (1888). Two further areas of study produced *The Authoress of the 'Odyssey'* (1897), arguing that Homer was a woman, and *Shakespeare's Sonnets Reconsidered* (1899).

Byars, Betsy (Cromer) 1928– American writer of CHILDREN'S LITERATURE. The success of *The Summer of the Swans* (1970) established her as a prolific novelist with a strong line in racy humour allied to realistic dialogue. In her most famous novel, *The Summer of the Eighteenth Emergency* (1973), a bright pupil named Benjie deals with the repercussions of making one joke too many at the expense of a slow, thuggish classmate.

Byatt, A(ntonia) S(usan) 1936– Novelist and critic. *Possession* (1990), which won the BOOKER PRIZE, uses a biographical investigation of an imaginary 19th-century poet to explore the process of literary interpretation. Its predecessors are *Shadow of a Sun* (1964) and *The Game* (1967), and two parts of a projected sequence tracing English life from the mid-1950s, *The Virgin in the Garden* (1978) and *Still-Life* (1985). *Sugar* (1987) and *The Matisse Stories* (1993) are collections of short stories, while *Angels and Insects* (1992) consists of two novellas on Victorian themes. Byatt has also published a mono-

graph on IRIS MURDOCH (1965), a critical study of WORDSWORTH and COLERIDGE (1970) and *Passions of the Mind* (1991), a collection of essays. MARGARET DRABBLE is her sister.

Byng, The Honourable **John,** 5th Viscount Torrington 1742–1813 Travel-writer. He inherited his title from his brother only a few weeks before his own death, having lived the unremarkable life of a younger son, first as an army officer and then as a place-holder with the Inland Revenue. What is remarkable is the written record he left of his 15 tours through England and Wales between 1781 and 1794, unpublished until C. Bruyn Andrews's four-volume edition in 1934. The unaffected style of his journals finds room for both sharp local observation and pithy utterance of his own firmly held views about taste, architecture and society, which frequently anticipate COBBETT.

Byrd, William 1674–1744 American diarist and travel-writer. He lived for long periods in England as well as in Virginia. His writings, unpublished during his lifetime, provide a vivid and sometimes satiric picture of his milieu. Two portions of his journal, discovered in the 20th century, have been published as *The Secret Diary of William Byrd of Westover 1709–1712* (1941) and *Another Secret Diary 1739–1741* (1942). The most famous of his travel narratives, *The History of the Dividing Line*, reworks a journal he kept while serving on a surveying commission in 1728 to determine the boundary between Virginia and North Carolina. *The Secret History of the Dividing Line*, probably an earlier version, is shorter, and its humour more racy. *A Progress to the Mines in the Year 1732* and *A Journey to the Land of Eden in the Year 1733* were probably reworked from his journals of the late 1730s.

Byrom, John 1692–1763 Poet. Though his religious verse is forgotten, he is remembered for the hymn 'Christians Awake', and for his Jacobite EPIGRAM on King and Pretender: 'But who Pretender is, or who is King,/ God bless us all – that's quite another thing.' *The Private Journal and Literary Remains of John Byrom* (first published 1854–7) is an important source of information on WILLIAM LAW, whom he admired.

Byron, George Gordon, 6th Lord 1788–1824 Poet. His parents were Catherine Gordon, a Scottish heiress, and her husband, the profligate Captain 'Mad Jack' Byron, who fled from his creditors to France soon after his son's birth and died when the boy was only three. Byron was brought up in Aberdeen, ensuring that Scottish scenery and Scottish Calvinism both left their mark on his character. On the death of his great-uncle William, the 5th Baron, in 1798 he inherited the title and the family home at Newstead Abbey in Nottinghamshire but very little fortune.

His earliest poems were written while at Harrow and Trinity College, Cambridge, which he entered in 1805. The reputation he cultivated there for high-spirited and profligate behaviour belied his real achievements: *Fugitive Pieces* was quickly followed in 1807 by *Poems on Various Occasions* and *Hours of Idleness*. A savage notice of the last, by HENRY BROUGHAM in *THE EDINBURGH REVIEW*, prompted him to revise and extend his satirical poem *British Bards* as *English Bards and Scotch Reviewers* (1809). He was later generous in admitting the hastiness of its witty attacks on SOUTHEY, COLERIDGE, WORDSWORTH and SIR WALTER SCOTT.

In 1809, after taking his seat in the House of Lords, Byron left on a tour of the Mediterranean with his Cambridge friend, John Cam Hobhouse. Apart from some vivid letters describing Spain, Portugal and the eastern Mediterranean and another volume, *Hints from Horace* (1811), the tour also produced the beginnings of *CHILDE HAROLD'S PILGRIMAGE*. Its first two CANTOS were published in 1812, the third in 1816 and the fourth in 1818. From its first appearance the work made him not just a celebrity but the most sought-after figure in English society, though as usual Byron did not allow such pleasures to deflect him from poetry. Between 1812 and the uproar of 1816 he published *The Curse of Minerva* (1812), *The Giaour* and *THE BRIDE OF ABYDOS* (1813), *THE CORSAIR, Lara* and *Jacqueline* (1814), *Hebrew Melodies* (1815), and *The Siege of Corinth and Parisina* (1816). In 1815 Byron married Annabella (Anne Isabella) Milbanke, an unimaginative woman who was no more an ideal wife than he was an ideal husband. After the birth of their daughter and less than a year after the wedding, she left him and obtained a separation. The English public, seized with what MACAULAY called 'one of its periodical fits of morality', supported Lady Byron. Byron himself left England for good in April 1816.

In Switzerland, which prompted *The Prisoner of Chillon* (1816), he joined PERCY SHELLEY, MARY SHELLEY and Mary's stepsister, Claire Clairmont, who bore him a daughter, Allegra, in 1817. His move to Venice that year began a particularly productive period which saw *The Lament of Tasso* (1817), MANFRED (1817), *Beppo* (1818) *Mazeppa* (1819), as well as the completion of *Childe Harold* and the beginning of *DON JUAN*, the great satirical poem which would engage much of his energy and appear in instalments throughout his remaining years. In Venice he formed a lasting connection with Teresa, Countess Guiccioli, which took him in 1819 to Ravenna and in 1821 to Pisa, where he again met Shelley and made a new acquaintance in EDWARD TRELAWNY. Chiefly by interesting him in Italian nationalism and the cause of the militant Carbonari, the Countess inspired *The Prophecy of Dante* (1821). His tragedies, *MARINO FALIERO* and *THE TWO FOSCARI* (both 1821), take Venice as their subject. The latter was published with two more dramatic poems or CLOSET DRAMAS, *SARDANAPALUS* and *CAIN*. One result of his productivity was that Byron, once merely notorious in England, was now famous throughout Europe.

A literary quarrel with Southey, begun by a hostile article from the older poet in 1819 and fuelled by Byron's reply in *Some Observations* (1820), reached its head with the publication of Southey's *A VISION OF JUDGEMENT* (1821), an ill-judged encomium on the passing of George III prefaced with an almost hysterical attack on *Don Juan* and its author as the founder of 'the Satanic school'. Byron's answer was to satirize Southey's poem with devastating ease in *THE VISION OF JUDGEMENT*, published by LEIGH HUNT's magazine *THE*

LIBERAL in 1822. The same year brought news of the death of his daughter Allegra and saw the death of Shelley. After moving on to Genoa, Byron resumed work on *Don Juan* and published a domestic tragedy (*Werner*), a verse tale (*The Island*) and a satirical poem (*The Age of Bronze*), all in 1823. *The Deformed Transformed*, an unfinished drama, followed in 1824.

With the end of the Carbonari and of Italian aspirations to independence from their Austrian overlords in 1821, Byron embraced the cause of Greek liberation from centuries of Turkish oppression. In response to a request for help from an English committee, he set sail for Greece with Trelawny and Teresa's brother, Count Gamba, in 1823 and worked tirelessly with the Greek rebels first at Cephalonia and then at Missolonghi. He caught rheumatic fever there the following year and died. Though the Greeks wished to bury him in Athens, only his heart was kept in Greece. His body was returned to England, but refused burial in Westminster Abbey; it was laid to rest in the family vault in the church of Hucknall Torkard, near Newstead Abbey in Nottinghamshire.

It was Byron's achievement, as much by his life as his poetry, to organize the new feelings of ROMANTICISM into a stance that the wider public could easily recognize and secretly admire even while publicly condemning it. He bequeathed to posterity the image of the Byronic hero, a Childe Harold or Cain or Manfred, an outcast from his own kind and a wanderer in foreign lands, gloomily absorbed in the memory of his past sins and the injustices done him by society. Like all satisfying legends, it was no less powerful for bearing only a partial resemblance to the man and the poet who inspired it. In personal life, Byron was practical and resilient, fully engaged in social and political affairs. In poetry, he found his characteristic voice not in *Childe Harold* but in mature works like *The Vision of Judgement* and *Don Juan* where he presents himself as the poised and urbane satirist, heir to the tradition of DRYDEN and POPE.

Byron, Henry James 1834–84 Playwright. He contributed to the development of PANTOMIME by inventing Buttons and Widow Twankey. His contemporary reputation rested on prodigiously punning BURLESQUES like *The Maid and the Magpie* (1858), *Blue Beard from a New Point of Hue* (1860) and *Ali Baba: or, The Thirty-Nine Thieves* (1863). *The Lancashire Lass* (1867) is an unabashed MELODRAMA and *Our Boys* (1875) an accomplished comedy.

Byron, Robert 1905–41 Travel-writer and journalist. He travelled extensively in Greece, India, Tibet, Afghanistan, Persia, Russia, China and Egypt, and his books are enthusiastic appreciations of the ancient world. They include *The Byzantine Achievement* (1929), *An Essay on India* (1931) and *The Road to Oxiana* (1937), widely considered his best work.

Cabell, James Branch 1879–1958 American novelist. He is best known for the creation of a mythical French province Poictesme, whose 'history' from 1234 to 1750 he chronicled in a series of novels commenting obliquely on American life. It began with *The Soul of Melicent* (1913) and ended with *Straws and Prayer-Books* (1924). One volume, *Jurgen: A Comedy of Justice* (1919), was suppressed on the grounds of obscenity from 1920 to 1922. The case stirred public curiosity, and Cabell enjoyed a large popular following in the 1920s.

Cable, George Washington 1844–1925 American novelist and short-story writer. Born in New Orleans, he became one of the leading local-colour writers of the 'New South', producing 18 volumes of fiction between 1879 and 1918. The best of these are generally thought to be the collection of short stories entitled *Old Creole Days* (1879) and the novels *The Grandissimes* (1880) and *Madame Delphine* (1881). He also wrote a history, *The Creoles of Louisiana* (1884), and *The Silent South* (1885), a treatise advocating reforms for improving the lives of blacks. Because of the offence these books caused to some of his Southern neighbours Cable moved to Northampton, Massachusetts, in 1885. Several novels – *Dr Sevier* (1884), *Bonaventure* (1888), *John March, Southerner* (1894) and *Bylow Hill* (1902) – treat the collision between Northern and Southern manners and morals.

Cadenus and Vanessa A poem by SWIFT, written in 1713. Vanessa was Esther Vanhomrigh and Cadenus (an anagram of *decanus* or dean) was Dean Swift. Vanessa fell in love with Swift but he did not return her passion, though he treated her with respect. The poem gives an equivocal account of their relationship in mock-classical form. Esther Vanhomrigh preserved the poem and it was published in 1726.

Caedmon *fl.* 670–80 BEDE's *Historia Ecclesiastica* records that he was a simple herdsman inspired to sing and write poetry in a dream. He entered Whitby Abbey during the rule of Abbess Hild (657–80). The nine-line hymn in praise of God the Creator quoted by Bede is his only definite work, FRANCIS JUNIUS's attribution of other poems being no longer accepted. Bede's apparent claim that Caedmon was the first to write hymns in Old English has also been challenged.

caesura In Greek or Latin prosody, the division of a metrical foot between two words, usually toward the middle of the line. In English, it denotes the natural pause or breathing-space occurring almost anywhere in the line, though most often near the middle, as in these lines from SHAKESPEARE's Sonnet 73: 'This thou perceiv'st, || which makes thy love more strong,/ To love that well || which thou must leave ere long.'

Cahan, Abraham 1860–1951 American novelist and short-story writer. The realistic presentation of Jewish immigrants in his first novel, *Yekl: A Tale of the New York Ghetto* (1896), became the hallmark of his work. *The Imported Bridegroom and Other Stories of the New York Ghetto* (1898) further established him as a leading Jewish-American writer, a position exemplified by his best-known work, *The Rise of David Levinsky* (1917), about a rich but dissatisfied garment manufacturer.

Cain A CLOSET DRAMA by BYRON, published in 1821 to a storm of abuse. It was widely considered blasphemous, partly because of Byron's readiness to deploy Cuvier's arguments on the creation of the earth and partly because he so obviously preferred Cain to Abel.

Cain, James M(allahan) 1892–1977 American novelist, journalist and screenwriter. His work combined NATURALISM in the tradition of NORRIS and DREISER with features of the hard-boiled school of DETECTIVE FICTION. In both his best-known novels, *The Postman Always Rings Twice* (1934) and *Double Indemnity* (1936), an unmarried man and a married woman plot her husband's murder for money. Cain's other novels include *Serenade* (1937), *Career in C Major* (1938), *The Embezzler* (1940), *Mildred Pierce* (1941), *Love's Lovely Counterfeit* (1942), *The Butterfly* (1947) and *The Root of His Evil* (1951). *Past All Dishonor* (1946) and *Mignon* (1962) are set in the period following the Civil War.

Caine, Sir (Thomas Henry) Hall 1853–1931 Novelist. He became a trusted friend of DANTE GABRIEL ROSSETTI and was with him at his death in 1882. *Recollections of Rossetti* was published the same year. Caine's melodramatic novels, popular in their day but soon forgotten, include *The Shadow of a Crime* (1885), *The Deemster* (1887), *The Bondman* (1890), *The Scapegoat* (1891), *The Manxman* (1894), *The Prodigal Son* (1904) and *The Woman Thou Gavest Me* (1913).

Caird, Edward 1835–1908 Scottish philosopher. He succeeded BENJAMIN JOWETT as Master of Balliol College, Oxford, in 1893. He published *The Philosophy of Kant* (1878), *The Critical Philosophy of Kant* (1899), a monograph on Hegel (1883), *The Religious and Social Philosophy of Comte* (1885) and *The Evolution of Religion* (1893).

Caird, John 1820–98 Scottish theologian and elder brother of EDWARD CAIRD. *An Introduction to the Philosophy of Religion* (1880) seeks to demonstrate the rationality of religion.

Caldecott, Randolph 1846–86 Children's illustrator. His success in illustrating WASHINGTON IRVING's *Old Christmas* (1876) prompted Edmund Evans, who had previously engaged WALTER CRANE, to invite him to illustrate a series of picture-books: COWPER's *John Gilpin* (1876), *The House That Jack Built* (1878), GOLDSMITH's *Elegy on a Mad Dog* (1879), *Sing a Song of Sixpence* (1880), *The Fox Jumps over the Parson's Gate* (1883) and FOOTE's *The Great Panjandrum* (1885). Many of his works are still in print, popular not just because of his nostalgic evocation of former rural life but also because of his ingenious ways of commenting on a text. Caldecott died in America, where he is remembered by the Caldecott Medal, awarded annually to the artist of the most distinguished American picture-book.

Caldwell, Erskine 1903–87 American novelist and short-story writer. He is best known for his portrayal of poor whites and blacks in the rural deep South in novels such as *Tobacco Road* (1932; dramatized by Jack Kirkland in 1933), *God's Little Acre* (1933), *Journeyman* (1935), *Trouble in July* (1940), *A House in the Uplands* (1946), and *Jenny by Nature* (1961). Collections of stories include *American Earth* (1930), *Jackpot* (1940) and *The Courting of Susie Brown* (1952). *You Have Seen Their Faces* (1937) is a documentary study of Southern sharecroppers.

Caleb Williams, The Adventures of: *or, Things as They Are* A novel by GODWIN, first published in 1794. As the subtitle indicates, he intended the book as a radical critique of an unjust social system, but he went beyond his polemical purpose by effective use of conventions associated with the GOTHIC NOVEL. Caleb, who tells the story, rises from humble origins to become secretary to the polished and accomplished local squire, Falkland. Disturbed by his master's fits of melancholy, he enquires into Falkland's past and discovers that he has murdered a boorish neighbour, Tyrrel. Falkland falsely accuses Caleb of theft, has him imprisoned and, when he escapes, relentlessly hunts him down. Caleb at last confronts Falkland and forces him into public confession. He collapses and dies, leaving Caleb feeling not triumphant but guilty at what he has done.

Calendar of Modern Letters, The A monthly literary journal published from 1925 to 1927. Edited by EDGELL RICKWORD, Douglas Garman and Bertram Higgins, it published contributions by FORSTER, GRAVES, D. H. LAWRENCE, WYNDHAM LEWIS and EDWIN MUIR. Its 'Scrutinies' questioning the reputations of established writers inspired the founders of SCRUTINY. F. R. Leavis compiled a selection from *The Calendar* in 1933.

Caliban upon Setebos: *or, Natural Theology in the Island* A DRAMATIC MONOLOGUE by ROBERT BROWNING, published in *Dramatis Personae* (1864). Browning borrows the character of Caliban from SHAKESPEARE's *THE TEMPEST* and uses his primitive speculation about the character of his god, Setebos, to glance obliquely at several strands of religious thought: stern Calvinism, the HIGHER CRITICISM and the debate about evolution.

Calisher, Hortense 1911– American novelist and short-story writer. Her wide-ranging work includes notable studies of family relationships and racial conflict. *The Collected Stories of Hortense Calisher* (1975) gathers together many previous volumes of shorter work. *False Entry* (1962) began her equally prolific output of novels, which has included *Textures of Life* (1963), *Journal from Ellipsia* (1965), *The Railway Police and The Last Trolley Ride* (1966), *The New Yorkers* (1969) *Queenie* (1971), *The Bobby-Soxer* (1986) and *Age* (1987). *Kissing Cousins* (1988) is a memoir.

Calisto and Melibea: *A New Comedy in English in Manner of an Interlude* A comedy or INTERLUDE printed by John Rastell, who may also have been its author, in 1530. It is adapted from *Celestina* by Fernando de Rojas, a novel written entirely in dialogue, which MABBE again translated in 1631. The high-born Calisto enlists the help of the bawd Celestina in wooing Melibea, who originally shrinks from the violence of his passion, but his servants murder Celestina for the reward she has been given. Calisto dies accidentally during a secret meeting with Melibea. In the Spanish original Melibea kills herself, but the English play softens the ending: her father Danio intervenes, warns her of damnation and persuades her to step no further into vice.

Call of the Wild, The A novel by JACK LONDON, published in 1903. The 'hero' is Buck, a dog kidnapped and sold into service in the Klondike, where he suffers brutal mistreatment until he is rescued by a kind gold prospector, John Thornton. Buck's fierce loyalty to Thornton cannot prevent the man eventually being killed in an Indian raid. Masterless, but now at home in the Alaskan wilds, the dog abandons human civilization to become the leader of a wolf pack.

Callaghan, Morley (Edward) 1903–90 Canadian novelist and short-story writer. HEMINGWAY encouraged him to publish his first novel, *Strange Fugitive* (1928).

Other titles include *They Shall Inherit the Earth* (1935), *More Joy in Heaven* (1937), *The Loved and the Lost* (1951), *The Many-Coloured Coat* (1960), *Close to the Sun Again* (1975) and *A Wild Old Man on the Road* (1988). His distinctively spare prose is displayed to greatest advantage in the collections of short stories, *A Native Argosy* (1929), *No Man's Meat* (1931), *Now That April's Here* (1936) and *Morley Callaghan's Stories* (1959).

Calverley, Charles Stuart 1831–84 Poet and parodist. He made a reputation as a translator from Greek and Latin, publishing, among other volumes, *Theocritus Translated into English Verse* (1869). But he was best known for the PARODIES of poets such as TENNYSON, ROBERT BROWNING and JEAN INGELOW which appeared in *Fly Leaves* (1872).

Cambises, King of Persia A tragedy by Thomas Preston, published in 1569. It combines elements from earlier MORALITY PLAYS with a new interest in history, introducing abstract figures (Murder, Cruelty, Commons Cry), a Vice (Ambidexter) and his companions (Huf, Ruf and Snuff) into the story of the vengeful conqueror Cambises, drawn from Herodotus' *Histories*. Popular with Elizabethan audiences, the play was long remembered for its stilted and bombastic verse. Nothing is known of Preston, though he has often been confused with his namesake, the Vice-Chancellor of Cambridge. He may also have written the heroical romance *Sir Clyomon and Sir Clamydes*.

Cambridge Platonists A group of 17th-century Anglican divines, notably HENRY MORE, CUDWORTH, JOHN NORRIS and John Smith, who evolved a philosophical approach marking a path between High Anglicanism and Puritanism. The chief contemporary influence was Descartes, though they could not accept his materialistic view of the inanimate world. The Cambridge Platonists advocated tolerance and insisted on the need for comprehension, seeing reason as the arbiter of both natural and revealed religion. Morality itself is based on reason, and reason and religion are essentially in harmony.

Camden, William 1551–1623 Historian and antiquary. The friend of SPENSER and teacher of JONSON, Camden became second master at Westminster School in 1575 and headmaster in 1593. His travels round Britain and his knowledge of Welsh and Anglo-Saxon resulted in two major Latin works. *Britannia*, published in 1586 and translated into English by PHILEMON HOLLAND under Camden's supervision in 1610, was described in its subtitle as 'A Chorographical Description of the Most Flourishing Kingdoms of England, Scotland, and Ireland, and the Islands Adjoining, out of the Depth of Antiquity'. The first practical and historical guide to the British Isles, it treated not only topography and monuments (most famously Stonehenge), but also such subjects as language and coins, liberally illustrated with engravings, maps and genealogies. The *Annales* (published 1615–2; translated 1625–29), describe and eulogize the reign of Elizabeth I. Camden's minor works include editions of chronicles and other histories, an account of the trial of the conspirators in the Gunpowder Plot, a list of epitaphs in Westminster Abbey, a poem on the marriage of the Thames and the Isis, and his *Remains* (1605), which he described as the 'rubble' of a greater work. In 1621 he endowed a chair of history at Oxford. He is buried in Westminster Abbey.

Camilla: *or, A Picture of Youth* FANNY BURNEY's third novel, published in 1796. It involves a large cast of diverse characters but concentrates on Camilla Tyrold, daughter of a respectable but modestly placed rector, her sisters Eugenia and Lavinia, her brother Lionel, cousins Indiana and Clermont Lynmere, and her eligible suitor Edgar Mandlebert. With an eye to the market, Burney introduced tender sentiment, dramatic incident and Gothic colour, but without deflecting attention from 'the human heart in its feelings and changes'.

Campaspe A comedy by LYLY, probably his first, performed as *Alexander and Campaspe c.* 1584. An elegant dramatization of a story from Pliny, it tells how Alexander the Great is attracted by his Theban prisoner Campaspe and commissions Apelles to paint her portrait. Apelles and Campaspe fall in love. Alexander releases Campaspe to him and returns to war on the famous grounds that 'It were a shame Alexander should desire to command the world, if he cannot command himself.'

Campbell, Alistair 1925– New Zealand poet and novelist. Originally associated with the LOUIS JOHNSON and the 'Wellington group' of poets in the 1950s, he went on to make a distinctive reputation for himself. A latter-day Romantic and one of New Zealand's finest lyric poets, he has shown a strong empathy for nature since his first volume, *Mine Eyes Dazzle* (1950). He has also been deeply influenced by Maori oral culture, as *Sanctuary of Spirits* (1963) demonstrates. *The Dark Lord of Savaika* (1980) and *Soul Traps* (1985) return to the legends of his native Cook Islands. Other volumes include *Wild Honey* (1964), *Kapiti* (1972), *Dreams, Yellow Lions* (1975) and *Collected Poems* (1982). *Island to Island* (1984) is an autobiography of his early years. *The Frigate Bird* (1989) is the first novel in a projected trilogy. He has also written plays, television documentaries and CHILDREN'S LITERATURE.

Campbell, David 1915–79 Australian poet. Drawing heavily on his formative years on an isolated sheep-farm in New South Wales, his early work is mainly serene nature poetry, attempting to bring together the tradition of the Elizabethan lyric and the Australian ballad tradition of A. B. PATERSON. His treatment of the bush is notable for its incorporation of Aboriginal elements. Campbell's distinctive poetic manner changed in the 1960s, becoming more involved with contemporary social issues. Volumes include *Speak with the Sun* (1949), *The Miracle of Mullion Hill* (1956), *The Branch of Dodonna* (1970), *Selected Poems* (1973) and *Devil's Rock* (1974). He also translated several volumes of Russian poetry with ROSEMARY DOBSON.

Campbell, (Ignatius) Roy (Dunnachie) 1902–57 South African poet. Born in Durban, he first travelled to England in 1918 and later lived in France. *The Flaming Terrapin* (1924) is a long, visionary poem. Back in South Africa in 1924–7 he collaborated with PLOMER on a radical magazine, *Voorslag* ('Whiplash'), and wrote pungent verse collected as *The Wayzgoose* (1928). Literary London never forgave him for his attack on Georgian literature in *The Georgiad* (1931). *Adamastor* (1931) is calmer, leading to more contemplative poetry and tauter versification in *Flowering Reeds* (1933) and *Mithraic Emblems* (1936). *Talking Bronco* (1946) includes war themes and, in 'Luis de Camões', some of his best poetry. He handsomely repays his debts in translations of *Poems of St John of the Cross* (1951) and Baudelaire's *Les Fleurs du mal* (1952). His pro-Fascist stance in, for example, *Flowering Rifle* (1939) and his swaggering autobiography, *Light on a Dark Horse* (1951), encouraged his undervaluation as a poet.

Campbell, Thomas 1777–1814 Poet. *The Pleasures of Hope* (1799), his first success, has ensured his inclusion in dictionaries of quotations ('Tis distance lends enchantment to the view'). He is also remembered for such poems as 'The Battle of Hohenlinden', 'Lord Ullin's Daughter', and 'Ye Mariners of England'.

Campbell, Wilfred 1858–1918 Canadian poet. A clergyman who abandoned the ministry, he wrote poetry reflecting the religious doubt of the period. He justified its rough and uneven style on the grounds that it made for a more spontaneous expression. LONGFELLOW and the English Romantic poets were significant influences on his work, and during his time in New England he became familiar with TRANSCENDENTALISM. His volumes include *Snowflakes and Sunbeams* (1888), *Lake Lyrics and Other Poems* (1889) and *The Dread Voice* (1893), painting a very unromantic picture of a nonpantheistic Canadian Nature which represents a marked shift from the view taken in his earlier verse. Later work like *Sagas of Vaster Britain: Poems of the Race, the Empire and the Divinity of Man* (1914) advocated imperialist values. Campbell also wrote verse dramas, novels and travel books, contributed the Eastern Canada volume of *The Scotsman in Canada* (1911) and edited *The Oxford Book of Canadian Verse* (1913).

Campion, Thomas 1567–1620 Poet and musician. His lute songs, which make him a worthy rival to John Dowland, were published as *A Book of Airs* (in collaboration with Philip Rossiter, 1601), *Two Books of Airs* (?1613) and *The Third and Fourth Books of Airs* (?1617). They contain great variety: BALLADS, courtly airs, English versions of Horace, Virgil and Catullus, and religious songs. Among the most famous are 'Follow Your Saint', 'Break Now My Heart and Die' and 'There is a Garden in Her Face'.

Poemata (1595) was a collection of Latin poems, mainly ELEGIES and EPIGRAMS. *Observations in the Art of English Poesy* (1602), arguing against rhyme and vainly advocating the application of classical quantitative metres and forms to English verse, was answered by DANIEL. Campion also wrote MASQUES, including *The Lord Hay's Masque* (performed at court in 1607), *The Lords' Masque* for the wedding of Princess Elizabeth (1613) and *The Somerset Masque* for the marriage of the Earl of Somerset to the Countess of Essex (1613).

Can You Forgive Her? The first of TROLLOPE's PALLISER NOVELS, serialized in 1864–5. It deals with three related love-triangles, in each of which a woman hesitates between a 'wild' and a 'worthy' lover. In the main plot, Alice Vavasor breaks off her engagement to an honourable country gentleman, John Grey, for a reckless politician, George Vavasor, her cousin. Grey regains Alice after Vavasor flees to America, a ruined man. The second plot concerns Alice's cousin and friend, Lady Glencora, who has made a prudent marriage to Plantagenet Palliser, a rising Liberal politician, despite her continuing attraction to the charming wastrel Burgo Fitzgerald. Realizing that his devotion to politics has made married life dull for her, Palliser refuses the coveted post of Chancellor of the Exchequer to take her on an extended European holiday. The novel ends with the birth of their son, Lord Silverbridge, thus ensuring a succession to the Omnium title, and with Mr Grey's election to the Palliser pocket borough of Silverbridge, thereby satisfying Alice's political interests. In a third, comic plot Alice's aunt, a wealthy widow, chooses a dashing suitor in preference to a solid one.

Canning, George 1770–1827 Tory politician and writer. He served as Foreign Secretary in 1822–7 and, briefly, as Prime Minister in 1827. Canning also founded THE ANTI-JACOBIN, where some of his wittiest verse appeared, and contributed regularly to THE QUARTERLY REVIEW. His *Collected Poems* appeared in 1823.

Canon's Yeoman's Tale, The See CANTERBURY TALES.

Canterbury Tales, The CHAUCER's most famous poem, an unfinished collection of tales told in the course of a pilgrimage to Becket's shrine at Canterbury. A General Prologue briefly describes the 30 pilgrims and introduces the framework: each pilgrim will tell two tales on the way to Canterbury and two more on the way back, the teller of the best tale winning a free supper. There follow 24 tales, including two told by Chaucer himself. They are of various types – including VERSE ROMANCE, FABLIAU, EXEMPLUM, FABLE, HOMILY, SAINT'S LIFE – and from widely differing sources, though usually written in verse with rhyming couplets the favourite form. The use of a single framework to link a series of stories in this way was common in medieval literature and there is no reason to suppose Chaucer had a specific model for it. His work is remarkable, however, for its integration of framework and tales: the characters established in the General Prologue are developed through linking passages and the tales they tell, making the collection a sustained piece of social drama. The structure of *The Canterbury Tales* probably began to emerge *c.* 1387, but the individual stories cannot be dated. The final order Chaucer intended for them has not been definitely established; they are usually given in the order in which they appear in the Ellesmere manuscript.

The *General Prologue* introduces the pilgrims as they meet at the Tabard inn in Southwark and begin their journey under the guidance of the Host, Harry Bailly. They come from all sections of society. Some are described in vivid and realistic detail, combining elements from the traditional representation of social types with individual characterization.

The *Knight's Tale* is a romance based on Boccaccio's *Teseida*. Palamon and Arcite, sworn brothers, become rivals for Theseus' niece, Emelye, whom they first see from their prison window. Theseus arranges a tournament to decide their quarrel. Arcite prays to Mars for victory, while Palamon prays to Venus for Emelye. Both requests are granted, as the victorious Arcite falls from his horse and dies and Palamon marries Emelye.

The *Miller's Tale* is a bawdy fabliau told by a drunken and quarrelsome character. Like *The Reeve's Tale* which follows, it has several analogues but no known single source. It describes the cuckolding of an Oxford carpenter by Nicholas, a clerk. Nicholas tricks him into believing that Noah's flood is about to recur, and the carpenter sleeps in a tub suspended under the rafters, leaving Alisoun, his wife, free to sleep with Nicholas. The amorous Absolon also tries to win her love, and Alisoun and Nicholas humiliate him. When Absolon stands under the window craving a kiss, Alisoun thrusts out her backside. But when he returns and Nicholas does the same, Absolon brands him with a red-hot iron. His screaming wakes the carpenter, who cuts the cord suspending him and plunges from the attic.

The *Reeve's Tale* answers the Miller's abuse of carpenters, for the Reeve is himself a carpenter. It tells how a miller is tricked by two clerks whom he has cheated. One sleeps with the miller's daughter and the other rearranges the furniture so that the miller's wife gets into his bed instead of her husband's. The first clerk goes to the miller's bed thinking his companion is in it and boasts of his conquest. The furious miller finds his wife with the other clerk and she accidentally beats him. The clerks further beat him and escape with their retrieved flour, baked into a cake.

The *Cook's Tale* is only a 57-line fragment, whose opening tells how an apprentice loses his position because of riotous living and moves in with a prostitute and her husband.

The *Man of Law's Tale* begins the second fragment of the poem. After a prologue complaining that Chaucer has spoiled all the good stories and announcing his intention to speak in prose, the Man of Law tells the tale of the unfortunate Constance. She is married to a sultan, converted to Christianity, whose evil mother destroys all the Christians in the court and sets the widowed Constance adrift in a boat. She lands in Northumberland, where she performs miraculous cures, survives a false accusation of murder and marries the king, whom she has converted. While he is away, his evil mother sets Constance adrift again, with her child. The king returns, kills his mother and is eventually reunited with Constance in Rome. Chaucer's immediate source was Nicholas Trivet's Anglo-Norman CHRONICLE, though the story also appears in GOWER's *Confessio Amantis* and as the basis of *EMARE*.

The *Wife of Bath's Tale* begins the third fragment. Its prologue develops the Wife's strong and pleasure-seeking personality as she recounts her eventful life with five husbands. Her tale, a version of THE WEDDING OF SIR GAWEN AND DAME RAGNELL, continues the theme of women's mastery over men. As a punishment for rape the hero has to discover, within a year, what women most desire. Eventually he promises to grant a wish to an old hag in return for the right answer. When he has given the answer in court, 'maistrie' or sovereignty, she demands that he marry her. In bed she asks him if he would prefer her ugly and faithful or beautiful and faithless; he allows her the choice and is rewarded by having her beautiful and faithful all the time.

The *Friar's Tale*, an animated and original version of a fabliau from an unknown source, is an attack on the Summoner. A corrupt summoner enters into fellowship with a fiend. They see a carter cursing his horses but the fiend refuses to take them because the curse is not sincere. When the summoner tries to cheat an old woman, she sincerely wishes him damned and the fiend carries him off to hell.

The *Summoner's Tale* answers the Friar with another fabliau from an unknown source about a corrupt mendicant friar who angers a dissatisfied benefactor by asking for more donations. He promises to divide whatever he is given among all 12 members of his chapter, and the man tricks him into accepting a fart. A squire, Jankin, wins a new coat by explaining how it may be divided – by seating 12 friars around a cartwheel, each with his nose at the end of a spoke, and letting off the fart from the centre.

The *Clerk's Tale*, beginning the fourth fragment, gives a version of the folk-tale of Patient Griselda, derived from Petrarch's Latin translation of Boccaccio's version of it in the *Decameron*. In order to test her love and patience, Griselda's husband subjects her to various cruelties, including the feigned murder of her children and his intended divorce and remarriage. She bears his cruelty to the end, when her children are finally restored to her and her husband again accepts her as his wife. Six stanzas called *Lenvoy de Chaucer* which follow the tale plead with wives to show more independent spirit in the face of stupid, cruel or stubborn husbands.

The Merchant's Tale also has its source in folk-tale, richly elaborated and expanded. The ancient January marries the young May but is cuckolded by Damyan. Struck blind, he does not learn of the affair until Pluto miraculously restores his sight so that he can see May and Damian making love in a pear tree in the garden. Proserpina gives May the ability to convince January that she was only struggling with Damyan, because she had been told it would restore January's sight.

The Squire's Tale, at the start of the fifth fragment, is an unfinished romance similar to the story of Cleomades. The King of Arabia and India sends a magic horse, sword, mirror and ring to King Cambyuskan. The brass horse can carry its rider anywhere he wishes to go at incredible speed, the sword can cut through all armour and heal wounds, the mirror reveals future misfortunes and the ring gives its wearer the power to understand the speech of birds. The King's daughter wears the ring and hears a falcon complaining of her betrayal by a fickle lover. She takes the bird to court and nurses its self-inflicted wounds. The tale breaks off at this point.

The Franklin's Tale is introduced as a BRETON LAY but its source is in Boccaccio's *Filocolo*. Dorigen, wooed during her husband's absence by a clerk, Aurelius, refuses him but promises her love if he can make her husband's return safe by removing all the rocks from the coast of Brittany. Secure in her belief that the preposterous condition cannot be met, she is horrified when, by enlisting a magician's help, Aurelius makes the rocks disappear. On his return her husband Arverargus tells his distraught wife she must keep her promise; Aurelius, touched by her love and fidelity to him, releases her from her obligation. The tale ends with an appeal to the audience to say which character is most 'fre'.

The Physician's Tale, the first in the sixth fragment, adapts the story of Virginia from *Le Roman de la rose*. Her father kills the chaste Virginia rather than surrender her to the judge Apius. His corruption uncovered, Apius is imprisoned and kills himself; his conniving servant Claudius is exiled.

The Pardoner's Tale is preceded by a prologue in which he explains how he preaches against all types of sin but himself indulges in various vices and begs from the poor. His tale takes the form of an exemplum inserted in a rhetorically flamboyant sermon. Three drunken men set out to find and destroy Death after one of their friends has died of the plague. An old man directs them to an oak tree where they find a hoard of gold, but greed prompts them to kill each other by trickery and treachery. The Pardoner ends by displaying his false relics and appealing to the other pilgrims to buy them.

The Shipman's Tale, which begins the seventh fragment, is a fabliau. The merchant's wife borrows 100 francs from the monk, who in turn borrows it from her husband. In the merchant's absence his wife and the monk sleep together. On his return the monk tells him he gave the money to his wife; she tells her husband that she thought it a gift and spent it on clothes.

The Prioress's Tale follows the host's polite request to her to speak next. A Christian child is murdered by Jews but the Virgin gives his body the power of song, to reveal his whereabouts and explain how he came to his death.

Sir Thopas is the first tale of Chaucer's tales, a splen-

did pastiche of verse romance at its most trite. Sir Thopas rides in search of an elf-queen and is challenged by a giant. He retreats, promising to return. After a conventional arming scene he leaves court again, but the tale is interrupted by the Host in exasperation. *The Tale of Melibee*, Chaucer's second tale, is a prose homily closely translated from the *Livre de Melibé et de Dame Prudence* ascribed to Renaud de Louens. Long and unremittingly dull to the modern reader, but not the Host, it describes how Prudence – speaking largely in proverbs – persuades her husband Melibeus to abandon thoughts of revenge and be reconciled with the enemies who have attacked his house and killed their daughter.

The Monk's Tale follows a prologue in which the Host requests a tale in keeping with his character, perhaps about hunting. Instead the Monk relates a series of tragedies, interrupted by the Knight because he cannot bear such dismal stories. The sources of the biblical, classical and contemporary figures are Boccaccio's *De casibus virorum et feminarum illustrium*, *De mulieribus claris*, *Le Roman de la rose*, the Bible, Boethius and Dante.

The Nun's Priest's Tale is a vivid fable related to the French *Roman de Renart*. After a premonitory dream which the cock, Chauntecleer, repeats to his favourite hen, Pertelote, he is approached by a fox who appeals to his vanity to make him close his eyes and crow. The fox seizes him and carries him off, but Chauntecleer tricks him into speaking and so escapes from his mouth.

The Second Nun's Tale, the first of two in the eighth fragment, is a saint's life from the *Legenda aurea* (later translated by CAXTON as THE GOLDEN LEGEND). The virgin St Cecilia converts her husband, his brother and some of their persecutors to Christianity before her martyrdom. The invocation to the Virgin in the prologue is based in part on lines from Dante's *Paradiso*. After the tale the Canon and his Yeoman join the party, though the Canon soon leaves again.

The Canon's Yeoman's Tale tells of his own experiences helping his master in alchemy. The tale gives details of alchemical processes and relates how the canon cheated a priest by tricking him into believing he could transmute mercury into silver.

The Maniple's Tale, the only one in the ninth fragment, narrates the story of the tell-tale bird also found in THE SEVEN SAGES OF ROME, though Chaucer adapted it from Ovid's *Metamorphoses*. Phebus has a white crow which tells him of his wife's infidelity. He kills his wife but, overcome by anger and remorse, plucks and curses the bird so that all its descendants are black with a coarse voice.

The Parson's Tale, comprising the tenth fragment, is the final tale. A lengthy prose sermon on the Seven Deadly Sins, it derives from the *De poenitentia* of Raymond de Pennaforte and Guilielmus Peraldus' *Summa de vitiis*. It is followed by *Chaucer's Retracciouns*, a much-debated passage in which the poet renounces all his secular works except THE LEGEND OF GOOD WOMEN and asks that they may be excused on account of the moral works he has written. The sincerity and reliability of the *Retracciouns* must be considered in view of contemporary convention and Chaucer's projected character in *The Canterbury Tales*, as well as their position immediately after the overtly moral and didactic *Parson's Tale*.

canto A sub-division of a long poem, used by Dante in Italian and in English by, among others, SPENSER in THE

FAERIE QUEENE and BYRON in CHILDE HAROLD'S PILGRIMAGE and DON JUAN.

Cantos, The The major work of EZRA POUND, published in *A Draft of XVI Cantos ... for the Beginning of a Poem of Some Length* (1925), *A Draft of Cantos XVII to XXVII* (1928), *A Draft of XXX Cantos* (1933), *Eleven New Cantos, XXXI–XLI* (1934), *The Fifth Decad of Cantos* (1937), *Cantos LII–LXXI* (1940), *The Pisan Cantos* (1948), *Section: Rock-Drill: 85–95 de los Cantares* (1956) and *Thrones: 96–109 de los Cantares* (1959). A collection, *The Cantos of Ezra Pound*, appeared in 1970. A total of 117 thematically and stylistically varied poems, they deal with people and events in ancient, Renaissance and modern history, employ diverse languages, and comment on various political and moral problems.

Cantwell, Robert 1908–78 American novelist. He is best known as a proletarian writer. His first novel, *Laugh and Lie Down* (1931), describes life in a lumber mill. His second, *The Land of Plenty* (1934), about factory life, is widely considered one of the finest novels to come out of the left-wing movement in the USA. In addition to a few uncollected short stories, he also wrote biography and criticism.

Canute, The Song of [Canute Song] Four lines of Middle English verse said to have been composed by King Cnut as he rowed past Ely and heard the monks sing. Its date of composition is unknown, but it was recorded by a monk of Ely *c.* 1167.

Capell, Edward 1713–81 Scholar. *Prolusions: or, Select Pieces of Ancient Poetry* (1760) reprinted the anonymous *EDWARD III* and considered the case for SHAKESPEARE's authorship (see also SHAKESPEARE APOCRYPHA). Twenty years' work was brought to a triumphant conclusion with his 10-volume edition of Shakespeare's plays in 1767–8, though Capell never published his edition of the poems and a lack of subscribers delayed full publication of his three-volume commentary on the plays until 1783, after his death. He prepared an acting edition of *ANTONY AND CLEOPATRA* with GARRICK in 1758, though their friendship turned sour. STEEVENS and MALONE, it was later alleged, used his notes with unwarrantable freedom. He bequeathed the finer parts of his library to Trinity College, Cambridge.

Capgrave, John 1393–1464 Historian and religious writer. His *Chronicle of England*, written in plain, clear prose, is a valuable historical authority on the reign of Henry IV. Provincial of the Augustinian friars in England, Capgrave also wrote a verse life of St Catharine, a prose life of St Gilbert of Sempringham and a guide for pilgrims to Rome, together with many theological, historical, hagiographical writings and biblical commentaries in Latin.

Capote, Truman 1924–84 American novelist and short-story writer. His novels include: *Other Voices, Other Rooms* (1948), a study of youthful innocence in a decadent world; *The Glass Harp* (1951); and *Breakfast at Tiffany's* (1958), a comedy of life in New York. His stories appeared in *A Tree of Night and Other Stories* (1949) and *A Christmas Memory* (1966). He is best remembered, however, for *In Cold Blood* (1966), which combines the methods of journalism and fiction to investigate the apparently motiveless murder of a Kansas family by two youths. *Local Color* (1950), *Selected Writings* (1963), *The Dogs Bark* (1973) and *Music for Chameleons* (1981) are collections of journalism. *Answered Prayers*, a final, incomplete novel on which Capote had made desultory progress for many years, appeared to general disappointment in 1986.

Captain Singleton, The Life, Adventures and Piracies of the Famous A novel by DEFOE, published in 1720. It is a narrative of romantic adventure, culled from Defoe's wide reading, and told in the first person.

As a child Singleton is kidnapped and sent to sea. Put ashore off Madagascar after an unsuccessful mutiny, he crosses Africa, acquiring a fortune in gold on the way. He squanders it recklessly in England and turns to piracy, from which he acquires a second fortune. At the end of the novel he is back in England, married to the sister of his virtuous shipmate William Walters. Because of his upbringing, Singleton himself is a man without 'sense of virtue or religion'.

Cardinal, The A tragedy by SHIRLEY, first performed in 1641. Often considered Shirley's best tragedy, it has a conventional plot dominated by the evil title character. The Cardinal arranges the marriage of his nephew Columbo to Rosaura, but she persuades the King of Navarre to let her marry Alvarez. Columbo kills Alvarez on the wedding night. Rosaura takes her revenge by having the disaffected Hernando kill Columbo. The Cardinal becomes the new avenger, eventually succeeding in poisoning Rosaura. Hernando kills the Cardinal before committing suicide.

Caretaker, The A play by HAROLD PINTER, first performed in 1960. It is set in a shabby room which belongs to either or both of two brothers, Aston and Mick. A derelict, who may be called Davies, makes desperate but futile attempts to establish a role for himself and a hold on the room.

Carew, Thomas ?1595–?1639 CAVALIER POET. His name is pronounced 'Carey'. He saw foreign diplomatic service, some of it at Paris in the employment of LORD HERBERT OF CHERBURY. At court his reputation as a lyric poet and stylish personality won him the friendship of Charles I. His MASQUE, *Coelum Britannicum*, was performed before the king in 1634. Best remembered as a love poet (for 'The Rapture', in particular) on a par with the other court poets SUCKLING and LOVELACE, Carew was a disciple of DONNE and JONSON, with whom he was a fellow-member of FALKLAND's circle at Great Tew.

Carey, Henry *c.* 1681–1743 Poet. He is remembered for his song 'Sally in Our Alley'. He wrote *Poems on Several Occasions* (1713) and a BURLESQUE tragedy, *Chrononhotonthologos* ('the Most Tragical Tragedy that ever was tragediz'd'), produced in 1734. He invented the nickname 'Namby-Pamby' for AMBROSE PHILIPS, and may have been the author of 'God Save the King'.

Carey, Peter 1943– Australian novelist and short-story writer. His fantasies have a concrete particularity rare in POST-MODERNIST writing. Of his novels, *Bliss* (1981) is a sardonic black comedy and *Illywhacker* (1985) the story of a 139-year-old confidence trickster looking back over his life. *Oscar and Lucinda* (1988), which won the BOOKER PRIZE, begins in the world of 19th-century REALISM but crosses the seas to Australia and a fantastic adventure into the bush. *The Tax Inspector* (1991) is set during the audit of Catchprice Motors in the Sydney of the 1990s. The short stories in *The Fat Man in History* (1974) and *War Crimes* (1979) are brought together in *Exotic Pleasures* (1980).

Carleton, William 1794–1869 Irish novelist. His sketches of the Irish scene were collected as *Traits and Stories of the Irish Peasantry* (first series, 1832; second series, 1833) and *Tales of Ireland* (1834). *Fardorougha the Miser* (1839) is the best-known of his novels, which also include *The Misfortunes of Barry Branagan* (1841), *Valentine McClutchy* (1845) and *The Evil Eye* (1860).

Carlyle, Jane Welsh 1801–66 Letter-writer and wife of Thomas Carlyle. Her shrewdness and astringent wit made her an excellent letter-writer, and her circle of correspondents included many eminent Victorians. *The Letters and Memorials of Jane Welsh Carlyle*, edited by her husband, appeared in 1883.

Carlyle, Thomas 1795–1881 Historian, philosopher, essayist and critic. The son of a stonemason in the little village of Ecclefechan, near Dumfries, he was educated at Annan Grammar School and Edinburgh University, to which he returned to study law after working as a teacher and abandoning his original purpose of entering the ministry. His early writings, published in The Edinburgh Review and other journals, concentrated on German literature: most notable are his translation of Goethe's *Wilhelm Meister's Apprenticeship* (1824) and his life of Schiller (1825). At Craigenputtock, the farm inherited by his wife, Jane Welsh Carlyle, he turned his interest to contemporary issues in *Signs of the Times* (1829) and *Characteristics* (1831), and embarked on his spiritual autobiography, Sartor Resartus, serialized in Fraser's Magazine in 1833–4.

After moving to London in 1834 Carlyle made a wide range of friends in the literary world, John Stuart Mill, Emerson and Tennyson among them. As his reputation increased he became the centre of a circle of admirers which included Dickens and Ruskin. His history of The French Revolution (1837) was followed by several series of public lectures, the most significant being published as On Heroes, Hero-Worship and the Heroic in History (1841). *Chartism* (1839) dealt with contemporary agitation and outlined Carlyle's views on the political and social problems of the day. Past and Present (1843) invoked a comparison with medieval culture to argue that the proper regulation of society depended upon the leadership of a strong man of genius. His edition of *Oliver Cromwell's Letters and Speeches* (1845) again considered history with contemporary problems in mind. *Latter-Day Pamphlets* (1850) repeated his views more vehemently. A biography of John Sterling, the friend of Tennyson and Mill, followed in 1851 but a long silence lapsed before the appearance of his most ambitious work, *The History of Frederick the Great* (1858–65). After its completion he published one more book, *The Early Kings of Norway* (1875), and letters to *The Times*, but little of importance.

In his lifetime, and indeed until the end of the 19th century, Carlyle enjoyed a reputation in striking contrast to his present obscurity. His appeal lay in the affirmation of moral certainties in an age of profound change. Victorian England saw the social upheavals of industrialism, the political turbulence of the demand for wider democracy and the challenge to established religion from the natural sciences. Carlyle responded, not with a philosophical system nor with a political programme, but with a list of values to which people could adhere: work, duty and self-abnegation. Above all, in an age of mass movements and mass democracy, he refused to see society in these terms but insisted on the importance of the individual, the private life of service by the ordinary man and the public life of heroism by the leader. His search for the hero, stretching from his early lectures to his biography of Frederick the Great, at first inspired contemporaries but, by removing him from the liberal and democratic tendencies of his age, finally isolated Carlyle and paved the way for later neglect.

Carman, (William) Bliss 1861–1929 Canadian poet. A cousin of Sir Charles G. D. Roberts, he was a prolific and popular writer of vigorous poetry celebrating the outdoor life, in *Low Tide on Grand Pré* (1893), three works with Hovey – *Songs from Vagabondia* (1894), *More Songs from Vagabondia* (1896) and *Last Songs from Vagabondia* (1901) – and a series of ballads and myths, *The Pipes of Pan* (1898–1905). Other works include *Behind the Arras* (1895), *A Book of the Sea* (1897), *April Airs* (1916), *Later Poems* (1921), *Far Horizons* (1925) and *Sanctuary* (1929).

carpe diem Literally, a Latin imperative meaning 'seize the day', an exhortation to make the best use of time before it is too late. The motif derives from Horace, but was frequently imitated by the erotic and devotional poetry of the Renaissance and 17th century. Classic expressions of it include Marvell's 'To His Coy Mistress' and Herrick's 'Gather Ye Rose-Buds While Ye May', both of which cite the urgency of passing time to dissuade a lady from chastity.

Carpenter, Edward 1844–1929 Poet, author and socialist reformer. Influenced by Whitman, Thoreau, Ruskin and William Morris, he abandoned the church for his own brand of primitive communism, earning his living as lecturer, farmer and controversial advocate of progressive causes (sexual reform, women's rights, vegetarianism). His best-known prose works were *England's Ideal* (1887), *Civilization: Its Cause and Cure* (1889) and *Love's Coming of Age* (1896). Volumes of poetry included *Narcissus* (1873), *Towards Democracy* (1883–1902) and *Sketches from Life in Town and Country* (1908). His autobiography, *My Days and Dreams*, was published in 1916. Carpenter was an early influence on D. H. Lawrence, and E. M. Forster admired his overt homosexuality.

Carr, Emily 1871–1945 Canadian writer and painter. *The Book of Small* (1942) and the first part of her posthumously published 'autobiography', *Growing Pains* (1946), give vivid, though partly fictionalized, accounts of her early years in British Columbia. After studying art in San Francisco, London and Paris, she went on to become Canada's best-known woman painter, taking her subjects mainly from the culture of the Western Canadian Indians and developing a style characterized by vivid use of colour and sweeping brush-strokes. Recognition did not come easily and she supported herself by a variety of means, including running a boarding house in Victoria, an experience described in *The House of All Sorts* (1944). She had turned to writing only when bedridden in later life, beginning with *Klee Wyck* (1941), a volume of short stories about the Indians of British Columbia. She occupies a particular place in Canadian literature as a fond chronicler of late 19th-century and early 20th-century life, as well as for the close affinity she demonstrates for Indian peoples.

Carr, J(ames) (Joseph) L(loyd) 1912–94 Novelist. *A Month in the Country* (1980), his best-known novel, is an intricately symbolic love story involving a World War I veteran. His fiction is notable for its discreet articulation of Englishness, often found in sports like cricket (*A Season in Sinji*, 1967) or football (in *How Steeple Sinderby Wanderers Won the FA Cup*, 1975). Other novels include *The Battle of Pollocks Crossing* (1985), *What Hetty Did* (1988) and *Harpole and Foxberrow, Publishers* (1992). *Carr's Dictionary of Extraordinary Cricketers* (1977), one of the tiny pamphlets he published himself, won a deserved reputation.

Carroll, Lewis [Dodgson, Charles Lutwidge] 1832–98 Humorist and writer of children's literature. He studied mathematics at Christ Church, Oxford, obtaining a university post but lecturing and teaching with difficulty because of his habitual shyness and bad stammer. For the same reasons he preached only occasionally after his ordination in 1861. He produced mathematical textbooks and some occasional comic writing. Both he and his friends were surprised by the immediate success of his masterpiece, *Alice's Adventures under Ground* (now usually known as ALICE'S ADVENTURES IN WONDERLAND; 1865), a book which revolutionized children's literature by putting all previous literary pieties aside and opening the door to entertainment for its own sake. At this stage in his life he also took great interest in photography and in the company of young children, particularly girls. Later successes were equally original, notably THROUGH THE LOOKING-GLASS AND WHAT ALICE FOUND THERE (1871) and a long nonsense poem, THE HUNTING OF THE SNARK (1876). After these Dodgson's genius faded, although his fame continued to grow. Today, while his life has become a quarry for psychological speculation, his best works remain as fresh and ultimately elusive as they have always been.

Carroll, Paul Vincent 1900–68 Irish playwright. *Things That are Caesar's* (1932), *Shadow and Substance* (1937) and *The White Seed* (1939), which satirize clerical authoritarianism, put him worthily in the line of COLUM and THOMAS CORNELIUS MURRAY. Apart from two lightly satiric comedies, *The Devil Came from Dublin* and *The Wayward Saint* (1955), his later work is heavily didactic.

Carter, Angela 1940–92 Novelist and essayist. Her fiction, often cited as MAGIC REALISM, mounts a witty, resourceful attack on received notions of 'reality' by using extravagant fantasy, a baroque multiplicity of characters who change role, status and even sex, and pastiches of genres from SCIENCE FICTION to PICARESQUE. Outstanding novels include *Heroes and Villains* (1969), *Nights at the Circus* (1984) and *Wise Children* (1991). *Bloody Chamber* (1979) is a collection of stories retelling classic fairy tales, a recurrent preoccupation in her writing. Non-fiction includes: *The Sadeian Woman* (1979), a major feminist essay; *Nothing Sacred* (1982); and a posthumous collection, *Expletives Deleted* (1992).

Carter, Elizabeth 1717–1806 Translator, linguist and poet. Her verse appeared in *Poems upon Particular Occasions* (1738) and *Poems on Several Occasions* (1762). A friend of SAMUEL JOHNSON, she contributed Nos. 44 and 100 to THE RAMBLER. Other friendships resulted in two valuable collections, *A Series of Letters between Mrs Elizabeth Carter and Miss Catherine Talbot from the Year 1741 to 1770* (4 vols, 1809), and of *Letters from Mrs Elizabeth Carter to Mrs Montagu, between the Years 1755 and 1800* (3 vols, 1817). Her translations included: in 1739, Jean Pierre de Crousaz's discussion of POPE's ESSAY ON MAN, which prompted Warburton's defensive response, *A Vindication of Mr Pope's Essay on Man, from the Misrepresentations of Mr de Crousaz*; in 1739, Algarotti's *Newtonianismo per le dame* as *Sir Isaac Newton's Philosophy Explained for the Use of Ladies*; and in 1758, the works of Epictetus, her most important achievement.

Carter, Martin 1927– Guyanese poet. He made his reputation with *Hills of Fire Glow Red* (1951), *The Kind Eagle* (1952), *Returning* (1953) and particularly *Poems of Resistance* (1954). Later collections include *Poems of Shape and Motion* (1955), *Conversations* (1961), *Jail Me Quickly* (1963), *Poems of Succession* (1977) and *Poems of Affinity* (1980). Although there are many influences on his writing from American and European sources, he remains indisputably a Caribbean poet. It has been said that he

combines a tradition of public poetry with uncomfortable private anguish.

Cartwright, William 1611–43 Poet, playwright and preacher. He was claimed as a poetic 'son' by JONSON. His comedy, *The Ordinary* (c. 1634), is Jonsonian in style, while two tragicomedies, *The Siege* (c. 1636) and *The Lady-Errant* (c. 1636), are not without ingenuity. *The Royal Slave* (1636) was acted before Charles I and Henrietta Maria. Cartwright took holy orders in 1638 and became a preacher noted for his fiery loyalty to the King. The 1651 edition of his works contains 51 commendatory verses by fellow-writers.

Carver, Raymond 1939–88 American short-story writer and poet. A prime example of 'Dirty Realism', his fiction navigates the apparently contingent lives of its small-town protagonists in unadorned prose. His stories are collected in *Will You Please be Quiet, Please?* (1976), *What We Talk About When We Talk About Love* (1981), *Cathedral* (1983) and *Fires: Essays, Stories, Poems* (1983). His poetry appeared in *Near Klamath* (1968), *Winter Insomnia* (1970), *At Night the Salmon Move* (1976), *Where Water Comes Together with Other Water* (1985) and *Ultramarine* (1986).

Cary, Henry Francis 1772–1844 Translator of Dante. His BLANK-VERSE translation of the *Inferno* appeared in 1805–6 and of the *Purgatorio* and *Paradiso* in 1814.

Cary, (Arthur) Joyce (Lunel) 1888–1957 Novelist. His first four novels – *Aissa Saved* (1932), *An American Visitor* (1933), *The African Witch* (1936) and *Mister Johnson* (1939) – derive from his experience in the Nigerian colonial service and deal with the confrontation between African tribal culture and British administration. *Castle Corner* (1938) is the only completed volume of a planned trilogy about the decline of the British Empire, and *Charley is My Darling* (1940) and *House of Children* (1941) are about childhood. His best-known works are two trilogies: *Herself Surprised* (1941), *To be a Pilgrim* (1942) and *The Horse's Mouth* (1944), about the world of art; and *Prisoner of Grace* (1952), *Except the Lord* (1953) and *Not Honour More* (1955), about politics. In both trilogies the story is told through first-person narratives by each of the three main characters. The narrative by the amoral artist Gully Jimson in *The Horse's Mouth* holds a particular appeal. Cary also published poetry and works on politics and aesthetics.

Cary, Patrick ?1623–57 Poet and younger brother to LUCIUS FALKLAND. His poems, written in 1650 and 1651, were unpublished in his lifetime and first printed in 1771. His secular work, the *Trivial Ballads*, embraces satire, PASTORAL and love-lyric, and exhibits skilful metrical variety and gentlemanly wit. Cary, who inherited his mother's Catholicism and briefly entered a monastery, also wrote devotional meditations: deeply felt, if of uneven quality, they echo both DONNE's vigour and JONSON's elegance.

Caste A comedy by THOMAS WILLIAM ROBERTSON, first performed in 1867. It is the outstanding example of his innovative realism in presenting domestic detail. Esther and Polly Eccles are sisters impoverished by their idle, drunken father. Polly is content to love a gas-fitter, Sam Gerridge, but Esther is persuaded to marry the genteel George d'Alroy and finds herself ill at ease in Mayfair.

Castle Dangerous See SCOTT, SIR WALTER.

Castle of Indolence, The A poem in SPENSERIAN STANZAS by JAMES THOMSON, published in 1748, though he had begun it 15 years before. The first CANTO tells of the wizard, Indolence, and the castle into which he lures world-weary pilgrims. They surrender to idleness in an atmosphere of delicious ease until they degenerate and are thrown into the dungeons. The second tells of the Knight of Arts and Industry and his destruction of the castle. Thomson introduces himself ('A bard here dwelt, more fat than bard beseems') and several of his friends into the first canto.

Castle of Otranto, The: *A Gothic Story* A novel by HORACE WALPOLE, published in 1764. He originally presented it as a translation from an imaginary Italian original but later acknowledged his authorship. The circumstances suggest that the tale was playfully conceived, though it proved influential in establishing the fashion for the Gothic novel.

Set in the 13th century, the story concerns Manfred, who holds the princedom of Otranto only because his grandfather had poisoned the rightful prince, Alfonso. A prophecy has foretold that the usurpers would remain in power as long as they had male issue to continue their line and the castle remained large enough to hold the lawful ruler. Manfred's plan to marry his only son, Conrad, to Isabella is frustrated by Conrad's mysterious death and his subsequent plan to marry Isabella himself is thwarted by her escape with Theodore. Finally the ghost of Alfonso, grown too enormous to be contained by the castle, overthrows it and rises from the ruins. Manfred confesses the usurpation by his family, and the ghost proclaims Theodore the lawful prince. Theodore and Isabella marry.

Castle of Perseverance, The A MORALITY PLAY, *c.* 1405–25. A drawing in the surviving manuscript shows it performed in the round, with the castle (symbolizing Christian patience in the face of temptation) in the centre and scaffolds on the circumference housing Flesh, World, Belial, Covetousness and God. Beneath the castle there is a bench-bed for the protagonist, Humanum Genus (or soul of humankind), over whom the forces of Good and Evil dispute. Saved from the World by the Good Angel, he takes refuge in the castle, which withstands an assault by Satan. Covetousness draws him towards riches but Death proves their transitoriness. Defended at the throne of God by Mercy and Justice, he is admitted to Heaven.

Castle Rackrent A novel by MARIA EDGEWORTH, published in 1801. Thady Quirk, steward to the Rackrents, tells the story of the family's path to ruin, beginning three generations before with the hard-drinking Sir Patrick. Like *THE ABSENTEE*, it criticizes 18th-century Irish landlords, vividly depicting the results of profligacy and corruption.

Cat on a Hot Tin Roof A play by TENNESSEE WILLIAMS, produced in 1955, awarded a PULITZER PRIZE and revised for a revival in 1974. The action centres on the question of who will inherit the dying Big Daddy Pollitt's Mississippi estate. He has stipulated that to inherit their share each of his sons must have children. Gooper Pollitt and his wife Mae already have five and are expecting another. Brick, the younger son, has turned to drink in his guilt about his homosexuality. He and his wife Maggie, the 'cat' of the title, are childless. The play ends with the suggestion that Maggie will be able to seduce Brick and conceive a child.

catachresis The misapplication of a word, sometimes ineptly, as in mixed metaphors (see METAPHOR), but often with striking rhetorical effect (as in MILTON's 'Blind mouths!' in *LYCIDAS*).

catalexis (truncation) The omission of the last syllable or syllables from a line in a passage of generally regular verse (see METRE). Such a line is said to be catalectic when it is one syllable short, brachycatalectic when it is two short. The regular lines of the passage are acatalectic. A line with one or two syllables in excess of the regular number would be hypercatalectic.

Catch-22 A novel by JOSEPH HELLER, published in 1961. Captain John Yossarian, an American airmen, is determined to survive World War II but is prevented from getting a medical discharge by the 'Catch-22' rule, which says that anyone rational enough to want to be grounded cannot be insane and is therefore capable of returning to flight duty. A non-chronological narrative technique is intended to emphasize the displacements that war produces.

Catcher in the Rye, The A novel by J. D. SALINGER, published in 1951. The 16-year-old Holden Caulfield narrates his own story of rebellion against the banality and 'phoniness' of middle-class values. Expelled from private school, he goes by himself to New York City, where he has an unsuccessful encounter with a prostitute, a meeting with an old girlfriend, Sally Hayes, and an unsettling reunion with his former schoolteacher, Mr Antolini, who makes homosexual advances to him. Planning to 'go West' and wanting to say goodbye to his sister Phoebe, he is overwhelmed by his love for her and decides to stay. He then has a nervous breakdown, and tells his story as he is recovering.

catharsis From the Greek, a purging or cleansing. In Aristotle's theory of TRAGEDY, it refers specifically to the release of emotion caused in the audience by the fate of the tragic hero.

Cather, Willa (Siebert) 1873–1947 American novelist. Born in rural Virginia and brought up in Nebraska, she worked as a journalist and teacher in Pittsburgh before joining the staff of *McCLURE'S MAGAZINE* in New York. An early volume of poetry and a collection of short stories were followed by more stories in magazines and her first novel, *Alexander's Bridge* (1912). Her most important novels are commonly considered to be: *O Pioneers!* (1913), about Alexandra Bergson, a Swedish immigrant farmer in Nebraska; *My Ántonia* (1918), about Ántonia Shimerda, from a family of Bohemian immigrant farmers in Nebraska; and *Death Comes for the Archbishop* (1927), based on the careers of two French missionaries, Jean-Baptiste Lamy and Joseph Machebeuf, in mid 19th-century New Mexico. Others include: *The Song of the Lark* (1915); *One of Ours* (1922), her first popular success, which won a PULITZER PRIZE; *A Lost Lady* (1923), about the moral decline of a woman from a small Nebraska town; *The Professor's House* (1925), set in a small Midwestern college and in New Mexico in the post-war years; *My Mortal Enemy* (1926); *Shadows on the Rock* (1931); *Lucy Gayheart* (1935); and *Sapphira and the Slave* (1940), her only novel set in Virginia. The three tales that make up *Obscure Destinies* (1932) take place in the Midwest. *Not Under Forty* (1936; later retitled *Literary Encounters*) is a volume of critical essays.

Catherine: *A Story, by Ikey Solomons, Esq., Junior* A short novel by THACKERAY, serialized in 1839–40. Based on the career of Catherine Hayes, executed in 1726 for murdering her husband, it is a deliberately sordid tale written in reaction against the sentimental view of criminals offered by the NEWGATE NOVEL.

Catiline His Conspiracy A tragedy by BEN JONSON, first performed and published in 1611. Drawn from Roman history, it follows the last stage in the career of the ambitious but dissolute Catiline (Lucius Sergius

Catilina) after Cicero and Antonius have defeated him in elections for the consulship. With the secret encouragement of Caesar and Crassus, he plans to assassinate Cicero as the first step in a plot to overthrow the government. Fulvia warns Cicero and Catiline flees Rome for Faesulae, where his supporters have raised an army. The Senate condemns the conspirators to death, but Catiline dies in battle.

Catnach, James 1792–1841 Printer and publisher. From 1813 until 1838 he ran a prosperous business in Seven Dials, London, issuing cheap publications of many sorts, including ABCs, children's tracts, nursery rhymes and carols. Catnach was best known, however, for his output of topical and sensational material – on crimes, scandals, villainies, prize-fights and political events – which with its crude woodcut illustrations was widely distributed by itinerant hawkers.

Cato A tragedy in BLANK VERSE by ADDISON, produced and published in 1713. It deals with the last weeks of the republican, Marcus Porcius Cato, besieged in Utica by Caesar in 46 BC. He has been betrayed by Sempronius, a senator, and the Numidian general, Syphax; Juba, Prince of Numidia, remains faithful. Addison introduces romantic interest in the character of Marcia, Cato's daughter, whom Juba loves, and the rivalry of Cato's two sons for Lucia's hand. The contemporary parallel with Queen Anne's death and the dispute over succession to the British throne helped the play to considerable success, though it has not been revived.

Catriona See KIDNAPPED.

Caudwell, Christopher [Sprigg, Christopher St John] 1901–37 Critic, journalist, poet and detective novelist. He joined the Communist Party in 1935 and was killed fighting for the International Brigade in the Spanish Civil War. His literary reputation rests on the posthumously published *Illusion and Reality* (1937), which attempted to develop a Marxist theory of poetry as a product of the human struggle with nature. *Studies in a Dying Culture* (1938) contains analyses of Freud, SHAW and D. H. LAWRENCE. Other works include *The Crisis in Physics* (1939) and *Further Studies in a Dying Culture* (edited by EDGELL RICKWORD, 1949). The verse brought together in *Poems* (1939), superseded by *Collected Poems* (1986), is unsentimental but direct and urgent. Under his real name he wrote DETECTIVE FICTION and textbooks on aircraft, as well as editing his own aeronautics magazine.

Causley, Charles 1917– Poet. *Hands to Dance* (1951), his first collection, was followed by *Farewell, Aggie Weston* (1951), *Survivor's Leave* (1953), *Union Street* (1957), *Johnny Alleluia* (1961), *Underneath the Water* (1968), *Figgie Hobbin* (1970), *Collected Poems* (1975), *Early in the Morning* (1988) and *Collected Poems* (1992). Well known as a poet of the sea, he uses simple diction, firm rhythms and traditional forms, especially the BALLAD. These techniques, together with his recurrent interest in the survival of innocence, have helped to make his poetry for children immensely popular.

Cavalier poets A term loosely describing a group of lyric poets who flourished during the reign of Charles I (1625–49). These courtiers wrote about love and loyalty to the monarch, usually in complimentary poems or lighthearted lyrics. LOVELACE, SUCKLING and CAREW were the most prominent, while HERRICK and WALLER, though not of their social coterie, often resemble them in literary style and attitude. All owe a debt to DONNE and JONSON.

Cave, Edward See GENTLEMAN'S MAGAZINE, THE.

Cavendish, George 1500–?61 Author of *The Life of Cardinal Wolsey*, a biography in the medieval tradition of historical writing describing the fall of a great man. It was not printed until 1641 but manuscript copies circulated in the 16th century made it known to writers like JOHN STOW, who drew on it for his *Annales*. Cavendish joined the Cardinal's household as a gentleman usher in 1527 and was with him when he died at Leicester in 1530.

Caxton, William *c.* 1415/24–*c.* 1491/2 Printer and translator. After gaining experience in Cologne and Bruges, he set up his own press – the first in England – near Westminster Abbey in 1476–7. Though he had printed works in Latin on the Continent, Caxton's Westminster press concentrated largely on works in English, the Greek and Latin classics (Ovid, Virgil, Cato) appearing only in translation. The 100 or so items he issued include works by CHAUCER, GOWER and LYDGATE (but not LANGLAND), books on history and geography, SAINTS' LIVES and didactic works, prose romances (most notably *The Knight of the Tower*, 1483) and miscellaneous treatises. Caxton was a prolific translator with a vigorous and fluent style, and, except MALORY's *MORTE DARTHUR*, all the prose romances he printed were his own work. Best known are *REYNARD THE FOX* (1481), *THE GOLDEN LEGEND* (1483), and the FABLES of Aesop (1483/4). *The Game and Play of the Chess* (1474/5) had been printed in Bruges, where the first part of his *Recuyell of the Histories of Troy* (1471–6), based on the French of Raoul Lefevre, also appeared. On his death Caxton's press passed to WYNKYN DE WORDE.

Cecil, Lord (Edward Christian) David (Gascoyne) 1902–86 Critic and biographer. He wrote studies of COWPER (1929), Lord Melbourne (1939, 1954), HARDY (1943), THOMAS GRAY and TEMPLE's wife Dorothy Osborne (*Two Quiet Lives*, 1948), AUSTEN (1978) and CHARLES LAMB (1983), but is best remembered for *Early Victorian Novelists* (1934). His gentlemanly style earned him the scorn of the Cambridge School led by F. R. LEAVIS. Several of his Oxford lectures were collected in *The Fine Art of Reading* (1957).

Cecilia: or, Memoirs of an Heiress FANNY BURNEY's second novel, published in 1782. The story concerns the fortunes of Cecilia Beverley, victimized by her three unscrupulous guardians, Harrel, Briggs and the Hon. Compton Delvile. Driven by ill usage to insanity and the point of death, she eventually finds a modicum of happiness with her lover Mortimer Delvile. The novel was highly successful, confirming the reputation Burney had won for herself with *EVELINA*.

Celtic revival, the The reawakening of interest in the literature and culture of the Celtic people in the 19th and 20th centuries. 18th-century antiquarianism and ROMANTICISM produced various works exploiting what was perceived as the Gothic element in early Celtic literature, from GRAY's 'The Bard' (1757) and 'The Triumphs of Owen' (1768) onwards. Interest was fuelled by the forgeries of the Welsh antiquarian and poet Iolo Morganwg (Edward Williams, 1747–1826) and particularly by JAMES MACPHERSON's 'Ossian' poems. Ieuan Brydydd Hir (Evan Evans, 1731–88) provided the first substantial translation of Welsh poetry in 1764. It was joined in the 19th century by Lady Charlotte Guest's *THE MABINOGION* (1838–49), Hersart de la Villemarqué's rendering of Breton poetry and, for Irish literature, the work of EUGENE O'CURRY. English authors made use of Celtic material, real or imaginary, in works as various as

PEACOCK'S *THE MISFORTUNES OF ELPHIN* (1829), TENNYSON'S *IDYLLS OF THE KING* (1842–85) and GERARD MANLEY HOPKINS'S 'St Winifred's Well' (written 1879–85). MATTHEW ARNOLD'S 'Lectures on Celtic Literature' (1865–6) linked Irish, Welsh, Scottish, Cornish, Breton and Manx literature and helped to create the popular view of Celts as mysteriously romantic, with a gift for style, 'natural magic' and 'Celtic melancholy'.

At the same time Irish, Scottish and Welsh writers exploited the same material in their English writing. YEATS'S collection of stories and folklore, *The Celtic Twilight* (1893), provided a descriptive term for Irish literary activity in the 1890s and early 1900s, soon made to look anachronistic by the new generation of JOYCE and SEAN O'CASEY. In Scotland this kind of writing, with its implicit belief in ancient heroes and spirits, was produced by WILLIAM BLACK and WILLIAM SHARP. In the 20th century English writers have continued to make use of Celtic material, and there have been literary revivals – often linked with strongly nationalist feeling – in many of the Celtic countries, both in Celtic languages and in English. See also FOLK REVIVAL.

Cenci, The A tragedy by SHELLEY, published in 1819. It was first produced privately in 1886 and has been occasionally revived since then. It provided the French visionary Antonin Artaud (1896–1948) with the basis for a scenario which can be seen as the central text in his THEATRE OF CRUELTY.

The play is based on the savage history of a 16th-century Roman family. Count Francesco Cenci, a vicious husband and father with a sadistic taste for punishment, combines hatred for his daughter Beatrice with incestuous lust. The family conspires to have him killed. Suspected and tortured, they are brought to trial, and, despite the compassion aroused by their pitiful story and by Beatrice's conduct, they are executed.

Centlivre, Susannah 1669–1723 Playwright. Eighteen of her plays were produced, to considerable success, during her lifetime. They include *The Gamester* (1705), adapted from *Le Joueur* by Jean-François Regnard; *The Wonder: A Woman Keeps a Secret* (1714) ; and *A Bold Stroke for a Wife* (1718). The last two provided successful parts for GARRICK.

Century Magazine, The An American journal, begun as *Scribner's Monthly* in 1870. Under the editorship of Josiah Gilbert Holland, it published fiction and essays on politics, religion, and current affairs. Contributors included JOEL CHANDLER HARRIS, GEORGE MACDONALD, MARGARET OLIPHANT and Jules Verne. Under the editorship of Richard Watson Gilder it displayed an increased concern with public events but serialized novels by WILLIAM DEAN HOWELLS, HENRY JAMES, JACK LONDON and GEORGE WASHINGTON CABLE. It was merged with *Forum* in 1930.

Chamberlayne, William 1619–89 Poet. *Pharonnida* (1659) is a heroic romance in couplets, the poetic fashion of his day, running to 14,000 lines. His play *Love's Victory* was published in 1658.

Chambers, Sir **E(dmund) K(erchever)** 1866–1956 Scholar. His work on SHAKESPEARE, begun with an edition of *RICHARD II* (1891), was carried out during a career with the Education Department (later the Board of Education). In 1906–39 he served as first president of the Malone Society founded by GREG. His deliberative care in sifting evidence is shown in *The Medieval Stage* (2 vols, 1903), *The Elizabethan Stage* (4 vols, 1923) and

William Shakespeare: A Study of the Facts and Problems (2 vols, 1930). Chambers also wrote a survey of Arthurian legend (1927) and biographies of COLERIDGE and ARNOLD, as well as producing editions of DONNE and MILTON and editing *The Oxford Book of Sixteenth-Century Verse* (1932).

Chance A novel by JOSEPH CONRAD, published in 1913. Marlow is the chief of several narrators who tell the story of Flora de Barral. Her self-confidence is undermined by an uncaring governess and her father's financial ruin and imprisonment. Her marriage to Captain Roderick Anthony is blighted by doubts about her own worth and remains unconsummated. After her father's release from prison all three live on board Anthony's ship, *Ferndale*. But de Barral, regarding his daughter's marriage as a betrayal, tries to poison Anthony and takes his own life when discovered by Powell, the second mate. Though she is unaware of these facts, her father's death helps Flora communicate with Anthony. When Anthony dies in an accident several years later, there is some prospect of a romance between Powell and Flora.

Chances, The A comedy by JOHN FLETCHER, apparently written *c.* 1617 but not published until 1647. Based on a novel by Cervantes, it contains some of his best writing. The 'chances' are the coincidences and complications that beset Constantia and the Duke of Ferrara when they decide to elope.

Chandler, Raymond (Thornton) 1888–1959 American writer of DETECTIVE FICTION. Born in Chicago and brought up in England, he worked as a journalist and businessman before starting to write at the age of 45. His stories, regularly published in *THE BLACK MASK*, are collected in *Trouble is My Business* (1950), *Killer in the Rain* (1964) and *The Smell of Fear* (1965). His most famous character, the disillusioned but chivalric detective Philip Marlowe, appeared in a series of novels: *The Big Sleep* (1939), *Farewell, My Lovely* (1940), *The High Window* (1942), *The Lady in the Lake* (1943), *The Little Sister* (1949), *The Long Goodbye* (1953) and *Playback* (1958). Chandler discusses his work in *The Simple Art of Murder* (1950) and the posthumous *Raymond Chandler Speaking* (1962).

Changeling, The A tragedy by THOMAS MIDDLETON and WILLIAM ROWLEY, first performed in 1622 and published in 1653. Beatrice Joanna, daughter of the Governor of Alicant, loves Alsemero and wants to avoid her arranged marriage to Alonzo de Piracquo. She enlists the dangerous support of her father's physically repulsive servant, De Flores, who kills Alonzo. Beatrice Joanna is free to marry Alsemero but the need to silence her maid, Diaphanta, draws her further into complicity with De Flores. Alsemero grows suspicious and unmasks the pair. Bound together to the end, Beatrice Joanna and De Flores kill themselves. An uncertainly related sub-plot, possibly Rowley's contribution to the play, is often omitted in performance. It concerns Antonio's unsuccessful attempt to seduce Isabella by pretending to be an idiot (i.e. becoming a changeling) and gaining admission to the lunatic asylum run by her husband.

Channing, William Ellery 1780–1842 American minister and social reformer. Originally a Congregationalist, he played a leading role in the emergence of Unitarianism. His 'Baltimore Sermon' (*A Sermon Delivered at the Ordination of the Rev Jared Sparks*, 1819) and *The Moral Argument against Calvinism* (1820) reject strict Calvinist theology and the doctrine that man is essentially depraved. These revisionist ideas were common among Channing's circle, which included EMERSON, THOREAU, MARGARET FULLER and BRONSON ALCOTT. He set forth his ideas on pacifism, prison reform, child labour, education and slavery – which he opposed fiercely – in pamphlets and sermons.

chapbooks Popular literature, especially profuse during the 18th century, sold by wandering dealers ('chapmen') and comprising BALLADS, folk-tales, assorted tracts, fairy-tales, contemporary legends and short biographical pieces. Generally illustrated with woodcuts, they were priced at a few pennies.

Chapman, George c. 1560–1634 Poet, translator and playwright. Very little is known of his life, though the learning everywhere apparent in his work suggests he had a university education.

Of his poetry, the two hymns combined in *The Shadow of Night* (1594) are the earliest to have survived. *Ovids Banquet of Sence* (1595) obliquely advocates true Platonism as a counter to Ovidian eroticism, a point implicit in his correction and completion of MARLOWE's *HERO AND LEANDER* (1598). *Euthymiae Raptus* (1609), better known by its alternative title *The Teares of Peace*, is a carefully constructed defence of learning in which DREAM-VISION is the vehicle for Platonic, Stoic and Christian speculation. A much-quoted sonnet by KEATS has ensured the continuing fame of Chapman's translations of Homer. Brought together in the complete *Iliads* (1611) and *Homer's Odyssey* (1614–15), they are translations not only from one language to another, but also from one age and culture to another.

Chapman was involved with the theatre by 1595–6, when *The Blind Beggar of Alexandria* was produced, and was considered among the best poets for both tragedy and comedy in MERES's *Palladis Tamia* (1598). *An Humorous Day's Mirth* (1597) strongly supports claims that Chapman's friendship with JONSON was mutually influential. Other surviving comedies are *The Gentleman Usher* (c. 1602); *All Fools* (1599 or 1604), derived from Terence; *Monsieur D'Olive* (1604); *Sir Giles Goosecap, Knight* (c. 1604); *The Widow's Tears* (c. 1605), a sour comedy about women's fickleness; and *May Day* (1609). He was imprisoned for his part-authorship, with Jonson and MARSTON, of the splendid *EASTWARD HO* (1605). His tragedies present deeply flawed Titanic heroes, philosophically removed from the recent French history in which they figured. These overreachers give their names to *BUSSY D'AMBOIS* (1604), *THE CONSPIRACY AND TRAGEDY OF CHARLES, DUKE OF BYRON, MARSHAL OF FRANCE* (1608), *THE REVENGE OF BUSSY D'AMBOIS* (c. 1610) and *Chabot, Admiral of France* (c. 1613).

Chapone, Hester 1727–1801 Moralist and BLUESTOCKING. A friend of SAMUEL RICHARDSON, she is remembered chiefly for her CONDUCT BOOK, *Letters on the Improvement of the Mind* (1773), a seminal work in the moral education of generations of girls. Among Mrs Chapone's exhortations are the necessity for humility, sincerity and uprightness of heart; pride and vanity must be subdued by reason and grace, the affections 'regulated' and the temper 'governed'. She also published *A Letter to a New Married Lady* (1777), tales in verse and essays. Her correspondence and a memoir were published posthumously (1807, 1808).

Charles, Duke of Byron, Marshal of France, The Conspiracy and Tragedy of A double play by GEORGE CHAPMAN, first performed in 1608, when its reference to recent history (the Marshal of France had been executed in 1602) offended the French ambas-

sador, who succeeded in getting the play banned. In the first play, the restlessly ambitious Herculean hero is discovered in his conspiracy against the French king, Henri IV, asks forgiveness and is pardoned. In the second play he again conspires, is again discovered and dwindles into cringing despair before being executed.

Charley's Aunt An immensely successful FARCE, first staged in 1892, the only play by which its author, BRANDON THOMAS, is remembered. Lord Fancourt Babberly, an amiable Oxford aristocrat, is prevailed upon to aid the amorous designs of two friends by impersonating his rich aunt. The troubles begin when the real aunt arrives in Oxford.

Charlotte Temple: *A Tale of Truth* A novel by SUSANNA ROWSON, published in England in 1791 and in America in 1794. Modelled on SAMUEL RICHARDSON's *CLARISSA*, it sold poorly in England but was a great success in the USA. The story, a highly moral warning against the dangers of seduction, describes how Charlotte elopes from school to New York with Montraville. He soon deserts her for an heiress, Julia Franklin, and she eventually dies after giving birth to his illegitimate child, Lucy. Charlotte's father adopts Lucy.

Chaste Maid in Cheapside, A A CITIZEN COMEDY by THOMAS MIDDLETON, first performed in 1611 and published in 1630. The misfortunes and humiliation of the dissolute Sir Walter Whorehound link its several plots. He succeeds in marrying his discarded mistress (the 'chaste' maid of the title) to Tim Yellowhammer, the bird-brained son of an avaricious goldsmith, but fails in his hope of marrying Tim's sister Moll. She is eventally united with Touchwood Junior. Whorehound loses the fortune he had hoped to inherit from the childless Sir Oliver and Lady Kix when she is impregnated by Touchwood Senior. He turns for help to the Allwits (Allwit has condoned his affair with Mistress Allwit for many years) but is rejected. He is arrested for debt and the Allwits plan to support themselves by setting up a bawdy-house. The play's realistic vision is nicely conveyed by the fact that the complacent Allwit comes nearest to being its 'hero'.

Chatterton, Thomas 1752–70 Poet. The son of a Bristol schoolmaster, he published his first poem when he was 11 and went on to make 15th-century Bristol the setting for a series of pseudo-medieval verses he attributed to the fictitious Thomas Rowley. In April 1770 he went to London where, though he contributed work to the journals, he failed to impress either DODSLEY or HORACE WALPOLE with the Rowley poems. Only one, 'Elinoure and Juga', was published in his lifetime. Impoverished and depressed, he committed suicide a few months before his 18th birthday. The Rowley poems were collected and edited by TYRWHITT in 1777. He and many others were persuaded of their authenticity, though THOMAS GRAY, THOMAS PERCY and THOMAS WARTON THE YOUNGER were doubtful. Tyrwhitt himself was induced to reconsider, and his 1778 edition of the poem contained 'An Appendix Tending to Prove That They Were Written by Chatterton'.

With their archaic vocabulary and Spenserian style, the poems nonetheless reveal a genuine talent. Chatterton became an object of admiration to the Romantics, who recognized his youthful genius and were impressed by the histrionic circumstances of his death. WORDSWORTH remembered him as 'the marvellous boy ... that perished in his pride' and KEATS dedicated *ENDYMION* to his memory.

Chatwin, Bruce 1940–89 Travel writer and novelist. His *sui generis* works frequently challenged the boundaries between travel writing, autobiography, history and fiction. *In Patagonia* (1977) alternates between minute esoterica and vast imaginative leaps. *The Songlines* (1987) develops a partly fictionalized investigation of nomadism into speculation on the origins of human civilization. *The Viceroy of Ouidah* (1980) is a predominantly historical monograph about the African slave kingdom of Dahomey. *On the Black Hill* (1982) is a novel in PASTORAL mode and *Utz* (1988) a brief, lapidary novel about a collector of Dresden china. *What am I Doing Here* (1989) consists of posthumously gathered shorter pieces.

Chaucer, Geoffrey Before 1346–1400 Son of a wealthy London vintner, he was perhaps educated at St Paul's Cathedral School and later studied at the Inner Temple. He was page to Elizabeth, Countess of Ulster, and Prince Lionel, at least until military campaigns in France in 1359–60; he was ransomed in March 1360 but returned to France later that year. He married Philippa, probably in 1366, and apparently had two sons, Lewis and Thomas. The fact that Edward III granted him a pension in 1367 is first evidence of his career in royal service. Between *c.* 1368 and 1378, when he was also connected with John of Gaunt, foreign diplomatic missions took him to Italy (apparently for the first time *c.* 1373); its culture became a strong influence on his poetry. Increasingly important official appointments included a post as customs official, acquired in 1374 but resigned, perhaps along with his house in Aldgate, in 1385. He retired to Kent, serving as JP, knight of the shire and, for one session in 1386, MP. When Richard II took over from Gloucester in 1389, Chaucer became Clerk of the King's Works, a job that demanded constant travel supervising building, maintenance and renovation work. He left the post in 1391 and became deputy forester of the royal forest of North Petherton, Somerset, his last regular office, renewed in 1398. Late in 1399 he moved to Westminster, dying there the following year; his tomb in Westminster Abbey became the nucleus of Poets' Corner.

Generally considered the greatest English poet of the Middle Ages, Chaucer used English at a time when much court poetry was still written in Anglo-Norman or Latin. Since the 19th century his work has been separated from the CHAUCERIAN APOCRYPHA, with only a few short pieces and a translation, THE ROMAUNT OF THE ROSE, remaining doubtful. The chronology of his poetry is less certain; only THE BOOK OF THE DUCHESS can be attached to a definite event (in 1368). The order of other works is suggested by internal relations, dates of known sources and the influence of French and Italian culture. *The Book of the Duchess*, some of the short poems and *The ABC* were written before 1372 and show the influence of French poets. Italian influence appears in the works ascribed to 1372–80: THE HOUSE OF FAME, *Anelida and Arcite*, early versions of *The Second Nun's Tale* and *The Monk's Tale*, and some of the lyrics. THE PARLEMENT OF FOULES, TROILUS AND CRISEYDE, an early version of *The Knight's Tale*, THE LEGEND OF GOOD WOMEN and some short poems, written between 1380 and 1386, show Italian influence fully assimilated. *The General Prologue* and the early stories of THE CANTERBURY TALES were written in 1387–92.

Although frequently imitated, Chaucer's blend of realism and philosophical depth, his interest in virtu-

ally all the forms available to a medieval poet and his control of dialogue and character were never matched. As a storyteller he is supreme, and it is for this that he is known best. In the framework of *The Canterbury Tales* he develops both character and dialogue, while critics have likened *Troilus and Criseyde* to a novel. He often directs his pervasive humour at himself: he cannot tell a tale competently in *The Canterbury Tales* and appears naive, ignorant and foolish in the DREAM-VISIONS. Apart from *The Tale of Melibee* and *The Parson's Tale*, his prose includes *Boece* (*c.* 1380), a translation of the Roman philosopher Boethius' *De consolatione philosophiae*, and *A Treatise on the Astrolabe* (1391–2), an introduction to astronomy and astrology dedicated to his young son Lewis. Chaucer may also have written a more sophisticated treatise, *The Equatorie of the Planets*.

Chaucerian apocrypha More than 100 poems once attributed to CHAUCER and often included in editions of his work until the canon was revised in the 19th century. They include works by other known poets such as LYDGATE, HENRYSON, USK and GOWER. There are also additions to THE CANTERBURY TALES – THE PLOWMAN'S TALE, *The Tale of Beryn* and THE TALE OF GAMELYN – and anonymous pieces like THE ASSEMBLY OF LADIES, THE CUCKOO AND THE NIGHTINGALE, THE FLOWER AND THE LEAF and JACK UPLAND. Some resemble Chaucer's presently accepted work hardly at all.

Chaudhuri, Nirad C(handra) 1897– Indian writer. His literary career began late, with *The Autobiography of An Unknown Indian* (1951), described by V. S. NAIPAUL as 'the one great book to come out of the Anglo-Indian encounter'. Other works include: a massive second volume, *Thy Hand, Great Anarch!* (1987); a travel book, *A Passage to England* (1960); two biographies, *Clive of India* (1975) and an account of F. M. Muller, *Scholar Extraordinary* (1975); *The Continent of Circe* (1965); *Culture in the Vanity Bag* (1976); and *Hinduism: A Religion to Live By* (1979).

Cheever, John 1912–82 American short-story writer and novelist. Much of his work deals humorously and compassionately with the spiritually and emotionally impoverished life in materially affluent communities. His novels include *The Wapshot Chronicle* (1957), *The Wapshot Scandal* (1964), *Bullet Park* (1969), *Falconer* (1977) and *Oh, What a Paradise It Seems* (1982). His short stories, many of which appeared originally in THE NEW YORKER and THE NEW REPUBLIC, were published in various volumes and gathered in *The Stories of John Cheever* (1978). His posthumously published letters (edited by Benjamin Cheever; 1988) and journals (1991) reveal a tormented private life apparently at odds with the often urbane character of his fiction.

Chesney, Sir George Tomkyns 1830–95 Novelist. *The Battle of Dorking*, a fictional account of an enemy attack on England, was published by BLACKWOOD'S MAGAZINE in 1871 and frequently reprinted. Other novels were *The Dilemma* (1876), set at the time of the Indian mutiny, *The New Ordeal* (1879), *The Private Secretary* (1881) and *The Lesters* (1893).

Chesnutt, Charles W(addell) 1858–1932 Black American short-story writer and novelist. His first two collections of stories, *The Conjure Woman* and *The Wife of His Youth and Other Stories of the Color Line* (both 1899), display a fluent, urbane style aimed at a popular readership in which he nevertheless achieved a probing exploration of racial themes and a realistic view of slavery and Reconstruction. Later work concentrated on the problems of racial and class identity in a changing society. Chesnutt wrote three novels, *The House behind the Cedars* (1900), *The Marrow of Tradition* (1901) and *The Colonel's Dream* (1906), as well as essays and reviews.

Chester cycle See MIRACLE PLAYS.

Chesterfield, Philip Dormer Stanhope, 4th Earl of 1694–1773 Statesman and writer. In the course of his career in public life he served as ambassador to The Hague (1728–32), Secretary of State in Newcastle's cabinet (1744 and again in 1746–8) and Lord Lieutenant of Ireland (1745–6).

A kindly and witty man who mixed in literary circles, Chesterfield was one of the most pleasant letter-writers in English. His most famous letters were written to his illegitimate son Philip Stanhope (1732–68) and published by his son's widow as *Letters to his Son, Philip Stanhope, Together with Several Other Pieces on Various Subjects* (1774). Affectionate, spontaneous and shrewd, they are full of advice and guidance which amount to a CONDUCT BOOK in the ways of the world. A second and similar series of letters to his godson and heir, also Philip Stanhope, first appeared as *The Art of Pleasing: in a Series of Letters to Master Stanhope* (1774).

Chesterfield has also acquired an undeserved literary notoriety as the epitome of churlish patrons for his treatment of SAMUEL JOHNSON. On his publisher's advice Johnson addressed his original *Plan* (1747) for his *DICTIONARY OF THE ENGLISH LANGUAGE* to Chesterfield, who failed to respond but belatedly commended the work on its publication in 1755. Johnson expressed his anger in a famous letter of 7 February 1755: 'Is not a patron, my lord, one who looks with unconcern on a man struggling for life in the water, and, when he has reached ground, encumbers him with help? The notice which you have been pleased to take of my labours, had it been early, had been kind; but it has been delayed ... till I am known and do not want it.'

Chesterton, G(ilbert) K(eith) 1874–1936 Poet, novelist, writer of DETECTIVE FICTION, critic, journalist and essayist. He was closely identified with his friend BELLOC in temperament and belief: a dislike of imperialism, particularly during the Boer War; an opposition to modern industrialism and centralized power; and a love of celebrating the 'Englishness' of England. The last is a common theme in his verse, gathered in *Collected Poems* (1933). His novels, *The Napoleon of Notting Hill* (1904) and *The Man Who was Thursday: A Nightmare* (1908), are exuberant political fantasies which celebrate the romance of an earlier pre-industrial world. *The Innocence of Father Brown* (1911) started an enduringly popular series of detective stories about an unassuming Catholic priest whose gift for solving complex mysteries springs largely from his insight into evil. Chesterton himself became a Roman Catholic in 1922.

Of his literary criticism, Chesterton's book about DICKENS (1906) is particularly memorable; he also published studies of ROBERT BROWNING (1903), SHAW and BLAKE (both 1910), and CHAUCER (1932). Works on social, political and religious subjects include *Heretics* (1905), *Orthodoxy* (1909), *St Francis of Assisi* (1923) and *St Thomas Aquinas* (1933). Collections of his essays appeared as *All Things Considered* (1908), *A Miscellany of Men* (1912), *The Uses of Diversity* (1920), and *As I was Saying* (1936).

Chestre, Thomas See SIR LAUNFAL and LIBEAUS DESCONUS.

Chettle, Henry c. 1560–c. 1607 Playwright. He turned to writing when his printing business failed. His satirical

dream-fable *Kind Harts Dreame* (1593) is best remembered for its preface regretting GREENE's abuse of SHAKESPEARE. *Piers Plainnes Seaven Yeres Prentiship* (1595) is a picaresque romance better than many of its kind. Although Chettle had a hand in about 50 plays, most are lost and of the survivors only *Hoffman* (c. 1603), a REVENGE TRAGEDY, is believed to be his alone. *The Downfall of Robert, Earl of Huntingdon* and *The Death of Robert, Earl of Huntingdon* (both performed in 1598), written with MUNDAY, are generally regarded as his most interesting work, not only because they deal with ROBIN HOOD. As well as contributing to SIR THOMAS MORE, Chettle collaborated with William Haughton and DEKKER on *PATIENT GRISSEL* (1600) and with JOHN DAY on *The Blind Beggar of Bednal-Green* (1600).

chiasmus A type of ANTITHESIS. Where the contrasting parts of the normal antithesis stand in the relation ab/ab, those of a chiasmus form a mirror-image, ab/ba: 'A Fop[a] their Passion[b]/ but their Prize[b] a Sot[a]' (POPE, *MORAL ESSAYS*).

Child, F(rancis) J(ames) 1825–96 American scholar. Boylston professor of rhetoric at Harvard from 1851 and professor of English from 1876, he is remembered for his collections of BALLADS, particularly *English and Scottish Popular Ballads* (1883–98); see also FOLK REVIVAL. Child edited SPENSER and wrote philological studies of CHAUCER and GOWER.

Child, Lydia M(aria) 1802–80 American social reformer and novelist. A leading Abolitionist, she wrote an 'Appeal in Favor of that Class of Americans Called Africans' (1833) and letters to the governor of Virginia published as *Correspondence* (1860). Novels include *Hobomok* (1824), about the Indians of colonial Massachusetts, *The Rebels: or, Boston before the Revolution* (1825), and *Philothea* (1836), set in classical Greece.

Childe Harold's Pilgrimage A poem by BYRON, written in SPENSERIAN STANZAS. The first two CANTOS were published in 1812, the third in 1816, and the fourth in 1818. It describes the wanderings of a disillusioned young man who looks for distraction in foreign scenes: Spain, Portugal, Albania and Greece. The third canto follows him to Belgium on the eve of Waterloo, along the Rhine and to the Alps and Jura. Finally, speaking in his own voice, Byron describes a literary and historical tour of Italy. After the publication of the first two cantos Byron 'woke one morning and found myself famous'. His poem made the melancholy 'Byronic hero' one of the most recognizable figures in English and European ROMANTICISM.

Childe Roland to the Dark Tower Came A poem by ROBERT BROWNING published in *Men and Women* (1855). A masterful and enigmatic nightmare, it takes its title from SHAKESPEARE's *KING LEAR* (III, iv, 173).

Childers, (Robert) Erskine 1870–1922 Novelist and political pamphleteer. An Anglo-Irishman who took up the cause of Irish Home Rule, he was executed for his role in the Irish Republican Army after the establishment of the Irish Free State. His political pamphlets are forgotten but his one novel, *The Riddle of the Sands* (1903), is not. A slow-paced thriller, packed with yachting lore and warnings of Germany's military ambitions, it remains notable for its two well-contrasted heroes, Carruthers and Davies.

children's literature Stories and poems aimed at children have a long history. Lullabies were sung in Roman times, and a few nursery games and rhymes are almost as ancient. The history of printed literature for children is much shorter. Before 1700 the only titles specifically intended for children were a few instructional works and religious tracts. Keen child readers had no alternative but to raid adult literature (something they still do today), where they found translations of Aesop's fables, fairy-stories, BALLADS and romances. A boy or girl in the early 18th century could have read BUNYAN's PILGRIM's PROGRESS (1678), DEFOE's ROBINSON CRUSOE (1719) or SWIFT's GULLIVER'S TRAVELS (1726). The fact that these classics appeared in simplified form shows that publishers had noticed their popularity with young readers. By the middle of the 18th century children's books designed to entertain rather than educate began to be produced by publishers like NEWBERY, whose winning formula of rhymes, stories and games in works like A Little Pretty Pocket Book (1744) was pirated almost immediately in America.

Such pleasing levity did not last. Influenced by Rousseau, whose Émile (1762) decreed that all children's books except Robinson Crusoe were a dangerous diversion, contemporary critics saw to it that children's literature should become instructive and uplifting. Mrs Sarah Trimmer's magazine, The Guardian of Education (1802), carried the first regular reviews of children's books, condemning fairy-tales for their violence and absurdity. Her own stories, Fabulous Histories (1786), described talking animals who were models of sense and decorum. MARY SHERWOOD's The History of the Fairchild Family (1818–47) contained dark moral warnings and regular reference to biblical verses. But MARRYAT's adventure stories – Masterman Ready (1841) or Children of the New Forest (1847) – owed their popularity less to lengthy digressions on flora, fauna and British history than the exciting action which allowed reader and writer to forget about self-improvement.

So the moral story for children was always threatened from within, given the way children have of drawing out entertainment from the sternest moralist. But the greatest blow to the improving children's book came from an unlikely source: early 19th-century interest in folklore. Nursery rhymes, selected by HALLIWELL for a folklore society in 1842, and collections of fairy-stories by the scholarly Grimm brothers, swiftly translated into English in 1823, soon rocketed to popularity with the young. Later on American children also had the chance of enjoying the legends of ROBIN HOOD (1883) and King Arthur (1903) skilfully reworked by PYLE, another revivalist who provided rich fare occasionally worrying to the puritan conscience. Latter-day followers of Rousseau who still battled for 'sensible' stories still had some success, despite the wrath of DICKENS, but history was against them. LEAR's Book of Nonsense (1846), THACKERAY's ROSE AND THE RING (1855) and CHARLES KINGSLEY's WATER BABIES (1863) made an unanswerable case for fantasy, while LEWIS CARROLL's ALICE'S ADVENTURES IN WONDERLAND (1865) was a masterpiece that not only avoided didacticism but actually made fun of it.

From now on younger children could expect stories written for their particular interest and with the needs of their own limited experience of life kept to the fore. In Britain EWING, MOLESWORTH and YONGE produced excellent stories aimed at young girl readers in this spirit. Their success was repeated in America by COOLIDGE in What Katy Did (1872), WIGGIN in Rebecca of Sunnybrook Farm (1903), Eleanor H. Porter in Pollyanna (1913), and in Canada by L. M. MONTGOMERY in ANNE OF

GREEN GABLES (1908). THOMAS HUGHES's classic TOM BROWN'S SCHOOLDAYS (1857) spawned a new generation of school-stories for boys. Older child readers and adults still tended to share each other's principal fare: BALLANTYNE's adventure stories were popular with all ages, while Gladstone was an enthusiastic fan of ROBERT LOUIS STEVENSON's TREASURE ISLAND (1883). MACDONALD's strange, mystical stories such as At the Back of the North Wind (1871) also intrigued a wide audience, while SEWELL's BLACK BEAUTY (1877) was once set as compulsory reading material in prison. What eventually determined the reading of older children was often not the availability of special, children's literature as such but access to books that contained characters with whom they could easily identify and action that made little demand on adult maturity or understanding. Such a list encompassed HENTY's imperialistic adventures, FENIMORE COOPER's LEATHERSTOCKING TALES, STOWE's UNCLE TOM'S CABIN (1852), LOUISA M. ALCOTT's Little Women (1868), TWAIN's HUCKLEBERRY FINN (1884) and BURNETT's Little Lord Fauntleroy (1885). A poll taken as late as 1888 showed that Dickens was still easily the most popular author with older children.

In time, however, adults themselves moved on to a narrower spectrum of imaginative literature, leaving genres they had once freely enjoyed to a younger audience. In this way, masterpieces such as KIPLING's JUNGLE BOOK (1894), GRAHAME's WIND IN THE WILLOWS (1908) or LANG's collection of folk-stories would more often be found on children's than adults' bookshelves. At the same time magazines specifically directed at children sprang up in Britain and America, while a new generation of writers such as NESBIT took the children's story into details of family life, imaginative games and domestic adventures that adults found less relevant to their current interests. In America BAUM's The Wonderful Wizard of Oz (1900) was another determinedly child-centred success, despite its doctrinaire morality, while Australian children could enjoy a comic masterpiece without adult pretensions, NORMAN LINDSAY's The Magic Pudding (1918). In poetry Stevenson's A Child's Garden of Verses (1885) set a standard unequalled until DE LA MARE's Peacock Pie (1913). More knockabout fare was provided by BELLOC's The Bad Child's Book of Beasts (1896), only rivalled in popularity years later by T. S. ELIOT's Old Possum's Book of Practical Cats (1939). At the same time, sentimental verses for and about children touched bottom with the saccharine cadences of Rose Fyleman's Fairies and Chimneys (1918).

The inter-war period saw a further consolidation of children's literature as an exclusive empire, a process helped by the growing popularity of children's annuals, children's picture-books and the children's comic, now moving well away from its rougher, penny-dreadful origins. Plots were softened, the dangers of Kenneth Grahame's Wild Wood or Kipling's jungle giving way to the gentler concerns of MILNE's Ashdown Forest in Winnie-the-Pooh (1926) and LOFTING's amiably eccentric collection of humans and animals in The Story of Doctor Dolittle (1922). In RANSOME's adventure stories young people wrestled with sailing boats rather than with hostile enemies, while in STREATFEILD's Ballet Shoes (1936) the chief fear was failing an audition rather than encountering adult ostracism or family ruin. In America, though, LAURA INGALLS WILDER's The Little House series (1932–43) described a past that could be tough as well as warm and loving. Picture-books also lost some of the matter-of-fact treatment of danger and death found earlier in BEATRIX POTTER's stories for small children. Instead, ARDIZZONE and William Nicholson in Britain or Munro Leaf and later DR SEUSS in America painted a world safe and welcoming to all.

The final apotheosis of literary childhood protected from unpleasant reality came with the arrival in the late 1930s of child-centred best-sellers intent on entertainment at its most escapist. In Britain BLYTON and CROMPTON described children always free to have the most unlikely adventures, secure in the knowledge that nothing bad could ever happen to them in the end. The fact that war broke out again during her books' greatest popularity fails to register at all in Blyton's self-enclosed world, and for Crompton's mischievous creation, William, a country in arms provides him with further opportunities for being a nuisance. Reaction against such dream-worlds was inevitable after World War II, coinciding with the growth of paperback sales, children's libraries and a new spirit of moral and social concern. Urged on by committed publishers and progressive librarians, writers slowly began to explore new areas of interest, shifting their settings from the middle-class world. In the realms of fantasy a similar spirit of moral toughness is shown by C. S. LEWIS and TOLKIEN and later in the stories of ALAN GARNER and LEGUIN. Picture-books also began to experiment with off-beat stories and characters. Artist-illustrators such as SENDAK and BRIGGS explored the small child's timeless concern with death and aggression as well as lighter preoccupations.

Critical emphasis, during this development, has been divided. For some the most important task was to rid children's books of social prejudice and exclusiveness no longer found acceptable. Others concentrated more on the positive achievements of contemporary children's literature, in particular those of British novelists such as WILLIAM MAYNE, GARFIELD, PEARCE, JOAN AIKEN and BAWDEN, American novelists such as VIRGINIA HAMILTON, PAULA FOX and BYARS, and Australian novelists such as WRIGHTSON, SOUTHALL and Nan Chauncy. That such writers are now often recommended to adult as well as child readers echoes the 19th-century belief that children's literature can be shared by the generations, rather than being a defensive barrier between childhood and the necessary growth towards adult understanding.

Chillingworth, William 1602–44 Divine. A godson of Archbishop Laud, he published *The Religion of Protestants a Safe Way to Salvation* (1637), which prompted controversy by arguing that disagreements among Protestants were not a spiritual hazard. HAWTHORNE may have been remembering his reputation for Protestant polemic when he called one of his characters in *THE SCARLET LETTER* Chillingworth.

Chimes, The The second of DICKENS's Christmas stories, published in 1844 and collected in *CHRISTMAS BOOKS* (1852). Mesmerized by chiming bells and influenced by spirits, the simple, good-hearted Toby ('Trotty') Veck witnesses the hardships of his daughter Meg, the falsely accused Will Fern and the orphaned Lilian. They are maltreated or condescended to by Sir Joseph Bowley, Alderman Cute, Mr Filer and others. A final burst of goodwill effects a happy ending.

Chomsky, Noam (Avram) 1928– American linguist and political activist. As a linguist, he rehabilitated the study of grammar in such seminal works as *Syntactic Structures* (1957), *Aspects of the Theory of Syntax* (1965), *Cartesian Linguistics* (1966) and *Reflections on Language* (1976). Arguing that grammar is not learned but genetically innate, Chomsky's theory approximates to Cartesian theories of a 'universal grammar' in which psychological structures permit the formation of linguistic sentences. Later works include *Language and Problems of Knowledge* (1987) and *Language in a Psychological Setting* (1987). Chomsky became a prominent political activist by his opposition to America's role in the Vietnam War. *At War with Asia* (1970) has been followed by a number of trenchant polemical works, which include: *Towards a New Cold War* (1982), *The Fateful Triangle* (1983), *Turning the Tide* (1985), *Necessary Illusions* (1989) and *Deterring Democracy* (1991).

Chopin, Kate 1851–1904 American novelist and short-story writer. Born in St Louis, Missouri, she moved to New Orleans following her marriage and devoted herself to writing after the death of her mother and husband. *At Fault* (1890), a novel showing Maupassant's influence, was followed by two collections of short stories set among Creoles and Acadians in Louisiana, *Bayou Folk* (1894) and *A Night in Acadie* (1897). Her best-known work, *THE AWAKENING* (1899), provoked hostile criticism by its sympathetic portrayal of a woman who rejects the constraints of marriage and motherhood.

Christ An Old English poem in the EXETER BOOK. Its three parts deal with the Nativity, the Ascension and Doomsday. CYNEWULF's runic signature appears in the second section, while the dialogue between Mary and Joseph in the first is the earliest dramatic scene in English to survive.

Christ and Satan An Old English poem in the Junius manuscript (see JUNIUS, FRANCIS). Its three parts, or perhaps separate pieces, deal with the Fall of the Angels, the Harrowing of Hell (from the *GOSPEL OF NICODEMUS*) and the Temptation of Christ.

Christabel An unfinished poem by SAMUEL TAYLOR COLERIDGE, begun during the period of his collaboration with WORDSWORTH on the *LYRICAL BALLADS* (1798) but first published in *Christabel and Other Poems* (1816). Making evocative use of Gothic and supernatural themes, it tells how the enchantress Geraldine deceives all but the virtuous Christabel.

Christian Socialism A 19th-century religious and social movement. In response to the Chartist agitation of 1848, it set out to help the working man to help himself and to avert revolution by improving social conditions. Its practical outcome was the founding of the Working Men's College in 1854, the establishment of small self-governing workshops and a revival of the Co-operative Movement. The leader was FREDERICK DENISON MAURICE; his associates were CHARLES KINGSLEY, who wrote under the pseudonym Parson Lot, THOMAS HUGHES, author of *TOM BROWN'S SCHOOLDAYS*, and 'John Townsend', whose real name was John Malcolm Ludlow (1821–1911). The Christian Socialists produced several short-lived journals: *Politics for the People* (1848), *The Christian Socialist* (1850), *Tracts for Christian Socialists* (1850) and *The Journal of Association* (1852).

Christian Year, The See KEBLE, JOHN.

Christie, Dame Agatha (Mary Clarissa) 1890–1976 Writer of DETECTIVE FICTION. Her first novel, *The Mysterious Affair at Styles* (1920), introduced the Belgian private detective Hercule Poirot, whose career extended through many books to *Curtain* (1975). *The Murder at the*

Vicarage (1930) introduced the shrewd, gentle Miss Marple, whose career rivalled Poirot's in length and popularity, ending with *Sleeping Murder* (1976). Classic books – *The Murder of Roger Ackroyd* (1926), *Peril at End House* (1932), *Lord Edgeware Dies* (1933), *Murder on the Orient Express* (1934), *Why Didn't They Ask Evans?* (1934), *The ABC Murders* (1936) and *Ten Little Niggers* (1939) – are perfunctory in setting and characterization, concentrating almost exclusively on tantalizing ingenuity of plot. Of the several short stories she adapted for the stage, *The Mousetrap* (1952) and *Witness for the Prosecution* (1953) were prodigiously successful. She also wrote light romantic novels as Mary Westmacott.

Christmas Books A collection of Christmas stories by Dickens, published together for the first time in 1852: *A Christmas Carol* (1843), *The Chimes* (1844), *The Cricket on the Hearth* (1845), *The Battle of Life* (1846) and *The Haunted Man and the Ghost's Bargain* (1848).

Christmas Carol, A A novella by Dickens, published in 1843. The first and most popular of his Christmas stories, it was gathered with its successors in *Christmas Books* (1852). On Christmas Eve the miserly Ebenezer Scrooge is visited by the shade of his dead partner, Jacob Marley, and then by The Ghost of Christmas Past, The Ghost of Christmas Present, and The Ghost of Christmas Yet to Come. They show him the scenes of his youth, the family life of his loyal clerk, Bob Cratchit, whose household includes the sadly crippled Tiny Tim, and an ominous future. Chastened, he resolves to lead a better life, sending a turkey to the Cratchits, visiting his honest nephew, donating to charity and raising Bob's salary.

chronicle Medieval histories, written in Latin, English or Anglo-Norman, varying from the universal to the local record. Sometimes the work of several hands, they adapt and borrow freely from each other. The large mythic and fictional element does not prevent them from being valuable historical sources for contemporary and near-contemporary events. *The Anglo-Saxon Chronicle* is the earliest vernacular English example, and William of Malmesbury's *Historia regum Britanniae* (c. 1135) the first important Latin chronicle. Geoffrey of Monmouth developed William's sceptical reference to King Arthur into a full 'history' of the king and his court imitating the form of the ostensibly accurate historical chronicle, a process continued by Wace's Anglo-Norman *Roman de Brut* (1155) and its Middle English version, Layamon's *Brut* (c. 1190). See Arthurian literature.

Chronicles of the Canongate The inclusive title given by Sir Walter Scott to stories presented as the recollections of Mrs Bethune, Baliol of the Canongate in Edinburgh. They are written down by her friend Mr Chrystal Croftangry, whose own remarkable story serves as an introduction. The first series, consisting of *The Highland Widow*, *The Two Drovers* and *The Surgeon's Daughter*, was published in 1827 and the second, *St Valentine's Day: or, The Fair Maid of Perth*, in 1828. The fair maid is Catharine Glover, who lives during the reign of Robert III in the 14th century. Henry Smith, an armourer, loves her and defeats the evil designs of the worthless Duke of Rothsay, the king's son, and his friend, Sir John Ramorny. The gentle Catharine eventually accepts Henry after he sickens of combat.

Church, Richard (Thomas) 1893–1972 Poet and novelist. His novels include *The Porch* (1937) and *The Nightingale* (1952). His essentially Georgian poetry, in *The Flood of Life* (1917), *The Lamp* (1946), *Collected Poems* (1948), *The Burning*

Bush (1967) and other volumes, is characterized by sturdy craftsmanship and limited ambition.

Churchill, Caryl 1938– Playwright. She established her reputation with work, such as *Vinegar Tom* (1976) and *Light Shining in Buckinghamshire* (1976), written for left-wing and feminist companies. *Cloud Nine* (1979) deals with sexual role-playing, while *Top Girls* (1982) presents famous women from different epochs describing their struggles. *Serious Money* (1987) is a satire of City financiers. *Mad Forest* (1990), a play about Romania, was developed on site in the weeks following the downfall of the Ceausescus.

Churchill, Charles 1731–64 Satirist. A clergyman ill-suited to his profession, he achieved overnight success with *The Rosciad* (1761), a verse satire praising Garrick at the expense of other contemporary actors. It led to his friendship with Wilkes, whose rakish example he lost no time in following. *The North Briton*, Wilkes's political weekly, owed a great deal of its success to Churchill, who wrote at least half of it. Wilkes made sure that his friend escaped prosecution in the uproar which followed the publication of No. 45 of the paper. Churchill's social and political satires included *The Apology* and *Night* (1761), *The Ghost* (1762–3), *The Prophecy of Famine*, *The Conference*, *The Author* and *An Epistle to William Hogarth* (1763), and *The Duellist*, *The Candidate*, *Gotham*, *Independence*, *The Times* and *The Farewell* (1764). He died at Boulogne on his way to visit Wilkes. *The Journey*, a fragment, and some satirical verses directed at Bishop Warburton appeared in 1765.

Churchill, Sir Winston (Leonard Spencer) 1874–1965 Statesman and historian. He found the time to be a prolific writer in the course of his career which culminated in two terms as Prime Minister (1940–5 and 1951–5) and made him the most respected Conservative politician of the century. His multi-volume historical studies include *The World Crisis 1916–18* (1923–31), *The Second World War* (1948–54) and *A History of the English-Speaking Peoples* (1956–8). His biographies include *Lord Randolph Churchill* (1906) and *Marlborough: His Life and Times* (1933–8). He also wrote a novel, *Savrola* (1900), and several books dealing with his adventurous early career, among them *My African Journey* (1908) and *My Early Life* (1930). He was awarded the Nobel Prize for Literature in 1953.

Churchyard, Thomas ?1520–1604 Poet. He started writing in the reign of Edward VI and lived long enough to celebrate James I's public entry to Westminster. In *Colin Clout's Come Home Again*, Spenser portrayed him as Palaemon, who 'sung so long until quite hoarse he grew'. He wrote pageant verses, epitaphs, tracts and broadsides. His best works are the 'Legend of Shore's Wife' which appeared in *The Mirror for Magistrates*, the voluminous collection *The First Part of Churchyard's Chips* (1575) and *The Worthiness of Wales* (1587), which has some historical interest.

Cibber, Colley 1671–1757 Actor, playwright and poet. His provocative and sometimes outrageous good humour stood him in good stead during his controversial years as co-manager of Drury Lane (1708–32) and, from 1730, as Poet Laureate, an appointment that earned him the dubious immortality of Pope's scorn in *The Dunciad*. Cibber's services to the theatre have been often underrated. *Love's Last Shift* (1696), his first play, heralded the long reign of sentimental comedy on the English stage. It is among the best of its now unfashionable kind, together with *The Careless Husband* (1704), *The*

Lady's Last Stake (1707) and *The Provoked Husband* (1728), a completion of VANBRUGH's *A Journey to London*. Cibber also produced clever versions of SHAKESPEARE's *RICHARD III* (1700), long replacing the original on the stage, and of Molière's *Tartuffe* as *The Non Juror* (1717). His autobiography, *An Apology for the Life of Mr Colley Cibber, Comedian* (1740, revised 1750 and 1756), gives an unrivalled account of the English theatre over four decades.

citizen [city] **comedy** The term for Elizabethan and Jacobean plays whose setting is London and whose characters are predominantly tradesmen. The satire of mercantile values and financial opportunism is usually good-humoured, but no quarter is given to social overreaching or the pursuit of commercial success by fraud. Citizen comedy is characteristically moral and determined to castigate whatever or whoever discredits the good name of London. Outstanding examples include DEKKER's *THE SHOEMAKER'S HOLIDAY* (1599), *EASTWARD Ho* (1605), on which CHAPMAN, JONSON and MARSTON collaborated – and which outdoes the two joint works of Dekker and WEBSTER, *WESTWARD Ho* (1604) and *NORTHWARD Ho* (1605) – and THOMAS MIDDLETON's *A CHASTE MAID IN CHEAPSIDE* (1611). The combination of a romantic plot and plain characters was sufficiently familiar by 1607 to provoke the lively mockery of BEAUMONT's *THE KNIGHT OF THE BURNING PESTLE*.

City Madam, The A CITIZEN COMEDY by MASSINGER, first performed *c.* 1632 and published in 1659. Sir John Frugal is a successful merchant whose wife and daughters have grown in affectation and vanity as his wealth has increased. In exasperation he pretends to retire to a monastery and hands the management of the household over to Luke, his prodigal younger brother.

Luke's behaviour at once changes from humble gratitude to arrogant greed. He is even willing to sell Lady Frugal and her daughters for human sacrifice to three 'Indians', in fact Sir John and two young men, Lacy and Plenty, who unsuccessfully wooed the daughters. Luke is unmasked and driven unrepentant from the house. The relieved and repentant ladies promise to behave better in future. The play is notable for its vivid picture of the different levels of London society, ranging from the honest merchant Sir John to Shavem and Secret, prostitutes in the stews.

City of Dreadful Night, The A poem by JAMES THOMSON, first published in 1874. Written in contrasting sections of episodic and ruminative verse, it envisages London both topographically and as a terrifying City of Dis, dark, tenebrous and forbidding. It reflects on the meaninglessness of the human condition, on the death-in-life Thomson believed man must endure. Sinister imagery, dramatic scenes, and brooding despair (as in the arresting description of Dürer's 'Melancholia') make the poem unique in the literature of despondency as well as a landmark in late-Victorian pessimism.

Civil Disobedience, On the Duty of An essay by THOREAU, originally published as *Resistance to Civil Government* in 1849 and given its familiar title in 1866. Citing the controversial Mexican War, slavery and the treatment of Indians, and referring to the night he himself spent in gaol for refusing to pay his poll tax, Thoreau argues that an individual may refuse to participate in a government that does not uphold his or her moral standards.

Clampitt, Amy 1920–94 American poet. It was not until 1973 that *Multitudes*, her first, privately printed

volume appeared. A number of her poems were originally printed in *THE NEW YORKER*, a forum which brought her a wider audience and growing reputation. Her intelligent, elegiac, frequently intense verse then appeared in several commercially published volumes: *The Kingfisher* (1973), *What the Light was Like* (1985), *Archaic Figure* (1987), *Westward* (1990) and *Predecessors* (1991).

Clandestine Marriage, The A comedy by GEORGE COLMAN THE ELDER and GARRICK, produced in 1766. It is based on the first plate of HOGARTH's *Marriage à la Mode*. The wealthy merchant, Sterling, plans to marry his elder daughter to Sir John Melvil, nephew of the impecunious Lord Ogleby, but he prefers the younger daughter, Fanny. She, however, is secretly married to her father's clerk, Lovewell. A series of misfortunes culminates in Lovewell being found in Fanny's bedroom, and it is Lord Ogleby who unexpectedly saves the situation.

Clanvowe, Sir John *c.* 1341–91 Poet and religious writer. A knight of Welsh ancestry, he fought in France and held political offices under Edward III and Richard II. It is reported that when he died near Constantinople, his lover Sir William Neville refused food and himself died a few days later. Clanvowe's two known works are quite different. One is a prose tract condeming luxury; though Clanvowe is counted with Neville among the 'Lollard knights', it does not express LOLLARD sympathies. *THE CUCKOO AND THE NIGHTINGALE* is a poem about love modelled on *THE PARLEMENT OF FOULES*, included in the CHAUCERIAN APOCRYPHA.

Clare, John 1793–1864 Poet. He was born into poverty at Helpston, Northamptonshire, where he worked as a thresher, farm labourer and gardener. *Poems Descriptive of Rural Life* (1820) and *The Village Minstrel* (1821), a long poem in SPENSERIAN STANZAS, contain moving descriptions of the rural poor, together with poignant evocations of the old village landscape of open fields, transformed by enclosure during his youth. Dissatisfied with the poetic diction he had inherited from GOLDSMITH and THOMSON, he went on in *THE SHEPHERD'S CALENDAR* (1827), *The Rural Muse* (1835) and the posthumous collection *The Midsummer Cushion* to blend the physical with the linguistic textures of Helpston, using grammar, vocabulary and syntax that are pronouncedly, though by no means naively, athwart the dominant conventions of PASTORAL.

Clare married in 1820 and in 1832 moved to Northborough, three miles northeast of Helpston but in a landscape so different to a man of his intimate sense of place that the poetry he wrote there communicates a sense of estrangement and deep melancholy. These feelings, and the passing of the vogue for 'peasant' poetry that had briefly brought him recognition in the 1820s, contributed to his mental illness. He was admitted to an asylum in High Beach, Epping, in 1837 and, after his escape in 1841, to the county asylum at Northampton, where he spent the rest of his life, enjoying considerable freedom and continuing to write. His poetry, much of it distorted by his publisher's editorial tampering, remained virtually unread until this century, when its reception as a pre-figuration of modern, or 'alienated', aesthetic consciousness has done much to stimulate new editions based on the original manuscripts.

Clarendon, 1st Earl of [Hyde, Edward] 1609–74 Historian and statesman. He entered Parliament in 1640 and quickly modified his opposition to Charles I's policies. He followed the future Charles II into exile and, while in the Scilly Isles, began in 1646 to write his *True Historical Narrative of the Rebellion and Civil Wars in England* – the HISTORY OF THE REBELLION, as it is usually known. At the Restoration he became Lord Chancellor and was created Earl of Clarendon, serving as Charles's chief minister until 1667. The mismanagement of the war with the Dutch (which he had opposed) gave political enemies a chance to force him into a second exile, in France, where he died. His *History*, not published until 1702–4, eventually incorporated two other works written in exile, *The History of the Irish Rebellion and Civil Wars in Ireland* and his autobiography (separately published in 1759). His speeches, political tracts and essays were published as *A Collection of Several Tracts* (1727), while his criticism of HOBBES's LEVIATHAN appeared two years after his death. From the Restoration until his flight from England Clarendon was Chancellor of the University of Oxford, which inherited his manuscripts. The profits from publication of his work provided the funds for the Clarendon Press.

Clarissa: or, The History of a Young Lady A novel by SAMUEL RICHARDSON, the first two volumes published in 1747, the last five in 1748. Like *PAMELA*, it is an EPISTOLARY NOVEL, consisting of a four-way correspondence between the principal characters: Clarissa Harlowe's to her friend Miss Howe and Robert Lovelace's letters to his friend John Belford predominate.

Clarissa is a well-bred young lady attracted to the dashing Lovelace, an unscrupulous man of whom her parents strongly disapprove. In deference to their wishes, Clarissa resists his advances, but also refuses to marry the man they have selected instead, the detestable Mr Solmes. Confined to her room (for the first 500 pages of the plot) she secretly corresponds with Lovelace, and runs away with him, only to discover his real nature. He instals her under the watchful eye of Mrs Sinclair, a bawd, and woos her ardently. When his subtlety gives way to impatience he drugs and then rapes her. Denounced by her family, she rejects Lovelace totally, ignores the pleas of his family and friends to accept his proposal of marriage, and retires into solitude. She dies of shame and grief, and Lovelace is killed in a duel with her cousin. Belford, the libertine correspondent, turns over a new leaf, becomes Clarissa's executor, and edits her letters.

Though the action of the novel encompasses less than a year, the intense degree of characterization is extraordinarily sustained, buoyed up by Richardson's careful unification of the narrative elements. *Clarissa* is widely regarded as his masterpiece, and, running to over a million words, is the longest novel in the English language.

Clark Bekederemo, J(ohn) P(epper) [Clark, John Pepper] 1936– Nigerian poet and playwright. His crisp, economical verse appears in *A Decade of Tongues* (a selection from earlier volumes; 1981), *State of the Union* (1985) and *Mandela and Other Poems* (1988). His plays include: *Song of a Goat* (1961; reissued in *Three Plays*, 1964), a verse tragedy; *Ozidi* (1966), a verse play adapted from the Ijaw epic drama he also translated as *The Ozidi Saga* (1975); and *The Bikoroa Plays* (1985), a prose trilogy about family strife. *America, Their America* (1964) angrily describes a year at Princeton. The essays in *The Example of Shakespeare* (1970) include a seminal piece, 'The Legacy of Caliban'.

Clark, Kenneth (Mackenzie), Lord 1903–83 Art historian and critic. In the course of a long and distinguished career he was director of the National Gallery (1934–45), Surveyor of the King's Pictures (1934–44) and chairman of the Arts Council of Great Britain (1953–60). As a writer he first attracted attention with *The Gothic Revival* (1928). The many works which followed include *Florentine Painting* (1945), *Landscape into Art* (1949), *The Nude: A Study of Ideal Art* (1953), *Moments of Vision* (1954) and *Civilisation* (1969), based on a successful television series. *Another Part of the Wood* (1974) and *The Other Half* (1977) are volumes of autobiography.

Clarke, Arthur C(harles) 1917– Writer of SCIENCE FICTION. His early works, *Childhood's End* (1953) and *The City and the Stars* (1956), show the influence of OLAF STAPLEDON but most of his novels aim at technological realism. They include *Rendezvous with Rama* (1973), *Imperial Earth* (1975), *The Fountains of Paradise* (1979) and *The Songs at Distant Earth* (1986). Clarke worked closely with Stanley Kubrick on the film *2001: A Space Odyssey* (1968), carrying the story forward in *2010: Odyssey Two* (1982) and *2061: Odyssey Three* (1988). *Cradle* (1988) and *Rama II* (1989) were written with Gentry Lee.

Clarke, Austin 1896–1974 Irish playwright, poet and novelist. He aimed to revive poetic drama in plays which include: *The Son of Learning* (1927), based on a medieval Irish story; two Pierrot plays, *The Kiss* (1942) and *The Second Kiss* (1946); *The Moment Next to Nothing* (1958), based on a Gaelic story he had already used in a novel, *The Sun Dances at Easter* (1952), banned in Ireland; and *The Plot Succeeds* (1950). He was founder of the Dublin Verse-Speaking Society and the Lyric Theatre Company. *The Vengeance of Fionn* (1917) was the first of several volumes of verse to demonstrate his enthusiasm for Irish legend and folk-tales.

Clarke, Charles Cowden 1787–1877 Scholar and critic. A friend of KEATS, LEIGH HUNT, SHELLEY, HAZLITT and DICKENS, he wrote and lectured on SHAKESPEARE. With his wife MARY COWDEN CLARKE he wrote *Recollections of Writers* (1878).

Clarke, Gillian 1937– Poet. *Letter from a Far Country* (1982), *Selected Poems* (1985) and *Letting in the Rumour* (1989) have established her as a leading poet of her generation. Although strongly rooted in both the urban and rural experience of her native Wales, her work transcends regional concerns and approaches archetypal themes of love, death and family life from intimate, almost casual angles.

Clarke, Marcus 1846–81 Australian novelist. Born in London, he emigrated to Victoria in 1863 and worked as a journalist, publishing his first novel, *Long Odds* (1869), in his own magazine, *The Colonial Monthy*. His best-known work, *HIS NATURAL LIFE* (serialized, 1870–2; revised for book publication, 1874), presented a vivid picture of the penal settlement in Tasmania. Other works included collections of short stories – *Old Tales of a Young Country* (1871) and *The Man with the Oblong Box* (1878) – and a PANTOMIME, *Twinkle, Twinkle Little Star* (1873).

Clarke, Mary (Victoria) Cowden 1809–98 Scholar and critic. Her *Concordance to Shakespeare's Plays* appeared in 1844–5. *Recollections of Writers* (1878) was written in collaboration with her husband CHARLES COWDEN CLARKE.

Clarke, Samuel 1675–1729 Divine. His Boyle lectures, known in their published form as *A Discourse Concerning the Being and Attributes of God* (1716), make a carefully reasoned defence of rational theology against the empiricism of JOHN LOCKE.

Claverings, The A novel by TROLLOPE, serialized in 1866–7. Harry Clavering, a schoolmaster resolved to become an engineer, is jilted by Julia Brabazon in favour of Lord Ongar. He falls in love with Florence Burton, the daughter of a partner in his firm, but is again drawn into contact with Julia, now widowed, to protect her from the sinister Count Pateroff and his scheming sister Sophie Gordeloup. Harry is drawn into a second proposal before he realizes that Florence will be a better wife. Julia surrenders her claim and Harry finds himself heir to the Clavering estate.

Clayhanger A novel by ARNOLD BENNETT, published in 1910. The first of a trilogy, it was followed by *Hilda Lessways* (1911) and *These Twain* (1916). A fourth novel, *The Roll Call* (1918), is loosely connected with the series.

It follows 20 years in the life of Edwin Clayhanger, from the day he leaves school, concentrating on his struggle with his dominating father, Darius, and his dream of escaping the Potteries town of Bursley. Edwin falls in love with Hilda Lessways, whom he meets through the cultivated Orgreaves family, but she mysteriously disappears and he hears of her subsequent marriage. Years later, after his father's death, Edwin traces Hilda and her son to a Brighton boarding house and learns of her ruin at the hands of the bigamous George Cannon. The novel ends with their plan to marry.

Cleanness [*Purity*] A late 14th-century poem in ALLITERATIVE VERSE and the West Midlands dialect. Preserved in the same manuscript as SIR GAWAIN AND THE GREEN KNIGHT, PATIENCE and PEARL, it is grouped with them by similarities of dialect (West Midlands), style and diction. They are usually taken to be the work of the same, unidentified author, known for convenience as the GAWAIN-poet. The theme of this poem is the supreme value of 'cleanness', or spiritual purity: not simply chastity but freedom from all the vices which defile the soul in the eyes of God. The poet draws on biblical stories (the parable of the Guest without a Wedding Garment, the Flood, the destruction of Sodom and Gomorrah and finally Belshazzar's Feast), transferred to an English medieval setting and enlivened by vivid description and gentle humour.

Cleary, Jon (Stephen) 1917– Australian novelist. His many novels are adventure stories or DETECTIVE FICTION, generally set in exotic locations and often distinguished by their subtle psychology. They include *You Can't See Round Corners* (1947), *Just Let Me Be* (1950), *The Sun-downers* (1952), *Forests of the Night* (1963), *The High Commissioner* (1966), *Season of Doubt* (1968), *Remember Jack Hoxie* (1969), *The Safe House* (1975), *A Very Private War* (1980), *Spearfield's Daughter* (1982), *Phoenix Tree* (1984), *Now and Then Amen* (1988), *Murder Song* (1990) and *Pride's Harvest* (1991).

Cleland, John 1709–89 Novelist. He is best known for *Memoirs of a Woman of Pleasure* (1748–9), usually called *Fanny Hill*, for long suppressed as obscene, though it was one of the most popular novels of the 18th century. He also wrote *Memoirs of a Coxcomb: or, The History of Sir William Delamere* (1751) and *The Surprises of Love* (1764) as well as plays and philological studies.

Clemo, Jack (Reginald John) 1916–94 Poet. A novel, *Wilding Craft* (1948) and an autobiography, *Confession of a Rebel* (1949) were followed by two volumes of poetry, *The Clay Verse* (1951) and *The Wintry Priesthood* (1951), featuring a tortured Christian existentialism and devastated, metaphysical Cornish landscapes. A late discovery of MODERNISM is evident in *Cactus on Carmel* (1967).

Other volumes include *Broad Autumn* (1975), *The Bouncing Hills* (1983), *The Shadowed Bed* (1986), *Selected Poems* (1988), *Banner Poems* (1989) and *Approach to Murano* (1992). Although he was praised by DONALD DAVIE and CHARLES CAUSLEY, the unusual and individual directions Clemo took hindered proper assessment of his work.

Cleopatra A Senecan CLOSET DRAMA by DANIEL, published in 1594. Its action takes place after Antony's death, dealing with Cleopatra's conflict with Octavius and her suicide. Octavius murders Caesarion, her son by Julius Caesar, and extinguishes the line of Ptolemy.

clerihew A comic verse form invented by EDMUND CLERIHEW BENTLEY, consisting of two rhyming couplets designed to sum up a subject or character: 'The art of Biography/ Is different from Geography. Geography is about maps,/ Biography is about chaps.'

Clerk of Pennecuik, Sir **John** 1676–1755 Man of letters. His *Memoirs*, published in 1895, give an illuminating picture of his experience as one of the circle of friends grouped around ALLAN RAMSAY in the reviving literary life of Edinburgh in the early 18th century. A pupil of Corelli, Clerk composed a set of five cantatas for solo voice (1698), wrote a number of songs and published *Observations on the Present State of Scotland* (1730).

Clerk's Tale, The See CANTERBURY TALES.

Cleveland, John 1613–58 Poet. His robust loyalty to the Royalist cause cost him his fellowship at St John's College, Cambridge; he was imprisoned by the Parliamentarians in 1655–6, but released after a personal appeal to Cromwell. His best poems are 'The Rebel Scot' and 'The King's Disguise'. He was both formidable and popular as a poet and political satirist, though DRYDEN would soon ridicule the roughness of his effects. His love of extreme and far-fetched conceits gave rise to the term 'Clevelandism' to denote implausible comparison, or CATACHRESIS. He is sometimes regarded as the last METAPHYSICAL POET.

cliché From the French, 'a stereotype plate': a trite expression which has lost its cutting edge.

Clive, Caroline 1801–73 Poet and novelist. Under the pseudonym V she published *IX Poems* (1840), well received and followed by several other volumes. Her most popular work was a SENSATION NOVEL, *Paul Ferroll* (1855), whose wealthy and cultured hero is forced to confess to the murder of his wife many years after the event. A sequel, *Why Paul Ferroll Killed His Wife* (1860), describes the provocation that drove him to the crime.

Cloete, Stuart 1897–1976 South African novelist. Born in Paris, he was educated in England. A prolific author of non-fiction, adventure novels and short stories, he is at his best in a sequence of realistic, unsentimental novels covering 19th-century Afrikaner history: *Turning Wheels* (1937), *The Curve and the Tusk* (1953) and *The Abductors* (1970). *A Victorian Son* (1971) and *The Gambler* (1973) are autobiographies.

Cloister and the Hearth, The: *A Tale of the Middle Ages* A historical novel by CHARLES READE, published in 1861. Set in the 15th century, it concerns Gerard, a Dutch mercer's son, who loves Margaret, the daughter of a poor scholar, Peter Brandt. Both the burgomaster and Gerard's family oppose the marriage and contrive to have Gerard imprisoned. He escapes and wanders through Europe, the incidents of his exile enlivened by atmospheric scenes in taverns, stews, castles and monasteries. In Italy a false report of Margaret's death drives him into a Dominican monastery. Returning to Holland, he discovers Margaret; she has borne him a son who will grow up to be ERASMUS. No longer able to marry, he spends the rest of his life at Gouda near his family.

closet drama Plays written to be read rather than performed. English examples include MILTON'S *SAMSON AGONISTES*, SHELLEY'S *PROMETHEUS UNBOUND*, and HARDY'S *THE DYNASTS*.

Cloud of Unknowing, The A mystical treatise written in the second half of the 14th century by an unknown author, to whom six lesser treatises have also been attributed. The 'cloud' of the title is the gulf between man and God which only love can cross. Preparation of the mind and soul for mystical experience demands obliteration of the sense of self. The treatise aims to correct misleading notions drawn from RICHARD ROLLE and was itself criticized by WALTER HILTON. See also MYSTICAL WRITING.

Clough, Arthur Hugh 1819–61 Poet. Born in Liverpool, he was sent to Rugby, where MATTHEW ARNOLD (son of the headmaster, THOMAS ARNOLD) became a lifelong friend. After studying at Balliol College, Oxford, he was elected a fellow and tutor of Oriel College but resigned because of spiritual doubts in 1848. In the remainder of his short, restless life he was principal of a student hostel at University College, London, a tutor in Cambridge, Massachusetts (where he was friendly with EMERSON and CHARLES ELIOT NORTON) and examiner in the Education Office. Only two volumes appeared during his lifetime: *The Bothie of Tober-na-Vuolich* (1848), a verse-novel in hexameters, and *Ambarvalia* (1849), 29 shorter poems printed together with some verses by Thomas Burbidge. *AMOURS DE VOYAGE* first appeared in THE *ATLANTIC MONTHLY* in 1858 and the unfinished *DIPSYCHUS*, mostly written in 1850, was posthumously published in 1865. *Mari Magno* and *Adam and Eve*, two other longer poems, both unfinished, and some lesser prose round off a body of work notable for its lyric quality and its interpretation of the Victorian spiritual malaise. Clough is commemorated in Arnold's *THYRSIS*.

Cobbe, Frances Power 1822–1904 Religious writer and philanthropist. She published *The Theory of Intuitive Morals* (1855–7) and *Italics* (about her travels in Italy, 1864), as well as many works supporting women's suffrage and opposing vivisection. Her autobiography appeared in 1894.

Cobbett, William 1763–1835 Political activist, journalist, farmer and MP. The son of an innkeeper in Farnham, Surrey, he became first a gardener and then a soldier. The charges of corruption and peculation he unsuccessfully brought against his former officers in 1792 set the pattern for a lifetime spent in confrontation with authority. Always a loyalist and a patriot, and never a revolutionary, he became nevertheless 'a fiercely independent radical reformer'. In 1792–1800, first in Wilmington and then in Philadelphia, his writings as 'Peter Porcupine' made him the outstanding journalist in support of the Washington administration. But the outspokenness of his newspaper, *Porcupine's Gazette* (1797–9), and of pamphlets such as *Observations on the Emigration of Dr Joseph Priestley* (1794) brought the first phase of his career as a political journalist to an end in a flurry of court actions.

Back in England he regularly savaged the British government for corruption and incompetence in his newspaper, *The Political Register*. Tried by one of the infamous special juries in an action brought against him by Spencer Perceval, a cabinet minister, he was found guilty of seditious libel, fined heavily and sent to Newgate for two years, after which, Habeas Corpus having been suspended, he fled to Long Island. But he returned to England (with the disinterred mortal remains of TOM PAINE in his baggage) to re-engage fearlessly with British political life. His target now was to a much greater extent what he took to be the mismanagement of an economy characterized by alarming fluctuations in the price of wheat and the over-production of paper money. His work on his farm at Botley and, from 1805, his smallholding in Kensington made the ability, indeed the right, of a man to live off the soil by his own labour one of the principal tenets of his belief. At the same time he continued to write and publish practical primers, treatises and handbooks for the use of the literate poor. He had earlier published *A Grammar of the English Language* (1818) and *Cottage Economy* (1822). To these he now added *A French Grammar* (1824), *Cobbett's Poor Man's Friend* (1826–7), *The Woodlands* (1828), *The English Gardener* (1828), *Advice to Young Men and (Incidentally) Young Women* (1830) and *A Spelling Book* (1831), to give these only their short titles. Late in life he realized one of his principal ambitions by being elected MP for Oldham in the Reformed Parliament of 1832. By that time he had already engaged in the travels that resulted in his best-known work, *RURAL RIDES* (1830), expressing the social indignation of his earlier writing in more mellow terms. Indeed, for any reader who believes Cobbett's political battles to have been won, *Rural Rides* must stand as his literary masterpiece.

Cockburn, Henry 1779–1854 Scottish judge and writer of autobiography. Though he wrote a life of his friend FRANCIS JEFFREY (1852), he did not make his literary gifts widely known in his lifetime. A posthumously published volume of reminiscences, *Memorials of His Time* (1856), continued by two volumes of his *Journal* (1874) and one of *Circuit Journeys* (1888), established his reputation. He was the recorder of a rapidly vanishing Scotland whose characters, especially among Edinburgh legal dignitaries, he captured in memorable vignettes. The Cockburn Association was founded in his memory in 1875.

Cockney School, The An abusive label for LEIGH HUNT and his friends KEATS and HAZLITT, apparently coined by *BLACKWOOD'S EDINBURGH MAGAZINE* in October 1817 in the first of a series of venomous attacks which portrayed them as literary upstarts whose humble (i.e. lower middle-class) origins ill fitted them for the poetic calling. Hazlitt sued the editors, who settled out of court. Keats's work, notably *Poems* (1817) and *ENDYMION* (1818), was cruelly combed for immature verses and 'Cockney' rhymes, and the poet derided as an apprentice apothecary 'of pretty abilities, which he has done everything in his power to spoil'.

Cocktail Party, The A verse drama by T. S. ELIOT, produced in 1949. It is loosely based on the *Alcestis* of Euripides. Its outer shell concerns a quartet of lovers in fashionable society, but Eliot's deeper concern is with modes of spiritual reconciliation for individual Christians. A knowing psychoanalyst, Sir Henry Harcourt-Reilly, restores the unsatisfactory marriage of Lavinia and Edward Chamberlayne. This achievement requires the Christian martyrdom of Edward's lover Celia, a sacrifice which permits the predominantly secular life of the community to continue.

Cockton, Henry 1807–53 Novelist. He achieved temporary success with broadly comic novels in the manner of the early DICKENS, notably *The Life and Adventures of Valentine Vox the Ventriloquist* (1840).

Coetzee, J(ohn) M(ichael) 1940– South African novelist. Although he takes his themes from his political environment, his linguistically explosive writing is as much about language and the techniques of fiction. Works include: *Dusklands* (1974), two novellas; *In the Heart of the Country* (1977; as *From the Heart of the Country* in the USA), presenting the patricidal fantasies of an Afrikaner spinster; *Waiting for the Barbarians* (1980), about power-sickness; *Life and Times of Michael K* (1983), which won the BOOKER PRIZE, about its despised hero's almost epic survival; *Foe* (1986), about a woman castaway excluded from DEFOE's *ROBINSON CRUSOE*; and *Age of Iron* (1990), narrated by a woman dying of cancer. His criticism includes *White Writing* (1988).

Cogswell, Fred 1917– Canadian poet and editor. He was editor of the magazine *Fiddlehead* from 1952 to 1967 and founded Fiddlehead Books, a publishing house which provided an outlet for many young Maritime writers. His poetry includes *The Stunted Strong* (1954), *Descent from Eden* (1959), *Lost Dimension* (1960), *Star-People* (1968), *A Long Apprenticeship: Collected Poems* (1980) and *The Best Notes Merge* (1988). His best work describes the lives of Maritime villagers in a witty, laconic style. His translations, which include *One Hundred Poems of Modern Quebec* (1970) and *Confrontations* (1976), have helped stimulate interest in Quebec poetry in anglophone Canada. With Jo-Anne Elder he has edited *Unfinished Dreams: Contemporary Poetry of Acadie* (1990).

Cohen, Leonard 1934– Canadian poet, novelist and composer-singer. Internationally known as an entertainer, he has also published poetry and fiction. His poetry includes *The Spice-Box of Earth* (1961), *Flowers for Hitler* (1964), *Selected Poems* (1968), *The Energy of Slaves* (1972), *Death of a Lady's Man* (1978) and *Book of Mercy* (1984). Like his songs, it explores contemporary mythologies but frequently uses traditional forms. His novels include *The Favourite Game* (1963) and *Beautiful Losers* (1968), a counter-cultural religious epic. Among his record albums are *Songs of Leonard Cohen* (1967), *Songs of Love and Hate* (1971), *New Skins for the Old Ceremony* (1974), *The Best of Leonard Cohen* (1975) and *Death of a Lady's Man* (1977).

Cohen, Matt 1942– Canadian novelist and short-story writer. After two experimental novels, *Korsoniloff* (1969) and *Johnny Crackle Sings* (1971), he turned to realism with his four 'Salem' novels, *The Disinherited* (1974), *The Colours of War* (1977), *The Sweet Second Summer of Kitty Malone* (1979) and *Flowers of Darkness* (1984). Other novels are: *Wooden Hunters* (1975); *The Spanish Doctor* (1984), an epic work about the Jewish diaspora in medieval Europe; *Emotional Arithmetic* (1990), about a woman scarred by her internment by the Nazis in World War II. He has also published several short-story collections: *Columbus and the Fat Lady* (1972), *Night Flights* (1978), *Café le Dog* (1983) and *Living on Water* (1988).

Coke [Cook], **Sir Edward** 1552–1634 Lawyer and legal writer. As Chief Justice of the Court of Common Pleas (from 1606) he waged a steady war against the courts of privilege, forcing acceptance of the principle that the King could not change the common law by proclamation. Adherents of the idea of government by *rex* were determined to overcome the champion of *lex*, and JAMES I 'promoted' Coke to Chief Justice of the King's Bench in 1613. He was dismissed in 1616 for his persistence in challenging the King's right to command the common-

law courts to desist from hearing cases pending, even if the royal interest was involved. Coke's *Reports* (13 vols, 1600–15) and *Institutes* (4 vols, 1628–44) contain a superb exposition of the rules of English common law.

Cold Comfort Farm The first and most famous novel by Stella Gibbons (1902–89). Published in 1932, it is an acute and witty PARODY of the rural fiction made popular by writers like MARY WEBB.

Colenso, John William 1814–83 Theologian. Appointed bishop of the new diocese of Natal in 1853, he caused controversy by his broadminded approach to race relations and to tribal customs in marriage but above all by his contributions to the HIGHER CRITICISM in *A Commentary on the Epistle to the Romans* (1861) and *The Pentateuch and Book of Joshua Critically Examined* (1862–79), which challenged the historical accuracy of those books and concluded that they were written during the post-Exile period. Colenso was deposed in 1863 but confirmed as holder of his see by the law courts in 1866; he continued in the affection of his diocese until he died.

Coleridge, Derwent 1800–83 Editor, biographer and poet. The son of SAMUEL TAYLOR COLERIDGE, he contributed poetry to *Knight's Quarterly Magazine* from 1822, as well as publishing *The Scriptural Character of the English Church* (1839) and a biography of his brother HARTLEY COLERIDGE (1849), whose works he edited (1851).

Coleridge, Hartley David 1796–1849 Poet. The eldest son of SAMUEL TAYLOR COLERIDGE, who named him after the philosopher DAVID HARTLEY, he published *Biographia Borealis* (1833), republished in 1852 as *Lives of Northern Worthies* with marginal observations by his father. Other works included a slight volume of *Poems* (1833), a biography of MARVELL (1835) and two volumes of *Poems* (1851), edited with a memoir by his brother DERWENT COLERIDGE.

Coleridge, Mary Elizabeth 1861–1907 Novelist, poet and great-granddaughter of SAMUEL TAYLOR COLERIDGE's brother, she published her first volumes of poetry, *Fancy's Following* (1896) and *Fancy's Guerdon* (1897), under the pseudonym Anodos. Her first novel, *The Seven Sleepers of Ephesus* (1893), was praised by ROBERT LOUIS STEVENSON; other titles include *The King with Two Faces* (1897), *The Fiery Dawn* (1901) and *The Lady on the Drawing Room Floor* (1906). *Poems Old and New* (1907) and *Gathered Leaves* (1910) appeared posthumously.

Coleridge, Samuel Taylor 1772–1834 Poet, critic and philosopher. The son of the vicar of Ottery St Mary, Devon, he attended Christ's Hospital in London and entered Jesus College, Cambridge, in 1791. After joining in the reformist fervour stimulated by the French Revolution, he abandoned Cambridge in 1793 to enlist in the Light Dragoons. Though rescued after two wretched months, he never completed his degree. In 1794 he joined SOUTHEY in an abortive scheme, called 'Pantisocracy', for establishing a commune in New England. *The Morning Chronicle* published his first poem in 1794. While lodging in Bristol with Southey he won the respect of local democrats by his lectures on politics, religion and education. After marrying Sara Fricker in 1795 (Southey married her sister Edith), he settled at nearby Clevedon, completing *Poems on Various Subjects* (1796), preaching, producing 10 issues of a radical Christian weekly called *The Watchman*, writing 'conversation poems' and studying German literature and philosophy. He also took opium during bouts of illness and depression.

His move to Nether Stowey in December 1796 brought him close to WILLIAM WORDSWORTH and his sister DOROTHY WORDSWORTH. The literary partnership that resulted laid the foundations of English ROMANTICISM and produced the *LYRICAL BALLADS* (1798), to which Coleridge's most important contribution was *THE RIME OF THE ANCIENT MARINER*. He also began but never completed three similar BALLADS, including *CHRISTABEL*, and produced more conversation poems, addressed to friends: 'This Lime-Tree Bower My Prison', 'Frost at Midnight', 'Fears in Solitude' and 'The Nightingale'. *KUBLA KHAN* was written in 1797. Other work included the verse tragedy *Osirio* (reworked and produced as *Remorse* in 1813), leading articles for *The Morning Post*, the political ode 'France' and the anti-war poem 'Fire, Famine, Slaughter: A War Eclogue'. Visitors included CHARLES LAMB and his sister Mary, and the young HAZLITT.

His trip in 1798–9 to Germany, where he studied at Göttingen, confirmed him as the most influential English interpreter of German Romanticism. Back in England, he translated part of Schiller's *Wallenstein* trilogy and planned an ambitious work of Romantic metaphysics. He also wrote some 50 articles for *The Morning Post*. By this time his personal affairs were approaching crisis, with the gradual failure of his marriage and his unhappy love for Sara Hutchinson, Wordsworth's sister-in-law, which casts its shadow over such poems as 'The Keepsake' (1800), 'On Revisiting the Seashore' (1801), 'To Asra' (1801), 'The Picture: or, The Lovers' Resolution' (1802) and 'A Daydream' (1801–2). 'Dejection: An Ode' (1802) was answered by Wordsworth's 'Intimations of Immortality' ode. Coleridge now became more or less addicted to opium. His energies flowed into the meditative, confessional *Notebooks*.

In 1804–6 he worked in the wartime Civil Service at Malta, leaving his family to Southey's care and formally separating from his wife on his return. Wordsworth's reading of the 'Poem to Coleridge', which became *THE PRELUDE*, prompted his conversation poem 'To William Wordsworth'. His 18 lectures 'On Poetry and the Principles of Taste' at the Royal Institute in 1808 were the first of many series in the next decade. Especially significant were those on SHAKESPEARE (published as *Shakespearean Criticism*, 1907). While staying with the Wordsworths at Grasmere, he produced *The Friend*, a 'literary, moral and political paper' running for 28 issues in 1809–10 and appearing in book form in 1812, perhaps the closest he came to fulfilling his dream of a synthesis. The final break with Wordsworth, and the last crisis of his relationship with Sara Hutchinson, came in 1810. Coleridge lodged in London and then Bath, suffering periods of near suicidal despair and ever-increasing opium addiction. The few poems of these years include 'The Visionary Hope' (1810), 'The Suicide's Argument' (1811) and 'Time, Real and Imaginary' (1812). To this period also belong the marginal commentaries added to *The Rime of the Ancient Mariner*, three short essays 'On the Principles of Genial Criticism Concerning the Fine Arts' and *BIOGRAPHIA LITERARIA*, one of the key texts of English Romanticism.

In 1816 Coleridge settled at the Highgate home of Dr James Gillman, remaining there for the rest of his life. A chastened but also clarified figure, he became the centre of a circle of friends and disciples, as well as a living legend to younger poets. *Christabel and Other Poems* (1816) printed 'Kubla Khan' and 'The Pains of Sleep' for the first time. *Sibylline Leaves*, his collected poems, was published in 1817 (and expanded in 1828 and 1834), along with the *Biographia* and a dramatic poem, *Zapolyta*. Though Coleridge's poetic career was largely over – 'Work without Hope', 'Constancy to an Ideal Object', 'Coeli Enarrant' and 'Love's Apparition' are among the most representative of his few late poems – his view of society, culture and religion became more concrete and programmatic. Two *Lay Sermons* (1816–17) develop ideas on morality, national education and the 'organic' structure of society. His 'Treatise on Method', included in the final three-volume edition of *The Friend* (1818), ranges through every conceivable branch of knowledge in dizzying fashion. His lectures on 'The History of Philosophy' and 'General Course on Literature' (1818–19) are described in *Literary Remains* (1836). *Aids to Reflection* (1824), emphasizing the importance of 'personal revelation', influenced the development of the Broad Church movement and CHRISTIAN SOCIALISM. *On the Constitution of the Church and State* (1830) proposed the removal of education from both ecclesiastical and state control and the establishment of teachers, scholars, scientists, artists and priests as an independent 'clerisy' or 'National Church'. Some idea of Coleridge's conversation is given in *Table Talk* (1836), edited by his nephew Henry Coleridge.

Coleridge's reputation as a poet is secured by a small, though radiant, corpus of major works. The distinctively Continental cast of his thought was excitingly new to British contemporaries. His theory of the poetic imagination as a unifying and mediating power within divided modern cultures provided one of the central ideas of Romantic aesthetics, and his dialectical juxtapositions of reason and understanding, culture and civilization, and mechanical and organic form shaped the vocabulary of its recoil from UTILITARIANISM. Yet much of Coleridge's work is shot through with a metaphysical anxiety that seems to anticipate modern existentialism.

Coleridge, Sara 1802–52 Miscellaneous writer. She was the only daughter of SAMUEL TAYLOR COLERIDGE. Her most important work was a romantic fairy-tale in prose and verse, *Phantasmion* (1837). She also wrote *Pretty Lessons for Good Children* (1845), published translations from Latin and French, and edited her father's *Poems* (1852) with her brother DERWENT COLERIDGE.

Colet, John ?1467–1519 Humanist and scholar. A close friend of ERASMUS and THOMAS MORE, he was influenced by Platonic and neo-Platonic thought and, in his biblical expositions delivered at Oxford in 1496–1504, abandoned the minute exegesis and allegorical interpretation of the schoolmen. As Dean of St Paul's, he founded St Paul's School (*c*. 1509) with William Lily as its first headmaster. Always an advocate of pure classical Latin, Colet collaborated on a Latin grammar, later revised by Erasmus.

Colin Clout's Come Home Again A PASTORAL poem (1595) by SPENSER. Colin, the major character in *THE SHEPHEARDES CALENDER*, describes his adventures to his fellow shepherds. The poem compliments Queen Elizabeth (Cynthia) and SIR WALTER RALEIGH (the Shepherd of the Ocean), laments the death of SIR PHILIP SIDNEY (Astrophel), and alludes to the Countess of Pembroke (Urania) among others. Ambivalent towards the court which it alternately compliments and criticizes, it is one of Spenser's most autobiographically allusive poems.

Colleen Bawn, The A MELODRAMA by BOUCICAULT, first performed in New York in 1860. It is based on GERALD GRIFFIN's 'true-life' crime novel, *The Collegians* (1829). In order to marry an heiress Hardress Cregan plans to murder his secret wife, Eily O'Connor, the poor but honest colleen bawn (Anglo-Irish for 'fair girl'). The attempt is frustrated by the comic vagabond Myles-na-Coppaleen, a character who gave new life to the figure of the stage Irishman.

Collier, Arthur 1680–1732 Churchman and philosopher. *Clavis Universalis: or, A Demonstration of the Non-Existence and Impossibility of the External World* (1713) shows that Collier had arrived independently at the same conclusions as BERKELEY's *Principles of Human Knowledge*.

Collier, Jeremy 1650–1726 Moralist and divine. He is best known for his controversial *Short View of the Immorality and Profaneness of the English Stage* (1698), an attack on the leading playwrights of the day, including DRYDEN, CONGREVE, VANBRUGH, JOHN DENNIS and D'URFEY. Both Congreve and Vanbrugh replied. A man of unwavering courage who suffered imprisonment and exile for his principles, Collier also wrote *Essays upon Several Moral Subjects* (1698–1705), *The Great Historical, Geographical, Genealogical and Poetical Dictionary* (1701) and *The Ecclesiastical History of Great Britain* (1708–14).

Collier, John Payne 1789–1883 Scholar and forger. His writings on SHAKESPEARE and Renaissance drama were supported by researches in noblemen's private libraries and vigorous work for various literary and historical publishing societies. The basis for his later work and reputation was a Second Folio Shakespeare (1632) with supposedly contemporary annotations, exposed as forgeries only after embittered controversy. The presumption that Collier was perpetrator rather than victim of the fraud blighted the end of his life, as well as rendering his previous work permanently suspect.

Collins, Anthony 1676–1729 Philosopher. A close friend and admirer of JOHN LOCKE, Collins became a freethinker and influential advocate of DEISM in his own right. His *Essay Concerning the Use of Reason* (1707) denied the accepted separation between those things that are beyond human reason and those that are not. *A Discourse of Freethinking, Occasioned by the Rise and Growth of a Sect Call'd Freethinkers* (1713) attacked ministers of all denominations and was in turn attacked by many churchmen. *A Philosophical Inquiry Concerning Human Liberty and Necessity* (1715) is a statement of determinism.

Collins, John Churton 1848–1908 Critic. He wrote damaging attacks on EDMUND GOSSE and even on his friend SWINBURNE, and offended Oxford University with his agitation for the establishment of an English school in *The Study of English Literature* (1891) and earlier articles for *THE PALL MALL GAZETTE*. He edited works by ROBERT GREENE, TOURNEUR, LORD HERBERT OF CHERBURY and MILTON, and published *Ephemera Critica* (1901) and *Studies in Shakespeare* (1904). He became professor of English at Birmingham in 1904.

Collins, (William) Wilkie 1824–89 Novelist. Son of the landscape painter William Collins, he was named after his father's friend Sir David Wilkie. He began by writing a memoir of his father (1848); *Antonina; or, The Fall of Rome* (1850), a historical novel in the manner of BULWER LYTTON; and the charming *Rambles beyond Railways* (1851), about Cornwall. He first met DICKENS in 1851,

joining him in amateur theatricals and contributing to *HOUSEHOLD WORDS*. They collaborated on, among other pieces, *The Lazy Tour of Two Idle Apprentices* (1857) and two MELODRAMAS, *The Lighthouse* (1855) and *The Frozen Deep* (1857). A succession of short stories and several novels, *Basil: A Story of Modern Life* (1852), *Hide and Seek* (1854) and *The Dead Secret* (1857), were the prelude to his work of the 1860s, when Collins emerged as the most skilful writer of SENSATION NOVELS with *THE WOMAN IN WHITE* (1860), *No Name* (1862), *Armadale* (1866) and *THE MOONSTONE* (1868). Collins's subsequent determination to tackle social issues disconcerted his audience and, at times, dispersed his narrative powers. He attacked athleticism in *Man and Wife* (1870), attitudes to fallen women in *The New Magdalen* (1873), the Jesuits in *The Black Robe* (1881) and vivisection in *Heart and Science* (1883). *The Evil Genius* (1886) dealt with adultery and divorce, *The Legacy of Cain* (1889) with heredity and environment. Collins also returned to mystery and suspense, with varying success, in *Poor Miss Finch* (1872), *The Law and the Lady* (1875), *My Lady's Money* (1878) and *I Say No* (1884). *Blind Love* (1890) was completed by WALTER BESANT.

Collins, William 1721–59 Poet. He published *Persian Eclogues* (1742) and *Odes on Several Descriptive and Allegoric Subjects* (1746) during a prolific career troubled by financial worries; for most of his life he was 'doubtful of his dinner and trembling at a creditor'. He became insane in 1750 and died in his sister's care in his native Chichester at the early age of 38. A planned translation of Aristotle's *Poetics* never materialized. Technically fluent and sometimes hinting at an originality which rises above the conventions of the time, his verse shows him above all a master of the ODE: 'Ode to Simplicity', 'Dirge in Cymbeline', 'Ode to Evening', 'How Sleep the Brave' ('Ode, Written in the Beginning of the Year 1746') and especially the posthumous 'Ode on the Popular Superstitions of the Highlands' (1788) have an honoured place in English poetry.

Colman, George, the elder 1732–94 Playwright, journalist and theatre manager. He become involved in the theatre through his friendship with GARRICK, writing a charming one-acter, *Polly Honeycombe* (1760), and achieving success with *The Jealous Wife* (1761), inspired by FIELDING's *TOM JONES*. His translation of *The Comedies of Terence* (1765) enhanced his reputation, as did a successful collaboration with Garrick in *THE CLANDESTINE MARRIAGE* (1766). The need to make money – Colman was profligate and inherited less than he had hoped from his uncle, the Earl of Bath – prompted him to buy a share in COVENT GARDEN, chief rival to Garrick's DRURY LANE, which he managed in 1767–74. His own plays during this period were mostly adaptations, though *The Man of Business* (1774) was a notable exception. On FOOTE's death in 1776 he took over the HAYMARKET, where his last two considerable plays, *The Suicide* (1778) and *The Separate Maintenance* (1779), were performed. Increasingly subject to bouts of insanity, Colman eventually surrendered its management to his son, GEORGE COLMAN THE YOUNGER, in 1790.

Colman, George, the younger 1762–1836 Playwright and theatre manager. He took over management of the HAYMARKET from his father, GEORGE COLMAN THE ELDER, in 1790. *Inkle and Yarico* (1787), his fourth play, is a comedy with songs, humanely if uninsistently critical of the slave trade. Colman's talent for comic verse, apparent in a collection of 'tales in verse', *My Nightgown and Slippers* (1797), also enlivens his historical romances, *The Battle of*

Hexham (1789) and *The Surrender of Calais* (1791), and colours his adaptation of GODWIN'S *CALEB WILLIAMS*, *The Iron Chest* (1796). *The Heir at Law* (1797), *The Poor Gentleman* (1801) and *John Bull* (1803) are more traditional five-act comedies. It is ironic that his work as Examiner of Plays in 1824–36 should have left him with the reputation of a spoiler of other people's entertainment.

Colonel Jack [*The History and Remarkable Life of the Truly Honourable Colonel Jacque, Commonly Called Colonel Jack*] A novel by DANIEL DEFOE, published in 1722. Like *CAPTAIN SINGLETON*, it is a romantic adventure told in the first person. Abandoned by his parents, 'Colonel Jack' falls into bad company, becomes a pickpocket, and reaches early manhood living on his wits. He enlists as a soldier but soon deserts. Next he is abducted and shipped to Virginia, where he is sold as a slave to a planter. Promoted to overseer and then freed, he succeeds as a planter himself. By the end of the tale he is back in England, prosperous and mellow.

Colton, Charles Caleb ?1780–1832 Author of *Lacon: or, Many Things in Few Words* (1820), a popular collection of aphorisms, EPIGRAMS and essays.

Colum, Padraic 1881–1972 Irish poet, playwright, folklorist and writer of CHILDREN'S LITERATURE. Early plays such as *Broken Soil* (1903), *The Land* (1905) and *Thomas Muskerry* (1910) are sombrely realistic pieces prompted by his association with YEATS and LADY GREGORY at the ABBEY THEATRE. *Wild Earth* (1907) is the first of many collections of poems distinguished by their simple rhythmic lyricism. After leaving Ireland in 1914 he lived chiefly in the USA, where he studied Polynesian folklore in Hawaii, lectured on comparative literature and published many volumes for children retelling Irish, Welsh, classical and Scandinavian myths and legends, while also continuing to write poems and plays. *The Flying Swans* (1957) is an ambitious, neglected novel.

Colvin, Sir Sidney 1845–1927 Critic of art and literature. He was Slade Professor of Fine Art at Cambridge (1873–85), director of the Fitzwilliam Museum (1876–84) and Keeper of Prints and Drawings at the British Museum (1884–1912). In addition to art criticism, he published volumes on LANDOR (1881) and KEATS (1887) for the English Men of Letters series, a biography of Keats (1917), and memorials to his friend ROBERT LOUIS STEVENSON in the *Vailima Letters* (1895), and in editions of Stevenson's works (1894–7) and Stevenson's correspondence (1899–1911).

Combe, William 1741–1823 Satirical poet and writer of miscellaneous prose. After squandering a substantial inheritance, he worked successively as a common soldier, a waiter, a teacher of elocution, a cook and a private in the French army before turning to writing in about 1772. *The Diaboliad* (1776), his first success as a satirist, settled a private score with Lord Imham. It was followed by *Diabo-lady* (1777), *Anti-diabolady* (1778), and many other works in verse and prose, including *The Devil upon Two Sticks* (1790) and the topographical *Microcosm of London* (1808). His most famous works – *The Tour of Dr Syntax in Search of the Picturesque* (1809), *The Second Tour of Dr Syntax in Search of Consolation* (1820) and *The Third Tour of Dr Syntax in Search of a Wife* (1821) – satirized the fashion for PICTURESQUE tours in general and the work of GILPIN in particular. Thomas Rowlandson's illustrations contributed greatly to their popularity. Combe again collaborated with Rowlandson in *The English Dance of Death* (1815–16), which contains some of his best verse;

The Dance of Life (1816); and *Johnny Quae Genius* (1822), the last, and feeblest, of the Syntax series.

comedy A term applied to a great variety of plays in which the common denominator is a happy ending; a more complex feature is a greater interest in society and its values than in individuals and their destiny.

The Greek word from which 'comedy' derives originally described a choric song of celebration. Its transition to describing a kind of play distinct from TRAGEDY was complete by the 5th century BC. The 'old comedy' of Aristophanes (c. 448–c. 380 BC) found room for satire, parody, personal abuse and obscenity. 'New comedy', exemplified by Menander (c. 342–293 BC) and his Roman successors, Plautus (c. 254–184 BC) and Terence (c. 190–159 BC), made plot central and developed stock characters. Much more easily imitable, 'new comedy' lies behind British and Continental traditions. *RALPH ROISTER DOISTER*, the earliest substantial example in English, imitates Terence, while Plautus gave SHAKESPEARE the plot of his early success, *THE COMEDY OF ERRORS*. By exaggerating Terentian stereotypes, JONSON created the immensely popular 'humours' comedy. Shakespeare's later comedies may depart from strict classical form, but English comedy followed Jonsonian lines. The comedy of manners dominating the stage after the Restoration rests on a Jonsonian contrast between true and false wit.

Too bawdy and too mordant for its critics, RESTORATION COMEDY gave way to 18th-century SENTIMENTAL COMEDY, which shifts emphasis from exposing folly and villainy to rewarding virtue and prudence. Criticism has tended to neglect such writers as STEELE, CIBBER, CUMBERLAND, O'KEEFFE, T. W. ROBERTSON, PINERO and HENRY ARTHUR JONES in favour of those who challenged the dominance of sentimental comedy in the 18th and 19th centuries: GOLDSMITH, RICHARD BRINSLEY SHERIDAN and WILDE. SHAW carried the reputation of comedy into the 20th century, but a distinctive kind of play formally classifiable as comedy is hard to identify in the modern theatre. It survived longer in Ireland, where SYNGE and FITZMAURICE nurtured a uniquely Irish comic drama.

Comedy of Errors, The An early comedy (perhaps the earliest) by SHAKESPEARE. It was first performed c. 1593, apparently with great success, and published in the First Folio of 1623. Its source is Roman comedy and particularly the *Menaechmi* of Plautus. Antipholus of Syracuse arrives in Ephesus unaware that the city holds his twin brother, another Antipholus. To complicate matters further the two Antipholuses are served by twins, both named Dromio. The whole purpose of the plot is thus to create scenes of mistaken identity – handled dexterously and with a mature sense of comic timing – before the confusions are finally resolved in an ending which reunites the brothers and frees their father Egeon from sentence of death.

Comical Revenge, The: *or, Love in a Tub* A comedy by ETHEREGE, produced and published in 1664. A slight comic plot concerns Sir Frederick Frolick's wooing by a rich widow, the impudence of a valet, Dufoy, who is wedged into a tub by his fellow servants, and the cheating of a country knight, Sir Nicholas Cully, by Palmer and Wheadle. The serious plot, in rhymed couplets, is almost a satire on heroic drama. Aurelia loves Colonel Bruce, who loves Aurelia's sister Graciana, who loves Lord Beaufort. Beaufort wins a duel against Bruce and takes Graciana. Bruce is comforted by Aurelia.

commedia dell'arte A style of comedy which flourished in Italy from the mid-16th to the mid-18th century and influenced drama throughout Europe. Performances were based, not on an established text (though some set speeches were learned by heart), but on a scenario which left room for improvised action and dialogue. The actors wore masks and played stock characters such as Arlecchino, Pantalone, the pedantic Dottore and the bragging Capitano. New masks were frequently added: Scaramuccia, who was adopted in France as Scaramouche, and Cetrulo, who was modified into Pulcinella and reached England as Punchinel in about 1650, becoming familiar as the fairground Punch. Though derived from the quick-witted Italian Arlecchino, the English Harlequin was utterly unlike him. It is in the evolution of the harlequinade and the PANTOMIME that the influence of *commedia dell'arte* in England can be most clearly seen. A divergent tradition is that of Pierrot, derived from the mask of Pedrolino by way of Paris.

Commentaries on the Laws of England See BLACKSTONE, SIR WILLIAM.

Common Sense A pamphlet by THOMAS PAINE, published anonymously in Philadelphia in January 1776. The first public statement to urge America's immediate and unqualified separation from Britain, it sold over half a million copies and helped to galvanize the forces which only seven months later began to fight the American Revolution. The first part insists that Britain's economic and political enslavement of the colonies has violated its mandate to protect the freedom and security of its citizens. The second rejects hereditary succession in favour of democratic election. The third and fourth parts celebrate America's economic security and its potential to safeguard, by example, the inalienable rights of all people.

complaint A conventional poetic expression of personal complaint common in the Middle Ages and used also by the CAVALIER POETS in the 17th century. A first-person narrator describes his sorrow and its causes, often by telling his story. The theme is frequently unrequited or betrayed love, but may also be some other personal grief or a general dissatisfaction with the state of the world or the vicissitudes of Fortune.

Compleat Angler, The: or, *The Contemplative Man's Recreation* WALTON's classic work on fish and fishing (1653), one of the most reprinted books in the history of British letters. A fisherman (Piscator, Walton himself), a huntsman (Venator) and a fowler (Auceps), travel north from Tottenham to Ware along the river Lea, discussing the relative merits of their respective pastimes. Piscator systematically introduces Venator to the art of angling, along with lore about watercraft and the countryside. The fifth edition (1676) added a second part concerning fly-fishing on the river Dove, a subject Walton himself knew little about, by his friend CHARLES COTTON. Often assumed to be the first of its kind in the language, the book in fact contains many borrowings and adaptations from the long tradition of piscatorial literature, as well as some 40 songs and verses and PASTORAL and devotional interludes. Everywhere flavoured by the personality of its author, it is a unique combination of manual and meditation.

Compton-Burnett, Dame **Ivy** 1884–1969 Novelist. Her first novel, *Dolores* (1911) was a pale imitation of GEORGE ELIOT, and it was not until *Pastors and Masters* (1925) that her distinct and highly individual style emerged. From the late 1920s until her death she produced a new novel almost every two years: *Brothers and Sisters* (1929), *Men and Wives* (1931), *More Women than Men* (1933), *A House and Its Head* (1935), *Daughters and Sons* (1941), *A Family and a Fortune* (1939), *Parents and Children* (1941), and so on, a total of over 20 novels. *Mother and Son* (1955) won the James Tait Black Memorial Prize. As their titles suggest, the novels are preoccupied with domestic scenes and family strife; their central theme is the abuse of power. The plots are realized almost exclusively through dialogue, dispensing with conventional authorial comment.

Comus The popular title for a PASTORAL entertainment by MILTON, published in 1637. Its original title explains the circumstances of its first production: *A Masque Presented at Ludlow Castle 1634: On Michaelmas Night, Before the Right Honourable, John Earl of Bridgewater, Viscount Brackley Lord President of Wales* ... Milton wrote it at the request of his friend Henry Lawes, who provided the music, to celebrate the earl's appointment as Lord President and the parts of the lady and her brothers were taken by the earl's children. *Comus* is not a MASQUE in the court sense, in which singing and spectacle were more important than words. Its theme, the confrontation between virtue and evil, is both serious and recurrent in the rest of Milton's poetry.

Separated from her two brothers in the forest at night, a young lady falls into the hands of Comus, son of Circe and Bacchus, an evil sorcerer who lies in wait for travellers. The benign Attendant Spirit, in the form of the shepherd Thyrsis, warns her brothers of her plight. They enter Comus' palace and subdue his rout, but Comus himself escapes and the Attendant Spirit needs to invoke Sabrina, goddess of the River Severn, to free the lady from the spell. After a song of thanks to Sabrina the lady and her brothers, guided by the Spirit, complete their journey to Ludlow Castle.

conceit A metaphorical figure which makes ingenious comparison between two apparently incongruous things or concepts. Originating from the Italian '*concetto*', it featured prominently in Petrarch's love poetry (see PETRARCHAN). In England it became one of the exercises of fancy admired by 16th-century poets and was developed by the METAPHYSICAL POETS, particularly DONNE.

concrete poetry An experimental form of poetry, flourishing in the 1960s, which concentrated on isolated and particular aspects of visual, phonetic or kinetic structure, abandoning normal forms of meaning for those disclosed at or below the level of the single word. Its pioneers were Eugen Gomringer and the Brazilian Noigandres group, though the *Calligrammes* (1918) of Apollinaire were perhaps equally influential and some critics have located concrete poetry in the long tradition of poems whose visual aspects contributed to their meaning. The leading British practitioner was IAN HAMILTON FINLAY, whose work has notably moved on to other fields.

Condition of England novel A type of novel reflecting concern about the 'Condition of England' in the 19th century, particularly in the 1840s. The concern was largely stimulated by CARLYLE's message in *Chartism* (1839) and *PAST AND PRESENT* (1843) that *laissez-faire* policies, combined with neglect of the industrial poor, were driving the ranks of society further apart and could easily lead to revolution. Recurrent preoccupations of the Condition of England novel are: the use of power, mechanical and social; the sense of a breach between man and man and the importance of healing it; the need for education; and the fear of revolution. Examples include: Disraeli's *Coningsby* (1844) and *Sybil* (1845); Charles Kingsley's *Yeast* (1848) and *Alton Locke* (1850); Gaskell's *Mary Barton* (1848) and *North and South* (1855); Charlotte Brontë's *Shirley* (1849); Dickens's *Hard Times* (1854); and Dinah Mulock's *John Halifax, Gentleman* (1857).

conduct books 'Improving reading' urged upon young people, particularly girls of the leisured class, especially in the 18th century. Like the Renaissance COURTESY BOOK, they touch on manners and deportment, but in the main deal with religion, morality and self-control. Probably the most famous and influential conduct books were Fordyce's *Sermons to Young Women* (1767) and Chapone's *Letters on the Improvement of the Mind* (1773). Other widely read examples include Henry Home's *Loose Hints upon Education* (1781), Reeve's *Plans of Education* (1792) and Hannah More's didactic novel, *Coelebs in Search of a Wife* (1809). Against this background, Wollstonecraft's *A Vindication of the Rights of Woman* (1792) may be seen as both traditional in its concerns and revolutionary in its stance.

Conduct of the Allies, The A pamphlet by Swift, published anonymously in 1711 under the full title *The Conduct of the Allies, and of the Late Ministry, in Beginning and Carrying on the Present War*.

Swift's most famous political pamphlet, it was also the single most polished contribution to the propaganda machine controlled by Robert Harley's Tory ministry in its determination to end the ruinous war with France. In *The Examiner* Swift had already alleged a Whig conspiracy by the Duke of Marlborough and others at the expense of Britain's true interests. *The Conduct* extends the theory to implicate the Allies (the Dutch, Austrians and Portuguese) as fellow conspirators of the Whig grandees. Swift artfully builds up the case for peace, portraying Britain as the losing party and playing down the fact that she would emerge with distinct advantages. The pamphlet greatly strengthened the Tory case, helping to smooth the way for Marlborough's dismissal at the end of 1711 and the Treaty of Utrecht in 1713.

Confessio Amantis [*The Lover's Confession*] Gower's major English poem, probably written in 1386–90 but later revised, replacing the dedicatory preface in praise of Richard II with praise of Henry of Lancaster. A major contribution to the literature of COURTLY LOVE in English, it describes how Amans (or the Lover), feeling that he has served love too long, confesses to Genius, the priest of Venus, and is answered by instruction and exposition, each point being explained through the use of tales drawn from medieval and classical sources. One of the tales supplied the source for SHAKESPEARE's *Pericles*, in which Gower appears as the Chorus. Amans is finally won over to reason and abandons his cause. The use of a framework designed to embrace various stories was common in the Middle Ages and, indeed, several used by Gower also appear in CHAUCER's *Canterbury Tales*.

confessional poetry Verse which reveals intimate details of the poet's life. It has played a major part in American poetry since the 1950s, in the work of such writers as W. D. Snodgrass, Robert Lowell, Theodore Roethke, John Berryman, Sylvia Plath, Anne Sexton and Adrienne Rich. They focus on particularly painful moments or experiences, often related to more general historical or cultural problems.

Confessions of an English Opium Eater An autobiographical work by De Quincey, published in two parts in *The London Magazine* in 1821 and as a single volume (with an appendix) in 1822. In 1856 he expanded it for the collected edition of his works, without enhancing the original slender text.

The account of his addiction is open to interpretation as an apology for opium-taking in that it advocates the drug as the most efficient means of inducing intellectual clarity and, above all, visionary waking dreams. The tumultuous symbolic actions facilitated by the opium are a retelling of the experiences of childhood, more often than not terrifying, that have moulded the adult mind. The work was an overnight success and quickly established De Quincey's reputation. Among his more famous disciples were Branwell Brontë and Francis Thompson, though he had a deterrent effect on the more cautious Carlyle. He profoundly influenced Poe, while a large part of Baudelaire's *Paradis artificiels* consists of verbatim translations of the *Confessions* and *Suspiria de Profundis*. A slight aura of scandal hangs over the *Confessions* to this day.

Confidence-Man, The: *His Masquerade* A novel by Herman Melville, published in 1857, the last to appear during his lifetime. It takes place on the Mississippi river steamer *Fidèle*. Many of the characters are different manifestations of the confidence-man, who appears successively as a deaf mute, herb doctor, salesman of phoney stock, beggar, collector for charity and, for the second half of the novel, as Frank Goodman, who engages in philosophical conversations with other passengers. The book ends with a discussion about the status of the apocryphal scriptures, fusing the book's thematic concern with trust with the literary issue of narrative as a bearer of meaning.

Congreve, William 1670–1729 Playwright. He led a fashionable and leisured life, numbering SWIFT (a former schoolfellow), POPE and STEELE among his friends, and the actress Anne Bracegirdle and Henrietta, Duchess of Marlborough, among his lovers. After publishing a novel, *Incognita* (1692), he achieved fame with his first play, *The Old Bachelor* (1693), shaped for performance with the help of DRYDEN. Two further comedies, *The Double Dealer* (1693) and *Love for Love* (1695), and his single tragedy, *The Mourning Bride* (1697), confirmed his status. The comedies are distinguished by the wit and elegance of their dialogue as well as by their skilful plotting and the crafty deployment of contrasting characters and themes. They are mannered explorations of social values, marital practices and the scope given to intrigue and deceit by prurience in high places. Jeremy Collier concentrated his fury on Congreve and Vanbrugh in his *Short View of the Immorality and Profaneness of the English Stage* (1698). That Congreve was stung by Collier's attack is evident in his own *Amendments of Mr Collier's False and Imperfect Citations* (1698) and, regrettably, in his diminishing interest in the theatre. The comparatively disappointing reception of his masterpiece, *The Way of the World* (1700), further encouraged him to turn away from the stage. His 18th-century work includes a MASQUE, *The Judgement of Paris* (1701), an operatic piece, *Semele* (1710), which, with additions by Pope, provided Handel with the libretto of his secular oratorio (1744), a prose tale, *An Impossible Thing* (1720), an edition of Dryden's plays (1717) and several poems.

Coningsby: *or, The New Generation* A novel by Benjamin Disraeli, published in 1844. It addresses the problem of leadership for England under a regenerated, idealistic Conservative Party. The answer, for Disraeli, lies in the symbolic marriage of his hero, the aristocratic Harry Coningsby, with a daughter of the 'millocracy', Edith Millbank. Edith's father originally opposes the match but later consents. The true hero, however, is the aloof Sidonia, fiercely proud of his Jewishness, who combines wealth, wisdom and cosmopolitan culture. While Coningsby and his brother-in-law, Oswald Millbank, go into Parliament, Sidonia reverts to the faith of his fathers, thus cutting him off from his place as a natural leader in England, and guards the purity of his race by not marrying.

Connecticut Wits, The A group of 18th-century American poets, often called the Hartford Wits because they were centred in Hartford, Connecticut. Drawn together at Yale, they advocated a revision of the curriculum to include American literature and sought in their own poetry to proclaim America's literary independence. They also adhered to orthodox Calvinism and conservative Federalism. Members included TRUMBULL, DWIGHT, BARLOW, Lemuel Hopkins, David Humphreys, Richard Alsop, Theodore Dwight, E. H. Smith and Dr Mason F. Cogswell. The most important of their collaborative efforts were: *The Anarchiad*, MOCK-HEROIC verse papers serialized in 1786-7; *The Echo* (1791-1805), a verse satire against anti-Federalists and JEFFERSON; and *The Practical Greenhouse* (1799), a Federalist satire.

Connecticut Yankee in King Arthur's Court, A A satirical fantasy by MARK TWAIN, published in 1889. Hank Morgan, chief superintendent at the Colt arms factory, awakes to find himself in Camelot. Originally conceived as a comic experiment in anachronistic contrast, the novel gradually develops into a darker, more violent story. Hank's introduction of 19th-century 'enlightenment', with its ideology of progress and its powerful gadgets, leads to civil war in Arthur's England, and to an apocalyptic last battle in which both sides are destroyed by advanced technology.

Connelly, Marc(us) (Cook) 1890–1980 American playwright. His first success came in a series of 10 collaborations with GEORGE S. KAUFMAN, beginning with *Dulcy* (1921), including *Merton of the Movies* (1922) and ending with *Beggar on Horseback* (1924), a notable piece of EXPRESSIONISM. His only important subsequent work was *The Green Pastures* (1930; PULITZER PRIZE), based on Roark Bradford's stories of Louisiana blacks.

Connolly, Cyril (Vernon) 1903–74 Critic and literary editor. His reputation for intellectual precocity set him a target of promise that his output consistently failed to fulfil. His main books are: *The Rock Pool* (1936), a novel; the partly autobiographical *Enemies of Promise* (1938); and *The Unquiet Grave* (1944), nostalgic-hedonist maxims by 'Palinurus'. Connolly founded and edited the influential *Horizon* (1939–50) and became principal book reviewer for *The Sunday Times*.

Conquest, (George) Robert (Acworth) 1917– Poet, historian and critic. His anthology, *New Lines* (1956), helped to establish the poets of the MOVEMENT. His own verse, gathered in *New and Collected Poems* (1988), shows him a typical Movement poet in his concern for traditional forms and ordinary language, less so in his variety of subjects, which include SCIENCE FICTION. He has also written and edited many works on Marxism and the USSR.

Conrad, Joseph [Korzeniowski, Jozef Teodor Konrad] 1857-1924 Novelist and short-story writer. He was born in Podolia in the Ukraine, the child of Polish parents opposed to the Tsarist domination of their country. His father's involvement in political conspiracy resulted in exile to Volgoda, north-west of Moscow, where Conrad's mother died when he was seven. His father died in Poland four years later and Conrad was guided through youth by his uncle Tadeusz. In 1874 he went to Marseilles and began a 20-year career as a sailor. After a reckless and improvident period, which involved gun-running for the Carlists in Spain and culminated in a suicide attempt in 1878, Conrad made steady progress. Serving on English ships, he passed his second mate's examination in 1880 and his first mate's examination in 1884. He became a naturalized British subject in 1886, and received his master's certificate from the Board of Trade.

He abandoned the sea in 1894 and married Jessie George in 1896, settling permanently in England and embarking on a second career as a writer. He was, he said, adopted by the genius of the English language. *Almayer's Folly's* (1895), published with the help of EDWARD GARNETT, and *An Outcast of the Islands* (1896) mark his literary apprenticeship. THE NIGGER OF THE 'NARCISSUS' (1897), recalling a voyage from Bombay to Dunkirk in 1884, ushered in his mature period. It was followed by LORD JIM (1900); HEART OF DARKNESS (published with *Youth*, 1902), using his experiences as a river captain in the Congo; and *Typhoon* (1903). While declaring their debt to a long tradition of maritime adventure which he had first encountered when he read MARRYAT as a child, Conrad's 'sea novels' frequently hinge on a decisively testing moment or experience which exposes the individual's fallibility. NOSTROMO (1904), THE SECRET AGENT (1907) and UNDER WESTERN EYES (1911) increasingly connect such private failures with the public world of politics and political ideologies, presented in an unblinkingly sceptical fashion. These works earned Conrad little money or popularity, but brought him the respect of leading contemporaries such as BENNETT, GALSWORTHY and FORD MADOX FORD, with whom he wrote *The Inheritors* (1901) and *Romance* (1903), as well as his fellow expatriates in Sussex and Kent, STEPHEN CRANE and HENRY JAMES. Wider public recognition came with CHANCE (1913) and VICTORY (1915). *The Shadow Line* (1917), *The Arrow of Gold* (1919), *The Rescue* (1920) and *The Rover* (1923) were among his later works. *The Mirror of the Sea* (1906) and *A Personal Record* (1912) are reminiscences.

Conroy, Jack 1899–1980 American novelist and editor. His novel *The Disinherited* (1933) is a classic of proletarian literature, exploring working-class life in the Depression with unsentimental directness. Other works include *A World to Win* (1935), *Anyplace but Here* (with ARNA BONTEMPS; 1966) and CHILDREN'S LITERATURE with Arna Bontemps. Conroy also founded *The Anvil* and *The New Anvil*, left-wing magazines which published work by writers such as RICHARD WRIGHT, ERSKINE CALDWELL, FRANK YERBY, JAMES T. FARRELL, MICHAEL GOLD, LANGSTON HUGHES and MERIDEL LE SUEUR, and published *Writers in Revolt: The Anvil Anthology* (with Curt Johnson, 1973).

Conscious Lovers, The A comedy by STEELE, performed at DRURY LANE in 1722 and published the following year. Though the plot derives from Terence's *Andria*, Steele softened his original to create an ethical hero in Bevil, who behaves with exemplary virtue in preferring his own ward, Indiana, to the wealthy heiress Lucinda.

Bevil's refusal of a challenge from his outraged friend Myrtle permits him (and Steele) to ridicule the fashion for duelling. The complexities are resolved when Indiana and Lucinda turn out to be half-sisters, sharing the same fortune and free to marry as they wish. Soon translated into French, the play influenced the development of the *comédie larmoyante*. In England, its success helped to oust the comedy of manners from the stage and to pave the way for SENTIMENTAL COMEDY.

Conservationist, The A novel by NADINE GORDIMER, published in 1974 and awarded the BOOKER PRIZE. The title is ironic since Mehring, a wealthy white businessman, is concerned with preserving the land on his weekend retreat near Johannesburg for his own use and enjoyment only. Preoccupied with the ecology of his farm, he tries to ignore the interdependence of human beings and is indifferent to the uprooting and dislocation of whole groups of peoples within South Africa. The novel portrays his increasing self-removal from meaningful human contact, leading to paranoia, mental breakdown and, finally, his flight from the country.

consonance See ALLITERATION.

Constable, Henry 1562–1613 Poet. A Catholic convert, he spent much of his life on the Continent, dying at Liège. *Diana*, his collection of SONNETS, was printed in 1592 and reissued in 1594 with additional sonnets dubiously ascribed to Constable and contributions by other poets. He also wrote sonnets to such noble ladies as the Countess of Pembroke and Penelope Rich, and 16 'Spiritual Sonnets', not printed until 1815. His work is represented in ENGLAND'S HELICON.

Constantine, David (John) 1944– Poet. Influenced by ROBERT GRAVES, he brings a classical and European sensibility to his work. *A Brightness to Cast Shadows* (1980), *Watching for Dolphins* (1983), *Madder* (1987) and *Selected Poems* (1991) are erudite and culturally wideranging. *Space Displaced* (1992) contains translations from Henri Michaux. An initial work on Hölderlin (1979) has been followed by a major critical study (1988). Constantine has also published *Early Greek Travellers and the Hellenic Ideal* (1984).

Contarini Fleming: *A Psychological Romance* A novel by BENJAMIN DISRAELI, published in 1832. It purports to be the autobiography of Contarini Fleming, son of a Venetian noblewoman and an aristocratic British politician. After a failed marriage to his cousin, Alceste, and a prolonged tour of Europe and the East, he settles in Rome, devoting himself to art.

Contrast, The A play by TYLER, produced in 1787 and published in 1790. The first comedy by a native American writer to be staged professionally, it is indebted to the 18th-century English comedy of manners, particularly SHERIDAN'S THE SCHOOL FOR SCANDAL. The contrast of the title is between two rivals in love: Bill Dimple, the representative of European affectation, and Colonel Manly, the representative of American straightforwardness and honesty. The subplot echoes the contrast between national manners in the amorous rivalry of Dimple's servant, the devious and conceited Jessamy, and Manly's servant Jonathan, the prototype of the naïve, goodhearted Yankee.

Cook, Eliza 1818–89 Poet. Her first volume, *Lays of a Wild Harp*, was published in 1835. *Melaia* (1838) and *New Echoes* (1864) followed. Her best-known poem, 'The Old Arm Chair', appeared in *The Weekly Dispatch* in 1836. She conducted *Eliza Cook's Journal* from 1849 to 1854.

Cook, Captain James 1728–79 Navigator. As well as writing *Sailing Directions* (1766–8), Cook left records of his three principal voyages, published as: *Journal during His First Voyage* (1893), edited by Captain W. J. L. Wharton; *A Voyage towards the South Pole and round the World in 1772–1775* (1777); and *A Voyage to the Pacific Ocean in 1776–1780* (1784), completed by Captain T. King after Cook's death in Hawaii.

Cook, Michael 1933– English-born Canadian playwright. His works are passionate and unsubtle celebrations of 'the elemental and instinctive', particularly as found in indigenous cultures. *Colour the Flesh the Colour of Dust* (1972) is a Brechtian examination of the political turmoil in 18th-century Newfoundland. *Head, Guts and Soundbone Dance* (1974) is a folk play capturing both Newfoundland speech and the fatalistic attitudes engendered by the island's harsh life. *The Gayden Chronicles* (1979) tells the story of a British Navy rebel hanged in St John's in 1812. Other plays include *Jacob's Wake* (1975), *Quiller* (1975), *On the Rim of the Curve* (1977) and *This Damned Inheritance* (1983).

Cook's Tale, The See CANTERBURY TALES.

Cooke, John (Esten) 1830–86 American novelist. He wrote a series of novels about the Civil War and historical novels of colonial Virginia in the manner of JAMES FENIMORE COOPER: *Leather Stocking and Silk* (1854), *The Virginia Comedians* (1854), *Henry St John, Gentleman* (1859), *Her Majesty the Queen* (about the Cavaliers; 1872), *Canolles* (about Virginia during the Revolution; 1877) and *My Lady Pokahontas* (1885). He wrote a life of Stonewall Jackson (1863) while fighting for the Confederates in the Civil War and a life of Robert E. Lee (1871).

Coolbrith, Ina Donna 1842–1928 American poet. *A Perfect Day* (1881), *The Singer of the Sea* (1894) and *Songs from the Golden Gate* (1895), written in a simple lyrical style, are the first published verses from California. She also shared the editorship of the OVERLAND MONTHLY with BRET HARTE.

Coolidge, Susan [Woolsey, Sarah Chauncy] 1845–1905 American writer of CHILDREN'S LITERATURE. She became popular with several generations of young readers for the heroine introduced in her second book, *What Katy Did* (1872), the tall, rebellious daughter of a small-town family very much like its creator's own. Katy's adventures in succeeding books cover her schooldays, foreign travel and engagement.

Cooper, Giles (Stannus) 1918–66 Playwright. Although best known in his lifetime as a prolific adapter for television (notably the *Maigret* series, which won him a Writer of the Year award in 1961), he produced 70 original plays for radio, television and the stage. He had some critical success in the theatre with *Everything in the Garden* (1962) and created one of the most spectacular television plays of its time, *The Other Man* (1964), an alternative history of Anglo-Nazi relations. But his best work, like *Unman, Wittering and Zigo* (1958), was in radio, a medium which suited his acerbic mixture of the absurd and the naturalistic. A prestigious award for radio drama bears his name.

Cooper, James Fenimore 1789–1851 American novelist. His first novel was *Precaution* (1820), a study of manners in the tradition of JANE AUSTEN. *The Spy* (1821), set during the American Revolution, and *The Pilot* (1823), a tale of the sea, were more characteristic of the vein of romance he would develop. *The Pioneers* (1823) began the LEATHERSTOCKING TALES, the series of novels for which he is chiefly remembered; subsequent volumes were *The Last of the Mohicans* (1826), *The Prairie* (1827), *The*

Pathfinder (1840) and *The Deerslayer* (1841). *Lionel Lincoln* (1825) is a story of Boston during the Revolution.

Cooper soon established a reputation as one of America's leading authors. The long stay in Europe which he began in 1826 made him one of the first American writers to become widely popular outside his own country, hailed as an American counterpart of SIR WALTER SCOTT. While in Europe he wrote: *The Red Rover* (1827), a sea story; *The Wept of Wishton-Wish* (1829), a novel of early American frontier life; *The Water Witch* (1830), another sea story; *Notions of America* (1828), an essay partly inspired by his friend the Marquis de Lafayette; and a historical trilogy, *The Bravo* (1831), *The Heidenmauer* (1832) and *The Headsman* (1833). After his return to the USA he damaged his popularity by the conservative views advanced in non-fictional works such as *The Monikins* (1835) and *The American Democrat* (1838) and dramatized in the novels *Homeward Bound* (1838) and *Home as Found* (1838). The 21 books he produced during the last decade of his life include two more sea novels, *Afloat and Ashore* and *Miles Wallingford*, and a historical trilogy about a New York family, known as the *Littlepage Manuscripts* and consisting of *Satanstoe* (1845), *The Chainbearer* (1845) and *The Redskins* (1846).

Cooper, Thomas 1805–92 Poet. A Chartist imprisoned for sedition in 1842, he wrote *The Purgatory of Suicides* (1845), an epic on political themes, and *Wise Saws and Modern Instances* (1845). He also published an *Autobiography* in 1872.

Cooper, William [Huff, Harry Summerfield] 1910– Novelist. His most important novel is *Scenes from Provincial Life* (1950), a seminal influence on JOHN BRAINE and the ANGRY YOUNG MEN generation. *Scenes from Married Life* (1961), *Scenes from Metropolitan Life* (1982) and *Scenes from Later Life* (1983) are sequels.

Coover, Robert (Lowell) 1932– American novelist. *The Origin of the Brunists* (1966), *The Universal Baseball Association, Inc., J. Henry Waugh, Prop.* (1968), *The Public Burning* (1977), *Spanking the Maid* (1981), *Gerald's Party* (1986) and *Pinocchio in Venice* (1991) are representative of POST-MODERNISM in their preoccupation with popular culture and the movements, particularly the extreme religious movements, which emerge from it. Coover has also published short stories in *Pricksongs and Descants* (1969), *You Must Remember This* (1987) and *Whatever Happened to Gloomy Gus of the Chicago Bears?* (1988).

Coppard, A(lfred) E(dgar) 1878–1957 Short-story writer and poet. His first volume of poetry, *Hips and Haws*, appeared in 1922. He is chiefly remembered for the collections of short stories that began with *Adam and Eve and Pinch Me* (1921) and included *The Black Dog and Other Stories* (1923), *Fishmonger's Fiddle: Tales* (1925) and *The Field of Mustard* (1926). They contain tales as diverse as the rich and mysterious 'Dusky Ruth' and 'The Presser', about a 10-year-old boy apprenticed to a Whitechapel tailor, but above all Coppard's work conveys the flavour of the English countryside.

Corbett [Corbet], **Richard** 1582–1635 Poet. He became chaplain to JAMES I, Dean of Christ Church, Bishop of Oxford and finally Bishop of Norwich. Convivial and witty, he included DONNE, JONSON and CORYATE among his friends and wrote sprightly occasional verse collected in *Certain Elegant Poems* (1647) and *Poëtica Stromata* (1648). 'Farewell, Rewards and Fairies' is a nostalgic, accomplished poem on England's past.

Corelli, Marie 1855–1924 Novelist. The daughter of CHARLES MACKAY, she achieved extraordinary popularity with wildly over-written romantic novels, of which *Barabbas* (1893) and *The Sorrows of Satan* (1895) were perhaps the most famous. Others include *Vendetta* (1886), *Thelma* (1887), *Ardath* (1889), *The Soul of Lilith* (1892), *The Mighty Atom* (1896), *The Master Christian* (1900) and *Temporal Power* (1902). A habit of creating exotic legends about her own life and an unfailing talent for publicity-seeking helped to keep her in the public eye.

Coriolanus A tragedy by SHAKESPEARE, first performed *c*. 1608 and published in the First Folio of 1623. The main source, NORTH's Plutarch, supplied a story much less familiar than the stories of *JULIUS CAESAR* or *ANTONY AND CLEOPATRA*, plays with which this stark political tragedy has little in common.

Rome's plebeians are on the verge of rebellion against their patrician rulers. Mollified by the tactful Menenius Agrippa, they are incensed again by the arrogance of Caius Martius. Five Tribunes of the People are appointed and Caius Martius is sent to put down a Volscian uprising. His victory at the Volscian city of Corioli wins him the name of Coriolanus. Election to the Senate seems certain until Coriolanus' pride makes him incapable of observing the traditional rites of public humility. His mother Volumnia finally persuades him to ask the plebeians for their support, but his outburst in the Forum forces the Tribunes to demand his banishment. Coriolanus presents himself to his sworn enemy, the Volscian leader Tullus Aufidius, either as a sacrifice or as an ally. He becomes the leader of the Volscian army against Rome, rejects the desperate pleas of the Senators and is persuaded to spare the city only after an astonishing confrontation with Volumnia. Aufidius sees the peace treaty as a betrayal and, when Coriolanus taunts him, he and the Volscians kill him as an enemy.

Corkery, Daniel 1878–1964 Irish critic, short-story writer and man of letters. Professor of English at University College, Cork, from 1931 to 1947, he was mentor to younger writers such as FRANK O'CONNOR and SEAN O'FAOLAIN as well as a critic whose work made a most sustained attempt to formulate a nationalist version of the Irish literary tradition. His own best stories can be found in the collections *A Munster Twilight* (1916), *The Stormy Hills* (1929) and, to a lesser extent, in *Earth out of Earth* (1939). He also published a number of plays, of which those in *The Yellow Bittern and Other Plays* (1920) are the most notable.

Corn Law Rhymer, The See ELLIOTT, EBENEZER.

Cornford, Frances 1886–1960 Poet. She was the granddaughter of CHARLES DARWIN and the mother of JOHN CORNFORD. Her *Collected Poems* (1954) includes the famous TRIOLET 'To a Fat Lady Seen from a Train'.

Cornford, (Rupert) John 1915–36 Poet and writer on politics. He joined the Communist Party in 1933 and was killed in the Spanish Civil War. His poetry was at first much influenced by his mother, FRANCES CORNFORD, but kept its clarity and direct simplicity after he rebelled in favour of MODERNISM. A few love-poems and 'Poems from Spain, 1936' are the best. Jonathan Galassi has edited *Understand the Weapon, Understand the Wound: Selected Writings of John Cornford* (1976).

Cornhill Magazine, The A monthly periodical founded by GEORGE SMITH in 1860. THACKERAY was its first editor and LESLIE STEPHEN a distinguished successor. Contributors included ELIZABETH BARRETT BROWNING, ROBERT BROWNING, SWINBURNE, ELIZABETH GASKELL, RUSKIN, GEORGE ELIOT, CHARLES READE,

MATTHEW ARNOLD, TROLLOPE and HARDY. It survived until 1975.

Cornwall, Barry [Procter, Bryan Waller] 1787–1874 Poet. He published several volumes, chiefly lyrics and songs, among them *Dramatic Scenes* (1819), *Marcian Colonna* (1820), *The Flood of Thessaly* (1823) and *English Songs* (1832). He also wrote a tragedy, *Mirandola* (1821). His daughter was ADELAIDE ANNE PROCTER.

Corsair, The A poem by BYRON, published in 1814. It belongs with *THE BRIDE OF ABYDOS* in its use of the pirate as Romantic hero. Conrad, an Aegean pirate, is captured by his enemy, the Turkish Pasha Seyd, but chivalrously refuses Gulnare's offer to kill her master. She kills the Pasha herself and flees with Conrad, who finds that his beloved Medora has died of grief after a mistaken report of his death. He leaves home and disappears, but returns in disguise as the title character of *Lara* (1814).

Corso, Gregory (Nunzio) 1930– American poet. His work, associated with that of the BEATS in its concern with political and social issues, often adopts the stance of a sophisticated child who looks upon a world gone mad. His first volume, *The Vestal Lady on Brattle and Other Poems* (1955), was followed by *Gasoline* (1958), *Bomb* (1958), *The Happy Birthday of Death* (1960), *Long Live Man* (1962), *Selected Poems* (1962), *There is Yet Time to Run Back through Life and Expiate All That's been Sadly Done* (1965), *Egyptian Cross* (1971), *Ankh* (1971), *The Night Last Night was at its Nightest ...* (1972), and *Earth Egg* (1974). Later volumes include *Writings from Ox* (1981) and *Mindfield: New and Selected Poems* (1989). One of his most important volumes is *Elegiac Feelings American* (1970), dedicated to JACK KEROUAC, which assembles completed poems, drafts of poems and casual drawings.

Corvo, Baron See ROLFE, FREDERICK WILLIAM.

Cory, William Johnson 1823–92 Poet. *Ionica*, a collection of lyrics, was published anonymously in 1858. His *Letters and Journals* appeared in 1897. His best-known works are the poem 'Heraclitus', paraphrasing Callimachus, and the 'Eton Boating Song', written in 1863.

Coryate, Thomas *c.* 1577–1617 Traveller and writer. His lively account of his European travels entitled *Coryats Crudities, Hastily Gobbled up in Five Months Travels* (1611), an entertaining mishmash of curiosities and opinionated reportage, was prefaced by commendations from several leading poets of the day; these were reprinted separately as *The Odcombian Banquet* (1611). The following year he embarked on an overland expedition to India by way of Greece, Turkey, Egypt, Mesopotamia and Persia. He reached Agra in 1616 but died exhausted in Surat on his way home. His notes on the journey were preserved in his correspondence and *Thomas Coriate Traveller for the English Wits: Greeting from the Court of the Great Mogul* (1616).

Cotton, Charles 1630–87 Poet, translator and angler. Son of a landowner and *literatus*, he passed most of his life in retirement, numbering DONNE, JONSON and HERRICK among his friends. He published burlesques of the *Aeneid* (*Scarronnides*, 1664) and Lucian (*The Scoffer Scoft*, 1675), and an excellently racy version of Montaigne's *Essays* (1685) which largely supplanted FLORIO's translation until this century. The bulk of his original poetry appeared posthumously, in *Poems on Several Occasions* (1689); it is a true miscellany, but his particular gifts are best represented in burlesques, conversational epistles and poems of retirement. These last bear eloquent witness to his love of angling, and his enduring fame has been as WALTON's friend and protégé, and as author of the additions to the fifth edition of *THE COMPLEAT ANGLER* (1676).

Cotton, John 1584–1652 American Puritan minister. He resigned from the living of St Botolph's in Boston, Lincolnshire, and in 1633 emigrated to Massachusetts Bay, where he became minister of the Boston church. INCREASE MATHER was his son-in-law and COTTON MATHER his grandson.

A Brief Exposition on the Whole Book of Canticles (1642) justifies the Puritan enterprise in Massachusetts by reference to the Song of Solomon, while the sermons collected in *Christ the Fountain of Life: or, Sundry Choice Sermons on Part of the Fifth Chapter of the First Epistle of St John* (1651) describe his ideas about religious conversion. *The Keys of the Kingdom of Heaven* (1644) and *The Way of Churches of Christ in New England* (1645) were widely read theological tracts, while his catechism, *Milk for Babes, Drawn from the Breasts of Both Testaments* (1646), was used throughout the 17th century in America. Cotton also replied to ROGER WILLIAMS's criticisms of New England church policies with *The Bloody Tenet Washed and Made White in the Blood of the Lamb* (1647) and disputed with Roger Baille. *A Survey of the Sum of Church Discipline* (1648) is his most thorough ecclesiastical statement.

Cotton, Sir **Robert Bruce** 1571–1631 Author of political tracts, antiquary and collector of manuscripts. He was less important for his own writings than for his library of manuscripts from the dissolved monasteries, precious material which might otherwise have been destroyed or lost. It was left to the nation by his grandson, Sir John Cotton, but suffered a disastrous fire in 1731. The remainder passed to the British Museum in 1753. Among the treasures to survive are the single manuscript of *BEOWULF*, the manuscripts of *SIR GAWAIN AND THE GREEN KNIGHT* and *PEARL*, several biblical manuscripts and the Lindisfarne Gospels.

Coulter, John 1888–1980 Irish-Canadian playwright. His best-known work is *Riel* (1950), an epic play about the leader of the 19th-century Métis rebellion in Western Canada. The same episode also yielded *The Crime of Louis Riel* (1966) and *The Trial of Louis Riel* (1968). Earlier work included the prize-winning *House in the Glen* (1937) and libretti for two operas by Healey Willan, *Transit through Fire* (1942) and *Deirdre* (1946). He was married to the Canadian writer Oliver Clare Primrose.

Count Robert of Paris See SCOTT, SIR WALTER.

Country Wife, The A comedy by WYCHERLEY, produced and published in 1675. One of the greatest examples of RESTORATION COMEDY, the play gave some offence even in its own day, and was toned down by GARRICK when he presented it as *The Country Girl* (1766). Horner, a cynical libertine, lets it be known that he is impotent, encouraging husbands to entrust their wives to his company. In this fashion, he exploits Pinchwife's jealousy to seduce his innocent young wife, Margery. The couple have come to London for the marriage of Pinchwife's sister, Alithea, to the mercenary Sparkish, who takes her for granted and so eventually loses her to Harcourt. In a brilliant conclusion the wives whom Horner has seduced discover to their wrath that they all share the same secret, but close ranks and swear to his impotence. Pinchwife has to make do with this assurance. The curtain comes down to a dance of cuckolds.

court theatres The entertainments staged at the Tudor

and Stuart courts were often elaborate enough to demand the temporary adaptation of indoor spaces, such as the Great Hall at Hampton Court, the Banqueting House and the Great Chamber at Whitehall and the Great Halls at Greenwich, Richmond and Windsor. More permanent structures were adapted or built under Charles I, notably Inigo Jones's Cockpit-in-Court (1629–30) and, to gratify the Stuart delight in MASQUES, the Masquing House (1637). The court theatres dwindled into insignificance under Charles II and his successors.

courtesy book A type of literature particularly popular in the Middle Ages, defining the rules of polite behaviour and the general demeanour and duties of a courtier. Baldessare Castiglione's dialogue *Il libro del cortegiano* (1528), translated into English by Sir Thomas Hoby as *The Courtier* (1561), introduced a Renaissance concern with an ideal man who combined a wide variety of attributes and skills, practical as well as intellectual. Its immediate influence is discernible in such educational treatises as ELYOT's *The Book Named the Governor* and ASCHAM's *The Schoolmaster*. The last courtesy book in the traditional mould is Lord CHESTERFIELD's *Letters to His Son* (1774).

courtly love The modern name for a literary and social concept, originating in the Middle Ages, of a particular kind of love between men and women, involving service and veneration on the part of the man, and a nominal or actual domination on the part of the woman. This reversal of the usual medieval marital relationship took place between a lady who might or might not be married and a man sometimes but not invariably her social inferior. Descriptions consequently insist on its private, discreet and secret nature, on the frustrations and obstacles intensifying it, and on the dangers of its discovery by spies and slanderers. Its aristocratic system of values envisaged love as an educative and ennobling experience, the source of prowess and refinement, and consequently beneficial to society.

Some critics have denied that such a concept ever existed and point to Gaston Paris's coining of the term *amour courtois* in 1883. More widely held is the view that some such variation of romantic love was discussed, and existed as an ideal, if not as a historical fact, from the 12th century onwards, though usually called fine (or *verai*, or *bon*) *amour*. Definitions of it have varied according to literary fashion and have proliferated in the 20th century, when increasingly specialized knowledge of the Middle Ages has also resulted in scepticism and an unwillingness to make grandiose hypotheses. Theories on the origins of courtly love have also proliferated. Dronke has asserted that it is a timeless human experience that transcends geographical boundaries (thus removing its 'courtly' label), and can be found in the earliest poetry. But C. S. LEWIS and most critics have seen it as a phenomenon arising, from multiple influences, in the courts of Southern France at the end of the 11th century.

The Troubadour ideal of *cortesia* as a high moral code of behaviour based on profane love spread to the Northern French lyric poets and to England, to the *lais* of MARIE DE FRANCE (fl. 1160–90) and the story of Tristan, both based on Celtic legends. The uncourtly material of legend has been modified or used to enhance other powerful constituents of courtly love. Hopeless passion makes young men accomplish all kinds of deeds; their suffering due to separation is intensified by all kinds of obstacles – mountains, jealous husbands, jealous wives. The Tristan story, above all, contributes three details endlessly imitated in courtly literature: the body/heart (*cors/cuers*) pun expressing Iseut's dilemma of body possessed by husband and heart by lover; the words '*En vus e ma mort e ma vie*'; and the love potion, expressing the sudden and inexorable force of passion. The romances of Chrétien de Troyes (fl. 1170–81) likewise link Celtic material and the terminology of courtly love but, despite the great, controversial exception of *Lancelot*, much of his work portrays married lovers. Andreas Capellanus's popular and much-translated treatise, *De arte honeste amandi* (1175–80), expounds courtly love, its rules and etiquette, but then claims that it should be rejected as harmful to the soul. Is it a scholastic joke, a seduction manual, a moralistic work or an early documenting of the game of love? The hugely influential 13th-century *Roman de la rose* by Guillaume de Lorris and Jean de Meun (which CHAUCER translated as *THE ROMAUNT OF THE ROSE*), used ALLEGORY for the first time to convey the courtly experience of love: it presents a garden of love which excludes old age and poverty but is open to the rich and leisured.

Expressions of the courtly ideal of love appear less often in medieval English literature than on the Continent. The 14th-century *IPOMADON* and *WILLIAM OF PALERNE* faithfully reflect the preoccupations of their French sources, while other romances – *SIR EGLAMOUR OF ARTOIS*, *THE EARL OF TOULOUS*, *SIR DEGREVANT*, *SIR TORRENT OF PORTYNGALE* and *GUY OF WARWICK* – portray the hero in love with his social superior. But English VERSE ROMANCES are not in general notably courtly, showing less interest in love problems than adventures. *YWAIN AND GAWAIN* (c. 1350), a version of Chrétien's *Yvain*, omits the long self-questioning monologues of the original, and the late 13th-century *SIR TRISTREM* is not predominantly a love story. The Lancelot story is not taken up till around 1400, in the stanzaic *LE MORTE ARTHUR*, where although love is the chief source of Lancelot's greatness, it is also firmly established as responsible for the fall of Arthur and the Round Table. SIR THOMAS MALORY too, who used the stanzaic *Morte* in his *LE MORTE DARTHUR*, was not entirely happy with the relationship of Lancelot and Guinevere and at times seems to deny the possibility of any carnal union between them.

The work of the greatest 14th-century English writers, however, shows them thoroughly familiar with and sympathetic to the aristocratic ideal of love. The relationship between Gawain and Bertilak's lady in *SIR GAWAIN AND THE GREEN KNIGHT* may remind us of Jan Huizinga's theory of courtly love as an aristocratic game. In GOWER's *CONFESSIO AMANTIS* the Lover 'confesses' his sentiments and experiences, and demonstrates his refined manners and 'fair speech' in his long and devoted service to his lady. But the Lover has grown old in this service and by the end of the poem Love will have no more of him. This realistic and clear-sighted attitude that accompanies a sympathetic depiction of courtly love is also shared by Gower's friend CHAUCER. The contrast between his first poem, *THE BOOK OF THE DUCHESS*, breathing the atmosphere of French love-visions, and *THE PARLEMENT OF FOULES*, taking a more detached and comic view of courtly relationships, anticipates the method of his mature work. In *THE CANTERBURY TALES* 'courtly' contributions – notably *The Knight's Tale* and *The Franklin's Tale* – are juxtaposed with others expressing sensual and bawdy attitudes to love. *TROILUS AND CRISEYDE* is Chaucer's most extended portrayal of a courtly love affair, ending in grief because one of the partners fails to adhere to *trouthe*, the highest standard of honourable behaviour. With that ending constantly in mind, Chaucer paints a complex, critical picture of his lovers and the ideals by which they talk and strive to act. Courtly behaviour in love is both high-principled and silly, noble and ineffectual. It satisfies the aspirations of both mind and body, yet cannot survive too much pressure from the violent world of war. Seen from the cosmic viewpoint Troilus is granted after death, it is indistinguishable from fleshly lust. Seen from the Christian perspective which closes the poem, it is infinitely surpassed by Divine love.

Covent Garden, Theatre Royal A theatre built and opened in 1732 by John Rich, who brought from his previous theatre in Lincoln's Inn Fields the patent entitling him to share with DRURY LANE the monopoly of legitimate drama in London (see PATENT THEATRES). The rivalry with Drury Lane continued until the abolition of the monopoly in 1843. By then, the first theatre had been replaced by a second, designed by Richard Smirke and opened in 1809. Under the management of John Philip Kemble and later Macready it struggled to overcome the costliness of its ambition, and soon after 1843 became primarily an opera-house. A fire destroyed the building in 1856 and a much-altered third theatre on the site, designed by Sir Edward Barry, now bears the name of the Royal Opera House.

Coventry, Francis d. ?1759 Satirist. His prose tale, *The History of Pompey the Little* (1751), gives a lap-dog's observation of life as he is passed from one owner to another.

Coventry cycle See MIRACLE PLAYS.

Coverdale, Miles ?1488–1569 Protestant reformer and translator of the Bible. A priest and Augustinian friar, he developed enthusiasm for reform and by 1528 was preaching against the Mass and devotion to images. A fellow worker with TYNDALE, he published the first complete English Bible to be printed (Cologne, 1535) and edited the Great Bible (1539). His contributions included the English version of the Psalms preserved in the BOOK OF COMMON PRAYER. Expelled from his bishopric of Exeter during Queen Mary's reign, he joined the group of exiles working on the Geneva Bible presented to Queen Elizabeth in 1560. Coverdale returned to England in 1559 but his Puritanism prevented his ever regaining a bishopric. See also BIBLE IN ENGLISH and PSALTERS.

Coward, Sir Noël (Pierce) 1899–1973 Playwright, actor, lyricist and composer. His distinctive theatrical voice was announced in *The Young Idea* (1922), the first of a succession of stylish comedies which includes *Fallen Angels* (1925), *HAY FEVER* (1925), *PRIVATE LIVES* (1930), *Design for Living* (1933), *Blithe Spirit* (1941) and *Present Laughter* (1942). He further made his name as a gifted actor, a showman who learned how to sell a song without singing it and a master of revue. Except in *Bitter-Sweet* (1929), he found it hard to sustain a whole piece with his own music, but individual tunes linger ('Some Day I'll Find You', 'I'll See You Again') and some of his lyrics are among the best of their kind, particularly those about English eccentricity ('The Stately Homes of England', 'Mad Dogs and Englishmen', 'Let's Not be Beastly to the Germans'). *The Coward Song-Book* (1953) and *The Lyrics of Coward* (1965) are useful collections.

Of Coward's patriotic plays, the ambitious *Cavalcade*

(1931) has more admirers than *This Happy Breed* (1942) and *Peace in Our Time* (1947). The best of his later work includes *Look after Lulu* (1959), an adaptation of a Feydeau farce, and the three plays performed under the general title *Suite in Three Keys* (1966). Coward also published two lively autobiographies, *Present Indicative* (1937) and *Future Indefinite* (1954), several volumes of short stories (*The Collected Short Stories*, 1962) and a novel, *Pomp and Circumstance* (1960).

Cowley, Abraham 1618–67 Poet. A Royalist, he spent the years 1644–54 in France as secretary to Henrietta Maria but submitted to Cromwell on his return to England (though he may have been a Royalist spy). At the Restoration he was reappointed to the fellowship at Trinity College, Cambridge, which he had originally been awarded in 1640. Thereafter he lived a retired life, studying botany and writing essays.

Cowley had begun writing at the age of 10 and had published two romantic epics by the time he was 15. His first collection of verse was *The Mistress: or, Several Copies of Love Verses* (1647). A multiple collection (1656) added *Miscellanies*, *Pindaric Odes* and four books of an Old Testament epic, *Davideis*. Later works included an 'Ode upon the Blessed Restoration' (1660), *A Discourse by Way of Vision Concerning the Government of Oliver Cromwell* (1661) and his *Proposition for the Advancement of Experimental Philosophy* (1661). A folio edition of his works (1668) contained *Several Discourses by way of Essays, in Verse and Prose*, the essays that kept his name alive. His reputation earned him a splendid tomb beside CHAUCER and SPENSER in Westminster Abbey, and JOHNSON made him the first subject of *THE LIVES OF THE POETS*, but Cowley's fame as a poet soon dwindled. His imitations of DONNE's high metaphysical style and the difficult measures of Pindar are energetic, learned and difficult to read.

Cowley, Hannah 1743–1809 Playwright and poet. In an age of generally turgid SENTIMENTAL COMEDY, her plays are refreshingly sprightly. *The Runaway* (1776), her first, was dedicated to GARRICK, who may have 'improved' it. *Who's the Dupe?* (1779) remained popular as a two-act afterpiece until the end of the century. *The Belle's Stratagem* (1780), her best work, held its own on the 19th-century stage. Hannah Cowley's career as poet involved her in a sentimental verse correspondence with Robert Merry, leader of the so-called DELLA CRUSCANS.

Cowper, William 1731–1800 Poet. His unhappy experiences at Westminster School gave him a vehement dislike of public school education, later voiced in 'Tirocinium' (1785). Though he studied law at the Inner Temple and was called to the Bar in 1754, he made no attempt to practise. Already suffering from bouts of depression, he deteriorated into unmistakable mania when, at the age of 32, he attempted suicide on the eve of a formal examination for a sinecure as Clerk of the Journals of the House of Lords. Throughout his life, the poet was fortunate to have a wide circle of friends who cared for his welfare, first with the Unwins in Huntingdon and then in Olney, Buckinghamshire. Here the widowed Mary Unwin was his companion, though the couple never married, and the Evangelical pastor John Newton became an influential friend. Cowper made several notable contributions to Newton's *Olney Hymns* (1779), including 'God Moves in a Mysterious Way'. Much of his best energy went into his direct and personal letters which show him, when not unwell, cheerfully intent upon a simple country existence. He also returned to poetry with *Anti-Thelyphthora: A Tale in Verse* (1781) and the series of eight satires contained in *Poems* (1782), which also includes 'The Shrubbery', 'Boadicea' and *Verses Supposed to be Written by Alexander Selkirk*. At the suggestion of his friend Lady Austen, he wrote *THE TASK*, in six books, published in 1785 in a volume which included *THE DIVERTING HISTORY OF JOHN GILPIN* (1782), also the result of Lady Austen's initiative.

Cowper and Mary Unwin moved in 1786 to nearby Weston Underwood, where he wrote a number of short poems published after his death, including 'The Poplar Field', 'On the Loss of the Royal George' and the fine sonnet 'To Mrs Unwin', and embarked on various translations, notably of the *Iliad* (1791). Mary Unwin's death in 1794 reduced him to the status of a physical and mental invalid for the rest of his life. He died at East Dereham, Norfolk, his last years yielding the depressingly powerful poem, 'The Castaway'. It is sometimes thought that Cowper did not take seriously enough his vocation as a poet, yet his quiet, direct verse addressing simple human and rural themes marked the point at which English poetry moved away from the concerns of NEO-CLASSICISM towards those of ROMANTICISM.

Cozzens, James Gould 1903–78 American novelist. His novels explore the social order of American life and its potential for stability and hierarchy, by portraying professional men caught in moral and cultural dilemmas. *The Last Adam* (1933) is about the medical profession, *Men and Brethren* (1936) is about the ministry, and *The Just and the Unjust* (1942) and *By Love Possessed* (1957), his most controversial novel, are about the law. *Guard of Honor* (1948) is an ambitious novel set during World War II. His last publications were *Children and Others* (children's stories; 1964) and *Morning, Noon and Night* (a novel; 1968).

Crabbe, George 1755–1832 Poet. Much of his life belonged to Suffolk. He was born at Aldeburgh and, after being educated and apprenticed elsewhere in the county, returned there in 1775 to practice as a surgeon. In the same year he published his first significant poem, *Inebriety*, a didactic SATIRE in the manner of POPE on the perils of drink. Committed to a literary career, he went to London in 1780 and, with EDMUND BURKE's help, published *The Library* (1781), another work showing Pope's influence. After a brief period as curate at Aldeburgh, he took holy orders and became chaplain to the Duke of Rutland at Belvoir in 1782–5. *THE VILLAGE* (1783) was praised by SAMUEL JOHNSON and established his reputation.

Though Crabbe continued to be intellectually active, there followed a period of more than 20 years during which Crabbe published nothing of importance. He held the living of Muston in Leicestershire from 1789 to 1814, though with long absences in Suffolk. *The Parish Register* (1807) inaugurated the second phase of his literary career, in which he emerged as a gifted exponent of verse narrative. The main part of the collection narrates the memories of a country parson as he leafs through the register of births, marriages and deaths. It includes 'Sir Eustace Grey', a remarkable poem portraying the hallucinations of a patient in a madhouse. *THE BOROUGH* (1810) consists of 24 'letters' describing the scenery and life of a country town based on his native Aldeburgh; *Peter Grimes* is the most memorable. *Tales* followed in 1812. After the death of his wife he became vicar of Trowbridge, Wiltshire, in 1814, though he kept in contact with London and literary circles, in which his friends included THOMAS MOORE, SAMUEL ROGERS,

SOUTHEY, WORDSWORTH and SIR WALTER SCOTT. His *London Journal* of 1817 was later printed in the *Life* by his son. *The World of Dreams* was written in 1817, while 1819 saw the publication of *Tales of the Hall*. In 1822 he wrote *In a Neat Cottage*, and in 1823 a collected edition of his *Works* appeared. Some of his unpublished work was incorporated into the last volume of his eight-volume *Poetical Works* (1834).

Although Crabbe first made his reputation as a poet in the age of Johnson, his best work was contemporary with that of the Romantics. He was not, however, simply a survival from the AUGUSTAN AGE, despite his almost unbroken fidelity to the HEROIC COUPLET and his firm commitment to that period's values of sense, judgement, moderation and balance. His tales are an original achievement in a new art form, probing the psychological, social and moral textures of the post-classical epoch. He was much admired by Scott, AUSTEN and BYRON, who saw him as 'Nature's sternest painter yet the best'.

Cradle Will Rock, The A musical drama of social protest, with lyrics and music by MARC BLITZSTEIN, produced in 1937. It brings techniques of classical opera together with elements of popular music to tell the story of a strike in 'Steeltown, USA'. The characters – like the owner of the steel mill, Mr Mister – are representative types rather than realistic individuals.

Craik, Dinah Maria See MULOCK, DINAH.

Crane, (Harold) Hart 1899–1932 American poet. In a career cut short by his suicide at the age of 33, he produced a significant body of poetry strongly influenced by French SYMBOLISM and by T. S. ELIOT. Using dramatic rhetoric and exotic diction, it often drew on images of water and the sea as material for symbolic and psychological speculations. His first book of poetry, *White Buildings*, was published in 1926, his *Collected Poems* in 1933. Crane is best known for *THE BRIDGE* (1930), a long poem written partly in response to the negativism of *THE WASTE LAND*.

Crane, Stephen 1871–1900 American novelist and short-story writer. Born in New Jersey, he worked as a journalist while writing his first novel, eventually published as *MAGGIE* (1893). It was not widely noticed but *THE RED BADGE OF COURAGE* (1895) achieved critical and popular success. A collection of short stories, *The Little Regiment* (1896) again dealt with the Civil War, while another novel, *George's Mother* (1896), turned to working-class life in New York. *The Third Violet* (1897) is a short novel about a young artist. *The Monster* (1898) is a volume of short stories. The novel *Active Service* (1899) derived from his experience of the Graeco-Turkish War. *The Black Rider* (1895) and *War is Kind* (1900) are collections of poetry. Until his health betrayed him Crane continued to work as a journalist, travelling to the Southwest, Mexico, Cuba and Greece. His experience after a shipwreck on his Cuban trip formed the basis for one of his most famous stories, the title piece of *The Open Boat and Other Stories* (1898). After settling in England he met JOSEPH CONRAD and HENRY JAMES, two of his most distinguished admirers. Posthumous publications include the sketches and stories from his life as a correspondent in *Wounds in the Rain* (1900); and *Whilomville Stories* (1900), about a childhood in a small town in New York state.

Crane, Walter 1845–1915 Artist and illustrator of CHILDREN'S LITERATURE. A friend of WILLIAM MORRIS, he designed mosaics, friezes and wallpapers and became the first president of the Arts and Crafts Society. He is best remembered for the children's picture-books commissioned by the pioneer colour printer Edmund Evans, which include classics like *The Railroad Alphabet*, *The House That Jack Built* and *Sing a Song of Sixpence*. Most popular of all, and still in print today, was *The Baby's Opera* (1877), a collection of traditional nursery rhymes where text, music and illustration come together in one diminutive but pleasing whole.

Cranford A novel by ELIZABETH GASKELL, serialized in *HOUSEHOLD WORDS* in 1851–3. Set in the early 19th century, it describes the warm-hearted Miss Matilda (Miss Matty) Jenkyns and her little circle of genteel spinsters and widows. A tenuous narrative takes Miss Matty from quiet satisfaction to adversity resolved by the reappearance of a long-lost brother. This is less important than the series of vignettes which gently reveal Miss Matty's essential virtue and the small foibles of the other characters: the pompous Mrs Jamieson and her awesome butler, Mulliner; the genial, straightforward Captain Brown, killed while looking up too late from reading; Miss Deborah Jenkyns, Miss Matty's elder sister and an ardent Johnsonian; and Martha, the cumbersome but loyal housemaid.

Cranmer, Thomas 1489–1556 Divine. Appointed Archbishop of Canterbury in 1533, he remained in office through the Reformation, thus becoming Canterbury's first Anglican archbishop. In co-operation with Thomas Cromwell he promoted publication of the BIBLE IN ENGLISH and wrote a prologue to the Great Bible of 1539. He composed a litany for the reformed church of 1545, was responsible for the publication of the *Homilies* in 1547 and supervised the first and second Edwardian prayer-books of 1549 and 1552 (see BOOK OF COMMON PRAYER). His other works include a controversy with Stephen Gardiner, a catechism and a treatise on the Eucharist. Under Queen Mary he was condemned for treason in 1553, degraded from ecclesiastical office and burned as a heretic.

Crashaw, Richard 1612–49 Poet. Deprived of his fellowship at Peterhouse, Cambridge, with the defeat of the Royalists in the Civil War, he went into exile on the Continent, became a Roman Catholic, and ended his days in a minor office at the Cathedral of Loreto. His chief collection of verse, *Steps to the Temple. Sacred Poems with Other Delights of the Muses* (1646; enlarged edition, 1648), was made more complete by the posthumous *Carmen Deo Nostro* (1652), edited by his friend Miles Pinkney. Except for the secular lyric 'Wishes: To His (Supposed) Mistress' and some translations, notably 'Love's Duel' (from the Latin), his poetry is religious. It is notable for CONCEITS carried to the extreme of baroque extravagance.

Crawford, Francis Marion 1854–1909 American novelist. The nephew of JULIA WARD HOWE, he had a cosmopolitan upbringing and travelled widely, becoming an accomplished linguist. *Mr Isaacs: A Tale of Modern India* (1882) was the first of almost 50 successful romances, historical novels and tales of adventure. They include *A Tale of a Lonely Parish* (1886), *Don Orsini* (1891), *Corleone: A Tale of Sicily* (1896), *Via Crucis* (1898), *In the Palace of the King: A Love Story of Old Madrid* (1900) and *The White Sister* (1909). *The Novel: What It Is* (1893) identified his purpose as being simply to entertain. Many of his novels were adapted for the stage, and the play *Francesca da Rimini* (1902) was written for Sarah Bernhardt.

Crawford, Isabella Valancy 1850–87 Canadian poet. She was born in Dublin, but her parents settled in

Canada in about 1858. Though well reviewed in England, *Old Spookses' Pass, Malcolm's Katie and Other Poems* (1884) only sold some 50 copies and her reputation depended on the posthumous *Collected Poems* (1905). Exuberant and vigorous, her poetry frequently uses mythological material drawn from classical legends, the Bible and folk-stories.

Creeley, Robert 1926– American poet. He has been associated with both the BLACK MOUNTAIN SCHOOL and the BEATS. *The Collected Poems of Robert Creeley, 1945–1975* (1982) brings together all his important early work. Prose works include: a novel, *The Island* (1963); a collection of short stories, *The Gold Diggers* (1954); *Was That a Real Poem and Other Essays* (1979), edited by Donald Allen; and *The Collected Prose* (1984). *Charles Olson and Creeley: The Complete Correspondence* (1980–3), a five-volume edition by George F. Butterick, is invaluable.

Creevey, Thomas 1768–1838 Politician. *The Creevey Papers* (1903), a selection from his gossip, irreverent letters and diaries, sheds light on the political and social life of his era.

Creighton, Mandell 1843–1901 Historian. Professor of ecclesiastical history at Cambridge (1884), Bishop of Peterborough (1891) and Bishop of London (1897), he made his reputation with *A History of the Papacy during the Period of the Reformation* (1882–94), praised for its detachment and erudition, and became first editor of *The English Historical Review* in 1886.

Crèvecoeur, J. Hector St John de 1735–1813 American essayist. Born in Normandy, and educated in France and England, he went to Quebec to serve in Montcalm's army in 1754. Subsequent travels are described in *Voyage dans la Haute Pennsylvanie et dans l'état de New York* (1801). Naturalized as an American colonial citizen, he settled on a farm in Orange County, New York, in 1769. *LETTERS FROM AN AMERICAN FARMER* was written while in exile from America during the Revolution; it was first published in London in 1782 and in Philadelphia in 1793. Crèvecoeur returned to America in 1783 and served as French consul, retiring to France in 1790. Further letters and essays eventually appeared as *Sketches of Eighteenth Century America* (1925).

Cricket on the Hearth, The A Christmas story by DICKENS, published in 1845 and collected in *CHRISTMAS BOOKS* (1852). After he introduces an elderly stranger into his house, John Peerybingle becomes jealous of his younger wife Dot but is prevented from wreaking vengeance by the 'Cricket on the Hearth in Faery shape'. Meanwhile, the villainous Tackleton woos Dot's friend, May Fielding, but is forestalled by the stranger, really her fiancé, the young Edward Plummer. Another narrative strand concerns Edward's blind sister Bertha and their father, the simple Caleb, who works for Tackleton. The story ends with reconciliation and rejoicing, in which even Tackleton joins.

Criterion, The A literary quarterly founded and edited by T. S. ELIOT, published from 1922 to 1939. *THE WASTE LAND* appeared in its first issue. Eliot's editorial 'Commentary' expounded his right-wing, Anglo-Catholic and classicist doctrine of order, and at times expressed admiration for fascism. This did not prevent him from publishing younger writers of different persuasions, such as AUDEN, HART CRANE, EMPSON, D. H. LAWRENCE and SPENDER.

Critic, The: or, *A Tragedy Rehearsed* A comedy-burlesque by RICHARD BRINSLEY SHERIDAN, first produced in 1779. Modelled on BUCKINGHAM'S *THE REHEARSAL* (1671), it is given added point by the exasperation Sheridan must often have felt as manager of DRURY LANE. In the first act, Dangle, a man obsessed with theatrical affairs, reads the paper and discusses the issues of the day; various figures are mocked, in particular CUMBERLAND as Sir Fretful Plagiary. In the second and third acts, Puff introduces and then exhibits a rehearsal of his appalling tragedy, the hilarious *Spanish Armada*.

Critical Quarterly, The A literary journal founded by C. B. Cox and A. E. Dyson in 1959. It publishes poems, reviews and critical articles with a strong emphasis on modern literature. Contributing poets have included LARKIN, TED HUGHES, R. S. THOMAS and CHARLES TOMLINSON.

Crockett, S. R. See KAILYARD SCHOOL.

Croker, John Wilson 1780–1857 Essayist and critic. A founder of THE QUARTERLY REVIEW, he is remembered for his savage review of KEATS's *Endymion*. *Essays on the Early Period of the French Revolution* (1857) was a collection of *Quarterly* papers. He also edited *Royal Memoirs of the French Revolution* (1823) and BOSWELL's LIFE OF JOHNSON (1831). Croker is said to have been the model for Rigby in DISRAELI's CONINGSBY.

Croker, T(homas) Crofton 1798–1854 Irish folklorist. *Fairy Legends and Traditions of the South of Ireland* (1825) is valuable both as an act of preservation and as a stimulus to further researches and to writers such as Wilhelm Grimm, SIR WALTER SCOTT, MARIA EDGEWORTH and YEATS.

Croly, George 1780–1860 Poet and playwright. Apart from his tragedy, *Catiline* (1822), he wrote narrative poems: *Salathiel* (1829), using the theme of the 'wandering Jew' to describe life in Rome under Nero and Jerusalem at the time of its destruction by Titus, and *Marton* (1846), set in the French Revolution and Napoleonic wars.

Crompton, Richmal [Lamburn, Richmal Crompton] 1890–1969 Novelist and writer of CHILDREN'S LITERATURE. The mischievous small boy called William, his irritable father, long-suffering mother and permanently suspicious older brother and sister were introduced in short stories for magazines, first collected in *Just William* (1922). At first, the 'William' stories were also aimed at a grown-up audience, allowing her creator to enjoy the mayhem he brings to his family and its suburban environs without adding any admonitory note. More 'William' books followed in quick succession after the success of *Just William*, outshining Richmal Crompton's modestly successful adult fiction. By the time of her death more than 8 million copies had been sold, and William had also been featured on radio, film and television.

Cronin, A(rchibald) J(oseph) 1896–1981 Novelist. After the success of *Hatter's Castle* (1931) he abandoned medicine for popular novels drawing on his Scottish childhood and experience of the Welsh coal-mining valleys. Like *Hatter's Castle*, many became successful films: *The Stars Look Down* (1935) in 1939, *The Keys of the Kingdom* (1942) in 1944 and *The Green Years* (1944) in 1946. *Jupiter Laughs* (1940) is a play, and *Adventures in Two Worlds* (1952) an autobiography. Later works included *The Judas Tree* (1961) and *A Pocketful of Rye* (1969).

Crossing the Bar A short poem by TENNYSON, published in 1889. Written while crossing the Solent (he lived on the Isle of Wight), it contemplates the prospect of death. It was his wish that it should appear at the end of all editions of his poems.

Crotchet Castle A novel by PEACOCK, published in 1831. As in NIGHTMARE ABBEY and GRYLL GRANGE, the plot is minimal and subordinate to a conversation about conservatism and progress which serves as vehicle for Peacock's highly individual brand of SATIRE. The chief participant is the Rev. Dr Folliott, gourmet, classicist and Tory, who disputes with other characters, notably Mr Skionar, a transcendental philosopher resembling COLERIDGE, Mr MacQuedy, a Scottish political economist, and Mr Chainmail, in love with the Middle Ages.

Crothers, Rachel 1878–1958 American playwright. She wrote many box-office successes during her long career. They include *The Three of Us* (1906), *A Little Journey* (1918), *He and She* (1920), *Nice People* (1921), *Mary the Third* (1923), *Let Us be Gay* (1929) and *Susan and God* (1937), all concerned with the possibility of freedom for women in a world dominated by men. Other notable works are *A Man's World* (1910), *Young Wisdom* (1914), *Old Lady 31* (1916), *39 East* (1919), *Expressing Willie* (1924), *A Lady's Virtue* (1925), *As Husbands Go* (1931) and *When Ladies Meet* (1932).

Crowe, Catherine 1800–76 Novelist, short-story writer and writer of CHILDREN'S LITERATURE. Her novels included *Susan Hopley* (1841) and *Lilly Dawson* (1847), but her most popular work was a collection of stories on ghostly and supernatural themes, *The Night Side of Nature* (1848).

Crowne, John c. 1640–1712 Playwright. His dislike of court manners may have resulted from his service as a gentleman usher to a London lady. Nevertheless, he wrote an impressive court MASQUE, *Calisto* (1675). His comedies, much better than his tragedies, are unusually firm in their moral judgements. They include *The Country Wit* (1676), *City Politiques* (1683), the excellent *Sir Courtly Nice* (1685) and *The Married Beau* (1694).

Crucible, The A play by ARTHUR MILLER, first performed in 1953. It deals with the Salem witch-trials of 1692. To cover their misdeeds, Abigail and her friends denounce their neighbours to the witch-finders. One by one the weak and the virtuous are brought to trial, condemned, and hanged. The strongest resistance comes from John Proctor, whom Abigail had seduced when she was working for his wife. His wife lovingly denies his confession of adultery and Proctor dies knowing that society has lost its ability to distinguish between good and evil. Written at the height of Senator McCarthy's campaign against Communists, the play draws a clear analogy between McCarthyism and the Salem witch-hunt.

Cruden, Alexander 1701–70 Compiler of *Cruden's Concordance* to the Bible, first published in 1737, a standard word-guide to the Authorized Version (see BIBLE IN ENGLISH). Thorough and accurate, but eccentric and sometimes mad, Cruden embarked on 'Alexander the Corrector's' campaign against proof errors. He died disappointed.

Cruelty, Theatre of A style of theatre advocated by the French actor Antonin Artaud in two manifestoes (1932 and 1933). Believing that 'the theatre only exists on a level which is not quite human', Artaud sought to uproot the complacency of audiences and to present human behaviour under extreme threat of provocation. No prominent English playwrights can be properly called his disciples, though he himself enlisted in the prospective repertoire of his theatre SHELLEY's THE CENCI, TOURNEUR's THE REVENGER'S TRAGEDY and JOHN FORD's 'TIS PITY SHE'S A WHORE.

Cruikshank, George 1792–1878 Caricaturist and illustrator. In addition to a long and successful career in political caricature, and the impassioned advocacy of temperance which occupied much of his later years, he also illustrated books by many contemporaries. These include: PIERCE EGAN'S *LIFE IN LONDON* (with his brother Robert, 1821); DICKENS'S *SKETCHES BY BOZ* (1836–7) and *OLIVER TWIST* (1839), in which he is reputed to have used himself as the model for Fagin; *Jack Sheppard* (1839) and other novels by AINSWORTH; and HARRIET BEECHER STOWE'S *UNCLE TOM'S CABIN* (1853).

Cuckoo and the Nightingale, The [*The Boke of Cupide*] A poem probably written between 1390 and 1403, generally attributed to Sir JOHN CLANVOWE. It formed part of the CHAUCERIAN APOCRYPHA because of its debt to *THE PARLEMENT OF FOULES*. In a DREAM-VISION the narrator overhears a cuckoo, against love, debating with a nightingale, who praises it; he sides with the nightingale.

Cudworth, Ralph 1617–88 Philosopher. His chief work, *The True Intellectual System of the Universe* (unfinished but published 1678), is also the chief exposition of the principles of the CAMBRIDGE PLATONISTS; it argues that the Christian religion is the only real source of knowledge. His *Treatise concerning Eternal and Immutable Morality* was published posthumously (1731).

Cullen, Countee 1903–46 Black American poet and leading figure of the HARLEM RENAISSANCE. His volumes include: *Color* (1925); *Copper Sun* (1927); *The Ballad of the Brown Girl: An Old Ballad Retold* (1927); *The Black Christ, and Other Poems* (1929), the title piece of which recounts the lynching of a black youth for a crime he did not commit; and *The Medea and Some Poems* (1935), a collection of SONNETS and short lyrics together with a translation of Euripides' tragedy. His only novel, *One Way to Heaven* (1932), is a social comedy of lower-class blacks and the bourgeoisie in New York. He also edited the magazine *Opportunity* and an anthology of black poetry, *Caroling Dusk* (1927).

Culture and Anarchy: *An Essay in Political and Social Criticism* A volume by MATTHEW ARNOLD, published in 1869. It portrays the England of his time as being in political, social and religious ferment, and seeks to show that the remedy lies in culture, the supreme realization of the human spirit under reason, defined in the opening chapters as 'a study of perfection' whose purpose is 'To render an intelligent being more intelligent' and 'To make reason and the will of God prevail'. Succeeding chapters chart the drift towards anarchy through an excess of liberty, unrestrained by any centre of authority. None of the various classes – barbarians (aristocracy), philistines (middle class) and populace (lower class) – provides an adequate centre of authority. Similarly, the two great traditions of Hebraism, with its 'strictness of conscience', and Hellenism, with its 'spontaneity of consciousness', have vied with each other in English life down the centuries instead of being complementary.

Cumberland, Richard 1732–1811 Playwright. His SENTIMENTAL COMEDIES, or 'bastard tragedies' as GOLDSMITH called them, often avert disaster only because of a villain's unlikely change of heart in the fifth act. Plays popular in their own time, like *The Brothers* (1769), *The West Indian* (1771) and *The Jew* (1794), can best be read as transitional pieces, carrying sentimental comedy towards MELODRAMA. Cumberland wrote nearly 50 plays as well as three novels, *Arundel* (1789), *Henry* (1795) and *John de Lancaster* (1809), a few vol-

umes of negligible verse, two volumes of *Memoirs* (1806–7), scores of journalistic essays and two books on Spanish painters and painting.

cummings, e(dward) e(stlin) 1894–1962 American poet. He created a memorable and idiosyncratic style, first announced in *&* and *is 5* (both 1925), influenced by jazz and contemporary slang and characterized by innovative use of punctuation and typography, as in the use of lower case letters for his own name. His other works include *Tulips and Chimneys* (1923), *XLI Poems* (1925), *Vi Va* (1931), *No Thanks* (1935), *1/20* (1936), *Collected Poems* (1938), *50 Poems* (1940), *1 x 1* (1944), *Poems 1923–1954* (1954), *Ninety-Five Poems* (1958), *73 Poems* (1963) and *Complete Poems 1913–1962* (1972). He also published a novel, *The Enormous Room* (1922), based on his mistaken imprisonment in a French detention centre during World War I, two plays, a book of drawings and paintings, a travel book, and *i, six nonlectures* (1953).

Cunningham, Alan 1784–1842 Miscellaneous writer. His first volume, *Remains of Nithsdale and Galloway Songs* (1810), innocently published as authentic old Scottish BALLADS, was followed by *Songs, Chiefly in the Rural Dialect of Scotland* (1813), *Traditional Tales of the English and Scottish Peasantry* (1822), *Songs of Scotland, Ancient and Modern* (1825) and *Lives of the Most Eminent British Painters, Sculptors and Architects* (1829–33) and an edition of BURNS'S poety with important new material. His romances and longer dramatic poems are little read today and he is chiefly remembered by a handful of poems and ballads, which include 'A Wet Hat Sheet and a Flowering Sea' and 'Hame, Hame, Hame'.

Cunningham, J(ames) V(incent) 1911–85 American poet. The poems in his first three volumes – *The Helmsman* (1942), *The Judge is Fury* (1947) and *Doctor Drink* (1950) – are notable for their economy of presentation, and their use of precise METRES and traditional verse forms. An accomplished Renaissance scholar, Cunningham was drawn to the EPIGRAM, publishing *Trivial, Vulgar, & Exalted: Epigrams* (1957). *The Collected Poems and Epigrams of J. V. Cunningham* and *Selected Poems* were both published in 1971. *Collected Essays* appeared in 1976.

Cunninghame Graham, R(obert) B(ontine) 1852–1936 Short-story writer, essayist, traveller and social reformer. He entered Parliament as a Liberal but became a socialist and disciple of WILLIAM MORRIS, receiving a six weeks' prison sentence for assaulting the police during a demonstration. He is chiefly remembered for *Mogreb-el-Aksa* (1898), an extraordinary account – much admired by SHAW and CONRAD – of his journey to discover the forbidden city of Tarudant in Morocco. Other works include *Thirteen Stories* (1900), *A Vanished Arcadia* (the story of the Jesuit settlements in Paraguay; 1901), *Success* (1902) and *Scottish Stories* (1914).

cup-and-saucer drama See ROBERTSON, THOMAS WILLIAM.

Curnow, Allen 1911– New Zealand poet, playwright, critic and editor. Early volumes such as *Not in Narrow Seas* (1939), *Island and Time* (1941) and *At Dead Low Water* (1949) set out to create a national tradition or myth. Two anthologies, *A Book of New Zealand Verse* (1945) and *The Penguin Book of New Zealand Verse* (1960), defined a canon in terms of his belief that the best poetry must be local. This poetic has been the biggest single influence on post-World War II poetry in New Zealand. Influenced by WALLACE STEVENS, Curnow's own work became more personal in *Poems 1949–57* (1957) and *A Small Room with*

Large Windows (1962). Later volumes such as *An Incorrigible Music* (1979), *You Will Know When You Get There* (1982), *The Loop in Lone Kauri Road* (1986) and *Continuum* (1988) together constitute the most sustained achievement in New Zealand poetry. Without abandoning the concerns of his earlier work, they treat them less self-consciously, with greater openness of form and in language more obviously influenced by MODERNISM. Curnow has also published four verse dramas and satirical verse under the pseudonym Whim-Wham.

Cursor Mundi [*The Course of the World*] An anonymous Middle English poem, probably early 14th-century. A spiritual history of the world from the Creation to Doomsday, it deals at length with the principal episodes of both Testaments as well as apocryphal material. The poet succeeds in maintaining unity and purpose despite the length and diversity of his material; his language is plain, his verse skilful and his sense of humanity evident. The work was widely known, and survives in several manuscripts.

Curzon, Robert, 14th Baron Zouche 1810-73 Traveller, writer and manuscript collector. His early travels resulted in *Visits to Monasteries in the Levant* (1849) and *Armenia* (1854). The manuscripts he collected were deposited in the British Museum after his death. Curzon's life and interests are well documented by a collection of unpublished letters to his friend the Rev. Walter Sneyd, now in Keele University Library.

Cymbeline A play by SHAKESPEARE, first performed *c.* 1610 and published in the First Folio of 1623. Of its various sources, HOLINSHED's *Chronicles* is primary only in the sense that it deals with the reign of the early Christian king, Cymbeline. The play stands with *PERICLES, THE WINTER'S TALE* and *THE TEMPEST*, all written to satisfy the new fashion for spectacle and romance. Its emotional centre is the love of Imogen, Cymbeline's daughter, and Posthumus Leonatus, whom the King has raised. Angered by their marriage, Cymbeline banishes Posthumus, and the intrigues and complications that delay his reunion with Imogen make the matter of the plot, which can be seen as a prolonged testing of their love. In Rome he meets the cynical Iachimo, who wagers he can seduce Imogen. He fails but provides circumstantial evidence to convince Posthumus he has succeeded. Posthumus swears vengeance and sails for England intent on killing her. Cymbeline's second wife, another schemer against the marriage, wants Posthumus dead so that her oafish son Cloten can marry Imogen. Imogen disguises herself as a boy (Fidele) and flees to Wales, where she becomes page to Belarius and Cymbeline's two lost sons, Guiderius and Arviragus. They protect her from Cloten and other hazards until, in a last act which has to work hard to achieve all the necessary reconciliations, Imogen and Posthumus are reunited and Cymbeline regains both his daughter and his two sons.

Cynewulf An Old English poet of the late 8th and early 9th centuries, Cynewulf is known through runic inscription of his name after four poems in the EXETER BOOK and the VERCELLI BOOK. One of them, *ELENE*, gives the only information known about him: that he had experienced some form of spiritual enlightenment, and was old at the time of writing. The other three poems are *The Ascension* (the second part of *CHRIST*), *JULIANA*, and *The Fates of the Apostles*.

Cynthia's Revels: *or, The Fountain of Self Love* A comedy by JONSON (performed in 1600 and published in 1601), which contributed to the 'war of the theatres'. It is chiefly memorable for its self-portrait of Jonson as Crites, judge of social and artistic standards, and for the lyric hymn to Diana, 'Queen and huntress, chaste and fair'.

dactyl See METRE.

Dafydd ap Gwilym *c.* 1320–80 Welsh poet, 'David son of William'. He was born, at Llanbadarn Fawr near Aberystwyth, into the influential landed gentry (*uchelwyr*) who maintained their prestige after the English conquest of Wales in 1284. He wrote in Welsh, his surviving works consisting of about 150 poems. Composed within a bardic tradition which had been absorbing Continental themes at least since the Norman Conquest, his poems have affinities with the HARLEY LYRICS and CHAUCER. His themes cover almost the entire range of medieval genres and *topoi*: COURTLY LOVE, dialogues between lovers, nature description, DREAM-VISION, humorous poems in a FABLIAU style. Most of his lyrics use: the *cywydd*, a traditional Welsh bardic metre widely practised in the 14th and 15th centuries; *cynghanedd*, an obligatory bardic device consisting of a complex and highly specific set of alliterative and rhyming patterns; *dyfalu*, compressed and striking images; and extended metaphors which develop a witty central image throughout the poem. The recurrent motifs of bardic patronage, the desirability of possessing women and land and the unremitting satire against bourgeois values all point to a context in which a traditional Welsh nobility guarded its privileges while aligning itself with the governing English aristocracy.

Dahl, Roald 1916–90 Writer of CHILDREN'S LITERATURE. *James and the Giant Peach* (1961), a good-humoured fantasy, was followed by the best-selling *Charlie and the Chocolate Factory* (1964). Its apparent cruelty upset many adult critics but young readers relished its excesses, and the verbal facility of *Revolting Rhymes* (1982) and *Dirty Beasts* (1984). The *BFG* (1982) won Dahl his first literary prize, although some critics objected to what they saw as sexism in *The Witches* (1983) and snobbery in *Matilda* (1988). *Boy* (1984) and *Going Solo* (1986) are vivid autobiographies of his early years.

Dahlberg, Edward 1900–77 American novelist and critic. *Bottom Dogs* (1929) is a semi-autobiographical novel about a childhood in slums and orphanages. A man of wide-ranging interests, Dahlberg went on to publish: *From Flushing to Calvary* (1932), about the slums of New York; *Those Who Perish* (1934), about the effects of Nazism on American Jews; studies of myth in *The Sorrows of Priapus* (1957) and *The Carnal Myth* (1968); essays on literature and society in *Do These Bones Live?* (1941), *The Flea of Sodom* (1950), *Truth is More Sacred* (1961) and *Alms for Oblivion* (1964); poetry; correspondence; and a richly eloquent autobiography, *Because I was Flesh* (1964).

Daily News, The A radical newspaper founded by DICKENS and edited by him from January until October 1846, when he was succeeded by JOHN FORSTER. It was absorbed by *The Daily Chronicle* in 1930 and became *The News Chronicle*, continuing under this name until 1960.

Daisy Miller A short novel by HENRY JAMES, published in 1879. Daisy tours Europe with her mother and brother. The expatriate American community interprets her lack of concern for social convention as immodesty, though one of its number, Frederick Winterbourne, is also charmed by her innocence. In Rome Daisy takes up with Giovanelli, a young Italian without social position, and visits the Coliseum with him at night. On meeting them, Winterbourne berates her. She returns to her hotel, contracts malaria and dies after a week.

Dallas, E(neas) S(weetland) 1828–79 Journalist and literary critic. He worked for *The Times* when J. T. DELANE was editor. His critical writing, *Poetics: An Essay on Poetry* (1852) and *The Gay Science* (1866), take a scientific approach to aesthetics, viewing the aim of art as pleasure and the imagination as a function of the unconscious mind.

Dalrymple, Sir David, Lord Hailes 1726–92 Scottish jurist, historian and man of letters. Political and religious differences did not deter him from becoming a friend of SAMUEL JOHNSON, BURKE, WALPOLE and Bishops Hurd, PERCY and Warburton. It was Dalrymple who fired the young BOSWELL with the desire to know Johnson. He contributed to *The World* and *THE GENTLEMAN'S MAGAZINE*, edited BALLADS and other ancient Scottish poetry, and produced his most significant historical work in *Annals of Scotland* (1776–9). Dalrymple took issue with EDWARD GIBBON, who approved his diligence and accuracy as a historian, in *An Inquiry into the Secondary Causes Which Mr Gibbon Has Assigned for the Rapid Growth of Christianity* (1786).

Daly, (John) Augustin 1838–99 American playwright and theatre manager. *Leah the Forsaken* (1862) was the first of about 100 plays which he wrote or, more often, adapted in regular collaboration with his brother Joseph. The best include spectacular MELODRAMAS like *Under the Gaslight* (1867), *The Flash of Lightning* (1868) and *The Red Scarf* (1868), and comedies about American high society like *Divorce* (1871), *Pique* (1875) and *Love on Crutches* (1884). *Horizon* (1871) is a frontier drama. At the Fifth Avenue Theatre from 1869 to 1873, and then at Daly's Theatre from 1879 until his death, he established the finest ensemble companies in America.

Dame Sirith A Middle English FABLIAU written *c.* 1272–83. It tells how the resourceful Dame Sirith helps Wilekin seduce Margery in her husband's absence. Much of the poem is in dialogue: it may have been intended for performance by several actors or, perhaps more likely, by a minstrel using mime to distinguish the different characters.

Damnation of Theron Ware, The See THERON WARE, THE DAMNATION OF.

Dana, Richard Henry, Jr 1815–82 American social reformer. He is chiefly remembered for *Two Years before the Mast* (1840), describing a voyage from Boston around Cape Horn to California with a vivid eye for the sufferings of his fellow seamen. It was followed by *The Seaman's Friend* (1841; as *The Seaman's Manual* in Britain), instructing sailors in their rights as well as their duties, and a less successful account of a later voyage, *To Cuba and Back* (1859). Dana had turned to the sea during an interlude in his studies at Harvard. After qualifying as a lawyer, he became a champion of the underprivileged and a vigorous opponent of slavery. His hopes of a political career were dashed by accusations of plagiarism levelled at his edition of Henry Wheaton's *Elements of International Law* (1866), and his appointment as ambassador to Great Britain was withdrawn by the Senate. He died, disappointed, in Europe.

Dance to the Music of Time, A A sequence of 12 novels by POWELL, consisting of *A Question of Upbringing* (1951), *A Buyer's Market* (1952), *The Acceptance World* (1955), *At Lady Molly's* (1957), *Casanova's Chinese Restaurant* (1960), *The Kindly Ones* (1962), *The Valley of Bones* (1964), *The Soldier's Art* (1966), *The Military Philosophers* (1968), *Books do Furnish a Room* (1971), *Temporary Kings* (1973) and *Hearing Secret Harmonies* (1975). The sequence is a ROMAN FLEUVE, constituting a history of 20th-century English life among artists and fashionable society as observed by the narrator, Nicholas Jenkins. His own life takes place 'off stage', but he is constantly present as the selective recorder of the temporal flow of events, eventually formalizing them into the pattern of a dance like the painting by Poussin from which the sequence takes its title. Among the most memorable characters in this epic enterprise is the power-hungry Kenneth Widmerpool.

Dane, Clemence [Ashton, Winifred] 1888-1965 Playwright and novelist. Her first and second novels, *Regiment of Women* (1917) and *Legend* (1919), were widely acclaimed, but she turned her attention to drama before returning to fiction with *Broome Stages* (1931), *The Moon is Feminine* (1938) and *He Brings Great News* (1944). Her first play, *A Bill of Divorcement* (1921), is about a woman who divorces her husband on grounds of insanity. Its success was never quite repeated by *Will Shakespeare* (1921), *Granite* (1926) and *Wild Decembers* (1932), about the BRONTËS.

Daniel An Old English poem in the Junius manuscript (see JUNIUS, FRANCIS), closely following the story of Daniel in Exodus. Though the style is generally flat and uninspiring, there are occasional vigorous passages like the description of the ordeal in the furnace.

Daniel, Samuel 1562/3–1619 Poet, translator, literary critic, historian and playwright. He tutored the future Earl of Pembroke, SHAKESPEARE's patron, and Lady Anne Clifford, daughter of the Countess of Cumberland. His literary range and choice of forms invite comparison with DRAYTON.

He is best remembered for *Delia*, a SONNET sequence influenced by Desportes and Tasso. Originally issued in 1592, it was revised and expanded over the years, swelling the number of sonnets from 50 to 57 by the 1601 edition of his *Works*. In 1592 Daniel also published *The Complaint of Rosamond*, in the manner of the poems in *THE MIRROR FOR MAGISTRATES*, adding to it his Senecan closet tragedy *CLEOPATRA* in 1594. *Civil Wars* (1595 and 1609), an incomplete verse epic about the Wars of the Roses, influenced Shakespeare's *RICHARD II* and the *HENRY IV* plays. Daniel's *Poetical Essays* (1599) included two new works: *Musophilus*, a verse colloquium on the literary life, and *Octavia*, a verse epistle in the manner of Ovid's *Heroides*. *A Defence of Rhyme* (1603) made sensible answer to CAMPION's *Observations in the Art of English Poesy*. *Certain Small Poems* (1605) contains *Philotas*, a tragedy on the story of a rebellion against Alexander the Great, which got Daniel into trouble because of its apparent sympathy with Essex's rebellion. It did not permanently damage his position at court, where his MASQUES were popular: *The Vision of the Twelve Goddesses* (1604), *Tethys' Festival* (1610), and *Hymen's Triumph* (1615). His last work was the ambitious *Collection of the History of England*, a prose narrative which had reached the reign of Edward III by the enlarged edition of 1618.

Daniel Deronda GEORGE ELIOT's last novel, published in 1876. It is principally concerned with the destinies of Daniel Deronda, the adopted child of an English aristocrat, and Gwendolen Harleth, the spoiled and selfish elder daughter of a widow. In order to avoid penury as her family approaches destitution, Gwendolen agrees to marry Henleigh Grandcourt, fully aware that he has children by his mistress. The marriage proves unhappy and Gwendolen finds herself drawn to Deronda for spiritual guidance. Deronda, who has rescued the Jewish girl, Mirah Lepidoth, from suicide, gradually discovers a dense Jewish world through Mirah and her brother, Mordecai. He eventually learns that he too is a Jew and the novel ends with his determination to seek for his ancient racial and religious roots in Palestine.

Although the novel has seemed awkward and unbalanced to some critics, it has also been acknowledged to be George Eliot's most ambitious work, combining scholarship and a challenging shape which contrasts the lax, aristocratic mores of her English characters with the fervour and moral intensity of her Jewish ones.

Dark, Eleanor 1901-85 Australian novelist. Her novels frequently explore the results of catastrophes and experiment with time. They include *Slow Dawning* (1932), *Prelude to Christopher* (1933), *Sun Across the Sky* (1937), *Waterway* (1938), *Return to Coolami* (1935) and *The Little Company* (1945). *The Timeless Land* (1941), *Storm of Time* (1948) and *No Barrier* (1953), a trilogy covering the first 25 years of the Sydney settlement, have been recognized as masterpieces of carefully researched historical REALISM.

Darley, George 1795-1846 Irish poet and critic. From the 1820s he contributed essays, mainly on drama, to *THE LONDON MAGAZINE* and later to *THE ATHENAEUM*. His poetry includes *The Errors of Ecstasie: A Dramatic Poem, with Other Pieces* (1822), *Sylvia: or, the May Queen: A Lyrical Drama* (1827) and *Nepenthe* (1835). His tragedy *Thomas à Becket: A Dramatic Chronicle* and his notable edition of the plays of BEAUMONT and FLETCHER appeared in 1840. He also published four popular guides to mathematics.

Darwin, Charles (Robert) 1809-82 Natural historian. The grandson of ERASMUS DARWIN, he attended Christ's College, Cambridge, in 1828-31. The most important formative period of his intellectual life was the five years (1831-6) he spent as naturalist on the survey ship *Beagle*. His *Journal of Researches into the Geology and Natural History of the Various Countries Visited by HMS Beagle* (1839) gives a thoughtful and highly readable account of his response to the tropics, his encounters with 'primitive' peoples, and his realization of how complex are the relations between living forms within an environment. MALTHUS's *Essay on Population* precipitated his theory of natural selection in the late 1830s. Recognizing from the start that 'descent with modification' removed humankind from its centrality in the natural order and undermined the time-honoured religious myths of Genesis, Darwin long delayed publication of his findings, wishing to buttress them with the most impregnable evidence. *THE ORIGIN OF SPECIES* (1859) was written rapidly, under the impetus of knowing that Alfred Russel Wallace had reached similar conclusions. Public response to his theories immediately recognized their implications for humankind and took offence at the implied kinship with other species.

Much of Darwin's later work emphasizes this kinship. *The Descent of Man and Selection in Relation to Sex* (1871) and *The Expression of the Emotions in Man and Animals* (1872) juxtapose material from anthropology, primate studies and sociology, disciplines which had themselves been partly formed by *The Origin of Species*. The emphasis on 'sexual selection' opened up connections between evolutionary theory and aesthetics and cultural studies. It also stimulated 'social Darwinism', developed by HERBERT SPENCER as much as Darwin himself, which redefined 'fitness' as physical and mental power. The result stressed a hierarchical order in society, a constant struggle for dominance by strong individuals, and a readiness to jettison the weak.

GEORGE ELIOT, SAMUEL BUTLER, THOMAS HARDY and JOSEPH CONRAD were among the 19th-century writers who responded to – and in Butler's case, contended against – Darwin's work. SHAW, H. G. WELLS and VIRGINIA WOOLF demonstrate how differently Darwin could be read in literary terms. In the 20th century his ideas have become part of the apparatus of assumptions to a degree which makes it difficult to track them independently, though their power is still manifest, particularly among writers of SCIENCE FICTION such as ISAAC ASIMOV and Stanislaw Lem.

Darwin, Erasmus 1731–1802 Botanist, poet and grandfather of CHARLES DARWIN. A physician, he practised for most of his life at Lichfield, where he established a botanical garden and wrote *The Botanic Garden*, a poem embodying Linnaeus' system. Part 2, *The Loves of the Plants*, appeared first, in 1789 and Part 1, *The Economy of Vegetation*, in 1791. It was ridiculed by FRERE and CANNING in *The Loves of the Triangles*, published in *THE ANTI-JACOBIN*. Darwin published his theory of the laws of organic life on the evolutionary principle in *Zoonomia* (1794–6) and *Phytologia* (1799).

Daryush, Elizabeth 1887–1977 Poet. The daughter of ROBERT BRIDGES, she ignored the innovations of POUND and ELIOT, clinging to traditional poetic procedures and archaic diction in *Charitessi 1911* (1912), seven books of *Verses* (1930–71), *The Last Man* (1936), *Selected Poems* (1972) and *Collected Poems* (1976). She is nevertheless important for her pioneering technical experiments with syllabic verse (see METRE).

Das, Kamala 1934– Indian poet. Her work can be both acerbic and tempestuous, radical and traditionally minded. Collections of verse in English include *Summer in Calcutta* (1965), *The Descendants* (1968), *The Old Playhouse and Other Poems* (1973) and a volume of poems, *Tonight, This Savage Rite* (with Pritish Nandy; 1979). Her work in Malayalam includes many short stories and an autobiography, *Ente Katha* ('My Story'; 1975).

D'Avenant, Sir William 1606–68 Playwright, poet and theatre manager. The son of an Oxford innkeeper, he took pains to encourage the rumour that SHAKESPEARE was his true father. In fact, he was the poet's godson. FULKE GREVILLE encouraged an interest in the theatre which resulted in *The Tragedy of Albovine* (1629), *The Cruel Brother* (1630) and *The Wits* (1636) as well as successful court MASQUES such as *The Temple of Love*. *Madagascar, with Other Poems* appeared in 1638, when D'Avenant succeeded JONSON as unofficial POET LAUREATE. He fought as a Royalist in the Civil War and continued work on his verse epic *Gondibert* (1651) while imprisoned in the Tower. MILTON may have helped him gain his pardon in 1654.

D'Avenant used his freedom to organize clandestine or 'private' theatrical performances, most notably *The Siege of Rhodes* (1656). It combined heroic drama with opera, both newcomers to the English stage. When the drama officially revived at the Restoration D'Avenant received one of Charles II's Letters Patent to form a com-

pany of players (see PATENT THEATRES). His theatre in Lincoln's Inn Fields brought Shakespeare back to the stage, albeit in a much-altered form, and introduced new ideas of presentation such as the proscenium, elaborate scenery, and the use of machinery. D'Avenant's patent passed in the next century to John Rich, who invested it in COVENT GARDEN.

David Copperfield A novel by DICKENS, published in monthly parts in 1849–50 and in volume form in 1850 as *The Personal History, Experience and Observations of David Copperfield the Younger, of Blunderstone Rookery, Which He Never Meant to be Published On Any Account*. David traces his childhood and youth, marred by his widowed mother's remarriage to Mr Murdstone and death, and by his experience working in a London factory (an incident modelled on Dickens's own boyhood suffering). Escaping from London, he takes refuge at Dover with his aunt, Betsey Trotwood, and, after a period of conventional schooling and a brief legal career, becomes a novelist. His marriage to Dora Spenlow proves unhappy but David is nonetheless devastated by her early death. His friendship for James Steerforth is equally disturbed by Steerforth's elopement with Emily, the niece of the Yarmouth fisherman, Mr Peggotty. He finally finds happiness with the faithful Agnes Wickfield, whom he has known since childhood and whose own future had seemed to be threatened by the wiles of her father's sometime clerk, Uriah Heep. The improvidence and verbal extravagance of Wilkins Micawber, with whom David lodges during his unhappy London days, is to some extent modelled on that of Dickens's own father.

David Simple, The Adventures of: Containing an Account of His Travels through the Cities of London and Westminster in the Search of a Real Friend. A novel by SARAH FIELDING, first published in 1744. Learning that his younger brother has tried to rob him of his inheritance, David sets out on a journey to rediscover honest friendship. Encounters with Mr Orgueil and his insolent wife, Mr Spatter and Mr Varnish nearly drive him to despair. Then he makes friends with three fellow victims of injustice, Cynthia, Camilla and Camilla's brother Valentine. David falls in love with Camilla, Valentine with Cynthia. The two couples settle down in a happy community established by David's generosity.

Davidson, Donald (Grady) 1893–1968 American poet, critic and historian. A member of the FUGITIVES, he edited the group's magazine, *The Fugitive* (1922–5). His poems were published in *An Outland Piper* (1924), *The Tall Men* (1927), *Lee in the Mountains, and Other Poems* (1938), *The Long Street* (1961) and *Poems, 1922–1961* (1966). Other writings include *The Attack on Leviathan: Regionalism and Nationalism in the United States* (1938), *Still Rebels, Still Yankees, and Other Essays* (1957), *Southern Writers in The Modern World* (1958) and *The Spyglass: Views and Reviews, 1924–1930* (1963).

Davidson, John 1857–1909 Poet, playwright, novelist and essayist. Although he wrote from an early age, he did not abandon his uncongenial teaching job in Scotland until 1889, the year he published a volume of plays which included a striking fantasy, *Scaramouch in Naxos*. Settled in London, he contributed to *THE YELLOW BOOK*, attended meetings of the RHYMERS' CLUB and, as well as novels, published several important volumes of poetry: *Fleet Street Eclogues* (1893), *Ballads and Songs* (1894), *A Second Series of Fleet Street Eclogues* (1896), *New Ballads* (1897) and *The Last Ballad* (1899). 'Thirty Bob a Week' is the best-known poem to show his satiric bent, colloquial language and fascination with the meaner aspects of urban life. The decade before his death by suicide was exceptionally fertile. As well as short stories, adaptations from the French, journalism, prose sketches and a series of poetic dramas, Davidson produced *Testaments* propounding his philosophy of life, fashioned from contemporary science, revolt against Christianity and perhaps his reading of Nietzsche: *The Testament of a Vivisector* (1901), *The Testament of a Man Forbid* (1901), *The Testament of an Empire-Builder* (1902), *The Testament of a Prime Minister* (1904) and *The Testament of John Davidson* (1908).

Davie, Donald (Alfred) 1922– Poet and critic. *Purity of Diction in English Verse* (1952; revised, 1992) and *Articulate Energy* (1955) established him as the major theorist of the MOVEMENT by their advocacy of 'Augustinian' discipline in poetic language. Davie subsequently modified his position, as exposure to European and American literature made him critical of 'Little-Englandism' among his contemporaries. His own poetry, gathered in successive versions of *Collected Poems* (1972, 1983 and 1990), charts a similar development from a cerebral to a more experimental style. Other critical studies include books on POUND (1964) and HARDY (1972), *Czesław Miłosz and the Insufficiency of Lyric* (1986), *Under Briggflatts: A History of Poetry in Britain 1940–1980* (1989) and *Slavic Excursions* (1990). *These the Companions* (1982) is a volume of memoirs.

Davies, Idris 1905–53 Poet. One of the few genuinely working-class poets to emerge from the 1930s, he produced two sequences about the Welsh valleys, *Gwalia Deserta* (1938) and *Angry Summer* (1943), as well as *Tonypandy* (1945) and *Selected Poems* (1953).

Davies, John c. 1565–1618 Poet, usually called John Davies of Hereford (his birthplace) to distinguish him from his contemporary SIR JOHN DAVIES. He wrote a philosophical poem, *Mirum in Modum: A Glimpse of God's Glory and the Soul's Shape* (1602), the physiological and psychological *Microcosmos* (1603) and *Humours Heaven on Earth* (1605), a description of the plague of 1603. *The Scourge of Folly* (c. 1610) is a book of complimentary EPIGRAMS addressed to SHAKESPEARE, DONNE, JONSON and DANIEL, among others.

Davies, Sir John 1569–1626 Poet. Davies was a lawyer who became, thanks to royal favour, Solicitor General of Ireland and Speaker of the Irish Parliament but died the day before he was to have become Lord Chief Justice of England.

His most intense period of poetic activity was between 1593 and 1599. *Orchestra: or, A Poem of Dancing* (1596) has traditionally been read as a solemn celebration of the harmonious and hierarchical 'Elizabethan world picture', although Davies's contemporaries saw it as a frivolous poem, and the author himself invokes 'Terpsichore, my light muse'. *Nosce Teipsum* ('Know Thyself', 1599) is an expository poem on natural philosophy and the immortality of the soul, its faculties and its relation to the body and to the senses. *Hymns of Astraea* (1599) is a collection of ACROSTIC poems spelling out 'Elisabetha Regina'. Davies's other poetry includes the usual SONNETS produced by poets in the 1590s, and also 'Gulling Sonnets' which mock PETRARCHAN convention. He was also a writer of occasional verse, verse paraphrases of the Psalms, and satirical EPIGRAMS which earned for him the description of 'our English Martial'.

Davies, Robertson 1913– Canadian novelist, essayist and playwright. He has achieved distinction in several fields during a long and varied career. As editor of *The Peterborough Examiner*, a paper previously owned by his father, he contributed articles under the pseudonym of Samuel Marchbanks, collected as *The Diary of Samuel Marchbanks* (1947), *The Table Talk of Samuel Marchbanks* (1949) and *Marchbanks' Almanack* (1967). His commitment to the theatre made him a successful stage director, taking an important part in the Ontario Stratford Shakespeare Festival. His plays include *Fortune, My Foe* (1949), *A Jig for the Gypsy* (1954) and *Hunting Stuart and Other Plays* (1972). His major reputation is as a novelist, even though he was 38 before he published *Tempest-Tost* (1951). Together with *Leaven of Malice* (1954) and *A Mixture of Frailties* (1958), it makes up *The Salterton Trilogy*, the first of three major trilogies. The second and finest is THE DEPTFORD TRILOGY: *Fifth Business* (1970), *The Manticore* (1972) and *World of Wonders* (1975). *The Cornish Trilogy* consists of *The Rebel Angels* (1981), *What's Bred in the Bone* (1985) and *The Lyre of Orpheus* (1988). *Murther and Walking Spirits* (1991) makes thoughtful, witty use of the supernatural. Strongly influenced by his interest in Jungian archetypes, his fiction is about myth, magic and miracles, contrasting the limited perspectives offered by provincial Canada with the psychic fulfilment to be discovered through encounters with the 'world of wonders'.

Davies, W(illiam) H(enry) 1871–1940 Poet and writer of autobiography. He is usually remembered for his *Autobiography of a Super-Tramp* (with a preface by SHAW, 1908), describing his itinerant adventures in the USA, Canada and England. A prolific poet, he published *The Soul's Destroyer* (1905) at his own expense and went on to win praise from EDWARD THOMAS among others with *New Poems* (1907) and *Nature Poems and Others* (1908). His *Collected Poems* (1943) contained both nature lyrics and poems reflecting the harsher side of his life on the road. *Complete Poems* (1963) was introduced by OSBERT SITWELL. Davies also wrote two novels, *A Weak Woman* (1911) and *Dancing Mad* (1927), and more autobiography in *Beggars* (1909), *The True Traveller* (1912), *A Poet's Pilgrimage* (1918) and *Later Days* (1925). *Young Emma*, posthumously published in 1980, describes his courtship and marriage to his young wife in 1923.

Davin, Dan(iel) 1913–90 New Zealand novelist and short-story writer. He went to Oxford as a Rhodes Scholar in 1936 and returned there after World War II to work for Oxford University Press. He established his reputation as a leading New Zealand writer with a series of realistic novels: *Cliffs of Fall* (1945); *For the Rest of Our Lives* (1947), about his war experiences; *Roads from Home* (1949); and *The Sullen Bell* (1956), about New Zealanders in post-war London. *The Gorse Blooms Pale* (1947) is a volume of short stories. Later work, sometimes judged not to fulfil his early promise, included: *Not Here, Not Now* (1970) and *Brides of Price* (1972), both novels; *Breathing Spaces* (1975), short stories; and *Closing Times* (1975), a volume of memoirs.

Daviot, Gordon See MACKINTOSH, ELIZABETH.

Davis, Dick 1945– Poet. His work in *Shade Mariners* (with ROBERT WELLS and Clive Wilmer; 1970), *In the Distance* (1975), *Seeing the World* (1980), *The Covenant: Poems 1979–1983* (1984) and *Devices and Desires* (1988) uses a deliberately 'plain style' and traditional forms and METRE. He has also edited a selection of TRAHERNE's writings (1980), written a study of YVOR WINTERS (1983) and with his wife, Alkham Darbandi, translated *The*

Conference of the Birds (1984) from a 12th-century Persian ALLEGORY by Farid Attar.

Davis, Jack (Leonard) 1917– Australian Aboriginal playwright and poet. The poetry in *The Firstborn* (1970), *Jagardoo (Poems from Aboriginal Australia)* (1978), *John Pat and Other Poems* (1988) and *Black Life: Poems* (1992) expresses Aboriginal attitudes in a direct and personal way. He is best known, however, as a playwright. *Kullark (Home)* (1979) portrays the devastating impact of European settlers on his people, the Nyoongarah, and *The Dreamers* (1982) portrays the squalor of contemporary Aboriginal life. *No Sugar* (1985), *Barungin: Smell the Wind* (1989) and *Our Town* (1990) continue the revision of Aboriginal history.

Davis, Rebecca (Blane) Harding 1831–1910 American novelist and short-story writer. Much of her fiction is set in her native Philadelphia, including her best-known story, 'Life in the Iron Mills' (1861), about the tragic life of Hugh Wolfe, a furnace-tender in a mill. One of the earliest exponents of American realism, she portrayed the bleak lives of industrial workers in *Margaret Howth* (1862) and of blacks in *Waiting for the Verdict* (1868). *John Andross* (1874) is a tale about political corruption.

Davis, Richard Harding 1864–1916 American journalist, novelist, short-story writer and playwright. The son of REBECCA HARDING DAVIS, he became one of the most prolific and popular writers of his day. His travels and work as a war correspondent provided the material for a succession of books, in addition to seven novels, over 80 short stories and 25 plays – successful in their day, though quickly forgotten. His novels include *Soldiers of Fortune* (1897), *The Bar Sinister* (1903) and *Vera the Medium* (1908); *Ranson's Folly* (1902) and *Miss Civilization* (1905) were among his most popular plays.

Davis, Thomas (Osborne) 1814–45 Irish poet and journalist. He emerged in the early 1840s as the leading literary exponent of romantic nationalism in verse and prose. Despite the historically well-informed reasonableness of his essays, his verse could be bombastic and even racialist in its attempt to provide new songs and BALLADS popularizing the spirit and sentiment of the old Gaelic tradition. His best work, such as 'Lament for Eoghan Ruadh O'Neill' and *The Patriot Parliament of 1689* (1843), explores the disasters and achievements of the Irish past as a stirring commentary on present possibilities.

Dawe, (Donald) Bruce 1930– Australian poet. His inventive, witty poems use the everyday structures of Australian speech with new resourcefulness and achieve a simple nobility. 'Drifters' and 'Homecoming', an elegy for the dead of the Vietnam War, are well known. Major collections include *Sometimes Gladness: Bruce Dawe. Collected Poems 1954–1978* (1978), *Towards Sunrise: Poems 1979–1986* (1986) and *This Side of Silence: Poems 1978–90* (1990). He has also published *Over Here, Harv and Other Stories* (1983) and *Bruce Dawe: Essays and Opinions* (1990).

Day, Clarence (Shepard) 1874–1935 American humorist. A regular contributor to THE NEW YORKER, he is best known for his autobiographical writings about upper-class life in 19th-century New York. They include *God and My Father* (1932), *Life with Father* (1935), *Life with Mother* (1937) and *Father and I* (1940). *Life with Father* was dramatized by Howard Lindsay and Russel Crouse in 1939 and became a long-running success.

Day, John 1574–1640 Playwright and poet, active in the London theatre for a decade after 1598. Of six extant plays in which he is known to have had a hand, four are probably his alone: the satiric comedies *Law Tricks* (1604) and *The Isle of Gulls* (1606); the attractive *Humour out of Breath* (c. 1608); and the fanciful pastoral dialogues of *The Parliament of Bees* (published in 1641). With CHETTLE, he wrote *The Blind Beggar of Bednal-Green* (1600) and with WILLIAM ROWLEY and George Wilkins a patriotic picaresque piece, *The Travails of the Three English Brothers* (1607). THE PARNASSUS PLAYS have also been attributed to him.

Day, Thomas 1748–89 Educationalist and writer of CHILDREN'S LITERATURE. An early and eccentric disciple of Rousseau, he published the influential *History of Sandford and Merton* (three parts; 1783, 1786 and 1789). Totally didactic in purpose, it follows the contrasting fortunes of Tommy Merton, the idle son of a rich gentleman, and Harry Sandford, the industrious son of a hardworking farmer. Day also wrote another moral tale, *The History of Little Jack* (1788), about a child suckled by goats and raised by a God-fearing old man before returning to civilization to make his fortune.

Day-Lewis, C(ecil) 1904–72 Poet and writer of DETECTIVE FICTION. He was the only member of of AUDEN's circle at Oxford to join and become active in the Communist Party. *Transitional Poem* (1929) and *From Feathers to Iron* (1931) are lyric sequences. In *The Magnetic Mountain* (1933) and *A Time to Dance* (1935) his Marxist politics clash with a tendency to Romanticism. *Overtures to a Death* (1938) contains his best political poems, 'Newsreel' and 'The Bombers'. His reputation declined after the war, as conflict was replaced by dry formalism in volumes such as *Pegasus* (1957), *The Gate* (1962) and *The Room* (1965). Increasing respectability brought many honours: he delivered the Clark lectures at Cambridge in 1946 (*The Poetic Image*, 1947), served as professor of poetry at Oxford in 1951–6 and became POET LAUREATE in 1968. *The Poems of C. Day-Lewis 1925–1972* appeared in 1977. He also published verse translations of Virgil and, as Nicholas Blake, wrote some 20 detective novels whose hero, Nigel Strangeways, was originally modelled on Auden. *The Buried Day* (1960) is a volume of autobiography.

De Boissière, Ralph 1907– Trinidadian novelist of French Creole descent. In Trinidad he was involved in both trade union activity and the influential Beacon Group, which helped to promote a sense of local cultural identity. His novels were published in Australia after he emigrated there in 1948. The best is *Crown Jewel* (1952), set in Trinidad on the eve of World War II, a long-neglected work successfully republished in 1981. Later novels are *Rum and Coca-Cola* (1956), a sequel to *Crown Jewel*, and *No Saddles for Kangaroos* (1964).

De Forest, John W. 1826–1906 American novelist. His *History of the Indians of Connecticut* (1851) was marked by the same objectivity which characterized his fiction. *Miss Ravenel's Conversion from Secession to Loyalty* (1867), a romance set during the Civil War and Reconstruction, includes grimly realistic battle scenes which anticipate those of STEPHEN CRANE. Later novels include *Kate Beaumont* (1872), about South Carolina plantation society, and *Honest John Vane* (1875), a SATIRE of political corruption. De Forest's Civil War memoirs, *A Volunteer's Adventures*, appeared posthumously in 1946, and *A Union Officer in the Reconstruction* in 1948.

De Jong, Meindert 1906– American writer of CHILDREN'S LITERATURE. *The Wheel on the School* (1954), *Far out the Long Canal* (1964) and *Journey from Peppermint Street*

(1968) are set in his native Holland. *The House of Sixty Fathers* (1956) memorably describes the plight of an abandoned Chinese boy during World War II.

de la Mare, Walter 1873–1956 Poet, writer of CHILDREN'S LITERATURE and anthologist. He wrote poems for children and poems about childhood for adults, exploiting a great variety of verse forms. EDWARD THOMAS described them as 'the most original featherweight poetry of our time'. De la Mare's first volume, *Songs of Childhood*, appeared in 1902 under the pseudonym Walter Ramal. The best-known of subsequent volumes preceding the definitive *The Complete Poems of Walter de la Mare* (1969) are *Peacock Pie: A Book of Rhymes* (1913), *Memory and Other Poems* (1938), *The Burning Glass and Other Poems* (1945) and *Winged Chariot* (1951). Volumes of short stories include *Broomsticks* (1925), *The Lord Fish* (1933) and *The Scarecrow* (1945). De la Mare's anthologies are *Come Hither* (1923), for children; *Behold This Dreamer* (1939); and *Love* (1943). He also published three novels, *Henry Brocken* (1904), *The Return* (1910) and *Memoirs of a Midget* (1921); critical works on RUPERT BROOKE and CARROLL; and an edition of CHRISTINA ROSSETTI.

de la Roche, Mazo 1879–1961 Canadian novelist. Her childhood on a farm in Ontario provided the background and setting for her popular and optimistic regional idylls. Success came with *Jalna* (1927), set in an old house of that name, and its sequel, *The Whiteoaks of Jalna* (1929). Another 14 novels were eventually added to the series. She also wrote CHILDREN'S LITERATURE, one-act plays, historical studies and an autobiography, *Ringing the Changes* (1957).

de Morgan, William (Frend) 1839–1917 Artist and novelist. A friend and colleague of WILLIAM MORRIS in the Arts and Crafts Movement, he made stained glass and decorative tiles. Only in retirement did he turn to writing, achieving considerable success with *Joseph Vance* (1906) and eight more novels, the last two completed by his wife, which cast a Dickensian eye over the London of his youth.

De Profundis An extended letter by OSCAR WILDE to LORD ALFRED DOUGLAS ('Bosie'), written during the author's imprisonment in Reading Gaol. It complains of Bosie's selfishness, shallowness, parasitism, greed, extravagance, tantrums, pettiness and neglect, while praising the selfless devotion of Robert Ross ('Robbie'). Ross, who became Wilde's literary executor, gave the work its present title (from the opening line of Psalm 130) and published an edited version in 1905. A fuller text appeared in 1949.

De Quincey, Thomas 1785–1859 Essayist and critic. Born in Manchester, he was educated at Bath, Winkfield and Manchester Grammar School, from which he ran away in 1802. After touring Wales he arrived destitute in London, an experience described in the first part of his *CONFESSIONS OF AN ENGLISH OPIUM EATER*.

In 1803, reconciled with his mother and guardians, he entered Worcester College, Oxford, where read voraciously, made few friends and began to take opium, to which he became thoroughly addicted in 1812–13. An ardent admirer of *LYRICAL BALLADS* since adolescence, he finally met COLERIDGE in 1806 and overcame the diffidence which had earlier prevented him introducing himself to WORDSWORTH and DOROTHY WORDSWORTH at Grasmere. He soon became devoted to his new friends, performing numerous literary services for Wordsworth and Coleridge and taking over the lease of Dove Cottage

when the Wordsworths moved to Allan Bank in 1808. He held it until 1834, though he earned the Wordsworths' disapproval by his opium addiction and his affair with Margaret Simpson, a local farmer's daughter, whom he married in 1817.

But for the need to support a family, De Quincey might never have become a writer. His work consisted almost entirely of contributions to magazines, and was collected only in the last years of his life in *Selections Grave and Gay from Writings Published and Unpublished* (1853–60). From 1821 to 1824 he wrote mainly for *THE LONDON MAGAZINE*, where *Confessions of an English Opium Eater* appeared in 1821, bringing him immediate notoriety and recognition. His 48 pieces for the periodical, remarkably varied in quality and character, include articles on Goethe, Herder, Richter, MALTHUS, Rosicrucians and Freemasons, English and German dictionaries, education, and one of his best critical essays, 'On the Knocking at the Gate in Macbeth'. He then turned to Edinburgh for his living, always precarious despite his relentless productivity. The appearance of the first part of his article on Lessing in *BLACKWOOD'S EDINBURGH MAGAZINE* in 1826 began an association which produced some of his best work in the next 23 years. It included: his long historical series, *The Caesars*; *The Last Days of Immanuel Kant*; an important article on rhetoric; one of his humorous masterpieces, *ON MURDER CONSIDERED AS ONE OF THE FINE ARTS*; *The Revolt of the Tartars* (1837); the incomplete *Suspiria de Profundis* (1845) with its magnificent dream-visions; and the two remarkable articles on *The Glory of Motion* and *The Vision of Sudden Death*, which make up *The English Mail Coach* (1849). A GOTHIC NOVEL, *Klosterheim*, appeared as a separate volume in 1832 and *The Logic of Political Economy* in 1844. In *Tait's Edinburgh Magazine* he published: the 'Sketches ... from the Autobiography of an English Opium Eater' (later entitled *Autobiographic Sketches*); *RECOLLECTIONS OF THE LAKES AND THE LAKE POETS* (1834–9), which effectively set the seal on his alienation from Wordsworth, Coleridge and SOUTHEY; an account of his gradual estrangement from Wordsworth and a criticism of his poetry; and articles on GODWIN, HAZLITT, SHELLEY, KEATS and POPE.

De Vere, Aubrey Thomas 1814–1902 Irish poet and essayist. He was the son of another poet, Sir Aubrey de Vere, and a close friend of TENNYSON and BROWNING. A Catholic covert, he became professor of social and political science at the new Catholic University in Dublin, where NEWMAN was rector, in 1854. His works include *The Waldenses and Other Poems* (1842), *English Misrule and Irish Misdeeds* (1848) and three volumes of *Critical Essays* (1887–9). *Recollections* appeared in 1897.

De Vries, Peter 1910–93 American novelist. From 1941 until 1987 he worked on the staff of *THE NEW YORKER*. His most popular works, typified by their worldly satire of suburban mores and sexual intrigue, include *The Tunnel of Love* (1955), *Madder Music* (1978) and *Slouching Towards Kalamazoo* (1983). *The Mackerel Plaza* (1958) has enjoyed the most consistent regard.

Death of a Salesman A play by ARTHUR MILLER, performed and published in 1949 and awarded a PULITZER PRIZE. After 35 years as a travelling salesman, measuring his own worth by the volume of his sales, Willy Loman is not the success he claims to be and is beginning to lose his grip. His wife, Linda, and his sons, Biff and Happy, worry about him. After he is fired, he starts to hallucinate about the past, particulary his unsatisfactory relations with his sons. Finally, deciding that he is worth more dead than alive (the insurance money will support his family and help Biff get a new start in life), he kills himself in his car on a last trip. Critics have disagreed whether his suicide is a last desperate and tragic assertion of the American dream or an act of cowardice and selfishness.

Death's Jest-Book: or, the Fool's Tragedy A play by BEDDOES, begun in 1825, continually revised and posthumously published in 1850. A REVENGE TRAGEDY in the Jacobean manner, its convoluted plot centres on two brothers, Wolfram and Isbrand, who enter the service of Duke Melveric in order to pursue their vengeance against him for the death of their father and the dishonour of their sister. Apart from its macabre atmosphere, the play is striking for some fine BLANK VERSE and some lyrics influenced by SHELLEY, notably the song 'Dream Pedlary' and the dirges for Sibilla and Wolfram.

debate poem A medieval poetic form in which two characters uphold opposing viewpoints. The characters are often animals, birds, inanimate objects or allegorical personifications, and the subjects of their debate range from spiritual problems to love. The contest may be inconclusive or resolved by a third party. The debate poem was used for serious philosophical discussion, political ALLEGORY and SATIRE (as in *WYNNERE AND WASTOURE*), and humour (*THE OWL AND THE NIGHTINGALE*). The parliament involving more than two participants is a related form: see *THE PARLIAMENT OF THE THREE AGES, THE PARLEMENT OF FOULES*.

Decline and Fall EVELYN WAUGH's first novel, published in 1928. Sent down from Oxford through no fault of his own, Paul Pennyfeather teaches at Llanabba Castle, a Welsh boarding school hopelessly administered by a staff which includes Mr Prendergast, a former clergyman, and Captain Grimes, a one-legged drunkard and bigamist. He is taken up by the sophisticated Margot Beste-Chetwynde, mother of one of his pupils. They become engaged but he is arrested for having unwittingly involved himself in her activities in the white-slave trade. In prison he meets Captain Grimes, a fellow prisoner, and Prendergast, now the prison chaplain. Margot engineers his escape and transports him to her villa in Corfu. He returns to Oxford as his own very distant cousin.

Decline and Fall of the Roman Empire, The History of the EDWARD GIBBON's great work of classical history, published in three instalments: vol. 1 in 1776, vols 2 and 3 in 1783, and vols 4, 5 and 6 in 1788. These correspond to the major divisions in his narrative: from Trajan and the age of the Antonines to the reign of Constantine; from the foundation of Constantinople to the Western Empire of Charlemagne; from the revival of the Western (Holy Roman) Empire to the long history of the Eastern (Byzantine) Empire and the capture of Constantinople by the Turks in 1453. The vast subject is finely organized, the narrative power unflagging, and the viewpoint elegantly detached, nowhere more so than in the sceptical treatment of Christianity – an aspect of the book which provoked much contemporary criticism.

deconstruction A practice of reading developed mainly by Jacques Derrida (1930–) and taken up by the 'Yale school' of critics, including Paul de Man, Geoffrey Hartman and J. Hillis Miller. Key Derridean concepts include 'logocentrism', 'phonocentrism', 'presence', 'differance', [*sic*] and 'supplement'. Derrida rejects 'logocentrism', the attempt to centre discourses and, by privileging one term over another, to permit distinctions between truth and falsehood. 'Phonocentrism', the 'violent hierarchy' imposed by Rousseau and others, places speech above writing. The deconstructor begins by reversing it and then by displacing the new hierarchy, thus leaving a certain indeterminacy in the particular discursive field. 'Difference', the process which prevents signs from achieving a full 'presence', combines two meanings: to 'differ' and to 'defer'. Signs acquire meanings within a system of differences, and at the same time meaning is deferred by the endless chain of signifiers which is generated as soon as we begin to interpret. The 'supplement' describes the unstable relationship which exists between terms like 'speech' and 'writing'. One term both takes the place of and supplements the other.

Deeping, (George) Warwick 1877–1950 Novelist. A prolific writer, he produced 70 novels and five volumes of short stories, which attempt to keep alive the idea and spirit of Edwardian Britain. Deeping's experiences in the Royal Army Medical Corps during World War I were the inspiration for his most famous work, *Sorrell and Son* (1925), the moving story of Captain Sorrell trying to make a life for his son Kit.

Deerslayer, The See LEATHERSTOCKING TALES, THE.

Defence of Poetry, The An essay by SHELLEY, written in 1821 and posthumously published in 1840. His most famous prose work, it amplifies arguments first advanced elsewhere (notably the first two chapters of *A Philosophical View of Reform*) in answer to PEACOCK's *The Four Ages of Poetry* (1820).

Shelley's use of 'poetry' is inclusive, referring to literature in general and poetry considered as a human faculty. The essay is essentially aimed against UTILITARIAN definitions of value and happiness accompanying the growth of industrial culture. As distinct from Reason's neutral observation, poetry is the 'expression of the Imagination', whose operations unify and synthesize. The case for the 'Defence' as a whole rests on poetry's role as a force for social freedom and creative eros: 'We want the creative faculty to imagine that which we know ... we want the poetry of life.' In burnished passages on CHAUCER, Dante and MILTON, he argues that, with their special capacity to sense connections between individual experience and social and intellectual change, poets both anticipated and provided the ideas by which subsequent ages lived. The celebrated (though often misunderstood) peroration hails them as unconscious 'ministers' of a beneficent 'Power which is seated on the throne of their own soul', as 'mirrors of the gigantic shadows which futurity casts upon the present' and as 'the unacknowledged legislators of the World'.

Defoe, Daniel 1660–1731 Novelist, journalist and entrepreneur. Born Daniel Foe, he attended the Stoke Newington Academy for Dissenters and remained a Presbyterian throughout his life. In youth he went into trade (business projects never ceased to fascinate him), travelled widely in Europe until his marriage in 1683, took part in Monmouth's rebellion in 1685 and joined William III's army in 1688 – the first of several changes of allegiance that earned him a mercenary reputation. His first writing, the *Essay on Projects* (1697), was on economics but his first literary success was *The True-Born Englishman* (1701), a satiric poem championing the cause of the foreign-born monarch. Afterwards he abandoned SATIRE to cultivate his skills in stylistic impersonation and IRONY. A pamphlet, *The Shortest Way with the Dissenters* (1702), mimicked the extreme attitudes of High Anglican Tories by advocating the extermination of Dissenters. Neither party was amused. Defoe was fined, imprisoned and pilloried – experiences prompting a mock ODE, *Hymn to the Pillory* (1703) – but became a popular hero.

In 1704 ROBERT HARLEY, Earl of Oxford, helped Defoe to publish his first issue of *THE REVIEW*, a thrice-weekly newspaper which survived until 1713. Defoe contributed articles on topics ranging from the commercial to the moral, pioneering examples of the literary essay which was emerging as one of the distinctive genres of the period. Harley also employed him as an undercover field-agent, a clandestine occupation suiting his personality. His own political beliefs remained resolute, however, irrespective of changes in party policies. A committed anti-Jacobite, he published *Reasons against the Succession of the House of Hanover* (1712), another satire misunderstood by the authorities and leading to a second term of imprisonment. He went on to edit *Mercator*, a trade journal, and supported free trade in *A General History of Trade* (1714). After the death of Queen Anne and the accession of the Hanoverians he became agent to Lord Townshend, the Whig Secretary of State, and may have operated in a double capacity as informer, reporter and monitor of events.

By 1720 Defoe had abandoned political controversy. He wrote instead a CONDUCT BOOK, *The Family Instructor* (1715–18), and several histories, *The History of the Wars of His Present Majesty Charles XII King of Sweden* (1715), *Memoirs of the Church of Scotland* (1717) and *The Life and Death of Count Puktil* (1717). His earliest venture into fiction had been *A True Relation of the Apparition of One Mrs Veal* (1706), an embroidered account of a current ghost story, but in his 60th year Defoe seems to have discovered a new well of talent for narrative. During the next five years he produced a flow of novels, beginning with *ROBINSON CRUSOE* and *The Farther Adventures of Robinson Crusoe* (1719), followed shortly by *The Serious Reflections ... of Robinson Crusoe*, *MEMOIRS OF A CAVALIER* and *CAPTAIN SINGLETON* (1720), *MOLL FLANDERS*, *A JOURNAL OF THE PLAGUE YEAR* and *COLONEL JACK* (1722), and *ROXANA* (1724). As if these were not enough, he also produced: *The Great Law of Subordination Considered* (1724), an examination of the treatment of servants; *A Tour Thro the Whole Island of Great Britain* (3 vols, 1724–7), an outstanding guide book; *The Complete English Tradesman* (1726), which identifies the new respectability of the merchant classes; and *Augusta Triumphans* (1728), an optimistic Utopian project.

It has proved difficult to establish the full extent of his output but, with over 500 verified publications to his name, Defoe is the most prolific author in the language. His enduring reputation rests on his novels, the form in which he was one of the great innovators. Concerned with social man rather than individual psychology, his fiction reveals a swashbuckling love of travel, adventure and piracy that subsequently became the stock material of the genre. As an essayist he was recognizably unlike most of his important contemporaries in the AUGUSTAN AGE, street-wise where they tended to be aesthetic, and a master of the plain style rather than the politely allusive mode cultivated by SWIFT and POPE.

Deirdre of the Sorrows A tragedy by SYNGE, posthumously produced at the ABBEY THEATRE in 1910. Had he lived, he would certainly have revised the text, written during illness and depression. The story comes from the Saga of Cuchulain; Synge would have known the verse plays on the same subject by YEATS and AE (GEORGE WILLIAM RUSSELL) as well as SIR SAMUEL FERGUSON'S poem. Deirdre, destined to be the wife of Conchubor, High King of Ulster, runs away with her lover Naisi. After seven years in Alban they are enticed back to Conchubor's court, where Naisi and his brothers are killed and Deirdre kills herself with Naisi's knife.

Deism A theological position which accepted the Supreme Being as the source of finite existence but denied the supernatural element in Christianity, as well as rejecting Christian revelation as the only way to salvation. EDWARD HERBERT (Lord Herbert of Cherbury) was the first English philosopher to advance these ideas, and JOHN LOCKE's *The Reasonableness of Christianity* (1695) gave support by its contention that man and his use of reason are evidence enough for the existence of God. Deism played an important role in 18th-century thought and controversy, influencing Voltaire, Rousseau and Diderot in France and spreading to Germany through a translation of TINDAL's *Christianity as Old as the Creation* (1730). See also JOSEPH BUTLER, SAMUEL CLARKE, ANTHONY COLLINS, CONYERS MIDDLETON and TOLAND.

Dekker, Thomas *c.* 1570–1632 Playwright and pamphleteer. His vivid accounts of London life make it plausible that he was a Londoner by birth and upbringing. Nothing certain is known of Dekker until his appearance on the theatrical scene in 1598. Despite his prodigious industry, money problems seem to have been constant and imprisonment for debt intermittent. Of the 50 or so plays linked to his name, only 20 survive, together with various MASQUES. The earliest, *OLD FORTUNATUS* (?1598), is a rambling moral tale. The second, *THE SHOEMAKER'S HOLIDAY* (1599), is Dekker's masterpiece, its variety and its boisterous portraits of London's citizens advancing the development of a distinctive comic form. The other plays of which he was sole author are, in comparison, disappointing. *SATIROMASTIX* (1601) is an unattractive rejoinder to some wittier abuse from JONSON. Its structural weaknesses are shared by *The Whore of Babylon* (c. 1606), *If It be Not Good the Devil is in It* (c. 1610) and *The Wonder of a Kingdom* (published in 1636). Of Dekker's many collaborations the most effective include: with WEBSTER, *WESTWARD HO* (1604), *The Famous History of Sir Thomas Wyatt* (c. 1604) and *NORTHWARD HO* (c. 1605); with THOMAS MIDDLETON, *THE HONEST WHORE* (1604; a second part, probably by Dekker alone, was produced in 1605) and *THE ROARING GIRL* (1610); with MASSINGER, *THE VIRGIN MARTYR* (1620); with JOHN FORD and WILLIAM ROWLEY, *THE WITCH OF EDMONTON* (c. 1621); and with CHETTLE and William Haughton *PATIENT GRISSEL* (1600). He was also one of the several playwrights who had a hand in *SIR THOMAS MORE* (c. 1593–5).

The moralizing occasionally observable in his plays becomes explicit in his pamphlets, of which the best were written in 1603–10. *The Wonderful Year* (1603) describes the effects of the plague on London. *The Seven Deadly Sins of London* (1606) gives a bustling picture of city life and the seven-day triumph of the traditional sins, with new names and in modern guise. *The Bellman of London* (1608) exposes the criminal underworld, and finds nothing to choose between the town and the country for villainy. A continuation and Dekker's greatest publishing success, *Lantern and Candlelight* (1608), includes an early account of English gypsies in its description of low life. *Work for Armourers* (1609) describes the assault by the army of Poverty on the army of Money. *The Gull's Horn-Book* (1609) parodies COURTESY BOOKS, giving satiric instructions to gallants on how to behave in taverns and playhouses. *The Four Birds of Noah's Ark* (1609) is a collection of prayers, the birds being the eagle, dove, phoenix and pelican. At his best Dekker writes with exuberance, and always with affection for erring humanity.

Delafield, E. M. [Dashwood (*née* De La Pasture), Edmée Elizabeth Monica] 1890–1943 Novelist. She wrote mildly satiric novels about the day-to-day upheavals of provincial life. *Messalina of the Suburbs* (1923) was based upon a famous murder case. The success of *The Diary of a Provincial Lady* (1930) launched a series which provided the basis for popular films. Delafield's other works included: *Faster! Faster!* (1936) and *Nothing is Safe* (1937); three plays, *To See Ourselves* (1930), *The Glass Wall* (1933) and *The Mulberry Bush* (1935); and a study of the BRONTËS (1938).

Delane, J(ohn) T(haddeus) 1817–79 Newspaper editor. As editor of *The Times* from 1841 to 1877 he assembled a distinguished team of journalists and took an influential public role, particularly in his attacks on the mishandling of the Crimean War.

Delaney, Shelagh 1939– Playwright. Her first and best-known play, *A Taste of Honey* (1958), owed its success to its unadorned contemporaneity. Neither Delaney's second play, *The Lion in Love* (1960), nor her later work has achieved equal acclaim, though since adapting *A Taste of Honey* for the screen in 1961 she has produced notable screenplays for *Charlie Bubbles* (1968) and *Dance with a Stranger* (1985).

Delany, Mary 1700–88 Letter-writer. Her reputation rests upon her six-volume *Autobiography and Correspondence* (1861–2), which includes letters to and anecdotes of JONATHAN SWIFT, and her correspondence on literary and social matters with other BLUESTOCKINGS such as ELIZABETH CARTER, ELIZABETH MONTAGU and CHAPONE.

Delany, Samuel R(ay) 1942– Black American writer of SCIENCE FICTION. Early novels, *Babel-17* (1966), *The Einstein Intersection* (1967) and *Nova* (1968), and the short stories in *Driftglass* (1971) and *Distant Stars* (1981), display a vivid romanticism. He broke new ground with a counter-cultural epic, *Dhalgren* (1975). Critical writings, including *The Jewel-Hinged Jaw* (1977), *The American Shore* (1978) and *Starboard Wine* (1984), show his interest in the language of science fiction. Explorations in SEMIOTICS and POST-STRUCTURALISM have influenced the fantasy series which includes *Tales of Nevèrÿon* (1979), *Neverÿóna* (1983), *Flight from Nevèrÿon* (1985) and *The Bridge of Lost Desire* (1987). An autobiography, *The Motion of Light in Water* (1988), documents the homosexual subculture.

DeLillo, Don 1936– American novelist. Widely recognized as leading examples of American POST-MODERNISM, his novels are highly self-aware evocations of a contemporary society which defines itself through the pseudo-religious rituals of its subcultures. They include: *Americana* (1971); *End Zone* (1973); *Great Jones Street* (1974); *Ratner's Star* (1976); *Players* (1977); *Running Dog* (1979); *The Names* (1983); *White Noise* (1986); *Libra* (1988), about the assassination of President Kennedy; and *Mao II* (1991), about the relations between literature and terrorism.

Dell, Floyd 1887–1969 American novelist. A radical journalist, he edited *The Masses* (1914–17) and *The Liberator* (1918–24). *Moon-Calf* (1920), its sequel *The Briary-Bush* (1921), *Janet March* (1923) and *Runaway* (1925) are about the disillusionment of the postwar generation and the turmoil of the Jazz Age. Other works include *An Old Man's Folly* (1926), *Upton Sinclair* (1927) and *Love in the Machine Age* (1930). With Thomas Mitchell, he dramatized his novel *An Unmarried Father* (1927) as *Little Accident* (1928). *Homecoming* (1933) is his autobiography.

Della Cruscans A short-lived school of sentimental poetry founded by Robert Merry (1755–98), who managed to join the Accademia della Crusca ('of the chaff' or 'bran') in Florence. There he edited two miscellanies, the *Arno* (1784) and the *Florence* (1785), containing his own effusions and those of Mrs Piozzi and other dilettanti. He returned to England in 1787 and published his 'Adieu and Recall to Love' over the signature 'Della Crusca' in *The World*. Its depth of sentiment moved HANNAH COWLEY to respond with 'The Pen', signed 'Anna Matilda'. Pseudonymous imitators rushed to swell the poetical correspondence, and the English Della Cruscans were launched. Merry and Mrs Cowley met, apparently for the first time, in 1789. Thereafter 'Della Crusca' produced 'The Interview' and 'Anna Matilda' replied in saddened strain, but their literary affair, their influence on poetry and their school soon ended. GIFFORD satirized their excess and nonsense in *The Baviad* (1791) and *The Maeviad* (1795).

Deloney, Thomas ?1543–1600 Author of prose fiction. A silk-weaver by trade, he began by writing BALLADS and BROADSIDES, including three on the Spanish Armada, of the popular but poorly regarded kind Autolycus sells in *THE WINTER'S TALE*. *Canaan's Calamity* is an attempt at a poem of greater length and sustained construction. His prose fiction draws on such popular works as jestbooks, the chronicles of EDWARD HALL and HOLINSHED and FOXE's *ACTS AND MONUMENTS*, with occasional excursions into fashionable EUPHUISM and romance, to describe and glorify the English artisan. *Thomas of Reading* (licensed 1602) depicts the clothier's craft, *Jack of Newbury* (licensed 1597, first extant edition 1619) that of the weaver, and *The Gentle Craft* (licensed 1597, first extant edition 1637) shoemakers. The last contains his finest creation, Long Meg of Westminster and also the story of Simon Eyre, a shoemaker who became Lord Mayor of London, which served as the source for DEKKER's *THE SHOEMAKER'S HOLIDAY*. Despite being dismissed by better-educated contemporaries and neglected by critics, Deloney has good claim to have formed the English 'novel'.

Democracy in America (*La Démocratie en Amérique*) A classic interpretation of American civilization by Comte Alexis de Tocqueville (1805–59), published in two parts in 1835 and 1840. The first part discusses America's geography, political institutions and processes, and society, arguing that Anglo-Americans have the habit of democratic self-government he considers essential to civilization. Equality is more advanced in the USA than anywhere else. The second part analyses the effect of democracy on intellectual movements, art, religion, taste and mores, concluding that it will lead to greater mediocrity of individual achievement, even as it makes possible greater general comfort and greater achievements by the state.

Demos: *A Story of English Socialism* A novel by GISSING, published in 1886. It is in fact an attack on the validity of socialism, portraying working-class agitators like Richard Mutimer and Daniel Dabbs as short-sighted, self-deceived, self-serving and ultimately corrupt. The story hinges on the establishment by Mutimer of an ironworks in an unspoiled valley, a model community in the tradition of ROBERT OWEN. It is finally closed, through a complex plot involving the loss and rediscovery of a will, and the money reverts to the rightful, aristocratic owner.

Denham, Sir John 1615–69 Poet. He was a staunch Royalist whose fortunes rose and fell with those of Charles I and flourished again at the Restoration. A blank-verse tragedy, *The Sophy*, and his most famous work, the poem *Cooper's Hill*, appeared when he was 26. Set near his home at Egham and concentrating on landscape description, *Cooper's Hill* influenced the topographical poetry of the 18th century and, in JOHNSON's words, conferred on Denham 'the rank and dignity of an original author'. Denham also worked on translations of Homer and Virgil.

Denis Duval An unfinished novel by THACKERAY, published in *THE CORNHILL MAGAZINE* in 1864, the year after his death. The setting is Rye in the late 18th century, and the book would have attempted the sort of full-scale historical novel he had handled so successfully in *HENRY ESMOND*. Denis Duval describes his involvement with smugglers and his love for Agnes de Saverne.

Dennis, Clarence Michael James 1876–1938 Australian poet and journalist. *Backblock Ballads* (1913), followed by *The Songs of a Sentimental Bloke* (1915) and *The Moods of Ginger Mick* (1916) became immensely popular, particularly with soldiers in the trenches, through their everyday language, teasing humour and use of bush themes. Later volumes were *Digger Smith* (1918) and *Rose of Spadgers* (1924), a sequel to *Ginger Mick*.

Dennis, John 1657–1734 Critic. A member of DRYDEN's circle and failed dramatist, Dennis had more success as a critic, though he became cantankerous in later life and was ridiculed by Pope in *THE DUNCIAD*. His principal essays are *The Impartial Critic* (1693), an attack on RYMER; *The Advancement and Reformation of Modern Poetry* (1701); *The Grounds of Criticism in Poetry* (1704); and *Three Letters on the Genius and Writings of Shakespeare* (1711). *Original Letters, Familiar, Moral and Critical* (1721) contains valuable information about the literary world of his day.

Dennis, Nigel (Forbes) 1912–89 Novelist, playwright and journalist. After making a reputation as a satirical novelist with the inventive *Cards of Identity* (1955), he turned to writing plays which deplored debased standards under facile democracies and denounced left-wing totalitarianism. They include an adaptation of *Cards of Identity* (1956), *The Making of Moo* (1957) and *August for the People* (1961), about the declining aristocracy. He also co-edited *ENCOUNTER*.

dénouement The final resolution (literally, 'untying' or 'unravelling') of a complex plot. Though the term refers most accurately to the formula of the WELL-MADE PLAY, it is also broadly applied to the closing scenes of many plays, and indeed of novels and other narratives. See also ANAGNORISIS.

Deor A short Old English poem in the EXETER BOOK. Deor the minstrel tells of five well-known miserable situations from history or mythology and then of his own misfortune, probably fictional, in losing his position as official poet. The refrain offers solace: these other sorrows passed and so will his own.

Deptford Trilogy, The A trilogy of novels by ROBERTSON DAVIES, consisting of *Fifth Business* (1970), *The Manticore* (1972) and *World of Wonders* (1975). Events in the fictional village of Deptford, Ontario, link the lives of the three central characters from childhood onwards: Dunstan Ramsay, narrator of the first volume and the central arbitrating consciousness of the sequence; Percy 'Boy' Staunton, whose flamboyant career ends in his mysterious death; and Paul Dempster, son of the disgraced wife of the Baptist minister, who transforms himself into the master-magician Magnus Eisengrim. All three volumes focus on metamorphoses of identity, on characters who are 'born again', whether through the agency of myth, magic, theatre or Jungian psychology.

Desai, Anita 1937– Indian novelist. Her work, which describes surface realities sharply while using them as markers for her characters' interior lives, includes *The Village by the Sea* (1982), *Cry, the Peacock* (1963), *Voices in the City* (1965), *Bye-Bye, Blackbird* (1971), *Where Shall We Go This Summer?* (1975), *Fire on the Mountain* (1977), *Clear Light of Day* (1980), *In Custody* (1984) and *Baumgartner's Bombay* (1988).

Desani, G(ovindas) V(ishnoodas) 1909– Indian novelist. He is ranked among the most important 20th-century Indian writers in English on the strength of one novel, *All About H. Hatterr* (1948), an eccentric and comic book about an Anglo-Indian in search of wisdom which combines linguistic dexterity and philosophical curiosity. Its admirers include T. S. ELIOT, ANTHONY BURGESS and SALMAN RUSHDIE.

Deserted Village, The A poem by GOLDSMITH, published in 1770. It takes as its theme the vanished rural past of England, destroyed by the Enclosure Acts and the depopulation of agrarian communities as the Industrial Revolution concentrated workers into the cities. Revisiting an idealized village, Auburn, the poet laments that money and progress should have become more important than human destinies. CRABBE'S *THE VILLAGE* was in part a reaction to this poem.

Desperate Remedies The first published novel by HARDY, appearing in 1871. Having failed to find a publisher for *The Poor Man and the Lady*, he deliberately adopted the popular formulas of the SENSATION NOVEL. Set mainly in Dorset, the complicated narrative of intrigue, violence and deception follows the welfare of Cytherea Graye, forced to become lady's maid and later companion to the imperious Miss Aldclyffe, mistress of Knapwater House. Cytherea is in love with Edward Springrove, a fledgling architect, but Miss Aldclyffe hopes she will marry her illegitimate son, Aeneas Manston. Manston's villainy fuels most of the interest and much of the plot. He is finally brought to book for murdering his first wife, Eunice, and hangs himself in his cell. Miss Aldclyffe dies and Cytherea and Springrove are reunited.

detective fiction A sub-genre of fiction which presents a mysterious event or crime, usually but not necessarily murder, at first concealing the solution from the reader but finally revealing it through the successful investigations of a detective. AUDEN summarizes a typical plot: 'a murder occurs; many are suspected; all but one suspect, who is the murderer, are eliminated; the murderer is arrested or dies'.

Historians of the form have tried to trace its origin to the puzzle tales of the Enlightenment (Voltaire's *Zadig*) or even to the Bible (Daniel, Susanna and the elders), but there is a general agreement that its real history starts in the 19th century. POE brought all the basic ingredients together in his 'tales of ratiocination' of the 1840s. His detective, the brilliant and eccentric Dupin, is accompanied by an obligingly imperceptive friend who narrates the story; he confronts mystery with a coherent, though not exclusively scientific, methodology of detection; and he produces the solution with a triumphant flourish that surprises and satisfies the reader. Without providing either a murder or an infallible detective, WILKIE COLLINS showed in *THE MOONSTONE* (1868) how the formula could be expanded to fit the requirements of the full-length novel. In his SHERLOCK HOLMES STORIES, begun in the late 1880s, ARTHUR CONAN DOYLE masterfully orchestrated the hints Poe had sketched out.

The success of Sherlock Holmes bred imitation ranging from distinguished contributions like CHESTERTON's Father Brown stories and E. C. BENTLEY's *Trent's Last Case* (1913) to forgotten works like ARTHUR MORRISON's Martin Hewitt stories and SHIEL's tales of Prince Zaleski. It also bred new awareness of the form, distinguishing detective fiction from all the other types of popular fiction which dabble in crime and mystery. According to Monsignor Ronald Knox (1888–1957) and his followers in the Detection Club, it should be concerned with puzzles rather than crime as such, and should elaborate its puzzles in strict obedience to the rules of logic and fair play. From such prescriptions arose the so-called Golden Age of the detective novel in the 1920s and 1930s. Writers became known for their expert refinements of the puzzle: R. Austin Freeman (1862–1943) for scientific expertise; Freeman Wills Crofts (1879–1957) for juggling with timetables and alibis; John Dickson Carr (1905–77) for variations on the locked-room mystery; and, most famous of all, CHRISTIE for her ingenuity in making the least likely suspect turn out to be the murderer.

Setting and characterization inevitably took second place, but they, too, followed well-worn paths. Detectives tended to be gentlemen amateurs rather than policemen or private enquiry agents. H. C. Bailey (1878–1961) was perhaps the first, in his Reggie Fortune stories, to make his gentleman amateur a facetious dandy. Fortune was soon joined by a lengthening list of detectives who owed as much to SAKI and WODEHOUSE as to Conan Doyle: Lord Peter Wimsey (SAYERS), Albert Campion (MARGERY ALLINGHAM) and even Nigel Strangeways (Nicholas Blake, the pseudonym of DAY-LEWIS). Settings were equally genteel, with country houses and Oxbridge colleges among the favourites, and the work of Michael Innes (J. I. M. STEWART) offering perhaps the best representative selection.

Detective stories in this classic mould were not confined to England, as the popularity of S. S. Van Dine (Willard Huntington Wright, 1880–1939), Ellery Queen (Frederic Dannay, 1905–82, and Manfred B. Lee, 1905–71) and Rex Stout (1886–1975) in America showed. Nor did they entirely disappear after the 1930s. Christie, Allingham, Blake, Innes and NGAIO MARSH all continued their careers after the war, with some adjustment to the change in public taste, joined by Edmund Crispin (Robert Bruce Montgomery, 1921–78) and Michael Gilbert (1912–). Contemporaries like P. D. JAMES in England

and Emma Lathen (Mary J. Latsis and Martha Henissart) in America can still follow the classic formula. But it came increasingly under challenge from writers who, whatever else they may not have shared, were agreed in finding it restrictive and in wishing to break down the barriers that separated detective fiction from other popular forms like the thriller, adventure story, chase novel and spy story, or from the concerns of serious literature.

By far the most significant challenge came from America, where HAMMETT, CHANDLER and other contributors to *THE BLACK MASK* pioneered 'hard-boiled' detective fiction. Its aims were succinctly indicated by Chandler when he praised Hammett for putting murder back in the hands of people who commit it with real weapons for real reasons, not just to provide the reader with a puzzle. With its tough, down-at-heel private eyes and its sleazy urban world of vice and hoodlums, hard-boiled detective fiction now dominates the American approach as thoroughly as Conan Doyle once did the English. In England itself the form has never properly taken root, but two other tendencies – both with international ramifications – are worth noting. The first is the 'crime novel', so called because an interest in the criminal and criminal psychology can overshadow or even replace the element of mystery. Pioneered by Anthony Berkeley Cox (1893–1971), writing as Francis Iles in the 1930s, it has since attracted distinguished adherents in the American PATRICIA HIGHSMITH, Julian Symons (1912–) and RUTH RENDELL. The second is the 'police novel', in which a determination to make good the genre's earlier neglect of the police can produce works ranging from strictly procedural novels like those of John Creasey (1908–73) or the American Ed McBain (EVAN HUNTER), to the atmospheric fiction of NICOLAS FREELING.

deus ex machina (The god from the machine) It refers to the practice on the classical Greek stage of lowering the gods in a large crane, or 'mechane', as if they were flying down to earth. It was often their task to resolve problems insoluble by human agency, and so the phrase has become more widely applied to describe any character or device used arbitrarily by a playwright to bring a plot to its desired end.

Devil is an Ass, The A comedy by JONSON, first performed in 1616 but not published until 1631. Meercraft, a 'projector' or confidence trickster, uses a scheme for reclaiming land to dupe Fitzdottrel, who parts with his estate on the promise of being made Duke of Drowndland. Fitzdottrel, in turn, deceives the law by pretending to be bewitched. Pug, a minor devil allowed out by Satan to practise his wickedness on earth for a day, is completely outwitted by human knaves and ends up in Newgate.

Dewey, John 1859–1952 American philosopher and educationalist. His influential writings on reform in education include *Psychology* (1887), *Moral Principles in Education* (1909), *Interest and Effort in Education* (1913), *Democracy and Education* (1916), *Experience and Education* (1938), *The Public Schools and Spiritual Values* (1944). His philosophical position, which he termed 'instrumentalism', emphasized the practical problems of social construction. It is elaborated in such works as *Outlines of a Critical Theory of Ethics* (1891), *Studies in Logical Theory* (1903), *Reconstruction in Philosophy* (1920), *Human Nature and Conduct* (1922), *Experience and Nature* (1925), *The Quest for Certainty* (1929), *Art as Experience* (1934) and *Freedom and Culture* (1939).

Dial, The A New England quarterly magazine (1840–4), expressing the views of TRANSCENDENTALISM. Its editors were EMERSON, MARGARET FULLER and THOREAU. Contributors included JONES VERY and WILLIAM ELLERY CHANNING.

Dialogues concerning Natural Religion A work by DAVID HUME, written in the 1750s and posthumously published in 1779. The narrator is Pamphilus, and the interlocutors are the philosopher Cleanthes, the sceptic Philo and the orthodox Christian Demea. Concentrating on the nature of God, the dialogues probe questions raised in the essay on miracles in AN ENQUIRY CONCERNING HUMAN UNDERSTANDING and THE NATURAL HISTORY OF RELIGION. In particular, divine providence is debated and held in doubt.

Diana of the Crossways A novel by GEORGE MEREDITH published in 1885. Diana Warwick is accused of adultery by her husband, a government official of limited sensibilities, and, though an action for divorce fails, they agree to live apart. Diana has an affair with a rising young politician, Percy Dacier, and marries an old admirer, Thomas Redworth, after her husband's death. The nervous, impulsive, inconsistent heroine is said to have been modelled on CAROLINE NORTON.

Diaper, William c. 1686–1717 Poet. *Nereides: or, Sea-Eclogues* (1712) is a whimsical production in which the speakers are mermaids and mermen. Diaper is best known for his translation of the first part of Oppian's *Halieuticks*, a Greek poem of epic proportions describing and classifying fish and methods of fishing.

Diary of a Nobody, The A comic novel of late-Victorian manners by GEORGE AND WEEDON GROSSMITH, published in 1892. The humour derives from the accident-prone Charles Pooter's unconsciousness of how ridiculous he makes himself by his petty snobberies, and from his invariably unsuccessful wrangles with his rebellious son Lupin. Nevertheless, a character of respectability and even integrity emerges, so that the reader rejoices in the eventual rise in the fortunes of Pooter and his faithful, though frequently irritated, wife Carrie.

Dibdin, Charles 1745–1814 Playwright, actor and composer. His first comic opera, *The Shepherd's Artifice* (1764), was produced before he was 20. Much of his early work was in collaboration with BICKERSTAFFE, for whose *The Padlock* (1768) he wrote the music and created the role of Mungo. He provided both text and music for *The Wedding Ring* (1773), *The Deserter* (1773), the excellent BALLAD OPERA *The Waterman* (1774) and upwards of 40 subsequent pieces. A series of one-man shows helped to restore his uncertain fortunes in later years. 'Tom Bowling' has proved the most durable of the many ballads for which he was famous. His prose work included a five-volume *History of the Stage* (1795) and several forgotten novels, of which *Henry Hooka* (1806) was the last.

Dick, Philip K(endred) 1928–82 American writer of SCIENCE FICTION. *The World Jones Made* (1956) and *Eye in the Sky* (1957) are striking among early paperback novels written for money. His mature work often studies the gradual mechanization of the environment and deals with false realities created by hallucinogenic drugs or schizophrenic delusion. It includes *The Man in the High Castle* (1962), *Martian Time-Slip* (1964), *Now Wait for Last Year* (1966), *Do Androids Dream of Electric Sheep?* (1969), *Flow My Tears, the Policeman Said* (1974) and *A Scanner Darkly* (1977). Dick turned with deepening interest to metaphysics and hypothetical theology in *Valis* (1981)

and *The Divine Invasion* (1981). Non-science fiction work, including *Confessions of a Crap Artist* (1975) and *The Transmigration of Timothy Archer* (1982), shows his concern for the plight of the meek.

Dickens, Charles (John Huffam) 1812–70 Novelist. Born at Portsmouth, the son of John Dickens, a clerk in the Navy Office, and his wife Elizabeth, he had an unsettled childhood in London, Chatham and London again. After the family's second move to London his parents slid into financial difficulties which resulted in John Dickens's imprisonment for debt in the Marshalsea. Two days after his 12th birthday Dickens was put to work in Warren's blacking factory, a humiliating experience which he nursed in memory until the end of his life. On his release John Dickens sent his son to Wellington House Academy, where he remained until early 1827. He then became office boy in a firm of attorneys, rising swiftly to work as reporter in Doctors' Commons. Characteristically alert to self-advancement, he went on to work for his uncle's Hansard-style *Mirror of Parliament* and for *The True Sun* before becoming parliamentary journalist for the THE MORNING CHRONICLE in 1833. Deeply wounded by his unsuccessful courtship of Maria Beadnell, Dickens finally married Catherine Hogarth in April 1836.

By this time he was more than a mere reporter. *SKETCHES BY BOZ* (1836–7) gathered his early work into a book anticipating his novels in its fascination with the variety of London life. The month of his marriage saw the unpromising start of THE PICKWICK PAPERS (1836–7). The introduction of Sam Weller in its fourth number made Dickens famous. With success assured, he worked and lived with even greater intensity than before. Overlapping with the serialization of *Pickwick Papers* came first OLIVER TWIST (1837–9) and then NICHOLAS NICKLEBY (1838–9). As *Nicholas Nickleby* came to its conclusion he conceived MASTER HUMPHREY'S CLOCK, a weekly miscellany whose failure forced him to expand a story originally designed for the miscellany into a full-length serial, THE OLD CURIOSITY SHOP (1840–1); this he quickly followed with BARNABY RUDGE (1841). Always prickly with publishers, he quarrelled with John Macrone and friction with RICHARD BENTLEY caused him to resign the editorship of BENTLEY'S MISCELLANY in 1839. He enlarged his family, rescued his parents from financial difficulties, met his future biographer JOHN FORSTER and widened his circle of friends beyond journalism.

Dickens made his first visit to America in 1842, though the criticisms expressed in AMERICAN NOTES (1842) and his next novel, MARTIN CHUZZLEWIT (1843–4), caused lasting resentment among his American audience. In 1843 he produced his first and most famous Christmas story, A CHRISTMAS CAROL. In the spring of the next year he went to live in Genoa, returning to England in 1845 and publishing PICTURES FROM ITALY. In the mid 1840s, too, Dickens produced THE CHIMES, THE CRICKET ON THE HEARTH, THE BATTLE OF LIFE and THE HAUNTED MAN, republished together with A Christmas Carol as CHRISTMAS BOOKS (1852). As a journalist, he edited the newly founded DAILY NEWS for a mere 17 numbers in 1846 before a disagreement with the publishers caused him to withdraw. In 1850 he founded his own magazine, HOUSEHOLD WORDS, succeeded by ALL THE YEAR ROUND in 1859. More important was the publication of DOMBEY AND SON (1846–8), the novel which ushered in the mature period of his art, followed in the next decade by *DAVID COPPERFIELD* (1849–50), *BLEAK HOUSE* (1852–3), *HARD TIMES* (1854), *LITTLE DORRIT* (1855–7) and *A TALE OF TWO CITIES* (1859). Where his early work had overflowed with improvisatory energy, the novels of the 1850s and beyond are more tightly controlled. No less wide-ranging in their subjects, they are unified by theme, image and symbol as much as by their complex and ramifying plots.

Outside literature, Dickens's energy continued unabated. He indulged his love of travel and of amateur theatricals, acting in *The Frozen Deep* (written in collaboration with his friend WILKIE COLLINS) and other pieces. He also concerned himself with capital punishment, the reform of prostitutes and model flats in Bethnal Green among other issues. By the late 1850s he had been captivated by the young actress Ellen Ternan; his marriage came to a publicly acrimonious end in 1858. The same year saw the first of his public readings from his work, successfully repeated throughout England and on a second visit to the United States in 1867, before the strain forced him to give them up. It is ironic that the 1860s should also have produced some of his best work: *GREAT EXPECTATIONS* (1860–1), *OUR MUTUAL FRIEND* (1864–5) and the tantalizingly incomplete *MYSTERY OF EDWIN DROOD*, halted in its serialization by his death.

It is hard to accept that in the space of 58 years Dickens should have written even as much as the foregoing, though his canon also includes: pamphlets such as the anti-Sabbatarian *Sunday under Three Heads* (1836); *A Child's History of England* (1851–3); short stories such as 'To be Read at Dusk' (1852), 'Hunted Down' (1859), 'A Holiday Romance' (1868) and 'George Silverman's Explanation' (1868); pieces for *Household Words* and *All the Year Round*, some of them gathered in *The Uncommercial Traveller* (1860; enlarged in 1865 and 1875); several comic plays; and speeches and letters which have occupied the attention of modern editors. So prolific is his output and so frenzied his life, it seems miraculous he lived as long as he did.

Dickey, James (Lafayette) 1923– American poet and novelist. Much of his work is concerned with the guilt arising from the cruelties of life in the Southern backwoods and from the collective cruelties of nations. His first volume of poetry was *Into the Stone and Other Poems* (1960) but his reputation was secured by *Drowning with Others* (1962) and *Helmets* (1964), dealing with his experiences as a pilot in the US Air Force during World War II. His prolific output is gathered in *Whole Motion: Collected Poems, 1948–1992* (1992). He is probably best known, however, for his first novel, *Deliverance* (1970), a bestseller about a violent Georgia canoe trip; his screenplay for the film version was published in 1981. *Alnilam* (1987) is his second novel.

Dickinson, Emily 1830–86 American poet. She was born and lived all her life in Amherst, Massachusetts. By the age of 30 she had become an almost total recluse in her father's house, using correspondence to conduct her friendships with, for example, HELEN HUNT JACKSON, the Reverend Charles Wadsworth and her mentor, Thomas Wentworth Higginson, a minister, author and critic. Only seven of her poems were published during her lifetime, though over a thousand were found at her death. Almost all were short lyrics, typically consisting of just two four-line stanzas. Most were untitled and undated, and some survived in several versions. Higginson and Mabel L. Todd, an Amherst friend, made various corrections to the texts and pub-

lished the first volumes of her poetry in 1890 and 1891. Other volumes, also marred by unnecessary editing, were published by Dickinson's niece, Martha Dickinson Bianchi, and Alfred Leete Hampson, and published in 1914, 1924, 1929, 1930, 1935 and 1937. *Bolts of Melody: New Poems of Emily Dickinson* (1945), edited by Todd and her daughter, Millicent Todd Bingham, was more faithful. Thomas H. Johnson prepared an authoritative variorum edition, containing all 1775 known poems, in 1955. Johnson and Theodora Ward edited *The Letters of Emily Dickinson* (1958).

The subjects of Dickinson's poetry are the traditional ones of love, nature, religion and mortality, seen through Puritan eyes, or, as she described it, 'New Englandly'. Much of the tension stems from religious doubt, and many lyrics mix rebellious and reverent sentiments. The eccentricities and technical irregularities which alarmed her early editors and reviewers include: frequent use of dashes; sporadic capitalization of nouns; convoluted and ungrammatical phrasing; off-rhymes; broken metres; bold, unconventional and often startling metaphors; and aphoristic wit. These have greatly influenced 20th-century poets and contributed to Dickinson's reputation as one of the most innovative poets of 19th-century American literature.

dictionaries See ENGLISH DICTIONARIES.

Dictionary of the English Language, A A monumental work by SAMUEL JOHNSON, first published in 1755. He first announced the project in a *Plan* (1747), dedicated to the EARL OF CHESTERFIELD; his uneasiness about patronage was justified by his later quarrel with Chesterfield. The extent of his purpose is indicated in the *Dictionary*'s full title: *A Dictionary of the English Language: In Which the Words are Deduced from Their Originals, and Illustrated in Their Different Significations by Examples from the Best Writers. To Which are Prefixed a History of the Language, and an English Grammar*. In the 18th century there was only scant etymological knowledge to help Johnson but he brought to his task massive common sense, just as he brought his extraordinary wealth of reading to bear on the choice of illustrative quotations, SIR PHILIP SIDNEY and SPENSER being his earliest authorities. He set himself to reject all the 'Gallick structure and phraseology' which the language had absorbed since the Restoration and which threatened to make the English 'babble a dialect of France'. He also honoured, as fully as the knowledge of his time permitted, provincialisms and dialect. The result was not definitive but pioneering, a dictionary which has influenced and inspired all later attempts in the field. See also ENGLISH DICTIONARIES.

Didion, Joan 1934– American essayist and novelist. She is perhaps best known for her essays, prime examples of the New Journalism which coolly explore the spookier fringes of American society and politics: *Slouching toward Bethlehem* (1969), *The White Album* (1979), *Salvador* (1983), *Miami* (1988) and *Sentimental Journeys* (1993). Three novels – *Run, River* (1964), *Play It As It Lays* (1971) and *Democracy* (1984) – chronicle exhausted marriages and peripatetic lives on the edge of violence. *A Book of Common Prayer* (1977) takes place in a fictional South American republic.

Digby, Sir **Kenelm** 1603–65 Writer on science and religion. After toying with Protestantism, he published a reaffirmation of his Catholic faith, *Conference with a Lady about Choice of Religion* (1638), and a criticism of BROWNE's *RELIGIO MEDICI* (*Observations upon Religio*

Medici) in 1643. Other works were *Of the Immortality of Man's Soul* (1644), *On the Cure of Wounds* (1658) and *A Discourse concerning the Vegetation of Plants* (1660), an address to the Royal Society, of which he was a founder-member, on the necessity of oxygen to plant life.

Digby, Kenelm Henry ?1797–1880 Enthusiast for medieval culture. A descendant of SIR KENELM DIGBY, he combined admiration for medieval religion with a love of chivalry. *The Broad Stone of Honour: or, Rules for the Gentlemen of England* (1822) set forth his ideals at greater and greater length, swelling to four volumes in 1828–9 and five in 1877. It had considerable influence on the cult of medievalism, particularly among the PRE-RAPHAELITES. The 11-volume *Mores Catholici: or, Ages of Faith* (1831–42) dealt with the Catholic virtues. Digby later turned to verse and religious painting.

Dilke, Charles Wentworth 1789–1864 Critic and editor. His liberal sympathies and literary interests brought him into contact with LEIGH HUNT and his circle, and he is particularly remembered for his close friendship with KEATS. His continuation and completion of DODSLEY's *Old Plays* (1814–16) made an important contribution to the rediscovery of forgotten Elizabethan dramatists. Although most of his numerous contributions to periodicals were on literary topics, he wrote a pamphlet calling for the repeal of the Corn Laws in 1821. He was editor-in-chief of THE ATHENAEUM from 1830 to 1846, when he was called in to manage the affairs of THE DAILY NEWS following DICKENS's departure. He is best known for his detective work on JUNIUS and his researches into POPE's early life and career.

Dillon, Wentworth, 4th Earl of Roscommon *c.* 1633–85 Translator. The nephew and godson of Thomas Wentworth, Earl of Strafford, he wrote an *Essay on Translated Verse* (1684) and made a blank-verse translation of Horace's *The Art of Poetry* (1680). He was among the first to recognize the greatness of MILTON's *PARADISE LOST*.

dimeter See METRE.

Dinesen, Isak [Blixen (*née* Dinesen), Karen Christentze] 1885–1962 Danish-born writer. She wrote in English, rewriting her work for Danish publication. Born in Rungsted, she went to East Africa in 1913 to marry her cousin, Baron Blor von Blixen-Finecke, and farmed coffee outside Nairobi. After the failure of the marriage and the farm she returned to Denmark in 1937. *Seven Gothic Tales* (1934) is a collection of sometimes portentous neo-Gothic stories. *Out of Africa* (1937), drawing on her own experiences, is remarkable for its clarity and intellectual breadth; *Shadows on the Grass* (1960) continued the same theme. Other collections, *Winter's Tales* (1942), *Last Tales* (1957) and *Anecdotes of Destiny* (1958), deal with provincial as well as sophisticated situations and the insoluble difficulty of reconciling art and nature.

Dipsychus A verse drama by CLOUGH, written in 1850 and published in 1865. Set in a Venetian palazzo, it takes the form of a near-plotless duologue of 13 scenes between Dipsychus (an individual of two natures) and the Spirit. The discussion ranges across problems of society, religion, the professions and the contemplative life, as the protagonist searches his inner self. Like Clough's other writings, it is essentially a work of introspection articulating the role of the intellectual adrift in the world.

Disch, Thomas M(ichael) 1940– American writer of SCIENCE FICTION. The characteristic mode of his writing is satirical black comedy. His novels include: an apocalyptic novel, *The Genocides* (1965); *Camp Concentration* (1968); *Black Alice* (as 'Thom Demijohn', with John Sladek; 1968); *Clara Reeve* (as 'Leonie Hargrave', 1975), a pastiche GOTHIC NOVEL; *On Wings of Song* (1979); *Neighbouring Lives* (with Charles Naylor; 1981), about the world of Victorian letters; *The Businessman: A Tale of Terror* (1984); and *The M. D.: A Horror Story* (1990). Among his short stories are *Under Compulsion* (1968; also known as *Fun with Your New Head*), *334* (1972), *Getting into Death* (1973), *Fundamental Disch* (1980) and *The Man Who Had No Idea* (1982). His poetry includes *The Right Way to Figure Plumbing* (1971), *Burn This* (1982) and *Here I am, There You are, Where were We?* (1984).

Disraeli, Benjamin, 1st Earl of Beaconsfield 1804–81 Novelist and politician. The eldest son of ISAAC D'ISRAELI, he was baptized at the age of 13, despite his Jewish descent. After losing money on the Stock Exchange and in trying to found a newspaper, *The Representative*, he published his first novel, *VIVIAN GREY* (1826), which gave the youthful hero his own wit and arrogance. It was followed by a satirical work, *The Voyage of Captain Popanilla* (1827) and another society novel, *The Young Duke* (1831). A tour of Spain, Greece, Albania and Egypt left its mark on his writing, including his next novels, *CONTARINI FLEMING* (1832) and *Alroy* (1833). Despite his increasing involvement in politics, he continued to publish throughout the 1830s: a light-hearted SATIRE of contemporary politics, *The Infernal Marriage* (1834), and two more novels, *HENRIETTA TEMPLE* (1837) and *Venetia* (1837), a fictionalized account of events in the lives of SHELLEY and BYRON. In 1837 he succeeded in becoming Conservative MP for Maidstone, marrying the widow of the previous member two years later. During his early years in the Commons Disraeli showed his concern for the condition of the working class and associated himself with other reforming Tories in the 'Young England' group. The same attitudes underlie the trilogy of novels for which he is best known: *CONINGSBY: or, The New Generation* (1844), *SYBIL: or, the Two Nations* (1845) and *TANCRED: or, The New Crusade* (1847).

Disraeli first achieved political office in Lord Derby's Conservative administration of 1852. He was twice Prime Minister, in 1868 and in 1874–80. In 1876 he took the title Earl of Beaconsfield, one he had invented for a character in his first novel. His success in politics overshadowed but did not end, his writing career. *LOTHAIR* (1870) is about religious conflict, *ENDYMION* (1880) about politics. He also left a fragment of an unfinished novel, *Falconet*.

d'Israeli, Isaac 1766–1848 Man of letters and father of BENJAMIN DISRAELI. His published works are *Curiosities of Literature* (1791), *Essay on the Literary Character* (1795), *Miscellanies, or Literary Recreations* (1796), *The Calamities of Authors* (1812–13) and *Quarrels of Authors* (1814). He also wrote historical works on JAMES I (1816) and Charles I (1828–31); *The Genius of Judaism* (1833); three volumes of projected history of English literature, *Amenities of Literature* (1841); and four unsuccessful novels.

dissociation of sensibility A term coined by T. S. ELIOT in his essay 'The Metaphysical Poets' (1921). Eliot argued that writers of the late 16th and early 17th centuries, particularly DONNE, possessed a unity of thought and feeling, making for 'a direct sensuous apprehension of thought'. With the influence of MILTON and DRYDEN, English poetry was impoverished by a dissociation of sensibility. Poets of the 18th and

19th centuries, Eliot concluded, thought but could not feel their thoughts.

dithyramb Originally a Greek choric hymn accompanied by music and describing the adventures of Dionysus. The term is now used for verse or prose of a wild, passionate or excited nature, or for any wild chant or song. Perhaps the finest English example of dithyrambic verse is DRYDEN's 'Alexander's Feast'.

Dixon, H(enry) H(all) 1822–70 Sporting journalist. Writing as 'The Druid', he carved himself a niche in the middle ground between the aristocratic world of C. J. APPERLEY ('Nimrod') and the debased pugilistic arena of PIERCE EGAN THE ELDER. His best-known books are *Post and Paddock* (1856), *Silk and Scarlet* (1859), *Scott and Sebright* (1862), *Field and Fern* (1865) and *Saddle and Sirloin* (1870).

Dixon, Richard Watson 1833–1900 Poet. At Oxford he associated with WILLIAM MORRIS, Burne-Jones and DANTE GABRIEL ROSSETTI. After his ordination he taught at Highgate School, where his pupil GERARD MANLEY HOPKINS became a lifelong friend. Dixon's own first collection of verse, *Christ's Company* (1861), was praised by Rossetti and SWINBURNE. Later volumes include *Historical Odes* (1864), *Odes and Eclogues* (1884) and *Lyrical Poems* (1887). *Mano: A Poetical History* (1883) is a narrative poem set in the 10th century. Favourite anthology pieces include 'Dream', 'The Wizard's Funeral' and 'Love's Consolation'. ROBERT BRIDGES edited a selection, *The Last Poems* (1905).

Dobell, Sydney (Thompson) 1824–74 Poet. *The Roman: A Dramatic Poem* (1850) supported the cause of Italian nationalism. *Balder* (1853) was left unfinished, so damaging was the ridicule inflicted by AYTOUN, who parodied its plot in *Firmilian* and identified its author as part of the SPASMODIC SCHOOL OF POETRY. Dobell's other volumes included *Sonnets on the War* (with ALEXANDER SMITH; 1855) and *England in Time of War* (1856), about the Crimean campaign. *Thoughts on Art, Philosophy, and Religion* appeared posthumously in 1876.

Dobson, Austin (Henry) 1840–1921 Poet and biographer. His knowledge of the 18th century is apparent in his biographies of HOGARTH (1879), STEELE (1886), GOLDSMITH (1888), HORACE WALPOLE (1890), RICHARDSON (1902) and FANNY BURNEY (1903). His verse often used French forms such as the TRIOLET and RONDEAU. Volumes include *Vignettes in Rhyme* (1873), *Proverbs in Porcelain* (1877) and *At the Sign of the Lyre* (1885). *Collected Poems* appeared in 1897, and a collection of later essays in 1921.

Dobson, Rosemary 1920– Australian poet. She is the granddaughter of AUSTIN DOBSON. Though it has not received a great deal of popular attention, her detached, reflective verse has few rivals in Australian literature for its craftsmanship and formal elegance. Her training in art frequently manifests itself in poems about painters, painting and design. Later poetry is increasingly concerned with personal experiences, especially that of motherhood, and Greek themes. It is gathered in two volumes of *Collected Poems* (1973 and 1991). She has also translated several volumes of Russian poetry with DAVID CAMPBELL and edited a feminist anthology, *Sister Poets* (1979).

Doctor Faustus, The Tragical History of A tragedy by MARLOWE, first produced *c.* 1589 but not published until 1604. An edition of 1616 is more reliable, though both are faulty. The story comes from a medieval legend which first found its way into print at Frankfurt in 1587, when the student who makes a bargain with the Devil

was identified with a Doctor Georg (or Johann) Faust, a German necromancer of the late 15th and early 16th centuries. Weary of science, Faustus turns to magic and invokes the aid of the Devil. His agent Mephistophilis appears and Faustus strikes his bargain: Lucifer will give him 24 years of power, with Mephistophilis as his servant, before claiming him, body and soul. Faustus's guardian angel goes on trying to redeem him, while a Bad Angel goes on persuading him he is damned. Lucifer himself comes to Faustus and shows him the pleasures of the seven deadly sins. After a confrontation with the Pope and cardinals in Rome, Faustus invokes the ghost of Helen of Troy and embraces her. The climax of the play is Faustus's monologue anticipating the terrors that await him in his last hour of mortal life ('See, see, where Christ's blood streams in the firmament!') and his descent into hell. Despite its collapse into crude farce in the middle section – charitably regarded as the additions for which SAMUEL ROWLEY was paid in 1602 – *Faustus* is a magnificent poem, a great theme expressed in language that is equal to it.

Dr Jekyll and Mr Hyde, The Strange Case of A novel by ROBERT LOUIS STEVENSON, published in 1886. Apart from TREASURE ISLAND, it is probably his best-known work. The mystery is gradually revealed to the reader through the narratives of Mr Enfield, Mr Utterson, Dr Lanyon and Jekyll's butler, Poole. Seeking to separate the good and evil aspects of his nature, the doctor secretly develops a drug which frees his evil propensities into the repulsive form of Mr Hyde. It grows harder and harder for Jekyll to return to his own personality. With his supply of the drug exhausted and Hyde wanted for murder, Jekyll kills himself. The body discovered in his sanctum is that of Hyde, but the confession Jekyll leaves behind establishes the common identity of the two men. The story has attracted much commentary, being read as a version of the Scottish Arminianism of JAMES HOGG's PRIVATE MEMOIRS AND CONFESSIONS OF A JUSTIFIED SINNER, a variant of the *Doppelgänger* myth, and a pre-Freudian study of ego and libido.

Dr Syntax in Search of the Picturesque, The Tour of See COMBE, WILLIAM.

Doctor Thorne The third of TROLLOPE's BARSETSHIRE NOVELS, published in 1858. Trollope's best-selling work in his own lifetime, it extends the range of the sequence to take in the life of county society. The unmarried Dr Thorne, a country practitioner, lives in Greshamsbury with Mary, illegitimate child of his brother Henry. The plot deals with her love for Frank Gresham, son of the local squire's family, and the obstacles posed by the Greshams and their aristocratic relatives, the De Courcys. The death of Sir Roger Scatcherd, brother of Mary's mother, and Scatcherd's son Louis brings Mary a fortune which enables her to marry Frank. A subsidiary plot deals with the relations between Frank's sister and a social-climbing lawyer, and his eventual marriage to her treacherous De Courcy cousin.

Dr Wortle's School A novel by TROLLOPE, serialized in 1880 and published in volume form in 1881. Dr Jeffrey Wortle, a high-spirited and worldly clergyman, runs a successful private school to which he appoints Mr Peacocke as an assistant master and Peacocke's beautiful American wife as matron. It emerges that the couple had married in the mistaken belief that her first husband was dead. Dr Wortle's courage in standing by his conviction of the Peacockes' integrity against pressure from his bishop, the press and the malevolent gossip of an ex-parent is rewarded when Peacocke goes to America and returns with proof that the first husband has subsequently died. The couple are married again in London. Conventional love interest is provided by a romance between the doctor's daughter Mary and one of his former pupils, Lord Carstairs.

Doctorow, E(dgar) L(awrence) 1931– American novelist. *Welcome to Hard Times* (1960; as *Bad Man from Bodie* in Britain) was followed by *The Book of Daniel* (1971), about the espionage trial of Julius and Ethel Rosenberg and its aftermath. He remains best known for *Ragtime* (1975), set in early 20th-century America, which exemplifies his technique of mixing fictional characters with historical figures. Other novels are *Big as Life* (1966), *Loon Lake* (1980), *World's Fair* (1985) and *Billy Bathgate* (1989), about the New York gangland of the 1930s. *Lives of the Poet, Six Stories and a Novella* (1984) addresses the position of the writer.

Doddridge, Philip 1702–51 Nonconformist divine. A major influence on the unification of Nonconformist groups, he wrote *The Rise and Progress of Religion in the Soul* (1745), *Some Remarkable Passages in the Life of Colonel James Gardiner* (1747), an account of a reformed rake, and over 350 hymns, which may be compared to those of ISAAC WATTS. His collected works appeared in 10 volumes in 1802–5.

Dodgson, Charles Lutwidge See CARROLL, LEWIS.

Dodsley, Robert 1703–64 Publisher and author. He began as a servant but came to the attention of literary London with his poem, *Servitude* (1729). The modest success of his play, *The Toyshop: A Dramatic Satire* (1735), and the financial help of POPE enabled him to open a bookshop in Pall Mall. Dodsley published work by Pope, THOMAS GRAY, AKENSIDE, WILLIAM COLLINS, EDWARD YOUNG, SHENSTONE, SAMUEL JOHNSON and GOLDSMITH. His great service to the poets of his time was the publication of their work in permanent volumes called *A Collection of Poems by Various Hands*, the first of which was published in 1748; six volumes appeared in 10 years. They are valuable to students of the period, as his collection of *Old Plays* (12 vols, 1744) is to students of drama. In 1758, the same year his tragedy *Cleone* was produced, Dodsley founded THE ANNUAL REGISTER with BURKE.

Dombey and Son A novel by DICKENS, published in monthly parts in1846–8 and in volume form in 1848, as *Dealings with the Firm of Dombey and Son, Retail, Wholesale and for Exportation*. It is commonly taken to herald the start of Dickens's maturity, for its careful planning marks a break from the high-spirited improvisation which often sustains his early fiction.

The stern, unbending Mr Dombey, preoccupied with his desire for a son and heir to the firm, ignores and resents his daughter Florence. Mrs Dombey dies at the beginning of the book in giving birth to a son, Paul, but he proves weak and dies in the fifth number (chapter 16). The bereavement further alienates Florence from her father. Dombey's second marriage, to Edith Grainger, proves loveless and childless. She finally runs away with Dombey's business manager, Carker, though she soon abandons him and he dies in a railway accident. Dombey's ensuing mental and physical decline parallels his business difficulties. Only as a ruined man can he at last respond to Florence's love. The novel contrasts the cold unhappiness of the Dombey household with the cheerful homes of the Toodle family and of Sol Gills and his nephew Walter Gay, Florence's future husband.

Domett, Alfred 1811–77 Politician and poet. He emigrated to New Zealand, where he became Prime Minister. After his return to England in 1871 he published two books of poetry reflecting his experiences, *Ranolf and Amohia* (1872) and *Flotsam and Jetsam* (1877). 'A Christmas Hymn' was once a familiar anthology piece. Domett is the 'Waring' of his friend ROBERT BROWNING's well-known poem (1842).

Don Juan BYRON's unfinished 'epic satire' in OTTAVA RIMA, published in 16 CANTOS between 1819 and 1824. Cantos 1–2 appeared in 1819, 3–5 in 1821, 6–14 in 1823 and 15–16 in 1824. Byron's central character is not the aggressive libertine of tradition, but a passive, if unprincipled, innocent who learns through the variety of his complex international adventures: a youthful intrigue with Donna Julia in his native Seville; a shipwreck in which the survivors are reduced to eating first his spaniel and then his tutor, Pedrillo; a love affair on a Greek island with a pirate's daughter, Haïdée; slavery in Constantinople; service in the Russian army; and finally a diplomatic mission to England. The last cantos contain much satirical comment on contemporary English society, politics and literature.

Don Juan is Byron's most sustained masterpiece. Its tone is varied and its loose structure allows the poet to intermix his gifts as a lyrical, satirical, comic and narrative writer, but above all to offer wide-ranging ironic comment on human passions, whims and shortcomings. It also contains the much-anthologized lyric 'The Isles of Greece' (Canto 3), Byron's powerful song to a nation still occupied by the Ottomans.

Donleavy, J(ames) P(atrick) 1926– Novelist, short-story writer and playwright. Born of Irish parents in New York, he settled in Ireland. He remains best known for a determinedly Rabelaisian novel of Dublin literary life, *The Ginger Man*, first published in Paris in 1955, then in a revised edition in New York in 1958 and in a unexpurgated edition in New York in 1965. Other novels include *A Singular Man* (1961).

Donne, John c. 1572–1631 METAPHYSICAL POET and divine. The grandson of the dramatist JOHN HEYWOOD and the son of a prosperous London ironmonger, he was brought up as a Roman Catholic – a reason for leaving Oxford in 1584 without taking a degree. The following years were clearly unsettled: he entered Lincoln's Inn in 1592, sailed with the Cadiz expedition in 1596 and the Azores expedition in 1597 (see 'The Calm'), womanized and wrote verse. The dating of his poetry is largely problematic, but to the 1590s apparently belong: most of the love poems contained in *Songs and Sonnets* (including 'The Good Morrow', 'The Canonization', 'The Bait' and songs such as 'Go and Catch a Falling Star'); the *Elegies*, characteristically sinuous, colloquial and racy poems which have none of the smoothness later identified with the ELEGY; and his five verse *Satires*, among the first formal verse satires in the language. In 1601 he published an ambitious but unfinished poem, *Metempsychosis*, a complicated explanation of the nature of good and evil as manifested in the progressive metamorphoses of the soul, from its vegetable origins in Eden to its embodiment in mankind.

On his return from the Azores expedition Donne had become secretary to Sir Thomas Egerton, Lord Keeper of the Great Seal, and through his influence MP for Brackley. In 1601 he secretly married Egerton's niece Ann Moore, then only 17. Before her early death in 1617 the couple had 12 children, of whom seven survived;

Constance, the eldest daughter, grew up to marry the actor EDWARD ALLEYN. The immediate consequences of Donne's marriage were drastic, earning him a brief spell of imprisonment and dismissal from Egerton's service. He cultivated a convivial circle of acquaintances including JONSON, DRAYTON and Inigo Jones, travelled briefly abroad, and sought vainly for advancement. He wrote two notable poems commemorating the death of Elizabeth Drury, the daughter of his friend and patron Sir Robert Drury, 'The First Anniversary' (1611) and 'The Progress of the Soul' (1612). In general, his writings record a preoccupation with religion and a movement away from Catholicism. *Biathanatos* (1607) is an erudite prose-work about Christianity and suicide. *Pseudo-Martyr* (1610), his most notable prose-work, urged English Catholics to take the Oath of Supremacy, while *Ignatius His Conclave* (1611) satirized the Jesuits. The *Holy Sonnets* reveal spiritual struggle and, at times, near-despair, as well as the hard-won triumph of the famous 'Death, be Not Proud'.

He was finally ordained in 1615, soon establishing a reputation as a fine preacher. He became a chaplain to JAMES I and reader in divinity at Lincoln's Inn, acquired livings in Kent and Huntingdon, and ended his life as Dean of St Paul's as well as vicar of St Dunstan's-in-the-West. Widowed and plagued increasingly by the ill health which had always dogged him, Donne gained in power as a religious writer. *Devotions upon Emergent Occasions* (1624) consists of meditations, expostulations and prayers; Meditation 17, which begins 'Perchance he for whom the bell tolls', has become one of the best-known passages of English prose. In his final illness, movingly described in the biography by his friend WALTON, he insisted on preaching his last sermon, 'Death's Duel', before Charles I at Whitehall. His monument in St Paul's, which he designed himself, survived the Great Fire.

Very little of Donne's verse appeared in print during his lifetime, and the posthumous *Collected Poems* (1633) was by no means complete. His verse is generally divided into the love poetry of his youth and the religious poetry of later years, though both clearly belong to the same process of organic development. The love poetry is original, energetic and highly rhetorical, full of passionate thought and intellectual juggling, paradox and punning designed to work forcefully against the tired conventions of the PETRARCHAN school. It is often erotic and physically urgent: Donne was the first writer to use 'sex' in its present sense. The same adroitness in argument and dramatic skill in impersonating different states of mind that make his love poetry intense and often riddling animate his religious verse. But as a devotional poet Donne is less stylistically arresting, less facetious, and less sure of his direction: the poems mirror what was evidently a fierce struggle of the spirit to conquer doubt and achieve faith. As a writer of religious prose he is best known for his *Sermons*, 160 of which were published after his death, in 1640, 1649 and 1660 successively. They are often brilliant and severe.

Doolittle, Hilda 1886–1961 American poet, who used the pseudonym H. D. She went to live in Europe in 1911, marrying RICHARD ALDINGTON and, through her association with POUND, becoming involved with IMAGISM. *Sea Garden* (1916) was the first of many volumes of poetry whose most abiding theme was her passion for classical Greek literature. They include: *Hymen* (1921); *Heliodora*

and Other Poems (1924); *Red Roses for Bronze* (1929); *Trilogy*, a long poem consisting of *The Walls Do Not Fall* (1944), *Tribute to the Angels* (1945) and *The Flowering of the Rod* (1946), deriving from her psychoanalysis by Freud (1933–4) and her experience of London during World War II; *Helen in Egypt* (1961), about Helen of Troy; and *Hermetic Definition* (1972). She also published novels: *Palimpsest* (1926), a three-part work set in classical Rome, post-war London and the Egypt of the excavators; *Hedylus* (1928), set in ancient Alexandria; and *Bid Me to Live* (1960), about life in London during World War I. Other works include: *Hippolytus Temporizes* (1927), a drama in classical form; *By Avon River* (1949), a tribute in verse and prose to SHAKESPEARE and the Elizabethans; three memoirs, *Tribute to Freud* (1956), *End to Torment: A Memoir of Ezra Pound* (1979) and *The Gift* (1982); and *Hermione* (1981), posthumously published writings on lesbian themes.

Dorn, Ed(ward) 1929– American poet. Associated with the BLACK MOUNTAIN SCHOOL, he established himself with *From Gloucester Out* (1964) as the most important younger poet extending the possibilities of CHARLES OLSON's theories of 'projective verse'. *What I See in the Maximus Poems* (1961) is a critical study of Olson. *The Collected Poems, 1956–1974* (1975) reprints all the verse from the first 18 years of his career except *Gunslinger* (1968–72), a dramatic narrative which first appeared as four separate books and then as *Slinger* (1975). Later volumes are *Hello La Jolla* (1978), *Selected Poems* (1978), *Views* (1980), *Abhorrence* (1990) and *By the Sound* (1991). *The Rite of Passage* (1965) is a novel.

Dos Passos, John (Roderigo) 1896–1970 American novelist. His early works include a collection of essays, a volume of poems and two novels, *One Man's Initiation: 1917* (1920) and *Three Soldiers* (1921), deriving from his experiences as an ambulance driver in France and Italy during World War I. He came to prominence with *Manhattan Transfer* (1925), a novel whose aim of providing a 'collective' portrait of New York embodied his left-wing views. A similar purpose underlay his most important work, *USA*, a trilogy consisting of *The 42nd Parallel* (1930), *1919* (1932) and *The Big Money* (1936), which together seek to provide a portrait of American life in the first decades of the century. *The Moon is a Gong* (1926; later renamed *The Garbage Man*), *Airways, Inc.* (1928) and *Fortune Heights* (1934) are plays stemming from his involvement with experimental theatre. His disillusionment with communism is made clear in *The Adventures of a Young Man* (1939), the first volume of another trilogy, *District of Columbia*, completed by *Number One* (1943), about the dangers of demagogy, and *The Grand Design* (1949), about the threat of bureaucracy. Later novels include *Chosen Country* (1951) and *Midcentury* (1961). Dos Passos's many works of non-fiction include a biography of Thomas Jefferson (1954). *The Fourteenth Chronicle* (1973) contains selections from his letters and diaries.

Double Dealer, The A comedy by CONGREVE, first performed in 1693. More satirical and more rigidly classical in form than its predecessor, THE OLD BACHELOR (1693), it was also less immediately popular. Mellefont, Lord Touchwood's nephew and heir, is about to marry Cynthia, daughter of Sir Paul Plyant. Lady Touchwood, who wants Mellefont for herself, sets out to obstruct his marriage by enlisting the aid of her former lover Maskwell, the double dealer of the title. He tricks both Sir Paul Plyant and Lord Touchwood into suspecting that Mellefont is having affairs with their wives, but comes unstuck when he claims Cynthia for himself. Lord Touchwood overhears the jealous Lady Touchwood upbraiding him and their plotting is discovered. Mellefont and Cynthia are at last free to marry.

Douce, Francis 1757–1834 Antiquary. A former keeper of manuscripts at the British Museum, he became an outstanding collector of books, manuscripts, prints and coins to the Bodleian Library. His *Illustrations of Shakespeare* (1807) was a collection of the principal sources and analogues of the plays.

Doughty, Charles Montagu 1843–1926 Travel-writer and poet. After settling in Damascus in 1875 in order to learn Arabic, he made the pilgrimage to Mecca in 1876 by joining a camel caravan, which he followed to Jedda. The account of his journey is contained in his most famous work, *Travels in Arabia Deserta* (1888). Doughty's poetry includes *The Dawn in Britain* (6 vols, 1906–7), *Adam Cast Forth* (1908), *The Clouds* (1912) and *Mansoul: or, The Riddle of the World* (1920).

Douglas A blank-verse tragedy by JOHN HOME, first performed in Edinburgh in 1756 and in London the following year to great success. It remained popular for almost a century, the parts of Young Norval (Douglas) and Lady Randolph being favourites with tragedians of the day. The plot is based on an old Scottish ballad. Young Norval, brought up by a shepherd, is briefly united with his long-lost mother, once Lady Douglas and now Lady Randolph. Glenalvon, Lord Randolph's heir, plots against him. Norval kills Glenalvon and Lord Randolph kills Norval. Lady Randolph commits suicide.

Douglas, Lord Alfred (Bruce) 1870–1945 Poet. His intimacy with OSCAR WILDE eventually provoked his father, Lord Queensberry, to intervene; Wilde's unsuccessful suit against Queensberry brought about his own downfall. In prison Wilde addressed the bitter *DE PROFUNDIS* to Douglas. Apart from his translation of *SALOME* into English (1894), *Oscar Wilde and Myself* (1914) and *Oscar Wilde: A Summing-Up* (1940), Douglas produced several volumes of undistinguished verse. He edited *THE ACADEMY* from 1907–10.

Douglas, Gavin ?1475–1522 Scottish poet. The son of the Earl of Angus, he became Bishop of Dunkeld in 1515 and played an ambitious role, frustrated by political rivalries, at the court of James IV's widow, the dowager Queen Margaret. The Scottish Council of Lords charged him with treason in 1522 and he died in exile, probably of plague. As a poet he is usually grouped with the SCOTTISH CHAUCERIANS. He says that he finished his translation of the *Aeneid* on 22 July 1513. His other major work, *The Palace of Honour*, was probably complete by 1501, though it was not printed until *c.* 1553. An allegorical DREAM-VISION designed for a courtly audience and dedicated to James IV, it describes the pageants of Minerva, Diana and Venus, the poet's trial by the Court of Venus on a charge of blasphemy and, in the third part, his eventual achievement of his quest at Honour's Palace. *Conscience*, probably by Douglas, is an attack on the cupidity of churchmen. *King Hart*, first printed in 1786 and doubtfully ascribed to him, is a homiletic ALLEGORY resembling *EVERYMAN*.

Douglas, George [Brown, George Douglas] 1869–1902 Scottish novelist. He earned his living contributing short stories and boys' stories to magazines but is remembered for his realistic story of Scottish life, *THE HOUSE WITH GREEN SHUTTERS* (1901).

Douglas, Keith (Castellain) 1920–44 Poet. During World War II he served in North Africa and Normandy, where he died. His war poems face the prospect of death without heightened rhetoric or mournful sentiment. *Selected Poems* appeared in 1943 and *Alamein to Zem Zem*, an account of his experience in the desert campaign, was published posthumously in 1946. TED HUGHES's enthusiastic introduction to a selection of Douglas's verse (1964) brought him a wider audience. *Complete Poems* appeared in 1979.

Douglas, (George) Norman 1868–1952 Novelist and travel-writer. He achieved his first and only popular success with *South Wind* (1917), a novel describing how the Bishop of Bambopo, Thomas Heard, is caught by the pagan spell of the sirocco (south wind) during a visit to the Mediterranean island of Nepenthe (Capri). Its frank discussion of moral and sexual questions caused considerable debate. *Siren Land* (1911), *Fountains in the Sand* (about Tunisia, 1912) and *Old Calabria* (1915) are travel books reflecting Douglas's wide-ranging interests as biologist, geologist, art lover, archaeologist and classicist. *They Went* (1920) and *In the Beginning* (1927) are fantasies about early mankind, and *Looking Back* (1933) is a fragmentary autobiography.

Douglass, Frederick 1817–95 Black American writer. Born into slavery on a Maryland plantation, he escaped to Massachusetts in 1838. One of the most eloquent anti-slavery orators of his day, he established two journals *The North Star* (1847–64), later called *Frederick Douglass' Paper*, and *Douglass' Monthly* (1858–63) and organized two black regiments for the Union during the Civil War. Three works of autobiography confirmed his reputation: the *Narrative of the Life of Frederick Douglass, an American Slave* (1845), *My Bondage and My Freedom* (1855) and *The Life and Times of Frederick Douglass* (1881). Late in life he served as recorder of deeds for the District of Columbia (1881–6) and as US minister to Haiti (1889–91). BOOKER T. WASHINGTON wrote his biography (1906).

Dover Beach A poem by MATTHEW ARNOLD, published in *New Poems* (1867). Despite its brevity, it is probably the best known of all his works. The poem contemplates the sea, finding in it melancholy reminders of the uncertainties of belief brought about by modern life. He turns instead to faith in human relationships: 'Ah, love, let us be true to one another!'

Dowden, Edward 1843–1913 Critic and scholar. The editor of 12 SHAKESPEARE plays for the original Arden edition, he also wrote *Shakespeare: A Critical Study of His Mind and Art* (1875) and *A Shakespeare Primer* (1877). Other works include a study of SOUTHEY (1879) and biographies of SHELLEY (1886) and BROWNING (1905).

Dowson, Ernest (Christopher) 1867–1900 Poet. A friend of BEARDSLEY, WILDE and RICHARD LE GALLIENNE, he attended meetings of the RHYMERS' CLUB and contributed verse to *THE YELLOW BOOK* and *The Savoy*. He first achieved attention with *Poems* (1896). *Decorations* (1899) included some experiments with prose-poems, and *The Pierrot of the Minute* (1897) was a one-act verse play. The poems are written in a variety of stanza-forms, and express *ennui* (as in 'Non Sum Qualis Eram' and 'Vitae Summa Brevis') and a correspondingly idealized love (in 'Poet's Road'). His *Poetical Works* appeared in 1934 and his *Letters* were edited by H. Maas and D. Flower (1967).

Doyle, Sir Arthur Conan 1859–1930 Novelist and writer of DETECTIVE FICTION and SCIENCE FICTION. The nephew of RICHARD DOYLE, he had abandoned his family's Roman Catholicism by the time he completed his medical studies at Edinburgh. *The Stark Munro Letters* (1894) reflects his experiences as a general practitioner. His SHERLOCK HOLMES STORIES began with two novels, *A Study in Scarlet* (1887) and *The Sign of Four* (1890), though their popularity dated from the short stories in *THE STRAND MAGAZINE*, collected as *The Adventures of Sherlock Holmes* (1892) and *The Memoirs of Sherlock Holmes* (1894). Doyle's attempt to kill off his creation was unsuccessful and Holmes reappeared in two novels, *The Hound of the Baskervilles* (1902) and *The Valley of Fear* (1915), and several collections of short stories, *The Return of Sherlock Holmes* (1905), *His Last Bow* (1917) and *The Case-Book of Sherlock Holmes* (1927).

To Doyle's own annoyance, the popularity of Sherlock Holmes overshadowed the other fruits of his versatile and hardworking career. His historical fiction comprises *Micah Clarke* (1889), *The White Company* (1891), *Rodney Stone* (1896), *The Exploits of Brigadier Gerard* (1896), *Uncle Bernac* (1897), *The Adventures of Gerard* (1903) and *Sir Nigel* (1906). *The Tragedy of the 'Korosko'* (1898) is an adventure story. Doyle also wrote SCIENCE FICTION in his Professor Challenger stories, *The Lost World* (1912), *The Poison Belt* (1913) and *The Land of Mist* (1926). The last of them reflects the belief in spiritualism which preoccupied much of his later life.

Doyle, Sir Francis Hastings Charles 1810–88 Poet. MATTHEW ARNOLD's successor as professor of poetry at Oxford, he wrote popular BALLADS, notably the patriotic 'Private of the Buffs' and 'The Red Thread of Honour', and one about racing, 'The Doncaster St Leger'.

Doyle, Richard 1824–83 Cartoonist and illustrator. The uncle of SIR ARTHUR CONAN DOYLE, 'Dicky' Doyle worked for *PUNCH* (he designed its famous cover) before becoming a distinguished book illustrator. His light, playful sketches accompanied RUSKIN's *King of the Golden River* (1851) and THACKERAY's *THE NEWCOMES* (1853–5), among other works.

Doyle, Roddy 1958– Irish novelist. North Dublin is the setting for his fiction, which has been highly praised for its picaresque evocation of Irish working-class life, largely through pithy, colloquial dialogue. *The Commitments* (1988), about an Irish soul band's bid for stardom, *The Snapper* (1990) and *The Van* (1991) form a trilogy dealing with the Rabbitte family. *Paddy Clarke Ha Ha Ha* (1993) won the BOOKER PRIZE.

Drabble, Margaret 1939– Novelist. Often preoccupied with the individual's struggle against a conventional or repressive background, her fiction has grown steadily broader in its consideration of the contemporary social climate. It includes: *A Summer Birdcage* (1963), *The Garrick Year* (1964), *The Millstone* (1965), *Jerusalem the Golden* (1967), *The Waterfall* (1969), *The Ice Age* (1977), and a trilogy following the friendship of three women, *The Radiant Way* (1987), *A Natural Curiosity* (1989) and *The Gates of Ivory* (1991). In the course of a prolific career which has included public work for literary causes, she has also written a biography of ANGUS WILSON (1995) and studies of WORDSWORTH (1966), ARNOLD BENNETT (1974) and the relationship between writers and landscape in *A Writer's Britain* (1979), as well as editing *The Oxford Companion to English Literature* (1984). Her sister is A. S. BYATT and her husband the biographer Michael Holroyd.

Dracula A novel by BRAM STOKER, published in 1897. Presented in diaries, letters and news items, its story of a bloodsucking vampire who preys on the living and can be repelled by garlic and crucifixes, is both absurd and powerful. Like *FRANKENSTEIN*, it has become modern myth – the subject of many film versions, imitations and parodies.

Jonathan Harker, a London solicitor, falls victim to Count Dracula in his Transylvanian castle. The Count then travels to England, arriving at Whitby, where the story is taken up in accounts by Harker's fiancée Mina Murray, her friend Lucy Westenra and Dr John Seward. Van Helsing, a Dutch doctor and expert in vampirism, leads the fight against Dracula. When Lucy becomes his victim a stake is driven through her heart so that she can rest in peace. Dracula turns his attention to Mina, but is pursued to Transylvania and vanquished.

dramatic irony See IRONY.

dramatic monologue A poem consisting of a speech by a single character who reveals his thoughts, character and situation. In the 19th century, when literature became increasingly preoccupied with the individual viewpoint, ROBERT BROWNING found it an ideal form and TENNYSON used it several times. T. S. ELIOT and others turned to it in the 20th century.

Drapier's Letters, The A group of seven pamphlets by SWIFT, five published in 1724 and two in 1735, written in the character of a Dublin draper, M. B. Drapier. The original five attack the patent acquired by William Wood, an 'obscure Ironmonger', for supplying Ireland with copper coinage. The scheme to coin 'Wood's ha'pence' was withdrawn and the satirist became a national hero. Swift's interest in the matter was part of his campaign against the arrogant and thoughtless treatment of Ireland by the English.

Drayton, Michael 1563–1631 Poet and playwright. His career covered a wide span (nearly 40 years) and explored nearly all the poetic genres then available. Drayton's interest in history makes a continual theme, his habit of revising and reissuing his work a constant mannerism.

He responded to the fondness for PASTORAL in the 1590s with *Idea: The Shepherds' Garland* (1593), whose nine ECLOGUES show the strong influence of SPENSER's *THE SHEPHEARDES CALENDER*. It was revised and reissued in 1606. *Idea's Mirror* (1594) is the first version of the SONNET sequence *IDEA*, Drayton's contribution to the sonnet vogue of the 1590s. *Endimion and Phoebe* (1595) is a fashionable EPYLLION, revised and retitled *The Man in the Moon* (1606 and 1619). The 1590s also saw Drayton's first attempts at historical poetry with 'legends', often drawn from HOLINSHED: *Piers Gaveston* (?1594), *Matilda* (1594), *Robert of Normandy* (1596, revised 1605 and 1619) and *Mortimeriados* (1596, rewritten and much altered as *The Barons' Wars*, 1603 and 1619), much indebted to MARLOWE's *EDWARD II*. *The Legend of Great Cromwell* (1607), a later work drawn from FOXE's *ACTS AND MONUMENTS*, is remarkable for its detached view of the reign of Henry VIII and its refusal of an easy 'Protestant' bias. It is the only one of Drayton's historical legends to be included in *THE MIRROR FOR MAGISTRATES* (1610 edition).

The First Part of Sir John Oldcastle (1600), Drayton's only extant play, cashed in on the success of Shakespeare's *HENRY IV* plays. Like other, lost plays, it seems to have been collaborative work. *England's Heroical Epistles* (1597) earned for Drayton the title of 'our English Ovid', though characteristically he replaced Ovid's mythological characters with figures from English history (Henry II and Fair Rosamond, Richard II and Isabel, etc.). *The Owl* (1604 and 1619) emulates the medieval FABLE. *Poems Lyric and Pastoral* (1606) contains imitations of Horace's *Odes*, the first attempted by an English Renaissance poet. *POLY-OLBION*, with *Idea* Drayton's major work, appeared in two parts in 1612 and 1622.

A number of new poems appeared together in 1627. *The Battle of Agincourt* is an attempt at epic which again draws on chronicle sources, and *The Miseries of Queen Margaret* is indebted to Holinshed and Shakespeare's *HENRY VI* plays. *Nimphidia*, in the same volume, has won Drayton more popularity than any of his other works. It is a MOCK-HEROIC series of 'Nimphalls' or fairy poems influenced by *A MIDSUMMER NIGHT'S DREAM*. *The Muses' Elizium* (1630) sees Drayton, like Shakespeare, returning to pastoral at the end of his career.

Dream of Gerontius, The A poem by NEWMAN, published in two parts in 1865 and in book form in 1866. It is the DRAMATIC MONOLOGUE of a just soul on the point of death. Sir Edward Elgar's oratorio setting was composed in 1900.

Dream of John Ball, A A tale by WILLIAM MORRIS, serialized in 1886-7 and published in book form in 1888. The dream takes Morris back to the Peasants' Revolt of 1381 and an encounter with the dissenting priest John Ball. As Morris describes the Industrial Revolution and 19th-century society, Ball realizes he is himself dreaming of the future course of history and still unfulfilled ideals. *A Dream of John Ball* is the forerunner of Morris's greatest socialist work, *NEWS FROM NOWHERE*.

Dream of the Rood, The An Old English religious poem, found in the VERCELLI BOOK and probably dating from 750 or earlier. In a dream the narrator sees the Holy Cross, both a beautiful symbol and a historical, blood-stained object. It speaks, describing the Crucifixion in terms of its own experience and its own emergence as a symbol of Christ's Passion.

dream-vision A medieval poem about a dream. Its substance is allegorical, and may be secular or religious, comic or serious. Despite their wide differences medieval dream-visions are usually told in the first person, contain a supernatural or surreal element, and instruct the dreamer. Sometimes the dreamer is naive, is accompanied by a guide and encounters a beautiful landscape. The chief influences on the form were classical and biblical traditions of revelation and vision, Cicero's *Somnium Scipionis* and Macrobius' commentary, and the *Roman de la rose* by Guillaume de Lorris and Jean de Meun. CHAUCER, LANGLAND and the GAWAIN-poet all wrote dream-visions. Chaucer's poems were widely copied and the form was continued into the 16th century by GAVIN DOUGLAS, SKELTON and DUNBAR. Later dream-visions, like MORRIS's *NEWS FROM NOWHERE*, are usually the result of deliberate medievalizing. The preoccupation with dreams in modern literature – JOYCE's *FINNEGANS WAKE*, for example – often acknowledges the medieval tradition but is influenced by psychological theory.

Dreiser, Theodore (Herman Albert) 1871-1945 American novelist. Born in Terre Haute, Indiana, he worked as a journalist in New York. *SISTER CARRIE* (1900) and *JENNIE GERHARDT* (1911) were attacked for their candid and uncompromising NATURALISM. *The Financier* (1912) and *The Titan* (1914) were the first two volumes of Dreiser's *Cowperwood* trilogy, based on the life of the business magnate, Charles T. Yerkes; it was completed by *The Stoic*, posthumously published in 1947. *The Genius* (1915) is a partly autobiographical novel examining the artistic temperament. Dreiser at last earned popular

acclaim with *AN AMERICAN TRAGEDY* (1925), based on the Chester Gillette–Grace Brown murder case of 1906. *The Bulwark* appeared posthumously in 1946.

Dreiser Looks at Russia (1928) describes a visit to the Soviet Union, while *Tragic America* (1931) and *America is Worth Saving* (1941) express his belief in socialism. Dreiser also published plays, verse, short stories, essays and an autobiography.

Drennan, William 1754-1820 Irish pamphleteer and poet. A founder of the society of United Irishmen, he withdrew from active politics after its defeat in the rising of 1798. He made a mark as a political writer with *Letters of an Irish Helot* (1784). His verse is lyrical, witty, iconoclastic or fiercely patriotic by turns. One of his best poems, 'The Wake of William Orr' (1797), is an ELEGY for the first United Irishman to be executed. His most famous poem, 'Erin to Her Own Tune and Words' (1795), set to a traditional air, is the source of the phrase 'the Emerald Isle'. His *Fugitive Pieces in Verse and Prose* appeared in 1815, a translation of Sophocles' *Electra* in 1817 and *Glendalloch and Other Poems*, incorporating poems by his two sons, posthumously in 1859. A selection of his vividly informative letters was published in 1931.

Drinkwater, John 1882-1937 Playwright and poet. His early verse plays are mostly short experimental pieces. His major achievement is a sequence of historical plays written in prose: *Abraham Lincoln* (1918), *Mary Stuart* (1921), *Oliver Cromwell* (1921) and *Robert E. Lee* (1923). *Bird in Hand* (1927) is a comedy. His verse includes *The Death of Leander and Other Poems* (1906), *Lyrical and Other Poems* (1908), *Cromwell and Other Poems* (1913) and a wartime volume, *Swords and Ploughshares* (1915). Critical work includes a study of WILLIAM MORRIS (1912) and biographies of PEPYS (1930) and SHAKESPEARE (1933).

Drummond, William Henry 1854-1907 Canadian poet. His family emigrated from Ireland to Canada when he was 11. *The Habitant* (1897), *Johnny Courteau* (1901), *The Voyageur* (1905) and *The Great Fight* (1908) show his fascination with the patois and culture of the French-Canadians of the Rivière des Prairies. A collected volume, *The Poetical Works*, was published in 1912.

Drummond of Hawthornden, William 1585-1649 Poet and pamphleteer. He is remembered less for his own work than the invaluable record he made of JONSON's conversation during a visit to his manor near Edinburgh in the winter of 1618-9. It was eventually published in 1832. Though Jonson was not among its warm admirers, Drummond's poetry reflects his wide reading and travels. *Tears on the Death of Moeliades*, on the death of Prince Henry, appeared in 1613 and *Poems, Amorous, Funeral, Divine, Pastoral, in Sonnets, Songs, Sextains, Madrigals* in 1616, the year after the death of his fiancée Mary Cunningham. A collection of religious verse, *Flowers of Sion* (1623), contains the sonnets 'Saint John Baptist' and 'For the Magdalene', which are among his best-known works, and the prose essay on death *A Cypress Grove*.

Drury Lane, Theatre Royal It originally opened as a PATENT THEATRE in 1662, housing the KING'S MEN under KILLIGREW's management. A second, enlarged building (possibly by Wren, 1674) prospered in the 18th century, particularly under the management of CIBBER and then GARRICK. RICHARD BRINSLEY SHERIDAN began his tenure with a production of *THE SCHOOL FOR SCANDAL* and later entrusted the management to the actor John Philip Kemble, who supervised rebuilding in 1791-4 to a design by Henry Holland. This third theatre burned down in 1809 and was replaced by a fourth building (by Benjamin Wyatt, 1812) which, though much altered, still stands. After the loss of its monopoly in 1843, Drury Lane became famous as the home of spectacle and PANTOMIME during the successive managements of Augustus Harris (1879–96) and Arthur Collins (1896–1923). It is now reliant on musicals.

Dry White Season, A A novel by ANDRÉ BRINK, published in 1979. Like many of his novels, it charts the gradual distancing of an ordinary Afrikaner from the conservative attitudes of his community. Ben Du Toit is moved by the distress of a black servant to investigate her husband's disappearance and death in police custody. He continues despite threats from the police and the hostility of his wife and daughter, becoming increasingly caught up in the black community and involved with a white journalist. *A Dry White Season* was filmed in 1989.

Dryden, John 1631–1700 Poet and playwright. Born at Aldwinkle in Northamptonshire, he attended Westminster School and Trinity College, Cambridge. He published his first verses while still at school. In 1659 he wrote his impressive 'Heroic Stanzas' on the death of the Lord Protector but soon welcomed the return of Charles II in *Astraea Redux* (1660). Though modest and well-liked as a person, Dryden has often been chastised as a mere opportunist. In fact, he was from the start an exponent of the golden mean in art, politics and morality – values that ideally equipped him to write public verse. The 'wonders' of 1666, the year of the naval war with the Dutch and the Fire of London, were commemorated in *Annus Mirabilis* (1667), which was instrumental in securing him the position of POET LAUREATE on the death of D'AVENANT in 1668. He was the first poet officially to hold the title.

He had already begun to write for the busy and fashionable playhouses. Early comedies like *Secret Love* (1667), a favourite of Charles II, were followed by the more durable *MARRIAGE À LA MODE* (1672). *The Indian Emperor* (1665) announced a distinctive style of heroic drama, a form he went on to explore in *Tyrannic Love* (1669), about St Catherine; the two-part *Conquest of Granada* (1670–1), about religious and civil disorder; *Aureng-Zebe* (1675), set in Mogul India; *ALL FOR LOVE* (1678), adapting SHAKESPEARE's *ANTONY AND CLEOPATRA*; and Dryden's first play in blank verse. Of less value were *The State of Innocence* (1664), a musical adaptation of MILTON's *PARADISE LOST*, unperformed, and his unfortunate adaptation (1679) of SHAKESPEARE's *TROILUS AND CRESSIDA*. It added to the ridicule he had already received in ROCHESTER's lampoons and BUCKINGHAM's *THE REHEARSAL* (1671).

By 1681 Dryden was beginning to direct his interests towards politics and that quickly maturing political adjunct, SATIRE. He effectively discredited Shaftesbury and the supporters of Monmouth during the Exclusion Crisis with *ABSALOM AND ACHITOPHEL* (1681), a miniature epic of ingenious exactitude supporting the legitimacy of James, Duke of York, to succeed his brother to the throne despite his Catholic sympathies. The attacks it provoked were further encouraged by *The Medal* (1682), a satire on Shaftesbury's supporters. SHADWELL's *The Medal of John Bayes*, the sharpest reply, prompted Dryden's most entertaining poem, *MAC FLECKNOE*, pirated in 1682 and officially published in 1684.

Religio Laici (1682) turned serious attention to religion. Its second part champions Anglicanism over Catholicism, though Dryden in fact embraced Catholicism in 1686, the year after the Catholic James II ascended the throne. Apart from several 'official' ODES in this period, he composed a movingly lyrical ode 'To the Pious Memory of ... Mrs Anne Killigrew' (1686), and began to translate from the classics. *The Hind and the Panther* (1687) is a lengthy allegorical fable about Catholicism (the 'milk-white Hind') and Anglicanism (the aggressive panther). With the Revolution of 1688 and the accession of William and Mary, he was deprived of the Laureateship. It went, ironically, to Shadwell.

Dryden turned afresh to the theatre, producing the libretto to Purcell's *King Arthur* (1691); a tragicomedy about sin, *Don Sebastian* (1690); a comedy of errors, *Amphitryon* (1690); *Cleomenes: The Spartan Hero* (1692); and finally the unsuccessful *Love Triumphant* (1694). In his later years he devoted himself largely to translations: most significant was his Virgil (1697), but his satires of Persius and Juvenal (1693) is additionally valuable for its preface, the excellent *Discourse concerning the Original and Progress of Satire*. In 1693 he also published his second ode for St Cecilia's Day, 'Alexander's Feast'. His last major achievement was *Fables, Ancient and Modern* (1700), paraphrases of Ovid, Boccaccio and CHAUCER, with a fine preface. Indeed, much of his prose is distinguished for its critical acuity: his *ESSAY OF DRAMATIC POESY* (1668) and *Essay of Heroic Plays* (1672) are outstanding.

A self-critical and civilized writer, Dryden brought to the language a clarity and balance of phrase that influenced many of the 18th century who followed him in his admiration of reasonableness and common sense, as well as his stringent cultivation of the HEROIC COUPLET. Nowadays, he is admired but not quite enjoyed. He summarized his aesthetic in his preface to the play *Evening's Love*: 'The employment of a poet is like that of a curious gunsmith, or watchmaker: the iron or silver is not his own; but they are the least part of that which gives the value: the prize lies wholly in the workmanship.'

Du Bois, W(illiam) E(dward) B(urghardt) *c.* 1868–1963 Black American writer. He became famous for his studies of the status of black people: *John Brown* (1909), *The Negro* (1915), *The Gift of Black Folk* (1924) and *Black Reconstruction* (1935). Sketches and verses about the life of blacks make up *The Souls of Black Folk* (1903) and *Darkwater* (1920). *Color and Democracy: Colonies and Peace* (1945) argues for the rights of small nations and rejects all aspects of imperialism. He also wrote a novel, *Dark Princess* (1928), and the autobiographical *Dusk of Dawn* (1940), as well as editing the magazine *Crisis* for 24 years and co-editing the *Encyclopedia of the Negro* (1945) with Guy Benton Johnson. A founder of the National Association for the Advancement of Colored People, Du Bois joined the Communist Party in 1961, the year he also went to live in Ghana.

Du Maurier, Dame Daphne 1907–89 Novelist. Daughter of Sir Gerald Du Maurier and granddaughter of GEORGE DU MAURIER, she spent most of her adult life in Cornwall, whose wild weather and scenery contribute the setting and atmosphere for her tense romances. The most famous are *Jamaica Inn* (1936), *Rebecca* (1938) and *My Cousin Rachel* (1951). Her short story, 'The Birds', was given a classic film treatment by Alfred Hitchcock (1963). Her memoirs appeared in *Vanishing Cornwall* (1967).

Du Maurier, George (Louis Palmella Busson) 1834–96 Novelist and artist. He regularly contributed drawings to *Punch*. Apart from *Trilby* (1894), he wrote *Peter Ibbetson* (1891), *The Martian* (1897) and humorous verse. He was father of the actor Gerald Du Maurier and grandfather of Daphne Du Maurier.

Dubliners A volume of short stories by Joyce, published in 1914 after delays caused by the printer's objections to a passage in 'Two Gallants'. The stories present Dublin in four aspects – childhood, adolescence, maturity and public life – and Joyce claimed to have written them in a style of 'scrupulous meanness'. The last, 'The Dead', is commonly considered the volume's masterpiece.

Duchess of Malfi, The A tragedy by Webster, published in 1623 but apparently first produced before 1614. The plot comes from a story by Matteo Bandello, though the striking central characters belong to Webster's own dark vision at its most powerful. The widowed Duchess of Malfi secretly marries her steward Antonio. Her insanely jealous and acquisitive brothers, the Cardinal and Duke Ferdinand, hire an ex-galley slave, Bosola, to spy on her. He discovers her pregnancy and betrays her. She and Antonio separate and flee. The Duchess is captured and confined to her house, where she and her children are eventually murdered. Ferdinand and the Cardinal decide to remove Bosola, who has been moved to remorse by the Duchess's courage and now regards his masters with loathing. He decides to kill the Cardinal but first kills Antonio by mistake before finding the right victim. Bosola is himself killed by the mad Ferdinand; his single dying consolation is to see Antonio's friends kill Ferdinand.

Duck, Stephen 1705–56 Poet. A self-taught agricultural labourer, he began to write doggerel verse based on ballads as well as classical models. Most of his poetry is occasional and much is absurd, though there is some merit in his early *The Thresher's Labour*, which earned him the nickname of the 'thresher poet'. Queen Caroline settled him at Windsor with a pension. After her death in 1737 he became a clergyman and as a preacher at Kew Chapel drew considerable crowds with his preaching. He eventually drowned himself in a trout stream outside the Black Lion Inn at Reading.

Dudek, Louis 1918– Canadian poet and critic. Early work, such as *East of the City* (1946), is realistic and shows strong egalitarian sympathies. Markedly different, his later poetry is influenced by modernism and particularly by Pound. His best work is to be found in his long poems, *Europe* (1954), *En Mexico* (1958) and *Atlantis* (1967). Other volumes include *The Transparent Sea* (1956), *Laughing Stalks* (1958), *Collected Poetry* (1971), *Cross-Section* (1980), *Continuation 1* (1981) and *Infinite Worlds* (1988). In 1952, with Raymond Souster and Irving Layton, he founded Contact Press, the leading publisher of Canadian poetry in the 1950s. From 1957 to 1966 he published a literary magazine, *Delta*. Literary criticism includes *Literature and the Press* (1960), *Selected Essays and Criticism* (1978) and *Technology and Culture* (1979).

Duenna, The A comic opera with text by Richard Brinsley Sheridan and music by Thomas Linley, produced and published in 1775. Don Jerome wants his daughter Louisa to marry Isaac. But Louisa is in love with Antonio and enlists the help of her duenna as intermediary with him. Isaac is eventually deceived into marrying the duenna and bringing about the marriage of Louisa to her Antonio.

Duffy, Maureen (Patricia) 1933– Novelist and poet. Intensely literary yet capable of simplicity and directness, her wide-ranging novels include: *That's How It Was* (1962), about an illegitimate child's relationship with her mother; *The Paradox Players* (1967), about a bitter winter on a Thames houseboat; *The Microcosm* (1966), a study of lesbianism which became her best-known work; *Gorsaga* (1981), a venture into science fiction; *Change* (1987), about young people in wartime Britain; and *Illuminations* (1991). *Collected Poems* appeared in 1985. She has also written a major study of Aphra Behn, *The Passionate Shepherdess* (1977).

Dugdale, Sir William 1605–86 Antiquary. *The Antiquities of Warwickshire* (1656) is regarded as the most accurate of its kind until that date, setting a new standard for local antiquarianism. *Monasticon Anglicanum* (1655–73) deals with monastic foundations; his valuable record of old St Paul's appeared in 1658. *The History of Imbanking and Drayning of Divers Fenns and Marshes* (1662) goes far beyond its brief to include an account of Hereward the Wake. Other works were *Origines Juridicales* (1666), a history of the administration of law in England, and *A Short View of the Late Troubles in England* (1681), expressing his Royalist principles.

Duggan, Eileen 1894–1972 New Zealand poet. Her work is characterized by its Roman Catholicism, its interest in Maori culture and its attempt to pioneer a sense of a local identity – an important influence on the following generation of poets. Volumes include *New Zealand Bird Songs* (1929), *Poems* (1937), *New Zealand Poems* (1940) and her best collection, *More Poems* (1951), transcending the Georgian simplicities of her early work. She was one of the first New Zealand poets to establish an international reputation.

Duke's Children, The The sixth and last of Trollope's Palliser Novels, serialized in 1879–80 and published in volume form in 1880. The Duke of Omnium (Plantagenet Palliser) is widowed and no longer Prime Minister. His eldest son, Lord Silverbridge, finds a gambling partner in the disreputable Major Tifto, stands for Parliament as a Conservative rather than a Liberal and further disappoints his father by falling in love with the beautiful and wealthy American girl, Isabel Boncassen. The duke's daughter, Lady Mary Palliser, also disappoints him by falling in love with Frank Tregear, a promising man without wealth or social rank. Gradually Isabel's charm and Silverbridge's determination win the duke over. He surrenders gracefully and the novel ends with both his children marrying. This closing harmony is shadowed by the loneliness of Lady Mabel Grex, who loses both the man she loves, Tregear, and the man who could have given her wealth and social position, Silverbridge. Isabel Boncassen anticipates Henry James's American girl, Isabel Archer, in *The Portrait of a Lady* (1881).

dumb show A feature of Tudor tragedies, flourishing in the actionless plays which followed in the wake of Gorboduc. Early dumb shows were typically allegorical, using symbolic figures rather than characters from the play itself, but later playwrights used them to focus the audience's attention on significant deeds outside the strict time-sequence of the play. There are famous examples in Kyd's *The Spanish Tragedy* and in Shakespeare's *Hamlet*. During the Jacobean period the dumb show became increasingly associated with the masque, though Webster and Thomas Middleton continued to exploit it to sensational effect.

Dunbar, Paul (Laurence) 1872–1906 Black American poet and novelist. The son of former slaves, he published *Oak and Ivy* (1893), *Majors and Minors* (1895), *Lyrics* of *Lowly Life* (1896), *Lyrics of the Hearthside* (1899), *Lyrics of Love and Laughter* (1903) and *Lyrics of Sunshine and Shadow* (1905). WILLIAM DEAN HOWELLS wrote the preface to the third volume. Known in his day primarily as a writer of dialect verse, he has been severely criticized for his sentimental depiction of black life in the South, though some of his work reveals a concern with the troubled social climate of his times. He also wrote four novels: *The Uncalled* (1898), *The Love of Landry* (1900), *The Fanatics* (1901) and *The Sport of the Gods* (1902).

Dunbar, William ?1465–?1530 The uncertain dates of his birth and death reflect how little is known about Dunbar's life. He graduated MA from St Andrews in 1479, probably became a Franciscan novice and travelled abroad at some point between 1479 and 1500. He visited England, probably in connection with arrangements for the marriage between James IV of Scotland and Henry VII's daughter Margaret, in 1501.

Usually considered one of the most important SCOTTISH CHAUCERIANS, Dunbar wrote in several well-established medieval forms: court poem, DREAM-VISION and moralizing reflection. His debt to 'noble CHAUCER' is most apparent in the court poetry. *The Thrissil and the Rois*, a song for the marriage of James IV (the thistle) and Margaret Tudor (the rose) in 1503, takes the form of an allegorical DREAM-VISION sometimes reminiscent of *THE PARLEMENT OF FOULES*. *The Goldyn Targe* is another allegorical dream, in which the poet-dreamer finds himself insecurely defended by the golden shield of reason at the Court of Venus. Though also probably intended for a courtly audience, *The Flyting of Dunbar and Kennedie* stands at the opposite extreme from the aureate diction of *The Goldyn Targe*. It is a stylized *tour de force* of mutually exchanged abuse – which may not indicate real personal hostility, since Dunbar's fellow poet Walter Kennedy is referred to fondly in *Lament for the Makaris*. SIR WALTER SCOTT thought it the most repellent poem he knew in any language. *The Tretis of the Twa Mariit Wemen and the Wedo* begins on a courtly note but mixes high and low styles by introducing a cynical discussion of marriage and sex.

Dunbar's other longer poems include *Dance of the Sevin Deidly Synnes*, a dream, or rather trance, in which the poet sees the devil Mahoun goading unshriven sinners into a *danse macabre*. *Lament for the Makaris* (also known by its liturgical refrain, 'Timor mortis conturbat me') is a familiar medieval meditation on the transitoriness and mutability of life; among the makers, or poets, taken by death we find Chaucer, HENRYSON and GOWER.

Dunbar also wrote religious poems, some of them macaronic lyrics (mixing the vernacular with Latin). They include 'Et Nobis Puer Natus Est' on the Nativity and a poem on the Resurrection with a splendid opening line, 'Done is a battell on the dragon blak'.

Duncan, Robert (Edward) 1919–88 American poet. Associated with the BLACK MOUNTAIN SCHOOL, he was preoccupied with mysticism and major writers of the past, as *The Opening of the Field* (1960), which he said announced the beginning of his mature work, shows. *Ground Work: Before the War* (1984) broke a long, self-imposed silence after his prolific output during the 1960s. With *Ground Work II* (1987), it contains improvisations on Dante and the METAPHYSICAL POETS expressing his horror at his country's involvement in Vietnam. Duncan also wrote plays and several volumes of prose, the most important of which are *Fictive Certainties: Five* *Essays in Essential Autobiography* (1979) and *Towards an Open Universe* (1982).

Duncan, Sara Jeanette 1861–1922 Canadian novelist. She was married to Everard Charles Cotes, a British journalist in India, the setting for some of her novels. Of more than 20 titles, the most notable are *A Social Departure: or, How Orthodocia and I Went Round the World by Ourselves* (1890), *An American Girl in London* (1891), *The Imperialist* (1904), set in the small Canadian town of 'Elgin', and *Cousin Cinderella: A Canadian Girl in London* (1908).

Dunciad, The A satirical poem by POPE, first published in three books in 1728. It was expanded in 1729 and a fourth book, *The New Dunciad*, added in 1742. The complete work was republished in 1743. Pope's original object was to retaliate against THEOBALD, who had castigated his edition of SHAKESPEARE, though in the final version Theobald is replaced as 'hero' by CIBBER. The body of the satire ridicules writers who had earned the poet's displeasure, but it is also a brilliantly wrought attack on literary vices.

The four books describe the triumph of Dullness. In Book I Bayes (Cibber) is anointed POET LAUREATE on the death of EUSDEN. Book II describes the celebrations following Bayes's enthronement as King of the Dunces, presiding over the empire of Emptiness and Dullness. The celebrations are a BURLESQUE of the funeral games for Anchises in the *Aeneid*, just one of the poem's many MOCK-HEROIC features. Everyone falls asleep while poetry is being read. In Book III Bayes sees in his dreams the past and future triumphs of the empire of Dullness extended to all arts and sciences, the theatre, and the court. His guide is SETTLE, one of DRYDEN's literary opponents. Book IV sees the dream realized. Thought is discouraged and Dullness triumphs in a final vision of cultural chaos, part comic and part serious, which is a triumph of Pope's art.

Dunlap, William 1766–1839 American playwright. The first American to make a profession of the theatre, he showed his patriotism in *The Father: or, American Shandyism* (1789) and his military tragedy, *André* (1798), about an incident in the Revolutionary War. Many of his more than 65 plays adapt foreign works, particularly the dramas of the German August von Kotzebue. He abandoned the theatre in 1811, resuming his early career as a painter. His advocacy of native art is voluminously represented in *A History of the American Theatre* (1832) and *A History of the Rise and Progress of the Arts of Design in the United States* (1834).

Dunn, Douglas (Eaglesham) 1942– Poet. The detailed observation of underprivileged lives in *Terry Street* (1969), influenced by LARKIN, has been followed by *The Happier Life* (1972), *Love or Nothing* (1974), *Barbarians* (1979), *St Kilda's Parliament* (1981), *Elegies* (1985), which mourned the death of his wife and won him a wider audience, *Selected Poems 1964–83* (1986) and *Northlight* (1988). He has also published *Secret Villages* (1985), a volume of stories, and edited *A Rumoured City: New Poets from Hull* (1982) and *The Faber Book of Twentieth-Century Scottish Poetry* (1992).

Duns Scotus, John ?1265–1308 Schoolman. He was born in Scotland, possibly at Duns near Berwick, and died at Cologne shortly before the Church examined his opinions for lack of orthodoxy. His commentaries, particularly those on the *Sentences* of Peter Lombard delivered at Cambridge, Oxford and Paris in the early 1300s, present a complex synthesis of Aristotelian, Thomistic and Augustinian ideas. Scotus rejected the Aristotelian emphasis on knowledge and intellect in favour of freedom, love and the will. He is thought of as a philosopher of 'realism', positing the close correspondence between our concepts and what is 'real', and seeking to establish a more perfect foundation for universal concepts (such as God). HOPKINS relied heavily on Scotus's *haecceitas*, the individuating difference between things as opposed to their shared attributes with other things.

Dunton, John 1659–1733 Bookseller. A characteristic publisher of his times, he strove to satisfy the newly expanding readership of the AUGUSTAN AGE. He started *The Athenian Gazette* (later *The Athenian Mercury*) in 1690, a journal where SWIFT first appeared in print. Dunton also wrote many political pamphlets and *The Life and Errors of John Dunton* (1705).

Durang, Christopher 1949– American playwright and actor. He is known for anarchic and satirical pieces which, particularly when they attack religion, have provoked controversy and attempts at censorship. They include *A History of the American Film* (1976), the Obie-Award winning *Sister Mary Ignatius Explains It All for You* (1979), *The Actor's Nightmare* (1981), *Beyond Therapy* (1981), *Baby with the Bath Water* (1983) and *The Marriage of Bette and Boo* (1973; revised 1985).

D'Urfey, Thomas 1653–1723 Playwright and songwriter. He is chiefly remembered for a collection of BALLADS, *Wit and Mirth: or, Pills to Purge Melancholy* (1719–20). An intimate of both Charles II and James II, he was a versatile dramatist. *Madame Fickle* (1676) and *A Fond Husband* (1677) follow WYCHERLEY and ETHEREGE, *Squire Oldsapp* (1678) and *The Virtuous Wife* (1679) lean towards FARCE, *Sir Barnaby Whigg* (1681) and *The Royalist* (1682) offer political satire. His best plays, *Love for Money* (1691) and *The Richmond Heiress* (1693), reflect the move towards higher moral standards.

Durrell, Gerald (Malcolm) 1925–95 Traveller and naturalist. The younger brother of LAWRENCE DURRELL, he founded the Jersey Zoo (1959) and Jersey Wildlife Trust (1964) to breed rare and threatened species. Although he wrote novels, journalism and programmes for television and radio, he remains best known for light-hearted, informative books about his travels and experiences with animals. They include *The Overloaded Ark* (1951), *The Bafut Beagles* (1953), *The Drunken Forest* (1955) and *My Family and Other Animals* (1956).

Durrell, Lawrence (George) 1912–90 Novelist, poet and travel-writer. He was elder brother of GERALD DURRELL and a friend of HENRY MILLER and ANAÏS NIN in Paris. The Eastern Mediterranean, where he spent much of his life, is the subject or setting of his best-known work, notably his books on Greece, *Prospero's Cell* (1945) and *Bitter Lemons* (1957), and the four novels forming the *Alexandria Quartet*: *Justine* (1957), *Balthazar* (1958), *Mountolive* (1958) and *Clea* (1960). Subsequent fiction includes *Tunc* (1968), *Nunquam* (1970) and the posthumously collected *Avignon Quintet* (1992): *Monsieur* (1974), *Livia* (1978), *Constance* (1982), *Sebastian* (1983) and *Quinx* (1985). His poetry, which began precociously with *Quaint Fragment: Poems Written between the Ages of Sixteen and Nineteen* (1931), includes *Collected Poems* (1960), *The Ikons* (1966) and *Vega and Other Poems* (1973).

Dutch Courtesan, The A comedy by MARSTON, first performed before Elizabeth I's death and published in 1605. The Dutch courtesan is Franceschina. Her protector Freevill is one of the most unpleasant characters in Jacobean drama; his presence, commenting on the other characters and manipulating them, gives the comedy its dark tone. He decides to end his liaison with Franceschina when he falls in love with Beatrice, the daughter of Sir Hubert Subboys. Freevill's friend Malheureux has conceived a violent passion for Franceschina and she promises to give herself to him in return for Freevill's death. He recoils from the proposal and reveals it to Freevill, who pretends to be dead. Franceschina denounces Malheureux as a murderer to Sir Hubert and Freevill's father. Malheureux finds himself sentenced to the gallows, but Freevill reappears in time to rescue him.

Dutchman A one-act play by AMIRI BARAKA, first performed in 1964, when the author was still known as LeRoi Jones. Set in the New York subway in summer, it depicts the fatal encounter between Lula, a provocative white woman, and Clay, a middle-class black man whom she taunts into expressing his suppressed racial hatred and then stabs to death. At the end Lula orders the other subway riders to remove his body and begins the process again with another black man who enters the car.

Dwight, Timothy 1752–1817 American poet. The grandson of JONATHAN EDWARDS and a founding member of the CONNECTICUT WITS, he is best known for poems advocating Calvinist and Federalist values: *The Conquest of Canaan* (1785), providing theological justification for the American Revolution, which he claimed as the first American EPIC; *Greenfield Hill* (1794); and *The Triumph of Infidelity* (1788). As president of Yale from 1795, he successfully advocated the enlargement of the curriculum and published a number of statements of his political views, among them *The True Means of Establishing Public Happiness* (1795) and *The Duty of Americans, at the Present Crisis* (1798). *Theology, Explained and Defended* (1818–19), a five-volume collection of 173 sermons, makes a complete statement of his theology.

Dyce, Alexander 1798–1869 Scholar. As an editor he was mainly concerned with FLETCHER, WEBSTER, GREENE, SHIRLEY, MIDDLETON, MARLOWE and especially SHAKESPEARE (9 vols, 1857). Other publications include an edition of SIR THOMAS MORE for the Shakespeare Society (1844). His library, strong in classical and European verse as well as Elizabethan authors, was bequeathed to the Victoria and Albert Museum.

Dyer, Sir Edward 1543–1607 Poet, courtier and diplomat. He gained access to the court as the Earl of Leicester's protégé and became a close friend of SIR FULKE GREVILLE and SIR PHILIP SIDNEY. A man of speculative interests, he helped to back Frobisher's expeditions in the 1570s. Later he became fascinated by alchemy, and developed a strong friendship with the magus John Dee. Only a handful of his poems survive, preserved in commonplace-books. He liked a plain style, but his lyrics have sweetness and good measure; their prevailing character is introspective and melancholy. Like so much Elizabethan courtier verse, his lines require a musical accompaniment to achieve their full effect. The most famous lyric ascribed to him, 'My Mind to Me a Kingdom Is' (printed in 1588) was set to music by William Byrd.

Dyer, John *c.* 1700–58 Poet. He is remembered for *Grongar Hill* (1727), a poem celebrating the valley of the River Towy in his native Dyfed. It brings freshness of observation to topographical poetry, anticipating some of the spirit of ROMANTICISM. Later, unsuccessful poems were *The Ruins of Rome* (1740) and *The Fleece* (1757), a faintly absurd treatment of the wool trade.

Dylan, Bob [Zimmerman, Robert Allen] 1941– American singer, song-writer and poet. Since making a reputation with the folk songs, protest songs and country blues on early albums such as *Bob Dylan* (1962), he has turned to rock music, Country and Western, and gospel music. *Bob Dylan's Greatest Hits* appeared in 1967 and *Bob Dylan's Greatest Hits, Volume 2* in 1971. *Biograph* (1987) is the most synoptic compilation of his work. The words to his songs, which have much in common with the work of the BEATS, have received considerable attention as poetry in their own right. *Lyrics, 1962–1985* (1985) collects his lyrics from the 20 or so years of his greatest achievement. Other books include: *Tarantula* (1966), a series of verbal collages; *Approximately Complete Works* (1970); *Writings and Drawings* (1971); *Poem to Joanie* (1972); *XI Outlined Epitaphs and Off the Top of My Head* (1981); and *Road Drawings* (1992).

Dynasts, The HARDY's 'Epic-Drama of the War with Napoleon', a long poem or CLOSET DRAMA, published in 1904–8. Its 19 acts and 130 scenes trace Napoleon's career from 1805 until his defeat at Waterloo some 10 years later. The structure embodies what Hardy liked to call his philosophical 'impressions'. The actions of the huge cast of human characters, from Napoleon down to the common soldiers and ordinary people of Wessex, are subject to the Immanent Will, the controlling power of the universe and a blind, unheeding force which bears no resemblance to the Christian God.

Earl of Toulous, The A VERSE ROMANCE written *c.* 1400
in the north-east Midlands, calling itself a BRETON LAY.
The story is based loosely on historical fact. The Earl
promises a prisoner freedom in exchange for a meeting
with his beautiful Empress, wife of the Earl's enemy,
and goes disguised as a hermit. She gives him a ring as a
love-token. When she is falsely accused of adultery by
jealous knights who have hidden a naked youth in her
chamber, the Earl appears disguised as a monk to
defend her. The Emperor accepts the Earl's friendship
and on his death the couple marry.

Earle, John *c.* 1601–55 Essayist. *Microcosmography: or, A
Piece of the World Discovered in Essays and Characters* (1628)
is a collection of 'characters', or descriptions of behav-
ioral types, a form much in fashion at the time. A
devout Royalist and tutor to the future Charles II, Earle
translated *EIKON BASILIKE* into Latin during his 16 years'
exile. At the Restoration he became Dean of
Westminster and later Bishop of Salisbury.

Earthly Paradise, The A poem by WILLIAM MORRIS,
published in three volumes in 1868–70. It consists of 24
tales, with linking narrative and a prologue offering
the reader an escape from industrial society: 'Forget six
counties overhung with smoke,/ Forget the snorting
steam and piston stroke.' A group of Norsemen searching for the Earthly Paradise where nobody grows old at
last arrive at 'a nameless city in a distant sea' where
Greek culture and civilization have been preserved.
Twice a month they meet their hosts at a feast and
exchange stories. One of the Norsemen tells a tale of
their past and one of their hosts relates a classical legend. Lyric poems connect the months and describe the
changing year.

East Lynne A novel by MRS HENRY WOOD, published in
1861. Immensely popular in its day, it was also dramatized with great success. Lady Isobel Vane deserts her
husband, Archibald Carlyle, for Sir Francis Levison but
returns, unrecognizably disfigured by a train crash, to
work as governess to her own children. She asks for
Carlyle's forgiveness on her deathbed.

Eastman, Charles (Alexander) 1858–1939 Native
American writer. Born of mixed Santee Sioux and white
parentage, he collaborated with his wife, Elaine
Goodale, on books describing the life, customs and
legends of his people for a primarily white audience.
Only *Wigwam Evenings: Sioux Folktales Retold* (1909),
one of several specifically aimed at children, bears
both their names. *The Soul of the Indian: An Interpretation*
(1911) describes the Indian system of ethics and Indian
attitudes toward nature. *The Indian To-day: The Past
and Future of the First Americans* (1915) is an overview
of Indian history. Other titles include *From the Deep
Woods to Civilization: Chapters in the Autobiography of
an Indian* (1916) and *Indian Heroes and Great Chieftains*
(1918).

Eastman, Max 1883–1969 American critic, poet and
essayist. *Enjoyment of Poetry* (1913), a critical study, is still
his best-known work. In his youth he co-founded and
edited the *The Masses* (1913–17) and *The Liberator*
(1918–22), and published *Marx, Lenin, and the Science of
Revolution* (1926). *Artists in Uniform: A Study of Literature
and Bureaucratism* (1934), *Marxism, is It Science?* (1940) and

Reflections on the Failure of Socialism (1955) chart a growing disillusionment with the Left. *Heroes I Have Known*
(1942) and *Great Companions* (1959) contain memoirs of
Isadora Duncan, Anatole France, Charlie Chaplin and
Trotsky. His poems were collected as *Poems of Five Decades*
(1954). *Love and Revolution* (1964) is an autobiography.

Eastward Ho A comedy by CHAPMAN, JONSON and
MARSTON, published in 1605. A passage in Act III about
the Scots so offended James I that Chapman and Jonson
were briefly imprisoned. The plot tells of Touchstone, a
goldsmith, his two daughters, Mildred and Gertrude,
and his two apprentices, Golding and Quicksilver.
Gertrude marries Sir Petronel Flash, a penniless adventurer who filches her dowry and sends her off on a
coach to an imaginary castle before setting off for
Virginia in company with the idle apprentice,
Quicksilver, who has robbed his master. They are
arrested when their ship is wrecked on the Isle of Dogs
and brought up before Golding, the industrious apprentice, who has married Mildred. A term in prison makes
them repent and they are eventually released through
Golding's good offices.

Eberhart, Richard 1904– American poet. His poetry,
often seen as in open combat with MODERNISM, has
doggedly pursued a personal, neo-Romantic style which
tends to be contemplative and lyrical. Themes range
from confrontation with death to meditations inspired
by nature; later work is frequently concerned with the
poetic process itself. *A Bravery of Earth* (1930), his first
volume, has been followed by many volumes, summarized in *Collected Poems* (1988), published by Oxford
University Press.

Ecce Homo See SEELEY, J. R.

eclogue From the Greek word for 'selection', hence
originally referring to a short poem or section of a
longer poem. The term was later applied to the PAS-
TORAL poems of Virgil and, in the Renaissance, to verse
dialogues on pastoral themes, like SPENSER'S *THE
SHEPHEARDES CALENDER*. By the 18th century a distinction was drawn between pastoral, which described a
context, and eclogue, which described a verse form. The
term can also mean merely a dramatic argument in
verse.

Eden, Richard ?1521–76 Collector and translator of
accounts of travel. His translations include: part of
Munster's *Cosmographiae* as *A Treatise of the New India*
(1553); *The Decades of the New World* (1555), a collection of
travels mainly from Peter Martyr of Angleria; Martin
Cortes's *Arte de navegar* as *The Art of Navigation* (1561); and
The History of Travel in the West and East Indies (1577).

Edgar, David 1948– Playwright. After a string of lively
agit-prop plays, he tackled more ambitious subjects in
his work for the ROYAL SHAKESPEARE COMPANY, with
whom his greatest success was his adaptation of
DICKENS'S *NICHOLAS NICKLEBY* (1981). His reputation as
the most skilled socialist playwright in contemporary
Britain now rests largely on: *Destiny* (1976), about the
rise of a neo-fascist group; *Maydays* (1983), about the
growing disillusion of British socialists; *That Summer*
(1987), about the effect of the failure of the 1984 Miners'
Strike; and *The Shape of the Table* (1990), about changes in
Eastern Europe. Another aspect of his work is shown by

Mary Barnes (1979), based on a case study of a disturbed child by R. D. Laing. Edgar also adapted STEVENSON's *THE STRANGE CASE OF DR JEKYLL AND MR HYDE* for the ROYAL NATIONAL THEATRE in 1991.

Edgeworth, Maria 1767–1849 Novelist. Her father, the eccentric Richard Lovell Edgeworth, was a wealthy landowner in Ireland and a powerful influence on his daughter's interests and literary career. She collaborated with him on *Practical Education* (1798), adapting and modifying Rousseau's theories, and completed the second volume of his *Memoirs* in 1820. Her first work, *Letters to Literary Ladies* (1795), was a defence of female education. *The Parent's Assistant* (1796–1800) is a collection of stories for children, to which she later added a volume of *Little Plays*. *CASTLE RACKRENT* (1800), *THE ABSENTEE* (in the second series of *Tales of Fashionable Life*, 1812) and *Ormond* (1817) are novels of Irish life, which won the admiration of SIR WALTER SCOTT and influenced his 'Waverley' novels. *Belinda* (1801), *Leonora* (1806), *Patronage* (1814) and *Helen* (1834) deal with English society.

Edinburgh Review, The A quarterly magazine founded in 1802 by FRANCIS JEFFREY, SYDNEY SMITH, HENRY BROUGHAM and FRANCIS HORNER. It became the most influential journal of its day, setting new standards for outspoken and deliberate criticism. Its attacks on WORDSWORTH, COLERIDGE and SOUTHEY, the so-called LAKE POETS, were particularly harsh, while Brougham's review of BYRON's *Hours of Idleness* provoked the poet's *English Bards and Scotch Reviewers*. Contributors included SIR WALTER SCOTT (a Tory, who withdrew to play a part in founding the *QUARTERLY REVIEW*), HAZLITT, HENRY HALLAM, FRANCIS HORNER and, in later years, MACAULAY, CARLYLE and THOMAS ARNOLD. The *Edinburgh Review* ceased publication in 1929.

Education of Henry Adams, The: *A Study of Twentieth-Century Multiplicity* The autobiography of HENRY ADAMS, privately printed in 1907, published in 1918 and awarded a PULITZER PRIZE. Writing about himself in the third person, he deliberately presents his own life and experiences as representative of modernity. A crucial chapter contrasts the dynamo, symbol of the accelerating forces of modern life, with the Virgin, symbol of the 13th century and the subject of his earlier book, *MONT-SAINT-MICHEL AND CHARTRES*.

Edward II, King of England, The Troublesome Reign and Lamentable Death of A tragedy by MARLOWE, first performed *c.* 1592 and published in 1594. Though its detractors complain it lacks the grandeur and lofty language associated with Marlowe, it is also the best constructed of all his works. It follows the grim events that succeed Edward's recall of his favourite Gaveston on his accession to the throne: the growing hatred of his queen, Isabella of France (the She-Wolf); the revolt of the barons culminating in their capture and murder of Gaveston; the rise of Hugh le Despenser in Edward's affections; the Queen's alliance with her lover Mortimer; the execution of Despenser and his father; and the confinement of Edward in Berkeley Castle and his degradation and murder.

Edward III, The Reign of An anonymous chronicle play published in 1596. The suggestion that SHAKESPEARE had a hand in it has not been completely rejected (compare SHAKESPEARE APOCRYPHA). Apart from its historical content, the Hundred Years War, the play is concerned with the King's unwelcome attentions to the Countess of Salisbury.

Edwards, Jonathan 1703–58 American Puritan minister and religious philosopher. In 1727 he was ordained minister of the church in Northampton, Massachusetts, where he served with his grandfather, SOLOMON STODDARD. His preaching helped precipitate the religious revival that swept through western Massachusetts in 1734–5, and later contributed to the 'Great Awakening' (1740). His *Faithful Narrative of Surprising Conversions* (1737) and *The Distinguishing Marks* (1741) describe and defend the 1735 revival and the Awakening respectively. His most famous sermon, *Sinners in the Hands of an Angry God* (1741), tries to move its hearers with the force of Calvinist doctrine to feel the first stirrings of conversion. *Some Thoughts concerning the Present Revival* (1743) speculates on the millennial possibilities raised by the Awakening. *A Treatise concerning Religious Affections* (1746) is his systematic exposition of religious psychology, while his diary and *Personal Narrative* (*c.* 1740, not intended for publication) trace his own conversion.

Dismissed by his Northampton congregation in 1750 for unorthodox views, he ministered to an Indian mission in Stockbridge. During this period he wrote *Freedom of the Will* (1754), *The Great Christian Doctrine of Original Sin Defended* (1758), *The Nature of True Virtue* (1765) and *The Great End for Which God Created the World* (1765). Fusing an orthodox Calvinism with Lockean psychology and Newtonian physics, he explains religious conversion in 18th-century rationalist terms. At the time of his death, when he was president of the College of New Jersey (later Princeton University), he was working on his systematic sacred history, *The History of the Work of Redemption*, based on sermons delivered in 1739 and eventually published in 1774.

Egan, Pierce, the elder 1772–1849 Comic writer and sporting journalist. He became known for his sports reports in the newspapers and *Boxiana: or, Sketches of Modern Pugilism* (1818–24) but is remembered for *LIFE IN LONDON* (1820–1), a comic portrait of Regency manners. Egan's weekly newspaper, *Life in London and Sporting Guide*, later merged into *Bell's Life in London*, first appeared in 1824.

Egan, Pierce, the younger 1814–80 Novelist and son of PIERCE EGAN THE ELDER. His many historical novels include *Wat Tyler* (1841) and *Paul Jones* (1842). He was a pioneer of cheap literature.

Eger and Grime A mid-15th-century VERSE ROMANCE from the North of England, surviving only in 17th-century copies. It is notable for its use of direct speech, often humorous and realistic. Questing for adventures to impress his mistress Winglaine, Eger is wounded by the giant knight Gray-steele and cared for by Loosepaine. Eger's sworn brother Grime kills Gray-steele with Loosepaine's help. Eger marries Winglaine on the strength of his supposed victory, and Grime marries Loosepaine.

Egerton, George [Dunne, Mary Chavelita] 1859–1945 Short-story writer. *Keynotes* (1893), her first and best collection, was published by John Lane with illustrations by BEARDSLEY. It was followed by *Discords* (1894) and contributions to *THE YELLOW BOOK*. She published two more volumes, *Symphonies* (1896) and *Fantasies* (1898), and two novels, *The Wheel of God* (1898) and *Rosa Amorosa: The Love-Letters of a Woman* (1901) which, like her stories, drew heavily on her own varied and colourful life. Her work blends realistic elements with Utopian fantasies of self-realization and freedom for the 'new woman'. She also translated *Hunger* by Knut Hamsun, to whom she dedicated *Keynotes*.

Eggleston, Edward 1837–1902 American novelist. The older brother of GEORGE EGGLESTON, he abandoned the Methodist ministry at the age of 37 to found a Church of Christian Endeavour in Brooklyn, New York, and later to write. His first success, and still his best-known novel, was *The Hoosier Schoolmaster* (1871), a realistic if pious portrait of rural Indiana. His next novels were *The End of the World* (set in Indiana; 1872), *The Mystery of Metropolisville* (set in Minnesota; 1873), *The Circuit Rider* (set in Ohio; 1874) and *Roxy* (set in Indiana; 1878). After turning his attention to history and biography, he published three more novels: *The Hoosier Schoolboy* (1883), a boy's view of the life described in *The Hoosier Schoolmaster*; *The Graysons: A Story of Illinois* (1888), about Abraham Lincoln; and *The Faith Doctor* (1891), a SATIRE of Christian Science.

Eggleston, George Cary 1839–1911 American novelist and journalist. The younger brother of EDWARD EGGLESTON, he taught in Indiana and practised law before editing the New York *Evening Post* and working on the *New York World*. He also wrote books for boys and several novels set in the South, including *A Man of Honour* (1873), *Dorothy South* (1902), *The Master of Warlock* (1903) and *Evelyn Byrd* (1904). With Dorothy Marbourg he co-wrote the novel *Juggernaut* (1891), set in Indiana. *A Rebel's Recollections* (1874) is based on his experiences during the Civil War.

Eglinton, John [Magee, William K.] 1868–1961 Irish essayist and critic. A friend of many leading figures of the Irish revival and founder-editor of the literary magazine *Dana* (1904–5), he worked as a librarian at the National Library, Dublin, appearing in this role in the 'Scylla and Charybdis' chapter of JOYCE's *ULYSSES*. YEATS published a selection of his criticism as *Some Essays and Passages by John Eglinton* (1905), though his best work appeared in *Anglo-Irish Essays* (1917). *Irish Literary Portraits* (1935) and *Memoir of AE* (1937) were written in England, where he lived after the founding of the Irish Free State in 1922.

Egoist, The A novel by GEORGE MEREDITH, published in 1879. The central character of this elegant comedy is Sir Willoughby Patterne, rich, selfish and conceited. He is loved by Laetitia Dale but proposes to Constantia Durham, who learns in time what sort of man he is and elopes with an officer of Hussars. Sir Willoughby then turns his attention to Clara Middleton and enlists her epicurean father Dr Middleton on his side. She remains equivocal and he proposes to Laetitia, but is overheard and exposed by the boy Crossjay. Clara has in any case fallen in love with Vernon Whitford, a handsome scholar. Stripped of his pretensions, Sir Willoughby finally persuades Laetitia to marry him.

The character of Dr Middleton is modelled on PEACOCK, Meredith's father-in-law, and that of Vernon on LESLIE STEPHEN. ROBERT LOUIS STEVENSON thought he recognized himself in Sir Willoughby, but Meredith insisted he was all of us.

Egoist, The: *An Individualist Review* A feminist journal founded in 1913 by Dora Marsden and REBECCA WEST as *The New Freewoman*. At the prompting of POUND and ALDINGTON it changed its name in 1919 and became, under the editorship of Harriet Shaw Weaver, a vehicle for Pound's IMAGISM. HILDA DOOLITTLE, Aldington and T. S. ELIOT served as assistant editors. *The Egoist's* most notable achievement was its serialization of JOYCE's *A*

PORTRAIT OF THE ARTIST AS A YOUNG MAN in 1914–15. After its closure in 1919, its name survived in Harriet Shaw Weaver's Egoist Press, which published *ULYSSES* in 1922.

Eikon Basilike 'The royal image', subtitled *The Portraiture of His Sacred Majesty in His Solitudes and Sufferings*. It was presented as the prayers and meditations of Charles I during his imprisonment and was published on the day of his burial, 9 February 1649, running to 40 editions before the Restoration. John Gauden, Bishop of Winchester, who later claimed authorship, probably compiled it from Charles's notes and memoranda. It was translated into Latin by EARLE and prompted a reply from MILTON.

Ekwensi, Cyprian 1921– Nigerian novelist. A popular writer, he dramatizes the attitudes of ordinary people buffeted by historical change. His works include: *People of the City* (1954); *Jagua Nana* (1962), his best-known novel, about a Lagos prostitute; *Beautiful Feathers* (1963); *Burning Grass* (1962); *Iska* (1966); *Survive the Peace* (1976); and *For a Roll of Parchment* (1976), set in London. He has also written short stories and CHILDREN'S LITERATURE.

Eldershaw, M. Barnard [Eldershaw, Flora Sydney Patricia (1897–1956) and Barnard, Marjorie Faith (1897–1987)] Australian novelists. Their best-known novels, *A House is Built* (1929) and *Green Memory* (1931), are set in 19th-century Australia. They also wrote short stories, histories and literary criticism. Barnard published a seminal biography of MILES FRANKLIN (1967) and a collection of stories, *The Persimmon Tree* (1943), frequently anthologized.

elegy In Greek and Roman literature, any poem using the 'elegiac couplet' (a dactylic hexameter followed by a dactylic pentameter). Since the Renaissance it has come to mean a sustained poetic meditation on a solemn theme, particularly death (e.g. MILTON's *LYCIDAS*, SHELLEY's *ADONAIS*). The 'elegiac stanza' (a quatrain of iambic pentameters, rhyming abab) takes its name from GRAY's *ELEGY WRITTEN IN A COUNTRY CHURCHYARD*.

Elegy Written in a Country Churchyard A poem by THOMAS GRAY, published in 1751. The churchyard is at Stoke Poges, Buckinghamshire, where Gray himself is now buried. Melancholy and reflective, the poet muses on rural life, human potential, and mortality. At the close, he looks forward to the prospect of his own death and considers the possibility that art might offer a durable memorial against time. The elegy's gentle gloominess is characteristic of the style cultivated by the so-called GRAVEYARD POETS, though their work rarely achieved such refinement elsewhere.

Elene An Old English poem by CYNEWULF preserved in the VERCELLI BOOK, about St Helena's discovery of the Cross in the Holy Land. The story occupies 14 sections of the poem; a 15th provides the only information known about Cynewulf and contains his runic signature.

Eliot, George [Evans, Mary Anne (Marian)] 1819–80 Novelist, critic and poet. Born at Arbury, Warwickshire, the daughter of a land agent, she attended schools in Nuneaton and Coventry, where she went to live with her father on his retirement in 1841. Having already read widely in theology, the Romantic poets and German literature, she was drawn to an intellectual circle that included Charles Bray and Charles Hennell, whose influences directed her towards free-thinking in religious opinion. In 1842 she refused to attend church with her father and in 1846 she completed a translation of Strauss's *Leben Jesu*, a central document of the HIGHER

CRITICISM. In London she was closely associated with John Chapman, proprietor of THE WESTMINSTER REVIEW, of which she was assistant editor in 1852–4. Her next publication of consequence was a translation of Feuerbach's *Essence of Christianity* (1854). By this time she had met GEORGE HENRY LEWES, with whom she went to live in 1853. Their union, happy despite Lewes's irregular marital situation, lasted until his death in 1878.

George Eliot's interest in writing fiction went back to her schooldays in the early 1830s but she did not make her début until the serialization of 'The Sad Fortunes of the Reverend Amos Barton', 'Mr Gilfil's Love-Story' and 'Janet's Repentance' in BLACKWOOD'S EDINBURGH MAGAZINE in 1857. These tales were collected, and well received, as SCENES OF CLERICAL LIFE (1858). They were followed by ADAM BEDE (1859), THE MILL ON THE FLOSS (1860) and SILAS MARNER (1861). After a brief Florentine visit George Eliot deserted her native literary landscapes to publish ROMOLA in THE CORNHILL MAGAZINE in 1862–3. Next came FELIX HOLT THE RADICAL (1866) in some respects anticipating MIDDLEMARCH, published in independent parts in 1871–2, and DANIEL DERONDA, which appeared in the same way in 1874–6. Her last work was *The Impressions of Theophrastus Such* (1879), a series of essays linked by a narrator. George Eliot also wrote some novellas and a surprising amount of poetry, including THE SPANISH GYPSY (1868), the product of a trip to Spain in 1867, and *The Legend of Jubal and Other Poems* (1874). In addition, she was one of the finest letter-writers in the language.

After the death of Lewes, she married John Walter Cross, a man many years her junior, in the spring of 1880; she died in December of the same year. Cross's biography was published in 1885. In a century of gifted women writers George Eliot stands pre-eminent.

Eliot, John 1604–90 American Puritan minister. Born in England, he emigrated to Massachusetts in 1631 and became minister at the church in Roxbury. He contributed to the BAY PSALM BOOK (1640). Known as the 'Apostle to the Indians', he established the first of a series of 'praying Indian Towns' at Natick in 1651, setting out his ideas for their governance in *The Christian Commonwealth* (1659). He also compiled a reading primer for the Indians and translated the Bible into the Algonquian dialect. COTTON MATHER, who knew him in his old age, included a biography of him in the *Magnalia Christi Americana*.

Eliot, T(homas) S(tearns) 1888–1965 Poet, critic and playwright. Born and brought up in St Louis, Missouri, he attended Harvard University, where he was influenced by SANTAYANA and BABBITT, as well as his reading in French SYMBOLISM. He began but did not complete a doctorate, his thesis eventually being published as *Knowledge and Experience in the Philosophy of F. H. Bradley* (1964). Eliot left America in 1914, settling in London and becoming a British citizen in 1927, the same year he joined the Church of England. His troubled marriage to Vivien Haigh-Wood lasted from 1915 until their separation in the early 1930s. He married Valerie Fletcher in 1957. During his early years in London he taught at Highgate School, worked for Lloyds Bank and reviewed for various journals before becoming editor of THE CRITERION (1922–39). As a director of Faber and Faber in later life he helped many younger poets.

He himself had begun to publish poetry with POUND's encouragement. THE LOVE SONG OF J. ALFRED PRUFROCK (1915) was collected in his first volume, *Prufrock and Other Observations* (1919). Two more collections followed: *Poems* (1919), which contained 'Gerontion', printed by LEONARD WOOLF and VIRGINIA WOOLF, and *Ara Vos Prec* (1920). THE WASTE LAND (1922) provoked controversy by its innovatory technique and apparently pessimistic tone but came to be accepted as a central text of MODERNISM. Eliot's reputation was confirmed by critical essays offering a theoretical counterpart to the example of his own poetry. *The Sacred Wood* (1920) reprinted his essay on HAMLET (with its concept of the OBJECTIVE CORRELATIVE) and the highly influential 'Tradition and the Individual Talent', arguing for the 'impersonality' of poetry. *Homage to John Dryden* (1924) contained essays on MARVELL and the METAPHYSICAL POETS, praised for their unified sensibility in contrast to the DISSOCIATION OF SENSIBILITY afflicting later generations.

For Lancelot Andrewes: Essays on Style and Order (1928), in which Eliot described himself as 'classical in literature, royalist in politics, and Anglo-Catholic in religion', emphasized the main direction of his development during the 1920s. The increasingly religious tendency of his poetry can be traced in *Poems 1909–25* (1925), which includes 'The Hollow Men', and *Collected Poems 1909–35* (1936), which added 'The Journey of the Magi' (1927) and 'Ash Wednesday' (1930). Its chief fruit was FOUR QUARTETS, published separately between 1935 and 1942 and together in 1943. *Old Possum's Book of Practical Cats* (1939) is a collection of humorous verse for children. *Collected Poems 1909–62* appeared in 1963.

His later prose writings include *The Use of Poetry and the Use of Criticism* (1933), the incautious *After Strange Gods: A Primer of Modern Heresy* (1934), *The Idea of a Christian Society* (1939), the influential *Notes Towards a Definition of Culture* (1948), *On Poetry and Poets* (1957) and *To Criticize the Critic* (1965). The preoccupation with authority and control in his approach to literary and cultural issues made his position increasingly unfashionable. More popular in its time was his attempt to revive verse drama, foreshadowed in *Sweeney Agonistes: An Aristophanic Fragment* (1932) and *The Rock* (1934), and seen at its most successful in MURDER IN THE CATHEDRAL (1935). In *The Family Reunion* (1939), THE COCKTAIL PARTY (1950), *The Confidential Clerk* (1954) and *The Elder Statesman* (1959) the burden of philosophical ideas and the conventions of the contemporary stage sit uneasily together.

In 1948 Eliot received both the Nobel Prize for Literature and the Order of Merit. Such honours acknowledged his vital role in showing poetry how to become modern. With its dense, even riddling, allusions to earlier literature *The Waste Land* had crucially redefined the traditions of use to the modern poet. Eliot's praise of the Elizabethan dramatists and the metaphysical poets in his criticism confirmed a preference for intellectual toughness, energy and WIT that left its mark on most of his immediate successors. Yet the rightwards tendency of his beliefs in politics and religion limited his influence over younger writers from AUDEN onwards.

elision In verse, the slurring or omission of an unstressed syllable so that a line may conform to the METRE, or the omission of part of a word for ease of pronunciation. It is most often accomplished by omitting a final vowel preceding an initial vowel, as in 'th'Eternal', but also occurs between syllables in a single word, as in 'ne'er' for 'never'.

Elkin, Stanley (Lawrence) 1930– American novelist and short-story writer. His work often explores the nature of evil through comedy. Novels include *Boswell* (1964), *A Bad Man* (1968), *The Dick Gibson Show* (1971), *The Franchiser* (1976), *The Living End* (1980), *The Magic Kingdom* (1985), *The Rabbi of Lud* (1987), *The MacGuffin* (1991) and *Pieces of Soap* (1993). *Searches and Seizures* (1973; published in Britain as both *Eligible Men*, 1974, and *Alex and the Gypsy*, 1977); and *Van Gogh's Room at Arles* (1993) are collections of novellas. *Stanley Elkin's Greatest Hits* (1980) is an omnibus collection of his stories.

Elliott, Ebenezer 1781–1849 The Corn Law Rhymer. A Chartist, he derived his nickname from his simple, direct verses attacking the Corn Laws and describing rural poverty: *The Village Patriarch* (1829), *Corn-Law Rhymes* (1831) and *The Splendid Village* (1833–5).

Ellis, (Henry) Havelock 1859–1939 Sexual scientist. A qualified doctor, he rarely practised medicine. He edited the Contemporary Science series and the Mermaid unexpurgated reprints of Elizabethan and Jacobean drama. *The New Spirit* (1890) reflected his interest in scientific and social progress and, particularly, the concern with sex which produced: *Man and Woman* (1894), *Sexual Inversion* (which included the case history of J. A. SYMONDS, 1897), *Studies in the Psychology of Sex* (1897–1910) and *The Erotic Rights of Women* (1918). These works were at once influential and notorious. *My Life* was published posthumously in 1940.

Ellison, Ralph (Waldo) 1914–94 Black American novelist, essayist and short-story writer. His reputation as the most important literary heir to RICHARD WRIGHT – matched only by that of JAMES BALDWIN – depends on his novel *INVISIBLE MAN* (1952), which weathered critical controversy to hold its place as a central text of the 20th-century Afro-American experience. Parts of an incomplete second novel, including a section entitled 'And Hickman Arrives', have appeared in print. 'Flying Home' and 'King of the Bingo Game' are widely anthologized short stories. *Shadow and Act* (1964) and *Going to the Territory* (1986) collect some of his many essays on black music, literature and American culture.

Ellwood, Thomas 1639–1713 Poet. An early Quaker and friend of PENN, he was reader to the blind MILTON, to whom he suggested the theme of *PARADISE REGAINED*. He was himself the author of *Davideis* (1712), a poem about King David, as well as *A Collection of Poems on Various Subjects* (1710) and *The History of the Life of Thomas Ellwood* (1714), an account of his imprisonment for his religious beliefs.

Elyot, Sir Thomas ?1499–1546 Lexicographer and administrator, best known for *The Book Named the Governor* (1531), remembered by his remote descendant and near-namesake T. S. ELIOT in 'East Coker', second of his *FOUR QUARTETS*. Dedicated to Henry VIII and drawn in part from Castiglione's *The Courtier* (see COURTESY BOOK), Elyot's work sets out a plan for bringing up gentlemen's sons and manifests the usual humanist concern for education. Perhaps as a result of the favourable reception of this book Elyot was made ambassador to Emperor Charles V. Elyot's Latin-English Dictionary (1538) is as important as *The Book Named the Governor*; it was revised as the *Bibliotheca Eliotae* (1542). He also produced translations and a medical treatise, *Castle of Health* (1539).

Emare A VERSE ROMANCE of c. 1400, claiming to be derived from a BRETON LAY, though no French version of the story survives. It is substantially the same as that of the 'constant' Constance, well known in the Middle Ages. Emare suffers first from the incestuous advances of her father, a widowed emperor, and then, after her marriage to the king of Galys, from her mother-in-law's hostility. She and her son Segramour are eventually reunited with both the king and emperor when they come to Rome on pilgrimages.

emblem book A book of symbolic pictures or engravings to which mottoes and verbal explanations of a proverbial or gnomic nature are attached. Offering religious and moral instruction, emblem books also became valuable sources for poetic imagery. Andrea Alciati's *Emblematum Liber* (1531) was the earliest European example, and Geoffrey Whitney's *Choice of Emblemes* (1586) the first to appear in English. The most popular was QUARLES's *Emblems* (1635).

Emecheta, Buchi 1944– Nigerian novelist. She moved to Britain in 1962, an experience reflected in *In the Ditch* (1972) and *Second-Class Citizen* (1974), published together as *Adah's Story* (1983). Her championship of women's rights gives compassion and anger to her other novels, mostly set in West Africa: *The Bride Price* (1976), *The Slave Girl* (1977), *The Joys of Motherhood* (1979), *Destination Biafra* (1982), *Naira Power* (1982), *Double Yoke* (1982) and *The Rape of Shavi* (1983).

Emerson, Ralph Waldo 1803–82 American essayist, philosopher and poet. Born in Boston and educated at Harvard, he followed in his father's footsteps and became a Unitarian minister in 1829 but resigned in 1832. In the same year he made the first of several visits to Europe, which sharpened his interest in religion and philosophy as well as forging a lifelong friendship with THOMAS CARLYLE. On his return to America he lectured widely and then, after settling in Concord, Massachusetts, in 1835, became a leading figure in TRANSCENDENTALISM, whose circle included HAWTHORNE, BRONSON ALCOTT, THOREAU and MARGARET FULLER. He was instrumental in founding the Transcendentalist magazine, *THE DIAL*, which he also edited. His own philosophical position – OLIVER WENDELL HOLMES called it an 'intellectual declaration of independence' – broke with tradition in asserting that human thought and action proceed from Nature and that the individual's intuitive spiritual experience is more important than any formal church. His writings include: *NATURE* (1836); *The American Scholar* (1837), an oration applying Transcendentalism to national and cultural questions; two volumes of essays (1841 and 1844); *REPRESENTATIVE MEN* (1850), based on lectures delivered in England; *English Traits* (1856); *The Conduct of Life* (1860); *Society and Solitude* (1870); and *Poems* (1847) and a subsequent volume of verse, *May-Day and Other Pieces* (1867). His *Journals* were published in 10 volumes (1909–14).

Emma A novel by JANE AUSTEN, written in 1814–15 and published in 1816. It follows Emma Woodhouse's slow, painful progress toward maturity. Left alone with her hypochondriacal father when her governess, Miss Taylor, marries a neighbour, Mr Weston, Emma makes a protégée of Harriet Smith, an illegitimate girl of no social status, and sets about arranging her life. She makes sure that Harriet rejects a proposal from a young farmer, Robert Martin. Emma's brother-in-law, George Knightley of Donwell Abbey, frowns on this manipulation but, undeterred, she tries to marry Harriet to Mr Elton, a young clergyman. Elton, however, despises Harriet and has set his sights on Emma herself. For her part, Emma half fancies herself in love with Mr Weston's son by his first marriage, Frank Churchill. Harriet, meanwhile, has become interested in Knightley's unaffected warmth and intelligence. Emma, reassuring Harriet after Elton's departure, is now considering Frank Churchill for her. Without giving the thought expression, she has always regarded Knightley as hers and the realization that Harriet might supplant her in Knightley's affections, together with the discovery that Frank Churchill is engaged to Jane Fairfax, forces her to examine her own conduct and resolve to behave better. Knightley proposes to her while Harriet, left to decide for herself, marries Robert Martin.

Empedocles on Etna A poem by MATTHEW ARNOLD, published in 1852. The despairing philosopher Empedocles (c. 450 BC) is not dissuaded by the physician Pausanias or the poet Callicles from killing himself in the volcano's crater.

Empson, Sir William 1906–84 Critic. His best-known critical work, *Seven Types of Ambiguity* (1930), encouraged the trend towards close verbal analysis by its detailed study of multiple shades of meaning in poetry. Empson's own poetry, especially in *Poems* (1935), is in the tradition of the METAPHYSICAL POETS in its use of scientific conceits and cerebral puzzles. A second volume, *The Gathering Storm* (1940), draws upon his experiences in the East. He revised these works for *Collected Poems* (1955). As critic, Empson remained a maverick: *Some Versions of Pastoral* (1935) extends the definition of PASTORAL to embrace proletarian fiction and *ALICE'S ADVENTURES IN WONDERLAND*; *The Structure of Complex Words* (1951) outlines an elaborate system for analysing the different senses of certain versatile words; and *Milton's God* (1961) launches an assault on Christianity. The essays in *Using Biography* (1984) defend the use of biographical information in criticism against the dogmas of NEW CRITICISM.

encomium Originally a Greek choral song in praise of a hero and now any composition in verse or prose which praises a person, idea or occasion. Encomiastic poetry enjoyed a minor vogue in the 17th and 18th centuries, DRYDEN's 'A Song for Saint Cecilia's Day' being a famous example.

Encounter A political, cultural and literary journal founded in 1953. Editors and co-editors have included STEPHEN SPENDER, NIGEL DENNIS, Frank Kermode, ANTHONY THWAITE and Melvin Lasky. It is notable for having published NANCY MITFORD's treatise on 'U and non-U' behaviour (1955) and C. P. SNOW's defence of his 'Two Cultures' thesis (1959–60), as well as much distinguished modern poetry.

end-stopped line A line of verse in which both the sense and grammatical structure are self-contained, without the need for ENJAMBEMENT, or running-on. End-stopped couplets occur frequently in 18th-century poetry, as in these lines from the fourth of POPE's *MORAL ESSAYS*: 'Who then shall grace, or who improve the soil?/ Who plants like Bathurst, or who builds like Boyle./ 'Tis use alone that sanctifies expense,/ And splendour borrows all her rays from sense.'

Endgame A play by BECKETT, first performed in French (as *Fin de partie*) in 1957 and in Beckett's English translation in 1958. Hamm sits in a room, immobile and dependent on his servant Clov for everything from painkillers to conversation. They are locked in resentful symbiosis: if Hamm cannot stand, Clov cannot sit.

Towards the end, Clov says he can see a boy in the wasteland outside and on his last exit claims that he is leaving for ever. The audience does not have enough confidence in an ending to believe him.

Endymion BENJAMIN DISRAELI's last novel, published in 1880. It describes the rise to eminence of Endymion and Myra Pitt Ferrars, twin children of a promising politician who dies penniless. Myra's husband, the Foreign Secretary Lord Roehampton, is able to help Endymion. Roehampton is modelled on Palmerston and St Barbe on THACKERAY.

Endymion: A Poetic Romance A poem in four books by KEATS, published in 1818. It was savagely attacked by *BLACKWOOD'S EDINBURGH MAGAZINE* and by CROKER in *THE QUARTERLY REVIEW*. Keats combined the Greek legend of Endymion, the young shepherd loved by the moon goddess, with the stories of Venus and Adonis, Glaucus and Scylla, and Arethusa, as well as an ambitious, if not completely successful, ALLEGORY of the quest for perfection and the distraction of human beauty. The famous 'Hymn to Pan' is in Book 1; the roundelay 'O Sorrow', leading into the lovely song of the Indian maid, 'Beneath My Palm Trees, by the River Side', is in Book 4.

Endymion: The Man in the Moon A comedy by LYLY, first performed in 1588. An elaboration of the classical myth of the sleeping shepherd, *Endymion* owed its contemporary reputation to its easily read ALLEGORY of court intrigue: Endymion (the Earl of Leicester) abandons Tellus, the earth (Mary, Queen of Scots), for love of Cynthia, the moon (Queen Elizabeth). Lyly exploited the skills of his chorister-actors by incorporating several songs as well as a DUMB SHOW and a dance of fairies; stage directions reveal the importance of scenic effects and costume.

Engel, Marian 1933–85 Canadian novelist. Most of her novels focus on the roles of women in contemporary consumer society. Her best-known work, *Bear* (1976), is a female quest novel which has affinities with MARGARET ATWOOD's *SURFACING*. Other novels include: *The Honeymoon Festival* (1970), a study of motherhood; *Monodromos* (1973; reissued as *One-Way Street*, 1974), a tragicomic account of a Canadian woman's life on a Greek island; and *The Glassy Sea* (1978), in which the protagonist joins an Anglican order of nuns. She also published two short-story collections, *Inside the Easter Egg* (1975) and *The Tattooed Woman* (1985).

England's Helicon A collection of mainly PASTORAL poems (1600). Generally acknowledged as the finest of the Elizabethan poetic miscellanies, it contains verses by SIR PHILIP SIDNEY, SPENSER, MARLOWE, DRAYTON, PEELE, GREENE, BRETON, CONSTABLE and THOMAS WATSON. Some poems are taken from Elizabethan songbooks and their titles ('jig', 'roundelay' and 'madrigal') testify to their musical nature.

English dictionaries The first, Robert Cawdrey's *A Table Alphabetical, Containing and Teaching the True Writing, and Understanding of Hard Usual English Words* (1604), grew out of earlier teaching manuals, works on grammar and orthography, foreign-language dictionaries and the long tradition of glossing Latin. In their turn Bullokar's *An English Expositor* (1616), Cockeram's *The English Dictionary* (1623), Blount's *Glossographia* (1656) and Phillips's *New World of English Words* (1658) depend on one another for basic materials, growing in bulk and pretension but still concentrating on difficult words. In the next century, recognizing the need for general treatment of the vocabulary, compilers admitted more everyday words into their dictionaries.

SAMUEL JOHNSON's DICTIONARY OF THE ENGLISH LANGUAGE (1755) continued this trend and moved on from the 'difficult words' tradition, to mark a monumental achievement in its own right. His *Plan* (1747) announcing the project reads almost like a programme for an English Academy, and marks the culmination of a long campaign for just such a body on the French or Italian model. The most notable innovation of the *Dictionary* itself was the systematic use of quotations, taken largely from literature 1560–1660, to illustrate usage and justify definitions. (The next major step was taken by Charles Richardson's inclusion of quotations from 1250 onwards in his *Encyclopaedia Metropolitana*, 1819.) Some contemporaries labelled Johnson 'the man who has conferred stability on the language of his country', but he himself recognized that a dictionary cannot 'embalm' language or 'secure it from corruption and decay'. That if nothing else assured that his achievement was pioneering, not definitive, though its status was not challenged until the appearance of the OXFORD ENGLISH DICTIONARY and, to a lesser extent, WEBSTER'S DICTIONARY.

English Review, The A literary periodical founded by FORD MADOX FORD in 1908. During his brief editorship (little more than a year) he published work by THOMAS HARDY, HENRY JAMES, H. G. WELLS and WYNDHAM LEWIS, and introduced the poems of D. H. LAWRENCE. It was finally absorbed into *The National Review* in 1937.

enjambement From the French, 'in-striding'. In English poetry it refers to the continuation of the sense and grammatical structure from one line (or couplet) to the next. Enjambement thus gives, for example, the BLANK VERSE of SHAKESPEARE's plays much of its fluidity and forward movement. The opposite practice is the END-STOPPED LINE.

Enoch Arden A poem by TENNYSON, published in 1864. In its day it was among his most popular works. Enoch Arden is forced to leave his wife, Annie Lee, and set sail on a merchantman. The ship is wrecked and he is reported dead. Annie finally marries Philip Ray, his former rival, but Enoch has survived and returns. Seeing the happiness of Annie, Philip and the children, he quietly resolves to leave them be. Nobody recognizes him but he confides his secret to Miriam, the local innkeeper, when he knows he is dying. She conveys his last blessing to his wife and children, and to Philip.

Enquiry concerning Human Understanding, An A philosophical work by DAVID HUME, originally published as *Philosophical Essays concerning Human Understanding* in 1748 and retitled in 1758. It recasts the arguments in Book I of *A TREATISE OF HUMAN NATURE* and adds a sceptical essay on miracles, once notorious, denying that they can be proved with any amount or type of evidence and excluding them from the reasonable foundation for a religious system.

Enquiry concerning Political Justice A libertarian philosophical treatise by GODWIN, published in 1793. Godwin's major theoretical work, it brought him immediate, though short-lived, fame during the critical years of the French Revolution. Its influence on the Romantic generation of writers was profound, and its themes echo in the writings of Tolstoy, Proudhon, Kropotkin and THOREAU.

It represents the fulfilment of the anarchic potential of classical enlightenment rationalism: itself system-atic to the point of pedantry, it is essentially a repudiation of political systems as such. Although its political programme was revolutionary in that it projected the abolition of law, government, marriage and all apparatuses of inequity and coercion, there could be no question of achieving these ends by insurrection, political agitation or even group solidarity. Reason's means could not differ from reason's end, which was the universal rejection of institutionalized justice itself rather than the violent or inflammatory confrontation of specific cases of its fallibility. People might, therefore, influence each other to embrace the good solely through informal reasoned persuasion. The ultimate triumph of rationality and correct moral sentiment was inevitable, however, and with it injustices would fall away of themselves.

Enright, D(ennis) J(oseph) 1920– Poet. An anthology, *Poets of the 1950s* (1955), helped to establish the MOVEMENT. His own work, beginning with *The Laughing Hyena* (1953), is gathered in *Collected Poems* (1981; reissued 1987). *Memoirs of a Mendicant Professor* (1969) relates his experiences teaching abroad, from post-war Berlin to Thailand and Singapore. He has also edited a selection of MILTON (1975), JOHNSON's RASSELAS (1976), *The Oxford Book of Contemporary Verse 1945–80* (1980), *The Oxford Book of Death* (1987) and *The Oxford Book of Friendship* (1991).

Entail, The See GALT, JOHN.

epic One of the earliest literary forms, it has been discussed by critics from Aristotle to the present. Most agree that an epic should be a long narrative, normally in verse, dealing with one important major action or theme, though it may be amplified or buttressed by subsidiary actions. A certain sublimity of style and grandeur of content are also expected. Homer and Virgil provide the main classical precedents; major English examples include *BEOWULF*, SPENSER's *THE FAERIE QUEENE* and MILTON's *PARADISE LOST*.

epic simile (or Homeric simile) A SIMILE, characteristic of EPIC but not confined to the genre, so long and elaborate that it seems to function as a small inserted lyric, or separate ornament in itself. The comparison between Satan and Leviathan in MILTON's *PARADISE LOST* (Book I) is a famous example.

Epicoene: or, The Silent Woman A comedy by JONSON, performed in 1609 and published in 1616. The plot concerns the deception of Morose, a self-centred bachelor who hates noise. His barber, Cutbeard, introduces him to the soft-spoken Epicoene but as soon as Morose marries her she becomes talkative and quarrelsome. His house is invaded by noisy well-wishers, including Sir Jack Daw and Sir Amorous LaFoole, who claim to have enjoyed Epicoene's favours in the past. Morose is forced to accept the help of his nephew, Sir Dauphine Eugenie, whom he had excluded from his will. Sir Dauphine removes Epicoene's wig to reveal that 'she' is a youth trained for the deception.

epigram 'Her whole life is an epigram, smart, smooth and neatly penn'd,/ Platted quite neat to catch applause with a sliding noose at the end.' This example by BLAKE both exploits and defines what the epigram has come to signify: a witty and well-turned saying with a sting in its tail. The word's Greek derivation means simply an 'inscription', and *The Greek Anthology* (6000 poems from 7th century BC to 10th century AD) includes many non-satirical items. Greatest and most influential of the classical epigrammatists is the Latin poet Martial (*c.* AD 38–104), who, with Catullus, provided the model for the Renaissance, with THOMAS MORE (writing in Latin) as the acknowledged master and HARINGTON, JONSON and HERRICK lively practitioners. Later epigrammatists include PRIOR, POPE, SWIFT, GOLDSMITH, COWPER, BURNS, BYRON, LANDOR, COLERIDGE and, in this century, BELLOC, ROBERT GRAVES and STEVIE SMITH.

Epigrams A collection of poems by JONSON, published in the 1616 edition of his works. The EPIGRAMS themselves satirize contemporary manners. Better known are the sweeter-toned addresses, compliments and epitaphs (which include 'On My First Son' and 'On Salomon Davy, a Child of Queen Elizabeth's Chapel').

epistolary novel A novel in which the story is told through letters between the characters. The form was made fashionable in the 18th century by SAMUEL RICHARDSON; SMOLLETT's *EXPEDITION OF HUMPHRY CLINKER* shows that it was still popular towards the end of the century. Since then it has been less often used.

Epithalamion SPENSER's marriage song, published together with *AMORETTI* (1595) and perhaps intended as the culmination of the sequence. Spenser himself had married Elizabeth Boyle in 1594. The poem begins with the invocation of the muses before dawn, describes the wedding and ends with a prayer in the bridal chamber for 'fruitful progeny'. Blending classical formulae with Christian sentiment, it is a work of jubilant festivity.

epyllion From the Greek, 'little epic', first used in the 19th century to describe classical poems telling a story about love, with mythological allusions and at least one major digression. The tradition dated from the time of Theocritus (d. 250 BC). Examples from Renaissance poetry include SHAKESPEARE's *VENUS AND ADONIS* and MARLOWE's *HERO AND LEANDER*.

Erasmus, Desiderius ?1466–1536 Humanist and scholar. Born in Rotterdam, he went to school in Deventer, became an Augustinian canon and was ordained priest in 1492, but throughout his life obtained dispensations allowing him to leave the cloister and live in the world. He studied for the degree of Doctor of Theology at Paris (1495–9), worked as Latin secretary to the Bishop of Cambrai and became tutor to boys of noble families.

His achievements won him recognition as the greatest humanist of the northern Renaissance. He edited or translated classical authors (Pliny, Seneca, Lucian) and Church fathers (Jerome, Cyprian, Hilary, Ambrose, Chrysostom, Origen). His edition of Lorenzo Valla's *Adnotationes* on the New Testament appeared in 1505. The *Novum instrumentum*, an edition of the Greek New Testament with a parallel Latin version which superseded the Vulgate in its elegance and accuracy, was printed in 1516. It gave impetus to Biblical translators like TYNDALE both by the purity of its text and by the appeal for dissemination of Scripture in its preface. The *Adagia*, a collection of Greek and Latin proverbs, grew to more than 3000 by the Venetian Aldine edition of 1508. The *Apophthegmata* (1531) is a similar collection of classical anecdotes, translated into English by UDALL. The *Enchiridion militis Christiani* (1503) is a manual of simple piety intended, in Erasmus' words, to kindle a warm love of the scriptures in generous hearts. An English translation, *The Manual of the Christian Knight* (1533), is attributed to TYNDALE; COVERDALE's *A Short Recapitulation of the Enchiridion* appeared in 1545. *Institutio principis Christiani* (1516) discusses the education of the Christian prince, while the *Colloquia* are dialogues on various subjects.

On visits to England in 1499–1500, 1505 and 1509–14 Erasmus found congenial friends in humanists like GROCYN, LINACRE, COLET and above all THOMAS MORE. During his last visit, when he lectured at Cambridge on Greek and theology, he wrote the *Moriae encomium* (1511; translated by Chaloner as *Praise of Folly*, 1549), whose title puns on the name of his greatest English friend. Its paradoxical self-praise by Folly herself satirizes clerical abuses, corruption and ignorance, and ends with praise of Christian folly, the simple Christian and the ultimate folly of Christ's crucifixion. Despite his criticisms of the Church, Erasmus could never bring himself to join Luther, finally opposing him in *De libero arbitrio* (1524), a treatise on free will. Yet there is much truth in the cliché that the Reformation was an egg laid by Erasmus and hatched by Luther.

Erewhon A satirical novel by SAMUEL BUTLER, published in 1872. Erewhon (an anagram of 'nowhere') is discovered by Higgs, the narrator, on the far side of a chain of unexplored mountains. His description embodies Butler's attack on the stagnation and hypocrisy of England, and particularly on attitudes to crime, religion and child-rearing. Higgs escapes in a balloon, accompanied by the girl with whom he has fallen in love. In a belated sequel, *Erewhon Revisited* (1901), he returns 20 years later to discover that his ascent in the balloon has inspired a religion, Sunchildism.

Ervine, St John (Greer) 1883–1971 Irish playwright. Works staged at the ABBEY THEATRE, of which he was briefly manager, include *Mixed Marriage* (1911), *Jane Clegg* (1913) and *John Ferguson* (1915). They obey the fashion for the WELL-MADE PLAY, while still addressing serious problems seriously. After World War I he settled in London where he continued to write social dramas but also produced comedies like *The First Mrs Fraser* (1929), almost in the style of NOËL COWARD, and *Boyd's Shop* (1936), a gentle study of Irish village life. He also wrote drama reviews, novels and biographies.

Essay concerning Human Understanding A philosophical treatise by JOHN LOCKE, published in 1690. Further editions, with important revisions by the author, were published in 1694, 1700 and 1706. *Some Thoughts on the Conduct of the Understanding in the Search of Truth*, originally designed as a chapter of the *Essay*, was published posthumously in 1762. Locke rejects the doctrine that knowledge is inborn, maintaining that it derives from experience. His examination of the nature and limits of knowledge threw light on the working of the human mind and the association of ideas, thereby influencing generations of poets and novelists.

Essay of Dramatic Poesy A critical symposium by DRYDEN, published in 1668. Those taking part are CHARLES SACKVILLE (Eugenius), SIR ROBERT HOWARD (Crites), Sedley (Lisideius) and Dryden himself (Neander). They discuss English drama past and present, comparing it with the French theatre. There is lively discussion of the use of rhyme and a fine appreciation of SHAKESPEARE.

Essay on Criticism, An A poem in HEROIC COUPLETS by POPE, published in 1711. It describes and illustrates the rules of taste and the principles by which a critic should be guided. Horace's *Ars poetica* is its classical inspiration. The poem's concentrated, witty utterance made Pope famous, and some lines have achieved proverbial status: 'A little learning is a dangerous thing' and 'Some praise at morning what they blame at night;/ But always think the last opinion right.'

Essay on Man A poem by POPE, in four epistles, the first three published in 1733 and the fourth in 1734. They were partly inspired by the philosophical writings of BOLINGBROKE, to whom they are addressed. The first deals with the nature of man and his place in the universe; the second with man as an individual; the third with man in society; and the fourth with man and the pursuit of happiness. The purpose is to demonstrate the essential rightness of the world as ordered by God. Though conventional in its thought, the poem is enlivened by witty aphorism.

Essays, The: or, Counsels, Civil and Moral FRANCIS BACON's essays were first published in a book of 10 in 1597, followed by a book of 38 in 1612, and a third in 1625 containing 58. Mostly reflections and observations shaped into advice for the conduct of a successful life, they deal with such topics as government ('Greatness of Kingdoms'), architecture ('Of Building') and aspects of human behaviour, including ambition and cunning. The essays use numerous quotations from earlier writers and an aphoristic turn of phrase. The essay on 'Atheism' first appeared in the 1612 edition.

Essays and Reviews A collection of theological essays, published in 1860. The editor was Henry Bristow Wilson and his contributors were BENJAMIN JOWETT, MARK PATTISON, Baden Powell, Frederick Temple, Rowland Williams and C. W. Goodwin. Influenced by the HIGHER CRITICISM, they argued for a liberal Christianity and were nicknamed the 'Seven against Christ' in the ensuing controversy. The book was condemned by a meeting of bishops in 1861 and by the Synod of the Church of England in 1864.

Essays in Criticism Two collections of essays by MATTHEW ARNOLD, the first published in 1865 and the second posthumously in 1888. In the first volume, mainly devoted to Continental and classical subjects, the most important essay is 'The Function of Criticism at the Present Time', a sustained attempt to broaden and elevate the role of criticism. The second collection likewise begins with a challenging essay, 'The Study of Poetry', notable for its theory of 'touchstones' of poetic excellence: one should 'have always in one's mind lines and expressions of the great masters ... and apply them as a touchstone to other poetry'. Otherwise, the volume is more narrowly informative than its predecessor. It includes essays on Tolstoy, Amiel, MILTON, GRAY, KEATS, WORDSWORTH, BYRON, and SHELLEY.

Essays in Criticism A quarterly journal founded by the Oxford critic F. W. BATESON in 1951, partly in emulation of and partly in rivalry with the Cambridge-based SCRUTINY. The title is borrowed from MATTHEW ARNOLD.

Essays of Elia, The Essays by CHARLES LAMB, pseudonymously contributed to THE LONDON MAGAZINE in 1820-3. The first collection was published in 1823; the remainder appeared, with other essays, as The Last Essays of Elia (1833). They are chiefly prized for reminiscences of childhood ('Christ's Hospital Five and Thirty Years Ago', 'Blakesmoor in H—shire') and descriptions of Lamb's wide range of acquaintances. Also included are purely fanciful or melancholy exercises which have become famous anthology pieces: 'Dream Children', 'A Dissertation upon Roast Pig' and 'A Chapter on Ears'.

Esson, (Thomas) Louis (Buvelot) 1879-1943 Australian playwright. He was one of the founders of a distinct Australian drama, particularly in work for the Pioneer Players in Melbourne in 1922-6. His work includes: a one-acter, The Woman Tamer (1910); a political comedy, The Time is Not Yet Ripe (1912); The Bride of Gospel Place (1926); and Mother and Son (1923) and two one-act tragedies, Dead Timber (1911) and The Drovers (1920), all set in the outback.

estates satire A medieval form expounding the characteristics, duties and failings of the different social 'estates', typical categories being pope, priest, prince, knight, nun and wife. The religious classes are at the top of the hierarchy, with laymen beneath them and women at the bottom. Works dealing solely in estates satire are mostly Latin, but English works indebted to it include PIERS PLOWMAN, the General Prologue to THE CANTERBURY TALES, MUM AND THE SOTHSEGGER and WYNNERE AND WASTOURE.

Esther Waters A novel by GEORGE MOORE, first published in 1894. Strongly influenced by French literature and particularly by Zola's NATURALISM, it was his first great success and is still regarded as his most important work. Esther Waters, a member of the Plymouth Brethren, goes into service at Woodview, the home of the Barfields. When William Latch, the footman, seduces and deserts her, she is dismissed and only Mrs Barfield – a fellow member of the Brethren – tries to be kind. Esther endures a bitter, humiliating struggle to bring up her son. William Latch returns and she marries him for their son's sake. He makes a good husband and father, but his life as a Soho publican and bookmaker ruins his health and his death leaves his family penniless. Esther returns to Woodview, where Mrs Barfield now lives alone, and at last finds peace.

Ethan Frome A novel by EDITH WHARTON, published in 1911. Ethan Frome and his slatternly wife Zeena (Zenobia) are joined by her cousin, Mattie Silver, on their poor farm in western Massachusetts. Ethan and Mattie are attracted to each other, and Zeena drives her off the farm. As he takes Mattie to the railroad station, Ethan tries to kill them both in an accident. They survive and spend the rest of their lives as invalids under Zeena's care.

Etherege, Sir George c. 1635–91 Playwright. His work profoundly influenced the development of RESTORATION COMEDY. His first play, THE COMICAL REVENGE (1664), won him a place in rakish society. ROCHESTER became an intimate. His second play, SHE WOULD IF SHE COULD (1668), may have contributed to his being appointed secretary to the ambassador to Constantinople in 1668-71. The responsibility did nothing to reform him and he resumed his wild life on his return. His last and greatest play, THE MAN OF MODE (1676), is a fully fledged Restoration comedy, more intolerant of dullness and affectation than of libertinism. On Charles II's death in 1685 Etherege was appointed ambassador to the Imperial Court at Ratisbon. The letters he wrote to friends in England, first collected in The Letterbook of Sir George Etherege (1928), are among the best of the period. A fuller selection of Letters (1974) and a volume of slight but elegant Poems (1963) complete his output.

Ettrick Shepherd, The See HOGG, JAMES.

Eugene Aram A novel by EDWARD BULWER LYTTON, published in 1832. A NEWGATE NOVEL based on a real crime, it tells how Aram, a scholar, is denounced and arrested on his wedding day for a murder to which he had been an accomplice some 14 years earlier. The portrait of the high-minded, guilt-ridden murderer was condemned in some quarters as immoral, but the book confirmed Bulwer's standing as England's most popular novelist.

Euphues: or, The Anatomy of Wit A prose romance by LYLY, probably first published in 1578. With its equally popular sequel, *Euphues and His England* (1580), it gave its name to the style known as EUPHUISM. Lyly probably found the word 'euphues', Greek for 'well-endowed', in ASCHAM's *The Schoolmaster*. *The Anatomy of Wit* takes its slight plot from Boccaccio, as well as the parable of the Prodigal Son. Euphues leaves his native Athens to visit Naples, where he pledges friendship with Philautus. Rivalry over Lucilla causes the friends to reproach each other but they are reconciled when he transfers her affections to Curio. These events are only the skeleton of a book fleshed out with discourses on WIT, religion and education, as well as love, friendship and the possible conflicts between them, all expressed in elaborate rhetorical artifices. *Euphues and His England* chronicles the friends' visit to England and Philautus' love-affairs there. Euphues ends the story by entering a Greek monastery, while Philautus gets married. ROBERT GREENE attempted a continuation in *Euphues, His Censure of Philautus* (1587).

euphuism A prose style fashionable in the late 16th century. It takes its name from LYLY's *EUPHUES*, where it first appears in full flower, though there are earlier hints of it in NORTH's *Dial of Princes* and PETTIE's *Petite Palace of Pettie His Pleasure*. Its characteristic quality is an obvious and exaggerated artifice, which exploits the figures and 'flowers' of rhetoric, and a fondness for *sententiae* (moral maxims), allusions to myth and history, and what SIR PHILIP SIDNEY calls 'strange similes'. Lyly has an especial liking for balanced antitheses, often reinforced by alliteration: 'Here may you see, gentlemen, the falsehood in fellowship, the fraud in friendship, the painted sheath with the leaden dagger, the fair words that make fools vain.'

Europeans, The A novel by HENRY JAMES, published in 1878. Felix Young, an artist, and his sister Eugenia, the estranged wife of a German nobleman, arrive in Massachusetts to visit their relatives, the Wentworths. Mr Wentworth's daughter Gertrude falls in love with Felix, despite her understanding with the Unitarian minister, Mr Brand; his son Clifford Wentworth becomes infatuated with Eugenia, who is looking for a wealthy husband. Matters are further complicated by Robert Acton, who is drawn to Eugenia, and Lizzie Acton, drawn to Clifford. In the end Felix marries Gertrude, Clifford marries Lizzie and Mr Brand marries Gertrude's sister Charlotte. Robert Acton does not marry Eugenia, who returns to Europe alone.

Eusden, Laurence 1688–1730 POET LAUREATE from 1718 until his death. His minor verse is dwarfed by the work of contemporaries like POPE, who assigned him a place in the realms of Dullness in THE DUNCIAD.

Eustace Diamonds, The The third of TROLLOPE's PALLISER NOVELS, serialized in 1871–3 and published in volume form in 1873. One of Trollope's darker novels, it is a study in moral duplicity with a plot that owes something to COLLINS's THE MOONSTONE. When she is widowed, the beautiful Lizzie Eustace claims the Eustace family diamonds but is opposed by the family lawyer, Mr Camperdown. She turns for help first to Lord Fawn, a dull but ambitious politician to whom she becomes engaged, and then to her cousin Frank Greystock. She claims the diamonds have been stolen but her dishonesty becomes apparent when they are really stolen. Lord Fawn breaks his engagement and she loses the disillusioned Frank, who finally marries Lucy Morris. Rejected even by the Byronic Lord George Carruthers, Lizzie ends by marrying the shady Mr Emilius, a converted Jew turned fashionable preacher.

Evan Harrington A novel by GEORGE MEREDITH, published in 1861. Evan is the son of Melchisedec ('the Great Mel') Harrington, an exquisitely mannered tailor. The plot centres on Evan's determination to clear his father's debts and the efforts of his sisters, who have all married well, to secure his marriage to the eligible Rose Jocelyn of Beckley Court. He finally gains both Rose and a diplomatic post in Naples. Though too long to sustain its attenuated narrative, the book is notable for its crispness of language, comedy, analysis of snobbery and the lively characterization of lesser figures like Jack Raikes, George Uploft and Mr Parsley, as well as Evan's sister Louisa, the wily Countess.

Evangeline: A Tale of Acadie A narrative poem by LONGFELLOW, published in 1847. Set in Acadia, a Canadian province roughly corresponding to present-day Nova Scotia, it recounts the frustrated love of Evangeline Bellefontaine and Gabriel Lajeunesse, separated by the French and Indian Wars. Evangeline finally becomes a Sister of Mercy in Philadelphia, where she recognizes an old man dying during a pestilence as her lover. She dies of grief and they are buried together.

Eve of St Agnes, The A narrative poem in SPENSERIAN STANZAS by KEATS, published in 1820. It is set in the distant past in a medieval mansion. Madeline has learned that a virgin may be granted a vision of her lover on St Agnes's Eve. She steals away from the revelry to her bedchamber, where her lover Porphyro, son of her family's deadliest enemy, has persuaded the sympathetic Angela to hide him. Enticed by his lute-playing, Madeline emerges from her dreams to find him by her bedside. Silently they slip through the sleeping halls and 'away into the storm'.

The poem is a skilful Romantic montage of popular legend, SHAKESPEARE's *ROMEO AND JULIET*, motifs from CHAUCER and Boccaccio, and the atmospherics of the GOTHIC NOVEL. Most striking of all, is the richness and radiant sensuousness of the imagery, particularly in the central bed-chamber sequence.

Evelina: or, A Young Lady's Entrance into the World An EPISTOLARY NOVEL by FANNY BURNEY, published anonymously in 1778. In seven months (and three volumes) the young Evelina undergoes her education in self-knowledge, prudence and discretion under the tutelage of her guardian Villars, the sensible Lady Howard and the judicious Lord Orville, whom she eventually marries. The vivid portraits of her undesirable relatives, Sir John Belmont, Mme Duval and the Branghtons, typify the book's accomplished and witty style. Burney's first novel, *Evelina* rapidly became a fashionable success and attracted the admiration of BURKE, JOSHUA REYNOLDS and JOHNSON, who said that it gave the impression of 'long experience and deep and intimate knowledge of the world'.

Evelyn, John 1620–1706 Diarist. The inevitable comparison with the diaries secretly kept at the same time by PEPYS is unhelpful, since the two records are totally different. Evelyn's annals, started as a series of jottings and memoirs which he began to organize in 1660, cover the whole of his life without ever being intimate. The chief interest of the *Kalendarium* lies in the sketches of contemporary events and public figures. It was not published until 1818, when it was rediscovered by the antiquarian William Upcott and edited by William Bray as *The Memoirs of John Evelyn*. The immediate interest in Evelyn led directly to the rediscovery of Pepys's diaries in Cambridge shortly afterwards. The definitive edition, by E. S. de Beer, was published in 1955.

An early Fellow of the Royal Society, Evelyn published *Fumifugium: or, The Inconvenience of the Air and Smoke of London Dissipated* (1661), proposing remedies for pollution, none of which was implemented. *Sculptura* (1662) is about engraving. The impending shortage of timber for shipbuilding resulted in his influential and informed *Sylva: or, A Discourse of Forest Trees* (1664). Evelyn submitted constructive proposals for the rebuilding of the capital after the Great Fire of 1666, and wrote a treatise on *Navigation and Commerce* (1674), as well as essays on topics from vineyards to medals. The death of his son at the age of five prompted a translation from the Greek, *The Golden Book of St John Chrysostom* (1659), about the education of children. Its 'Epistle Dedicatory' is an early example of the evocative powers of his style.

Every Man in His Humour A comedy by JONSON, first performed in 1598 by the Lord Chamberlain's Men (see KING'S MEN) with SHAKESPEARE apparently in the cast. A revised version (published 1616) changed the names and the setting from Italy to London. It created the fashion for 'humours' comedy, dealing in grotesquely obsessive characters governed by a single dominant emotion or 'humour'.

Irrationally jealous, the merchant Kitely suspects the boisterous crowd which flocks to his house of having designs on his young and pretty wife. One of them, Edward Knowell, woos Kitely's sister Bridget while another, Captain Bobadil, is a cowardly soldier forever boasting of his valour. Knowell's servant, Brainworm, plays on Kitely's jealousy and Dame Kitely's credulity to bring about a confrontation between them. Captain Bobadill's pretensions are exposed. Justice Clement, a shrewd observer of human folly, resolves the misunderstandings and Knowell wins Bridget's hand.

Every Man out of His Humour (performed in 1599), though much less attractive, nevertheless captures foolish 'humours' in Fungoso, Sogliardo and Sir Fastidious Brisk, and satirizes MARSTON and DEKKER, Jonson's adversaries in the war of the theatres, as Clove and Olive.

Everyman The best known of English MORALITY PLAYS, written around the end of the 15th century. It is closely related to a Flemish play printed in 1495. *Everyman* dramatizes the hero's progress from complacency through fear at the prospect of death to Christian resignation; Good Deeds proves the only friend willing to accompany him all the way to the grave.

Ewart, Gavin (Buchanan) 1916– Poet. A skilful writer of light, comic verse and PARODY, he has published a succession of volumes culminating in *Collected Poems* (1991). They include *Poems and Songs* (1939), the erotic *Pleasures of the Flesh* (1966), *The Collected Ewart 1933–80* (1980), *Other People's Clerihews* (1983), *Cluster of Clerihews* (1986) and *Penultimate Poems* (1989). *The Learned Hippopotamus* (1988) is a book of children's poetry. He has also edited *The Penguin Book of Light Verse* (1980).

Ewing, Juliana (Horatia) 1841–85 Writer of CHILDREN'S LITERATURE. She began by contributing to YONGE's magazine *The Monthly Packet* and *Aunt Judy's Magazine*, edited by her mother, MARGARET GATTY. *Mrs Overtheway's Remembrances* (1869) is a family story told with conviction and a rare feeling for domestic ups and

downs. *Jan of the Windmill* (1876) told the story of a foundling later to become a celebrated artist. Mrs Ewing is best remembered now by association, in that *The Brownies and Other Tales* (1870) influenced Sir Robert Baden-Powell and gave him the name for the junior section of the Girl Guide Movement.

Examiner, The A weekly journal begun in August 1710, as an instrument of Tory propaganda, by ROBERT HARLEY with the help of BOLINGBROKE, ATTERBURY, PRIOR and other Tory pens. SWIFT edited it anonymously from 2 November 1710 to 14 June 1711, contributing 33 issues before he was replaced by MANLEY. *The Examiner* survived until 1716.

Examiner, The A radical weekly magazine founded in 1808 by LEIGH HUNT and his brother John. It introduced the poetry of KEATS and SHELLEY to the public, thus identifying Hunt and his friends in the eyes of their detractors as the COCKNEY SCHOOL of poetry. *The Examiner* survived until 1881.

Excursion, The A poem in nine books by WILLIAM WORDSWORTH, published in 1814. The only completed part of a projected philosophical poem, it is still his longest work. *THE PRELUDE* was originally conceived as a 'sort of portico' to *The Recluse*.

Travelling with the Wanderer, the poet meets the Solitary, an enthusiast for the French Revolution now dispirited by events in France. The Solitary is reproved for his lack of faith and loss of confidence in man. A Pastor offers the consolations of virtue and faith. At the Pastor's house the Wanderer presents his conclusions, philosophical and political. The last two books embody Wordsworth's hostile view of the Industrial Revolution. He makes a strong plea for the education of children.

exemplum Short narrative illustrating a moral point. Exempla frequently appear in medieval didactic works, homilies and sermons, and in secular works like GOWER's *CONFESSIO AMANTIS*.

Exeter Book, The A collection of Old English poems compiled *c.* 975. It includes some of the most important surviving poems from the period: *CHRIST, DEOR, JULIANA, THE PHOENIX, THE SEAFARER, THE WANDERER, WIDSITH, THE WHALE, WULF AND EADWACER, THE HUSBAND'S MESSAGE, THE WIFE'S COMPLAINT*, and riddles.

Exodus An Old English poem preserved in the Junius manuscript, retelling the story of the Exodus from Egypt. FRANCIS JUNIUS wrongly attributed it to CAEDMON.

Expedition of Humphry Clinker, The See *HUMPHRY CLINKER, THE EXPEDITION OF*.

expressionism A term coined by the French painter Julien-Auguste Hervé in 1901 to describe a new approach to painting, and later applied to movements in the other arts. In painting it signified the rejection of impressionism and its goal of depicting external reality in favour of an attempt to convey private experience, seen in the work of Van Gogh and Matisse and most memorably embodied in Edvard Munch's *The Scream*. As a literary term, expressionism has most often been applied to the theatre, beginning with German plays but spreading to the USA in the work of EUGENE O'NEILL, particularly in *THE EMPEROR JONES* (1920) and *The Hairy Ape* (1922), and ELMER RICE in *THE ADDING MACHINE* (1923), and to Britain in the later work of O'CASEY. The term 'expressionism' has also been applied to poetry (such as parts of ELIOT's *THE WASTE*

LAND) and fiction (such as the Nighttown episode of JOYCE's *ULYSSES*).

extravaganza A form of 19th-century theatrical spectacle. The finest exponent, PLANCHÉ, based his work on well-known myths or fairy-tales, embellished with punning rhyming couplets and frequent songs. They shadow the rise of the English PANTOMIME.

Eyeless in Gaza A novel by ALDOUS HUXLEY, published in 1936. The title and epigraph are from MILTON's *SAMSON AGONISTES*: 'Eyeless in Gaza at the mill with slaves'. Largely autobiographical, it uses flashbacks covering the years 1902–35 to chart the career of Anthony Beavis and friends, including Brian Foxe (a sensitive and intellectual schoolfriend who later commits suicide), Hugh Ledwidge and his wife Helen (who becomes Beavis's lover) and Mark Staithes (who turns to Marxism). The main purpose is to reveal Beavis's increasing sense of the futility and meaninglessness of his life – and by extension, of contemporary Western society. Finally an anthropologist, James Miller, introduces him to mysticism and pacifism.

Ezekiel, Nissim 1924– Indian poet. Reacting deliberately against the oratorical transcendentalism of Aurobindo Ghose (1872–1950), Ezekiel cultivated a direct, often conversational English to convey his predominant moods of questioning and scepticism. His early verse, in *A Time to Change* (1951), *Sixty Poems* (1953) and *The Third* (1958), is rational and reflective. Restrained, tautly articulated confession of personal failure, even though apprehended as part of a whole generation's collapse of faiths, makes the poems in *The Unfinished Man* (1960) the most impressive he has written, though he continued to produce finely-turned satirical and confessional poems in *The Exact Name* (1965) and *Hymns in Darkness* (1976). *Latter-Day Psalms* (1982) includes poems from earlier volumes.

Faber, Frederick William 1814–63 Poet and hymn-writer. An Anglican clergyman, he converted to Roman Catholicism under NEWMAN's influence in 1845 and established the London Oratory in 1849. His verse includes *The Styrian Lake and Other Poems* (1842), *The Rosary and Other Poems* (1845) and *Hymns* (1848). *Collected Hymns* appeared in 1862.

fable A short narrative using anthropomorphized animals to point a moral. The form is said to have originated with Aesop (6th century BC), but the earliest known fable is by Hesiod (c. 8th century BC). Medieval collections were derived from Latin versions. The oldest of them is the work of MARIE DE FRANCE (12th century). Single fables appear in English in *THE OWL AND THE NIGHTINGALE, PIERS PLOWMAN, THE CANTERBURY TALES* (*Nun's Priest's Tale*). Fables were also used and collected as religious EXEMPLA. Aesopian collections by HENRYSON and CAXTON appeared at the end of the 15th century. Later exponents include DRYDEN, GAY, SMART, COWPER, ORWELL and THURBER.

Fable for Critics, A A verse SATIRE by JAMES RUSSELL LOWELL, published in 1848. On Olympus a critic reports to Apollo about contemporary American writers. Particularly memorable are the sketches of EMERSON ('A Greek head on right Yankee shoulders'), HAWTHORNE ('with genius so shrinking and rare/ That you hardly at first see the strength that is there'), and POE ('with his raven, like Barnaby Rudge,/ Three fifths of him genius and two fifths sheer fudge').

Fable of the Bees, The See MANDEVILLE, BERNARD DE.

fabliau A medieval comic tale with a plot about trickery and sex, told from a cheerfully amoral viewpoint. The genre emerged in late 12th-century France. English examples, all in verse, include CHAUCER's *The Miller's Tale* and *The Reeve's Tale* (in *THE CANTERBURY TALES*) and the anonymous *DAME SIRITH*.

Faerie Queene, The SPENSER's longest, most complex and greatest poem. The first three books appeared in 1590, indicating a plan – apparently never completed – for 12 books. An edition of 1596 added Books IV–VI, and the first folio edition (1609) added the two Mutability cantos, cautiously stating that they seemed to be part of some subsequent book. The main story is the quest of Arthur, who appears intermittently throughout, for Gloriana, one of several projections of Elizabeth I, who also appears as Belphoebe, 'a most virtuous and beautiful lady'.

Book I depicts the knight of holiness, Redcross. His mission is to protect Una and free her besieged parents from a dragon, but he is distracted by the magician Archimago and the disguised Duessa, imprisoned in the castle of the giant Orgoglio and freed by Arthur. He is healed in the House of Celia, kills the dragon and finally marries Una. The book is concerned with the fate of the individual Christian seduced by false religion (Rome). In Book II Spenser draws on the Aristotelian definition of virtue as the mean between defect and excess in describing Guyon, the patron of temperance, and his journey to Acrasia's Bower of Bliss, which he destroys. Book III changes the nature of the quest. Britomart, the female knight of chastity, does not have the primary mission of destroying evil, but of finding Arthegall, her future husband. Interlaced with her story we find the beginnings of the stories of the estranged lovers, Amoret and Scudamour, Florimell and Marinell. Centrally placed in this book is the fruitful Garden of Adonis. Britomart frees Amoret from the enchanter Busirane, and in the 1590 edition Amoret and Scudamour are reunited. Spenser changed the ending in 1596, to delay the reunion until the next book.

Book IV, the book of friendship, continues the stories of the separated lovers and reunites most of them. Britomart and Arthegall pledge their love, but their story is not concluded until Book V. Book IV, meanwhile, is taken up with the story of Cambel and Triamond and their respective loves for Cambina and Canacee, a complicated quartet of relationships which suggests the book's theme of concord. Book V concerns the quest of Arthegall, the knight of justice, to destroy the giant Grantorto and rescue Irena. Incidents allude to Elizabeth's dealings with the Netherlands, France, Spain and Ireland. Book VI recounts the mission of Calidore, the knight of courtesy, to capture the Blatant Beast. Towards the end of the book, in a pastoral interlude, he meets Colin Clout, the poet-shepherd of *THE SHEPHEARDES CALENDER*, piping to the three Graces dancing on Mount Acidale. At the end of the book the Blatant Beast escapes from the world of the poem and threatens the poet's own work.

The Mutability cantos apparently contain no knight and no quest, but describe the threat of the giantess Mutability to claim the created universe. She is arraigned on Arlo Hill before Nature, who enigmatically pronounces that the giantess is evidence of constancy and stability, since change itself is a constant phenomenon. In the last two stanzas the poet turns from this 'state of life so tickle' to contemplate eternity. The poem reaches its tremendous climax in a prayer to 'the God of Sabaoth'.

No account of *The Faerie Queene* can do justice to its variety, complexity and richness. Spenser blends heroic poetry with ALLEGORY, an Aristotelian scheme of virtues with Platonic overtones. The poetic techniques include epic formulas, rhetorical devices and emblematic representations, and Spenser's sources for his imagery range from medieval descriptions of the virtues and vices to court pageants and MASQUES. Some 19th-century readers admired the visual element in *The Faerie Queene* but found its moralism distasteful. Spenser would not have understood, for his work is a sustained example of the speaking pictures intended to delight and instruct that PHILIP SIDNEY talks of in his *APOLOGY FOR POETRY*.

Fair Maid of the West, The A romantic 'adventure' play by THOMAS HEYWOOD. Its first part may have been performed before 1610 and its second as late as 1630. Spencer kills a man in protecting Besse Bridges, 'the flower of Plymouth', and makes her proprietress of the Windmill Tavern in Fowey before leaving the country with Essex's expedition to the Azores (1597). Wounded and apparently dying, he writes a farewell letter leaving her all his property. She sets out to retrieve his body, finds him alive but imprisoned by the Spaniards, and finally rescues him.

Fair Quarrel, A A comedy by THOMAS MIDDLETON and WILLIAM ROWLEY, published in 1617 and probably performed a year or two earlier. Captain Ager challenges a fellow officer to a duel for an insult to his mother's virtue but, to prevent the duel, his mother acknowledges the truth of the accusation. When Ager withdraws, his opponent brands him a coward, giving new grounds for a confrontation. Ager fights and wounds his opponent; the two men are reconciled. The story of Ager's moral dilemma is supported by a bawdy sub-plot, probably Rowley's work.

Fairburn, A(rthur) R(ex) D(ugard) 1904–57 New Zealand poet and personality. A journalist, radio scriptwriter and university tutor (in art history), he was a restless, ardent publicist for good causes (art galleries, New Zealand wine, good sewage) and a sharp satirist of small-minded prejudice. In the 1930s he joined friends such as DENIS GLOVER and R. A. K. MASON in the attempt to establish a distinctively local voice and forms. He used some of Glover's BALLAD forms and much of Mason's IRONY in an idiom which ranged from the epigrammatic to the lyric. *Dominion* (1938; reprinted in *Three Poems*, 1952) and *Strange Rendezvous* (1952) contain his best work. *Collected Poems* appeared posthumously in 1966, and a selection of his letters in 1984.

Fairfax, Edward ?1568–1635 Translator and poet. He was acclaimed for his translation of Tasso's *Gerusalemme liberata* as *Godfrey of Bulloigne* (1600). Other works, unpublished in his lifetime, include ECLOGUES, epitaphs and *Daemonologia*, an account of witchcraft as sensationally practised on his own family.

Faithful Shepherdess, The A pastoral comedy by JOHN FLETCHER, first produced *c.* 1608 and published *c.* 1610. Unsuccessful on the stage, it is nevertheless acknowledged as his poetic masterpiece. The faithful shepherdess is Clorin, who lives faithfully in the forest by her dead lover's grave. Thenot is attracted by her exemplary devotion. Amarillis loves Perigot, who loves Amoret. Repulsed by Perigot, Amarillis tries to seduce him by assuming the form of Amoret, with the help of the Sullen Shepherd. Cloe, a wanton shepherdess, abandons the retiring Daphnis in favour of Alexis. Misunderstandings abound, and virtue and chastity are sorely tried.

Falconer, William 1732–69 Poet. His own adventure off the mainland of Greece resulted in a narrative poem *The Shipwreck* (1762), briefly popular and admired by BURNS. *An Universal Dictionary of the Marine* appeared in 1769, the year Falconer was drowned.

Falkland, Lucius Cary, 2nd Viscount 1610–43 Royalist. His house at Great Tew, near Oxford, became the meeting place for a circle including JONSON, CAREW and WALLER. Falkland argued forcibly for moderation, for the preservation of the reformed Anglican church, and for the ideal of a constitutional monarchy. CLARENDON suggests that the outbreak of hostility in 1642, when he was Charles I's Secretary of State, left him permanently disillusioned. He died at the Battle of Newbury, aged 33.

Falkner, J(ohn) Meade 1858–1932 Writer of CHILDREN'S LITERATURE. His first novel, *The Lost Stradivarius* (1895), was soon eclipsed by *Moonfleet* (1898), an adventure story about smuggling set in the 18th century and obviously indebted to STEVENSON'S *TREASURE ISLAND*. Nothing Falkner wrote afterwards had the same power.

Fall of Hyperion, The See HYPERION.

Fallon, Padraic 1905–74 Irish poet and playwright. His verse plays for Radio Éireann, notably *Diarmuid and Grainne* (1950) and *The Vision of Mac Conglinne* (1953), treat legendary Gaelic material. They are considered among the most successful of their kind. Recognition of Fallon's stature began only with the collection *Poems* (1974) and he remains unfairly overlooked.

Fanny Hill (*The Memoirs of a Woman of Pleasure*) See CLELAND, JOHN.

Fanshawe, Sir Richard 1608–66 Translator and poet. A Royalist active in Charles I's service, he was elected MP for Cambridge University after the Restoration and subsequently sent as ambassador to Portugal and to Spain. His widow, Lady Ann Fanshawe (1625–80), piously recorded his adventurous life in her *Memoirs*, not published in full until 1829. Fanshawe's most important literary work was in translating Guarini's *Il pastor fido* (1647), a Renaissance pastoral drama, and in providing the first English version of the great Portuguese national epic, Camoens's *Lusiadas* (1655). His versatility as a translator can also be seen in *Selected Parts of Horace* (1652), Mendoza's *Querer por solo querer* and *Fiestas de Aranjuez* (1654, published 1671) and in his version, in SPENSERIAN STANZAS, of the fourth book of Virgil's *Aeneid* (1648), together with shorter poems and translations in the second edition of *Il pastor fido*.

Far from the Madding Crowd A novel by HARDY, published in 1874. The first of his books to achieve popular success, it was also the first to use the name WESSEX for its fictional territory. The title is taken from GRAY's *ELEGY WRITTEN IN A COUNTRY CHURCHYARD*. The capricious but strong-minded Bathsheba Everdene is wooed by three men: the loyal Gabriel Oak, who becomes her shepherd and then bailiff after his own farm fails; the braggart Sergeant Troy, who has already abandoned the pregnant Fanny Robin; and a neighbouring farmer, Boldwood. She marries Troy, but he deserts her and is thought drowned. She then yields to Boldwood's frenetic attentions, but Troy reappears at their engagement party. Boldwood shoots him and then unsuccessfully turns the gun on himself; his death sentence is later commuted to life imprisonment. Soon afterwards Oak, her first suitor, who has been overseeing the farms of Bathsheba and Boldwood, again proposes and is accepted.

Farah, Nuruddin 1945– Somali novelist. He has written in Somali as well as English, following the creation of a written form of the Somali language in the early 1970s. *From a Crooked Rib* (1970), about a Somali girl's resistance to the traditional life she is expected to lead in a nomadic community, has been hailed as one of the best portrayals of a woman in African fiction. It has been followed by novels presenting Somali society as a corrupt and repressive patriarchal tyranny: *A Naked Needle* (1976); *Sweet and Sour Milk* (1979), *Sardines* (1981), and *Close Sesame* (1983), which form a trilogy entitled *Variations on the Theme of an African Dictatorship*; and *Maps* (1984).

farce A type of broad COMEDY in which extreme crisis for the characters makes the audience laugh. Although its techniques were familiar from folk-drama and INTERLUDES by such writers as JOHN HEYWOOD, the word 'farce' did not enter the language until after the Restoration. It derived, by way of the French theatre, from the Latin *farcire*, 'to stuff' – reflecting the highbrow assumption that such horseplay could be no more than spice to something more serious in its totality. The broad comic episodes of MARLOWE's *DOCTOR FAUSTUS* are a model for this kind of farce. It established an independent popularity with 18th- and 19th-century audiences, but its lowly status in the dramatic hierarchy delayed its development until PINERO, *CHARLEY'S AUNT* and WILDE's *THE IMPORTANCE OF BEING EARNEST* established new possibilities. A study of farce in the 20th century must take account, not only of TRAVERS, AYCKBOURN and COWARD, but also of SHAW, STOPPARD, ORTON, PETER BARNES and BECKETT's *WAITING FOR GODOT*.

Farewell to Arms, A A novel by ERNEST HEMINGWAY, published in 1929. Set mainly in war-torn Italy in 1917-18, it is about the love-affair between Frederic Henry, an American ambulance driver for the Italian army, and Catherine Barkley, a young English nurse. Eventually, Frederic deserts and flees to neutral Switzerland with Catherine. He is left desolate when their son is stillborn and Catherine dies soon afterwards.

Farjeon, Eleanor 1881-1965 Writer of CHILDREN'S LITERATURE. *A Nursery in the Nineties* (1935) memorably records her childhood. *Nursery Rhymes of London Town* (1916) gathers early stories and poems, while *Martin Pippin in the Apple Orchard* (1921), mixing prose with verse, is steeped in folk-song and country lore. Other works include *The Glass Slipper* (1944), a play written with her brother Herbert, and a collection of stories, *The Little Bookroom* (1955). A close friend of EDWARD THOMAS, she published selections from their correspondence in *Edward Thomas: The Last Four Years* (1958).

Farnol, (John) Jeffery 1878-1952 Novelist. *The Broad Highway* (1910) was the first of his romantic cloak-and-dagger novels, often set in the Georgian or Regency period. He is probably best remembered for *The Amateur Gentleman* (1913). Other works include *Our Admirable Betty* (1918), *The Crooked Furrow* (1939), *The Happy Harvest* (1939) and *The Glad Summer* (1951).

Farquhar, George c. 1677-1707 Playwright. Born in Ireland, he spent the last 10 years of his short life in England except for a brief military campaign in Holland (1700). A derivative intrigue-comedy, *Love and a Bottle* (1698), was followed by *The Constant Couple* (1699), which introduced a popular character in Sir Harry Wildair. Anxious to capitalize on his success, Farquhar wrote an untidy sequel, *Sir Harry Wildair* (1701), and then adapted JOHN FLETCHER's *THE WILD GOOSE CHASE* as *The Inconstant* (1702). He turned away from RESTORATION COMEDY towards a more demure morality in *The Twin-Rivals* (1702). Its failure was only partially redeemed by the successful afterpiece, *The Stage Coach* (1704). Farquhar, who married in 1703 only to find his wife not the heiress he had fondly hoped, was forced to support his new family by joining the grenadiers. His experience in the Midlands prompted the first of his great comedies, *THE RECRUITING OFFICER* (1706). Like its brilliant successor, *THE BEAUX' STRATAGEM* (1707), it is animated by the values of romantic love rather than by its occasional cynicism. Both plays extend Restoration comedy by removing it from London to the provinces, where he celebrates a boisterous low and middle life. Their popularity did not prevent Farquhar dying in poverty.

Farrar, Frederick William 1831-1905 Religious writer and author of CHILDREN'S LITERATURE. A headmaster of Marlborough (1871-6) influenced by THOMAS ARNOLD's example at Rugby, and finally Dean of Canterbury, he published many sermons and theological writings, including *The Life of Christ* (1874). He was chiefly famous,

however, for heavily moralistic children's stories: *Eric: or, Little by Little* (1858), *Julian Home: A Tale of College Life* (1859) and *St Winifred's: or, The World of School* (1862).

Farrell, J(ames) G(ordon) 1935-79 Novelist. His second novel, *The Lung* (1965), drew on his experience as a polio victim. The 'Empire trilogy', his major achievement, dramatized episodes from the history of the British Empire: the Irish civil disturbances during the 1920s in *Troubles* (1969), the Indian Mutiny in *The Siege of Krishnapur* (BOOKER PRIZE, 1973) and the fall of Singapore in *The Singapore Grip* (1978). It combines scrupulous research with a multiplicity of characters and quirky comedy. A novel about British India, *The Hill Station* (1981), was unfinished at his death.

Farrell, James T(homas) 1904-79 American novelist. He supported the Communist Party from 1932 to 1935 but was one of the first American intellectuals to break with it over the totalitarian character of Stalin's regime. He is best known for *The Studs Lonigan Trilogy*, consisting of *Young Lonigan: A Boyhood in Chicago Streets* (1932), *The Young Manhood of Studs Lonigan* (1934) and *Judgment Day* (1935). Set on the South Side of Chicago and charting the short, violent and dissolute life of its protagonist, it is a powerful indictment of the American Dream. Other series of novels in Farrell's prolific output include: *A World I Never Made* (1936), *No Star is Lost* (1938), *Father and Son* (1940), *My Days of Anger* (1943) and *The Face of Time* (1953), contrasting the middle-class O'Flahertys and the working-class O'Neills; and *Bernard Clare* (1946), *The Road Between* (1949) and *Yet Other Waters* (1952), chronicling the difficulties faced by radical literary intellectuals after World War II.

Fast, Howard 1914– American novelist. He became known with novels such as *Conceived in Liberty* (1930), *The Unvanquished* (1942), *Citizen Tom Paine* (1943), *The Proud and the Free* (1950) and *April Morning* (1961), often set during the American Revolution and reflecting his left-wing politics. Other works dealing with remote or recent American history include *The Last Frontier* (1941), *Freedom Road* (1944), *The American* (1946) and *Clarkton* (1947). Novels about the ancient world include *My Glorious Brothers* (1948), *Spartacus* (1951), *Moses, Prince of Egypt* (1958) and *Agrippa's Daughter* (1964). *The Naked God* (1957), a work of non-fiction, describes his disenchantment with the Communist Party during the Stalinist era.

Fatal Curiosity, The A tragedy by LILLO, produced and published in 1736. Like *THE LONDON MERCHANT*, it deals with humble people but is in BLANK VERSE rather than prose. The play is set in Jacobean England and based on an old Cornish murder story. The elderly Wilmot is persuaded by his wife to murder a stranger who turns out to be their son, believed drowned at sea.

Fatal Dowry, The A tragedy by MASSINGER and FIELD, first published in 1632. The exact date of its first performance is unknown. Believing that his wife Beaumelle is continuing an affair with her former suitor Novall, Charalois kills him in a duel. Called upon to judge Beaumelle, her father, Rochfort, finds her guilty but is shocked when Charalois kills her. Handed over to justice as a double murderer, Charalois is acquitted, but a friend of Novall kills him in revenge. ROWE refashioned the play as *The Fair Penitent* (1703), much admired on the 18th-century stage. Beaumelle becomes Calista, the fair penitent of the title, and Novall the libertine Lothario.

Father and Son See GOSSE, SIR EDMUND.

Faulkner, William (Cuthbert) 1897-1962 American

novelist. His work combines a commitment to MOD-ERNISM, notably in the use of STREAM-OF-CONSCIOUS-NESS, and to his native South, the fictional Yoknapatawpha county (based on his native Mississippi) serving as a recurrent location.

Soldiers' Pay (1926) centres on the return of a disabled soldier from World War I. *Mosquitoes* (1927) is about artists and intellectuals in New Orleans. *Sartoris* (1929; reissued under its original title as *Flags in the Dust*, 1973) was his first novel to be set in Yoknapatawpha. His most productive period began with THE SOUND AND THE FURY (1929), about another Yoknapatawpha family, and *As I Lay Dying* (1930). *Sanctuary* (1931) was aimed at a popular audience. *LIGHT IN AUGUST* (1932), though set in Yoknapatawpha county, differs from his other early novels in not concentrating on a single family. *Pylon* (1935) is about aviation. *ABSALOM, ABSALOM!* (1936) concerns the frustrated attempts of Thomas Sutpen to found a Southern dynasty in 19th-century Mississippi. Following *The Unvanquished* (1938), *The Wild Palms* (1939) and *The Hamlet* (1940) – the first of three novels about the Snopes family – came *Go Down Moses* (1942), composed of several interrelated stories about Southern blacks; one of them, 'The Bear', is among his most frequently reprinted pieces. *Intruder in the Dust* (1948) tells the story of Lucas Beauchamp, a black man unjustly accused of murder. *Requiem for a Nun* (1951), a sequel to *Sanctuary*, offers a less brutal treatment of sexual themes than its horrifying predecessor.

A more optimistic tone emerges in *A Fable* (1954), an ALLEGORY of Jesus in a World War I setting. It won Faulkner a belated PULITZER PRIZE. *The Town* (1957) and *The Mansion* (1959) complete the Snopes family trilogy. *The Reivers* (1962) is a mildly comic portrait of several characters from earlier books. Other works include: *Knight's Gambit* (1949), a collection of DETECTIVE FICTION; *Collected Stories* (1950) and *Uncollected Stories of William Faulkner* (1979); *Mayday* (1976), stories about a medieval knight; and *Vision in Spring* (1984), poems originally written for his wife. His Hollywood screenplays include HEMINGWAY'S *To Have and Have Not* (1945) and CHANDLER'S *The Big Sleep* (1946). Faulkner received the Nobel Prize for literature in 1950.

Fauset, Jessie R(edmon) 1882–1961 Black American novelist. As editor of W. E. B. Du Bois's magazine *Crisis* she published many writers of the HARLEM RENAISSANCE. Her four novels, *There is Confusion* (1924), *Plum Bun* (1929), *The Chinaberry Tree* (1931) and *Comedy: American Style* (1934), depict the experience of black women.

Fearing, Kenneth (Flexner) 1902–61 American poet. His first collection, *Angel Arms* (1929), announced his preoccupation with an urban and mechanized society lacking compassion. Other volumes include *Dead Reckoning: A Book of Poetry* (1938), *Afternoon of a Pawnbroker and Other Poems* (1943), *Stranger at Coney Island and Other Poems* (1948) and *New and Selected Poems* (1956). His novels include *The Hospital* (1939) and *The Big Clock* (1946).

Federal Theatre Project A branch of President Roosevelt's Works Project Administration, founded in 1935 to employ out-of-work actors and theatrical workers and to create an uncensored forum for innovative productions. Employing over 10,000 people altogether, it mounted approximately 1000 shows in 30 states. Controversial productions included the 'Living Newspapers' originated by ELMER RICE and MARC BLITZSTEIN'S *THE CRADLE WILL ROCK* (1937). Congress abolished the Project in 1939.

Feinstein, Elaine 1930– Novelist, poet and translator. *The Circle* (1970), about a woman's attempt to reconcile the needs for independence and marriage, and *The Amberstone Exit* (1972), in which dreams, images and memories pass through the mind of a woman about to give birth, have been followed by *The Survivors* (1982), an epic incorporating part of her own history into the story of two Jewish émigré families, *The Border* (1984), *Mother's Girl* (1988), *All You Need* (1989) and *Loving Brecht* (1992). Volumes of poetry include *The Celebrants and Other Poems* (1973), *Some Unease and Angels* (1977), *Feast of Eurydice* (1980) and *Cuty Music* (1989). She has also published translations of Marina Tsvetayeva, Margaret Aliger, Yunna Moritz and Bella Akhmadulina and a biography of Tsvetayeva (1987).

Felix Holt, the Radical A novel by GEORGE ELIOT, published in 1866. The respectably educated Felix Holt returns to his native village and maintains his mother. He burns to participate in politics so that he may improve the lot of his fellow artisans. Contrasted with Felix Holt is the intelligent, economically secure Harold Transome, who intends to enter Parliament as a Liberal, contrary to his family's traditional Toryism. He is opposed to the electioneering practices of the time and his growing disdain for his agent, the dishonest lawyer Jermyn, forms an important narrative line. Much of the action centres upon the hustings and the drunken behaviour of the mob, whose violent activities Felix tries unsuccessfully to quell. His efforts earn him a prison sentence for alleged manslaughter. Both Felix and Transome vie for the hand of Esther, supposed daughter of the quixotic Dissenting minister, Rufus Lyon. She has a legitimate claim to the Transome estates but resigns it shortly before marrying Felix. The story is enhanced by character studies of Harold Transome's mother and the corrupt political agent Johnson, as well as Mr Christian, Sir Maximus Debarry and the loyal servant Denner.

Female Quixote, The See LENNOX, CHARLOTTE.

feminist criticism Not a school, but a set of influential lines of enquiry encouraged by the growth of feminism since the 1960s. Forgotten women writers, whose work lacked a modern reprint or a properly informed readership, have been rediscovered. Several publishers (Virago, Pandora, The Women's Press) have built up impressive lists and laid the ground for major reassessment. Critics have interpreted the texts and explained their neglect. One notable result has been to challenge the habit of tracing the rise of the novel through great male writers. Women's experience as reflected in various kinds of writing has also been reinterpreted, an approach that has yielded some powerful revisionist accounts of 19th-century fiction in particular.

Both achievements have raised an obvious question: is there such a thing as 'feminine writing', marked by certain characteristic features of language or style? Some feminists have agreed with VIRGINIA WOOLF's notion of the 'woman's sentence', glimpsed in occasional, fragmentary forms but holding out the promise of deliverance from male habits of thought, and the idea of an *écriture féminine*, departing from standard language patterns, developed by French critics such as Hélène Cixous. According to this view, women's writing draws on libidinal energies and drives which find no place in the regimented discourse of male (patriarchal) reason. Men may perhaps gain access to such writing, and may even themselves produce it in certain rare cases (perhaps Molly Bloom's soliloquy in JOYCE's *ULYSSES*, for example). Other feminists reject the very notion of some essential difference between male and female writing, pointing out that it runs the risk of simply inverting the old, hierarchical distinction between male and female, leaving its terms still securely in place. For these critics, sexual difference is a matter of biological fact and nothing more.

Fenton, Sir **Geoffrey** ?1539–1608 Translator. An administrator in Ireland, he translated Guicciardini's *La historia d'Italia*, from a French version, as *The History of Guicciardin concerning the Wars of Italy* (1597). *Certain Tragical Discourses* (1567) translates Bandello's stories from Belleforest's French version, loading them with rhetorical devices, proverbs and maxims. *Golden Epistles* (1575) gathers pieces from Guevara and others.

Fenton, James 1949– Poet and journalist. His first collection was *Terminal Moraine* (1972) but his reputation rests on *The Memory of War* (1982), poems based on his experience as a war reporter, and *Out of Danger* (1993). He became professor of poetry at Oxford in 1994. His journalism includes *All the Wrong Places: Adrift in the Politics of Asia* (1990).

Ferdinand Count Fathom, The Adventures of A novel by SMOLLETT, published in 1753. Though among his weaker works, it is notable for moving away from the PICARESQUE and anticipating features of the GOTHIC NOVEL. An amoral, self-seeking villain, Ferdinand adopts the title of Count Fathom and is received into the family of a benevolent German nobleman, Count de Melville, which he proceeds to plunder. His wickedness is eventually revealed but forgiven, and he reforms.

Ferguson, Adam 1723–1816 Philosopher and historian. He was successively professor of natural philosophy, of moral philosophy and of mathematics at Edinburgh University. His *Essay on the History of Civil Society* (1767) attributed social decline to the failure of citizens to play their part in public affairs. *The History of the Progress and Termination of the Roman Republic* (1783) provided an introduction to GIBBON's great work.

Ferguson, Sir **Samuel** 1810–86 Irish poet and antiquary. An undistinguished poet in his own right, he played an important role in translating ancient Irish literature. *Lays of the Western Gael* (1864) contained 'The Tain-Quest', his version of the *Tain Bó Cúaigne* (The Cattle Raid of Cooley), and brought the myth of Cuchulain and Queen Maev of Connaught back into circulation. Other poems concerned Fergus, Conor, Deirdra and Dermid (in Ferguson's spelling). *Congal* (1872) is a poem on the last heroic stand of Celtic paganism against Christianity. Other works include *Deirdra* (1880), *The Forging of the Anchor* (1883) and *Ogham Inscriptions in Ireland, Wales and Scotland* (1887). A collection of prose tales was edited by Lady Ferguson as *Hibernian Nights' Entertainment* (1887).

Fergusson, Robert 1750–74 Scottish poet. He was born and lived in Edinburgh, the smoky city to which he gave a nickname in his most famous poem, 'Auld Reekie'. He began by imitating English styles in lyrics for Scots airs and did not find his true voice until he turned to the vernacular in works like 'The Farmer's Ingle'. A volume of poems appeared in 1773. His wit and sociability made him sought after in Edinburgh literary circles, but he fell victim to religious mania and died insane at an early age. His admirer BURNS sometimes feared his own career might come to the same end.

Ferlinghetti, Lawrence 1919– American poet, editor and publisher. He was a leading figure in the BEAT movement in the 1950s. His work, experimental and often light or satiric in tone, includes *Pictures from the Gone World* (1955), *A Coney Island of the Mind* (1958), *Starting from San Francisco* (1961; revised 1967), *The Secret Meaning of Things* (1969), *Open Eye, Open Heart* (1973), *Landscapes of Living and Dying* (1979), *The Populist Manifestos* (1981) and *Endless Life: The Selected Poems* (1981).

Ferrar, Nicholas 1592–1637 Scholar. In 1625 he retired from Parliament and Cambridge to Little Gidding, near Huntingdon, where he founded a community of some 30 people based on Anglican principles. A Parliamentary raid ended it in 1646. Ferrar's manuscripts were destroyed, so his only surviving works are his published translations of Lessius' treatise *On Temperance* and Valdez's *Divine Considerations*, the latter with notes by GEORGE HERBERT, a close friend who entrusted Ferrar with publication of his poems. SHORTHOUSE remembered Little Gidding in *John Inglesant* and T. S. ELIOT in *FOUR QUARTETS*.

Ferrier, Susan (Edmonstone) 1782–1854 Novelist. She knew the literary society of Edinburgh through her father's friends and was warmly esteemed by SIR WALTER SCOTT. Her three novels of Scottish life – *MARRIAGE* (1818), *THE INHERITANCE* (1824) and *Destiny* (1831) – mix comedy resembling JANE AUSTEN's with explicit didacticism.

Field, Nathan 1587–c. 1620 Actor and playwright. Praised by JONSON, in whose plays he acted, Field graduated from a BOYS' COMPANY to the adult theatre, where he played the hero of CHAPMAN's *BUSSY D'AMBOIS* and ended his career with the KING's MEN. His two London comedies, *A Woman is a Weather-Cock* (c. 1609) and *Amends for Ladies* (c. 1610), are fashionably bawdy. He is known to have collaborated with MASSINGER in *THE FATAL DOWRY* (c. 1618) and with FLETCHER in several plays, including *The Honest Man's Fortune* (1613) and *The Knight of Malta* (c. 1618).

Fielding, Henry 1707–54 Novelist and playwright. Born in Somerset, of aristocratic descent, he studied law in London during the late 1720s and briefly attended Leyden University. But his first ambition was the theatre, and between 1728 and 1737 he produced some 25 plays, ranging in form from the BALLAD OPERA to conventional comedy. An early success, *Tom Thumb: A Tragedy* (1730; revised as *The Tragedy of Tragedies*, 1731), is a BURLESQUE of heroic drama, set in an absurd court of King Arthur. Its attack on Sir Robert Walpole's Whig administration was continued in *The Historical Register for the Year 1736*, a satire produced in 1737, the year when the authorities imposed stage censorship by introducing the Licensing Act.

Aged 30 and with a wife to support (he had married Charlotte Cradock in 1734), Fielding was effectively barred from the drama. He resumed his legal studies – eventually being called to the Bar in 1740 – and threw himself into political journalism as vigorous in its satire as his plays had been. Adept at PARODY too, he responded to the success of RICHARDSON's *PAMELA* (1740) with *An Apology for the Life of Mrs Shamela Andrews* (1741), a skilful squib which makes the innocent virtue of Richardson's heroine appear scheming. His first – and funniest – novel, *JOSEPH ANDREWS* (1742), followed up the idea by making Pamela's brother the central character. Its shapely narrative follows the mishaps of the innocent Joseph and his equally innocent companion, Parson Adams, as they travel through the predatory world of Georgian England. The third volume of Fielding's *Miscellanies* (1743) presented THE LIFE OF JONATHAN WILD THE GREAT, a finely ironic fable inspired by the famous contemporary thief and thief-taker, pretending to equate goodness with greatness. The *Miscellanies* also contained *A Journey from this World to the Next*, a spirited satire in the Lucianic mould which describes the progress of the soul. Some time after the death of his beloved Charlotte in 1744 and his marriage to her former maid, Mary Daniel, Fielding began work on what is probably his greatest achievement, THE HISTORY OF TOM JONES, A FOUNDLING (1749). Ambitious in scope and scrupulous in design, it presents a refreshingly un-idealized hero and a narrator who is virtually a character in his own right. His last novel, AMELIA (1751), is less exuberant, reflecting his own grim experience of social hardships in the metropolis.

In 1748 Fielding had been appointed a Justice of the Peace for Westminster and for Middlesex. His concern at social abuses and judicial corruption is reflected in *A Charge Delivered to the Grand Jury* (1749), *An Enquiry into the Causes of the Late Increase of Robbers* (1751), *Examples of the Interposition of Providence in the Detection and Punishment of Murder* (1752) and *A Proposal for Making an Effectual Provision for the Poor* (1753). As a magistrate, Fielding was both dedicated and effective: together with his blind half-brother, John, he was responsible for Britain's first organized detective police force, the Bow Street Runners. A return to journalism as editor of *The Covent Garden Journal* in 1752 brought him into conflict with SMOLLETT. Fielding was already badly ill, with asthma and gout, when he set sail in 1754 for Lisbon, where he died. *The Journal of a Voyage to Lisbon* (1755) is sharply observed but unavoidably depressing.

Despite the legends of his rakish life-style, Fielding also had a deserved reputation for generosity of spirit and natural sympathy for his fellow man. As a novelist, he was a committed critic of society's corruptions and hypocrisy and a strong believer in benevolence or 'good nature'. In formal terms, he drew eclectically on various traditions – classical epic prose romances, the European PICARESQUE, and the learned fooling of the Scriblerian satirists – while also managing to create a new degree of psychological realism and a linear narrative strength. Though their wealth of topical allusion has prevented his plays from being revived, SHAW paid tribute to Fielding as 'the greatest practising dramatist, with the single exception of SHAKESPEARE, produced by England between the Middle Ages and the nineteenth century'.

Fielding, Sarah 1710–68 Novelist and sister of HENRY FIELDING. THE ADVENTURES OF DAVID SIMPLE (1744) scored a considerable success. *Familiar Letters between the Principal Characters in David Simple* and a second edition of *The Adventures* appeared in 1747, both with prefaces by her brother. *The Governess: or, The Little Female Academy* (1749) preceded *David Simple: Volume the Last* (1753). Other works were *The Cry: A New Dramatic Fable* (with Jane Collier; 1754), *The Lives of Cleopatra and Octavia* (1757), *The History of the Countess of Dellwyn* (1759) and *The History of Ophelia* (1760). She also translated Xenophon's *Memorabilia* and *Apologia* (1762).

Fiennes, Celia 1662–1741 Travel-writer. From 1685 until about 1703 she travelled around England, recording her experiences in journals intended for family reading. The fullest description of the country since CAMDEN, they were roughly transcribed and published in 1888 and edited by Christopher Morris in 1947. Her style is natural and personal, opinionated and sometimes quirky, but full of enthusiastic observations on topics ranging from gardening to manufacture.

Fiesta See SUN ALSO RISES, THE.

Figes, Eva 1932– Novelist. A lyrical writer who has been compared to VIRGINIA WOOLF in her preoccupation with the inner self, she has published *Equinox* (1966), *Winter Journey* (1968), *Nelly's Version* (1977), *Light* (1983), *The Seven Ages* (1986), *Ghosts* (1988) and *The Tree of Knowledge* (1990). She has also written several radio plays and translated works by Martin Walser, Bernhard Grzimek and George Sand.

Fight at Finnsburh, The A fragment of Old English verse preserved in a corrupt 18th-century copy from a lost manuscript. The poem apparently told the well-known story of a feud between the Danes and Frisians, which forms the subject of the minstrel's song in *BEOWULF*. The fragment describes Hnaef and his men defending their hall from attack.

Findley, Timothy 1930– Canadian novelist. He is best known for *The Wars* (1977), the story of a young Canadian officer in World War I. Other novels include: *The Last of the Crazy People* (1967), a study of a decaying southern Ontario family; *The Butterfly Plague* (1969), about a Hollywood family; *Famous Last Words* (1981), the fictional story of EZRA POUND's Hugh Selwyn Mauberley; and *Not Wanted on the Voyage* (1984), a highly imaginative account of the Great Flood. *Dinner along the Amazon* (1984) and *Stones* (1988) are collections of short stories. With his collaborator William Whitehead he has won several awards for television scripts.

Finlay, George 1799–1875 Historian. A supporter of Greek independence who had been with BYRON in Missolonghi, he bought an estate in Attica and eventually died in Athens. His histories of Greece, originally published between 1844 and 1861 and collected as *A History of Greece from Its Conquest by the Romans to the Present Time: 146 BC to AD 1864* (1877), supplemented the work of GROTE and THIRLWALL. Many of Finlay's letters from Greece were published in *The Times* (1864–70).

Finlay, Ian Hamilton 1925– Poet and artist. The leading British exponent of CONCRETE POETRY in the 1960s, he began his work with inscriptions and landscape gardening at Stonypath, Lanarkshire, in 1969. It is shown to good effect in *Selected Ponds* (1976). His work is represented in the Tate Gallery and the Scottish National Gallery of Modern Art, but is still primarily involved with the poetic use of language.

Finnegans Wake A novel by JOYCE, published in 1939. He began it in 1922 and published individual sections as *Work in Progress* during the 17 years of its composition. Joyce's last work, it embodies his most extreme experiments with language and narrative. Puns, verbal compounds, and foreign words are combined with allusions from every conceivable source to create an obscure and densely structured text. Its aim is to relate the minimal central story to a historical, psychological, religious and artistic cosmology, a procedure which has been likened to that of scholasticism and medieval ALLEGORY.

On a literal level, the novel presents the dreams and nightmares of Humphrey Chimpden Earwicker (a Dublin tavern-keeper) and his family (wife Anna, their sons Shem and Shaun, and daughter Isabel) as they lie asleep throughout one night. This, however, provides only a rationale for what is really a novel without narrative or plot, and in which all human experience is ultimately viewed as fragmentary. Major sources of influence have been identified in Vico's ideas of cyclical repetition, Freud's dream psychology, and Bruno's theory of the complementary but conflicting nature of opposites. The title is itself a compound of Finn MaCool, the Irish folk-hero who is supposed to return to life at some future date to become the saviour of Ireland, and Tim Finnegan, the hero of a music-hall BALLAD, who sprang to life in the middle of his own wake.

Firbank, (Arthur Annesley) Ronald 1886–1926 Novelist. Eccentric and delicate in health, he was wealthy enough to indulge his own way of life and develop his own distinctive style of fiction: witty, sinister and meticulous, even artificially, written. He is best known for *Vainglory* (1915), *Inclinations* (1916), *Caprice* (1917), *Valmouth: A Romantic Novel* (1919), the short story *Santal* (1921), *The Flower beneath the Foot* (1923), *Prancing Nigger* (1924) and *Concerning the Eccentricities of Cardinal Pirelli* (1926). A play, *The Princess Zoubaroff: A Comedy* (1920), was not produced during his lifetime, and several short poems were published posthumously. His friend OSBERT SITWELL describes him in *Noble Essences*.

Fisher, St John 1459–1535 Humanist and Roman Catholic martyr. A priest and confessor to Lady Margaret Beaufort, he encouraged her patronage of the University of Cambridge and took a leading role in the foundation of Christ's College (1505) and its sister college, St John's (1511). He himself became president of Queens' College, chancellor of the university, Bishop of Rochester and, in the last year of his life, cardinal. A staunch supporter of Catholicism, he preached against Luther, whom he also attacked in controversialist Latin works like *Assertionis lutheranae confutatio* (1523). His opposition to the break with Rome finally led him to the scaffold. Fisher was beatified in 1886 and canonized in 1935.

Fisher, Roy 1930– Poet. Although he is influenced by the American BLACK MOUNTAIN SCHOOL, his deliberately experimental approach makes his work hard to categorize or identify with a particular movement. *Poems 1955–1987* (1988) brings together new work and work from earlier volumes, including the prose poems of which he is a master. His best-known poem is probaby 'City', a study in urban desolation discussed by DONALD DAVIE in his study of HARDY (1972).

Fitch, William Clyde 1865–1909 American playwright. *Beau Brummel* (1890) was the first of nearly 60 plays which earned him a fortune and Broadway a new status as the home of American drama. The best are society MELODRAMAS combining superficial realism with emotional excess. They include *A Modern Match* (1892), *Barbara Frietchie* (1899), *The Climbers* (1901), *Captain Jinks of the Horse Marines* (1901), *The Girl with the Green Eyes* (1902), *The Truth* (1906) and *The Woman in the Case* (1909).

Fitzball, Edward 1793–1873 Playwright. Born Edward Ball, he produced at least 150 plays as well as four novels, six volumes of bouncy verse and an informative autobiography, *Thirty-Five Years of a Dramatic Author's Life* (1859). Most famous for spectacular MELODRAMAS like *The Flying Dutchman* (1827), he wrote nothing better than *Jonathan Bradford* (1833), based on a recent murder. His titles record his quest for gallery-gripping effects: *The Burning Bridge* (1824), *The Earthquake* (1828), *The Negro of Wapping* (1838) and *The Wreck and the Reef* (1847).

FitzGerald, Edward 1809–83 Poet and translator. After becoming the friend of THACKERAY and TENNYSON at Trinity College, Cambridge, he pursued no particular career and passed most of his life in his native county of Suffolk. Its even tenor was disturbed only by an incautious marriage in 1856 to the daughter of the Quaker poet, BERNARD BARTON, of whom he had supplied a striking *Memoir* for a collection of Barton's writings in 1849. His first separate publication was *Euphranor* (1851), a Platonic dialogue about the Victorian obsession with the rebirth of chivalry. Next came *Polonius: A Collection of Wise Saws and Modern Instances* (1852) and in 1853 the first of several translations of Calderón's work. His Oriental studies resulted in two translations, *Salámán and Absal: An Allegory Translated from the Persian of Jami* (1856) and his major literary work, THE RUBÁIYÁT OF OMAR KHAYYÁM, published as an anonymous pamphlet in 1859. In later years he translated *Agamemnon*, *Oedipus Tyrannus* and *Oedipus Coloneus*, as well as continuing to write witty, sympathetic letters and to sail his yacht off the Suffolk coast.

Fitzgerald, F(rancis) Scott (Key) 1896–1940 American novelist and short-story writer. He established himself as a leading spokesman of 'The Jazz Age' (his own phrase) with the critical and financial success of his early works: *This Side of Paradise* (1920), a loosely autobiographical novel; *Flappers and Philosophers* (1920), a collection of stories; *The Beautiful and Damned* (1922), a disappointing second novel; and *Tales of the Jazz Age* (1922), which includes 'The Diamond as Big as the Ritz'. THE GREAT GATSBY (1925), which many consider his masterpiece, was followed by *All the Sad Young Men* (1926), a third collection of stories.

During these years he and his wife Zelda travelled back and forth between America and Europe, becoming friends of HEMINGWAY and GERTRUDE STEIN in Paris. Their boisterous, decadent existence was undermined by alcoholism and a series of nervous breakdowns which periodically hospitalized Zelda from 1930 until her death in 1948. TENDER IS THE NIGHT (1934), his fourth novel, reflected a new and subdued mood of self-revaluation, continued, after another collection of stories, *Taps at Reveille* (1935), in a series of confessional essays 'The Crack-Up', 'Pasting It Together' and 'Handle with Care'. These were eventually included in *The Crack-Up* (1945), a selection of Fitzgerald's essays, notes and letters edited by his friend EDMUND WILSON. From 1927 onwards Fitzgerald worked sporadically and unsuccessfully in Hollywood, completing only one screenplay, *Three Comrades* (1938), and still suffering from his drinking problem. He returned to fiction in his last months, producing the pieces gathered as *The Pat Hobby Stories* (1962) and starting a novel about a Hollywood producer, *The Last Tycoon*, published in its unfinished state in 1941.

Fitzgerald, Robert D(avid) 1902–87 Australian poet. Preoccupied with philosophical issues, his work helped to bridge the gap between the 'difficult' poetry of CHRISTOPHER BRENNAN and the more accessible poetry of THOMAS SHAPCOTT or LES MURRAY. A strong humanitarian concern is always evident. His best work includes 'The Hidden Bole', an ELEGY for Pavlova in *Moonlight Acre* (1938). *Heemskerk Shoals* (1949) considers time and art more colloquially. *Between Two Tides* (1952) describes a struggle between two Tongan chiefs and meditates on how choices are made. *The Wind at Your Door* (1959), his finest achievement, attempts to come to terms with the opposing strains in Australian ancestry: free settler and convict, victor and victim. Fitzgerald's other poetry includes *The Greater Apollo* (1927), *To Meet the Sun* (1929), *This Night's Orbit* (1953), *Southmost Twelve* (1962), *Forty Years' Poems* (1965) and *Product* (1978).

Fitzmaurice, George 1877–1963 Irish playwright. The ABBEY THEATRE produced his first play, *The Country Dressmaker* (1907), about Irish peasants, and his idiosyncratic one-act tragicomedies, *The Pie-Dish* (1908) and *The Magic Glasses* (1913). Increasingly reclusive after service in World War I, he resisted performance of his later work and slipped from public notice until the appearance of *Collected Plays* (1967–70). His tragedy, *The Moonlighter*, and such comic fantasies as *The Enchanted Land*, *The Ointment Blue* and *The Dandy Dolls*, show his range and originality.

Flecker, James (Herman) Elroy 1884–1915 Poet and playwright. He contributed to GEORGIAN POETRY and published volumes of lyric poetry influenced by the last years of the AESTHETIC MOVEMENT: *The Bridge of Fire* (1907), *Forty-Two Poems* (1911) and *The Golden Journey to Samarkand* (1913). *The Grecians* (1910) is a dialogue on education, and *The King of Alsander* (1914) an experimental novel. Two plays, *HASSAN* (1922) and *Don Juan* (1925), appeared after his early death. J. C. SQUIRE edited his *Collected Poems* (1947).

Flecknoe, Richard *c.* 1600–*c.* 1678 Poet and playwright. He was made a memorable target of DRYDEN's satire in MAC FLECKNOE and MARVELL's in 'An English Priest at Rome', provoked by his *Short Discourse on the English Stage* (1664). Other works include a *Relation of Ten Years Travels in Europe, Asia, Africa and America* (1654); five plays, of which only *Love's Dominion* (1654) was performed; *Enigmatical Characters*, a collection of prose sketches (1658); and a book of verse, *Epigrams of All Sorts* (1670).

Fleming, Ian (Lancaster) 1908–64 Novelist. *Casino Royale* (1952) was the first of 13 thrillers whose knowing, exotic detail and racy adventure made their hero, James Bond, one of the most popular secret agents in the history of spy fiction. Film adaptations starring, successively, Sean Connery, Roger Moore and Timothy Dalton increased Fleming's and Bond's reputations. After Fleming's death KINGSLEY AMIS (in *Colonel Sun*, 1968) and John Gardner continued Bond's career in pastiche thrillers.

Fletcher, Giles, the elder 1546–1611 Poet and diplomat. He was father of the poets PHINEAS FLETCHER and GILES FLETCHER THE YOUNGER, and uncle of JOHN FLETCHER. *Of the Russe Commonwealth* (1591), the most important description of Russia by a 16th-century Englishman, resulted from his mission as ambassador to Tsar Fyodor I in 1588. It remained popular long enough to include MILTON, as well as JONSON, among its readers. *Licia* (1593) is chiefly a collection of SONNETS influenced by PHILIP SIDNEY's *ASTROPHIL AND STELLA*, though it also contains an ODE, a dialogue, some ELEGIES and a monologue by Richard III. Fletcher's attempt to gain Burghley's patronage for a Latin history of the reign of Elizabeth was unsuccessful.

Fletcher, Giles, the younger 1585–1623 Poet. The younger son of GILES FLETCHER THE ELDER, he is remembered for *Christ's Victory and Triumph in Heaven and Earth, over and after Death* (1610), a baroque religious poem influenced by SPENSER and popular in its day.

Fletcher, John 1579–1625 Playwright. He was the son of a bishop of London and a nephew of GILES FLETCHER THE ELDER. It was probably through JONSON's circle that he met FRANCIS BEAUMONT. Together they took over as leading dramatists for the KING's MEN in the PRIVATE THEATRE at the Blackfriars. The success of their partnership, notably in *PHILASTER* (*c.* 1609), *THE MAID's TRAGEDY* (*c.* 1610) and *A KING AND NO KING* (1611), encouraged their

contemporaries and immediate successors to ascribe to them far more work than the seven or eight confidently allowed by modern scholars. See the entry about Beaumont for further details.

The most important plays of which Fletcher is widely accepted as the sole author include: THE FAITHFUL SHEPHERDESS (*c.* 1609), *VALENTINIAN* (1610–?14), THE CHANCES (*c.* 1617), THE HUMOROUS LIEUTENANT (*c.* 1619), THE WILD-GOOSE CHASE (*c.* 1621) and RULE A WIFE AND HAVE A WIFE (1624). However, he remained a willing collaborator after Beaumont's retirement, with SHAKESPEARE in HENRY VIII (1613) and THE TWO NOBLE KINSMEN (1613), with FIELD in *The Honest Man's Fortune* (1613), *The Knight of Malta* (*c.* 1618) and other plays, and with MASSINGER in more than 20 plays. These include: *The Tragedy of Sir John van Olden Barnavelt* (1619), *The Custom of the Country* (*c.* 1619), *The Beggar's Bush* (*c.* 1622) and *The Spanish Curate* (*c.* 1622).

Fletcher, John Gould 1886–1950 American poet. He lived in England from 1909 to 1933. His early work, in volumes such as *Irradiations: Sand and Spray* (1915) and *Goblins and Pagodas* (1916), is associated with IMAGISM. His later work, which continues his interest in Eastern mysticism, also reflects his connection with the FUGITIVES. *Selected Poems* (1938) won a PULITZER PRIZE.

Fletcher, Phineas 1582–1650 Poet. He was the elder son of GILES FLETCHER THE ELDER. *The Locusts or Apollyonists* (1627) is typical of his anti-Catholic verse. Like his brother GILES FLETCHER THE YOUNGER, he also imitated SPENSER, to whom his erotic narrative, *Britain's Ida* (1628), was mistakenly ascribed. *The Purple Island* (1633) is a convoluted ALLEGORY about mind and body. A pastoral play, *Sicelides: A Piscatory* (published in 1631), never received its intended performance at court.

Flint, F(rank) S(tuart) 1885–1960 Poet. His first collection, *In the Net of Stars* (1909), featured conventional love poems but *Cadences* (1915), published after he had met POUND and T. E. HULME, made an important contribution to IMAGISM. It observes his theory of 'unrhymed cadence'. A final volume, *Otherworld: Cadences* (1920), reverted to his initial Romanticism. Flint was also an authority on contemporary French poetry.

Flores and Blancheflour One of the earliest English VERSE ROMANCES (*c.* 1250), it is based on a lost French version. Flores, son of the King of Spain, and Blancheflour fall in love and triumph over his parents, who disapprove, and the Emir of Babylon, who holds her captive in his harem.

Florio, John ?1553–1625 Translator and lexicographer. The son of an Italian Protestant refugee, he studied at Oxford and was groom of the privy chamber to the Queen in 1604–19. His greatest work was the translation of Montaigne's *Essais* (1603, revised 1613) which SHAKESPEARE read. *Florio His First Fruits* (1578) and *Florio's Second Fruits* (1591) are grammars and dialogues in English and Italian; *A World of Words* (1598) is an Italian–English dictionary, enlarged as *Queen Anne's New World of Words* (1611). *Giardino di Ricreazione* (1591) collects Italian proverbs.

Flower and the Leaf, The An anonymous poem dating from the third quarter of the 15th century, once part of the CHAUCERIAN APOCRYPHA and sometimes, unconvincingly, attributed to the author of THE ASSEMBLY OF LADIES. The narrator, though not necessarily the poet, is a woman. She observes the followers of the Flower (the idle and pleasure-seeking) and the Leaf (the faithful and chaste). She favours the latter.

folk revival, the The researches of THOMAS PERCY, ALLAN RAMSAY, BURNS and SCOTT in the late 18th century and of the German Grimm brothers in the early 19th century had become influential throughout the English-speaking world in the late 19th century, when middle-class intellectuals were anxious to preserve a traditional peasant culture which they saw as threatened by industrialization, urbanization and the spread of mechanical forms of entertainment.

Much of this energy was devoted to Celtic culture and forms part of the CELTIC REVIVAL. The folk revival was spearheaded in England by SABINE BARING-GOULD, who collected and published Devonian folk songs, and Frank Kidson, and in the USA by FRANCIS J. CHILD's *The English and Scottish Popular Ballads* (1882–98). In the early 20th century the work of collecting was continued by Cecil J. Sharp (1859–1924), who operated widely throughout England and the Eastern USA, and musicians such as Ralph Vaughan Williams, Percy Grainger and E. J. Moeran. The second phase of the revival, following World War II, was brought about largely by left-wing thinkers, often working-class, who saw folk song as a means of politicizing the working class. A. L. Lloyd, who edited the influential *Penguin Book of English Folksongs* (1959) with Vaughan Williams, approached his subject in Marxist terms in *Folk Song in England* (1967). He was joined by Ewan MacColl in England, Hamish Henderson in Scotland and Pete Seeger in the USA in placing as much emphasis on performance as on scholarship and in freeing songs from the bowdlerization forced on earlier editors. Many singers steeped in traditional song, such as MacColl, Cyril Tawney, Peter Bellamy, Bob Pegg and Peter Coe, created new songs in the traditional idiom which the revival had brought to a wider audience.

Fool of Quality, The A SENTIMENTAL NOVEL by HENRY BROOKE, published in 1766–72. The title-character is Henry, son of the Earl of Moreland, rejected by his parents because he seems dull and unintelligent in comparison with his elder brother. He grows into a young man of strength, beauty and virtue who spends his time helping the unfortunate. On this slender framework Brooke hangs a number of discourses on various aspects of the human condition and, in the latter part, on Christian mysticism.

foot See METRE.

Foote, Samuel 1720–77 Playwright and actor. The plays which he wrote as vehicles for his acting exploited his considerable talent for mimicry. Almost all include satiric portraits of living individuals, most famously George Whitefield and the Methodists in *The Minor* (1760). A riding accident led to his having a leg amputated in 1766 and, in compensation, aristocratic friends procured a summer licence for Foote to perform plays at the HAYMARKET. Still determined to act, he wrote 'cripple' plays, including *The Devil upon Two Sticks* (1768) and *The Lame Lover* (1770). His last considerable play, *Piety in Pattens* (1773), vigorously attacked fashionable sentimentalism. The Duchess of Kingston's fury at her portrait as Lady Kitty Crocodile in *A Trip to Calais* (1775) indirectly brought his theatrical career to an end. Tried on a trumped-up charge of homosexual rape, Foote was acquitted but effectively silenced.

For the Term of His Natural Life See HIS NATURAL LIFE.

Ford, Ford Madox [Hueffer, Ford Hermann] 1873–1939 Novelist and literary journalist. He was the grandson of the painter Ford Madox Brown and the nephew of WILLIAM MICHAEL ROSSETTI, and changed his name from Hueffer in 1919. In the course of a turbulent life, punctuated by various romantic liaisons, he lived in France and the USA as well as Britain. At several points he exerted a powerful and benign influence on contemporary writers. During his brief editorship of *THE ENGLISH REVIEW*, founded in 1908, he managed to sponsor POUND, D. H. LAWRENCE and WYNDHAM LEWIS as well as publishing work by JAMES, HARDY, BENNETT, GALSWORTHY and YEATS. *The Transatlantic Review*, which he founded in Paris in 1924 with HEMINGWAY as his deputy editor, included Pound, JOYCE, GERTRUDE STEIN, E E CUMMINGS and JEAN RHYS among contributors. He also gave support to many of the younger American Southern Agrarians such as ALLEN TATE, CAROLINE GORDON, KATHERINE ANNE PORTER and ROBERT LOWELL. Ford collaborated with CONRAD on two novels, *The Inheritors* (1901) and *Romance* (1903). His own novels include: a trilogy of historical romance, *The Fifth Queen* (1906–8); *A Call* (1910); *THE GOOD SOLDIER* (1915); and a tetralogy, *PARADE'S END* (1924–8). *It was the Nightingale* (1933), about his years in Paris, is one of many works of personal recollection. His last work, *The March of Literature* (1939), is a monumental survey of ancient literature and Mediterranean culture.

Ford, John *c.* 1586–*c.* 1640 Playwright. Little is known of his life, and the precise dates of his plays are debated by scholars. He began, probably, as a collaborator with DEKKER and WILLIAM ROWLEY on *THE WITCH OF EDMONTON* (*c.* 1621), working again with Dekker on *The Welsh Ambassador* (1623) and a MASQUE, *The Sun's Darling* (1624). The most important works of which he was sole author are two tragedies, *THE BROKEN HEART* (*c.* 1629) and *'TIS PITY SHE'S A WHORE* (*c.* 1625–33), together with *PERKIN WARBECK* (published 1634). *Love's Sacrifice* (*c.* 1632) is a tragedy of almost unrelieved gloom, notable for a magnificent villain in D'Avalos. *The Lover's Melancholy* (1628) is comedy edging towards tragedy. *The Fancies, Chaste and Noble* (*c.* 1636) and *The Lady's Trial* (1638), are slight comedies.

Forest, The A collection of poems by JONSON, published in the 1616 edition of his works. It includes 'That Women are But Men's Shadows', 'To Penshurst', 'Come My Celia, Let Us Prove' and 'Song: To Celia' ('Drink to Me Only, with Thine Eyes').

Forester, C(ecil) S(cott) 1899–1966 Novelist. He was best known for his popular 'Hornblower' series, starting with *The Happy Return* (1937), which, in the dozen novels that followed, charted the hero's rise from midshipman to admiral during the Napoleonic Wars. Other novels include: *Payment Deferred* (1926), set during World War I; *Brown on Resolution* (1929); *Death to the French* (1932) and *The Gun* (1933), both set during the Peninsula War; *The African Queen* (1935), which became a famous film in 1952; and *The General* (1936), reworking his favourite theme of individual fortitude in war.

formalism A term applied both to a generalized tendency and to certain specific schools and movements of literary criticism. His analysis of TRAGEDY made Aristotle the precursor of formalist method. Since then, criticism has fluctuated between a concern with systematic theory and a more subjective, less methodical style of approach. In the present century formalism has enjoyed a widespread revival of interest among critics determined to rescue their discipline from the vagaries of individual taste.

The Russian Formalists of the 1920s concentrated on the language of poetry and the structure of narrative. They saw poetry as a special kind of language with the power of 'making strange' (*ostranenie*), which 'defamiliarizes' the normal relation between language and reality, word and world, and prevents us reading straight 'through' the text to its paraphrasable content. In narrative the Formalists detected deep regularities amounting to a 'grammar' of types. Criticism is then employed in deducing these structures and not in piling up of new interpretations. It then achieves a truly scientific, co-operative basis, as well as being able to profit from advances in neighbouring disciplines like structural linguistics.

STRUCTURALISM revived and developed the Formalist legacy. NEW CRITICISM has also been described as a type of formalism, but it preferred to operate with a handful of non-technical terms ('ambiguity', 'IRONY', 'paradox') whose loose definition created flexibility.

Fors Clavigera A miscellany by RUSKIN, published as monthly letters to the workmen and labourers of England in 1871–8 and intermittently thereafter. The enigmatic title suggests more than 'Fortune with the nail'. 'Fors' he associates with 'Force' (the power of doing good work), with 'Fortitude' (the bearing of pain) and with 'Fortune' (the 'necessary fate of man'). Similarly, 'Clavigera' means the 'Club', the 'Key' and the 'Nail' – Herculean strength, patience and the law, respectively. While *Fors Clavigera* includes many urgent messages on social issues, it digresses into a dazzling show of linguistic pyrotechnics.

Forsaken Merman, The A poem by MATTHEW ARNOLD, published in *The Strayed Reveller and Other Poems* (1849). A merman laments his wife, a girl from the land who bore him children and then left him, feeling the call of her own world in the sound of church bells at Easter.

Forster, E(dward) M(organ) 1879–1970 Novelist, short-story writer and essayist. Born in London, he was educated at Tonbridge School, which he hated, and King's College, Cambridge, where he was elected to the APOSTLES and met future members of the BLOOMSBURY GROUP. He returned to King's on a three-year fellowship in the 1920s and as a permanent honorary fellow after his mother's death in 1945.

Although *WHERE ANGELS FEAR TO TREAD* (1905), *THE LONGEST JOURNEY* (1907) and *A ROOM WITH A VIEW* (1908) were widely noticed, it was *HOWARDS END* (1910) that fully established his reputation. However, *The Celestial Omnibus* (1911), a relatively minor volume of short stories, was followed by more than a decade of silence, during which he wrote *MAURICE*, about a successful homosexual relationship, not published until 1971. During World War I he served in the International Red Cross in Alexandria. *Alexandria: A History and a Guide* (1922; revised 1938) was followed by *Pharos and Pharillon* (1923), a collection of Alexandrian essays which included translations of poems by his friend C. P. Cavafy. A second visit to India in 1921–2 as secretary and companion to the Maharajah of Dewas Senior prompted him to complete *A PASSAGE TO INDIA* (1924), his most acclaimed novel but also his last. Thereafter he published: *Aspects of the Novel* (1927), a shrewd piece of criticism based on his Clark lectures; *The Eternal Moment* (1928), a volume of pre-war short stories about the supernatural; two volumes of essays, *Abinger Harvest* (1936) and *Two Cheers for Democracy* (1951), whose mildness of tone does not conceal the commitment to toler-

ance and individual liberty which characterized his thinking; and *The Hill of Devi* (1953), about his second visit to India. He also wrote, with Eric Crozier, the libretto for Benjamin Britten's *Billy Budd* (1949). *The Life to Come* (1972), a collection of earlier short stories which, like *Maurice*, treated the homosexual theme, also had to await posthumous publication.

Forster, John 1812–76 Essayist and biographer. A lawyer attracted to journalism and the literary life, he succeeded his friend DICKENS as editor of *THE DAILY NEWS* in 1846. He also edited *The Foreign Quarterly Review* (1842–3) and *THE EXAMINER* (1847–55). Though he wrote a number of literary studies, he is remembered for his biographies of Dickens (1872–4) and another friend, LANDOR (1869).

Forsyte Saga, The A sequence of novels by GALSWORTHY, comprising *The Man of Property* (1906), *In Chancery* (1920) and *To Let* (1921; with two interludes, 'Indian Summer of a Forsyte', 1918, and *Awakening*, 1920), published together in 1922.

It follows three generations of the Forsyte family, from the 1880s to the early 1920s. Soames Forsyte, a successful solicitor, builds a house at Robin Hill. His wife Irene deserts him for the architect, Bosinney, but returns after Bosinney dies in a street accident. *In Chancery* describes how she deserts Soames and marries his cousin, Jolyon. They have a son, Jon. The embittered Soames marries Annette Lamotte, who gives birth to Fleur. In *To Let* the young Jon and Fleur fall in love but, learning of the family past, he leaves her and goes to America, where Irene joins him after Jolyon's death. Fleur throws herself at an admirer, Michael Mont. Soames learns that Annette has been unfaithful. Robin Hill is left empty and Timothy Forsyte, last of the old generation, dies at the age of 100.

Fortescue, Sir John c. 1394–c. 1476 Legal writer. Appointed Chief Justice in 1442, he supported Henry VI but submitted to Edward IV after the battle of Tewkesbury (1471). *A Declaration upon Certain Writings* (1471–3) formally retracted his support for the Lancastrian cause. *The Governance of England* (c. 1473), his most important work, is the earliest constitutional treatise in English, written in a straightforward style which benignly influenced the development of English prose. Of his Latin treatises, *De laudibus legum Angliae* (1468–70), published 1546) was written for the education of the young Prince Edward; *De natura legis naturae* (1461–3) was rendered into English as *Monarchia; or, The Difference between an Absolute and a Limited Monarchy*.

Fortnightly Review, The A periodical founded in 1865 by ANTHONY TROLLOPE, the publisher Frederic Chapman and others as a platform for liberal opinion. G. H. LEWES, its first editor, elicited contributions from BAGEHOT, GEORGE ELIOT, FREDERIC HARRISON and HERSCHEL, as well as Trollope. Its second editor, JOHN MORLEY (1867–82) published work by MEREDITH, MILL, HUXLEY, ARNOLD, SWINBURNE, SPENCER and LESLIE STEPHEN. FRANK HARRIS, editor in 1886–94, rescued it from decline partly by flouting respectable taste. Under W. L. Courtney (1894–1928) the *Fortnightly* was urbane, academic and distinguished. It ceased publication in 1954.

Fortunes of Nigel, The A novel by SIR WALTER SCOTT, published in 1822, set in the reign of James I. Impoverished by his father's loan to the king, Nigel Oliphaunt, Lord Glenvarloch, comes to London to recover the debt but is opposed by Prince Charles, the

Duke of Buckingham and their favourite, Lord Dalgarno. Margaret Ramsay, a London clockmaker's daughter, succeeds in saving him from their schemes and in securing reparation for Dalgarno's wronged wife, Lady Hermione. Nigel marries Margaret and returns to Scotland. Dalgarno pursues him but is killed by robbers on the way.

42nd Parallel, The See USA.

Four Hymns A group of poems (1596) by SPENSER, in honour of Love, Beauty, Heavenly Love and Heavenly Beauty. The double pairing reflects Platonic and neo-Platonic theory. Platonic influence can also be detected in the parentage of Love in the first hymn and its account of Love as the agent of creation. The second pair is explicitly Christian, describing God's love in the Incarnation and the mysterious figure of Sapience enthroned in heaven. All four demonstrate a typically complex Renaissance synthesis, mingling Platonic philosophy and Renaissance commentary with theological language and Protestant piety and, in the first poem, the pains of the suffering poet-lover.

Four Quartets Four poems by T. S. ELIOT, published between 1935 and 1942 and collected in 1943. Together, they make a meditative or devotional sequence, linked by recurrent motifs and common themes: consciousness and memory, the individual's relation to time and the transcendent experience of timelessness. Each poem is firmly anchored in a place. 'Burnt Norton' (1935) meditates on a country house in the Cotswolds with a rose garden pervaded by children, or the memory of children. 'East Coker' (1940) takes its title from the Somerset village of Eliot's ancestors, a fitting scene for meditation on transience and eternity. 'The Dry Salvages' (1941), named after a group of rocks off the Massachusetts coast, evokes memories of America, including Eliot's boyhood in St Louis. 'Little Gidding' (1942), referring to the religious community established by NICHOLAS FERRAR, contemplates war, destruction and reconciliation.

fourteeners See METRE.

Fowler, Henry Watson 1858–1933 Lexicographer and grammarian. With his brother Francis George Fowler (1870–1918) he produced a four-volume translation of Lucian (1905) and The King's English (1906). His Concise Oxford Dictionary of Current English (1911), an abridgement of THE OXFORD ENGLISH DICTIONARY, was the first of a series of Oxford dictionaries, the best known being the Dictionary of Modern English Usage (1926; re-edited by SIR ERNEST GOWERS, 1965), long considered authoritative for both word usage and grammar.

Fowler, Katherine 1632–64 Poet, also known by her married name, Katherine Philips. HENRY VAUGHAN, ABRAHAM COWLEY and JEREMY TAYLOR were among the circle who attended her salons for discussing poetry and religion. As 'Matchless Orinda' she was the subject of several verses. Her own work includes verses prefixed to Vaughan's Poems (1651), a translation of Corneille's Pompée (1663) and a posthumous collection (1667). Cowley wrote her ELEGY.

Fowles, John (Robert) 1926– Novelist and essayist. Superficially diverse in both subject and manner, his fiction is preoccupied with the possibilities of genuinely free action. The Collector (1963) is a psychological thriller; The Magus (1966, revised 1977) is a long, compulsive masquerade of sexual enticement on a Greek island; and The French Lieutenant's Woman (1969), still his best-known work, is a pastiche of Victorian fiction

undercut by 20th-century literary and social insight. Its heroine, the governess Sarah Woodruff, is one version of the inscrutable woman who appears throughout his work, notably in the title novella of The Ebony Tower (1974), a collection of shorter fiction. Later works include: Daniel Martin (1977), a dense, realistic BILDUNGSROMAN; Mantissa (1983), a sexual jeu d'esprit and SATIRE of STRUCTURALISM; and A Maggot (1985), an 18th-century murder mystery. Of his non-fiction, The Aristos (1964, revised 1980) is a 'self-portrait in ideas' and The Tree (1979) an autobiographical essay attesting to his interest in the natural world.

Fox, George 1624–91 Founder of the Society of Friends. His remarkable Journal, prepared for publication by a committee of fellow Quakers in 1694, tells the story of his spiritual search simply and with vivid vignettes. A Collection of Epistles was published in 1698, Gospel Truth in 1706.

Fox, Paula 1923– American novelist and writer of CHILDREN'S LITERATURE. Her children's novels mark a distinct break with the more secure world described by earlier authors. In How Many Miles to Babylon? (1967) a small black boy is kidnapped by older children. In The Slave Dancer (1973) a boy is kidnapped into slavery in 1840. The Lost Boy (1987) is a troubling story set on a Greek island.

Fox and the Wolf, The A Middle English poem (c. 1250–75). Apart from The Nun's Priest's Tale in CHAUCER'S CANTERBURY TALES, it represents the only branch of the Renard cycle in Middle English before the appearance of CAXTON'S REYNARD THE FOX. It narrates an episode in which the fox dupes the wolf Sigrim into helping him esape from the bottom of a well. The story has energy and humour, and the anthropomorphism of the two animals is skilfully handled.

Foxe, John 1516–87 Martyrologist. On the accession of Queen Mary in 1553 he lost his post as tutor to the Earl of Surrey's children and fled to the Continent, taking with him the beginnings of the work of Protestant history and propaganda published as ACTS AND MONUMENTS in 1563 but popularly known as 'Foxe's Book of Martyrs'. Latin versions appeared at Strasburg and Basle, which with Frankfurt made his places of refuge. In exile he also produced a crude apocalyptic play, Christus triumphans, translated into English in 1578, and an appeal for resistance to Mary in Ad inclytos ac praepotentes Angliae proceres (1557). On his return to England after Elizabeth's accession he took holy orders, though his radical Protestantism prevented his advancement. Later works include the anti-Catholic A Sermon of Christ Crucified (1570), an edition of Anglo-Saxon texts of the Gospels (1571) and a Latin treatise on the Eucharist (?1580).

Fra Lippo Lippi A DRAMATIC MONOLOGUE by ROBERT BROWNING, published in Men and Women (1855). Filippo Lippi (c. 1406–69), Florentine painter and Carmelite monk, expresses his discontent with the constraints of monasticism and with the purely spiritual art demanded by his superiors. Instead, he prefers a realism which attends to fleshly details of the world around him.

Frame, Janet 1924– New Zealand novelist, short-story writer and poet. Misdiagnosed schizophrenic, she spent most of her time between 1947 and 1955 in psychiatric hospitals. She was saved by her writing: her first collection of stories, The Lagoon (1951), won the Hubert Church award shortly before she was due to have a leucotomy. After her release she lived in Ibiza, Andorra, Britain and the USA before returning to New Zealand. Her works include: *Owls Do Cry* (1957), in which the protagonist has her imagination cut away by a leucotomy; *Faces in the Water* (1961), fictionalizing her experience of psychiatric hospitals; *The Edge of the Alphabet* (1962); *Scented Gardens for the Blind* (1963); *The Adaptable Man* (1965); *Intensive Care* (1970), an ambitious future-fiction; *Daughter Buffalo* (1972) and *Living in the Maniototo* (1979), complex metafictional experiments set in North America; and *The Carpathians* (1988). Two themes dominate her work: the clash of inner and outer worlds, often expressed through the figure of the misfit (epileptic, mental patient, artist); and the complexity of language, crucial to identity but also perilously unstable. Generally recognized as her country's finest novelist, she reached a wider audience with *To the Island* (1982), *An Angel at my Table* (1984) and *The Envoy from Mirror City* (1985), autobiographical works which uncover the sources of her writing. She has also published several volumes of short stories, a collection of poetry, *The Pocket Mirror* (1967), and a children's book.

Framley Parsonage The fourth of TROLLOPE'S BARSETSHIRE NOVELS, serialized in 1860–1. It features familiar Barsetshire characters – the Grantlys and their daughter Griselda (who marries Lord Dumbello), Bishop and Mrs Proudie, and the Rev. Josiah Crawley – but concentrates on the fortunes of Mark Robarts. Given the living of Framley by the widowed Lady Lufton through his friendship with her son, Lord Ludovic Lufton, he becomes involved with the spendthrift Mr Sowerby and the disreputable Duke of Omnium. Ludovic helps to rescue him from these unsuitable acquaintances and, overcoming his mother's opposition, marries Mark's sister Lucy. The rich Miss Dunstable, whom Sowerby had hoped to marry, marries Dr Thorne.

Francis, Sir Philip 1740–1818 Civil servant and politician. A former councillor to the Governor General of India who joined BURKE in the unsuccessful prosecution of Warren Hastings, he later entered Parliament. There is evidence for identifying him as the JUNIUS of the letters published by his old schoolfellow Henry Sampson Woodfall in THE PUBLIC ADVERTISER in 1769–71. However, Woodfall denied Francis's authorship and the letters treat some of Francis's friends harshly.

Frank, Waldo (David) 1889–1967 American novelist and critic. *City Block* (1922), *Holiday* (1923), *The Death and Birth of David Markand* (1934) and *The Bridegroom Cometh* (Britain, 1938; USA, 1939) are novels advocating social and political reform. *Chalk Face* (1924) is a horror novel and *New Year's Eve* (1929) a play influenced by EXPRESSIONISM. He also wrote a good deal of historical and social criticism.

Frankenstein: or, The Modern Prometheus A GOTHIC NOVEL by MARY SHELLEY, published in 1818. Frankenstein, a student of natural philosophy in Geneva, builds a creature in the semblance of a man and gives it life. Possessed of unnatural strength, it inspires horror but is miserably eager to be loved. It pursues Frankenstein to Chamonix, where he agrees to make a mate. When he changes his mind, the creature kills Frankenstein's bride on their wedding night. Frankenstein's father dies of grief, and the scientist's mind gives way. Eventually he recovers and sets out to destroy his creation. After a chase across the world, the two confront each other in the Arctic wastes. Frankenstein dies and the creature disappears into the frozen wilderness, hoping for annihilation.

Franklin, Benjamin 1706–90 American politician and man of letters. Born in Boston and trained as a printer, he moved to Philadelphia and then, for two years, to England, where he wrote and published *A Dissertation on Liberty and Necessity, Pleasure and Pain* (1725). On his return to Philadelphia in 1726 he became a major force in the city's affairs, as well as publisher of a newspaper, *The Pennsylvania Gazette* (1729–1766), and author of the popular POOR RICHARD'S ALMANAC (1732–58). *Experiments and Observations on Electricity* (1751–3) reported on his famous kite experiments.

Though Franklin founded the American Philosophical Society in 1769 , he spent many years during the 1760s up to 1775 lobbying in England for colonial representation in Parliament, later serving in the Continental Congress and on the committee which ordered the drafting of the Declaration of Independence, and representing the Congress in France during the War of Independence. On his return to America from France in 1785 he was appointed president of the Executive Council of Pennsylvania. He signed the Constitution in 1787.

His many tracts discuss politics, legal theory, education, language and population control. Along with his large and varied correspondence, they constitute a witty, informative history of 18th-century America. Writings of note include *A Scheme for a New Alphabet and Reformed Mode of Spelling* (1768); *Edict of the King of Prussia* (1773) and *Rules by Which a Great Empire May be Reduced to a Small One* (1773), both of which oppose the Townshend Acts; *Remarks concerning the Savages of North America* (1784); 'On The Slave Trade' (1790), a memorandum advocating the abolition of slavery; and his *Autobiography*, begun in 1771 but not completed.

Franklin, (Stella Maria Sarah) Miles 1879–1954 Australian novelist. *My Brilliant Career* (1901), described as 'the very first Australian novel', and its sequel *My Career Goes Bung* (1946) describe the adventures and misadventures of Sybylla Melvyn, who aspires to the cultivated life of a writer but is hampered by the backwardness of bush society. The author denied that Sybylla, with her determined independence, fiery self-confidence and inopportune blundering, was a self-portrait. Other novels include *Some Everyday Folk – and Dawn* (1909), *Old Blastus of Bandicoot* (1931), *Bring the Monkey* (1933) and *All That Swagger* (1936). A prestigious Australian award for fiction bears her name.

Franklin's Tale, The See CANTERBURY TALES.

Fraser, G(eorge) S(utherland) 1915–80 Critic and poet. *The Fatal Landscape* (1941) and *Home Town Elegy* (1944) show a lyrical clarity free from the excesses of the NEW APOCALYPSE movement, with which he was associated. Later volumes include *The Traveller Has Regrets* (1948), *Conditions: Selected Recent Poetry* (1969) and the posthumous *Collected Poems* (1981). They were less important than the criticism contained in *The Modern Writer and His World* (1953) and *Vision and Rhetoric: Studies in Modern Poetry* (1959).

Fraser's Magazine A monthly magazine founded by WILLIAM MAGINN and Hugh Fraser in 1830. It was at its wittiest and most challenging under Maginn's editorship, when contributors included CARLYLE and THACKERAY, as well as JOHN GALT, CHARLES KINGSLEY, JAMES ANTHONY FROUDE and JAMES SPEDDING. Maginn was succeeded by FRANCIS SYLVESTER MAHONY (Father Prout), Froude, WILLIAM ALLINGHAM and others. The magazine ceased publication in 1882.

Frayn, Michael 1933– Playwright, novelist and journalist. First known for gently satirical newspaper columns and novels, he established himself as a writer of stage comedy: *Alphabetical Order* (1975), about mayhem in a newspaper cuttings library; *Donkeys' Years* (1976), about university loves; and *Clouds* (1976), about journalists on a visit to Cuba. *Balmoral* (1978), re-titled *Liberty Hall* (1979), satirizes a writers' collective. Major commercial success came with *Noises Off* (1982), a backstage comedy about an appalling touring company. The less popular *Look, Look!* (1990) offers an equally jaundiced impression of audiences. Frayn has also made distinguished translations and adaptations of work by Chekhov and Tolstoy.

Frazer, Sir James (George) 1854–1941 Anthropologist and classical scholar. *The Golden Bough* (1890; expanded in 1900 and 1911–15, abridged in 1922) describes the religious behaviour of the primitive world from a rationalistic and evolutionary point of view. Its thesis is that everywhere a belief in magic preceded religion, which in turn was followed in the West by science. Frazer's analysis constituted an effective, because well-written, attack on what he regarded as the outworn absurdities of religion in general and Christianity in particular. Images drawn from his work (like that of the Fisher King) attained general intellectual currency in, for example, ELIOT'S *THE WASTE LAND* (1922). Since then Frazer's standing as a classical scholar, in his commentary on Pausanias (1898) and his edition of Ovid's *Fasti* (1929), has fared better than his reputation as an 'armchair' anthropologist.

Frederic, Harold 1856–98 American novelist. *Seth's Brother's Wife* (1886) portrays life on an American farm and examines the worlds of politics and journalism. *The Lawton Girl* (1890) and *The Return of the O'Mahoney* (1892) extended his reputation as a local colourist. *In the Valley* (1890) deals with the American Revolution, *The Copperhead* (1893) and *Marsena and Other Stories* (1894) with the Civil War. His best-known novel, *THE DAMNATION OF THERON WARE* (1896), depicts the religious and psychological decline of a Methodist minister. His last three novels – *March Hares* (1896), and the posthumously published *Gloria Mundi* (1898) and *The Market Place* (1899) – are historical tales set in England.

free verse See METRE.

Freeling, Nicolas 1927– Writer of DETECTIVE FICTION. His immersion in European culture gives his work its characteristic locations, richly reflective style and increasing indifference to generic labels. *Love in Amsterdam* (1962) began a series featuring the Dutch detective Van der Valk, who quickly outgrew the model of Simenon's Maigret. *A Long Silence* (1972; *Auprès de Ma Blonde* in USA) killed off Van der Valk, though he has been revived in *Sand Castles* (1989). *A Dressing of Diamonds* (1974) introduced Henri Castang, a French policeman who has regularly appeared in subsequent novels, sometimes joined by Van der Valk's widow Arlette, herself the central character of *The Widow* (1979).

Freeman, Edward Augustus 1823–92 Historian. He became Regius Professor of Modern History at Oxford in 1884. His best-known books are *The History of the Norman Conquest of England: Its Causes and Its Results* (1867–79) and *The Reign of William Rufus and the Accession of Henry I* (1882), eccentric in style and quickly superseded by more thorough research. A fierce controversialist and regular contributor to periodicals, including *THE SATURDAY REVIEW*, he published four collections of *Historical Essays* (1871, 1873, 1879 and 1892).

Freeman, Mary (Eleanor) Wilkins 1852–1930 American short-story writer and novelist. Her first collections, *A Humble Romance and Other Stories* (1887) and *A New England Nun and Other Stories* (1891), focus on women in small New England villages who are forced to defend their values against the community. *Pembroke* (1894), one of her more successful novels, is a study of New England character and life. Other works include *Giles Corey, Yeoman: A Play* (1893), *Madelon* (a novel, 1896), *Silence and Other Stories* (1898), *The Heart's Highway: A Romance of Virginia* (1900) and *The Fair Lavinia and Others* (1907).

French, David 1939– Canadian playwright. His most highly praised work, *Jitters* (1979), is a backstage comedy offering an affectionate view of theatrical life. *Leaving Home* (1972), *Of the Fields Lately* (1973) and *Salt-Walter Moon* (1984) explore conflicts among the Mercers, an 'immigrant' Newfoundland family in Toronto. His other plays include *One Crack Out* (1975), *The Riddle of the World* (1981) and *1949* (1989).

French Revolution, The A history by CARLYLE, published in 1837. This formidable warning to the British aristocracy opens with the death of Louis XV in 1774 and closes with Bonaparte's defeat of the Insurrection of Vendémiaire in 1795. An epic work tracing with dramatic power the end of a long-established régime, the consequent Terror and the inevitable decline of insurrection, it is rich in portraits (Robespierre and Mirabeau, for example) and descriptive set-pieces (the murder of Marat, the flight to Varennes, the mutiny at Nancy).

Freneau, Philip (Morin) 1752–1832 American poet. At the College of New Jersey (later Princeton University) he met BRACKENRIDGE, with whom he collaborated on *Father Bembo's Pilgrimage to Mecca* (1770), a prose SATIRE on American manners, and a patriotic poem, *The Rising Glory of America* (1772). A short collection, *The American Village* (1772), was followed by 'Pictures of Columbus' in 1774. The patriotic poetry he produced during the War of Independence included 'George the Third's Soliloquy', 'The Loyalists' and 'America Independent'. His brief but harsh imprisonment by the British on board the *Scorpion* in New York harbour prompted a BROADSIDE, *The British Prison Ship* (1781). The essays and poems he contributed to the *Philadelphia Freeman's Journal* (1781–2) and his *National Gazette* (1791–3), which he founded and edited at THOMAS JEFFERSON's urging, continued to celebrate American heroes and attack the British. The poems in *Journeys from Philadelphia to New York* (1787) and the essays in *Letters on Various Interesting and Important Subjects* (1799) used the humorous persona of a weaver, Robert Slender. *Poems on American Affairs* (1815) contained verses about the war of 1812, as well as poems influenced by DEISM, among them 'On the Universality and Other Attributes of the God of Nature'.

Frere, John Hookham 1769–1846 Translator and poet. Combining literature with a diplomatic career, he joined GEORGE CANNING in publishing *THE ANTI-JACOBIN*, played a part in founding *THE QUARTERLY REVIEW* and published translations from Spanish and Greek. His MOCK-HEROIC poem, *Prospectus and Specimen of an Intended National Work by William and Robert Whistlecraft of Stowmarket in Suffolk, Harness and Collar*

Makers. Intended to Comprise the Most Interesting Particulars Relating to King Arthur and His Round Table (1817), revived OTTAVA RIMA and prompted BYRON to adopt it in *BEPPO* and *DON JUAN*.

Freudian criticism See PSYCHOANALYTIC CRITICISM.

Friar Bacon and Friar Bungay, The Honourable History of A comedy by GREENE, printed in 1594 and probably produced a few years before. The title characters are based on ROGER BACON and his fellow Franciscan Thomas Bungay. Bacon makes a brass head and gives it the power of speech with the Devil's help. It will utter at some time in the course of a month but they must be present to hear it speak. After a three-week vigil Bacon hands the watch over to his servant Miles and falls asleep. Miles does not wake him when the head speaks three times ('Time is', 'Time was', 'Time is past') before falling to the floor and shattering into pieces. A sub-plot tells of the love of Lord Lacy and the Prince of Wales for Margaret, a gamekeeper's daughter.

Friar's Tale, The See CANTERBURY TALES.

Friel, Brian 1929– Irish playwright. The wistfulness and traces of sentimentality in *Philadelphia, Here I Come!* (1964), a bitter-sweet comedy about dreams of emigration, continue in *The Loves of Cass McGuire* (1966), *Lovers* (1967), *Crystal and Fox* (1968) and *Aristocrats* (1979). Plays about modern Ireland include *The Freedom of the City* (1974) and *The Volunteers* (1975). *Faith Healer* (1979) describes the life and death of a charlatan. With *Translations* (1980) and *The Communication Chord* (1984) Friel emerged as the poet of the Troubles, tracing the downward steps of an increasingly rocky path, but without the hostility of the committed underdog. The highly successful *Dancing at Lughnasa* (1990) is a tender evocation of his own boyhood. In 1980 Friel helped to found the theatre company Field Day in a town – Derry to Catholics and Londonderry to Protestants – whose name reveals the divisions of which he writes.

Frost, Robert (Lee) 1874–1963 American poet. Although he was born and raised in San Francisco and lived from 1912 to 1915 in England, where he made friends with POUND and EDWARD THOMAS, he was most deeply connected with New England and particularly with the New Hampshire farm which he made his home from 1915. Like many great national poets, Frost relied heavily on the language of the people, using and transforming New England patterns of speech to create some of the most accessible (and widely read) modern poetry. Its central theme is the quest of the solitary individual to make sense of the world. His first volumes were *A Boy's Will* (1913) and *North of Boston* (1914), though he did not begin to attract national attention until *Mountain Interval* (1916). Succeeding volumes which confirmed his reputation include *New Hampshire* (1923), *West-Running Brook* (1928), *Collected Poems* (1930), *A Further Range* (1936), *A Witness Tree* (1942), *A Steeple Bush* (1947) and *In the Clearing* (1962). They won him a total of four PULITZER PRIZES. *A Masque of Reason* (1945) and *A Masque of Mercy* (1947) are dramatic poems in BLANK VERSE, portraying biblical characters and exploring the relation of man to God in the modern world.

Froude, James Anthony 1818–94 Historian. The younger brother of RICHARD HURRELL FROUDE, he escaped the influence of NEWMAN to become the disciple, lifelong friend and eventually literary executor of THOMAS CARLYLE. His Carlylean *History of England from the Fall of Wolsey to the Death of Elizabeth* (1858–70) and *The English in Ireland in the Eighteenth Century* (1872–4) were

popular but tinged by controversy which anticipated the literary storm he created with his commendably frank memoirs of Carlyle in *Thomas Carlyle: A History of the First Forty Years of His Life* (1882), *Thomas Carlyle: A History of His Life in London* (1884) and *My Relations with Carlyle* (1886).

Among his other works were *Shadows in the Clouds* (1847) and *The Nemesis of Faith* (1848), essays in semi-fictional autobiography describing his loss of religious belief; studies of BUNYAN (1880) and DISRAELI (1890); and *Oceana: or, England and Her Colonies* (1886) and *The English in the West Indies: or, The Bow of Ulysses* (1888), both readable and interesting for the contemporary view. He was appointed Regius Professor of Modern History at Oxford in 1892.

Froude, Richard Hurrell 1803–36 Religious controversialist. The elder brother of JAMES ANTHONY FROUDE and an early leader of the OXFORD MOVEMENT, he contributed to *TRACTS FOR THE TIMES* and was the intimate friend of NEWMAN, who wrote a preface to his *Remains* (1838–9), chiefly extracts from his private diary. It caused a disturbance in the Movement by its hostility to the leaders of the Reformation.

Fry, Christopher 1907– Playwright. *A Phoenix Too Frequent* (1946), a lively version of the Widow of Ephesus story, proclaimed the arrival of a new contributor to the revival of verse drama. *The Firstborn* (1948) is one of several plays using biblical themes to celebrate life's beauty and mystery. Fry's delight in language is shown at its best in *The Lady's Not for Burning* (1948), a comedy about the developing love between Jennet Jourdemayne, falsely accused of murder by witchcraft, and the world-weary Thomas Mendip. Fry later described it as the 'spring' piece in a seasonal cycle, completed by an 'autumn' play, *Venus Observed* (1950), the 'winter' *The Dark is Light Enough* (1954) and *A Yard of Sun: A Summer Comedy* (1970). *A Sleep of Prisoners* (1951) is among the best of his subsequent work, together with several adaptations of French plays.

Frye, (Herman) Northrop 1912–91 Canadian critic. He passed his academic career at Toronto, as the first University Professor of English from 1967 and chancellor of Victoria University from 1978. The leading exponent of archetypal (or mythopoeic) criticism, he demonstrated his characteristic concern with the role of myth and SYMBOL in his first book, *Fearful Symmetry* (1947), a study of BLAKE. His most important work, *Anatomy of Criticism* (1957), elaborates an ambitiously comprehensive theory of literary models and genres which in his view reflect the processes of the human mind. It divides literature into four categories with a mythic or archetypal basis in the seasonal cycle: COMEDY (spring), romance (summer), TRAGEDY (autumn) and IRONY (winter). Some of his many subsequent works applied his theories to SHAKESPEARE (*A Natural Perspective*, 1965; *Fools of Time*, 1967; *The Myth of Deliverance*, 1983), MILTON (*The Return of Eden*, 1965), T. S. ELIOT (1963), English ROMANTICISM (1968) and, controversially, the Bible (*The Great Code*, 1982; *Words with Power*, 1990). *The Bush Garden* (1971) and *Divisions on a Ground* (1982) collect his essays on Canadian literature.

Fugard, Athol (Harold Lanigan) 1932– South African playwright, director and actor. His innovative drama has been forged under 'poor theatre' conditions with black-township groups. Works dealing with black families in the ghetto and white, lower middle-class households include *The Blood Knot* (1963), *Hello and*

Goodbye (1966) and *Boesman and Lena* (1973). 'Workshop plays' confronting the apparatus of apartheid include *SIZWE BANSI IS DEAD* and *Statements after an Arrest under the Immorality Act*, published together in 1974. Later solo plays include: *'Master Harold' ... and the Boys* (1983), a semi-autobiographical revelation of youthful racial arrogance; *The Road to Mecca* (1985), about an Afrikaner woman's rejection of conformity; and *A Place with the Pigs* (1988), a 'personal parable' about a Russian Army deserter who hid in his pigsty for 41 years. He has also written a novel, *Tsotsi* (1981), film scripts and *Notebooks 1960-1977* (1983).

Fugitives, The A group of 20th-century American poets and writers committed to preserving a distinctively Southern literature and the traditional rural economy of the South. It included JOHN GOULD FLETCHER, JOHN CROWE RANSOM, LAURA RIDING, ALLEN TATE, ROBERT PENN WARREN and DONALD DAVIDSON, who edited its magazine, *The Fugitive* (1922-5). Other notable publications include *Fugitives: An Anthology of Verse* (1928) and *I'll Take My Stand: The South and the Agrarian Tradition* (1930), a collection of essays edited by Ransom.

Fulgens and Lucrece A two-part play or INTERLUDE by HENRY MEDWALL. First performed *c.* 1497 and published *c.* 1515, it is the first secular drama in English to have survived in full. The main plot is an illustrated debate about gentility. Its pretext is the choice of a suitable husband for Lucrece, daughter of the Roman senator Fulgens. More interesting is the sub-plot in which two servants involuntarily parody their betters in their rivalry for Lucrece's waiting-maid.

Fuller, Henry Blake 1857-1929 American novelist and short-story writer. He was born in Chicago and lived there all his life except for a two-year tour of Europe. His best-known novel is probably *The Cliff-Dwellers* (1893), satirizing the social ambitions of people living in a skyscraper apartment. *With the Procession* (1895) also deals with social climbers, in this case the middle-class Marshalls. *Bertram Cope's Year* (1919) takes up the topic of homosexuality. All three novels are striking examples of American REALISM. In addition to other novels, Fuller also wrote plays and short stories.

Fuller, John (Leopold) 1937- Poet and novelist. He is the son of ROY FULLER. His many volumes of diverse, technically sophisticated poetry include *Fairground Music* (1961), *Lies and Secrets* (1979), *Waiting for the Music* (1982), *The Beautiful Inventions* (1983) and *The Mechanical Body* (1991). His novels include *Flying to Nowhere* (1983) and *Look Twice* (1991). He has also written a valuable guide to the SONNET (1972) and edited *The Chatto Book of Love Poetry* (1990).

Fuller, (Sarah) Margaret 1810-50 American writer. A leading figure in TRANSCENDENTALISM and the BROOK FARM experiment, she was BRONSON ALCOTT's assistant, editor of *THE DIAL* (1841-2) and literary critic of HORACE GREELEY's New York *Tribune*, to which she contributed distinguished 'letters from abroad'. Her monumental *Woman in the Nineteenth Century* (1845) reflects her feminism. She was drowned with her husband, the Marquis Angelo Ossoli, and infant son on the return journey to New York. She inspired the character of Zenobia in HAWTHORNE's *THE BLITHEDALE ROMANCE* and the heroine of OLIVER WENDELL HOLMES's *ELSIE VENNER*.

Fuller, Roy (Broadbent) 1912-91 Poet and novelist. Influenced by AUDEN, the early work in *Poems* (1939), *The Middle of a War* (1942), *A Lost Season* (1944) and *Epitaphs and Occasions* (1949) is left-wing in sympathy and concerned with man as a social animal. His many subsequent volumes, culminating in *New and Collected Poems* (1985) and *Consolations* (1987), are more interested in outlining individual psychologies. He developed into a master technician, urbane, detached and ironic. His novels, more than an interesting sideline, include *Fantasy and Fugue* (1954), *Image of a Society* (1956), *The Ruined Boys* (1959), *The Father's Comedy* (1961), *The Perfect Fool* (1963), the excellent *My Child My Sister* (1965) and *Stares* (1990). His lectures as professor of poetry at Oxford in 1968-73 appeared in *Owl and Artificers* (1971) and *Professors and Gods* (1974). *Spanner and Pen* (1991) is an autobiography. His son is JOHN FULLER.

Fuller, Thomas 1608-61 Antiquarian and divine. His most famous work was *The History of the Worthies of England*, unfinished and published posthumously in 1662. By no means as dull as its title suggests, it makes a county-by-county survey of England, describing topography, natural curiosities, local history and famous people associated with the different counties, all memorably treated in a frequently witty style. A celebrated preacher and royal chaplain, Fuller also wrote prolifically. *The History of the Holy War* (1639-40) dealt with the Crusades. *Good Thoughts in Bad Times* (1645), *Good Thoughts in Worse Times* (1647) and *The Cause and Cure of a Wounded Conscience* (1647) were topical tracts, later praised by COLERIDGE but less popular than *The Holy State and The Profane State* (1642), a book of 'characters' and essays on diverse subjects. Later works were *A Pisgah-Sight of Palestine* (1650) and *The Church History of Britain: From the Birth of Christ till 1648* (1655).

Furnivall, F(rederick) J(ames) 1825-1910 Philologist and scholar. He joined the Philological Society in 1847, proposing, organizing and in 1861 becoming editor of the Society's *New English Dictionary*, a project which became the *OXFORD ENGLISH DICTIONARY*. He helped to found the Working Men's College in 1854 and founded the Early English Text Society (1864), the Chaucer Society (1868), the Ballad Society (1868), the New Shakspere Society (1873), and societies dedicated to WYCLIF (1881), BROWNING (1881) and SHELLEY (1886). He also edited SHAKESPEARE and medieval texts.

Furphy, Joseph 1843-1912 Australian novelist. Furphy described his work as being of 'Temper democratic; bias offensively Australian'. *Such is Life: Being Certain Extracts from the Life of Tom Collins* (1903) is a picaresque novel with no formal plot and many digressions, which one critic has described as 'a primary document for any student of Australian attitudes'. The rich material trimmed from the unwieldy manuscript of *Such is Life* created two more books, published after Furphy's death: *Rigby's Romance* (1946) and *The Buln-Buln and the Brolga* (1948).

G

Gaddis, William 1922– American novelist. *The Recognitions* (1955) focuses on a group of artists and poets in Greenwich Village during the late 1940s and early 1950s. *JR* (1975) is written entirely in dialogue and takes place mostly at a school on Long Island. *Carpenter's Gothic* (1985) examines the impact of the Vietnam war on those who endured it.

Gaines, Ernest J. 1933– Black American novelist and short-story writer. *Catherine Carmier* (1964) describes the difficulties encountered by a black college graduate on returning home to Louisiana. *Of Love and Dust* (1967) is set on a Louisiana plantation in the 1940s. *Bloodline* (1968) is a collection of stories. His best-known novel, *The Autobiography of Miss Jane Pitman* (1971), presents the recollections of a 110-year-old black woman whose experiences range from slavery to the civil rights movement of the 1960s. Gaines's concern with the effects of racism is further revealed in *My Father's House* (1978), examining the conflict between a black preacher and his more radical son.

Gale, Zona 1874–1938 American novelist and short-story writer. She rose to prominence as a writer in the 'local colour' vein with *Romance Island* (1906), a novel, and *Friendship Village* (1908), a collection of stories. Her sentimental tendencies gave way to sterner realism in *Birth* (1918), *Miss Lulu Bett* (1920), her best-known novel, and *Faint Perfume* (1923). Her stage adaptation of *Miss Lulu Bett* won a PULITZER PRIZE in 1922. Later novels, such as *Preface to a Life* (1926) and *Borgia* (1929), reflect her interest in Eastern mysticism. *Papa La Fleur* (1933), *Light Woman* (1937) and the posthumously published *Magna* (1939) share a concern with the gap between the pre-war and post-war generations. Some of her best stories are collected in *Yellow Gentians and Blue* (1927) and *Bridal Pond* (1930).

Gallant [née Young], Mavis 1922– Canadian short-story writer and novelist. An expatriate writing with a mercilessly detached awareness about isolation and displacement, in Paris, Montreal or in post-war Germany, she has won recognition in Britain and the USA as well as Canada. Collections of stories include *The Other Paris* (1956), *My Heart is Broken* (1964; as *An Unmarried Man's Summer* in Britain), *The Pegnitz Junction* (1973), *The End of the World and Other Stories* (1974), *From the Fifteenth District* (1979), *Home Truths* (1981), *Overhead in a Balloon* (1985) and *In Transit* (1988). She has also written two novels, *Green Water, Green Sky* (1959) and *A Fairly Good Time* (1970), and a play, *What is to be Done?* (1983).

Galsworthy, John 1867–1933 Novelist and playwright. He wrote over 31 full-length plays and several successful one-acters, many commenting on social injustice. *The Silver Box* (1906) introduced his favourite device of parallel and contrasted families, one rich and the other poor. *Justice* (1910) led to reform of solitary confinement in prisons. *Strife* (1909) is about the effects of a strike, and *The Skin Game* (1920) about privilege and social snobbery. *Collected Plays* appeared in 1929.

His novels show him less uncomfortable with his own privileged background. His first success was *The Man of Property* (1906), which together with *In Chancery* (1920) and *To Let* (1921, with two interludes, 'Indian Summer of a Forsyte', 1918, and *Awakening*, 1920) made up *THE FORSYTE SAGA*, published complete in 1922. A second Forsyte chronicle, *A Modern Comedy* (1929), included *The White Monkey* (1924), *The Silver Spoon* (1926), *Swan Song* (1928) and two interludes, 'A Silent Wooing' and 'Passers By'. Other work included a trilogy, *End of the Chapter* (1925), on the family history of the Charwells (relatives of the Forsytes) and *Collected Poems* (1934). Galsworthy received the Nobel Prize for Literature in 1932.

Galt, John 1779–1839 Novelist and essayist. *Voyages and Travels in the Years 1809, 1810 and 1811* (1812) describes his Continental wanderings, which included a visit to Greece and Turkey in the company of BYRON, of whom he later wrote a biography (1830). Galt is best remembered for his ironic, richly observant novels about Lowland Scots life. They include: *The Ayrshire Legatees* (1820), in the form of letters from a Scottish minister, Dr Zachariah Pringle, and his family in London to their friends; *The Annals of the Parish* (1821), told by the Rev. Micah Balwhidder; *The Provost* (1822), told by Mr Pawkie; and *The Entail* (1823), about the disastrous consequences of Claud Walkinshaw's decision to disinherit his eldest son.

Game at Chess, A A comedy by THOMAS MIDDLETON, first performed in 1624. Its anti-Spanish satire proved immensely popular but led to its being banned and a warrant issued for Middleton's arrest. Diplomacy and confrontation are cleverly presented in terms of chess, with the Black Knight representing Gondomar, the Spanish Ambassador who had tried to secure an alliance between Protestant England and Catholic Spain through the marriage of the Prince of Wales to a Spanish princess.

Gamelyn, The Tale of A VERSE ROMANCE probably written around 1350–70. It has been called *The Cook's Tale of Gamelyn*, and was at one time attributed to Chaucer (see CHAUCERIAN APOCRYPHA). One of the relatively few verse romances with an English source, it was in turn used by LODGE in his *ROSALYNDE* (1590), which formed the basis of SHAKESPEARE's *As You Like It*. A vigorous and violent tale with few courtly elements, it tells how Gamelyn reclaims the inheritance of which his eldest brother has cheated him.

Gamester, The A comedy by SHIRLEY, first performed in 1633 and published in 1637. Wilding is addicted to gambling and in love with his wife's ward, Penelope; his resourceful wife cures him of his adulterous love and exposes him to the dangers of his addiction. *The Gamester* is also the title of a tragedy (1753) by EDWARD MOORE.

Gammer Gurton's Needle A comedy, possibly written in 1553, which vies with *RALPH ROISTER DOISTER* as the first English comedy. The favourite candidate for authorship is William Stevenson, who produced plays at Christ's College, Cambridge, in 1550–4. The printed edition of 1575 survives but an earlier edition, *c.* 1563 has been lost. Written in rhymed doggerel, the play is totally English and shows no trace of the influence of Terence or Plautus, hitherto inescapable. Its action turns on the loss of Gammer Gurton's needle, with which she mends the clothes of Hodge, her servant; the resolution is the finding of the needle in the seat of

Hodge's breeches. Among the characters are: Diccon of Bedlam, who enjoys mischief-making; Gammer Gurton's enemy Dame Chat; Doctor Rat the curate; the servants Tib, Doll and Spendthrift; and Gib the cat.

Garden of Proserpine, The A poem by SWINBURNE, published in *Poems and Ballads* (1866). One of his most anthologized pieces ('Here, where the world is quiet'), it is deliberately pagan in spirit. A note says that it was intended to capture 'that brief total pause of passion and of thought, when the spirit, without fear or hope of good things or evil, hungers and thirsts only after the perfect sleep'.

Gardiner, Samuel Rawson 1829–1902 Historian. Professor of Modern History at King's College, London and, later, Ford Lecturer at Oxford, he chronicled the early Stuart and Commonwealth periods in *The History of England from the Accession of James I to the Outbreak of the Civil War* (1883–4), *The History of the Great Civil War* (1886–91) and *The History of the Commonwealth and Protectorate* (1894–1901), completed by C. H. Firth with *The Last Years of the Protectorate* (1909).

Gardner, Dame Helen (Louise) 1908–86 Scholar and critic. She was Merton Professor of English Literature at Oxford in 1966–75. Her editions of DONNE's *Divine Poems* (1952) and *Elegies, and Songs and Sonnets* (1965) are important for both text and commentary; *The Art of T. S. Eliot* (1949) and a textual examination of ELIOT's *FOUR QUARTETS* (1978) are pioneering studies. Her *New Oxford Book of English Verse 1250–1950* (1972) replaced QUILLER-COUCH's anthology.

Gardner, John 1933–82 American novelist, short-story writer and scholar. His most highly praised book, *Grendel* (1971), retells *BEOWULF* from the monster's point of view and focuses on the potential meaninglessness of life, a theme also examined in *The Sunlight Dialogues* (1972). His other novels include: *The Wreckage of Agathon* (1970), set in Sparta; *Nickel Mountain* (1973), about a middle-aged motel proprietor's struggle against loneliness and the fear of death; *October Light* (1976), about ageing; *Freddy's Book* (1980); and *Mickelsson's Ghosts* (1982). Collections of stories include *The King's Indian Stories and Tales* (1974) and *The Art of Living and Other Stories* (1981). Gardner also wrote: an epic poem, *Jason and Medea* (1973); three libretti, *William Wilson, Frankenstein* and *Rumpelstiltskin* (collected in *Three Libretti*, 1979); *Poems* (1978); and *The Forms of Fiction* (1962), *On Moral Fiction* (1978) and *The Art of Fiction: Notes on Craft for Young Writers* (1984).

Garfield, Leon 1921– Writer of CHILDREN'S LITERATURE. *Jack Holborn* (1964), *Smith* (1967) and *Black Jack* (1968) are strongly imaginative, rambling adventure stories owing something to FIELDING and DICKENS. The larger-than-life villains who populate his earlier books give way to more ambiguous characterizations in later works such as *The Strange Affair of Adelaide Harris* (1971), a comic, fast-moving FARCE set in Regency Brighton, the stories in *Garfield's Apprentices* (1976–8), and *The Empty Sleeve* (1982), about a pair of twins who are spiritually opposite but also mutually dependent.

Garioch, (Sutherland) Robert 1909–81 Scottish poet and translator. He spent most of his life in Edinburgh, writing urban poetry in a form of Scots which brings together contemporary colloquial speech and literary diction. Many of his best-known poems combine a gift for comic impersonation with satirical observations of civic follies, hypocrisy and pretence. He also translated into Scots the SONNETS of 19th-century Roman dialect

poet Belli and the FREE VERSE of Apollinaire. *Collected Poems* appeared in 1977. Robin Fulton has edited his *Complete Poetical Works* (1983) and *A Garioch Miscellany* (1986).

Garland, (Hannibal) Hamlin 1860–1940 American short-story writer and novelist. He is chiefly remembered for *MAIN-TRAVELLED ROADS* (1891), stories and sketches about the Midwest. Two further collections, *Prairie Folks* (1892) and *Wayside Courtships* (1897), were combined as *Other Main-Travelled Roads* (1910). His writing often tended towards propaganda, especially in his novels. *Jason Edwards, An Average Man* (1892) is a plea for HENRY GEORGE's Single Tax Theory, while *A Spoil of Office* (1892) campaigns for the Populist Party. Less political novels include two books about life in Dakota farm country, *A Little Norsk* (1892) and *Rose of Dutcher's Coolly* (1895). *The Captain of the Gray-Horse Troop* (1902) and *Cavanagh, Forest Ranger* (1910) are novels about the Far West. *A Son of the Middle Border* (1917) and *A Daughter of the Middle Border* (1921) are autobiographical narratives. His essays on his theory of realistic fiction, which he called 'veritism', appeared as *Crumbling Idols* (1894).

Garner, Alan 1934– Writer of CHILDREN'S LITERATURE. His first children's book, *The Weirdstone of Brisingamen* (1960), is a powerful mixture of fantasy and everyday reality. *Elidor* (1965) and *The Owl Service* (1967), partly inspired by *THE MABINOGION*, concentrate on the role which myth and legend can still play. *Red Shift* (1973), another technically innovatory novel, presents three parallel stories of intolerance. *The Stone Book Quartet* (1976–8) contains stories drawn from his own family of local craftsmen, told in Cheshire dialect.

Garner, Helen 1942– Australian novelist and short-story writer. She achieved overnight fame with her first novel, *Monkey Grip* (1977), written in the fragmentary post-modernist manner which typifies all her work. It was filmed in 1981. She has secured her reputation in subsequent works chronicling contemporary Australian lifestyles at home and abroad. They include: *Honour and Other People's Children* (1980), two novellas; *The Children's Bach* (1984), a novel; *Postcards from Surfers* (1985), a collection of short stories; and *Cosmo Cosmolino* (1992), a novel.

Garner, Hugh 1913–79 Canadian novelist and short-story writer. Born in Batley, Yorkshire, he was taken to Toronto in 1919. *Storm Below* (1949) was based on his wartime experience in the navy. *Cabbagetown*, written earlier, appeared in a butchered version in 1950 and a complete version in 1968. His finest novel, it gives a vivid account of the working-class district where he grew up. Other works include *The Silence on the Shore* (1962), *A Nice Place to Visit* (1970), *The Intruders* (1976) and three detective novels. His short stories are collected in *The Yellow Sweater* (1952), *Hugh Garner's Best Stories* (1963), *Men and Women* (1966), *Violation of the Virgins* (1971) and *Hugh Garner Omnibus* (1978). *One Damn Thing after Another* (1973) is his autobiography.

Garnett, David 1892–1981 Novelist. The son of Constance and EDWARD GARNETT, he was associated with the BLOOMSBURY GROUP. His first novel, *Lady into Fox* (1922), is a fantasy about a young wife, Sylvia Tebrick, who is changed into a vixen. *A Man in the Zoo* (1924) and *The Grasshoppers Come* (1931) were not as successful and Garnett abandoned fantasy. *A Rabbit in the Air* (1932) drew on his early attempts to become an aviator. *Aspects of Love* (1955) is a delicate and bizarre love story. Later works include *A Shot in the Dark* (1958) and *A*

Net for Venus (1962). His non-fiction included editions of the letters of T. E. LAWRENCE (1938), the novels of PEACOCK (1924–34) and his own correspondence with T. H. WHITE (1968). *The Golden Echo* (1953), *The Flowers of the Forest* (1955) and *The Familiar Faces* (1962) comprise his autobiography.

Garnett, Edward (William) 1868–1937 Man of letters. He was the son of RICHARD GARNETT and the husband of Constance Garnett, translator of the Russian classics. An influential publisher's reader who encouraged CONRAD, FORSTER and D. H. LAWRENCE, he wrote critical biographies of HOGARTH (1911) and Turgenev (1917), a volume of essays, *Friday Nights* (1922), and *The Trial of Jeanne d'Arc and Other Plays* (1931).

Garnett, Eve 1900–91 Writer and illustrator of CHILDREN'S LITERATURE. She is remembered for *The Family from One End Street* (1937), about the Ruggles family, one of the first 20th-century children's books to discuss the realities of domestic poverty. Two sequels produced some years later were less successful.

Garnett, Richard 1835–1906 Scholar and short-story writer. He is chiefly remembered for his collection of short stories, *The Twilight of the Gods* (1888), many of which had originally appeared in THE YELLOW BOOK. A prodigious memory and a career working for the British Museum Library (as Superintendent of the Reading Room in 1875–84) gave him an encyclopaedic knowledge of the classics and international literature. He published short biographies of MILTON, CARLYLE and EMERSON, edited *Relics of Shelley* (1862) and wrote a *History of Italian Literature* (1897). His son and grandson, EDWARD GARNETT and DAVID GARNETT, both became writers.

Garrick, David 1717–79 Actor, playwright and adapter of work by other playwrights. He moved to London with his former schoolmaster, SAMUEL JOHNSON, in 1737. He led theatrical taste from 1741, when his performance in CIBBER's version of SHAKESPEARE's RICHARD III caused a sensation, until his retirement in 1776, above all during his 30 years as manager of DRURY LANE (1747–76). Though sporadically challenged, his superiority as an actor was never decisively defied.

Garrick's writings have been too readily neglected. His lively FARCES and afterpieces include *The Lying Valet* (1741), *Miss in Her Teens* (1747), *The Irish Widow* (1772) and *Bon Ton: or, High Life above Stairs* (1775). Of a dozen or so Shakespearean adaptations, *Florizel and Perdita* (1756), based on THE WINTER'S TALE, and a musical version of THE TEMPEST (1756) are of some interest. His collaboration with GEORGE COLMAN THE ELDER on *THE CLANDESTINE MARRIAGE* (1766) was his most important work. Garrick's letters (1963) give some indication of his wit and the uncertainty of his wisdom.

Garrison, William Lloyd 1805–79 American Abolitionist leader, editor and lecturer. He founded THE LIBERATOR in 1831 and edited it until 1865. His books include *Thoughts on African Colonization* (1832), *Sonnets* (1843), and a collection of essays and speeches, *Selections* (1852).

Garth, Sir **Samuel** 1661–1719 Physician and poet. A member of the KIT-CAT CLUB, he wrote *The Dispensary* (1699), a burlesque poem praised by POPE, which poked fun at apothecaries.

Gascoigne, George ?1525–77 Poet, playwright and translator. His significance in Renaissance literature is that he did many things for the first time, or almost the first time, especially in domesticating foreign literary forms. *The Posies of George Gascoigne* (1575) is an authorized printing of a miscellany which had previously appeared without his authority as *A Hundred Sundry Flowers* (1573). Its most important contents are two plays: *Supposes*, the first successful English adaptation of Italian comedy, based on Ariosto's *I suppositi*, and *Jocasta*, the first Greek tragedy played on the English stage. Gascoigne also wrote *The Glass of Government* (1575), a CLOSET DRAMA in the form of a Roman comedy, and various court MASQUES. *The Steel Glass* (1576), a satire, makes an early use of non-dramatic blank verse; its companion piece, *The Complaint of Philomene*, is an Ovidian narrative. *The Grief of Joy* (written in 1576 but unpublished until 1869) imitates Petrarch's *De remediis utriusque fortunae*, on the vanity of beauty and strength. *The Spoil of Antwerp* (1576) is war journalism and *The Drum of Doomsday* (1576), treating the frailties and miseries of life, a translation of part of a treatise by Innocent III. The poet NICHOLAS BRETON became Gascoigne's stepson.

Gascoyne, David (Emery) 1916– Poet. He published his first volume at the age of 16 and became an *habitué* of London's literary Fitzrovia. A critical survey (1935) established him as the leading British authority on surrealism, and *Man's Life is This Meat* (1936) as one of its leading British practitioners. The remainder of his writing career, broken by long silences, has culminated in a revised edition of *Collected Poems* (1988), as well as *Three Translations* (1988) and *Hymns to the Night* (1989). *Collected Journals 1936–42* appeared in 1991.

Gaskell, Elizabeth (Cleghorn) 1810–65 Novelist and biographer. After a peripatetic youth she married William Gaskell, a Unitarian parson and professor of English history and literature at Manchester New College, in 1832. Her response to life in Manchester dominates her first novel, *MARY BARTON* (1848), a tale of industrial strife and unrest. It earned her the friendship and respect of DICKENS, who encouraged her to continue contributing to HOUSEHOLD WORDS. CRANFORD, which appeared in its pages in 1851–3, is a gentle tale about a spinster and her circle. *RUTH* (1853) boldly takes an unmarried mother's problems as its subject. NORTH AND SOUTH (1855) is another industrial story. An eight-year interval in novel-writing closed with SYLVIA'S LOVERS (1863). WIVES AND DAUGHTERS, not quite finished before her death and posthumously published in 1866, stands in striking contrast to her early work by allying itself with the tradition and style of JANE AUSTEN. Mrs Gaskell also wrote longer short stories bordering on the novella, collected in volumes such as *Life in Manchester* (1848), *Lizzie Leigh and Other Tales* (1855), *Round the Sofa* (1859) and *Cousin Phillis and Other Tales* (1865). Given her close friendship with CHARLOTTE BRONTË, whom she first met in 1850, it was not surprising that she should have undertaken a biography after Charlotte's early death in 1855. *The Life of Charlotte Brontë* (1857) ran into difficulties because of its account of the Brontë children at the Clergy Daughters' School at Cowan Bridge and, in particular, its indiscreet allusions to Branwell's relations with Mrs Edmund Robinson. These resulted in threats of legal action and, ultimately, the withdrawal of questionable passages.

In a century rich in women writers Mrs Gaskell stands to the forefront in her sympathy for the deprived, her evocations of nature, her gentle humour and her narrative pace. Of note is her exceptionally direct development from loosely structured melodramatic writing to the urbanity and balanced form of her later work, particularly *Wives and Daughters*.

Gass, William 1924– American novelist, short-story writer and scholar. *Omensetter's Luck* (1966), a novel, and *Willie Masters' Lonesome Wife* (1971), a novella, are notable for their experimental use of language. *In the Heart of the Heart of the Country and Other Stories* (1968), *The First Winter of My Married Life* (1979) and *Culp* (1985) are collections of short stories. Non-fiction includes *Fiction and the Figures of Life* (1970), *On Being Blue: A Philosophical Inquiry* (1975), *The World Within the Word* (1978) and *Habitations of the Word: Essays* (1985).

Gatty, Margaret 1809–73 Writer of CHILDREN'S LITERATURE. She founded the enormously popular *Aunt Judy's Magazine* in 1866, editing it until she died. Best known for her *Parables from Nature* (five books; 1855–71), she also published *The Fairy Godmothers* (1851), *Aunt Judy's Tales* (1859) and *Aunt Judy's Letters* (1862).

Gawain-poet, The Author of SIR GAWAIN AND THE GREEN KNIGHT, to whom are attributed also three other poems surviving in the same manuscript: CLEANNESS, PATIENCE and PEARL. His identity is not known, and the theory of common authorship is based on similarities of dialect (West Midlands), diction and style.

Gay, John 1685–1732 Poet and playwright. Born in Barnstaple, he was apprenticed to a London silk merchant. Socially at ease from the start of his urban life, he soon began to move in literary circles and to attract attention with *Wine* (1708), an anonymous BLANK-VERSE poem, and an essay, *The Present State of Wit* (1711). His appointment as secretary to the Duchess of Monmouth in 1712 took care of his immediate financial worries. 1713 saw the publication of *The Fan*, a pale imitation of his friend POPE'S *THE RAPE OF THE LOCK*, and the more accomplished *Rural Sports*, a GEORGIC poem celebrating the English countryside. Success came with his wittiest poem, *THE SHEPHERD'S WEEK* (1714), a PASTORAL cycle that is partly PARODY and partly true to life, designed to support Pope's opposition to AMBROSE PHILIPS. In 1714 Gay became secretary to Lord Clarendon on a mission to Hanover, but his hopes of advancement collapsed with the death of Queen Anne and the fall of Harley's Tory government.

One of his distinctive strengths as a writer was a quick ear for speech rhythms, which, combined with his lively interest in BALLADS and street literature, contributed much to the success of *TRIVIA: or, The Art of Walking the Streets of London* (1716). *Poems on Several Occasions* (1720), containing various ECLOGUES and songs, made him some money, which he promptly invested in the South Sea Company. Gay was ruined when the 'Bubble' burst, and his health had also begun to deteriorate. In a final attempt to secure preferment at court he began work in 1726 on his *Fables*, addressed to young Prince William. The first volume appeared in 1729; the second part, more serious, was published posthumously.

Gay's early attempts at drama in *The Mohocks* (1712), *What D'ye Call It* (1715) and *THREE HOURS AFTER MARRIAGE* (1717), written with Pope and ARBUTHNOT, yielded only mixed results. There was nothing in this record to prepare for the astonishing success of *THE BEGGAR'S OPERA* (1728), a BALLAD OPERA poking fun at Italian opera and inverting the heroic values of polite society by translating hypocrisy into the underworld of London's criminals. The sequel, *POLLY* (1729), became a *cause célèbre* when it was suppressed by Walpole and the printed version sold quickly. It was finally produced in 1777.

Gay's literary reputation has proved difficult to determine. The runaway success of *The Beggar's Opera* has overshadowed his other plays. As a poet, he was a master of the HEROIC COUPLET, and his songs and fables continued to be read after his death, for their sweetness of sound and neatness of phrase. His refusal to be solemn is epitomized by the epitaph he composed for himself: 'Life is a jest, and all things show it; I thought so once – and now I know it.'

Gee, Maurice 1931– New Zealand novelist, short-story writer and writer of CHILDREN'S LITERATURE. He secured his reputation with *Plumb* (1978), marking a break with the realism of his earlier work. It became the first volume of a trilogy, completed by *Meg* (1981) and *Sole Survivor* (1983), chronicling three generations of a family during this century and exploring the effects of New Zealand's Puritan inheritance on individual and social relations. Later novels include *Prowlers* (1987) and *The Burning Boy* (1990). His fine stories for children include *Under the Mountain* (1979) and *The Fire-Raiser* (1986).

Gelber, Jack 1932– American playwright. Although a dozen or so of his plays have been produced in New York, he is best known for *The Connection* (1959), about four heroin addicts waiting for a 'connection' to bring their drugs. Its use of improvisatory techniques to collapse the traditional distance between audience and actors is typical of his work.

Generides A late-14th-century VERSE ROMANCE. The story incorporates many themes and motifs common in medieval romance and, despite its setting, is unlikely to be Eastern in origin. Generides, illegitimate son of King Aufreus and Princess Sereyne, travels to Persia and falls in love with the Sultan's daughter, Clarionas, whom he eventually succeeds in marrying. The obstacles to overcome include a rival who kidnaps Clarionas and Aufreus' Queen, who with his treacherous steward has taken over his kingdom. Aufreus marries Sereyne, Generides defeats the steward and the Queen dies.

Genesis An Old English poem attributed to CAEDMON by FRANCIS JUNIUS. It is now known to be a composite of two poems, neither of them by Caedmon. The major part, *Genesis A*, is the work of an 8th-century monk: beginning with the war in Heaven, it follows the Book of Genesis up to chapter 22. Interpolated are over 600 lines of a 9th-century poem about Satan, *Genesis B*, translated from German.

Gent, Thomas 1693–1778 Printer, poet and writer of topographical works. The only master printer in York and, it is thought, in the North of England, he produced a number of topographical works, of which the most important are his *History of York* (1730) and *History of Ripon* (1734), which contains a poem in praise of Fountains Abbey by Peter Aram, father of the murderer Eugene Aram. Gent's autobiography (1832) provides much information about the printing trade and literary world and also shows him to have been extraordinarily cantankerous.

Gentleman's Magazine, The A periodical founded in 1731 by Edward Cave (1691–1754). It began as a review of news, essays and comment from other journals but, partly through SAMUEL JOHNSON's influence, assumed a more serious tone, publishing parliamentary reports, maps, reviews of publications and music. The magazine survived until 1914.

Geoffrey of Monmouth d. ?1155 Chronicler. Probably born in Monmouth and having some connection with

Caerleon-on-Usk, he lived in Oxford and London, and became Bishop Elect of Asaph in 1151. Three works of his survive, all written in Latin: *Historia regum Britanniae* (c. 1135), *Propheti Merlini* and *Vita Merlini*. The *Prophecies* and *Life* were conceived separately but finally incorporated into the *History*. Deriving from the work of BEDE, Gildas and Nennius, it traces events from the legendary founding of Britain by Brutus, grandson of Aeneas, to the death of the last British king, Cadwallader, in 689. Although some of the narrative bears a remote resemblance to actual events, the majority is pure invention. It relates the lives of, among others, Kings Cole, Lear, Cymbeline and Arthur, Julius Caesar, Claudius, Vespasian and Gorboduc, and events such as the founding of London, the moving of Stonehenge to Salisbury Plain by Merlin, and the coming of St Augustine to Britain. But it is for the history of King Arthur, occupying more than a fifth of the work, that the *History* is best known. His marriage to Guinevere, Mordred's treason, his disappearance to Avalon and the exploits of Gawain, Bedevere, Cador and Kay are all related, though Lancelot does not appear. Geoffrey's *History* formed the basis of Wace's *Roman de Brut* and of the vast ensuing body of ARTHURIAN LITERATURE.

Geoffrey of Vinsauf d. *c.* 1210-20 Rhetorician. Little is known about him except that he taught the future Richard I, visited Rome at least once and may have studied in Paris. Three major works survive: the *Documentum de modo et arte dictandi et versificandi*, the *Summa de coloribus rhetoricis* and the influential *Poetria nova* cited by CHAUCER in *THE CANTERBURY TALES*. A valuable source of information about the devices and techniques prescribed by medieval theoreticians, the *Poetria nova* treats poetry as an aspect of rhetoric, recommending a thorough knowledge of the rules of poetic composition (*ars*), study of past poetry (*imitatio*) and steady practice (*usus*).

George, Henry 1839–97 American journalist and political reformer. An editorial in *OVERLAND MONTHLY* in 1868 argued that the railroad industry would serve only to make the rich richer and the poor poorer. His Single Tax theory, announced in *Our Land and Land Policy* (1871), was developed in *Progress and Poverty* (1879) and subsequent works, arguing that the gap between the rich and the poor could be closed by replacing the various taxes levied on labour and capital with a tax on the rental value of property. Lecture tours made his theories even more influential in Europe than in the USA.

George Barnwell See *LONDON MERCHANT, THE*.

Georgian Poetry A five-volume anthology published between 1912 and 1922, planned by its publisher HAROLD MONRO, RUPERT BROOKE and SIR EDWARD MARSH, the editor. The early, influential volumes included Brooke, LASCELLES ABERCROMBIE, GORDON BOTTOMLEY, W. H. DAVIES, DE LA MARE, DRINKWATER, RALPH HODGSON, D. H. LAWRENCE and MASEFIELD. Though later volumes included BLUNDEN, GRAVES, ROSENBERG and SASSOON, the predominant tone of *Georgian Poetry* – colloquial and lightly shocking in its realism – was criticized by Graves himself, POUND, ELIOT and the SITWELLS, whose anthology *Wheels* was a MODERNIST alternative.

georgic A poem offering instruction about some branch of skill or art, the most famous example being the *Georgics* of Virgil, which discuss the conditions of life in the countryside and various aspects of farming. The 17th and 18th centuries produced many imitations, about sheep-shearing, cider-making, physical health and country sports, and ADDISON's *Essay on the Georgic* (1697), which distinguishes it from PASTORAL.

Gerard, John 1545–1612 Herbalist. He supervised Lord Burleigh's gardens in the Strand, as well as his own gardens in Holborn, of which he issued a catalogue in 1596. His *Herbal* (1597; revised by Thomas Johnson, 1633) in fact completed an unfinished translation by a Dr Priest of Dodoenus' *Stirpium historiae pemptades sex* (1583), illustrated with woodcuts largely borrowed from Tabernaemontanus' *Eicones plantarum*. The description of plants, for which Gerard often gives the old English names, includes their habitat, times of flowering and 'virtues': the lettuce cools heartburn and causes sleep, narcissus root pounded with honey is good for burns.

Gerhardie, William 1895–1977 Novelist. He changed the spelling of his name from 'Gerhardi' in old age. Born into a family of English merchants in St Petersburg, he was still an Oxford undergraduate when he published his first novel, *Futility* (1922), and a study of Chekhov (1923), a central influence on his own fiction. Extravagantly plotted, his novels disconcertingly juxtapose the absurd and the profound, the comic and the tragic. *Futility*, *The Polyglots* (1925) and their successors, notably *Pending Heaven* (1930), *Resurrection* (1934) and *Of Mortal Love* (1936), enjoyed brief critical success. Gerhardie published no more books after 1940 and the major novel on which he was rumoured to be working during the years of his obscurity never materialized.

Germ, The The literary magazine of the PRE-RAPHAELITES. It lasted for only four issues, published between January and April 1850, and contained poetry by DANTE GABRIEL ROSSETTI (*THE BLESSED DAMOZEL*), CHRISTINA ROSSETTI and COVENTRY PATMORE, Rossetti's short story *Hand and Soul* and reviews of contemporary verse by his brother, WILLIAM MICHAEL ROSSETTI, who was also the editor.

Gest Hystoriale of the Destruction of Troy A VERSE ROMANCE written in the second half of the 14th century, the longest Middle English poem in ALLITERATIVE VERSE. A free version of Guido's *Historia destructionis Troiae*, it treats the history of Troy from the story of Jason and the destruction of the Old Troy to the destruction of the New Troy and the death of Ulysses. It includes the story of Troilus and Briseida, invented by Benoît de Sainte-Maure and used by CHAUCER in *TROILUS AND CRISEYDE*.

Gesta Romanorum A popular collection of tales, originally in Latin, accumulated during the 14th century. Few of the stories are about Rome and some are Eastern in origin. Each was designed to point a moral. Several translations appeared, including one in Middle English. WYNKYN DE WORDE issued the first printed version in English (1510).

Ghose, Zulfikar 1935– Indian/Pakistani poet and novelist. His verse includes *The Loss of India* (1964), *Jets of Orange* (1967) and *The Violent West* (1972). The stories in *Statement against Corpses* (1964), with B. S. JOHNSON, and the novels *Contradictions* (1966) and *The Murder of Aziz Khan* (1969) seek a 'still point' between Western rationality and Eastern 'nothingness'. Two critical works, *Hamlet, Prufrock, and Language* (1978) and *The Fiction of Reality* (1984), point to the nature of his sophisticated and challenging novels since 1972: a trilogy, *The Incredible Brazilian* (1972), *The Beautiful Empire* (1975), and *A Different World* (1979); *Hulme's Investigations into the Bogart Script* (1981); *A New History of Torments* (1982); and *Don Bueno* (1983). *Confessions of a Native-Alien* (1965) is an autobiography.

Gibbon, Edward 1737–94 Historian. Born into comfortable circumstances, he left Magdalen College, Oxford, in disappointment to study by himself. His conversion to Roman Catholicism in 1753 caused his alarmed father to send him to Lausanne, where a Calvinist minister reversed the damage. His attachment to Suzanne Curchod, the only romantic attachment of his life, was broken off because of his father's disapproval. Gibbon returned home in 1758, served in the Hampshire militia and published his first work, *Essai sur l'étude de la littérature* (1761; English version, 1764). After completing the Grand Tour he produced a mass of miscellaneous reviews and exercises, including the *Observations of the Design of the VIth Book of the Aeneid* (1770), and established himself in London. He became an MP in 1774, steadfastly supporting Lord North's government, and was appointed Commissioner of Trade and Plantations in 1779–82.

On its appearance in 1776 the first volume of *The History of the Decline and Fall of the Roman Empire* was greeted with general praise, except from orthodox Christians. Gibbon replied to his critics in *A Vindication of Some Passages in the Fifteenth and Sixteenth Chapters* (1779), without silencing them. Their attacks did not deter him from continuing a book whose scope, ambitious in the original conception, grew as he proceeded. Volumes 2 and 3 appeared in 1783 and volumes 4, 5 and 6 in 1788. By this time he was again living in Lausanne. A subsequent project, *The Antiquities of the House of Brunswick*, was never completed. On his return to England in 1791 he accepted the hospitality of the Earl of Sheffield, who prepared his *Memoirs of My Life and Writings* for publication in 1796, as well as the *Miscellaneous Works*.

Gibbon, Lewis Grassic [Mitchell, James Leslie] 1901–35 Scottish writer. Mitchell used the pseudonym for his specifically Scottish undertakings, most notably *A Scots Quair*, a trilogy of novels set in his native Howe of Mearns: *Sunset Song* (1932), *Cloud Howe* (1933) and *Grey Granite* (1934). He collaborated with Hugh MacDiarmid on *Scottish Scene: or, The Intelligent Man's Guide to Albyn* (1934), an important contribution to the Scottish renaissance. Under his own name Mitchell published seven English novels, many short stories and works of history, archaeology and anthropology.

Gibbons, Stella See *Cold Comfort Farm*.

Gibson, Graeme 1934– Canadian novelist. *Five Legs* (1969), *Communion* (1971) and *Perpetual Motion* (1982) are experimental but carefully constructed works, all set in southern Ontario and concerned with man's relation to nature and spirit. A prominent figure in Canadian cultural politics, Gibson has also published a collection of interviews, *Eleven Canadian Novelists* (1973).

Gibson, Wilfred Wilson 1878–1962 Poet. From *Urlyn the Harper and Other Songs* (1902) onwards he wrote prolifically, his commonest subject being the plight of the unfortunate, particularly ordinary men and women at the mercy of industrial and political change. *Collected Poems* (1926) was followed by another dozen collections before his death. *Within Four Walls* (1950) contains five verse plays.

Gibson, William 1948– American writer of science fiction. Most of his work – including the novels *Neuromancer* (1984), *Count Zero* (1985), *Mona Lisa Overdrive* (1988) and the short stories collected in *Burning Chrome* (1986) – is typical of so-called 'Cyberpunk' fiction, which deals with the intimate interaction of people and electronic machinery in an overpopulated, decadent near future. *The Difference Engine* (with Bruce Sterling; 1990) is an alternative history novel in which Victorian England undergoes a technological revolution thanks to Charles Babbage's mechanical computer.

Gifford, William 1756–1826 Satirist and critic. He first attracted notice with two satires of the Della Cruscans, *The Baviad* (1791) and *The Maeviad* (1795). A sour and conservative critic, he became editor of *The Anti-Jacobin* in 1797 and of *The Quarterly Review* in 1809. He was caricatured by Peacock as Mr Vamp in *Melincourt* (1817) and rebuked by Hazlitt in *A Letter to Gifford* (1819). Gifford also translated the satires of Juvenal (1802) and Persius (1812), and prepared editions of several Jacobean dramatists.

Gilbert, Sir Humphrey ?1539–83 Soldier, navigator and stepbrother of Sir Walter Raleigh. His suggestions for voyages to discover the Northwest Passage, including those in *A Discourse of a Discovery for a New Passage to Cataia* (written in 1566, printed in 1576), received only grudging support from Elizabeth, who eventually granted him a charter to settle heathen lands not yet settled by any Christian ruler. He claimed Newfoundland for the Queen in 1583 but was lost at sea on the journey home. The scene is described in Hakluyt's *Voyages*.

Gilbert, William 1544–1603 Scientist and physician to Elizabeth I and James I. He agreed with Copernicus that the earth revolved on its axis. *De magnete* (1600) coined the term 'electrical force'. At his death Gilbert left manuscripts which were edited by his brother and published as *De mundo nostro sublunari philosophia nova* (1651).

Gilbert, Sir W(illiam) S(chwenck) 1836–1911 Playwright, librettist and lyricist. His early humorous verse was collected in *The Bab Ballads* (1868) and *More Bab Ballads* (1872). After considerable apprentice work for the theatre, particularly in the field of burlesque, he achieved popularity with a verse play, *The Palace of Truth* (1870), followed by *Pygmalion and Galatea* (1871), *The Wicked World* (1873), *Sweethearts* (1874) and *Engaged* (1877). A career as a librettist was founded on his partnership with Arthur Sullivan, beginning uncertainly with *Thespis* (1871) but flourishing from *Trial by Jury* (1875) onwards to produce the series known as the Savoy Operas. Gilbert's prominence as a librettist reduced his output as a playwright, though he wrote several ambitious later plays, including *Broken Hearts* (1875) and *Gretchen* (1879). Unlike his mentor T. W. Robertson, he avoided realism and the contemporary scene, developing a style marked by formality and paradox. His profoundly pessimistic view of human nature (expressed in its purest form in *The Palace of Truth* and *Engaged*) was made more palatable in comic opera, and it is by his collaboration with Sullivan that his work survives in the theatre.

Gillette, William (Hooker) 1855–1937 American actor and playwright. He gained a considerable reputation, writing parts for himself in which his restrained acting style could be exploited. His best-known works are two melodramas about the Civil War, *Held by the Enemy* (1886) and *Secret Service* (1895). He starred for over 30 years in *Sherlock Holmes* (1899), his own dramatization of the Sherlock Holmes stories.

Gilman, Charlotte Perkins 1860–1935 American feminist writer. *This Our World* (1893) is a collection of poems about 19th-century womanhood and *Women and*

Economics (1898) an indictment of patriarchal culture. Other reforming works, including *Concerning Children* (1900) and *The Home: Its Work and Influence* (1903), discuss the detrimental effects that restrictions on women have on the family. *The Yellow Wallpaper* (1899) is a semi-autobiographical treatment of a woman writer's breakdown. Two novels, *What Diana Did* (1910) and *The Crux* (1911), originally published in her journal, *The Forerunner*, developed her ideas about sexual relations and oppression in modern society. Her autobiography appeared in 1935.

Gilmore, Dame **Mary** 1865–1962 Australian poet. A member of William Lane's idealistic experimental community in Paraguay, she returned to Australia after its failure and conducted the women's page of *The Sydney Worker* for 23 years. Her 10 books of verse, which include *Married and Other Verses* (1910), *The Passionate Heart* (1918) and *The Wild Swan* (1930), are enthusiastic and radical in tone.

Gilpin, William 1724–1804 Travel-writer. The vicar of Boldre, Hampshire, he achieved considerable success with accounts of tours through Britain and established himself as a leading authority on the PICTURESQUE. His books, delicately illustrated by himself and showing as great a concern for abstract principles of beauty as for the particular scene, covered the following areas: the Wye Valley and South Wales (1782), the Lake District (1786), the Highlands (1789), the New Forest (1791), the West Country and the Isle of Wight (1789), the coasts of Hampshire, Sussex and Kent (1804), Cambridge, Norfolk, Suffolk, Essex and North Wales (1809). Also notable is the collection *Three Essays: On Picturesque Beauty, On Picturesque Travel, On Sketching Landscape* (1792). The vogue he helped to encourage was satirized in COMBE's *Tour of Dr Syntax in Search of the Picturesque*.

Ginsberg, Allen 1926– American poet. His first collection, *Howl and Other Poems* (1956), secured his reputation as a leader of the BEATS. Other volumes include *Kaddish and Other Poems, 1958–1960* (1961), *Reality Sandwiches, 1953–1960* (1963), *Planet News* (1964), *Wichita Vortex Sutra* (1966), *Ankor Wat* (1968), *The Fall of America: Poems of These States, 1965–1971* (1972), *Mind Breaths: Poems 1972–1977* (1978), *Poems All Over the Place: Mostly Seventies* (1978), *Straight Hearts' Delight: Love Poems and Selected Letters* (1980), *Collected Poems 1947–1980* (1984) and *White Shroud: Poems 1980–1985* (1986). Ginsberg's verse derives its long-cadenced line from WILLIAM BLAKE and WALT WHITMAN, to whom 'A Supermarket in California' is a kind of comic tribute.

Giovanni, Nikki (Yolande Cornelia) 1943– Black American poet. *Black Feeling, Black Talk* (1968) and *Black Judgment* (1969), two militant volumes, were followed by *Recreation* (1970) and *Spin a Soft Black Song* (1971), which mingle personal concerns with social and political statement. Her examination of the black experience is developed in *My House* (1972), *Ego-Tripping and Other Poems for Young People* (1974), *The Women and the Men* (1975), *Cotton-Candy on a Rainy Day* (1983) and *Sacred Cows ... and Other Edibles* (1988). *Gemini: An Extended Autobiographical Statement on My First Twenty-Five Years of Being a Black Poet* appeared in 1971.

Gissing, George (Robert) 1857–1903 Novelist. After being expelled from Owens College (later the University of Manchester) for stealing, he spent a month in prison, wandered for a year in America and then settled in London, where he survived by private coaching. He married two working-class girls in succession.

Consciousness of his humble origins made him proud and lonely; his only close friend in the literary world was H. G. WELLS.

Hardworking, prolific and obsessed with his vocation, he became respected as an exponent of NATURALISM in the French manner, usually taking poverty and failure as his subjects. His first novel, *WORKERS IN THE DAWN* (1880), was followed by *The Unclassed* (1884), *Eve's Ransom* (1885), *Isabel Clarendon* and *Demos* (both 1886), *Thyrza* (1887), *A Life's Morning* (1888), *The Nether World* (1889), *The Emancipated* (1890), *NEW GRUB STREET* (his best-known novel, 1891), *Born in Exile* (1892), *Denzil Quarrier* (1892), *THE ODD WOMEN* (1893), *Sleeping Fires* (1895), *The Whirlpool* (1897), *Human Odds and Ends* (short stories, 1897), *The Town Traveller* and a critical study of DICKENS (both 1898), *The Crown of Life* (1899), *Our Friend the Charlatan* (1901) and *By the Ionian Sea* (impressions of Italy, 1900). *THE PRIVATE PAPERS OF HENRY RYECROFT* (1903) is semi-autobiographical. After his death came a historical romance of 6th-century Italy, *Veranilda* (1904), *Will Warburton* (1905), *The House of Cobwebs* (short stories, 1906), *The Sins of the Fathers* (1924), *The Immortal Dickens* (1925), *A Victim of Circumstances* (1927), *Brownie* (1931), *Notes on Social Democracy* (1968), *George Gissing's Commonplace Book* (edited by J. Korg; 1962) and *The Diary of George Gissing, Novelist* (edited by P. Coustillas; 1978). In recent years he has received increasing critical attention.

Glanvill, Joseph 1636–80 Philosopher and theologian. A clergyman who ended his days with the living of the Abbey Church in Bath, he was 25 when he published *The Vanity of Dogmatizing* (1661; revised as *Scepsis scientifica*, 1665), arguing for a scientific approach to learning. It contains the story which inspired MATTHEW ARNOLD's *THE SCHOLAR-GIPSY*. *Plus Ultra* (1668) emphasizes further the value of experimental science. *Saducismus triumphatus* (1681) attempts to prove the existence of witchcraft.

Glasgow, Ellen 1874–1945 American novelist. She is best remembered for *Barren Ground* (1925), in which Dorinda Oakley struggles with the 'barren ground' of her Virginia farm and the unpropitious conditions of her life, and *Vein of Iron* (1935), about the Fincastles, a Scottish-Irish family in Shut-In Valley, Virginia. The old agrarian South is the subject of a series of historical novels, beginning with *The Voice of the People* (1900) and including *The Battle-Ground* (1902), *The Deliverance* (1904), *The Wheel of Life* (1906), *The Ancient Law* (1908), *The Romance of a Plain Man* (1909) and *The Miller of Old Church* (1911). *Virginia* (1913) and *Life and Gabriella* (1916) examine the position of women in the modernization of the Old South. Other novels include *The Builders* (1919), *One Man in His Time* (1922), *The Romantic Comedians* (1926), *They Stooped to Folly* (1929), *The Sheltered Life* (1932) and *In This Our Life* (1941), about the decay of an aristocratic Virginia family. Her short stories are found in *The Shadowy Third* (1923) and *Collected Stories* (1963), and the prefatory essays to her novels in *A Certain Measure* (1943). *The Woman Within* (1954) is autobiographical.

Glaspell, Susan 1882–1948 American playwright, novelist and short-story writer. With her husband, George Cram Cook, she was a founder of the Provincetown Players (see EUGENE O'NEILL). Her plays include one-act pieces, such as *Trifles* (1916), as well as full-length works, such as *Inheritors* (1921), *The Verge* (1921), about a woman simultaneously on the verge of madness and true discovery, and *Alison's House* (1930; PULITZER PRIZE), about EMILY DICKINSON. Her novels are unimpressive but the short stories collected in *Lifted Masks* (1912) and *A Jury of Her Peers* (1927) display the intensity of her quest for social justice. *The Road to the Temple* (1927) is an evocative account of her life with Cook.

Glass Menagerie, The A play by TENNESSEE WILLIAMS, produced in 1944. Described as a 'memory play', it is framed by the recollections of Tom Wingfield, whose impressionistic narratives, accompanied by images projected on a screen, introduce a number of the scenes. Tom recalls his life in St Louis with his mother Amanda, a faded Southern belle who clings persistently to glamorous illusions about her past, and his sister Laura, a crippled, painfully shy young woman whose intensely private world is centred on a treasured collection of small glass animals.

Globe Theatre The home of the KING'S MEN, the leading Elizabethan and Jacobean theatre company, to which SHAKESPEARE and RICHARD BURBAGE belonged. They were among the shareholders who in 1599 supervised the salvage of timber from the company's old home, the Theatre, to build the first Globe, on the south bank of the Thames, a short distance west of what is now Southwark Cathedral. It was here that most of the great plays of Shakespeare's maturity were first performed. Destroyed by fire in 1613, the Globe was reconstructed and reopened in 1614. It remained in use until the closing of the theatres under Cromwell, and was torn down in 1644.

Glover, Denis 1912–80 New Zealand poet. As founder of the Caxton Press in 1936 he provided a significant outlet for New Zealand writers during the years of growth which followed. He first achieved recognition as a poet himself in the 1930s when, with his close associate ALLEN CURNOW, he was a member of the Phoenix Group. Works like *Six Easy Ways of Dodging Debt Collectors* (1936) and his contributions to *A Caxton Miscellany* (1937) are witty reflections on the local cultural situation. Glover was always a champion of directness but, despite their apparently rough-hewn quality, his poems show considerable craftsmanship. Among the best-known of more than 20 volumes are *Recent Poems* (1941), *Sings Harry* (1951), *Arawata Bill* (1953), a highly popular sequence about a wandering prospector, and *Since Then* (1957). *Selected Poems* appeared in 1981.

Glover, Richard 1712–85 Poet and playwright. He wrote three tragedies – *Boadicea* (1753), *Medea* (1767) and *Jason* (unproduced and posthumously published, 1799) – as well as a good deal of indifferent BLANK VERSE, including *Leonidas* (1737) in nine books and *The Athenaid* in 30 books (posthumously published, 1787). *Admiral Hosier's Ghost* (1740), a popular BALLAD, was included in THOMAS PERCY's *Reliques of Ancient English Poetry*.

Glyn, Elinor 1864–1943 Novelist. Her 21 romantic novels were popular and controversial for their treatment of sex, particularly women's sexual feelings. *Three Weeks* (1907), the best known because of erotic scenes played out on a tiger-skin, describes the sensual awakening of Paul, a young English nobleman, in his affair with a Slavonic beauty of noble rank. The ending punishes the lovers.

Go-Between, The A novel by L. P. HARTLEY, published in 1953. In old age Leo Colston recalls the summer of 1900, when he stayed with a schoolfriend, Marcus Maudsley, at a Norfolk country house. He became a go-between, innocently carrying messages for a local farmer, Ted Burgess, and Marcus's older sister Marian, who were conducting a secret affair despite Marian's engagement

to Lord Hugh Trimingham. In the process he slowly became aware of adult sexuality. Marian's mother grew suspicious and forced Leo to witness her discovery of the couple making love. Marian married Trimingham and Burgess killed himself. In an epilogue Leo visits Marian 50 years later and agrees to contact her grandson to explain what really happened.

Goblin Market A poem by CHRISTINA ROSSETTI, published in 1862. A cryptic fairy-tale, notable for its verbal and metrical inventiveness, it tells the story of two sisters, Lizzie and Laura, who are tempted by goblins to eat their delicious but dangerous fruit.

Godber, John 1956– Playwright and director. Since 1984 he has been artistic director of Hull Truck, for whom he has staged comedies, closely in touch with their northern audience, which delight in physical and athletic gags and in jibes against the Establishment. They include *Up 'N' Under* (1984), *Bouncers* (1985), *Teechers* (1987), *Salt of the Earth* (1990), *Happy Families* (1991) and *April in Paris* (1992). His work for TV includes *Blood Sweat and Tears* (1986), adapted from his stage play, and *The Ritz* (1987).

Godden, (Margaret) Rumer 1907– Novelist and writer of CHILDREN'S LITERATURE. Beginning as an adult author, she won acclaim with a series of successful novels including *Black Narcissus* (1939), *Breakfast with the Nickolides* (1942) and *The Greengage Summer* (1958), a story of first love set in France and now also considered a children's book. Her books written expressly for children include *The Dolls' House* (1947) and *The Mousewife* (1951), based on a note in DOROTHY WORDSWORTH's diary. Other successful books include *The Diddakoi* (1972) and *Peacock Spring* (1978), another tale of disappointed love, set in India, and suitable for both old and young readers.

Godolphin, Sidney 1610–43 Poet and translator. A devoted Royalist, he died in a skirmish at Chagford. A friend of FALKLAND and CLARENDON, he is characterized as 'little Sid' in SUCKLING's *Sessions of the Poets*. WALLER completed his translation of Book IV of Virgil's *Aeneid* (1658). His love lyrics and devotional poems were first collected in 1906.

Godric, St d. ?1170 Author of three verse fragments written before 1170, important as the earliest examples of native popular verse in Middle English. Godric was an uneducated pedlar before becoming a hermit at Finchdale, near Durham. A contemporary Latin life alleges that the words and music of his first and best-known poem, 'Cantus beati Godrici', were inspired by the Virgin. A four-line hymn was given to him by his dead sister in a vision and the third poem, 'Cantus Sancto Nicholao', was inspired by an Easter vision of St Nicholas.

Godwin, William 1756–1836 Philosopher and novelist. He began by becoming a Dissenting minister but his reading of Rousseau, d'Holbach and Helvetius undermined his faith and he embraced atheism in 1783. The French Revolution stirred his interest in political philosophy and emancipatory politics. *ENQUIRY CONCERNING POLITICAL JUSTICE* (1793), his response to the debates and polemics of the time, was an immediate success and included the young WORDSWORTH, SOUTHEY and COLERIDGE among its admirers. The inner social and psychological drama masked by its elaborate philosophical method is impressively externalized in his novel, *CALEB WILLIAMS* (1794). Godwin was the anarchist of the Age of Reason. Nothing if not consistent in his rationalistic individualism, he opposed both all existing institutions and all organized resistance to them. He never revised his model of reason, and jealously defended his system against the slightest imputation of activism. Although this position alienated him from radical groups like the London Corresponding Society, it did not prevent him becoming the scapegoat of the loyalist reaction orchestrated by Pitt. By the time he published *The Enquirer* (1797) he had been thoroughly and systematically defamed. It was a blow from which he never recovered intellectually and which permanently soured his personal relations.

His wife, MARY WOLLSTONECRAFT, died a few days after the birth of their daughter, the future MARY SHELLEY, in 1797. He wrote her biography, *Memoirs of the Author of the Vindication of the Rights of Woman* (1798), edited her posthumous works and portrayed her in his novel *St Leon* (1799). His subsequent remarriage to Mrs Clairmont was largely an alliance of convenience. In 1814 SHELLEY eloped with Mary and Claire Clairmont, eventually marrying Mary in 1816. Godwin's adroit manipulation of the poet's generosity helped to alleviate his financial problems. During the last two decades of his life he repudiated many of the more radical aspects of *Political Justice* – in, for example, *Thoughts on Man* (1831) – and in the late 1820s he spoke out against the increasingly powerful movement for reform. The only significant work of this period was *Of Population* (1820), an answer to MALTHUS's *Essay on the Principle of Population*. His substantial output also includes a life of CHAUCER (1803–4) and the novels *Fleetwood* (1805), *Mandeville* (1817), *Cloudesly* (1830) and *Deloraine* (1833).

Gogarty, Oliver St John 1878–1957 Irish man of letters and poet. He was a friend of JOYCE, who portrayed him as Buck Mulligan in *ULYSSES*. His poetry in *An Offering of Swans* (1923), *Wild Apples* (1928) and *Selected Poems* (1933) was over-rated by YEATS in the *Oxford Book of Modern Verse* (1936). He also published several volumes of memoirs, notably *As I was Going Down Sackville Street* (1937), and an autobiography, *It isn't That Time of Year at All* (1954), written after he settled in the USA. *Collected Poems* appeared in 1950.

Golagros and Gawain A late 15th-century Middle Scots romance in ALLITERATIVE VERSE, freely adapted from the First Continuation of the *Conte du Graal* by Chrétien de Troyes. It exemplifies the contrast between Kay's churlishness and Gawain's courtesy that had become conventional in ARTHURIAN LITERATURE. In the first episode Kay's request for hospitality on behalf of Arthur and his knights is refused while Gawain's is granted. In the second, Gawain defeats Golagros but treats him generously.

Gold, Herbert 1924– American novelist. Several novels are autobiographical: *Therefore Be Bold* (1960) tells of his experience growing up in Cleveland; *Fathers: A Novel in the Form of a Memoir* (1967) draws on his experiences as a father and son; and *Family: A Novel in the Form of a Memoir* (1981) is about a Jewish immigrant family. *The Man Who was Not with It* (1956), probably his best-known work, is the story of a drug-addicted carnival barker. Others are *Birth of a Hero* (1951), *The Prospect before Us* (1954), *The Optimist* (1959), *Salt* (1963), *The Great American Jackpot* (1971), *Swiftie the Magician* (1974), *He/She* (1980), *True Love* (1982), *Mister White Eyes* (1984), *A Girl of Forty* (1986) and *Dreaming* (1988). His short stories and essays have been collected in *15 × 3* (1957), *Love and Like* (1960), *The Age of Happy Problems* (1962) and *The Magic Will: Stories and Essays of a Decade* (1971).

Gold, Michael 1894–1967 American journalist and novelist. His best-known book, *Jews without Money* (1930), is a fictionalized autobiography about Jewish ghetto life which ends with the protagonist's conversion to Communism. A contributor to *The Masses* and editor of *The Liberator*, Gold also founded their successor, *THE NEW MASSES*, in 1926. His fiery columns have been collected in *The Mike Gold Reader* (1954) and *Mike Gold: A Literary Anthology* (1972), which also reprints articles from *120 Million* (1929) and *Change the World* (1937), his earlier collections of *New Masses* prose.

Golden Bough, The See FRAZER, SIR JAMES.

Golden Bowl, The A novel by HENRY JAMES, published in 1904. Maggie is the daughter of Adam Verver, an American millionaire and art collector living in Europe. Her friend Fanny Assingham finds her an Italian prince, Amerigo. Charlotte Stant, prevented from marrying Amerigo by their lack of money, wants to buy a gilded crystal bowl as a present for Amerigo but he declines the gift because it is flawed. Adam Verver marries Charlotte, but Charlotte and Amerigo have not forgotten their feelings for each other and meet in secret. Maggie buys a bowl for her father's birthday but learns from the dealer that it is the same one Amerigo and Charlotte had rejected. Maggie makes clear to Fanny that she knows the whole truth about Charlotte and Amerigo, and smashes the bowl. Amerigo stops seeing Charlotte; Adam gives no hint to her that he knows of her liaison; Maggie conducts herself with unruffled serenity. Charlotte is left wondering at her lover's withdrawal and Adam finally resolves the situation by returning to America with her.

Golden Legend, The A collection of biblical narratives and SAINTS' LIVES. Originally the 13th-century *Legenda aurea* of Jacobus de Voragine, it was translated into English in the 15th century. The best-known English version was printed by CAXTON *c.* 1487.

Golden Treasury, The See PALGRAVE, FRANCIS TURNER.

Golding, Arthur ?1536-1605 Translator. His most important translation was of Ovid's *Metamorphoses* (1565–67), one of the finest and most faithful of Elizabethan classical translations, to which SHAKESPEARE among others was indebted. Golding also translated Caesar's *De bello gallico* (1565), Seneca's *De beneficiis* (1578) and commentaries and sermons by Calvin, as well as finishing SIR PHILIP SIDNEY's translation of de Mornay's *Trueness of the Christian Religion* (1587).

Golding, Sir William (Gerald) 1911–93 Novelist. Much of his writing explores moral dilemmas at the centre of human existence, and he often places his characters in extreme situations to suggest a 'mythological' dimension to their lives. Preoccupied with evil and original sin, he treated these subjects in a way that transcends the boundaries of orthodox Christianity. He achieved success with his first novel, *LORD OF THE FLIES* (1954), now regarded as a modern classic. It was followed by: *The Inheritors* (1955), about primeval man; *Pincher Martin* (1956), in which a drowning man is tormented by his past life; *Free Fall* (1959); *The Spire* (1964), a densely symbolic account of the building of Salisbury Cathedral spire; *The Pyramid* (1967); *The Scorpion God* (1971); *Darkness Visible* (1979); and *The Paper Men* (1984), an uncharacteristically comic account of a famous author plagued by an American academic. *The Ends of the Earth* (1991) brings together a trilogy of powerful historical novels reflecting his abiding fascination with the sea: *Rites of Passage* (1980), which won the BOOKER PRIZE, *Close Quarters*

(1987) and *Fire Down Below* (1989). *The Double Tongue* appeared posthumously in 1995. Other works include a play, *The Brass Butterfly* (1958), and collections of essays, *The Hot Gates* (1965) and *A Moving Target* (1982). He was awarded the Nobel Prize for Literature in 1983.

Goldsmith, Oliver ?1730–74 Playwright, poet, novelist and essayist. A son of the Irish Protestant clergy on both sides of the family, he studied at Trinity College, Dublin, and spent a few months each at Edinburgh and Leiden Universities. The authenticity of the medical degree he later claimed has not been established. While busking his way through France, Switzerland and Italy in 1755–6 , playing Irish tunes on his flute, he started his poem *THE TRAVELLER* (1764).

On arriving in England in 1756 he scraped a living in menial jobs before devoting himself to work as a GRUB STREET hack. *An Enquiry into the Present State of Polite Learning in Europe* (1759), his first important work, attacked university education as inadequate, poetry as divorced from nature and drama as bound by the rules of current taste. His 'Chinese Letters' for NEWBERY's *The Public Ledger*, republished as *The Citizen of the World* (1762), gave a satirical view of contemporary English life and manners through the eyes of an imaginary foreigner. Goldsmith's finances were never stable, and he was about to be arrested for debt when his friend and near-neighbour SAMUEL JOHNSON negotiated the sale of the manuscript of his only novel, *THE VICAR OF WAKEFIELD* (1766). During the years that remained to him before his early death he continued his diverse output with, among other work, *An History of England in a Series of Letters from a Nobleman to His Son* (1764); two anthologies, *Poems for Young Ladies* (1766, dated 1767) and *The Beauties of English Poesy* (1767); *The Roman History* (1769); and biographies of THOMAS PARNELL and BOLINGBROKE (1770). His *Grecian History* and his *History of the Earth and Animated Nature* both appeared posthumously in 1774. None of these books is as important as his work for the stage, notably his first comedy, *THE GOOD-NATURED MAN* (1768), and its more famous successor, *SHE STOOPS TO CONQUER* (1773). His best-known poem, *THE DESERTED VILLAGE*, which draws in part on his childhood memories of Ireland, appeared in 1770. *The Haunch of Venison*, posthumously published in 1776, is a lively expression in comic verse of gratitude for a gift from his friend Lord Clare.

Gone with the Wind The only novel by the American writer Margaret Mitchell (1900–49), published in 1936 and awarded a PULITZER PRIZE. An immediate best-seller, it has sold more than 25 million copies, been translated into 27 languages and inspired an enduringly popular film (1939) starring Vivien Leigh and Clark Gable. Set largely on a Georgia plantation, Tara, the story follows the fortunes of a wilful Southern belle, Scarlett O'Hara, against the backdrop of the Civil War, the defeat of the South and reconstruction.

Good Soldier, The: *A Tale of Passion* A novel by FORD MADOX FORD, published in 1915. The narrator, John Dowell, controls the reader's view of what he calls 'the saddest story', an account of his entangled relations with his wife Florence, their friend Edward Ashburnham (the good soldier) and his Irish-Catholic wife Leonora, and Nancy Rufford, ward of Edward and Leonora. The story moves towards a DÉNOUEMENT at once melodramatic and formally ordered.

Good-Natured Man, The A comedy by GOLDSMITH, produced and published in 1768. The generous and improvident Honeywood loves the wealthy Miss Richland but lacks the self-confidence to propose. Sir William, his uncle, has him arrested for debt to show him who his true friends are. Miss Richland secures his release but Honeywood insists on believing that Lofty, a government official, is responsible. The exasperated heroine and uncle between them expose Lofty's imposture and secure the marriage of Honeywood and Miss Richland. The sub-plot concerns Croaker, Miss Richland's guardian, and the defeat of his ambition to arrange for his son, Leontine, to marry the heroine.

Goodman, Paul 1911–72 American social critic and novelist. His many non-fictional works include: *Utopian Essays and Proposals* (1962), on political theory; *Gestalt Therapy* (1951), on psychology; *Communitas* (with his brother Percival; 1947), on city planning; *Compulsory Mis-Education* (1964); *Growing Up Absurd* (1960), an influential study of youth and deliquency. His novels include *The Empire City* (1959), set in New York from 1930 to 1950, and the autobiographical *Making Do* (1963). He also wrote for *PARTISAN REVIEW* and *THE NEW REPUBLIC. Five Years: Thoughts during a Useless Time* (1966) is autobiographical. *Collected Poems* appeared in 1974.

Googe, Barnabe 1505–94 Poet and translator. He was a long-lived kinsman of William Cecil, Elizabeth I's minister, who employed him in Ireland for 10 years. An industrious translator of Latin anti-Catholic pieces, he also displayed his Puritanism in *Eclogues, Epitaphs and Sonnets* (1563), which – with the work of his near-contemporary ALEXANDER BARCLAY – are among the earliest examples of PASTORAL poetry in English.

Gorboduc: or, The Tragedy of Ferrex and Porrex A tragedy by THOMAS NORTON (Acts 1–3) and THOMAS SACKVILLE (Acts 4 and 5), first acted in 1561 and printed in 1565. Though adhering to the Senecan model, it abandoned both the tradition of MORALITY PLAYS and the Aristotelian unities of time and place, moving towards the flexible action of plays in the great age of English drama. The story (from GEOFFREY OF MONMOUTH) takes place in legendary Britain. When Ferrex and Pollux, sons of Gorboduc and his queen Videna, quarrel over the division of the kingdom, the country is plunged into civil war and the royal line finally extinguished.

Gordimer, Nadine 1923– South African novelist and short-story writer. She received the Nobel Prize for Literature in 1991. Instants, symptoms and symbols of the South African malaise are captured by the short stories in volumes beginning with *Face to Face* (1949) and including, in her later career, *Livingstone's Companions* (1972), *Selected Stories* (1975), *Some Monday for Sure* (1976), *A Soldier's Embrace* (1980), *Something out There* (1984), *Why Haven't You Written?* (1990) and *Jump* (1991). Early novels – *The Lying Days* (1953), *A World of Strangers* (1958), *Occasion for Loving* (1963) and *The Late Bourgeois World* (1966) – chart the fluctuations of hope and disillusion in her view of South Africa. *A Guest of Honour* (1971) and *THE CONSERVATIONIST* (1974) announce the maturity of her fiction, successfully integrating the personal with the political. Later novels have included: *Burger's Daughter* (1979), about the child of devout Afrikaner Marxists; *July's People* (1981); *A Sport of Nature* (1987); and *My Son's Story* (1990), about a young coloured man trying to come to terms with his heritage. *The Black Interpreters* (1973) and *The Essential Gesture – Writing, Politics and Places* (1988) are collections of essays.

Gordon, Adam Lindsay 1833–70 Australian poet. A classical education and the background of a cultured home encouraged an interest in poetry which stayed with him throughout his short but adventurous life in Australia, where he arrived in 1853 and achieved fame as a steeplechase rider. His first published work, *The Feud*, appeared in 1864 and he contributed regularly to *Bell's Life in Victoria* and *The Australasian*. A collection was published as *Sea Spray and Smoke Drift* (1867). *Ashtaroth: A Dramatic Lyric*, an unsuccessful exercise on the Faust theme, appeared in the same year. Further poems were published in MARCUS CLARKE's paper, *The Colonial Monthly*, and in *Bush Ballads and Galloping Rhymes* (1870). He committed suicide at the age of 37.

Gordon, Caroline 1895–1981 American novelist and short-story writer. Born in Kentucky, she treated the history of the South in novels such as *Penhally* (1931), *Aleck Maury Sportsman* (1934) and *None Shall Look Back* (1937). Her short story 'Old Red', awarded the O. Henry Prize in 1934, reappeared in *The Forest of the South* (1945), *Old Red and Other Stories* (1963) and *The Collected Stories of Caroline Gordon* (1981).

Gore, Mrs Catherine Grace 1799–1861 Novelist and playwright. Of the 70 assorted works she produced in under 40 years, the best-known were SILVER-FORK NOVELS of fashionable life and high society. They include *Manners of the Day* (1830), *Mrs Armytage: or, Female Domination* (1836), *Cecil: or, The Adventures of a Coxcomb* (1841) and *The Banker's Wife* (1843).

Gorges, Sir Arthur 1557–1625 Poet and translator. A close companion of SIR WALTER RALEIGH, he entered royal service in his early twenties but fell from favour under JAMES I. SPENSER praised his love songs and SONNETS, several of which appeared in Elizabethan miscellanies. He prepared a manuscript collection, 'his vanities and toys of youth', which also includes a chivalric narrative, *The Olympian Catastrophe* (1612), modelled on Spenser's FAERIE QUEENE. Gorges also translated Lucan's *Pharsalia* in 1614 and, in 1619, BACON's *De sapientia veterum* and *Essays*, the latter into French.

Gospel of Nicodemus, The An apocryphal gospel which provided medieval theology, art and literature with the story of the Harrowing of Hell. First appearing around AD 400, it exists in an Old English translation and a version in Middle English verse and prose.

Gosse, Sir Edmund (William) 1849–1928 Critic and essayist. He is best remembered for *Father and Son* (1907), 'A Study of Two Temperaments' which blends sympathy and irony in its account of his bleak childhood with his widowed father Philip H. Gosse, distinguished zoologist and devout member of the Plymouth Brethren. He also wrote studies of THOMAS GRAY (1882), JEREMY TAYLOR (1903) and SIR THOMAS BROWNE (1905) for the English Men of Letters series, as well as a biography of SWINBURNE (1917). These are less important than his interest in Scandinavian culture, expressed in *Studies in the Literature of Northern Europe* (1879), a study of Ibsen (1907) and influential translations of *Hedda Gabler* (1891) and *The Master Builder* (with WILLIAM ARCHER; 1893). Gosse was a central figure in London literary life, the friend of SWINBURNE, ROBERT LOUIS STEVENSON, THOMAS HARDY and HENRY JAMES.

Gosson, Stephen 1554–1624 Pamphleteer and clergyman. Although he is known to have written pastoral plays in youth, Puritanism made him an opponent of the theatre. *The School of Abuse* (1579) was dedicated without permission to PHILIP SIDNEY, whose APOLOGY FOR POETRY was written partly to confute its attack on poets and actors. *Plays Confuted in Five Actions* (1582) continued the controversy.

Gothic novel A type of romance popular in the late 18th and early 19th centuries. 'Gothic' had come to mean 'wild', 'barbarous' and 'crude', qualities which writers cultivated in reaction against the NEOCLASSICISM of earlier 18th-century culture. Gothic novels were usually set in the past (most often the Middle Ages) and in foreign countries (particularly the Catholic countries of southern Europe). Monasteries, castles, dungeons and mountainous landscapes were made settings for plots which hinged on suspense or mystery and flirted with the fantastic or supernatural. WALPOLE's *THE CASTLE OF OTRANTO* (1764), the first Gothic novel proper, influenced the work of RADCLIFFE, BECKFORD, M. G. LEWIS and MATURIN. The wider ramifications of the taste for Gothic fiction continued in some Romantic poetry, MARY SHELLEY's *FRANKENSTEIN*, the stories of POE and the novels of the BRONTË sisters.

Gould, Nathaniel ['Nat'] 1857–1919 Sporting novelist. His first novel, *The Double Event* (1891), written while he was working in Australia, combined his knowledge of the country with his love of racing. Later fiction includes *Banker and Broker* (1893), *The Famous Match* (1898) and *Left in the Lurch* (in *Nat Gould's Annual*, 1903).

Gower, John c. 1330–1408 Poet. Little is known of Gower's life, but he apparently lived in Kent and London. Ranked during the 15th century with CHAUCER (who dedicated *TROILUS AND CRISEYDE* to him) and LYDGATE as one of the greatest English poets, he wrote in French, Latin and English. His first major work, *Le Mirour de l'omme* or *Speculum meditantis* (1376–9) is a moral poem in French about the effects of sin. The Latin *Vox clamantis* (1379–82) attacks the corruption of society under Richard II; its first book offers an apocalyptic vision provoked by the Peasants' Revolt of 1381. The *Cronica tripertita* is a sequel added after Richard's deposition in 1399. *CONFESSIO AMANTIS*, written in 1386–90 and revised in 1393, makes a notable contribution to the literature of COURTLY LOVE in English. One of its tales supplied the source for SHAKESPEARE's *PERICLES*, in which Gower appears as the Chorus. His only other English work is the poem 'To King Henry IV, in Praise of Peace'; he also wrote short Latin verses and, in French, the *Cinkante Balades*.

Gowers, Sir Ernest (Arthur) 1880–1966 Writer on writing. A distinguished civil servant, he originally produced *Plain Words: A Guide to the Use of English* (1948), a brief paper on writing English, for Civil Service use. It was republished with its successor, *ABC of Plain Words* (1951), as *The Complete Plain Words* (1954). Gowers also compiled a second edition of HENRY FOWLER's *A Dictionary of Modern English Usage* (1965). *A Life for a Life? The Problem of Capital Punishment* (1956) grew out of his work as chairman of the Royal Commission of 1949–53.

Grace, Patricia 1937– New Zealand short-story writer and novelist. *Waiariki* (1975) was the first collection of stories by a Maori woman writer. Since then she has published two further collections, *The Dream Sleepers* (1980) and *Electric City* (1987), and two novels, *Mutuwhenua: The Moon Sleeps* (1978) and *Potiki* (1986). Her writing explores the opposition of Maori and Pakeha (European) worlds from a point of view within contemporary Maori culture. She has also collaborated with the Maori artist Robyn Kahukiwa in producing CHILDREN'S LITERATURE.

Graham, W(illiam) S(ydney) 1918–86 Poet. Although essentially a Scottish poet, he stood outside the tradition of his friend HUGH MACDIARMID and was open to the influence of Rimbaud and HART CRANE. The early poems in *Cage without Grievance* (1942), *The Seven Journeys* (1944) and *The White Threshold* (1949) mix imagery from industrial and rural scenes. In later work, such as *The Nightfishing* (1955), *Malcolm Mooney's Land* (1970) and *Implements in Their Place* (1977), he went on to develop the extended metaphor of the voyage, inward and outward, to examine language and being. By the time *Collected Poems 1942–77* appeared in 1979 he had begun to receive a measure of the critical attention he deserved.

Grahame, Kenneth 1859–1932 Essayist and writer of CHILDREN'S LITERATURE. His book of essays, *The Golden Age* (1895), and its sequel, *Dream Days* (1898), paint a convincingly unsentimental picture of childhood. After his marriage in 1899 Grahame took to telling stories to his young son Alastair, continued in a series of letters. These formed the basis for THE WIND IN THE WILLOWS (1908), which – after several rejections by publishers – came out to scant critical acclaim. Its fame quickly grew and the addition of illustrations by E. H. SHEPARD and ARTHUR RACKHAM helped it to classic status. Grahame wrote nothing else of substance, becoming something of a recluse after his son's suicide at the age of 19.

Grammar of Assent, The A theological essay by NEWMAN, published in 1870. It argues that religious certainty comes not from logic but from intuition, the conscience and the heart – what he calls the 'illative sense'. The *Grammar* is an attempt to show that 'common sense' is as much a part of religious faith as it is of 'science and progress'.

Grand Guignol A particularly lurid and violent form of drama, in which the violence threatened but characteristically averted in MELODRAMA is carried through into performance. The name is derived from the 19th-century French marionette, Guignol. There are few notable examples in English. JAMES ELROY FLECKER's *HASSAN* has elements of the genre, as does Patrick Hamilton's proficient thriller, *Gaslight* (1938), but it is film that most insistently preserves the decadence of Grand Guignol.

Granta A Cambridge University student magazine from 1889 until the mid-1970s, it published early work by FORSTER, A. A. MILNE, TED HUGHES and SYLVIA PLATH. It was resurrected in 1979 under the editorship of Bill Buford as a quarterly literary magazine, publishing a range of distinguished fiction, journalism and travel writing.

Granville-Barker, Harley 1877–1946 Actor, director, playwright and scholar. Born Harley Granville Barker, he hyphenated his name in 1918. His acting work for the eccentrically single-minded Shakespearean director William Poel influenced his own productions of SHAKESPEARE in 1912–14 and his sensitive *Prefaces to Shakespeare* (1927–47). His role as Marchbanks in SHAW's *Candida* introduced a second major influence. The Barker-Vedrenne seasons at the ROYAL COURT THEATRE (1904–7) established Shaw as a major force in the theatre, while Barker's own plays, particularly *The Voysey Inheritance* (1905), *Waste* (1907) and *The Madras House* (1910), show a Shavian commitment to intelligent debate.

Grapes of Wrath, The A novel by JOHN STEINBECK, published in 1939 and awarded a PULITZER PRIZE. Forced to leave their Oklahoma farm, the Joads drive to California, which they imagine to be a land of plenty. The grandparents die on the journey and in California the Joads suffer the hard life of migrant fruit-pickers. Tom Joad joins Jim Casy, a minister turned labour orga-

nizer, and, when Casy is killed, himself kills a man in revenge. Ma Joad finally decides that Tom must leave for the good of the family. In a controversial end to the novel, Rose of Sharon, the eldest daughter, who has just given birth to a stillborn child, nurses a starving man with her own milk.

Graves, A(lfred) P(ercival) 1846–1931 Irish essayist, songwriter, poet and editor. He contributed to the Irish literary revival with anthologies of Irish poetry and song, *Irish Literary and Musical Studies* (1913) and a valuable chapter on Anglo-Irish literature in the *Cambridge History of English Literature* (1916). Though he knew little Irish and no Welsh he made good use of translations from both languages in popular works such as *A Celtic Psaltery* (1917) and *Songs of the Gael* (1925). His own poetry dealt increasingly with the heroic world of Irish myth and legend popularized by YEATS and LADY GREGORY. His lively autobiography *To Return to All That* (1930) is in part a response to *Goodbye to All That* by his son ROBERT GRAVES.

Graves, Richard 1715–1804 Novelist. He is best remembered for *The Spiritual Quixote: or, The Summer's Ramble of Mr Geoffry Wildgoose: A Comic Romance* (1773), a SATIRE in which Wildgoose sets out with the village cobbler, Jerry Tugwell, to preach the Gospel and meets his hero, George Whitefield (whom Graves had known at Oxford). Other novels, interesting for their portrayal of social conditions, are *Columella: or, The Distressed Anchoret* (1779), *Eugenius: or, Anecdotes of the Golden Vale* (1785) and *Plexippus: or, The Aspiring Plebeian* (1790). The rector of Claverton, near Bath, and a popular figure in local society, he was a friend of SHENSTONE, whom he portrayed in *Columella* and made the subject of *Recollections* (1788).

Graves, Robert (von Ranke) 1895–1985 Poet, novelist and critic. He was the son of A. P. GRAVES. The early poems in *Over the Brazier* (1916), *David and Goliath* (1916), *Fairies and Fusiliers* (1917) and EDWARD MARSH's *GEORGIAN POETRY* were dominated by his experiences in World War I. Subsequent work, gathered successively in *Poems 1914–26* (1927), *Poems 1926–30* (1931), *Poems 1938–45* (1946) and two editions of *Collected Poems* (1938 and 1975), records the development of a highly individual style, continually evolving yet always returning to classical literature and mythology for inspiration. Many of the finest poems use a plain diction, refuse public themes and concentrate on love. His poetry went hand in hand with a mass of other work. A controversial memoir, *Goodbye to All That* (1929), ends with his departure from England with his partner during this period, LAURA RIDING, for a largely expatriate life which took him to Italy, France, the USA and, most famously, Mallorca. Critical books include *A Survey of Modernist Poetry* (with Laura Riding; 1928), attacking both popular attitudes to poetry and MODERNISM in its more fashionable forms. *The White Goddess* (1948) elaborates his mythology of poetic inspiration in erudite, passionate, sometimes baffling terms. His interest in myth and classical culture also prompted, among many other books, the two most famous of his 13 novels, *I, Claudius* (1934) and *Claudius the God* (1934), and a minor classic in *The Greek Myths* (1955). *The Anger of Achilles: Homer's Iliad* (1957) is among his translations from the classics.

graveyard poets 18th-century writers, never a formal school, who found inspiration in graveyards and the contemplation of mortality. They were especially fashionable in the 1740s and 1750s but also fed the therapeutically melancholic side of ROMANTICISM. A brief selection of graveyard writing would include Parnell's 'Night-Piece on Death' (1721); Blair's *The Grave* (1743); Young's *Night Thoughts* (1742–6); James Hervey's prose *Meditations among the Tombs* (1746–7); and Gray's *Elegy Written in a Country Churchyard* (1751), the *locus classicus* of its kind.

Gravity's Rainbow A novel by Pynchon, published in 1973. A lengthy and extremely dense text, it involves more than 400 characters and concerns itself with the historical trends identifiable in American society since World War II, particularly those arising from scientific and technological discoveries. Its allusions range from classical music theory to film and comic-strip characters. The literary figures evoked include Faulkner, Dickinson, Rilke, Borges and Joyce, to whose *Ulysses* the novel has often been compared.

Gray, Alasdair 1934– Scottish novelist. He is the most prominent member of a new wave in Scottish writing. Glasgow, his home city, provides the location for *Lanark* (1981) and *1982, Janine* (1984), huge, sprawling picaresque narratives indebted to Sterne and Joyce. His shorter fiction is collected in *Unlikely Stories, Mostly* (1983). Other works include: *The Fall of Kelvin Walker* (1985); *McGrotty and Ludmilla* (1990), a short political satire issued by his own publishing imprint, the Dog and Bone Press; *Something Leather* (1990); *Poor Things* (1992); and *A History Maker* (1994).

Gray, Simon (James Holliday) 1936– Playwright. Publishing and university life make the setting for several of his plays, which sustain a flow of comedy while exploring the nature of suffering. They include *Butley* (1971), *Otherwise Engaged* (1975), *Close of Play* (1978), *Quartermain's Terms* (1981), *The Common Pursuit* (1984), *Melon* (1987) and *Hidden Laughter* (1990). *An Unnatural Pursuit* (1985) and *How's That For Telling 'Em, Fat Lady?: A Short Life in the American Theatre* (1988) describe why it is easy to lose faith in the theatre.

Gray, Thomas 1716–71 Poet. At Eton he formed a lifelong friendship with Horace Walpole which survived their quarrel during a Continental tour in 1739–41. Gray had entered Peterhouse, Cambridge, in 1734. He returned in 1742 and, though he moved to Pembroke College in 1756, was based in Cambridge for the rest of his life. The only interludes were a two-year stay in London (1759–61) researching a projected history of English poetry and several tours in England and Scotland. His second visit to the Lake District (1769), recorded in letters to Thomas Warton the younger, had a major influence on the picturesque appreciation of landscape. Other literary friends included Christopher Smart, William Mason and Conyers Middleton. In 1768 Gray was appointed Regius Professor of Modern History at Cambridge.

Gray's poetic output was slim and he never felt under pressure to publish. Youthful work included Latin verses, the *Ode to Spring, Agrippina* (a tragedy) and a translation of Locke's *Essay concerning Human Understanding* into Latin. At his mother's house in Stoke Poges he wrote the *Sonnet on the Death of Richard West*, his ode *On Adversity*, the *Ode on a Distant Prospect of Eton College* and the unfinished *Hymn to Ignorance*. In 1747 the death of Walpole's cat prompted him to the delicately comic *Ode on the Death of a Favourite Cat, Drowned in a Tub of Gold Fishes*. The *Elegy Written in a Country Churchyard*, published in 1751, marked his rise to fame and secured his posthumous reputation. Apart from a small collection, *Designs by Mr R. Bentley for*

Six Poems by Mr T. Gray (1753), which included *A Long Story* as well as the *Ode to Adversity*, he published little more. Two Pindaric odes, *Progress of Poesy* and *The Bard*, appeared in 1757, the same year Gray was offered but declined the post of Poet Laureate on the death of Cibber. *The Fatal Sisters* and *The Descent of Odin*, written in imitation of Norse and Celtic verse, appeared in a collected volume of his *Poems* (1768). In 1769 he wrote a masterful ode on the installation of the Duke of Grafton as chancellor of the University of Cambridge.

Polished and exact, Gray's verse bears witness to his wide reading, particularly in the classics. Yet his own voice is distinctive in its balance between introspection and sentiment, qualities which marked the shift from neoclassicism to the taste for the picturesque. His finest work, like the *Elegy Written in a Country Churchyard*, has a delicacy admired by the Romantic poets and still accessible today.

Great Expectations A novel by Dickens, serialized in *All the Year Round* in 1860–1 and published in volume form in 1861. Despite its melodramatic plotting and its gallery of comic characters, it is a work of sober and sustained purpose.

Philip Pirrip (Pip) describes the three stages of his 'great expectations'. He spends an orphaned childhood on the Kentish marshes with his harsh sister and her kindly blacksmith husband, Joe Gargery. When young, he helps an escaped convict, Abel Magwitch, who is soon recaptured. Later he is summoned to Satis House, where Miss Havisham has lived in seclusion since being jilted by her fiancé, and becomes devoted to her ward, the coldhearted Estella. The lawyer Jaggers arrives with news that Pip has been awarded a generous allowance, which he mistakenly assumes to come from Miss Havisham. In London he lives with Herbert Pocket and falls into extravagant ways in the attempt to become a gentleman. Magwitch reappears and announces that he is Pip's benefactor. Pip's attempt to get him safely out of the country fails and Magwitch dies in prison. Estella, dramatically revealed as Magwitch's daughter, marries an upper-class lout, Bentley Drummle, who mistreats her before his early death. Pip, learning both loyalty and humility from his experiences, meets Estella again some years later. In the original ending the two remain separate, but Dickens altered it to provide a conventionally happy ending.

Great Gatsby, The A novel by F. Scott Fitzgerald, published in 1925. The narrator, Nick Carraway, is fascinated by Jay Gatsby, his neighbour in West Egg, Long Island, who makes his mansion the scene of extravagant nightly parties. Many of those who attend are uninvited and none seem to know the truth about Gatsby's past or the source of his wealth. Nick learns that Gatsby is obsessed with winning back Daisy, whom he had loved before she married the rich but boring Tom Buchanan. The tensions in the group of characters reach a climax when Daisy, driving Gatsby's car, accidentally runs over Tom's mistress Myrtle Wilson. Tom tells Myrtle's husband that Gatsby was the driver, and Wilson kills Gatsby before committing suicide. Nick is left to piece together Gatsby's past and to arrange the funeral, which hardly anyone attends.

Great Hoggarty Diamond, The A story by Thackeray, published in *Fraser's Magazine* in 1841. The gift of the Diamond from his aunt involves Samuel Titmarsh with swindlers, shady dealings and misfortunes, from which his wife rescues him.

Greeley, Horace 1811–72 American journalist. He founded the New York *Tribune*, which he edited from 1841 until his death. He was chosen as the Democratic presidential candidate in 1872 but was defeated by Ulysses S. Grant. His writings include: *Glances at Europe* (1851) and *An Overland Journey* (1860), travel books; *The American Conflict* (1864–6), an important contemporary history of the Civil War; and *Recollections of a Busy Life* (1868), an autobiography.

Green, Henry [Yorke, Henry Vincent] 1905–73 Novelist. While still at Oxford he attracted attention with his first novel, *Blindness* (1926). His work is distinguished by elegant impressionist prose, oblique dialogue, rapid cutting from scene to scene, and a vein of poetry most strongly evident in his second novel, *Living* (1929). This is set in the sort of engineering works he knew well from his own work as foundryman, engineer and managing director of his family's company in Birmingham. *Party Going* (1939) portrays an upper-class group with wealth but without responsibility. Other works include *Caught* (1943), about the Auxiliary Fire Service in World War II, *Loving* (1945), set in a remote castle in Ireland, *Back* (1946), *Concluding* (1948), *Nothing* (1950) and *Doting* (1952). Green also wrote *Pack My Bag: A Self Portrait* (1940).

Green, John Richard 1837–83 Historian. His appointment as librarian of Lambeth Palace in 1869 gave him the opportunity for research. *A Short History of the English People* (1873; expanded as *A History of the English People*, 1877–80) proved the most popular history since MACAULAY's. Green also wrote a collection of essays, *Stray Studies from England and Italy* (1876), and, with the help of his wife, Alice Stopford Green, *The Making of England* (1881) and *The Conquest of England* (1883). He was a frequent contributor to THE SATURDAY REVIEW.

Green, Matthew 1696–1737 Poet. *The Spleen* (1737) discusses boredom or depression and offers suggestions for its prevention and cure.

Green, Paul (Eliot) 1894–1981 American playwright. He began with realistic folk-plays about blacks and poor whites in his native North Carolina. The short pieces in *Lonesome Road* (1926) included *White Dresses* (1923) and a play expanded as *In Abraham's Bosom* (1926), an angry story of persecution and lynching. *The House of Connelly: A Drama of the Old South and the New* (1931), produced by the GROUP THEATRE, deals with the deteriorating fortunes of a white landowning family. *Tread the Green Grass* (1932) is one of several 'symphonic dramas' using dance and music, while *Johnny Johnson* (1936) is an anti-war musical with a score by Kurt Weill. *Hymn to the Rising Sun* (1936) exposes state penitentiaries. Green later wrote pageant-dramas about American history, dramatized RICHARD WRIGHT's NATIVE SON (1941) and wrote 11 screenplays, including an adaptation of John Howard Griffith's *Black Like Me* (1964).

Green, Thomas Hill 1836–82 Philosopher. His principal work was *Prolegomena to Ethics* (1883), though he had earlier written extended introductions to an edition of DAVID HUME's TREATISE OF HUMAN NATURE in 1874, presenting detailed criticisms of LOCKE, BERKELEY and HUME, and arguing that neither JOHN STUART MILL nor HERBERT SPENCER had advanced beyond Hume. Green became White's Professor of Moral Philosophy at Oxford in 1878.

Green Carnation, The See HICHENS, ROBERT.

Green Mansions: *A Romance of the Tropical Forest* A novel by W. H. HUDSON, published in 1904. Abel Guevez de Argensola (Mr Abel), a political refugee, settles in the Venezuelan jungle (the 'green mansions') with the Indian tribe of his friend Runi. He falls in love with Rima, a girl whose spirit has strong affinities with that of the forest itself, and sets out with her grandfather, Nuflo, to try to locate Rima's mother. They return to discover that the Indians have destroyed Rima's hut and burnt her to death. Abel revenges himself by attacking the Indians' village and slaying Runi. He returns to civilization with Rima's ashes. The Hudson Memorial in Hyde Park presents a sculpture of Rima by Sir Jacob Epstein, commissioned in 1925.

Greenaway, Kate 1846–1901 Illustrator and writer of CHILDREN'S LITERATURE. Her first major success was *Under the Window* (1879), printed in colour and selling over 100,000 copies. Her pictures of demure little girls, accompanied by her own verses, helped popularize a particular fashion for high-waisted, frilly dresses and sun-bonnets. Many of her other best-sellers remain in print today. Particularly good are her alphabet book, *A Apple Pie* (1886), and *Mother Goose: or, The Old Nursery Rhymes* (1881), although her essentially decorative style of drawing was unequal to the demands of the more vigorous nursery rhymes.

Greene, (Henry) Graham 1904–91 Novelist, short-story writer, playwright, travel writer, essayist and critic. His preoccupation with pursuit, guilt, treachery and failure is already apparent in his first novel, *The Man Within* (1929), though popular success did not come until *Stamboul Train* (1932), a more topical thriller and the first of the novels which he termed 'entertainments'. These continued with *It's a Battlefield* (1934), *England Made Me* (1935), *A Gun for Sale* (1936), *The Confidential Agent* (1939), *Loser Takes All* (1955) and *Our Man in Havana* (1958). A convert to Catholicism in 1926, he tackled explicitly Catholic themes in BRIGHTON ROCK (1938), THE POWER AND THE GLORY (1940), THE HEART OF THE MATTER (1948), *The End of the Affair* (1951) and THE QUIET AMERICAN (1955). Four more novels deal with the committed and the uncommitted in a political context: *A Burnt-Out Case* (1961), set in the Belgian Congo; *The Comedians* (1966), in Haiti; *The Honorary Consul* (1973), in Argentina; and *The Human Factor* (1978), in the underworld of spies. Later novels include *Doctor Fischer of Geneva* (1980) and *The Captain and the Enemy* (1989). *Travels with My Aunt* (1969) and *Monsignor Quixote* (1982) are ventures into comedy. His short stories appeared in *The Basement Room and Other Stories* (1935), *Nineteen Stories* (1947), *Twenty-One Stories* (1954), *May We Borrow Your Husband?* (1967) and *The Last Word* (1990).

Two travel books – *Journey without Maps* (1936), about Liberia, and *The Lawless Roads* (1939), about the visit to Mexico which also prompted *The Power and the Glory* – stand out from the mass of his other work. Particularly memorable, too, is the screenplay for Carol Reed's *The Third Man* (1949). *A Sort of Life* (1971) and *Ways of Escape* (1980) are autobiographical.

Greene, Robert c. 1558–92 Pamphleteer and playwright. Associated with the UNIVERSITY WITS and particularly with PEELE, he led a dissipated life charted in autobiographical pamphlets ranging from the superior journalism of *The Art of Conny-Catching* (1591) to the self-excoriating penitence of *Greene's Groatsworth of Wit, Bought with a Million of Repentance* (1592), famous for its attack on SHAKESPEARE. Early pamphlets imitating LYLY culminated in his continuation of EUPHUES in *Euphues, His Censure of Philautus* (1587). Prose romances modelled on SIDNEY's *ARCADIA* included *Pandosto* (1588), on which Shakespeare based *THE WINTER'S TALE*, and *Menaphon* (1589), which contains the lyric, 'Weep not, my wanton'. Of his surviving plays, the earliest is *Alphonsus, King of Aragon* (c. 1587), a shameless imitation of MARLOWE, and the best *FRIAR BACON AND FRIAR BUNGAY* (c. 1589). A *Looking-Glass for London and England* (c. 1590), written with LODGE, is a satirical treatment of material handled more lightheartedly in Greene's pamphlets. *James the Fourth* (c. 1591) combines the chronicle play with fairy fantasy.

Greenwood, Walter 1903–74 Novelist. His first novel and only commercial success was *Love on the Dole* (1933), about the misfortunes of a Lancashire family, the Hardcastles, during the Depression. It was dramatized (1934) and filmed (1941). *There was a Time* (1967) is Greenwood's autobiography.

Greg, Sir W(alter) W(ilson) 1875–1959 Scholar. A private income enabled him to devote his life to bibliography and textual criticism, although he was librarian at Trinity College, Cambridge, in 1907–13. In 1906 he founded the Malone Society for the reproduction of early English plays (i.e. pre-1640), acting as general editor until 1939, when he succeeded E. K. CHAMBERS as president. As well as editions of *SIR THOMAS MORE* (1911) and other plays, he published *Dramatic Documents from the Elizabethan Playhouses* (1931) and *English Literary Autographs 1550–1650* (1925–32). The great task of his later years was *A Bibliography of the English Printed Drama to the Restoration* (1939–59); his major editorial achievement was the two texts of MARLOWE's *DOCTOR FAUSTUS* (1950).

Gregory, Lady (Isabella) Augusta 1852–1932 Playwright. Her friendship with YEATS, a frequent visitor to her Coole Park estate, led to the foundation of the Irish Literary Theatre in 1899 and to the renaissance of Irish drama at the ABBEY THEATRE from 1904. She was one of the Abbey's most prolific playwrights, as well as director, occasional stage manager and frequent adviser. Her one-act plays about the Irish peasantry include *Spreading the News* (1904), *The Rising of the Mood* (1906), the tragedy *The Gaol Gate* (1906) and *The Workhouse Ward* (1908). Of her Irish folk-history plays, the best are *The White Cockade* (1905), *The Canavans* (1906) and *The Deliverer* (1911). *Hyacinth Halvey* (1906) is a contemporary comedy that shares the affectionate patriotism of her adaptations of Molière, published in *The Kiltartan Molière* (1910). *Our Irish Theatre* (1913) and *Lady Gregory's Journals 1916–30* (1946) are valuable records.

Gregory, Horace (Victor) 1898–1982 American poet. His early verse was strongly influenced by Marxism but he later angered other left-wing writers by asserting that art should be apolitical. Throughout his career, however, he remained concerned with the plight of the poor and dispossessed. Volumes include *Collected Poems* (1964) and *Another Look* (1976). With his wife, MARYA ZATURENSKA, he edited various poetry anthologies and wrote *A History of American Poetry 1900–1940* (1946).

Grenfell, Julian (Henry Francis) 1888–1915 Poet. He is usually remembered for 'Into Battle', published in *The Times* on the day he was killed in May 1915. Grenfell's output was small and his poems are usually found in anthologies, such as T. STURGE MOORE's *Some Soldier Poets* (1919).

Greville, Charles Cavendish Fulke 1794–1865 Politician. Clerk to the Council in 1821–59 and an intimate of Wellington and Palmerston, he knew every politician of account in his lifetime and put his knowledge superbly to use in *The Greville Memoirs* (originally published in 1874–87; re-edited in 1938). His portraits of famous contemporaries are indispensable to students of English history and politics. He also wrote *The Past and Present Policy of England to Ireland* (1845), advocating a more liberal policy for religious endowments.

Greville, Sir Fulke, 1st Baron Brooke 1554–1628 Courtier, poet and playwright. He enjoyed a long and distinguished career under both Elizabeth and James I. None of his work was published in his lifetime. The most famous, probably written between 1610 and 1614 and first published in 1652, is a biography of SIR PHILIP SIDNEY, his close friend and exact contemporary. (Other friends included fellow members of the AREOPAGUS: DANIEL, BACON, CAMDEN and EDWARD COKE.) The sequence of songs and SONNETS called *Caelica* contains love poems as well as religious and philosophical verses. It was first published in 1633, together with two tragedies, *Alaham* and *Mustapha*. A third, on Antony and Cleopatra, reflected his feelings about the fall of his friend the Earl of Essex, but Greville destroyed it. He also wrote verse treatises on political subjects.

Grey, (Pearl) Zane 1872–1939 American novelist. In 60 books, which sold over 15 million copies in his lifetime, he developed the Western novel in the tradition of OWEN WISTER. *Riders of the Purple Sage* (1912), *To the Last Man* (1922), *Nevada* (1928), *Wild Horse Mesa* (1928) and *Code of the West* (1934) present the West as a moral landscape which destroys or redeems characters according to their response to its violent code. Over 100 films were based on his stories.

Grierson, Sir Herbert J(ohn) C(lifford) 1866–1960 Scholar and critic. A professor at Aberdeen and then Edinburgh, he produced an edition of DONNE's poetry (1912) and an anthology of *Metaphysical Lyrics and Poems of the Seventeenth Century* (1921). His introduction prompted T. S. ELIOT and others to a major reassessment of the METAPHYSICAL POETS. He also co-edited SIR WALTER SCOTT's letters (1932–7) and wrote his biography (1938).

Grieve, Christopher Murray See MACDIARMID, HUGH.

Griffin, Gerald 1803–40 Novelist and poet. The fame of his novel, *The Collegians* (1829), was eclipsed by BOUCICAULT, who dramatized it as *THE COLLEEN BAWN* (1860). It also inspired an opera, *The Lily of Killarney* (1863), by Julius Benedict.

Griffiths, Trevor 1935– Playwright. He was born and educated in Manchester. His debate plays, which reveal his training in Marxist dialectic, include *Occupations* (1970), *Sam, Sam* (1972), *Comedians* (1975), *The Party* (1973) and *The Gulf between Us* (1992). His work for TV includes the series *Bill Brand* (1976) and *Fatherland* (1986).

Grigson, Geoffrey (Edward Harvey) 1905–85 Poet and man of letters. His poetry is overshadowed by his work as founder and editor of an influential modernist periodical, *New Verse* (1933–9), and his sharp-tongued literary journalism. His austere early poetry, in *Several Observations: Thirty-Five Poems* (1939), *Under the Cliff* (1943) and *The Isles of Scilly* (1946), gave way to more emotional work, which includes a sequence of love-poems, *Legenda Suecana* (1953), *Collected Poems 1963–1980* (1982) and *Montaigne's Tree* (1984). He wrote an autobiography, *The Crest on the Silver* (1950), and many books on nature, literature and art, as well as editing influential selections of JOHN CLARE and WILLIAM BARNES.

Grimald, Nicholas 1519–62 Translator and poet. His main significance lies in the 40 poems he contributed to *TOTTEL'S MISCELLANY*, which he may have edited. He also translated Cicero's *De officiis* (?1556), made a Latin paraphrase of Virgil's *Georgics* (1591) and wrote two Latin plays, *Christus redivivus* (1543), about the Resurrection, and *Archipropheta* (1548), about John the Baptist.

Grocyn, William ?1446–1519 Humanist. He introduced the study of Greek at Oxford, belonged to the circle surrounding ERASMUS and THOMAS MORE, his student, and preached at St Paul's at the invitation of JOHN COLET. His only known works are a letter to the Venetian printer Aldus Manutius, prefaced to LINACRE's *Sphaera Procli* (*c.* 1499), and an EPIGRAM on a lady who threw a snowball at him.

Grose, Francis ?1731–91 Antiquary and draughtsman. He was best known for the 'tinted drawings, chiefly of architectural remains' in his *Antiquities of England and Wales* (1773–87), *The Antiquities of Scotland* (1789–91) and the posthumous *Antiquities of Ireland* (1791–5). *Essays on Gothic Architecture* (1800) contained work by, among others, Grose and THOMAS WARTON THE YOUNGER. Armour, the art of caricature, local proverbs and superstitions all caught the interest of this 'antiquarian Falstaff'. He also pioneered the lexicography of slang in *A Classical Dictionary of the Vulgar Tongue* (1785), many times reprinted and re-edited, notably as *Lexicon Balatronicum: A Dictionary of Buckish Slang, University Wit and Pickpocket Eloquence* (1811) and in an edition by PIERCE EGAN (1823).

Grosseteste, Robert ?1167–1253 Churchman and scholar. Regarded by contemporaries as one of 'the greatest clerics in the world', he studied at Paris and Oxford (where he was rector of the Franciscans and perhaps the university's first chancellor) before becoming a reforming Bishop of Lincoln in 1235. An equally energetic writer, Grosseteste produced letters, sermons, biblical and Aristotelian commentaries, translations from the Greek, scientific treatises and a long Anglo-Norman allegorical poem on the history of salvation from the Fall of Adam to the Resurrection of Christ. Matthew Paris's *Chronicle* contains fascinating anecdotes of his life.

Grossmith, George 1847–1912 and **Grossmith, Weedon** 1854–1919 Joint authors of *THE DIARY OF A NOBODY* (1892), which Weedon also illustrated. George started his career as a police court reporter for *The Times*, Weedon as an artist. Both later became actors, George creating many of the most famous baritone *buffo* roles in GILBERT and Sullivan's SAVOY OPERAS. Weedon also wrote a novel, *A Woman with a History* (1896), and several plays, of which the most successful was *The Night of the Party* (1901). George published two volumes of memoirs, *Reminiscences of a Clown* (1888) and *Piano and I* (1910).

Grote, George 1794–1871 Historian. After retiring from Parliament and banking he devoted himself to completing his 12-volume *History of Greece* (1845–6), which surpassed a similar work by CONNOP THIRLWALL, his friend from Charterhouse days. He wrote two works on Greek philosophy, *Plato and the Other Companions of Sokrates* (1865) and *Aristotle* (1872).

Group, The An informal circle of poets which flourished from the mid-1950s until 1965 under the impetus of HOBSBAUM and LUCIE-SMITH, who edited *A Group Anthology* (1963). Members included PETER PORTER, MACBETH, REDGROVE and BROWNJOHN. The participants' critical perspective demanded poems that were immediately and easily understood, and poems were accordingly written to be read aloud, giving attention to the possibilities of the spoken voice. From 1965, under the influence of MARTIN BELL, the Group transmuted into the Poets' Workshop.

Group of Noble Dames, A Ten short stories by HARDY, collected in 1891. Largely romantic and melodramatic, they are derived from Dorset local history and set in various mansions and castles. Hardy rewrote and bowdlerized a good deal in gathering them together.

Group Theatre, The A New York theatrical organization founded in 1931 by a group including Lee Strasberg, Harold Clurman and Cheryl Crawford. They were committed to the stage as a forum for the open discussion of political and social issues. Before its demise in 1940, the Group helped to launch the careers of CLIFFORD ODETS and MARC BLITZSTEIN.

Grove, Frederick Philip 1871–1948 Canadian novelist and essayist. Born in Russia and brought up in Europe, he eventually became a teacher in Manitoba. Written despite considerable hardship, *Over Prairie Trails* (1922), *The Turn of the Year* (1923) and the powerful and controversial *Settlers of the Marsh* (1925) established him as Canada's first accomplished exponent of realism. His later works were *A Search for America* (1927), *Our Daily Bread* (1928), *It Needs to be Said* (a volume of essays; 1929), *The Yoke of Life* (1930), *Fruits of the Earth* (1933), *Two Generations* (1939), *The Master of the Mill* (1944) and *Consider Her Ways* (1946). *In Search of Myself* (1946) is an autobiography. 'Felix Powell's Career' and 'The Seasons', which he thought his best work, were unfinished at his death.

Grub Street A term for busy hack writers and impoverished scribblers on the fringes of the professional literary industry, derived from an actual street in Moorfields which no longer exists. It is particularly applied to certain categories of minor Renaissance and Augustan literature – almanacs, verses, pamphlets, BROADSIDES – of indifferent quality. Pat Rogers's *Grub Street* (1972) is a definitive study.

Grundy, Sydney 1848–1914 Playwright. His normal practice was to adapt, and if necessary clean up, French plays. Bowdlerized and reshaped versions of the works of Alexandre Dumas, *père* – *A Marriage of Convenience* (1897), *The Silver Key* (1897), *The Musketeers* (1898), *The Black Tulip* (1899) – are typical, as is his best-known work, *A Pair of Spectacles* (1890), from *Les Petits Oiseaux* by Labiche and Delacour. An outspoken opponent of the 'demoralizing' Ibsen, he nevertheless provided Lillie Langtry with a *succès de scandale* in *The Degenerates* (1899), and played with fire in *A Fool's Paradise* (1889), a response to the Maybrick trial, and *Slaves of the Ring* (1894), about Tristan and Isolde.

Gryll Grange PEACOCK's last novel, published in 1860–1. The setting is a house party held at the edge of the New Forest. The host, Mr Gryll, personifies the England of the immediate rosy past, as it exists in the minds of those who dislike the present. Taking part in the conversations which make up much of the book are: Dr Opimian, an amiable clergyman; Mr Falconer, a romantic without delusions about reforming mankind; and Miss Ilex, an old maid of real charm.

Guardian, The A daily journal of essays, letters and news, founded and mainly edited by RICHARD STEELE during its short life from March to October 1713. ADDISON, who took over for July, restored some of the political neutrality which in Steele's hands had given way to attacks on the Tory *EXAMINER*. The authorship of the 175 numbers has still not been satisfactorily established but, apart from Addison and Steele, contributors included: TICKELL, who wrote a series of papers on PASTORAL; POPE, who wrote at least eight issues, the most famous (No. 40) being an ironic paean on the pastorals of AMBROSE PHILIPS; BERKELEY; and GAY.

Guare, John 1938– American playwright. Major works since he gained recognition with *Muzeeka* (1968) and *The House of Blue Leaves* (1970) include *Rich and Famous* (1974), *The Landscape of the Body* (1977), *Bosoms and Neglect* (1979) and his most successful play, *Six Degrees of Separation* (1990). *Lydie Breeze* (1982), *Gardenia* (1982) and *Women and Water* (1984–5) belong to a projected tetralogy set in 19th-century New England. Though some critics have found his work too cerebral, few have failed to praise the lyrical and theatrical use of language. His screenplay for Louis Malle's *Atlantic City* (1981) shows his taste for SATIRE.

Guest, Lady Charlotte See CELTIC REVIVAL and *MABINOGION, THE.*

Guest, Edwin 1800–80 Historian and philologist. He passed his career at Gonville and Caius College, Cambridge, of which he became master in 1852. With THOMAS ARNOLD, A. P. STANLEY and CONNOP THIRLWALL he was a founder of the Philological Society in 1842. He wrote *A History of English Rhythms* (1838) and papers on philology and Romano-British history.

Guilpin, Everard *fl.* 1595–1600 Satirist. *Skialetheia* (1598), a collection of EPIGRAMS, displays intimate knowledge of contemporary theatre.

Gulliver's Travels *(Travels into Several Remote Nations of the World, in Four Parts, by Lemuel Gulliver* ...*)* A prose SATIRE by SWIFT, published in 1726.

In Book I Lemuel Gulliver, the ship's surgeon who narrates the story, is shipwrecked on the island of Lilliput, where he is taken prisoner by the population, who are only six inches tall. The Emperor and his court offer a physical counterpart to the small-minded attitudes underlying human behaviour, for they are suspicious, deceitful and petty. There are specific satires on contemporary topics such as religious disputes (which end an egg should be opened) and in-fighting at court (rope-dancing). In Book II Gulliver finds himself stranded in Brobdingnag, a kingdom where the gigantic inhabitants are twelve times taller than himself. His own attitudes and pomposity are exposed when, after a series of undignified adventures, he boasts to the King about the marvels of European civilization, such as gunpowder and the judicial system.

Book III, the last to be written, is less unified and has always held least appeal. Gulliver visits Laputa, a flying island where the nobles quite literally have their heads in the clouds. So immersed are they in impractical theories of knowledge that nothing works properly. He visits nearby Lagado and its Academy (a satire on the Royal Society), full of 'projectors' working on outlandish scientific schemes such as breeding sheep with no wool and extracting sunbeams from cucumbers. Gulliver visits Glubbdubrib, the Island of Sorcerers, where famous historical figures are summoned from the past, and meets the terrifying race of immortals, the Struldbruggs, whose fate is to become increasingly decrepit. Book IV is perhaps the most intellectual in concept, describing the country of the Houyhnhnms, coldly rational horse-like creatures who govern their nature dispassionately, and keep in subservience the filthy brutes called Yahoos, in whom Gulliver finds an unwelcome resemblance to himself. The two races represent the extremes of human potential, bestial physicality and remote rationality. Gulliver returns home thoroughly imbalanced, and passes most of his time in the stable, preferring the company of his horse to that of his family.

Gulliver's Travels is a seriously reductive work, a satire on pride and folly. Gulliver himself is a human ambassador: gullible, snobbish and servile, holding ridiculous yet common opinions. The book is also lastingly funny, the hero's antics arising entertainingly from the bizarre proportions of his various surroundings. This element of the fantastic has maintained the book's appeal for children in many languages.

Gunn, Mrs Aeneas 1870–1961 Australian novelist. Out of her brief exposure to the outback in the Northern Territory she created two popular books, *The Little Black Princess* (1905) and *We of the Never Never* (1908), presenting an idealized picture of Aboriginal life and of relations between the white farmers and the native population.

Gunn, Neil M(iller) 1891–1973 Scottish novelist. A friend of HUGH MACDIARMID, he was a socialist involved in the politics of nationalism. Like many of his novels, *Highland River* (1937) and *Morning Tide* (1930) are set in his native Highlands. *Sun Circle* (1933) deals with the Viking invasion, *Butcher's Broom* (1934) with the Highland Clearances, and *The Silver Darlings* (1941), widely considered his best novel, with the aftermath of the Clearances. After the pastoral idyll of *Young Art and Old Hector* (1942) he responded to the dangers of fascism with *The Green Isle of the Great Deep* (1944), in which Art and Hector find their way to a dystopian world. His later fiction culminates in a more 'metaphysical' vision of existence in *The Well at the World's End* (1951). He also produced essays, short stories, travel writings and an autobiography, *The Atom of Delight* (1956).

Gunn, Thom(son) (William) 1929– Poet. The tight verse forms and anti-romanticism of *Fighting Terms* (1954) identified him with the MOVEMENT, though he lacked its reductive IRONY. Subsequent collections, published after he moved to the USA, and not always well received, testify to a relentless, unpredictable development. They include: *The Sense of Movement* (1957); *My Sad Captains* (1961); *Touch* (1967); *Moly* (1971); *Jack Straw's Castle* (1976); *Selected Poems 1950–1975* (1979); *The Passages of Joy* (1982), relaxed, anecdotal and open about his homosexuality; and *The Man with the Night Sweats* (1992), ending with a series of poems about the death of friends from AIDS. *Collected Poems* appeared in 1994. He has also published *The Occasions of Poetry: Essays in Criticism and Autobiography* (1982) and acknowledged his roots in the 16th and 17th centuries by editions of FULKE GREVILLE (1968) and JONSON (1974).

Gurney, Ivor (Bertie) 1890–1937 Poet and composer. *Severn and Somme* (1917) and *War's Embers* (1919) deal with the countryside of his native Gloucestershire (in, for example, 'Only the Wanderer') and his experience of World War I. In 1922 Gurney was committed to the City of London Mental Hospital, Kent, where he remained for the rest of his life, still writing and composing. The poems written in hospital were published in selections by BLUNDEN (1954) and Leonard Clark (1973) and in P. J. KAVANAGH's edition of the *Collected Poems* (1982). They are uneven, apparently lacking in control but often recovering vision and language. Gurney set six of EDWARD THOMAS's poems to music in *Lights Out* (1918–25) and composed two cycles on poems by A. E. HOUSMAN, *Ludlow and Teme* and *The Western Playland* (both 1919).

Gustafson, Ralph 1909– Canadian poet. The conventional romantic verse which he wrote in Britain during the 1930s yielded to the new sardonic style he found in New York, apparent in *Flight into Darkness* (1944). Since his return to Canada in 1960 his work, especially that dealing with his travel experiences, has often been confessional. It includes *Rivers among Rocks* (1960), *Rocky Mountain Poems* (1960), *Sift in an Hourglass* (1966), *Ixion's Wheel* (1969), *Corners in the Glass* (1977), *Soviet Poems* (1978), *Conflicts of Spring* (1981) and *The Celestial Corkscrew and Other Strategies* (1988). *The Moment is All* (1983) is a selection of his verse from 1944 to 1983. Gustafson has also edited several anthologies, including *The Penguin Book of Canadian Verse* (1958, revised 1967).

Guthlac Two Old English poems describe the life of the hermit and saint who died at Crowland in 714 or 715. *Guthlac A* was probably written during his life or shortly after his death; *Guthlac B* is based on the Latin *Vita Guthlaci* by Felix of Crowland.

Guy Mannering A novel by SIR WALTER SCOTT, published in 1815. It is set in the 18th century. The title notwithstanding, it tells the story of Harry Bertram, dispossessed of his estate of Ellangowan by the lawyer Glossin. Serving with the army in India, he falls in love with Julia, the daughter of his colonel, Guy Mannering. A misunderstanding between the two men leads to a duel in which Harry is left for dead. On his journey to Ellangowan he meets the Lowland farmer Dandy Dinmont and the gypsy Meg Merrilies, who help frustrate Glossin's murderous schemes. The novel ends happily with Harry regaining his inheritance and Guy Mannering's good opinion, thus leaving the way clear for his marriage to Julia.

Guy of Warwick An early 14th-century VERSE ROMANCE, ultimately derived from an Anglo-Norman romance (*c.* 1232–42) rendered several times into Middle English. It resembles *BEVIS OF HAMPTON* in its popular tone and its incident-packed plot. After an adventurous career abroad, Guy returns home to marry Felice, who had originally rejected him because of his lowly status; he soon leaves again, on a pilgrimage of atonement for his life as a warrior and returns disguised as a hermit, revealing himself to Felice shortly before his death. The poem also describes the adventures of Guy's son Reinbrun, stolen by pirates at the age of seven, and the steward who searches for him.

Habington, William 1605–54 Poet. *Castara*, a book of verse celebrating his marriage to Lucy Herbert, first appeared in 1634. Later editions (1635, 1640) added an ELEGY on a friend and religious verse. With his father, Thomas, he also wrote *The History of Edward the Fourth* (1640), *Observations upon History* (1641) and a play, *The Queen of Aragon* (1640).

Hadrian the Seventh See ROLFE, FREDERICK WILLIAM.

Haggard, Sir **Henry Rider** 1856–1925 Novelist and agricultural reformer. Born into the Norfolk squirearchy, he joined the colonial service as personal aide to Sir Henry Bulwer, the designated Lieutenant-Governor of Natal. His two periods of residence in South Africa (1875–9 and 1880–1) convinced him of British imperial responsibility. He was distracted from his study of the law by the runaway success of *KING SOLOMON'S MINES* (1885), *ALLAN QUATERMAIN* (1887) and *SHE: A HISTORY OF ADVENTURE* (1887). They established him as co-founder, with ROBERT LOUIS STEVENSON, of a new 'school of romance' which was praised as a healthy antidote to analytic fiction and NATURALISM. Haggard's fascination with Zulu culture continued in *Nada the Lily* (1892) and a trilogy, *Marie* (1912), *Child of Storm* (1913) and *Finished* (1917). By no means simply paternalist or racist, his versions of the 'primitive' draw on a considerable knowledge of history, tradition and mythographic theory, probably encouraged by his friendship with ANDREW LANG, with whom he collaborated in *The World's Desire* (1890). Apart from his African romances, his best works are *Eric Brighteyes* (1891), a recreation of the spirit of the Icelandic sagas, and *Montezuma's Daughter* (1893), a version of Cortes's conquest of Mexico. Haggard's experience farming his wife's Norfolk estate prompted *A Farmer's Year* (1899) and, more importantly, *Rural England* (1902), a survey of agricultural decline which brought him into contact with HARDY.

Hakluyt, Richard ?1552–1616 Historian and travel-writer. In publishing and collecting accounts of voyages he deserved DRAYTON's epithet 'industrious'. *Divers Voyages Touching the Discovery of America* was published in 1582 and a translation from the French, *A Notable History concerning Four Voyages Made by Certain French Captains into Florida*, in 1587. In support of RALEIGH's plan for colonizing Virginia he wrote *A Discourse concerning the Western Planting* in 1584, although it was not printed until 1831. His major work, *The Principal Navigations, Voyages and Discoveries of the English Nation* (1589), was enlarged to three volumes in 1598–1600 and was continued after his death by PURCHAS. As well as containing information useful to his contemporaries, Hakluyt's *Voyages* are full of adventurous stories: Cabot's discovery of Hudson Bay, Drake's raid on Cadiz and the last fight of the *Revenge* under Sir Richard Grenville. Hakluyt also corresponded with the mapmakers Ortelius and Mercator, gave information to the newly founded East India Company, delivered public lectures on exploration and is regarded as the first professor of modern geography at Oxford.

Haldane, J(ohn) B(urdon) S(anderson) 1892–1964 Writer on science. A biochemist and geneticist, he taught at Oxford, Cambridge and London before emigrating to India in 1957. His strictly scientific works include *Enzymes* (1930) and *The Causes of Evolution* (1932). He is better known for his imaginative speculations about the future in *Possible Worlds* (1927), which influenced HUXLEY's *BRAVE NEW WORLD*, and for the active commitment to Marxism expressed in *The Marxist Philosophy and the Sciences* (1938), *Science and Everyday Life* (1939) and *Everything Has a History* (1951). He also wrote a collection of children's stories, *My Friend Mr Leakey* (1937).

Hale, Sir **Matthew** 1609–76 Judicial writer. Successively a judge in the Court of Common Pleas (1654), Baron of the Exchequer (1660) and Chief Justice of the King's Bench (1671), he is best known as a writer for his *History of the Common Law in England* (1713). GILBERT BURNET wrote his biography.

Hale, Sarah 1788–1879 American humanitarian. She edited *The Ladies' Magazine* in 1828–37 and *Godey's Lady's Book* for the next 40 years. Her massive *Women's Record* (1853; expanded 1855 and 1870) details the achievements of over 1500 women. By no means a radical feminist, she was a forceful advocate of education for women, as well as child welfare. Her novel *Northwood: A Tale of New England* (1827) attacked slavery. Her short stories were collected in *Sketches of American Character* (1829).

Hales, John 1584–1656 Scholar and divine. 'One of the greatest scholars in Europe', according to CLARENDON, he opposed both the coercion of Rome and the extremism of Calvinism, contending that guidance of Scripture was the rightful way for each individual. His sermons and tracts were collected by JOHN PEARSON as *Golden Remains* (1659).

Haliburton, Thomas Chandler 1796–1865 Canadian satirist and humorist. His 'Sam Slick' papers, observations by a shrewd itinerant clockmaker, were collected as *The Clockmaker: or, the Sayings and Doings of Samuel Slick* (1837) and *The Attaché: or, Sam Slick in England* (1843–4). They influenced the American homespun philosophy and frontier humour practised by ARTEMUS WARD, TWAIN and JOSH BILLINGS. Among other titles are *The Letter Bag of the Great Western: or, Life in a Steamer* (1840) and *The Old Judge: or, Life in a Colony* (1849). A judge of the supreme court of Nova Scotia, Haliburton retired to England in 1856.

Hall [née Fielding], Anna Maria 1800–81 Irish novelist. She was married to SAMUEL CARTER HALL. Her most successful works were delicate and humorous portraits of Irish life, among them *Sketches of Irish Character* (1829), *Lights and Shadows of Irish Life* (1838), *Marian* (1839) and *The White Boy* (1845).

Hall, Edward ?1498–1547 Historian. *The Union of the Two Noble and Illustre Families of Lancaster and York* (1542) traced a providential pattern supporting the Tudor interpretation of English history. It was a source for HOLINSHED and SHAKESPEARE.

Hall, John 1627–56 Essayist, poet and translator. He earned praise from HERRICK, HENRY MORE and THOMAS HOBBES in the course of his short career. His work included a book of lively essays, *Horae vacivae* (1646), *Poems* (1647) and the first English translation of Longinus. *An Humble Motion to the Parliament of England concerning the Advancement of Learning: and Reformation of the Universities* was written when he was 22.

Hall, Joseph 1574–1656 Satirist and divine. The verse SATIRES in *Virgidemiarum* (1597 and 1598) are, with those of DONNE, among the first in English to follow classical models. Hall also wrote a prose satire, *Mundus alter et idem* (1605), translated into English by J. Healey (1609). His religious writings include devotional works, notably *Meditations and Vows* (1605), and *Episcopacy by Divine Right, Asserted by J. H.* (1641), a reply to SMECTYMNUUS which brought him into conflict with MILTON. Hall was successively Bishop of Exeter and Bishop of Norwich, but was among 13 bishops imprisoned by Parliament in 1642 and was evicted from his palace in 1647.

Hall, (Marguerite) Radclyffe 1886–1943 Novelist and poet. She is chiefly known for her novel, *The Well of Loneliness* (1928), a sympathetic study of lesbianism which was successfully prosecuted for obscenity. It has since been frequently reprinted. Later works include *The Master of the House* (1932), *The Sixth Beatitude* (1936) and a volume of short stories, *Miss Ogilvie Finds Herself* (1934).

Hall, Samuel Carter 1800–89 Journalist and art critic. He was founder and editor of *The Art Journal*, author of *A Book of Memoirs of Great Men and Women* (1871) and co-author (with his wife ANNA MARIA HALL) of several volumes, including *Ireland: Its Scenery, Character etc.* (1841–3).

Hallam, Arthur Henry 1811–33 Poet and essayist. At Trinity College, Cambridge, he was elected to the APOSTLES and became the close friend of ALFRED TENNYSON, who mourned his early death in *In Memoriam*. His *Remains in Verse and Prose* (1834) was edited by his father, HENRY HALLAM. An essay on Tennyson's early poems (1831) proves him one of the poet's most discerning critics.

Hallam, Henry 1777–1859 Historian. *A View of the State of Europe during the Middle Ages* (1818), which took 10 years to complete, was notable for its pioneering use of primary sources. It was followed by *The Constitutional History of England from the Accession of Henry VII to the Death of George II* (1827), and *An Introduction to the Literature of Europe in the 15th, 16th and 17th Centuries* (1837–9). He also edited the *Remains in Verse and Prose* (1834) of his son, ARTHUR HENRY HALLAM.

Halleck, Fitz-Greene 1790-1867 American poet and member of the KNICKERBOCKER GROUP. He was born in Guilford, Connecticut. He collaborated with Joseph Rodman Drake on the satirical 'Croaker' poems, published anonymously in 1819 and collected as *The Croaker Papers* in 1860. His long poem *Fanny* (1819) satirized New York society in the manner of BYRON, who, with SCOTT, influenced 'Alnwick Castle', collected in 1827. Other notable poems include 'Red Jacket' (1827), 'The Field of Grounded Arms' (1831), and 'Young America' (1865).

Halliwell [Halliwell-Phillipps], **J(ames) O(rchard)** 1820–89 Scholar. Of his numerous works about SHAKESPEARE the most important are a biography (1848), *New Boke about Shakespeare and Stratford-on-Avon* (1850) and an edition of Shakespeare (1853–65).

Halper, Albert 1904–84 American novelist. His books include *Union Square* (1933); *On the Shore* (1934); *The Foundry* (1934), about electrotype workers in Chicago just before the 1929 crash; *The Chute* (1937), about workers in a mail-order house; *Sons of the Fathers* (1940) about a Jewish immigrant; *The Little People* (1942), short stories; *Only an Inch from Glory* (1943); *The Golden Watch* (1953); *Atlantic Avenue* (1956); and *Goodbye, Union Square* (1970), his memoir of the 1930s.

hamartia From the Greek, 'error', and in Aristotle's theory of TRAGEDY, the mistake or failing which brings about the hero's downfall. 'Tragic flaw', the usual English translation, can mislead by its concentration on moral weakness, since hamartia can also be ignorance or mistaken judgement. Aristotle's term for the hero's realization of error is ANAGNORISIS.

Hamburger, Michael (Peter Leopold) 1924– Poet, translator and critic. Born in Berlin, he was brought to Britain in 1933. The poems in volumes such as *Collected Poems* (1984), *Trees* (1988), *Selected Poems* (1988), *Testimonies* (1989) and *Roots in the Air* (1991) are often concerned with rootlessness and draw on the European tradition as much as the English. He has also translated Hofmannsthal (1961), Grass (1966), Hölderlin (1966) and Celan (1980). His criticism includes *The Truth of Poetry* (1969), *After the Flood: Essays on Post-War German Literature* (1986) and *A Proliferation of Prophets: German Literature from Nietzsche to Brecht* (1986).

Hamilton, Charles (Harold St John) 1876–1961 Writer of CHILDREN'S LITERATURE. The more than 72 million words he wrote under various pseudonyms make him the most prolific author in the history of juvenile fiction. Published in boy's magazines and comics, his stories usually concerned fictional public schools (of which he invented more than 50). As Frank Richards he created Harry Wharton and Billy Bunter of Greyfriars school for *The Magnet*. He made a well-argued reply to ORWELL's criticism of such stories in the essay 'Boys' Weeklies' (1939). A Billy Bunter revival after World War II kept him fully occupied until his death.

Hamilton, (Robert) Ian 1938– Poet, critic and editor. He founded and edited *The Review* (1962–72), succeeded by the glossy, controversial *NEW REVIEW* (1974–9). His own poetry, distinctive in its density and compression, has appeared in *The Visit* (1970) and *Fifty Poems* (1988). He is better known for his criticism: *A Poetry Chronicle: Essays and Reviews* (1963); *The Little Magazines: A Study of Six Editors* (1976); a biography of ROBERT LOWELL (1982); a study of J. D. SALINGER (1989); *Writers in Hollywood* (1990); and *Literary Estates and the Rise of Biography* (1992).

Hamilton, Thomas 1789–1842 Scottish novelist. The younger brother of SIR WILLIAM HAMILTON, he wrote *Cyril Thornton* (1827), a popular novel about university and military life.

Hamilton, Virginia (Esther) 1936– Black American writer of CHILDREN'S LITERATURE. Her most famous story, *M. C. Higgins the Great* (1974), concerns a boy who lives on top of a high steel pole set deep in the mountainside. Other novels include a SCIENCE-FICTION trilogy, *The Planet of Junior Brown* (1971) and *Sweet Whispers, Brother Rush* (1987).

Hamilton, Sir William 1788–1856 Scottish philosopher. He was elected professor of logic and metaphysics at Edinburgh in 1836. *Discussions on Philosophy and Literature, Education and University Reform* (1852), *Lectures on Metaphysics and Logic* (posthumously published, 1859–60) and his edition of THOMAS REID (completed by H. L. Mansel; 1846) are notable for their contribution to the study of German philosophy and for Hamilton's theories of the association of ideas, unconscious mental modifications and the inverse relation of perception and sensation. J. S. MILL attacked him as a representative of the 'intuitional' school in his *Examination of Sir W. Hamilton's Philosophy* (1865).

Hamlet, Prince of Denmark A tragedy by

SHAKESPEARE, first performed *c.* 1601. A bad, perhaps pirated, Quarto (Q1) was published in 1603. Modern editors use a second Quarto (Q2), published in 1604, and the text in the First Folio of 1623. Various sources have been proposed, among them a lost play, or *Ur-Hamlet*, perhaps by KYD. Standing at the very centre of Shakespeare's dramatic career, *Hamlet* has been performed and discussed more than any other play in the language; the centre of its fascination resides in Hamlet himself, by turns witty and melancholy, introspective and histrionic.

The death of King Hamlet brings his brother Claudius to the Danish throne, hastily married to the old king's widow, Gertrude. Prince Hamlet, spectacularly mourning both his father's death and his mother's remarriage, hears from his friend Horatio that his father's ghost has been seen on the battlements of Elsinore. Hamlet keeps watch, encounters the ghost and learns that Claudius poisoned his father. He swears vengeance but also defers it, alternating between self-doubting soliloquies and displays of feigned madness intended to confirm Claudius's guilt. He denounces Ophelia, whom he had loved, and succeeds in convincing her father, the court chamberlain Polonius, of his madness. The arrival of a company of actors at the Danish court provides Hamlet with further opportunity. He persuades them to revive a play which offers a persuasive parallel to Claudius's murder of the king. Claudius betrays himself, and orders Hamlet to go to England, where he plans to have him killed. Hamlet escapes his pursuers, confronts Gertrude in her chamber and stabs to death the eavesdropping Polonius, apparently on the assumption that he is Claudius. Determined to avenge Polonius's death, his son Laertes returns to Denmark, where he finds Ophelia mad. News reaches Claudius that Hamlet is back in Denmark. He plots with Laertes a duel in which Hamlet's death will be assured by a poison-tipped sword. News of Ophelia's death by drowning strengthens Laertes's resolve. The duel takes place and culminates in the death of Gertrude, Laertes, Claudius and Hamlet. The play ends with Fortinbras of Norway, newly proclaimed King of Denmark, ordering a military funeral for Hamlet.

Hammett, (Samuel) Dashiell 1894–1961 American writer of DETECTIVE FICTION. His experience working as an investigator for the Pinkerton Agency in San Francisco served him well when he turned to writing. He published short stories in *THE BLACK MASK*, collected in *The Adventures of Sam Spade* (1944), *The Creeping Siamese and Other Stories* (1950) and *The Continental Op* (1974). His novels are *Red Harvest* (1929), *The Dain Curse* (1929), *The Maltese Falcon* (1930), *The Glass Key* (1931), *The Thin Man* (1934) and an unfinished autobiographical novel, *Tulip*, included in a selection from his work, *The Big Knockover* (1966), by his longtime companion LILIAN HELLMAN. Hammett's unadorned, realistic style, perfectly suited to his material, was later christened the 'hard-boiled' style.

Hammon, Jupiter 1720–1800 America's first published black poet. A slave in a Long Island household, he wrote *An Evening Thought* (1760) and an essay, *An Address to the Negroes of the State of New York* (1787), urging fellow slaves to be patient and owners to free slave children. His work helped generate support for the Abolitionist movement.

Hammond, Henry 1605–60 Theologian. Works like his *Paraphrase and Annotations on the New Testament* (1653)

have led some to call him the father of English biblical criticism. His sermons are highly regarded for their clarity and tolerant spirit.

Hampton, Christopher (James) 1946– Playwright. Early work includes: *When Did You Last See My Mother?* (1966); *Total Eclipse* (1968), about the relationship between Rimbaud and Verlaine; *The Philanthropist* (1970); and *Savages* (1973). He has also sought to provide modern, actable versions of European classics, including work by Chekhov, Ibsen, Molière, Laclos (whose *Les Liaisons dangereuses*, 1986, was Hampton's greatest success) and the Austrian dramatist Odon von Horvath, barely known in Britain before Hampton adapted *Tales from the Vienna Woods* (1977), *Don Juan Comes Back from the War* (1978) and *Faith, Hope and Charity* (1989). Horvath appears with Thomas Mann, Heinrich Mann and Brecht in *Tales from Hollywood* (1983), set in the émigré community in California during World War II. He has also adapted GEORGE STEINER's *The Portage to San Cristobal of A.H.* (1982).

Hand of Ethelberta, The: *A Comedy in Chapters* A novel by HARDY, published in 1876. His only venture into social comedy, it is among the least read of his works. Despite being a butler's daughter, Ethelberta Chickerel marries the son and heir of Sir Ralph and Lady Petherwin. When he dies on the honeymoon, she turns to making her living as a 'Professed Story-Teller'. Three suitors pay her court: the painter Eustace Lovell, Alfred Neigh and the elderly Lord Mountclere, whom she marries. An earlier suitor, the organist Christopher Julian, marries her sister Picotee.

Handful of Dust, A A novel by EVELYN WAUGH, published in 1934. Tony Last is the proud owner of a Victorian gothic country house, Hetton. His wife, Lady Brenda, becomes infatuated with a young socialite, John Beaver, and deserts Tony after their son, John Andrew, is killed in a hunting accident. Refusing to grant her a divorce, Tony departs for an extended trip to Brazil and accompanies a casual acquaintance, Dr Messinger, on a disastrous journey up the Amazon. He is rescued from near-death by a mad recluse, Mr Todd, who forces him to become his 'companion' and spend his life reading aloud the works of Dickens. In England Tony is reported dead and Brenda marries a politician, Jock Grant-Menzies. In an 'Alternative Ending' Tony returns to be greeted by a repentant Brenda.

Handley Cross A novel by SURTEES, first published in book form in 1843; an expanded version (1854) was illustrated by JOHN LEECH. It continues the adventures of John Jorrocks, the sporting grocer who appeared in *JORROCKS'S JAUNTS AND JOLLITIES* (1838) and returns in *HILLINGDON HALL* (1845). Here his position as master of the Handley Cross foxhounds provides the excuse for hunting scenes described with Surtees's usual dash and authenticity. Jorrocks's public lectures on hunting, though delivered in the broadest cockney, are replete with technical knowledge and common sense.

Handy Andy: *A Tale of Irish Life* A comic novel by SAMUEL LOVER, published in 1842. It tells of Andy Rooney, the hopelessly inefficient servant of Squire Egan, who proves to be the heir of Lord Scatterbrain.

Hannay, James 1827–73 Novelist and journalist. He contributed to *PUNCH*, edited the Edinburgh *Evening Courant* in 1860–4 and published two novels of naval life, *Singleton Fontenoy* (1850) and *Eustace Conyers* (1855).

Hanrahan, Barbara 1939–91 Australian novelist and artist. Her paintings hang in the National Gallery of

Australia. As a writer, she remains best known for *The Scent of Eucalyptus* (1973), an autobiographical first novel giving an evocative account of an adolescent girl's growth. *Sea-Green* (1974) is another highly personal work and *Kewpie Doll* (1984) an equally poetic sequel to *The Scent of Eucalyptus*. Other novels in her short but highly prolific career include a group set in the 19th and early 20th centuries: *The Albatross Muff* (1977), *Where the Queens All Strayed* (1978), *The Peach Groves* (1979), *The Frangipani Gardens* (1980) and *Dove* (1982).

Hansberry, Lorraine 1930–65 American playwright. Her best-known play, *A Raisin in the Sun* (1959), is about a family of black Chicagoans who plan to move into a white neighbourhood. *Raisin*, a musical adaptation, was produced in 1973. *The Sign in Sidney Brustein's Window* (1964) is set in New York's Greenwich Village. After her death her husband assembled *To be Young, Gifted and Black* (1969) from her letters, diaries and other unpublished material.

Happy Days A play by SAMUEL BECKETT, performed in English in 1961. The French version is *Oh! les beaux jours*. Buried first to her waist and then to her neck in sand, Winnie joyfully itemizes the trivial details of her existence. Her only witness is her silent partner, Willie.

Hard Times: For These Times A novel by DICKENS, serialized in *HOUSEHOLD WORDS* in 1854. It contrasts Fact, Dickens's name for the coldness and lovelessness he associated with UTILITARIANISM, and Fancy, which represents the warmth of the imagination. The fable traces the life of the warm-hearted Sissy Jupe, a circus child deserted by her father and adopted into the household of the fact-ridden Thomas Gradgrind, whose children Tom and Louisa are reared in ignorance of love and affection. Louisa is driven to a miserable marriage with the boastful, wealthy Josiah Bounderby and then almost to an affair with the dandified James Harthouse. Tom descends to thieving and is saved only through Sissy and the circus folk. Of comparable significance is the story of Stephen Blackpool, the honest worker in Bounderby's mill, driven out of the community and suspected in his absence of Tom Gradgrind's crime. He is exonerated only after death.

Hardy, Thomas 1840–1928 Poet and novelist. The son of a builder and master mason, he was born in Higher Bockhampton, near Dorchester, a town which remained the centre of his life and became the centre of his fictional WESSEX. A precocious child, he was given a thorough education at the village school and in Dorchester but still remained close to rural culture, playing beside his father in the village band. While apprenticed to the local architect John Hicks in 1856–62 he became a friend of WILLIAM BARNES, who helped complete his classical education, and the brilliant but unstable Horace Moule, who later committed suicide. During these years he was first exposed to the unsettling influences of DARWIN's *ORIGIN OF SPECIES* and *ESSAYS AND REVIEWS*. After a five-year stint (1862–7) working for the architect Arthur Blomfield in London he returned, his health undermined, to Hicks's office and soon afterwards began the lost and partly cannibalized novel, *The Poor Man and the Lady*. GEORGE MEREDITH, then a reader for Chapman and Hall, saw merit in it but advised against publication. While working for the firm of Crickmay in Weymouth, Hardy began a more acceptable novel, *DESPERATE REMEDIES* (1871). In the same year he met Emma Lavinia Gifford while surveying the church at St Junot in Cornwall. They were married in 1874.

Desperate Remedies launched Hardy on a hard-working career as a novelist, with *UNDER THE GREENWOOD TREE* (1872), *A PAIR OF BLUE EYES* (1873) and his first real success, *FAR FROM THE MADDING CROWD* (1874). During the years when Hardy and his wife led a wandering existence in London, Swanage, Sturminster Newton, London again and then Wimborne he wrote *THE HAND OF ETHELBERTA* (1876), *THE RETURN OF THE NATIVE* (1878), *THE TRUMPET-MAJOR* (1880), *A LAODICEAN* (1881) and *TWO ON A TOWER* (1882). *THE MAYOR OF CASTERBRIDGE* (1886) followed his return to Dorchester. Max Gate, the house he built for himself, remained home for the rest of his life, though he continued to spend a few months in London each year for 'the season'. *Wessex Tales* (1888), *A GROUP OF NOBLE DAMES* (1891), *Life's Little Ironies* (1894), and a later volume, *A Changed Man and Other Tales* (1913), are short stories. The major novels continued with *THE WOODLANDERS* (1887), *TESS OF THE D'URBERVILLES* (1891), *THE WELL-BELOVED* (1897, but written several years earlier) and *JUDE THE OBSCURE* (1895).

The increasing pessimism and the handling of sexual relations in *Tess* and *Jude* provoked a storm of controversy which encouraged Hardy to give up novels and return to poetry, which he had always regarded as his first calling. The volumes he published in the last 30 years of his life began with *WESSEX POEMS AND OTHER VERSES* (1898) and *POEMS OF THE PAST AND PRESENT* (1902). His epic verse-drama, *THE DYNASTS* (1903–8), was followed by *TIME'S LAUGHINGSTOCKS AND OTHER VERSES* (1909), *SATIRES OF CIRCUMSTANCE, LYRICS AND REVERIES* (1914), a collection of particular interest for the elegiac 'Poems of 1912–13', written out of remorse and expiatory sadness at the sudden death of Emma Hardy in 1912. The poetry continued with *MOMENTS OF VISION AND MISCELLANEOUS VERSES* (1917), *LATE LYRICS AND EARLIER* (1922), *HUMAN SHOWS, FAR PHANTASIES, SONGS AND TRIFLES* (1925) and the posthumous *WINTER WORDS IN VARIOUS MOODS AND METRES* (1928). The *Famous Tragedy of the Queen of Cornwall* (1923) is a verse-drama about Tristram and Iseult.

Increasingly the mantle of the Grand Old Man of English Letters tightened across Hardy's shoulders as distinctions and accolades – the Order of Merit and various honorary degrees – came to him. He continued to live simply in the melancholy twilight of Max Gate, and in 1914 married Florence Emily Dugdale (1879–1937). With her he destroyed many letters, notes and writings of a personal nature, received the inevitable admirers and receded into old age until death came peacefully. *The Early Life of Thomas Hardy, 1840–1891* (1928) and *The Later Years of Thomas Hardy, 1892–1928* (1930), two sometimes misleading volumes which Hardy himself had compiled in his last years, were published under his wife's name.

Hare, David 1947– Playwright. Cambridge, where he was a student, makes the setting for *Teeth 'n' Smiles* (1975), following the sordid progress of a pop group hired to play at a May Ball. *Fanshen* (1975) presents an alternative social system, Revolutionary China, less sceptically than his plays about British power politics. *Plenty* (1978) is a bleak encounter with the moral bankruptcy of post-war Europe, more effective than the ambitious *Map of the World* (1983). *Pravda* (1985), a study of the corruptions of newspaper ownership written in collaboration with BRENTON, scored a striking success at the ROYAL NATIONAL THEATRE. Hare's work in other media includes *Licking Hitler* (TV, 1978) and two films of which he was writer-director, *Wetherby* (1985) and *Paris by Night* (1988).

Harington, Sir **John** ?1560–1612 Courtier, wit, epigrammatist and translator. The godson of Elizabeth I, he is chiefly remembered for his EPIGRAMS and his translation of Ariosto's *Orlando furioso* (1591). *A New Discourse of a Stale Subject, Called the Metamorphosis of Ajax* (1596) announced the invention of a water closet ('a jakes') with a display of erudition, indecency and SATIRE that identifies him as an early English imitator of Rabelais. The satire, rather than the indecency, gave offence and he fell from royal favour.

Hariot [Harriot], **Thomas** 1560–1621 Mathematician and astronomer. He was an associate of MARLOWE and SIR WALTER RALEIGH, who sent him as scientific adviser on Sir Richard Grenville's expedition to Roanoke Island in 1585–6. His account of the journey appeared as *A Brief and True Report of the New Found Land of Virginia* (1588). He contributed to the development of algebra through his posthumously published treatise on equations, *Artis analyticae praxis ad aequationes algebraicas novo methodo resolvendas* (1631). This work also introduced the signs > (greater than) and < (less than). As an astronomer he observed sunspots and, independently of Galileo, the moons of Jupiter.

Harland, Henry 1861–1905 American novelist. Under the pseudonym of Sidney Luska he wrote several realistic novels about Jewish immigrants in New York: *As It was Written: A Jewish Musician's Story* (1885), *Mrs Peixada* (1886), *The Yoke of the Thorah* (1887) and *My Uncle Florimund* (1888). Migrating to Paris in 1889 and to London the following year, he dropped the pseudonym for his later short stories and novels, of which the most successful were *The Cardinal's Snuff Box* (1900) and *My Friend Prospero* (1904). He is best remembered as the first editor of *THE YELLOW BOOK*.

Harlem Renaissance A term (like the 'Black Renaissance' or 'New Negro') for the period of cultural activity by black American artists in the 1920s and 1930s. In his introduction to the anthology *The New Negro* (1925), which served as a manifesto, ALAIN LOCKE noted a new spirit of 'group expression and self-determination' among black writers, in contrast to the solitary efforts of earlier figures. The Renaissance was also marked by its emphasis on the African heritage of American blacks. Leading writers associated with it include CLAUDE MCKAY, JEAN TOOMER, COUNTEE CULLEN, LANGSTON HUGHES, ZORA NEALE HURSTON, JESSIE REDMON FAUSET, ARNA BONTEMPS and STERLING A. BROWN.

Harley, Edward, 2nd Earl of Oxford 1689–1741 Patron of literature and book collector. From his father, ROBERT HARLEY, 1st Earl of Oxford, he inherited important literary friendships with POPE, SWIFT and PRIOR (who died at Harley's country house, Wimpole Hall in Cambridgeshire). He also inherited a fine library which he further improved at immense cost. Most of the collection was sold at his death. The printed material, 50,000 books, 41,000 prints and 350,000 pamphlets, was bought by Thomas Osborne, the bookseller, and catalogued in the five-volume *Catalogus bibliothecae Harleianae* (1743–5) with an introduction by SAMUEL JOHNSON. The manuscripts, in 7639 volumes, together with over 14,000 rolls, charters and similar legal material, were sold to the nation and now form the Harleian Collection in the British Library. Among these volumes are the HARLEY LYRICS, the finest extant collection of Middle English lyric poetry.

Harley, Robert, 1st Earl of Oxford 1661–1724 Politician. Leader of the Tory Party and effectively Prime Minister under Queen Anne, he survived impeachment proceedings on the accession of George I in 1714. When in power he was an effective manipulator of propaganda, employing DEFOE and STEELE among others, and helping to found *THE EXAMINER*, which SWIFT first edited. He was also a member of the SCRIBLERUS CLUB and an avid book collector, founding the library enlarged by his son EDWARD HARLEY.

Harley Lyrics, The A collection of MEDIEVAL LYRICS, preserved in the British Library, first assembled by ROBERT HARLEY and EDWARD HARLEY. It contains more than half the secular lyrics surviving from before the 15th century. They range from the humorous 'Man in the Moon' to the love song 'Alysoun' and the evocative 'Suete Iesu, King of Blysse'.

Harper, Frances E(llen) (Watkins) 1825–1911 Black American poet. *Poems on Miscellaneous Subjects* (1854), largely devoted to attacking slavery, proved extremely popular. Her other works include *Moses: A Story of the Nile* (1869), *Poems* (1871), *Iola Le Roy: or, Shadows Uplifted* (1892), about the tragic life of a young octoroon woman before and during the Civil War, and *Atlanta Offering: Poems* (1895).

Harper's New Monthly Magazine It was founded in 1850, as *Harper's Monthly Magazine*, by the New York publishing firm of Harper and Brothers. It initially concentrated on publishing established British authors but under the editorship of Henry M. Alden (1869–1919) drew on American writers as well, JOHN DE FOREST, HAMLIN GARLAND, WILLIAM DEAN HOWELLS and SARAH ORNE JEWETT among them. Though fiction remained its main offering, it later devoted more space to political and social issues. It changed its name to *Harper's New Monthly Magazine* in 1900 and to *Harper's Magazine* in 1925; it is now commonly known as *Harper's*.

Harpur, Charles 1813–68 Australian poet. He has been called 'the grey forefather' of Australian poetry because of his early use of Australian subjects in 'The Creek of the Four Graves', 'The Bushfire' and 'Ned Connor'. His volumes include *Thoughts: A Series of Sonnets* (1845) and *The Bushrangers: A Play and Other Poems* (1853), the first play by an Australian-born author to be printed in the colony, followed by *A Poet's Home* (1862), *The Tower of the Dream* (1865) and *Poems* (edited by Henry Maydwell Martin; 1883).

Harraden, Beatrice 1864–1936 Novelist and suffragette. *Ships That Pass in the Night* (1893), set in the Kurhaus at Petershof, a winter resort for consumptive patient, reflects many of her feminist beliefs. *In Varying Moods* (1894) was a collection of short stories written in Sussex, Cannes and Menton. Other titles include *Hilda Strafford* (1897), *The Fowler* (1899), *Katharine Frensham* (1903), *Interplay* (1908), *Youth Calling* (1924) and *Search Will Find It Out* (1928).

Harrington [Harington], **James** 1611–77 Political theorist. *The Commonwealth of Oceana* (1656), a political romance in the manner of MORE's UTOPIA, describes an ideal state dedicated to liberty and equality and ruled by a democratically elected 'Archon'. In sharp contrast to the scheme set down in HOBBES's LEVIATHAN (1651), it later influenced the early settlers of America. Harrington was imprisoned for his views at the Restoration.

Harris, Frank (James Thomas) 1856–1931 Journalist and literary editor. He gained a considerable reputation on the London literary scene, editing *The Evening News* (1882–6), THE FORTNIGHTLY REVIEW (1886–94) and *THE SATURDAY REVIEW* (1894–8), which he transformed into the leading weekly with a new bias towards the arts. His notoriety as a braggart and liar was epitomized in *My Life and Loves* (1922–7), highly unreliable memoirs of his early life as a precocious intellectual and sexual buccaneer. Other publications included short stories (*Elder Conklin*, 1894; *Montes the Matador*, 1900), novels (*The Bomb*, 1908; *Great Days*, 1914), two plays (*Mr and Mrs Daventry*, 1900; *Shakespeare and His Love*, 1910), popular literary studies (*The Man Shakespeare*, 1909; *The Women of Shakespeare*, 1911), biographies of WILDE (1916) and SHAW (1931), and *Contemporary Portraits* (1915–23).

Harris, George Washington 1814–69 American short-story writer. A Tennessee River steamboat captain before he turned to writing, he is best known for *Sut Lovingood: Yarns spun by a 'Nat'ral Born Durn'd Fool'* (1867), a collection of tall tales and sketches full of Southwestern frontier dialect and humour.

Harris, Joel Chandler 1848–1908 American short-story writer. He is best known as the creator of the black storyteller, Uncle Remus, and the humanized animals, Br'er Rabbit, Br'er Fox and Br'er Wolf. *UNCLE REMUS: His Songs and Sayings* (1881) was followed by several other collections: *Nights with Uncle Remus* (1883), *Uncle Remus and His Friends* (1892), *Mr Rabbit at Home* (1895), *The Tar Baby and Other Short Rhymes of Uncle Remus* (1904) and *Uncle Remus and Br'er Rabbit* (1906). They offer traditional black folk-wisdom in what MARK TWAIN considered a flawless duplication of Southern black speech. *On the Plantation* (1892) recounts the childhood experiences in Georgia that inspired much of his work.

Harris, (Theodore) Wilson 1921– Guyanese novelist. He published two volumes of verse, *Fetish* (1951) and *Eternity to Season* (1954), before moving to London in 1959. He is known particularly for *Palace of the Peacock* (1960), later grouped with *The Far Journey of Oudin* (1961), *The Whole Armour* (1962) and *The Secret Ladder* (1963) as *The Guyana Quartet* (1985). Other 'Guyanese' novels, fusing a poetic imagination, wide reading and passionate response to landscape, include *Heartland* (1964), *The Eye of the Scarecrow* (1965), *The Waiting Room* (1967), *Tumatumari* (1968) and *Ascent to Omai* (1970). Since volumes of salvaged or imagined pre-Columbian legends, *The Sleepers of Roraima* (1970) and *The Age of the Rainmakers* (1971), he has written novels set in Scotland, South America, Mexico and London: *Black Marsden* (1972), *Companions of the Day and Night* (1975), *Da Silva da Silva's Cultivated Wilderness* with *Genesis of the Clowns* (1977), *The Tree of the Sun* (1978), *The Angel at the Gate* (1982) and his *Carnival* trilogy, *Carnival* (1985), *The Infinite Rehearsal* (1987) and *The Four Banks of the River of Space* (1990). Critical writings include *Tradition, the Writer and Society* (1967), *Explorations* (1981), *The Womb of Space: The Cross-Cultural Imagination* (1983) and *The Radical Imagination* (1992).

Harrison, Frederic 1831–1923 Philosopher and critic. A leading advocate of POSITIVISM, he published, among other works, *Order and Progress* (1875), *Victorian Literature* (1895), *Carlyle and the London Library* (1907), *The Philosophy of Common Sense* (1907), *The Positive Evolution of Religion* (1912) and *Autobiographical Memoirs* (1911). His contemptuous remarks on culture stimulated ARNOLD to reply in *CULTURE AND ANARCHY* (1869).

Harrison, Tony 1937– Poet, translator and playwright. An accomplished verse writer for the stage, he is perhaps best known for his adaptations of *The Oresteia* (1981) and *The Mysteries* (1985). *Theatre Works 1973–1985* (1986) is a collection. His disciplined, vernacular poetry has appeared in *The Loiners* (1970), *Palladas: Poems* (1975), *From 'The School of Eloquence' and Other Poems* (1978), *A Kumquat for John Keats* (1981), *US Martial* (1981), *Selected Poems* (1984) and *A Cold Coming* (1991). A 1987 television version of *V.* (1985), about the desecration of his parents' grave, brought an overwhelming response.

Harrison, William 1534–93 Historian and topographer. His *Description of England*, incorporated in HOLINSHED's *Chronicles*, gives a vivid picture of social conditions in Elizabethan England with its food, institutions, customs, inns and fairs.

Harrower, Elizabeth 1928– Australian novelist. Most of her fiction deals with struggles in personal relationships and with conflicting moral issues. *Down in the City* (1957) and *The Long Prospect* (1958) appeared while she was living in Britain. *The Catherine Wheel* (1960), published after her return to Australia, describes the experiences of a young Australian woman in London. The title of *The Watch Tower* (1966) refers to an elegant house in a Sydney suburb which proves an emotional and intellectual prison for the heroine and her sister.

Hart, Moss 1904–61 American playwright and director. His first successes were written in witty partnership with GEORGE S. KAUFMAN: *Once in a Lifetime* (1930), *You Can't Take It with You* (1936) and *The Man Who Came to Dinner* (1939). On his own he wrote the book for a musical about psychoanalysis, *Lady in the Dark* (1941), and a comedy about the theatre, *Light Up the Sky* (1948).

Harte, (Francis) Bret(t) 1836–1902 American short-story writer. He went to California at the age of 18, working as prospector, teacher, Wells Fargo expressman, secretary of the US Mint in San Francisco and journalist. In 1868 he helped to establish OVERLAND MONTHLY, which he edited for its first two-and-a-half years. His own contributions included his most famous collection, *The Luck of Roaring Camp and Other Sketches* (1868–70). Apart from the title-piece, its sharply naturalistic portraits of frontier life in the American West include 'The Outcasts of Poker Flats', 'Tennessee's Partner' and 'Miggles'. After returned to the East, he served as US consul in Germany and then in Glasgow, spending his last years in London. His stories are collected in *Mrs Skaggs's Husbands* (1873), *Tales of the Argonauts* (1875), *An Heiress of Red Dog, and Other Sketches* (1878), *A Sappho of Green Springs, and Other Stories* (1891) and *Colonel Starbottle's Client, and Some Other People* (1892). He also published poetry, comic BALLADS and PARODIES; several novels, including *Gabriel Conroy* (1876) and *Jeff Briggs's Love Story* (1880); and two plays, *Two Men of Sandy Bar* (1876) and *Ah Sin* (1877), the latter in collaboration with TWAIN.

Hartford Wits See CONNECTICUT WITS.

Hartley, David 1705–57 Philosopher. He is remembered for one of the earliest attempts at psychological enquiry in English, *Observations on Man: His Frame, His Duty and His Expectations* (1749), which relates psychology to physiology and contributed to the development of the 'association of ideas' theory. Its influence on COLERIDGE can be seen in his poetry and in his decision to name his eldest son HARTLEY COLERIDGE.

Hartley, L(eslie) P(oles) 1895–1972 Novelist and short-story writer. He established himself as a leading writer of short stories with many collections, including *Night Fears* (1924), *The Killing Bottle* (1932), *The Travelling Grave* (1951), *The White Wand* (1954) and *Two for the River*

(1961). His first novel, *Simonetta Perkins* (1925), was set in Venice, where he spent much of his life. *The Shrimp and the Anemone* (1944), *The Sixth Heaven* (1946) and *Eustace and Hilda* (1947) are a trilogy, indebted to HENRY JAMES and Freud, following the lives of a brother and sister from childhood. Childhood is also a central preoccupation of THE GO-BETWEEN (1953), his best-known novel. Other novels include *A Perfect Woman* (1955), *The Hireling* (1957), *Facial Justice* (1960), *The Brickfield* (1964) and its sequel *The Betrayal* (1966), *Poor Clare* (1968) and *The Love Adept* (1969).

Harvey, Gabriel ?1550–1631 Scholar. A Cambridge don, he pursued learned interests in rhetoric, neo-Aristotelian philosophy and law, leaving copious marginalia in the books in his library. His friendship with SPENSER led to an exchange of letters, printed in 1580, partly dealing with metrics and referring to the coterie known as the AREOPAGUS. With his brother, the astrologer Richard Harvey, he became embroiled in a bitter exchange of pamphlets with NASHE, described under the entry for that author.

Harvey, William 1578–1657 Physician. He expounded his theory of the circulation of the blood in 1616 but did not publish it until *Exercitatio anatomica de motu cordis et sanguinis in animalibus* ('On the Movement of the Heart and Blood in Animals'; 1628). His theories, the result of observation and experiment carried out without the help of a microscope, were substantiated only after 200 years of slow acceptance. Harvey also made contributions to embryology and comparative anatomy. He was physician to Charles I.

Harwood, Gwen(doline) [Nessie] 1920– Australian poet. Tense, controlled pieces like 'In the Park', 'Prize-Giving' and 'Cocktails at Seven', sketching scenes of middle-class despair and vacillating between rage and ELEGY, have made her one of Australia's foremost lyric poets. Her volumes are *Poems* (1963), *Poems: Volume Two* (1968), *New and Selected Poems* (1975), *Lion's Bride* (1981), *Bone Scan* (1990) and *Collected Poems* (1991).

Harwood, Lee (Travers Rafe) 1939– Poet. His first major collection, *The White Room* (1968), which won praise from JOHN ASHBERY, has been followed by *Landscapes* (1969), *The Sinking Colony* (1970), *Monster Masks* (1985), *Rope Boy* (1988), *Crossing the Frozen River: Selected Poems* (1988) and translations from Tzara (1975).

Harwood, Ronald 1934– Playwright. Born in South Africa, he came to Britain and joined Sir Donald Wolfit's touring Shakespearean company, the inspiration for his first stage success, *The Dresser* (1980). His mixture of affection and despair is reflected in *J. J. Farr* (1987) and *Another Time* (1989). *Reflected Glory* (1992) describes the rivalry between a restaurant-owner and his more successful playwright-brother.

Hassan A play in highly charged prose, interspersed with poetry, by JAMES ELROY FLECKER, written in 1913–14, published in 1922 and performed in 1923 with music by Delius and a balletic choreography by Fokine. Hassan, a middle-aged confectioner in old Baghdad, becomes embroiled in the cruel and corrupt court of the Caliph as a result of his love for the courtesan, Yasmin. Influenced by GRAND GUIGNOL, the play contains enough voyeurism and sadism to explain the Lord Chamberlain's hesitation to grant it a licence in 1923.

Hau'ofa, Epeli 1939– Tongan short-story writer and novelist. One of the most distinctive voices in South Pacific literature, he is unusual in his comic treatment of post-colonial themes. The stories in *Tales of the Tikongs* (1983) draw on the Tongan oral tradition of the tall tale to create a fictional world in which contemporary South Pacific society is gently ridiculed. His novel *Kisses in the Nederends* (1987) is a *tour de force* of comic-grotesque realism in which the central character searches for a cure to his ulcerated anus through all the region's problem-solving agencies. Hau'ofa has also written poetry and works of social anthropology.

Haunted Man and the Ghost's Bargain, The A Christmas story by DICKENS, published in 1848 and collected in *CHRISTMAS BOOKS* (1852). An evil phantom visits the sadly reflective Mr Redlaw and makes a compact with him to obliterate the sorrows, wrongs and troubles he has known. In return, Redlaw agrees to transmit this oblivion to others but his influence is baleful upon everyone he encounters. Ultimately, through the goodness embodied in William Swidger's wife Milly, the unhappy man's bargain is terminated.

Havelok the Dane A VERSE ROMANCE of *c.* 1280–1300. Although it has an Anglo-Norman source in Gaimar's *Histoire des Engles*, no European romance of Havelok survives and his story is English in character. He has not been convincingly identified with any historical figure. Son of the Danish king, he survives his guardian's attempt to kill him. The fisherman Grim takes him to England, where he works as a scullion and grows up to be the strongest man in the land. Godrich, guardian of Goldborough, the heir to the English throne, marries her to Havelok in the hope of gaining the throne for himself. Magic tokens reveal Havelok's identity, allowing him to defeat both guardians and become king of Denmark and England.

Hawes, Stephen d. ?1523 Poet. By his own account he was groom of the chamber to Henry VII. Though his concern with the education of princes shows the influence of the 'New Learning', his poetry belongs to the tradition of CHAUCER, GOWER and especially LYDGATE. *The Pastime of Pleasure* (1509), *The Example of Virtue* (earliest surviving edition, 1510) and *The Comfort of Lovers* (earliest surviving copy, ?1510) are love-allegories. They were printed by WYNKYN DE WORDE, together with *The Conversion of Swearers* (1509), attacking blasphemy, and *A Joyful Meditation* (1509), celebrating Henry VIII's coronation.

Hawker, R[obert] S[tephen] 1803–75 Poet. Twice married, a High Churchman who converted to Rome on his deathbed, the eccentric 'Passon' Hawker spent most of his adult life as vicar of Morwenstow on the North Cornish coast. His best-known poem is 'Song of the Western Men'. Volumes include *Records of the Western Shore* (1832), *Poems* (1836), *Ecclesia* (1841), *Reeds Shaken with the Wind* (1st series, 1843; 2nd series, 1844), *Cornish Ballads* (1869) and *The Quest of the Sangraal* (1864), generally acknowledged as his most ambitious work and often compared with TENNYSON's IDYLLS OF THE KING, another Victorian contribution to ARTHURIAN LITERATURE. Often cast as BALLADS, Hawker's poems deal with saints' legends, smuggling, village life and other motifs closely associated with Cornwall; there are also verses dedicated to the Christian life. He wrote on antiquarian subjects, dabbled in translation and contributed to a number of prominent journals. His prose work, *Footprints of Former Men in Far Cornwall* (1870), deals with the mysterious, the supernatural and the forbiddingly unusual in Cornish lore and legend.

Hawkes, John (Clendennin Burne), Jr 1925– American novelist. *The Cannibal* (1949), about World War II, has been followed by novels using nightmarish surrealism to explore violence and eroticism: *The Beetle Leg* (1951), *The Goose on the Grave* (1954), *The Lime Twig* (1961), *Second Skin* (1964), *Death, Sleep and the Traveller* (1974), *Travesty* (1976), *The Owl* (1977), *The Passion Artist* (1979), *Virginie: Her Two Lives* (1981), *Innocence in Extremis* (1985), *Adventures in the Alaskan Skin Trade* (1985) and *Whistlejacket* (1989).

Hawkins, Sir **Anthony Hope** See HOPE, ANTHONY.

Hawkins, Sir **John** 1532–95 Sailor. A relative of Drake, he was a naval commander and, in his reconstruction of the fleet, architect of the Elizabethan navy. His early career was as a slave-trader, running slaves from Guinea to the West Indies in 1562–9. The last voyage is described in *A True Declaration of the Troublesome Voyage of Mr John Hawkins* (1569). He died on a raiding expedition with Drake to the Spanish West Indies.

Hawthorne, Nathaniel 1804–64 American novelist and short-story writer. Born in Salem, Massachusetts, into a prominent family whose ancestors were among the earliest settlers of the colony, he was brought up in seclusion by his widowed mother. When he was 11 they moved to Maine, where he attended Bowdoin College. In 1825 he returned to Salem, producing a weak first novel, *Fanshawe* (1828), and the historical and allegorical stories later collected in *Twice-Told Tales* (1837; expanded 1842), exploring the impact of Puritanism on the guilty conscience of New England. He then worked as editor and hack writer for the publisher Samuel Goodrich and as surveyor for the Boston Custom House, and involved himself in the BROOK FARM experiment, before moving with his wife Sophia Peabody to Concord in 1842. Here he wrote *Mosses from an Old Manse* (1846), which contains the story 'Young Goodman Brown'. After serving as customs surveyor at Salem in 1846–9 he finally produced his first significant novel, THE SCARLET LETTER (1850). It was rapidly followed by: THE HOUSE OF THE SEVEN GABLES (1851); *The Snow Image and Other Tales* (1851), which includes such stories as 'Ethan Brand' and 'My Kinsman Major Molineux'; *A Wonder Book* (1852), which retells Greek myths for children; THE BLITHEDALE ROMANCE (1852); and *Tanglewood Tales* (1853).

Hawthorne never equalled such productivity again. In 1853 he was appointed US consul at Liverpool, living in England for four years and in Italy for two. On his return to the USA he published his final novel, THE MARBLE FAUN (1860), and *Our Old Home* (1863), a book of essays on England. Four unfinished novels eventually appeared as *Septimius Felton: or, the Elixir of Life* (1872), *The Dolliver Romance* (1876), *Dr Grimshawe's Secret* (1882) and *The Ancestral Footstep* (1883). His wife edited his notebooks as *Passages from the American Notebooks* (1868), *Passages from the English Notebooks* (1870) and *Passages from the French and Italian Notebooks* (1871).

Hay, Ian [Beith, John Hay, Major-General] 1876–1952 Novelist and playwright. His light-hearted novels about life in boys' boarding-schools include *A Man's Made* (1909), *A Safety Match* (1911), *The Middle Watch* (1930) and *The Housemaster* (1936). As well as adapting his own work for the stage, he dramatized stories by his friend P. G. WODEHOUSE.

Hay Fever A comedy by NoëL COWARD, produced in 1925. It is a skilfully composed account of a weekend at the home of the eccentric Bliss family, who have all invited guests without telling each other. The guests, bewildered by the Bliss version of bickering hospitality, creep away at breakfast on the second day, leaving the family arguing about the exact topography of Paris.

Haydon, Benjamin Robert 1786–1846 Painter and diarist. After considerable success producing large canvases in the Renaissance manner, he alienated patrons and influential well-wishers with his often intemperate advocacy of otherwise sound and progressive schemes for promoting art education, decorating public buildings and establishing design schools. Among the first to appreciate the Elgin Marbles, he was instrumental in securing their purchase for the British Museum. Although consumed to the point of madness by the desire for glory with the brush, he was a better writer and lecturer than painter, and is now best known for his *Lectures on Painting and Design* (1846) and his posthumously published *Autobiography and Journals* (1853), a treasure-trove of anecdote and vivid observation of his friends, who included David Wilkie, KEATS, WORDSWORTH, HAZLITT, LEIGH HUNT, MARY RUSSELL MITFORD and ELIZABETH BARRETT BROWNING. His extravagant personality intrigued DICKENS, who used him, along with Leigh Hunt, as the model for Skimpole in *BLEAK HOUSE*.

Hayley, William 1745–1820 Poet and biographer. His poetry was widely read in its day, and the popular success of his two most ambitious works, *The Triumphs of Temper* (1781) and *The Triumphs of Music* (1805), earned him BYRON's ridicule in *English Bards and Scotch Reviewers*. BLAKE, who enjoyed his patronage in 1800–3, illustrated *Ballads Founded on Anecdotes of Animals* (1805). Other literary friends included COWPER, of whom he wrote a *Life* (1803), and SOUTHEY, who thought him good in everything 'except his poetry'. Other biographies include lives of MILTON and the portrait painter Romney. He declined the chance to become POET LAUREATE in 1790.

Haymarket Theatre Successively called the Little Theatre in the Haymarket, the Theatre Royal, Haymarket, and the Haymarket Theatre, it opened in 1720 as a speculative challenge to the monopoly of the PATENT THEATRES. HENRY FIELDING staged anti-Walpole satires there. During FOOTE's management (1747–76) it acquired a licence for performing plays when the Patent Theatres were closed in the summer and thus became an important testing-ground for new work. Foote's licence was acquired by GEORGE COLMAN THE ELDER, whose regime was continued by his son, GEORGE COLMAN THE YOUNGER, until 1817. The first building was replaced in 1820 by a larger theatre, designed by John Nash.

Hayward, Sir **John** ?1564–1627 Historian. He was imprisoned for his account of Richard II's deposition in *The First Part of the Life and Reign of King Henry IV* (1599), flatteringly dedicated to Essex. FRANCIS BACON, who found its politics unobjectionable, thought its borrowings from Tacitus felonious. Hayward later wrote *The Lives of the Three Normans, Kings of England* (1613) and *The Life and Reign of King Edward VI* (1630). Another edition (1636) contains *The Beginning of the Reign of Queen Elizabeth*, part of a larger work which remained in manuscript until it was printed in 1840. *The Sanctuary of a Troubled Soul* (1616) is a collection of prayers and meditations, *David's Tears* (1622) a commentary on three of the penitential psalms.

Haywood, Eliza *c.* 1693–1756 Hack. In a career spanning nearly 40 years she wrote a few unsuccessful plays and collaborated with William Hatchett on *Tom Thumb the Great* (1733), a comic opera adapted from FIELDING's *Tragedy of Tragedies*, edited *The Female Spectator*, a monthly collection of essays, in 1744–6, and produced many novels. These ranged from *The Life of Mr Duncan Campbell* (1720), written in collaboration with DEFOE, through the ROMAN À CLEF, *Memoirs of a Certain Island Adjacent to Utopia* (1725), to *The History of Jemmy and Jenny Jessamy* (1753), praised in SCOTT's OLD MORTALITY. Though she consistently asserted her moral purpose, POPE condemned her as 'the libellous Novelist' and SWIFT as a 'stupid, infamous, scribbling woman'.

Hazard of New Fortunes, A A novel by WILLIAM DEAN HOWELLS, published in 1890. The title refers to Basil March's decision to move his family from Boston to New York and work for *Every Other Week*, a new magazine financed by Jacob Dryfoos. Dryfoos's son Conrad also works for the magazine, though he really wants to become a minister. He loves Margaret Vance, a young society woman he has met through his charitable work. When Dryfoos learns that Lindau, whom March has hired, is a socialist, he demands that he be sacked. March refuses but Lindau resigns in outrage at having been employed by a strike-breaking capitalist. Conrad is killed by a stray police bullet during a streetcar-workers' strike and Lindau dies later from his injuries. Disheartened, Jacob sells the magazine and takes his family to Europe. Margaret Vance becomes an Episcopalian nun.

Hazlitt, William 1778-1830 Essayist, journalist and critic. An intellectually precocious boy (his first essay, 'A Project for a New Theory of Criminal and Civil Legislation', appeared in 1792), he was intended for the Unitarian ministry but soon developed an 'extreme distaste' for the religious life and turned instead to painting. Though his acquaintances in the literary world included COLERIDGE, WORDSWORTH, LAMB (a lifelong friend) and GODWIN, it was not until 1804-5 that he decided his real talents lay in philosophy and literature.

An Essay on the Principles of Human Action (1805), a systematic defence of the unity of the mind against prevailing doctrines of sense impressions, was followed by his *Reply* (1807) to MALTHUS's *Essay on Population*, which sides with Godwin, and *The Eloquence of the British Senate*, a selection of parliamentary speeches by BURKE, Chatham, Fox, the younger Pitt and others. In 1810 he lectured *On the Rise and Progress of Modern Philosophy* and published his *New and Improved Grammar of the English Language*, based on the linguistic theories of HORNE TOOKE. He then exchanged philosophy for journalism, working as parliamentary reporter and theatrical critic for THE MORNING CHRONICLE, and writing essays for *The Champion*, LEIGH HUNT's EXAMINER, THE LIBERAL and THE EDINBURGH REVIEW. His *Characters of Shakespeare* (1817) established him as a Shakespearean critic second only to Coleridge and found an ardent admirer in KEATS, who was also deeply impressed by *The Round Table* (with Leigh Hunt; 1817) and, above all, by the *Lectures on the English Poets* (1818), which immediately anticipate Keats's idea of the poet as an individual of NEGATIVE CAPABILITY. *Lectures on the English Comic Writers* (1819) appeared in the same year as his *Political Essays* addressing the conditions of the poor.

Table Talk (1821-2) was followed in 1823 by *Characteristics*, in imitation of La Rochefoucauld, and *Liber amoris*, an embarrassingly transparent description of the love for his landlord's daughter, Sarah Walker, which led Hazlitt to divorce his wife, whom he had married in 1808, and brought him close to insanity. His second marriage, to a Mrs Bridgewater in 1824, came to a mysteriously abrupt end in 1825. Two collections, THE

SPIRIT OF THE AGE (1825) and *The Plain Speaker* (1826), contained some of his best work. *Boswell Redivivus* (1827) recounts his conversations with the painter Northcote. The major project of his solitary last years was his poorly researched and one-sided *Life of Napoleon* (1828-30).

Hazlitt's claim to literary fame is founded almost exclusively on his work as descriptive and critical essayist. Although he was often condemned as a hack, his ideas on art and creativity were highly regarded by later 19th-century writers and critics. Taken as a whole, his writing represents an early attempt at a critical history of English literature and the establishment of the criteria for a canon. Whilst his judgements are based on conspicuously 'Romantic' ideas, he was hostile to Wordsworth's subjectivism and Coleridge's system-building, and fought against their tendency to exempt the artist from social and political responsibilities. Although his sympathies were radical and republican, his temperament precluded precisely defined loyalties, and he was always something of a one-man political party.

Hazzard, Shirley 1931- Australian novelist and short-story writer. She lives in Manhattan but pays frequent visits to Italy, the setting of *The Evening of the Holiday* (1966) and *The Bay of Noon* (1970), two early but formally assured works in the tradition of Flaubert and HENRY JAMES. She first achieved recognition for the short stories in *Cliffs of Fall* (1963). *People in Glass Houses* (1967), a series of interconnected satirical portraits of people working for a dehumanizing institution, confirmed her stature. Her reputation further increased with *The Transit of Venus* (1980), an account of the odyssey of two sisters in Australia and England.

He Knew He was Right A novel by TROLLOPE, serialized in 1868-9 and published in volume form in 1869. Louis Trevelyan marries Emily Rowley but the couple separate because of his unreasonable jealousy of Colonel Osborne. Sure that he is right in his suspicions, Trevelyan hires a private detective to watch Emily and abducts their young son with his help. They go to Italy where Trevelyan declines into complete mental and physical breakdown; Emily persuades him to return to England, where he dies. In one of several sub-plots Emily's sister Nora falls in love with Trevelyan's friend Hugh Stanbury, choosing him in preference to a wealthy aristocratic suitor, Mr Glascock. The novel's interest in the question of women's independence is reflected in the hostile portrait of an American feminist, Wallachia Petrie.

Head, Bessie 1937-86 South African novelist. *When Rain Clouds Gather* (1968), *Maru* (1971) and *A Question of Power* (1974) examine lonely people in corporate environments, probing connections between personal morality and political integrity. *The Collector of Treasures* (1977) retells village tales, *Serowe: Village of the Rain Wind* (1981) recreates the history of the Bamangwato capital in Botswana from oral tradition, and *A Bewitched Crossroad* (1984) is a novel about peace and security under the benevolent Bamangwato king, Khama III (1875-1923). Posthumous publications include *A Woman Alone: Autobiographical Writings* (1990), *A Gesture of Belonging: Letters from Bessie Head, 1965-79* (1990) and *Tales of Tenderness and Power* (1990).

Head, Richard ?1637-?1686 Bookseller and hack. His most famous work is a licentious PICARESQUE novel, *The English Rogue: Described in the Life of Meriton Latroon, A*

Witty Extravagant (1665), much of it autobiographical. His many other productions include an eccentric comedy of Irish life, *Hic et ubique: or, The Humours of Dublin* (1663).

Headlong Hall PEACOCK's first satirical novel, published in 1816. The guests debating civilization and progress over Christmas at Squire Headlong's Welsh country house include: Mr Foster the perfectibilian, who rehearses the rational optimism of Condorcet and GODWIN; Mr Escot the deteriorationist, a blend of Rousseau, MALTHUS and the notes to SHELLEY's *QUEEN MAB*; Mr Jenkison the status quo-ite; and the gourmandizing Reverend Doctor Gaster. They are joined by Dr Cranium, the phrenologist, and his daughter Cephalis; Mr Milestone, the landscape gardener; Mr Panscope the polymath; and assorted musicians, poets, and marriageable daughters. In a finely worked comic episode Mr Milestone's criticism of the unimproved gardens causes his host to blow away an offending rock with near-fatal consequences for two guests. The Squire again proves true to his name at the end, when he arranges no fewer than four marriages, including his own.

Heaney, Seamus (Justin) 1939– Irish poet. Born in County Derry, he migrated to the Republic of Ireland in 1972. He became Boylston Professor of Rhetoric and Oratory at Harvard University in 1984 and professor of poetry at Oxford in 1989. The early poetry in *Death of a Naturalist* (1966) and *Door into the Dark* (1969) draws on childhood experience as well as his enduring sense of habitat and environment. *Wintering Out* (1972), *North* (1975) and *Field Work* (1979) are more political, beginning his intense concentration on the cultural and historical implications of words. They have been followed by *Station Island* (1984), *Haw Lantern* (1987) and *Seeing Things* (1991). *Selected Poems 1965–75* appeared in 1980, *Selected Poems 1966–87* in 1990. *Sweeney Astray* (1983) is a version of the medieval Irish *Buile Suibhne*. His wide-ranging criticism includes *Preoccupations* (1980), *The Government of the Tongue and Other Critical Writings* (1988) and *The Redress of Poetry* (1990).

Hearn, (Patricio) Lafcadio (Tessima Carlos) 1850–1904 Journalist, travel-writer, novelist and writer about Japan. Born in Greece of Irish-Greek parentage, and educated in France and England, he emigrated in 1869 to the USA, where his writings included colourful descriptions of Creole life in New Orleans. *Gombo Zhebes* (1885) is a collection of proverbs in French from Louisiana and the West Indies, and *Chita* (1889) a novel set on the Gulf Coast of Louisiana. *Two Years in the French West Indies* (1890) is about his experience of Martinique. In 1890 he went to Japan, becoming a Japanese citizen, adopting the name Yakimo Koizumi and writing *Gleanings in Buddha-Fields* (1897), *In Ghostly Japan* (1899), *A Japanese Miscellany* (1901) and *Japan: An Attempt at Interpretation* (1904).

Hearne, John 1926– Jamaican novelist. Articulate, middle-class characters respond generously to calls on their humanity, but with disastrous personal consequences, in *Voices under the Window* (1955), *Stranger at the Gate* (1956) and *The Autumn Equinox* (1959). The latter two novels and *The Faces of Love* (1957) and *Land of the Living* (1961) are about the fictional Caribbean island of Cayuna. *The Sure Salvation* (1981), his finest novel to date, is set on a slave-ship. As John Morris, Hearne has written thrillers with Morris Cargill.

Hearne, Thomas 1678–1735 Antiquary. He wrote *Reliquiae Bodleianae: or, Some Genuine Remains of Sir Thomas*

Bodley (1703) and *Ductor historicus: or, A Short System of Universal History and an Introduction to the Study of It* (1704–5), and edited the works of LELAND, CAMDEN and earlier chroniclers. His Jacobite convictions lost him the post of keeper of the Bodleian Library in 1716. He appears as Wormius in POPE's *DUNCIAD*.

Heart of Darkness A story by CONRAD, published in the same volume as *Youth* in 1902. It is told mainly by Marlow to his friends on a yacht in the Thames estuary. He had been hired by a European trading company to replace a steamship captain on a great African river. The Westerners he meets at the trading post and the Central Station are interested only in extracting ivory and do not notice the suffering of the native workers. Marlow is sent upriver to rescue Kurtz, an agent, now seriously ill, whose commercial success is matched by his reputation for idealism. Expecting to meet an apostle of Western civilization, he finds a man who has made himself the natives' god. His depravity is signalled by the human heads which decorate the posts outside his hut. His deathbed cry – 'The horror! The horror!' – intimates a kind of desperate self-knowledge.

Heart of Midlothian, The A novel by SIR WALTER SCOTT, published in 1818 as the second series of *Tales of My Landlord*. The heart of Midlothian is the Tolbooth prison in Edinburgh, focal point of the Porteous Riots of 1736. Effie Dean, imprisoned there on a charge of child murder, is sentenced to death when her half-sister Jeanie refuses to lie on her behalf. But Jeanie walks to London and secures a royal pardon for Effie. Robertson, one of the rioters, is revealed as George Staunton, a wild son of good family and the father of Effie's son. He persuades Effie to marry him and, as Lady Staunton, she learns that her son is still alive, left with a band of robbers after being stolen by the crazed Madge Wildfire. Staunton is unwittingly killed by his own son when he tries to rescue him. Modern readers and critics have usually agreed that *Heart of Midlothian* is the finest of Scott's novels and that Jeanie Deans is his best-realized character. The book is notable, too, for the lyric, 'Proud Maisie', sung by the dying Madge Wildfire.

Heart of the Matter, The A novel by GRAHAM GREENE, published in 1948. It takes place in West Africa, a harsh physical and moral wilderness, during World War II. Scobie, the deputy commissioner of police, becomes the victim of his compassion for others: first for his unstable wife, Louise, then for a young widow, Helen, with whom he has an affair. He falls into debt, and inadvertently causes the death of his servant Ali. Resolving to commit suicide, a mortal sin in terms of his Catholic creed, he tries to conceal this from his wife by fabricating his diary. His fate is observed throughout by a young intelligence agent, Wilson, who is in love with Louise but acts in his official capacity to uncover Scobie's posthumous deceit.

Heartbreak House: *A Fantasia in the Russian Manner on English Themes* A play by SHAW, published in 1919 and produced in New York in 1920 and at the ROYAL COURT THEATRE in 1921.

Shaw's portrait of 'cultured, leisured Europe before the war' presents a series of extraordinary encounters and mistaken identities in a crazy house owned by the aged and eccentric Captain Shotover and presided over by one of his daughters, Mrs Hector Hushabye. Her friend, Ellie Dunn, is dutifully engaged to Boss Mangan, an oafish millionaire, but has fallen in love with Marcus Darnley; he turns out to be Hector Hushabye, a pathological liar and philanderer. Captain Shotover wonders if Ellie's father, Mazzini Dunn, is the boatswain and ex-pirate he once employed. But that man, Billy Dunn, turns up to burgle the house and be killed with Mangan in the air raid which closes the play. Another visitor is Shotover's daughter Lady Utterword, whose husband has been governor of all the Crown Colonies in succession.

Heath, Roy (Aubrey Kelvin) 1926– Guyanese novelist, who lives in London. Calling himself 'a chronicler of Guyanese life in this century', he has written about slum poverty in *A Man Come Home* (1974), psychotic behaviour in *The Murderer* (1978), middle-class respectability in the trilogy, *From the Heat of the Day* (1979), *One Generation* (1981) and *Genetha* (1981), rural destitution in *Kwaku* (1982), the clash between the values of 'civilization' and the hinterland in *Orealla* (1984). His narrative technique successfully blends social realism with the Amerindian, African and Indian folk legend and myth in Guyanese popular beliefs.

Heath-Stubbs, John (Francis Alexander) 1918– Poet. His first poems appeared with the work of KEITH DOUGLAS and SIDNEY KEYES in *Eight Oxford Poets* (1941). Subsequent work, gathered in *Collected Poems* (1988) and *Selected Poems* (1990), established him as a traditionalist with an interest in classical subjects and forms. His many translations include a version of THE RUBÁIYÁT OF OMAR KHAYYÁM (1979). He has also edited *The Faber Book of Twentieth-Century Verse* (with DAVID WRIGHT; 1953), and written studies of BEDDOES, JOHN CLARE and GEORGE DARLEY, in *The Darkling Plain* (1950), and of CHARLES WILLIAMS (1955).

Heber, Reginald 1783–1826 Bishop and hymn-writer. He was appointed Bishop of Calcutta in 1822. The author of a *Narrative of a Journey through the Upper Provinces of India 1824–1825* and a few volumes of poetry, he is best known for his hymns, which include: 'Brightest and Best of the Sons of the Morning!', 'From Greenland's Icy Mountains', 'The Son of God Goes Forth to War' and 'Holy, Holy, Holy! Lord God Almighty!'.

Hecht, Ben 1894–1964 American playwright, screenwriter and novelist. He scored a huge success with *The Front Page* (co-written with CHARLES MACARTHUR; 1928), about Chicago newspapermen. He and MacArthur also wrote the popular comedy *Twentieth Century* (1932) and several successful screenplays, including *Nothing Sacred* (1937), *Wuthering Heights* (1939), *Spellbound* (1945) and *Notorious* (1946).

Heinlein, Robert A(nson) 1907–88 American writer of SCIENCE FICTION. His understanding of technology and enthusiasm for the conquest of space made him an outstanding pulp writer. He was one of the first science fiction authors to break into more respectable markets. *The Past through Tomorrow* (1967) gathered the short stories which form a coherent future history, featuring as an 'alternate world' in some of his subsequent work. Novels include a political fantasy, *Double Star* (1956), a future war story, *Starship Troopers* (1959), and, in abrupt change of direction, *Stranger in a Strange Land* (1961), about a messianic hero. *The Cat Who Walked Through Walls* (1985) and its sequel *To Sail Beyond the Sunset* (1987) are typical examples of his later work.

Heiress, The A comedy by BURGOYNE, produced with great success in 1786. Clifford woos Lady Emily Gayville. Her brother, Lord Gayville, is reluctant to marry a vulgar heiress, Miss Alscrip, and falls in love with the poor Miss Alton instead. All ends well when she is discovered to be Clifford's long-lost sister and the true heiress to the Alscrip fortune.

Heller, Joseph 1923– American novelist. He is still best known for *CATCH-22* (1961), an anti-war SATIRE which drew on his own military experience, as he did again for his play *We Bombed in New Haven* (1968). It has given the language a term for self-contradicting illogic. His subsequent novels are *Something Happened* (1974), *Good as Gold* (1979), *God Knows* (1984), *Picture This* (1988) and *Closing Time* (1994), a belated sequel to *Catch-22*. His experience as a victim of Guillain-Barré syndrome, a debilitating virus, is described in *No Laughing Matter* (with Speed Vogel; 1986).

Hellman, Lillian (Florence) 1907–84 American playwright. She began an acclaimed career with *The Children's Hour* (1934), about a malicious schoolgirl's invention of a lesbian relationship between her two teachers. Her second stage success, *The Little Foxes* (1939), dealt with the breaking-up of a Southern family, the Hubbards. It was followed by: *Watch on the Rhine* (1941) and *The Searching Wind* (1944), two anti-Nazi dramas; *Another Part of the Forest* (1946), about the earlier history of the Hubbard family; *The Autumn Garden* (1951); and *Toys in the Attic* (1960). Three volumes of autobiography, *An Unfinished Woman* (1969), *Scoundrel Time* (1976) and *Pentimento* (1973), treat, *inter alia*, her long-standing relationship with DASHIELL HAMMETT and her experience of McCarthyism in the early 1950s.

Helps, Sir Arthur 1813–75 Essayist, historian and novelist. A friend of Queen Victoria, he edited *Speeches and Addresses of the Prince Consort* (1862) and Victoria's *Leaves from the Journal of our Life in the Highlands* (1868). He also published: three novels, including the popular *Realmah* (1868); a book of aphorisms, *Thoughts in the Cloister and the Crowd* (1835); three plays; essays and dialogues; biographies of Columbus and Cortes; and a history of the Spanish conquest of America (1855–61).

Helwig, David 1938– Canadian poet, novelist and short-story writer. The early poems in *Figures in a Landscape* (1967) deal mainly with everyday subjects, but subsequent work has tended towards the sinister and violent. It includes *The Sign of the Gunman* (1969), *The Best Name of Silence* (1972), *Atlantic Crossings* (1974), *A Book of the Hours* (1979) and *Talking Prophet Blues* (1989). *The Glass Knight* (1976), *Jennifer* (1979), *It is Always Summer* (1982) and *A Sound like Laughter* (1983) form a tetralogy of novels set in Kingston. Other novels are *The Day before Tomorrow* (1971), *A Postcard from Rome* (1988), *Old Wars* (1989) and *Of Desire* (1990). *The Streets of Summer* (1969) is a collection of short stories. He has also edited *A Book about Billie* (1972), from interviews with a habitual criminal.

Hemans, Felicia Dorothea 1793–1835 Poet. An accomplished scholar and acknowledged beauty, she was the friend of SCOTT and WORDSWORTH. Her best-known poems are 'The Better Land', 'The Landing of the Pilgrim Fathers in New England' and 'Casablanca' ('The boy stood on the burning deck'). Volumes include *The Domestic Afflictions* (1812), *The Forest Sanctuary* (1825), *Records of Woman* (1828) and *Songs of the Affections* (1830). Of her two plays, *The Siege of Valencia* and *The Vespers of Palermo* (both published in 1823), only the latter was produced, with little success.

Hemingway, Ernest (Miller) 1898–1961 American novelist and short-story writer. In an adventurous life, lived increasingly in the public eye, he moved from his native Illinois to Kansas, Chicago, Toronto, Europe and, finally, Cuba. His years in Paris, where he was part of the circle including POUND, GERTRUDE STEIN and FORD MADOX FORD, were his most creative period. It produced two significant collections of stories, *In Our Time* (1925; expanded 1930), partly looking backward to his childhood in the Great Lakes, and *Men without Women* (1927), as well as two significant novels, THE SUN ALSO RISES (1926; called *Fiesta* in Britain), and *A Farewell to Arms* (1929). Their laconic, disillusioned stance captured the mood of the 'lost generation' who had survived World War I, and their spare style helped to refresh 20th-century prose. *Death in the Afternoon* (1932), a study of bullfighting, was followed by: *Winner Take Nothing* (1933), a collection of stories; *Green Hills of Africa* (1935), about big-game hunting; *To Have and Have Not* (1937), a short novel about smuggling in the Key West–Havana region; and *The Fifth Column and the First Forty-Nine Stories* (1938), in which the title-piece is a play about the Spanish Civil War and the stories include 'The Snows of Kilimanjaro'. The Spanish Civil War also provided the subject of *For Whom the Bell Tolls* (1940), an ambitious novel whose title (borrowed from DONNE) implies that the loss of freedom anywhere diminishes it everywhere.

Across the River and into the Trees (1950), his first novel in a decade, was poorly received but *The Old Man and the Sea* (1952), a parable of inner strength and courage, won Hemingway a belated PULITZER PRIZE and helped to earn him the Nobel Prize for Literature in 1954. Consciousness of his literary decline, as well as ill health, contributed to his suicide. Posthumous publications include: a memoir of his years in Paris, *A Moveable Feast* (1964); two novels, *Islands in the Stream* (1970) and *The Garden of Eden* (1986); and *The Dangerous Summer* (1985), about a trip to Spain in 1959.

Henderson, Hamish 1919– Scottish poet, songwriter, folklorist and translator. *Elegies for the Dead in Cyrenaica* (1948; reissued, 1977) is a tribute to 'the dead, the innocent' on both sides of the war in the 'brutish desert'. He has edited *Ballads of World War Two* (1948) and recorded a collection of songs, *Freedom Come All Ye* (1977). His best-known pieces – 'The John Maclean March' and 'Free Mandela' – show his strong socialist and republican sympathies. He is also a distinguished translator of Italian poetry.

Hendry, J(ames) F(indlay) 1912–86 Poet and anthologist. A central figure in the NEW APOCALYPSE movement, he introduced the first of its three major anthologies, *The New Apocalypse* (1939), and edited the other two, *The White Horseman* (1941) and *The Crown and the Sickle* (1943), with HENRY TREECE. *Myth and Social Integration* (1940) is the major statement of the movement's aims. A minor poet himself, he also published *The Bombed Happiness* (1940), *The Orchestral Mountain* (1943), *Marimarusa* (1979), *A World Alien* (1980) and *Fernie Brae* (1987).

Henley, Beth 1952– American playwright and actress. *Crimes of the Heart* (1981), about three Mississippi sisters who rally round after one has shot her husband, typifies her flair for witty, absurd comedy in the tradition of Southern Gothic. Other plays include *The Wake of Jamey Foster* (1982), *Am I Blue?* (1982), *The Miss Firecracker Contest* (1984), *The Debutante Ball* (1985), *The Lucky Spot* (1986) and *Abundance* (1990). She has also written screenplays for *Crimes* and *Miss Firecracker*.

Henley, W(illiam) E(rnest) 1849–1903 Poet, critic and editor. While convalescing after the amputation of his leg, he began the 'In Hospital' poems (1875), sometimes hailed as early examples of free verse. He is best known

for 'Invictus' (1875): 'I am the master of my fate:/ I am the captain of my soul.' His collections include *A Book of Verses* (1888), *The Song of the Sword* (1892), *London Voluntaries* (1893), *For England's Sake* (1900) and *Hawthorn and Lavender* (1901). He also published two volumes of art and literary journalism, *Views and Reviews I* and *II* (1890 and 1892), a selection of verse for boys, *Lyra heroica* (1891), an edition of BURNS (1896–7) and *Tudor Translations* (1892–1903). As editor of *The Magazine of Art* from 1882 he brought the work of Whistler and Rodin to a wider public, and as editor of *The Scots Observer* (later *The National Observer*) from 1889 he published KIPLING. Before their friendship soured he wrote several plays with STEVENSON, who used him as model for Long John Silver in *TREASURE ISLAND*.

Henri, Adrian See LIVERPOOL POETS.

Henrietta Temple A novel by BENJAMIN DISRAELI, published in 1837. It follows the tangled love affairs of the poor but noble Ferdinand Armine, who proposes to his wealthy cousin, Katherine Grandison, but also becomes engaged to the penniless Henrietta Temple. When his treachery is exposed Henrietta deserts him and agrees to marry Lord Montfort. Katherine, meanwhile, forgives Ferdinand and, with the help of Count Mirabel, disentangles the situation. She marries Lord Montfort and Henrietta, who inherits a fortune, helps Ferdinand.

Henry, O. [Porter, William Sidney] 1862–1910 American short-story writer. He was a popular and prolific writer of stories characterized by a twist of plot which turns on an ironic or coincidental circumstance and by a surprise ending. They were collected in *Cabbages and Kings* (1904), *The Four Million* (1906), *Heart of the West* (1907), *The Trimmed Lamp* (1907), *The Gentle Grafter* (1908), *The Voice of the City* (1908), *Options* (1909), *Roads of Destiny* (1909), *Whirligigs* (1910), *Strictly Business* (1910) and four posthumous volumes, *Sixes and Sevens* (1911), *Rolling Stones* (1912), *Waifs and Strays* (1917) and *Postscripts* (1923).

Henry IV, King A history play in two parts by SHAKESPEARE. The shaping of the plot, drawn largely from HOLINSHED's *Chronicles*, suggests that he had the second part in mind when he prepared the first. Even so, they are distinct and can be performed separately.

Part One, probably first performed in 1597, was first published in Quarto (Q1) in 1598; editors collate this text with that in the First Folio of 1623. The historical events begin with Owen Glendower's uprising and the defeat of the invading Scots by Henry Percy (Hotspur) and culminate in the defeat and death of Hotspur at the Battle of Shrewsbury (1403). Bolingbroke, the decisive usurper of *RICHARD II*, has become a careworn king, further troubled by his son's waywardness. Prince Hal beguiles the time in the company of the fat knight, Sir John Falstaff, drinking in taverns and plotting practical jokes. By comparison, Hotspur seems all the more a hero. But when Hotspur joins forces with Glendower, it is Hal who saves the day at Shrewsbury, killing him in single combat.

Part Two, probably first performed in 1598, was first published in a censored Quarto (Q1) in 1600; editors collate this text with that in the First Folio of 1623. The play covers the period from the Battle of Shrewsbury to Henry IV's death in 1413. Hal has returned to the company of Falstaff and his cronies, but takes up arms when the rebel forces gather again. Falstaff, recruiting in the Cotswolds, finds a welcome with his old friend Justice Shallow. Prince John, the king's younger son, defeats the rebels by trickery. The dying King hears of this success, and is reconciled with Hal. Falstaff is overjoyed to hear of Hal's succession, but the transformed Henry V publicly spurns him during his coronation procession. Falstaff proved popular enough for Shakespeare to use him again in THE MERRY WIVES OF WINDSOR.

Henry V, The Life of A history play by SHAKESPEARE, concluding the sequence begun by RICHARD II and HENRY IV. It was first performed *c.* 1599 and first published in a corrupt (probably pirated) Quarto (Q1) in 1600. The text in the First Folio of 1623 is probably taken from Q2 (1602). Shakespeare's main source was HOLINSHED's *Chronicles.*

This most obviously patriotic of the English history plays is the only one that openly celebrates the achievements of a successful monarch, 'the mirror of all Christian kings'. Mocked by the French, he displays his political astuteness by quelling a rebellion at home before going on to demonstrate his military prowess in a French campaign of which the Battle of Agincourt is the highlight. Magnanimous in victory, he charmingly woos the French princess, Katharine, and the play ends with their marriage plans sealed with a kiss. A low-life sub-plot involves, first, the reported death of Falstaff and then the unruly conduct of various of his old associates, Pistol, Bardolph and Nym. Symbolizing the bonds of loyalty that hold Henry's united kingdom, but oddly ill at ease in both main and sub-plot, are four English, Welsh, Irish and Scottish commanders, Gower, Fluellen, Macmorris and Jamie.

Henry VI A history play in three parts, of which SHAKESPEARE was the main, but almost certainly not the sole, author. It may contain his first surviving work for the stage. The first part may date from as early as 1590, and Elizabethan theatre practice would suggest that the second and third parts followed fairly closely; ROBERT GREENE's attack on Shakespeare as 'an upstart crow', which parodies a line from Part 3, was published in 1592. The only reliable text is that of the First Folio (1623).

Henry VI gives an episodic account of the king's reign, based largely on HOLINSHED's *Chronicles* and EDWARD HALL's *The Union of the Two Noble and Illustre Families of Lancaster and York.* It begins with Henry V's funeral and ends with Henry VI's murder by Richard, Duke of Gloucester, paving the way for Edward IV's accession to the throne and the events depicted in the altogether more inventive *RICHARD III.* Whereas Part 1 divides its attention between factional quarrels in England and the war in France, the last two parts confine themselves to the dynastic struggles between Yorkists and Lancastrians that have come to be known as the Wars of the Roses. The complex history of plot and counter-plot is uncertainly controlled, and the trilogy is less successful as a whole than it is memorable for a handful of episodes and characters (most notably perhaps Henry's wife Margaret of Anjou).

Henry VIII, The Life of King A historical play, probably written collaboratively by SHAKESPEARE and JOHN FLETCHER. It was apparently first performed in 1613, and it was first published in the First Folio of 1623. HOLINSHED's *Chronicles* is a main source. The play is at its most impressive in chronicling the guile of Wolsey and his sudden downfall, and the anguish of Queen Katharine over the question of the royal divorce. Otherwise, the history was perhaps too recent (the infant Elizabeth I is christened at the end) to allow the authors' imaginations sufficient freedom. If this was

Shakespeare's last work for the theatre, it made a disappointingly half-hearted end.

Henry Esmond, The History of A novel by THACKERAY, published in 1852. Set in the reign of Queen Anne, it is generally considered the finest Victorian historical novel.

Henry Esmond tells the story of his life, though predominantly in the third person. Believing he is the illegitimate son of the 3rd Viscount Castlewood, he spends a lonely childhood in Jacobite circles, lightened when his cousin Francis Esmond inherits the title and comes to live at Castlewood with his young wife Rachel and their two children, Frank and Beatrix. He returns from Cambridge to find the dissolute Lord Mohun a regular guest, gambling with Lord Castlewood and pursuing his wife. The two lords fight a duel in London and Castlewood is killed, leaving a confession which reveals Henry to be the true heir of Castlewood. He burns the document. Imprisoned and rejected by Rachel for his part in the duel, he goes abroad to fight in the War of the Spanish Succession. On visits home he is reconciled with Rachel and falls in love with the proud and beautiful Beatrix. She becomes engaged to the Duke of Hamilton, who fights a duel with Lord Mohun. Both men die. In a last effort to please Beatrix, Henry joins in a plot to restore James Edward Stuart, the Old Pretender, to the throne but it fails because of the Prince's reckless pursuit of Beatrix to Castlewood. Disillusioned with power and worldliness, Esmond marries Rachel and retires with her to a life of domestic tranquillity in Virginia. THE VIRGINIANS continues the story of the Esmond family.

Henryson, Robert d. *c.* 1508 Scottish poet. All that is known of him is that he lived in Dunfermline and, according to DUNBAR, was dead by 1508. It has been suggested that he was a schoolmaster and studied medicine or law (or both), perhaps at Bologna. Although he is classed with the SCOTTISH CHAUCERIANS, Henryson's originality is the outstanding feature of his best-known work. THE TESTAMENT OF CRESSEID provides an alternative ending to CHAUCER's TROILUS AND CRISEYDE. Drawing on a long European tradition of Aesopic writing, *The Morall Fabillis of Esope the Phrygian* describes animal life in sympathetic detail. *Orpheus and Eurydice* adapts the classical story as a moral ALLEGORY of the vulnerability of affection and the relationship between reason and affection. *Robene and Makyne,* owing something to both the *pastourelle* and the debate poem, tells how the shepherd Robene refuses Makyne's love but is scorned in turn when he later falls in love with her. Henryson also wrote a number of shorter works, several of them meditations on mortality, and two didactic allegories. *The Bludy Serk* is a brief narrative about a knight killed in rescuing a maiden from a giant's castle; the bloody shirt he leaves for her to remember him by is interpreted in terms of Christ's sacrifice. *The Garmont of Gud Ladeis* is similar, describing an allegorical garment made up of various virtues.

Henty, G(eorge) A(lfred) 1832–1902 Writer of CHILDREN'S LITERATURE. His experience as a war correspondent in the Crimean War and other conflicts served him well when he started writing adventure stories for boys. Henry produced about 80 novels (sometimes at the rate of three per year), usually concentrating on action-packed episodes from British history. Typical titles include *Under Drake's Flag* (1883), *The Lion of the North* (1885) and his last book, *With the Allies in Pekin* (1904).

heptameter See METRE.

Heraud, John Abraham 1799–1887 Poet. His powerful, grandiose style is best represented in *The Descent into Hell* (1830) and *The Judgement of the Flood* (1834). He also wrote a successful play, *Videna: or, the Mother's Tragedy* (1854).

Herbert, A(lan) P(atrick) 1890–1971 Humorist and reformer. His experiences in World War I resulted in two volumes of poetry (1916 and 1918) and a novel, *The Secret Battle* (1919). He joined the staff of *PUNCH* in 1924. His mock law reports were collected as *Misleading Cases in the Common Law* (1929). *Holy Deadlock* (1934), a novel, exposed the need for reform of the divorce law, one of several campaigns he undertook as Independent MP for Oxford University (1935–50). The battle over his Marriage Bill was related in *The Ayes Have It* (1937). *Independent Member* (1950) described his years in Parliament. His most popular novel, *The Water Gipsies* (1930), reflected his long-standing love for the English waterways. He also wrote libretti for several successful musicals, including *Riverside Nights* (1926), *Tantivy Towers* (1930) and *Bless the Bride* (1947). *APH: His Life and Times*, his autobiography, appeared in 1970.

Herbert, Edward, 1st Baron Herbert of Cherbury 1583–1648 Philosopher, poet and diplomat. The elder brother of GEORGE HERBERT, he moved in court circles, served as ambassador to France (1619–24) and was a reluctant Royalist soldier before submitting to Parliament in 1645. His career was one of early promise but no ultimate greatness. Herbert's foremost work was *De veritate* (1625), a philosophical treatise in Latin aligning him with the CAMBRIDGE PLATONISTS; the principles of natural religion he propounded have earned him the title the 'Father of DEISM'. *The Life and Reign of Henry VIII* (1644) is not outstanding but, even though it stops at 1624, his *Autobiography* (first published in 1764 by HORACE WALPOLE) is an interesting revelation of the times. He also published spirited English verse.

Herbert, Frank 1920–86 American writer of SCIENCE FICTION. He caught the mood of the day with the intense ecological mysticism of his epic novel *Dune* (1965), describing the advent of a messiah-figure in a desert world. Five sequels were added. *The Green Brain* (1966) and *Hellstrom's Hive* (1973) developed his interest in ecology. His fascination with religion continued in *The God Makers* (1972) as well as *The Jesus Incident* (1979), *The Lazarus Effect* (1983) and *The Ascension Factor* (1988), the sequels which he and Bill Ransom added to his solo novel *Destination: Void* (1966).

Herbert, George 1593–1633 Poet and divine. He was the younger brother of EDWARD HERBERT and a member of the noble family that included the earldoms of Pembroke and Montgomery among its holdings. An outstanding scholar, he was educated at Westminster and Trinity College, Cambridge, where he became a fellow at 22, and Public Orator to the University in 1619–27. He was MP for Montgomery in 1624–5 but became a deacon in 1626 and a priest in 1630, obtaining the living of Bemerton, Wiltshire, and staying there until his death. *The Temple: Sacred Poems and Private Ejaculations* (1633) was posthumously published by his friend NICHOLAS FERRAR and went through 13 editions by 1680. These 160 poems, among the finest work by any of the METAPHYSICAL POETS, are short but often exquisite, distinguished by their carefully wrought shapes, the ingenuity of their images, and their calm and subtle religious faith. Herbert's short prose work, *A Priest to the*

Temple (1652), offered guidance to country priests. WALTON wrote his biography (1670).

Herbert, (Alfred Francis) Xavier 1901–84 Australian novelist. His best-known work is *Capricornia* (1938), a sprawling chronicle of Aborigines and white men set in the Northern outback. Other novels are *Seven Emus* (1958) and *Soldiers' Women* (1960). In *Poor Fellow My Country* (1975) he returned to the outback with a massive saga notable for passages dealing with Aboriginal life. He is also the author of *Larger Than Life* (short stories; 1963) and *Disturbing Element* (autobiography; 1963).

Herbst, Josephine (Frey) 1897–1969 American novelist and journalist. Like many of her generation, she aligned herself with the political left. *Pity is Not Enough* (1933), *The Executioner Waits* (1934) and *Rope of Gold* (1939) form a trilogy about the decay of capitalism and the failure of a revolutionary movement to bring about the new Communist social order it seeks. Other novels include *Nothing is Sacred* (1928), *Money for Love* (1929), *Satan's Sergeants* (1941) and *Somewhere the Tempest Fell* (1947).

Herd, David 1732–1810 Scottish collector and anthologist of BALLADS. He accumulated a good deal of older Scottish traditional verse, notably in *Ancient and Modern Scottish Songs ... Collected from Memory, Tradition, and Ancient Authors* (1776).

Herne, James A. 1839–1901 American playwright, manager and actor. His collaborative work with DAVID BELASCO included *Chums* (1879; retitled *Hearts of Oak*, 1880), a MELODRAMA which nevertheless showed hints of the REALISM which distinguished his most important work, *Margaret Fleming* (1891). A study of a woman's response to her husband's infidelity, it was influenced by Ibsen and acclaimed by WILLIAM DEAN HOWELLS. *Shore Acres* (1892) is an equally realistic but happier story of life in New England. Herne also wrote: *The Minute Men of 1774–75* (1886); *Drifting Apart* (1888), an unconventional temperance drama; *The Reverend Griffith Davenport* (1899), a Civil War story based on Helen H. Gardner's *An Unofficial Patriot* (1894); and *Sag Harbor* (1900), a reworking of the themes of *Hearts of Oak* .

Hero and Leander An erotic poem (or EPYLLION) left incomplete by MARLOWE at his death in 1593 and finished by CHAPMAN. Marlowe's share of the poem, published by itself in 1598, is its first two 'sestiads' (a word coined by Chapman by analogy with 'Iliad'). All six sestiads appeared later in 1598. Marlowe took the story of the meeting and wooing of Hero and Leander from Musaeus, an Alexandrian poet of the 5th century AD, but his tone and manner are Ovidian. His fragment ends with the dawn breaking after a night of love. Chapman's continuation does not preserve Marlowe's wry, detached narrative voice and is more concerned with morality and decorum.

Heroes, Hero-Worship, and the Heroic in History, On A group of six lectures by CARLYLE, delivered in May 1840 and published the following year. After asserting that 'The History of the World is but the Biography of great men', he describes the different forms taken by the hero in different phases of human history: Divinity (Odin), Prophet (Mahomet), Poet (Dante and SHAKESPEARE), Priest (Luther and Knox), Man of Letters (JOHNSON, Rousseau and BURNS) and King (Cromwell and Napoleon).

heroic couplet In English verse, a pair of rhyming iambic pentameters (see METRE). The form was developed by CHAUCER and championed by DRYDEN against the BLANK VERSE of much English tragic drama. He also promoted its use in non-dramatic verse, cultivating the poised, epigrammatic effects which predecessors like JONSON, DONNE and WALLER had occasionally managed and which 18th-century successors like POPE and SAMUEL JOHNSON emulated. The 'closed couplet' uses the END-STOPPED LINE, but the 'open couplet' uses ENJAMBEMENT.

Herrick, Robert 1591-1674 Poet. After mixing in the artistic circles of London, where he became a friend of JONSON, he was ordained and, in 1629, appointed to the living of Dean Prior in Devon. Ejected in 1647 for refusing the Solemn League and Covenant, he returned to London, but was reinstated in 1662. He died, a bachelor, at the age of 83, in his parish. His major collection, *Hesperides* (1648), consists of 1200 poems, many of them short, tackling an impressive variety of forms: ELEGIES, epitaphs, EPIGRAMS, ANACREONTICS, hymns, songs (many later set to music), imitations of Horace and Catullus, and, in the sub-section *Noble Numbers*, devotional verse. Some of the epigrams are positively vile, but elsewhere Herrick is capable of beautifully wrought lyrics which have invited analogies with goldsmith's work, a craft to which he had originally been apprenticed. 'The Funeral Rites of the Rose' and 'The Lily in a Crystal' demonstrate the intricate style of his more delicate lyrics. There is a whimsical grace in much of his love poetry – such as his classic exposition of the CARPE DIEM theme, 'To the Virgins, To Make Much of Time' – which allies him with the CAVALIER POETS as well as their common master, Jonson. 'Oberon's Feast' and 'Oberon's Palace' are two of his fantasy pieces about faeries. Never a profound poet, Herrick was a distinguished verbal craftsman, and his erotic poems can be highly sensory.

Herrick, Robert 1868-1938 American novelist. Many of his novels depict men who find that worldly success leaves them unfulfilled, though Van Harrington, the hero of his best-known novel, *Memoirs of an American Citizen* (1905), makes a fortune and wins a seat in the Senate without experiencing regret. *The Man Who Wins* (1897), his first novel, and *Web of Life* (1900) are about doctors, and *The Common Lot* (1904) is about an architect; *The Real World* (1901; republished as *Jock O'Dreams*, 1908), *A Life for a Life* (1910) and *Waste* (1924) tell the stories of business executives. Herrick also published short stories and *Sometime* (1933), a satirical Utopian novel.

Herschel, Sir John Frederick William 1792-1871 Astronomer. A founder of the Royal Astronomical Society and Secretary to the Royal Society in 1824-7, he discovered many new stars, clusters and nebulae. His writings include *Outlines of Astronomy* (1841) and *Familiar Lectures on Scientific Subjects* (1867).

Hervey, James 1714-58 Essayist. A prominent member of early Methodist circles, he published several popular books – *Meditations among the Tombs* (1746-7), *Reflections on a Flower Garden* and *Contemplations on the Night* (both 1747) – appealing to the same tastes as the work of the GRAVEYARD POETS.

Hervey, John, Baron Hervey of Ickworth 1694-1743 Politician. A supporter of Sir Robert Walpole, he became Vice-Chamberlain to George II in 1730, served as Lord Privy Seal in 1733-42, and enjoyed the confidence of Queen Caroline. As a friend of the accomplished LADY MARY WORTLEY MONTAGU, he became a hated enemy of POPE, who attacked him in *THE DUNCIAD* and as Sporus in the *Epistle to Dr Arbuthnot*. His attempt to respond in

kind did not efface Pope's portrait of him as a dangerously pernicious fop. *Memoirs of the Reign of George the Second* (1848) offers a frank and satirical portrait of his times.

Herzog A novel by BELLOW, published in 1964. Moses Herzog, a 47-year-old scholar, undergoes an emotional, intellectual and moral crisis. From his summer home in the Berkshire Mountains he writes letters, in his head or on paper, to friends, relatives, his psychiatrist, politicians, philosophers (such as Heidegger and Nietzsche), the public and even God. Flashbacks provide the reader with information about Herzog's relations with his family, his two ex-wives (Daisy and Madeleine), his Japanese mistress Sono, and his current lover, Ramona. A trip to Chicago, to avenge himself on Madeleine and her lover, Valentine Gersbach, ends in humiliation. At the end, he rejects his brother's suggestion that he go into a mental hospital, plans for the future and feels relative peace.

Hewett, Dorothy (Coade) 1923- Australian playwright, poet and novelist. For many years a member of the Communist Party, she drew on her experience of factory work in her novel, *Bobbin' Up* (1959). Her second novel, *Playwright*, appeared in 1993. In the interval Hewett concentrated on the theatre, producing mainly expressionistic works which feature music and poetry. They include *This Old Man Comes Rolling Home* (1967), *The Chapel Perilous* (1971), *Bon Bons and Roses for Dolly* (1972), *The Tatty Hollow Story* (1974), *Pandora's Cross* (1978), *The Man from Muckinupin* (1979) and *The Fields of Heaven* (1982). *Selected Poems* (1991) draws on her several previous volumes. Structural weaknesses in most of her writing are overridden by a powerful Rabelaisian personality which is fully revealed in *Wild Card: An Autobiography* (1990).

Hewitt, John (Harold) 1907-87 Irish poet. Born in Belfast, he first gained attention as a nature poet and celebrant of local landscapes. His inherited Nonconformity and his reading of radical writers prompted a quest for an Ulster identity based on the dialect and idiom generated by local history and environment, rather than on Protestant unionism or the traditions of Catholic and Celtic nationalism. Formally disciplined and understated, his verse is gathered in Frank Ormsby's edition of the *Collected Poems* (1991). Hewitt's lifelong concern with his native province is also reflected in an anthology, *The Rhyming Weavers and Other Country Poets of Antrim and Down* (1974), and *Ancestral Voices: The Selected Prose of John Hewitt* (edited by Tom Clyde, 1987).

Hewlett, Maurice (Henry) 1861-1923 Novelist and poet. *The Forest Lovers* (1898), a medieval romance which became an immediate success, was followed by *Richard Yea and Nay* (1900) and *The Queen's Quair* (1904). A trilogy of modern life, *Halfway House* (1908), *Open Country* (1909) and *Rest Harrow* (1910), centre on John Maxwell Senhouse, a gentle itinerant scholar. *The Song of the Plow* (1916) is a poem considering the agricultural labourer's lot.

hexameter See METRE.

Heylyn, Peter 1600-62 Religious controversialist. A supporter of Archbishop Laud, he wrote *Ecclesia Restaurata; or, The History of the Reformation of the Church of England* (1661); *Cyprianus Anglicus; or, The History of the Life and Death of Archbishop Laud* (1668), in answer to WILLIAM PRYNNE's attacks; *Aerlus Redivivus; or, The History of Presbyterianism* (1670), which sees Calvinism as the cause of religious strife; and *Microcosmus: A Little Description of the Great World* (1621), enlarged as *Cosmography* (1652).

Heyward, Dorothy 1890-1961 and **Heyward, (Edwin) DuBose** 1885-1940 American playwrights. Their husband-and-wife partnership is remembered for *Porgy* (1927) and *Mamba's Daughters* (1929), both based on novels by DuBose Heyward and both notable for their vivid use of Southern black folklore. *Porgy* became enduringly famous in George Gershwin's operatic adaptation, *Porgy and Bess* (1935).

Heywood, John c. 1497–c. 1580 Playwright. His marriage to THOMAS MORE's niece helped his career at the court of Henry VIII, where he was a singer and musician. A zealous Roman Catholic, he was convicted of treason for his role in a conspiracy against CRANMER in 1544, but returned to favour under Queen Mary. On the accession of Elizabeth he went into exile and was last heard of at Malines, in the Netherlands, in 1578. His daughter became JOHN DONNE's mother.

Heywood published several collections of EPIGRAMS and proverbs, and contributed to court MASQUES for Edward VI and Mary. But his importance lies in his short dramatic INTERLUDES, which abandon ALLEGORY and instruction for Chaucerian comedy. They include *The Play of the Weather* (1533), *A Play of Love* (1533), *A Dialogue concerning Witty and Witless* (first printed 1846) and, closest to true stage comedy, *The Play Called the Four PP* (c. 1544), about a debate between Palmer, Pardoner, 'Pothecary and Pedlar.

Heywood, Thomas 1573-1641 Playwright, actor, poet and pamphleteer. Of the 220 plays to which he claimed to have contributed, some 30 have survived. They include: *A WOMAN KILLED WITH KINDNESS* (1603), an outstanding domestic tragedy; *THE FAIR MAID OF THE WEST* (published 1631), a frolicsome adventure play; *If You Know Not Me, You Know Nobody* (1605), a chronicle play; *The Golden Age, The Silver Age, The Brazen Age* and the two parts of *The Iron Age* (1611–13), from Greek mythology; *The Four Prentices of London* (published 1615), a chivalric romance satirized in *THE KNIGHT OF THE BURNING PESTLE*; and *The Late Lancashire Witches* (with BROME; 1634). *An Apology for Actors* (1612) vigorously defends the theatre against Puritan attack.

Hiawatha, The Song of A narrative poem by LONGFELLOW, published in 1855. Hiawatha is reared by Nokomis, daughter of the moon, to become an Indian hero and leader. When his wife Minnehaha dies, he follows her spirit to the land of the North Wind, advising his people to accept the coming of the white man. Longfellow based the METRE on that of a Finnish epic, *The Kalevala*. Its hypnotic effect has made it a frequent target for PARODY.

Hibberd, Jack 1940– Australian playwright and novelist. A director as well as writer, he joined DAVID WILLIAMSON and others in the movement to create a new Australian drama in the 1960s. Early plays like *White with Wire Wheels* (1967) use a rough vernacular style. *Dimboola* (1969) is an affectionately satirical treatment of a country wedding. *A Stretch of the Imagination* (1972), a monologue by an old man facing death, blends comedy and pathos. Its use of Australian popular folklore also informs *Captain Midnite VC* (1972), *A Toast to Melba* (1974) and *The Les Darcy Show* (1975). Since abandoning the theatre he has published novels: *Memoirs of an Old Bastard* (1989), *The Life of Riley* (1991) and *Perdita* (1992).

Hichens, Robert (Smythe) 1864-1950 Journalist and novelist. Of his 66 books, the most famous is his first

novel, *The Green Carnation* (1894), an amiable ROMAN À CLEF in which OSCAR WILDE appears as Esme Amarinth and LORD ALFRED DOUGLAS as Lord Reggie. The slight plot, which has Lord Reggie toying with the idea of marriage to Lady Locke but offering a green carnation to her son, is less memorable than the cunning PARODY of Wilde's style.

Higgins, Matthew 1810-68 Journalist. He often used the pseudonym of Jacob Omnium, from the title of a satire on mercantile dishonesty (1845). He showed his skill as a controversialist in his pamphlets and writings on the Irish question in 1847. His many letters to *The Times* (up to 1863) and his periodical contributions had a high reputation. A friend of THACKERAY, he moved widely in sporting as well as literary society.

Higher Criticism, The The historical and literary study of the Bible, pioneered by 18th- and 19th-century German scholars. David Friedrich Strauss's *Das Leben Jesu* (1835–6), translated into English by GEORGE ELIOT, denied the historicity of all supernatural elements in the Gospels. Joseph Ernest Renan's *Vie de Jésus* (1863) also demythologized Christ by portraying Him as an amiable rabbi. The Higher Criticism implied that the Bible was not the directly inspired word of God but a human artifact; it was less a repository of incontrovertible truth than an anthology of literary beauties. This tendency in biblical studies was part symptom, part cause of the 19th-century decline in religious belief. See also JOHN WILLIAM COLENSO and *ESSAYS AND REVIEWS*.

Highsmith, Patricia 1921–95 Novelist and short-story writer. Born in Texas and brought up in New York, she lived alternately in the USA and Europe. The ingenious symmetry of her first novel, *Strangers on a Train* (1950), encouraged reviewers to label her work DETECTIVE FICTION, which did not help it find its best audience. Her real preoccupation is with guilt, unease and the refuges offered by obsession and fantasy. The last theme marks *The Cry of the Owl* (1962), *The Glass Cell* (1964), *The Story-Teller* (1965; as *A Suspension of Mercy* in UK) and *The Tremor of Forgery* (1969). Her unjudging authorial stance generates irony and black comedy in several collections of short stories and the novels about the likeable psychopath Tom Ripley: *The Talented Mr Ripley* (1955), *Ripley under Ground* (1970), *Ripley's Game* (1974), *The Boy Who Followed Ripley* (1980) and *Ripley under Water* (1991).

Hill, Aaron 1685-1750 Theatre manager, playwright and versifier. Youthful travels resulted in *A Full Account of the Ottoman Empire* (1709). His first play, *Elfrid* (1709), flopped and was only fractionally more successful as *Athelwold* (1731). *Rinaldo* (1710) was his translation of Rossi's libretto to music by Handel. His astonishing belief in his own ability led him to write letters advising GARRICK how to act, Walpole how to conduct political life, and POPE how to write. Pope put him in *THE DUNCIAD*. Most of his writings are quite properly forgotten. His two lasting achievements were in stage scenery: a practicable mountain in *Rinaldo* and the first practicable bridge in his production of *HENRY V* at DRURY LANE in 1723.

Hill, Geoffrey 1932– Poet. His first volume, *For the Unfallen* (1959), has been followed by *King Log* (1968), *Mercian Hymns* (1971), *Tenebrae* (1978), *The Mystery of the Charity of Charles Péguy* (1983) and *Collected Poems* (1986). Disciplined and rigorous, his poetry gives passionate voice to historical figures, both distant and recent. Although his attitude to Christianity is ambivalent, religious and moral themes play as prominent a role as his preoccupation with music. He has also published criticism: *Lords of Limit: Essays on Literature and Ideas* (1984), *Enemy's Country: Words, Contextures and Other Criticisms of Language* (1991) and *Illuminating the Shadows: Mythic Power of Film* (1992).

Hill, Susan 1942– Novelist and short-story writer. Her work treats loneliness with psychological precision and narrative composure: *In the Springtime of the Year* (1974) explores a woman's bereavement; *A Change for the Better* (1969) depicts a group of damaged, isolated people; and *I'm the King of the Castle* (1970), probably her best-known book, exposes the brutality latent in childhood innocence. Several years' self-imposed literary silence were broken by *The Woman in Black* (1983) and *The Mist in the Mirror* (1992), both pseudo-Victorian ghost stories, and a novel, *Air and Angels* (1991).

Hillingdon Hall A novel by SURTEES, published in volume form in 1845. The third in the Jorrocks trilogy begun with *JORROCKS'S JAUNTS AND JOLLITIES* and *HANDLEY CROSS*, it deals with his life in retirement. He becomes a JP and we leave him when he has just been elected to Parliament; the appalling Mrs Jorrocks is *grande dame* of the village.

Hillyer, Robert (Silliman) 1895–1961 American poet, novelist and critic. His verse, gathered in *Collected Poems* (1961), favours traditional forms, notably the SONNET and HEROIC COUPLET. He also wrote novels (*Riverhead*, 1932; *My Heart for Hostage*, 1942) and a critical study, *First Principles of Verse* (1938).

Hilton, James 1900–54 Novelist. He made his name with *Goodbye, Mr Chips* (1934), a sentimental tale about an English public school master, and *Lost Horizon* (1933), which described 'Shangri-La', an imaginary land where the inhabitants are liberated from the stresses of normal life. The name has since been used for any idyllic retreat from the world.

Hilton, Walter *c.* 1340–96 Author of *The Scale* (or *Ladder*) *of Perfection*, a devotional treatise. After studying at Cambridge, he became a hermit and then an Augustinian canon. The first part of *The Scale of Perfection* shows how the soul must replace the image of sin with the image of Christ and practise virtue to attain perfection; the second, written much later, explains the distinction between the active and contemplative religious lives. Though familiar with *THE CLOUD OF UNKNOWING*, Hilton is unlikely to have been its author.

Himes, Chester (Bomar) 1909–84 Black American novelist and writer of DETECTIVE FICTION. He is most widely known for richly detailed, extravagantly plotted detective novels, set in Harlem and usually following the exploits of Coffin Ed Johnson and Gravedigger Jones. They include *For Love of Imabelle* (1957; retitled *A Rage in Harlem*, 1965), *The Real Cool Killers* (1959), *All Shot Up* (1960), *Cotton Comes to Harlem* (1965), *The Heat's On* (1966), *Blind Man with a Pistol* (1969). They belong to the last phase of a writing career begun while serving a prison sentence. Earlier work includes: *If He Hollers Let Him Go* (1945), about racial conflict in Los Angeles defence plants during World War II; *Lonely Crusade* (1947), about racial discrimination and violence in the wartime labour unions of California; and *Cast the First Stone* (1952), based on his prison experiences.

His Natural Life A novel by MARCUS CLARKE, serialized in 1870–2 and revised and shortened in 1874. A longer title, *For the Term of His Natural Life*, was first used in 1885, four years after Clarke's death. In the original version Rufus Dawes is wrongly convicted of murder and trans-ported to the Norfolk Island settlement in Australia. His cousin Maurice Frere, the sadistic commandant, marries and destroys Dora, whom Dawes has loved since she was a child. After 30 years of suffering Dawes clears his name and is reunited with his wife. Dorcas, the child of Dora and Frere, marries his upright nephew Arthur Devine. The revised version shortens the prologue explaining Dawes's sentence, changes Dora's name to Sylvia, and ends as Dawes dies reunited with her while escaping from Norfolk Island.

History of Great Britain, The DAVID HUME's most popular work, published in 1754–62. It extends from Caesar's invasion to the flight of James II in 1688, though his chief concern is the 17th century and the progress of society, by which he largely means the development of political liberty. His analysis of the social and economic conditions which make liberty possible, and of the relations between liberty and necessary authority, is conducted from a broadly Whig standpoint but without conspicuous partisan loyalties.

History of the Rebellion, The The title usually given to CLARENDON's *True Historical Narrative of the Rebellion and Civil Wars in England*. It was begun in 1646, when Edward Hyde (as he then was) accompanied the future Charles II into exile in the Scilly Isles, but not completed until his second exile, begun in 1667, and not published until 1702–4. It is a landmark in English historical literature, written by an eyewitness with a lawyer's training in considered judgement and a gift for characterization.

Hoadly, Benjamin 1676–1761 Churchman and theologian. His sermon (1717) arguing that the Gospels afford no warrant for any visible church authority provoked the 'Bangorian controversy', so called because both Hoadly and his main opponent, THOMAS SHERLOCK, at different times held that see. His other works include *A Plain Account of the Nature and End of the Lord's Supper* (1735), maintaining that the Last Supper was merely commemorative.

Hoadly, Benjamin 1706–57 Playwright. Son of Bishop BENJAMIN HOADLY, he was a physician in the royal household and a friend of GARRICK, who staged his comedy, *The Suspicious Husband* (1747). No other play by Hoadly was produced, though he is believed to have written a total of three. He also published medical textbooks.

Hoban, Russell 1925– Novelist and writer of CHILDREN'S LITERATURE. For many years an illustrator, he became a writer for children before turning to adult fiction as well. *The Mouse and His Child* (1969) is regarded as a modern children's classic. Many of his lively picture-books have been illustrated by Quentin Blake. His novels include: *Turtle Diary* (1975); *Riddley Walker* (1980), ostensibly a scenario of a Britain reverted to primitivism after a late 20th-century holocaust; *Pilgermann* (1983), continuing his metaphysical and mystical fabulation; and *The Medusa Frequency* (1987).

Hobbes, John Oliver [Craigie (*née* Richards), Pearl Mary Teresa] 1867–1906 Novelist and playwright. Born in Boston, she finally settled in England. She is chiefly remembered for her first novel, *Some Emotions and a Moral* (1891), and for her play *The Ambassador* (1898). Another play, *The Wisdom of the Wise* (1900), achieved some contemporary success. She also published essays on GEORGE ELIOT (1901) and George Sand (1902).

Hobbes, Thomas 1588–1679 Philosopher. He served as tutor, then secretary and companion to William

Cavendish (later 1st Earl of Devonshire), met Galileo and Descartes while travelling on the Continent, and spent five years (1621–6) working with FRANCIS BACON. He left England for Paris with the first group of Royalist émigrés in 1640 and became tutor to the future Charles II in 1647. In exile he wrote LEVIATHAN (1651), his most famous expression of the systematic philosophy, especially of society and government, elsewhere explored in *De cive* (1642; translated as *Philosophical Rudiments concerning Government and Society*, 1651), *De corpore politico: or the Elements of Law, Moral and Politic* (1650) and *Questions concerning Liberty, Necessity and Chance* (1656). A materialist who argued from first principles, Hobbes had been confirmed in a reliance on 'the rules and infallibility of reason' by his early study of science and geometry. The application of his ideas to society and government, particularly in the sharp and clear prose of *Leviathan*, gave offence to many shades of political opinion and to the religious by its subordination of the church to civil power. A Bill in the House of Commons later listed *Leviathan* as a blasphemous book. In old age Hobbes turned to translating Homer, publishing his *Odyssey* at the age of 85 and his *Iliad* at 86. Posthumously published works include *Behemoth: The History of the Civil Wars of England* (1679–81) and *A Dialogue between a Philosopher and a Student of the Common Laws of England* (1681).

Hobsbaum, Philip (Dennis) 1932– Poet. He was the founder of the GROUP and, with EDWARD LUCIE-SMITH, editor of *A Group Anthology* (1963). His own poetry, which includes *The Place's Fault* (1964), *In Retreat* (1966), *Coming Out Fighting* (1969) and *Women and Animals* (1972), is influenced by ROBERT LOWELL and LARKIN and characterized by tones of loss and regret.

Hobson's Choice A comedy by HAROLD BRIGHOUSE, first produced in 1915. Maggie Hobson breaks down her dominating father's resistance to her marrying her downtrodden employee Will Mossop at the same time as she makes Will aware of his own potential.

Hoccleve [Occleve]**, Thomas** *c.* 1368/9–*c.* 1437 Poet, active from 1402 until 1422. Born perhaps in Hockliffe, Bedfordshire, he was a clerk in the office of the Privy Seal. Autobiographical or pseudo-autobiographical material about his youthful excesses, poverty, illnesses and mental breakdown appears in many of his best-known poems: *La Male Regle*, a confessional and begging poem; *Hoccleve's Complaint*; *Dialogus cum amico*; and *De regimine principum*, which combines a description of his life and over 30 EXEMPLA with political complaint and advice on good government. He also wrote: a poem in praise of women, *Lepistre de Cupide*, freely adapted from Christine de Pisan's *L'Epistre au Dieu d'Amours*; *Ars sciendi mori*, an adaptation of part of Heinrich Suso's *Horologium sapientiae* on the art of dying; the *Tale of the Emperor Jerelaus*, a version of the story of LE BONE FLORENCE OF ROME; and many short, mostly religious, pieces.

Hodgins, Jack 1938– Canadian novelist and short-story writer. His fiction combines a strong regional flavour (much of it is set on his native Vancouver Island) and a post-modernist approach that has affinities with MAGIC REALISM. Novels include *The Invention of the World* (1977), *The Resurrection of Joseph Bourne* (1979), *The Honorary Patron* (1987) and *Innocent Cities* (1990). *Spit Delaney's Island* (1976) and *The Barclay Family Theatre* (1981) are volumes of short stories. He has also written a children's book, *Left Behind in Squabble Bay* (1988), and an Australian travel journal, *Over Forty in Broken Hill* (1992).

Hodgson, William Hope 1877–1918 Novelist. He used his youthful experience of the sea in short stories for magazines, many of them horror stories featuring monstrous life-forms. Two novels, *The Boats of the 'Glen Carrig'* (1907) and *The Ghost Pirates* (1909), are in the same vein, but *The House on the Borderland* (1908) is a visionary ALLEGORY extending over vast reaches of time and space and *The Night Land* (1912) is a bizarre far-future fantasy. The cosmic perspective of his more ambitious work is a remarkable, if eccentric, product of the age which also produced H. G. WELLS's THE TIME MACHINE. Hodgson was killed in World War I.

Hoffman, Charles Fenno 1806–84 American poet, novelist and travel-writer. *A Winter in the West* (1835) describes a journey on horseback through the scarcely settled regions of Illinois and Michigan. It was followed by *Wild Scenes in the Forest and Prairie* (1839) and *Greyslaer* (1840), a novel about a Kentucky murder case. Many of his poems, originally published in the 1840s and collected in 1873, evoke the Hudson River setting of his home.

Hofmann, Michael 1957– Poet. He is the son of the German novelist Gert Hofmann. *Nights in the Iron Hotel* (1983) and *Acrimony* (1986) mark him out as an unusual talent, given to off-beat, anecdotal meditation on such subjects as the detritus of urban society, loneliness and personal disappointment or failure.

Hogarth, William 1697–1764 Painter. His major literary work was *The Analysis of Beauty* (1753), arguing that it is possible to explicate beauty in geometric terms: the best paintings observe the principle of the pyramid (the major features being bounded by an isosceles triangle), inside which the eye is led by a serpentine 'line of beauty'. The idea was taken up by STERNE in TRISTRAM SHANDY in his description of Trim reading the sermon, and Hogarth provided a plate illustrating the scene. A close friend of FIELDING, Hogarth was praised in the preface to JOSEPH ANDREWS and produced in return a plate illustrating the essential differences between character and caricature that Fielding had laid down. From a literary point of view his main achievement was a legal victory in the matter of COPYRIGHT. The Act 8 Geo. II, c. 13 (1735), laying down the principle of copyright in engravings, was passed mainly at his instigation and is sometimes known as Hogarth's Act.

Hogg, James 1770–1835 Poet, journalist and novelist. The son of a poor farmer at Ettrick Forest, Selkirkshire, he worked as a shepherd and sheep-farmer. His early collection, *Scottish Pastorals, Poems, Songs etc.* (1801), attracted the attention of SIR WALTER SCOTT, for whose *Minstrelsy of the Scottish Border* he supplied traditional BALLADS. *The Mountain Bard* (1807) was his first volume of original ballads. After moving to Edinburgh he established his reputation as a poet with THE QUEEN'S WAKE (1813). It led to friendships with BYRON, SOUTHEY and WORDSWORTH, who remembered him in a fine ELEGY, 'Extempore Effusion upon the Death of James Hogg'. He joined the editorial board of BLACKWOOD'S EDINBURGH MAGAZINE, to which he made many contributions and in which he appeared as the 'Ettrick Shepherd' in the *Noctes Ambrosianae*. Hogg later claimed credit for devising the notorious *Chaldee MS* (1817), which earned the magazine a fine and much useful publicity. *Pilgrims of the Sun* (1815) was followed by *The Poetic Mirror: or, the Living Bards of Great Britain* (1816), deft PARODIES of the Romantic poets. *The Jacobite Relics of Scotland* (1819) includes some of Hogg's own best lyric poetry. His chief works of fiction are *The Three Perils of Man* (1822) and its weaker sequel, *The Three Perils of Women* (1823), and *THE PRIVATE MEMOIRS AND CONFESSIONS OF A JUSTIFIED SINNER* (1824), for long neglected but now recognized as his masterpiece. He also produced *The Domestic Manners and Private Life of Sir Walter Scott* (1834) and, with MOTHERWELL, an edition of BURNS (1834–5).

Hoggart, Richard 1918– Critic of literature and contemporary culture. With the work of RAYMOND WILLIAMS, his writings – especially *The Uses of Literacy* (1957) – have helped to broaden the scope of literary study to include questions of working-class culture, education and the communications media. Other books include *Auden* (1951), *The Critical Moment* (1964), *Speaking to Each Other* (1970) and his Reith Lectures, *Only Connect* (1972).

Holcroft, Thomas 1745–1809 Playwright and novelist. His *Memoirs* (edited by HAZLITT; 1816) describe his early struggles as pedlar, Newmarket stable-boy, tutor and strolling actor. His acting experiences furnished material for his first novel, *Alwyn: or, The Gentleman Comedian* (1780). *Anna St Ives* (1792) and *Hugh Trevor* (1794), reflect his friendship with PAINE and GODWIN. Though acquitted of high treason in 1794, he remained under suspicion as a freethinker for the rest of his life. Holcroft's dramatic writing began with a comedy, *Duplicity* (1781), and continued with an adaptation of Beaumarchais's *The Marriage of Figaro* as *The Follies of a Day* (1784), *The School for Arrogance* (1791), the outstandingly successful *THE ROAD TO RUIN* (1792) and *Love's Frailties* (1794). *A Tale of Mystery* (1802), adapted from Pixérécourt's *Coelina*, was the first English play to be called a MELODRAMA.

Holden [née Gibbert], **Molly (Winifred)** 1927–81 Poet. Volumes include *A Hill Like a Horse* (1963), *The Bright Cloud* (1964), *To Make Me Grieve* (1968), *Air and Chill Earth* (1974) and *The Country Over* (1975). Her unflamboyant, fragile poems belong to the tradition of CLARE, HARDY and EDWARD THOMAS. The posthumous *New and Selected Poems* (1987) contains 36 of more than 400 uncollected poems.

Holinshed, Raphael d. ?1580 Chronicler. His *Chronicles* (1577) of British history up to 1575 made a favourite source-book for SHAKESPEARE, not just in his history plays but also in *MACBETH*, *KING LEAR* and *CYMBELINE*, and for MARLOWE in *EDWARD II*. Holinshed took the project over when the London printer Reginald Wolfe died in 1573. RICHARD STANIHURST was engaged to continue the description of Ireland and WILLIAM HARRISON to help with the description of England and Scotland. The description of Scotland draws on HECTOR BOECE's *Scotorum historiae*, that of England on EDWARD HALL's *Union of the Two Noble and Illustre Families of Lancaster and York*. On Holinshed's death the printers employed John Hooker and various assistants to continue the work; the 1587 edition inserted many new passages and continued the chronicles to 1586.

Holland, Philemon 1552–1637 Translator. He translated Livy (*Roman History*, 1600), Pliny (*Pliny's Natural History of the World*, 1601), Plutarch (*The Philosophy, Commonly Called the Morals*, 1603), Suetonius (*The History of the Twelve Caesars*, 1606), Ammianus Marcellinus (1609), CAMDEN's *Britannia* (1610) and Xenophon's *Cyropaedia* (1632), an account of Persia. His work, combining scholarship with a lively, popular style, won him recognition as one of the foremost translators of his age.

Holland, Sir Richard *fl.* 1450 Scottish poet. Little is known about him except that he supported the Douglases at James II's court; *THE BUKE OF THE HOWLAT*, his only surviving poem, contains a passage praising the family. After its fall he may have retired to Shetland.

Hollander, John 1929– American poet and critic. Poignant and witty, formally strict and sometimes esoteric, his verse has appeared in *Movie-Going* (1962), *Visions from the Ramble* (1965), *The Night Mirror* (1971), *The Head of the Bed* (1974), *Tales Told of the Fathers* (1975), *Spectral Emanations: New and Selected Poems* (1978), *Powers of Thirteen* (1983), *In Time and Place* (1986), *Blue Wine and Other Poems* (1979) and *Harp Lake* (1988). Critical works, scholarly yet engaged with contemporary poetry, include *The Untuning of the Sky* (1961) and *Melodious Guile: Fictive Pattern in Poetic Language* (1988).

Hollo, Anselm (Paul Alexis) 1934– Poet and translator. Born in Helsinki, he lived in Britain from 1958 and moved to the USA in 1967. His English poems, gathered in *Maya: Works 1959–1969* (1970) and *Sojourner Microcosms: New and Selected Poems 1959–1979* (1979), have strong ecological concerns. American volumes include *Sensation* (1972), *Finite Continued* (1980) and *no complaints* (1983). He has also translated Russian and European poetry into English and American poetry into Finnish.

Holme, Constance 1881–1955 Novelist. Born at Milnthorpe on Morecambe Bay, she set many of her novels in her native region. They include *The Lonely Plough* (1914), *The Splendid Faring* (1916), *The Old Road from Spain* (1916), *Beautiful End* (1918), *The Trumpet in the Dust* (1921), *The Things Which Belong* (1925) and *He-Who-Came* (1930).

Holmes, John Clellon 1926–88 American novelist, essayist and poet. He recorded the lifestyle of the BEATS in his first novel, *Go* (1952; as *The Beat Boys* in Britain), as well as *Nothing More to Declare* (1967), a collection of essays, and a memoir of JACK KEROUAC (1980). *The Horn* (1958) describes the jazz scene. He published two collections of poems, *The Bowling Green Poems* (1977) and *Death Drag: Selected Poems* (1979).

Holmes, Oliver Wendell 1809–94 American essayist, novelist and poet. He was Parkman Professor of Anatomy and Physiology at Harvard in 1847–82. A popular teacher and entertaining after-dinner speaker, he achieved considerable success with *THE AUTOCRAT OF THE BREAKFAST TABLE* (1858), a collection of humorous essays, poems and occasional pieces originally published in *THE ATLANTIC MONTHLY*, which he had co-founded with JAMES RUSSELL LOWELL in 1857. Later collections include *The Professor at the Breakfast Table* (1860), *The Poet at the Breakfast Table* (1872) and *Over the Teacups* (1891). Holmes's other light verse includes 'The Chambered Nautilus' and 'The Deacon's Masterpiece'. He also wrote three novels exploring the biological and psychological factors determining human behaviour: *Elsie Venner* (1861), *The Guardian Angel* (1867) and *A Mortal Antipathy* (1885). The heroine of *Elsie Venner* is modelled on MARGARET FULLER.

Holtby, Winifred 1898–1935 Novelist. Her pithy style is best savoured in her last novel, *South Riding* (1936), whose heroine, Sarah Burton, is a strong-willed headmistress. Most notable among her earlier works are: *The Crowded Street* (1924); *The Land of Green Ginger* (1927); *Poor Caroline* (1931), an indictment of moribund charities; and *Mandoa! Mandoa!* (1933), satirizing the effects of European civilization on Africa. Other works include a study of VIRGINIA WOOLF (1932) and two volumes of short stories, *Truth is Not Sober* (1934) and *Pavements at Anderby* (1937). Her life and achievement are commemorated in BRITTAIN's *Testament of Friendship* (1940).

Holy War, The: *Made by Shaddai upon Diabolus* BUNYAN's last major work, published in 1682. A complex religious ALLEGORY, it links the conversion of the individual soul to the early history of the world, events in recent and contemporary history, and the forthcoming millennium. The City of Mansoul (man's soul), built by King Shaddai, is alternately conquered by Diabolus and recaptured by Emmanuel.

Holy Willie's Prayer A satirical poem by BURNS, published in *Poems Chiefly in the Scottish Dialect* (1786). It is a DRAMATIC MONOLOGUE by a bigoted elder of the Kirk who exposes himself as a canting hypocrite. Holy Willie is based on William Fisher, an elder of the church at Mauchline, who fell from grace in 1790.

Homage to Catalonia An account by GEORGE ORWELL of his experiences in the Spanish Civil War, published in 1938. He went to Spain in December 1936, enlisted as a militiaman in the far-left Workers' Party of Marxist Unity (POUM), witnessed the battle of Barcelona in May 1937 and was wounded at the front line. He left Spain in July 1937. Parts of the book record his personal experiences of boredom and frustration and, occasionally, danger. Other parts analyse the politics of the struggle, the 'racket' of newspaper reports and the suppression of the POUM by the Soviet-backed forces.

Home, Henry, Lord Kames 1696–1782 Scottish judge and philosopher. Apart from writings on law, ethics, history and agricultural improvement, his works include the three-volume *Elements of Criticism* (1752), an influential analysis of literary style. He was a prominent figure in the Edinburgh enlightenment.

Home, John 1722–1808 Scottish playwright. A Presbyterian minister, he resigned his living after outraging church dignitaries by the success of his tragedy, *DOUGLAS* (1756). *The Siege of Aquileia* (1760) is probably the best of five tragedies that followed. The last was *Alfred* (1778). Supported by a pension from George III, whom he had tutored, he broke the silence of his later years only with his *History of the Rebellion of the Year 1745* (1802).

Home, William Douglas 1912–92 Playwright. His comedies of upper middle-class and political life, successful in the post-war West End theatre, include *The Chiltern Hundreds* (1947), *The Manor of Northstead* (1954), *The Reluctant Peer* (1964), *The Jockey Club Stakes* (1970), *Lloyd George Knew My Father* (1972) and *The Dame of Sark* (1974). *Now Barabbas ...* (1947) tackles a serious theme about prison life, while *The Secretary Bird* (1968) is a thoughtful comedy about a *ménage à trois*.

Homecoming, The A play (1965) by PINTER. Teddy returns from America with his wife Ruth to the all-male household run by his cantankerous father, Max. The presence of a woman excites the rivalries and competitiveness of the family. At the end, Teddy goes back alone to his university job, leaving Ruth as mother or whore to his family.

Homeric simile See EPIC SIMILE.

homily A didactic address or sermon, usually expounding a biblical text.

Honest Whore, The A play by DEKKER in two parts, the first published in 1604 and the second, to which THOMAS MIDDLETON contributed, in 1630. The setting is apparently Italy but the atmosphere breathes Dekker's London. The honest whore is the beautiful Bellafront, prompted to change her life by Count Hippolito. She falls in love with him, but he goes on to fulfil his ambition of marrying the Duke's daughter, Infelice. The Duke arranges the marriage of Bellafront to Matheo,

her first seducer. In the second part, Bellafront's beauty arouses Hippolito. The vicious Matheo suggests that she resume her old life to supply him with money. But his servant Orlando is in fact Bellafront's father: he saves her when she is unjustly committed to a house of correction and proves her innocent when Matheo accuses her of betraying him with Hippolito.

Hood, Hugh 1928– Canadian novelist and short-story writer. He is essentially a novelist of ideas and his intellectual Catholicism frequently manifests itself in the form of religious ALLEGORY. Artists are the central figures in several early novels: *White Figure, White Ground* (1964), *The Camera Always Lies* (1967) and *A Game of Touch* (1970). *You Can't Get There From Here* (1972) is a political novel. *The Swing in the Garden* (1975), *A New Athens* (1977), *Reservoir Ravine* (1979), *Black and White Keys* (1982), *The Scenic Art* (1984), *The Motor Boys in Ottawa* (1986) and *Tony's Book* (1988) belong to an ambitious projected sequence of 12 novels, entitled *The New Age/Le Nouveau Siècle*. His volumes of short stories include *Flying in a Red Kite* (1962), *Around the Mountain* (1967), *The Fruit Man, the Meat Man and the Manager* (1971), *Dark Glasses* (1976), *None Genuine without This Signature* (1980) and *August Nights* (1985). He has also published *The Governor's Bridge* (1973), a volume of essays.

Hood, Thomas 1799–1845 Poet. He wrote his first volume, *Odes and Addresses to Great People* (1825), in collaboration with a fellow comic spirit, JOHN HAMILTON REYNOLDS. Hood is now chiefly known for verbal dexterity and, particularly, the love of punning which makes poems like 'Faithless Nelly Gray' and 'The Ballad of Sally Brown and Ben the Carpenter' (in the first series of *Whims and Oddities*, 1826–7) excruciatingly memorable. In 'Miss Kilmansegg', a grotesque SATIRE on Victorian worship of money, the heroine is eventually murdered for her artificial gold leg. His major serious poem, 'The Song of the Shirt', appeared anonymously in *PUNCH* in 1843 to immediate acclaim. Based on an account by DOUGLAS JERROLD of a woman accused of pawning articles belonging to her employer, it makes a powerful attack on exploitation. In the course of a busy careeer Hood edited, founded or worked for several journals, including *THE LONDON MAGAZINE*, as well as producing plays and a novel, *Tylney Hall* (1834).

Hook, Theodore Edward 1788–1841 Journalist, novelist, playwright and wit. Editor of the Tory *John Bull*, he moved in the fashionable society he described in SILVER-FORK NOVELS such as *Maxwell* (1830), *Gilbert Gurney* (1836) and *Jack Brag* (1837). He was the model for Mr Wagg in THACKERAY's *PENDENNIS*.

Hooker, Richard, ?1554–1600 Anglican theologian. *Of the Laws of Ecclesiastical Polity* is an apology for the Elizabethan religious and political settlement, prompted partly by the controversy started by the Puritan *Admonition to Parliament* (1572). Books I–IV were published in 1594 and Book V in 1597; Books VI and VIII (1648) and VII (1661) are of doubtful authority. For Hooker the Anglican tradition relied on the Bible, the church and reason, which pronounces on those matters where the voices of the Bible and the church are silent or unclear. Natural law, which governs the universe, and whose voice is 'the harmony of the world', is an expression of God's reason. *Ecclesiastical Polity* also insists on the unity of church and state and suggests a contractual theory of political government. His monument at Bishopsbourne, Kent, where he was vicar at the time of his death, remembers him as 'judicious' Hooker. WALTON wrote his biography (1665).

Hooker, Thomas 1586–1647 American Puritan minister. He emigrated to Massachusetts in 1633 and moved to Hartford in the Connecticut Valley in 1636. He was the most thorough exponent of the theory of preparation, or the set of steps a Christian goes through during conversion, set forth in *The Soul's Preparation for Christ* (1632) and *Application of Redemption, by the Effectual Work of the Word, and the Spirit of Christ, for the Bringing Home Lost Sinners to God* (posthumously published, 1656). Other works include *A Survey of the Sum of Church Discipline* (1648), an exposition of independent Congregational church polity, and *The Poor Doubting Christian Drawn unto Christ* (1629), a manual for dealing with religious melancholy or 'cases of conscience'.

Hope, A(lec) D(erwent) 1907– Australian poet. *The Wandering Islands* (1955), his first collection, was welcomed for its skilful use of traditional verse forms and shrewd commentary on modern values. *Poems* (1960), *New Poems 1965–1969* (1969), *Dunciad Minor: An Heroick Poem* (1970), *Collected Poems 1930–1970* (1972), *A Late Picking: Poems 1965–1974* (1975), *A Book of Answers* (1978), *The Drifting Continent* (1979), *The Age of Reason* (1985), *Ladies from the Sea* (1987) and *Orpheus* (1991) have given him a leading place in modern poetry. A prolific and influential critic, he has published *Australian Poetry* (1960), *Australian Literature 1950–1962* (1963), *The Cave and the Spring* (1965), *A Midsummer Eve's Dream: Variations on a Theme by William Dunbar* (1970), *Native Companions* (1974), a study of JUDITH WRIGHT (1975), *The Pack of Autolycus* (1978) and *The New Cratylus: Notes on the Craft of Poetry* (1979).

Hope, Anthony [Hawkins, Sir Anthony Hope] 1863–1933 Novelist. He achieved success in 1894 with *The Dolly Dialogues*, a series of witty sketches of the London season, and a romance, THE PRISONER OF ZENDA, which earned high praise from ROBERT LOUIS STEVENSON and ANDREW LANG. A sequel, *Rupert of Hentzau* (1898), proved equally popular. Other novels include *Tristram of Blent* (1901), *Sophy of Kravonia* (1906) and *Lucinda* (1920). His reminiscences appeared as *Memories and Notes* (1927).

Hope, Christopher (David Tully) 1944– South African-born novelist and poet. He has been based in London since 1975. *Cape Drives* (1974), his first volume of poems published in Britain, has been followed by *In the Country of the Black Pig* (1981) and a single poem, *Englishmen* (1985), subsequently dramatized by the BBC. But his main output has been fiction. His first novel, *A Separate Development* (1980), written in his robust satirical style, has been followed by *Kruger's Alp* (1984), *The Hottentot Room* (1986), the novella *Black Swan* (1987), *My Chocolate Redeemer* (1989) and *Serenity House* (1992). His early stories, *Private Parts* (1981), have been reissued with additions as *Learning to Fly* (1990). A play, *Ducktails*, televised in 1977, deals with his youth in Pretoria, as does his semi-autobiographical *White Boy Running* (1988). His journalism includes *Moscow! Moscow!* (1990).

Hope, Thomas ?1770–1831 Novelist and art connoisseur. A wealthy collector who patronized major contemporary artists, he also wrote on ancient costume and on taste and design. His most important work, however, was *Anastasius: or, Memoirs of a Greek* (1819), a lively PICARESQUE novel which drew on his knowledge of the Near East. Published anonymously, it was once attributed to BYRON.

Hopkins, Gerard Manley 1844–89 Poet. He was received into the Roman Catholic Church by NEWMAN in 1866, whilst an undergraduate at Balliol College, Oxford. After briefly teaching at Newman's Oratory School in Birmingham, he became a novitiate of the Society of Jesus in 1868, passing the next decade at Manresa House in Roehampton, Stonyhurst College in Lancashire and St Beuno's in North Wales. After his ordination in 1877 he ministered to parishes in Chesterfield, London, Oxford, Liverpool and Glasgow, returned to Stonyhurst as teacher of Greek and Latin in 1882–4, and spent his last years as Professor of Classics at University College, Dublin.

Hopkins burned most of his early work and abandoned writing when he became a Jesuit. He broke his silence in 1875 with 'The Wreck of the *Deutschland*', an ODE dedicated to the memory of five Franciscan nuns drowned in the Thames estuary. *The Month*, a Jesuit periodical, accepted the poem but then decided against printing it. 'The Loss of the *Eurydice*' (1878) met a similar fate. Hopkins wrote 'God's Grandeur', 'The Windhover' and 'Pied Beauty' before his ordination, and ended his poetic career with the 'terrible' sonnets, 'Tom's Garland' and 'That Nature Is a Heraclitean Fire'. He circulated his poems in letters to his friends RICHARD WATSON DIXON and ROBERT BRIDGES but made no attempt to publish them. A few appeared in anthologies after his death, but Hopkins did not gain an audience until Bridges's edition in 1918.

His small body of work dwells chiefly on his spiritual relations with God, manifest not just in the agonized questioning of his later poems but also in the subtle yet ecstatic response to nature which is perhaps his most characteristic note. His view of the created world is controlled by what he called 'instress' and 'inscape' – respectively, the animating energy in art, nature and God, and the distinctive organic form of a thing. His pursuit of a language of inspiration that would capture experience afresh led him to break with the conventional poetic diction of his time, reviving archaisms, borrowing dialect words and using coinages of his own. The emphatic or 'oratorical' rhythm of his poems he called 'sprung rhythm', an attempt to reconcile speech rhythms with the greatest possible poetic emphasis, which is scanned by stresses rather than by the number of syllables (see also METRE).

Hopkinson, Francis 1737–91 American essayist. He served in the Second Continental Congress (signing the Declaration of Independence) and in a variety of positions in the revolutionary government. His writings include: *A Pretty Story* (1774), an ALLEGORY of a family of sons (the colonies) wronged by their wicked stepmother (Parliament); 'The Battle of the Kegs' (1778), a BALLAD ridiculing the British; *The Temple of Minerva*, a MASQUE performed for General Washington in Philadelphia in 1781; and 'The New Roof' (1787), one of several further SATIRES in support of the Constitution. He spent his last years as a judge, and also published some volumes of songs. His revised *Miscellaneous Essays* appeared posthumously in 1792.

Horne, Richard Henry [Hengist] 1803–84 Poet and essayist. He is chiefly known for *Orion* (1843), an EPIC poem which he priced at one farthing as a satirical comment on the contemporary valuation of poetry. His report on the employment of children in mines and factories provoked ELIZABETH BARRETT BROWNING to write 'The Cry of the Children'. *A New Spirit of the Age* (1844), to which ROBERT BROWNING and Elizabeth Barrett Browning contributed, remains an illuminating account of contemporaries. *Australian Autobiography and Australian Facts and Prospects* (1859) describes his experiences in the Australian gold rush.

Horner, Francis 1778–1817 Lawyer, politician and economist. A highly capable product and exponent of Scottish UTILITARIANISM, he was thrice elected to Parliament in the liberal Whig interest, and earned a distinguished reputation as a speaker on economic affairs and the slave trade. With HENRY BROUGHAM, FRANCIS JEFFREY and SYDNEY SMITH he founded THE EDINBURGH REVIEW in 1802. His *Memoirs* were edited by his brother, Leonard Horner, in 1843.

Hornung, E(rnest) W(illiam) 1866–1921 Novelist and short-story writer. The brother-in-law of ARTHUR CONAN DOYLE, he created A. J. Raffles, the gentleman-burglar whose exploits are related by his faithful friend Bunny in several collections of short stories, *The Amateur Cracksman* (1899), *The Black Mask* (1901) and *A Thief in the Night* (1905), and a novel, *Mr Justice Raffles* (1909). Raffles was also popular on the stage and in the cinema. Other books, notably *Stingaree* (1905), use an Australian background.

Horovitz, Frances 1938–83 Poet. Her books include *Poems* (1967), *The High Tower* (1970), *Water over Stone* (1980) and *Snow Light, Water Light* (1983). She is also represented in *Children of Albion* (1969) and its successor, *Grandchildren of Albion* (1992), edited by her husband MICHAEL HOROVITZ.

Horovitz, Michael 1935– Poet and anthologist. Always anti-establishment, he has found a forum for his radical views in his magazine, *New Departures*, and two well-known anthologies, *Children of Albion: Poetry of the Underground in Britain* (1969) and *Grandchildren of Albion* (1992). In keeping the spirit of 1960s poetry alive, he also created the Poetry Olympics, public readings in which many poets took part. His own work includes *The Wolverhampton Wanderer* (1971) and *Growing Up: Selected Poems and Pictures 1951–79* (1979). He was married to FRANCES HOROVITZ.

Hospital, Janette Turner 1942– Australian novelist, resident in North America. Her novels, variously set in India, Australia and North America, include *The Ivory Swing* (1982), *The Tiger in the Tiger Pit* (1983), *Borderline* (1985) and the complex post-modernist *Charades* (1988). *Dislocations* (1986) and *Isobars* (1990) are collections of short stories. She writes about nomads, whom she describes as 'characters who cross borders, who straddle cultures and countries, who live with a constant sense of dislocation'. She also publishes DETECTIVE FICTION under the pseudonym of Alex Juniper.

Houghton (William) Stanley 1881–1913 Playwright. He is remembered for *Hindle Wakes* (1912), a comedy of Lancashire life with an independent-minded heroine, Fanny Hawthorne. Other plays are *The Dear Departed* (1908) and *The Younger Generation* (1910).

Hound of the Baskervilles, The See SHERLOCK HOLMES STORIES.

House at Pooh Corner, The See MILNE, A. A.

House of Fame, The An unfinished poem by CHAUCER, c. 1374–80, sometimes read as an ALLEGORY of incidents in his life or at court. A DREAM-VISION transports the narrator to a glass temple with images of famous warriors and lovers. He emerges into a desert and is carried off by a talking eagle, which promises to take him where he may learn about love. A tower of ice bears the names of the famous, now melting and unreadable. In a castle of beryl the dreamer sees Fame, a woman of varying

height with numerous eyes, ears and tongues, indiscriminately rewarding or rejecting petitioners. The eagle then takes him to the house of Rumour, built of sticks, where the poem breaks off.

House of Life, The A SONNET sequence by DANTE GABRIEL ROSSETTI, first published in full in *Ballads and Sonnets* (1881). The title derives from astrology. The 101 poems are a perplexing mixture of love, mysticism, Dantesque lore, exaltation, natural phenomena, deep despair and, in particular, autobiography. As often with Rossetti, there are eccentric rhymes and arcane diction as well as obscure phraseology.

House of Mirth, The A novel by EDITH WHARTON published in 1905. Set in New York society during the first years of the 20th century, it records the disastrous social career of Lily Bart, a penniless orphan related to some of the city's prominent families. Having failed to secure a rich husband, she is unjustly accused of having an affair with another woman's husband, disinherited by her wealthy aunt and forced to take a job as a milliner. The novel ends with her death from an overdose of a sedative.

House of the Seven Gables, The A novel by HAWTHORNE, published in 1851. It is set in the mid-19th century. Generations earlier, 'Wizard' Maule cursed Colonel Pyncheon before being hanged for witchcraft. His death allowed Pyncheon to take possession of a disputed plot of land and build the House of the Seven Gables. The current owner is the hypocritical Judge Pyncheon, who lets his poor cousin Hepzibah and her debilitated brother Clifford live there. Clifford has just been released from 30 years' wrongful imprisonment, to which the judge sentenced him for murdering their rich uncle. Clifford and Hepzibah are joined by Phoebe, a young cousin from the country, and Holgrave, a daguerreotypist. The Judge's sudden death ends his persecution of Clifford, and leaves him and Hepzibah wealthy. Holgrave reveals that he is the last descendant of 'Wizard' Maule and explains how both the 'murdered' uncle and the Judge were victims of the Maule curse, not of human wrongdoing. The curse will be lifted by his marriage to Phoebe.

House with the Green Shutters, The A novel by GEORGE DOUGLAS, published in 1901. A sharp and unsentimental study of small-town life in Scotland, it centres on John Gourlay, an arrogant and mean-spirited businessman who is finally killed by his own son.

Household, Geoffrey (Edward West) 1900–88 Novelist. He achieved fame with his second novel, *Rogue Male* (1939), a thriller in which the hero attempts to assassinate a foreign dictator (presumably Hitler) and is himself hunted by an enemy agent. Most of the 20 novels that followed explore the psychology of the chase, notably *Watcher in the Shadows* (1960), *Dance of the Dwarfs* (1968) and the belated sequel *Rogue Justice* (1982).

Household Words A weekly magazine owned and edited by DICKENS from 1850 until 1859, when it was superseded by ALL THE YEAR ROUND. The name (from SHAKESPEARE'S *Henry V*) announced its intention of providing family entertainment. Dickens published his own novels in the journal as well as work by BULWER LYTTON, WILKIE COLLINS, ELIZABETH GASKELL and CHARLES LEVER.

Housman, A(lfred) E(dward) 1859–1936 Poet and scholar. Despite his brilliant reputation at St John's College, Oxford, he achieved only a pass degree. While working for the Patent Office he published the scholarly work on Propertius, Ovid and Juvenal which earned him the professorship of Latin at London University in 1892. His definitive edition of Manilius appeared in 1902–30. He became Kennedy Professor of Latin at Cambridge, and a fellow of Trinity College, in 1911.

A Shropshire Lad (1896), his collection of nature and love poems, combined an idealized vision of the English countryside with lyric pessimism – a blend that made it extremely popular during World War I. Despite this success Housman largely turned away from poetry, though he did publish Last Poems (1922). More Poems appeared posthumously in 1936 and 18 additional poems were published in the memoir (1937) by LAURENCE HOUSMAN, his brother. Collected Poems appeared in 1939. Housman is also known for his lecture, The Name and Nature of Poetry (1933).

Housman, Laurence 1865–1959 Artist, art critic, poet and playwright. Brother of A. E. HOUSMAN, he was a protean figure, writing on feminism, socialism and pacifism, publishing volumes of light verse, popular novels (including Thimblerigg, a SATIRE of Lloyd George, in 1924) and the notorious and much-parodied An English Woman's Love Letters (1900). He is best known for his plays, which included Bethlehem (1902), Angels and Ministers (1921), The Little Plays of St Francis (1922) and Victoria Regina (1934). He also published an autobiography, The Unexpected Years (1937), and a memoir of his brother (1937). Collected Poems appeared in 1937.

Hovey, Richard 1864–1900 American poet. He collaborated with BLISS CARMAN on three volumes celebrating life on the open road: Songs from Vagabondia (1894), More Songs from Vagabondia (1896) and Last Songs from Vagabondia (1901). Along the Trail (1898) was published in the year of the Spanish-American War. The Holy Graal (1907) contains fragments of an uncompleted cycle of poetic dramas drawn from ARTHURIAN LITERATURE. A posthumous collection, To the End of the Trail, appeared in 1908.

How They Brought the Good News from Ghent to Aix A poem by ROBERT BROWNING published in Dramatic Romances and Lyrics (1845). Despite appearances, this favourite anthology piece does not refer to any historical event. Browning admitted that he simply wanted to evoke the rhythm of horses galloping.

Howard, Bronson (Crocker) 1842–1908 American playwright. He first succeeded with Saratoga (1870), a comedy of upper-class life produced by AUGUSTIN DALY and adapted for the London stage as Brighton (1874). The Banker's Daughter (1878), a revised version of Lillian's Last Love (1873), and Young Mrs Winthrop (1882) confirmed his reputation. His plays deal with the shaping power of American society and convention on human relationships. After its initial failure, his Civil War drama, Shenandoah (1888), became one of the most successful of its kind. His last popular work was The Henrietta (1887), a SATIRE of Wall Street.

Howard, Edward See RATTLIN THE REEFER.

Howard, Sir Robert 1626–98 Playwright, courtier and politician. A fervent Royalist, he was imprisoned during the Commonwealth and honoured after the Restoration. His first play, The Blind Lady (1660), is halfway between Jacobean tragedy and the new heroic tragedy, but The Indian Queen (1664) is fully fledged heroic drama, the first of its kind. The best of his four comedies is The Committee (1662). He abandoned theatre for politics after 1668.

Howard, Sidney (Coe) 1891–1939 American playwright. His first success was They Knew What They Wanted (1924; PULITZER PRIZE), based on the story of Paolo and Francesca. His most experimental play, Yellow Jack (with Paul de Kruif; 1924), deals with the research into the cause of yellow fever. Other works include Lucky Sam McCarver (1925), The Silver Cord (1926), Salvation Nell (with CHARLES MACARTHUR; 1928) and The Late Christopher Bean (1932).

Howards End A novel by E. M. FORSTER, published in 1910. It centres on the cultured Schlegel sisters, Margaret and Helen, and the materialistic Wilcox family, which consists of Henry, his sons Charles and Paul, his daughter Evie and the dying Mrs Wilcox. She leaves Margaret her house, Howards End, in a note which the surviving Wilcoxes destroy. Margaret and Henry become engaged. Helen arrives angrily at the Wilcoxes' second home at Oniton with Leonard Bast, a young clerk whom she and Margaret have tried to help but whom Henry has treated with indifference. Bast's wife Jacky and Henry Wilcox recognize each other as ex-lovers. Margaret forgives his past adultery and they marry. Helen is pregnant by Leonard. Charles thrashes him to death for what he takes to be callous seduction and goes to prison. The sisters are reunited at Howards End. 'Only connect', the epigraph to the novel, expresses Forster's lifelong belief in salvation through fraternal sympathy.

Howe, E(dgar) W(atson) 1853–1937 American novelist and editor. He owned and edited the Daily Globe of Atchison in Kansas (1877–1911), and E. W. Howe's Monthly (1911–37). Despite its melodramatic plot, his novel The Story of a Country Town (1883) drew high praise when it first appeared and is recognized as a landmark of American realism.

Howe, Julia Ward 1819–1910 American poet and humanitarian. A tireless worker for women's suffrage, prison reform and the abolition of slavery, she is best remembered as the author of THE BATTLE HYMN OF THE REPUBLIC (1861).

Howell, James c. 1594–1666 Miscellaneous writer. A minor diplomat and loyal Royalist imprisoned in 1643–51, he was appointed Historiographer Royal at the Restoration. His diverse publications include: Dodona's Grove (1640), a political allegory; Instructions for Foreign Travel (1642); and the satiric Perfect Description of the Country of Scotland (1649) and Londinopolis: An Historical Discourse or Perlustration of the City of London (1657). His most important work is Epistolae Ho-Elianae: Familiar Letters (1645–55), written to imaginary correspondents and an arresting source of detail about contemporary events.

Howell, Thomas fl. 1560–80 Poet. Little is known of him, but he spent his life in service to the Herbert family, whom he celebrates in New Sonnets, and Pretty Pamphlets (undated but licensed in 1567–8), The Arbour of Amity (1568) and H. His Devices (1581).

Howells, William Dean 1837–1920 American novelist, journalist, editor and critic. He was born and brought up in Ohio, where he began his career as a journalist. His work as US consul in Venice in 1861–5 provided the basis for two travel books, Venetian Life (1866) and Italian Journeys (1867). On his return to the USA he settled in Boston and worked as assistant editor and then editor-in-chief of THE ATLANTIC MONTHLY, amongst other prestigious journalist posts. The first of his 40 or so novels were Their Wedding Journey (1872) and A Chance Acquaintance (1873), drawing on his travel experiences. A

Foregone Conclusion (1874) and *The Lady of the Aroostook* (1879) deal with the contrast between Americans and Europeans. Thereafter Howells moved away from the comedy of manners to tackle larger social issues, in works such as *The Undiscovered Country* (1880), a novel about spiritualism and the Shakers, *A MODERN INSTANCE* (1882), *A Woman's Reason* (1883) and *THE RISE OF SILAS LAPHAM* (1885). *INDIAN SUMMER* (1886) is a delicately handled story of romance in middle age. *A HAZARD OF NEW FORTUNES* (1890), written after he had moved to New York, announced a stronger political awareness while affirming his commitment to REALISM. His later fiction includes: *The Quality of Mercy* (1892), about embezzlement; *An Imperative Duty* (1892), which has a black heroine; *The World of Chance* (1893), examining the lack of causality in human affairs; and *A Traveller from Altruria* (1894), a Utopian novel. Among his critical works are *Criticism and Fiction* (1891) and *Life and Literature: Studies* (1902). *Literary Friends and Acquaintance: A Personal Retrospect of American Authorship* (1900) and *My Mark Twain: Reminiscences and Criticism* (1910) document his wide-ranging friendships in the literary world. His achievements in journalism and fiction earned him the title of the 'dean of American letters'.

Hoyt, Charles Hale 1860–1900 American playwright. Between 1883 and 1899 he wrote and produced 17 FARCES and one comic opera. Later works, like the comical MELODRAMA *A Midnight Bell* (1889) and the political SATIRE *A Texas Steer* (1890), are more socially aware. As lessee of the Madison Square Theatre in New York, known as Hoyt's Theatre, he wrote and produced: *A Trip to Chinatown* (1891), about the Bowery; *A Temperance Town* (1893), about the Prohibition movement; *A Milk White Flag* (1894), about home guard companies; *A Runaway Colt* (1895), about corruption in baseball teams; and *A Contented Woman* (1897), about women's suffrage.

Huchown of the Awle Ryale He is mentioned in ANDREW OF WYNTOUN's *Cronykil* (c. 1420) as the author of the *Geste of Arthure*, *Awntyre of Gawayn* and *Pistel of Swete Susan*. The first two have been dubiously identified as the alliterative *MORTE ARTHURE* and the *AWNTYRS OF ARTHURE*. The last is probably the extant *SUSANNA: OR, THE PISTIL OF SWETE SUSAN*. The identification of Huchown as the Hew of Eglinton mentioned in DUNBAR's *Lament for the Makaris* is no longer accepted.

Huckleberry Finn, The Adventures of A novel by MARK TWAIN, published in 1884. A sequel to *THE ADVENTURES OF TOM SAWYER*, it achieves a moral dimension lacking in its predecessor by its SATIRE and its treatment of slavery.

Huck narrates the story. He has been adopted by Widow Douglas and her sister Miss Watson but his blackguard father returns and kidnaps him. He frees himself by making it appear as if he has been murdered and meets Jim, Miss Watson's goodhearted slave, who has decided to run away. Together they travel down the Mississippi on a raft, undergoing a series of encounters with feuding clans, murderers, lawless 'aristocrats' and mobs, all of which they survive by luck, wit and determination. A dense fog causes them to miss Cairo, where Jim planned to leave the Mississippi and travel up the Ohio River to freedom. Finally, in Arkansas, Jim is captured and sold to a farmer and his wife, who by coincidence are Tom Sawyer's Uncle Silas and Aunt Sally Phelps. Tom himself arrives and involves Huck in an absurdly romantic plan to rescue Jim, even though he knows that Miss Watson's death has left Jim a free man.

The arrival of Tom's Aunt Polly sets matters straight. At the end Huck decides to 'light out' for the territories rather than face life with Aunt Sally, who plans to 'sivilize' him.

Hudibras A satiric poem by SAMUEL BUTLER in three parts, published in 1663, 1664 and 1678. Its distinctive octosyllabic couplets and MOCK-HEROIC style gave rise to the term 'Hudibrastics'. It was immensely popular in its time for its SATIRE (partly inspired by Cervantes and Rabelais) against Puritanism and the Commonwealth. The name 'Hudibras' comes from *THE FAERIE QUEENE* but the character was based on the zealous Sir Samuel Luke, whom Butler had served as secretary.

In Part 1 Hudibras rides out, bickering with his squire Ralpho. They skirmish with bear-baiters (Puritans disapproved of the sport) and land up, still quarrelling, in the stocks. In Part 2 Hudibras is visited in the stocks by a widow whose money he covets. He consults the astrologer Sidrophel (based on Sir Paul Neale of the Royal Society) about his suit before discovering, to his rage, that Sidrophel is a fraud. In Part 3 Hudibras gives a false account of his adventures to the widow before Ralpho exposes him and the astrologer's friends humiliate and terrify him. He decides to continue his courtship by letter. At this point Hudibras is forgotten and the last two CANTOS of Part 3 turn to the activities of the Republicans just before the Restoration. Butler gives a notable study of the Earl of Shaftesbury, the Achitophel of DRYDEN's *ABSALOM AND ACHITOPHEL*.

Hudson, W(illiam) H(enry) 1841–1922 Novelist and naturalist. Born to American parents in Argentina, he emigrated to England in 1869. *The Purple Land That England Lost* (1885), a series of stories set in South America, later became famous. Other stories and two novels, *A Crystal Age* (1887) and *Fan* (1892), followed but most of his writing during the 1890s was the work of a naturalist with an attractive, clear-cut style. *The Naturalist in La Plata* (1892), *Birds in a Village* and *Idle Days in Patagonia* (both 1893), *British Birds* (1895), *Birds in London* (1898), *Nature in Downland* (1900) and *Birds and Man* (1901) earned some acclaim but his first real success came with a romance, *GREEN MANSIONS* (1904). Hudson published 12 more books, of which *A SHEPHERD'S LIFE* (1910) and the autobiographical *Far Away and Long Ago* (1918) established his place in literature.

Hughes, Langston 1902–67 Black American novelist, short-story writer, poet and playwright. He emerged as a leading figure of the HARLEM RENAISSANCE with poetry, *The Weary Blues* (1926) and *Fine Clothes to the Jew* (1927), and a novel, *Not Without Laughter* (1930). *The Ways of White Folks* (1934) is a collection of satiric short stories; two later collections, *Laughing to Keep from Crying* (1952) and *Something in Common* (1963), again highlight the absurdities of racial prejudice. Later poetry includes *Shakespeare in Harlem* (1942), *Fields of Wonder* (1947), *Montage of a Dream Deferred* (1951), and *Ask Your Mama* (1961). Hughes also produced: plays, collected in *Five Plays* (1963); two autobiographies, *The Big Sea* (1940) and *I Wonder as I Wander* (1956); another novel, *Tambourines to Glory* (1958); books, essays and articles on society, history and music; collections of black folklore, poetry and stories; and *Simple Speaks His Mind* (1950), *Simple Takes a Wife* (1953), *Simple Stakes a Claim* (1957) and *Simple's Uncle* (1965), in which a seemingly slow-witted black outsmarts his antagonists.

Hughes, Richard (Arthur Warren) 1900–76 Novelist

and playwright. He is chiefly remembered for *A High Wind in Jamaica* (1929; as *The Innocent Voyage* in USA), an unsentimental and disturbing novel about seven English schoolchildren kidnapped by Captain Jonsen and his crew of pirates during a voyage to England. *In Hazard: A Sea Story* (1938) tells of men at sea whose lives are threatened first by a hurricane and then by fears of a mutiny. Hughes later broke a long silence with two novels launching an ambitious multi-volume sequence, *The Human Predicament*, which was to include historical as well as fictional characters. It was never completed. *The Fox in the Attic* (1961) opens in Wales at the end of World War I. *The Wooden Shepherdess* (1973) met with little critical enthusiasm. Hughes's plays include *The Sister's Tragedy* (1922) and *A Comedy of Good and Evil* (1924).

Hughes, Ted (Edward James) 1930– Poet. Since *Hawk in the Rain* (1957) his poetry has appeared in *Lupercal* (1960), *Wodwo* (1967), *Crow* (1970), *Season Songs* (1974), *Gaudete* (1977), *Cave Birds* (1978), *Remains of Elmet* (1979), *Moortown* (1979) and *Selected Poems 1957–81* (1982). His forms owe something to D. H. LAWRENCE and HOPKINS but his version of the animal world is quite his own, isolating cruel and predatory instincts and projecting them on creatures of his own invention. The family poems in *Wolfwatching* (1989) may signal a change in direction. Hughes succeeded SIR JOHN BETJEMAN as POET LAUREATE in 1984, gathering his Laureate verse in *Rain Charm for the Duchy* (1992). He has also written CHILDREN'S LITERATURE, edited selections of KEITH DOUGLAS (1964) and EMILY DICKINSON (1968), and published criticism which includes *Dancer to God: Tributes to T. S. Eliot* (1992), *Shakespeare and the Goddess of Complete Being* (1992) and *Winter Pollen* (1994). He was married to SYLVIA PLATH.

Hughes, Thomas 1822–96 Miscellaneous writer and author of CHILDREN'S LITERATURE. While studying for the Bar he became a supporter of CHRISTIAN SOCIALISM, with his friends F. D. MAURICE and CHARLES KINGSLEY. He helped to found the Working Men's College in London and acted as its principal in 1872–83. His most famous work, *TOM BROWN'S SCHOOLDAYS* (1857), is a lightly fictionalized account of Rugby, his old school, under the headmastership of THOMAS ARNOLD. Hughes did not repeat the success in *Tom Brown at Oxford* (1861) or an intervening novel, *The Scouring of the White Horse* (1861), a slight compilation of legends connected with the countryside round Uffington, his birthplace. In later years, when he was a Liberal MP and a circuit judge in Chester, he wrote admiring biographies, *Alfred the Great* (1869) and *David Livingstone* (1889), a book on his religious views (*The Manliness of Christ*; 1879), and the touching *Memoir of a Brother* (1873) in tribute to George Hughes.

Hulme, Keri 1947– New Zealand novelist, short-story writer and poet. She published stories and poems in magazines and a volume of poetry, *The Silences Between (Moeraki Conversations)* (1982), before becoming internationally famous with *The Bone People* (1984), a novel which won the BOOKER PRIZE. Its insistence on the hybrid nature of New Zealand society and its exploration of Maori culture continue to be debated. She has also published a collection of stories, *Te Kaihau: The Windeater* (1986) and two volumes of poetry, *Lost Possessions* (1985) and *Strands* (1992).

Hulme, T(homas) E(rnest) 1883–1917 Poet, essayist and 'philosophic amateur'. Only six of his poems were published before his early death in World War I, five of them as 'The Complete Poetical Works of T. E. Hulme' in

Orage's *NEW AGE* (1912). He also published articles on 'Romanticism and Classicism' and Bergson in the same magazine in 1911. Much of his work survived only in notebooks, edited by HERBERT READ as *Speculations* (1924) and *Notes on Language and Style* (1929). His rejection of ROMANTICISM and his advocacy of the 'hard, dry image' influenced IMAGISM.

Human Shows, Far Phantasies, Songs and Trifles
The penultimate volume of verse by HARDY, published in 1925. It gathers old, revised and recently written poems commemorating past affections, among them his first wife Emma, his sister Mary, and his long-dead friend Horace Moule. It also includes poems of philosophical reflection, narrative, love and contemporary events (the hanging of Edith Thompson in 1923).

Hume, David 1711–76 Philosopher and historian. Born in Edinburgh, he left Edinburgh University without a degree to study privately at home and then in France (1734–7). There he began *A TREATISE OF HUMAN NATURE* (1739–40, with an abstract added later in 1740), received with indifference and some hostility. The five-volume *Essays, Moral and Political* appeared between 1741 and 1748. By this time Hume had begun to combine the role of man of affairs with man of letters: he was tutor to the Marquis of Annandale in 1745 and accompanied General St Clair on a disastrous expedition to Port L'Orient in 1747 and diplomatic missions to Vienna and Turin in 1748. *AN ENQUIRY CONCERNING HUMAN UNDERSTANDING* (originally called *Philosophical Essays concerning Human Understanding*, 1748; retitled 1758) included a sceptical discussion of miracles which damaged his reputation with the orthodox. *An Enquiry concerning the Principles of Morals* appeared in 1751.

In 1752–7 Hume was Advocates' Librarian in Edinburgh. *Political Discourses* (1752) helped his growing reputation in Europe. *THE HISTORY OF GREAT BRITAIN* (1754–62) was his most popular work. *Four Dissertations* (1757) contained *THE NATURAL HISTORY OF RELIGION*, *Of the Passions*, *Of Tragedy* and *Of the Standard of Taste*; dissertations on suicide and immortality appeared anonymously after his death as *Two Essays* (1777). Hume's sceptical stance created a bond with French intellectual and literary life, confirmed by a period (1763–5) as secretary to the Embassy in Paris. He returned to England with Rousseau, whose bitter public quarrel forced him to publish their correspondence in his own defence (1766). After serving as Under-Secretary of State (1767–8) he finally settled in Edinburgh. ADAM SMITH published the curiously detached *Life of David Hume, Written by Himself* (1777). *DIALOGUES CONCERNING NATURAL RELIGION* appeared in 1779.

Hume, Fergus (Wright) 1859–1932 New Zealand writer of DETECTIVE FICTION. His first novel, *The Mystery of a Hansom Cab* (1886), was immediately popular and sold some half a million copies in his lifetime. None of the 140 detective and mystery novels that followed equalled its success.

Humorous Lieutenant, The: or, Generous Enemies
An eccentric comedy of intrigue by JOHN FLETCHER, first performed *c.* 1619 and published in 1647. The title character suffers from a mysterious infirmity that makes him courageous in battle. The main plot concerns Celia, a captive at the court of King Antigonus, loved by both Antigonus and his son Demetrius. Antigonus tells Demetrius that Celia is dead and tries to obtain a response from her with a love philtre. The humorous lieutenant accidentally drinks the philtre and falls in

love with Antigonus. Celia eventually persuades Antigonus to restore her to Demetrius.

humour See WIT.

Humphrey, William 1924– American novelist and short-story writer. His novels, set primarily in the Red River country of north-east Texas, are *Home from the Hill* (1958), *The Ordways* (1965), *Proud Flesh* (1973), *Hostages to Fortune* (1984) and *No Resting Place* (1989). He has also published: *The Collected Stories of William Humphrey* (1985); *Ah! Wilderness! The Frontier in American Literature* (1977), a volume of criticism; and *Open Season* (1986), about sport.

Humphry Clinker, The Expedition of An EPISTOLARY NOVEL by SMOLLETT, published in 1771. Matthew Bramble, a cranky but kind-hearted Welsh squire, travels through England and Scotland with his family: his unpleasant, husband-hunting sister Tabitha; his amiable nephew Jerry; his teenage niece, Lydia; and Tabitha's maid, Winifred Jenkins. Humphry Clinker, an ostler, becomes their resourceful and devoted servant. The family's travels take them to Bristol, Bath, Harrogate, York, Scarborough and Durham, where they are joined by Lieutenant Obadiah Lismahago, an impecunious Scots soldier. Humphry, a Methodist, converts Tabitha, who succeeds in marrying Lismahago. Lydia falls in love with a handsome young actor who proves to be of good family. Winifred and Humphry fall in love, and he turns out to be Matthew Bramble's long-lost son. These adventures allow Smollett to comment on contemporary life and manners, especially in the spa towns and resorts, more gently than in earlier work. *Humphry Clinker* has often been considered his finest novel.

Hunt, (James Henry) Leigh 1784–1859 Poet, journalist and critic. A precocious writer who published his first volume of poems when he was only 17, he went on to pursue a busy and varied career as man of letters. *THE EXAMINER*, a radical weekly which he and his brother John founded in 1808, introduced the work of KEATS and SHELLEY to the public. When the brothers were fined and sentenced to two years' imprisonment for an uncomplimentary article about the Prince Regent, he continued to edit the journal from his cell. After conducting another journal, *The Indicator*, in 1819–21 he went to Italy in 1822 to join BYRON and Shelley in founding a new periodical, *THE LIBERAL*. Although Shelley's death and Byron's departure for Greece brought *The Liberal* to an end after only four issues, it managed to publish Byron's *VISION OF JUDGEMENT* during its short life. *Lord Byron and Some of His Contemporaries* (1828) offers a jaundiced view of Byron's part in the affair. Hunt went on to edit several more journals· and to publish essays, criticism (*Imagination and Fancy*, 1844), an entertaining autobiography (1850), as well as a play (*A Legend of Florence*, 1840) and volumes of poetry. 'Abou Ben Adhem' and 'Jenny Kissed Me' (about JANE WELSH CARLYLE) are favourite anthology pieces. His personality gave DICKENS the hint for his portrait of Skimpole in *BLEAK HOUSE*.

Hunt, Violet 1866–1942 Novelist. The daughter of the painter Alfred William Hunt, she wrote several novels – *The Maiden's Progress: A Novel in Dialogue* (1894), *Unkist, Unkind* (1897) and *The Tiger Skin* (1924) – and interesting if unreliable reminiscences of the PRE-RAPHAELITES in *Those Flurried Years* (1926) and *The Wife of Rossetti* (1932).

Hunter, Evan [Lombino, Evan] 1926– American novelist. He has also written under the pseudonyms of Ed McBain, Hunt Collins and Richard Marsten. His best-known novel is probably *The Blackboard Jungle* (1954), about an urban high school. Other novels written as Evan Hunter generally deal with social problems, including *Second Ending* (1956), *Mothers and Daughters* (1961), *Sons* (1969) and *Love, Dad* (1981) . He has also produced plays and screenplays. As Ed McBain he writes DETECTIVE FICTION in a popular series of novels about the police of the 87th Precinct.

Hunting of the Snark, The A nonsense poem by LEWIS CARROLL, published in 1876. It describes the quest, led by the lugubrious Bellman, for a mysterious Snark who finally turns out to be a dangerous Boojum instead. Further précis is impossible, given the poem's deliberate lack of logic and its specially invented vocabulary.

Huon of Bordeaux A translation by JOHN BOURCHIER of a 13th-century *chanson de geste*. It was printed after his death, apparently by WYNKYN DE WORDE, in 1534. Huon earns reprieve from execution by performing seemingly impossible tasks with the help of Oberon, king of the fairies, a character whom the work introduced to English readers.

Hurston, Zora Neale 1903–60 Black American novelist and folklorist. *Mules and Men* (1935) and *Tell My Horse* (1938) gather black traditions of the American South and the Caribbean. Her best-known novel, *Their Eyes were Watching God* (1937), portrays the life of Janie Crawford, an independent black woman and folk heroine. Another novel, *Moses: Man of the Mountain* (1939), examines Moses as he appears in the Old Testament and black myth. *Dust Tracks on a Road* (1942) is an autobiography. *I Love Myself When I am Laughing* (1979) is a collection edited by ALICE WALKER and *Spunk* (1984) is a collection of short stories.

Husband's Message, The An Old English poem in the EXETER BOOK. Apparently carved on a staff in runic letters, the message is from a man forced to flee by a vendetta, assuring his wife of his love and asking her to join him. The poem may be connected with *THE WIFE'S LAMENT*.

Hutchinson, Lucy b. 1620 Author of *The Memoirs of the Life of Colonel Hutchinson*, a biography of her husband John Hutchinson (1615–64), a prominent Parliamentarian soldier in the Civil War. Written for the interest of her descendants, it was not published until 1806, when it appeared with a fragment of Lucy Hutchinson's autobiography. The book is valuable for its picture of a distinguished Puritan family.

Hutchinson, R(ay) C(oryton) 1907–75 Novelist. *The Unforgotten Prisoner* (1933) deals with poverty and distress in post-war Germany, *Testament* (1938) with the Russian Revolution, and *A Child Possessed* (1964) with the love of a French *routier* for his idiot child. His finest work grappled with grand themes, often of tragedy in foreign countries he did not know well. It attracted a small but loyal readership.

Hutton, R(ichard) H(olt) 1826–97 Journalist, theologian and literary critic. In 1855 he joined WALTER BAGEHOT in editing *The National Review*, and in 1861 he became joint editor and part owner of *The Spectator*, contributing incisive reviews of contemporary literature. *Essays on Some of the Modern Guides of English Thought in Matters of Faith* (1877), which considers CARLYLE, MATTHEW ARNOLD, GEORGE ELIOT, F. D. MAURICE and NEWMAN, is one of several books reflecting his preoccupation with problems of faith.

Huxley, Aldous (Leonard) 1894–1963 Novelist and short-story writer. He was the grandson of T. H. HUXLEY, the nephew of MRS HUMPHRY WARD and the younger brother of SIR JULIAN HUXLEY. In youth he wrote journalism, poetry and a collection of short stories, *Limbo* (1920), but made his name as a witty and satirical commentator on contemporary events with a novel, *Crome Yellow* (1921). It was followed by *Antic Hay* (1923), *Those Barren Leaves* (1925) and *Point Counter Point* (1928), which contains portraits of D. H. LAWRENCE and JOHN MIDDLETON MURRY. *BRAVE NEW WORLD* (1932) turned its attention to the threat posed by scientific totalitarianism. Subsequent novels, equally marked by Swiftian despair and disgust, include *EYELESS IN GAZA* (1936) and, after Huxley moved to California in 1937, *Time Must Have a Stop* (1944), *Ape and Essence* (1948) and *The Genius and the Goddess* (1955). *Island* (1962), about a Utopian community, reflects his search for an extension of awareness. This quest, begun with *The Perennial Philosophy* (1946), led to the experiments with mescalin described in *The Doors of Perception* (1954) and *Heaven and Hell* (1956).

Huxley's other works include *The Devils of Loudon* (1952), a study of demonic possession during the reign of Louis XIII (adapted by JOHN WHITING as *The Devils*), and many essays (in *Collected Essays*, 1959). He also wrote two travel books (*Jesting Pilate*, 1926; and *Beyond the Mexique Bay*, 1943) and edited *The Letters of D. H. Lawrence* (1932). Huxley's short stories, which many class with his best work, were reprinted in *Collected Short Stories* (1957).

Huxley, Sir **Julian (Sorell)** 1887–1975 Biologist and elder brother of ALDOUS HUXLEY. His books include *Essays of a Biologist* (1923), *Religion without Revelation* (1927), *The Captive Shrew and Other Poems* (1932), *Man in the Modern World* (1947), *Evolution in Action* (1953) and *New Bottles for New Wine* (1957).

Huxley, Thomas Henry 1825–95 Scientist. A powerful supporter of CHARLES DARWIN and an advocate of free investigation and enquiry, he coined the word 'agnostic' to describe himself. His books include *On the Educational Value of the Natural History Sciences* (1854), *On Races, Species and their Origin* (1860), *Evidence as to Man's Place in Nature* (1863), *On the Methods and Results of Ethnology* (1865), *The Evidence of the Miracle of Resurrection* (1876), *The Advance of Science in the Last Half-Century* (1887), *Social Diseases and Worse Remedies* (1891), *Evolution and Ethics* (1893) and *Collected Essays* (1893–4).

Hyde, Douglas 1860–1949 Irish scholar, poet and translator. He was a founder and in 1893–1915 first president of the Gaelic League, dedicated to preserving and spreading the Irish language, Irish games and Irish dancing. *Love Songs of Connacht* (1893), his most influential publication, printed the Irish originals with verse translations and carefully literal prose versions. His *Literary History of Ireland* (1899) was deliberately confined to literature in Irish. He wrote verse and plays in Irish, including *Casadh an tSugain* (1901), translated by LADY GREGORY as *The Twisting of the Rope*, as well as compiling volumes of folk-stories, songs and religious poems translated from the Irish. Hyde was the first president of the Irish Republic in 1938–44.

Hyde, Robin [Wilkinson, Iris Guiver] 1906–39 New Zealand novelist and poet. Her fiction includes *Passport to Hell* (1936), an account of the early life of Douglas Stark, a World War I bomber pilot, and its sequel, *Nor the Years Condemn* (1938), which give a vivid picture of New Zealand life in the opening years of this century. The interaction between private and public history is also the theme of her two best works, *Check to Your King* (1936), a fictionalized biography of Charles, Baron de Thierry, who attempted to establish a Utopian community for English settlers and Maoris in early 19th-century New Zealand, and the autobiographical *The Godwits Fly* (1938). *Persephone in Winter* (1937) is the most substantial volume of verse she published in her lifetime but her best-known poetry is found in the posthumous *Houses by the Sea* (1952), a sequence recreating the natural and social environment of her youth.

Hydriotaphia: or, Urn Burial A treatise by SIR THOMAS BROWNE, published with *The Garden of Cyrus* (1658) and taking as its point of departure the discovery of some ancient grave urns at Walsingham in Norfolk. Browne broadens his enquiry to consider the many ways mankind has disposed of its dead, and his zestful, idiosyncratic scholarship ranges over a wide field. His theme is brought to a close with an eloquent chapter expressing the Christian view of mortality.

Hymn to Proserpine A DRAMATIC MONOLOGUE by SWINBURNE, published in *Poems and Ballads* (1866). Addressed to Proserpine, Queen of the Underworld, by a pagan Roman (possibly Julian the Apostate) of the 4th century of the Christian era, it sets forth the Heraclitan doctrine of flux and change as forcefully as it challenges fundamental Christian beliefs.

Hypatia: or, New Foes with an Old Face A historical novel by CHARLES KINGSLEY, serialized in 1852–3 and published in volume form in 1853. The setting is Alexandria in the 5th century AD, a city governed ineffectually by the pagan prefect, Orestes, and threatened by the barbarian tribes advancing from the heart of Europe. Philammon, a young monk from the desert, is repelled by the fanaticism of the Christian church, led by the patriarch Cyril, and drawn to the beautiful Hypatia, who teaches neo-Platonic philosophy. He witnesses a Christian mob cutting Hypatia to pieces and returns, disillusioned, to the desert.

hyperbole An exaggerated or extravagant statement designed to command attention or provoke reaction. A famous example is the question asked of Helen of Troy by the hero of MARLOWE'S *DR FAUSTUS*: 'Is this the face that launched a thousand ships/ And burned the topless towers of Ilium?'

Hyperion Two unfinished poems by KEATS, written in 1818–19. The first, subtitled *A Fragment*, appeared in 1820 and the second, called *The Fall of Hyperion: A Dream*, was published by MONCKTON MILNES in 1856. Both use the Greek legend of the fall of the Titans and their replacement by the gods, particularly Apollo. The first version tells how Saturn and the other Titans place their hopes in the only Titan who remains undeposed, the sun-god Hyperion. In the second version the poet has a dream in which Moneta, the Titan's priestess, describes the fall of Hyperion and the coming of Apollo.

iamb See METRE.

iambic pentameter See METRE.

Iceman Cometh, The A play by EUGENE O'NEILL, produced in 1946. The men who gather in Jimmy-the-Priest's saloon, as well as its owner Harry Hope, are good-natured and trusting in the value of love and honour. When the salesman Hickey tries to persuade them to abandon their illusions and return to reality, the truths they discover cause them to despair. Only the cynical philosopher Larry Slade can stand up to Hickey.

Idea A SONNET sequence by DRAYTON, first published as *Idea's Mirror* (1594) but reissued with substantial changes and additions in 1599, 1600, 1602, 1605 and 1619, and also in Drayton's collections. The changes, often in response to criticism from fellow poets, usually reject the extravagant CONCEITS of earlier versions and increase the clarity of logic and poetic structure, though later editions also contain work akin to that of the METAPHYSICAL POETS. 'Since There's No Help' (added in 1619) is usually considered Drayton's finest sonnet.

Idea of a University, The Lectures by NEWMAN, published in 1873. They arose from his experience as rector of the new Roman Catholic university in Dublin. The justification of a 'liberal education' is the 'enlargement of the mind'. Knowledge, despite having absolute value for Newman, is not the highest good. He argues that knowledge and reason are 'sure ministers to Faith' and that 'Right Reason ... leads the mind to the Catholic Faith.'

Ideal Husband, An A play by OSCAR WILDE (1895). The most strongly plotted of his earlier works for the theatre, it deals with political corruption, public and private honour, blackmail, repentance and forgiveness.

Idler, The A series of papers, largely by SAMUEL JOHNSON, contributed to *The Universal Chronicle or Weekly Gazette* in 1758-60. The papers are similar in character to *THE RAMBLER* but shorter in length and generally lighter in tone. Of the 12 papers not by Johnson, three are by JOSHUA REYNOLDS (Nos. 76, 79 and 82) and three by THOMAS WARTON THE YOUNGER (Nos. 33, 93 and 96).

A monthly journal edited by JEROME K. JEROME and Robert Barr, appearing in 1892–1911, was also called *The Idler*.

idyll From the Greek, 'little picture': a descriptive piece of poetry or prose, usually with a PASTORAL or rural scene.

Idylls of the King, The A sequence of poems by TENNYSON, his most ambitious work as well as the most ambitious contribution to ARTHURIAN LITERATURE since MALORY'S *LE MORTE DARTHUR*. It was written at different stages in his career. The reception of his early 'Morte d'Arthur' (1842) discouraged him from returning to the subject until 1859, when he published *The Idylls of the King*, containing 'Vivien', 'Enid', 'Elaine' and 'Guinevere'. 'The Coming of Arthur', 'The Holy Grail', 'Pelleas and Ettarre' and 'The Passing of Arthur' appeared in 1869, 'The Last Tournament' in 1871 and 'Gareth and Lynette' in 1872. The Imperial Library edition gathered up all the *Idylls* and added the Epilogue, 'To the Queen'. 'Balin and Balan' was published in *Tiresias and Other Poems* (1885). 'Enid' was later divided into 'The Marriage of Geraint' and 'Geraint and Enid'. In its final order the sequence runs as follows:

The Coming of Arthur. The newly crowned king sets out to restore order and falls in love with Guinevere. Her father Leodegran, King of Cameliard, hesitates to allow the marriage until Bellicent, wife of King Lot of Orkney, tells him the truth about Arthur's birth, upbringing and coronation, and about Merlin and Excalibur. The source is Malory.

Gareth and Lynette. Gareth, son of King Lot and Queen Bellicent of Orkney, is allowed to go to Arthur's court on condition that he works in the kitchens for a year. He serves his allotted term under Kay, the Seneschal. When Lynette, a noble lady, arrives asking Lancelot to rescue her sister Lyonors, Gareth claims the adventure and Arthur grants his wish. Lynette is disgusted and treats him with contempt, but he defeats the four knights besieging Lyonors; the fourth, dressed in hideous armour as Death, proves to be a mere boy. Malory says that Gareth marries Liones, the lady he rescues. Tennyson leaves the matter undecided.

The Marriage of Geraint and *Geraint and Enid*. Geraint decides to withdraw from the court and remove his wife Enid from Guinevere's influence. Believing her faithless, he keeps her with him during his adventures but forbids her to speak to him. Her devotion finally reassures him of her fidelity. The sources were the story of *Gereint and Enid* in *THE MABINOGION* (translated by Lady Charlotte Guest, 1838–49) and *Erec* by Chrétien de Troyes.

Balin and Balan. The last of the *Idylls* to be written, it was intended to introduce the story of Merlin and Vivien. Balin is an irascible knight devoted to Queen Guinevere. Disturbed by her friendship with Lancelot, he leaves the court, kills Sir Garlon for dishonouring her name, and escapes pursuit by Garlon's father, King Pellam. Vivien finds him in the forest and maliciously confirms his unease about the Queen, making him destroy the tokens of her favour in a fury. His brother Balan, hunting a forest demon, hears the wild cries and mistakes Balin for his quarry. The brothers die in combat and Vivien rides away, unconcerned. The source is Malory.

Merlin and Vivien. Vivien arrives at Arthur's court from the court of King Mark of Cornwall begging protection from the Queen. She tries to sow suspicion and to seduce the King but decides that the magician Merlin will serve her purpose better. She succeeds in extracting a charm from him and seals him up for ever in a giant oak tree. The story of Merlin's enchantment is in Malory but Vivien is Tennyson's own invention.

Lancelot and Elaine. The story of Elaine, 'the lily maid of Astolat', and her hopeless love for Lancelot (which Tennyson had already used in *THE LADY OF SHALOTT*) closely follows the French prose *Lancelot* and the English *MORTE ARTHUR*, but does not continue to Agravain's betrayal of Lancelot and Guinevere.

The Holy Grail. The quest is related by Sir Percivale, whose sister, a nun, has the first vision of the Grail and recognizes the requisite purity of character in Galahad, youngest of the knights. Galahad occupies the Siege Perilous, the vision of the Grail is seen by the knights of the Round Table, and the quest begins.

Pelleas and Ettarre. On his way to Arthur's court the

idealistic Pelleas meets and falls in love with the vain Ettarre, but she rebuffs him after he has gained his knighthood and won the prize at a tournament. She refuses to admit him to her castle and sends her knights to attack him. Gawain undertakes to further Pelleas's suit but betrays him with Ettarre. Pelleas is further embittered when he learns from Percivale that Lancelot and Guinevere, too, are false. He attacks Lancelot, scorns the Queen and leaves the court. Guinevere and Lancelot foresee 'the dolorous day to be', while Modred watches and waits.

The Last Tournament. The Tournament of Dead Innocence takes place when the glory of Arthur's court is fading. Lancelot presides, Arthur having taken the younger knights to quell the growing disorder in the kingdom. Tristram wins the prize and presents it not to his wife but to Isolt, King Mark's wife. Mark surprises and executes him. Arthur encounters the hate-filled Pelleas as the Red Knight and returns to his castle to find that Guinevere has departed. Tennyson was particularly pleased with his creation of the 'half-humorous half-pathetic fool' Dagonet who greets Arthur in tears at the end.

Guinevere. Tennyson's account of the progress of Guinevere's remorse is his own invention. Overwhelmed by guilt, she implores Lancelot to leave the court and arranges a last meeting. The lovers are overheard by Vivien and surprised by Modred. Lancelot returns to his own land and Guinevere seeks sanctuary in a nunnery at Almesbury, where, after begging Arthur's forgiveness, she dies.

The Passing of Arthur. Bedivere tells the story of Arthur's last days. All the knights are slain in the great battle except Bedivere, Modred and Arthur. Arthur overcomes Modred in single combat but himself receives a mortal wound. Bedivere cannot bring himself to throw Excalibur into the lake until the third time the command is given. He carries Arthur down to the water's edge to await the barge, with its three queens, which will bear the dying king to Avilion. Arthur comforts Bedivere as best he can, in the lines beginning: 'The old order changeth, yielding place to new,/ And God fulfils himself in many ways ...'

Ieuan Brydydd Hir See CELTIC REVIVAL.

Ignoramus A farcical comedy by George Ruggle, produced at Cambridge during a visit by King James and Prince Charles in 1615 and repeated on a later visit. It was published in 1630. Ruggle (1575–1622) was a fellow of Clare College and *Ignoramus* is his only surviving play. It satirizes lawyers and particularly Francis Brackyn, the Recorder of Cambridge, also a target of *THE PARNASSUS PLAYS*.

Ihimaera, Witi 1944– New Zealand novelist and short-story writer. The first significant Maori writer in English, he has published *Pounamu, Pounamu* (1972), a collection of short stories, and two novels, *Tangi* (1973) and *Whanau* (1974), defending what is most valuable in traditional Maori culture. The stories in *The New Net Goes Fishing* (1977) deal with the city. Later works include *The Matriarch* (1986), an ambitious attempt at a modern epic, *The Whale Rider* (1987) and *Dear Miss Mansfield* (1989), which rewrites stories by KATHERINE MANSFIELD. He has also co-edited *Into the World of Light: An Anthology of Maori Writing* (1982) and written opera libretti.

Il Penseroso A poem by MILTON, the companion piece to *L'ALLEGRO*, written in 1632 and published with other early work in a volume of 1645. Milton had not then gained his later fluency in Italian and the title is a mistaken form of 'Il pensieroso', meaning 'the contemplative'. The poem invokes the goddess Melancholy and celebrates the delights of solitude, withdrawal, music, drama and epic poetry.

Imaginary Conversations of Literary Men and Statesmen A series of dialogues by LANDOR, published in 1824–29. It ranges from classical times to Landor's own day, covering a wide field of topics: dramatic, satirical, idyllic, social, political and literary. Among the best known are: 'Epicurus and Leantion and Ternissa', 'Leofric and Godiva', 'Dante and Beatrice', 'Leonora d'Este and Father Panigarola', 'Princess Mary and Princess Elizabeth', 'Lord Bacon and Richard Hooker', 'Calvin and Melanchthon' and 'Aesop and Rhodope'. *Pericles and Aspasia* (1836) and *Imaginary Conversations of Greeks and Romans* (1853) are in the same style.

imagism An early 20th-century movement in British and American poetry. Influenced by T. E. HULME, it found its leading spokesman in EZRA POUND who, with F. S. FLINT, wrote an imagist 'manifesto' published in POETRY magazine in 1913. It advocated a free choice of subject matter (often dealing with concentrated moments of experience), conciseness of expression, concreteness of imagery, and rhythm composed 'in sequence of the musical phrase, not in sequence of a metronome'. Pound's anthology, *Des Imagistes* (1914), included work by RICHARD ALDINGTON, HILDA DOOLITTLE, FORD MADOX FORD, JOYCE, WILLIAM CARLOS WILLIAMS and AMY LOWELL, who assumed leadership of the movement, helping to publish three further anthologies, all entitled *Some Imagist Poets* (1915, 1916, 1917).

imitation A form distinct from translation, allowing the writer considerably more poetic licence in reworking the structure and theme of an earlier writer's work. The most notable examples in English date from the late Renaissance, the Restoration and the AUGUSTAN AGE, when POPE produced his *Imitations of Horace* and SAMUEL JOHNSON his imitations of Juvenal in *LONDON* and *THE VANITY OF HUMAN WISHES*.

The Latin *imitatio* and its Greek counterpart, *mimesis*, have a different connotation, referring to the whole process of representing reality through the written word.

Imlay, Gilbert 1754–1828 American novelist and radical. He lived in London during the 1790s, publishing *A Topographical Description of the Western Territory of North America* (1792) and *The Emigrants* (1793), an EPISTOLARY NOVEL about the frontier area of Pennsylvania. In France Imlay frequented the radical circles of JOEL BARLOW and THOMAS PAINE and lived for a time with MARY WOLLSTONECRAFT, who bore him a daughter.

Importance of Being Earnest, The: *A Trivial Comedy for Serious People* A comedy by OSCAR WILDE, first produced in 1895. His last play, it has proved his most enduringly popular. The slender but deftly worked plot concerns two fashionable young gentlemen, John Worthing (Jack) and Algernon Moncrieff (Algy), and their eventually successful courtship of Gwendolen Fairfax and Cecily Cardew. More important is the continual flow of witty, uncompromisingly artificial dialogue and the characterization, especially of Gwendolen's mother, Lady Bracknell, and also of Miss Prism and Canon Chasuble.

In a Glass Darkly A book of short stories by LE FANU, published in 1872. It is presented as a collection of cases investigated by Dr Martin Hesselius, who explores the supernatural in terms of psychopathology. 'Green Tea', 'The Watcher', 'The Room in the Dragon Volant' and 'Carmilla', about vampirism, have become classics of occult literature.

In Memoriam A. H. H. A poem by TENNYSON, consisting of 132 connected lyrics, published in 1850. Though reaching out to consider many topics of contemporary intellectual debate, and everywhere tinged with religious doubt, it is essentially an ELEGY for Tennyson's friend ARTHUR HENRY HALLAM, who met an early death in 1833. It encompasses the fluctuating states of shock, despair, resignation and reconciliation as the poet explores his experience of bereavement. The three Christmas lyrics (XXVIII, LXXVIII and CIV) locate the process in a lengthy three-year cycle. Among the many remarkable passages is lyric CIII, which describes a symbolic voyage ending in a vision of Hallam as Tennyson's muse. The epilogue, in the form of a prothalamion on the marriage of the poet's sister Cecilia, was designed to bring the work to an optimistic close. In many ways the cornerstone of Tennyson's reputation with his contemporaries, In Memoriam remains his most highly regarded work.

Inchbald, Elizabeth 1753–1821 Playwright and novelist. She ran away from home in 1772, defying a speech impediment to become an actress but devoting herself to writing after 1789. She is best remembered for a novel, A SIMPLE STORY (1791). Her first play, A Mogul Tale (1784), cleverly exploiting the current craze for hot-air balloons, was followed by comedies, notably I'll Tell You What (1785), and two more ambitious pieces: The Child of Nature (1788) and Lovers' Vows (1798), an adaptation of Kotzebue which plays a memorable role in AUSTEN's MANSFIELD PARK. She also edited three multi-volume collections, The British Theatre (1808), Farces (1809) and The Modern Theatre (1809).

Indian Summer A novel by WILLIAM DEAN HOWELLS, published in 1886. In Florence a middle-aged American newspaper publisher, Theodore Colville, encounters a friend from his childhood, Evalina Bowen, now widowed. Her young friend Imogene Graham is attracted to Colville and her feelings are strengthened when she learns of his suffering in an unhappy youthful romance. Eventually, however, she falls truly in love with a young clergyman, Morton, leaving the way clear for Colville and Evalina, who have secretly loved one another almost from the beginning, to marry.

Inge, William 1913–73 American playwright. His plays include: Come Back, Little Sheba (1950), about a married couple's fruitless battle with alcoholism; Picnic (1950), about a stranger's relationships with several lonely women in a small Kansas town; Bus Stop (1955), about a love-affair between a nightclub singer and a lonely cowboy; The Dark at the Top of the Stairs (1957), about the Flood family; and The Last Pad (1970), about three men on death row. He also wrote the screenplay for Splendor in the Grass (1961), adapted from his own Glory in the Flower (1959), and two novels, Good Luck, Miss Wyckoff (1971) and My Son is a Splendid Driver (1972).

Ingelow, Jean 1820–97 Poet, novelist and writer of CHILDREN'S LITERATURE. Mopsa the Fairy (1869) was a children's favourite for many years. Several of her poems became anthology pieces, notably 'The High Tide on the Coast of Lincolnshire, 1571' and 'Divided' from Poems (1863) and 'A Story of Doom' from the collection of that name (1867). Her novels are Off the Skelligs (1872), Fated to be Free (1875) and Sarah de Beranger (1879).

Ingoldsby Legends, The See BARHAM, R. H.

Inheritance, The A novel by SUSAN FERRIER, published in 1824. The Earl of Rossville repudiates his son when he marries beneath him, but after the son's death acknowledges his daughter-in-law and makes his granddaughter, Gertrude, heiress presumptive. She falls in love with the profligate Colonel Delmour and becomes engaged to him after the Earl's death. He abandons her when she turns out to be an adopted child and hence not an heiress. Her cousin, the faithful Edward Lyndsay, eventually wins her.

Inn Album, The A dramatic poem by ROBERT BROWNING, published in 1875. The visitors' book at the inn is used by two couples whose fates are unavoidably intertwined to convey messages, make assignations and record threats. Though it draws on the career of a notorious Regency rake for its plot, the poem has a contemporary setting.

Innes, Michael See STEWART, J. I. M.

Innocents Abroad, The: or, The New Pilgrim's Progress A travel book by MARK TWAIN, published in 1869 and based on his visit to Europe and Palestine in 1867. It took shape from letters he wrote to the San Francisco Alta California and the New York Herald and Tribune. Shrewd and often humorous, it marked the beginning of the most productive phase of Twain's career.

inscape and **instress** See HOPKINS, GERARD MANLEY.

Intelligencer, The A Dublin weekly started in 1728 by SWIFT and written with help from Thomas Sheridan. It ran to only 19 numbers, the contents ranging from discussion of the state of Ireland (particularly its poverty) to a famous defence of GAY's THE BEGGAR'S OPERA.

The Intelligencer was also the name of a newspaper published by ROGER L'ESTRANGE in the 1660s.

interlude The name, from the Latin interludium, for short dramatic sketches performed during intervals at banquets in the 15th and 16th centuries. The work of JOHN HEYWOOD, in particular, illustrates their importance in the evolution of English drama.

Invisible Man A novel by RALPH ELLISON, published in 1952. Set in the 1930s, it details the often incoherent experiences of its nameless black narrator as a bright high-school student in the South, a disoriented college student who is eventually expelled from his Southern 'negro' college, a factory worker in New York and a rising figure in left-wing politics. He eventually realizes that his black skin makes him 'invisible' to white eyes and retreats to an underground sewer, where he lives while writing his book. The Invisible Man is also the title of a novel (1897) by H. G. WELLS.

Iolo Morganwg See CELTIC REVIVAL.

Ipomadon A late 14th-century VERSE ROMANCE translated from Hue de Rotelande's Anglo-Norman Ipomédon (c. 1190), unusual for an English medieval romance in retaining the preoccupation with the psychology and etiquette of COURTLY LOVE from its source. It is written in 12-line TAIL-RHYME stanzas. There are two other English versions: Ipomedon, in prose, and The Lyfe of Ipomydon, in couplets. A humorous and entertaining story packed with description and detail, it tells how the Duke of Calabria's daughter vows to marry the most proficient knight in the world. Ipomadon, King of Apulia, finally wins her hand after many adventures and exploits, usually carried out in disguise.

Ireland, David 1927– Australian novelist. He wrote plays and verse before turning to fiction. Using discontinuous narrative, surrealism and a range of metafictive techniques, it is frequently highly political and frequently concerned with gender stereotypes and subcultures. His novels include: *The Chantic Bird* (1968), the confession of a youthful outsider which has been compared to CATCHER IN THE RYE; *The Unknown Industrial Prisoner* (1971), about the pressures of working for a multinational oil company; *The Flesheaters* (1972), adapted from his best-known play, *Image in the Clay* (1964); *Burn* (1974); *The Glass Canoe* (1976); *A Woman of the Future* (1979); *City of Women* (1981); *Archimedes and the Seagle* (1984); and *Bloodfather* (1988), which has been called Joycean in its range of characters and structural invention.

Ireland, William Henry 1777–1835 Forger. He began forging SHAKESPEARE items in his teens, producing the whole of *KING LEAR* and excerpts from *HAMLET* in the poet's hand as well as legal documents and signatures. In 1795 an exhibition was held by his father, the engraver Samuel Ireland (d. 1800), who naively insisted on accepting the forgeries until the end of his life. They were initially admired by BOSWELL and HENRY PYE, the POET LAUREATE, among others. William Henry overreached himself with two entirely new Shakespeare plays, *Vortigern and Rowena* and *Henry II*, of which the former was accepted by RICHARD BRINSLEY SHERIDAN for performance but denounced by RITSON, STEEVENS and MALONE.

Iron Heel, The A novel by JACK LONDON, published in 1908. A socialist vision of the future, it is presented as a manuscript written by Avis Cunningham Everhard in 1912–32 about the fight against the Oligarchy, the Iron Heel of the title, a proto-fascist conglomeration of major trusts and their private militias. A socialist revolution is crushed and the manuscript breaks off on the eve of a second uprising, with Avis's husband Ernest already dead and Avis apparently about to be executed. Iron Heel's eventual defeat is recorded by the editor, Anthony Meredith, writing 700 years later in the fourth century of the Brotherhood of Man. The novel proved controversial and was banned in several parts of America.

irony A mode of discourse, whether lyric, narrative or dramatic, which purports to convey a latent meaning different from or opposite to the ostensible one. The term has been stretched to cover understatement, naivety, HYPERBOLE, pun, paradox, contrast or ambiguity – in fact, to cover anything other than literal statement. But, on both etymological and practical grounds, these are better regarded as means of irony or, according to the literary circumstances, as overlapping concepts. If irony is thought of as a dissembling, in keeping with its origin in the *eiron* (a dissembler), then it becomes a term still broad but limited enough to be critically useful. Like Socrates, though, the *eiron* dissembles not to deceive but to enlighten. So irony, properly speaking, is a dissembling that is meant to be seen through.

The dissembling element, however, is not a husk to be discarded when the real meaning is perceived. The fact of opposition is as central to the ironic experience as the fact that it is overcome. Only then will there be the characteristic effect of inward amusement, smiling enlightenment, through the release of tension. The perception of irony thus involves both discernment and detachment – a fact which renders it the most effective weapon of SATIRE and (as tragic irony, a form of dramatic irony) the saving grace of TRAGEDY, distancing us from horror.

All irony is necessarily either textual or structural: inherent either in verbal constructions, making an immediate impression, or in the memory-dependent constructions of plot or story. These two kinds of irony are normally distinguished as verbal and dramatic irony, the one relying on treatment, the other on content. Sarcasm is verbal irony that is crude rather than clever; it is rightly regarded as inferior since it denies the reader the higher pleasures of discernment and detachment. Dramatic irony presents a state of affairs very different from what the protagonists think. The audience usually sees this disparity throughout and is thus, to some extent, detached from the action. Sophocles' *Oedipus Rex* provides the classic example: his pursuit of the criminal leads Oedipus to himself.

Irving, Edward 1792–1834 Minister. A friend of THOMAS CARLYLE, he was expelled from the Church of Scotland for publishing *Homilies on the Sacraments* (1828). His new 'Irvingite' sect, or 'Catholic Apostolic Church', espoused the principles of the early Christian church and revived the gift of tongues.

Irving, John 1942– American novelist. *Setting Free the Bears* (1969), *The Water-Method Man* (1972) and *The 158-Pound Marriage* (1974) found little attention but he made his name with *The World According to Garp* (1978), a long, energetic BILDUNGSROMAN. It has been followed by *The Hotel New Hampshire* (1981) and, moving away from the comic exuberance and surreal invention of his earlier fiction, *The Cider House Rules* (1985), *A Prayer for Owen Meany* (1989) and *A Son of the Circus* (1994).

Irving, Washington 1783–1859 American essayist and short-story writer. His early humorous works include *The Letters of Jonathan Oldstyle, Gent.* (1803), *SALMAGUNDI* (1807–8) and the highly successful *History of New York* (1809), a BURLESQUE. The last was written under the pseudonym of Dietrich Knickerbocker, a name adopted by the KNICKERBOCKER GROUP, of which he was a leading member. His arrival in England in 1815 began a 17-year stay in Europe, during which he formed friendships with several writers – notably SIR WALTER SCOTT – and himself became the first American writer to enjoy an international reputation. His success was largely due to *THE SKETCH BOOK OF GEOFFREY CRAYON, GENT.* (1820), a collection of tales and sketches which included 'Rip Van Winkle' and 'The Legend of Sleepy Hollow', and *BRACEBRIDGE HALL* (1822). *Tales of a Traveller* (1824) was less well received. His stay in Spain as diplomatic attaché to the American embassy in Madrid inspired several historical works: *Life and Voyages of Columbus* (1828), *Conquest of Granada* (1829), *Voyages and Discoveries of the Companions of Columbus* (1831) and *The Alhambra* (1832). *The Crayon Miscellany* (1835), published after his return to America, combines memories of Europe in 'Abbotsford and Newstead Abbey' and 'Legends of the Conquest of Spain' with impressions of America in 'A Tour of the Prairies'. Later books include *Astoria* (1836), an ill-judged book about the Astor fur-trade empire, *Adventures of Captain Bonneville, USA* (1837), *Mahomet and his Successors* (1850), *Wolfert's Roost* (1855) and a life of George Washington (1855–9).

Isabella: or, the Pot of Basil A poem in OTTAVA RIMA by KEATS, published in 1820. The story is drawn from Boccaccio's *Decameron*. Isabella loves the lowly Lorenzo but her proud brothers murder him. He appears to Isabella in a vision to describe his fate and tell where his body is buried in the forest. She finds the grave, removes his head and places it in a pot of basil, which flourishes as she wastes away. Their suspicions aroused, her brothers steal the pot of basil and, horrified at their discovery, flee from Florence. Isabella loses her reason and dies.

Isherwood, Christopher (William Bradshaw) 1904–86 Novelist, short-story writer and playwright. He is best remembered for *Mr Norris Changes Trains* (1935) and *Goodbye to Berlin* (1939), episodic, semi-autobiographical works about the Bohemian society of Berlin, where he lived in 1929–33. The latter contains 'Sally Bowles', a sketch about a cabaret artiste, later dramatized by John van Druten as *I am a Camera* (1951) and turned into a musical, *Cabaret* (1968). Isherwood collaborated with AUDEN on three plays, *The Dog beneath the Skin* (1935), *The Ascent of F6* (1936) and *On the Frontier* (1939), and an account of their visit to China, *Journey to a War* (1938). After emigrating to the USA in 1939 he wrote screenplays, took an increasing interest in Indian philosophy and religion, and published several novels: *Prater Violet* (1945), *The World in the Evening* (1954), *Down There on a Visit* (1962) and *A Single Man* (1964). His autobiography, *Christopher and His Kind* (1972), gives a frank account of his homosexuality.

Ishiguro, Kazuo 1954– Novelist. A former student of MALCOLM BRADBURY's creative writing course at the University of East Anglia, he began with two novels on Japanese themes, *A Pale View of Hills* (1981) and *An Artist of the Floating World* (1986). *The Remains of the Day* (1990), which won the BOOKER PRIZE, is a deadpan first-person account of an ageing butler's motoring tour of England in the 1950s, using minute ironies to reveal a familiar English ferment of emotional starvation.

Israel Potter: His Fifty Years of Exile A novel by HERMAN MELVILLE, serialized in 1854–5 and published separately in 1855. Loosely based on an anonymous tract, *Life and Remarkable Adventures of Israel R. Potter* (1824), it follows its hero's adventures during the Revolutionary War. He enlists in the Revolutionary army, is captured by the British, escapes, meets George III, takes messages to BENJAMIN FRANKLIN and serves under John Paul Jones. He finally settles in London and is prevented by poverty from revisiting Boston until he is in his 80s.

Ivanhoe SIR WALTER SCOTT's most popular novel, and the first of his works to be set in England, published in 1819. The period is the reign of Richard I.

Wilfred of Ivanhoe loves Rowena, but his father Cedric plans to marry her to Athelstane of Coningsburgh. Ivanhoe serves with Richard in the crusades. Returning after his imprisonment in Austria to confront his usurping brother John, Richard appears at the tournament at Ashby-de-la-Zouch, where he helps Ivanhoe defeat the knights of John's party, among them the Templar, Sir Brian de Bois-Guilbert. Bois-Guilbert falls in love with Rebecca, a beautiful and courageous Jewess, who loves Ivanhoe. Rebecca, her father Isaac, Rowena, Cedric and the wounded Ivanhoe are taken captive by the Norman barons and imprisoned in Torquilstone Castle. The King and a Saxon force, with the help of Locksley (ROBIN HOOD) and his band of outlaws, take the castle and release the prisoners except Rebecca, who is carried off by Bois-Guilbert. Though his designs are frustrated, Rebecca is further imperilled by a trial for witchcraft at which Ivanhoe appears as her champion and Bois-Guilbert as her reluctant accuser. Bois-Guilbert falls dead, a victim of his conflicting emotions. Seeing Ivanhoe's love for Rowena, Rebecca leaves England with her father.

Iyayi, Festus 1947– Nigerian novelist. Representative of the new generation of Nigerian novelists which has turned away from anti-colonial and often village-based themes, he has presented the poverty, corruption and alienation of city life in *Violence* (1979), *The Contract* (1982) and *Heroes* (1986), about the Nigerian Civil War.

Jack Juggler (*A New Interlude for Children to Play, Named Jack Juggler*) A comedy written in the late 1550s and printed in 1562. Attributed without much evidence to UDALL, it tones down the *Amphitruo* of Plautus for performance by schoolboys. Jupiter and Amphitryon are removed from the plot entirely and Mercury becomes the trickster Jack Juggler; the other characters are as English as the London street in which the action takes place.

Jack Upland The first of three anonymous pieces in a style somewhere between prose and rough ALLITERATIVE VERSE, tentatively dated 1390, 1420 and 1450. *Jack Upland*, usually classified as prose, is a LOLLARD attack on the greed and hypocrisy of friars, particularly mendicant Franciscans. *Friar Daw's Reply* answers the charges and condemns the Lollards. *Jack Upland's Rejoinder*, the third and coarsest piece, is a personal attack on Friar Daw.

Jackson, Helen (Maria) Hunt 1830–85 American novelist and poet. Her poetry is collected in *Verses by H. H.* (1870) and *Sonnets and Lyrics* (1886). Concern for the American Indians prompted her to write *A Century of Dishonor* (1881), a historical study, and *Ramona* (1884), a novel. Other works include CHILDREN'S LITERATURE, a travel book and magazine articles, some written under the pseudonym Saxe Holm. Her novel *Mercy Philbrick's Choice* (1876) is probably a fictionalized portrait of her friend EMILY DICKINSON.

Jackson, Holbrook See *NEW AGE, THE*.

Jackson, Laura Riding See RIDING, LAURA.

Jackson, Shirley 1919–65 American novelist and short-story writer. Her best-known story, 'The Lottery' (1948), and her second novel, *The Hangsaman* (1951), typify her interest in the dark side of human nature. She also produced humorous stories and articles, some collected in *Life among the Savages* (1953) and *Raising Demons* (1957). Other works include *The Bird's Nest* (1954), *Witchcraft of Salem Village* (1956), *The Bad Children* (1959), *The Sundial* (1958), *The Haunting of Hill House* (1959), *Special Delivery* (1960), *We Have Always Lived in the Castle* (1962), *Nine Magic Wishes* (1963) and two collections edited by her husband, *The Magic of Shirley Jackson* (1966) and *Come Along with Me* (1968).

Jacob's Room A novel by VIRGINIA WOOLF, published in 1922. Her first move towards the experimentation for which she was later recognized, it attempts to evoke the inner life of Jacob Flanders (a character based on her brother Thoby) through various impressionistic scenes, some involving STREAM OF CONSCIOUSNESS. After Cambridge, Jacob is glimpsed at social gatherings in London, with his mistress, and abroad at Versailles and in Athens. The novel ends during World War I, when Jacob has been killed and two friends are visiting his room in Bloomsbury to dispose of his possessions.

Jacobs, W(illiam) W(ymark) 1863–1943. Author of some 20 volumes of humorous stories about barge crews, night-watchmen and other coastal workers. His first was *Many Cargoes* (1896); others are *The Skipper's Wooing* (1897), *Light Freights* (1901) and *Sea Whispers* (1926). He also wrote tales of horror, the best known being 'The Monkey's Paw'.

Jacobson, Dan 1929– South African novelist and short-story writer. He settled in Britain in 1958. His fic-

tion, often concerned with uncontrolled states of mind in varying relationships with personal or political power, includes *The Trap* (1955), *A Dance in the Sun* (1956), *The Price of Diamonds* (1957), *Evidence of Love* (1960), *The Beginners* (1966), *The Rape of Tamar* (1970), *The Wonder-Worker* (1973), *The Confessions of Joseph Baisz* (1977), and *Her Story* (1987), set in the future. His volumes of short stories include *Beggar My Neighbour* (1964). *Time and Time Again* (1985) is an autobiography.

Jago, Richard 1715–81 Poet. He is remembered for *Edgehill: or, The Rural Prospect Delineated and Moralised* (1767), which describes the view at various times of day from the ridge where the battle took place during the Civil War.

James I of England 1566–1625 King of Scotland, as James VI, from 1567 and of England from 1603. A scholarly man, if exaggeratedly vain of his learning, he published several important works. *The Essays of a Prentice, in the Divine Art of Poesy* (1584) contains poems, translations from Du Bartas and Lucan, and, most significantly, the first Scots contribution to literary criticism in the Renaissance. *His Majesty's Poetical Exercises at Vacant Hours* (1591) includes further translations from Du Bartas. *The True Lawe of Free Monarchies* (1598) and *Basilikon Doron* (1599) set forth his philosophy of government. A fascination with witchcraft bore fruit in *Daemonologie* (1597), which attacks the sceptical REGINALD SCOT. Perhaps his most enduring work is *A Counterblast to Tobacco* (1604). Both as writer and as patron, particularly of the development of the English MASQUE by JONSON and Inigo Jones, he exercised a considerable influence on the culture of Stuart England.

James I of Scotland See *THE KINGIS QUAIR*.

James, Alice 1848–92 American diarist. The sister of HENRY JAMES and WILLIAM JAMES, she suffered the first of several neurasthenic breakdowns when she was 19. Her diary, apparently intended for publication, was begun in 1886, after she had settled in England. It shows her to have been an astute critic of the work and careers of her brothers, as well as of the issues of the day. A major theme is her awareness of approaching death from breast cancer. The diary appeared as *Alice James: Her Brothers – Her Journal* (1934) and has been republished as *The Diary of Alice James* (1964). A selection of her letters, *The Death and Letters of Alice James*, appeared in 1983.

James, G(eorge) P(ayne) R(ainsford) 1799–1860 Author of over 100 historical novels. They include *Richelieu* (1829), *The Huguenot* (1838), *The Man-at-Arms* (1840), *Arabella Stuart* (1844), *The Cavalier* (1859) and *The Man in Black* (1860). His style was parodied by THACKERAY in *PUNCH'S PRIZE NOVELISTS*.

James, Henry 1843–1916 American novelist, short-story writer, playwright, critic and essayist. The brother of WILLIAM JAMES and ALICE JAMES, he was born in New York and attended schools in Boulogne, Paris, Geneva, Bonn and Newport, Rhode Island. After a brief spell at Harvard Law School he concentrated on writing, encouraged by CHARLES ELIOT NORTON and WILLIAM DEAN HOWELLS, publishing reviews and essays in THE NORTH AMERICAN REVIEW and THE ATLANTIC MONTHLY. His first novel, *Watch and Ward*, was serialized in the latter journal in 1871. *A Passionate Pilgrim and Other Tales* (1875) and *Transatlantic*

Sketches (1875) reflect his experiences of Europe on extended visits in 1869 and 1872–4. After spending 1875 in Paris he settled in England in 1876, making London his base for over 20 years before moving to Lamb House in Rye, Sussex. He became a British subject in 1915.

Deeply influenced by Continental literature (he had met Turgenev, Daudet, Flaubert, the Goncourts and Zola in Paris), James took the American experience of Europe as the theme of his first important works: *RODERICK HUDSON* (1876), *THE AMERICAN* (1877), *THE EUROPEANS* (1878), *DAISY MILLER* (1879), *An International Episode* (1879) and, his masterpiece of this period, *THE PORTRAIT OF A LADY* (1881). *WASHINGTON SQUARE* (1880) and *THE BOSTONIANS* (1886) use an American setting, and *THE PRINCESS CASAMASSIMA* (1886) studies the political underworld of London, while *THE ASPERN PAPERS* (1888) returns to his 'international theme'. In addition to short stories, essays and travel writings, he also published significant critical studies of French poets and novelists (1878), of *HAWTHORNE* (1879) and of 'The Art of Fiction' (1884).

James continued to publish short stories: *The Lesson of the Master* (1892), which includes 'The Pupil', 'The Solution', and 'Sir Edmund Orme', *The Real Thing and Other Tales* (1893), *Terminations* (1895), which includes 'The Altar of the Dead', and *Embarrassments* (1896), which includes 'The Figure in the Carpet'. But he spent much of the early 1890s in a fruitless preoccupation with the drama, culminating in the failure of *Guy Domville* (1895). The novels which followed – notably *THE SPOILS OF POYNTON* (1897), *WHAT MAISIE KNEW* (1897), *THE AWKWARD AGE* (1899) and *THE SACRED FOUNT* (1901) – abandon his 'international theme', though it returns in his last three major works: *THE WINGS OF THE DOVE* (1902), *THE AMBASSADORS* (1903) and *THE GOLDEN BOWL* (1904). *THE TURN OF THE SCREW* (1898) is his most famous venture into the uncanny. James revised his novels for the New York Edition (1907–9) and contributed 18 new prefaces which form a major statement of his approach to fiction. *The American Scene* (1907) records his impressions of his native country after long absence. His last completed novel was *The Outcry* (1911); *The Ivory Tower* and *The Sense of the Past* were left unfinished.

James, M(ontague) R(hodes) 1862–1936 Scholar and writer of ghost stories. In the course of his distinguished career he became Provost of King's College, Cambridge (1905) and Provost of Eton (1918), serving also as director of the Fitzwilliam Museum (1893–1908) and Vice-Chancellor of the University of Cambridge (1913–15). His broad interests embraced biblical studies, palaeography and medieval art and literature. Beyond the scholarly world he is best remembered for *Ghost Stories of an Antiquary* (1904), *More Ghost Stories of an Antiquary* (1911), *A Thin Ghost, and Others* (1919), *The Five Jars* (1922) and *A Warning to the Curious, and Other Ghost Stories* (1925). The first volume contained the much-anthologized 'Oh, Whistle and I'll Come to You, My Lad'. *Collected Ghost Stories* appeared in 1931.

James [White], P(hyllis) D(orothy), Baroness James of Holland Park 1920– Writer of DETECTIVE FICTION. Her experience working for the National Health Service and the Home Office is clearly reflected in the settings of her novels. They feature two recurrent detectives: the policeman Adam Dalgliesh (*Cover Her Face*, 1962; *A Mind to Murder*, 1963; *Unnatural Causes*, 1967; *Shroud for a Nightingale*, 1971; *The Black Tower*, 1975; *Death of an Expert Witness*, 1977; *A Taste for Death*, 1986; *Devices and Desires*,

1989) and the private detective Cordelia Gray (*An Unsuitable Job for a Woman*, 1972; *The Skull beneath the Skin*, 1982). By comparison with the classic efficiency of her early work, *Innocent Blood* (1980) and *Original Sin* (1994) mark a dissatisfaction with the conventional boundaries of detective fiction. *The Children of Men* (1992) ventures into SCIENCE FICTION.

James, William 1842–1910 American philosopher. The elder brother of HENRY JAMES, he qualified as a doctor and opened a pioneering laboratory of psychology at Harvard in 1876, becoming professor of psychology (1889–97) and professor of philosophy (1897–1907). His chief works are: *THE PRINCIPLES OF PSYCHOLOGY* (1890), a classic in its field; *THE WILL TO BELIEVE* (1897), a collection of essays defining his position as a 'radical empiricist'; *THE VARIETIES OF RELIGIOUS EXPERIENCE* (1902); and *PRAGMATISM* (1907), arguing that an idea has meaning only in relation to its consequences in feeling and action. *The Meaning of Truth* (1909) answered his critics. *A Pluralistic Universe* (1909) explained his metaphysical principles. Posthumous publications were *Some Problems of Philosophy: A Beginning of an Introduction to Philosophy* (1911), *Memoirs and Studies* (1911) and *Essays in Radical Empiricism* (1912).

Jameson, Anna Brownell 1794–1860 Art and literary critic. Her books include *Loves of the Poets* (1829), *Characteristics of Women* (1832; later called *Shakespeare's Heroines*), *Memoir of the Early Italian Painters* (1845) and *Sacred and Legendary Art* (1848). *Diary of an Ennuyée* (1826) describes her experiences touring Europe as a governess. *Winter Studies and Summer Rambles* (1838) describes the lives and customs of the Canadian Indian tribes.

Jane Eyre A novel by CHARLOTTE BRONTË, published in 1847. Jane is an orphan whose independent spirit does not fit the household of her unpleasant aunt, Mrs Reed, and cousins. As pupil and then teacher at Lowood Asylum she suffers appalling physical conditions but learns self-control from her friend Helen Burns, who dies of consumption. She leaves Lowood to become governess at Thornfield Hall. Its master, Edward Rochester, is attracted by her wit and self-possession, and proposes marriage. Their wedding is interrupted by the revelation that Rochester is already married and that his wife, now mad, is secretly confined at the Hall. Jane leaves and is finally taken in by a clergyman, St John Rivers, and his sisters Diana and Mary. They turn out to be her cousins and Jane to be heir to a fortune, which she shares with them. The dedicated but narrow-minded St John proposes that she accompany him to India as his wife. She almost consents but Rochester's voice calls to her out of the air. Returning to Thornfield, she discovers that a fire has destroyed it and the first Mrs Rochester, leaving Rochester himself maimed and blind. At last they can marry.

Contemporary praise for *Jane Eyre* was mixed with criticism of its harsh portrait of Lowood and its Evangelical headmaster, Brocklehurst, and a more general unease about the book's morality. While observing the conventional code of female behaviour, Jane's actions still make a powerful statement of women's claim to independence.

Jane Shore, The Tragedy of A play by ROWE, one of his three 'she-tragedies', produced and published in 1714. It traces the fall from favour of Edward IV's mistress Jane Shore, making her an unlikely image of domestic virtue and providing her jealous friend, Alicia, with a conclusion in eloquent madness.

Janet's Repentance See *SCENES OF CLERICAL LIFE*.

Jarrell, Randall 1914–65 American poet and critic. His verse is colloquial, emphasizing the grotesqueness of a reality made more chaotic by modern science. War is an important theme, notably in 'The Death of the Ball Turret Gunner'. Volumes include *Blood for a Stranger* (1942), *Little Friend, Little Friend* (1945), *Losses* (1948), *The Seven-League Crutches* (1951), *Selected Poems* (1955; expanded 1964); *Uncollected Poems* (1958); *The Woman at the Washington Zoo* (1960), *The Lost World* (1965), *Complete Poems* (1969) and *Jerome: The Biography of a Poem* (1971). His critical writings include *Poetry and the Age* (1953), *The Third Book of Criticism* (1969) and *Kipling, Auden, & Co.: Essays and Reviews 1935–1964* (1979). Jarrell also wrote CHILDREN'S LITERATURE, translations and a novel, *Pictures from an Institution* (1954), as well as holding editorial positions on several periodicals, including *THE NATION* (1946) and *PARTISAN REVIEW* (1949–51).

Jason, The Life and Death of A narrative poem by WILLIAM MORRIS, published in 1867. It follows the familiar adventures of the hero's career, including his voyage in the *Argo*, his theft of the Golden Fleece and his flight with Medea. Jason ends in melancholy loneliness, musing in the shadow of his rotting ship.

Jebb, Richard Claverhouse 1841–1905 Greek scholar. Professor of Greek at Glasgow and then at Cambridge, he published *The Attic Orators from Antiphon to Isaeus* (1876–80), editions and translations of Theophrastus (1870), Sophocles (1883–96) and Bacchylides (1905), and a biography of RICHARD BENTLEY (1882).

Jefferies, (John) Richard 1848–87 Journalist and novelist. He is mostly remembered for novels and essays celebrating the countryside of southern England. He established himself in the public view during the early 1870s with articles on wild life for *THE PALL MALL GAZETTE* and a long letter to *The Times* on the plight of the agricultural labourer in Wiltshire, his native county. His fiction began with melodramatic and for the most part unsuccessful works: *The Scarlet Shawl* (1874), *Restless Human Hearts* (1875) and *The World's End* (1877). More convincing are his last novel, *Amaryllis at the Fair* (1887), with its portrait of his father in the character Iden, and, among earlier works, the autobiographical *Bevis, the Story of a Boy* (1882) and his actual autobiography, *The Story of My Heart* (1883). Books of essays reflecting his close engagement with rural England include *The Amateur Poacher* (1879), *The Gamekeeper at Home* (1880), *Hodge and His Masters* (1880), *Greene Ferne Farm* (1880), *The Open Air* (1885) and the posthumous *Field and Hedgerow* (1889). Present but not precisely visible in these works is the thoroughgoing distaste for 19th-century industrialism implicit in *After London* (1885), a novel presenting a vision of future disaster which forces people to trust in their knowledge of the earth, animals and plants for survival.

Jeffers, (John) Robinson 1887–1962 American poet. Calling for a poetry of 'dangerous images', he often used biblical stories or Greek and Roman myths, and wrote with classical directness and clarity. He first achieved his distinctive voice in *Tamar and Other Poems* (1924); numerous other volumes include *Roan Stallion* (1924), *The Woman at Point Sur* (1927), *Cawdor and Other Poems* (1928), *Dear Judas and Other Poems* (1929), *Give Your Heart to the Hawks and Other Poems* (1933), *Be Angry at the Sun* (1941), *The Double Axe* (1948) and *Hungerfield, and Other Poems* (1954). *Medea* (1947) was his best-known play.

Jefferson, Thomas 1743–1826 Third president of the USA. Born in Virginia, he emerged as a leading voice of the colonies' grievances with *A Summary View of the Rights of British America* (1774). As a member of the Second Continental Congress he drafted the Declaration of Independence in 1776. During the American Revolution he served in the Virginia legislature (1776–9) and as the state's governor (1779–81). He espoused a vision of an agrarian society based on an independent yeomanry, defended individual freedom against privilege and government encroachment, and supported the gradual abolition of slavery. *NOTES ON THE STATE OF VIRGINIA* (1785) is a clear expression of his ideals. After serving as American minister to Paris (1785–9), he became Washington's Secretary of State (1789–93), Adams's Vice-President (1797–1801) and then President (1801–9).

Jefferson had lifelong interests in science, architecture and education. He was president of the American Philosophical Society in 1797–1814 and founded the University of Virginia, chartered in 1819. His library formed the nucleus of the Library of Congress. He also wrote *Observations on the Whale-Fishery* (1788), *A Manual of Parliamentary Practice* (1801) and a *Life of Captain Lewis* (1814). Among papers unpublished at his death were his *Autobiography*, the *Anas* (political memoirs) and 'The Morals of Jesus of Nazareth', reflecting his DEISM.

Jeffrey, Francis 1773–1850 Lawyer, editor and critic. One of some Whig Edinburgh lawyers who supported reform, he became MP for Edinburgh in 1832 and Lord of Session in 1834, as Lord Jeffrey. With SYDNEY SMITH, HENRY BROUGHAM and FRANCIS HORNER he founded *THE EDINBURGH REVIEW* in 1802. He became its editor in 1803 and held the post for 25 years, establishing himself as an influential critic who (despite his dislike of WORDSWORTH's poetry) raised the standard of public taste. A selection from his papers appeared in 1844.

Jellicoe, Ann 1927– Playwright. She wrote and directed her comedies, *The Sport of My Mad Mother* (1958) and *The Knack* (1961), as well as the less successful *Shelley* (1965) for the ROYAL COURT THEATRE. In a second phase of her career she has written and directed community plays for the Colway Theatre Trust in the south-west of England, including *The Reckoning* (1978), *The Tide* (1980), *The Western Women* (with FAY WELDON and JOHN FOWLES; 1984) and *Under the God* (1989).

Jenkins, (John) Robin 1912– Scottish novelist. One of the most prolific post-war Scottish writers, he has often been neglected, perhaps because of his distance from both the SCOTTISH RENAISSANCE and MODERNISM. His novels, often autobiographical in origin, include *Happy for the Child* (1953), *The Cone-Gatherers* (1955), *The Changeling* (1958), *Guests of War* (1956), *A Would-be Saint* (1978) and a comic masterpiece, *Fergus Lamont* (1979). Spells of teaching abroad prompted *Dust on the Paw* (1961), *The Sardana Dancers* (1964), *The Holy Tree* (1969) and *A Figure of Fun* (1974). His short stories were collected in *A Far Cry from Bowmore* (1973).

Jennie Gerhardt A novel by DREISER, published in 1911. Jennie, pretty but poor, is forced to leave home when she becomes pregnant by Senator George Brander. She works as a maid for the Bracebridges and meets Lester Kane, who persuades her to live with him. His wealthy family disapproves and his father makes his inheritance conditional on his abandoning Jennie. He eventually marries Letty Pace Gerald, a widowed socialite. Jennie's daughter, Vesta, dies and she adopts two orphans. The dying Lester summons her to express his regret at leaving her. She attends his funeral, masked behind a veil.

Jennings, Elizabeth (Joan) 1926– Poet. *Poems* (1955) identified her with the MOVEMENT, though her Catholicism gave her work a quiet vulnerability and made faith rather than IRONY its dominant quality. Early work, in *A Way of Looking* (1955), *A Sense of the World* (1958) and *Song for a Birth or a Death and Other Poems* (1961), shows simplicity and a belief in traditional formal properties. *Recoveries* (1964) and *The Mind Has Mountains* (1966) come from a period of mental illness. Later work, in *Growing Points* (1975), *Consequently I Rejoice* (1977), *Moments of Grace* (1977), *Celebrations and Elegies* (1982), *Extending the Territory* (1985), a second *Collected Poems* (1986), *Tributes* (1989) and *Times and Seasons* (1992), gains authority from the sense of triumph over disruptive forces. She has also written studies of religion and poetry.

Jenny A DRAMATIC MONOLOGUE by DANTE GABRIEL ROSSETTI, begun in 1847 and eventually published in 1870. Jenny is a prostitute, scorned by her virtuous sisters and, more tellingly, by the men who use her. Rossetti's only poem with a contemporary subject, it has a close connection with his only painting on a contemporary theme, the unfinished 'Found'.

Jerome, Jerome K(lapka) 1859–1927 Humorist and novelist. *On Stage and Off* (1885) and *Idle Thoughts of an Idle Fellow* (1886) were lighthearted essays which set the tone for his most enduring work, *Three Men in a Boat* (1889), about an accident-prone rowing holiday on the Thames. *Three Men on the Bummel* (1900) took the same characters on a tour of Germany. He founded *The Idler*, a humorous periodical, in 1892, and wrote many plays, the most successful being *The Passing of the Third Floor Back* (1907). His own favourite work was *Paul Kelver* (1902), an autobiographical novel.

Jerrold, (William) Blanchard 1826–84 Journalist. He succeeded his father, DOUGLAS JERROLD, as editor of *Lloyd's Weekly Newspaper*. He wrote four plays, published a biography of his father (1859) and provided the text for Gustave Doré's volume of illustrations, *London: A Pilgrimage* (1872).

Jerrold, Douglas (William) 1803–57 Playwright and journalist. He scored his major success in the theatre with *Black-Eyed Susan* (1829). Other popular works included a FARCE (*Paul Pry*, 1827) and several MELODRAMAS (*Fifteen Years of a Drunkard's Life*, 1828; *The Mutiny at the Nore*, 1830; *The Rent Day*, 1832), though his characteristic vein was comedy (*The Bride of Ludgate*, 1831; *Beau Nash*, 1834; *Time Works Wonders*, 1845). He joined the staff of the newly founded PUNCH in 1841, became a regular contributor under the signature of 'Q', and helped to establish the paper's popularity with *Mrs Caudle's Curtain Lectures* (serialized, 1845; book form, 1846), the diatribes of a nagging wife. He edited *Lloyd's Weekly Newspaper* from 1852 until his death.

Jew of Malta, The Famous Tragedy of the Rich A tragedy by MARLOWE, first produced *c.* 1590 but not published until 1633. The text is believed to contain alterations made during production, usually attributed to THOMAS HEYWOOD. The successful Jewish merchant Barabas has his wealth and house confiscated by the governor when the Turks demand tribute from Malta. In a campaign of revenge against his enemies he disposes of his daughter Abigail and her Christian lover, poisons wells and destroys the entire nunnery, his former house, with poisoned porridge. But his plan to destroy the Turkish commander and his retinue at a banquet by means of a collapsible floor goes awry. He is betrayed and meets his death in a cauldron.

Jewett, Sarah Orne 1849–1909 American novelist and short-story writer. Her fiction was shaped by youthful observation of the decaying farms and fishing towns of Maine and by the example of HARRIET BEECHER STOWE's stories of New England. *Deephaven* (1877), a collection of stories, takes its name from a harbour town based on York, near her home town of South Berwick. It was followed by two novels, *A Country Doctor* (1884) and *A Marsh Island* (1885), and further collections of stories: *A White Heron* (1886), *The King of Folly Island* (1888), *A Native of Winby* (1893) and *The Life of Nancy* (1895). *The Country of the Pointed Firs* (1896), set in the imaginary town of Dunnet Landing, gained a lasting place in American literature. Later work included two books for children; a historical romance, *The Tory Lover* (1901); and the posthumous *Verses* (1916).

Jewsbury, Geraldine Endsor 1812–80 Novelist. The friend of THOMAS and JANE CARLYLE, she produced several unjustly neglected novels: *Zoe: The History of Two Lives* (1845), *The Half-Sisters* (1848), *Marian Withers* (1851), *Constance Herbert* (1855), *The Sorrows of Gentility* (1856) and *Right or Wrong* (1859).

Jhabvala, Ruth Prawer 1927– Indian novelist. Though a satirically minded outsider, she has also experienced Indian joint family life, and skilfully exploits this duality in novels such as *To Whom She Will* (1956), *The Nature of Passion* (1957), *The Householder* (1960), *Esmond in India* (1958), *Heat and Dust* (1975), *A New Dominion* (1973; as *The Travelers* in the USA), *A Backward Place* (1963) and *In Search of Love and Beauty* (1983). *Like Birds, Like Fishes* (1963), *A Stronger Climate* (1968), *An Experience of India* (1971) and *How I Became a Holy Mother* (1976) are collections of stories. Part of the Merchant–Ivory film-making team, she has written several scripts, of which *Autobiography of a Princess* and *Shakespeare Wallah* were outstanding international successes.

Jocelin of Brakelond *fl.* 1173–1215 Chronicler. He entered the abbey at Bury St Edmunds in 1173 and held increasingly important posts there until 1215, when his name disappears from the records. His Latin *Chronicle* about life in the monastery is notable for a vivid portrait of Abbot Samson. The account covers Samson's early career, his election in 1182 and his repair of the abbey church, but ends eight years before his death in 1211 at the age of 77. First published in 1840, the *Chronicle* was made famous by CARLYLE's use of it in *PAST AND PRESENT* (1843); as a result, an English translation appeared in 1844.

John Bull, The History of A group of pamphlets by ARBUTHNOT, first published in 1712 and rearranged for publication in POPE and SWIFT's *Miscellanies* (1727). A SATIRE against the war with France, it marks the first appearance of the typical Englishman, John Bull, 'an honest plain-dealing Fellow' who honours his mother (the Church of England) but is easily deceived by partners, apprentices and servants.

John Gilpin, The Diverting History of A comic BALLAD by COWPER, published anonymously in *The Public Advertiser* in 1782 and in the same volume as *THE TASK* (1785). The real John Gilpin was a linen draper of Cheapside who owned land at Olney, Buckinghamshire. The poem tells how he and his wife decide to celebrate their wedding anniversary at The Bell, Edmonton. She and the children travel by chaise and pair, while he rides a borrowed horse which runs out of control, carrying him 10 miles further, to Ware, and back again.

John Halifax, Gentleman See MULOCK, DINAH.

John Inglesant See SHORTHOUSE, JOSEPH HENRY.

John of Salisbury c. 1115–80 Philosopher. A student of Peter Abelard and, from 1176, Bishop of Chartres, he was at the centre of intellectual life in the medieval church. His *Policraticus* deals, often satirically, with the ethics of politics and the state. The *Metalogicus* combines the studies of logic and metaphysics. The *Historia pontificalis* is a delightful account of life in Rome, where John had worked in the papal curia. Two biographies of leading churchmen, Anselm and Thomas Becket, and a collection of his letters also survive.

Johns, W(illiam) E(arle) 1893–1968 Writer of CHILDREN'S LITERATURE. An ex-RAF officer and pilot in the Royal Flying Corps during World War I, he introduced his most famous hero, Biggles (Captain James Bigglesworth), in short stories published in the magazine, *Popular Flying*, he founded in 1932. Along with his companions Ginger, Algy and Bertie, Biggles provided young readers with an idealized image of toughness, honesty and stoicism in over 70 novels. Johns also created a slightly less popular commando hero, Gimlet, and a female Biggles, Worrals of the WAAF.

Johnson, B(rian) S(tanley) 1933–73 Novelist. *Travelling People* (1963), *Albert Angelo* (1964), *Trawl* (1966), *The Unfortunates* (1969), *Christie Malry's Own Double Entry* (1973) and *See the Old Lady Decently* (1975) ran counter to the realistic bias of post-war British fiction, turning instead to the example of JOYCE, BECKETT, FLANN O'BRIEN and STERNE. The extremity of Johnson's technical adventures occasionally earned him the charge of gimmickry.

Johnson, Colin See MUDROOROO.

Johnson, Edward 1598–1672 American historian. He emigrated to Massachusetts in 1636 and held many influential civic positions. *The Wonder-Working Providence of Sion's Saviour in New-England* (1654) is a history covering the period 1628–52 and cataloguing instances of divine intervention which, Johnson argues, show God's approval of the New England Way.

Johnson, Emily Pauline 1862–1913 Canadian poet. The daughter of an Indian chief and an Englishwoman, she contributed to periodicals and recited her verse under her Indian name of Tekahionwake. Her best works, *White Wampum* (1895), *Canadian Born* (1903) and *Flint and Feathers* (1913), demonstrate a keen understanding of Indian life.

Johnson, James Weldon 1871–1938 Black American novelist and poet. While practising law in Florida, he collaborated with his brother in writing popular songs and spirituals. 'Lift Every Voice and Sing' became known as the black anthem. His first novel, *Autobiography of an Ex-Colored Man* (1912), is about a light-skinned black man who poses as a white. *Black Manhattan* (1930) is a black history of New York. Other volumes of poetry are *Fifty Years and Other Poems* (1917), *God's Trombones: Seven Negro Sermons in Verse* (1927), *Saint Peter Relates an Incident at the Resurrection Day* (1930) and *Selected Poems* (1935). His autobiography is *Along This Way* (1933).

Johnson, Linton Kwesi 1952– Poet. Born in Jamaica, he came to Britain in 1963. His work, mostly dub poetry, is often urban in theme and filled with street-wise aggression. It enjoys a large popular following. His recorded poems give a better idea of his talents, but Johnson has also published several collections: *Voices of the Living and the Dead* (1974), *Dread Beat and Blood* (1975), *Inglan is a Bitch* (1980) and *Tings and Times* (1991). Records include *Dread Beat An' Blood* (1978), *Forces of Victory* (1979), *Bass Culture* (1980) and *Making History* (1984).

Johnson, Lionel (Pigot) 1867–1902 Poet and critic. A Roman Catholic convert, he was a member of the RHYMERS' CLUB and a close friend of W. B. YEATS, whose early poetry he influenced. His study of HARDY (1894) was followed by *Poems* (1895) and *Ireland with Other Poems* (1897), which included 'Ways of War'. *Posliminium*, a posthumous collection of essays, appeared in 1912 and his *Complete Poems*, edited by I. Fletcher, in 1953. Although his poems about Ireland are rhetorical, his other work 'conveys an emotion of joy, of intellectual clearness, of hard energy', as Yeats wrote. Johnson acknowledged his alcoholism in 'Mystic and Cavalier': 'Go from me, I am one of those who fall.'

Johnson, Louis 1924–88 New Zealand poet and editor. In 1951–64 he edited *Poetry Yearbook*, the focus of a 'Wellington school', including JAMES K. BAXTER and ALISTAIR CAMPBELL, which advocated a romantic-universalist approach against ALLEN CURNOW's insistence that New Zealand poetry should engage with local reality. Johnson's own poetry includes *The Sun among the Ruins* (1951), *New Worlds for Old* (1957) and *Bread and a Pension* (1964). He also wrote poems satirizing the Puritan ethos of New Zealand society. Later work, especially the posthumous *Last Poems* (1990), is sparser in diction and tighter in form.

Johnson, Pamela Hansford 1912–81 Novelist and critic. Her talent for light SATIRE is best revealed in the 'Dorothy Merlin' trilogy: *The Unspeakable Skipton* (1959), *Night and Silence, Who is Here* (1962), and *Cork Street, Next to the Hatter's* (1965). Non-fictional works include studies of IVY COMPTON-BURNETT, Proust and THOMAS WOLFE, and *On Iniquity* (1967), about the Moors Murders. She married C. P. SNOW in 1950.

Johnson, Samuel 1709–84 Critic, scholar, lexicographer, poet and man of letters. The son of a Lichfield bookseller, he went to Pembroke College, Oxford, in 1728 but left without taking a degree. His later achievements earned him an MA in 1755 and an honorary doctorate of civil law in 1775, though Oxford was anticipated by Trinity College, Dublin, in entitling him to the 'Dr' by which the world came to know him. After leaving Oxford, Johnson taught at the grammar school in Market Bosworth and then lived in Birmingham, where he completed *A Voyage to Abyssinia* (1735), a translation from the French version of the travels of Father Jerome Lobo. In 1735 he married Mrs Elizabeth Porter ('Tetty'), a widow 20 years his senior; the couple harboured an enduring affection for each other. After the failure of the school they founded at Edial, near Lichfield, they moved to London in 1737, accompanied by GARRICK, a former pupil.

Johnson found steady work contributing in a wide variety of forms to Edward Cave's GENTLEMAN'S MAGAZINE. LONDON (1738), his IMITATION of Juvenal, was approved by POPE. The death of his erstwhile friend RICHARD SAVAGE prompted the first of his biographical pieces (1744). Although the *Plan of a Dictionary of the English Language* he addressed to CHESTERFIELD in 1747 fell on deaf ears he continued, without a patron, to work intermittently on the project for the next eight years. He published his longest and most enduring poem, *THE VANITY OF HUMAN WISHES*, in 1749, the same year Garrick kept a promise by staging his indifferent tragedy *Irene*, completed 12 years earlier. In 1750 Johnson embarked on THE RAMBLER, a twice-weekly periodical of moral essays and commentaries, which ran until 1752 with Johnson writing, anonymously, all but four of its 208 numbers himself. His grief at Tetty's death in 1752 exacerbated the bouts of depression from which he suffered throughout his life.

A DICTIONARY OF THE ENGLISH LANGUAGE, his most substantial scholarly achievement and still a milestone in English lexicography, finally appeared in 1755. It was greeted with acclaim and belated endorsement from Chesterfield, whom Johnson vigorously rebuffed. He was still struggling to earn his bread, writing numerous political articles, reviews and essays for the periodicals, lives of SIR THOMAS BROWNE (1756) and ASCHAM (1761), and THE IDLER (1758–60), a series of papers contributed to the *Universal Chronicle*. His philosophical romance, *The Prince of Abyssinia: A Tale*, later known as RASSELAS, appeared shortly after his mother's death in 1759.

The award of an annual pension by George III in 1762 somewhat relaxed his straitened circumstances. The following year he first met JAMES BOSWELL, who was later to become his biographer. In 1764 he and JOSHUA REYNOLDS founded 'the Club', an artistic coterie whose meetings were attended by BURKE, GOLDSMITH, Garrick, Boswell and Charles James Fox. Hester Thrale, the wife of a prosperous and cultured brewer, became a close and generous friend who offered him hospitality during a period of depression. After considerable delay, his eight-volume edition of SHAKESPEARE appeared in 1765; subsequent scholarship may have superseded most of the editorial work, but its *Preface* remains a model of good sense. By now a famous literary figure whose opinions on a variety of subjects were eagerly noted in metropolitan circles, Johnson finally agreed to Boswell's proposal that they tour Scotland together. Johnson's observations appeared as A JOURNEY TO THE WESTERN ISLANDS OF SCOTLAND (1775), his friend's as THE JOURNAL OF A TOUR TO THE HEBRIDES (1785). At the suggestion of a number of London booksellers, Johnson began work on a series of 'little prefaces' for an edition of the works of the English poets; these penetrating essays were published separately as THE LIVES OF THE POETS (1781), his last major work.

Johnson's reputation as the greatest man of letters England has produced was helped by Boswell's LIFE OF SAMUEL JOHNSON LL.D. (1791), which fused its subject's personality with his writings and raised him to legendary status. A pioneering scholar, famous conversationalist in an age when conversation was considered a minor art form, and eloquent sage, Johnson is sometimes wrongly considered a reactionary embodying the High Tory principles of the dwindling AUGUSTAN AGE. Though famous in later life, he kept both his humility and his scepticism, and never forgot the real hardships of his early years as a struggling hack. He was not a philosopher who discovered an original system of thought, but his wisdom shaped a stern and practical critique of both human behaviour and literature. Pathologically lazy himself, he chastised idleness in others; fearful of insanity, he was fascinated by irrationality in others. He applauded originality, clarity, honesty and the perception of general truths, demonstrating these values in his life as well as in his writings.

Johnston, Sir Charles (Hepburn) 1912–86 Poet and translator. He combined a diplomatic career with literature. His highly regarded translation of Pushkin's *Eugene*

Onegin (1977) was followed by privately printed volumes, *Poems and Journeys* (1979), *Rivers and Fireworks* (1980), *Talk about the Last Poet* (1981), *Choiseul and Talleyrand* (1982) and *The Irish Lights* (1983), mixing new and old poems with translations from Latin and Russian. His wide range includes EPIGRAMS, autobiographical poems, DRAMATIC MONOLOGUES and narrative verse.

Johnston, George (Henry) 1912–70 Australian novelist. His work includes *The Darkness Outside* (1959), *The Far Face of the Moon* (1964) and a trilogy of self-examining novels, *My Brother Jack* (1964), *Clean Straw for Nothing* (1969) and *A Cartload of Clay* (1971), the last volume left incomplete at his death. Together they brilliantly present aspects of 20th-century Australian life, depicting archetypal qualities in the Australian male character. Johnston also wrote thrillers under the pseudonym of Shane Martin.

Johnston, Jennifer 1930– Irish novelist. She is the daughter of the playwright Denis Johnston. Her best work – *The Captains and the Kings* (1972), *How Many Miles to Babylon?* (1974) and *The Invisible Worm* (1991) – continues the tradition of the Irish 'Big House' novel, centring on the decay of the Protestant gentry and their embattled position in modern Ireland. *Shadows on Our Skin* (1977) and *Fool's Sanctuary* (1987) depict divided loyalties in families caught up in the Northern Irish troubles.

Johnstone, Charles *c.* 1719–1800 Journalist and satirist. *Chrysal: or, The Adventures of a Guinea* (1760–5), satirical episodes from the life of the times, is told by a guinea as it is passed from hand to hand. Most notable are the scenes at the Hellfire Club and the manoeuvres of an ambitious wife on behalf of her clergyman husband.

Jolley, Elizabeth 1923– Australian novelist, short-story writer and radio playwright. Her habit of tinkering with several projects simultaneously for several years resulted in an apparently late start followed by a rush of publications which belies the care bestowed on her work. She first became known for radio plays and the short stories in *Five Acre Virgin* (1976), *The Travelling Entertainer* (1979) and *Woman in a Lampshade* (1983). The first two volumes were combined in *Stories* (1984). Her recognition was completed by novels, of which the most important may well prove to be *Mr Scobie's Riddle* (1983), a comedy of old age, and *Miss Peabody's Inheritance* (1983) and *Foxybaby* (1985), both about women novelists. The play between different kinds of textual reality in the latter makes it a classic of POST-MODERNISM.

Jolly Beggars, The A verse cantata by BURNS, published in a Glasgow chapbook in 1799. A group of wretched folk enjoy themselves singing and drinking the evening away. The songs are linked by precise and evocative descriptions of the singers.

Jonathan Wild the Great, The Life of A novel by HENRY FIELDING, published in 1743. It gives a fictionalized version of the life of the infamous criminal executed in 1725, ironically presenting him as an example of heroism and greatness. Wild's success in the underworld is compared to the values at work in polite society and government. Sir Robert Walpole is the chief target for this aspect of the SATIRE. After showing an early propensity for crime, Wild becomes chief of a gang of thieves, safeguarding himself by turning over to the law any subordinates who question his leadership. He concentrates on ruining the jeweller Heartfree, his virtuous former schoolfellow. Heartfree is rescued from the scaffold by the exposure of Wild, who is hanged in his stead, a 'hero' and 'great man' to the last.

Jones, (Walter) David (Michael) 1895–1974 Poet and artist. Combining verse, prose, illustration and lettering, his work makes highly allusive and associative use of a variety of sources in ritual and romance. *In Parenthesis* (1937) relates the experience of Private John Ball in World War I to chivalric antecedents, and the modern waste land to MALORY'S *MORTE DARTHUR*. *The Anathemata* (1952), a much wider chronicle, was admired by AUDEN, KATHLEEN RAINE and EDWIN MUIR. Later works include *The Sleeping Lord and Other Fragments* (1974), *The Kensington Mass* (1975) and *The Roman Quarry and Other Sequences* (1981). *Epoch and Artist* (1959) and *The Dying Gaul* (1978) are collections of essays and articles.

Jones, Henry Arthur 1851–1929. Playwright. After *It's Only Round the Corner* (1878; later called *Harmony*, 1884), he established his reputation with *THE SILVER KING* (1882), a spectacular MELODRAMA, but then turned to more serious theatre. He adapted Ibsen's *A Doll's House* as *Breaking a Butterfly* (with Henry Herman; 1884) and showed a talent for naturalistic dialogue and portrayal of character in his own work. It included *Saints and Sinners* (1884), *The Dancing Girl* (1891), *The Case of Rebellious Susan* (1894), *The Triumph of the Philistines* (1895), *Michael and His Lost Angel* (1896), *THE LIARS* (1897) and *Mrs Dane's Defence* (1900). The last two are occasionally revived.

Jones, James 1921–77 American novelist. *From Here to Eternity* (1951), his first and best-known novel, is a realistic story of army life in Hawaii on the eve of the attack on Pearl Harbor. His career continued with *Some Came Running* (1957), *The Pistol* (1959), *The Thin Red Line* (1962), *Go to the Widow-Maker* (1967) and *A Touch of Danger* (1973). His short stories are collected in *The Ice Cream Headache* (1968) and *The Merry Month of May* (1971). *Viet Journal* (1974) describes a visit to Vietnam.

Jones, LeRoi See BARAKA, AMIRI.

Jones, Sir **William** 1746–94 Jurist and orientalist. Though he published several books on law and oriental languages, he is best remembered for his mastery of Sanskrit and his insistence, in his essay in *Asiatic Researches* (1786), on its study as the common source of Greek and Latin. Jones's work, together with JOHN HORNE TOOKE's advocacy of the study of Gothic and Anglo-Saxon (published in the same year), brought the science of comparative philology into being.

Jonson, Ben(jamin) 1572–1637 Playwright and poet. Probably born in Westminster and educated at Westminster School, he may have worked with his stepfather, a master bricklayer. He had probably fought in Flanders and was certainly married by 1597, when he may have been among those imprisoned for performing *The Isle of Dogs*. Jonson's outspoken, combative temperament assured him a lifetime of conflict with authority. The next year he killed a fellow actor in a duel but escaped execution by pleading benefit of clergy.

EVERY MAN IN HIS HUMOUR (1598), his second known play, made him famous and created a brief fashion for 'humours' comedy. The less successful *Every Man out of His Humour* (1599) and *CYNTHIA'S REVELS* (1600) are satirical comedies displaying classical scholarship and delight in formal experiment. Jonson's quickness to take offence inevitably drew him into the war of the theatres: MARSTON and DEKKER were his chief adversaries and *THE POETASTER* (1601) his major contribution. *SEJANUS, HIS FALL* (1603) and his later tragedy, *CATILINE HIS CONSPIRACY* (1611), are too ponderous to stand comparison with SHAKESPEARE's Roman plays. A play by a Catholic (Jonson had converted in 1598) about conspiracy and assassination, *Sejanus* brought a summons from the Privy Council on charges of 'popery and treason'. Together with his contribution to *EASTWARD HO* (1604), for which he was again briefly imprisoned, it jeopardized his role as court poet and MASQUE writer to JAMES I. *The Masque of Blackness* (1605) was the first of many collaborations with Inigo Jones, threatened and finally destroyed by rivalry.

His enduring reputation rests on the four comedies he wrote between 1605 and 1614: *VOLPONE* (1605), *EPICOENE: OR, THE SILENT WOMAN* (1609), *THE ALCHEMIST* (1610) and *BARTHOLOMEW FAIR* (1614). Their artfully controlled stagecraft still leaves an air of improvisatory spontaneity. The 'image of the times', promised in the Prologue to the revised *Every Man in His Humour* (1616), is uncomfortable, peopling the stage with deceivers and dupes, and leaving the virtuous or intelligent an unusually small part to play. Pug, a junior devil allowed a day on earth in *THE DEVIL IS AN ASS* (1616), finds himself out of his depth among humans.

The comparative failure of this play may have discouraged Jonson. Nine years passed before his next comedy, *The Staple of News* (1625), and his effective dramatic output was completed by *The New Inn* (1629) and *A Tale of a Tub* (1633). But he was never inactive. His vivid sense of his own stature was announced by the publication of his dramatic and poetic *Works* (1616) and his continuing provision of court masques. He was rewarded with a royal pension and appointment as POET LAUREATE. The songs and poems in the masques, together with the collected verse of *EPIGRAMS* and *THE FOREST* (both 1616) and *UNDERWOODS* (1640), explain his influence among younger poets, the self-styled 'tribe' or 'sons' of Ben. His prose style is memorably sketched in the notes of DRUMMOND OF HAWTHORNDEN (1632) and the posthumously published *TIMBER* (1640). One of the loyal friends who attended his funeral in Westminster Abbey inscribed the words 'O rare Ben Jonson' on his gravestone.

Jorrocks's Jaunts and Jollities A collection of 10 stories by SURTEES, published in book form in 1838, with illustrations by HABLOT K. BROWNE, and enlarged in 1869. They describe the adventures of John Jorrocks, a sporting London grocer, his vulgar wife, his friend Charlie Stubbs and his servant Binjimin. Apart from hunting, there is also racing, shooting, fishing, eating, drinking and a jaunt to France. *HANDLEY CROSS* (1843) and *Hillingdon Hall* (1845) continue the story.

Joseph Andrews *(The History of the Adventures of Joseph Andrews, and of his Friend Mr Abraham Adams. Written in Imitation of Cervantes, Author of Don Quixote)* A novel by HENRY FIELDING, first published in 1742. Joseph is the brother of Pamela Andrews, heroine of RICHARDSON's *PAMELA*, and a footman to Lady Booby. When she and her companion, Mrs Slipslop, show designs on his chastity he decides to return to his sweetheart, Fanny, and takes to the road. He is accompanied by Parson Adams, an absent-minded and gullible curate intent on getting his sermons published. The pair suffer a long series of scrapes, embarrassments and encounters with rogues and hypocrites. The main characters converge for a final show-down at the Boobys' country seat. Squire Booby has meanwhile married Pamela (Joseph's sister), and the novel ends by revealing that Joseph is actually the son of a respectable couple and not Pamela's brother.

Joseph Andrews quickly outgrows the BURLESQUE of

Richardson and develops a shape of its own. Though Fielding describes himself in his 'Preface' as 'the founder of a new province of writing', his main achievement is to synthesize earlier narrative forms (EPIC, romance and, above all, PICARESQUE) with contemporary realism and an eye for telling detail.

Journal of a Tour to the Hebrides with Samuel Johnson, The A narrative by JAMES BOSWELL, published in 1785, describing the journey he had undertaken with his friend in 1773. In *A JOURNEY TO THE WESTERN ISLANDS OF SCOTLAND* Johnson himself gave a formal account of their itinerary. Boswell, by contrast, writes informally about the discomforts, hazards and passing incidents of the journey, and concentrates in particular on sketching the character of his travelling companion.

Journal of a Voyage to Lisbon, The See FIELDING, HENRY.

Journal of the Plague Year, A An imaginatively reworked account, part fact and part fiction, of the Great Plague in 1664–5, written by DEFOE and published in 1722. The narrator is 'H.F.', a Whitechapel saddler who remains in London throughout the epidemic and provides a graphic commentary on its rise, the public reaction, the precautions taken by the authorities and the drastically changing atmosphere of the capital as it becomes depopulated. Defoe skilfully weaves plague bills of mortality, statistics, historical accounts, anecdotes and hearsay into the lively and colloquial narrative. The result is both a study in human isolation and a life-affirming work that examines a city under threat.

Journal to Stella A collection of private letters written by SWIFT from London in 1710–13 to his close friend Esther Johnson (later nicknamed Stella) and her companion Rebecca Dingley in Dublin. Swift gives an intriguing inside view of the world of political intrigue, party wrangling, gossip and literary chitchat. His use of baby-talk (or 'little language') shows his softer side. Though the letters were not designed for publication, a selection appeared in 1766 and an edition was prepared by his cousin, Deane Swift, in 1768.

Journey to the Western Islands of Scotland, A SAMUEL JOHNSON's description, published in 1775, of the three-month tour he made with JAMES BOSWELL in 1773. Boswell took him north from Edinburgh to St Andrews and Aberdeen. They paid a visit to Lord Monboddo, an eccentric law lord, and then travelled west to Inverness, Glenelg, Skye, Iona and Oban. They were guests of the Duke of Argyll at Inverary, of the faculty at Glasgow University and of Boswell's father, Lord Auchinleck, at the family seat.

Where Boswell's *JOURNAL OF A TOUR TO THE HEBRIDES WITH SAMUEL JOHNSON* is casual and anecdotal, Johnson offers a formal survey. His interest lay in exploring the variety and extent of nature, particularly of human nature, and his aim was to record local differences in a scientific spirit and universal truths in a philosophical one. Apart from being more sympathetic to Scotland than popular legend supposes Johnson to be, the book is one of the great achievements of 18th-century travel literature.

Journey's End See SHERRIFF, R. C.

Jowett, Benjamin 1817–93 Scholar and divine. Regius Professor of Greek at Oxford from 1855 and Master of Balliol College from 1870, he taught PATER and GERARD MANLEY HOPKINS and showed a sympathetic interest in SWINBURNE's undergraduate career. A theological liberal, he took a fresh and original approach in *Epistles of Paul to the Thessalonians, Galatians and Romans* (1835; revised 1855 and 1859). 'The Interpretation of Scripture' in *ESSAYS AND REVIEWS* (1860) caused angry debate and cast suspicion on his orthodoxy. Jowett also translated Plato (1871), Thucydides (1881) and Aristotle's *Politics* (1885).

Joyce, James (Augustine Aloysius) 1882–1941 Irish novelist, short-story writer and poet. Born in Dublin, he was educated at Jesuit schools and University College. While an undergraduate he made the acquaintance of YEATS, SYNGE, LADY GREGORY and GEORGE WILLIAM RUSSELL (A. E.) and others fostering the Irish cultural renaissance, but, eager to escape his family and dissatisfied with the narrowness of Irish life, he went to Paris after graduating in 1902. His mother's terminal illness obliged him to return the following year. During this visit he met Nora Barnacle, who became his permanent companion (they finally married in 1931) in a life of exile, wandering and poverty dictated by his unwavering dedication to his art. They left Ireland together in 1904 and first settled in Trieste, moving to Zurich during World War I and to Paris in 1920. During the 1930s he was increasingly beset by family worries – his daughter Lucia was diagnosed schizophrenic in 1932 – and by problems with deteriorating eyesight. The outbreak of World War II forced him to return to Zurich, where he died.

Youthful publications included an essay on Ibsen (1900) in the *THE FORTNIGHTLY REVIEW* and a volume of poetry, *Chamber Music* (1907). His first significant work was *DUBLINERS* (1914), a collection of short stories, whose very title announced a central if paradoxical feature of his mature art: for all his Continental wanderings and cosmopolitan sensibility, his subject would always remain the city he had left. *A PORTRAIT OF THE ARTIST AS A YOUNG MAN*, begun as *Stephen Hero* in 1903, was serialized in *THE EGOIST* in 1914–15 and published in volume form in 1916. An autobiographical novel, it used the technique of STREAM OF CONSCIOUSNESS which he had encountered in Dujardin's *Les Lauriers sont coupés* (1888).

Joyce subsequently published an unsuccessful play, *Exiles* (1918), and a slight volume of verses, *Pomes Penyeach* (1927), but these were mere asides during the creation of the two great works which occupied his remaining life. *ULYSSES*, begun in 1914 and finished in 1921, used the character of Stephen Dedalus and the technique of stream of consciousness from the *Portrait*, while subduing both to a more radically ambitious purpose: nothing less than to recreate a day in the life of Dublin in painstaking detail while also locating it in the widest possible context of history and myth. The novel was serialized in *THE LITTLE REVIEW* from 1918 until a prosecution for obscenity in 1920, and was first published in volume form in Paris by Harriet Shaw Weaver's Egoist Press in 1922. It was banned in the USA until 1933 and in Britain until 1937. *FINNEGANS WAKE*, begun in 1923, was serialized in 12 parts as *Work in Progress* in 1928–37 and published complete in 1939. The radical experimentalism which dissolves narrative into dream and the English language into polyglot puns has given it an exaggerated reputation for inaccessibility, yet it takes its place with *Ulysses*, not just as a central text of MODERNISM, but as a work which can outlive fluctuating critical judgements of modernism.

Jude the Obscure A novel by HARDY, published in 1895. Jude Fawley, a stonemason with a talent and passion for scholarship, is trapped into marriage by Arabella Donn. When she deserts him he makes his way to Christminster (Oxford) and earns his living as a labourer while aspiring to be a student. He meets and is attracted to his cousin Sue Bridehead. She marries Phillotson, Jude's former schoolmaster, but flees his sexual advances and lives with Jude. Two children are born to them and they also take care of 'Father Time', Jude's son by Arabella. As impoverished social outcasts, they become bitterly unhappy: Sue retreats into morbid Christianity while Jude moves towards atheism. 'Father Time' kills the two children and himself. In a misguided attempt at expiation Sue returns to Phillotson. Jude declines, resentfully cared for by Arabella, and eventually dies alone.

Many contemporary readers and reviewers were outraged by the pessimism of the novel and its depiction of the 'deadly war waged between flesh and spirit'. Hardy wrote no more fiction afterwards.

Judith An Old English poem preserved in the same manuscript as *BEOWULF*. It is incomplete, but it is not certain how much has been lost. The surviving fragment of 350 lines gives a free, often dramatic rendering of the biblical story of Judith's execution of Holofernes, her flight and the Hebrew defeat of the Assyrians.

Julian and Maddalo: *A Conversation* A poem by SHELLEY, published in 1824. The conversation, presented as a dialogue in couplets, is between Shelley (Julian) and BYRON (Maddalo) as they wander through Venice and its environs discussing religion, progress and freedom. Through the intervention of a child, innocence and virtue are proposed as lasting values, but the poem retains its presiding cynicism.

Julian of Norwich 1342–after 1429 Author of *A Revelation of Divine Love*. Little is known about her besides the information she gives in her single work, an account of mystical experience which, being illiterate, she dictated to a scribe some time after 1393. Her revelations were concerned with God's love for mankind and how the Christian should love God. The first 15 occurred during a period of sickness and hysteria in 1373; the last, many years later, confirmed that her experience had been a token of Christ's love. By 1394 she had become an anchorite attached to St Julian's Conesford in Norwich, where she was visited by MARGERY KEMPE in about 1413. See also MYSTICAL WRITING.

Juliana A short Old English poem by CYNEWULF, preserved (except for a few missing pages) in the EXETER BOOK. Closely following a Latin source, it describes the martyrdom of a Christian virgin in AD 303. Refusing marriage and paganism, Juliana is tortured and put in prison, where she survives a devil's attempt to trick her, before being executed.

Julius Caesar A tragedy by SHAKESPEARE, first performed in 1599 and published in the First Folio of 1623. He relied on NORTH's Plutarch for the story and much of the language. Though Caesar's defeat of Pompey makes him popular with the majority of Romans, he is mistrusted by Pompey's former supporters and a group of patricians led by Cassius, who fear that he wishes to be crowned. Cassius persuades Brutus, the most respected republican, to join their conspiracy. Ignoring a soothsayer's warning, Caesar goes to the Capitol and is assassinated. After justifying the murder to the people, Brutus allows Mark Antony to speak. His rhetoric turns them against the conspirators. Brutus and Cassius flee

Rome and gather their forces, while Antony, Lepidus and Caesar's great-nephew Octavius form a triumvirate and prepare for war. After quarrelling with Brutus, Cassius learns that Brutus' wife, Portia, has committed suicide. Partly out of remorse, he accepts Brutus' decision to march and confront Antony at Philippi. Brutus and Cassius lose the battle and kill themselves. The play ends with Octavius' ominously ambiguous proposal that he and Antony should 'part the glories of this happy day'. Critics have noted the play's shift from the tragedy of Caesar to that of Brutus; it is equally possible to read it as a sophisticated REVENGE TRAGEDY, with Antony becoming Caesar's avenger.

Jungle Book, The and **Second Jungle Book, The** Collections of short stories and poems by KIPLING, published in 1894 and 1895 respectively. Their core is the sequence of stories about the boy Mowgli, accidentally thrust out of the human community into the jungle. His growth to dominance over the animals and his eventual return to human service as a forest ranger provide the basic framework. The code of conduct in the animal world is severe and requires a high level of responsibility; humanity is unruly and undignified by comparison.

Junius The pseudonym adopted by the author of a series of letters which appeared in *THE PUBLIC ADVERTISER* in 1769–71, making shrewd and unsparing political attacks from a Whig viewpoint. The Duke of Grafton, Lord North, Lord Mansfield and George III were all targets, and WILKES was defended. The identity of Junius has never been discovered, though SIR PHILIP FRANCIS has for long been a favourite candidate. An edition of the letters appeared in 1772.

Junius, Francis [Dujon, François] 1589–1677 Antiquary. Born in Heidelberg, he was librarian to the 2nd Earl of Arundel and a friend of MILTON. The Junius Manuscript was his collection of the manuscripts of Old English scriptural poems he attributed to CAEDMON, notably *GENESIS*, *EXODUS*, *DANIEL* and *CHRIST AND SATAN*. He presented it to the Bodleian Library in Oxford, together with his philological collections. As well as editing Caedmon (1655), Junius wrote an *Etymologicum Anglicanum*, published in 1743, which helped JOHNSON with his *DICTIONARY OF THE ENGLISH LANGUAGE*.

Juno and the Paycock A play by O'CASEY, produced at the ABBEY THEATRE in 1924. It is set in Dublin during the civil war of 1922. The idle Jack Boyle ('Captain') lives in a tenement with his wife Juno and their children Mary and Johnny. On the strength of a promised inheritance, he borrows money and spends it drinking with his crony, Joxer Daly. He remains comically and horrifyingly unaffected by the domestic tragedies around him. Charles Bentham gets Mary pregnant and abandons her when Boyle's inheritance comes to nothing. Johnny is revealed as an informer and taken off to be executed by the Republican Army. Juno finally abandons Boyle, who is still talking with Joxer in the empty flat when the play ends.

Just So Stories A collection of 12 stories and 12 poems by KIPLING, published in 1902. It was written to be read aloud by adults to children, and the interplay between human and animal worlds in the first seven stories is simpler and more playful than in *THE JUNGLE BOOK*. An element of teasing is most obviously apparent in such stories as 'How the Leopard Got Its Spots', where Kipling travesties the theory of evolution.

kailyard school A group of late 19th-century Scottish writers who wrote, often in the vernacular, about home-spun topics and promoted a sentimental image of small-town life. 'Kailyard', meaning 'cabbage patch', was used by Ian Maclaren (born John Watson, 1850–1907) as the motto for a collection of his stories, *Beside the Bonnie Briar Bush* (1894). The group also included BARRIE and S. R. Crockett (1860–1914), author of *The Stickit Minister* (1893).

Kangaroo A novel by D. H. LAWRENCE, published in 1923. Set in Australia, it is principally a vehicle for Lawrence's reactions to the country and to post-World War I politics. Richard Lovat Somers, a writer, and his wife Harriet meet Benjamin Cooley ('Kangaroo'), a Jewish barrister and leader of a radical political party, who tries unsuccessfully to enlist Somers's support for his programme, a combination of fascism and Lawrentian 'blood consciousness'. After a meeting in Canberra Hall has been violently disrupted, the couple leave for America.

Kaufman, George S(imon) 1889–1961 American playwright and director. All but one of his 40 plays, half of them Broadway hits, were written in collaboration: with MARC CONNELLY (*Dulcy*, 1921; *Merton of the Movies*, 1922; *Beggar on Horseback*, 1924); Edna Ferber (*The Royal Family*, 1927; *Dinner at Eight*, 1932; *Stage Door*, 1936); Morris Ryskind (*The Cocoanuts*, 1925, and *Animal Crackers*, 1928, for the Marx Brothers, and *Of Thee I Sing*, 1931; PULITZER PRIZE); and MOSS HART (*Once in a Lifetime*, 1930; the Pulitzer Prize-winning *You Can't Take It with You*, 1936; *The Man Who Came to Dinner*, 1939). Kaufman's distinctive contribution was the wisecrack, timed with the same precision he brought to his work as a director.

Kavanagh, Julia 1824–77 Novelist. Born in County Tipperary, she spent much of her early life in France. Works include *Madeleine* (1848), *Nathalie* (1850), *Daisy Burns* (1853), *Adele* (1858), *Bessie* (1872) and *Woman in France during the Eighteenth Century* (1850).

Kavanagh, Patrick (Joseph) 1904–67 Irish poet. His early life on a peasant farm in County Monaghan is treated in an autobiography, *The Green Fool* (1938), and more cynically in a novel, *Tarry Flynn* (1948). The poetry which followed *Ploughman and Other Poems* (1936) includes *The Great Hunger* (1942), a grimly compassionate account of Irish rural life, in partially rhymed free verse influenced by the early T. S. ELIOT. *Come Dance with Kitty Stobling* (1960) announced a renewal of poetic power after difficulty and ill health. *Complete Poems* appeared in 1972. Kavanagh's realistic treatment of rural life, in deliberate reaction against YEATS's view of the peasantry, and his confidence that local subject matter need not entail a narrowly 'provincial' treatment influenced R. S. THOMAS and subsequent Irish poets such as SEAMUS HEANEY.

Kavanagh, P(atrick) J(oseph) (Gregory) 1931– Poet and novelist. Formally traditional and influenced by WORDSWORTH, YEATS and EDWARD THOMAS, his poems are preoccupied with the pains and joys of life, the hope given by love, and death – particularly the death of his wife, also the informing event behind his autobiography, *The Perfect Stranger* (1966). His volumes, from *One and One* (1959) onwards, include *Selected Poems* (1982), *Presences: New and Selected Poems* (1987) and *Collected Poems* (1988). Novels include *A Song and Dance* (1968) and *A Happy Man* (1973).

Kaye-Smith, Sheila 1887–1956 Novelist. *The Tramping Methodist* (1908) started a series of rural novels focusing on a Sussex family, the Alards. The best known are *Sussex Gorse* (1916), *Tamarisk Town* (1919), *Green Apple Harvest* (1920), *Joanna Godden* (1921) and *The End of the House of Alard* (1923). Later work includes *The History of Susan Spray* (1931), *Ember Lane* (1940), *Mrs Gailey* (1951) and an autobiography, *Three Ways Home* (1937).

Keary, Annie 1825–79 Novelist and writer of CHILDREN'S LITERATURE. She wrote two notable children's books, *The Heroes of Asgard* (with her sister Eliza Keary; 1857) and *Sidney Grey* (1857). Adult novels include *Oldbury* (1869), *Castle Daly* (1875) and *A Doubting Heart* (1879), unfinished at her death.

Keats, John 1795–1821 Poet. He was born at Moorfields, London, the oldest of four children. His father, who managed a livery stables, died in 1804 and, after an unhappy second marriage, his mother died at Edmonton in 1810. Keats went to school in Enfield, where the headmaster's son, CHARLES COWDEN CLARKE, became an important friend. He was apprenticed to a local surgeon-apothecary in 1814 and went to study at Guy's Hospital in 1815. Although he became a licentiate of the Society of Apothecaries in 1816 he soon effectively abandoned any thought of pursuing the profession.

During his last two years at school he had begun to read voraciously, particularly about Greek mythology, and started a translation of Virgil's *Aeneid*. His discovery of SPENSER's *FAERIE QUEENE* is reflected in his first poem, 'Lines in Imitation of Spenser' (1814). To the following year belong the ODES 'To Hope' and 'To Apollo', the 'Sonnet Written on the Day after Mr Leigh Hunt Left Prison', three SONNETS on Woman and, showing the influence of WORDSWORTH, the sonnet 'O Solitude'. In 1816 he wrote 'I Stood Tiptoe upon a Little Hill', 'Sleep and Poetry' and the sonnet 'On First Looking into Chapman's Homer'. With 'O Solitude', the last was printed in THE EXAMINER. Its editor, LEIGH HUNT, took Keats under his wing and helped to broaden his literary acquaintance. New friends included JOHN HAMILTON REYNOLDS, the painter HAYDON (to whom he addressed the sonnet 'Great Spirits Now on Earth are Sojourning') and SHELLEY, whom, however, he always treated with a certain reserve. In the 'Young Poets' issue of *The Examiner* (November 1816) Hunt hailed Keats, Shelley and Reynolds as the most promising writers of their generation, a public endorsement which made *BLACKWOOD'S EDINBURGH MAGAZINE* greet Keats's first collection, *Poems* (1817), by dismissing him as a member of the COCKNEY SCHOOL of poetry.

In the years 1817–18 he undertook tours to the Isle of Wight, Oxford and the Lake District, Scotland and Northern Ireland. He also enlarged his acquaintance to include CHARLES LAMB, as well as his neighbours in Hampstead, CHARLES WENTWORTH DILKE and Charles Armitage Brown. His letters to friends such as Reynolds, his brothers George and Tom and his sister Frances (Fanny) became the vehicle of his most considered thoughts on poetry, love, philosophy, his own personality and the people and events around him. They show him wrestling with large critical ideas such as his concept of the poet as an individual of NEGATIVE CAPABILITY. Vivid, witty and revealing, they have come to be almost as highly regarded as the poems themselves, which during this period include ENDYMION and ISABELLA: OR, THE POT OF BASIL. On its appearance in print in 1818 Endymion was savagely mauled by Blackwood's and THE QUARTERLY REVIEW. To this professional discouragement, which made Keats briefly consider giving up poetry, was added a list of private pains: the departure of his brother George for America, the death of his other brother Tom from tuberculosis, the onset of the disease in himself and his jealous, unhappy love for his Hampstead neighbour Fanny Brawne.

Keats's astonishing poetic development and productivity during the next year is comparable to Shelley's in Italy at roughly the same time. In the winter of 1818–19 he worked mainly on HYPERION. THE EVE OF ST AGNES and the fragmentary Eve of St Mark were composed during a visit to Sussex at the end of January. Returning to Hampstead in early February, he wrote the enigmatic BALLAD LA BELLE DAME SANS MERCI, the two sonnets on 'Fame', 'Why Did I Laugh Tonight?' and several of the reflective ODES which have done more than anything else to secure him his place among the English poets: 'On Indolence', 'On a Grecian Urn', 'To Psyche', 'To a Nightingale' and 'On Melancholy'. In the second half of 1819 he wrote the tragedy Otho the Great with Charles Brown, began another play on the subject of King Stephen, and finished LAMIA, which was followed by the beautiful 'Ode to Autumn' and the second version of Hyperion, called The Fall of Hyperion. Lamia, Isabella, The Eve of St Agnes and Other Poems (1820), which brought together most of the great odes, Hyperion, Fancy and other works, was generously praised by the reviewers. But Keats's illness was taking its toll. Though he began 'The Cap and Bells', he soon found himself too weak to write and never completed it. After being nursed by the Hunts and then by Fanny and Mrs Brawne, he put his affairs in order and sailed for Italy with the painter Joseph Severn in September 1820. He died in Rome the following February.

Keats's reputation continued to grow during the 19th century, when his admirers included TENNYSON, MATTHEW ARNOLD and the PRE-RAPHAELITE BROTHERHOOD. In the 20th century he is, together with Wordsworth, perhaps the most widely read and familiar of the English Romantics, and some of his odes ('To Autumn', for example, or 'On a Grecian Urn') are as well-known as anything by SHAKESPEARE, to whom he has, indeed, often been compared. Recent biographical studies have, in many respects, deepened the tragedy of his life by showing him to have been in many ways the precise opposite of the overburdened, sensitive soul of posthumous legends.

Keble, John 1792–1866 Poet and clergyman. A leading figure in the OXFORD MOVEMENT, he wrote nine of the TRACTS FOR THE TIMES. The Christian Year (1827), poems for Sundays and holy days, became perhaps the most popular religious verse of the age. Its success led to his appointment as professor of poetry at Oxford in 1831. Later volumes included Lyra apostolica (with NEWMAN and ISAAC WILLIAMS; 1836), an English Psalter (1839) and Lyra innocentium (1846). Keble also published an edition of RICHARD HOOKER (1836) and a translation of St Irenaeus in the Library of the Fathers (posthumously pub-

lished, 1872). He became vicar of Hursley, Hampshire, in 1836 and never sought preferment. Keble College, Oxford, was founded in his memory in 1870.

Keillor, Garrison 1942– American short-story writer, novelist and humorist. His radio programme, 'A Prairie Home Companion', introduced a long-running series of tales, gently comic and confidentially anecdotal, about the fictional Minnesota town of Lake Wobegon. These have been collected in Happy to be Here (1985), Lake Wobegon Days (1985), Leaving Home (1987) and, with other short fiction, essays and verse, We are Still Married (1989). WLT: A Radio Romance (1992) is a novel.

Kelly, George (Edward) 1887–1974 American playwright. His works include: The Torchbearers (1922), about a stagestruck woman; The Show-Off (1924), about a braggart; Craig's Wife (1925), about a grasping, self-centred woman; Daisy Mayme (1926) and Behold the Bridegroom (1927), about rich and wilful women; Maggie, the Magnificent (1929) and Philip Goes Forth (1931), about conflict between the generations; Reflected Glory (1936), about the conflict between the theatre and family responsibilities; and The Deep Mrs Sykes (1945) and The Fatal Weakness (1946), about suspicion and self-deception in marriage.

Kelly, Hugh 1739–77 Playwright. His journalism made him more enemies than friends by its time-serving support of the government against WILKES. Thespis (1766), written in emulation of CHARLES CHURCHILL'S The Rosciad, is a gossipy account of DRURY LANE's leading actors and actresses. He owed his brief reputation to the success of a SENTIMENTAL COMEDY, False Delicacy (1768), and a version of Molière's The School for Wives (1773). A Word to the Wise (1770) and The Man of Reason (1776) were unsuccessful.

Kelman, James 1946– Novelist and short-story writer. The short stories in Not Not While The Giro (1983) blend deadpan humour with the demotic of Scottish working-class life. Subsequent work, like the collection Greyhound for Breakfast (1987), has become more serious in tone. His novels include The Busconductor Hines (1984), A Disaffection (1989) and How Late It was, How Late (BOOKER PRIZE, 1994), an ex-convict's monologue.

Kemble, Fanny [Frances] **(Anne)** 1809–93 Actress, playwright, poet and autobiographer. The daughter of Charles Kemble and niece of Sarah Siddons and John Philip Kemble, she was more ambitious to write than to act. She left her American husband Pierce Butler in 1845 after disagreements over slavery. Back in England she made provincial tours and then supported herself by public readings from SHAKESPEARE. Her Poems appeared in 1844 and her Plays in 1863. In retirement she supplemented her Journal (also called Journal of a Residence in America; 1835) and Journal of a Residence on a Georgian Plantation in 1838–39 (1863) with several frank and discerning volumes of reminiscence, Record of a Girlhood (1878), Records of Later Life (1882) and Further Records (1890), and a novel, Far Away and Long Ago (1889).

Kemble, John Mitchell 1807–57 Philologist and historian. The son of the actor Charles Kemble and the elder brother of FANNY KEMBLE, he published The Anglo-Saxon Poems of Beowulf (1833–7) and a work on the early history of England, Codex diplomaticus aevi saxonici (1839–48). The Saxons in England (1849) argued that England's stability was owing to the principles and institutions inherited from Teutonic invaders.

Kempe, Margery Mystic and autobiographer active in the early 15th century. All that is known of her is recorded in her single work, *The Book of Margery Kempe*. She abandoned her brewing business in her native King's Lynn, persuaded her husband to allow her to live in chastity and undertook pilgrimages in England, Europe and the Holy Land. Her mystical experiences, divinely inspired advice and hysterical weeping did not make her universally popular; she was sometimes accused of being a charlatan and a hypocrite. Valuable as autobiography, her book is disappointing as MYSTICAL WRITING. It records a visit to JULIAN OF NORWICH in her travels.

Kempinski, Tom 1938– Playwright. Psychoanalysis and Freudian theory are prominent features of his work, which includes: *Duet for One* (1980), about a concert violinist stricken with multiple sclerosis and attempting to cope with her illness through therapy; *Self-Inflicted Wounds* (1985); *Separation* (1987); and *When the Past is Still to Come* (1992), an account of his own 'struggle against the fear which kills', including family memories of the Holocaust. *Sex Please, We're Italian* (1991) ventures unconvincingly into popular comedy.

Ken, Thomas 1637–1711 Poet and prelate. Partly brought up by WALTON, a relation by marriage, he was appointed chaplain to Charles II in 1680 and Bishop of Bath and Wells in 1684 but lived a life of retirement after his refusal to swear allegiance to William and Mary. Ken was renowned for his piety, charity and asceticism, and it was widely believed that DRYDEN modelled his 'Character of a Good Parson' (1700) on him. He wrote several devotional works, in both prose and verse, most notably his *Hymns on the Christian Festivals* (1721) and the famous 'Morning, Evening and Midnight Hymns' (1695).

Kendall, Henry (Clarence) 1839–82 Australian poet. The appearance of his poems in THE ATHENAEUM in 1862 marked the first recognition of an Australian poet by an English journal. Volumes include *Poems and Songs* (1862), *The Bronze Trumpet: A Satirical Poem* (1866), *Leaves from Australian Forests* (1869), *Songs from the Mountains* (1880), *Orara: A Tale* (1881) and *Poems* (1886). At its best his work is a vivid realization of Australia and the natural beauty which appealed to his lyric gifts.

Keneally, Thomas (Michael) 1935– Australian novelist. His best-known work, *Schindler's Ark* (1982), about a German Catholic factory owner rescuing Jews in World War II, was conceived and written as a documentary but read sufficiently like a novel to receive the BOOKER PRIZE. It was retitled *Schindler's List* after the success of Steven Spielberg's film version. The book typifies Keneally's interest in journalistic research, strong storytelling and settings, contemporary or historical, of war, violence and their aftermath. This informs *Blood Red, Sister Rose* (1974), *Gossip from the Forest* (1975), *Season in Purgatory* (1976), *Confederates* (1979), *Cut-Rate Kingdom* (1980), *A Family Madness* (1986), *Towards Asmara* (1989) and *Flying Hero Class* (1991). His prolific output also includes three early Catholic novels, *The Place at Whitton* (1964), *The Fear* (1965) and *Three Cheers for the Paraclete* (1968), and several novels with typically Australian subjects: convicts in *Bring Larks and Heroes* (1967), bush life in *A Dutiful Daughter* (1971) and Aborigines in *The Chant of Jimmie Blacksmith* (1972). He has also written plays and travel books.

Kenilworth A novel by SIR WALTER SCOTT, published in 1821. The story interprets events leading to the mysterious death of Amy Robsart in 1560. Secretly married to Elizabeth I's favourite, the Earl of Leicester, she is kept at Cumnor Place, near Oxford, by the villainous Richard Varney, whom her rejected suitor Edmund Tressilian believes to be her lover. Tressilian's attempts to free her finally result in her meeting the Queen at Kenilworth. Elizabeth extracts a confession of the truth from Leicester, who, suspecting Tressilian's relation with his wife, orders Varney to murder her. Tressilian arrives too late at Cumnor Place to prevent her death.

Kennedy, Adrienne (Lita) 1931– Black American playwright. Her work blends symbols, historical figures, racial images and myths to surreal, highly personal effect. *Funnyhouse of a Negro* (1964) and *The Owl Answers* (1969) both portray mulatto women unable to cope with their mixed racial heritage. Other plays include *A Rat's Mass* (1966), a fantasy of war and prejudice; *The Lennon Play: In His Own Write* (1967); and *A Lancashire Lad* (1980), a children's play based on the early life of Charlie Chaplin.

Kennedy, John Pendleton 1795–1870 American novelist and essayist. His first and best-known novel, *Horse-Shoe Robinson* (1835), is set during the Revolutionary War. It was followed by *Rob of the Bowl* (1838). Kennedy had earlier produced two collections of sketches, *The Red Book* (1818–19) and, under the pseudonym of Mark Littleton, *Swallow Barn* (1832). A friend of WASHINGTON IRVING and OLIVER WENDELL HOLMES, and the American host to THACKERAY, he was also one of the first to recognize POE.

Kennedy, Margaret (Moore) 1896–1967 Novelist. Her second novel, *The Constant Nymph* (1924), made her famous, and a poised style, cool wit and skilful characterization kept her novels welcome for three decades: *Red Sky at Morning* (1927), *The Fool of the Family* (1930), *Return I Dare Not* (1931), *A Long Time Ago* (1932), *Together and Apart* (1936), *The Midas Touch* (1938), *The Feast* (1950), *Lucy Carmichael* (1951), *Troy Chimneys* (James Tait Black Memorial Prize; 1953), *The Oracle* (1955), *The Heroes of Clone* (1957), *A Night in Cold Harbour* (1960), *The Forgotten Smile* (1961) and *Not in the Calendar* (1964). She also wrote several plays, a book on JANE AUSTEN (1950) and *The Outlaws on Parnassus* (1958), a study of the art of fiction.

Kenyon Review, The A literary magazine founded by JOHN CROWE RANSOM in 1939. It soon became a leading organ for the NEW CRITICISM, publishing work by ALLEN TATE, CLEANTH BROOKS, R. P. Blackmur, WILLIAM EMPSON and many others. In the 1950s its emphasis shifted from criticism to poetry and fiction.

Ker, W(illiam) P(aton) 1855–1923 Critic and scholar. His high reputation as an authority on medieval literature was established by *Epic and Romance* (1897), *The Dark Ages* (1904) and *Essays on Medieval Literature* (1905). Ker was professor of English language and literature at University College, London, and later director of the University's School of Scandinavian Studies as well as professor of poetry at Oxford.

Kerouac, Jack 1922–69 American novelist. *The Town and the City* (1950) was the first of his semi-autobiographical novels. ON THE ROAD (1957), his best-known book, describes the often aimless search for significant experience of the BEATS. *The Subterraneans* and *The Dharma Bums* (both 1958), *Tristessa* (1960), *Big Sur* (1962) and *Desolation Angels* (1965) are all products of the Beat consciousness; *Doctor Sax* and *Maggie Cassidy* (both 1959) and *Visions of Gerard* (1963) are evocations of Kerouac's boyhood. *Satori in Paris* (1966) is an account of his quest for his Breton ancestors. Other books include *Lonesome*

Traveller (1960; travel sketches), *Mexico City Blues* (1959; verse) and *Book of Dreams* (1961). *Visions of Cody*, written in 1951–2, was published posthumously in 1972.

Kesey, Ken 1935– American novelist. He is still best known for his first novel, ONE FLEW OVER THE CUCKOO'S NEST (1962). *Sometimes a Great Notion* (1964) focuses on a logging family in the Northwest and *Sailor Song* (1993) is set in Alaska in the near future. *Kesey's Garage Sale* (1973) and *Demon Box* (1986) are collections of essays, letters, interviews, stories and drawings. TOM WOLFE's *The Electric Kool-Aid Acid Test* (1968) records his wild lifestyle in the 1960s.

Keyes, Sidney (Arthur Kilworth) 1922–43 Poet. While an undergraduate he introduced *Eight Oxford Poets* (1942), containing work by himself, JOHN HEATH-STUBBS and KEITH DOUGLAS. *The Iron Laurel* (1942) included 'The Buzzard', 'William Wordsworth' and 'The Foreign Gate'. *The Cruel Solstice* (1943), published after his death in battle in Tunisia, included 'War Poet' and 'To Keep off Fears'. Michael Meyer edited *Collected Poems* (1945); *Minos of Crete: Plays and Stories* appeared in 1948. His most enduring poems ('The Migrant', 'The Kestrels') are those in which landscapes, seascapes and birds appear in their least symbolically forced settings.

Keynes, J(ohn) M(aynard), 1st Baron Keynes of Tilton 1883–1946 Economist. *A General Theory of Employment, Interest, and Money* (1936), his most important work, revolutionized the approach to unemployment by arguing for greater government spending on public works. It was a major influence on the creation of the Welfare State. A member of the BLOOMSBURY GROUP, Keynes founded and endowed the Arts Theatre in Cambridge and became first chairman of the Arts Council of Great Britain in 1945. Among his more general contributions to literature were *Essays in Persuasion* (1931), *Essays in Biography* (1933) and *Two Memoirs* (posthumously published 1949), which revealed a lively prose style combined with novelistic powers of character drawing.

Kickham, Charles J(oseph) 1828–82 Irish novelist. A Fenian and one of the editors of *The Irish People*, he served four years in English prisons, during which he wrote *Sally Cavanagh* (1869). His real fame as a novelist depends on *Knocknagow: or, The Homes of Tipperary* (1879), a tale of depopulation, land-laws and landlord greed which became one of the most popular novels in Irish literary history.

Kidnapped* and *Catriona A novel and its sequel by ROBERT LOUIS STEVENSON, published respectively in 1886 and 1893. After his father's death David Balfour turns for help to his miserly uncle, Ebenezer, who has him kidnapped and put aboard a ship for the Carolinas. His subsequent adventures, with the Jacobite rebel Alan Breck, include shipwreck, accidental involvement in Colin Campbell's murder, and flight across the Highlands. Eventually Ebenezer is exposed and David's estate restored. In the sequel David is in love with Catriona, daughter of the renegade James More. He tries to help James Stewart of the Glens, falsely accused of Colin Campbell's murder, but finds himself in danger. He survives the plot, and Alan Breck finally escapes to safety in France.

Killigrew, Thomas 1612–83 Playwright and theatre manager. He went into exile with the future Charles II, a lifelong friend who, at the Restoration, granted him Letters Patent to form a company of players (see PATENT THEATRES). Killigrew established the reconstituted

KING's MEN at DRURY LANE in 1662. His coarse and uninhibited comedy, *The Parson's Wedding*, based on the Spanish of Calderón, had originally been staged before the closing of the theatres in 1642. Published and revived in 1664, it contributed to the emergence of RESTORATION COMEDY. His brother William, and his son Thomas, both wrote plays; another son, Charles, took over the management of the Theatre Royal in 1671.

Kilvert, (Robert) Francis 1840–79 Clergyman and diarist. He served as curate at Langley Burrell, Clyro, in 1865–72 and vicar of Bredwardine, Herefordshire, from 1877 until his sudden death. Three volumes of his *Diary*, covering the period 1870–9, were discovered by WILLIAM PLOMER, published in 1938–40 and abridged in 1944. It is a sensitive document of life in the Welsh border country, depicting in vivid detail the landscape in which he delighted as well as the pains and pleasures of rural parish society. Kilvert's style reflects his gentle and attractively unworldly personality.

Kim A novel by KIPLING, published in 1901. It exploits many of his childhood memories of India. Kim (Kimball O'Hara), the orphan son of an Irish colour-sergeant and a nursemaid in a colonel's family, learns self-reliance and resourcefulness early in life on the streets of Lahore. He encounters Mahbub Ali, who works for the British Secret Service, and a Tibetan lama, on a quest to be freed from the Wheel of Life, staying in touch with them even after he is recognized by the chaplain of his father's old regiment and sent to the school for Anglo-Indian children at Lucknow. He plays an active role in the great game of imperial espionage against the Russians but is united with the lama at the end of the latter's quest for the sacred River of the Arrow.

King, Francis (Henry) 1923– Novelist and short-story writer. His many novels, combining fluent narrative with an interest in decadent, sometimes horrific, behaviour, include *To the Dark Tower* (1946), *The Dividing Stream* (1951), *The Widow* (1957), *The Custom House* (1961), *Flights* (1973), *The Action* (1979), *Acts of Darkness* (1983), *Voices in an Empty Room* (1984) and *The Ant Colony* (1991). Short stories include *The Brighton Belle and Other Stories* (1968) and *Hard Feelings and Other Stories* (1976). He has also published a biography of FORSTER (1978) and edited LAFCADIO HEARN's *Writings from Japan* and the diaries of J. R. ACKERLEY.

King, Henry 1592–1669 Poet. He was an impressive preacher and resolute opponent of Puritanism, ejected from the see of Chichester by the Parliamentarians in 1643 but restored to it in 1660. His occasional verses include ELEGIES on DONNE (whose executor he was), JONSON, RALEIGH and, most memorably, his first wife in *The Exequy*. His work first appeared in book form in 1657.

King, William 1663–1712 Poet and polemicist. A High Church Tory, he contributed to the 'Battle of the Books' with *Dialogues of the Dead* (1699), an attack on RICHARD BENTLEY written with Charles Boyle, but is best remembered for his urbane and witty poem *The Art of Cookery, in Imitation of Horace's Art of Poetry* (1708), and for the BURLESQUES and light verse collected in *Miscellanies in Prose and Verse* (1709) and *Useful Miscellanies* (1712).

King Alisaunder An anonymous early 14th-century VERSE ROMANCE, telling the mythical history of Alexander the Great from the magical circumstances surrounding his conception to his death. The first part deals with Alexander's life up to his defeat of Darius; the second describes his travels and conquests in the East, with many pseudo-geographical descriptions.

King and No King, A A tragicomedy by BEAUMONT and FLETCHER, performed in 1611 and published in 1619. Arbaces, King of Iberia, defeats Tigranes of Armenia and offers him liberty if he will marry his sister Panthea, who has grown up during Arbaces' absence at war. Tigranes declines because he loves Spaconia, whom he sends to Panthea to enlist her help in opposing the match. When Panthea appears, her beauty disturbs both Tigranes and Arbaces, who discovers that his incestuous passion is returned. Gobrias, the Lord Protector, resolves matters by disclosing that he is Arbaces' real father. Arbaces is free to marry Panthea, and Tigranes to marry Spaconia.

King Horn A VERSE ROMANCE written c. 1225. Despite its Anglo-Norman source, the vigorous and straightforward narrative has its origins in Old English storytelling. Horn, the King of England's son, is set adrift by the pirates who killed his father and brought up at the court of King Aylmer of Westnesse, where he falls in love with the king's daughter Rymenhild. Slandered and exiled, he succeeds in avenging his father's death and returns to prevent Rymenhild being married to King Mody. He kills Mody, avenges his betrayal at Aylmer's court, marries Rymenhild and regains his kingdom. Two related poems, *Horn Child* and the *Ballad of Hind Horn*, are less successful.

King James Version, The See BIBLE IN ENGLISH.

King John, The Life and Death of An early history play by SHAKESPEARE, published in the First Folio of 1623 and apparently based on the anonymous *The Troublesome Reign of John, King of England* (1591). John is determined to keep his throne despite the better claims of his nephew, Arthur, who has the support of the King of France. Harassed also by Arthur's mother Constance and by Cardinal Pandulph, the papal legate, John bribes Hubert de Burgh to blind Arthur but, in a memorable scene, the boy's pleas move Hubert to spare him. Arthur later jumps to his death while trying to escape. The French invade and the defeated king takes refuge in Swinstead Abbey, where he dies of poison. The play's chief splendour is the loyal but outspoken Bastard, Faulconbridge, under whose guidance the new king, Henry III, must try to restore England after the ravages of John's reign.

King Lear A tragedy by SHAKESPEARE, first performed c. 1605. The text of the First Folio edition (1623) differs considerably from that of the 1608 Quarto. For this most titanic of his tragedies, Shakespeare used various sources, including HOLINSHED's *Chronicles* and SIDNEY's *ARCADIA*. The aged king decides to share his kingdom between his daughters but his youngest (and favourite) daughter, Cordelia, refuses to join her elder sisters, Regan and Goneril, in exaggerated public declarations of love for him. In anger he gives the kingdom to Goneril and Regan, banishes the Duke of Kent for defending Cordelia and leaves Cordelia to marry the King of France. Annoyed by Goneril's grudging hospitality, Lear leaves for Regan, only to find her imposing even stricter limits on his entertainment. Incredulous, he denounces their cruelty and is driven out on the heath during a storm. With him go his Fool and the loyal Kent, serving him in disguise. They meet 'poor Tom', apparently a mad beggar but really Edgar, son of the Duke of Gloucester, who has fallen from his father's favour through the lies of his illegitimate brother Edmund. Lear goes mad, and, in his madness, encounters his own unprotected humanity. When Goneril, Regan, Edmund

and Regan's husband the Duke of Cornwall hear that a French army has landed, and that Lear is being taken to Dover to be reunited with Cordelia, they blind Gloucester, who has helped him escape. Edgar, still posing as poor Tom, tends his father until death. Lear finds Cordelia at Dover and is restored to sanity; but the French lose the battle and Cordelia and Lear are captured. Edmund, powerful because he is the lover of both Regan and Goneril, orders that they be put to death. He is defeated in single combat by Edgar but his dying confession comes too late to save Cordelia. Lear dies cradling her body and insisting she is still alive.

King Solomon's Mines A novel by HAGGARD, published in 1885. Sir Henry Curtis, Captain John Good RN and the narrator, Allan Quatermain, set off with their native servant, Umbopa, to find Curtis's brother George, who has gone to look for the treasure of King Solomon's mines in the lost land of the Kukuanas. After journeying over waterless desert and freezing mountains, they encounter the villainous King Twala and the witch-doctor Gagool. Umbopa turns out to be the rightful king and wins the civil war which breaks out. Twala dies in single combat with Curtis. Gagool pretends to guide the heroes to Solomon's mines but leaves them to die in an underground vault. They escape and return to civilization, finding George Curtis on the way.

King's Men, The The finest of Elizabethan theatre companies, formed as the Lord Chamberlain's Men in 1594 but taken into his personal patronage by JAMES I in 1603. In 1599 the shareholders, who included BURBAGE and SHAKESPEARE, moved the company from the Theatre in Shoreditch to the GLOBE in Southwark, where the repertoire included work by JONSON, WEBSTER, TOURNEUR, THOMAS MIDDLETON, MARSTON, BEAUMONT and FLETCHER as well as Shakespeare. After his retirement, Fletcher and then MASSINGER became the 'attached' playwrights of the King's Men. In 1608 the company added the indoor Blackfriars Theatre to the outdoor Globe, continuing to perform at both until the closure of the theatres in 1642. A different and less remarkable company assembled at DRURY LANE in 1662 under the nominal leadership of KILLIGREW and the patronage of Charles II.

King's Tragedy, The A poem by DANTE GABRIEL ROSSETTI, published in *Ballads and Sonnets* (1881). Catherine Douglas (Kate Barlass) tells the story of the murder of James I of Scotland and her vain attempt to save him.

Kingis Quair, The ('The King's Book') A poem attributed to JAMES I OF SCOTLAND (1394–1437). The central part is a DREAM-VISION in which the imprisoned king learns about love and fortune. On waking, he receives a message carried by a dove foretelling his fortune in love and eventually weds. The verse is strongly influenced by CHAUCER and its philosophical content derived from Boethius. RHYME-ROYAL stanzas are probably so called because of their use in this poem.

Kinglake, Alexander William 1809–91 Historian and travel-writer. A successful barrister, he is best remembered for *Eothen: or, Traces of Travel Brought Home from the Near East* (1844), a brilliant and evocative account of his adventures. He followed the British army to the Crimea and wrote a meticulous history, *The Invasion of the Crimea* (1863–87).

Kingsley, Charles 1819–75 Clergyman, novelist and writer of CHILDREN'S LITERATURE. The influence of THOMAS CARLYLE and F. D. MAURICE, leader of the movement for CHRISTIAN SOCIALISM, is clearly apparent in his contributions to *Politics for the People* (1848) and *The Christian Socialist* (1850–1) under the pseudonym of Parson Lot, and in his novels, *YEAST* (serial, 1848; volume, 1850) and *ALTON LOCKE* (1850), which expose the injustices suffered by agricultural labourers and workers in the clothing trade. *HYPATIA* (1843), a novel about early Christianity, is regarded by many as his finest work. *WESTWARD HO!* (1855) turned to the Elizabethan era and the landscape of his Devon childhood. *Two Years Ago* (1857) has a contemporary setting. Other works include: *Glaucus: or, The Wonders of the Shore* (1855), a volume of natural history; *The Heroes* (1856), retelling the legends of Perseus, Theseus and Jason, and *THE WATER BABIES* (1863), a fantasy, both for children; *The Roman and the Teuton* (1864), lectures at Cambridge; *Hereward the Wake* (1866), a novel about the 'Last of the English' and his defeat by William the Conqueror at Ely; *At Last* (1871), an account of his journey to the West Indies; and *Prose Idylls* (1873), a volume of essays. Kingsley was notable for applying Christian ethics to contemporary social problems while stopping well short of radicalism. 'Muscular Christianity', his brand of hearty Protestantism, often led him into quarrels, like the one in 1864 which prompted NEWMAN to write *APOLOGIA PRO VITA SUA*.

Kingsley, Henry 1830–76 Novelist and younger brother of CHARLES KINGSLEY. He spent five years in Australia, the setting for the novel he published on his return, *Geoffrey Hamlyn* (1859). Subsequent works include *Ravenshoe* (1862), a romance about the mystery of the hero's birth which includes episodes set in the Crimean War; *Austin Elliott* (1863); and *The Hillyars and the Burtons* (1865), another Australian novel.

Kingsley, Mary 1852–1931 See MALET, LUCAS.

Kingsley, Mary (Henrietta) 1862–1900 Travel-writer and niece of CHARLES KINGSLEY. *Travels in West Africa* (1897) gives an original, informative account of an expedition made in 1893 to study primitive religion.

Kingsley, Sidney 1906–95 American playwright. He made his name with *Men in White* (produced by the GROUP THEATRE; 1933; PULITZER PRIZE), about a young doctor's experiences in a hospital, and *Dead End* (1935), about young people in the slums. Subsequent work includes: *The Patriots* (1943), about the conflict between JEFFERSON and Alexander Hamilton; *Detective Story* (1949), about police brutality; and an adaptation (1951) of KOESTLER's *Darkness at Noon* .

Kingsmill, Hugh 1889–1949 Man of letters. The second son of Sir Henry Lunn, the travel agent, he lived precariously by his literary earnings. Biographies of MATTHEW ARNOLD (1928), FRANK HARRIS (1932), SAMUEL JOHNSON (1933), DICKENS (1934) and D. H. LAWRENCE (1938), and *The Return of William Shakespeare* (1929), earned him a reputation for irreverence. Among Kingsmill's anthologies are *Invective and Abuse* (1929), *Made on Earth* (on marriage; 1937) and *The High Hill of the Muses* (studies of Johnson 'without Boswell'; 1955). He collaborated with WILLIAM GERHARDIE on *The Casanova Fable* (1934), with Malcolm Muggeridge on two books of PARODIES, *Brave Old World* (1936) and *Next Year's News* (1938), and with Hesketh Pearson on a series of 'conversational travel books'. *The Progress of a Biographer* (1949), a collection of essays, contains much of his best work.

Kinnell, Galway 1927– American poet. *What a Kingdom It Was* (1960), *Flower Herding on Mount Monadnock* (1964) and *Body Rags* (1968) established him as a contemporary master of free verse. *The Book of Nightmares* (1971) confirmed the sacramental dimension apparent in all his work. Other collections are *First Poems, 1946–54* (1970), *The Shoes of Wandering* (1971), *The Avenue Bearing the Initial of Christ into the New World: 1946–1964* (1974), *Mortal Acts, Mortal Words* (1980), *Selected Poems* (1982, PULITZER PRIZE) and *When One Has Lived a Long Time* (1990). He has also published: a novel, *Black Light* (1966); a collection of interviews, *Walking Down the Stairs* (1978); and translations of French writers.

Kinsella, Thomas 1928– Irish poet and translator. One of the most prolific and respected of contemporary Irish poets, his published volumes range from *Poems* (1956) to *Songs of the Psyche* (1985) and *One Fond Embrace* (1988). The characteristic themes of his calmly objective and predominantly personal early poetry have given way to a sense of personal and cultural disarray, signalled by *Nightwalker* (1968) and the ambitious experiments of later work. Translations from the Irish include *An Duanaire: Poems of the Dispossessed* (with Seán O'Tuama; 1981), a version of the ancient *Cattle Raid of Cooley* (*The Táin*, 1985) and items in his edition of *The Oxford Book of Irish Verse* (1986).

Kipling, Rudyard 1865–1936 Poet, short-story writer and novelist. Son of the artist John Lockwood Kipling, he was born in Bombay and sent back to England with his sister in 1871. His unhappiness at Southsea was relieved by visits to his maternal uncle, Edward Burne-Jones, who, with WILLIAM MORRIS, inspired his move in 1878 to the United Services College at Westward Ho! in Devon. Kipling's relatively happy years there underlie his popular *STALKY & CO.* (1899). He returned to India in 1882 to work as a journalist in Lahore. His familiarity with all ranks of the Anglo-Indian community gave freshness to the poems and tales published in newspapers or as booklets by the Indian Railway Library, gathered in *Departmental Ditties* (1886), *Plain Tales from the Hills* (1888), *The Phantom Rickshaw* (1888), *Wee Willie Winkie* (1888) and *SOLDIERS THREE* (1892).

After his return to England in 1889 he rapidly established himself in literary London, winning the friendship of HENRY JAMES, HAGGARD and HENLEY. *BARRACK-ROOM BALLADS AND OTHER VERSES* (1892), with two collections of short stories, *LIFE'S HANDICAP* (1891) and *MANY INVENTIONS* (1893), set the pattern for his major writings. Two novels, *The Light That Failed* (1891) and *The Naulahka* (with Wolcott Balestier; 1892), were relative failures. After marrying Balestier's sister, Caroline, he spent the years 1892–6 near her family in Vermont, USA, where the stories of *THE JUNGLE BOOK* (1894) and *The Second Jungle Book* (1895) were written. By the time his best-known novel, *KIM*, appeared in 1901 the family was back in England. Kipling settled in Sussex in 1902. The *JUST SO STORIES* (1902), *PUCK OF POOK'S HILL* (1906) and *Rewards and Fairies* (1910) show an unusual sympathy with children, though he continued to publish stories for adults in *TRAFFICS AND DISCOVERIES* (1904), *Actions and Reactions* (1909), *A Diversity of Creatures* (1917), *Debits and Credits* (1926) and *Limits and Renewals* (1932). The posthumous *Something of Myself* (1937) is autobiographical.

Kipling's high reputation, as 'Poet of Empire' and the first English writer to receive the Nobel Prize for literature (1907), had begun to wane before his death. Later generations have rediscovered the craft of his poetry and the stern realism of his fiction.

Kipps: *The Story of a Simple Soul* A novel by H. G. WELLS, published in 1905. Arthur Kipps's feelings for Ann Pornick, a childhood sweetheart, prove a saving grace in the years of deadening apprenticeship to Mr Shalford, a Folkestone draper. A legacy from his grandfather begins a bitterly comic process of social initiation, with Helen Walshingham, his wood-carving teacher, playing a leading part in his loss of self-esteem. He marries Ann but soon learns that his money has been embezzled by Helen's brother. The unexpected success of his friend Chitterlow's play, in which Kipps had invested, restores the fortunes of Kipps, Ann and their child.

Kit-Cat Club A coterie of 18th-century Whig writers, including ADDISON, CONGREVE, STEELE, VANBRUGH and the physician GARTH. It originally met at the London house of a pastry-cook, Christopher Katt (or Catling), whose mutton pies were called kit-cats, but later moved to the home of TONSON, its secretary.

Kizer, Carolyn (Ashley) 1925– American poet. Her work is notable for its exploration of feminist issues, begun in *Poems* (1959) and continued in collections such as *The Ungrateful Garden* (1961), *Knock upon Silence* (1965), *Midnight was My City: New and Selected Poems* (1971), *Mermaids in the Basement: Poems for Women* (1984), *Yin: New Poems* (1984, PULITZER PRIZE) and *Carrying Over* (1992). *Proses: Selected Essays, Reviews, and Conversations* appeared in 1992.

Klein, A(braham) M(oses) 1909–72 Canadian poet. One of the so-called Montreal group, he is highly regarded for *Hath Not a Jew* (1940) and *The Rocking Chair* (1948). *The Second Scroll* (1951) is a short novel accompanied by poems and brief scenes of verse drama.

Knickerbocker Group An early 19th-century school of American writers, mainly living in New York. Deriving its name from WASHINGTON IRVING's pseudonym, Diedrich Knickerbocker, it tended towards sophistication in style and conservatism in politics. Members included Irving, WILLIAM CULLEN BRYANT, JAMES KIRKE PAULDING, FITZ-GREENE HALLECK and Joseph Rodman Drake. Much of their work appeared in *THE KNICKERBOCKER MAGAZINE*.

Knickerbocker Magazine, The A monthly magazine founded in New York by Lewis G. and Willis G. Clark in 1833. It survived until 1865. Although dominated by the KNICKERBOCKER GROUP, it published most living American writers of distinction, IRVING, LONGFELLOW, HAWTHORNE, WHITTIER, WILLIAM DEAN HOWELLS, HOLMES and WILLIAM CULLEN BRYANT among them.

Knight, Ellis Cornelia 1757–1837 Miscellaneous writer. Her youthful association with SAMUEL JOHNSON and his circle prompted *Dinarbas* (1790), a romantic continuation of *RASSELAS*. Her *Autobiography*, posthumously edited from her diaries and published in 1861, is discreet about her connection with Nelson's mistress Lady Hamilton but notable for its account of her experience of court life as companion to Queen Charlotte and Princess Charlotte.

Knight, G(eorge) (Richard) Wilson 1897–1985 Critic. Although he also wrote studies of Ibsen, BYRON and JOHN COWPER POWYS, his life's work was devoted to SHAKESPEARE, about whom he wrote 13 books. The most important, *The Wheel of Fire* (1930), pioneered a major new movement in interpretation by reading the plays as expanded poetic metaphors. This approach was taken up by L. C. KNIGHTS and others, and applied to prose fiction by F. R. LEAVIS and Q. D. LEAVIS. Knight's other principal works on Shakespeare are *The Imperial Theme* (1931), *The Shakespearean Tempest* (1932), *The Crown*

of Life (1947) and *The Mutual Flame* (1955). He also wrote *Principles of Shakespearean Production* (1936).

Knight, Richard Payne See PICTURESQUE.

Knight of the Burning Pestle, The A comedy, first performed in 1607, formerly attributed to BEAUMONT and FLETCHER but now believed to be by Beaumont alone. It gives a precious glimpse of stage practices in the PRIVATE THEATRES and a wittily critical view of the merchant class. A grocer and his wife interrupt a performance of 'The London Merchant' to demand that their apprentice, Ralph, take part. The action continues but interspersed with scenes written by the grocer himself to satisfy Ralph's histrionic pretensions and renamed 'The Knight of the Burning Pestle'. They are a BURLESQUE of the romantic knight errantry in plays such as HEYWOOD's *The Four Prentices of London*. Ralph becomes a 'grocer errant', with a burning pestle as his device, and has wild adventures that include the defeat of Barbaroso, a villainous barber.

Knight's Tale, The See CANTERBURY TALES.

Knights, L(ionel) C(harles) 1906– Critic. He ended his career as Edward VII Professor of English Literature at Cambridge (1965–73), where he had originally founded and co-edited *SCRUTINY* in 1932. His best-known work is the essay 'How Many Children Had Lady Macbeth?' (1933), a milestone in SHAKESPEARE criticism attacking the literal-mindedness of A. C. BRADLEY and clearing the ground for *Some Shakespearian Themes* (1959) and *An Approach to Hamlet* (1961). *Drama and Society in the Age of Jonson* (1937) shows a strong sociological interest. His essays were published as *Explorations* (1946), *Further Explorations* (1965) and *Explorations 3* (1976).

Knolles, Richard ?1550–1610 Historian. His *General History of the Turks* (1603) was one of the earliest English examinations of the Ottoman Empire. It gave D'AVENANT the basis for his spectacular entertainment, *The Siege of Rhodes*, and influenced BYRON.

Knowles, James Sheridan 1784–1862 Playwright. His sanctimonious *Lectures on Dramatic Literature* (1873) are pulpit pieces written with the brief authority of a playwright whose tragedies were in their day considered to rival SHAKESPEARE's, but are too mawkish to survive 20th-century appraisal. They include *Virginius* (1820), *William Tell* (1825) and *John of Procida* (1840). More successful are his romances modelled on JOHN FLETCHER, which include *The Beggar's Daughter of Bethnal Green* (1828; revised as *The Beggar of Bethnal Green*, 1834), and *The Hunchback* (1832), and best of all are his comedies, *The Love-Chase* (1837) and *Old Maids* (1841).

Knox, John ?1514–72 Scottish Protestant reformer. He trained for the priesthood but converted to Protestantism and was preaching the reformed religion by 1547. On Mary I's accession he fled to Frankfurt am Main and then Geneva, publishing *A Faithful Admonition* (1554) to the English Protestants and *The First Blast of the Trumpet against the Monstrous Regiment of Women* (1558), arguing that women in authority are contrary to religion and natural law. Knox's belief that magistracy and nobility may resist a ruler endangering true religion did not endear him to Elizabeth I, who banned him from England. Recalled to Scotland by the Protestant party in 1559, he was instrumental in organizing and establishing a liturgy for the Scottish Reformed Church, with its moderately Calvinist faith, elected ministry and prohibition of the mass. His *First Book of Discipline* (1559) advocated a national system of education. Knox's stormy audiences with Mary Queen of

Scots are described in his major work, *The History of the Reformation of Religion within the Realm of Scotland* (1587).

Koch, Christopher 1932– Australian novelist. He first came to the fore, with PATRICK WHITE and RANDOLPH STOW, in challenging the NATURALISM which dominated Australian fiction until the 1950s. Never a prolific writer, he is a meticulous stylist whose prose aims towards poetry in its symbolic density. His themes are an encounter with a romantic 'otherland' and an exploration of the dualities he finds at the heart of the human condition. *The Boys in the Island* (1958) and *The Doubleman* (1985) are notable for graphic evocations of his native Tasmania. *Across the Sea Wall* (1965) was inspired by his experience of India, and *The Year of Living Dangerously* (1978), generally regarded as his best work, is set in Sukarno's Indonesia. Both explore the alternative spiritual possibilities which Eastern religions and cultures offer the Australian psyche. Koch has also written *Chinese Journey* (with Nicholas Hasluck; 1985) and a collection of essays, *Crossing the Gap* (1987).

Koch, Kenneth 1925– American poet. With FRANK O'HARA and JOHN ASHBERY, he emerged in the 1950s as a leading member of the NEW YORK SCHOOL. Influenced by the French surrealist Jacques Prévert, his work demonstrates the School's preoccupation with urban settings and metaphors. It includes *Ko: or a Season on Earth* (1959), a comic EPIC in verse which simultaneously approximates to being a novel. Other work can be sampled in *Selected Poems, 1952–1982* (1985). *Rose, Where Did You Get That Red? Teaching Great Poetry to Children* (1973) and *I Never Told Anybody: Teaching Poetry in a Nursing Home* (1977) reflect his interest in teaching the writing of poetry to children and the elderly. He has also written several off-Broadway plays, collected in *Bertha and Other Plays* (1969) and *One Thousand Avant-Garde Plays* (1988).

Koestler, Arthur 1905–83 Novelist and thinker. It is entirely fitting that his most widely read book should be *Darkness at Noon* (1940), a novel condemning Stalin's totalitarianism, written in German and translated into English by another hand. His early life was essentially a paradigm of the turmoil Europe suffered in the years before World War II, and his writings were essentially a commentary, always engaged but increasingly oblique and reflective, on the nature and roots of that turmoil. Born in Budapest and educated in Vienna, he lived in Palestine, worked as a journalist in Berlin, joined the Communist Party, visited the Soviet Union, reported the Spanish Civil War, and suffered imprisonment in Spain, Paris and again after his escape to Britain. His first book in English, *The Scum of the Earth* (1941), recounts these experiences; *Arrow in the Blue* (1952) and *The Invisible Writing* (1954) continue the autobiographical process. Other works, diverse yet plotting a relentless course, include: *The Yogi and the Commissar* (1945), essays about contemporary politics; *Thieves in the Night* (1946), a novel, and *Promise and Fulfilment* (1949), a work of history, both about the Jewish state; and *The Age of Longing* (1951), a novel about the threat of nuclear extermination. *The Sleepwalkers* (1959), *The Act of Creation* (1964) and *The Ghost in the Machine* (1967) are about the nature of mind. *The Roots of Coincidence* (1972) and *The Challenge of Chance* (with Sir Alister Hardy and Robert Harvie; 1973) investigate ESP. He left a bequest in his will to promote academic study of psychic phenomena.

Kogawa, Joy 1935– Japanese-Canadian poet and novelist. She has published several collections of poetry – *The Splintered Moon* (1967), *A Choice of Dreams* (1974) and *Jericho Road* (1977) – though she is known best for *Obasan* (1981), a novel which combines documentary realism and lyrical protest against the silences of official history about the Japanese-Canadian experience.

Kolatkar, Arun 1932– Indian poet. His reputation as a poet in English is based mainly on *Jejuri* (1976), pithy and sharply observed poems conveying a true sense of Indian regional life. Kolatkar also writes in Marathi and translates between his two languages of expression.

Kopit, Arthur L(ee) 1937– American playwright. His best-known work, *Oh Dad, Poor Dad, Mama's Hung You in the Closet and I'm Feelin' So Sad* (1960), is a PARODY of the THEATRE OF THE ABSURD in its style and of the Oedipal complex in its subject. Other plays have included: *The Day the Whores Came Out to Play Tennis* (1965), about social-climbing country-clubbers; *Indians* (1968), about the genocide of the Indians; *Wings* (1978), about a stroke victim; and *The Road to Nirvana* (1990), about Hollywood.

Kroetsch, Robert 1927– Canadian novelist, poet and critic. Virtually all his fiction is located in his native Alberta and concerned with the specifics of Western Canadian place and identity. Drawing heavily on classical and native Canadian myths, it frequently involves quests. Perhaps the most notable examples are *The Studhorse Man* (1969), *Gone Indian* (1973), *Badlands* (1975) and *Alibi* (1983). Other novels are *But We are Exiles* (1965), *The Words of My Roaring* (1966) and *What the Crow Said* (1978). His many volumes of verse have been gathered into a poetic autobiography, *Field Notes* (1981, 1985, 1989). A leading critic, influenced by POST-MODERNISM, he has published *The Lovely Treachery of Words* (1989). Other works include: *Alberta* (1988), a travel book; *The Crow Journals* (1980), a literary diary; *Labyrinths of Voice* (1982), interviews; and *Excerpts from the Real World* (1986), a prose poem.

Kubla Khan: or, A Vision in a Dream A 54-line fragment of an unfinished poem by SAMUEL TAYLOR COLERIDGE, published in *Christabel and Other Poems* (1816). Vaguely oriental in its setting, it presents a sequence of suggestive but cryptic images. In the preface Coleridge gave a famous description of how he came to write it and why it was never completed. While staying near Porlock in 1797 he took an anodyne and fell asleep over a copy of PURCHAS's *Pilgrimage*. In his dream he composed some 200–300 lines. He hastened to write them down as soon as he woke, but was interrupted by 'a person on business from Porlock' and found that the rest of the poem had passed from his memory.

Kumin, Maxine (Winokur) 1925– American poet, novelist and short-story writer. Her verse, which includes *Up Country: Poems of New England* (1972; PULITZER PRIZE), can be sampled in *New and Selected Poems* (1982). It focuses on loss and survival, and frequently emphasizes the importance of family bonds; recent writing has stressed the role of the poet and dealt with the threat of Armageddon. Kumin's fiction includes novels – *Through Dooms of Love* (1965), *The Passions of Uxport* (1968), *The Abduction* (1971) and *The Designated Heir* (1974) – and the stories in *Why Can't We Live Together Like Civilized Human Beings?* (1982). She wrote two books for children with ANNE SEXTON.

Kunene, Mazisi 1930– South African poet. He writes in Zulu and makes his own English version. *Zulu Poems* (1970) and *The Ancestors and the Sacred Mountain* (1982) combine the oral tradition with political dissent. His major achievements, identifying him as probably the most ambitious poet in modern Africa, are two long epic works, *Emperor Shaka the Great* (1979) and *Anthem of the Decades* (1981), which aim to dignify the modern African by extolling the Zulu cultural and historical inheritance.

Kunitz, Stanley 1905– American poet. *Intellectual Things* appeared as early as 1930. A second volume, *Passport to the War: A Selection of Poems* (1944), brought him a wider audience but it was with *Selected Poems: 1928–58* (1958, PULITZER PRIZE) that he began to command general esteem. His poetry is admired for its frequently extravagant lyricism. *The Poems, 1928–1978* (1979), introducing the full range of his work, has been followed by *The Wellfleet Whale and Companion Poems* (1983) and *Next to Last Things* (1985). He has also published literary anthologies, translations from the Russian and *A Kind of Order, A Kind of Folly: Essays and Conversations* (1975).

Kuppner, Frank 1951– Poet. An eccentric, unpredictable talent, he has published: *A Bad Day for the Sung Dynasty* (1984), a sequence based on Chinese paintings; *The Intelligent Observation of Naked Women* (1987); *A Very Quiet Street* (1985), which transforms his native Glasgow into a series of surreal images; *Ridiculous, Absurd, Disgusting* (1989); and *A Concussed History of Scotland* (1990).

Kyd, Thomas 1558–94 Playwright. Little is known about his life, though he was arrested for heresy in 1593 because of his association with MARLOWE, probably suffered torture, and died soon after his release. Even the belief that he wrote *THE SPANISH TRAGEDY* (c. 1589), an influential adaptation of Senecan tragedy for the English stage, rests on a remark by THOMAS HEYWOOD. The only other surviving play which we can be fairly certain he wrote is *Cornelia* (1594), a version of Robert Garnier's *Cornélie*. Some scholars have suggested that he wrote a lost *Ur-Hamlet* of which SHAKESPEARE's *HAMLET* made use.

Kynaston, Sir **Francis** 1587–1642 Author of a romance in verse, *Leoline and Sydanis* (1642), and translator into Latin of CHAUCER's *TROILUS AND CRISEYDE*.

La Belle Dame sans Merci A poem closely translated from the French of Alain Chartier (*c.* 1424) by Richard Ros of Leicestershire *c.* 1450, though it was once attributed to CHAUCER (see CHAUCERIAN APOCRYPHA). It consists of a debate about COURTLY LOVE between a lover and his cruel lady. See also next entry.

La Belle Dame sans Merci A BALLAD by KEATS, published in 1820. The title derives from Alain Chartier's *La Belle Dame sans Merci* (*c.* 1424), which Keats probably read in the Middle English translation (see previous entry). It tells of a knight's fatal enthralment by a beautiful lady, part witch and part fairy. Though Keats thought it only a slight piece, its medievalism and its rehearsal of the morbid aspect of Romantic love strongly influenced later poets, particularly the PRE-RAPHAELITES.

La Guma, Alex 1925–85 South African novelist. His fiction presents the iniquities of apartheid in scrupulously realistic language, while also asserting a romantic faith in his characters' potential for compassion. It includes: *A Walk in the Night* (1962), about a Cape Town slum, District Six; *And a Threefold Cord* (1964), about a shantytown; *The Stone Country* (1967), set in prison, a precise metaphor for South Africa itself; *In the Fog of the Season's End* (1972), about underground resistance; and *Time of the Butcherbird* (1979), set in a tribal area. *A Soviet Journey* (1978) is a travel book.

La Ramée, Louise de See OUIDA.

Lady Audley's Secret A SENSATION NOVEL by MARY ELIZABETH BRADDON, serialized in 1861–2 and published in volume form in 1862. Written in haste but with a breathlessly readable plot, it has a striking central character in Lady Audley, who murders her first husband, George Talboys, on his return from Australia in order to protect her bigamous second marriage and position as mistress of Audley Court. Her crime is uncovered by Robert Audley, Sir Michael's nephew, and she is committed to a private asylum. In a final twist to the story, Talboys turns out to be alive, having secretly left the country after surviving the attempted murder.

Lady Chatterley's Lover A novel by D. H. LAWRENCE, written and privately printed in Florence in 1928. Constance (Connie) marries Sir Clifford Chatterley, a mineowner left paralysed and impotent by a war wound. After a superficial affair with Michaelis, a playwright, she enters into a passionate relationship with Sir Clifford's gamekeeper, Oliver Mellors, a forthright man uncontaminated by industrial society. When she becomes pregnant, Connie asks for a divorce but Sir Clifford refuses to release her. Though separated, the lovers wait hopefully for the obstacles between them to be surmounted.

Lady Chatterley was denied full publication in Britain for over 30 years. An expurgated version (1932) eliminated the four-letter words and detailed sexual descriptions. The unexpurgated text became available in 1960 after Penguin Books survived a prosecution under the Obscene Publications Act in 1959. The earlier versions of the novel have been published as *The First Lady Chatterley* (1944) and *John Thomas and Lady Jane* (1972).

Lady of Shalott, The A poem by TENNYSON, published in 1832 and revised for the 1842 edition of his *Poems*. The setting is Arthurian. The lady leads an isolated life, never looking out of her window but weaving pictures from a mirror's reflection of the scene. When Sir Lancelot passes by, she is tempted to gaze directly on reality and dies. Tennyson gave the story a different treatment in 'Lancelot and Elaine', one of the *IDYLLS OF THE KING*.

Lady of the Lake, The A poem in six CANTOS by SIR WALTER SCOTT, published in 1810. The period is the early 16th century, the lady is Ellen, daughter of the outlawed James of Douglas, and the lake is Loch Katrine, where the Highland chief Roderick Dhu entertains the King of Scotland, disguised as a knight, James Fitz-James. The king joins Roderick and Malcolm Graeme as a suitor of Ellen, kills Roderick in a duel and pardons Douglas. Ellen marries Malcolm. The poem includes her song, 'Rest, Warrior, Rest', and the beautiful funeral lament, 'He is Gone on the Mountain'.

Lady Windermere's Fan A play by OSCAR WILDE, performed in 1892. His first theatrical success, it deals with a blackmailing divorcée driven to self-sacrifice by maternal love. The dialogue uses the paradoxical, witty comments on society which made Wilde famous.

Lai le Freine A fragment of an early-14th-century VERSE ROMANCE, perhaps by the author of *SIR ORFEO*. One of the better Middle English BRETON LAYS, it is loosely adaped from MARIE DE FRANCE's *Lai le Fresne*. The heroine's mother abandons her in an ash tree and the nuns who bring her up christen her Freine, 'ash'. She lives as the mistress of a knight, Guroun, who eventually marries Freine's twin sister. The fragment ends here, but in the source Freine's robe is recognized by her mother, who confesses her crime. Guroun's marriage is dissolved and he weds Freine.

Laing, B(ernard) Kojo 1946– Ghanaian novelist and poet. His fiction is surreal, inventive and technically accomplished. *Search Sweet Country* (1986) is set in Accra in the mid 1970s, while *Woman of the Aeroplanes* (1988) and *Major Gentl and the Achimota Wars* (1992) take place in the near future. The poems in *Godhorse* (1989) also display witty combinations of imagery and formal invention.

Lake Poets [Lake School], The A term applied to WORDSWORTH, COLERIDGE and SOUTHEY because of their close association with the Lake District. It was apparently first used by *THE EDINBURGH REVIEW* in 1817.

Lalla Rookh: *An Oriental Romance* Four narrative poems, with a connecting tale in prose, by THOMAS MOORE, published in 1817. In its day it was one of the most popular examples of Orientalism. On her way from Delhi to her arranged marriage in Cashmere, Lalla Rookh, the daughter of the Emperor Aurungzebe, listens to stories told by a young poet Feramorz, who eventually turns out to be her prospective husband, the King of Bucharia. 'The Veiled Prophet of Khorassan' and 'The Fire-Worshippers', the first and third stories, are about tragic love. In 'Paradise and the Peri' a *peri*, or child of a fallen angel, finally gains admission to paradise by bringing the tear of a repentant criminal. In 'The Light of the Haram' Nourmahal wins back the love of her husband, Selim, with a magic song she learns from the enchantress Namouna.

L'Allegro A poem by MILTON, written in 1632 and published with other early work in 1645. Its title means 'the cheerful man' and it celebrates mirth, in the delights of rustic scenery and also in the city. Its companion piece is *Il Penseroso*.

Lamb, Charles 1775–1834 Essayist and poet. Born in London, he was educated at Christ's Hospital, where he formed a lifelong friendship with COLERIDGE. From 1789 until his retirement in 1825 he worked for the South Sea House and then the East India House. In 1796 his sister Mary Ann Lamb (1764–1847) murdered their mother in a fit of insanity and was confined to an asylum, at length being released into her brother's care. Lamb's burden of responsibility and his gentle, engaging personality attracted many friends and made him the popular host of gatherings which included Coleridge, SOUTHEY, LEIGH HUNT, HAYDON, CRABB ROBINSON and TALFOURD, who published a volume of his letters with a biographical sketch (1834) and *Memorials of Charles Lamb* (1848).

He contributed four SONNETS to Coleridge's *Poems on Various Subjects* (1796) and published *Blank Verse* (with Charles Lloyd; 1798), which included 'The Old Familiar Faces'. *A Tale of Rosamund Gray and Old Blind Margaret* (1798) was followed by a tragedy, *John Woodvil* (1802; initially entitled 'Pride's Cure'), and a FARCE, *Mr H* (1806). *Tales from Shakespeare* (1807), a classic for several generations of young readers, was written jointly with his sister Mary, though her name did not appear on the title-page until 1838. She contributed 14 of the 20 prose summaries of SHAKESPEARE's plays. Other children's books were: *The Adventures of Ulysses* (1808); *Mrs Leicester's School* (1809), written with Mary and containing reminiscences of their childhood; *Poetry for Children* (1809); and *Prince Dorus* (1811), a fairy-tale in verse. Lamb's contributions to journals included 'On the Character and Genius of Hogarth' and 'On the Tragedies of Shakespeare', but he is best remembered for THE ESSAYS OF ELIA, first published in THE LONDON MAGAZINE in 1820–3. They were collected in 1823 and a second series, *The Last Essays of Elia*, appeared in 1833.

Lamb, Mary Ann See LAMB, CHARLES.

Lamia A poem by KEATS, published in 1820. Hermes transforms the serpent Lamia into a beautiful maiden who enchants Lycius, a young man of Corinth. They retire to an exquisite palace, but Lycius insists on inviting his friends to a feast at which the philosopher Apollonius recognizes Lamia's true nature. She vanishes and Lycius dies. Keats borrowed the subject from BURTON's ANATOMY OF MELANCHOLY.

Lamming, George 1927– Caribbean novelist. His highly successful first novel, *In the Castle of My Skin* (1953), draws on his boyhood in Barbados. Its successors include: *The Emigrants* (1954), about West Indian disillusion with life in Britain; *Of Age and Innocence* (1958), which contrasts peasant wisdom and youthful tolerance with violent, Caribbean, pre-Independence politicking; *Season of Adventure* (1960), in which the heroine painfully achieves Caribbean identity; the ambitious *Water with Berries* (1971); and his masterpiece, *Natives of My Person* (1972), set aboard a 17th-century slave ship. *The Pleasures of Exile* (1960) consists of Lamming's essays. He also edited an anthology of black writing, *Cannon Shots and Glass Beads* (1974).

Lampman, Archibald 1861–99 Canadian poet. His reputation rests on *Among the Millet* (1888) and *Lyrics of Earth* (1893), which emphasize natural themes and use a Canadian setting. *Alcyone* (1899), which includes 'The

City of the End of Things', was in preparation at the time of his death. *At the Long Sault* (1943), hitherto unpublished poems, was edited by his friend DUNCAN CAMPBELL SCOTT in collaboration with E. K. BROWN.

Land of Cockaygne, The A Middle English poem written in Ireland during the second half of the 13th century. It presents a lively parody of the Christian Paradise and the Earthly Paradise of European tradition, describing a land where buildings are edible, monks and nuns enjoy a licentious life and geese fly ready-roasted.

Landon, Letitia Elizabeth 1802–38 Poet and novelist, who generally used the initials L. E. L. She was among the most popular and prolific writers of her day. Volumes of poetry include *The Fate of Adelaide* (1821), *The Improvisatrice* (1824), *The Troubadour* (1825), *The Venetian Bracelet* (1829) and *The Vow of the Peacock* (1835). Her most successful novel was *Ethel Churchill* (1837); others were *Romance and Reality* (1831), *Francesca Carrara* (1834) and *Duty and Inclination* (1838).

Landor, Walter Savage 1775–1864 Poet and essayist. He is chiefly remembered for his prose dialogues, IMAGINARY CONVERSATIONS OF LITERARY MEN AND STATESMEN (1824–9), *Pericles and Aspasia* (1836) and *Imaginary Conversations of Greeks and Romans* (1853). His poetry is largely forgotten, though much of it displays a distinguished simplicity: 'Lately Our Poets Loitered in Green Lanes', 'Dying Speech of an Old Philosopher', 'Mother I Cannot Mind My Wheel', 'Rose Aylmer' and 'To Ianthe'. An extraordinary and irascible man whose temper periodically made life in England untenable, he spent much of his life in Italy and died in Florence, where his admirer ROBERT BROWNING attempted to protect and care for him. He was tolerantly caricatured by DICKENS as Boythorn in BLEAK HOUSE.

Lane, Edward William 1801–76 Arabic scholar. He published the classic *Account of the Manners and Customs of the Modern Egyptians* (1836). Other works were a translation of the *Arabian Nights' Entertainments* (1838–40) and *Selections from the Kur-an* (1843).

Lang, Andrew 1844–1912 Poet, scholar and man of letters. There was almost no type of writing that he did not touch: essays, reviews, literary controversy, plays, novels and biographies all form part of his collected works. His first volume of poetry, *Ballads and Lyrics of Old France* (1872), was followed by *Ballades in Blue China* (1880 and 1881), *Helen of Troy* (1882), *Rhymes à la Mode* (1885), *Grass of Parnassus* (1888), *Ban and Arrière Ban* (1894) and *New Collected Rhymes* (1905). As a classical scholar he worked mostly on Homer. As a historian he was chiefly concerned with Scotland, though he also wrote a book on Joan of Arc (1908). As a biographer he wrote lives of Sir Stafford Northcote (1890) and J. G. LOCKHART (1896). As an anthropologist he published *Custom and Myth* (1884), *Myth, Ritual and Religion* (1887) and *The Making of Religion* (1898).

Lang's controversy with Max Müller about folk-tales led to his best-remembered work: *The Blue Fairy Book* (1889) and 11 subsequent volumes, known by the colours in their titles, the last appearing in 1910. Taken from many different sources, the stories were rewritten by Lang's wife and a committee of ladies, who also bowdlerized his *Arabian Nights' Entertainments* (1898). Lang edited one of the best anthologies of nursery rhymes, *The Nursery Rhyme Book* (1897).

Langland, William Author of the religious poem PIERS PLOWMAN, surviving in three versions (known as the A-, B- and C-texts) which together span the period 1360–87.

Nothing is known of his life beyond what can be deduced from the poem and a few details from notes in a 15th-century manuscript of the C-text. Traditionally he is supposed to have been the son, perhaps illegitimate, of Stacy de Rokayle and to have been educated at the priory of Great Malvern. The poem implies a knowledge of the Malvern Hills and suggests that he lived in London. His connection with the church is not known, though he was passionately concerned with the corruption of the regular clergy and the mendicant orders. His familiarity with the Scriptures is abundantly clear, although his knowledge of biblical commentaries, patristic writers and other areas of scholarship was patchy. SKEAT's attribution of *Richard the Redeless* (see *MUM AND THE SOTHSEGGER*) to Langland is no longer accepted and no other poem is now associated with his name.

Lanier, Sidney 1842–81 American poet and critic. His verse – collected in 1884, with expanded editions in 1891 and 1916 – was greatly influenced by his work as a professional musician. A lecturer at Johns Hopkins University from 1879, he published many critical works, including a study of METRE, *The Science of English Verse* (1880).

Laodicean, A: *A Story of Today* A novel by HARDY, published in 1881. Paula Power, the Laodicean or vacillator, inherits Stancy Castle in Somerset. She falls in love with George Somerset, a young architect, but cannot agree to an engagement. She does, however, eventually accept Captain de Stancy, a member of the family which once owned the castle. He is helped by his illegitimate son, the conniving Will Dare. On discovering Dare's villainy Paula breaks her engagement and is reconciled with Somerset. Dare contrives to burn the castle to the ground.

Lardner, Ring(gold) (Wilmer) 1885–1933 American short-story writer. A sports reporter, he became famous with the witty, vernacular letters he wrote as 'Jack Keefe', a newcomer to a professional baseball team. They were collected as *You Know Me, Al: A Busher's Letters* (1914). *Bib Ballads* (1915) is a volume of poetry, *Gullible's Travels* (1917) and *Treat 'em Rough* (1918) are collections of satirical stories, and *The Big Town* (1921) is Lardner's only novel. He had a large and enthusiastic following by the time he published *How to Write Short Stories (with Samples)* (1924). His later works are the collections *What of It?* (1925), *The Love Nest* (1926), *Round Up* (1929) and *First and Last* (1934).

Larkin, Philip (Arthur) 1922–85 Poet, novelist and essayist. His early volumes were *The North Ship* (1945), written under the influence of the early YEATS, and the more mature *XX Poems* (1951). His reputation rests on what PETER LEVI has called the '85 perfect poems' in his three major collections: *The Less Deceived* (1955); *The Whitsun Weddings* (1964), whose title-poem, describing a train journey from Hull to London, is his best-known work; and *High Windows* (1964), which contains 'The Old Fools' and 'The Building', about ageing, illness and death. Working with traditional, often ingeniously constructed poetic forms, Larkin extended the territory of poetry in his wry treatment of contemporary English life. The arrangement of his work in *The Collected Poems* (1988), edited by ANTHONY THWAITE, did not please all readers.

He also published two understated novels, *Jill* (1946) and *A Girl in Winter* (1947). The jazz reviews collected in *All What Jazz?* (1970) are prompted by the same dislike of

MODERNISM which informs his edition of *The Oxford Book of Twentieth-Century English Verse* (1973). *Required Writing* (1983) is a selection of occasional articles and reviews. *Collected Letters 1940–1985*, edited by Anthony Thwaite, appeared in 1992.

Last Chronicle of Barset, The The final volume in TROLLOPE'S BARSETSHIRE NOVELS, published in 1867. Josiah Crawley, the intractable curate of Hogglestock, is falsely accused of stealing a £20 cheque from Lord Lufton's agent, Mr Soames. The bishop's wife, Mrs Proudie, plays a leading part in the persecution. Archdeacon Grantly's son, Major Henry Grantly, breaks with his father in insisting on becoming engaged to Crawley's daughter Grace. Mrs Arabin (the former Eleanor Harding) establishes Crawley's innocence and resolves the affair. Crawley is appointed to the parish of the late Mr Harding, and Archdeacon Grantly is won over when he meets Grace. The novel also contains the death of Mrs Proudie and follows Johnny Eames's ever-hopeful pursuit of Lily Dale.

Last Days of Pompeii, The A novel by BULWER LYTTON, published in 1834. The action takes place just before and during the eruption of Vesuvius in AD 79. There are lively pictures of Roman life (including an early Christian sect) and a memorable villain, Arbaces, the Priest of Isis.

Last of the Barons, The A novel by EDWARD BULWER LYTTON, published in 1843. The hero is the medieval Earl of Warwick, known as 'the kingmaker'. The book was intended as a political ALLEGORY: Warwick's defeat at the Battle of Barnet represents the overthrow of the hereditary feudal order by the new commercial classes.

Last of the Mohicans, The See LEATHERSTOCKING TALES, THE.

Late Lyrics and Earlier A collection of poems by HARDY, published in 1922. Its main theme is music, and many poems evoke the rhythms of the BALLAD or the folksong.

Latimer, Hugh ?1485–1555 Preacher and Protestant martyr. Graphic, engaging and anecdotal sermons – such as 'Sermon on the Card' (c. 1529) and 'Of the Plough' (1548) – established his reputation as a reforming cleric. He became Bishop of Worcester in 1535 but resigned his see rather than subscribe to the Six Articles (1539) designed to halt the further spread of reforming ideas. Briefly restored to favour during Edward VI's reign, he was committed to the Tower of London on Queen Mary's accession. After defending his opinions at Oxford with CRANMER and Ridley, he was condemned as a heretic, excommunicated and burned with Ridley. Two collections of his sermons, *Twenty-Seven Sermons* (1562) and *Fruitful Sermons* (1571), were reprinted many times in the 16th century.

Lauder, William d. 1771 Literary hoaxer. A classical scholar, he tried to convict MILTON of plagiarizing from Masenius' poem *Sarcotis* and Grotius' *Adamus exil* in *PARADISE LOST*. His allegations, made in *THE GENTLEMAN'S MAGAZINE* and repeated in *An Essay on Milton's Use and Imitation of the Moderns in his 'Paradise Lost'* (1749), impressed SAMUEL JOHNSON, who contributed a prospectus for the proposed publication of *Adamus exil*. Lauder's forgery, which consisted of inserting passages from a Latin translation of *Paradise Lost* into the works of Masenius and Grotius, was exposed by John Douglas in 1750. An apology appeared in 1751, though Lauder subsequently retracted it.

Laurence, (Jean) Margaret 1926–87 Canadian novelist. Her most important achievement is the 'Manawaka' sequence, five works set in a fictional Canadian small town and dealing largely with the lives of women: *The Stone Angel* (1964), *A Jest of God* (1966), *The Fire-Dwellers* (1969), *A Bird in the House* (short stories, 1970) and *The Diviners* (1974), the most impressive volume. She also published several works about Africa: *This Side Jordan* (1960), a novel set at the time of Ghanaian independence; *The Tomorrow-Tamer* (1963), short stories; *The Prophet's Camel Bell* (1963), a non-fictional account of her life in Somaliland; and *Drums and Cannons* (1968), a study of Nigerian novelists and playwrights. *Heart of a Stranger* (1976) is a collection of personal essays. *Dance of the Earth* (1989) is an autobiographical memoir.

Laus Veneris A poem by SWINBURNE, published in *Poems and Ballads* (1866). Both a peroration on physical love and a treatment of the Tannhäuser legend, *Laus Veneris* (Praise of Venus) reworks the medieval tale to stress the tragedy of Tannhäuser's return to Venus.

Lavengro: The Scholar – The Gypsy – The Priest A fictionalized autobiography by GEORGE BORROW, published in 1851. 'Lavengro' is the gipsy name for a philologist. Borrow conceals his early family life behind irresistibly romantic portraits of his father and mother, draws a veil over his early attempts to establish himself as a writer and says nothing of Russia, where he lived in 1833–5. Instead he writes episodically and without regard for chronology about an almost penniless young man who, leaving London in 1825, wanders round England for a year or more, consorting with tinkers, innkeepers, Nonconformist ministers, eccentric old gentlemen, chaste young women and gipsies. Though many contemporaries distrusted the book, it was soon recognized as a masterpiece. *THE ROMANY RYE* (1857) is a sequel.

Lavin, Mary 1912– Irish short-story writer and novelist. Her work deals with the small tensions of Irish middle-class life. Although she has published novels, *The House in Clewe Street* (1945) and *Mary O'Grady* (1950), her preferred form is the short story. Volumes include *Tales from Bective Bridge* (1942), *The Long Ago and Other Stories* (1944), *The Becker Wives and Other Stories* (1946), *At Sallygap and Other Stories* (1947) and *In The Middle of the Fields* (1967). *Collected Stories* appeared in 1971.

Law, William 1686–1761 Religious writer. A nonjuror who refused to take the Oath of Allegiance to George I, he was deprived of his Cambridge fellowship and forbidden to take up any church appointment. In 1717 he published the first of *Three Letters to the Bishop of Bangor*, a reply to HOADLY's defence of the church's submission of loyalty to George I. *Remarks on a Late Book Entitled The Fable of the Bees* (1723) is a reply to BERNARD DE MANDEVILLE. *The Absolute Unlawfulness of the Stage Entertainment* (1726) attacked the contemporary theatre.

His two most influential books, admired by SAMUEL JOHNSON and JOHN WESLEY, were *A Practical Treatise on Christian Perfection* (1726) and *A Serious Call to a Devout and Holy Life* (1728). Vigorously written, with a strong appeal in the simplicity of their teaching, they constitute a guide to the full practice of Christian ideals in everyday life. *The Case of Reason* (1731) replied to the Deists (see DEISM). Later, mystical writings which estranged Law from some of his former disciples include *The Spirit of Prayer* (1749–50), *The Way to Divine Knowledge* (1752), and *The Spirit of Love* (1752–54).

Lawler, Ray(mond) (Evenor) 1921– Australian playwright. *SUMMER OF THE SEVENTEENTH DOLL* (1955)

stands unchallenged as the first sign of a new movement in the Australian theatre. Later, less successful works include: *The Piccadilly Bushman* (1959); two experimental plays, *The Unshaven Cheek* (1963) and *The Man Who Shot the Albatross* (1972), about Captain Bligh; *Breach in the Wall* (1967); *Kid Stakes* (1975) and *Other Times* (1976), treating earlier years in the lives of the characters in *Summer of the Seventeenth Doll*; and *Godsend* (1982).

Lawless, Emily 1845–1913 Irish poet and novelist. Her novels, generally studies of the Irish peasantry, include *A Millionaire's Cousin* (1885), *Hurrish* (1886) and *Grania* (1892). *With the Wild Geese* (1902), a volume of poetry, was well received by contemporary critics.

Lawrence, D(avid) H(erbert) (Richards) 1885–1930 Novelist, short-story writer, poet, critic, playwright, essayist and painter. He was born at Eastwood, Nottinghamshire. His father was a coal-miner and his mother came from a family with genteel aspirations. He left Nottingham High School in 1901 and worked as a clerk and pupil-teacher before taking a training course at University College, Nottingham. Subsequently he taught in Croydon until illness forced him to resign. His writing was first encouraged by his friend Jessie Chambers and FORD MADOX FORD, who published his poetry in *THE ENGLISH REVIEW* and helped with the publication of his first novel, *The White Peacock* (1911). Set in what is recognizably the countryside around Eastwood, it contains a striking character in the gamekeeper Annable. *The White Peacock* was followed by *The Trespasser* (1912), based on the experiences of his friend Helen Corke, and his first major work, the autobiographical *SONS AND LOVERS* (1913).

In 1912 Lawrence met Frieda Weekley (*née* von Richthofen), daughter of a German baron and wife of a professor at Nottingham. They went to Germany together and married after her divorce in 1914. During World War I they lived in London and Cornwall, until expelled on suspicion of spying for the Germans. By this time Lawrence had formed close friendships with, among others, DAVID GARNETT, ALDOUS HUXLEY, BERTRAND RUSSELL, LADY OTTOLINE MORRELL, KATHERINE MANSFIELD, JOHN MIDDLETON MURRY and RICHARD ALDINGTON. His next novel, *THE RAINBOW* (1915), was prosecuted and banned on grounds of obscenity. Its successor, *WOMEN IN LOVE*, had difficulty finding a publisher. It was finally printed privately in New York in 1920; a censored English edition followed in 1921.

In 1919 Lawrence and Frieda left England for Italy, where he wrote *The Lost Girl* (1920), *Aaron's Rod* (1922) and *Mr Noon*, an incomplete novel carrying forward his life following *Sons and Lovers*. It was eventually published in 1984. Subsequent works reflect the travels of a writer who had become a permanent exile from his native country. *KANGAROO* (1923) was written during a four-month stay in Australia, where Lawrence met M. L. Skinner (with whom he collaborated on *The Boy in the Bush*, 1924). *THE PLUMED SERPENT* (1926) was inspired by his stays in Mexico. His last novel, *LADY CHATTERLEY'S LOVER*, was published in Florence in 1928. An expurgated edition appeared in England and the USA in 1932 but the original version had to await favourable court verdicts in 1959 and 1960 respectively. The first two versions of the novel were published independently as *The First Lady Chatterley* (1944) and *John Thomas and Lady Jane* (1972).

Lawrence died of tuberculosis at Vence, in France, at the age of 44. Given the brevity of his writing career, the sheer amount of his output is remarkable. His short stories, which include some of his finest work, appeared in *The Prussian Officer* (1914), *England, My England* (1922), *The Woman Who Rode Away* (1928), *Love among the Haystacks* (1930) and *The Lovely Lady* (1933). His novellas, also among his best work, include *The Ladybird, The Fox, The Captain's Doll* (1923); *St Mawr* and *The Princess* (1925); *Sun* (1926); *The Escaped Cock* (also known as *The Man Who Died*; 1929) and *The Virgin and the Gipsy* (1930). His poetry, first collected in 1928, includes *Love Poems* (1913), *Amores* (1916), *Look! We Have Come Through!* (1917), *New Poems* (1918), *Bay* (1919), *Birds, Beasts and Flowers* (1923), *Pansies* (1929), *Nettles* (1930) and *Last Poems* (1932). In addition Lawrence wrote plays, several about mining families, collected in *The Complete Plays* (1965).

His non-fictional prose covers a broad spectrum. *Psychoanalysis and the Unconscious* (1921) and *Fantasia of the Unconscious* (1922) stand in intimate relationship to the thinking which informs his major novels. His literary criticism includes the ground-breaking *Studies in Classic American Literature* (1923) and a study of HARDY (first published in *Phoenix*). *Reflections on the Death of a Porcupine* (1925) and *Assorted Articles* (1930) are collections of essays. His travel books include *Twilight in Italy* (1916), *Sea and Sardinia* (1921), *Etruscan Places* (1932) and *Mornings in Mexico* (1927). *Movements in European History* (1921) is a school history book written under the pseudonym of Lawrence H. Davison. Many of his uncollected stories, essays, reviews and introductions were included in *Phoenix: The Posthumous Papers* (1936) and *Phoenix II: Uncollected, Unpublished and Other Prose Works* (1968). Most of his pictures were reproduced in *The Paintings of D. H. Lawrence* (1929). The Cambridge edition of his complete works and letters promises to be definitive.

Lawrence, George Alfred 1827–76 Novelist. *Guy Livingstone* (1857) introduced 'muscular blackguardism' (as opposed to CHARLES KINGSLEY's 'muscular Christianity') in the character of its brutally strong and unprincipled hero. Eight other novels followed, including *Sword and Gown* (1859), *Barren Honour* (1862), *Breaking a Butterfly* (1869) and *Hagarene* (1874).

Lawrence, T(homas) E(dward) 1888–1935 Soldier and author, commonly known as 'Lawrence of Arabia'. After a distinguished career at Oxford, he worked in the intelligence section of the Arab Bureau during World War I, organizing the Arab revolt against the Turks in 1916. He found it difficult to deal with his almost legendary reputation and enlisted in the Royal Air Force under the names of Ross and later Shaw. His Oxford thesis was eventually published as *Crusader Castles* (1936). *The Seven Pillars of Wisdom: A Triumph* (privately printed, 1926; abbreviated as *Revolt in the Desert*, 1927), his account of his war years, has alternately been praised as a masterpiece and condemned as an exercise in self-aggrandizement. Lawrence also published a translation, *The Odyssey of Homer* (1932), and *The Mint* (limited edition, 1936), about his life in the ranks. DAVID GARNETT edited his letters (1938).

Lawson, Henry 1867–1922 Australian poet and short-story writer. The best of his bush ballads and stories, based on his experience of the outback in New South Wales, were written by the turn of the century. After 1901 he seemed unable to recapture his laconic humour and fine balance of style, and his later work is marred by sentimentality. Lawson's first collection was *Stories in Prose and Verse* (1894), followed by *While the Billy Boils* (1896), *On the Track* (1900) and *Joe Wilson and His Mates* (1901). A collection, *The Stories of Henry Lawson*, was edited by Cecil Mann (1965).

Lawson, John Howard 1894–1977 American playwright. He helped to shape the theatre of social consciousness in the 1920s and 1930s with *Processional* (1925), about a coal strike in West Virginia, and *Marching Song* (1937), about the triumph of labour's solidarity over an uncaring management. His career was cut short when he was summoned before the House Un-American Activities Committee. As one of the 'Hollywood Ten', he served a one-year prison sentence (1950–1). *Parlor Magic* (1963) was his only subsequent play.

Lay of the Last Minstrel, The A poem in six CANTOS by SIR WALTER SCOTT, published in 1805. The 16th-century story which the minstrel tells was suggested to Scott by the Border legend of the goblin Gilpin Horner. He appears in the poem as the page to Lord Cranstoun, mischievously thwarting but eventually helping his master's efforts to overcome a family feud and marry Margaret, daughter of the lady of Branksome Hall.

Layamon Author of *Brut*, a late 12th-century CHRONICLE in ALLITERATIVE VERSE, adapted from the French of Wace's *Le Roman de Brut* (1155), itself an adaptation of GEOFFREY OF MONMOUTH's Latin *Historia regum Britanniae* (*c.* 1135). It narrates the history of England from its foundation by the legendary Brutus, great-grandson of Aeneas. King Lear and Cymbeline both appear, but the narrative is memorable for being the first to tell the story of King Arthur in English (see ARTHURIAN LITERATURE). *Brut* lacks much of Wace's courtliness, resembling the vigorous epic character of Old English poetry. All that is known of Layamon comes from an early version of his work, in which he says he decided to write the poem while a priest at Areley Kings in the Severn valley.

Layard, Sir Austen Henry 1817–94 Archaeologist. His excavations resulted in *Nineveh and Its Remains* (1848–9) and *The Ruins of Nineveh and Babylon* (1853). A close friend of DICKENS, he became Under-Secretary for Foreign Affairs and later ambassador to Madrid and Constantinople.

Lays of Ancient Rome, The A sequence of poems by MACAULAY, published in 1842. These simple, vigorous verses for long remained favourites of the anthology and the classroom. 'Horatius' tells of the defence of the Sublician Bridge against the Etruscans by Horatius Cocles; 'The Battle of Lake Regillus' describes the Romans' defeat of the Latins (*c.* 496 BC); 'Virginia' concerns the maiden killed by her father, Virginius, to save her from the lust of Appius Claudius; and 'The Prophecy of Capys' looks forward to the future greatness of Rome.

Layton, Irving 1912– Canadian poet. *Here and Now* (1945), *In the Midst of My Fever* (1954), *The Bull Calf and Other Poems* (1956), *A Red Carpet for the Sun* (1959), *The Swinging Flesh* (1961), *The Shattered Plinths* (1968) and *Droppings from Heaven* (1979) are among his many volumes. *A Wild Peculiar Joy* (1982) collects his verse from 1945 to 1982. Layton's early work was designed to oppose the austerity of Canadian poetry; later work shows an increasing resentment of social inequality and a deepening sensitivity. *Wild Gooseberries* (1989) is a selection of his letters. He founded Contact Press, the leading publisher of Canadian poetry, with LOUIS DUDEK and RAYMOND SOUSTER in 1952.

Le Bone Florence of Rome An anonymous late-14th-century VERSE ROMANCE written in the north Midlands.

It is notable for the portrayal of its heroine and the vivid attention to detail in describing her sufferings before becoming a famous healer, respected by those who wronged her and reunited with her long-lost husband Esmere. Florence's patience recalls the popular story of the 'constant' Constance (see EMARE).

Le Carré, John [Cornwell, David John Moore] 1931– Novelist. His novels about the grey, duplicitous world of spying have increasingly come to be regarded less as thrillers than as perceptive documentations of the Cold War. *The Spy Who Came In from the Cold* (1963), his third novel, made his reputation and remains his most concentrated study. *Call for the Dead* (1961) had already introduced George Smiley, who has reappeared several times, notably in *Tinker, Tailor, Soldier, Spy* (1974) and *Smiley's People* (1980). Other novels include: *The Looking-Glass War* (1965); *A Small Town in Germany* (1968); *The Honourable Schoolboy* (1977); *The Perfect Spy* (1986); *The Little Drummer Girl* (1983); and *The Russia House* (1989), in response to the end of the Cold War.

Le Fanu, (Joseph) Sheridan 1814–73 Novelist. In all, he published some 20 books including novels, stories and verse, the latter including a drama, 'Beatrice', 'The Legend of the Glaive' and 'Song of the Bottle'. He is best known for his ingenious tales of mystery and terror, notably *The Cock and Anchor* (1845), *The House by the Churchyard* (1863), UNCLE SILAS (1864) and a volume of short stories, *IN A GLASS DARKLY* (1872).

Le Gallienne, Richard (Thomas) 1866–1947 Poet and essayist. *My Lady's Sonnets* (1887) and his best-known book of verse, *The Lonely Dancer* (1913) are characteristic of the 1890s, being uncompromisingly mannered and artificial. *The Romantic Nineties* (1926) gives a valuable account of the circle which included WILDE, SYMONS and BEARDSLEY. Other volumes of reminiscences are *Quest for the Golden Girl* (1896) and *From a Paris Garret* (1936).

Le Guin, Ursula K(roeber) 1929– American novelist, poet and critic. Her SCIENCE-FICTION novels include: *The Left Hand of Darkness* (1969), about a society of hermaphrodites; *The Lathe of Heaven* (1971), about dreams which alter reality; *The Word for World is Forest* (1972), about colonialism; *The Dispossessed* (1974); and *Always Coming Home* (1986), about future inhabitants of northern California. *The Wind's Twelve Quarters* (1975) and *The Compass Rose* (1982) are short stories. Her non-fantastic fiction, including *Orsinian Tales* (1976) and *Malafrena* (1979), is usually set in the imaginary past. Her CHILDREN'S LITERATURE includes the much-acclaimed 'Earthsea' fantasy series: *A Wizard of Earthsea* (1968), *The Tombs of Atuan* (1971), *The Farthest Shore* (1972) and *Tehanu* (1990). Her critical essays are collected in *The Language of the Night* (1979; revised 1989) and *Dancing at the Edge of the World* (1989). Her poetry includes *Wild Angels* (1975), *Hard Words and Other Poems* (1981) and *In the Red Zone* (1983). *Buffalo Gals and Other Animal Presences* (1987) mixes prose and verse.

Leacock, Stephen 1869–1944 Canadian humorist. A political economist, he spent his career at McGill University and wrote a standard college textbook, *Elements of Political Science* (1906). Beginning with *Literary Lapses* (1910), he published an average of one humorous book a year for the remainder of his life. These include *Nonsense Novels* (1911), *Sunshine Sketches of a Little Town* (1912), *Arcadian Adventures with the Idle Rich* (1914), *Moonbeams from the Larger Lunacy* (1915), *Further Foolishness* (1916), *Frenzied Fiction* (1918), *Winnowed*

Wisdom (1926), *My Remarkable Uncle* (1942) and *Last Leaves* (1945). *My Discovery of England* (1922) and *My Discovery of the West* (1937) grew out of highly successful lecture tours. A master of the short sketch or extended anecdote, he belongs in the tradition of such North American humorists as ARTEMUS WARD, TWAIN and, in Canada, HALIBURTON.

Leader, The A weekly periodical founded by G. H. LEWES and Thornton Leigh Hunt, published from 1850 to 1866.

Lear, Edward 1812–88 Artist, travel-writer and nonsense poet. A commission to draw the parrots in the Zoological Gardens led to his being engaged as an artist by the Earl of Derby, who kept a menagerie at Knowsley Hall. There Lear began his most enduring work: nonsense poems accompanied by nonsense drawings. They appeared as *A Book of Nonsense* (1845; enlarged 1861, 1863, 1870), *A Book of Nonsense and More Nonsense* (1862), *Nonsense Songs, Stories, Botany and Alphabets* (1871), *More Nonsense, Pictures, Rhymes, Botany, Etc.* (1872) and *Laughable Lyrics, a Fresh Book of Nonsense Poems* (1877). *Queery Leary Nonsense* (1911), compiled by Lady Strachey, contained new material; *Teapots and Quails* (1953), edited by P. Hofer and A. Davidson, contained unpublished fragments. Holbrook Jackson edited *The Complete Nonsense of Edward Lear* (1947). Lear's well-known poems include 'The Owl and the Pussycat', 'The Jumblies' and 'The Courtship of the Yongy-Bonghy-Bo'. He was also an accomplished exponent of the LIMERICK.

Successfully established as an artist, he was engaged to give drawing lessons to Queen Victoria. His wide travels resulted in some fine landscapes and books: *Illustrated Excursions in Italy* (1846), *A Tour in Sicily* (1847), *Journal of a Landscape Painter in Albania, Illyria etc.* (1851), *Journal of a Landscape Painter in Southern Calabria* (1852), *Journal of a Landscape Painter in Corsica* (1870) and *Italian Journal* (1873–5). He finally settled at San Remo in Italy.

Leatherstocking Tales, The A series of novels by JAMES FENIMORE COOPER, consisting of *The Pioneers: or, The Sources of the Susquehanna* (1823), *The Last of the Mohicans: A Tale of 1757* (1826), *The Prairie: A Tale* (1827), *The Pathfinder: or, The Inland Sea* (1840) and *The Deerslayer: or, The First War Path* (1841).

Set in the early frontier period of American history, they take their name from the protagonist, Natty Bumppo, variously called Leatherstocking, Deerslayer, Hawkeye and Pathfinder. The chronological sequence differs from the dates of composition. *The Deerslayer* relates Bumppo's experiences as a young man in upstate New York in the early 1740s. *The Last of the Mohicans* is set during the Seven Years War between the French and the British in 1757. *The Pathfinder* takes place soon after *The Last of the Mohicans*, in the same conflict between the French and Indians and the British colonials. *The Pioneers* is set in 1793 in Otsego County, part of the recently settled region of New York state. *The Prairie* is set on the frontier of the great plains in 1804, when Natty Bumppo is in his 80s. Several figures emerge with almost mythic clarity from the densely complicated romantic plots: Bumppo himself, continually pushing forward the frontiers of a civilization which he avoids and his creator apparently despises, and the Red Indians, alternately noble savages and primordial villains, memorably embodied in Bumppo's companion, Chingachgook (Indian John).

Leaves of Grass A volume of poems by WALT WHITMAN, first published in 1855 and expanded until the 'Deathbed' edition of 1891–2. Its elaboration was the masterwork of his career. The first edition included the poems eventually titled 'Song of Myself', 'I Sing the Body Electric', and 'The Sleepers'. 'Song of Myself', over 1300 lines long in its final version, celebrates the poet's self and its relation to common men and women, announcing the presence of the cosmic 'I' who sings the poem. Later editions added 'Crossing Brooklyn Ferry', 'Song of the Open Road', 'Out of the Cradle Endlessly Rocking', 'When Lilacs Last in the Dooryard Bloom'd' and 'O Captain! My Captain!' (ELEGIES for Lincoln) and 'Passage to India'. The form and content of *Leaves of Grass* were revolutionary. Whitman's sprawling lines and cataloguing technique, as well as his belief that poetry should include the lowly, the profane, even the obscene, have had enormous influence. His intention, he said, was to create a truly American poem, 'proportionate to our continent, with its powerful races of men, its tremendous historic events, its great oceans, its mountains, and its illimitable prairies'.

Leavis, F(rank) R(aymond) 1895–1978 Critic. He spent most of his life in Cambridge, pursuing a career which was always both influential and controversial. *Mass Civilization and Minority Culture* (1933), *For Continuity* (1933), and *Culture and Environment* (with Denys Thompson, 1933) proposed the study of English literature to counter the threats posed by industrialism, especially the cinema, advertising and the spread of 'mass' culture. These arguments underlie the critical campaign undertaken by SCRUTINY, which he co-edited in 1932–53. Leavis began a thorough revision of the English literary tradition in *New Bearings in English Poetry* (1932), which championed GERARD MANLEY HOPKINS, T. S. ELIOT, POUND and YEATS, and *Revaluation* (1936), which opposed a 'line of WIT' from DONNE to Eliot to the line running from MILTON to SWINBURNE. Extending his approach to the novel, *The Great Tradition* (1948) praised AUSTEN, GEORGE ELIOT, HENRY JAMES and CONRAD for their life-enhancing moral seriousness. The rehabilitation of DICKENS in *Dickens the Novelist* (with his wife, Q. D. LEAVIS; 1970) identified a complementary tradition linking BLAKE and D. H. LAWRENCE, whose work he had defended in *D. H. Lawrence: Novelist* (1955).

Leavis refused to define the theoretical basis of his judgements, though it can be inferred from numerous asides. Historically considered, he belongs to the tradition of ARNOLD, RUSKIN and other writers on 'the condition of England'. The almost religious seriousness which he introduced to criticism inspired a generation of followers ('Leavisites') with a sense of vocation.

Leavis, Q(ueenie) D(orothy) 1906–81 Critic. She married F. R. LEAVIS in 1929. Her only book, *Fiction and the Reading Public* (1932), made an early attempt at a sociological approach to literature, tracing the split between a 'highbrow' minority interested in the art of the novel and a mass audience consuming popular romances. It influenced her husband's work and the ethos of SCRUTINY, to which she was a regular contributor. She wrote important critical reassessments of DICKENS in *Dickens the Novelist* (with F. R. Leavis; 1970) and of JANE AUSTEN, CHARLOTTE and EMILY BRONTË, HAWTHORNE and EDITH WHARTON in essays gathered, with other work, in three posthumous volumes (1983–89).

Lecky, William Edward Hartpole 1838–1903 Historian. *A History of the Rise and Influence of the Spirit of Rationalism in Europe* (1865), influenced by BUCKLE, argued that progress is due to rationalism and the tolerance demanded by reason, and is always impeded by theological dogmatism and bigotry. Lecky followed it with *The History of European Morals from Augustus to Charlemagne* (1869) and *A History of England in the Eighteenth Century* (1878–92).

Lee, (Nelle) Harper 1926– American novelist. Her only novel is *To Kill a Mockingbird* (1960), a story of racial prejudice set in a Southern town like her hometown of Monroeville, Alabama. A white lawyer, Atticus Finch, defends a black man, Tom Robinson, falsely accused of raping a white girl. The action is presented from the viewpoint of Finch's six-year-old daughter, Jean Louise ('Scout').

Lee, Laurie 1914– Autobiographer and poet. He is best known for *Cider with Rosie* (1959), a lyrical memoir of his Gloucestershire childhood. It was followed by *As I Walked Out One Midsummer Morning* (1969), about his youthful adventures on the road to London and in Spain, and *A Moment of War* (1991), about his experiences in the Spanish Civil War. *The Sun My Monument* (1944), *The Bloom of Candles* (1947) and *My Many Coated Man* (1955) are among many volumes of poetry showing his love of the countryside.

Lee, Nathaniel c. 1653–92 Playwright and actor. *Nero* (1674), *Sophonisba* (1675) and *Gloriana* (1676) were tragedies in HEROIC COUPLETS, but his masterpiece, *The Rival Queens* (1677), led the return to BLANK VERSE for tragedy. Lee could create complex characters and portray political motives acutely enough for *Lucius Junius Brutus* (1680) to be banned. A member of the dissipated circle surrounding ROCHESTER, whom he portrays as Nemours in the satiric sex-comedy, *The Princess of Cleve* (1681), he was confined to Bedlam in 1684–9.

Lee, Sir Sidney 1859–1926 Scholar and biographer of SHAKESPEARE. He assisted SIR LESLIE STEPHEN with the *Dictionary of National Biography*, succeeding him and seeing the main project to its conclusion in 1900. His biography of Shakespeare (1898), grew from his *DNB* contributions; several times revised, it gave a full statement of the sparse biographical facts, set in a wide literary and historical context. Having written on the Queen for the *DNB* he prepared a prompt and frank *Queen Victoria, a Biography* (1902) and was later commissioned to write a *Life of King Edward VII* (1925–7).

Leech, John 1817–64 Comic artist and illustrator. He was a founding member of *PUNCH* and remained its chief artist until his death. Outstanding among the 50 books he illustrated are DICKENS's *A CHRISTMAS CAROL* (1844), the novels of SURTEES and GILBERT À BECKETT's *The Comic History of England* (1847) and *The Comic History of Rome* (1852).

Left Book Club A publishing venture launched in 1936 by Victor Gollancz, the Labour MP John Strachey and Harold Laski to combat the rise of fascism. Its membership rose to 50,000 by 1939 but declined after the Nazi-Soviet Pact. The Club was dissolved in 1948. The majority of its publications were factual and, except for ORWELL's *THE ROAD TO WIGAN PIER* (1937) and ODETS' *Waiting for Lefty* (1937), did not achieve lasting success.

Legend of Good Women, The An unfinished poem by CHAUCER. It narrates the lives of women who suffered or died as a result of their faithful love: Cleopatra, Thisbe, Dido, Hypsipyle and Medea, Lucrece, Ariadne, Philomela, Phyllis and Hypermnestra. A rather more lively prologue, surviving in two versions, uses a debate about the supremacy of the flower or the leaf (see also *THE FLOWER AND THE LEAF*) to proclaim allegiance to the daisy, which the poet says is a transformation of Alceste, the leader of 'Good Women', and explains that the God of Love has required him to write in praise of women after libelling them in TROILUS AND CRISEYDE and his translation, THE ROMAUNT OF THE ROSE. It is not known whether the poem was actually a response to criticism of Chaucer's earlier work.

Legend of Montrose, A A novel by SIR WALTER SCOTT, in the third series of *Tales of My Landlord*, published in 1819. Its setting is the rising of the Highland clans against the Covenanters and in support of Charles I in 1644. The novel is more successful in its portrait of the free-booting soldier of fortune, Dugald Dalgetty, than in its account of Allan M'Aulay's tragic love for Annot Lyle.

Lehmann, (Rudolph) John (Frederick) 1907–87 Poet and man of letters. Brother of ROSAMOND LEHMANN, he edited *New Writing* (1936–9), *New Writing and Daylight* (1942–6) and *Penguin New Writing* (1940–50), which featured the work of ROY FULLER, LAURIE LEE and HENRY REED. He was also editor of THE LONDON MAGAZINE in 1954–61. His eponymous publishing imprint (1946–51) issued Sartre's *La Nausée* and SAUL BELLOW's *Dangling Man*. Lehmann's verse, which includes *A Garden Revisited and Other Poems* (1931), *The Noise of History* (1934), *The Sphere of Glass* (1944) and *Poems New and Selected* (1986), is now neglected.

Lehmann, Rosamond (Nina) 1903–90 Novelist. Her studies of developing womanhood and the subtle shades of emotional relationships include *Dusty Answer* (1927), *A Note in Music* (1930), *Invitation to the Waltz* (1932) and its sequel *The Weather in the Streets* (1936), *The Ballad and the Source* (1944) and *The Echoing Grove* (1953). *The Gypsy's Baby* (1946) is a volume of short stories and *The Swan in the Evening* (1967) an autobiography. She was the sister of JOHN LEHMANN.

Leigh, Mike 1943– Playwright and director. His first play, *The Box Play* (1966), evolved through improvisation with actors – a technique which he has developed in work for the stage, television and film. His best-known play, *Abigail's Party* (1977), is a satire on middle-class manners. Other work includes *Bleak Moments* (1970), *Babies Grow Old* (1974), *Goose Pimples* (1981), *It's a Great Shame* (1993), and the films *High Hopes* (1988) and *Naked* (1993). Despite writing 'by proxy', as he puts it, Leigh has a distinctive style: mordant, witty and analytical.

Leland [Leyland]**, John** ?1506–52 Antiquary and poet. The earliest of the 16th-century antiquarians, he toured the country in 1534–43 researching documents in the libraries of monasteries and colleges, intending to write a work called 'History and Antiquities of this Nation'. An English version of the account he presented to Henry VIII was published by his friend BALE as *The Laborious Journey and Search of John Leland* (1549). He became insane in 1547 and his great work was still in notes when he died. They were used by later topographers and historians such as WILLIAM HARRISON, HOLINSHED and CAMDEN, as well as DRAYTON in POLYOLBION, before appearing as the *Itinerary* (1710–12). Leland also wrote a defence of the Arthurian legends, *Assertio inclytissimi Arthuri* (1544), translated as *A Learned and True Assertion of the Original Life, Acts and Death of … Arthur* (1582). He wrote a few Latin poems: on the death of WYATT (1542) and the birth of Prince Edward (1543); *Cygnea cantio* (1545), which has been suggested as a model for SPENSER's PROTHALAMION; and *Laudatio pacis* ('Praise of Peace'; 1546).

Lemon, Mark 1809–70 Co-founder, with HENRY MAYHEW, and first editor of PUNCH. He nursed *Punch* to success and lived to see it established as a national institution. At first he subsidized it by his earnings from the theatre, for which he wrote over 60 pieces. He also wrote songs, lyrics, novels, Christmas fairy-stories, a joke-book and a one-act FARCE with DICKENS, *Mr Nightingale's Diary* (1851).

Lennox, Charlotte (Ramsay) 1720–1804 Novelist. Daughter of the lieutenant governor of New York, she arrived in England at the age of 15. *The Life of Harriot Stuart* (1750) was a SENTIMENTAL NOVEL but she achieved success with *The Female Quixote: or, The Adventures of Arabella* (1752), a SATIRE whose heroine is saturated in French romances of the previous century. She dramatized it as *Angelica: or, Quixote in Petticoats* (1758). *The History of Henrietta* (1758) was followed by *Sophia* (1762) and *Euphemia* (1790). *The Sister* (1769) is a play.

Leonard, Hugh [Byrne, John Keyes] 1926– Irish playwright. His work for television, including the series *Me Mammy*, shows the same knowledge of FARCE apparent in his work for the stage. *The Patrick Pearse Motel* (1971) and *Time Was* (1976) use the genre to satirize Dublin's fashionable outer suburbs. *Da* (1973) is a serio-comic treatment of the same location. *A Life* (1976) retraces its main character's path to his desiccated marriage, accounting for and perhaps disturbing his defensive reserve.

Lessing, Doris (May) 1919– Novelist. Her prolific and varied output has been marked by its interest in the private action of the mind and its willingness to challenge narrative convention. *The Grass is Singing* (1950), reflecting her childhood in Southern Rhodesia, was followed by *Martha Quest* (1952), *A Proper Marriage* (1954), *A Ripple from the Storm* (1958), *Landlocked* (1965) and *The Four-Gated City* (1969), forming a sequence called *The Children of Violence*. *The Golden Notebook* (1962), hailed if not conceived as the expression of feminist politics, examines the experience of a woman writer. Two experimental novels, *Briefing for a Descent into Hell* (1971) and *The Memoirs of a Survivor* (1974), anticipate *Canopus in Argos: Archives*, a 'space fiction' series: *Re: Colonised Planet 5, Shikasta* (1979), *The Marriages between Zones Three, Four and Five* (1980), *The Sirian Experiments* (1981), *The Making of the Representative for Planet 8* (1982) and *Documents Relating to the Sentimental Agents in the Volyen Empire* (1983). She has since returned to realistic narrative with *The Diary of a Good Neighbour* (1983) and *If the Old Could* (originally published under the pseudonym of Jane Somers, 1984), *The Good Terrorist* (1985) and *The Fifth Child* (1988), a bleak novella. In addition to short stories, she has also published poetry, travel books, personal writings and the first volume of her autobiography, *Under My Skin* (1994).

L'Estrange, Sir Roger 1616–1704 Journalist and translator. An active Royalist, he began by writing political pamphlets against the army leaders and the Presbyterians from exile on the Continent. Appointed Surveyor of the Press in 1663, he published a series of newspapers: *The Intelligencer* and *The News* (neither as successful as MUDDIMAN's *London Gazette*), the *City Mercury* and, after another period of Continental exile, *The Observator*. The accession of William and Mary ended his career as a journalist. In later life he supported himself by translations, including ERASMUS' *Colloquies* (1680 and 1689), *The Fables of Aesop and Other Eminent Mythologies* (1692) and the works of Josephus (1702).

Letters from an American Farmer A collection of 12 essays by CRÈVECOEUR, published in London in 1782 and in Philadelphia in 1793. Writing to a British correspondent as 'Farmer James', he describes American agrarian life and the virtue, independence, industry, and prosperity of the American farmer in glowing terms. The experience of immigration, the process of 'Americanization' and the relation between the geography of various regions and the character of their people are all discussed. A disillusioned final essay, 'Distresses of a Frontier Man', describes his realization that the agrarian idyll is no longer possible in the midst of frontier raids and Revolutionary violence.

Lever, Charles (James) 1806–72 Novelist. He made his name with a succession of lively novels about Ireland and the army: *The Confessions of Harry Lorrequer* (1837), *Charles O'Malley* (1840), *Jack Hinton the Guardsman* (1842), *Tom Burke of Ours* (1844), *Arthur O'Leary* (1844) and *The O'Donoghe* (1845). Their tone was well parodied by THACKERAY in *PUNCH'S PRIZE NOVELISTS*. Later novels were more subdued, partly through an attempt at greater realism and partly through fatigue; they include *Roland Cashel* (1850), *Sir Jasper Carew* (1855), *The Fortunes of Glencore* (1857), *Luttrell of Arran* (1865) and *Lord Kilgobbin* (1872).

Leverson, Ada 1865–1936 Novelist. A member of the circle which included WILDE, GEORGE MOORE and BEERBOHM, she contributed to *THE YELLOW BOOK*. Her novels are *The Twelfth Hour* (1907), *Love's Shadow* (1908), *The Limit* (1911), *Tenterhooks* (1912), *Bird of Paradise* (1914) and *Love at Second Sight* (1916).

Levertov, Denise 1923– American poet. She was born in Britain, where she published *The Double Image* (1946) before emigrating to the USA. Subsequent work has been associated with the BLACK MOUNTAIN SCHOOL and the influence of WILLIAM CARLOS WILLIAMS, with whom she shares a preference for sparing use of METAPHOR and allusion. Written in the rhythms of speech, her poems often concern the nature of the creative process itself and have concentrated increasingly on political and feminist themes. Volumes which review her career include *Collected Earlier Poems, 1940–1960* (1979), *Poems 1960–1967* (1983) and *Selected Poems* (1986). *In the Night* (1968) is a work of fiction, and *The Poet in the World* (1973) and *Light up the Cave* (1981) are volumes of essays.

Levi, Peter (Chad Tigar) 1931– Poet, critic and translator. His tranquil, indirect poetry has gained a steadily growing reputation. The mature work gathered in *Collected Poems* (1976), *The Echoing Green* (a volume of ELEGIES; 1983) and *Shadow and Bone* (1989), merges PASTORAL with SYMBOLISM, presenting landscape and the seasons in a cryptic, subtly disjunctive manner. He has also published: translations of Eastern European poetry; criticism in *The Noise Made by Poems* (1977) and *The Art of Poetry* (1991), based on his lectures as professor of poetry at Oxford; an autobiography, *The Flutes of Autumn* (1983); travel books, including *The Light Garden of the Angel King: Journeys in Afghanistan* (1983); and DETECTIVE FICTION.

Leviathan*: or, *The Matter, Form, and Power of a Commonwealth Ecclesiastical and Civil A treatise on political philosophy by THOMAS HOBBES, published in 1651. Its title refers to the principle of sovereign rule. Hobbes's fundamental tenet is that, since man is not inherently peaceful nor prone to communal society in any stable fashion, the basis of government must be practical consent. Voluntary adherence to 'articles of peace' would result in a 'commonwealth' in which each individual acknowledged his obligation to the peaceful liberty of others on an equal basis to his own. Communal security would be vested in a person or assembly – the sovereign and indivisible power – ruling under a covenant between each individual governed, and subordinating all other potential power (such as the church) to its absolute influence. Without this cohesive contract, 'the life of man is solitary, poor, nasty, brutish and short'.

Levine, Norman 1923– Canadian short-story writer and novelist. His fiction evokes place and often concentrates on social outsiders, the problems of the writer's life and his own Jewish-Canadian upbringing. Volumes of short stories include *One Way Ticket* (1961), *I Don't Want to Know Anyone Too Well* (1971), *Thin Ice* (1979), *Why Do You Live So Far Away?* (1984) and *Something Happened Here* (1991). *Champagne Barn* (1984) is a collection drawn mainly from his earlier volumes. *The Angled Road* (1952) and *From a Seaside Town* (1970) are novels. Although he is best known for his fiction, he has also published poetry and an abrasive memoir, *Canada Made Me* (1958).

Levine, Philip 1928– American poet. *On the Edge* (1961), *Silent in America: Vivas for Those Who Failed* (1965) and *Not This Pig* (1968) established him as a bitter and ironic chronicler of the working classes of Detroit and southern California. *New Selected Poems* (1991) introduces the full range of his work. Levine has also translated contemporary Spanish poetry and published a collection of essays and interviews, *Don't Ask* (1981).

Lewes, George Henry 1817–78 Journalist, philosopher, scientist and critic. He is now best remembered as the companion of GEORGE ELIOT from 1854 until his death. His previous marriage prevented them from marrying. In his own right, Lewes founded and edited *THE LEADER* and *THE FORTNIGHTLY REVIEW*, as well as writing two novels, ten plays, books of dramatic criticism and a biography of Robespierre. His most important work was *The Life and Works of Goethe* (1855). Other writing include: on philosophy, *A Biographical History of Philosophy* (1845), *Comte's Philosophy of the Sciences* (1853) and *Problems of Life and Mind* (completed by George Eliot, 1873–9); and on science, *Seaside Studies* (1858) and *Studies of Animal Life* (1862).

Lewis, Alun 1915–44 Poet and short-story writer. He died in Burma from a wound which may have been self-inflicted. *Raiders' Dawn* (1942) contains poems about the identity and environment of industrial Wales, as well as love and wartime Britain. *The Last Inspection* (1942) contains wry and observant stories. Poems, stories and letters from India were collected in *Ha! Ha! Among the Trumpets* (introduced by ROBERT GRAVES; 1945) and *In the Green Tree* (1948).

Lewis, C(live) S(taples) 1898–1963 Critic, theologian, writer of SCIENCE FICTION and CHILDREN'S LITERATURE. He passed most of his academic career at Oxford, where his circle of friends ('The Inklings') included TOLKIEN, Hugo Dyson and CHARLES WILLIAMS. Between 1929 and 1931 he was converted back to Christianity, an experience charted in his spiritual autobiography, *Surprised by Joy* (1955), and the mainspring of all his subsequent writing, starting with *The Pilgrim's Regress* (1933) and his science-fiction trilogy, *Out of the Silent Planet* (1938), *Perelandra* (1939) and *That Hideous Strength* (1945). The first and still most famous of his scholarly books is *The Allegory of Love* (1936), a study of COURTLY LOVE, but others remain influential: *A Preface to Paradise Lost* (1942), the third volume of the Oxford History of English Literature, *English Literature in the Sixteenth Century, Excluding Drama* (1954), *Studies in Words* (1960) and *The Discarded Image* (1963). What brought him wide popularity, however, were his radio talks on Christianity during World War II (collected as *Mere Christianity*) and *The Screwtape Letters* (1942). The seven 'Narnia' stories for children, combining strong imagination and lively adventure with artfully concealed Christian parable, secured him another large audience; they began with *The Lion, the Witch and the Wardrobe* (1950) and closed with *The Last Battle* (1956). Lewis moved to Cambridge to occupy the first chair of medieval and Renaissance English in 1954 and in 1956 married Joy Davidman, who brought him much happiness before her death in 1960.

Lewis, Leopold 1828–90 Playwright. His single claim to fame was his adaptation of *Le Juif polonais* by Erckmann and Chatrian as THE BELLS (1871). None of his three later plays succeeded.

Lewis, M(atthew) G(regory) 1775–1818 Novelist, playwright and poet. After serving as attaché at the British Embassy at The Hague, he entered Parliament in 1796, the same year he published his GOTHIC NOVEL, *THE MONK*. Its sensational success earned him the nickname of 'Monk' Lewis and encouraged him to seek out the company of the rich, titled and famous. It is now almost the only work by which he is remembered, but Lewis wrote other novels (*The Bravo of Venice*, 1804; *Feudal Tyrants*, 1806), plays (*The Castle Spectre*, 1796; *The East Indian*, 1799; *Alphonso, King of Castile*, 1801; *The Wood Demon*, 1807) and several volumes of verse – though his best poem, 'Alonzo the Brave and the Fair Imogine', appeared in *The Monk*. His *Journal of a West Indian Proprietor*, posthumously published in 1834, describes his efforts to manage the Jamaican sugar plantations he had inherited and to improve conditions for the slaves.

Lewis, Norman 1908– Travel writer and novelist. One of the least egotistical travel writers, he has sought out countries and communities on the brink of radical, irreversible change: Cambodia, Laos and Vietnam in the final years of the French administration in *A Dragon Apparent* (1951) and Burma in *Golden Earth* (1952). His best books, perhaps, are *Naples '44* (1978), a compassionate war diary, and *Voices of the Old Sea* (1984), about the ancient fishing community at Farol in southern Spain. Lewis has also written: *The Honoured Society* (1964), a history of the Sicilian Mafia; *Jackdaw Cake* (1985), a characteristically quirky autobiography; and *The Missionaries* (1988), an attack on the activities of Christian evangelists among the tribes of the Amazon. *A View of the World* (1986) collects shorter travel pieces. His novels are unpretentious thrillers.

Lewis, (Harry) Sinclair 1885–1951 American novelist. His first success, *MAIN STREET* (1920), is a satirical portrayal of smalltown Midwestern life which looks back to his own roots in Sauk Center, Minnesota. *BABBITT* (1922), which continued his critique of provincial America, was followed by *Arrowsmith* (1925), about an altruistic doctor, *Elmer Gantry* (1927), about a sham revivalist minister, and *Dodsworth* (1929), about a retired car manufacturer travelling in Europe. In 1930 Lewis became the first American writer to receive the Nobel Prize. Though it demonstrates his continuing commitment to social and political change, his later work marked a decline in strength. *It Can't Happen Here* (1935), a warning about the possibility of fascism in the USA, was dramatized and produced by the FEDERAL THEATRE

PROJECT throughout the country with Lewis himself playing the lead. *Cass Timberlane* (1945), *Kingsblood Royal* (1947) and *The God-Seeker* (1949) return to the Minnesota setting of *Main Street*.

Lewis, (Percy) Wyndham 1882–1957 Artist, novelist and critic. The leading spirit of VORTICISM, he conducted its short-lived journal, *BLAST* (1914–15), with the help of EZRA POUND. His first novel, *Tarr* (1918), is an intellectual comedy set in pre-war Paris. *The Childermass* (1928), a remarkable fantasy located in a waste land outside heaven's gate, began a sequence eventually continued by *Monstre Gai* and *Malign Fiesta* (both 1955) and called *The Human Age*. *The Apes of God* (1930), a SATIRE mocking the fashionable racket of art and literature in the London of the 1920s, is often considered his best work. *The Revenge for Love* (1937) is set against the background of the Spanish Civil War. *Self Condemned* (1954), his last major novel, is semi-autobiographical. It reflects the disillusionment and isolation to which Lewis was increasingly condemned, not just by his fascist sympathies in the 1930s but by his gift for making enemies among his contemporaries. His political and critical essays, which embody this gift quite as markedly as his fiction, include *The Art of Being Ruled* (1925), *Time and Western Man* (1927), *Men without Art* (1934), *The Mysterious Mr Bull* (1938) and *The Writer and the Absolute* (1952). His short stories were collected in *The Wild Body* (1927) and *Rotting Hill* (1951). Chapters of his autobiography were published in *Blasting and Bombardiering* (1937) and *Rude Assignment* (1950).

Leyden, John 1775–1811 Polymath. He moved easily from composing a discourse on the colonization of North Africa to contributing 'The Elf King', a BALLAD, to M. G. LEWIS's *Tales of Wonder* (1801). A passion for ancient Scottish literature enabled him to help SIR WALTER SCOTT with *The Minstrelsy of the Scottish Border* (1802). Meanwhile, he qualified as a doctor in order to take up the post of assistant-surgeon in Madras, where he became a professor of Hindustani and also Judge of the Twenty-four Pergunnahs and Commissioner of the Court of Requests, and concerned himself with the agriculture, geology, public health and languages of the Mysore provinces. Scott wrote a memoir for *The Edinburgh Annual Register* of 1811 and commemorated him in *The Lord of the Isles* (1815). William Erskine completed Leyden's *Commentaries of Baber* (1826). Other posthumous works were *Poetical Remains* (1819), a translation of *Malay Annals* (1821) and *Poems and Ballads* (1858).

Liars, The A social comedy by HENRY ARTHUR JONES, performed in 1897. It elaborates on the need to lie in a hypocritical society, which turns an innocent friendship into a serious threat to the marriage of Lady Jessica Nepean.

Libeaus Desconus ('The Fair Unknown') A mid-14th-century VERSE ROMANCE perhaps by THOMAS CHESTRE, who wrote SIR LAUNFAL. It is an uninspired treatment of a story current in several European languages. Gawain's illegitimate son Gingelein (or Gauinglain) is brought up ignorant of his identity but distinguishes himself as a knight at Arthur's court, where he is called Libeaus Desconus. He encounters a serpent with a woman's face, bewitched until she kisses Gawain or one of his line. The kiss transforms her into a beautiful woman, and they marry.

Libel of English Policy, The A poem (or 'little book') provoked by the attack on Calais in 1436 and written in that year or 1437. It stresses the importance of maritime trade, and hence the need to control Dover and Calais with a powerful navy.

Liberal, The A periodical founded by SHELLEY and BYRON and edited by LEIGH HUNT. Only four issues appeared, from September 1822 to June 1823, before it succumbed to the problems created by Shelley's death, hostility between Byron and Hunt, Byron's departure for Greece and legal difficulties arising from the publication of Byron's THE VISION OF JUDGEMENT.

Liberator, The An American Abolitionist weekly journal founded by WILLIAM LLOYD GARRISON in 1831 and edited by him until 1865. Its circulation was never higher than 3000, but its radical stance aroused vocal and violent antagonism in South and North alike.

Liberty, On An essay by JOHN STUART MILL, first published in 1859. He regarded it as his most important work. It is based on the realization that democracy does not of itself guarantee freedom, since public opinion could be as repressive of minority rights as any other form of dictatorship. Mill therefore sought to devise a principle by which individual liberty might be legitimated and interference with this liberty limited only to those occasions where its exercise would involve harm to others.

Life in London: or, The Day and Night Scenes of Jerry Hawthorn Esq. and His Elegant Friend Corinthian Tom, Accompanied by Bob Logic, The Oxonian, in Their Rambles and Sprees through the Metropolis A boisterously comic description of life in Regency London by PIERCE EGAN THE ELDER, serialized in 1820–1 and published in book form in 1821, with illustrations by Robert and GEORGE CRUIKSHANK. In a series of cheerfully coarse episodes Corinthian Tom, a Regency rake, helped by his facetious friend Bob Logic, shows the sights of the capital to his country cousin, Jerry Hawthorn. The book was enormously popular with young men who aspired to a dashing life, though Egan himself seems to have had second thoughts. In The Finish to the Adventures of Tom, Jerry and Logic, in Their Pursuits through Life in and out of London (1828) all the characters except Jerry come to miserable ends.

Life of Samuel Johnson LL.D., The JAMES BOSWELL's biography of his friend, published in 1791. It remains by common consent the greatest biography in the language.

Because of the date of their meeting, the treatment of the last 20 years of Johnson's life occupies three-quarters of the book, but his skill in reconstructing the early years is quite remarkable. He worked always with a master-plan in mind and was tireless in his search. His training as a lawyer helped him sift the evidence of friends and to operate forensically on Johnson himself: he was able to draw him out as no one else could. Johnson was actually made more 'Johnsonian' by Boswell's transformation of his conversation and doings into the scenic forms and polished prose of the published Life. One important aspect of the Life's greatness is suggested by its full title: 'The whole exhibiting a view of literature and literary men in Great-Britain, for near half a century, during which he flourished'. Johnson's centrality in 18th-century letters is established not only by Boswell's record of his life and conversation, but also by the book's success in placing him in a literary and cultural context.

Life on the Mississippi A book by MARK TWAIN published in 1883. Part history, part geography, part memoir and part travelogue, it opens with a brief history of

the river before turning to Twain's own childhood, youth and life as a river pilot. A second half, added in 1890, describes a return trip to the scenes of his youth and ruminates on the detrimental effects of Southern romanticism, which he links to the historical romances of SIR WALTER SCOTT.

Life's Handicap: Being Stories of Mine Own People A collection of 27 stories by KIPLING, published in 1891. Almost all reflect his experiences of India. One group, which includes 'The Courting of Dinah Shadd' and 'On Greenhow Hill', deals with the characters who also appear in SOLDIERS THREE. Another, which includes 'The End of the Passage' and 'The Limitations of Pambe Serang', consists of horror stories.

Light in August A novel by WILLIAM FAULKNER, published in 1932. Pregnant and unwed, Lena Grove arrives in Jefferson, Mississippi, in search of Lucas Burch, her baby's father. Instead she finds Byron Bunch, a hard-working, dependable bachelor who falls in love with her. Flashback scenes provide an account of the early life of Joe Christmas, an orphan unsure of his racial origins, and of the circumstances which drive him to kill his lover Joanna Burden. He is denounced by Lucas Burch and captured. He escapes and takes refuge with Gail Hightower, a disgraced and reclusive minster, but is shot by the National Guard. Hightower withdraws again into private reverie. With her baby and Byron Bunch, Lena continues her search for Burch.

Lilliburlero An anti-Catholic song which first became popular with the army in Ireland in the 1680s. Lord Thomas Wharton probably wrote the words and perhaps the tune, which was also once attributed to Purcell. It is a favourite of Uncle Toby's in STERNE's TRISTRAM SHANDY, and is included in THOMAS PERCY's Reliques of Ancient English Poetry (1786). Radio listeners know it as the identifying tune of the BBC World Service.

Lillo, George c. 1693–1739 Playwright. His most important works, THE LONDON MERCHANT (1731) and THE FATAL CURIOSITY (1736), were pioneering examples of bourgeois or domestic TRAGEDY, abandoning the world of kings and courtiers to insist on the seriousness of high emotion in ordinary people lower down the social ladder. Lillo also wrote: Sylvia: or, The Country Burial (1730), a BALLAD OPERA; The Christian Hero (1735); Marina (1738), based on SHAKESPEARE's PERICLES; Elmerick: or, Justice Triumphant (1740); and an adaptation of the Elizabethan tragedy, ARDEN OF FEVERSHAM (1759). Britannia and Batavia, a MASQUE, was not performed.

Lilly, William 1602–81 Astrologer. He wrote a number of pamphlets containing 'Prophesies' and published an annual almanac from 1644. Monarchy, or No Monarchy, in England (1651) claimed to have foretold the execution of Charles I.

limerick A form of nonsense verse with a strict rhyme scheme (aabba). Its name is said to derive from parties where each guest contributed a verse followed by the chorus 'Will you come up to Limerick?' The form was first used in the 1820s and made popular by EDWARD LEAR. An example is: 'There was a young lady of Clyde/ 'Twas of eating green apples she died./ The apples fermented/ Inside the lamented/ And made cider inside her inside.'

Linacre, Thomas ?1460–1524 Scholar and founder of the Royal College of Physicians (1518). He was a friend of ERASMUS and THOMAS MORE who, with Henry VIII and Cardinal Wolsey, were also his patients. One of the first

English scholars to cultivate the study of Greek, he translated many of Galen's works into Latin. His Latin grammar, *Rudimenta graminatices*, was originally written for the future Queen Mary, to whom he was Latin tutor.

Lindsay, Lady **Anne** 1750–1825 Scottish poet and diarist. Her journals, edited by D. Fairbridge as *Lady Anne Barnard at the Cape, 1797–1802* (1924), are a valuable source of information on the first British occupation of the Cape. She is also known as the author of the BALLAD 'Auld Robin Gray' (1771) and 'Why Tarries my Love?' (1805).

Lindsay, Sir **David** See LYNDSAY.

Lindsay, Jack 1900–90 Australian writer, editor and publisher. The son of NORMAN LINDSAY, he lived in England after 1926. A prolific writer who published over 120 books, as well as editing literary journals and founding the Fanfrolico Press, he received numerous awards in Australia and elsewhere but comparatively little critical recognition. His works include translations of Aristophanes, Petronius and other classical authors and a number of historical novels and verseplays. *The Roaring Twenties* (1960), which gives a vivid portrait of Sydney literary life in the early 1920s, is among his most interesting works. It has been reissued as the second part of his autobiographical trilogy, *Life Rarely Tells* (1982).

Lindsay, Norman (Alfred William) 1879–1969 Australian artist, novelist and writer of CHILDREN'S LITERATURE. His first novel, *A Curate in Bohemia* (1913), was followed by an enduring fantasy for children, *The Magic Pudding* (1918). *Redheap* (1930), *Saturdee* (1933) and *Halfway to Anywhere* (1947) form a trilogy about boyhood and adolescence. Lindsay also published three volumes of essays, *Creative Effort* (1920), *Hyperborea: Two Fantastic Travel Essays* (1928) and *Madam Life's Lovers* (1929).

Lindsay, (Nicholas) Vachel 1879–1931 American poet. *General William Booth Enters Into Heaven and Other Poems* (1913), *The Congo and Other Poems* (1914), *The Chinese Nightingale and Other Poems* (1917) were welcomed for their dramatic, incisive rhythms and vivid imagery drawn from a broad American background. His *Golden Book of Springfield* (1920), about a Utopia based on the 'Gospel of Beauty', expressed his idealistic belief in the need to reconcile 'culture and manliness'. Lindsay enjoyed a brief popularity as a reader of his own poetry before sinking into relative obscurity. His last published work before his suicide was a volume of political essays, *The Litany of Washington Street* (1929). *Collected Poems* (1923) was revised in 1925. A volume of *Letters* appeared in 1979.

Lindsay of Pittscottie, Robert ?1500–?65 Author of *The History and Chronicles of Scotland*, or at least of that part from the accession of James II in 1437 until 1565. The continuation of the narrative up to 1604 is by another hand. The work is Protestant in sympathy, and shows considerable inaccuracy and confusion over dates. It exists in several early manuscript copies and was first printed in Robert Freebairn's edition (1728).

Lingard, John 1771–1851 Historian. *The History of England from the First Invasion of the Romans to the Accession of William and Mary* (1819–30) enjoyed considerable success for its objectivity, careful use of original documents and balanced view of the Reformation. A Catholic priest, Lingard also wrote a *New Version of the Four Gospels* (1836).

Linklater, Eric 1899–1974 Novelist and writer for radio. His most successful novel was *Private Angelo* (1946), a comic account of post-war reorganization in Italy. *White Maa's Saga* and *Poet's Pub* (both 1929) are set in the Orkney Islands, and *Juan in America* (1931) is satirical. His work for radio includes 'conversation pieces' such as *The Great Ship* and *Rabelais Replies* and a play, *Crisis in Heaven* (all 1944). *Husband of Delilah* (1962) is the best known of his later works. *The Man on My Back* (1941) and *A Year of Space* (1953) are autobiographical.

Linton, Eliza Lynn 1822–98 Novelist. She worked for THE MORNING CHRONICLE, THE SATURDAY REVIEW and ALL THE YEAR ROUND. Her best novels are *The True History of Joshua Davidson* (1872), *Patricia Kenball* (1874) and *The Autobiography of Christopher Kirkland* (1885). In spite of her own success in an independent life, she was a vehement anti-feminist, as *The Girl of the Period and Other Essays* (1883) shows.

Lippard, George 1822–54 American novelist. He was best known for sensational books about the immorality of large cities, such as *The Quaker City: or, The Monks of Monk Hall* (1844) and *New York: Its Upper Ten and Lower Million* (1854). He also wrote romantic historical novels, including *Blanche of Brandywine* (1846) and *Legends of Mexico* (1847).

Lippmann, Walter 1889–1974 American journalist. In the course of his long career, which twice earned him the PULITZER PRIZE, he established himself as an important spokesman for liberalism. Of his books, *A Preface to Politics* (1913), *Drift and Mastery* (1914), *The Stakes of Diplomacy* (1915), *The Political Scene* (1919), *Public Opinion* (1922), *The Phantom Public* (1925), *A Preface to Morals* (1929), *The Method of Freedom* (1934) and *The Good Society* (1937) advocate public virtue, individual freedom and *laissez-faire* economics. Later works include studies of foreign policy.

Listener, The A weekly magazine published by the BBC in 1929–91. It had a strong literary bias, printing articles, talks and poems by many established writers, particularly during the editorship of J. R. ACKERLEY in 1935–59.

litotes A figure of speech which uses understatement for rhetorical effect, a positive being expressed by the negative of an opposite, e. g. 'Shakespeare's was no mean achievement'.

Little Dorrit A novel by DICKENS, published in monthly parts in 1855–7 and in volume form in 1857.

Amy, 'Little Dorrit', is born in the Marshalsea, the debtors' prison where her father William Dorrit has spent so many years that he is called 'the father of the Marshalsea'. They are befriended by Arthur Clennam, recently returned from a long period abroad, whose mother employs her as a seamstress. William Dorrit inherits a fortune, leaves the Marshalsea and travels in style to Italy, where he dies, finally unable to remember anything but his years in prison. Clennam, fighting his own battles with the Circumlocution Office, becomes victim of a gigantic fraud perpetrated by the financier Merdle and is sentenced to the Marshalsea. Little Dorrit finds him there, and the couple eventually marry. A complex sub-plot involves Clennam's mother, a gloomy and bigoted paralytic, and two villains, the Frenchman Rigaud (alias Blandois) and Jeremiah Flintwich. The latter's wife Affery is a memorable character, as are Flora Finching and 'Mr F's aunt', Little Dorrit's lovesick suitor John Chivery, the self-tormenting Miss Wade and the highly correct Mrs General.

Little Lord Fauntleroy See BURNETT, FRANCES HODGSON.

Little Review, The A periodical based successively in Chicago, New York and Paris from 1914 to 1929, and edited by Margaret Anderson and Jane Heap. It published work by T. S. ELIOT, HEMINGWAY, POUND (also its foreign editor) and YEATS, and gained notoriety when the editors were found guilty of obscenity in 1920 for publishing a portion of JOYCE's ULYSSES.

Little Women See ALCOTT, LOUISA MAY.

Lively [née Greer]**, Penelope (Margaret)** 1933- Novelist and writer of CHILDREN'S LITERATURE. A preoccupation with the effect of the past on the present, often manifested in a supernatural manner, is the hallmark of her books. She began as a writer for children with *Astercote* (1970), *The Wild Hunt of Hagworthy* (1971), *The Whispering Knights* (1971) and *The Ghost of Thomas Kempe* (1973), in which the ghost of a 17th-century sorcerer returns to haunt a present-day family. In *A Stitch in Time* (1976) the heroine becomes obsessed with a sampler embroidered by a girl who lived in the house more than 100 years before. Stories for younger children include *A House Inside Out* (1987). Her first adult novel, *The Road To Lichfield* (1977), was followed by *Judgement Day* (1980), *According to Mark* (1984) and *Moon Tiger* (1987), which won the BOOKER PRIZE.

Liverpool poets A group of poets, Adrian Henri (1932-), Roger McGough (1937-) and Brian Patten (1946-), committed to reviving poetry as a public, performed art. They flourished in the 1960s in Liverpool, strongly influenced by pop music and culture. *The Mersey Sound* (1967), in the Penguin Modern Poets series, is an anthology.

Lives of the Poets, The Biographies by SAMUEL JOHNSON, published in 1779-81. He originally proposed to begin with CHAUCER, though in the event the *Lives* started with COWLEY. Even so, they ran to 52 in all and amounted to a comprehensive review of the previous century of verse – a major undertaking for a writer then in his 70s. They combine biographical sketch, analysis of character and subjective opinion. Many pieces have become landmarks of literary criticism: the lives of DRYDEN and GAY, for example, and the dissection of METAPHYSICAL POETRY in the life of Cowley. Others, like the life of SOMERVILLE, are masterly achievements of Johnson's style of prose.

Livesay, Dorothy 1909- Canadian poet. Her first collection, *Green Pitcher* (1928), was followed by works like *Day and Night* (1944) reflecting her left-wing activism during the 1930s and 1940s. *Collected Poems: The Two Seasons* (1972) provides the most comprehensive sample of her work up to this date. Later volumes include *Ice Age* (1975), *The Woman I Am* (1977), *The Phases of Love* (1983), a retrospective collection of previously unpublished love poems, and *Feeling the Worlds* (1985). *The Self-Completing Tree* (1986) is her selection from almost 60 years of writing. She has also published a volume of autobiographical short stories, *A Winnipeg Childhood* (1973), a memoir, *Right Hand, Left Hand* (1977) and a novel, *The Husband* (1989).

Livings, Henry 1929- Playwright. His anarchically cheerful plays, which show special sympathy for the underdog and a feeling for North Country life, include *Stop It, Whoever You Are* (1961), *Big Soft Nellie* (1961), *Nil Carborundum* (1962), *Kelly's Eye* (1963), *Eh?* (1964) and *Stop the Children's Laughter* (1992).

Liyong, Taban lo 1939- Ugandan essayist and poet. His first book, *The Last Word* (1969), introduced an idiosyncratic writer who argues for what he calls 'cultural synthesism', an attempt to make sense out of the fragmented present. *Eating Chiefs: Lwo Culture from Lolwe to Malkal* (1970) sets out to create a new medium which can call on African traditional culture and yet be appropriate to the modern world. He has also written short stories, *Fixions* (1969), and poetry, including *Frantz Fanon's Uneven Ribs* (1971), *Another Nigger Dead* (1972), *Ballads of Underdevelopment* (1976) and a 'funeral dirge', *Meditations of Taban lo Liyong* (1978).

Llewellyn, Richard [Lloyd, Richard Dafydd Vivian Llewellyn] 1907-83 Novelist and playwright. He achieved early success with plays, *Poison Pen* (1937) and *Noose* (1947), but gained lasting recognition with his novel, *How Green was My Valley* (1939), set in a Welsh mining community. Its blend of lyricism, realism and humour has represented something quintessentially 'Welsh' for many readers. Other novels included *None But the Lonely Heart* (1943) and *A Few Flowers for Shiner* (1950), both about the London slums. A sequence of spy novels, *The End of the Rug* (1968), *But We Didn't Get the Fox* (1969), *White Horse to Banbury Cross* (1971) and *The Night is a Child* (1972), concerned a British agent turned industrialist, Edmund Trothe. *A Night of Bright Stars* (1979), about a Brazilian pioneer aviator, was set in *fin-de-siècle* Paris.

Locke, Alain (Leroy) 1886-1954 Black American editor, critic, philosopher, art historian and educator. He is usually remembered for his contribution to the HARLEM RENAISSANCE in editing 'Harlem, Mecca of the New Negro', a special edition of *The Survey* magazine, and *The New Negro*, the first literary anthology of the Renaissance. Both appeared in 1925. Other work includes *Plays of Negro Life* (with Montgomery Gregory; 1927), *The Negro and His Music* (1936), *Negro Art: Past and Present* (1936) and *The Negro in Art: A Pictorial Record of the Negro Artist and of the Negro Theme in Art* (1940).

Locke, John 1632-1704 Philosopher. As student and teacher at Oxford he interested himself in Greek, rhetoric, medicine and the new experimental science being developed by NEWTON, ROBERT BOYLE, WILLIAM HARVEY and others. In 1667 he became physician to the 1st Earl of Shaftesbury's household, a position which led to his exile in 1682-8 for suspected complicity in Shaftesbury's plots. He held various government appointments on his return to England. *Letters concerning Toleration* (1689-92) advocated religious freedom for all except atheists and Catholics. *Two Treatises on Government* (1690) rejected the theory of Divine Right, proposing a social contract between governors and governed. His *ESSAY CONCERNING HUMAN UNDERSTANDING* (1690) began as the attempt to answer the question, 'what objects our understandings were, or were not, fitted to deal with'. Locke also wrote on money and education, and considered faith in *The Reasonableness of Christianity As Delivered in the Scriptures* (1695), which contributed to the development of DEISM. Attacks on his work prompted him to two *Vindications* (1695 and 1697). His last years found him increasingly preoccupied with religion; two posthumous publications were *A Paraphrase and Notes on the Epistle of St Paul to the Galatians* (1705) and *A Discourse on Miracles* (1716).

Locke's view of society was based on his belief in religious toleration, parliamentary democracy and the *laissez-faire* system of commerce and trade. In religion, he was an analytical Christian whose contempt for traditional theological argument earned him the wrath of the church. As befitted a man who had become a Fellow of the Royal Society in 1666, he followed the principles of the new experimental science in his investigation of the mind. Though he stimulated later metaphysics, he was not concerned with speculation, appealing constantly to experience, from which reason and knowledge proceed.

Lockhart, John Gibson 1794–1854 Biographer, critic and novelist. As a shaping influence on BLACKWOOD'S EDINBURGH MAGAZINE during its early years and as editor of THE QUARTERLY REVIEW from 1824 to 1853, he earned himself the nickname of 'The Scorpion' by his savage and uncompromising criticism, most notoriously of the so-called COCKNEY SCHOOL of writers. The author of a famous biography of his father-in-law, SIR WALTER SCOTT (1838), he also published a life of BURNS (1828) and several novels.

Locksley Hall A poem by TENNYSON, published in *Poems* (1842). Beyond its narrative of the hero's frustrated love for his cousin Amy, it is invested with ideas which shaped the Victorian frame of mind: the middle-class intellectual's fear of encroaching democracy, material optimism, emigration, and a touch of Carlylean thought implicit in the doctrine of active participation.

Lodge, David (John) 1935– Novelist and critic. He was professor of modern English literature at the University of Birmingham from 1976 to 1987. The literary criticism in *The Language of Fiction* (1966), *The Novelist at the Crossroads* (1971), *Working with Structuralism* (1981) and *After Bakhtin* (1990) combines the same fundamental adherence to a traditionally humanist definition of literature with a prolonged flirtation with STRUCTURALISM and successive critical movements apparent in his fiction. Notable experiments include: *Changing Places* (1975), a satirical 'campus' novel, and its sequel *Small World* (1983), whose structure mimics Arthurian romance; *Nice Work* (1988), an industrial novel self-consciously in the tradition of ELIZABETH GASKELL; *Paradise News* (1991), about tourism; and *Therapy* (1995). *How Far Can You Go?* (1978), about the problems of Catholicism, returns to an earlier mode of realism.

Lodge, Thomas ?1557–1625 Pamphleteer, poet, playwright and author of prose romances. His life seems to have been as adventurously miscellaneous as his writings. After Oxford, he briefly studied law, took part in privateering expeditions to the Canaries (1588) and South America (1591), qualified as a doctor, converted to Catholicism and spent periods of exile on the Continent, particularly after the Gunpowder Plot in 1605. His earliest work is a pamphlet, *A Defence of Poetry, Music and Stage Plays* (1580), answering GOSSON's *The School of Abuse*. It was followed by various pamphlets and sermons on moral and religious themes, less significant than his poetry: an EPYLLION, *Scillae's Metamorphosis* (1589; republished as *Glaucus and Scilla*, 1610); a sonnet cycle, *Phillis* (1593); and a collection of satires, *A Fig for Momus* (1595). His most successful prose romance is *ROSALYNDE* (1590), the source for *As You Like It*. It was preceded by *Frobonius and Prisceria* (1584) and followed by *Robert Second Duke of Normandy* (1591), *William Longbeard* (1593) and *A Margarite of America* (1596), a story he claimed to have found in South America. Lodge wrote two undistinguished plays: *The Wounds of Civil War* (printed in 1594, probably performed *c.* 1586), about Roman history, and *A Looking Glass for London and England* (1594), a morality play in collaboration with GREENE. He apparently wrote little after 1600.

Lofting, Hugh (John) 1886–1947 Writer of CHILDREN'S LITERATURE. His stories originated in the illustrated letters he sent to his family from the front in World War I. In *The Story of Dr Dolittle* (1920) the vague, benign hero learns how to address the many animals who share his home and dominate his surgery. They all sail to Africa to cure a deadly monkey disease. Further adventures are described in many other books, all illustrated with Lofting's simple drawings.

Logue, Christopher 1926– Poet, translator and playwright. *Wand and Quadrant* (1953) and *Devil, Maggot and Son* (1958) were followed by *Songs* (1959), which revealed his conversion to radical socialism and his debt to Brecht, also apparent in stage plays like *Jazzetry* (1959) and *Antigone* (1960). *Ode to the Dodo: Poems 1953–78* (1981) confirms him as a writer of populist lyric and SATIRE with a strong sense of the possibilities of the voice. *War Music* (1981), *Kings* (1991) and *The Husbands* (1994) are free adaptations of Homer's *Iliad*.

Lolita A novel by VLADIMIR NABOKOV, published in France in 1955 and in the USA in 1958. Between these dates it had begun its rise from the status of underground classic, supposedly pornographic in its account of Humbert Humbert's hopeless love for the underage Lolita, to that of a work exploring the discrepancies of texts, languages and cultures and belonging more to the literature of COURTLY LOVE than to any other defined category. It is presented as a confession, edited and introduced by an unhelpful Freudian psychiatrist, written by Humbert before his death in prison while awaiting trial for the murder of his rival, Clare Quilty.

Lollards, The Originally a group of Oxford followers of WYCLIF (*c.* 1320–84). It grew despite continual persecution, as well as recantations by several members, but was driven underground after suffering military defeat by Henry V in 1414. It resurfaced several times well into the 16th century. The Lollards' main demands were for freely available vernacular translations of the Bible (see also BIBLE IN ENGLISH), and a reduction in the materialism and powers of the Church. They denied the value of pilgrimages and prayers for the dead, the necessity of confession and the validity of the doctrine of transubstantiation.

The most important Lollard writings are the two translations of the Bible (*c.* 1375–96), though Wyclif's own contribution seems to have been limited to an unfinished version of the New Testament. Many sermons, tracts and commentaries attributed to Wyclif are apparently by followers such as his secretary, John Purvey, drawing partly on Wyclif's Latin writings. They attack the worldliness and corruption of the orthodox Church, and especially friars. See also JACK UPLAND.

London A poem by SAMUEL JOHNSON in IMITATION of Juvenal's Third Satire, published in 1738. The Latin original, a popular model for Augustan poets, presents a dialogue with a friend leaving the metropolis for the country. In Johnson's version the poet Thales, about to leave London for Wales, delivers an eloquent tirade against the 'thoughtless age' in which he lives, denouncing courtiers and flatterers as well as fashion.

London, Jack [Chaney, John Griffith] 1876–1916 American novelist, short-story writer and essayist. In his restless, adventurous youth, begun on the Oakland waterfront, he sailed on a sealing voyage, agitated for socialist reform and took part in the Klondike gold rush (1897). The Klondike is the setting for his first collection of stories, *The Son of the Wolf* (1900), his first novel, *A Daughter of the Snows* (1902), and his first great popular success, THE CALL OF THE WILD (1903), which – like the later *White Fang* (1906) – has a dog as its hero. Subsequent collections of short stories include *Love of Life* (1907), *Lost Face* (1910), *South Sea Tales* (1911), and *The Red One* (1918). A second novel, *The Cruise of the Dazzler* (1902), was based on his experiences as an oyster pirate. *The People of the Abyss* (1903) draws on his observation of the slums of London. THE SEA-WOLF (1904) chronicles the voyage of a ship run by a ruthless captain. *The War of the Classes* (1905) is a socialist treatise and *The Game* (1905) a novel about prizefighting. *Before Adam* (1906) attempts to recreate a prehistoric community while THE IRON HEEL (1908) is set in the near future. MARTIN EDEN (1909), more directly autobiographical, deals with his attempts to become a successful writer and to come to terms with his success. *Burning Daylight* (1910) returns to the Klondike, *Smoke Bellew* (1912) to the Yukon. *The Valley of the Moon* (1912), another socialist novel, is about a working-class couple who escape from the harshness of industrial life in Oakland to an idyllic life on the land. *John Barleycorn* (1913), an autobiographical memoir, deals with London's struggle against alcohol. *The Star Rover* (1915) is the story of a San Quentin lifer's spiritual struggles. Hugely successful but never at ease with his success, he worked as a foreign correspondent, travelled widely and died at the age of 40, perhaps by suicide. *The Human Drift*, a socialist treatise, appeared posthumously in 1917.

London Assurance A comedy by BOUCICAULT, staged in 1841. Sir Harcourt Courtly, a vain widower, plans to marry Grace Harkaway, an heiress 45 years his junior, and goes to Oak Hall to meet her. He is anticipated by his son Charles who, with the help of the sporting Lady Gay Spanker, eventually wins both Grace and his father's forgiveness.

London Labour and the London Poor See MAYHEW, HENRY.

London Lickpenny A satirical poem from the first half of the 14th century, surviving in two versions. It was at one time wrongly attributed to LYDGATE. The adventures of a countryman who comes to London serve as the occasion for vivid descriptions of street life.

London Magazine, The The earliest journal of this name was published in 1732–85. Its more famous successor, edited by John Scott, appeared in 1820–9 in rivalry with *BLACKWOOD'S EDINBURGH MAGAZINE*. During its brief life it published DE QUINCEY's *CONFESSIONS OF AN ENGLISH OPIUM-EATER* and LAMB's *ESSAYS OF ELIA*, as well as poetry by KEATS and CLARE. Its staff included HAZLITT, THOMAS HOOD and MARY RUSSELL MITFORD.

The *London Magazine* is also the name of a monthly journal with a strong international bias, founded by JOHN LEHMANN in 1954. TONY HARRISON and Jaroslav Seifert are among the writers whose work it has discovered and propagated.

London Merchant, The: *or, The History of George Barnwell* A tragedy by LILLO, produced and published in 1731. It is often called *George Barnwell*, after the BALLAD from which its plot is taken. It follows the downward path of an apprentice seduced into robbery and murder by a courtesan, Millwood, with whom he is eventually hanged. Barnwell is contrasted with his fellow apprentice, Trueman, who remains faithful to their master, the honest Thorowgood. Written in prose, *The London Merchant* was a pioneering example of bourgeois or domestic tragedy (see TRAGEDY).

London Review of Books, The A fortnightly paper devoted to literature, the arts and political philosophy, modelled on the prestigious *NEW YORK REVIEW OF BOOKS* and founded by Karl Miller in 1979.

Long Day's Journey Into Night A play by EUGENE O'NEILL, produced in 1956 and awarded a PULITZER PRIZE. It takes place during a single day in 1912 at the summer home of the Tyrone family. Its members, to some extent modelled on O'Neill's own family, are: James Tyrone, an actor; the drug-addicted mother, Mary; and their children, the alcoholic James Jr and Edmund.

Longest Journey, The A novel by E. M. FORSTER, published in 1907. The title comes from SHELLEY's *Epipsychidion*: 'Who travel to their home among the dead ... / With one chained friend ... / The dreariest and the longest journey go.' It refers to the unhappy marriage between the lame and delicate Frederick Elliot, nicknamed Rickie, and Agnes Pembroke, whose original fiancé, the athletic Gerald Dawes, dies in a sporting accident. On leaving Cambridge, Rickie accepts a teaching post from Agnes's brother Herbert at Sawston, a minor public school. His growing disillusionment with the values of Sawston and the Pembrokes coincides with his interest in the drunken but amiable Stephen Wonham, who turns out to be his half-brother, the son of Rickie's mother. Resolved to help Stephen, Rickie leaves Agnes but is killed trying to rescue him from an accident.

Longfellow, Henry Wadsworth 1807–82 American poet. A professor of languages at Bowdoin College and then, in 1836–54, at Harvard, he became one of the most popular poets of his day in Britain as well as America. The mixture of sentiment and didacticism in such pieces as 'A Psalm of Life', 'Footsteps of Angels' and 'The Reaper and the Flowers' in *Voices of the Night* (1839) and 'The Wreck of the Hesperus' and 'The Village Blacksmith' in *Ballads and Other Poems* (1842) perfectly expressed the atmosphere of the Victorian parlour and fireside. Longfellow's later work reflects his reading of European epics and his interest in establishing an American mythology. It includes EVANGELINE (1847); THE SONG OF HIAWATHA (1855); *The Courtship of Miles Standish* (1858); three series of *Tales of a Wayside Inn*, modelled on CHAUCER's *CANTERBURY TALES*, the first (1863) containing the famous 'Paul Revere's Ride'; and a trilogy, *Christus* (1872). His translation of Dante appeared in 1867.

Longley, Michael 1939– Irish poet. His relatively slender output includes *Poems 1963–1983* (1985), combining earlier collections and new work, and *Gorse Fires* (1991). A versatile lyric poet, he explores strange moments of fulfilment or misgiving and describes love, grief, visited landscapes, country lore, birds and animals. In his imaginative recoil from contemporary political violence and celebration of nature's permanencies he seeks identification not only with his friends SEAMUS HEANEY and DEREK MAHON but also with the lyric poets of Greece and Rome and the poets of World War I. He has also edited a symposium on the arts in Ulster (*Causeway*; 1971) and an anthology of children's verse.

Longstreet, Augustus Baldwin 1790–1870 American writer. He was at various times a college president, editor of the *States Rights Sentinel* (which he founded in 1834), clergyman and jurist. He is best remembered for his *Georgia Scenes, Characters and Incidents, &c., in the First*

Half Century of the Republic (1835), a collection of humorous sketches. A pioneering regionalist, he also wrote short stories and a novel, *Master William Mitten* (1864).

Lonsdale, Frederick 1881–1954 Playwright. He made his reputation with social comedies dealing ironically with polite manners and modern marriage. *The Last of Mrs Cheney* (1925) remains popular.

Look Back in Anger A play by OSBORNE, performed at the ROYAL COURT THEATRE in 1956, when it spearheaded the post-war revival of the British theatre. Its contemporary importance was not dependent on its flimsy plot – in which Jimmy Porter, a redbrick graduate, deserts his wife for her middle-class actress friend and is precariously reconciled with his wife at the end – but on Porter's articulate anger. His tirades against the complacency of the English establishment won Osborne a reputation as leader of the ANGRY YOUNG MEN.

Looking Backward: 2000–1887 An influential Utopian novel by EDWARD BELLAMY, published in 1888. It is narrated by Julian West, a Bostonian, who falls asleep in 1887 and wakes in the year 2000 to find himself in a brilliant new society. Dr Leete explains how America came to adopt a rigorous socialist programme which has organized labour according to a system like military service. Great political, technological and sociological achievements are described in vivid detail. Edith Leete, a descendant of his former fiancée, returns his love.

Lord Jim A novel by CONRAD, published in 1900. Its crux is Jim's betrayal of his duty as chief mate of the *Patna* in deserting the steamship and its cargo of pilgrims after it has struck a submerged object. In Aden the narrator, Marlow, observes Jim at the Court of Inquiry where he has elected to face the consequences of his action. Being stripped of his master's certificate brings public but not spiritual atonement. Jim takes a variety of jobs ashore but only a position as agent at the remote trading post of Patusan promises him real freedom. There he becomes Tuan, or Lord Jim, and is helped towards serenity by his relationship with Jewel. When Gentleman Brown and his fellow thieves arrive, he pledges to the elderly chief, Doramin, that they will leave without bloodshed. His misplaced trust leads to the death of Doramin's son and, accepting responsibility, Jim allows Doramin to shoot him.

Lord of the Flies WILLIAM GOLDING's first novel, published in 1954. It is an inverted Victorian boys' adventure story, with savage knowledge rather than blithe innocence at the core of the fable. Marooned on a desert island after a plane crash, a party of English schoolboys quickly degenerates into vindictive barbarism. The roguish Jack emerges as a ruthless dictator, while the fat and clumsy Piggy is eventually killed with the Christlike Simon. It is only when the boys are rescued by a British destroyer that Piggy's well-meaning friend Ralph realizes the true extent of their depravity.

Lord of the Rings, The See TOLKIEN, J. R. R.

Lorna Doone: *A Romance of Exmoor* A novel by R. D. BLACKMORE, published in 1869. It is set on Exmoor during the late 17th century. Monmouth's rebellion and Judge Jeffreys form part of the background to the story. Young John Ridd, a yeoman, is determined to avenge his father's death at the hands of the Doones, an evil clan which pursues a career of murder and theft from a nearby valley. He also falls in love with Lorna, daughter of the clan's chieftain. He and his friends bring the Doones to account and rescue the girl. The discovery that she is really the daughter of a noble family makes

him acutely aware of the difference in their positions, but his reluctance is overcome and the story ends happily.

Lothair A novel by BENJAMIN DISRAELI, published in 1870. Lothair is an orphaned nobleman whose guardians are Lord Culloden and Grandison, a clergyman who embraces Catholicism and becomes a cardinal. Lothair joins Garibaldi's campaign in Italy, where his wealth makes him a target for the Catholics. Cardinal Grandison, Clare Arundel and Monsignor Catesby try to convert him. Their influence is resisted by Lord Culloden, Lady Corisande and Theodora, who dies fighting for Garibaldi. Lothair eventually returns to England, unconverted, and marries Lady Corisande.

Lotos-Eaters, The A poem by TENNYSON, published in 1832 and revised for *Poems* (1842). Its subject comes from Book IX of the *Odyssey*, where Odysseus' sailors find an island inhabited by people who eat only the fruit of the lotos plant, which fills them with languorous contentment. Tennyson uses all his skill with verbal music in evoking the desire to withdraw from the world of work and competitive struggle.

Love, Nicholas Translator. The scanty records suggest that he came to prominence in 1409–10, when he was made rector, and then prior, of the Carthusian house at Mount Grace, Yorkshire. His translation of the *Meditationes vitae Christi* (once attributed to Bonaventura) as the *Mirror of the Blessed Life of Jesu Christ* omits some of the doctrinal material of its source to concentrate on Christ's humanity, treating the Gospels with simple realism and emotional intensity. The late medieval church used it to combat the LOLLARDS and the general demand for the translation of the Bible.

Love and Mr Lewisham A novel by H. G. WELLS, published in 1900. As a young schoolmaster, Lewisham dreams of being a scholar and man of influence. His ambition is matched, and appears threatened by, his attraction to the more experienced Ethel Henderson. His idealism is also offset by inadequate figures of authority in the adult world: Bonover, the shallow headmaster who dismisses him, and Ethel's father, the devious Chaffery. Later, Lewisham follows a principled pathway as a gifted student in London, although distracted by the attentions of the bluestocking, Miss Heydinger. When he meets Ethel again after a three-year gap, he sees that she is a victim of her unscrupulous father. Their courtship, Ethel's pregnancy and their marriage are traced with sympathy for the pains as well as pleasures of married life.

Love for Love A comedy by CONGREVE, produced and published in 1695. Valentine is a fashionable man-about-town whose extravagance has led him into debt. His father, Sir Sampson Legend, agrees to pay the debts only if Valentine will sign his inheritance away to his younger brother, Ben, a sailor. Valentine has to agree but, realizing that he faces ruin, pleads and even feigns madness to avoid signing the bond. He is rescued by the resourceful Angelica, whom he had been unsuccessfully courting. Meanwhile, the independent-minded Ben has baulked at Sir Sampson's plan to marry him to Miss Prue, a foolish country girl. The plot involves some diverting minor characters, including Valentine's resourceful servant Jeremy and the amorous Mrs Frail.

Love Song of J. Alfred Prufrock, The A poem by T. S. ELIOT, published in *POETRY* in 1915 and reprinted in his first collection, *Prufrock and Other Observations* (1917). The title is ironic, for the middle-aged Prufrock shows himself too timid to make the significant gesture that might free him from the empty social rituals of his genteel world. Both the use of the DRAMATIC MONOLOGUE and the setting, with the seamier side of city life glimpsed at the edges of bourgeois life, anticipate *THE WASTE LAND*.

Love's Labour's Lost A comedy by SHAKESPEARE, first performed *c.* 1594. The text of the First Folio (1623) is based on a Quarto edition of 1598. No source has been identified, so the story may be one of the few Shakespeare invented. Having forsworn the company of women for three years, Ferdinand, King of Navarre, and his three lords, Berowne, Dumain and Longaville, are sorely tried and eventually overcome by the embassy of the Princess of France with her three ladies, Rosaline, Katharine and Maria. The news that the princess's father has died forestalls the expected ending, for the ladies require their suitors to wait a year, and the play concludes with the delightful song 'When Icicles Hang by the Wall'. The complications of the plot are wittily prolonged and the language the most ornate that Shakespeare wrote. This is a play that has been understandably called Mozartian, though LYLY's *EUPHUES* and the fashion it created were the immediate influence and the object of Shakespeare's affectionate SATIRE. The extravagant conceits of the courtly lovers are a feature of the play, but Shakespeare has also created a gallery of notable minor characters in the fantastical Spaniard Armado, the pedantic schoolteacher Holofernes, Dull the constable and Costard the clown. They are of the kind that JONSON would later develop into 'humours'.

Love's Last Shift A comedy by CIBBER, first performed in 1696. Loveless deserts his wife Amanda after only six months and resumes a rakish life in London. She wins him back by courting him in disguise and appealing to his better nature. VANBRUGH's *THE RELAPSE* is a cynical sequel, in which Loveless reverts to type.

Lovel the Widower A story by THACKERAY, published in *THE CORNHILL MAGAZINE* in 1860. Lovel lives with his overbearing mother-in-law, Lady Baker, and a charming governess, Miss Prior. When Lady Baker discovers that Miss Prior had been a dancer she orders her out of the house, but Lovel asks her to marry him.

Lovelace, Earl 1935– Trinidadian novelist. Expert in varieties of Trinidadian speech, his novels penetrate serious contemporary issues. They include *While Gods are Falling* (1966), *The Schoolmaster* (1968) and his two finest works, *The Dragon Can't Dance* (1979) and *The Wine of Astonishment* (1984). *Jestina's Calypso and Other Plays* appeared in 1984. He has also published *A Brief Conversion and Other Stories* (1988) and a dramatized version of *The Dragon Can't Dance* (1989).

Lovelace, Richard 1618–58 CAVALIER POET. The handsome and dashing son of a wealthy Kentish knight, he gained a romantic reputation in the eyes of contemporaries by his proud devotion to the Royalist cause, for which he was twice imprisoned. He was freed after Charles I's execution and spent the rest of his life in relative poverty. During his second imprisonment (1648–9) he had prepared for publication the collection of verses called *Lucasta: Epodes, Odes, Sonnets, Songs, etc.*, which includes 'On Going to the Wars'. Another volume, *Lucasta: Posthume Poems*, was published by his brother a year after his death. (Lucasta was his fiancée, Lucy Sacheverell.) His work was almost forgotten until 1765, when PERCY included the lovely 'To Althea from Prison' in his *Reliques of Ancient English Poetry*. Lovelace was not

prolific, and his poetic reputation depends on a handful of elegant lyrics.

Lover, Samuel 1796–1868 Novelist and songwriter. A Protestant Irishman, he is best remembered for 'Rory O'More', a BALLAD developed into a novel in 1836 and a play in 1837. *Songs and Ballads* appeared in 1839. As a humorous novelist working in the same vein as CHARLES LEVER, he scored his greatest success with *HANDY ANDY* (1842). Lover also wrote several plays, successful in their time, and stories about Irish life.

Loves of the Angels, The A poem by THOMAS MOORE, published in 1823. The source was the Koran and the tradition of the angels Harut and Marut, whose purpose is to tempt men and teach them sorcery. Moore elaborated this into a story of three fallen angels who loved mortal women.

Lowell, Amy 1874–1925 American poet. A champion of modern poetry, she introduced IMAGISM to America in what some critics felt was a bastardized form. Her first volume of verse, *A Dome of Many-Colored Glass*, appeared in 1912; *The Complete Poetical Works of Amy Lowell* appeared in 1955. She is best remembered for poems such as 'Lilacs' and 'Patterns'.

Lowell, James Russell 1819–91 American poet and man of letters. As a poet, he is chiefly remembered for two works of SATIRE: *A FABLE FOR CRITICS* (1848) and *The Biglow Papers*, of which the first series (1848) attacked the Mexican War and the second (1867) the Confederacy in the Civil War. His post as LONGFELLOW's successor at Harvard did little to check his prolific writing. As well as publishing seven volumes of essays, he also edited *THE ATLANTIC MONTHLY*, which he co-founded with OLIVER WENDELL HOLMES, in 1857–61 and jointly edited *THE NORTH AMERICAN REVIEW* with CHARLES ELIOT NORTON in 1864. As US minister in Spain (1877–80) and Britain (1880–5) he did much to interpret American aspirations and ideals to the Old World.

Lowell, Robert 1917–77 American poet. The great-grandnephew of JAMES RUSSELL LOWELL, he was preoccupied with the legacy of New England and his own family. His early work, in volumes such as *Land of Unlikeness* (1944), *Lord Weary's Castle* (1946; PULITZER PRIZE) and *The Mills of the Kavanaughs* (1951), is formal and highly symbolic. *Life Studies* (1959) introduced the loose form and sharp IRONY which characterize his mature style. It is also usually identified as a major example of CONFESSIONAL POETRY, though Lowell did not confine himself to purely personal subjects. *Imitations* (1961) included translations of classical and European poets, while later volumes, such as *For the Union Dead* (1964) and *Near the Ocean* (1967), linked an understanding of the self to politics and history. Other works are *The Voyage, and Other Versions of Poems by Baudelaire* (1968), *Notebook 1967–68* (1969), *Notebooks* (1970), *History* (1973), *For Lizzie and Harriet* (1973), *The Dolphin* (1973; Pulitzer Prize), *Selected Poems* (1976), *Day by Day* (1977) and several plays, including *The Old Glory* (1965). *Collected Prose* appeared in 1987.

Lowndes, Marie (Adelaide) Belloc 1868–1947 Novelist, short-story writer and playwright. The sister of HILAIRE BELLOC, she published over 40 novels. Most are skilfully plotted and observed stories of crime or mystery, and several derive from real-life criminal cases. Her most famous book, *The Lodger* (1913), describes how landlady Mrs Bunting comes to realize that her genteel lodger is in fact Jack the Ripper. It inspired several film versions, including one by Alfred Hitchcock (1926).

Lowry, (Clarence) Malcolm 1909–57 Novelist. In youth he sailed to China as a deckhand on a merchant ship and studied at St Catharine's College, Cambridge. Then, an alcoholic and a wanderer, he lived in Mexico and British Columbia before returning to Britain. *Ultramarine* (1933) is a novel of seafaring. His second novel, *UNDER THE VOLCANO* (1947), is widely regarded as his masterpiece. A volume of short stories, *Hear Us, O Lord, from Heaven Thy Dwelling Place* (1961), *Selected Poems* (1962), *Lunar Caustic* (1968), *Dark as the Grave Wherein My Friend is Laid* (1968) and *October Ferry to Gabriola* (1971) have been published from the mass of work he left behind.

Lubbock, Percy 1879–1965 Critic. His writings range from autobiography (*Earlham*, 1922) to fictional travelogue (*Roman Pictures*, 1923) and biographies of PEPYS (1909) and EDITH WHARTON (1947). A friend and disciple of HENRY JAMES, he edited the novelist's *Letters* (1920) and the 35 volumes of his *Novels and Stories* (1921–3) while working on his own best-known book, *The Craft of Fiction* (1920), which is also his fullest homage to James.

Lucie-Smith, (John) Edward (McKenzie) 1933– Poet, art critic and anthologist. Although he was chairman of the GROUP in 1959–65 and edited *A Group Anthology* (1963) with PHILIP HOBSBAUM, his own poetry has reflected a considerable variety of influences: the MOVEMENT in *A Tropical Childhood* (1961); ROBERT BROWNING and DRAMATIC MONOLOGUE in *Confessions and Histories* (1964); and the BLACK MOUNTAIN SCHOOL in *Towards Silence* (1968) and *The Well Wishers* (1974). His interest in *avant-garde* poetry is shown not only in this later work but in his *Primer of Experimental Poetry* (1971). *Beasts with Bad Morals* (1984) contains comic poems. In recent years he has concentrated mainly on critical studies developing a wide range of subjects in 19th- and 20th-century art.

Lucky Jim The first novel by KINGSLEY AMIS, published in 1954. The plot is a catalogue of the misadventures which beset Jim Dixon in the first term of his new job teaching history at a provincial university. Virtuoso comic sequences include Jim setting his bed on fire with his cigarette while staying at the home of the professor of English and his disastrous lecture to the faculty at the end of term. As well as being a work of sustained, often farcical comedy, the novel also mocks 'phoniness' and pretension.

Ludlow, Edmund 1617–92 Author of *Memoirs*, written from exile in Switzerland and published in 1698–9. They give a first-hand account of the Civil War and the Interregnum, and of Ludlow's turbulent career as anti-Royalist, soldier in Cromwell's army and regicide.

Ludlow, John Malcolm See CHRISTIAN SOCIALISM.

Ludus Coventriae See MIRACLE PLAYS.

Lurie, Alison 1926– American novelist. Her poised, witty novels explore the subversive effects of change on comfortable, middle-class Americans, often academics exposed to the world outside the campus. They include *Love and Friendship* (1962), *The Nowhere City* (1965), *Imaginary Friends* (1967), *Real People* (1970), *The War Between the Tates* (1974), *Only Children* (1979), *Foreign Affairs* (1985; PULITZER PRIZE); and *The Truth about Lorin Jones* (1988). *Women and Ghosts* (1994) is a volume of short stories. *Don't Tell the Grown-Ups* (1990) is a study of CHILDREN'S LITERATURE.

Luska, Sidney See HARLAND, HENRY.

Luttrell, Narcissus 1657–1732 Diarist, historian and collector. MP for Bossiney (1679–80) and Saltash (1690–5), he was a Whig at heart but also on terms with Tories such as ROBERT HARLEY. He published nothing during his lifetime, but began early to collect the books and ephemera on which he based his two *Popish Plot Catalogues* (published 1956) and *A Brief Historical Relation of State Affairs from September 1678 to April 1714* (6 vols., 1857). The latter compilation and his *Abstract* (edited by Henry Horwitz in 1972 as *The Parliamentary Diary of Narcissus Luttrell 1691–1693*) are now appreciated as indispensable source books for parliamentary and political history.

Lyall, Sir Alfred Comyn 1835–1911 Poet. A civil servant in India, he wrote two books about Hinduism, *Asiatic Studies* (1882 and 1899), a biography of Warren Hastings (1889), *The Rise of the British Dominion in India* (1893) and a study of TENNYSON (1902). *Verses Written in India* (1889; revised, enlarged and reprinted as *Poems*, 1907), enjoyed some success.

Lyceum Theatre Of the several theatres on the site, just off London's Strand, the first was opened in 1772. A second, built in 1816, was destroyed by fire in 1830. The third Lyceum, opened in 1834, was famous from 1878 to 1902 as the 'temple' of Sir Henry Irving, who staged SHAKESPEARE and indifferent MELODRAMAS, while resisting the new movement in drama initiated by TOM ROBERTSON. Irving's Lyceum was demolished in 1904.

Lycidas An ELEGY by MILTON on the death of Edward King, a Cambridge contemporary drowned in the Irish Sea while returning to Dublin in August 1637. It first appeared in a volume of memorial verses to King published in 1638. The poem moves from personal grief at the loss of this promising man to a larger consideration of the meaning of death, eventually finding consolation in the immortality and resurrection of the soul. It prefigures later works like *PARADISE LOST* in its skilful union of classical and Christian traditions (of PASTORAL as well as elegy) and its pointed contemporary references (to the sad state of the church).

Lydgate, John *c.* 1370–1449 Poet. Born in the village of Lidgate, Suffolk, he entered the nearby Benedictine abbey at Bury St Edmunds in or before 1382. He remained there for most of his life, although he is known to have spent some time in London, Oxford and Paris, and was prior of Hatfield Broad Oak, Essex, in 1421–32. His works range from brief occasional poems to the long translations from French and Latin by which he is best known. *The Troy Book* (1412–21), a version of Guido delle Colonne's *Historia troiana* (1287), begins with Jason's search for the Golden Fleece and ends with the death of Ulysses. The debt to CHAUCER is even more apparent in *The Siege of Thebes*, drawn from a lost French work and presented as an addition to *THE CANTERBURY TALES*. In 1426 Lydgate began a translation of *Le Pèlerinage de la vie humaine* by Guillaume de Deguileville, a long and mediocre moral ALLEGORY, though with some humorous touches, which describes the Christian's quest for salvation. *The Fall of Princes* (1431–8) is a RHYME-ROYAL translation of a French version of Boccaccio's *De casibus virorum illustrium*, giving the tragic stories of all the major historical and mythical figures from Adam to King John of France. *Reason and Sensuality* (*c.* 1408), an allegory on chastity translated from French, is less austere, as are the love-allegories in Chaucer's manner, *The Temple of Glass* and *The Complaint of the Black Knight*. Lydgate also wrote lyrics, specially commissioned occasional pieces, SAINTS' LIVES (including one of St Edmund), versions of Aesop's fables, and a short prose work on Julius Caesar, *The Serpent of Division* (1422). Although his immediate successors considered him the equal of Chaucer and GOWER, he has never returned to popularity, damned by his ragged METRE, his love of cliché and aureate diction, and the sheer length of his works.

Lyly, John ?1554–1606 Playwright and author of prose romances. *EUPHUES: OR, THE ANATOMY OF WIT* (?1578) and its sequel *Euphues and His England* (1580), the two prose romances that began his career, were instant successes that made EUPHUISM, as prose modelled on his own elaborate and elegant style was called, the fashionable mode of the 1580s. The stage comedies that followed, all written for BOYS' COMPANIES and aimed at a courtly audience, achieve a patterned artifice combining Italian pastoralism with intrigue derived from Plautus and Terence. *CAMPASPE* (early 1580s), *Sapho and Phao* (early 1580s), *Gallathea* (1584), *ENDYMION: THE MAN IN THE MOON* (1586–7), *Love's Metamorphosis* (1589), *Midas* (1589) and *Mother Bombie* (1589) helped establish prose as a medium for comedy. *The Woman in the Moon* (?1594) is his only play in verse. *Pap with a Hatchet* (1589) is Lyly's contribution, on the side of the bishops, to the Marprelate controversy (see MARPRELATE, MARTIN).

Lyndsay [Lindsay], **Sir David** 1490–1555 Poet and dramatist. A courtier and close companion of James V of Scotland, he continued his diplomatic career after the king's death in 1542 at the English and Danish courts. Though his literary career started late, he became one of the important 'makaris' of early-16th-century Scottish poetry. *The Dreme* (finished 1528, printed 1558) is a DREAM-VISION in which Dame Remembrance shows the poet hell, purgatory and heaven, from which he sees the kingdoms of the earth, including Scotland. *The Testament and Complaynt of Our Soverane Lordis Papingo* (finished 1530, printed 1538) puts advice to the king and characteristic satire against ecclesiastics into an animal's mouth, a technique he used again in *The Complaynt and Publict Confessioun of the King is Auld Hound* (c. 1536). An *Answer Quhilk Schir David Lyndsay Maid to the Kingis Flyting* (1536) is an example of the poetic abuse of which DUNBAR was master. Lyndsay had shown an early interest in drama by acting before James and Margaret Tudor at Holyrood in 1511; his play, *SATIRE OF THE THREE ESTATES*, was produced for Epiphany 1540. Other poems include: *The Tragedy of the Cardinal* (1547), a warning to princes and prelates; *The History and Testament of Squire Meldrum* (?1550, first printed 1582), a romance about a Scottish laird; *The Monarchie* (1554), an ambitious anti-Catholic work; and *Kitteis Confessioun*, satirizing the confessional.

lyric A term, originally from the Greek ('for the lyre'), now commonly used to describe any short poem, especially one expressing the poet's personal sentiments.

The lyric mode covers a wide range of topics ranging from the experience of love, to pastoral description and praise of God. See also MEDIEVAL LYRIC.

***Lyrical Ballads*, with a Few Other Poems** A collection by WORDSWORTH and COLERIDGE, published in 1798. A second edition in two volumes, with a preface by Wordsworth in place of his original short 'Advertisement', appeared in January 1801 (though it is usually dated 1800), and a third in 1802.

One of the abiding reference points of English ROMANTICISM, it originally consisted of 23 anonymous poems. Only four are by Coleridge: *THE RIME OF THE ANCIENT MARINER*, 'The Nightingale', 'The Foster-Mother's Tale' and 'The Dungeon'. Wordsworth's contribution includes BALLADS, songs and narratives such as 'Goody Blake and Harry Gill', 'The Idiot Boy', 'The Thorn', 'The Mad Mother', 'Simon Lee', as well as other lyrical and personal poems: 'The Tables Turned', 'Lines Written in Early Spring' and 'Lines Composed a Few Miles above Tintern Abbey'. The 'Advertisement' characterizes these works as experiments in adapting 'the language of conversation in the middle and lower classes of society' to poetry and challenges readers to rethink their criteria of poetic decorum.

The second edition includes a further poem by Coleridge, 'Love', but omits his name from the title-page. Wordsworth contributed many new poems, including important works such as the 'Lucy' poems, 'The Old Cumberland Beggar', and 'Michael, a Pastoral Poem' and the long new preface which expounds his ideas on poetic diction and the origin of poetry in 'emotion recollected in tranquillity'. In the expanded version prepared for the 1802 edition, Wordsworth managed to accommodate some of his collaborator's reservations about the preface, but in *BIOGRAPHIA LITERARIA* Coleridge explicitly distanced himself from its ideas.

Lyrical Ballads paved the way for Wordsworth's later fame as a poet. Its preference for subjects drawn from 'low and rustic life', and the self-mythologizing poetic persona, were often ridiculed and lampooned, yet no poet of the Romantic generation was to escape the underlying force of its call for a poetic reinterpretation of the world.

Lyttelton, George, 1st Baron 1709–73 Poet and patron. The owner of Hagley Hall, Worcestershire, he is remembered in literature as a minor poet and a generous patron, the friend of HENRY FIELDING, POPE, THOMSON and SHENSTONE. His poetry includes *Monody* (1747) to the memory of his wife, and *Dialogues of the Dead* (1760). He also published *The History of the Life of Henry the Second* (1767–71).

Lytton, Edward Bulwer See BULWER LYTTON, EDWARD.

Mabbe, James 1572–c. 1642 Translator from the Spanish. His first work was *The Rogue: or, The Life of Guzman de Alfarache* (1622), from Mateo Alemán (see PICARESQUE). He is best remembered for *The Spanish Bawd* (1631), from Fernando de Rojas's *Celestina*, which had already served as the basis for the play *CALISTO AND MELIBEA*, and his translation of Cervantes's *Novelas ejemplares* as *Exemplary Novels* (1640), the most famous of which is *The Spanish Lady*.

Mabinogion, The The collective name for a group of 11 medieval Welsh prose tales first published in an English translation (1838–49) by Lady Charlotte Guest. They date from the late 11th and 12th centuries, and may have been written down as early as 1200. The complete *Mabinogion* is found in the Red Book of Hergest (c. 1400), although fragments in the White Book of Rhydderch (c. 1350) suggest this was an earlier complete version. The word *mabinogion* occurs once in the manuscripts but is clearly an error for *mabinogi*, apparently derived from the Welsh *mab*, 'boy' or 'youth'.

In modern scholarship, *Mabinogi* refers to a group of four of the tales known as 'Pedair Cainc y Mabinogi' (*The Four Branches of the Mabinogi*): 'Pwyll', 'Branwen', 'Manawydan' and 'Math'. Located in a pre-Norman past where independent Welsh rulers vie for power, they commemorate ancient strata of Celtic myth and history. Of the other tales, 'Culhwch ac Olwen' (*Culhwch and Olwen*) is the longest and oldest, possibly antedating the Norman Conquest. It is set at Arthur's court and describes a sequence of feats which the hero, Culhwch, must accomplish in order to win Olwen, daughter of the giant Ysbaddaden. Written before GEOFFREY OF MONMOUTH's *Historia regum Britanniae*, it is a crucial text in ARTHURIAN LITERATURE. Though the *Tair Rhamant* (*Three Romances*) of 'Owain', 'Peredur' and 'Geraint' also have a native Arthurian context, they are strongly influenced by Continental Arthurian literature and correspond to the 12th-century French romances of 'Yvain', 'Perceval' and 'Erec et Enide' by Chrétien de Troyes; it is likely that both groups derive from French or Breton versions of original Welsh material.

The remaining tales, 'Breuddwyd Rhonabwy' (*The Dream of Rhonabwy*), 'Breuddwyd Macsen' (*The Dream of Maxen*) and 'Cyfranc Lludd a Llefelys' (*The Tale of Lludd and Llevelys*), are 12th-century versions of native historical legends. Arthur and Owain appear in 'Breuddwyd Rhonabwy'. Two tales, using material found in Geoffrey of Monmouth's *Historia* and its Welsh translations, hark back to the achievements of British Celts in the pre-Saxon era.

Mac Flecknoe: or, *A Satire upon the True-Blue-Protestant Poet T.S.* A satirical poem by DRYDEN, written about 1678, pirated in 1682 and officially published in 1684. Its target is SHADWELL, who had attacked Dryden, the POET LAUREATE, in *The Medal of John Bayes*. Dryden's poem describes how Shadwell assumes the mantle of literary dullness from FLECKNOE, and makes him into the epitome of the absurdly untalented poet. The climax is a coronation scene which influenced POPE's *THE DUNCIAD*.

MacArthur, Charles 1895–1956 American playwright. *Salvation Nell* (1928), an exposé of a female revivalist, was written with SIDNEY HOWARD. MacArthur's long collaboration with BEN HECHT began with *The Front Page* (1928), a play about Chicago newspapermen, and continued with a comedy, *Twentieth Century* (1932), as well as various screenplays, including *Nothing Sacred* (1937), *Wuthering Heights* (1939), *Spellbound* (1945) and *Notorious* (1946).

Macaulay, Dame (Emilie) Rose 1881–1958 Novelist, essayist and travel-writer. She first attracted attention with *Potterism* (1920), a satire of modern journalism and commercialization. *They were Defeated* (1932) is a historical novel about ROBERT HERRICK. Her two post-war novels, *The World My Wilderness* (1950) and *The Towers of Trebizond* (1956), are also her best-known. She also published collections of essays and travel books, including *The Pleasure of Ruins* (1953). Constance Babington Smith edited her correspondence with her religious adviser as *Letters to a Friend* (1961–2), as well as *Letters to a Sister* (1964).

Macaulay, Thomas Babington 1800–59 Historian and essayist. The son of Zachary Macaulay, an anti-slavery campaigner and 'Clapham Sect' Evangelical, he distinguished himself at Trinity College, Cambridge, of which he was elected a fellow in 1824. He made his reputation with articles in THE EDINBURGH REVIEW, notably essays on MILTON (1825) and UTILITARIANISM (1829) and an attack on SOUTHEY's *Colloquies* (1830), a classic expression of the Whig belief in progress. These launched him on a career in public life, first as an MP supporting the Reform Bill of 1831–2 and then as a member of the new Supreme Council for India with responsibility for drafting legislation. During his four years there he initiated major reforms in education and the penal code. He entered the Cabinet as Secretary-at-War after returning to England in 1838. His essay on FRANCIS BACON (1837) and *LAYS OF ANCIENT ROME* (1842), mostly written in India, were followed by essays on Clive (1840), Warren Hastings (1841) and ADDISON (1843). The first collected edition of his *Critical and Historical Essays* appeared in 1843.

The immediate and spectacular success of the first two volumes of his *History of England* in 1849 encouraged him to devote himself mainly to writing, though he sat in the Commons again in 1852–5. The third and fourth volumes of his *History* appeared in 1855 and a posthumous volume, edited by his sister, in 1861. Macaulay's original plan was to pursue the narrative from 1685 to the threshold of the First Reform Bill, thus dealing with the development of Britain 'between the revolution, which brought the crown into harmony with the parliament, and the revolution which brought the parliament into harmony with the nation'. Though the final work deals only with the period 1685–1702, its progressive thrust and conviction of the rightness and adaptability of the English constitution survive.

McAuley, James Phillip 1917–76 Australian poet. *Under Aldebaran* (1946) and *A Vision of Ceremony* (1956) show his commitment to control, formality and sophistication. McAuley's poetic theories were further shown by the hoax he concocted with Harold Stewart in 1944, publishing the 'posthumous' works of 'Ern Malley' in the modernist journal *Angry Penguins*. The verses were in fact a PARODY of contemporary verse, particularly that of DYLAN THOMAS and TREECE.

McBain, Ed See HUNTER, EVAN.

Macbeth A tragedy by SHAKESPEARE, first performed *c.* 1606 and published, in an imperfect text, in the First Folio of 1623. In turning to Scottish history (as described in HOLINSHED's *Chronicles*) and making witchcraft an element of the tragedy, Shakespeare clearly intended some flattery to JAMES I.

Macbeth and Banquo, generals to King Duncan, meet three witches who prophesy that Macbeth will become Thane of Cawdor and King of Scotland and that Banquo's heirs will be kings. Almost at once Macbeth learns that he has been made Thane of Cawdor. When Duncan visits his castle, Lady Macbeth urges her husband to kill him, overriding his hesitation and helping him in the aftermath of the murder. Suspicion falls on Duncan's sons, Malcolm and Donalbain, who flee. As king, Macbeth feels no safety. The witches' prophecy prompts him to have Banquo and one of his sons killed, but the murderers let the son escape and Banquo's ghost haunts Macbeth at a banquet. He seeks out the witches, finding comfort in their assurance that he will not be defeated until Birnam Wood comes to Dunsinane and that no man born of woman can harm him. Scotland is suffering under his guilty reign and Macduff, the Thane of Fife, seeks out Malcolm in England. Macbeth orders the slaughter of Macduff's family. As Malcolm's army advances, Lady Macbeth walks in her sleep, obsessed with Duncan's murder. Macbeth is so isolated that he hardly reacts to the news of her death. When Malcolm's army camouflages its attack with branches from Birnam Wood, he loses part of the reassurance he had taken from the witches' words. The rest goes when he learns that Macduff was not 'born' but 'untimely ripped' from his mother's womb. Macduff kills him and establishes Malcolm on the Scottish throne.

MacBeth, George (Mann) 1932–92 Poet. A central figure in the GROUP in the 1950s and involved in performance poetry in the 1960s, he took suffering, death, war and violence as his themes, though later work is simpler and more genuinely moving. Volumes include *The Broken Places* (1963), *The Colour of Blood* (1967), *Collected Poems 1958–70* (1971), *Shrapnel* (1973), *The Long Darkness* (1983), *Anatomy of a Divorce* (1988) and *Trespassing: Poems from Ireland* (1991). *Another Love* (1990) is a novel.

MacCaig, Norman (Alexander) 1910– Scottish poet. Widely regarded as Scotland's finest contemporary poet, he dabbled with the influence of the NEW APOCALYPSE before starting on what he calls 'the long haul towards lucidity' with *Riding Lights* (1955). Since then he has published a succession of slim volumes and his prize-winning *Collected Poems* (1985, revised 1990). Often centring on Edinburgh or north-west Sutherland, his poetry has moved from tight traditionality to more open forms, characterized by sharp WIT and playfulness; much of it is 'metaphysical', concerned with the nature of perception. *As I Say It* (1971) is a fine recording of MacCaig reading his own poems.

MacCarthy, Sir (Charles Otto) Desmond 1877–1952 Literary and dramatic critic. A brilliant conversationalist of whom great things were expected by his friends in the BLOOMSBURY GROUP, he worked as drama critic and then literary editor of *The New Statesman* and, from 1928 until his death, as senior literary critic of *The Sunday Times*. He was among the first to recognize the significance of Ibsen and Chekhov, and wrote admired portraits of SAMUEL BUTLER, MEREDITH, HENRY JAMES, SHAW, CONRAD, RUSKIN and Asquith. His essays were collected in 10 volumes.

McCarthy, Justin 1830–1912 Irish journalist, novelist, historian and politician. A youthful supporter of the Young Ireland movement, he later embarked on a successful career in fiction, publishing some 20 now-forgotten novels. The best is probably *Mononia: A Love-Story of 'Forty-Eight'* (1901), reflecting the country life and political enthusiasms of his Munster youth, though *Dear Lady Disdain* (1875) and *Miss Misanthrope* (1878) were also very popular. He entered Parliament in 1879. His immensely popular *History of Our Own Times* (1879–1905), covering Queen Victoria's reign, was supplemented by *The Reign of Queen Anne* (1905) and *The History of the Four Georges and William IV* (1884–1901) and shorter studies of Peel (1891) and Gladstone (1898).

McCarthy, Mary 1912–89 American novelist, short-story writer, essayist and critic. Her best-selling novel, *The Group* (1963), follows eight Vassar women after their graduation. *The Groves of Academe* (1952) draws on her experiences as a university teacher, and *Memories of a Catholic Girlhood* (1957) describes her childhood. Her political interests are evident not just in *Vietnam* (1967) and *Hanoi* (1968) but also her travel books, *Venice Observed* (1956) and *The Stones of Florence* (1959). She also wrote literary criticism (*The Writing on the Wall*, 1970; *Ideas and the Novel*, 1981) and many more novels, short stories, and essays, including *Birds of America* (1971), *The Mask of State: Watergate Portrait* (1974), *Cannibals and Missionaries* (1979), *The Hounds of Summer and Other Stories* (1981) and *Occasional Prose: Essays* (1985). EDMUND WILSON was her second husband.

McClure's Magazine An American literary and political magazine founded by Samuel Sydney McClure and John Sanborn Phillips in 1893. It published fiction by RUDYARD KIPLING, O. HENRY, WILLA CATHER and JACK LONDON, and in the first decades of the 20th century pioneered reformist non-fiction, later called muckraking journalism. It merged with *New Smart Set* in 1929.

McCrae, Hugh Raymond 1876–1958 Australian poet. Seeing the poet's task as 'to live in making others live', he created a vivid mythological world in *Satyrs and Sunlight* (1909), *Columbine* (1920), *Idyllia* (1922) and *The Mimshi Maiden* (1938). The *Dr Poissey Anecdotes* (1922) are fictional revelations in the 18th-century manner, and *My Father and My Father's Friends* (1935) is a biography of George Gordon McCrae and his friends MARCUS CLARKE, HENRY KENDALL and ADAM LINDSAY GORDON.

McCullers, Carson (Smith) 1917–67 American novelist. Her work often deals with spiritual isolation and the attempt to overcome it through love. She was also one of the first American writers to deal openly with homosexuality. *The Heart is a Lonely Hunter* (1940), which won immediate recognition, was followed by *Reflections in a Golden Eye* (1941), *The Ballad of the Sad Café* (1951), *Clock without Hands* (1961) and *The Mortgaged Heart* (1971), a collection of stories. ALBEE dramatized *The Ballad of the Sad Café* and she herself dramatized *The Member of the Wedding* (1946), as well as writing another play, *The Square Root of Wonderful* (1958).

MacDiarmid, Hugh [Grieve, Christopher Murray] 1892–1978 Scottish poet and critic. He published his first book, *Annals of the Five Senses* (1923), under his own name but in 1922–3 began to publish poems in revived or synthetic Scots and, as Hugh MacDiarmid, became the central figure of the SCOTTISH RENAISSANCE. A Communist and nationalist, he became a founder-member of the Scottish National Party in 1928 and was involved in political controversy throughout his life. From the early 1960s he began to enjoy growing recognition as a major poet.

He established his reputation with poems like 'The Watergaw' and 'The Eemis Stane'. Two collections, *Sangschaw* (1925) and *Penny Wheep* (1926), were followed by *A Drunk Man Looks at the Thistle* (1926), a sequence usually regarded as his masterpiece. He extended the use of Scots throughout the 1920s and 1930s in such works as *To Circumjack Cencrastus* (1930) and in styles ranging from the political *First Hymn to Lenin* (1931) to the meditative 'By Wauchopeside', 'Whuchulls' and 'Depth and the Chthonian Image'. In the mid 1930s he began to experiment with what he called 'synthetic English', most impressively in 'On a Raised Beach' (*Stony Limits*, 1934), continuing the experiment in two major works, *In Memoriam James Joyce* (1954) and *The Kind of Poetry I Want* (1961). MacDiarmid's *Complete Poems 1920–76* (1978, revised 1982) was edited by Michael Grieve and W. R. Aitken. He also produced translations, short stories, critical and political essays and the prose autobiography *Lucky Poet: A Self-Study in Literature and Political Ideas* (1943; reissued in 1972). Alan Bold edited his letters (1984).

MacDonagh, Donagh 1912–68 Irish poet and playwright. The son of THOMAS MACDONAGH, he was probably best known for his play *Happy As Larry* (1947). With LENNOX ROBINSON he edited *The Oxford Book of Irish Verse* (1958).

MacDonagh, Thomas 1878–1916 Irish Poet. Professor of English literature at University College, Dublin, he wrote books of criticism, plays and several well-regarded volumes of verse gathered in *Collected Poems* (1917), with an introduction by JAMES STEPHENS. He was executed for his part in the Easter Rising and mourned by YEATS in 'Easter 1916'.

MacDonald, George 1824–1905 Scottish novelist and writer of CHILDREN'S LITERATURE. His fairy-stories are shot through with an unmistakable blend of Christian symbolism and mystical imagination. In the most famous, *At the Back of the North Wind* (1871), a cabdriver's son called Diamond travels the world each night in the company of the North Wind, pictured as a beautiful lady. Subsequent classics include *The Princess and the Goblin* (1872), a powerful ALLEGORY of good and evil, and *The Princess and Curdie* (1883), where the miner's son Curdie again braves dangers to save the princess. MacDonald's adult fiction – the allegorical *Phantastes* (1858) and *Lilith* (1895), and novels such as *David Elginbrod* (1863) – is less well remembered.

McEwan, Ian 1948– Novelist and short-story writer. Two collections of short stories, *First Love, Last Rites* (1975) and *In between the Sheets* (1977), and a short novel, *The Cement Garden* (1978), announced his ability to combine the graphic or shocking with a cerebral, modulated prose style. Subsequent works, increasingly more substantial, are: *The Comfort of Strangers* (1981), owing its location and claustrophobic concentration to Mann's *Death in Venice*; *The Child in Time* (1987), a study of bereavement; *The Innocent* (1990), set in Berlin during the 1950s; and *Black Dogs* (1992), using the memory of Nazi atrocities for an investigation of evil. McEwan is also the author of a TV play, *The Imitation Game* (1981); an oratorio about nuclear war, *Or Shall We Die?* (1983); and the screenplay for *The Ploughman's Lunch* (1983).

MacEwen, Gwendolyn 1941–87 Canadian poet, novelist and short-story writer. A prolific writer in a wide range of forms, she was preoccupied with myth, magic and a sacrificial view of life. Her poetry includes *Selah* (1961), *The Drunken Clock* (1961), *The Shadow-Maker* (1969), *The Armies of the Moon* (1972), *The T. E. Lawrence Poems* (1982) and *Earthlight: Selected Poems 1963–1982* (1982). Other works are: *Julian the Magician* (1963) and *King of Egypt, King of Dreams* (1971), novels; *Noman* (1972), *The Honey Drum: Seven Tales from Arab Lands* (1984) and *Noman's Land* (1985), collections of stories; *The Trojan Women* (1979), a version of Euripides' play; and translations from Y. Ritsos.

McGahern, John 1934– Irish novelist and short-story writer. He writes about Ireland in astringent, measured, often bleak fiction, which includes: *The Barracks* (1963); *The Dark* (1965); *The Leavetaking* (1975), about the love affair between an Irish Catholic schoolteacher and an American divorcée; *The Pornographer* (1979), contrasting the protagonist's facility at writing pornography with the gauche failure but also the tenderness of his private life; and *Amongst Women* (1990) about an ageing farmer. McGahern's economy of style lends itself ideally to short stories, gathered in *Collected Stories* (1992).

McGee, Thomas D'Arcy 1825–68 Irish journalist and poet. He wrote hurried but pioneering studies of *The Irish Writers of the Seventeenth Century* (1846) and *The Life and Conquest of Art McMurrough* (1847). The facile popular poetry he wrote for *The Nation*, chiefly on nationalist or historical themes, was admired by YEATS. Actively involved in the Young Ireland rising of 1848, he escaped to North America, where he continued to lecture and write indefatigably if controversially. His best-remembered poems are the dreamily nostalgic 'The Celts' and 'Salutation to the Celts'. Several touching elegies for Irishmen include a tribute to THOMAS MOORE, to whose influence his own metrical virtuosity and lyric grace are largely attributable.

McGonagall, William 1830–1902 Scottish versifier, self-styled 'Poet and Tragedian'. The unscanned doggerel and painful rhymes of *Poetic Gems* (1890) made him a butt for audiences. He specialized in shipwrecks, battles and beauty spots; his most frequently quoted work is perhaps 'The Tay Bridge Disaster'.

McGough, Roger See LIVERPOOL POETS.

McGuane, Thomas (Francis) 1939– American novelist. Comic and energetic, his fiction includes *The Sporting Club* (1969), *The Bushwacked Piano* (1971), *Panama* (1978), *Nobody's Angel* (1979), *Something to be Desired* (1984) and *Nothing But Blue Skies* (1993). *Ninety-Two in the Shade* (1973) was filmed in 1975. He has also written the screenplays for *Rancho Deluxe* (1973), *The Missouri Breaks* (1976) and *Tom Horn* (1980).

Machen, Arthur (Llewellyn) 1863–1947 Novelist. He is chiefly remembered for supernatural tales such as *The Great God Pan* (1894) and *The Hill of Dreams* (1907), steeped in Welsh folklore and occult philosophy. He also published translations of *The Heptameron* (1886) and *The Memoirs of Casanova* (1894), and a volume of criticism, *Hieroglyphics* (1902). *Far Off Things* (1922) and *Things Near and Far* (1923) were both autobiographical. The Caerleon Edition of his works (1923) resulted from the 'rediscovery' of Machen after many years of neglect.

McIlvanney, William 1936– Scottish novelist, writer of DETECTIVE FICTION and poet. His reputation rests particularly on two novels examining the Scots tradition of the 'hard man': *Docherty* (1975), about an Ayrshire miner in the early years of the century, and *The Big Man* (1985), about bare-knuckle fighting. Earlier works include *Remedy is None* (1966) and *A Gift from Nessus* (1968). *Laidlaw* (1978), *The Papers of Tony Veitch* (1983) and *Strange Loyalties* (1991) are equally tough and gritty detective novels. He has also published two books of poetry, *The Longships in Harbour* (1970) and *These Words: Weddings and After* (1984).

MacInnes, Colin 1914–76 Novelist and journalist. Son of the popular novelist Angela Thirkell and a descendant of KIPLING, he grew up in Australia, where his first novel, *June in Her Spring* (1952), is set. He is now remembered for his 'London trilogy' – *City of Spades* (1957), *Absolute Beginners* (1959) and *Mr Love and Justice* (1960) – which vividly evokes a London just beginning to become multi-racial and to develop a militant youth culture. MacInnes's incisive, wide-ranging essays are collected in volumes such as *England, Half English* (1961).

Mackay, Charles 1814–89 Scottish songwriter. He published several volumes of verse, beginning with *Songs and Poems* (1834). Many of his poems were set to music; it was said that 400,000 copies were sold of 'A Good Time Coming'. His daughter was the novelist MARIE CORELLI.

McKay, Claude 1890–1948 Black American poet and novelist. Born in Jamaica, he emigrated to the USA in 1912. A collection of poetry, *Harlem Shadows* (1922), established his popular reputation. His novels include: *Home to Harlem* (1928), about a black soldier's return to the USA; *Banjo: A Story without a Plot* (1929), about a vagabond's life on the Marseilles waterfront; and *Banana Bottom* (1933), about a black woman's return to Jamaica. Other publications include: a collection of stories, *Gingertown* (1932); an autobiography, *A Long Way from Home* (1937); and a study of the black community, *Harlem* (1940).

MacKaye, Percy (Wallace) 1875–1956 American playwright. His works include: *The Canterbury Pilgrims* (1903), about the Wife of Bath's amorous pursuit of CHAUCER; *Jeanne d'Arc* (1906); *Sappho and Phaon* (1907); *The Scarecrow* (1908), based on HAWTHORNE's story 'Feathertop'; and *The Mystery of Hamlet, King of Denmark – or, What We Will* (1949), an ambitious verse tetralogy about the characters before the beginning of SHAKESPEARE's *HAMLET*. MacKaye also wrote community masques and emphasized the communal functions of drama in several books about the theatre.

Mackenzie, Sir (Edward Montague) Compton 1883–1972 Novelist. The best of his many works include the grimly realistic *Carnival* (1912), the semi-autobiographical *Sinister Street* (1913–14), *Guy and Pauline* (1915), *Sylvia Scarlett* (1918), *Extraordinary Women* (1928), *Our Street* (1931), *The Four Winds of Love* (1937–45) and the well-known Scottish novels, *The Monarch of the Glen* (1941) and *Whisky Galore* (1947). He also published memoirs of his experience in the Dardanelles during World War I and the ten-volume *My Life and Times* (1963–71).

Mackenzie, Henry 1745–1831 Novelist, playwright and man of letters. An Edinburgh lawyer who played a leading role in the city's learned and literary circles, he made a significant contribution to the SENTIMENTAL NOVEL with *THE MAN OF FEELING* (1771), about a man whose morality is too delicate for a harsh world. It was followed by *The Man of the World* (1773), about the selfish pursuit of happiness, and an EPISTOLARY NOVEL, *Julia de Roubigné* (1777). In 1805 a committee chaired by Mackenzie decided that MACPHERSON's *Ossian* was not the true Gaelic epic it claimed to be. Mackenzie's complete works (1808) included several plays: two tragedies,

The Spanish Father and *The Prince of Tunis*, and a comedy, *The White Hypocrite*. His *Anecdotes and Egotisms* (edited by Harold William Thompson; 1927) give a vivid picture of Edinburgh life, with gossip about the lordly and the famous.

Mackenzie, Seaforth [Mackenzie, Kenneth Ivo] 1913–54 Australian novelist and poet. He published two novels, *The Young Desire It* (1937) and *Chosen People* (1938), and two volumes of poetry, *Our Earth* (1937) and *The Moonlit Doorway* (1944).

Mackintosh, Elizabeth 1897–1952 Author of DETECTIVE FICTION under the pseudonym of Josephine Tey and of plays and novels under the pseudonym of Gordon Daviot. *The Man in the Queue* (1929, first published as being by Gordon Daviot) introduced the genteel police detective Alan Grant who reappeared in several thrillers, of which the best is probably *The Daughter of Time* (1951), an investigation of the character of Richard III. *The Franchise Affair* (1948) is based on an 18th-century *cause célèbre*. The same interest in history informed her best-known plays as Gordon Daviot, *Richard of Bordeaux* (1932) and *Queen of Scots* (1934).

Macklin, Charles 1699–1797 Irish actor and playwright. Of his ten plays, some are specifically about the stage, like *The New Play Criticized* (1747) and *Covent Garden Theatre* (1752), and all are clearly written from an actor's viewpoint. *Love à-la-Mode* (1759) is a satirical afterpiece, while *The True-Born Irishman* (1762) and *The Man of the World* (1781), a revised version of *The True-Born Scotsman* (1764), ridicule national characteristics.

Maclaren, Ian See KAILYARD SCHOOL.

Maclean, Sorley 1911– Gaelic poet. He led Gaelic poetry into the 20th century with *Dain do Eimhir Agus Dain Eile* (1943), chiefly a book of love poems. Many reappeared in *Reothairt is Contraigh, Taghadh de Dhain 1932–72* (1977) with new work which included his most admired single poem, 'Hallaig', about a township depopulated during the Highland Clearances. Later books are *Ris a' Bhruthaich* (1985), a collection of critical essays particularly concerned with 16th- and 17th-century Gaelic songs, and *From Wood to Ridge: Collected Poems in Gaelic and English* (1989).

MacLeish, Archibald 1892–1982 American poet and playwright. His highly subjective early poetry, in *The Happy Marriage* (1924), *The Pot of Earth* (1925), *Streets in the Moon* (1926) and *The Hamlet of A. MacLeish* (1928), owed much to T. S. ELIOT and POUND. Later volumes include: *New Found Land* (1930), written after his return to the USA from Paris; *Conquistador* (1932), about the conquest of Mexico; *Frescoes for Mr Rockefeller's City* (1933); and *Collected Poems* (1952). Among his verse plays are: *Nobodaddy* (1926); *Panic* (1935), about the Wall Street crash; *The Fall of the City* (1937), *Air Raid* (1938) and *The Trojan Horse* (1952), written for radio; *J. B.* (1958), about a modern Job; and *Herakles* (1967), about the conflict between human needs and science. MacLeish also pursued an active career in public and academic life.

MacLennan, (John) Hugh 1907–90 Canadian novelist and essayist. His first and best-known novels, *Barometer Rising* (1941) and *Two Solitudes* (1945), blend REALISM and symbolism in their examination of early 20th-century Canadian identity. Other works are *The Precipice* (1948), *Each Man's Son* (1951), *The Watch That Ends the Night* (1959), *Return of the Sphinx* (1967) and *Voices in Time* (1981). An accomplished essayist, he argued for a view of civilization in which classical humanist and contemporary materialist values are brought together.

Macleod, Fiona See SHARP, WILLIAM.

McMurtry, Larry (Jeff) 1936– American novelist. His first novel, *Horseman, Pass By*, was published in 1961. Books like *The Last Picture Show* (1966), *Terms of Endearment* (1975) and *Texasville* (1987) explore life in the kind of small-town Texas communities which have been mythologized into emblems of American identity in legends of the Wild West. *Lonesome Dove* (1986; PULITZER PRIZE), set in 1876, looks directly at those legends. Later works include *The Evening Star* (1992) and a sequel to *Terms of Endearment, Streets of Laredo* (1993).

McNally, Terrence 1939– American playwright. Born in St Petersburg, Florida, he attended Columbia University. Although he began by expressing the out-raged, turbulent mood of the late 1960s and early 1970s, he has since developed a more lyrical and positive style, offering unsentimental hope. Plays include *And Things That Go Bump in the Night* (1964), *Where Has Tommy Flowers Gone?* (1971), *The Ritz* (1975), *Broadway* (1979), *It's Only a Play* (1982), *The Lisbon Traviata* (1985), *Frankie and Johnny in the Clair de Lune* (1987) and *Lips Together, Teeth Apart* (1991).

MacNeice, (Frederick) Louis 1907–63 Poet. At Oxford he was part of AUDEN's circle. *Blind Fireworks* (1929), his first volume, was followed by several plays, *Poems* (1935), a widely praised translation of the *Agamemnon* (1936), *Letters from Iceland* (with Auden; 1937), *The Earth Compels* (1938) and *Autumn Journal* (1938), superbly capturing the mood of the Munich weeks. From 1941 until his death he worked for BBC radio, writing dozens of feature pro-grammes and plays, including *Christopher Columbus* (1944) and *The Dark Tower* (1947). Notable post-war vol-umes of poetry included *Solstices* (1961) and *The Burning Perch* (1963). His unfinished autobiography, *The Strings are False*, appeared in 1965, his *Collected Poems* in 1966, and a volume of *Selected Literary Criticism* in 1987.

The 'Macspaunday' tag which permanently linked him with Auden, DAY-LEWIS and SPENDER is misleading. Always technically adroit, often debonair and detached, MacNeice's poetry at its best achieved a taut intensity which expressed a pervasive sense of loss. As a love poet, a poet of urban rhythms and delights, and as a reporter with an educated, sensuous intelligence, his reputation stands high.

McNickle, D'Arcy 1904–77 American Indian novelist. *The Surrounded* (1936) is about a youth torn between his Flathead Indian and Spanish ancestry, while *Wind from an Enemy Sky* (1978) deals with the conflicts between Indian and non-Indian cultures. *Runner in the Sun: A Story of Indian Maize* (1954) is CHILDREN'S LITERATURE. McNickle also wrote a biography of Oliver LaFarge and several histories of Indian culture.

Macpherson, James 1736–96 Scottish poet and trans-lator. After publishing *The Highlander* (1758), a poem in HEROIC COUPLETS, he used his knowledge of Gaelic poetry to produce *Fragments of Ancient Poetry Collected in the Highlands of Scotland and Translated from the Gaelic or Erse Language* (1760), warmly received by Edinburgh lit-erary society. Its preface spoke of a Gaelic epic which Macpherson could recover for literature. The result of his labours appeared as *Fingal: An Ancient Poem* (1762), closely followed by *Temora: An Ancient Epic Poem* (1763). A collection attributing the originals to Ossian, a leg-endary Gaelic bard, appeared in 1765.

Macpherson went on to publish works of history and a prose version of *The Iliad* (1773), without repeating the success of his Ossianic poems. Those, like JOHNSON and

HUME, who challenged the poems' authenticity were strengthened in their doubts by Macpherson's failure to produce the originals. After his death a committee of inquiry headed by HENRY MACKENZIE concluded that he had treated the Gaelic poems in a free and selective fashion, adding much verse of his own invention. Such considerations did not check the enormous influence of Macpherson's Ossianic poems. Their popularity spread beyond Britain to include Napoleon, Goethe and Herder among admirers. By turning attention to wild nature, the mythic past and folk culture, the poems played a crucial role in the emergence of ROMANTICISM and, in particular, the CELTIC REVIVAL.

Macpherson, Jay 1931– Canadian poet. Born in Britain, she went to Canada at the age of nine. *Nineteen Poems* (1952) and *O Earth Return* (1954) were collected in a poetic cycle, *The Boatman* (1957), which was in turn expanded by another collection, *Welcoming Disaster* (1974), and republished as *Poems Twice Told* (1981). Her concentrated, allusive lyrics swing confidently within the tradition of English poetry, supplemented by the oral tradition of BALLAD and nursery rhyme. Her fasci-nation with biblical and classical myth suggests her double affinities with European MODERNISM and the Canadian mythopoeic tradition exemplified by NORTHROP FRYE. Her imaginative response to landscape finds overt expression not in her poetry but in a schol-arly study, *The Spirit of Solitude: Conventions and Continuities in Late Romance* (1982).

***McTeague:** A Story of San Francisco* A novel by FRANK NORRIS, published in 1899. McTeague (Mac) is a dentist absorbed in the physical pleasures of eating, drinking and smoking. His friend Marcus Schouler introduces him to Trina Sieppe, whom he courts and marries. Trina wins $5000 in a lottery and Marcus becomes jealous of Mac's good fortune. The two men fight and Marcus takes his revenge by revealing that Mac has been prac-tising dentistry without a licence. Mac depends on Trina for money and their relationship becomes sado-masochistic. Eventually he beats her to death and flees, with her gold coins and a canary in a gold cage. Marcus, who has joined the posse searching for him, tracks him down to Death Valley. They fight and Mac kills him, but not before Marcus has handcuffed himself to Mac. The novel ends with him still handcuffed to the corpse, with his canary but without water.

Madge, Charles (Henry) 1912– Poet and sociologist. A Marxist influenced by both AUDEN and surrealism, he produced two notable collections, *The Disappearing Castle* (1937) and *The Father Found* (1941). The founder of Mass Observation with Humphrey Jennings in 1937, he has also published Mass Observation surveys and socio-logical studies, including *Inner City Poverty in Paris and London* (with P. Willmott; 1981).

***Maggie:** A Girl of the Streets* A novel by STEPHEN CRANE, privately printed in 1893 under the pseudonym Johnston Smith and entitled *A Girl of the Streets*. A pio-neer work of American NATURALISM, it describes the sor-did and almost hopeless existence of Maggie Johnson in the Bowery area of New York. Alternately neglected and abused in childhood, she is seduced and abandoned, becomes a prostitute and finally drowns herself.

magic realism A term for one manifestation of POST-MODERNISM, first applied to the large body of spectacu-lar, fantastic fiction produced in South American countries since World War II, notably the work of Gabriel Garcia Márquez, whose *One Hundred Years of*

Solitude (trans. G. Rabassa; 1970) is generally regarded as its paradigm. It juxtaposes apparently reliable, realistic reportage with extravagant fantasy, not just in a spirit of inscrutable playfulness but also in response to the manipulation of fact and information in South American politics. Indeed, magic realism assumes that truth is best viewed as a communal, collaborative construct, rather than as residing in the integrity of individual perceptions, whose authority tends merely to that of caprice and rumour. Such emphasis makes it an essentially comic genre.

Magic realism has since been identified in other literatures, including the work of the Czech novelist Milan Kundera and the Italian Italo Calvino. The chief examples in English are the novels of RUSHDIE, ANGELA CARTER, GRAHAM SWIFT and PETER CAREY. In the European tradition, it is possible to see Rabelais and Kafka as precursors of the magic realist idiom, while Rushdie's work points back through the English novel to DICKENS and *TRISTRAM SHANDY*.

Maginn, William 1793–1842 Journalist. A lively, witty writer, he joined LOCKHART and JOHN WILSON on the staff of *BLACKWOOD'S EDINBURGH MAGAZINE*, signing his contributions as Ensign O'Doherty. In 1830 he helped Hugh Fraser to launch *FRASER'S MAGAZINE* and became its first editor, publishing his own *Homeric Ballads* and *Illustrious Literary Characters* in the magazine. He was the model for Captain Shandon in THACKERAY's *PENDENNIS*.

Mahapatra, Jayanta 1928– Indian poet. He writes both in English and Oriya, but it is as an outstanding writer in English that he has received international recognition. His best collections of poetry include *A Rain of Rites* (1976), *Waiting* (1979), *The False Start* (1980), *Relationship* (1980), *Life Signs* (1983) and *Burden of Waves and Fruit* (1988).

Mahon, Derek 1941– Irish poet. He first came to prominence, with SEAMUS HEANEY and MICHAEL LONGLEY, as a leading Belfast poet in the 1960s. Urban and urbane, his work is deeply influenced by LOUIS MACNEICE. The Northern Irish crisis has deepened its sense of estrangement and doom, goading him to question the relationship between poetry and public troubles. His chief collections are *Night-Crossing* (1968), *Lives* (1972) and *The Snow Party* (1975), gathered with revisions in *Poems 1962–1978* (1979), and *The Hunt by Night* (1982), *Antarctica* (1985) and *Selected Poems* (1991). His translations include Molière's *The School for Wives* (1986), *The Selected Poems of Philippe Jacottet* (1988) and *The Bacchae of Euripides* (1991).

Mahony, Francis Sylvester 1804–62 Poet under the pseudonym of Father Prout. *The Reliques of Father Prout* (1836), his contributions to *FRASER'S MAGAZINE*, consisted of writings about the life of a parish priest interspersed with literary dialogues, verse translations, prose and the supposed discovery of original stanzas in French, Latin and Greek of the songs and verses of such popular melodists as THOMAS MOORE.

Mahy, Margaret 1936– New Zealand writer of CHILDREN'S LITERATURE. She has moved from producing inventive picture-books to writing stories for older readers, vividly original in their language and plotting, which combine fantasy and magic with psychological realism. In *The Haunting* (1982) a shy young boy has to coexist with the real world and the ghosts which haunt him. *The Changeover* (1985) describes how a schoolboy becomes supernaturally possessed.

Maid Marian A novel by PEACOCK, published in 1822. It introduces the characters of Robin Hood and Richard I into a SATIRE of oppression and extreme doctrines of social order. Coming hard on the heels of SIR WALTER SCOTT's *IVANHOE* (1819), which had portrayed Robin Hood as Robin of Locksley, it confirmed the Romantics' interest in the legendary outlaw and contributed much to his present image in popular culture.

Maid's Tragedy, The A sensational tragedy by BEAUMONT and FLETCHER, first performed *c.* 1610 and published in 1619. Amintor obeys the king in abandoning Aspatia to marry Evadne, but on their wedding night she reveals she is the king's mistress. Though Amintor agrees to remain silent, Evadne's brother Melantius persuades her to kill the king. The rejected Aspatia, disguised as her brother, provokes Amintor into killing her in a duel. Evadne kills herself when Amintor rejects her, and Amintor kills himself on discovering he has killed Aspatia.

Mailer, Norman 1923– American novelist and journalist. His war service in the Pacific prompted *THE NAKED AND THE DEAD* (1948), which made him famous on both sides of the Atlantic. His critical view of society also informed *Barbary Shore* (1951) and *The Deer Park* (1955; dramatized in 1967). A pioneer of the New Journalism, he registered changes in the American sensibility in *Advertisements for Myself* (1959), *An American Dream* (1965), *Why are We in Vietnam?* (1967), *Armies of the Night* (1968; PULITZER PRIZE), *Miami and the Siege of Chicago* (1969), *Of a Fire on the Moon* (1969), *The Prisoner of Sex* (1971), *Marilyn: A Biography* (1973) and *The Fight* (1975), about Muhammad Ali. *The Executioner's Song* (1979; Pulitzer Prize), recreates events surrounding the execution of Gary Gilmore. Though versatile, his later fiction has found less favour. It includes *Ancient Evenings* (1983), *Tough Guys Don't Dance* (1984) and *Harlot's Ghost* (1991).

Main Street A novel by SINCLAIR LEWIS, published in 1920, and his first great success. After working as a librarian in St Paul, Minnesota, Carol Milford marries Dr Will Kennicott and moves to Gopher Prairie, where she initially rebels against the complacent small-town values but finally submits to them.

Main-Travelled Roads A collection of short stories by HAMLIN GARLAND, published in 1891 and expanded in 1899 and 1922. It depicts life in the rural Midwest as drab and monotonous. 'Under the Lion's Paw' is about the economic survival of the fittest or the most ruthless. In 'Up the Coulee' an actor returns to the Midwestern farm where he grew up. Contrasted with the harshness and squalid poverty are the 'silent heroism' of some characters and the panoramic beauty of the prairies.

Mais, Roger 1905–55 Jamaican novelist. Concentrating on 'the dreadful condition of the working classes', he gave social-realist accounts of human despair in the Kingston slums in his collections, *Face and Other Stories* (1942) and *And Most of All Man* (1943), and the novels, *The Hills were Joyful Together* (1953) and *Brother Man* (1954). The more fluid, non-realist *Black Lightning* (1955) suggests that poverty and suffering do not totally preclude fulfilment.

Maitland, Sir Richard 1496–1586 Scottish lawyer, statesman and poet. His collection of Scottish poetry in the Maitland Folio (begun *c.* 1570), continued by his daughter in the Maitland Quarto, is second in importance only to BANNATYNE's. It contains his own poems (mainly satires and reflections on the disturbed state of

Scotland) as well as work by WILLIAM DUNBAR, GAVIN DOUGLAS and HENRYSON. The manuscripts passed into several hands, including those of PEPYS. A selection appeared in 1786.

Major Barbara A play by SHAW, produced in 1905. Major Barbara has joined the Salvation Army in revolt against her father, the armaments manufacturer Andrew Undershaft. Quite as much a rebel against the social conventions, Undershaft weakens her faith by argument and by showing her the model conditions in which his workers live. Barbara is forced to realize that her own fight against poverty is less successful than her father's.

Malamud, Bernard 1914–86 American novelist. His first novel, *The Natural* (1952), deals with baseball. *The Assistant* (1957), *A New Life* (1961), *The Fixer* (1966, PULITZER PRIZE) and *Pictures of Fidelman* (1969) all explore aspects of the personal struggle involved in the Jewish experience. Later novels are *The Tenants* (1971), *Dubin's Lives* (1979) and *God's Grace* (1982). Malamud's short stories are collected in *The Magic Barrel* (1958), *Idiots First* (1963) and *Rembrandt's Hat* (1973).

Malcontent, The A tragicomedy by MARSTON, commonly regarded as his most accomplished play. It was published (with revisions probably by WEBSTER) and performed in 1604, but may originally have been produced a few years earlier. Altofronto loses the duchy of Genoa to Pietro but returns disguised as Malevole, a licensed philosopher-buffoon. He is helped by Pietro's first minister, Mendoza, an ambitious rogue who has seduced Pietro's willing wife Aurelia and has designs on Malevole's wife Maria. Malevole persuades Pietro to go into hiding and then announces his death. Mendoza seizes power but his duplicity is exposed during a ball at the ducal palace.

Malet, Lucas [Kingsley, Mary] 1852–1931 Novelist. She was the daughter of CHARLES KINGSLEY. Among her novels, *The Wages of Sin* (1891) and *The History of Sir Richard Calmady* (1901) were highly popular.

Mallet, David c. 1705–65 Poet. A Scot who went to London and anglicized his name from 'Malloch', he gained entrance to POPE's circle. He collaborated with JAMES THOMSON on a MASQUE, *Alfred* (1740), remembered only for 'Rule Britannia', in fact contributed by Thomson but claimed by Mallet. Mallet himself is remembered for *William and Margaret* (1724), a forerunner of Gothic and Romantic verse. It was developed from the fragment of an old BALLAD, 'Margaret's Ghost', which was later included in THOMAS PERCY's *Reliques of Ancient English Poetry*.

Mallock, W(illiam) H(urrell) 1849–1923 Conservative thinker. The nephew of J. A. FROUDE and RICHARD HURRELL FROUDE, he defended traditional values against liberal theology, the progress of science and new political ideologies. He is chiefly remembered for two satirical works in the manner of PEACOCK. *The New Republic: or, Culture, Faith, and Philosophy in an English Country House* (1877) pits the views of RUSKIN against those of T. H. HUXLEY, BENJAMIN JOWETT, MATTHEW ARNOLD and PATER. *The New Paul and Virginia: or, Positivism on an Island* (1878–9) takes Huxley, TYNDALL, FREDERIC HARRISON and HARRIET MARTINEAU as its particular targets.

Malone, Edmond 1741–1812 Scholar. Though remembered for his work on SHAKESPEARE, he was a man of many interests and friends in literary circles. Coming to London from Dublin in 1763, he struck up a lifelong friendship with JOHNSON and helped BOSWELL with *THE JOURNAL OF A TOUR TO THE HEBRIDES* as well as *THE LIFE OF SAMUEL JOHNSON*, which he edited from its third to its sixth edition. BURKE dedicated his *REFLECTIONS ON THE REVOLUTION IN FRANCE* to Malone and REYNOLDS, whose writings he later edited, painted his portrait in 1774. Malone's devotion to the methodical study of Shakespeare, which finally resulted in his 10-volume edition (1790), led him to quarrel with his bad-tempered mentor, STEEVENS. He died without finishing his biography of Shakespeare, though Boswell's son made some order out of Malone's completed work, notes and revisions in the 21-volume *Plays and Poems of William Shakespeare* (1821). He also played an important part in exposing the forgeries of CHATTERTON and IRELAND, and edited the works of GOLDSMITH (1780) and the prose of DRYDEN (1800).

Malory, Sir Thomas d. ?1471 Author of *LE MORTE DARTHUR*, a title taken from the epilogue of CAXTON's edition (1485). Malory's identity is uncertain and several possible figures have been suggested. The author himself provides only the following information: that his name was Thomas Malory, that he was a knight, and that he wrote most if not all of his work while imprisoned in Newgate, where he completed it in 1469–70.

Malouf, David 1934– Australian novelist and poet. His life has alternated between Australia and Europe, while his work juxtaposes different modes of existence and perception. He achieved recognition as a poet with *Bicycle and Other Poems* (1970), *Neighbours in a Thicket* (1974), *The Year of the Foxes* (1979), *First Things Last* (1980), *Wild Lemons* (1981), *Selected Poems* (1981) and *New and Collected Poems* (1991). He has, however, become better known as a novelist. *Johnno* (1975), his most conventional novel, explores the hero's rebellion against Brisbane society in the 1940s and 1950s. *12 Edmonstone Street* (1985) contains four more autobiographical explorations. Artists play central roles in *An Imaginary Life* (1978) – about Ovid – the title-novella of *Child's Play* (1982) and *Harland's Half Acre* (1984). *Fly Away Peter* (1982) and *The Great World* (1990), contrast the calm of Australia with the horrors of World War I.

Malthus, Thomas Robert 1766–1834 Economist. *On the Principle of Population as it Affects the Future Improvement of Society* (1798, second edition 1803), argued that population increases geometrically while food supply increases mathematically; population levels would outgrow the means of subsistence. His theory provoked controversy, largely because of his apparent acceptance (in the first edition) of poverty and disease as necessary checks on population growth, but exerted a lasting influence on 19th-century thought. Malthus's later writings were directly concerned with economics, notably *An Investigation of the Cause of the Present High Price of Provisions* (1800), *Observations on the Effect of the Corn Laws* (1814) and *The Principles of Political Economy* (1820).

Mamet, David 1947– American playwright. He first attracted attention with one-acters, such as *Duck Variations* (1972) and *Sexual Perversity in Chicago* (1974), and made his name with a Broadway production in 1977 of *American Buffalo*, a scathing attack on the decline of American values from the perspective of a Vietnam War veteran. Like all his work, it is minimally plotted and concentrates on character development. Other plays include: *A Life in the Theatre* (1977), contrasting an elderly and a youthful actor onstage and backstage; *All Men are Whores* (1977); *Glengarry Glen Ross* (1983;

filmed, 1992), about the world of real-estate salesmen; and *Speed-the-Plow* (1988). Subsequently much of his attention has been devoted to filmwriting and directing, and adapting Chekhov.

Man and Superman A comedy by SHAW, produced in 1905 and published in 1908. His ideas about the 'life force' are embodied in Ann Whitefield and her guardian, John Tanner. She decides to marry him and, though he struggles to evade it, her decision proves irresistible. Some of the play's liveliest encounters occur in Spain, where he dreams the scene (sometimes omitted in performance) 'Don Juan in Hell'.

Man of Feeling, The A SENTIMENTAL NOVEL by HENRY MACKENZIE, published in 1771. Harley, the quixotic hero, leaves home to seek his fortune and is educated in the harsh realities of the world by encounters with, among others, a pair of professional cardsharpers and a prostitute. In Bedlam he meets a girl who has gone mad for love. The novel is a critique of acquisitive society and a warning against being taken in by appearances, its sentimentality relieved by a pervasive, gentle IRONY.

Man of Law's Tale, The See *CANTERBURY TALES*.

Man of Mode, The: or, *Sir Fopling Flutter* The third and last comedy by ETHEREGE, produced and published in 1676. One of the first great examples of RESTORATION COMEDY, it reflects society as seen through the brilliant personification of its types. The characters include: Dorimant, a witty gentleman (perhaps modelled on ROCHESTER), and his follower Medley; the beautiful and intelligent Harriet; the poet Young Bellair and his love Emilia; the old-fashioned Lady Woodvill and the fashionable and wise Lady Townley; the remarkable Sir Fopling Flutter; and the sharply observed shoemaker and orange-woman. Dorimant meets his match in Harriet, with whom he falls in love.

Manciple's Tale, The See *CANTERBURY TALES*.

Mandeville, Bernard de 1670–1733 Satirist. A Dutchman, he practised medicine in England. His most famous work was a SATIRE in doggerel verse, published as *The Grumbling Hive: or, Knaves Turned Honest* (1705), reissued with prose commentaries as *The Fable of the Bees: or, Private Vices, Public Benefits* (1714 and 1723), expanded in 1728, and published complete in 1734. Its mordant view of society as a hive in which mankind flourished through mutual greed provoked replies from LAW and BERKELEY. Other writings include *A Modest Defence of Public Stews* (1724), *An Enquiry into the Causes of the Frequent Executions at Tyburn* (1725) and *An Enquiry into the Origin of Honour, and the Usefulness of Christianity in War* (1732).

Mandeville's Travels (*The Travels of Sir John Mandeville*) An account in Middle English prose of travels through Europe and the Near East, including the Holy Land, originally written in French (*c.* 1357) and translated into many European languages. It claims to be the work of Sir John Mandeville, who says he was born in St Albans, began his travels on 29 September 1322, and wrote his book from memory when suffering from arthritic gout. The identity of the real author is unknown and his account is compiled from previous sources, notably the itineraries translated into French by Jean de Long of St Omer (1351). Traditional stories and legends, as well as mythical animals, appear alongside accurate observation and scientific fact.

Manfred A dramatic poem by BYRON, published in 1817. The hero lives in the Alps as a guilty outcast. Neither the spirits of the universe nor the Witch of the Alps relieve his misery, though the spirits of Evil summon the shade of Astarte, the sister whom he loved and whose death is the cause of his guilt. She tells him that he will die the next day. When the evil spirits come to claim him, Manfred rejects his compact and they disappear. Though he dies at the predicted time, his resolution to remain master of his fate never falters.

Mangan, James Clarence 1803–49 Irish poet. *Anthologia Germanica* (1845) consists of translations from German poets. *The Poets and Poetry of Munster* (1849) was called translations but is more correctly versions in English. Mangan contributed to *Romances and Ballads of Ireland* (edited by E. Ellis; 1850) and left a version of the Irish satire, *The Tribes of Ireland* by Aenghus O'Daly (1852). His best-known poems, 'Dark Rosaleen' and 'The Nameless One', are often found in collections of Irish verse.

Manhire, Bill 1946– New Zealand poet, short-story writer, critic and editor. He was influenced by contemporary American poetry, particularly ROBERT CREELEY. Typically using a short line and combining clarity of diction with ambiguity of meaning, his poetry mixes different idioms and registers of language. Volumes include *The Elaboration* (1972), *How to Take Off Your Clothes at the Picnic* (1977), *Good Looks* (1982), *Zoetropes: Poems 1972–82* (1984) and *Milky Way Bar* (1991). *The New Land* (1990) is a collection of stories. He has also written a study of MAURICE GEE (1986) and co-edited several collections of stories.

Manley, Delarivière (Mary) 1663–1724 Novelist, playwright and political journalist. She wrote a comedy, *The Lost Lover*, and a tragedy, *The Royal Mischief* (both 1696), but is best known for pioneering the ROMAN À CLEF in English with: *The Secret History of Queen Sarah and the Sarazians* (1705–11); the notorious *Secret Memoirs and Manners of Several Persons of Quality, of Both Sexes*, usually known as *The New Atalantis* (1709), for which she, her publisher and printer were arrested; and *Memoirs of Europe towards the Close of the Eighth Century* (1710). In 1711 she took over the editorship of *THE EXAMINER* from SWIFT, with whom she collaborated in a number of polemic pamphlets. *The Power of Love, in Seven Novels* (1720) is a collection of conventional romances.

Manning, Olivia 1908–80 Novelist. Her wartime experiences in Bucharest, Athens, Egypt and Jerusalem form the basis of the six novels grouped into *The Balkan Trilogy* (*The Great Fortune*, 1960; *The Spoilt City*, 1962; *Friends and Heroes*, 1965) and *The Levant Trilogy* (*The Danger Tree*, 1977; *The Battle Lost and Won*, 1978; *The Sum of Things*, 1980). The fate of a newly married English couple, Harriet and Guy Pringle, is the central thread in a narrative which gives an ambitious and detailed portrait of the effects of war. Other novels include *School for Love* (1951) and *The Doves of Venus* (1955). She also published two collections of short stories.

Mannyng of Brunne, Robert *c.* 1283–1338 Author of *Handlinge Sin* and the *Story of England*. A native of Bourne in Lincolnshire, he was a Gilbertine canon at Sempringham Priory (*c.* 1302–17). *Handling Sin*, begun in 1303, translates the Anglo-Norman *Manuel des péchés* (*c.* 1250–70) usually ascribed to William of Wadington. The Ten Commandments, the seven deadly sins, sacrilege, the 12 requisites of penance and the 12 graces of shrift are all discussed, and illustrated with skilfully told EXEMPLA which are the work's chief interest. Thirteen of them were added to his source by Mannyng. The *Story of England* (1338) is a two-part verse CHRONICLE covering the period from the Flood to the death of Edward I (1307).

Mansfield, Katherine [Beauchamp, Kathleen Mansfield] 1888–1923 Short-story writer. Born in New Zealand, she settled in London in 1908, contributing to THE NEW AGE and *Rhythm*, an *avant-garde* quarterly founded by Michael Sadleir and JOHN MIDDLETON MURRY, who became her second husband in 1918. She died of tuberculosis in France.

Her penetrating and relentless intelligence, balanced by a sense of form, was ideally suited to the short story. Her first collection, *In a German Pension* (1911), was followed by *Prelude*, a story published singly in 1918, which like much of her best work drew on her childhood in New Zealand and showed the influence of Chekhov. Others appeared in *Bliss and Other Stories* (1919), *The Garden Party and Other Stories* (1920) and *Other Stories* (1922). Posthumous works included *Poems* (edited by Murry; 1923), *Something Childish and Other Stories* (1924) and *A Fairy Story* (1932). *The Collected Stories of Katherine Mansfield* (1945) was an omnibus volume. Murry also edited *The Letters of Katherine Mansfield* (1928) and *Katherine Mansfield's Letters to John Middleton Murry: 1913–1922* (1951).

Mansfield Park A novel by JANE AUSTEN, begun in 1811 and published in 1814. Sir Thomas and Lady Bertram of Mansfield Park have two daughters, Maria and Julia, and two sons, Tom and Edmund. Fanny Price, Lady Bertram's impoverished niece, is brought to live at Mansfield Park where she is patronized by three of her cousins, but finds a friend in Edmund. When Sir Thomas leaves for the West Indies, his children plan to stage a play (INCHBALD's *Lovers' Vows*) and engage in flirtations, from which Fanny alone stays aloof. Maria Bertram, though engaged to Mr Rushworth, is attracted to Henry Crawford; his sister Mary fascinates Edmund Bertram. But Maria decides after all to marry Rushworth, whereupon Henry turns his attention to Fanny. When she refuses his proposal, Sir Thomas, now back at Mansfield, is highly displeased at her apparent foolishness. The unhappy Fanny visits her own family in Portsmouth, though longing to be back at Mansfield Park. Meanwhile Maria, now Mrs Rushworth, runs off with Henry Crawford. Julia elopes with a Mr Yates. Edmund, who has taken orders, is rejected by Mary Crawford and at last begins to see her character clearly. Edmund and Fanny eventually find happiness together.

Many Inventions A collection of 14 stories by KIPLING, published in 1893. It includes six Indian tales, of which two concern characters who also appear in SOLDIERS THREE. In 'His Private Honour' Ortheris's conduct is dictated by a code which transcends the army rule book. Other notable stories are: 'The Disturber of Traffic', about the delusions and growing obsession of Dowse, a lighthouse keeper in the Java Straits; 'The Finest Story in the World', in which Charlie begins to recall moments of previous lives on a Roman galley and a Viking ship; and 'The Record of Badalia Herodsfoot', a realistic account of the London slums in the 1890s.

Mapanje, Jack 1945– Malawian poet. A single volume, *Of Chameleons and Gods* (1981), established him as one of Africa's most accomplished and distinctive poets. It draws on a wide range of subjects and techniques, including traditional forms and symbols, colloquial monologues, and satires on African politicians and intellectuals. His imprisonment without charge or trial in 1987–91 became an international *cause célèbre*. He now lives in Britain.

Marble Faun, The: or, The Romance of Monte Beni A novel by HAWTHORNE, published in 1860. In Britain it was entitled *Transformation*. Kenyon and Hilda are Americans studying art in Rome. With Miriam, an artist, they meet Donatello, an Italian nobleman who resembles the Marble Faun sculpted by Praxiteles. Donatello falls in love with Miriam, but she is troubled by some secret from the past and dogged by a mysterious Capuchin monk. Witnessed by Hilda and perhaps encouraged by Miriam, Donatello kills the monk. Agreeing with Miriam that they must bear the consequences, he gives himself up and goes to prison. She embarks on a penitential pilgrimage. After finding relief in a Catholic confessional, Hilda marries Kenyon. The secret of Miriam's past is never revealed: a 'Postscript' claims that to seek to know whether Donatello really is a faun and who Miriam really is, would destroy the poetry and beauty of the story.

Mardi and a Voyage Thither A novel by HERMAN MELVILLE, published in 1849. It begins as an adventure story in which the narrator, Taji, and Jarl, an older seaman, desert their ship and encounter a brigantine abandoned by all except a Polynesian couple, Samoa and Annatoo. After Annatoo is drowned the three survivors arrive at the islands of Mardi, where the story becomes a kind of ALLEGORY. Taji lives happily with Yillah. When she is kidnapped he sets out to find her, accompanied by a king, a historian, a philosopher and a poet. Their search takes them to various lands, whose societies are closely observed and discussed. Dominora apparently stands for Great Britain, Porpheero for Europe and Vivenza for the USA. They eventually reach Serenia, which is ruled by Alma (Christ), but Taji insists on continuing his search alone.

Marechera, Dambudzo 1952–87 Zimbabwean novelist and short-story writer. *The House of Hunger* (1978), consisting of a novella and short stories, is a cry of distress from one of the new generation of writers brought up amid war and injustice. *Black Sunlight* (1980), an intense post-modernist novel, deals with urban guerrillas. *An Articulate Anger: Dambudzo Marechera, 1952–87* (1988) contains interviews and statements. Previously unpublished, and sometimes unfinished, writings appear in *The Black Insider* (1990).

Marie de France Late 12th-century French poet who probably lived in England, writing in Anglo-Norman. Conjecture plausibly identifies her with the illegitimate daughter of Godefroy d'Anjou who was abbess of Shaftesbury by 1181 and died *c*. 1216. Her surviving works are the oldest definitely attributed to a woman in England or France. The *Lais* (written before 1189) collect 12 BRETON LAYS, ranging from a mere snippet of the Tristan legend ('Le Chevrefoil') to the lengthy 'Eliduc'. They exercised a powerful influence over the spread of COURTLY LOVE in England. The *Fables* are a collection of 102 Aesopic fables. The *Espurgatoire Saint Patrice* (written after 1189) retells the popular legend of St Patrick's vision of purgatory.

Marino Faliero A tragedy by BYRON, published and produced (against his wishes) in 1821. Set in Venice, like THE TWO FOSCARI, it deals with the conflict between the haughty 14th-century Doge, Marino Faliero, and Michele Steno, a gentleman of poor but distinguished family. *Marino Faliero* is also the title of a tragedy (1885) by SWINBURNE which presents the Doge as a symbol of liberty.

Marius the Epicurean A novel or philosophical romance by WALTER PATER, published in 1885. Set in ancient Rome, the story examines Marius' response to the philosophical influences of his time, Roman religion, the brutal spectacles of the amphitheatre and finally the growing power of Christianity. He dies to save the life of his friend Cornelius and is regarded as a martyr by the Christian church.

Mark, Jan(et) (Marjorie) 1943– Writer of CHILDREN'S LITERATURE. Norfolk is the setting for her early novels, *Thunder and Lightnings* (1976), and *Handles* (1983). *Nothing to be Afraid Of* (1980), and *Feet* (1983) are collections of short stories. Her SCIENCE-FICTION trilogy for older children, *The Ennead* (1978), *Divide and Rule* (1979) and *Aquarius* (1982), provides a bleak and despairing vision of a corrupt society and its victims. *Dream House* (1987) and *Man in Motion* (1989) strike a lighter note.

Markandaya, Kamala 1924– Novelist. She has shown herself an impressive explorer of human consciousness and of the convolutions of intimate relationships in *Nectar in a Sieve* (1954), *Some Inner Fury* (1955), *Possession* (1963), *A Silence of Desire* (1960), *The Coffer Dams* (1969), *A Handful of Rice* (1966), *Two Virgins* (1974), *The Golden Honeycomb* (1977) and *Pleasure City* (1982).

Markham, Edwin 1852–1940 American poet. His most famous piece, the title-poem of *The Man with the Hoe and Other Poems* (1899), was inspired by Millet's painting. This collection and *Lincoln and Other Poems* (1901) are largely concerned with the degrading conditions of the working classes. Less popular volumes include *California the Wonderful* (1915), *Gates of Paradise* (1920), *Ballad of the Gallows Bird* (1926), *New Poems: Eighty Poems at Eighty* (1932) and *Collected Poems* (1940).

Markham, Gervase *c.* 1568–1637 Miscellaneous writer. An ex-soldier, he wrote prolifically for a popular audience, supplementing *A Discourse on Horsemanship* (1593) and *Cavelarice: or, The English Horseman* (1610) with a veterinary work, *Markham's Masterpiece: or, What Doth a Horseman Lack* (1610), and books about husbandry and the art of war, as well as plays and poems.

Marlatt, Daphne 1942– Canadian poet and novelist. Concerned with the attempt to render the perceptual process in language, her poetry frequently relates mental states to exterior surroundings. *Rings* (1971), a long poem, offers a vivid picture of isolation. *Vancouver Poems* (1972) documents a personal response to the city. *Steveston* (1974), generally regarded as her most important work to date, meditates on the history of a Japanese-Canadian fishing town. Other volumes include *Frames* (1968), *Our Lives* (1975), *Net Work* (1980), *Here and There* (1981), *How Hug a Stone* (1983) and *Double Negative* (1988). *Zocalo* (1977) and *Ana Historic* (1988) are novels.

Marlowe, Christopher 1564–93 Playwright and poet. The son of a Canterbury shoemaker, he was awarded a scholarship at Corpus Christi College, Cambridge (BA 1584, MA 1587). Possibly while still there, he became an agent of Francis Walsingham and a favourite of Walsingham's brother, Thomas. Nothing is known about his work for the secret service, and only speculation links it with his violent death in a Deptford tavern. The manner of his death added spice to an already notorious reputation. Accused of atheism, blasphemy, subversion and homosexuality, Marlowe was certainly free-thinking and indiscreet.

On leaving Cambridge Marlowe almost at once presented the London theatre with the startling success of *TAMBURLAINE THE GREAT* (two parts, both probably performed in 1587). The chronological order of his work is uncertain, but he may already have written *Dido, Queen of Carthage*; whose first edition (1594) named NASHE as co-author. The play's use of Virgil confirms the careful apprenticeship in the classics suggested by Marlowe's translation of Lucan's *Pharsalia* (published in 1600, but possibly completed at Cambridge) and of Ovid's *Elegies* (published in 1595, but probably also student work). After *Tamburlaine*, Marlowe continued to dramatize the careers and aspirations of overreaching heroes whose defiance of social, political and religious morality prompts admiration as well as condemnation. THE JEW OF MALTA (*c.* 1590) is a grotesque comedy in which murderous excess and inflated rhetoric parody statesmanship and the posturings of Christian authority. *The Massacre at Paris* (*c.* 1589) resembles *The Jew of Malta* in its energetically sardonic treatment of the horrific St Bartholomew massacre of Protestants in 1572. *EDWARD II* (*c.* 1592), Marlowe's most accomplished play, depicts the defeat and eventual murder of a homosexual king with a new and unexpected plainness of style. The Marlovian overreacher comes to what, in retrospect, seems a logical conclusion in *DOCTOR FAUSTUS*, claimed as his last play. Marlowe spent the last months before his murder writing the narrative poem *HERO AND LEANDER* (published in 1598), which, together with the lyrical *THE PASSIONATE SHEPHERD*, is his poetic monument.

Marmion: A Tale of Flodden Field A poem by SIR WALTER SCOTT, published in 1808. It followed *THE LAY OF THE LAST MINSTREL* in Scott's immensely successful series of verse romances which take their subjects from legend and history. The title character is a fictitious favourite of Henry VIII who schemes to marry the rich and beautiful Lady Clare in spite of his entanglement with Constance de Beverley, a nun who has broken her vows. The climax takes place at the battle of Flodden, where Marmion is killed.

The poem includes the songs 'Where Shall the Lover Rest?' and 'Lochinvar'.

Marmion, Shakerley 1603–39 Poet, playwright and Royalist. He wrote three plays: *Holland's Leaguer* (1631), *A Fine Companion* (1633) and *The Antiquary* (*c.* 1635), his best work, mocking the foolishness of old age. *Cupid and Psyche* (1637), based on Apuleius' *The Golden Ass*, is among the best examples of Caroline narrative poetry.

Marprelate, Martin The name assumed by the author of a series of Puritan pamphlets attacking the bishops, issued from secret presses in 1588–9. The identity of Marprelate is in doubt, though John Penry and John Udall were arrested. Penry was executed in 1593, while Udall probably died in prison. Job Throckmorton denied complicity at Penry's trial and escaped punishment. Seven tracts survive: *The Epistle* (October 1588), *The Epitome* (November 1588), *Certain Mineral and Metaphysical Schoolpoints* (February 1589), *Hay* [i.e. have you] *Any Work for Cooper* (March 1589), *Martin Junior* (July 1589), *Martin Senior* (July 1589) and *The Protestation of Martin Marprelate* (September 1589). The bishops replied in *An Admonition to the People of England* (1589) by the Thomas Cooper alluded to in one of the tracts. They also employed professional writers, who never succeeding in matching Marprelate's satirical vigour. LYLY wrote *Pap with a Hatchet* (1589); *A Whip for an Ape* and *Mar-Martin* (both 1589) have also been attributed, although doubtfully, to him. Various pamphlets have been attributed to NASHE, but only *An Almond for a Parrot* (1590) with any certainty. Richard Harvey wrote *Plain Percival* (1589) and *A Theological Discourse of the Lamb of God* (1590).

Marriage A novel by SUSAN FERRIER, published in 1818. Lady Juliana, the Earl of Courtland's daughter, soon loses her romantic illusions after she elopes with Henry Douglas, a penniless young officer. She concentrates her energy on making sure her twin daughters do not repeat her own mistake of an imprudent marriage. Mary rejects her mother's ambitious plans and settles down contentedly with the man of her choice. Adelaide allows herself to be pushed into marriage with an elderly duke but soon deserts him for a worthless man.

Marriage à la Mode A comedy by DRYDEN, produced in 1672 and published in 1673. Its 'heroic' plot concerns the love of Palmyra, daughter of the usurping King of Sicily, and Leonidas, the rightful heir. A contrasting plot in the 'comedy of manners' style concerns Rhodophil and Doralice, married but bored with each other. Rhodophil's friend Palamede falls in love with Doralice, not knowing she is married to Rhodophil. Rhodophil pursues Melantha, not knowing she is intended for Palamede. The quadrille is played out until the characters discover they want their original partners after all.

Marriage of Heaven and Hell, The A prose work by BLAKE, usually dated 1790. It is prefaced by a poem, 'The Argument', declaring that the paths of truth have been corrupted by false religion. 'The Voice of the Devil' attacks the conventional religious distinction between body and soul, proclaims that 'Energy is Eternal Delight' and sides with Satan in MILTON's *PARADISE LOST*. 'Proverbs of Hell' explores this Romantic doctrine in a series of aphorisms, sometimes deliberately shocking.

Marryat, Captain **Frederick** 1792–1848 Novelist and writer of CHILDREN'S LITERATURE. His early novels – *The Naval Officer: or, Scenes and Adventures in the Life of Frank Mildmay* (1829), the highly successful *Peter Simple* (1834), *Jacob Faithful* (1834) and *Mr Midshipman Easy* (1836) – drew on his adventurous career in the navy. After *Japhet in Search of a Father* (1836) and *Snarleyyow* (1837) he turned to children's fiction with *Masterman Ready* (1841), a vigorous rebuke to Johann Wyss's romanticized *Swiss Family Robinson*. Marryat's other great success as children's writer, *The Children of the New Forest* (1847), is set in the Civil War, with heroic Royalist children hiding from their Roundhead oppressors in the forest.

Marsh, Sir **Edward (Howard)** 1872–1953 Civil servant and patron of the arts. For many years he served, in various guises, as private secretary to SIR WINSTON CHURCHILL. A connoisseur of English painting and poetry, he greatly helped Mark Gertler, John and Paul Nash, Stanley Spencer, FLECKER, DE LA MARE, D. H. LAWRENCE, GRAVES and BLUNDEN. The five volumes of Marsh's anthology, GEORGIAN POETRY (1912–22), first brought many of these writers to public notice. He edited the *Collected Poems* (1918) of his friend RUPERT BROOKE, whose literary executor he was.

Marsh, Dame **Ngaio** 1899–1982 New Zealand writer of DETECTIVE FICTION and playwright. She combined a career as a theatre producer with a succession of popular novels, starting with *A Man Lay Dead* (1934), featuring Superintendent Roderick Alleyn of Scotland Yard, her equivalent of CHRISTIE's Hercule Poirot and SAYERS's Lord Peter Wimsey. The settings are often theatrical and her plots show a tight dramatic construction. More than 30 in all, her novels include *Artists in Crime* (1938), *Died in the Wool* (1945), *Opening Night* (1951), *Killer Dolphin* (1966) and *Black as He's Painted* (1974). *A Surfeit of Lampreys*

(1950) and *False Scent* (1961) are plays adapted from her own novels. Her autobiography, *Black Beech and Honeydew* (1966), is primarily about her life in the theatre.

Marston, John 1576–1634 Playwright and poet. His verse SATIRE, collected in *The Metamorphosis of Pygmalion's Image* and *The Scourge of Villainy* (both 1598), earned him a reputation for bitter invective, reinforced by his disputes with JONSON in the 'war of the theatres', to which parts of *Histrio-mastix* (1599) refer. Marston had already written the dark comedy ANTONIO AND MELLIDA and its sequel ANTONIO'S REVENGE, a REVENGE TRAGEDY (both 1599 or 1600). The satiric comedies *Jack Drum's Entertainment* (1600) and *What You Will* (c. 1601) were followed by his best plays, THE DUTCH COURTESAN (before 1603), THE MALCONTENT (1604) and *Parasitaster: or, The Fawn* (c. 1605), all comedies, though *The Malcontent* in particular touches on tragedy. *The Wonder of Women: or, The Tragedy of Sophonisba* (1606) is an uneasy mix of austere Roman tragedy and theatrical spectacle. *The Malcontent* is dedicated to Jonson, his former adversary, whom he joined, with CHAPMAN, in writing the comedy EASTWARD HO (1605). Marston was imprisoned, for unknown reasons, in 1608, abandoned the theatre after his release and took holy orders.

Marston, John Westland 1819–90 Playwright and dramatic critic. His many verse tragedies include *The Patrician's Daughter* (1842). Marston's reviews for THE ATHENAEUM in the 1860s and his retrospective book, *Our Recent Actors* (1888), are substantial contributions to theatrical literature.

Marston, Philip Bourke 1850–87 Poet. The son of JOHN WESTLAND MARSTON, he published *Song-Tide and Other Poems* (1871), *All in All: Poems and Sonnets* (1875) and *Wind-Voices* (1883). *Garden Secrets* (1887), *For a Song's Sake and Other Stories* (1887) and *A Last Harvest* (1891) appeared posthumously.

Martian poets, The A term for a group of poets, first prominent in the late 1970s, whose work presents familiar objects in unfamiliar ways. The title poem of CRAIG RAINE's collection, *A Martian Sends a Postcard Home* (1979), which purports to be a Martian's uncomprehending reaction to everyday things, suggested the label. Disciples include CHRISTOPHER REID and David Sweetman.

Martin, Violet Florence See SOMERVILLE AND ROSS.

Martin Chuzzlewit A novel by DICKENS, published in monthly parts in 1843–4, as *The Life and Adventures of Martin Chuzzlewit, His Relatives, Friends and Enemies. Comprising All His Wills and His Ways, with an Historical Record of What He Did and What He Didn't; Shewing Moreover Who Inherited the Family Plate; Who Came in for the Silver Spoons, and Who for the Wooden Ladles. The Whole Forming a Complete Key to the House of Chuzzlewit.*

The selfish young Martin Chuzzlewit is articled to the hypocritical architect Pecksniff but dimissed at the request of his grandfather, old Martin. Jonas Chuzzlewit, old Martin's nephew, engineers his father's death, marries and maltreats Pecksniff's daughter Mercy, and draws Pecksniff into his dubious schemes. Meanwhile, Martin's disillusioning experiences in America with his irrepressible servant Mark Tapley have taught him valuable lessons. He returns to England determined to make peace with his grandfather but finds him apparently under Pecksniff's control. Eventually old Martin's purpose of testing both Pecksniff and his grandson is revealed, and Martin is able to marry Mary Graham, Chuzzlewit's companion and adopted daughter. Pecksniff is exposed and Jonas, arrested for murdering his partner in roguery, Montague Tigg, poisons himself. Pecksniff's assistant, the innocent Tom Pinch, is suitably employed by old Martin and further gratified when his beloved sister Ruth marries their friend John Westlock. Mrs Sarah Gamp, the drunken midwife, is one of Dickens's most memorable minor characters.

Martin Eden A novel by JACK LONDON, published in 1909. Martin Eden, a labourer and former sailor, educates himself and becomes a writer, aspiring to the life led by the wealthy Ruth Morse. She deserts him when a newspaper brands him a socialist but returns when his work enjoys success. He rejects her and becomes more depressed by the suicide of his friend Russ Brissenden. Despising the society that has finally honoured him, Martin kills himself during a sea voyage.

Martineau, Harriet 1802–76 Writer on religion and economics, and novelist. The sister of JAMES MARTINEAU, she began by writing on religion but became interested in economics, earning a reputation as a lively expositor of UTILITARIANISM in *Illustrations of Political Economy* (1832–4), *Poor Law and Paupers Illustrated* (1833) and *Illustrations of Taxation* (1834). A visit to the USA prompted *Society in America* (1837), which contains her comments on slavery, and *Retrospect of Western Travel* (1838). *Deerbrook* (1839) and *The Hour and the Man* (1841), which takes Toussaint L'Ouverture as its subject, are novels. In 1853 she produced a condensed version of Comte's *Cours de philosophie positive*. Her *Autobiographical Memoir* (1877) is valuable for its comments on her contemporaries.

Martineau, James 1805–1900 Theologian. The brother of HARRIET MARTINEAU, he was a Unitarian minister and professor of mental and moral philosophy at Manchester New College. His highly influential works include *Ideal Substitutes for God* (1879), *Study of Spinoza* (1882), *Types of Ethical Theory* (1885), *A Study of Religion* (1888) and *The Seat of Authority in Religion* (1888).

Martyn, Edward 1859–1923 Irish playwright. He was a prominent figure in the Irish cultural revival and a founder of the Irish Literary Theatre (see ABBEY THEATRE), to which he contributed *The Heather Field* (1899) and *Maeve* (1900). *Romulus and Remus* (1907) and *The Dream Physician* (1914) reflect his later disagreement with YEATS and his circle. *Grangecolman* (1912) was written for the Independent Theatre Company. In 1914 he founded the Irish Theatre to present plays in Gaelic.

Martyrs, Foxe's Book of See ACTS AND MONUMENTS.

Marvell, Andrew 1621–78 METAPHYSICAL POET and satirist. Born near Hull and brought up in the city, Marvell went to Trinity College, Cambridge, in 1633, and made a prolonged tour of the Continent in 1642–7. He wrote some commendatory verses for LOVELACE's *Lucasta* in 1648 and an elegy for Lord Hastings in 1649. His sometimes equivocal political affiliations expressed themselves in cautious approval of Cromwell in 'An Horatian Ode upon Cromwell's Return from Ireland' (1650). In 1651–3 he was tutor to Lord Fairfax's daughter at Nun Appleton House in Yorkshire, where he probably composed his finest poetry, including 'Upon Appleton House'. In 1653–6 he acted as tutor to William Dutton, later a ward of Cromwell's, and in 1657 secured the post of Assistant Latin Secretary to the Council of State, for which MILTON recommended him. He was MP for Hull from 1659 until his death.

With the Restoration, Marvell's moderate eulogies of Cromwell were converted into a reasonable acceptance of monarchical stability, but he rapidly became an outspoken opponent of Charles II's government for its failure to promote religious toleration and its inefficiency in military matters. His comprehensively withering SATIRE, *The Last Instructions to a Painter*, written in 1667, pilloried those who had influence on affairs of state. Other political and religious satires include 'Clarindon's House Warming', 'The Loyal Scot', 'The Statue in Stocks-Market' and a prose work, *The Rehearsal Transprosed* (1672–3), denouncing the opinions of Samuel Parker, Archdeacon of Canterbury.

Apart from his satires, little of his poetry was known or published before *Miscellaneous Poems* (1681). Marvell was 'discovered' in the 19th century as the writer of accomplished PASTORAL poetry and celebrated as 'the green poet'. These poems, probably written before 1653, include 'The Garden' (a complicated contemplation on sophistication and innocence), 'The Picture of Little T.C. in a Prospect of Flowers', and 'The Nymph Complaining for the Death of Her Fawn'. His chief influence was DONNE, whose metaphysical CONCEITS clearly impressed Marvell, though he is stylistically less brittle than his predecessor. His most famous poem is 'To His Coy Mistress', a seductive love poem of the CARPE DIEM mode, precisely constructed and erotically pitched.

Marxist criticism Never a single school of thought, but a set of changing responses to the ideas of Marx and Engels, who themselves had little time to elaborate a cultural theory explaining how social and economic forces condition or determine literature and art. From within the Socialist Realism which the Soviet Union adopted in the 1930s, Georg Lukács evolved a theory of 'reflection', by which a novel gives us a structural understanding of social development. The Frankfurt School developed a Hegelian strain of cultural theory; Adorno, Horkheimer and others believed that *avant-garde* literature and art give us a 'negative' knowledge of a hostile social world. Adorno's associate Walter Benjamin developed a personal mixture of fundamentalist Marxism and Cabbalistic lore. In the 1960s STRUCTURALISM helped Marxist criticism to a new phase of sophistication. Lucien Goldmann's 'genetic structuralism' revealed the 'homologies' (structural parallels) between literature, ideas and social groups. In contrast, Louis Althusser argued that the different levels within the social formation have no overall unity but possess their own 'specific effectivity'.

RAYMOND WILLIAMS and Terry Eagleton are the best-known English Marxist critics. The former developed late as a Marxist from an early socialist reinterpretation of F. R. LEAVIS, while Eagleton was influenced by Althusser's theories of ideology and then by the tradition of Brecht and Benjamin.

Mary Barton: A Tale of Manchester Life A novel by ELIZABETH GASKELL, published in 1848. Its close, sympathetic observation of the lives of factory workers and its portrayal of industrial unrest make it an important CONDITION OF ENGLAND NOVEL. John Barton, an active trade unionist, is chosen by his fellows to kill Henry Carson, son of one of their employers. Carson had been paying flattering attention to Barton's daughter Mary and she had briefly been diverted from her love for Jem Wilson, a young engineer. When Jem is charged with the murder, Mary manages to establish his innocence without revealing her father's guilt. Finally Barton, on the verge of death, confesses his crime to Henry Carson's father and obtains his forgiveness.

Masefield, John (Edward) 1878-1967 Poet, novelist, playwright, journalist and writer of CHILDREN'S LITERATURE. After youthful service in the merchant navy, he began his career as a poet with *Salt-Water Ballads* (1902), which included 'Sea Fever' ('I must go down to the sea again'). *Ballads and Poems* (1910) was followed by long narrative poems, *The Everlasting Mercy* (1911), *The Widow in the Bye Street* (1912), *The Daffodil Fields* (1913) and *Dauber* (1913). *Reynard the Fox* (1919) is a Chaucerian narrative of a fox-hunt. *Collected Poems* (1923) proved a great success and Masefield became POET LAUREATE in 1930, though his critical reputation then waned. In all, he published more than 50 books. Novels include *Sard Harker* (1924), *The Bird of Dawning* (1933), *Dead Ned* (1938) and *Live and Kicking Ned* (1939). Plays include *The Trial of Jesus* (1926) and *The Coming of Christ* (1928). *The Midnight Folk* (1927) and *The Box of Delights* (1933) are popular children's books. *So Long to Learn* (1952) and *Grace before Ploughing* (1966) are autobiographical.

Mason, A(lfred) E(dward) W(oodley) 1865-1948 Novelist. *The Four Feathers* (1902) is the best known of his many popular historical novels and adventure stories. He is also remembered for his contribution to DETECTIVE FICTION in creating Inspector Hanaud of the Sûreté, who appeared in *At the Villa Rose* (1910), *The House of the Arrow* (1924), *No Other Tiger* (1927) and *The Prisoner in the Opal* (1929).

Mason, R(onald) A(lison) K(ells) 1905-71 New Zealand poet and playwright. His poetry is strongly influenced by his classical education, but also contains a strong religious element. His best work is found in his early volumes: *The Beggar* (1924), *In the Manner of Men* (1923) – sometimes seen as marking the beginnings of modern New Zealand verse – and *No New Thing* (1934). Later volumes include *End of Day* (1936), *This Dark Will Lighten: Selected Poems 1923-1941* (1941) and *Collected Poems* (1962). *Squire Speaks* (1938), *China* (1943) and *Refugee* (1945) are political plays, reflecting the Marxism that also animated his journalistic work for the magazines *People's Voice* and *Challenge*, which he edited from 1943 to 1954. A modern Romantic, whose best poetry appears to be an urgent expression of spontaneous feeling, he is highly regarded, though seldom imitated, in New Zealand.

Mason, William 1725-97 Poet, playwright, gardener and musician. He was a friend of Thomas Arne, THOMAS GRAY, JOSHUA REYNOLDS, HORACE WALPOLE, MARY DELANY and GARRICK, but his own achievements were second-rate by comparison to theirs. His plays adopted old-fashioned forms: *Elfrida* (1752) and *Caractacus* (1759) are both historical tragedies in the classical mode. As a poet he produced rather plodding couplets, though the didactic *The English Garden* (1772-82) is in BLANK VERSE. It advocates the informality which he put into practice in his own designs. An avid musician, he invented the celestinette and wrote essays on cathedral music. He painted badly and translated Du Fresnoy's *Art of Painting* (1782). As Gray's literary executor, he published the poet's *Life and Letters* in 1774.

masque A spectacular entertainment, involving dance, drama, music, lavish costumes and elaborate scenery. It reached its height at the court of JAMES I and Charles I, where many of the finest masques resulted from the uneasy collaboration between JONSON and Inigo Jones, who introduced Italian perspective scenery to the English theatre. The origins of the masque lay in the entertainments provided for Queen Elizabeth during her 'progresses' to noblemen's seats; these retained features from the older 'disguisings', in which disguised guests would present gifts to their host.

Massinger, Philip 1583-1640 Playwright. His long association with the KING'S MEN, almost uninterrupted from 1613 to 1640, suggests the regard in which he was held. He thought his tragedy about the Emperor Domitian, *THE ROMAN ACTOR* (1626), to be his best work but it has not lasted as well as the bitter comedies *A NEW WAY TO PAY OLD DEBTS* (c. 1622) and *THE CITY MADAM* (c. 1632). An independent, satirical temperament is unmistakable in the works of which he is generally supposed to have been sole author, like *The Maid of Honour* (c. 1621), *The Bondman* (1623), *The Renegado* (1624) and *Believe As You List* (1631). He collaborated with FIELD in *THE FATAL DOWRY* (c. 1618), with DEKKER in *THE VIRGIN MARTYR* (1620) and with FLETCHER in more than 20 plays. These include: *The Tragedy of Sir John van Olden Barnavelt* (1619), *The Custom of the Country* (c. 1619), *The Beggar's Bush* (c. 1622) and *The Spanish Curate* (c. 1622).

Masson, David 1822-1907 Biographer. Professor of rhetoric and English literature at Edinburgh from 1865 until 1895, he founded *Macmillan's Magazine*, which he edited until 1867. Apart from his exhaustive life of MILTON (1859-94), he wrote studies of DRUMMOND OF HAWTHORNDEN (1873), CHATTERTON (1874), and DE QUINCEY (1881), *Essays Biographical and Critical, Chiefly on English Poets* (1856) and several volumes of memoirs.

Master Humphrey's Clock A weekly miscellany begun by DICKENS in 1840. It reintroduced Mr Pickwick and the Wellers, and served as a framework for *THE OLD CURIOSITY SHOP*, but was never in itself a commercial success. Dickens dropped the title when *BARNABY RUDGE* began to appear in 1841.

Master of Ballantrae, The: *A Winter's Tale* A novel by ROBERT LOUIS STEVENSON, published in 1889. It is set in Jacobite Scotland in the period after the 1745 Rebellion. The narrator, Ephraim Mackellar, recounts the lifelong feud between James Durie, the Master of Ballantrae, violent, charming and unscrupulous, and his younger brother Henry, quiet, dutiful and dull. When the Master is reported killed at Culloden, Henry inherits his title, estate and sweetheart, Alison Graeme. The Master returns, embittered by his exclusion, and suffers apparent death on two more occasions, each time at his brother's hand: first in a moonlit duel and then, when the scene has shifted to America, in a murderous attack. The shock of his last reappearance, literally from the grave, kills Henry. They are buried together. The wild melodrama of the plot is matched by the dark subtlety of the psychology.

Master of Game, The A hunting treatise (c. 1410) by Edward Plantagenet, 2nd Duke of York, widely copied during the 15th century. It is largely a translation of the *Livre de chasse* by Gaston Phoebus, Comte de Foix.

Masterman Ready See MARRYAT, CAPTAIN FREDERICK.

Masters, Edgar Lee 1868-1950 American poet and novelist. He became famous with *SPOON RIVER ANTHOLOGY* (1915), a book of epitaphs in free verse about the dead in a rural Illinois cemetery. He never repeated its success, but commanded attention with three dramatic poems, *Lee* (1926), *Jack Kelso* (1928) and *Godbey* (1931), three novels based on his youth, *Mitch Miller* (1920), *Skeeters Kirby* (1923) and *Mirage* (1924), and a hostile biographical study of Lincoln (1931). *The New Spoon*

River (1924) applied the technique of his first success to urban life. *Across Spoon River* (1924) is his autobiography.

Masters, John 1914–83 Novelist. His fast-moving, epic adventures about British India include *Nightrunners of Bengal* (1951), set during the Indian Mutiny, and *Bhowani Junction* (1954), about the strife immediately preceding Indian independence. Masters also wrote *Loss of Eden*, a trilogy about World War I comprising *Now, God be Thanked* (1979), *Heart of War* (1980) and *By the Green of the Spring* (1981).

Mather, Cotton 1663–1728 American Puritan minister, the eldest son of INCREASE MATHER and grandson of JOHN COTTON and RICHARD MATHER. His two most important works were *Magnalia Christi Americana* ('The Great Works of Christ in America', 1702), an ecclesiastical history of New England conceived as an epic account of a providentially guided community, and *Bonifacius: An Essay upon the Good* (1710), a treatise stressing that true Christians fulfil their callings for the good of the whole community in co-operative rather than competitive ways. Apart from many sermons expounding Puritan doctrine, he also wrote on witchcraft in *Memorable Providences, Relating to Witchcrafts and Possessions* (1689) and *The Wonders of the Invisible World* (1693), on the natural world in *The Christian Philosopher* (1721) and on medicine in *The Angel of Bethesda* (1722). *Parentator* (1724) is a biography of his father, 'Paterna' an unpublished autobiography written for his children. Among other religious works, *Biblia Americana*, a systematic commentary on the Bible that was his lifelong project, remained unpublished at his death.

Mather, Increase 1639–1723 American Puritan minister. The son of RICHARD MATHER and the husband of JOHN COTTON's daughter, he was minister of the Second Church of Boston as well as a fellow of Harvard University and eventually its president.

His election sermon, *The Day of Trouble is Near* (1674), was sometimes interpreted as prophesying the Indian wars. Two histories, *A Relation of the Troubles Which Have Happened in New England, by Reason of the Indians There* (1677) and *A Brief History of the War with the Indians* (about King Philip's War; 1676), view the wars as contests between the saints and the forces of the devil. His works on scientific subjects, like the *Kometographia* (1683) and other works on comets, as well as the *Essay for the Recording of Illustrious Providences* (1685), include detailed observations which point to the mysterious ways of God rather than to rational understanding. *Cases of Conscience concerning Evil Spirits* (1693) censured the judges at the Salem witchcraft trials for basing convictions on 'spectral evidence'. Other writings include sermons on conversion and church membership policy, speculations on the millennium, and an autobiography.

Mather, Richard 1596–1669 Puritan minister and father of INCREASE MATHER. Born in Lancashire, he emigrated to New England in 1635 and became one of the leading ministers in the Bay Colony, contributing to the translations of the Psalms in the BAY PSALM BOOK (1640). *Church Government and Church Covenant Discussed* (1643) is the most important of his treatises defending the New England congregational system against Presbyterian opponents. He was one of the main architects of the 1648 Cambridge Synod's *Platform of Church Discipline* (1649), which set out the main principles of New England church polity. His *Journal*, which includes an account of his Atlantic crossing, was published in the 19th century.

Maturin, Charles Robert 1782–1824 Novelist and playwright. Born in Dublin, he took holy orders after studying at Trinity College. He is remembered for *MELMOTH THE WANDERER* (1820), a powerful GOTHIC NOVEL. Other novels were *The Fatal Revenge* (1807), *The Wild Irish Boy* (1808), *The Milesian Chief* (1811), *Women: or, Pour et Contre* (1818) and *The Albigenses* (1824). His tragedy *Bertram* was produced with great success in 1816, but two other tragedies, *Manuel* (1817) and *Fredolfo* (1819), failed.

Maud A poem by TENNYSON, published in 1855 as *Maud: or, The Madness* but retitled *Maud: A Monodrama* in 1875. The narrator recounts the melancholy history of his life: his father's death and the ruin of his family, his love for Maud and the duel in which he killed her brother, his flight from home, his descent into insanity and his recovery through patriotic commitment to the Crimean War. Tennyson described the work as 'a little *HAMLET*'.

Maugham, (William) Somerset 1874–1965 Novelist, short-story writer and playwright. Born at the British Embassy in Paris, he travelled widely and from 1926 made his home in the South of France. His first novel, *Liza of Lambeth* (1897), was an experiment in NATURALISM based on his observations of slum life while qualifying as a doctor at St Thomas's Hospital. He first achieved success as a playwright, with *Lady Frederick* (1907), followed by a string of popular works which included *The Tenth Man* (1910), *Our Betters* (1917), *The Circle* (1921), *The Letter* (1927) and *For Services Rendered* (1932). His first really successful novel was the semi-autobiographical *Of Human Bondage* (1915), charting the life of a young man in 'Blackstable' (Whitstable) and 'Tercanbury' (Canterbury). *The Moon and Sixpence* (1919), set in Tahiti, is about a Gauguinesque artist. Other novels include: *The Painted Veil* (1925), *Cakes and Ale* (1930), a lighthearted comedy which contains a fictionalized portrait of HARDY, *The Razor's Edge* (1945) and *Catalina* (1948). His short stories, still the most widely praised aspect of his work, appeared in collections beginning with *Orientations* (1899) and ending with *Creatures of Circumstance* (1947). Particularly notable volumes are *The Trembling of a Leaf* (1921), *Ashenden: or, The British Agent* (1928) and *Six Stories in the First Person Singular* (1931). Maugham's views on life and art can be found in *The Summing Up* (1938), *Strictly Personal* (1942), *A Writer's Notebook* (1949) and *Points of View* (1958). In his own judgement he was one of the leading 'second-raters'. Critics have admired his narrative skill and anti-romantic powers of observation.

Maurice A novel by E. M. FORSTER, written in 1913–14 but not published until 1971, after his death. Maurice Hall slowly becomes aware of his homosexuality in the repressive world of public school and Cambridge. A clandestine relationship with a fellow undergraduate, Clive Durham, ends when Clive decides to become 'normal' and marries. On a visit to the newly-weds Maurice meets Alec Scudder, Clive's gamekeeper. They fall in love and Alec gives up his plan to emigrate in order to stay with Maurice. Forster's 'Terminal Note', added after the final revision in 1960, defends the happy ending and condemns the persecution of homosexuals in Britain.

Maurice, (John) Frederick Denison 1805–72 Clergyman and leader of CHRISTIAN SOCIALISM. Associating Christian practice with the need for social reform, he held that 'a true socialism is the necessary result of a sound Christianity'. The belief led to the formation of the Christian Socialist group and his connection with Ludlow, THOMAS HUGHES and CHARLES KINGSLEY. *Theological Essays* (1853) questioned the accepted doctrine of eternal punishment. He was dismissed from his post as professor of theology at King's College, London. In 1866 he became professor of moral philosophy at Cambridge. Maurice's lasting memorial is the Working Men's College, London, which arose from the organization of evening classes and was firmly established in 1854. His views are expressed in *The Religions of the World* (1847), *Social Morality* (1869) and *Moral and Metaphysical Philosophy* (1871–2).

Maurice, Furnley [Wilmot, Frank] 1881–1942 Australian poet. His work is fresh, vernacular, engaging and playful. Volumes include *Unconditioned Songs* (1913), *To God: From the Weary Nations* (1917), *The Bay and Padie Book* (1917), *Eyes of Vigilance* (1920), *Ways and Means* (1920), *The Gully and Other Verses* (1929), *Odes for a Curse Speaking Choir!* (1933) and *Melbourne Odes* (1934). *Poems by Furnley Maurice* appeared in 1944.

Maxwell, Gavin 1914–69 Writer, conservationist and traveller. He is chiefly remembered for *Ring of Bright Water* (1960), an account of his life with otters on the west coast of Scotland. Two sequels, *The Rocks Remain* (1963) and *Raven Seek Thy Brother* (1968), failed to recapture its note of innocence and joy. Other works include: *Harpoon at a Venture* (1952), about his attempt to set up a shark fishing industry on the island of Soay, off Skye; *A Reed Shaken by the Wind* (1956), a study of the Marsh Arabs of Southern Iraq; and *The House of Elrig* (1966), about his boyhood.

May, Thomas 1595–1650 Translator, playwright and poet. JONSON praised his translations of Lucan's *Pharsalia* (1627) and Virgil's *Georgics* (1628), which, with *Selected Epigrams of Martial* (1629) and a further instalment of Lucan, *Continuation* (1630), are regarded as his best work. He also translated JOHN BARCLAY's *Icon animorum* as *The Mirror of Minds* (1631), and wrote undistinguished plays and narrative poems dealing with English history. A Puritan who embraced the Parliamentary cause during the Civil War, May became secretary to the Long Parliament and wrote a valuable history of it (1647).

Mayhew, Henry 1812–87 Journalist. He is remembered for *London Labour and the London Poor*, an ambitious, detailed and compassionate survey which occupied him between 1849, when first instalments appeared in THE MORNING CHRONICLE, and 1864, when its final volume appeared. Mayhew himself considered *The Criminal Prisons of London and Scenes of Prison Life* (1862) his most important work of social criticism. In the course of a busy career he also founded PUNCH with MARK LEMON and produced more than a score of other books. *The Rhine and its Picturesque Scenery* (1856) and *German Life and Manners As Seen in Saxony* (1864) are worth mention.

Mayne, Rutherford [Waddell, Samuel J.] 1878–1967 Irish actor and playwright. Brother of HELEN WADDELL, he was a leading force in the ULSTER LITERARY THEATRE from its foundation in 1902. His plays include *The Turn of the Road* (1906), *The Drone* (1908) and two one-act tragedies, *The Troth* (1908) and *Red Turf* (1911), in which the Irish experience of eviction and land-grabbing is tersely recreated. *Peter* (1930) and his last play, *Bridge Head* (1934), were written for the ABBEY THEATRE.

Mayne, William (Cyril) 1928– Writer of CHILDREN'S LITERATURE. *A Swarm in May* (1955) is a gentle adventure story set in a choir school. Subsequent works, favouring understatement, include *Earthfasts* (1966), his first break with strict realism, the ambitious *A Game of Dark* (1971) and *The Jersey Shore* (1973), perhaps his most difficult book.

Mayor of Casterbridge, The, The Life and Death of the: *A Story of a Man of Character* A novel by HARDY, published in 1886. It endows the rise and fall in its hero's fortunes with the inevitability of tragic process. Michael Henchard, an out-of-work hay trusser, gets drunk and sells his wife, Susan, and child to a sailor named Newson. After 18 years, believing her sailor-husband drowned, Mrs Newson comes with her daughter, Elizabeth-Jane, to seek out Henchard, now sober and prospering as a grain merchant and mayor of Casterbridge. He agrees to break his engagement to Lucetta Le Sueur and to marry Mrs Newson anew. She dies soon afterwards and Henchard is embittered by the discovery that Elizabeth-Jane is Newson's daughter, not his own. She goes to live with Lucetta. Donald Farfrae, an energetic young Scot whom Henchard has hired, marries Lucetta. Henchard's pig-headedness makes Farfrae set up in business for himself and he thrives as Henchard declines. The old liaison between Henchard and Lucetta is publicized and she dies of shame. Newson returns, Elizabeth-Jane and Farfrae marry, and Henchard dies on Egdon Heath cared for by the loyal Able Whittle.

Mazeppa A poem by BYRON, published in 1819. It is based on a story told by Voltaire in his *Histoire de Charles XII* (1731). After their defeat at Pultowa in 1719 Ivan Stepanovitch Mazeppa tells the Swedish king and his officers the story of his life. Mazeppa is also the subject of Pushkin's *Pultowa*.

Measure for Measure A play by SHAKESPEARE, formally a comedy but so dark in tone that it is often classed among the PROBLEM PLAYS. It was first performed *c.* 1604 and published in the First Folio of 1623. The main source is the story of Promos and Cassandra which WHETSTONE had borrowed from Cinthio's *Hecatommithi* in a play (1578) and a collection of romances (1582).

Vincentio, Duke of Vienna, entrusts law-enforcement to his puritanical deputy, Angelo, and disguises himself as a friar to observe the consequences of his decision. Angelo orders the destruction of brothels and sentences Claudio to death for impregnating the woman to whom he is betrothed. Claudio asks his sister, Isabella, a novice in a nunnery, to intercede and Angelo offers Claudio's life as an exchange for Isabella's body. Outraged when Claudio begs her to accept the offer, Isabella abandons him, but is persuaded by the disguised duke to play a trick on Angelo. Angelo had broken a marriage-contract with Mariana when her dowry was lost; she would willingly take Isabella's place in Angelo's bed. The substitution is arranged, but the duke's scheme is ruined by Angelo's decision to have Claudio killed despite his promise to Isabella. The fortunate death in prison of a pirate resembling Claudio gives the duke another opportunity to thwart Angelo, whose villainy is unmasked when the duke reappears. Claudio can now marry the pregnant Juliet, Angelo's punishment is to marry Mariana, and the duke declares his love for the chaste Isabella.

medieval lyric A short poem originally written for musical accompaniment, or written as if to be sung. It usually has a repeated stanza form, forceful METRE, simple rhymes and a refrain. More religious than secular lyrics survive, largely because they were often recorded in the margins of manuscripts executed in religious houses. Penitential lyrics, prayers to the Virgin and meditations upon Christ's Passion predominate. Though humorous and satirical lyrics also survive, the most common secular topic is love. Many lyrics survive independently, but the most famous collection is the HARLEY LYRICS. The authors are generally not known.

Medwall, Henry c. 1462–1502 Playwright. Only two plays survive: *Nature* (printed in 1530), a MORALITY PLAY, and *FULGENS AND LUCRECE*, an INTERLUDE first performed c. 1497 and printed c. 1515. It is the first completely secular play in English. Little is known about Medwall beyond the fact that he was Cardinal Morton's chaplain and received various livings from the Crown, the last at Calais.

Mehta, Ved 1934– Indian essayist and autobiographer. Although he has written a short satirical novel, *Delinquent Chacha* (1967), he is best known as a shrewd and observant commentator on Indian society. *Face to Face* (1957) describes his childhood and his early struggle with blindness. *Walking the Indian Streets* (1963) deals with a journey round India after his years abroad. A more ambitious journey resulted in *Portrait of India* (1970). Mehta explores the intellectual life not only of India but also of Europe and the USA in *Fly and the Fly Bottle* (1963) and *John is Easy to Please: Encounters with the Written and Spoken Word* (1971). *Daddyji* (1972) and *Mamaji* (1979), touching studies of his parents, have been followed by more volumes of autobiography, now collectively titled *Continents of Exile: The Ledge between the Streams* (1977), *Sound Shadows of the New World* (1986) and *The Stolen Light* (1989).

Melibeus, The Tale of See CANTERBURY TALES.

Melincourt: *or, Sir Oran Haut-Ton* The second novel by PEACOCK, published in 1817. Rich Mr Sylvan Forester has educated the orang-outang of the title so that he appears to be a charming gentleman and has bought him a baronetcy and a seat in Parliament. The portrait of Forester himself owes something to SHELLEY. The book's targets include WORDSWORTH (Mr Paperstamp), COLERIDGE (Mr Mystic), SOUTHEY (Mr Feather-nest) and WILLIAM GIFFORD (Mr Vamp).

Melmoth the Wanderer A GOTHIC NOVEL by MATURIN, published in 1820. The hero has made a pact with Satan to prolong his life, but the debt can be transferred if he can find someone else willing to assume it. This situation provides a framework for a series of episodes in which Melmoth approaches various desperate people and tries to persuade them to take on his dreadful debt. Nobody agrees and Melmoth is doomed.

melodrama A type of play, popular in the Victorian theatre, which exposed the uncommonly virtuous to the threat of defeat by the uncompromisingly vicious, allowing good to win only after sensational risks had been taken or fearsome adventures undergone. Constant peril sustained the tension, and disaster for the good characters was almost always averted in the nick of time. Outstanding examples included DOUGLAS JERROLD's *Black-Ey'd Susan* (1829), TOM TAYLOR's *THE TICKET-OF-LEAVE MAN* (1863), BOUCICAULT's *THE SHAUGHRAUN* (1874) and HENRY ARTHUR JONES's *THE SILVER KING* (1882). Their influence can be felt in popular Victorian fiction, notably the NEWGATE NOVEL and the SENSATION NOVEL. The first English play to be advertised as a melodrama was HOLCROFT's *A Tale of Mystery*

(1802). It borrowed the term from France, where *mélodrames* – like Rousseau's *Pygmalion* (1770) – were works combining spoken words and music. In opera the term 'melodrama' still defines passages spoken to musical accompaniment.

Melville, Herman 1819–91 American novelist, short-story writer and poet. After working as a bank clerk, teacher and farm labourer, he became a sailor at the age of 19. He was encouraged to set down some of his more exotic experiences in *TYPEE* (1846). *OMOO* (1847), *MARDI* (1849), *REDBURN* (1849), and *WHITE-JACKET* (1850) also derived from his life at sea and won him a good deal of popular acclaim. In 1850 he and his wife moved to Pittsfield, Massachusetts, where wider reading and his friendship with HAWTHORNE prompted him to write *MOBY-DICK* (1851), the whaling adventure still considered by many to be the greatest work of American fiction. It was not well received, and from relative popularity he began to fade into obscurity. *PIERRE* (1852), a psychological and moral study based on his childhood, was followed by a short novel, *ISRAEL POTTER* (1855), *THE PIAZZA TALES* (1856), a collection of stories which includes 'Bartleby the Scrivener' and 'Benito Cereno', and his last novel, *THE CONFIDENCE-MAN* (1857). At the age of 40 he turned almost exclusively to poetry. *Battle-Pieces and Aspects of the War* (1866) was followed by *Clarel* (1876), a long poem of religious crisis, which was his last published work. *John Marr and Other Sailors* (1888) and *Timoleon* (1891) were privately printed and distributed among a small circle of acquaintants. Additional material was published from manuscript long after his death, when his reputation began to revive. *BILLY BUDD* appeared in 1924. *Journal up the Straits* (1935), *Journal of a Visit to London and the Continent* (1948), and *Journal of a Visit to Europe and the Levant* (1955), all record his travels in the 1850s. *Weeds and Wildings* (1924) is a collection of previously unpublished poetry. His letters were published in 1960.

Melville, James 1556–1614 Poet and diarist. A Scottish Presbyterian minister and educator, he became Moderator of the General Assembly of the Church of Scotland in 1589. He wrote poems, some on ecclesiastical affairs in Scotland, and *The Diary of Mr James Melville, 1556–1601*, published in 1829.

Memoirs of a Cavalier: *or, A Military Journal of the Wars in Germany, and the Wars in England, from the Year 1632 to the Year 1648* A novel by DEFOE, published in 1720. Andrew Newport, an English gentleman, accompanies the imperial army during the Thirty Years War and, after the sack of Magdeburg, joins the opposing army of Gustavus Adolphus, King of Sweden. After the king's death at the Battle of Lutzen in 1632, Newport returns to England and fights for Charles I, taking the narrative to the Battle of Naseby and the end of the Civil War.

Memoirs of a Woman of Pleasure (Fanny Hill) See CLELAND, JOHN.

Men at Arms See SWORD OF HONOUR.

Mencken, H(enry) L(ouis) 1880–1956 American essayist, editor and critic. With GEORGE JEAN NATHAN he edited the New York periodical *Smart Set* (1914–23), as well as founding the detective magazine *THE BLACK MASK* (1920) and *THE AMERICAN MERCURY* (1924), which he edited until 1933. His books include *The American Language* (1919), six volumes of witty, caustic essays called *Prejudices* (1919–27) and three volumes of autobiography, *Happy Days* (1940), *Newspaper Days* (1941) and

Heathen Days (1943). Mencken also published plays and critical works, including studies of SHAW and Nietzsche.

Menologium A poetical calendar in Old English prefixed to one version of the ANGLO-SAXON CHRONICLE. It combines descriptions of nature with an account of saints' days.

Mercer, David 1928-80 Playwright. Though his career included stage successes from *Ride a Cock Horse* (1965) onwards, he was best known for his television work, particularly the trilogy later published as *The Generations* (1964) and *A Suitable Case for Treatment* (1962; filmed as *Morgan*, 1965). A writer from the working-class North, he frequently took class conflict as his theme and chose rebellious or eccentric protagonists.

Merchant of Venice, The A comedy by SHAKESPEARE, first performed *c.* 1596, and published in 1600 as well as in the First Folio of 1623. A story by Giovanni Fiorentino was a main source; GESTA ROMANORUM supplied the casket episode. Shylock's theatrical impact has sometimes distorted the qualities of a play which belongs with *A MIDSUMMER NIGHT'S DREAM* among the 'middle comedies'.

When Bassanio needs money to woo the heiress Portia, his friend Antonio borrows it from the Jewish moneylender Shylock. Shylock hates Antonio and proposes that a pound of his flesh be the bond for failure to repay within three months. Confident that his ships will return from their trading, Antonio accepts. Bassanio wins Portia by choosing the right casket in a test stipulated in Portia's father's will, but their marriage celebrations are interrupted by the news that Antonio's fleet has foundered and Shylock has demanded his bond. Shylock's hatred of Christians has been sharpened by the elopement of his daughter Jessica with Bassanio's friend, Lorenzo. In court before the Duke of Venice, Antonio is represented by an unknown advocate and his clerk (Portia and her maid Nerissa in male disguise). Shylock rejects Portia's plea for mercy and demands his bond. But Portia insists that it mentions flesh only, no blood, and the Duke upholds the point. Shylock is pardoned on condition he give half his wealth to Antonio and become a Christian. The celebrations in Belmont are completed with news that Antonio's ships have, after all, returned safely.

Merchant's Tale, The See CANTERBURY TALES..

Meredith, George 1828-1909 Novelist and poet. The son of a naval outfitter in Portsmouth, he was articled to a London solicitor but quickly turned to writing. In 1849 he married Mary Ellen Nicholls, widowed daughter of THOMAS LOVE PEACOCK, who deserted him for the painter Henry Wallis in 1857. Her death in 1861 left him free to marry Mary Vulliamy. In 1864 he moved to Flint Cottage at Box Hill in Surrey, his home for the rest of his life.

After working as a journalist and publisher's reader (in which capacity he encouraged both HARDY and GISSING), Meredith published *Poems* (1851), which contained the first version of 'Love in the Valley'. After two fantasies, *The Shaving of Shagpat* (1856) and *Farina* (1857), came *THE ORDEAL OF RICHARD FEVEREL* (1859) and *EVAN HARRINGTON* (1861), the novels which established his distinctive voice, at once thoughtful and comic, wryly questioning and exuberant. *MODERN LOVE* (1862) earned him a permanent place as a poet. Over the next 20 years he published a steady flow of novels: *Sandra Belloni* (first called *Emilia in England*; 1864); *Rhoda Fleming* (1865);

Vittoria (1867), a sequel to *Sandra Belloni*; *The Adventures of Harry Richmond* (1871); *Beauchamp's Career* (1876); *THE EGOIST* (1879), the work that best exemplifies his epigrammatic wit and mastey of comic form; *The Tragic Comedians* (1880); and *DIANA OF THE CROSSWAYS* (1885). *Poems and Lyrics of the Joy of Earth* appeared in 1883.

With good reason, OSCAR WILDE described Meredith as 'a prose BROWNING'. His condensed and loaded prose, discovered in all his novels, is particularly notable in later works: *One of Our Conquerors* (1891), *Lord Ormont and His Aminta* (1894) and *The Amazing Marriage* (1895). His critical essay *On Comedy and the Uses of the Comic Spirit* (1897) is a highly regarded study. Further volumes of poetry included *Poems and Ballads of Tragic Life* (1887), *A Reading of Life* (1909) and *Last Poems* (1909).

Meredith, Owen See BULWER LYTTON, EDWARD ROBERT.

Meres, Francis 1565-1647 Author of *Palladis Tamia: Wit's Treasury* (1598), which contained brief comparisons between English and classical authors. SHAKESPEARE is praised as a modern Plautus and Seneca, 'the most excellent' for both comedy and tragedy. The list of plays includes the problematic *Love's Labour's Won*, lost sequel to *LOVE'S LABOUR'S LOST* or alternative title for one of the other comedies left unmentioned. MARLOWE 'for his epicurism and atheism had a tragical death'. DRAYTON comes out particularly well among the Renaissance poets, though the soul of Ovid lives in *VENUS AND ADONIS*, *THE RAPE OF LUCRECE* and Shakespeare's 'sugared sonnets'. CHAUCER, 'the god of English poets', is compared to Homer; PIERS PLOWMAN and SKELTON are also noticed. A clergyman, Meres also published a sermon and translations of Spanish religious works.

Merrill, James 1926– American poet. His earliest volume, *Jim's Book: A Collection of Poems and Short Stories* (1942), appeared while he was still in his teens but it was *First Poems* (1950) that gained the attention of the poetry-reading public. His reputation was secured by volumes such as *The Country of a Thousand Years of Peace and Other Poems* (1959, revised edition 1970) and *Water Street* (1962). Subsequent work has combined an autobiographical and confessional element with an interest in the visionary and esoteric, most apparent in the sequence begun by *The Divine Comedies* (1976; PULITZER PRIZE) and completed by *Santorini: Stopping the Leak* (1982), which attempts to mythologize the self in relation to a cosmic order. His prolific output can be sampled in *From the First Nine: Poems, 1947-1976* (1982) and *New Selected Poems* (1993).

Merry, Robert See DELLA CRUSCANS, THE.

Merry Wives of Windsor, The A comedy by SHAKESPEARE, first published in an unreliable Quarto (Q1) in 1602 and later in the First Folio of 1623. Tradition claims it was written to satisfy Elizabeth I's desire to see Falstaff (from *HENRY IV*) in love. Although Shakespeare was obviously interested in exploiting Falstaff's theatrical popularity, the story is no more certain than the suggestion that the play was first performed at the Garter feast of 1597. An equally likely date for the first performance is 1600. Since no source has been identified, the plot may be one of the few Shakespeare invented. Falstaff woos Mistress Ford and Mistress Page because they control their husbands' purses. But his disgruntled followers reveal his scheming to Page and the exaggeratedly jealous Ford, who thrashes him. The women add to the humiliation with a series of practical jokes culminating in his being pinched and punched by fairies (the Page family in disguise) in Windsor Forest, to which he has gone for an assignation. He is finally forgiven and taken home. In a slightly more serious plot, the Pages' daughter Anne succeeds in marrying the impoverished Fenton rather than the suitors her parents prefer.

Merwin, W(illiam) S(tanley) 1927– American poet. His poetry often reflects his concern with contemporary loss of belief in traditional myths and the sense of emptiness which ensues. *A Mask for Janus* (1952), his first volume, was followed by *The Dancing Bears* (1954), *Green with Beasts* (1956), *The Drunk in the Furnace* (1960) and *The Moving Target* (1963). The traditional structures of his early work are loosened in *The Lice* (1967), *The Carrier of Ladders* (1970; PULITZER PRIZE) and *Signs: A Poem* (1971). Later volumes include *The First Four Books of Poems* (1975), *Three Poems* (1975), *The Compass Flower* (1977), *Feathers from the Hill* (1978), *Opening the Hands* (1983), *Selected Poems* (1988), *The Rain in the Trees* (1988), *The Lost Upland* (1992) and *Travels: Poems* (1993). He has also produced plays and translations, particularly from French and Spanish.

mesostich See ACROSTIC.

metaphor Where SIMILE asserts the likeness of one thing to another, metaphor asserts their identity. Usually, though not always, something relatively abstract is identified with something relatively concrete, making it more vivid or accessible. Since the mind seems better able to understand a new concept through concrete illustration than abstract explanation, the language is full of dead metaphors, in which illustration has been fully absorbed into concept. 'Metaphor' itself (literally 'a carrying over') is one, and so are 'abstract' and 'explanation'. Certain metaphors, like 'head of State' and 'table leg', seem to inhabit the borderline between death and life.

The terms commonly used nowadays for the figurative or concrete element of a metaphor and its literal or conceptual element are those suggested by I. A. RICHARDS: 'vehicle' and 'tenor' respectively. In a good metaphor the two should have enough in common to avoid absurdity while being different enough for the vehicle to enrich the tenor as well as illustrating it. Where tenor and vehicle are particularly difficult to distinguish – as in BLAKE's 'The Sick Rose' – it is customary to speak of SYMBOL, or at least symbolic metaphor.

metaphysical poets A term used to group certain 17th-century poets, usually DONNE, GEORGE HERBERT, MARVELL, HENRY VAUGHAN and TRAHERNE, though other figures like ABRAHAM COWLEY are sometimes included. DRYDEN introduced the term when he accused Donne of affecting 'the Metaphysics' in his love poetry, and JOHNSON adopted it.

The metaphysical poets investigate the world by rational discussion rather than by intuition or mysticism. They share common characteristics of WIT, inventiveness and a love of elaborate stylistic manoeuvres, including extravagantly ingenious CONCEITS. Reacting against the deliberately smooth and sweet tones of much 16th-century verse, they adopted an energetic, uneven and vigorous style. In his essay, 'The Metaphysical Poets' (1921), which helped bring the poetry of Donne and his contemporaries back into favour, T. S. ELIOT argued that their work fuses reason with passion: it shows a unification of thought and feeling which later became separated in a 'DISSOCIATION OF SENSIBILITY'.

Metcalf, John 1938– Canadian novelist, short-story writer and critic. Born in Britain, he emigrated to Canada in 1962. His fiction uses a disciplined, sometimes spare, poetic style to capture the beauty and absurdity of modern life. Collections of stories include *The Lady Who Sold Furniture* (1970), *The Teeth of My Father* (1975), *Selected Stories* (1982), and *Adult Entertainment* (1986). Two novels, *Going Down Slow* (1972) and *General Ludd* (1980), satirize academic life. *Kicking Against the Pricks* (1982), critical essays, and *Writers in Aspic* (1988), an anthology, express his irritation at the Canadian literary establishment.

metonymy A figure of speech which replaces the name of an object by the name of an attribute or something closely connected with it. It is common not just in literary language but in everyday speech, when we use 'the Crown' for the monarchy or 'the Press' for journalism. See also SYNECDOCHE.

metre Language 'measured', usually by the foot, into line-lengths of patterned verse. Such measuring can be of four kinds: quantitative (by long and short sounds); syllabic (by syllable count); accentual (by stress count); and accentual/syllabic (by both stress and syllable count).

Since both sense and implication in English rely considerably on stress, quantitative and syllabic metre have never become naturalized, though the influence of classical poetry and French poetry, respectively, has encouraged a number of attempts. Accentual metre, with feet made up of one stressed syllable and a varying number of unstressed ones, was used in Anglo-Saxon and much pre-Chaucerian poetry and is still common in nursery rhymes, jingles and popular ballads. HOPKINS, who revived it, calls it sprung rhythm (and its unstressed syllables 'hangers' or 'outriders'); 'strong rhythm' is another, more recent name.

Accentual/syllabic metre, however, is by far the most common kind in English poetry. It accommodates itself easily to natural speech rhythms, as syllabic metre does not, and is less prone than accentual metre to lapse into jingle or singsong. The most common type of foot (or component unit of metre) is the iamb, consisting of one unstressed syllable followed by a stressed one: 'The cŭr|few tŏlls|the knĕll|ŏf part|ĭng daỹ'. The trochee is the reverse: 'Brĭght thĕ|vĭsion ...'. The anapaest has two unstressed syllables followed by a stressed one: 'Ănd hĭs cŏ|hŏrts were gleǎm|ĭng wĭth purp|lĕ aňd gold'. The dactyl is the reverse of the anapaest: 'Ófŏr thĕ|wĭngs ŏf a ...'. The feet often used to vary these metres are the spondee (——), the pyrrhic (˘˘) and two so-called 'rocking feet', the amphimacer (—˘—) and the amphibrach (˘—˘).

The four-foot line (tetrameter) and the five-foot line (pentameter) seem to provide the best setting for poetry's blend of formality and freedom, and are in fact by far the commonest verse lines. The iambic pentameter, in particular, has come close to dominating English poetry, used without rhymes in everything from Elizabethan drama and MILTON's *PARADISE LOST* to WORDSWORTH's *THE PRELUDE* and TENNYSON's *IDYLLS OF THE KING*, and rhymed in the Renaissance SONNET and the satirical verse of DRYDEN and POPE. The dimeter, trimeter and hexameter (two-, three- and six-foot lines) are less common. The iambic hexameter is usually known as an alexandrine, and Pope vividly demonstrated the reasons for its relative unpopularity among English poets: 'A needless Alexandrine ends the song/That like a wounded snake drags its slow length along'. The monometer (one-foot line) is rare, like the heptameter (seven-foot line), also called a 'fourteener' when its feet are iambic.

Perhaps surprisingly, these patterns are not restrictive. With both rhythm and arithmetic at its service, accentual/syllabic metre can play off freedom against order, emphasize by reinforcing sense with metrical stress or undercut by doing the opposite; it can add a musical or a hypnotic element by modulating or by formalizing its basic regularities; and it can structure the unorganized as in life we must structure the raw sense-experience presented to us. In fact, accentual/syllabic metre not only may but must make some accommodation with the rhythms of natural speech. In good verse, then, absolutely regular lines are probably rather less common than those where at least one foot departs from the norm. And in those lines that are entirely regular not all the stresses will be equal. What determines whether a syllable counts as stressed is not the actual amount of breath used but the amount used in relation to the adjoining syllables; the emphases of sense might even result in an unstressed syllable at one point of the line requiring more effort than a stressed one elsewhere. This is probably the main way in which metre makes its accommodation with the rhythms of prose.

metrical romance See VERSE ROMANCE.

Mew, Charlotte 1869–1928 Poet and short-story writer. Championed by HAROLD MONRO, she published *The Farmer's Bride* (1916) and *The Rambling Boy* (1929). Her colloquial diction and restrained expression of romantic passion was admired by VIRGINIA WOOLF and HARDY. V. Warner edited her *Collected Poems and Prose* (1981).

Meynell, Alice (Christiana Gertrude) 1847–1922 Poet, essayist and critic. She helped her husband, Wilfrid Meynell (1852–1948), to found the periodical *Merry England* in 1883 and to rescue FRANCIS THOMPSON from destitution. MEREDITH and PATMORE attended her literary gatherings. Her poetry, the best of which takes religious mystery as its theme, appeared in *Preludes* (1875), *Poems* (1893), *Other Poems* (1896), *Later Poems* (1902), *A Father of Women* (1917) and *Last Poems* (1923), together with a *Collected Poems* in 1912. Volumes of essays include *The Rhythm of Life* (1893), *The Colour of Life* (1896), *The Spirit of Place* (1899), *Ceres' Runaway* (1909) and *The Second Person Singular* (1921).

Michaelmas Term A comedy by THOMAS MIDDLETON performed by a BOYS' COMPANY *c.* 1606 and published in 1607. It satirizes materialism and mercantile affluence by portraying the self-defeating acquisitiveness of a London woollen-draper, Ephestian Quomodo, who has tricked Easy, an amiable gentleman from Essex, out of his estates.

Middlemarch: A Study of Provincial Life A novel by GEORGE ELIOT, published in 1871–2. Initially the narrative concentrates on the blighted marriage of the wealthy young Puritanical idealist, Dorothea Brooke, to the middle-aged pedant, Dr Edward Casaubon, labouring fruitlessly on his *Key to All Mythologies*. Upon his death, affection develops between Dorothea and her former husband's cousin, Will Ladislaw, whom she eventually marries. Another strand traces the career of the equally idealistic Dr Tertius Lydgate, devotee of scientific progress and the new medicine, and his marriage to the local mayor's daughter, Rosamund Vincy, whose foolish social ambitions ruin his life. A third narrative depicts the down-to-earth relationship between Rosamund's brother Fred and Mary Garth, daughter of the honest estate manager, Caleb Garth. The affairs of Bulstrode, the rich hypocritical banker who harbours a grim secret, are also followed to their humiliating end.

These narratives involve many sharply observed minor characters: Dorothea's uncle Mr Brooke, a characteristic early-19th-century landowner and source of much unintentional humour; Mrs Cadwallader, the witty wife of the Rector, himself hardly a fisher of souls; Sir James Chettam, a stolid local squire who marries Dorothea's sister, Celia; Mrs Bulstrode, a woman of dignity and integrity, and the billiard-playing vicar, Camden Farebrother. Beyond them is a huge gallery of briefer portraits of servants, auctioneers, clergymen, businessmen, housewives, labourers, tenants, medical men, schoolmistresses, children and apothecaries. Even those who appear fleetingly are fused into a portrait of English economic, social, and religious life during the pre-Reform years 1829–32. All the characters and the narrative strands in which they play their part serve George Eliot's purpose of examining the 'web of society' and asking whether it merely destroys or is eventually improved by ardent but flawed souls like Dorothea and Lydgate.

Middleton, Christopher 1926– Poet. *Torse 3* (1962) and *Woden Dog* (1962) began a poetic journey of experimentation unattached to any particular school or movement. Succeeding volumes, selected in *111 Poems* (1983), demand that the reader share his complete absorption in language, places, people and real or metaphorical journeys. Later work includes *Two Horse Wagon Going By* (1986), which contains his most 'American' poems, and *The Balcony Tree* (1992). *Pataxanadu and Other Prose* (1977) is a collection of prose poems, fables and fantasies on journeys. His translations include work by Robert Walser, Canetti, Goethe, Gert Hofmann, Balzac and *Andalusian Poems* (with Leticia Garza-Falcón; 1992). The essays in *Bolshevism in Art* (1978) and *The Pursuit of the Kingfisher* (1983) develop his poetic and his wide range of literary, political and cultural interests.

Middleton, Conyers 1683–1750 Theologian. He published a *Life of Cicero* (1741) but is best remembered for *A Free Inquiry into the Miraculous Powers Which are Supposed to Have Existed in the Christian Church through Several Successive Ages* (1748), rejecting the evidence for post-apostolic miracles. Controversially, the book showed that some principles of DEISM could find a sympathetic response in the ranks of the established church.

Middleton, Stanley 1919– Novelist. During a career as a Nottingham schoolmaster, he has produced a succession of quietly observed, 'implacably domestic' novels set in his native Potteries. They include *Holiday* (BOOKER PRIZE winner; 1974), *Entry into Jerusalem* (1982), *Valley of Decision* (1985), *Beginning to End* (1991) and *A Place to Stand* (1992).

Middleton, Thomas *c.* 1580–1627 Playwright. The son of a master bricklayer, he had already published three volumes of verse by 1600. The adroitly plotted CITIZEN COMEDIES of the next decade contain some of his best work. Those intended for BOYS' COMPANIES include *A Mad World, My Masters* (*c.* 1605), *A TRICK TO CATCH THE OLD ONE* (*c.* 1605) and *MICHAELMAS TERM* (*c.* 1606). For adult companies he wrote, with DEKKER, *THE HONEST WHORE* (1604) and *THE ROARING GIRL* (1610), and his own comic masterpiece, *A CHASTE MAID IN CHEAPSIDE* (1611). After 1613, Middleton was responsible for many City of London pageants, serving as City Chronologer from 1620 until his death, but continued to write plays. Three collaborations with WILLIAM ROWLEY are notable: *A FAIR QUARREL* (published 1617), *The World Tossed at Tennis* (published 1620) and the outstanding tragicomedy THE CHANGELING (1622). A GAME AT CHESS (1624) is a boldly anti-Spanish SATIRE and WOMEN BEWARE WOMEN (c. 1625) a tragedy whose bloody but almost mischievous conclusion has reinforced the argument of critics who believe Middleton also wrote THE REVENGER'S TRAGEDY.

Midsummer Night's Dream, A A comedy by SHAKESPEARE, first performed c. 1596 and published in 1600 as well as in the First Folio of 1623. The story is gathered from a number of sources and amplified by Shakespeare's own invention to create a comedy which subtly blends love-intrigue, fairy magic and farce. When Theseus, Duke of Athens, supports her father's attempt to make her marry Demetrius, Helena elopes with Lysander to a wood near Athens; they are followed by Demetrius who is in turn followed by Helena, who is in love with him. In the same wood Bottom the weaver and his fellow 'mechanicals' are rehearsing the play of 'Pyramus and Thisbe', which they hope to present at the wedding of Theseus and the Amazon queen Hippolyta. Both groups become accidentally embroiled in the quarrel between Oberon, king of the fairies, and his queen, Titania, and in the mischievous operations of Oberon's servant Puck. Puck's application of a magic love potion makes both Lysander and Demetrius fall in love with Helena. The same potion makes Titania fall in love with Bottom, whom Puck has endowed with an ass's head. Oberon's magic eventually unravels all and, at the wedding celebrations of Theseus and the Amazon queen Hippolyta, Hermia is matched with her Lysander and Helena with her Demetrius, while Bottom and his fellow actors perform their play to the assembled nobles.

Mill, James 1773–1836 Philosopher, economist and historian. A friend of BENTHAM and warm disciple of UTILITARIANISM, he became the leader of the 'philosophical radicals'. He encouraged the work of others, notably RICARDO, took an active part in founding THE WESTMINSTER REVIEW, and applied Benthamite principles to a wide range of subjects in such works as Elements of Political Economy (1821), Analysis of the Human Mind (1829) and Fragment on Mackintosh (1835). The Autobiography (1873) by his son JOHN STUART MILL provides a lasting testament to the way in which he put theory into practice with a rigorous educational programme intended to fit his son for future leadership of the Benthamite cause. The History of India (1817), which won him a position with the East India Company, is notable for concentrating not on wars and rulers but on social analysis.

Mill, John Stuart 1806–73 Philosopher, economist and administrator. His Autobiography (1873) describes the rigorous education given him by his father, JAMES MILL, to equip him as leader of the next generation of UTILITARIANISM. In youth he spent his spare time editing the papers of BENTHAM and writing articles for periodicals such as THE WESTMINSTER REVIEW. An acute attack of depression in 1826 led him to question Benthamite doctrines for neglecting cultivation of the emotions in favour of developing the intellect. The poetry of WORDSWORTH, with its emphasis upon the morally educative role of emotional association, played a restorative part in redressing the balance. By 1830 Mill had begun to revise his philosophical and economic thinking in the light of ideas drawn from COLERIDGE and POSITIVISM, among other sources, and to adopt a constructive eclecticism. As the essays on Bentham (1838) and Coleridge (1840) reveal, he saw the moral and mental improvement of mankind, to which he was dedicated, as emerging from synthesis and toleration of diversity.

Mill's influence, as the voice of 19th-century liberalism, sprang in part from his deep-seated conviction of the connection between theory and practice. His major works, therefore, often gained a readership far wider than their apparent subject matter would invite. Books such as THE SYSTEM OF LOGIC (1843) and Principles of Political Economy (1848) use the platform of theoretical discussion to present his unconventional views on contemporary society. Among the most noteworthy of his many essays are ON LIBERTY (1859), Utilitarianism (1861), 'Auguste Comte and Positivism' (1865), THE SUBJECTION OF WOMEN (1869) and Three Essays on Religion (1874).

After working for the East India Company from 1823 until 1858, Mill sat as independent MP for Westminster (1865–8), making notable contributions to debates on Irish land reform and women's suffrage. He enjoyed an intense but platonic relationship with Mrs Harriet Taylor, whom he claimed to be the dominant intellectual influence in his life, from 1830 until their marriage in 1851, two years after her first husband's death. Her unexpected death in 1858 cast a shadow over his remaining years.

Mill on the Floss, The A novel by GEORGE ELIOT, published in 1860. Maggie and Tom Tulliver are the children of the miller of Dorlcote, an honest but unimaginative man, and his weak and foolish wife. In this oppressive environment Maggie's intelligence, scholarly competence and wide-ranging imagination become liabilities, especially in a woman. She responds to Philip Wakem, the deformed son of the leading lawyer in the nearby town of St Ogg's. Tulliver regards the lawyer Wakem as his enemy and Tom, blindly supporting his father's cause, makes Maggie give up Philip's friendship. After Tulliver's death Maggie goes to St Ogg's to stay with her cousin Lucy, who is to marry Stephen Guest. He is attracted to Maggie and his irresponsible behaviour on a boating expedition compromises her reputation. Tom turns her out of his house and she is ostracized by local society, except for Lucy, Philip and the rector, Dr Kenn. Autumn brings a flood which threatens the mill, and Maggie attempts to rescue Tom. She fails, and brother and sister are drowned together, but not before they have briefly recaptured the affection they felt for each other as children.

Response to The Mill on the Floss has been divided between admiration of the skill with which George Eliot evokes the rural background to Maggie and Tom's childhood and criticism of the rushed and arbitrary ending.

Millay, Edna St Vincent 1892–1950 American poet. A Few Figs from Thistles (1920) and The Harp-Weaver and Other Poems (1923) established her as a representative voice of her generation in their freshness, gaiety and implied rebellion against established moral standards. Later works, showing a new political and social consciousness, include: Distressing Dialogues (1924), a book of satirical sketches written under the pseudonym of Nancy Boyd; Three Plays (1926); The King's Henchman (1927), a libretto; The Buck in the Snow and Other Poems (1928); Fatal Interview (1931), a SONNET sequence; Wine from These Grapes (1934); Conversation at Midnight (1937); Huntsman, What Quarry? (1939); and Make Bright the Arrow (1940).

Miller, Arthur 1915– American playwright. His interest in conflict between the generations informed All My

Sons (1947), about a veteran who discovers that his father sold faulty aeroplane parts to the government, and *DEATH OF A SALESMAN* (1949; PULITZER PRIZE), still his most famous play, about the unsuccessful salesman Willy Loman. Like Ibsen, whose *An Enemy of the People* he translated in 1950, Miller often explores the origins and consequences of shameful actions. *THE CRUCIBLE* (1953) connects the Salem witch trials with the McCarthyite era. *A View from the Bridge* (1955, revised 1956) examines the tragic consequences of Sicilian-American longshoreman Eddie Carbone's passion for his niece Catherine. After an absence Miller returned to the New York stage with: *After the Fall* (1964), a semi-autobiographical play about his marriage to Marilyn Monroe; *Incident at Vichy* (1964), about the Nazi persecution of the Jews; and *The Price* (1968), his last international success, again examining family conflict and filial disloyalty. Subsequent plays include *The Creation of the World and Other Business* (1972), *Up from Paradise* (1974), *The Archbishop's Ceiling* (1977) and *The American Clock* (1980). Among other work are the screenplay for *The Misfits* (1961) and the important *Theatre Essays* (1971).

Miller, Henry (Valentine) 1891–1980 American writer. His most famous work, *Tropic of Cancer* (1934), describes his promiscuous life in Paris. Considered pornographic, it was not published in the USA until 1961. *Black Spring* (1936), ten autobiographical stories, and *Tropic of Capricorn* (1939), about his years working for Western Union, were also suppressed. *The Colossus of Maroussi* (1941) is a travel book about Greece, while *The Air-Conditioned Nightmare* (1945) and *Remember to Remember* (1947) decry the spiritual and cultural desolation of his native land. Other works include *The World of Sex* (1940), *The Plight of the Creative Artist in the United States of America* (1944), *Books in My Life* (1951), *The Time of the Assassins: A Study of Rimbaud* (1956) and a trilogy – *Sexus* (1949), *Plexus* (1953; first published in French, 1952) and *Nexus* (1960) – collectively titled *The Rosy Crucifixion*.

Miller, Joaquin [Miller, Cincinnatus Hiner [Heine]] 1839–1913 American poet. *Specimens* (1868) was followed by *Joaquin et al.* (1869), a defence of the Mexican bandit, Joaquin Murietta, from whom he derived his nickname. *Pacific Poems* (1871) and *Songs of the Sierras* (1871), published while he was in London, won acclaim from the PRE-RAPHAELITES, especially DANTE GABRIEL ROSSETTI. Numerous other volumes of poetry, novels and plays include *The Danites of the Sierras* (1877), about the Mormons, and an autobiography, *Life amongst the Modocs* (1873).

Miller's Tale, The See *CANTERBURY TALES*.

Millin, Sarah Gertrude 1889–1968 South African novelist. *Adam's Rest* (1922), *God's Stepchildren* (1924), *Mary Glenn* (1925) and *The Sons of Mrs Aab* (1931) made a major contribution to South African fiction during the interwar period. Her novels show an awareness of the realities and complexities of racial conflict, a subject explored further in her study, *The South Africans* (1926, revised 1934). She also published biographies of Rhodes (1933) and Smuts (1936).

Milman, Henry Hart 1791–1868 Historian and poet. He was a fellow of Brasenose College, Oxford, and professor of poetry (1821). His poetry, which included dramatic poems and translations from the Sanskrit, is less important than his work as a historian. His *History of the Jews* (1830), *History of Christianity* (1840) and *History of Latin Christianity* (1854–5) reflect his admiration for the work of EDWARD GIBBON, whose *DECLINE AND FALL OF THE ROMAN EMPIRE* he edited (1838–9) and whose biography he wrote (1839).

Milne, A(lan) A(lexander) 1882–1956 Novelist, playwright, humorist and writer of CHILDREN'S LITERATURE. An assistant editor of *PUNCH*, he won additional good opinions with his plays, *Wurzel-Flummery* (1917), *Mr Pim Passes By* (1919; published, 1922), *The Truth about Blayds* (1921; published, 1922) and *The Dover Road* (1921; published, 1922). His great success came with children's books. *When We were Very Young* (1924) and *Now We are Six* (1927) were verses about his young son Christopher Robin. The works by which he will always be remembered are *Winnie-the-Pooh* (1926) and *The House at Pooh Corner* (1928), based on the imaginary conversations and adventures of Christopher Robin's toys. Each is given a distinctive characteristic: Pooh's greediness, Eeyore's misanthropy, Tigger's bounciness and Piglet's timidity. The stories are perfectly adapted to young readers' interests, concentrating on topics such as birthday presents, the quest for food and mini-adventures involving bad weather, mysterious footprints or getting lost. Pooh's 'hums' (or verses) and E. H. SHEPARD's illustrations are also memorable.

Milne came to resent the success of these little books at the expense of his adult work. This includes: DETECTIVE FICTION; two novels, *Two People* (1931) and *Chloë Marr* (1946); a plea against war, *Peace with Honour* (1934); and an autobiography, *It's Too Late Now* (1939). His last triumph was a stage adaptation of GRAHAME's *THE WIND IN THE WILLOWS* as *Toad of Toad Hall* (1929).

Milnes, Richard Monckton, 1st Baron Houghton 1809–85 Man of letters and poet. A member of the APOSTLES when it included TENNYSON and ARTHUR HALLAM, he became MP for Pontefract in 1837 and a peer in 1863. His five volumes of verse are less important than his role as patron of letters and generous host to writers at his home, Fryston Hall, in Yorkshire. He also helped to secure the reputation of KEATS in *Life, Letters and Literary Remains of John Keats* (1848).

Milton, John 1608–74 Poet. The son of a prosperous scrivener and amateur composer, he was born in London and spent his life there with only a few intermissions. The first came in 1625, when he left St Paul's School for an unsatisfactory undergraduate career at Christ's College, Cambridge. Although he had intended to join the clergy, he showed no anxiety to commit himself to a career after taking his BA in 1629 and MA in 1632, devoting himself instead to studious leisure and literary interests. While at Cambridge he had already begun to write poems in Latin, Italian and English, including 'At a Vacation Exercise' and his first great lyric in English, the 'Ode Upon the Morning of Christ's Nativity' (1629). *L'ALLEGRO* and *IL PENSEROSO*, among the poems gathered in his first collection of 1645, were written in 1632, the same year 'On Shakespeare' was published in the Second Folio of SHAKESPEARE's plays. Milton's musical interests found expression in two entertainments written in collaboration with the musician Henry Lawes: *Arcades* (1633) and *COMUS*, performed at Ludlow in 1634 and published in 1637. *LYCIDAS* appeared in a volume of memorial verses (1638) to Edward King, a Cambridge contemporary drowned while crossing the Irish Sea. *Epitaphium Damonis*, his most sustained Latin poem, memorializes his close friend Charles Diodati. It was written in 1639, shortly after his return to England from a Continental tour which had taken him to France and Italy.

Milton's return was prompted, apparently, by ecclesiastical controversies in England, but he took no part until the 'second Bishops' War' of 1641, which prompted five anti-episcopal pamphlets; they include *Animadversions* (1641) and *An Apology against a Pamphlet* (1642), in defence of SMECTYMNUUS, and *The Reason of Church Government* (1642). His marriage in 1642 to Mary Powell, his junior by 16 years, foundered when she returned to her Royalist relatives within six weeks. They were reconciled in 1645; she bore him two daughters and a son who died in infancy before dying herself in 1652. In the meantime her desertion had provoked four pamphlets of 1643–5, most notoriously *The Doctrine and Discipline of Divorce*, arguing for the legitimacy of divorce on the grounds of incompatibility. Despite the public storm they aroused, he also found time for *Of Education* (1644), a treatise inspired by his own wide humanism, and *AREOPAGITICA* (1644), pleading for freedom of the press.

His public role in the English Commonwealth was confirmed in 1649 by pamphlets attacking monarchy and justifying the execution of Charles I: *The Tenure of Kings and Magistrates* and *Eikonoklastes* ('Image Breaker'), a riposte to *EIKON BASILIKE*. In the same year he was appointed Secretary of Foreign Tongues to the Council of State, a post which required him to translate diplomatic documents and correspondence. He answered Royalist propaganda in *Pro populo anglicano defensio* (1651), *Defensio secunda* (1654) and *Defence of Himself* (1655). MARVELL was appointed to help him in 1657, assistance being all the more necessary since Milton had effectively been blind since 1651. His blindness and the death of his second wife, Katherine Powell, in 1658 are among the personal topics reflected in the SONNETS he wrote during the 1640s and 1650s. Other sonnets, including 'On the New Forcers of Conscience' and 'On the Late Massacre in Piedmont', dwell on the same public themes as his controversial pamphlets.

Defiantly, Milton published *The Ready and Easy Way to Establish a Free Commonwealth*, even as the Proectorate crumbled after Cromwell's death and the return of Charles II loomed in 1660. After the Restoration copies of his works were publicly burned. He was first a fugitive and then a prisoner, though after payment of a massive fine he was finally released into a life of relative retirement. In 1663 he married Elizabeth Minshull. With renewed leisure for poetry, he completed *PARADISE LOST*, probably begun before the Restoration. It appeared in 1667 and again, with signficant revision, shortly after his death in 1674. *PARADISE REGAINED* and the verse drama *SAMSON AGONISTES* were published jointly in 1671. Milton also issued a revised version of his first poetic collection (1673), and some pamphlets written at an earlier date: on grammar (1669), on Ramist logic (1672), on *The History of Britain* (1670) and *Of True Religion* (1673). *The History of Moscovia* was published posthumously in 1682.

Even by Renaissance standards, Milton was a polymath. Although he had asserted his conviction that his life should be dedicated to a great literary work, his early poems and letters show signs of self-doubt stemming from what he saw as his own dilatoriness. Immersed in controversy during the 1640s and 50s, he considered his pamphlets the work of his 'left hand' merely. Published towards the end of a life which had, superficially regarded, been spent in disparate, if distinguished, literary activity, *Paradise Lost* won Milton a

reputation that was largely posthumous. His eminence was confirmed by ADDISON's *SPECTATOR* papers (1712), the first substantial contribution to Milton criticism. Throughout the 18th century his style was considered a model for the 'Sublime' mode in English poetry, though JOHNSON's complaint that Milton's language was 'harsh and barbarous' anticipated 20th-century attacks by T. S. ELIOT and LEAVIS. In the Romantic period his radical politics, as well as his achievement in producing an English EPIC, attracted admiration.

Minot, Laurence The author of 11 fervently nationalist poems, all short and most in ALLITERATIVE VERSE, written during the 14th century, probably in Lincolnshire. Nothing is known of Minot's life. The poems describe battles and political events which took place between 1328 and 1352, and include accounts of Crécy (1346), Halidon Hill (1333), Sluys (1340), Neville's Cross (1346) and the defeat of the Spanish fleet at Winchelsea (1350).

miracle [mystery] **plays** Dramatized versions of biblical stories from the Creation to the Resurrection, popular in the Middle Ages. Although their early history cannot be confidently outlined, it is widely accepted that they outgrew the church in which they began. By the mid-14th century cycles of biblical plays were being performed all over England, with trade guilds contributing different episodes under the control of the corporation. Debate about techniques of staging continues: pageant wagons were used in York, Chester and Wakefield, though these were probably stationed at a fixed site or handful of fixed sites. Miracle plays lost their communal centrality with the Reformation.

The survival of certain cycles seems to be largely haphazard. The Chester cycle of 25 plays is probably the earliest. The York cycle contains 48 plays, in verse forms of varying sophistication. The Wakefield (or Towneley) cycle has 32 plays, five in the nine-line stanza associated with the anonymous Wakefield Master, the finest exponent of the form. His work, especially the *Second Shepherds' Play*, exemplifies the secularization that may have contributed to church hostility during the 15th and 16th centuries. The *Ludus Conventriae* (or Coventry or N-town cycle), of uncertain provenance but believed by many scholars to be East Anglian, uses ALLITERATIVE VERSE.

Mirror for Magistrates, A A 16th-century collection of didactic poetry illustrating the instability of fortune, the fall of the great and the punishment of the vicious. Its complicated publishing history began with the first edition in 1559, commissioned as a continuation of LYDGATE's *Fall of Princes*. William Baldwin and George Ferrers, the chief collaborators, drew on chronicles for 19 examples of the fall of famous men from the reigns of Richard II to Edward IV, many later made familiar by MARLOWE and SHAKESPEARE's history plays. The poems are connected by prose links. New editions in 1563 and 1578 added more stories from the reigns of Henry VI and Richard III, including those of Jane Shore by CHURCHYARD and of Buckingham by THOMAS SACKVILLE.

The First Part of the Mirror for Magistrates (1574) by John Higgins is the 'first part' in the sense that it gives 16 legends from early British history. *The Second Part of the Mirror for Magistrates* (1578) is by yet another hand, Richard Blennerhassett, and gives 12 legends of early British and Saxon characters. In 1587 Higgins brought together enlarged versions of his early British histories and the Sackville–Baldwin *Mirror*. A last reshaping

(1610), by Richard Niccols, omits the prose links and adds DRAYTON's legend of Thomas Cromwell.

Misfortunes of Arthur, The A tragedy by Thomas Hughes, published in 1587 and performed for Elizabeth I at Greenwich in 1588. Fully titled *The Misfortunes of Arthur (Uther Pendragon's Son) Reduced in to Tragical Notes*, it shows the interest in ARTHURIAN LITERATURE crossing the bridge from medieval romance to Elizabethan drama. Thomas Hughes of Gray's Inn had been a fellow of Queens' College, Cambridge.

Misfortunes of Elphin, The A romance by PEACOCK, published in 1829. He uses Welsh Arthurian legends to satirize literary affectations and political movements. Elphin succeeds to the kingdom of Ceredigion, which has suffered through Seithenyn's negligence. He is imprisoned by a neighbouring prince, Maelgon, but the bard Taliesin secures his release by appealing to King Arthur. The book contains many songs and set-piece speeches; some of them adapt or translate Welsh sources, while others, like 'The War-Song of Dinas Vawr', are original.

Misogonus A comedy acted at Trinity College, Cambridge, between 1568 and 1574 and printed in 1577. It varies the theme of the prodigal son by making the prodigal, Misogonus, stay at home and waste the fortune of his father Philogonus in dissipation – the most elaborately realized feature of a play notorious for its coarseness. Evidence points to Anthony Rudd (*c.* 1549–1615), later Bishop of St David's, as the author.

Mitchel, John 1815–75 Irish patriotic writer. PATRICK PEARSE venerated him as one of the four evangelists of Irish nationality. He joined O'Connell's Repeal Association, wrote for the Young Ireland paper *The Nation*, and founded his own more extreme paper, *The United Irishman*, in 1848. Convicted of treason, he was transported to Bermuda, South Africa and finally Tasmania, whence he escaped to the USA in 1853. These experiences were recorded in his most famous work, the *Jail Journal* (1854). In America he became notorious for his defence of slavery before and after the Civil War. Other writings include *The Life and Times of Aodh O'Neill* (1846), an edition of Irish pamphlets by SWIFT and BERKELEY (1847), *Letters to the Protestant Farmers ... of the North of Ireland* (1848; republished as a book, 1917) and a *History of Ireland* (1868). His savage account of the Irish famine and the Young Ireland insurrection of 1848, *The Last Conquest of Ireland (Perhaps)* (1861), invites comparison with Swift.

Mitchell, Adrian 1932– Poet, novelist and playwright. His accessible, witty, political poems have appeared in *For Beauty Douglas* (1982), bringing together work from earlier volumes, and *On the Beach at Cambridge* (1986), *Love Songs of World War II* (1989) and *Greatest Hits* (1991). Mitchell's novels include *If You See Me Comin'* (1962) and *The Bodyguard* (1970). Of his work for the stage, the best known is his adaptation of Peter Weiss's *Marat/Sade* (1966).

Mitchell, James Leslie See GIBBON, LEWIS GRASSIC.

Mitchell, Julian 1935– Playwright and novelist. He began by writing novels, most notably *An Undiscovered Country* (1968). Since then he has concentrated on drama, working for the stage and television. His stage plays include *Half-Life* (1977), *The Enemy Within* (1980), *Francis* (1983) and *After Aida* (1986), but he is perhaps best known for *Another Country* (1981; filmed 1984), about the making of a traitor.

Mitchell, Langdon (Elwyn) 1862–1935 American

playwright. His best-known play is *The New York Idea* (1906), a SATIRE of contemporary attitudes to love and marriage. His adaptations include *The Adventures of François* (1900), from a novel by his father, S. Weir Mitchell, and *Becky Sharp* (1899) and *Major Pendennis* (1916), from THACKERAY.

Mitchell, Margaret See GONE WITH THE WIND.

Mitchell, W(illiam) O(rmond) 1914– Canadian novelist and playwright. A popular raconteur and humorist with his roots in oral story-telling, he is a seminal figure in the development of recent western Canadian writing. His first novel, *Who Has Seen the Wind* (1947), is a classic account of a Prairie boyhood. *Jake and the Kid* (1961) collects 13 of the original stories from the more than 300 scripts he wrote for his series on Canadian Broadcasting Corporation radio in 1951–8. Other works include *The Kite* (1962), *The Vanishing Point* (1973), *How I Spent My Summer Holidays* (1981), *Ladybug, Ladybug* (1988), *According to James and the Kid* (1989), *Roses are Difficult* (1990), and the plays *The Devil's Instrument* (1973) and *Back to Beulah*, published in *Dramatic W. O. Mitchell* (1982).

Mitchison, Naomi (Mary Margaret) 1897– Novelist and short-story writer. Daughter of the physiologist J. S. Haldane and sister of J. B. S. HALDANE, she published some 70 books. The best are generally acknowledged to be those evoking classical Greece and Rome: *The Conquered* (1923), *When the Bough Breaks* (short stories; 1924), *Cloud Cuckoo Land* (1925), *Barbarian Stories* (1929), *Black Sparta* (short stories; 1928), *The Corn King and the Spring Queen* (1931); *The Delicate Fire* (short stories; 1933); and *The Blood of the Martyrs* (1939).

Mitford, Mary Russell 1787–1855 Author of sketches and short stories, novelist and playwright. The charming *Our Village: Sketches of Rural Life, Character and Scenery* began as a series of contributions to *The Lady's Magazine* in 1819 and appeared in five volumes in 1824–32. The village is Three Mile Cross, near Reading, which itself became the subject of *Belford Regis: Sketches of a Country Town* (1835). A novel, *Atherton and Other Tales* (1854), was less successful. Miss Mitford's plays include *The Foscari* (1826), *Rienzi* (1828) and *Charles I* (1834). *Recollections of a Literary Life* (1852) comments on her contemporaries.

Mitford, Nancy (Freeman) 1904–73 Novelist and biographer. She was the daughter of the 2nd Baron Redesdale. Her younger sister, Jessica, wrote an account of their family life in *Hons and Rebels* (1960). Her own novels generally describe Bohemian life in upper-class society, combining a satiric tone with a sharp ear for dialogue. The most successful include *The Pursuit of Love* (1945), *Love in a Cold Climate* (1949) and *The Blessing* (1951). Her biographies include *Madame de Pompadour* (1954), *Voltaire in Love* (1957), *The Sun King* (1966), and *Frederick the Great* (1970). With A. S. C. Ross she edited and contributed to *Noblesse Oblige* (1956), a collection of satirical essays on snobbery which gave the terms 'U' and 'non-U' to the language. She also edited family correspondence in *The Ladies of Alderley* (1938) and *The Stanleys of Alderley* (1939).

Mitford, William 1744–1827 Historian. His five-volume *History of Greece* (1784–1818) was suggested by EDWARD GIBBON and praised by MACAULAY.

Mittelholzer, Edgar 1909–65 Guyanese novelist. His 23 novels helped to create a genuine Caribbean consciousness incorporating Guyanese history and landscape. The Kaywana novels – *Children of Kaywana* (1952; including *Kaywana Heritage*, separately published from 1976), *The Harrowing of Hubertus* (1954; later published as

Kaywana Stock) and *Kaywana Blood* (1958) – are a family saga covering the years 1612–1953. Other works include: *Corentyne Thunder* (1941), about the Indian peasantry in Guyana; *A Morning at the Office* (1950), about Jamaican race relations; *Shadows Move among Them* (1952) and *The Mad MacMullochs* (1959), both about ideally free, sexually liberated communities; *Latticed Echoes* (1960); *The Life and Death of Sylvia* (1953); *The Pilkington Drama* (1965), which ends with a suicide by fire prefiguring the manner of Mittelholzer's own death.

Mo, Timothy 1950– Novelist. He was born in Hong Kong of English and Cantonese parents. *The Monkey King* (1978), set in Hong Kong, and *Sour Sweet* (1982), set in London's Chinese community, have been followed, more ambitiously, by: *An Insular Possession* (1986), about the Opium Wars; *The Redundancy of Courage* (1991), about a guerrilla movement in a fictional country modelled on the Philippines; and *Brownout of Breadfruit Boulevard* (1995).

Moby-Dick: or, The Whale A novel by HERMAN MELVILLE, published in New York and London in 1851. The British title was *The Whale*.

The central narrative thread is Ishmael's account of his whaling voyage from Nantucket on the *Pequod*. Before he goes aboard he befriends Queequeg, a harpooner from the South Sea Islands, and hears Father Mapple's sermon about Jonah. The crew of the *Pequod*, castoffs and refugees of all races and lands, is a microcosm of humanity. The harpooners are Queequeg, Tashtego (a Gay Head Indian) and Daggoo (an African); the three mates are Starbuck, Stubb and Flask. The mysterious Captain Ahab appears only after several days at sea, to reveal that he sees the purpose of the voyage as being to kill the white sperm whale known as Moby-Dick, which took off his leg on a previous voyage. The crew are drawn into his monomaniacal plan; only the business-like Starbuck demurs. The story culminates in a three-day chase of Moby-Dick, which ends when the enraged whale charges the ship. Ahab is caught in his harpoon line and drowned. The *Pequod* sinks, taking all the whaling boats and their crews down in the suction. The only survivor is Ishmael, clinging to the coffin that had been made for Queequeg.

The novel is by turns naturalistic and fantastic. Large sections dwell on the history and technique of whaling, the anatomy of whales, and the mythic significance of the whale, shaping these subjects – as well as virtually every aspect of life on board the *Pequod* – into obscure parables. The result, turbulent and highly complex, elevates Ahab's mad quest to the level of EPIC and TRAGEDY.

mock-heroic The use for comic effect of a high or epic style out of all proportion to its low or trivial subject matter (compare BURLESQUE). Late 17th- and 18th-century literature, in particular, offers many examples, including DRYDEN's *MAC FLECKNOE* and POPE's *THE RAPE OF THE LOCK* and *THE DUNCIAD*.

Modern Chivalry A novel by BRACKENRIDGE, published between 1792 and 1815. Captain John Farrago and his Irish servant, Teague O'Regan, American versions of Don Quixote and Sancho Panza, travel around Pennsylvania, their adventures providing the occasion for satirical observations about post-Revolutionary American life and manners. Farrago devotes much of his energy to discouraging or preventing the untrained, uneducated Teague from taking advantage of the opportunities offered by the new American society – as preacher, Indian treaty maker, potential husband for a

well-bred young lady and pupil to a French dancing master. The tensions between them thus dramatize the problem of authority and leadership in a democracy.

Modern Instance, A A novel by WILLIAM DEAN HOWELLS, serialized in 1881 and published in volume form in 1882. He referred to it as his 'New Medea', a 'modern instance' of what would happen to a gradually estranged couple. Marcia Gaylord's marriage to Bartley Hubbard, a Boston journalist, fails and she leaves him. They are eventually divorced and he dies in Arizona. She is courted by Ben Halleck, who nevertheless cannot decide whether or not to leave the ministry for her. The novel ends without giving his final decision.

Modern Painters A five-volume treatise on art by RUSKIN, published in 1843–60. The full title of the first volume was *Modern Painters: Their Superiority in the Art of Landscape Painting to All the Ancient Masters Proved by Examples of the True, the Beautiful and the Intellectual, from the Works of Modern Artists, Especially from Those of J. M. W. Turner, Esq., R.A.* It quickly transcends this goal to advocate Truth and Beauty, to consider art as a social force and to praise Nature. The second volume (1846) is a formidable treatise on ideas of beauty and the imaginative faculty. The third volume (1856), appropriately subtitled 'Of Many Things', sweeps the reader through commentary on painting and poetry, and on landscape modern, medieval and classical. It includes a famous chapter, 'Of the Pathetic Fallacy'. The fourth volume (1856) includes chapters on 'The Mountain Gloom' and 'The Mountain Glory', relating these natural phenomena to spiritual, social and aesthetic temperaments. The final volume (1860) is marked by its author's conviction that the entire series reveals Turner as the supreme landscape painter.

modernism The term for an international tendency in the arts brought about by a creative renaissance during the last decade of the 19th century and lasting into the post-war years. Strictly speaking, modernism cannot be reliably characterized by a uniform style or even described as a 'movement', since it embraced a wide range of artistic movements, including SYMBOLISM, impressionism, post-impressionism, futurism, constructivism, IMAGISM, VORTICISM, EXPRESSIONISM, dada, and surrealism. Technically, modernism was distinguished by its challenge to traditional representation and its highly self-conscious manipulation of form. Conventional narrative gave way to STREAM OF CONSCIOUSNESS and conventional poetic form to FREE VERSE. Such experiments were conducted with strong awareness of pioneering studies in other disciplines: in psychology, WILLIAM JAMES's *PRINCIPLES OF PSYCHOLOGY* (1890) and Freud's *The Interpretation of Dreams* (1899); in physics, Einstein's *General Principles of Relativity* (1915); and in anthropology, SIR JAMES FRAZER's *The Golden Bough* (1890–1915). The most notable landmarks in English literature are commonly understood to include HENRY JAMES's *THE AMBASSADORS* (1903), CONRAD's *NOSTROMO* (1904), T. S. ELIOT's *THE WASTE LAND* (1922), and JOYCE's *ULYSSES* (1922). The work of POUND, YEATS, FORD MADOX FORD, VIRGINIA WOOLF and, in America, FAULKNER, could be added to a list which would still be far from exhaustive.

Modest Proposal, A: *for Preventing the Children of Poor People from being a Burden to Their Parents, or the Country, and for Making Them Beneficial to the Public* A satirical pamphlet by SWIFT, published in 1729. The central proposal is that it would make sense if the offspring of the Irish poor were farmed for the table of the rich English. With the scrupulous reasoning of an economic 'projector', Swift adopts a dispassionate, even benevolent tone as he sets down the appallingly plausible plan. Its several advantages include the reduction of beggars, the year-round availability of tasty meat, profit to the mothers ('dams') and the certainty that husbands would look after their women, as a source of their livelihood. Swift by implication suggests that cannibalism on a commercial scale would be no less justifiable than the economic system which allows England to exploit Irish labour and trade. As a rhetorical performance in satiric impersonation, *A Modest Proposal* is probably unrivalled in English prose.

Moir, David Macbeth 1798–1851 Scots novelist. He contributed regularly to BLACKWOOD'S EDINBURGH MAGAZINE and other periodicals, signing his name with the Greek capital delta. His best-remembered book, *The Life of Mansie Wauch, Tailor in Dalkeith* (1828) is an imaginary autobiography containing much wry observation. It is dedicated to JOHN GALT.

Molesworth, Mary Louisa 1839–1921 Writer of CHILDREN'S LITERATURE. She published *Lover and Husband* (1869) and several other novels under the pseudonym Ennis Graham before turning to children's books with great popular success. Macmillan made a practice of issuing a book by Mrs Molesworth every Christmas, sometimes illustrated by WALTER CRANE. Among more than 100 titles are *The Cuckoo Clock* (1877), *The Tapestry Room* (1879), *The Adventures of Herr Baby* (1881), *The Children of the Castle* (1890), *The Carved Lions* (1895), *Peterkin* (1902), *The Little Guest* (1907) and *The Story of a Year* (1910).

Moll Flanders, The Fortunes and Misfortunes of the Famous A novel by DEFOE, published in 1722. Born in Newgate, she is taken in by the mayoress of Colchester, from whom she passes to another gentlewoman, whose son seduces her. She leads an adventurous love life and eventually marries. In Virginia with her husband, she finds her mother and discovers that her husband is in fact her brother. She leaves him and her children for England, where she falls into bad company and becomes a thief. Transported to Virginia, she renews her liaison with a former husband on the way. Moll inherits her mother's plantation and prospers. When their sentence runs out, she and her husband return to England, where she looks back from the age of 70 over 'the wicked lives we have lived'.

Moll Flanders owes much of its success and its importance in the development of English fiction to the fact that it is a novel of character rather than an adventurous romance. It may not be neat or shapely, but Moll herself is made an identifiable personality.

Momaday, N(atachee) [Navarre] Scott 1934– American Indian novelist, poet and scholar. He became known as editor of the poems of FREDERICK GODDARD TUCKERMAN (1965). His first novel, *House Made of Dawn* (1968) received a PULITZER PRIZE. He has since published: a collection of Kiowa folk-tales, *The Way to Rainy Mountain* (1969); a volume of poetry, *Angle of Geese and Other Poems* (1974); *The Gourd Dancer* (1976); *The Names: A Memoir* (1976); and a second novel, *The Ancient Child* (1989).

Moments of Vision and Miscellaneous Verses Poems by HARDY, published in 1917. A short poem, 'Moments of Vision', gives the volume its title and evokes its ambience of Wordsworthian introspection and inner searching. Yet much of the verse is contemporary in composition and one group of poems is given to

war and patriotism. The volume includes 'The Last Signal' (about WILLIAM BARNES), 'The Blinded Bird', 'During Wind and Rain', and 'Near Lanivet' (among those about Emma, his first wife) and 'Afterwards'.

Monastery, The A novel by SIR WALTER SCOTT, published in 1820. It is more interesting for its evocation of Kennaquhair, a monastery based on Melrose Abbey, in the time of Elizabeth I than for the romantic plot, which concerns the rivalry of Sir Piercie Shafton and the brothers Edward and Halbert Glendinning in their love for Mary Avenel. *The Abbot* (1820), set in the reign of Mary, Queen of Scots, was intended as a sequel.

Moncrieff, William Thomas 1794–1857 Playwright and theatre manager. Lessee at various times of the Queen's, Astley's Amphitheatre, the Coburg, Vauxhall Gardens and the City Theatre, he wrote over 100 hack plays. *The Lear of Private Life* (1820), from a novel by AMELIA OPIE, has some interest as a 19th-century domestication of SHAKESPEARE. *The Shipwreck of the Medusa* (1820) exploited the excitement created by Géricault's picture. *Tom and Jerry* (1821) was a particularly zestful adaptation of PIERCE EGAN'S *LIFE IN LONDON*. *The Cataract of the Ganges* (1823) was notable for the use of a horse troupe and lavish sets.

Money A comedy by EDWARD BULWER LYTTON, produced in 1840. After unexpectedly inheriting a fortune, Alfred Evelyn sorts out which of his friends are true and which of two women he should marry by pretending to have lost all the money. The reading of the will (Act One) and the gambling scene (Act Three) are highlights of this socially alert play.

Monk, The A GOTHIC NOVEL by M. G. LEWIS, published in 1796. It relies on horror rather than terror, and allows supernatural events to remain without natural explanation. The theme is the sexual repression at the heart of asceticism. Ambrosio, a devoted young monk, is tempted into depravity and eventually damned by his association with Matilda, the model for his own much beloved portrait of the Virgin Mary but in fact the Devil's emissary. Sub-plots compound the horror of a tale which many found both ridiculous and indecent, though it also enjoyed considerable popularity.

Monk's Tale, The See CANTERBURY TALES.

monometer See METRE.

Monro, Harold (Edward) 1879–1932 Publisher and poet. He is best remembered for the Poetry Bookshop which he established in 1913 to publish and sell work by contemporary poets and organize public readings. He also published EDWARD MARSH's GEORGIAN POETRY anthologies and founded *The Poetry Review* and its short-lived successor, *Poetry and Drama*. His own work includes *Chronicle of a Pilgrimage: Paris to Milan on Foot* (1909) and *Collected Poems* (1933), introduced by T. S. ELIOT.

Monroe, Harriet 1860–1936 American editor and poet. Her poetry appeared in *Valeria and Other Poems* (1891), *You and I* (1914), *The Difference* (1924) and *Chosen Poems* (1935). She also wrote verse dramas, five of them included in *The Passing Show* (1903). She founded POETRY: A Magazine of Verse in 1912 and edited it until her death, publishing work by EZRA POUND, T. S. ELIOT (*THE LOVE SONG OF J. ALFRED PRUFROCK*) and many other distinguished figures. Her autobiography, *A Poet's Life: Seventy Years in a Changing World* (1937), provides an informative account of the American literary scene. *Poets and Their Art* (1932) is a collection of essays.

Monsarrat, Nicholas (John Turney) 1910–79 Novelist. He is chiefly remembered for his novel of

World War II, *The Cruel Sea* (1951), made into a successful film; other works include *The Tribe That Lost Its Head* (1965) and *Richer Than All His Tribe* (1968). *Life is a Four-Letter Word* (1966–70) is autobiographical.

Mont-Saint-Michel and Chartres: *A Study of Thirteenth-Century Unity* A work of history by HENRY ADAMS, privately printed in 1904 and published in 1913. Adams identifies the dominant cultural power of the Middle Ages as the Catholic faith and, in particular, sees the unifying symbolic 'force' of the Virgin as having provided the spiritual impulse for the arts. The investigation of medieval culture is complemented by the discussion of modernity in *THE EDUCATION OF HENRY ADAMS*, subtitled 'A Study of Twentieth-Century Multiplicity'.

Montagu, Elizabeth 1720–1800 Leading member of the BLUESTOCKING circle. The wife of Charles, cousin of Edward Wortley Montagu (see LADY MARY WORTLEY MONTAGU), she held regular assemblies for intellectual and literary conversation at her London home. Members of her 'Blue Stocking Society' included BURNEY, CHAPONE, HANNAH MORE and HORACE WALPOLE. She was author of the *Essay on the Writings and Genius of Shakespeare* (1769), defending SHAKESPEARE against the attacks of Voltaire.

Montagu, Lady Mary Wortley 1689–1762 Poet and letter-writer. The eldest daughter of the 1st Duke of Kingston and the wife of Edward Wortley Montagu, she became well known in literary circles, associating with ADDISON and POPE. After their friendship soured Pope was malicious to her in print on several occasions. *Court Poems* (1716) are witty and perceptive *vers de société*. Her letters in 1716–18 from Turkey, where her husband was ambassador, give a sharp account of life at the Ottoman Court. A collection of her letters appeared in 1763–7 and a complete edition by Robert Halsband was published in 1965–7. She introduced the practice of inoculation against smallpox.

Montague, John 1929– Irish poet. A contemporary and friend of THOMAS KINSELLA, he introduced American and French influences into Irish poetry at a time when it was becoming introverted and provincial. Deeply affected by the crisis in Northern Ireland, his work has always sought a reconciliation between the intimacies of private life and the brutalities of public experience, most notably in *The Rough Field* (1972). Other volumes are *Poisoned Lands* (1961; revised edition, 1976), *A Chosen Light* (1967), *Tides* (1970), *A Slow Dance* (1975), *The Great Cloak* (1978), *Mount Eagle* (1989) and *New Selected Poems* (1990). He has also published a volume of stories, *Death of a Chieftain* (1964), and edited an important anthology, *The Faber Book of Irish Verse* (1974).

Montgomerie, Alexander ?1556–?1610 Scottish poet. He held office at the Scottish court, under the regent Morton and then James VI, before losing favour through his implication in a popish plot in 1594. His principal work is *The Cherrie and the Slae* (1597), an allegorical poem about the choice between the noble and virtuous cherry and the lowly sloe. The *Flyting betwixt Montgomerie and Polwart* (1621) is an example of the exchanged invective used by earlier Scottish poets such as DUNBAR.

Montgomery, L(ucy) M(aud) 1874–1942 Canadian novelist and writer of CHILDREN'S LITERATURE. *Anne of Green Gables* (1908), an immediate popular success, tells how a lively 11-year-old, Anne Shirley, wins the hearts of Matthew and Marilla Cuthbert, an elderly bachelor and his sister, when she is sent to their farm on Prince Edward Island. *Anne of Avonlea* (1909) and numerous other titles followed the scapegrace heroine's career from teaching college to marriage and domesticity, but without recapturing the charm of the original book.

Other novels include *The Blue Castle* (1926), *Kilmeny of the Orchard* (1910) and the melancholy, semi-autobiographical *Emily of New Moon* (1923), *Emily Climbs* (1925) and *Emily's Quest* (1927).

Moodie, Susanna 1803–85 Poet, novelist and essayist. The sister of CATHARINE PARR TRAILL and AGNES STRICKLAND, she emigrated to Canada in 1832. *Enthusiasm and Other Poems* (1831) was followed by other volumes written to help the family finances, including the novels *Mark Hurdlestone and the Gold Worshipper* (1853), *Geoffrey Monckton* (1853) and *Flora Lyndsay* (1854). Her most enduring works are *Roughing It in the Bush: or, Life in Canada* (1852) and *Life in the Clearings versus the Bush* (1853).

Moody, William Vaughn 1869–1910 American playwright and poet. Although only two of his plays were produced during his lifetime, He was important for choosing distinctively American subjects. *A Sabine Woman* (1906), later produced and published as *The Great Divide* (1909), treats the conflict between Eastern culture and frontier life. *The Masque of Judgment* (1900), *The Fire Bringer* (1904) and the uncompleted *The Death of Eve* (1912) are a trilogy of verse dramas. *The Faith Healer* (1909) was the last play in his brief career. *Poems* (1901) contains the often-anthologized pieces 'Gloucester Moors' and 'An Ode in Time of Hesitation'.

Moonstone, The A novel by WILKIE COLLINS, published in 1868. It uses features of the SENSATION NOVEL to create a pioneering example of DETECTIVE FICTION. The story is told through eyewitness accounts by the characters. Franklin Blake presents the Moonstone diamond, stolen from a Hindu holy place, to Rachel Verinder but it disappears by the next morning. Sergeant Cuff investigates the mystery. Suspicion falls variously on three Hindus lurking in the neighbourhood, the servant Rosanna Spearman and Rachel herself. She inexplicably turns against Franklin Blake and becomes engaged to the philanthropist Godfrey Ablewhite. Ezra Jennings, the local doctor's assistant, demonstrates that Blake unknowingly removed the diamond while under the influence of opium. The diamond, meanwhile, is traced to a London bank and Cuff exposes Ablewhite as the thief, but not before Ablewhite has been killed and the diamond retrieved by the Hindus.

Moorcock, Michael 1939– Writer of SCIENCE FICTION. He became editor of *New Worlds* in 1964, making it a forum for surreal, modernist science fiction. Among his own works are: the 'Jerry Cornelius' stories, including a tetralogy, *The Final Programme* (1968), *A Cure for Cancer* (1971), *The English Assassin* (1972) and *The Condition of Muzak* (1977); *Behold the Man* (1969); the 'Dancers at the End of Time' series, including *An Alien Heat* (1972), *The Hollow Lands* (1974) and *The End of All Songs* (1976); and many 'sword and sorcery' novels, of which *Gloriana* (1978) is the most substantial. His mildly surrealistic non-fantasy novels include *The Brothel in Rosenstrasse* (1982), *Byzantium Endures* (1983), *The Laughter of Carthage* (1984), *Mother London* (1988) and *Casablanca* (1989), set, like much recent work, in North Africa.

Moore, Brian 1921– Irish novelist. His experience of Catholicism and a divided Ireland frequently provides him with themes. The unflinchingly realistic surfaces of his novels belie an underlying engagement with phantasmagora, myth and ritual. Works include: *Judith Hearne* (1955; retitled *The Lonely Passion of Judith Hearne*), about the descent into delusion of a Belfast spinster; *The Feast of Lupercal* (1957; *The Luck of Ginger Coffey* (1960); *An Answer from Limbo* (1962); *The Emperor of Ice Cream* (1965); *I Am Mary Dunne* (1968), perhaps his best book, a study of imperilled identity; *Catholics* (1972); *The Great Victorian Collection* (1975); *The Mangan Inheritance* (1979); *Cold Heaven* (1983), about earthly reincarnation; *Black Robe* (1985), about 17th-century Jesuits and Canadian Indians; *The Colour of Blood* (1987), about Communist Poland; *Lies of Silence* (1990), a thriller about Ireland; and *No Other Life* (1993).

Moore, Edward 1712–57 Playwright and poet. Of his three plays, *The Foundling* (1748), *Gil Blas* (1751) and *The Gamester* (1753), only the last is of any enduring significance. A bourgeois or domestic TRAGEDY about the lure of gambling, it was influenced by LILLO and in turn influenced German drama, as well as encouraging the rise of MELODRAMA.

Moore, George (Augustus) 1852–1933 Anglo-Irish novelist and playwright. Born in Ireland and educated in Birmingham, he spent ten years in Paris, studying painting and publishing two books of verse, *Flowers of Passion* (1878) and *Pagan Poems* (1881). After his arrival in London in 1880 he published poems, plays, essays, art criticism, an autobiography and a stream of novels which clearly showed the influence of Zola's NATURAL-ISM: *A Modern Lover* (1883), *A Mummer's Wife* (1885), *A Drama in Muslin* (1886), *A Mere Accident* (1887), *Spring Days* (1888), *Mike Fletcher* (1889) and *Vain Fortune* (1891). He achieved a major success with ESTHER WATERS (1894), generally acknowledged as his finest work. His years in Ireland (1899–1911) are described in *Hail and Farewell* (1911–14), a trilogy of reminiscence valuable for its portrait of the Irish literary revival and the establishment of the ABBEY THEATRE. Back in London, he acquired a reputation as a literary sage. His last period as a writer was announced by *The Brook Kerith* (1916), a painstaking novel about Jesus. Other works include two more novels, *Héloïse and Abelard* (1921) and *Aphrodite in Aulis* (1930), and plays, *The Making of an Immortal* (1927) and *The Passing of the Essenes* (1930; a revised version of *The Apostle*, 1911).

Moore, G(eorge) E(dward) 1873–1958 Philosopher. A contemporary of BERTRAND RUSSELL at Trinity College, Cambridge, he became professor of philosophy in 1925–39 as well as a major influence on the BLOOMSBURY GROUP, which included many of his former students. 'The Refutation of Idealism' (1903; reprinted in *Philosophical Studies*, 1922) defended the independent reality of material objects, minds and their states. His major work, *Principia ethica* (1903), rejected the view that moral properties such as goodness can be reduced to 'naturalistic properties' such as happiness or evolutionary success. He argued for 'direct moral awareness' and claimed that the contemplation of beauty and affectionate personal relations are the only supremely good states of mind. Other works include 'A Defence of Common Sense' (1923) and 'A Proof of an External World' (1939), and *Some Main Problems of Philosophy* (1953).

Moore, Marianne (Craig) 1887–1972 American poet. Volumes include *Poems* (1921), *Observations* (1924), *Selected Poems* (1935), *The Pangolin and Other Verse* (1936), *What are Years* (1941), *Nevertheless* (1944), *A Face* (1949), *Collected Poems* (1951), *Like a Bulwark* (1956), *O, to be a*

Dragon (1959) and *Tell Me, Tell Me: Granite, Steel, and Other Topics* (1966) and *The Complete Poems of Marianne Moore* (1967). Her poetry is marked by an unconventional but disciplined use of METRE and a witty, often ironic tone. Exotic animals are favourite subjects. Other works include a volume of critical essays, *Predilections* (1955), and two volumes of translations from La Fontaine. *The Complete Prose of Marianne Moore* appeared in 1986.

Moore, Nicholas 1918–86 Poet. The son of G. E. MOORE, he edited *Seven* (1938–40) and *New Poetry* (1944–5) and was a central figure in the NEW APOCALYPSE movement, appearing in two of its anthologies, *The New Apocalypse* (1939) and *The White Horseman* (1941). Indebted to AUDEN, WALLACE STEVENS and BLAKE, his poetry has visual clarity and lyrical fluency. Principal volumes are *A Wish in Season* (1941), *A Book for Priscilla* (1941), *The Cabaret, the Dancer, the Gentleman* (1942), *The Glass Tower* (1944) and *Recollections of the Gala: Selected Poems 1943–48* (1950).

Moore, Thomas 1779–1852 Poet. *Odes of Anacreon Translated into English Verse, with Notes* (1801), his first work, and *Epistles, Odes and Other Poems* (1806) earned him the nickname 'Anacreon Moore'. He turned to light satire in *Intercepted Letters: or, The Twopenny Post Bag, by Thomas Brown the Younger* (1813) and *The Fudge Family in Paris, Edited by Thomas Brown the Younger* (1818). A sequel, *The Fudges in England*, appeared in 1835. Meanwhile, he was preparing the work which secured his reputation. *A Selection of Irish Melodies* (1808–34), offered a reassuringly sentimental view of Ireland and included 'The Last Rose of Summer'. *LALLA ROOKH: An Oriental Romance* (1817) and THE LOVES OF THE ANGELS (1823) were not only romantic but exotic, a combination for which the poetry of his friend BYRON had already created a large public.

On his death Byron left his manuscript 'Memoirs' to Moore, who destroyed the original but used some material from it to compile his controversial *Letters and Journals of Lord Byron, with Notices of His Life* (1830). Other works include lives of SHERIDAN (1825) and Lord Edward Fitzgerald (1831), *The Epicurean* (1827), a novel about the 3rd-century philosopher Alciphron, and *The History of Ireland* (1835–46).

Moore, T(homas) Sturge 1870–1944 Poet and art historian. He was the brother of G. E. MOORE. A wood engraver, he designed covers for several volumes by his friend YEATS. His own poetry, cordially received by the critics but neglected by the public, includes *The Vinedresser* (1899), *Danae* (1903), *The Gazelles* (1904), *Marianne* (1911), *Medea* (1920), *Judas* (1923) and his collected poems (1931–3). He also published studies of Altdorfer (1900), Dürer (1905), Correggio (1906) and Charles Ricketts (1933).

Moorhouse, Frank 1938– Australian short-story writer. As co-founder (with MICHAEL WILDING) and editor of the alternative fiction magazine *Tabloid Story*, he has had an influence beyond his own writing. This he began by describing as 'discontinuous narrative'. More traditional than some Australian post-modernists, he uses forms reflecting the fragmentation of contemporary urban life. His books include *Futility and Other Animals* (1969), *The Americans, Baby* (1972), *The Electrical Experience* (1974), *Conference-Ville* (1976), *Tales of Mystery and Romance* (1977), *The Everlasting Secret Family and Other Secrets* (1980), *Room Service* (1986), *Forty Seventeen* (1988) and *Lateshows* (1990). He has edited an important anthology of Australian contemporary fiction, *The State of the*

Art: The Mood of Contemporary Australia in Short Fiction (1983). Days of Wine and Rage (1980) documents the 1970s. He has also written several screenplays.

Moral Essays Four verse epistles by POPE, each addressed to a different acquaintance. Epistle I, Of the Knowledge and Characters of Men, is addressed to Viscount Cobham and sets out Pope's belief that each individual has a 'Ruling Passion' dictating his perspective on life. Epistle II, Of the Characters of Women, is addressed to Martha Blount and includes waspish verse-portraits, such as 'Atossa' (the Duchess of Marlborough), and satire of other contemporary women. Epistle III, Of the Use of Riches, to Lord Bathurst, takes the form of a dialogue praising Bathurst's house and gardens; it contains descriptions of the benevolent 'Man of Ross' (John Kyrle, the philanthropist) and the death of Buckingham. Epistle IV, to Lord Burlington, also considers the uses of wealth, equating good taste with good sense (morality) and contrasting Burlington's taste with 'Timon's villa', the embodiment of opulent vulgarity.

morality plays Where medieval MIRACLE PLAYS derived from the liturgy and celebrated God as manifest in the life and death of Jesus, morality plays took their inspiration from the sermon and treated the problems confronting Man. They were usually allegorical, with abstractions like Mercy or Justice and Envy or Lust competing for possession of the soul. The most remarkable collection is The Macro Plays, perhaps from the abbey at Bury St Edmunds: Mankind (c. 1473), Wisdom, Who is Christ (c. 1460) and the earliest and most elaborate, THE CASTLE OF PERSEVERANCE (c. 1425). EVERYMAN, probably an English version of the Dutch Elckerlijk (1495), is the most famous and belongs to the whole of western Europe. The form persisted in England up to the mid-16th-century, when it had grown flexible enough to accommodate SATIRE and COMEDY, as well as individual characterization.

Mordaunt, Elinor [Mordaunt, Evelyn May] 1877–1942 Novelist and traveller. The Venture Book (1926), Purely for Pleasure (1932) and Traveller's Pack (1933) describe her wide-ranging travels. Her many novels include The Rose of Youth (1915) and Reputation (1923). Sinabada (1937) is her autobiography.

More, Hannah 1745–1833 Playwright and religious writer. After publishing a pastoral play, The Search after Happiness (1773), she moved from Bristol to London, where she became friends with JOSHUA REYNOLDS, SAMUEL JOHNSON, GARRICK, HORACE WALPOLE and the BLUESTOCKING circle. Another play, Inflexible Captive, was published in 1774 and Garrick produced her tragedies, Percy and The Fatal Falsehood, in 1777 and 1779. In later life her strong Evangelical convictions caused her to abandon the theatre and devote herself to didactic writing, aimed largely at the poorer classes perceived as vulnerable to the ideas spread by the French Revolution. Village Politics (1793) was followed by the popular series of Cheap Repository Tracts (1795–8), which included 'The Shepherd of Salisbury Plain'. The Religious Tract Society was formed to continue her work, while she herself went on to support Wilberforce in his campaign against slavery, to pioneer the Sunday School movement and to write a didactic novel, Coelebs in Search of a Wife (1809). Her Letters appeared in 1834.

More, Henry 1614–87 Philosopher and leading member of the CAMBRIDGE PLATONISTS. Like his fellow Platonist CUDWORTH he was opposed to the materialism of THOMAS HOBBES and Descartes. More was an industri-

ous writer in both verse and prose. Psychozoia Platonica (1642) was enlarged and incorporated in Philosophical Poems (1647). His later works include Enthusiasmus Triumphatus (1656), a denunciation of Puritan 'enthusiasms' (extravagant claims for their faith and inspiration) and The Immortality of the Soul (1659).

More, St Thomas 1477–1535 Humanist, politician and Roman Catholic martyr. The son of a judge, he studied at Oxford under LINACRE and GROCYN, qualified as a barrister in 1501 and entered Parliament in 1504. More helped Henry VIII to write his Defence of the Seven Sacraments in answer to Luther, and with the King's favour his career prospered. Knighted in 1521, he became Speaker of the Commons in 1523, Chancellor of the Duchy of Lancaster in 1525 and Wolsey's successor as Lord Chancellor in 1529. His fall came rapidly. Opposing Henry's break with Rome, he refused to attend Anne Boleyn's coronation and to swear to the Act of Succession. Tried and condemned as a traitor, he was executed on 6 July 1535, asserting that he was dying for his faith. He was beatified in 1886 and canonized in 1935.

More's friendship with ERASMUS dated from the latter's first visit to England in 1499. During Erasmus' second visit they both produced Latin translations from Lucian, printed in 1506. On his third visit in 1509–14 Erasmus wrote Encomium Moriae (Praise of Folly), whose title quibbles with More's name, at his friend's house. More's English translation of a Latin life of the Italian humanist Giovanni Pico della Mirandola was printed in 1510. UTOPIA, his most influential work, was published in Latin at Louvain in 1516 and in an English translation by Ralph Robinson in 1551. In the late 1520s and early 1530s he produced controversial defences of the Catholic faith against the criticisms of TYNDALE. His predictably hostile History of Richard III, written in Latin and English c. 1513–18 but left unfinished, was imperfectly printed in English in Grafton's Chronicle (1543). It was used by JOHN STOW, EDWARD HALL and HOLINSHED, thus transmitting material to SHAKESPEARE for Richard III. While a prisoner in the Tower More wrote A Dialogue of Comfort against Tribulation (printed in 1553), a supposed English translation of a French version of a Latin dialogue between two Hungarians, Anthony and Vincent. If nothing else, his martyrdom ensured that he became a popular subject of biography: the most notable (not printed until 1626) was by his son-in-law, William Roper. Plays about him include SIR THOMAS MORE, to which Shakespeare contributed, and BOLT's A Man for All Seasons (1960).

Morgan, Charles (Langbridge) 1894–1958 Novelist and playwright. His 11 novels include: Portrait in a Mirror (1929); The Fountain (1932), sometimes considered his most successful work; The Voyage (1940); The Judge's Story (1947), a fable on the struggle between spiritual and material values, echoed in a collection of essays, Liberties of the Mind (1951); and Challenge to Venus (1957). His plays are: The Flashing Stream (1938); The River Line (1952), from his 1949 novel of the same title; and The Burning Glass (1954). He also wrote a tribute to his close friend George Moore (1935) and Ode to France (1942), a country where his work was much admired.

Morgan, Edwin (George) 1920– Scottish poet, translator and critic. His poetic career stretches from The Vision of Cathkin Braes (1952) to From the Video Box (1986) and You: Anti-War Poetry (1991). Collected Poems appeared in 1990. Although essentially a poet of

Glasgow, he has experimented with sound and CON-CRETE POETRY and embraced both the social observation of the *Glasgow Sonnets* (1972) and the playfulness of 'The Computer's First Christmas Card'. He has translated literature from several languages into Scots and English, showing a particular affinity with modern Italian poets such as Montale and Quasimodo. *Rites of Passage: Selected Translations* appeared in 1976. *Crossing the Border* (1990) is among the works which have established him as a notable critic of MACDIARMID and contemporary Scottish literature.

Morgan, Lady Sydney ?1783–1859 Novelist. She was known for Irish romances, the best being *The Wild Irish Girl* (1806), *O'Donnel* (1814) and *The O'Briens and the O'Flaherties* (1827). She also wrote two lively books on France and Italy, and a life of Salvator Rosa.

Morier, James Justinian *c.* 1780–1849 Traveller and novelist. Service with Sir Hartford Jones's mission to Persia led to his *Journey through Persia, Armenia and Asia Minor* (1812) and the more notable *Second Journey through Persia* (1818). Morier also used his experiences in several Oriental romances, of which the most successful is *The Adventures of Hajji Baba of Ispahan* (1824), a PICARESQUE novel whose uncomplimentary account of Persian society drew a protest from the Persian minister in London, later printed in a sequel, *The Adventures of Hajji Baba of Ispahan in England* (1828).

Morley, Henry 1822–94 Journalist and critic. He contributed to *HOUSEHOLD WORDS* and *ALL THE YEAR ROUND*, edited *THE EXAMINER* and published translations, biographies and miscellanies. He became professor of English at University College, London, and was active in the field of adult education, producing cheap editions of English classics and 11 volumes of an ambitious history of English literature, *English Writers*, begun in 1887.

Morley, John, 1st Viscount 1838–1923 Statesman, biographer and journalist. A supporter of Gladstone, he held office as Chief Secretary for Ireland (1886 and 1892), Secretary of State for India (1905) and Lord President of the Council (1910). His chief contribution to literature was his biography of Gladstone (1903). He edited the English Men of Letters series, to which he contributed the volume on EDMUND BURKE (1879), as well as *THE FORTNIGHTLY REVIEW*, to which he contributed the essays gathered as *Critical Miscellanies* (1871–1908), and *THE PALL MALL GAZETTE*.

Morning Chronicle, The A Whig journal founded in 1769 by William Woodfall. It became prominent at the turn of the century under the editorship of James Perry and John Black. Contributors included SHERIDAN, LAMB, THOMAS MOORE, RICARDO, JOHN STUART MILL, THACKERAY and MAYHEW. The young DICKENS was employed as a reporter and published part of *SKETCHES BY BOZ* in its pages. It ceased publication in 1862.

Morrell, Lady Ottoline 1873–1938 Literary patron and socialite. In the years before, during and after World War I she and her husband, the Liberal MP Philip Morrell, entertained a wide circle of political and literary celebrities at their London home and at Garsington Manor, near Oxford. It included BERTRAND RUSSELL, VIRGINIA WOOLF, T. S. ELIOT, YEATS, D. H. LAWRENCE and ALDOUS HUXLEY. Lawrence's *WOMEN IN LOVE* and Huxley's *Crome Yellow* both contain fictional portraits of her. Robert Gathorne Hardy edited her *Memoirs* (1963–74).

Morris, Sir Lewis 1833–1907 Poet. His cheerful and musical collection, *Songs of Two Worlds* (1871), was well received by the reading public; *The Epic of Hades* (1876–7) was still more popular. Other works included *Gwen* (1879), *Songs Unsung* (1883), *Gycia: A Tragedy* (1886) and *A Vision of Saints* (1890). *The New Rambler* (1905) is a volume of essays. He helped to found the University of Wales and was knighted in 1895.

Morris, Mervyn 1937– Jamaican poet. He has published several collections, among them *The Pond* (1973), *On Holy Week* (1976) and *Shadowboxing* (1979). His poems deal with precisely wrought moments of feeling or observation, showing that Caribbean poetry can be about private pains as well as about public causes. He has also played an important part in encouraging a younger generations of oral poets, editing volumes by MICHAEL SMITH and Jean Minta Breeze as well as several anthologies.

Morris, William 1834–96 Writer, artisan and socialist. As an undergraduate at Exeter College, Oxford, he first met his lifelong friend Edward Burne-Jones and fell under the influence of the PRE-RAPHAELITES. Lodging in London with Burne-Jones from 1856, he began to design furniture and, with encouragement from DANTE GABRIEL ROSSETTI, took up painting. Jane Burden, whom he married in 1859, appears as Queen Guinevere in his only extant oil painting; she became one of the most familiar Pre-Raphaelite models. His experience furnishing his new home, The Red House, prompted him in 1861 to found Morris, Marshall, Faulkner and Co. (later Morris and Co.) and thus begin a major revival of decorative arts and crafts. His own talents lay in designing patterns for wallpapers, chintzes, damasks, embroideries, tapestries and carpets; the firm is also famous for stained glass, stencilled mural decoration, painted tiles and furniture.

Morris published *THE DEFENCE OF GUENEVERE AND OTHER POEMS* in 1858. Only one further collection followed, *Poems by the Way* (1891), as his interest turned to ambitious narrative poetry. *THE LIFE AND DEATH OF JASON* (1867) is a greatly enlarged version of a tale originally intended for *THE EARTHLY PARADISE* (1868–70), which secured his reputation as a leading poet. Though he returned to classical poetry, translating *The Aeneids of Virgil* (1875) and *The Odyssey of Homer* (1887), Morris became absorbed with Northern European legend. His study of Icelandic, visits to Iceland and prose translations (with Eirikr Magnússon) from the sagas were preparatory work for *SIGURD THE VOLSUNG AND THE FALL OF THE NIBLUNGS* (1876), his great poetic version of the *Volsunga Saga*. He also translated *BEOWULF* (with A. J. Wyatt, 1895).

His outraged response to the Bulgarian atrocities in 1876 began a political pilgrimage that culminated in the foundation of the Socialist League in 1884 and the Hammersmith Socialist Society in 1890. Much of his writing was devoted to political polemic and his contiguous theories of art (as in *Hopes and Fears for Art*, 1882). His most important socialist works were the prose pieces *A DREAM OF JOHN BALL* (1886–7) and *NEWS FROM NOWHERE* (1890). For the Kelmscott Press, which he founded in 1891, he designed two typefaces, 'Golden' and 'Troy', and collaborated with Burne-Jones in designing books which include the great folio CHAUCER (1896). The most important of his last writings are romances: *The Wood beyond the World* (1894), *THE WELL AT THE WORLD'S END* (1896) and the posthumously published *The Water of the Wondrous Isles* and *The Sundering Flood* (both 1897).

Morris's importance in both the Arts and Crafts movement and the history of British socialism is not in doubt. However, little of his vast literary corpus is now read, with the exception of *News from Nowhere*. In the 20th century the influence of the prose romances has been greatest on YEATS, while in recent years they have acquired a new readership among devotees of TOLKIEN and C. S. LEWIS.

Morris, Wright 1910– American novelist. Preoccupied with the American Edenic myth and the influences of American history, his novels include *My Uncle Dudley* (1942), *The Man Who was There* (1945), *The World in the Attic* (1949), *The Works of Love* (1952), *A Field of Vision* (1956, National Book Award), *Love among the Cannibals* (1957), *Ceremony in Lone Tree* (1960), *Cause for Wonder* (1963), *In Orbit* (1967), *Fire Sermon* (1971), *A Life* (1973), *The Fork River Space Project* (1977) and *Plains Song* (1980). *Collected Stories: 1948–1986* appeared in 1986. He has published literary criticism and three volumes of memoirs, *Will's Boy: A Memoir* (1981), *Solo: An American Dreamer in Europe, 1933–34* (1983) and *A Cloak of Light: Writing My Life* (1985).

Morrison, Arthur 1863–1945. Novelist, short-story writer and writer of DETECTIVE FICTION. He spent most of his life in the East End of London, the setting for his best work. *Tales of Mean Streets* (1894) and two novels, *A Child of the Jago* (1894) and *The Hole in the Wall* (1902), portray the working people and criminals of the slums without sentimentality or didacticism. Despite the debt to Zola and GEORGE MOORE, they are works of considerable originality in their clear-eyed realism and unadorned prose style. Morrison's detective stories – *Martin Hewitt, Investigator* (1894), *Chronicles of Martin Hewitt* (1895) and *Hewitt: Third Series* (1896) – enjoyed a brief popularity in the wake of the SHERLOCK HOLMES STORIES. More interesting, and now equally little known, is a novel of witchcraft and smuggling in Napoleonic times, *Cunning Murrell* (1900). A collector of Japanese prints and paintings, Morrison also published an early and influential study, *The Painters of Japan* (1911).

Morrison, (Philip) Blake 1950– Poet, anthologist and critic. He has published a study of the MOVEMENT (1980), a monograph on SEAMUS HEANEY (1982) and, with ANDREW MOTION, the controversial *Penguin Book of Contemporary British Poetry* (1982). His work as a critic precedes and outweighs his poetry, which includes *Dark Glasses* (1984) and *The Ballad of the Yorkshire Ripper* (1987). *And When Did You Last See Your Father* (1993) is a memoir.

Morrison, Toni 1931– Black American novelist. She has won wide recognition for novels reaching back into the black American experience, particularly as it has affected women: *The Bluest Eye* (1970), about a year in the life of a young black girl who declines into insanity; *Sula* (1973), about the friendship between two young black women; *Song of Solomon* (1977), about Milkman Dead's exploration of his family history; *Tar Baby* (1981), about motherhood and the relationships between black and white cultures; and *Beloved* (1987; PULITZER PRIZE), which chronicles the return of a dead daughter to the mother who killed her when faced with a renewed term of slavery. She was awarded the Nobel Prize for Literature in 1993.

Morte Arthur A Middle English poem (c. 1400) derived from the French prose *Mort Artu*. It gave MALORY the source for the last two tales in LE MORTE DARTHUR, describing Lancelot's adultery with Guinevere and the destruction of the Round Table by the king's battle with Lancelot and Mordred's uprising. Arthur's body is borne to Avalon, while Lancelot and Guinevere end their lives in religious seclusion. The poem is remarkable amongst medieval ARTHURIAN LITERATURE in that the powerful, yet simple and concise, narrative moves towards the inexorable destruction of the society of the Round Table without digression or spurious incident.

Morte Arthure An alliterative poem (c. 1360) by an unknown author once thought to be HUCHOWN OF THE AWLE RYALE. The principal source was probably a version of Wace's *Roman de Brut*. Arthur dominates a narrative which tells, in epic style, of his early victories, defeat of Lucius and death as a result of Mordred's uprising. The poem was used by MALORY in LE MORTE DARTHUR; see also ARTHURIAN LITERATURE.

Morte Darthur, Le A prose version of the Arthurian legends by SIR THOMAS MALORY, completed in 1469–70. It survives in CAXTON's printed text of 1485 and a manuscript discovered at Winchester in 1934. Still the most comprehensive and ambitious contribution in English to ARTHURIAN LITERATURE, it derives from three French texts, the prose *Tristan*, the Vulgate Cycle and the *Roman du Graal*, and two English works, the alliterative MORTE ARTHURE and the stanzaic MORTE ARTHUR. Though Malory unravelled intertwined narratives and made the Arthuriad more compact by omitting extraneous material, the extent to which he succeeded in creating a unified narrative – or had this as his main purpose – has been a matter of debate.

The first tale (Books 1–4) relates Arthur's birth, accession and marriage to Guinevere, his begetting of Mordred by his half-sister Morgan and the establishment of the Round Table. The stories of Merlin and various knights also appear. The second tale (Book 5) describes Arthur's defeat of the Roman emperor Lucius and his coronation by the Pope. The third and fourth tales (Books 6 and 7) deal with Lancelot du Lake and Sir Gareth of Orkney. The fifth tale (Books 8–12), occupying almost half the work, is about Sir Tristram de Lyones. The love and jealousy of Tristram, Isode and Mark is combined with other exploits, including Lancelot's begetting of Galahad, but Malory omits the tragic end of the story. The 'Tale of the Sankgreall' (Books 13–17) deals with the quest for the Holy Grail and the fragmentation of the Round Table; only Galahad, Perceval and Bors succeeding in taking the Grail to Sarras. The seventh tale (Books 18–19) deals with Lancelot's adultery with Guinevere, while the final tale (Books 20–21) tells of the destruction of the Round Table through Arthur's discovery of Guinevere's adultery, the war between Lancelot and Arthur, and Mordred's revolt. After his death in the final battle, Arthur's body is carried to the Isle of Avalon, and Malory mentions the legend that king still lives, awaiting the time for his return.

Mortimer, John (Clifford) 1923– Playwright, journalist and barrister. Although his theatrical career began during the era of the ANGRY YOUNG MEN, he has maintained a cool, witty and professional tone in comedies such as *The Dock Brief*, staged with *What Shall We Tell Caroline?* in 1958, *The Wrong Side of the Park* (1960), *Two Stars for Comfort* (1962), *Come As You Are* (1970) and *Heaven and Hell* (1976). The semi-autobiographical *A Voyage round My Father* (1970) reveals greater emotional warmth and understanding. *A Flea in Her Ear* (1966) and *The Captain of Kopenick* (1971) are adaptations from, respectively, Feydeau and Zuckmayer. His highly successful TV career includes *Rumpole of the Bailey*, featuring a splendidly disreputable barrister introduced in a volume of stories (1978).

Morton, H(enry) V(ollam) 1892–1979 Travel-writer. The success of *The Heart of London* (1925) and, particularly, *In Search of England* (1927) launched a series of gently reflective travels books which covered Scotland (1929), Ireland (1930), Wales (1932), the Middle East (1941), South Africa (1948), Spain (1954), Rome (1957) and the Holy Land (1961). He finally settled in South Africa.

Morton, Nathaniel 1612–85 American colonial historian. Born in the pilgrim community in Leyden, he emigrated to Plymouth Colony in 1623 and lived with his uncle, WILLIAM BRADFORD. He served as the colony's secretary from 1647 until his death. His history, *New England's Memorial: or, A Brief Relation of the Most Memorable and Remarkable Passages of the Providences of God, Manifested to the Planters of New England, in America: With Special Reference to the First Colony Thereof Called New Plymouth* (1669), relied on Bradford's *History of Plymouth Plantation* and provided a source for COTTON MATHER's *Magnalia Christi Americana*.

Morton, Thomas 1764–1838 Playwright. He won his first success with a musical play, *The Children in the Wood* (1793), followed by a number of comedies, of which the best are *The Way to Get Married* (1796), *A Cure for the Heart Ache* (1797), *Secrets Worth Knowing* (1798), SPEED THE PLOUGH (1800) and *The School of Reform* (1805). The character of Tyke in the last play was as famous in its time as that of Mrs Grundy in *Speed the Plough*.

Mosley, Nicholas, Lord Ravensdale 1923– Novelist. His works include *Accident* (1966), filmed by Joseph Losey, and an abstract, experimental sequence consisting of *Catastrophe Practice: Plays Not for Acting, and Cypher: A Novel* (1979), *Imago Bird* (1980), *Serpent* (1981), *Judith* (1986, revised 1992) and *Hopeful Monsters* (1990). He has also written a study of JULIAN GRENFELL (1976) and a biography of his parents, Sir Oswald and Lady Cynthia Mosley (1982–3).

Motherwell, William 1797–1835 Poet. He published a collection of Scottish ballads, *Minstrelsy Ancient and Modern* (1827), and collaborated with JAMES HOGG in editing the poetry of BURNS (1834–6). *Poems Narrative and Lyrical* (1832) is a collection of his own work. The BALLAD 'Jeanie Morison' was widely popular.

Motion, Andrew (Peter) 1952– Poet. His volumes are: *The Pleasure Steamers* (1978), owing a good deal to EDWARD THOMAS, of whom he published a critical study in 1980; *Independence* (1981), centred on the year of Indian independence; *Secret Narratives* (1983); *Dangerous Play* (1984); *Natural Causes* (1987); and *Love in a Life* (1991). With BLAKE MORRISON he edited the controversial *Penguin Book of Contemporary British Poetry* (1982). He has also published a study of LARKIN (1982), whose official biographer he is, and a group biography of George, Constant and Kit Lambert (1986). *Pale Companion* (1990) is a novel.

Motley, John Lothrop *c.* 1814–77 American historian. A diplomat who served in Europe for many years, he is remembered as the author of *The Rise of the Dutch Republic* (1856), *The History of the United Netherlands* (1861–7) and *The Life and Death of John of Barneveld, Advocate of Holland* (1874).

Motley, Willard 1912–65 American novelist. His observation of the slums of Chicago served as material for his first novel, *Knock on any Door* (1947). *We Fished All Night* (1951) and *Let No Man Write My Epitaph* (1958) are also

critical examinations of the urban environment. *Let Noon be Fair* (1966) traces the gradual corruption of a Mexican tourist town.

Motteux, Peter Anthony 1663–1718 Journalist, translator and playwright. A Huguenot from Rouen, he fled to England at the Revocation of the Edict of Nantes in 1685. He seems to have brought the word 'journalist' into English. His *The Gentleman's Journal: or, The Monthly Miscellany* (1692–4), a sophisticated literary periodical using the epistolary form of the French *Mercure galant*, included contributions from Henry Purcell, SEDLEY, JOHN DENNIS, Tom Brown and PRIOR. Motteux completed URQUHART's translation of Rabelais and published a translation of *Don Quixote* which, in John Ozell's revision, was (like the Rabelais) to remain standard for many years. *Love's a Jest* (1696) was the first of many pieces for the theatre, of which the most significant were the tragedy *Beauty in Distress* (1698) and the libretto for *Arsinoë, Queen of Cyprus* (1705). Though sung in English, *Arsinoë* gave the London audience its first hint of the Italian opera which was to become so dominant as to be satirized by GAY's THE BEGGAR'S OPERA (1728).

Mottram, R(alph) H(ale) 1883–1971 Novelist. He first achieved recognition with *The Spanish Farm* (1924), the first part of a trilogy continued in *Sixty-four, Ninety-four* (1925) and *The Crime at Vanderlynden's* (1926). It is set on a farm near the Front during World War I. Many of his later novels are set in East Anglia, where he spent most of his life.

Mourning Becomes Electra A trilogy of plays by EUGENE O'NEILL, produced in 1931. It transfers the *Oresteia* of Aeschylus to the home of General Mannon in a small New England coastal town at the close of the Civil War.

Mourning Bride, The CONGREVE's only tragedy, produced and published in 1697. A considerable success, it provided a fine part for a tragic actress in the character of Sara. The play has been forgotten but two quotations are remembered: 'Music has charms to soothe a savage breast' and 'Heav'n has no rage, like love to hatred turn'd,/ Nor Hell a fury, like a woman scorn'd.'

Movement, The A loose grouping of poets who made their names during the 1950s, essentially those included in CONQUEST's anthology *New Lines* (1956): Conquest himself, KINGSLEY AMIS, DAVIE, ENRIGHT, GUNN, John Holloway, JENNINGS, LARKIN and WAIN. Conquest's introduction claimed that they shared a 'negative determination to avoid bad principles'. In practice, this meant a determination to re-establish the values of rational intelligence and skilful craftsmanship in English poetry. Their stance was ironic and anti-romantic, their manner at times literary and, to some tastes, academic. Yet no post-war anthology of new writers has included such an impressive proportion of subsequently distinguished poets as *New Lines*.

Mowat, Farley 1921– Canadian essayist, story-teller and writer of CHILDREN'S LITERATURE. His first book, *People of the Deer* (1952), denounced the treatment of the Inuit by government officials and missionaries. Its impassioned prose created an immense readership and considerable controversy, both of which have stayed with him throughout his career. Translated into 23 languages and published in more than 40 countries, he has written more than 30 books of 'subjective non-fiction', as he describes his writings, documenting his interest in the north, the wilderness, the animal kingdom and disadvantaged peoples. *The Desperate People* (1959),

Canada North (1967), and Canada North Now: The Great Betrayal (1976) study the Canadian north. Never Cry Wolf (1963) and A Whale for the Killing (1972) are his most famous animal books. Children's books include The Dog Who Wouldn't Be (1957), Owls in the Family (1961), Lost in the Barrens (1965) and The Boat Who Wouldn't Float (1968).

Mowatt, Anna Cora 1819–70 American playwright, novelist and actress. Born in Bordeaux, she married a New York lawyer at the age of 15. After publishing a verse romance, Pelayo (1836), and a verse SATIRE, Reviewers Reviewed (1837), she turned her hand to novels of New York social life, including The Fortune Hunter (1844) and Evelyn: or, A Heart Unmasked (1845). The success of Fashion (1845), a comedy about the newly rich Mr and Mrs Tiffany, encouraged her to go on the stage herself. She toured for nine years, retiring to write her Autobiography of an Actress (1854), Mimic Life (1856) and Twin Roses (1857) – romantic narratives of life in the theatre – and various historical sketches.

Mphahlele, Es'kia [Ezekiel] 1919– South African novelist, short-story writer, autobiographer and critic. The stories of the ghetto and the black experience in Man Must Live (1947), The Living and the Dead (1961) and In Corner B (1967), selected in The Unbroken Song (1981), sound a rising note of political protest. The Wanderers (1971), Chirundu (1979) and Father Come Home (1984) are novels, though his narrative skill is seen at its best in Down Second Avenue (1959), a vivid autobiography. Afrika My Music: An Autobiography 1957–1983 (1984) is less compelling. His criticism includes The African Image (1962, revised edition 1974), a pioneering study of African literature and its politico-cultural context, and Voices in the Whirlwind (1972).

Mr Badman, The Life and Death of A religious ALLEGORY by BUNYAN, published in 1680. It consists of a dialogue between Mr Wiseman and Mr Attentive about Mr Badman, who has recently passed over into damnation. The book shows a considerable degree of realism, especially in its vivid representation of a 17th-century market town and the lively credibility of Mr Badman's own character, making an unmistakable contribution to the development of the novel.

Mr Britling Sees It Through A novel by H. G. WELLS, published in 1916. Strongly autobiographical, it captured the national mood as World War I took its toll. Through Britling, a mature and successful writer, we are given a picture of Wells's early enthusiasm for the war and his growing disillusionment, as well as glimpses of his marital infidelities, generally considered among the novelist's less discreet reflections on his life.

Mr Gilfil's Love Story See SCENES OF CLERICAL LIFE.

Mr Midshipman Easy See MARRYAT, Captain FREDERICK.

Mr Polly, The History of A novel by H. G. WELLS, published in 1910. At the age of 37, Alfred Polly seems trapped in his unprofitable shop and his marriage to Miriam, but he escapes for a life on the road. Rural England, around the Potwell Inn and its plump landlady, prove a haven from the pressures of his class and its failed commercial prospects. Polly is able to settle at the Inn only after proving his manhood in a fight with the criminal Uncle Jim, and after Miriam has been awarded life insurance for the husband she thinks dead.

Mr Scarborough's Family A novel by TROLLOPE, serialized in 1882–3 and published in volume form in 1883.

The plot concerns the disappointment of Mr Scarborough who, after the birth of a son, Mountjoy, marries his wife again before the birth of a second son, Augustus, to ensure that he can declare the latter his heir, should Mountjoy not prove of responsible character. The novel is enlivened by the characters of Mr Grey, Scarborough's attorney, and his daughter, Dolly, who refuses to marry because all the men she meets compare unfavourably with her father.

Mr Sponge's Sporting Tour A novel by SURTEES, published in 1853 with illustrations by JOHN LEECH. Probably his best novel, it has more form and balance than the others and the central character is convincingly developed. Sponge lives up to his name by forcing himself on rich men and making up to their daughters, but his skill on horseback and genuine love of hunting redeem him. Mr Facey Romford's Hounds (1865) is a sequel.

Mrs Dalloway A novel by VIRGINIA WOOLF, published in 1925. Clarissa Dalloway, the wife of Richard Dalloway MP and a fashionable London hostess, is to give an important party. Her character is gradually revealed through her thoughts during the day and her memories of the past, rendered by STREAM OF CONSCIOUSNESS. The other people who have touched her life are her one-time suitor Peter Walsh, lately returned from India; her childhood friend Sally Seton; her daughter Elizabeth and spinster tutor Miss Kilman; and a political hostess, Lady Bruton. A complementary character is Septimus Warren Smith, a shell-shock victim who has retreated into a private world and ends the day by committing suicide.

Mrs Warren's Profession A play by SHAW, written in 1893, privately performed in 1902 but denied public performance until 1925. Mrs Warren's profession is prostitution: she runs a chain of brothels. Her brilliant and independent daughter, Vivie, is shaken to discover this and rejects both her suitors in favour of continuing actuarial work with her friend Honoria. Vivie is not prepared to learn what Mrs Warren is prepared to teach: that prostitution is economically determined by a society which only pretends to outlaw it.

Mtshali, Oswald Mbuyiseni 1940– South African poet. Sounds of a Cowhide Drum (1971) led the creative outburst of black 'township' poetry which broke a decade of post-Sharpeville silence and found voice in the work of SEROTE, SEPAMLA and the other poets in the anthology, Black Poets in South Africa (1974). He has also published Fireflames (1980).

Much Ado about Nothing A comedy by SHAKESPEARE, first performed c. 1598 and published in Quarto (Q1) in 1600 as well as in the First Folio of 1623. The Claudio/Hero plot was already familiar and could come from any number of sources. The unwilling love of Beatrice and Benedick, though formally a sub-plot, is more original and chiefly responsible for the play's success in the theatre.

Claudio, in the service of the Prince of Aragon, Don Pedro, falls in love with Hero, daughter of Leonato, Governor of Messina. Don Pedro's discontented brother, Don John, destroys the match by convincing Claudio that Hero is unfaithful. He rejects his intended bride at the altar; she faints away and Leonato gives out that she is dead. When Don John's henchman Borachio is overheard boasting of the trick, Claudio's horror is relieved by Leonato's forgiveness and Hero's return to life.

In what is formally a sub-plot, Claudio's friend Benedick and Leonato's niece Beatrice fight a duel of wit which, through the manoeuvres of their friends, is exposed as a disguise of their real love for each other. Outraged by Claudio's behaviour, Beatrice demands that Benedick kill him. He challenges Claudio, but the confrontation is averted by the discovery of Don John's villainy – accidentally brought about by the fumbling and incompetent constable, Dogberry.

Muddiman, Henry b. 1629 Journalist. Almost nothing is known of his personal life. He was licensed to write a news-sheet under the Long Parliament in 1659. *The Oxford Gazette*, which he began to publish in 1665, quickly became *The London Gazette* and enjoyed a monopoly of printed news until 1678.

Mudrooroo [Johnson, Colin] 1939– Australian Aboriginal novelist, poet and critic. He changed his name in protest against the bicentennial celebrations. He is still best known for his first novel, *Wild Cat Falling* (1965), a brief but intense book focusing on a 19-year-old half-Aboriginal, half-white 'anti-hero'. *Doin Wildcat* (1988) describes the filming of the novel. His other fiction includes *Long Live Sandawara* (1979), *Doctor Wooreddy's Prescription for Enduring the Ending of the World* (1983) and *Master of the Ghost Dreaming* (1990). His verse includes *The Song Circle of Jacky and Selected Poems* (1986) and *Dalwurra: A Poem Cycle* (1988). He has written the first theorizing account of Aboriginal literature, *Writing from the Fringe* (1990), and co-edited *Paperbark* (1990), the main collection of Aboriginal writings.

Muir, Edwin 1887–1959 Poet, novelist, translator and critic. Volumes include *First Poems* (1925), *Chorus of the Newly Dead* (1926), *Journeys and Places* (1937), *The Narrow Place* (1943), *The Voyage* (1946), *The Labyrinth* (1949), *One Foot in Eden* (1956) and *Collected Poems 1921–1958* (1960). His poetry became increasingly allegorical and philosophical, though he is perhaps best represented by the often-anthologized 'The Horses'. He also published three novels, several critical studies and, with his wife Willa, translations of Kafka. His autobiography, *The Story and the Fable* (1940), was revised as *An Autobiography* (1954).

Mulcaster, Richard ?1530–1611 Writer on education. He was the first headmaster of Merchant Taylors' School in 1561–86, when he may have taught SPENSER, and then high master of St Paul's School. *Positions* (1581) and *The First Part of the Elementary* (1582) propose advanced ideas: university education and adequate salaries for teachers, close contact between teachers and parents, and music in schools. His Latin verse includes an elegy on the death of Elizabeth (1603).

Muldoon, Paul 1951– Irish poet. He now lives in the USA. His adroit verse has appeared in *New Weather* (1973), *Mules* (1977) and, intensifying his humour and broadening his range, *Why Brownlee Left* (1980), *Quoof* (1984), *Madoc: A Mystery* (1990) and *The Annals of Chile* (1994). *Selected Poems* appeared in 1986. He has edited a controversial anthology, *Contemporary Irish Poetry* (1986), and translated contemporary Gaelic poetry.

Mulock, Dinah Maria [Mrs Craik] 1826–87 Novelist. *The Ogilvies* (1849), *Olive* (1850), *The Head of the Family* (1852) and *Agatha's Husband* (1853) were followed by her most popular work, *John Halifax, Gentleman* (1856). Set in Tewkesbury (called Norton Bury), it is a CONDITION OF ENGLAND NOVEL, concerned with class and industrial conflict. The hero is a poor, friendless orphan who succeeds in the world, and marries the heroine, through his own merit rather than advantages of birth. Later novels included *A Life for a Life* (1859), *Christian's Mistake*

(1865), *The Woman's Kingdom* (1869) and *Young Mrs Jardine* (1879). She also published poetry and some sensible and penetrating essays, including 'A Woman's Thoughts about Women' (1853).

Mum and the Sothsegger Two anonymous fragments of ALLITERATIVE VERSE from the first decade of the 15th century, generally assumed to belong to a single work. The first, once known as *Richard the Redeless* and attributed by SKEAT to LANGLAND, deals with Richard II's deposition in 1399 and criticizes the king for his folly. The second fragment, referring to events after 1402, presents a debate between Mum and the soothsayer (or truth-teller), Mum advocating discreet silence and the sooth-sayer adamant that criticism should be voiced. In a dream the narrator is assured that truth-telling is best.

mummers' play Folk-drama apparently surviving from festivals celebrating the death of winter and the birth of spring. More than 3000 texts have been recovered, divided into three groups: the Hero-Combat Play, the Sword Play and the Wooing Ceremony. Adapted over the centuries, the texts can accommodate heroes from St George to Churchill and villains from the Turkish Knight to Hitler. Whoever dies can be revived by the Doctor. HARDY described the performance of a mummers' play in THE RETURN OF THE NATIVE and borrowed from the form in *The Famous Tragedy of the Queen of Cornwall*.

Munby, A(rthur) J(oseph) 1828–1910 Poet and diarist. A reluctant lawyer who preferred the literary life, he published *Benoni* (1852), *Verses New and Old* (1865), *Vestigia retrorsum* (1891), *Vulgar Verses* (under the pseudonym of Jones Brown; 1891), *Poems: Chiefly Lyric and Elegiac* (1901), *Relicta* (1909) and several verse romances, notably *Susan* (1893). Their recurrent preoccupation with working women and the gentleman who falls in love with a servant reflects Munby's love for Hannah Cullwick, a maid of all work whom he secretly married in 1873. This side of his life is recorded in the diaries he kept from 1859 onwards, used by Derek Hudson in *Munby: Man of Two Worlds* (1972).

Munday, Anthony 1560–1633 Playwright. He was engaged in writing plays within a few years of his anti-theatrical tract, *A Second and Third Blast of Retreat from Plays and Theatres* (1580). Not many have survived. *Fedele and Fortunio* (c. 1584), a piece for court performance, and *John a Kent and John a Cumber* (1594) are now believed to be mostly his work. His hand is one of several at work in SIR THOMAS MORE (c. 1593–5) and Part One of *Sir John Oldcastle* (1599). MERES praised him as 'the best for comedy' and 'our best plotter' in 1598. The plotting is arguably better than the writing in *The Downfall of Robert, Earl of Huntingdon* and *The Death of Robert, Earl of Huntingdon* (with CHETTLE; both 1598), about Robin Hood. Munday also wrote pageants for the City of London and published vigorously Protestant pamphlets. His translations from French and Spanish prose romances helped the dispersal of Arthurian and semi-Arthurian stories, while *Zelauto* (1580) and *A True and Admirable History of a Maiden of Consolens in Poitiers* (1603) advanced the development of the novel.

Munera Pulveris Essays by RUSKIN, first published in *FRASER'S MAGAZINE* as 'Essays On Political Economy' in 1862–3 and then in book form as *Munera Pulveris* in 1872. They analyse the salient aspects of political economy, which Ruskin sees as 'a system of conduct' that cannot be achieved 'except under certain conditions of moral culture'. He defines the commercial cornerstones of Wealth, Money and Riches and in each case his definitions assume life-giving qualities, assert human principles and demonstrate adherence to a moral standard – an approach very different from that of Victorian *laissez-faire* capitalism.

Mungoshi, Charles 1947– Zimbabwean novelist and short-story writer. His best-known novel, *Waiting for the Rain* (1975), is set in rural, pre-independence Zimbabwe and draws on Shona and Christian traditions for its portrait of spiritual, political and material drought, as well as the ambivalent relationships between the older generations and two brothers, Lucifer and Gabhara. Other work in English includes the stories in *Coming of the Dry Season* (1972), banned before Zimbabwean independence, and *Some Kinds of Wounds and Other Short Stories* (1980), and the poetry in *The Milkman Doesn't Only Deliver Milk*. Work in Shona includes three novels and a play.

Munro, Alice 1931– Canadian short-story writer. Her low-key, understated stories question notions of 'normality' and make her provincial towns mythical places in which universal dramas are enacted. She is both an acute observer of small-town Canadian cultural codes – in particular how women are socialized – and a writer who describes patterns of growing up and behaviour that are common across cultures. Two books, *Lives of Girls and Women* (1971) and *Who Do You Think You Are?* (1978; as *The Beggar Maid* in Britain), are collections of short stories with common protagonists who provide a sense of novelistic unity. Other collections – *Dance of the Happy Shades* (1968), *Something I've been Meaning to Tell You* (1974), *The Moons of Jupiter* (1982), *The Progress of Love* (1987) and *Friend of My Youth* (1990) – are unified by recurrent themes and motifs.

Murder Considered as One of the Fine Arts, On An essay in black humour by DE QUINCEY, published in *BLACKWOOD'S EDINBURGH MAGAZINE* in 1827 and followed by a *Supplementary Paper* in the same periodical in 1839. It purports to be the text of a lecture given in London at a meeting of the Society of Connoisseurs in Murder. After surveying the history of his subject, the speaker subjects several recent murders to detailed aesthetic criticism, based absurdly but logically on BURKE's conceptions of the 'sublime'. The sustained poker-faced seriousness of the piece invites comparison with SWIFT, though its sequel about the Society's celebration dinner degenerates into rather laboured buffoonery.

Murder in the Cathedral A verse drama by T. S. ELIOT, produced at Canterbury Cathedral in 1935 and published the same year. It follows the events at Canterbury after Archbishop Thomas à Becket's return from exile in 1170. A Chorus of Women laments the absence of their archbishop and the schism between church and state. The priests welcome news of Becket's return, while doubting his reconciliation with Henry II. Becket wrestles with the Four Tempters, resolves to offer his life to 'the Law of God above the Law of Man' and delivers his Christmas morning sermon. The Four Knights arrive and threaten him. When he refuses to leave, they return and murder him. Afterwards each knight addresses the audience in justification of their deed. The stage is left to the priests, who offer thanks to God for giving Canterbury another saint.

Murdoch, Dame **Iris (Jean)** 1919– Novelist and philosopher. The casual humour of *Under the Net* (1954) was followed by the growingly emphatic symbolism of *The Flight from the Enchanter* (1955), *The Sandcastle* (1957)

and *The Bell* (1958), widely considered her most successful novel, about a declining religious community. Her prolific output has continued with *A Severed Head* (1961), *An Unofficial Rose* (1962), *The Unicorn* (1963), *The Italian Girl* (1964), *The Red and the Green* (1965), *The Time of the Angels* (1966), *The Nice and the Good* (1968), *Bruno's Dream* (1969), *A Fairly Honourable Defeat* (1970), *An Accidental Man* (1971), *The Black Prince* (1972), *The Sacred and Profane Love Machine* (1974), *A Word Child* (1975), *Henry and Cato* (1977), *The Sea, the Sea* (BOOKER PRIZE; 1978), *The Philosopher's Pupil* (1983), *The Book and the Brotherhood* (1987), *Message to the Planet* (1989) and *The Green Knight* (1993). Her plays include an adaptation of *A Severed Head* (with J. B. PRIESTLEY; 1963). Her philosophical works include *Sartre: Romantic Rationalist* (1953), *The Sovereignty of Good* (1970) and *The Fire and the Sun: Why Plato Banned the Artists* (1977).

Murphy, Arthur 1727–1805 Playwright, editor and critic. A man of unusually broad interests, he combined an active career as a barrister with a prodigious literary output. He was submitting contributions to FIELDING's *Covent Garden Journal* by 1752, though his committed Toryism – particularly his articles attacking WILKES and *THE NORTH BRITON* in 1762 – alienated progressive Londoners. *The Apprentice* (1756) was the first of several accomplished FARCES that were among the most popular 18th-century afterpieces. Others were *The Upholsterer* (1758), *The Citizen* (1761) and the excellent *Three Weeks after Marriage* (1776), a revised version of *What We Must All Come To* (1764). His unsentimental comedies include *The Way to Keep Him* (1760, revised 1761), *All in the Wrong* (1761) and particularly *Know Your Own Mind* (1777). Murphy's tragedies, even the best of them, *The Grecian Daughter* (1772), are less effective. Other work included the first edition of Fielding's works (1762), books on Samuel Johnson (1792) and GARRICK (1801), and a translation of Tacitus (1793).

Murphy, Richard 1927– Irish poet. His collections are *The Archaeology of Love* (1955), *Sailing to an Island* (1963), *The Battle of Aughrim* (1968), *High Island* (1974), *Selected Poems* (1979), *The Price of Stone* (1985), *New Selected Poems* (1989) and *Mirror Wall* (1989). In a sense he is the last of the Anglo-Irish poets, dwelling on a heritage similar to that of YEATS but also ranging beyond it in search of the other Ireland of hovels, famine and disaster. His most ambitious poem, 'The Battle of Aughrim', commissioned and broadcast by the BBC, coolly explores the battle fought between 'planters' and 'mere Irish' in 1691.

Murray, Sir **James A(ugustus) H(enry)** 1837–1915 Lexicographer. A tailor's son from Hawick, he became a schoolmaster. FURNIVALL, whom he met through the Philological Society, involved him in preparing medieval texts for the Early English Text Society. In 1878 he was appointed editor of *THE OXFORD ENGLISH DICTIONARY*, becoming the driving force behind that formidable project and continuing to pour his enthusiasm and compulsively hard work into it even in his seventies. His achievement brought him many honorary doctorates as well as the award of a Civil List pension (1884) and a knighthood (1908).

Murray, John 1778–1843 Publisher. He inherited the publishing firm, which still exists today, from its founder, John Murray I (born MacMurray, 1745–93), and made it one of the most prestigious and successful houses of the 19th century. Though he held an interest in *THE EDINBURGH REVIEW* and *BLACKWOOD'S*

EDINBURGH MAGAZINE at various points, he was chiefly associated with the Tory QUARTERLY REVIEW, which he founded with the encouragement and support of SIR WALTER SCOTT in 1809. His single most important author was his friend BYRON, though their alliance broke down because of Murray's growing doubts about DON JUAN. His other authors included JANE AUSTEN, CRABBE, SOUTHEY, COLERIDGE and BORROW. The famous series of guidebooks was inaugurated by Mariana Starke's Guide for Travellers on the Continent (1820) and continued by the third John Murray (1808–92).

Murray, Les(lie) A(llan) 1938– Australian poet. 'The Powerline Incantation' and 'An Absolutely Ordinary Rainbow' typify his adventurous and commanding poetry. 'Noonday Axeman' epitomizes his role as sage and as mythologizer of Australian landscape and culture. Volumes include The Ilex Tree (with Geoffrey Lehmann; 1965), The Weatherboard Cathedral (1969), Poems against Economics (1972), Lunch and Counter Lunch (1974), Ethnic Radio (1977), Daylight Moon (1980), Dog Fox Field (1990) and a verse novel, The Boys Who Stole the Funeral (1979). The continually expanded Selected Poems: The Vernacular Republic (1976, 1982, 1988) preserves what he regards as his essential canon. Collections of prose include Blocks and Tackles: Articles and Essays 1982–1990 (1990).

Murray, Thomas Cornelius 1873–1959 Irish playwright. With LENNOX ROBINSON, he was one of the 'Cork realists' who helped to determine the characteristic style of the ABBEY THEATRE in works such as Birthright (1910), Aftermath (1922), Autumn Fire (1924), and Michaelmas Eve (1932). They present a sombre vision of a small-farming society bound by Catholic teaching and obsessed by ownership of their harsh land.

Murry, John Middleton 1889–1957 Critic. As editor of THE ATHENAEUM in 1919–21 and founder-editor of THE ADELPHI in 1923–30, he was an energetic force behind the new wave of post-war literature, encouraging and publishing many of the younger writers associated with MODERNISM. He was a close friend of D. H. LAWRENCE and, from 1918, the husband of KATHERINE MANSFIELD. Murry's influence waned as his strongly mystical disposition came to the fore, but he is still remembered for The Problem of Style (1922) and particularly for Son of Woman (1931), an analysis of Lawrence's struggles with the female element in his nature.

Mwangi, Meja (David) 1948– Kenyan novelist. He belongs to a generation deeply affected by the Mau Mau emergency of the early 1950s, the subject of Carcase for Hounds (1974), filmed as Cry Freedom, and Taste of Death (1975). Most of his later fiction, most famously Going down River Road (1976), has been concerned with the social conditions of life in post-independence Kenya. Other books include Kill Me Quick! (1973), The Cockroach Dance (1979), The Bushtrackers (1979), Bread of Sorrow (1987), Weapon for Hunger (1989), The Return of Shaka (1990) and Striving for the Wind (1992).

My Last Duchess A DRAMATIC MONOLOGUE by ROBERT BROWNING, published in Dramatic Lyrics (1842). On the point of marrying again, the duke displays a strikingly life-like portrait of his previous wife. It soon becomes obvious that, in his jealous obsession, he had resented her vivacity and arranged her murder. The source is apparently an incident in the life of Alfonso II, 16th-century Duke of Ferrara.

Myers, F(rederic) W(illiam) H(enry) 1843–1901 Poet, critic and psychical researcher. He wrote much ardent, emotional verse on a note of unrest and baffled enquiry, notably St Paul (1867) and The Renewal of Youth (1882). As critic, he published a monograph on WORDSWORTH (1881) and Essays, Classical and Modern (1883). His dominant passion was the scientific study of paranormal phenomena and the evidence of life after death. A founder of the Society for Psychical Research in 1882, he contributed to Phantasms of the Living (1886) on the nature of apparitions; his papers on hallucination, mediumship and double personality were the first of their kind.

Myers, L(eopold) H(amilton) 1881–1944 Novelist. The son of F. W. H. MYERS, he is best known for a tetralogy set in 16th-century India at the court of the Mogul emperor Akbar: The Near and the Far (1929), Prince Jali (1931), The Root and the Flower (1935) and The Pool of Vishnu (1940), republished in one volume as The Near and the Far in 1943. It uses a past and idealized society to explore the poverty of contemporary existence, particularly its failure to reconcile material and spiritual values.

Mysteries of Udolpho, The A GOTHIC NOVEL by ANN RADCLIFFE, published in 1794. The setting is Gascony and the Italian Apennines at the end of the 16th century. Emily de St Aubert becomes the ward of her tyrannical aunt, Madame Cheron, who marries the sinister Montoni. She is carried off to Udolpho, Montoni's castle in the Apennines, where frightening and apparently supernatural occurrences are frequent. She manages to escape, however, and returns to Gascony and her lover, the Chevalier de Valancourt. Montoni is captured and brought to justice. The combination of terrifying incident and lavishly PICTURESQUE setting made Udolpho one of the most popular of all Gothic novels.

Mystery of Edwin Drood, The DICKENS's last novel, left half-finished at his death in 1870. In the cathedral city of Cloisterham, John Jasper leads a double life as choirmaster and opium addict. The story centres on the disappearance of his nephew Edwin Drood shortly after the young man has broken off his engagement to Rosa Bud, whom Jasper loves. Most attempts to complete the story presume that Jasper has murdered Drood. Other matters are less clear, notably the role to be played by Neville and Helena Landless, the twins who come to live with Mr Crisparkle, and the true identity of Dick Datchery, the detective who arrives in Cloisterham as Dickens's fragment breaks off.

mystery plays See MIRACLE PLAYS.

mystical writing Medieval religious prose dealing with personal spiritual experience. Though written in reaction against the absolute authority of the church and its involvement in secular politics, it nevertheless remains orthodox and does not seek doctrinal or social change. It is the only medieval genre in which women authors were prominent. See THE CLOUD OF UNKNOWING, WALTER HILTON, JULIAN OF NORWICH, MARGERY KEMPE, RICHARD ROLLE.

mythopoeic criticism See FRYE, NORTHROP.

N-town cycle See MIRACLE PLAYS.

Nabokov, Vladimir 1899–1977 American novelist, short-story writer and poet. Born in St Petersburg, he followed his family into exile, studying at Cambridge (1919–22) and producing critically acclaimed poems, short stories and novels written in Russian while living in Berlin and Paris. In the USA he published his first novels in English, *The Real Life of Sebastian Knight* (1941) and *Bend Sinister* (1947), and a memoir, *Conclusive Evidence* (1951; expanded and revised as *Speak, Memory*, 1966). The success of *LOLITA* (1955) enabled him to move to Switzerland. While working on his translation of Pushkin's *Eugene Onegin* (1964), he wrote three more novels: *Pnin* (1957), about an émigré teacher as baffled by the USA as the hero of *Lolita*; *Pale Fire* (1962), which explores the discrepancies between John Shade's autobiographical poem and the commentary by its posthumous editor, Charles Kinbote; and *Ada, or Ardor: A Family Chronicle* (1969), another 'edited' text of maze-like design, set in Amerussia on the planet Antiterra. *Nabokov's Dozen* (1958) and *Nabokov's Quartet* (1966) are collections of stories. He also supervised the translation of his Russian novels by his son Dimitri. *The Enchanter* (1987) is a belatedly published novella.

Nahal, Chaman 1927– Indian novelist. He is best known for a sequence dealing with Partition and its aftermath: *Azadi* (1975), *The Crown and the Loincloth* (1981) and *The Salt of Life* (1990). *The Last of the Tricolour* will complete the quartet. Nahal has also written a satirical novel, *The English Queens* (1979), and a volume of stories, *The Weird Dance* (1965).

Naipaul, Shiva(dhar) S(rinivasa) 1945–85 Trinidadian novelist and journalist. His novels are *Fireflies* (1970), *The Chip-Chip Gatherers* (1973) and the despairing *A Hot Country* (1983). *North of South* (1978) reports on Africa, *Black and White* (1980) on American subcultures and the People's Temple mass suicides in Guyana. *Beyond the Dragon's Mouth* (1984) collects journalism, autobiography and stories. He was the younger brother of V. S. NAIPAUL.

Naipaul, Sir V(idiadhar) S(urajprasad) 1932– Trinidadian novelist and travel writer, of Indian descent. He has lived in Britain since 1950. The genial SATIRE of Trinidadian life in *The Mystic Masseur* (1957), *The Suffrage of Elvira* (1958) and *Miguel Street* (1959) culminated in his comic masterpiece, *A House for Mr Biswas* (1961). Novels set in England are *Mr Stone and the Knights Companion* (1963), about the city, and *The Enigma of Arrival* (1987), about the countryside. While keeping his fastidious, sardonic tone, Naipaul has developed his preoccupation with 20th-century uncertainties and the damaging effects of imperialism in *The Mimic Men* (1967), *In a Free State* (BOOKER PRIZE; 1971); *Guerrillas* (1975) and *A Bend in the River* (1979), a work of tragic scope. *A Flag on the Island* (1967) collects his short stories, while *A Way in the World* (1994) consists of linked stories and prose pieces.

His non-fiction, largely based on his travels and closely related to his novels, includes: *The Middle Passage* (1962) and *The Loss of El Dorado* (1969), about the Caribbean; *An Area of Darkness* (1964), *India: A Wounded Civilization* (1977) and *India: A Million Mutinies Now* (1990);

A Turn in the South (1989), about the American South; and *Among the Believers* (1981), about Islam. *Finding the Centre* (1984) contains a memoir of his father, while *The Overcrowded Barracoon* (1972) and *The Return of Eva Perón* (1980) collect shorter pieces.

Nairne, Carolina, Baroness 1766–1845 Scottish poet. Her songs, plainly Jacobite in sympathy, include 'Will Ye No Come Back Again?', 'The Auld Hoose', 'The Rowan Tree', 'The Land o' the Leal', 'The Laird of Cockpen', 'Caller Herrin' and 'Charlie is My Darling'. They were gathered as *Lays from Strathearn* (1846). As a collector of Scottish songs, her tendency was to refine the robust lyrical strength which BURNS left intact.

Naked and the Dead, The A novel by MAILER, published in 1948. Set on a Pacific island during World War II, it focuses on 13 soldiers, whose civilian lives are recalled through flashbacks. Mailer's cynicism about America's past and his doubts about its post-war future are expressed largely through the clash between the rigid General Cummings and the liberal Lieutenant Hearn. Rough in language, violent in action, and hostile towards mainstream American values, the novel foreshadows much of Mailer's later writing.

Narayan, R(asipuram) K(rishnaswami) 1907– Indian novelist. His novels include *Swami and Friends* (1935), *The Bachelor of Arts* (1937), *The Dark Room* (1938), *The English Teacher* (1945; as *Grateful to Life and Death* in the USA, 1953), *Mr Sampath* (1949; as *The Printer of Malgudi* in the USA, 1955), *The Financial Expert* (1952), *Waiting for the Mahatma* (1955), *The Guide* (1958), *The Man-Eater of Malgudi* (1962), *The Sweet Vendor* (1967; as *The Vendor of Sweets* in the USA) and *The Painter of Signs* (1976). Deceptively simple English and an ironic outlook make him particularly accessible to Western readers, though the unobtrusive, wry moral thrust of his fiction also aligns it with traditional Indian story-telling. Transparently clear narrative itself becomes a device for satirizing human follies in a tiger's 'autobiography', *A Tiger for Malgudi* (1983). He has also published many volumes of short stories and a genial autobiography, *My Days* (1975).

Nasby, Petroleum V(esuvius) [Locke, David Ross] 1833–88 American humorist and journalist. A humorist in the style of ARTEMUS WARD and JOSH BILLINGS, he specialized in facetious letters to the editor. *The Nasby Papers* (1864) ridiculed the Confederate cause in the Civil War by proclaiming its righteousness in the silliest way possible. Abraham Lincoln was among its admirers. Locke also wrote a political novel, *The Demagogue* (1881).

Nash, Ogden 1902–71 American poet. His light verse shows him a master of IRONY, adept at questioning the commonplace in American life and finding humour in social assumptions, domestic problems, even the nature of grammar and prosody itself. His books include *Cricket of Cavador* (1925), *Free Wheeling* (1931), *The Bad Parents' Garden of Verse* (1936), *I'm a Stranger Here Myself* (1938), *Good Intentions* (1942), *Versus* (1949), *Family Reunion* (1950), *Everyone But Thee and Me* (1962), *Marriage Lines* (1964), *Merrill Lynch We Roll Along* (1965), *Bed Riddance: A Posy for the Indisposed* (1970) and the posthumous *A Penny Saved is Impossible* (1981).

Nashe [Nash], **Thomas** 1567–1601 Satirist, pamphleteer and playwright. A member of the circle that included GREENE, he began by contributing a stern review of recent literature as preface to Greene's *Menaphon* (1589) and continued the SATIRE in *The Anatomy of Absurdity* (1589). Various anti-Puritan pamphlets in the MARPRELATE controversy have been assigned to him, but only *An Almond for a Parrot* (1590) with any certainty. Nashe was also embroiled in controversy with GABRIEL HARVEY and his brother Richard. Richard attacked him for presumption in the preface to *Menaphon* and Nashe replied in *PIERCE PENNILESS HIS SUPPLICATION TO THE DEVIL* (1592). Gabriel gave a bitter account of Greene's last days in *Four Letters* (1592) and Nashe responded in *Four Letters Confuted* (also known as *Strange News of the Intercepting of Certain Letters*; 1593). *Christ's Tears over Jerusalem* (1593), his most serious prose work, contains an attempt at peace-making. Harvey returned to the attack in *Pierce's Supererogation* (1593) and Nashe in *Have with You to Saffron Walden* (1596). The quarrel was ended only by episcopal decree in 1599.

Nashe's prose writings manifest a racy and colloquial diction, grotesque characterizations, fantasy and a dislike of foreigners and Puritans. *THE UNFORTUNATE TRAVELLER* (1594), now his best remembered and most admired work, has a claim to be the first PICARESQUE novel in English. *The Terrors of the Night* (1594) is a series of visions and an account of demons, spirits and superstitions. *Nashe's Lenten Stuff* (1599), a mock panegyric of a red herring, contains a vivid description of Yarmouth.

His play, *Summer's Last Will and Testament* (1592), contains the poignant lyric, 'Adieu, Farewell Earth's Bliss'. The title-page of *The Tragedy of Dido Queen of Carthage* (1594) makes Nashe co-author with MARLOWE. *The Isle of Dogs* (1597), suppressed as lewd and seditious, is lost.

Nathan, George Jean 1882–1958 American editor and critic. With MENCKEN he edited *Smart Set* from 1914 and founded *THE BLACK MASK* in 1920 and *THE AMERICAN MERCURY* in 1924. A founder and, in 1937–9, president of the New York Drama Critics Circle, Nathan wrote several plays – *The Eternal Mystery* (1913), *Heliogabalus* (with Mencken, 1920) and *The Avon Flows* (1937) – and an annual record of the New York stage, *The Theatre Book of the Year* (1943–51).

Nation, The An American weekly, founded in 1865 as part of the campaign to secure full rights for American blacks. Originally it consisted almost entirely of political commentary and literary reviews, but by the 1920s it included original works of literature. Successors of E. L. Godkin, the first editor, have included WILLIAM LLOYD GARRISON and Paul Elmer More.

National Theatre See ROYAL NATIONAL THEATRE.

Native Son A novel by RICHARD WRIGHT, published in 1940. Bigger Thomas, a black from the Chicago ghetto, goes to work as chauffeur to a wealthy family, accidentally kills the daughter, Mary, and in his panicked flight, kills his girlfriend. Awaiting trial in prison, he feels a sense of freedom for the first time. His Communist lawyer, Max, shows him what real emotional connection with a white person can be. Max tries to make him talk about the social conditions which led to his acts, but Bigger is too proud to do anything more than affirm that 'what I killed for, I am!'

Natural History of Religion, The One of DAVID HUME's *Four Dissertations* (1757). It examines the theoretical argument that leads to theism and the mental processes from which religion arises. In primitive societies, religious beliefs spring from the fear of death or pain and the desire for security and pleasure: God is

simply a particular providence, not the author of nature. By further insisting that polytheism preceded monotheism, Hume concludes that God's existence cannot be proved by reason.

naturalism A term generally applied to art which seeks to adhere to nature. More strictly, it refers to the scientifically based extension of REALISM propounded by Émile Zola in the 1870s and 1880s. In naturalist writing, medical and evolutionary theories of 19th-century science inform readings of human character and social interactions, which are seen as being genetically and historically determined. The struggle of the individual to adapt to environment, the fight for the spouse and the Darwinian idea of the survival of the fittest become central concerns.

Naturalism influenced HARDY, GISSING and GEORGE MOORE, notably in *ESTHER WATERS* (1894), but it was less important in Britain than in the USA, where DREISER, LONDON and STEPHEN CRANE are the notable naturalist writers. Plays indebted to naturalism include SYNGE's *RIDERS TO THE SEA* (1904) and GALSWORTHY's *Strife* (1909).

Nature A book by EMERSON, published in 1836 and expanded in 1849. It sets forth the main principles of TRANSCENDENTALISM, postulating the need for 'an original relation to the universe' and viewing Nature as the expression of a divine will.

Neale, John Mason 1818–66 Church historian and hymn writer. A High Churchman in sympathy with the OXFORD MOVEMENT, in 1839 with Benjamin Webb he founded the Cambridge Camden Society for studying ecclesiastical art. He published *A History of the Holy Eastern Church* (1847–50) and *Theodora Pranza* (1857), a novel about the fall of Christian Constantinople. His hymns, eventually edited by M. S. Lawson as *Collected Hymns, Sequences and Carols* (1914), include 'O Happy Band of Pilgrims', 'Art Thou Weary?', 'Good Christian Men, Rejoice', 'Good King Wenceslaus' and 'Jerusalem the Golden'.

negative capability A term coined by KEATS to describe the quality he thought essential to the poet: 'when man is capable of being in uncertainties, Mysteries, doubts, without any irritable reaching after fact & reason' (letter of 21–7 December 1817). The letter goes on to cite SHAKESPEARE as the supreme example of negative capability and to note its absence in COLERIDGE, MILTON and WORDSWORTH.

Neilson, John Shaw 1872–1942 Australian poet. His life was dogged by poverty and ill health, and his poetry shows pity and tenderness for suffering. Volumes include *Old Granny Sullivan* (1916), *Heart of Spring* (1919), *Ballad and Lyrical Poems* (1923), *New Poems* (1927), *Collected Poems* (1934), *Beauty Imposes* (1938) and the posthumous *Unpublished Poems of Shaw Neilson* (1947).

Nemerov, Howard 1920– American poet, novelist, short-story writer and critic. *The Image and the Law* (1947) established many of the preoccupations which characterize his subsequent work, notably an interest in moral and philosophical complexities. His poetic career is largely summarized in *Collected Poems* (1977; PULITZER PRIZE) and *Trying Conclusions: New and Selected Poems, 1961–1991* (1991). His fiction, often exploring moral problems in modern society, includes *Commodity of Dreams and Other Stories* (1959), *Stories, Fables and Other Diversions* (1971) and three novels: *The Melodramatists* (1949), *Federigo, or The Power of Love* (1954) and *The Homecoming Game* (1957). He has also written plays, including *Endor* (1962). His criticism appears in *Poetry* and Fiction: Essays (1963), Reflexions on Poetry and Poetics (1972), Figures of Thought: Speculations on the Meaning of Poetry and Other Essays (1978) and New and Selected Essays (1985). Journal of the Fictive Life (1965) is a self-examination which throws light on his own work and the creative process.

neoclassicism A term for the ideas about art and literature which evolved during the 17th and 18th centuries under the influence of the classical (i.e. Graeco-Roman) tradition.

Although SIDNEY'S APOLOGY FOR POETRY (1595) advanced the classical theory of literature, it did not gain currency until the 17th century. JONSON imitated Martial and Juvenal and took an interest in theories of dramatic action derived from Aristotle. DRYDEN's plays and criticism, notably his ESSAY OF DRAMATIC POESY (1668), temper SHAKESPEARE's abundance by insisting on the neoclassical unities of time, place and action. Although there was never any concerted body of neoclassical principles as such, writers of the AUGUSTAN AGE shared a common response to the writings of the ancients. They agreed in admiring the concision, elegance, good taste and WIT of their classical predecessors. Their poetry emulated the intelligent articulacy of Horace's verse epistles, or the vituperative energy of Juvenal's SATIRE, or the heroic elevation of Homer's EPIC. Their theory of literature followed Aristotle's Poetics in making the classification of genres a foremost consideration and agreed with Horace's Ars Poetica in several vital tenets: the need to discipline the creative impulse by practice and self-control, the usefulness of imitating past models, the desirability of a literary decorum that matches content to style, and the aim of combining pleasure with instruction. POPE's ESSAY ON CRITICISM (1711) is representative of neoclassical concern with artistry and structure; as are FIELDING's Preface to JOSEPH ANDREWS (1742), several of JOHNSON's RAMBLER papers (1750–2) and his Preface to Shakespeare (1765).

Enquiry into the methods and rules of composition stimulated wider interests derived to some extent from the Graeco-Roman tradition: in the connection between nature and art and between the various sister arts, for example, and in the relations of imagination and reason, taste and sense, originality and imitation, beauty and pleasure. Behind such theorizing lay an essential fascination with systematic principles, but as the 18th century progressed an interest in the universal aspects of nature itself came to predominate over any notion of artistic rules. Poetry written by recipe and formulaic regulations became stale and outworn. Later generations concentrated attention on the poet rather than his audience, his mind rather than his medium, and nature rather than art, thus moving away from the general body of inherited classical principles towards ROMANTICISM.

Nesbit, E(dith) 1858–1924 Writer of CHILDREN'S LITERATURE. After doing literary hack work, she discovered her talent for writing lively family stories unburdened with moralizing. Her first success, The Story of the Treasure Seekers (1899), was about Bastable children and their mini-adventures, often in search of extra pocket money. Succeeding books (written quickly but with an ear for children's dialogue) mixed fantasy with reality, most successfully in The Phoenix and the Carpet (1904) and The Story of the Amulet (1906), both involving time-travel. Her most famous novel, The Railway Children (1906), has a more realistic setting. The title characters retreat to the countryside after their father is arrested on a trumped-up charge, and make friends with the local railway porter, Perks. The story involves a political refugee, theft, misplaced charity and fierce family loyalty – powerful ingredients for young readers, balanced by romantic adventures, fortunate coincidences and happy endings.

New Age, The A journal founded in 1907 by Holbrook Jackson (1874–1948) and A. R. Orage (1873–1934), with financial support from SHAW. Orage edited it until 1922. Regular contributors included Shaw, ARNOLD BENNETT and J. C. SQUIRE, though Orage also recruited new talents such as POUND, KATHERINE MANSFIELD, T. E. HULME and EDWIN MUIR. The New Age introduced Freud's theories to the British reading public.

New Apocalypse, The A literary movement which flourished just before and during World War II in reaction against the committed rationalism of AUDEN's generation. New Apocalypse writers reinterpreted Freud and Marx in the light of D. H. LAWRENCE's Apocalypse (1931) and accommodated diverse strands of a European non-rational impulse, principally EXPRESSIONISM and surrealism. Key figures were HENDRY, who introduced an anthology, The New Apocalypse (1939), and TREECE, who joined Hendry as editor of two further anthologies, The White Horseman (1941) and The Crown and the Sickle (1943). Poems by G. S. FRASER, NICHOLAS MOORE, MacCAIG and WATKINS appeared in their pages. DYLAN THOMAS was also associated with the movement.

New Atlantis, The An unfinished Utopian fiction by FRANCIS BACON, posthumously published in 1627. English mariners discover the Pacific island of Bensalem, a high civilization of great antiquity which has isolated itself from the world to preserve its integrity. The chief purpose of the story is to introduce Bacon's ideal design for a college of sciences, here called Salomon's House or the College of the Six Days' Works, its function being to study the entire physical creation. The work is experimental, and the results advance the knowledge and enhance the life of the people of Bensalem. Salomon's House represents the kind of institution that Bacon hoped JAMES I would establish to carry out the programme of experiments suggested in Sylva Sylvarum, following the methods of scientific enquiry laid out in THE ADVANCEMENT OF LEARNING and the NOVUM ORGANUM. His proposals were revived in the 1650s and in some measure fulfilled by the foundation of the Royal Society in 1660.

New Bath Guide, The See ANSTEY, CHRISTOPHER.

New Criticism A term first used by the American critic Joel Spingarn in 1910 and revived by RANSOM in 1941 to prescribe a new 'ontological' approach to literary studies, as distinct from traditional criticism which had generalized broadly from biographical data and influences. His qualified recognition of the contributions of I. A. RICHARDS, T. S. ELIOT, EMPSON and WINTERS had the (largely unintentional) effect of promoting them as a new Anglo-American 'movement'. Other critics – ROBERT PENN WARREN, ALLEN TATE, R. P. Blackmur, CLEANTH BROOKS and F. R. LEAVIS – were later conscripted, though the group always differed widely in its individual aims. As a general rule, the New Critics may be said to have initiated a view of the text as an autonomous whole, an object with its own inherent structure, which invited rigorous scrutiny. They encouraged an awareness of verbal nuance and thematic organization. Although rejected by many more recent schools, New Criticism still has influence: close reading of the text remains a dominant principle in most literary criticism.

New Grub Street A novel by GISSING, published in 1891. Its bleak portrait of the literary world is drawn from Gissing's own discouraging struggle. Despite writing two fine books, Edward Reardon is hampered by poverty and an unsympathetic wife, Amy. Her desertion of him, coupled with his failure, sends him to the grave. Alfred Yule is an unappreciated and embittered scholar. His daughter Marian falls in love with Jasper Milvain, a self-interested reviewer, but he abandons her when her expected legacy does not materialize, marries the widowed Amy and becomes, in worldly terms, a success. Other characters include Harold Biffen, earnestly polishing a novel of absolute realism, and Whelpdale, a failure who becomes an 'adviser to literary aspirants'.

New Masses, The An American journal founded in 1926 by MICHAEL GOLD, who became its sole editor in 1928. Until it ceased publication in 1948 The New Masses served as a forum for writers and intellectuals involved with left-wing politics and the Communist Party.

New Republic, The An American literary and political journal founded by Herbert Croly in 1914. Its literary editors have included EDMUND WILSON, Malcolm Cowley, Richard Gilman and Reed Whittemore. Since the 1950s, its emphasis has shifted to political commentary, usually from a liberal point of view.

New Review, The A monthly literary magazine published in 1974–9 and edited by IAN HAMILTON. Preferring short, minimalist poems, it included work by JAMES FENTON, CRAIG RAINE, JULIAN BARNES, Clive James and IAN McEWAN. The New Review Anthology appeared in 1985.

New Way to Pay Old Debts, A A comedy by MASSINGER, first performed c. 1622 and published in 1633. The plot is derived from THOMAS MIDDLETON'S A TRICK TO CATCH THE OLD ONE, though the monstrously greedy Sir Giles Overreach was based on Sir Giles Mompesson, a contemporary extortioner. Sir Giles has gained possession of the property belonging to his prodigal nephew, Frank Wellborn, but is persuaded to lend him money when Lady Allworth pretends that she means to marry Wellborn. Sir Giles opposes his daughter, Margaret, in her desire to marry Lady Allworth's stepson, Tom, until Lord Lovell outwits him. His unbalanced rage is toppled into madness when he learns that his claim on Wellborn's estate cannot be upheld, and he is carried off to Newgate. Lady Allworth marries Lord Lovell, and Wellborn takes a commission in Lovell's regiment.

New York Review of Books, The An American magazine, in newspaper format, originally founded by Robert Silvers and Barbara Epstein to provide book reviews during the New York newspaper strike of 1963. It specializes in extended essay reviews and articles on politics, often by writers of the left. THE LONDON REVIEW OF BOOKS is modelled on it.

New York School A group of American poets, including JOHN ASHBERY, KENNETH KOCH and FRANK O'HARA, which flourished in the 1950s in reaction against the academic austerity of mid-century American poetry. The name acknowledged its connection with the New York abstract-expressionist painters.

New Yorker, The An American weekly magazine founded in 1925 by Harold W. Ross. Under his editorship, contributors including JAMES THURBER, DOROTHY PARKER, ROBERT BENCHLEY, E. B. WHITE and Charles Addams established a light, witty style which epitomized literary New York in the 1930s. William Shawn, editor from 1951 until 1987, published notable short fiction, poetry, criticism and non-fiction, as well as maintaining The New Yorker's reputation for sophisticated cartoons. Shawn was succeeded by Robert Gottlieb and then Tina Brown.

Newbery, John 1713–67 Publisher specializing in CHILDREN'S LITERATURE. His large output of moral tales copiously illustrated with woodcuts had a major influence on educational publishing. Newbery also issued many works by CHRISTOPHER SMART, who married his stepdaughter. His friends JOHNSON and GOLDSMITH contributed to The Public Ledger, a periodical he started in 1759.

Newbolt, Sir Henry (John) 1862–1938 Poet. His many volumes of patriotic BALLADS and lyrics include The Island Race (1899), Admiral's All and Other Verses (1907), Clifton Chapel and Other School Poems (1908), Songs of Memory and Hope (1909) and Drake's Drum and Other Sea Songs (1919), the title poem of which was set to music by Charles Stanford in Songs of the Sea.

Newcastle, Margaret, Duchess of 1623–74 Biographer, poet and playwright. Born Margaret Lucas, she was an indefatigable writer, remembered only for her biography (1667) of her Royalist husband, William Cavendish, Duke of Newcastle (1592–1676). PEPYS dismissed it as ridiculous, but LAMB and VIRGINIA WOOLF praised it. It remains a notable document of its age.

Newcomes, The: Memoirs of a Most Respectable Family A novel by THACKERAY, published in parts in 1853–5. The story is told by Arthur Pendennis, the hero of PENDENNIS.

Colonel Thomas Newcome is a simple and honourable gentleman. His son Clive is in love with his cousin Ethel, daughter of the wealthy banker, Sir Brian Newcome. Their union is opposed by her relatives – notably her snobbish brother Barnes and her grandmother, the Countess of Kew – though she resists their pressure to marry her cousin, Lord Kew, or Lord Farintosh. Clive is manoeuvred into marrying Rosey, daughter of the scheming Mrs Mackenzie. When Colonel Newcome loses his fortune he is so bullied and reproached by Mrs Mackenzie that he takes refuge in the Greyfriars almshouse, where he dies. Clive's fortunes are restored by the discovery of a will, and his wife's death leaves him free to marry Ethel.

Newgate Calendar, The The title, or generic label, of various 18th- and 19th-century collections describing the careers of notorious criminals. Although they usually claimed to have a moral purpose, their main interest was always salacious and sensational. The first appeared in 1774 and the last in 1886. BORROW compiled a six-volume version in 1826.

Newgate novel A school of crime fiction popular in the 1830s. It took real-life cases as the source for plots and pointed to the treatment of crime by FIELDING, GAY and HOGARTH as a respectable precedent. Critics alleged that it sentimentalized or glamorized the criminal, making him the victim of social circumstances in BULWER LYTTON's Paul Clifford (1830), a conscience-stricken philosopher in the same author's EUGENE ARAM (1832) and a glamorous outlaw in AINSWORTH's Rookwood (1834) and Jack Sheppard (1839). DICKENS's OLIVER TWIST (1837–8) countered by offering a harshly realistic view of crime.

Newman, John Henry 1801–90 Theologian. At Oxford he was successively a Fellow (1822) and tutor (1826) of Oriel College and vicar of St Mary's (1827). His sermons in the 1830s made him, with KEBLE and PUSEY, a leading figure in the OXFORD MOVEMENT. During this period he defended the Anglican church as the *via media*, or middle way, between Romanism and popular Protestantism. His researches into early church history led to his publishing, in TRACTS FOR THE TIMES, the famous *Tract XC* (1841), which argued that the 39 Articles of the Anglican church were compatible with Catholicism. After it was condemned by the Bishop of Oxford, Newman ceased publishing tracts and gave up being editor of *The British Critic*. In 1842 he set up a monastic community at Littlemore, where he continued his studies of the early church. In 1845 he became the most famous 19th-century convert to Catholicism, drawing many Anglican clergy in his wake. In 1854 he went to Dublin as rector of a new Catholic university, work which occupied him for four disappointing years and prompted *THE IDEA OF A UNIVERSITY* (1873). CHARLES KINGSLEY's attack on his honesty provoked his *APOLOGIA PRO VITA SUA* (1864; revised 1865), describing the changing convictions which had led him to become a Catholic. *THE GRAMMAR OF ASSENT* (1870) presents his arguments for religious belief. His poem, *THE DREAM OF GERONTIUS*, and the hymn, 'Lead, Kindly Light', were written in 1832. The latter was first collected in the volume *Lyra Apostolica* (with Keble and ISAAC WILLIAMS; 1836). He also wrote two novels, *Loss and Gain* (1848) and *Callista* (1856). Newman became a cardinal in 1879.

News from Nowhere: *or, An Epoch of Rest, being Some Chapters from a Utopian Romance* A prose work by WILLIAM MORRIS, published in 1890. He dreams of waking amid a communist society in the early 21st century. The central chapters comprise a discussion with an aged historian, in which the course of history from the 19th century through violent socialist revolution and up to the Utopian present is described. The society envisaged is based on 'the religion of humanity', the sanctity of labour and its inseparability from art. In the concluding chapters Morris journeys up the Thames from London to Kelmscott for the hay-making season.

Newton, Sir Isaac 1642–1727 Scientist and philosopher. He passed his early career at Trinity College, Cambridge, where his teacher BARROW resigned the Lucasian Professorship of Mathematics in his favour in 1669. His theological interests allied him to the CAMBRIDGE PLATONISTS. From 1696 he was in London, rewarded with public honours and offices which included the presidency of the Royal Society. His *Principia* (*Philosophiae Naturalis Principia Mathematica*, 'The Mathematical Principles of Natural Philosophy'; 1687) marked a milestone in the history of science by announcing his theory of the law of universal gravitation. The *Opticks* (1704) established him as the founder of the modern science of optics; to this book was attached *Method of Fluxion*, the Newtonian calculus which caused a bitter dispute with Leibniz over priority of invention.

Ngugi wa Thiong'o [Ngugi, James] 1938– Kenyan playwright, novelist and critic. Plays such as *The Black Hermit* (1968), *This Time Tomorrow*, with *The Rebels* and *The Wound in the Heart* (1970), and *The Trial of Dedan Kimathi* (with Micere Mugo; 1976) dramatize peasant, proletarian and national struggles. *Detained* (1981) describes his year-long detention after the banning of *Nhaahika Ndeenda* (with Ngugi wa Mirii, 1977; English version, *I*

Will Marry When I Want, 1982). He has lived in exile since 1982. His novels, progressing from freshly written accounts of youthful idealism and disillusion to complex political analysis, include: *Weep Not, Child* (1964), *The River Between* (1965), *A Grain of Wheat* (1967), *Petals of Blood* (1977), *Devil on the Cross* (originally published in Gikuyu; 1982) and *Matigari* (originally published in Gikuyu; 1987). *Secret Lives* (1975) is a collection of short stories. *Homecoming* (1972), *The Writer and Politics* (1981) and *Barrel of a Pen* (1983) are collections of essays.

nichol, b p 1944–88 Canadian poet and writer of fiction. He first attracted attention with the CONCRETE POETRY in *The Year of the Frog* (1967), *Ballads of the Restless Are* (1968) and *Dada Lama* (1968). He later used a wide variety of modes – publicly performed sound-poetry, free verse and STREAM OF CONSCIOUSNESS prose among them – to challenge commonly held assumptions about language and the creative process. His best-known work is *The Martyrology*, a continuing poem in several parts, of which the first two books appeared in 1972 and the last book, as *gIFTS*, in 1990. Other works include *Two Novels* (1969), *Still Water* (1970), *ABC: The Aleph Beth Book* (1971), *Love: A Book of Remembrances* (1974), *Craft Dinner* (1978), *Journal* (1978) and *extreme positions* (1981).

Nicholas Nickleby A novel by DICKENS, published in monthly parts in 1838–9 and in volume form in 1839. Loosely structured, with frequent excursions into sentiment and MELODRAMA, it is nevertheless informed by the joyful energy that typifies Dickens's early work.

After the death of Nicholas Nickleby senior, his widow and children Nicholas and Kate turn for help to his brother Ralph, an unscrupulous financier. Kate is apprenticed to a dressmaker, Madame Mantalini, and Nicholas sent to teach at Dotheboys Hall in Yorkshire. He rebels against Wackford Squeers's ill-treatment of the pupils, particularly the half-witted orphan Smike. Nicholas and Smike run away, working where they can and travelling with Vincent Crummles's company of actors. Kate, meanwhile, is exposed to the unwelcome attentions of Ralph Nickleby's business associates, including Sir Mulberry Hawk. Alerted to her danger by Newman Noggs, Ralph's eccentric clerk, Nicholas returns to London with Smike, obtains a post in the business of the amiable Cheeryble brothers and thrashes Sir Mulberry. Squeers and Ralph Nickleby conspire to injure Nicholas through Smike, but their plan fails when Smike dies. Newman Noggs and the Cheerybles help defeat the villains completely and, with the revelation that Smike had been his own son, Ralph hangs himself.

Nichols, Grace 1950– Guyanese/British poet and novelist. She established herself as a writer of CHILDREN'S LITERATURE but reached a wider audience with the poetry in *i is a long memoried woman* (1983), *The Fat Black Woman's Poems* (1984) and *Lazy Thoughts of a Lazy Woman* (1989). Concern with race and gender are key topics, though she treats them with a measure of comedy. The vigorously oral quality of her work makes her public recitals popular. *Whole of a Morning Sky* (1986) is a novel, apparently based on her own growing-up in Guyana.

Nichols, Peter (Richard) 1927– Playwright. His first stage success came with *A Day in the Death of Joe Egg* (1967), about the parents of a spastic child. Subsequent works fall into two categories: expansive plays about social or historical themes, such as *The National Health* (1969), *The Freeway* (1974), *Privates on Parade* (1977) and *Poppy* (1983); and domestic plays, such as *Down Forget-Me-*

Not Lane (1971), *Chez Nous* (1974), *Born in the Gardens* (1980), *Passion Play* (1981) and *A Piece of My Mind* (1986). *Feeling You're Behind* (1984) is an autobiography.

Nichols, Robert (Malise Bowter) 1893–1944 Poet and playwright. He contributed to GEORGIAN POETRY and published two volumes, *Invocations* (1915) and *Ardours and Endurances* (1917), popular for their celebration of the 'loved, living, dying heroic soldier' in World War I. His friend ROBERT GRAVES wrote 'To Robert Nichols' in reply to 'Faun's Holiday'. Later volumes were *Aurelia* (1920), the satirical *Fisbo* (1934) and a selection, *Such was My Singing* (1942). His plays include *Guilty Souls* (1922) and *Wings over Europe* (1930).

Nicholson, Norman 1914–87 Poet, playwright and critic. He was born on the fringe of the Lake District, a region which informs books such as *The Lakes* (1977) as well as poetry in the tradition of COWPER and WORDSWORTH. Volumes include *The Pot Geranium* (1954), *Wednesday Early Closing* (1975), *A Local Habitation* (1972), *Sea to the West* (1981) and *Selected Poems, 1940–1982* (1982). Verse dramas, which include *The Old Man of the Mountains* (1946) and *Prophesy to the Wind* (1950), and critical writing such as *Man and Literature* (1943) owe much to T. S. ELIOT and his own Anglicanism.

Nicolson, Sir **Harold (George)** 1886–1968 Man of letters. The husband of VITA SACKVILLE-WEST, he served abroad as a diplomat before entering Parliament. His books include: two novels, *Sweet Waters* (1921) and *Public Faces* (1932); biographical and critical studies of Verlaine (1921), TENNYSON (1923), BYRON (1924), SWINBURNE (1926) and Sainte-Beuve (1957); *The Congress of Vienna: A Study in Allied Unity 1812–1822* (1946); and the official biography of King George V (1952). The three-volume *Diaries and Letters* (1966–8) edited by his son Nigel Nicolson give an interesting picture of political life between the two world wars.

Nigger of the 'Narcissus', The A novel by CONRAD, published in 1897. The preface is frequently cited as a manifesto of literary Impressionism and its chief aim: 'before all, to make you see'. Narrated by an anonymous seaman, the story reveals the tensions on board the *Narcissus* on its way from Bombay to London. Captain Alistoun and the veteran Singleton, primarily concerned with their duties, are increasingly at odds with the younger Donkin and the title character, Wait. During a storm which puts the safety of the entire ship at risk, five men chance their lives to save Wait from the cabin where he lies ill. In the end the captain calmly reasserts a seaman-like authority over Donkin, and Singleton's belief that Wait will die at the first sight of land comes true.

Night Thoughts The usual abbreviation by which EDWARD YOUNG's lengthy didactic poem, *The Complaint: or, Night-Thoughts on Life, Death and Immortality* (1742–6), is known. The first of its nine books is devoted to reflections by the poet. The following seven take the form of a soliloquy rebuking the worldly Lorenzo, who is exhorted to turn to faith and the virtuous life. The final book, called 'The Consolation', includes a vision of the Day of Judgement, a contemplation of eternity, a survey of the firmament, a last exhortation to Lorenzo and an invocation to God.

Nightmare Abbey A satirical novel by THOMAS LOVE PEACOCK, published in 1818. Its principal target is the contemporary literary intelligentsia, with its predilection for morbid subjects and unworldly philosophical systems. Mr Glowry is the master of Nightmare Abbey

on the edge of the Lincolnshire Fens, where he lives with his philosophical son Scythrop (SHELLEY) and a retinue of servants chosen for their depressing appearance or dismal names. He keeps open house for his fellow spirits and relatives. The most persistently mocked character is Mr Flosky (COLERIDGE), though Mr Cypress (BYRON) is also derided for his misanthropy and Scythrop for his illuminist politics. Their modish melancholy contrasts with the enthusiasm of the scientist Mr Asterias, dedicated to capturing a mermaid, and of Mr Hilary, whose protests against the prevailing 'conspiracy against cheerfulness', and advocacy of nature, Mozart and the life-affirming wisdom of the ancient Greeks, appear to have the author on their side.

Nin, Anaïs 1903–77 American diarist and novelist. She was born in Paris, to which she returned in 1923–39, becoming a friend of HENRY MILLER. The elegant sparsity of her *Diary* (1966–83), begun in 1931, and her volumes of erotica, *Delta of Venus: Erotica* (1977) and *Little Birds* (1979), are as much at odds with Miller's style as her fiction. Influenced by D. H. LAWRENCE (of whom she wrote a study in 1932) and psychoanalysis, this includes: *House of Incest* (Paris, 1936; USA, 1947); *The Winter of Artifice* (Paris, 1939; USA, 1942), a collection of three novelettes; *Under a Glass Bell* (1944), a volume of short stories; *Cities of Interior*, a five-part sequence (1946–58); and *Collages* (1964).

Nine Worthies, The Figures from myth and history often mentioned in medieval and early Renaissance literature. The group consists of three pagans (Alexander, Hector and Julius Caesar), three Jews (Joshua, David and Maccabeus) and three Christians (Arthur, Charlemagne and Godfrey of Bouillon).

Nineteen Eighty-Four A novel by GEORGE ORWELL, first published in 1949. In 1984 Britain has become Airstrip One in the superstate Oceania, perpetually at odds with Eurasia and Eastasia. It is ruled by the Party under the aegis of the possibly non-existent Big Brother, whose agents constantly rewrite history and redesign the language to control people's thoughts absolutely. A minor Party operative, Winston Smith, commits thought-crimes by keeping a secret diary and loving Julia, but is seduced into self-betrayal by his superior, O'Brien. Interrogation ultimately breaks his spirit. This brilliant, bitter novel provides a heavily ironic commentary on the state of the world in 1948. The development of world politics between then and 1984 did nothing to soothe the anxieties with which it plays.

1919 See *USA*.

Nkosi, Lewis 1936– South African novelist, playwright and critic. He worked on the staff of *Drum* magazine before leaving South Africa in 1961 for the USA, Britain and Zambia. His eloquent, often provocative essays about township life, the generation of 1950s writers in South Africa, apartheid, exile, and African literature were collected in *Home and Exile* (1964). A later collection, *Tasks and Masks* (1981), is concerned with contemporary African writing. He has also written *Rhythm of Violence* (1965), one of the first English-language plays by a black South African, and *Mating Birds* (1986), a novel about the interaction between sexual and racial politics in South Africa.

Noah, Mordecai Manuel 1785–1851 American playwright. His best-known work, *She would be a Soldier: or, The Plains of Chippewa* (1819), is a patriotic comedy about a young woman who disguises herself as a soldier to follow her lover in the War of 1812. Whether his subject was ancient or contemporary, Noah always wrote what he termed 'national plays', intended to represent the course of a nation's history.

Noctes Ambrosianae See BLACKWOOD'S EDINBURGH MAGAZINE.

Noonuccal [Nunukul]**, Oodgeroo** See OODGEROO.

Norman, Marsha 1947– American playwright. Characters in her plays confront devastation in their past to determine whether and how to survive. *Getting Out* (1978) dramatizes the internal conflict of a woman parolee, and *'night, Mother* (1983; PULITZER PRIZE) enacts the last night of a young woman as she prepares herself and her mother for her suicide. Other works include *Third and Oak, The Laundromat (and) The Pool Hall* (1978), *The Holdup* (1983), *Traveler in the Dark* (1984), *Winter Shakers* (1983), *Sarah and Abraham* (1988), a musical with Norman L. Berman, and *The Secret Garden* (1991), a musical based on FRANCES HODGSON BURNETT's novel.

Norris, (Benjamin) Frank(lin) 1870–1902 American novelist. Born in Chicago, he was partly brought up in San Francisco, where he later worked as a journalist. He also reported on the Boer War from South Africa and the Spanish-American War from Cuba. Early works such as his sea story, *Moran of the Lady Letty* (1898), first appeared in a San Francisco magazine, *The Wave*. Norris is chiefly remembered for his contributions to NATURALISM in *McTEAGUE* (1899) and his projected trilogy, *The Epic of the Wheat*, of which two volumes, *THE OCTOPUS* (1901) and *THE PIT* (1903), were completed before his early death from an appendix operation. The third part, *The Wolf*, which would have told of a wheat famine in Europe, was never written. Also published posthumously were *The Responsibilities of the Novelist* (1903), describing the type of naturalistic writing he had derived from Zola, and *Vandover and the Brute* (1914), a novel which he had started in 1895.

Norris, John 1657–1711 Philosopher. The last of the CAMBRIDGE PLATONISTS, he followed Nicholas Malebranche, the French philosopher, in combining the ideas of Descartes with a Platonic mysticism. His *Essay towards the Theory of the Ideal or Intelligible World* (1701 and 1704) criticizes LOCKE's *ESSAY CONCERNING HUMAN UNDERSTANDING*. Norris also wrote devotional verses.

North, Christopher See WILSON, JOHN.

North, Sir Thomas ?1535–?1601 Translator. His most important translation was of Plutarch's *Lives*, from a French version by Amyot, as *The Lives of the Noble Grecians and Romans* (1579; expanded in 1595 and 1603). It was SHAKESPEARE's main source of knowledge about ancient history and its great men; the Roman plays draw heavily on North, even reworking his language in (for example) Enobarbus' description of Cleopatra in *ANTONY AND CLEOPATRA*. North also translated Guevara's *El relox de príncipes* as *The Dial of Princes* (1557), in a style anticipating the EUPHUISM of the 1580s, and a volume of beast FABLES as *The Moral Philosophy of Doni* (1570).

North American Review, The An American journal, founded as a quarterly in Boston in 1815, though it later became a monthly and moved to New York. Originally a literary journal, it expanded its coverage to include articles on political and social matters. It reverted to quarterly publication after World War I and survived until 1940. Its editors included CHARLES ELIOT NORTON, JAMES RUSSELL LOWELL, HENRY ADAMS and Henry Cabot Lodge, and its contributors EMERSON, WASHINGTON IRVING,

LONGFELLOW, FRANCIS PARKMAN, WHITMAN, TWAIN, HENRY JAMES, Tolstoy, D'Annunzio, H. G. WELLS, Maeterlinck and ALAN SEEGER.

North and South A novel by ELIZABETH GASKELL, serialized in *HOUSEHOLD WORDS* in 1854–5 and published in volume form in 1855. Margaret Hale leaves the south and goes with her father to the grim industrial city of Milton-Northern, where he teaches aspiring millowners. She takes the side of the workers and confronts the millowner John Thornton. He is strongly drawn to her despite the difference in their views, but she coldly rejects his proposal of marriage. Their relationship is further complicated by his mistaken jealousy. Eventually Thornton's business problems modify his attitude to the workers, and the pair come together. An important CONDITION OF ENGLAND NOVEL for its portrait of the contrast between the comfortable south and industrial north, the book also has in Margaret a tough, wilful and self-confidently proud heroine, reflecting the influence of CHARLOTTE BRONTË.

North Briton, The A political weekly founded by WILKES in 1762 and edited with CHARLES CHURCHILL's help. Its chief aim was to oppose the Earl of Bute's paper, *The Briton*, edited by SMOLLETT. Wilkes risked prosecution by publishing the 'obscene' *Essay on Woman* and also for No. 45, which alleged that a speech from the throne had lied about the Peace of Paris. *The North Briton* was suppressed in 1763 and Wilkes, though avoiding prosecution by claiming parliamentary privilege, expelled from the Commons and banished.

Northanger Abbey A novel by JANE AUSTEN, published posthumously in 1818, though it had been begun in 1798 and accepted by a publisher in 1803. Her shortest major work, it makes fun of the fashion for the GOTHIC NOVEL, particularly the work of ANN RADCLIFFE. A guest of Mr and Mrs Allen at Bath, Catherine Morland meets the eccentric General Tilney, his son Henry and his daughter Eleanor. She is invited to their home, Northanger Abbey, where she imagines various gruesome secrets surrounding the General and his house. Henry proves that her suspicions are groundless but the General orders her out of the house. She returns home and is followed by Henry, who explains that the General had, mistakenly, come to believe her penniless. Restored to a sensible humour by the truth, the General finally consents to Henry's marriage to Catherine.

Northward Ho A comedy by DEKKER and WEBSTER, produced *c.* 1605 and published in 1607. Greenshield tries to seduce Mistress Maybury and libels her when he fails. Convinced of his wife's innocence, Maybury takes his revenge with the help of the old poet Bellamont (an amiable caricature of CHAPMAN).

Nortje, Arthur 1942–70 South African poet. In 1966 he came to Britain, where his death from a drug overdose ended a short but promising career. His one volume, *Dead Roots* posthumously published in 1973, contains supple free verse using a range of tones and images; it contrasts South African prison and township life with British life to express the consciousness of an African in exile.

Norton, Caroline Elizabeth Sarah 1808–77 Poet, novelist and pamphleteer. The granddaughter of RICHARD BRINSLEY SHERIDAN, she pursued a literary career with many volumes of poetry and several novels, including *Stuart of Dunleath* (1851) and *Old Sir Douglas* (1867). Though successful, they brought her less fame than the public failure of her marriage to George

Chapple Norton, who in 1836 brought an unsuccessful suit against Lord Melbourne for alienating her affections. Her marital wrongs prompted her to write *English Laws for Women* (1853) and other powerful pamphlets on womens' rights. The object of much abuse and much admiration, she is said to have provided the model for the heroine of MEREDITH's *DIANA OF THE CROSSWAYS*.

Norton, Charles Eliot 1827–1908 American man of letters, and professor of the history of fine art at Harvard from 1875 to 1898. A regular contributor to *THE ATLANTIC MONTHLY* and co-editor of *THE NORTH AMERICAN REVIEW*, he also helped to found *THE NATION* in 1865. Frequent visits to Europe gave him a wide acquaintance among British as well as American writers. He published discreet editions of CARLYLE's early letters (1886) and *Reminiscences* (1887) and of RUSKIN's letters to him (1904). Other works include a prose translation of Dante (1891–2), an edition of DONNE (1895) and *Notes of Travel and Study in Italy* (1859). His *Letters* (1913) are a valuable document of intellectual life in Massachusetts.

Norton, Mary 1903– Writer of CHILDREN'S LITERATURE. Her first novels, *The Magic Bedknob* (1943) and *Bonfires and Broomsticks* (1947), reissued together as *Bedknob and Broomstick* (1970), concern the adventures of three children and Miss Price, a village spinster who is also studying to be a witch. *The Borrowers* (1952) was the first in a series of five books about a family of tiny people who flee when they are discovered by the 'human beans' and embark on an epic journey across the countryside.

Norton, Thomas 1532–84 Playwright. With THOMAS SACKVILLE he wrote *Gorboduc*, acted in 1561 and printed in 1565, which has some claim to be the first proper English tragedy. He also translated Calvin, wrote Latin verses and contributed to *TOTTEL'S MISCELLANY*. A lawyer and CRANMER's son-in-law, Norton was active in examining Catholics during Elizabeth's reign.

***Nostromo**: A Tale of the Seaboard* A novel by CONRAD, published in 1904. It is set in the coastal province of Sulaco, the wealthiest region of the South American republic of Costaguana. Along with the San Tomé silver mine, the Englishman Charles Gould has inherited the instability of a civil war between Ribiera's legal government and Montero's populist party. To save the silver from the rebels he entrusts it to the journalist Martin Decoud and the Italian Nostromo ('our man'), Capataz de Cargadores, a local hero, who smuggle it out into the gulf. When they are forced to run aground on nearby islands, the Isabels, they hide the silver and Nostromo returns to Sulaco. Left alone, Decoud drowns himself. Though Dr Monygham persuades him to summon loyal forces to save Sulaco, Nostromo has been shocked into awareness that he is exploited by his employers. He allows people to believe that the silver has been lost and makes secret visits to retrieve it from the Isabels, where the lighthouse keeper is now Giorgio Viola, the father of his betrothed, Linda. Nostromo finds himself in love with Linda's sister Giselle. When Giorgio mistakes him for an intruder and shoots him, the secret of the silver is lost forever.

Notes on the State of Virginia A book by THOMAS JEFFERSON, published in 1785. It goes well beyond its original purpose, to answer questions about American landscape, customs and institutions from a French representative during the Revolutionary War, and is perhaps the best single expression of Jefferson's ideas. The programme he advocates for America includes religious toleration, the emancipation of the slaves and a society based on an agrarian ideal.

novel of sensibility See SENTIMENTAL NOVEL.

Novels by Eminent Hands See *PUNCH'S PRIZE NOVELISTS*.

Novum organum A Latin treatise (1620) by FRANCIS BACON, forming the second part of the great programme of intellectual and scientific reform proposed under the title of *Instauratio magna* ('Great Instauration'). *THE ADVANCEMENT OF LEARNING* had attacked the Aristotelian structures of knowledge and appealed for the development of new, systematic and profitable methods of enquiry into all areas of research. 'Novum organum' means 'the new instrument' that will be employed to advance learning. Bacon identifies the causes of ignorance and misunderstanding in sterile methods of enquiry and prejudices, which he calls Idols of the Mind. The method of enquiry he recommends is induction, the process of inferring a general law or principle from the observation of particular instances. Book II is given over to a practical investigation of the nature of heat.

Nowra, Louis 1950– Australian playwright. His plays, exotic in their settings and theatrical mode, depict private worlds of illusion, obsession and madness. They include *Albert Names Edward* (1975), *The Golden Age* (1975), *Inner Voices* (1977), *Visions* (1978), *The Song Room* (1980), *Inside the Island* (1980), *The Precious Woman* (1980), *Sunrise* (1983), *Capricornia* (based on the novel by XAVIER HERBERT; 1988), *Byzantine Flowers* (1990) and *Summer of the Aliens* (1992).

Noyes, Alfred 1880–1958 Poet, novelist, short-story writer and playwright. His poetry – which includes the epic in blank verse *Drake* (1906–8) and famous shorter poems like 'The Barrel Organ' ('Come down to Kew in lilac time') and 'The Highwayman' – was vigorously traditional. *The Torch-Bearers*, an ambitious trilogy about science and Christianity consisting of *The Watchers of the Sky* (1922), *The Book of Earth* (1925) and *The Last Voyage* (1930), reflected a growing preoccupation with religion. Notable among his fiction are the ventures into fantasy in *Walking Shadows* (1918), *The Hidden Player* (1924) and *The Last Man* (1940). *Two Worlds for Memory* (1953) is autobiographical.

Nun's Priest's Tale, The See *CANTERBURY TALES*.

Nunukul [Noonuccal], **Oodgeroo** See OODGEROO.

Nwapa, Flora (Nwanzuruahal) 1931–93 Nigerian novelist. *Efuru* (1966) and *Idu* (1969) established her as Nigeria's first woman novelist. Both study the lives of women in rural society and seek to portray the particular flavour of Igbo culture. Nwapa adopted a mode closer to popular romance in later books such as *This is Lagos and Other Stories* (1971), *Wives at War and Other Stories* (1981), *One is Enough* (1981), *Never Again* (1984) and *Women are Different* (1986), which often deal with urban women who have rejected traditional mores. She also wrote CHILDREN'S LITERATURE.

Oates, Joyce Carol 1938– American novelist, short-story writer, poet and critic. Her intense, often violent vision, sustained throughout a prolific career, is perhaps most powerfully expressed in *Wonderland* (1971), based on LEWIS CARROLL's Alice stories, and in the loosely arranged trilogy, *A Garden of Earthly Delights* (1967), *Expensive People* (1968) and *Them* (1969). Other works include: a trilogy of pastiche Gothic romances, *Mysteries of Winterhurn* (1984), *Solstice* (1985) and *Marya: A Life* (1986); *American Appetites* (1989); *Because It is Bitter, Because It is My Heart* (1990); and *Black Water* (1992), based on Edward Kennedy's accident at Chappaquiddick. Her short-story collections are *By the North Gate* (1963), *The Wheel of Love* (1970), *The Goddess and Other Women* (1974), *The Seduction and Other Stories* (1975), *Last Days* (1984) and *Raven's Wing* (1987). Volumes of poetry include *Women in Love, and Other Poems* (1968) and *Anonymous Sins, and Other Poems* (1969).

objective correlative A term coined by T. S. ELIOT in his essay on *HAMLET* (1919): 'The only way of expressing emotion in the form of art is by finding an "objective correlative"; in other words, a set of objects, a situation, a chain of events which shall be the formula of that *particular* emotion; such that when the external facts, which must terminate in sensory experience, are given, the emotion is immediately evoked.'

objectivism An American poetic movement of the 1930s. Finding the principles of IMAGISM too vague, OPPEN, ZUKOFSKY, REZNIKOFF and WILLIAM CARLOS WILLIAMS emphasized the importance of the poem as a physical object, paying attention to typography as well as more conventional poetic devices. The movement did not long outlive *An 'Objectivists' Anthology* (1932).

O'Brien, Edna 1932– Novelist and short-story writer. Much of her work is concerned with the position of women: their lack of fulfillment and the repressive nature of their upbringing. *The Country Girls* (1960), *The Lonely Girl* (1962) and *Girls in Their Married Bliss* (1963) follow the quest for 'life' of two Irish girls, 'Kate' Brady and 'Baba' Brennan. Other novels, often bleak but lightened by a lyrical quality associated with nostalgia for Ireland, include *August is a Wicked Month* (1965), *Casualties of Peace* (1966), *A Pagan Place* (1971), *Night* (1972), *Johnny I Hardly Knew You* (1977) and *The High Road* (1988). Collections of short stories include *The Love Object* (1968), *A Scandalous Woman and Other Stories* (1974), *Mrs Reinhardt and Other Stories* (1978; as *A Rose in the Heart* in USA) and *Lantern Slides* (1990).

O'Brien, Fitz-James *c.* 1828–62 Short-story writer. Born in Ireland, he emigrated to the USA and established a reputation for short stories in the fantastic vein. The most famous was 'The Diamond Lens' (1858). O'Brien also published a play, *A Gentleman from Ireland* (1858).

O'Brien, Flann [O'Nolan, Brian] 1911–66 Irish novelist. As 'Myles na Gopaleen' he also contributed a column to *The Irish Times* from 1940, in which he constantly argued against the use of clichés about Ireland. A collection, *The Best of Myles*, appeared in 1968. His first and most important novel, *At Swim-Two-Birds* (1939), combines REALISM and fantasy in a manner which places it

in a direct line of desent from JOYCE's *ULYSSES*. Other novels include *The Hard Life* (1961), *The Dalkey Archive* (1964), and *The Third Policeman* (1967). A novel in Gaelic, *An Béal Bocht* (1941), was translated by P. C. Power as *The Poor Mouth* (1973).

O'Casey, Sean 1880–1964 Irish playwright. He was born into a poor Protestant family in Dublin and worked, despite ill health, as a manual labourer, becoming involved with both trade union and nationalist politics. *THE SHADOW OF A GUNMAN* (1923), the first of his plays to be staged by the ABBEY THEATRE, was followed by *JUNO AND THE PAYCOCK* (1924), hissed by the intensely nationalistic audience, and *THE PLOUGH AND THE STARS* (1926), which provoked a full-scale riot led by objectors to its unheroic portrait of participants in the Easter Rising. Feeling rejected by the theatre whose fortunes his plays had sustained, O'Casey left Dublin for London. The decisive break with the Abbey came in 1928, when YEATS and his fellow directors rejected *THE SILVER TASSIE* because of the EXPRESSIONISM of its second act. It was staged in London in 1929 and, amid protest, at the Abbey in 1935. O'Casey had never wished to be limited to the tragicomic REALISM of his previous plays about the Dublin poor, as he showed in the wholly expressionistic *Within the Gates* (1943). His later plays, never rivalling the popularity of his Dublin work, included overtly Communist pieces, such as *The Star Turns Red* (1940) and *Red Roses for Me* (1943), and Irish plays, such as *Cock-a-Doodle Dandy* (1949), *The Bishop's Bonfire* (1955) and *The Drums of Father Ned* (1959). These last depict a joy-denying church obstructing the Irish instinct for happiness, a theme often referred to in six extraordinary volumes of autobiography, beginning with *I Knock on the Door* (1939) and ending with *Sunset and Evening Star* (1954).

Occleve, Thomas See HOCCLEVE, THOMAS.

O'Connor, Flannery 1925–64 American short-story writer and novelist. Before her early death from lupus she made a strong impression on the American literary scene with her portrayal of spiritual struggle in the rural South. Using grotesque humour and unnerving IRONY, her work exposes the religious poverty and crippled intellect of the modern world – a vision which reflects her own devout Catholicism. Her novels are *Wise Blood* (1952), about Hazel Motes, the lonely and self-tortured prophet of a 'church of Christ without Christ', and *The Violent Bear It Away* (1960). Equally influential are the stories collected in *A Good Man is Hard to Find* (1955; as *The Artificial Nigger and Other Stories* in Britain, 1959) and *Everything That Rises Must Converge* (1965).

O'Connor, Frank [O'Donovan, Michael Francis] 1903–66 Irish writer. Although he produced translations of Irish verse, plays for the ABBEY THEATRE (of which he was a director), novels and literary criticism, his reputation rests chiefly on the realistic short stories published in *Guests of the Nation* (1931), *The Saint and Mary Kate* (1932), *Bones of Contention* (1936), *Three Old Brothers* (1937), *The Big Fellow* (1937), *Crab Apple Jelly* (1944), *The Common Chord* (1947), *Traveller's Samples* (1950), *Domestic Relations* (1957) and *My Oedipus Complex* (1963). *An Only Child* (1961) and the unfinished *My Father's Son* (1968) are autobiographical.

Octavian A mid-14th-century VERSE ROMANCE existing in two versions. Both derive from the French, though the story appears in several other languages. A jealous mother-in-law (father in one version) drives Florence, the Emperor Octavian's wife, and her twin sons into the forest. The children are stolen by animals. Florence recovers one, the young Octavian, with his lioness stepmother, and they free the other, Florentyn, and his father when they are captured fighting the Saracens. The mother-in-law is burned.

Octopus, The: *A Story of California* The first volume of FRANK NORRIS's uncompleted trilogy *The Epic of the Wheat*, published in 1901. The second volume is THE PIT (1903); the third volume was never written. The octopus is the Pacific and Southwestern Railroad, which in the course of the story dispossesses the wheat farmers of California. The chief antagonists are Behrman, a railroad agent who is suffocated when he falls into the wheat he has plundered, and Magnus Derrick, a farmer eventually ruined when his son Lyman betrays him. Other characters include: Dyke, a railroad engineer who wants to be a farmer; Shelgrim, the railroad president; and the protesting poet, Presley.

Octoroon, The A MELODRAMA by BOUCICAULT, first performed in New York in 1859. It is based on CAPTAIN MAYNE REID's novel *The Quadroon*. The octoroon is Zoe, a freed slave and daughter of the late Judge Peyton. The Judge's widow, his nephew George and the virtuous Yankee Salem Scudder try to save Zoe and Peyton's plantation from the villainous M'Closky. Zoe kills herself in the American version, but Boucicault grudgingly provided English audiences with an alternative ending in which she survives.

O'Curry, Eugene 1796–1862 Irish scholar. Like GEORGE PETRIE and JOHN O'DONOVAN, he made pioneering scholarly contributions to the CELTIC REVIVAL, establishing the British Museum catalogue of Irish folk material. Appointed professor of Irish history and archaeology at Dublin's new Catholic University in 1850, he published *Lectures on the Manuscript Materials of Ancient Irish History* (1861).

Odd Women, The A novel by GISSING, published in 1893. Dr Madden's death leaves his three daughters stranded with very little money and no training of any kind. Their loneliness and poverty in London lodgings and their desperate maintenance of middle-class respectability are conveyed with considerable pathos. In contrast to them is Rhoda Nunn, an active feminist who believes in preparing women for some fate other than marriage.

ode A lyric poem in rhymed stanzas, generally in the form of an address and exalted in feeling and expression. Famous examples include KEATS's 'To a Nightingale' and 'On a Grecian Urn' and WORDSWORTH's 'Intimations of Immortality from Recollections of Early Childhood'. The Pindaric ode takes its name from the Greek poet Pindar (522–442 BC) whose work, designed to honour victors in the Greek games, used an elaborate stanzaic pattern of strophe, antistrophe and epode. ABRAHAM COWLEY introduced it into English, though he and successors such as DRYDEN and POPE loosened the stanzaic pattern. TENNYSON's 'Ode on the Death of the Duke of Wellington' is a fine late example.

O'Dell, Scott 1903–89 American writer of CHILDREN'S LITERATURE. His most famous work, *Island of the Blue Dolphin* (1960), tells how Karana, an Indian girl, survives for 18 years alone on a tiny island. *The King's Fifth* (1966), describes how foreign adventurers looted South America.

Odets, Clifford 1906–63 American playwright. He established himself as a left-wing writer and champion of the underprivileged with works produced by the GROUP THEATRE: *WAITING FOR LEFTY* (1935); the anti-Nazi *Till The Day I Die* (1935); *Awake and Sing!* (1935), about a Jewish family in the Bronx during the Depression; *Paradise Lost* (1935), about the disintegration of a middle-class family as a result of the Depression; *Golden Boy* (1937), his greatest popular success, about a talented young Italian violinist who chooses to become a prizefighter; *Rocket to the Moon* (1938), about a dentist's midlife crisis; and *Night Music* (1940), about distrustful love between alienated people in Hollywood. Later and largely less successful work includes *Clash by Night* (1941), *The Big Knife* (1949), *The Country Girl* (1950) and *The Flowering Peach* (1954).

O'Donovan, John 1809–61 Irish scholar and topographer. He contributed to the CELTIC REVIVAL by pioneering researches into ancient Irish civilization in *A Grammar of the Irish Language* (1845) and particularly his edition of *Annala Rioghacta Eireann: Annals of the Kingdom of Ireland by the Four Masters* (1848–51).

O'Dowd, Bernard 1866–1953 Australian poet. He corresponded with WHITMAN, who influenced his work. Volumes include *Dawnward?* (1903), *The Silent Land* (1906), *Dominions of the Boundary* (1907), *The Seven Deadly Sins* (1909), *The Bush* (1912) and *Alma Venus!* (1921). His poetic technique is discussed in the address *Poetry Militant: An Australian Plea for the Poetry of Purpose* (1909).

O'Faolain, Sean 1900–91 Irish novelist, short-story writer and biographer. His novels, *A Nest of Simple Folk* (1933), *Bird Alone* (1936) and *Come Back to Erin* (1940), deal with the tyranny and pathos of Irish life and politics, particularly the oppression of Irish Catholicism. *Midsummer Night Madness* (1932) is a book of short stories. He also wrote biographies of several leading Irish figures, literary criticism and an autobiography, *Vive-moi!* (1964).

Officers and Gentlemen See SWORD OF HONOUR.

O'Flaherty, Liam 1897–1984 Irish novelist and short-story writer. He is best known for his unsentimental short stories, many of them about his native Aran Islands. Volumes include *Spring Sowing* (1926) and *The Fairy Goose* (1929), collected in *The Short Stories of Liam O'Flaherty* (1956). *The Informer* (1925), generally considered his best novel, is about the last day of Gypo Nolan, a destitute Irish revolutionary who betrays a comrade. *The Martyr* (1927), *The Assassin* (1928), *The Puritan* (1931) and *Famine* (1937) are equally uncompromising and realistic accounts of the Irish condition. *Two Years* (1930), *I Went to Russia* (1931) and *Shame the Devil* (1934) are autobiographies which document O'Flaherty's wide travels.

O'Grady, Standish James 1846–1928 Irish historian. He was called to the Bar in 1872 but never practised, preferring to explore his country's past in works which helped to inspire the CELTIC REVIVAL. His *History of Ireland* (1878–80) and *The Early Bardic Literature of Ireland* (1879) aroused considerable interest. *Red Hugh's Captivity* (1889) and its sequel, *The Flight of the Eagle* (1897), are novels about Ireland in the days of Elizabeth I. Irish myth is the matter of *Cuculain: An Epic* (1882), *Finn and His Companions* (1892), *The Coming of Cuculain* (1894) and *The Departure of Dermot*, *The Triumph of Cuculain* and *The Passing of Cuculain* (all 1917). *The Bog of Stars* (1893) is a collection of stories about 16th-century Ireland; *Hugh Roe O'Donnell* (1902) is a play set in the same period.

O'Hara, Frank 1926–66 American poet and playwright. A leading figure in the NEW YORK SCHOOL, he assimilated a wide variety of influences – from painting as well as literature – to create a deceptively casual poetry in an American idiom. It appeared in *A City Winter and Other Poems* (1952), *Meditations in an Emergency* (1957), *Odes* (1960), *Lunch Poems* (1964), *Love Poems* (1965) and two posthumous volumes, *Collected Poems* (edited by Donald Allen; 1971) and *Poems Retrieved* (1977). His plays are *Try, Try!* (1951), *Changing Your Bedding* (1952), *Awake in Spain* (1960), *Love's Labor* (1960) and *The General Returns from One Place to Another* (1964). *Selected Plays* appeared in 1978.

O'Hara, John 1905–70 American novelist and short-story writer. His novels include: *Appointment in Samarra* (1934), about the suicide of Julian English in the stratified society of 'Gibbsville', based on the author's hometown of Pottsville, Pennsylvania; *Butterfield 8* (1935), about the experiences of a Manhattan newspaperman; and *Pal Joey* (1940), which he adapted as a musical in the same year, a comic series of letters from a nightclub entertainer. Like O'Hara's novels, the short stories collected in volumes stretching from *The Doctor's Son* (1935) to *Waiting for Winter* (1967) often focus on questions of class and social privilege. O'Hara also worked as a screenwriter in Hollywood and published *Five Plays* (1961).

Okai, Atukwei [John] 1941– Ghanaian poet. Although among the most metrically inventive African poetry, his work is little known outside Ghana, both because it incorporates local references and words and because it relies on an element of performance. He frequently reads publicly from unpublished collections such as 'Calabash Chorus' or unpublished sequences such as 'Rhododendrons in Donkeydom'. Volumes include *Flowerfall* (1969), *Fontonfrom, and Other poems* (1971), *Lorgorligi Logarithms, and Other poems* (1974) and *Selected Poems* (1979).

Okara, Gabriel (Imomotimi Gbaingbain) 1921– Nigerian poet and novelist. Though he has published little and did not issue his first collection, *The Fisherman's Invocation*, until 1978, he enjoys a high reputation for lyric poetry rooted in the oral tradition. Many of his best-known poems, such as 'The Snowflakes Sail Gently Down', are often anthologized. A novel, *The Voice* (1964), has been widely noticed for its attempt at a form of English which incorporates the structural principles of the Ijaw language.

O'Keeffe, John 1747–1833 Irish playwright, born in Dublin. Of the 60 plays and operas he wrote for the London stage only one, *Wild Oats* (1791), has achieved lasting fame. It is an artificial but quick-moving comedy about a strolling player called Rover. O'Keeffe had been blind for several years when he wrote it.

Okigbo, Christopher 1932–67 Nigerian poet. After his early death in the Nigerian Civil War, his poetry was gathered in *Labyrinths* (1971) and the fuller *Collected Poems* (1986). Among anglophone African writers, Okigbo has possibly the most fertile, and most mythopoeic, poetic imagination; he always rejoiced in unexpected correspondences between apparently disparate cultural references. In his own life he could reconcile Catholicism with being hereditary priest of a

traditional Igbo village deity, and this priesthood is subsumed in his function as a modern poet in English open to influences from the classics, the Bible, Catholic liturgy, and poets such as HOPKINS and T. S. ELIOT. Notable works include 'Heavensgate', 'Limits' and his last, 'drum' poems.

Okri, Ben 1959– Nigerian novelist and short-story writer. He belongs to a small group of younger writers who have largely abandoned the concerns of CHINUA ACHEBE's generation in favour of a more personal and introspective mode. His prodigious if slightly unwieldy talent was announced in two apparently autobiographical novels, *Flowers and Shadows* (1980) and *The Landscapes Within* (1981), and two collections of stories, *Incidents at the Shrine* (1986) and *Stars of the New Curfew* (1988). *The Famished Road* (1991), which won the BOOKER PRIZE, views urban Nigeria through the eyes of an *abiku*, or child returned from the dead.

Old Bachelor, The CONGREVE's first play, a comedy, produced and published in 1693. Heartwell, the old bachelor, is persuaded to marry Silvia, only to discover that she is Vainlove's discarded mistress. To his relief, he learns that the parson who married them is Vainlove's friend Belmour, in disguise to pursue an intrigue with Laetitia Fondlewife. Heartwell is still a bachelor, and a husband is found for Silvia by deceiving the foolish Sir Joseph Wittol. His companion, the bully Captain Bluffe, is similarly deceived into marrying Silvia's maid.

Old Curiosity Shop, The A novel by DICKENS, serialized in *MASTER HUMPHREY'S CLOCK* in 1840–1 and published in volume form in 1841. The prolonged deathbed sufferings of Little Nell made it immensely popular with contemporaries, though today it is among the least regarded of Dickens's works.

Little Nell (Nell Trent) lives in the shop of the title with her grandfather. When he falls into the clutches of the moneylender Daniel Quilp, an evil dwarf, they quit the shop and roam the countryside together, reduced to beggary. Quilp sets out in pursuit, while Kit Nubbles, the errand boy at the shop, does his best to find and help them. Nell's great-uncle, returned from abroad, succeeds only when it is too late. Exhausted by her troubles, Nell dies a lingering death, followed soon afterwards by her grandfather. Trying to evade arrest, Quilp drowns in the Thames.

Old Fortunatus, The Pleasant Comedy of A play by DEKKER, performed before Elizabeth I on Christmas night, probably 1598, and published in 1600. It comes from a story in the German *Volksbuch* (1509) already dramatized by Hans Sachs in 1553. Fortune offers the old beggar Fortunatus the choice of long life, wisdom, strength, health, beauty or riches. He chooses riches and receives an inexhaustible purse. He also acquires the miraculous hat of the Soldan of Turkey, which takes the wearer wherever he wants to go. When Fortunatus dies, his son Andelocia follows the same thoughtless way of life until Fortune withdraws the gifts.

Old Mortality A novel by SIR WALTER SCOTT, the second in the first series of his *Tales of My Landlord*, published in 1816 and for many years one of his most admired works. The title is the nickname of Robert Paterson who, at the end of the 18th century, wandered round Scotland caring for the graves of the Cameronians, or strict Covenanters. His stories of the 17th-century Covenanters persecuted by John Graham of Claverhouse form the basis of the novel. The hero is Henry Morton, driven to join the Covenanters by unjust treatment after he shelters John Balfour without knowing him to be involved in murdering the Archbishop of St Andrews. Against this background are set the vicissitudes of Morton's love for Edith Bellenden, who belongs to a royalist family, and his relations with his rival, Lord Evandale.

Old Vic Theatre A theatre in London's Waterloo Road, called the Royal Coburg when it opened in 1818, renamed the Royal Victoria in 1833, and soon nicknamed the 'Old Vic'. Originally a home for MELODRAMA, it established its reputation for performing SHAKESPEARE under the management of Lilian Baylis in 1912–37. Under the direction of Michael Benthall it presented all the plays in the Shakespeare First Folio in 1953–8. The Old Vic was the first home of the ROYAL NATIONAL THEATRE in 1962–76.

Old Wives' Tale, The A play by PEELE, published in 1595. It combines rhetoric, spectacle, robust humour and lyricism to satirize the romantic drama of the time. The wicked magician Sacrapant steals Delia and the two brothers who tried to rescue her, but he is overcome by a gallant knight, Sir Eumenides, aided in his quest by Jack's ghost. MILTON took the plot as the basis for *Comus*.

Old Wives' Tale, The A novel by ARNOLD BENNETT, published in 1908. It follows the lives of two sisters, Constance and Sophia Baines, from 1860 to their deaths in about 1906. Constance remains in Bursley, marries the family apprentice, Samuel Povey, and is left in lonely widowhood when her son Cyril goes to London. Sophia has a more adventurous but equally frustrated life. She elopes with Gerald Scales, a glamorous commercial traveller, but he deserts her in Paris, where she achieves independence as proprietor of the Pension Frensham. In old age she returns to Bursley to live with her sister. Sophia's journey to Manchester, where she is too late to speak to the dying Scales, strikes a grim keynote to the concluding section, 'What Life Is'.

Oldham, John 1653–83 Satirical poet. He impressed contemporaries (DRYDEN among them) as a writer of great promise before his early death from smallpox. *A Satire upon a Woman, Who by Her Falsehood and Scorn was the Death of My Friend* (1678), *A Satire against Virtue* (1679) and four *Satires upon the Jesuits* (1681) were written in the aftermath of the discovery of the 'Popish Plot' by Titus Oates. The manner is confident and the matter (especially in the attacks on the Jesuits) aggressive in the extreme. Other works include an ODE *Upon the Works of Ben Jonson*, SATIRES in the manner of Horace and two translations from Juvenal.

Oldmixon, John 1673–1742 Historian. *The British Empire in America* (1708) was the first history of that subject. *The Secret History of Europe* (1712–15) made unsparing criticism of the Tory party for its willingness to reach agreement with France. To the third edition (1727) of the *Critical History of England* (1724–6) Oldmixon added a fiercely anti-Tory 'Essay on Criticism' which made him a target for POPE and other hostile wits. *The History of England during the Reigns of the Royal House of Stuart* (1730) is sometimes regarded as his best work.

Oliphant, Laurence 1829–88 Travel-writer and journalist. One of the most remarkable travellers of his age, he published *Journey to Khatmandu* (1852), *The Russian Shores of the Black Sea* (1853), *Minnesota and the Far West* (1855) and a *Narrative of the Earl of Elgin's Mission to China and Japan in the Years 1857, 58, 59* (1859). As a correspondent for *The Times* he covered aspects of the Crimean

War, the Indian Mutiny, the Risorgimento and the Franco-Prussian War. *Piccadilly* (1866) is a pleasantly satirical novel about London life. In 1867 Oliphant became a disciple of the American 'prophet' Thomas Lake Harris. After this disillusioning experience he founded a community of Jewish immigrants at Haifa, where he wrote a second novel *Altiora Peto* (1883) and, with his wife, the curious *Sympneumata* (1885), which they believed to have been dictated by a spirit. The autobiographical *Episodes of a Life of Adventure* appeared in 1887, and his cousin MARGARET OLIPHANT wrote his biography.

Oliphant, Margaret 1828–97 Novelist and biographer. She wrote more than 100 books and some 200 contributions to BLACKWOOD'S EDINBURGH MAGAZINE. Of the *Chronicles of Carlingford*, a series of novels about Scottish life, *Salem Chapel* (1863) and *Miss Marjoribanks* (1866) received particular praise. Other Scottish novels included *The Minister's Wife* (1869), *Effie Ogilvie* (1886) and *Kirsteen* (1890). She also wrote histories, biographies (notably a life of her cousin LAURENCE OLIPHANT, 1892) and an *Autobiography* (1899).

Oliver Twist: *or, The Parish Boy's Progress* A novel by DICKENS, serialized in 1837–9 and published in book form in 1838. One of its aims was to correct the glamorous portrayal of criminals in the NEWGATE NOVEL of the day; another was to attack the inhumane New Poor Law of 1834.

Oliver's mother dies soon after giving birth to him in the workhouse. He outrages Mr Bumble, the parish beadle, by daring to 'ask for more' and is apprenticed to an undertaker, where he is no better used. He runs away to London and meets the Artful Dodger (Jack Dawkins), who takes him to the den where Fagin has a stable of boys trained as thieves. Fagin's associates are the burglar Bill Sikes and Nancy, a prostitute. Oliver is rescued by the benevolent Mr Brownlow but, prompted by the villainous Monks, the thieves kidnap him. When they send him out on a burglary with Bill Sikes, he is wounded and cared for by the inhabitants of the house, Mrs Maylie and her adopted daughter Rose. Nancy visits Rose to warn her that Monks is bribing Fagin to corrupt Oliver. With Mr Brownlow's help enquiries are begun. Nancy's betrayal is discovered and Bill Sikes murders her. In the hue and cry he accidentally hangs himself, and Fagin and the rest are taken. Monks is revealed to be Oliver's half-brother, seeking an inheritance of which Oliver was ignorant for himself, while Rose Maylie is Oliver's aunt. Fagin is hanged and Oliver is adopted by Mr Brownlow.

Olsen, Tillie 1913– American short-story writer and novelist. *Tell Me a Riddle* (1962) draws on her experience as a working-class wife, mother, wage-earner and labour activist in San Francisco. *Yonnondio: From the Thirties* (1974) tells the story of a poor family's journey to the slums of an industrial city in an unsuccessful search for a way out of poverty and despair. *Silences* (1978), a collection of essays, explains how social and economic pressures prevent members of oppressed groups from becoming writers.

Olson, Charles 1910–70 American poet. He inspired the BLACK MOUNTAIN SCHOOL, a group of poets attracted to the experimental Black Mountain College in North Carolina, where he taught from 1948. It included ROBERT CREELEY, DENISE LEVERTOV and ROBERT DUNCAN. Much of Olson's influence derived from his essay 'Projective Verse' (1950), advocating 'open forms' and 'composition by field' which abandoned conventional METRE. His own major work is the *Maximus Poems*, a sequence which appeared between 1953 and 1975 and was published in a complete edition in 1983. It concentrates on a single town – Gloucester, Massachusetts – in which the central figure, Maximus, attempts to discover the energies shaping both personal and social history. Other verse was gathered in *Archaeologist of Morning: The Collected Poems outside the Maximus Series* (1970). His wide-ranging prose works include *Projective Verse* (1959) and *Poetry and Truth: The Beloit Lectures and Poems* (1971).

Omnium, Jacob See HIGGINS, MATTHEW.

Omoo: *A Narrative of Adventures in the South Seas* A novel by HERMAN MELVILLE, published in 1847. A sequel to *TYPEE*, it proved equally controversial in its depiction of the failure of missionary work in Tahiti. After his flight from the Marquesas the narrator signs on with the crew of the *Julia*, an unseaworthy ship with a sick and unstable captain. The crew mutinies in Tahiti, and the narrator and the doctor, Long Ghost, find work on a plantation in Imeeo and then become beachcombers. The narrator finally ships out on the whaler *Leviathan*.

O'Neill, Eugene (Gladstone) 1888–1953 American playwright. The son of a popular actor, James O'Neill, he first came to notice with plays for the Provincetown Players based on his experience of life at sea. *Beyond the Horizon* (1920) and *Anna Christie* (1921; first produced as *Chris*, 1920) brought him a wider audience. O'Neill went on to become a major influence on modern American theatre, exploring difficult subjects and experimenting with a variety of styles. Black Americans made up the cast of *The Dreamy Kid* (1919); an interracial marriage is the subject of *All God's Chillun Got Wings* (1924); and in *The Emperor Jones* (1920) a black actor dominates the stage. Its EXPRESSIONISM is developed in *The Hairy Ape* (1922) and a mask-drama, *The Great God Brown* (1926). *Strange Interlude* (1928) portrays its central character, Nina Leeds, through dialogue and stylized internal monologue. O'Neill's interest in the familial patterns of Greek tragedy is evident in *Desire under the Elms* (1924) and *MOURNING BECOMES ELECTRA* (1931), a reworking of Aeschylus' *Oresteia*. After the failure of *Days without End* (1934) O'Neill suffered from increasing ill health. *THE ICEMAN COMETH* (1946), is set in a Bowery bar. *LONG DAY'S JOURNEY INTO NIGHT* (1956) is a tortured but compassionate portrait of his own family, a subject treated more lightly in *Ah, Wilderness!* (1933) and returned to in *A Moon for the Misbegotten* (1957). Of a projected 11-play cycle tracing the fortunes of an American family from the 18th to the 20th centuries, only *A Touch of the Poet* (1957) and the incomplete *More Stately Mansions* (1962) were written. *Hughie* (1958) is the single play of another projected series.

On the Road A semi-autobiographical novel by JACK KEROUAC, published in 1957. One of the most popular statements by the BEATS, it tells of a group of friends travelling around America in search of new and intense experiences. The headlong style of Sal Paradise's narrative captures the chaos, exhilaration and despair of their quest. Several characters are modelled on Kerouac's friends: Dean Moriarty is Neal Cassady and Carlo Marx is ALLEN GINSBERG.

Ondaatje, Michael 1943– Canadian writer, born in Sri Lanka. He first received critical acclaim for *The Dainty Monsters* (1967), *The Man with Seven Toes* (1969) and

Rat Jelly (1973), poetry characterized by a surreal vision in which macabre imagery and unexpected conjunctions force readers to reassess their habitual ways of viewing the world. Later volumes are *There's a Trick with a Knife I'm Learning to Do* (1979) and *The Cinnamon Peeler* (1990), a collection which brings together much of the best of his earlier poetry. *The Collected Works of Billy the Kid* (1970), *Coming through Slaughter* (1979) and *Running in the Family* (1982) experiment with a form combining prose, poetry and visual representation in discontinuous narratives. Two novels, *In the Skin of a Lion* (1987) and *The English Patient* (1992), co-winner of the BOOKER PRIZE, are considered his finest works to date. The former is set in Toronto during the 1920s and 1930s. The latter, set in war-torn Italy in 1945, brings together four characters, of different ages and backgrounds, whose lives have been affected by the larger forces of public history.

One Flew over the Cuckoo's Nest A novel by KEN KESEY, published in 1962. The story is told from the viewpoint of an Indian named Bromden, who pretends to be deaf and dumb. He is one of the inmates in a psychiatric ward ruled by Big Nurse. A new arrival, the defiant McMurphy, encourages them to rebel but is lobotomized by the doctors. Bromden smothers him out of rage and pity and escapes.

onomatopoeia The formation of a word by imitation of a sound associated with the thing described; for example, 'hurlyburly', 'lullabye', and many of our words for animal calls.

Oodgeroo [Walker, Kath] 1920–93 Australian Aboriginal poet, of the tribe Noonuccal or Nunukul. The title-poem of her highly successful *We Are Going* (1964) is a moving ELEGY on the dispossession of the Aboriginal people. Later collections are *Dawn is at Hand* (1966) and *My People* (1970). *Stradbroke Dreamtime* (1972) combines traditional Aboriginal stories with stories from her childhood. *Father Sky and Mother Earth* (1981) and *Australian Legends and Landscapes* (1990) also seek to make the Aboriginal view of the world accessible.

Opie, Amelia 1769–1853 Novelist and poet. The wife of the painter John Opie, and the friend of GODWIN and WOLLSTONECRAFT, she produced much popular fiction and poetry. Her novels included *Father and Daughter* (1801), *Adeline Mowbray* (suggested by Wollstonecraft's life; 1802), *Simple Tales* (1806), *Valentine's Eve* (1816) and *Madeline* (1822). She stopped writing novels after becoming a Quaker in 1825, devoting much of her energy to the Bible Society and the Anti-Slavery Society. Her last book, a volume of poetry, was *Lays for the Dead* (1833).

Opie, Peter (Mason) 1918–82 and **Opie, Iona (Margaret Balfour)** 1923– British folklorists and anthologists. The ground-breaking works on the culture of childhood include: *I Saw Esau* (1947), a collection of children's skipping and singing rhymes; *The Oxford Dictionary of Nursery Rhymes* (1951); *The Lore and Language of Schoolchildren* (1959), recording rhymes, chants and teases; and *Children's Games in Street and Playground* (1969), doing the same for non-verbal favourites. *The Singing Game* (1985) is a masterly survey of another aspect of children's oral culture, completed by Mrs Opie after her husband's death. She collaborated with Moira Tatem on *A Dictionary of Superstitions* (1989).

Oppen, George 1908–84 American poet. *Of Being Numerous* (1968; PULITZER PRIZE) contains his two best-known works: the title-poem and 'Route'. His work is gathered in *The Collected Poems of George Oppen, 1929–1975* (1975) and sampled in a selection by CHARLES

TOMLINSON (1990). Closely associated with OBJECTIVISM, Oppen's verse is concerned to realize concrete objects without drawing attention to itself formally; it uses clear images and lean, precise diction.

Orage, A. R. See (NEW AGE, THE.

Orczy, Baroness (Emma Magdalena Rosalia Marie Josefa Barbara) 1865–1947 Novelist, short-story writer and playwright. Born in Hungary, she arrived in London at the age of 15. *The Scarlet Pimpernel* (1905), which she and her husband successfully dramatized, introduced Sir Percy Blakeney and his exploits rescuing victims of the French Revolution. Its many popular sequels included *I Will Repay* (1906) and *The Elusive Pimpernel* (1908). Baroness Orczy also wrote DETECTIVE FICTION, notably stories about 'The Old Man in the Corner' (*The Case of Miss Elliott*, 1905; *The Old Man in the Corner*, 1909; *Unravelled Knots*, 1925).

Ordeal of Richard Feverel, The A novel by GEORGE MEREDITH, published in 1859. Deserted by his wife, Sir Austin Feverel brings up his son Richard according to his own system. Richard falls in love with Lucy Desborough, a farmer's niece whom Sir Austin thinks too humble. The couple marry in secret. Sir Austin ruthlessly manipulates Richard's feelings to separate him from Lucy, sending him to London where Lord Mountfalcon, who has designs on Lucy, puts him in the path of a 'fallen' woman. Richard is easily seduced and goes abroad in shame. He hurries home on learning that he is a father and that Sir Austin is at last reconciled to Lucy. Just when happiness seems within his grasp, he discovers Lord Mountfalcon's villainy, challenges him to a duel and is seriously wounded. Lucy loses her reason and dies.

Origin of Species, The A work of natural history by CHARLES DARWIN, published in 1859 as *On the Origin of Species by Means of Natural Selection: or, The Preservation of Favoured Races in the Struggle for Life.* With Marx's *Capital*, it is probably the work which has most transformed the explanatory systems of the past hundred years. Darwin's theory of 'descent with modification' challenged the notion that species are fixed and eternal. Change from the 'single progenitor' of life on earth has been impelled by several mechanisms, notably sexual selection and natural selection. Natural selection works by means of descent and relies on variation: individual organisms vary in differing degrees and across a spectrum of characteristics from the parent-generation. Those variations most apt to current physical conditions will prosper and produce offspring, which will in turn vary one from another and in some cases will intensify advantageous characteristics. By this slow means the highly specialized skills of current species have evolved.

Darwin's theory has been extrapolated into many fields, often in contradictory ways. We meet it in race-theory, NATURALISM, musical history, and politics, though Darwin always insisted on its entirely biological reference. Most commentators have represented it as a theory of competition, though it is now clearly recognized also as an ecological theory.

Orlando: *A Biography* A novel by VIRGINIA WOOLF, published in 1928. Dedicated to V. SACKVILLE-WEST, it used her ancestral home at Knole in Kent as its setting. The deliberately fanciful story traces the career of the androgynous Orlando from the late 16th century to the present day. He begins as an Elizabethan poet and playwright, and becomes Ambassador Extraordinary to Constantinople under Charles II, an 18th-century lady of high society, a mother, and, in the present day, a woman poet.

Orley Farm A novel by TROLLOPE, issued in monthly parts in 1861–2. Sir Joseph Mason's will leaves his estate to Joseph, his son by his first wife, and in a codicil reserves Orley Farm for Lucius, his son by his second wife. Though Joseph originally contests the codicil, the widowed Lady Mason and Lucius live comfortably at the Farm for 20 years until Dockwrath, a discontented attorney, persuades Joseph to revive his challenge. Mr Chaffanbrass appears successfully for Lady Mason in the suit, but afterwards she confesses her forgery to her elderly lover, Sir Peregrine Orme. Orley Farm reverts to Joseph Mason.

Ormulum A series of early 13th-century HOMILIES in verse. The dedication identifies the author as Orm, an Augustinian canon. He promises to give the gospels of the mass book for the entire year in English, each accompanied by its interpretations and applications. The table of contents lists 242 homilies but only 32 are extant; the series was probably never finished.

Oroonoko: *or, The Royal Slave* A novel by BEHN, published *c.* 1678 and included in *Three Histories* (1688). It was the first expression in English literature of sympathy for the plight of slaves. Oroonoko, grandson and heir of an African king, loves the beautiful Imoinda, daughter of the king's general. The old king himself falls in love with Imoinda and commands that she be taken to his harem, then sells her as a slave. Captured and sold by an English slaver, the grieving Oroonoko finds Imoinda in Surinam, where he rouses the other slaves to escape. They are eventually induced to surrender to Byam, the deputy governor, who has Oroonoko flogged. Determined to exact retribution but knowing he cannot escape its consequences, Oroonoko kills Imoinda, is discovered near her body and is cruelly executed. SOUTHERNE adapted the novel for the stage (1695).

Orphan, The: *or, The Unhappy Marriage* A tragedy by OTWAY, produced and published in 1680. Acasto has brought up Monimia, the orphaned daughter of a friend, with his own twin sons, Castalio and Polydore. They have both fallen in love with her. She loves Castalio, who, from consideration of Polydore's feelings, hesitates before declaring himself and secretly marrying her. Polydore overhears his brother arranging to meet Monimia during the night and contrives to take his place. Monimia accepts him. The deception is eventually revealed by Monimia's brother, Chamont, and the three unhappy lovers kill themselves.

Ortiz, Simon 1941– Native American poet and short-story writer. All his work reflects a strong concern for Native American civil rights. His volumes of poetry include *Naked in the Wind* (1970), *Going for the Rain* (1976), *Fight Back: For the Sake of the People, For the Sake of the Land* (1980), *From Sand Creek* (1981) and *Woven Stone* (1992). His stories include *Fightin': New and Collected Stories* (1983).

Orton, Joe (Kingsley) 1933–67 Playwright and actor. He developed a style of exuberantly tasteless black FARCE, partly derived from PINTER and Genet, in *The Ruffian on the Stair* (1964), *Entertaining Mr Sloane* (1964), *Loot* (1966), and *The Erpingham Camp* (1967). *What the Butler Saw* (1969) carried the farce tradition of threatened adultery into forbidden realms of incest and violence. Orton was murdered by his male lover, who subsequently killed himself.

Orwell, George [Blair, Eric Arthur] 1903–50 Novelist, essayist and journalist. He went from Eton into the Burmese Imperial Police and then to a deliberately chosen state of 'fairly severe poverty' described in *Down and Out in Paris and London* (1933). *Burmese Days* (1934), a novel, expressed his dislike of imperialism. A second novel, *A Clergyman's Daughter* (1935), is about a middle-class woman's brief period of freedom among tramps and hop-pickers. The aspirations and humiliations of Gordon Comstock, the hero of *Keep the Aspidistra Flying* (1936), closely paralleled Orwell's own. *Coming Up For Air* (1939) was written in the shadow of World War II.

THE ROAD TO WIGAN PIER (1937), a documentary account of unemployment in the north of England commissioned for the LEFT BOOK CLUB, was a milestone in literary journalism. It established Orwell's political outlook as an unaligned democratic socialist, a position emphasized by HOMAGE TO CATALONIA (1938), about his experiences in the Spanish Civil War, and the stream of lucid and colloquial journalistic essays he produced throughout the 1930s and 1940s. Originally reprinted in such volumes as *Inside the Whale* (1940), *Critical Essays* (1946) and *Shooting an Elephant* (1950), they were gathered in the four volumes of *Collected Essays, Journalism and Letters* edited by his second wife, Sonia Orwell, and Ian Angus (1968). ANIMAL FARM (1945) and NINETEEN EIGHTY-FOUR (1949), pessimistic SATIRES about the threat of political tyranny, have remained his most popular works.

Osborne, Dorothy See TEMPLE, SIR WILLIAM.

Osborne, John (James) 1929–94 Playwright. LOOK BACK IN ANGER, staged at London's ROYAL COURT THEATRE in 1956, established him as the leader of the ANGRY YOUNG MEN. Subsequent plays, more often nostalgically disgruntled than angry, include: *The Entertainer* (1957), about the declining career of a music-hall comedian; *Luther* (1961); *Inadmissible Evidence* (1964); *A Patriot for Me* (1966); *The Hotel in Amsterdam* (1968); *Time Present* (1968); *West of Suez* (1971); *A Sense of Detachment* (1972); *The End of Me Old Cigar* (1975); *Watch It Come Down* (1976); and *Déjàvu* (1992), returning to Jimmy Porter, the hero of *Look Back in Anger*. He wrote a vigorous autobiography, *A Better Class of Person* (1981).

O'Shaughnessy, Arthur William Edgar 1844–81 Poet. ROSSETTI and other PRE-RAPHAELITES were both friends and influences on his poetry. He published *An Epic of Women* (1870), *Lays of France* (1872), *Music and Moonlight* (1874) and, with his wife, a volume of verse for children, *Toyland* (1875). Today he is usually remembered only for the delicate 'Ode' in *Music and Moonlight* beginning 'We are the music-makers'.

Ossian See MACPHERSON, JAMES.

O'Sullivan, Vincent 1937– New Zealand poet, short-story writer, novelist, playwright and critic. His early poetry, in *Our Burning Time* (1965), *Revenants* (1969) and *Bearings* (1973), repeatedly turns to myth. *Butcher and Co.* (1977) and *The Butcher Papers* (1982) show his flair for drama and SATIRE, as well as his mastery of vernacular, qualities also apparent in his short stories, *The Boy, The Bridge, The River* (1978), *Dandy Edison for Lunch* (1981), *Survivals* (1985) and *The Snow in Spain* (1990). Later poetry includes *The Pilate Tapes* (1986). He has also written: *Miracle* (1976), a satirical novel; plays, including *Shuriken* (1985) and *Billy* (1990); and a study of JAMES K. BAXTER (1976).

Othello, the Moor of Venice A tragedy by SHAKESPEARE, first performed *c.* 1604 and published in Quarto (Q1) in 1622 as well as in the First Folio of 1623. The source is a story in Giraldo Cinthio's *Hecatommithi* (1565).

Othello, a Moor but also a trusted Venetian general, has secretly married Desdemona. His ensign Iago, whom he thinks loyal and 'honest', schemes against him, ostensibly because he preferred Michael Cassio as his lieutenant. Iago prompts the foolish Roderigo to report the marriage to Desdemona's father, the senator Brabantio, who nevertheless has to accept the whole-heartedness of Desdemona's love when she appears before the senate. News of a planned Turkish attack on Cyprus requires Othello's departure there. He is joined by Desdemona, Iago, Cassio and Roderigo. The dispersal of the Turkish fleet leaves Iago free to discredit Cassio, gain his place and insinuate that Desdemona has been unfaithful with him. He secretes a handkerchief Othello gave Desdemona as a love-token among Cassio's possessions, and Cassio gives it to his mistress, Bianca. When Othello sees her with it, he is convinced of Desdemona's infidelity and publicly humiliates her. Iago incites Roderigo to kill Cassio, but he botches the attack and Iago kills him to ensure his silence. Othello, overwhelmed by the horror of a tarnished love, kills Desdemona. Iago's troubled wife, Emilia, reveals the details that betray Iago's guilt. He kills her, is wounded by Othello and escapes. The remorseful Othello stabs himself, while the recaptured Iago is condemned to torture and prison.

Although affairs of state are prominent in *Othello*, the domestic tragedy of a marriage vindictively destroyed is the play's dominant concern. This makes it unique among Shakespeare's great tragedies, but its towering achievement is the relationship between Iago and Othello. No attempt to find motives for Iago's malice can adequately account for its impact.

ottava rima A verse form using stanzas of eight lines, each with 11 syllables, rhyming abababcc. Much used by Tasso, Ariosto, Pulci and other Italian masters, it entered English poetry in the Renaissance but did not fully come into its own until the Romantic period, when BYRON (after shortening the line to 10 syllables) found it ideally suited to his needs.

Otuel and Roland A VERSE ROMANCE (*c.* 1330–40) based on the French *Otinel*. It forms the second part of the compound *Charlemagne and Roland*, of which ROLAND AND VERNAGU is the first fragment. The Saracen emissary Otuel becomes a Christian and fights for the Emperor in his invasion of Lombardy. The poem then resumes the story of *Roland and Vernagu*, ending with Roland's death at Roncesvalles and the Emperor's subsequent defeat of the Saracens (subject of the Old French *Chanson de Roland*).

Otway, Thomas 1652–85 Playwright. His first two plays, *Alcibiades* (1675) and *Don Carlos* (1676), are tragedies in HEROIC COUPLETS and elevated rhetoric. Otway's emotional honesty, together with his satiric denial of hope, distinguishes his BLANK-VERSE tragedies, THE ORPHAN (1680) and VENICE PRESERVED (1682); they were written in sensitive response to Jacobean models and benefit from his encounter with the work of Racine, whose *Bérénice* he had adapted as *Titus and Berenice* in 1676. Comedies such as *The Soldier's Fortune* (1680) and its sequel, *The Atheist* (1683), are forgotten, though an adaptation of Molière's *The Cheats of Scapin* (1676) was popular in its time. He died in poverty, unable to secure a patron. The *Familiar Letters* collected by Tom Brown and Charles Gildon (1697) record his unrequited love for the actress, Elizabeth Barry.

Ouida [de la Ramée, Marie Louise] 1839–1908 Novelist. *Under Two Flags* (1867), her most famous work, is a story of the Foreign Legion. Among the rest of her 45 novels were *Tricotin* (1869), *Puck* (1870), *Two Little Wooden Shoes* (1874), *Moths* (1880) and *In Maremma* (1882). Her vivid brand of hot-house romanticism kept her novels popular until about 1890.

Our Mutual Friend DICKENS's last complete novel, published in monthly parts in 1864–5 and in volume form in 1865.

The chief of its several plots centres on John Harmon, thought drowned but in fact secretly evaluating Bella Wilfer, the girl he must marry if he is to receive his inheritance. As John Rokesmith, he becomes secretary to Mr Boffin (known as Noddy and the Golden Dustman), heir to the property if John does not marry Bella. When Harmon falls in love with Bella but is scornfully rejected, the worthy Boffin affects a miserly unpleasantness which eventually succeeds in reconciling her with Harmon. A second plot concerns Lizzie Hexam, daughter of the dishonest waterman Gaffer Hexam, who is accused of murdering Harmon. She is passionately loved by Bradley Headstone, schoolmaster of her brother Charley, but loves the indolent barrister Eugene Wrayburn, a friend of Mortimer Lightwood. The jealous Headstone tries to kill his rival but Lizzie saves him. Rogue Riderhood blackmails Headstone and they kill each other in a fight. Other characters enforcing a bleak and comprehensive vision of contemporary society include the faded aristocrats and parvenus gathered at the Veneerings' dinner table, the pauperized Betty Higden and the greedy Silas Wegg.

Our Town A play by THORNTON WILDER, produced in 1938 and awarded a PULITZER PRIZE. Its three acts treat Daily Life, Love and Marriage, and Death in the small New Hampshire town of Grover's Corners, focusing on two families in particular, the Gibbses and the Webbs. Each act is played without curtain or scenery and is introduced by the Stage Manager in a direct address to the audience.

Overland Monthly An American literary journal, founded in San Francisco in 1868. It was edited by BRET HARTE for the first two-and-a-half years, and published the work of writers such as JACK LONDON, EDWIN MARKHAM and FRANK NORRIS. It lasted until 1935.

Owen, Robert 1771–1858 Socialist and philanthropist. In 1799 he established the New Lanark mills in Scotland, a pioneering experiment in mutual co-operation which became an object of pilgrimage for social reformers, statesmen and royal personages. Its example helped to bring about the Factory Act of 1817. *A New View of Society* (1813) expounded Owen's ideas of social improvement. After attempting to repeat his experiment at New Harmony, Indiana, he returned to Britain and campaigned for the growing co-operative movement. *The Revolution in Mind and Practice of the Human Race* appeared in 1849.

Owen, Wilfred (Edward Salter) 1893–1918 Poet. Before World War I he worked as a lay assistant to an Anglican clergyman and taught English in Bordeaux, where he met and was influenced by the poet and pacifist Laurent Tailhade. He enlisted in October 1915, serving with the Artists' Rifles and then the Manchester Regiment, stationed at the Somme. In May 1917 he was diagnosed 'shell-shocked' and sent to Craiglockhart

Hospital, Edinburgh, where he met SIEGFRIED SASSOON and drafted and revised his best poems. After being posted to Ripon, he returned to the trenches in August 1918 and was killed on the Sambre Canal a week before the armistice.

Only four of his poems were published during his lifetime. A handful more appeared soon after his death, notably in EDITH SITWELL's *Wheels* (1919), but the bulk awaited publication in successively enlarged editions by Sassoon (1920), BLUNDEN (1931), DAY-LEWIS (1963) and Jon Stallworthy (1983). In a draft preface Owen wrote: 'My subject is War, and the pity of War. The Poetry is in the pity.' His best poems, such as 'Strange Meeting', 'Anthem for Doomed Youth', 'Dulce et Decorum Est', 'Futility' and 'Mental Cases', achieve a remarkable nightmare vision which becomes, by virtue of its power and detail, also a protest. His brother, Herbert Owen, published a three-volume memoir, *Journey from Obscurity* (1960–5). Benjamin Britten combined several of the poems with the Latin mass for the dead in his *War Requiem* (1962).

Owl and the Nightingale, The An anonymous DEBATE POEM written between 1189 and 1216. The narrator overhears the sombre owl and lighthearted nightingale disputing topics that range from theology to the different characteristics of their species. The debate is inconclusive, the birds leaving to consult the mysterious Nicholas of Guildford – perhaps the poet's patron – for an answer. The masterly evocation of the two 'characters' gives the debate an additional dimension and is the main source of its charm. The tone is comic and gently satiric.

Oxford English Dictionary, The The generic label (often abbreviated to OED) for the most ambitious of all ENGLISH DICTIONARIES. It has appeared under more than one title as well as in several editions. The first, originally called a *New English Dictionary on Historical Principles* (abbreviated as NED or HED), appeared in 125 parts in 1884–1928, fulfilling a project begun by the Philological Society in 1857. The nickname 'Murray's dictionary' acknowledges the unique contribution of JAMES MURRAY among its various editors and co-editors. *The Oxford English Dictionary*, a 12-volume edition, appeared together with the first supplements in 1933. A 20-volume second edition or *New Oxford English Dictionary* (1989) is known as the NOED, though it may also be nicknamed 'Burchfield's dictionary' in tribute to R. W. Burchfield's 4-volume *Supplement* (1972–86), which it incorporates. The most notable of many abridgements and adaptations is the two-volume *Shorter Oxford English Dictionary*, retaining the most essential historical information, first published in 1933.

Since its first publication the OED has been uniquely important in providing a full survey of the English vocabulary from 1150. Full dialect coverage is given into the 15th century. Each main entry identifies spelling, variant forms and pronunciation, and provides etymological information. Senses are listed according to their chronological emergence, illustrated by at least one or two quotations per century of usage. Conceived as an aid to reading English literature, the OED's bias has made it a valued quarry for writers and literary scholars.

Oxford Movement, The A 19th-century religious movement, so called because its leaders – KEBLE, PUSEY and NEWMAN – and many of its followers were connected with Oxford. Alternative names were the High Church Movement and the Tractarian Movement, the latter referring to TRACTS FOR THE TIMES (1833–41), the pamphlets which announced its doctrines. These included belief in the Church of England as a divinely inspired institution, in the validity of the Apostolic succession and in the importance of the BOOK OF COMMON PRAYER. Always controversial, the Movement was attacked by the bishops and liberal clergy. *Tracts for the Times* came to an end after Newman's *Tract XC* found the 39 Articles of the Church of England compatible with Catholic theology. Pusey was suspended from the office of university preacher after he declared his belief in the Real Presence. He hoped for a reunion of the English and Roman churches and did his best to prevent conversions to Rome, of which Newman's in 1845 was the most famous.

oxymoron A rhetorical device which deliberately joins apparently contradictory words. Oxymoron is a particularly notable feature of PETRARCHAN verse – for example, 'sweet enemy' and 'I burn and freeze like ice'.

Ozick, Cynthia 1928– American short-story writer and novelist. Her short stories include *The Pagan Rabbi and Other Stories* (1971) and *Bloodshed and Three Novellas* (1976), reflecting her interest in mysticism and the supernatural, and *Levitation: Five Fictions* (1981). Novels include *Trust* (1981), *The Cannibal Galaxy* (1983) and *The Messiah of Stockholm* (1987). *The Shawl* (1991) brings together a novella and a short story about the ordeal in later life of a Holocaust survivor. *Art and Ardor* (1983) and *Metaphor and Memory* (1989) are collections of essays.

Page, P(atricia) K(athleen) 1916– Canadian poet, novelist and painter. Born in Britain, she moved with her family to Alberta in 1919. Early work – which includes a novel, *The Sun and the Moon* (1944) originally published under the pseudonym of Judith Cape, and the verse collected in *As Ten As Twenty* (1946) and *The Metal and the Flower* (1954) – demonstrates strong political commitment and a concern with psychoanalytic themes. Later volumes include a children's book, *A Flask of Sea Water* (1989), and several poetry collections, *Cry Ararat!* (1967), *Evening Dance of the Grey Flies* (1981) and *The Glass Air* (1985), in which she turns to a spare economic verse and an interest in spiritual self-liberation.

Page, Thomas Nelson 1853–1922 American novelist, short-story writer, esssayist and biographer. Much of his writing sentimentalizes the aristocratic Old South. *Red Rock: A Chronicle of Reconstruction* (1898), about the hardships of Reconstruction, became a best-seller. Page was appointed US ambassador to Italy in 1913.

Paine, Thomas 1737–1809 Radical politician and writer. Born in Thetford, he worked as a staymaker, schoolteacher and then as excise officer until his dismissal for attempting to organize the workers. Later re-employed by the excise service he was again dismissed for publishing his first pamphlet, *The Case of the Officers of Excise* (1772). Already a confirmed radical, he went to America in 1774 armed with letters of introduction from BENJAMIN FRANKLIN. As editor of *The Pennsylvania Magazine* in Philadelphia he attacked slavery and advocated independence, an argument powerfully advanced in his most famous pamphlet, COMMON SENSE (1776). During the Revolutionary War he served in Washington's army and continued his political writing in a series of pamphlets, THE AMERICAN CRISIS (1776–83), and *Public Good* (1780), reiterating the case for federal union made in *Common Sense* and objecting to the Virginia Plan. After undertaking a diplomatic mission to France in 1781 he withdrew to his farm at New Rochelle, where he wrote *Dissertations on Government*, an attack on paper money and a warning against the dangers of inflation.

He returned to England in 1787. THE RIGHTS OF MAN (1791–2), his reply to BURKE'S REFLECTIONS ON THE REVOLUTION IN FRANCE, prompted Pitt's government to introduce a law against seditious publication, and Paine, who had fled to France, was convicted of sedition in his absence and outlawed. In Paris the revolutionary Assembly made him a citizen and a member of the Convention. A moderate republican, he opposed the King's execution and spent the years 1793–5 in prison. *A Letter to George Washington* (1796) criticizes the failure of the American minister to help him. While in prison he also completed THE AGE OF REASON (1794–6), a stark critique of accepted religious beliefs. The book confirmed hostility to Paine in England and alienated former friends in America, to which he returned in 1802. Refused burial in consecrated ground, his body was interred at his New Rochelle farm. COBBETT exhumed his bones 10 years later and brought them back to England; he was not allowed to bury them and they eventually disappeared.

Painter, William ?1540–94 Translator. His *Palace of Pleasure* (1566–7; enlarged, 1575) is a collection of tales based on classical and Italian writers such as Herodotus, Livy, Boccaccio and Bandello. WEBSTER, BEAUMONT and FLETCHER and SHIRLEY all quarried it for plots, and it also probably provided the version of the story of Giletta of Narbonne that SHAKESPEARE used in *ALL'S WELL THAT ENDS WELL*.

Pair of Blue Eyes, A A novel by HARDY, published in 1872. The setting, as well as the characters of Stephen Smith and Elfride Swancourt, echoes the circumstances of Hardy's courtship of Emma Gifford. Elfride, the daughter of the vicar of Endelstow on the north Cornish coast, falls in love with Stephen, a young architect who comes to restore the church. Her father opposes the marriage because of Stephen's humble origins. Elfride at first agrees to run away, then vacillates and in Stephen's absence becomes engaged to his friend and patron, the idealistic Henry Knight. When he learns of her previous engagement Knight leaves her heartbroken. When Stephen and Knight meet, they resolve their differences and hurry down to Cornwall, but their train also carries the corpse of Elfride, being transported home for burial after her marriage to a man she did not love.

Paley, William 1743–1805 Theologian and philosopher. His Cambridge lectures on ethics, much indebted to the theories of ABRAHAM TUCKER, were expanded and published as THE PRINCIPLES OF MORAL AND POLITICAL PHILOSOPHY (1785). *Horae Paulinae* (1790) sought to demonstrate the historical truth of the New Testament by a close examination of the life and epistles of St Paul. Like much of Paley's work, *A View of the Evidences of Christianity* (1794) earned its wide popularity by clear presentation and lucid style rather than originality of argument. *Natural Theology* (1802) made a more intensive examination of the same issues.

Palgrave, Sir Francis 1788–1861 Historian. *A History of the Anglo-Saxons* (1831) was the first of several works of medieval history, followed by *The Rise and Progress of the English Commonwealth* (1832), *An Essay on the Original Authority of the King's Council* (1834), *Truths and Fictions of the Middle Ages* (1837) and *The History of Normandy and England* (1851–64).

Palgrave, Francis Turner 1824–97 Poet, anthologist and son of SIR FRANCIS PALGRAVE. His own verse is less important than *The Golden Treasury* (1861), an anthology compiled with the help and advice of his friend TENNYSON. A classic statement of Victorian taste, it was reprinted many times and a second series appeared in 1896. Palgrave became professor of poetry at Oxford in 1895.

palindrome From the Greek, 'running back again': a word, phrase or verse which reads the same both forwards and backwards. 'Rotor' is such a word, 'Madam I'm Adam' such a phrase. Like the ACROSTIC, palindromic verse is occasionally used as an exercise of writer and reader's ingenuity.

Pall Mall Gazette, The An evening newspaper founded by GEORGE SMITH and Frederick Greenwood, its first editor, in 1865. Among subsequent editors were JOHN MORLEY (1880–3), W. T. STEAD (1883–90), Henry Cust (1892–6) and J. L. Garvin (1911–15). Contributors and reviewers included RUSKIN, ARNOLD, PATMORE,

WILDE, PATER, WELLS and KIPLING. After a long decline it was incorporated in *The Evening Standard* in 1923.

Palliser Novels, The A sequence of novels by ANTHONY TROLLOPE, about political and Parliamentary life. Plantagenet Palliser – the Liberal politician who first appeared in a BARSETSHIRE NOVEL, *THE SMALL HOUSE AT ALLINGTON* – and his wife Glencora are central presences. The sequence consists of *CAN YOU FORGIVE HER?* (1864–5), *PHINEAS FINN* (1867–9), *THE EUSTACE DIAMONDS* (1871–3), *PHINEAS REDUX* (1873–4), *THE PRIME MINISTER* (1875–6) and *THE DUKE'S CHILDREN* (1879–80).

Palmer, Nettie 1885–1964 Australian critic and woman of letters. As socialists and promulgators of a national Australian culture, she and her husband VANCE PALMER were among the most influential figures of their generation. After writing two volumes of early poetry, *The South Wind* (1914) and *Shadowy Paths* (1915), she devoted herself mainly to literary journalism, publishing *Modern Australian Literature, 1900–1923* (1924), a pioneering essay which argued for the development of an organic local literature, and the first major Australian study of HENRY HANDEL RICHARDSON (1950). Other books include a volume of essays, *Talking It Over* (1932), and *Fourteen Years: Extracts from a Private Journal, 1925–1939* (1948).

Palmer, Vance (Edward Vivian) 1885–1959 Australian novelist and critic. Eager to promote and contribute to a national literature, he first attempted to establish himself as a popular writer with plays and fiction. *The Man Hamilton* (1928) began his career as a serious novelist, continued by *Men are Human* (1930), *The Passage* (1930), *Daybreak* (1932) and *The Swayne Family* (1934). Later work included a trilogy about the mining community of Mount Isa, *Golconda* (1948), *Seedtime* (1957) and *The Big Fellow* (1959). Palmer also published poetry, essays, criticism and collections of short stories, among them *Let the Birds Fly* (1955) and *The Rainbow-Bird* (1957).

Paltock, Robert 1697–1767 Novelist. He is remembered for a fantasy, *The Life and Adventures of Peter Wilkins* (1751). The hero is shipwrecked in the far south and reaches a country inhabited by people who can fly. He falls in love with one of them, Youwarkee, marries her and rises to importance in the kingdom.

Pamela: *or, Virtue Rewarded* An EPISTOLARY NOVEL by SAMUEL RICHARDSON, its first part published in 1740 and its second part in 1741.

Pamela Andrews is a teenage maidservant in a household where her mistress has just died. The lady's son, Mr B., conceives a passion for her and, helped by his servants Mrs Jewkes and Monsieur Calbrand, tries to take advantage of her position. Pamela is partly revolted and partly attracted by Mr B., but at length his persistence makes her leave the house. Part of Pamela's journal which has been stolen by Mrs Jewkes enables Mr B. better to understand her character. He writes asking her to return and at length proposes marriage. The second, less inspiring part of the book depicts Pamela's acclimatization to her new position, the changing attitudes of Mr B.'s family, her husband's wayward behaviour and the dignified way she handles married life.

Pamela was the 18th-century equivalent of a runaway bestseller. An early example of the unified novel of character, it owed its success largely to the plight of the heroine and the strongly evocative atmosphere of domestic tension which Richardson creates. HENRY FIELDING was the most memorable of the contemporary parodists of Richardson, both in *An Apology for the Life of Mrs Shamela*

Andrews (1741), a skilful BURLESQUE on the values and mannerisms of the first part of *Pamela*, and in his use of Pamela's brother Joseph as the central character in *JOSEPH ANDREWS*.

pantomime A form of popular drama which combines COMMEDIA DELL'ARTE with a native delight in spectacular effects and storytelling dances. By the end of the 18th century, British folklore and nursery tales were nudging out Graeco-Roman myths. In the early 19th century Joseph Grimaldi shifted attention from the dumb Harlequin to the Clown, and the transvestite roles of dame and principal boy were established. PLANCHÉ and H. J. BYRON helped the taste for outrageous puns in rhyming couplets. By mid-century, pantomimes were increasingly associated with Christmas. The involvement of 19th-century music-hall stars and 20th-century TV stars has confirmed their hold on popular culture.

Paracelsus A poem by ROBERT BROWNING, published in 1835. It portrays an imaginary character based on the Swiss alchemist and philosopher (1493–1541). A man single-mindedly bent on searching out true knowledge, he sees, when he is discredited and dying, that his great learning was inadequate without the secret now known to him: love becomes the means of knowledge and intelligence the instrument of love.

Parade's End A tetralogy of novels by FORD MADOX FORD, consisting of *Some Do Not ...* (1924), *No More Parades* (1925), *A Man Could Stand Up* (1926) and *Last Post* (1928). It describes the struggle for survival by Christopher Tietjens in pre-war London and in action during World War I. Events enter into Christopher's consciousness impressionistically, and the impersonal narrator, using many time-shifts, is faithful to the characters' inner constructions of reality.

Paradise Lost MILTON'S EPIC poem, begun in 1658, completed in 1663 and published in 1667. A revised edition (1674) rearranged the 10 books as 12.

Book I. The argument concerns the Fall of Man, the origins of his disobedience to God being traced to Satan's efforts to exact revenge for his expulsion from Heaven. Satan and the rebel angels are first shown lying in the burning lake. He rouses his followers, organizes them into legions, and tells them of a new world being created somewhere in the darkness of Chaos. Then he summons a council and builds the palace of Pandemonium.

Book II. Satan and his followers debate whether to wage another war against Heaven. Instead it is decided that Satan will investigate the new world. He passes through Hell Gates past the twin sentinels, Death and Sin, and journeys through Chaos.

Book III. God observes Satan's journey and foretells how he will succeed in bringing about the Fall of Man and how God will punish Man for yielding to temptation. He accepts the Son of God's offer of himself as a ransom for Man and ordains his incarnation on a future day. Satan meanwhile has reached the outer rim of the universe. He passes the Limbo of Vanity and arrives at the Gate of Heaven, where he changes his form to deceive Uriel, Guardian of the Sun. He learns about the new world and Man.

Book IV. Satan arrives on earth and finds the Garden of Eden, where he observes Adam and Eve. He decides to concentrate his temptation on the Tree of Knowledge. Gabriel finds Satan at Eve's bower, trying to tempt her in a dream. Satan is ejected.

Book V. Eve wakes troubled by her dream and is comforted by Adam. God sends Raphael, who tells Adam about Satan and the need for obedience to God.

Book VI. Raphael continues his narrative, describing the war in Heaven and the defeat of Satan and his rebels. The passage where the Son mounts his attack on the rebels is the literal and thematic centre of the poem, Man's future disgrace being the indirect consequence.

Book VII. The archangel tells Adam that, after Satan's defeat, God decided on another world, from which Man may aspire to Heaven. He sent his Son to perform the Creation in six days.

Book VIII. Adam asks for knowledge of the celestial bodies but Raphael tells him that his first need is for knowledge of his own world. Adam then talks of Eve and the passion she arouses in him. The archangel warns him to attend also to his higher instincts, lest they become subordinate to his love for Eve. Then Raphael departs.

Book IX. Satan has returned to Eden as a mist by night and entered into a sleeping serpent. He finds Eve alone and praises her beauty. He tells her he gained the gift of speech by eating fruit from the Tree of Knowledge. At length he weakens her resolve and she eats the fruit. Satan slips out of the Garden and Eve, transformed in awareness, takes the fruit to Adam, who sees at once that she is lost. He eats the fruit in order to share her transgression, and their innocence vanishes.

Book X. The Son goes to Eden to deliver judgement on Adam and Eve. Before leaving, he clothes them out of pity for their shame in their nakedness. Satan has returned triumphant to Hell; henceforth a path is open for Sin and Death to enter the world of Man. Adam and Eve approach the Son in repentance, begging for mitigation of the doom pronounced upon their children.

Book XI. The Son intercedes with the Father, but God declares that Adam and Eve must be expelled from Paradise. Michael descends to the Garden and tells them they must go out into the world, which he shows Adam from the summit of a hill. Adam is also shown what will happen until the time of the Flood.

Book XII. Michael continues his account, describing Abraham and the Messiah promised in the Son's intercession. Adam is comforted by these revelations; he wakes the sleeping Eve and Michael leads them from the Garden.

The poem's greatness stems partly from its sheer sustained length, but also from its visual immediacy. Both Adam and Eve are archetypes with whom a reader can identify, and the network of abstract influences surrounding their central transgression rarely threatens to obscure their essential characteristics. As an embodiment of malicious cunning, Satan is a dramatic and almost recognizable character. Milton has been criticized for glossing over contemporary developments in scientific and intellectual thought (the astronomical ambiguities in Book VIII, for example) but the poem's realism is that of myth, and its credibility depends on the shapes of Christian belief rather than any specific historical details. It is a monumental achievement, both intellectually and for the powerful expanses of its verse which, with the strength of classical precedents behind it, proved inimitable.

Paradise of Dainty Devices, The One of the most popular of the Elizabethan miscellanies (1576), it includes verse by minor poets such as CHURCHYARD, VAUX, Jasper Heywood and William Hunnis.

Paradise Regained A poem by MILTON, published in 1671. The title suggests it is a sequel to *PARADISE LOST* and the subject – Satan's unsuccessful temptation of Christ, closely derived from the Gospel – is clearly a counterpart to Satan's successful temptation of Man. But *Paradise Regained* is shorter and prefers debate to epic splendour.

Book I. Jesus is baptized by John the Baptist and proclaimed the beloved Son by the Father's voice from Heaven. Satan resolves to outwit him. Disguised as an old countryman he approaches Jesus, fasting in the desert, and asks why he does not make bread of the stones? Jesus recognizes his tempter and resists him.

Book II. Mary awaits her son's return. Satan approaches Jesus in the guise of a rich man, offering food, wine and luxury, and, when these are rejected, all the riches of the world. Jesus still resists him.

Book III. Satan asks why Jesus will not free the kingdom of David from Roman yoke. Jesus answers that he is under his Father's rule and knows the tempter seeks his destruction. Satan takes him to a high mountain to show him the eastern kingdoms of the earth: he will ally any of them to Jesus and restore the kingdom of David to him.

Book IV. Satan takes Jesus to the other side of the mountain and looks towards Rome, offering to help overthrow Tiberius. Jesus rejects the offer and also turns his back on Athens. On the third day Satan makes his last try, tempting Jesus to prove his godhead by throwing himself from the pinnacle of the Temple. Jesus again spurns him. Satan falls back into the pit and angels come to bear Jesus away.

Pardoner's Tale, The See *CANTERBURY TALES*.

Parker [Rothschild]**, Dorothy** 1893–1967 American poet, short-story writer and critic. Her writings are characterized above all by sardonic wit and irreverent sophistication. She contributed reviews, articles, columns, poems and short stories to magazines such as *Vogue, VANITY FAIR, Esquire, THE NEW YORKER, THE NATION, THE NEW REPUBLIC, Cosmopolitan, The Saturday Evening Post* and *THE AMERICAN MERCURY*. Her first, best-selling book of verse, *Enough Rope* (1926), was followed by two more volumes, *Sunset Gun* (1928) and *Death and Taxes* (1931), and her collected poems, *Not So Deep As a Well* (1936). Her short stories appeared in *Laments for the Living* (1930), *After Such Pleasure* (1933) and *Here Lies* (1939). She collaborated with ELMER RICE on the play *Close Harmony* (1929) and with Arnaud d'Usseau on *Ladies of the Corridor* (1953).

Parker, Matthew 1504–75 Divine and scholar. Master of Corpus Christi College, Cambridge, from 1544 and, from 1559, Queen Elizabeth's first Archbishop of Canterbury, Parker was a moderate churchman. He concerned himself with issuing the 39 Articles and the 1568 translation of the Bible known as the Bishops' Bible (see BIBLE IN ENGLISH). As a scholar he produced editions of Gildas, ASSER, AELFRIC, Matthew of Westminster (1567–70), Matthew Paris (1571) and Thomas of Walsingham (1574). His most substantial work was a history of the early English church, *De antiquitate ecclesiae et privilegiis ecclesiae cantuarensis* (1572). He left his collection of books and manuscripts to Corpus Christi and founded scholarships there, one of which was held by MARLOWE.

Parker, Theodore 1810–60 American social reformer and Unitarian minister. He denied the authority of the Bible and the supernatural origin of Christ but affirmed the moral truths of Christianity in *The Transient and Permanent in Christianity*, a sermon delivered in 1841, and *A Discourse of Matters Pertaining to Religion* (1842). As pastor of the radical Twenty-Eighth Congregational Society of Boston from 1845, he sought to apply Christian morality to contemporary problems, championing prison reform, temperance, women's education and, particularly, the abolition of slavery – the subject of his *Letter to the People of the United States Touching the Matter of Slavery* (1848).

Parkes, Sir **Henry** 1815–96 Australian politician, journalist and poet. As Premier of New South Wales, he was one of the moving spirits behind the Australian Federal Commonwealth, which finally came into being in 1901. He also encouraged Australian poetry and wrote poetry himself as a recreation, *Murmurs of the Stream* (1857) being his most highly regarded volume. Other books were *Australian Views of England: Eleven Letters, 1861 and 1862* (1869) and *Fifty Years in the Making of Australian History* (1892).

Parkinson, John 1567–1650 Botanist and herbalist of the royal gardens. He published *Paradisi in Sole Paradisus Terrestris: or, A Garden of All Sorts of Pleasant Flowers Which Our English Air Will Permitt to be Nursed Up* (1629) and a massive herbal, *Theatrum Botanicum* (1640), dealing with nearly 4000 plants.

Parkman, Francis, Jr 1823–93 American historian. *The Oregon Trail* (1847–9) describes the 1700-mile trek across the prairies and into the Rocky Mountains he made with his cousin Quincy Adams Shaw in 1846. Despite a chronic nervous disorder, Parkman continued to travel widely, researching the great histories known collectively as *France and England in North America: Pioneers of France in the New World* (1865), *Jesuits in North America in the Seventeenth Century* (1867), *The Discovery of the Great West* (1869; revised and published as *LaSalle and the Discovery of the Great West* in 1878), *The Old Regime in Canada* (1874), *Count Frontenac and New France under Louis XIV* (1877), *Montcalm and Wolfe* (1884) and *A Half-Century of Conflict* (1892). Though Parkman greatly admired the courage and stamina of the French, his writings show a bias against what he perceived as Catholic despotism and in favour of Protestant democracy, represented by the English.

Parlement of Foules, The A DREAM-VISION by CHAUCER, probably written between 1374 and 1381. The negotiations for a marriage between Richard II and Anne of Bohemia (1381) and Princess Marie of France (1376–7), and even the poet's own marriage (1366?), have been suggested as its occasion. After reading the *Somnium Scipionis*, the narrator falls asleep and dreams that Africanus leads him to a garden, where he visits the temple of Venus and sees the birds gathered before the goddess Nature to choose their mates on St Valentine's Day. A tercel (male) eagle claims the formel (female) eagle on Nature's wrist but is challenged by two other tercels of lower rank. After debate, Nature rules that the formel herself shall choose. She asks for a delay of a year. The other birds choose their mates and sing a roundel in praise of St Valentine and the summer. The delightful comic debate has elements of social SATIRE and sometimes mocks the ideals of COURTLY LOVE.

Parliament of the Three Ages, The A poem (1370–90) in ALLITERATIVE VERSE, perhaps by the author of *WYNNERE AND WASTOURE*. The narrator falls asleep after a poaching expedition and witnesses a dull debate between Youth, Middle Age and Old Age, who asserts the inevitability of death and the transience of worldly bliss and describes the NINE WORTHIES.

Parnassus Plays, The A group of plays produced at St John's College, Cambridge, in about 1600, consisting of *The Pilgrimage to Parnassus* and the two-part *Return from Parnassus*; whose second part is called *The Scourge of Simony*. Their author is unknown, though they have been attributed to JOHN DAY. In *The Pilgrimage* Philomusus and his cousin Studioso achieve Parnassus by way of the Trivium (logic, grammar and rhetoric) and Philosophy. They meet Madido, the votary of wine, Amoretto, the voluptuary, and Ingenioso, who has burned his books. *The Return* is satirical and shows the characters on their way back to London, where they are reduced to working as shepherds. The satire continues in *The Scourge of Simony*, which considers the separation of town and gown, abuses Brackyn, the Recorder of Cambridge who also suffers in IGNORAMUS, and pokes fun at contemporary poets, including SHAKESPEARE and JONSON.

Parnell, Thomas 1679–1718 Poet. After moving from Dublin to London in 1712 he contributed to THE SPECTATOR, thereby attracting the attention of SWIFT and POPE and joining the SCRIBLERUS CLUB. He contributed *An Essay on the Life of Homer* to Pope's translation of the *Iliad* but published relatively little during his lifetime, apart from *An Essay on the Different Styles of Poetry* (1713). Pope was responsible for a posthumous selection of his friend's verse, *Poems on Several Occasions* (1721), which included 'A Night-Piece on Death' (anticipating the work of the GRAVEYARD POETS) and the 'Hymn to Contentment'. 'The Hermit', his narrative poem in HEROIC COUPLETS, was based on a story in the *GESTA ROMANORUM*.

parody A form of literary mimicry that holds up a glass in which writers may see their own worst potentialities realized. For the reader, it is literary criticism of a particularly palatable kind. Since outright bad literature may itself resemble a parody of better literature, parody usually mimics the mighty rather than the humble, and often mingles admiration with mockery. However, this is not always the case: witness the parodies of advertisements, newspaper styles, novelettes and so forth in JOYCE's ULYSSES. At its best, parody remains close to the original and is fairly good-natured. At one end of its spectrum it may approximate to BURLESQUE by exaggerating mimicry into caricature. At the other end it may approach SATIRE by permitting moral criticism to usurp its central function as literary criticism.

Parr, Samuel 1747–1825 Latin scholar. His learning gained him considerable distinction and the nickname of the 'Whig Johnson'. He wrote the Latin epitaph on JOHNSON in St Paul's Cathedral. His writings were collected and published in 1828.

Parson's Tale, The See CANTERBURY TALES.

Parsons, Clere (Trevor James Herbert) 1908–31 Poet. He produced only one slender volume, *Poems* (1932). Despite the occasional archaic phrase, poems such as 'Introduction', 'Suburban Nature Piece' and 'Garden Goddess' have a graceful elegance and a distinctive, original voice. They do not deserve the obscurity into which they have fallen.

Partisan Review An American literary and political journal, founded in 1934 with Philip Rahv and William Phillips as co-editors. Its originally Marxist position has long since been modified. The long list of distinguished contributors includes writers from Europe as well as the USA.

Partonope of Blois A 15th-century VERSE ROMANCE adapted from the French. The hero becomes the lover of an invisible empress, Melior, who promises to wed him if he does not attempt to see her for two and a half years. Though he breaks his promise, he is nursed back to health from despair and near-madness and eventually regains her.

Partridge, Eric (Honeywood) 1894–1979 Philologist and lexicographer. He specialized in slang and bawdy, areas of the English vocabulary not covered by *THE OXFORD ENGLISH DICTIONARY*. His most popular publications include the *Dictionary of Slang and Unconventional English* (1937), *Usage and Abusage* (1942), *Dictionary of the Underworld* (1950), *Origins* (1958) and *Shakespeare's Bawdy* (1947).

Passage to India, A A novel by E. M. FORSTER, published in 1924. Adela Quested visits Chandrapore with Mrs Moore to make up her mind whether to marry Mrs Moore's son Ronny, a narrow-minded magistrate. Adela's desire to understand the 'real India', shared by Mrs Moore, annoys the white community apart from the liberal Cyril Fielding, principal of the government college. Fielding's friend Dr Aziz takes Mrs Moore and Adela to visit the Marabar Caves. Mrs Moore suffers a nihilistic psychic experience and Adela believes she has been sexually assaulted by Aziz. He is arrested and committed to prison to await trial. Only Fielding continues to assert his innocence, but their friendship is irrevocably compromised. Mrs Moore dies on the voyage home, and Adela, under extreme psychological pressure, admits that she was mistaken. Some time afterwards, Aziz and Fielding meet for the last time and discuss the future of India. Aziz insists that he and Fielding can be friends only when the British are driven out of India.

Passionate Pilgrim, The A slim volume of poems, the earliest surviving complete edition of which is the second (1599), whose title-page claims it as the work of SHAKESPEARE. Five of the 20 poems are certainly his (three pieces from *LOVE'S LABOUR'S LOST* and versions of Sonnets 138 and 144). The rest include one by MARLOWE (*THE PASSIONATE SHEPHERD TO HIS LOVE*) and two by BARNFIELD. There is no reason to think Shakespeare the author of any of the unattributed poems, although claims have been made for the charming lyric 'Crabbed Age and Youth Cannot Live Together.'

Passionate Shepherd to His Love, The MARLOWE's invitation to the beloved to share life in an idyllic world first appeared in *THE PASSIONATE PILGRIM* (1599), but the text in *ENGLAND'S HELICON* (1600) is the commonly accepted one. RALEIGH's witty counter, *The Nymph's Reply to the Shepherd*, is almost as well known. Together they constitute a classic pairing of romantic extravagance and romantic realism.

Past and Present A prose work by CARLYLE, published in 1843. Its first two books contrast medieval and Victorian England. Drawing on JOCELIN OF BRAKELOND's 12th-century *Chronicle*, which described life in the abbey of St Edmund under Abbot Samson, Carlyle asks if the medieval peasant, secure in his place in the social order, is not happier and better off than his 19th-century counterpart. The third book, 'The Modern Worker', is in the main a satirical attack on Mammonism, Benthamism, politicians and similar forces that Carlyle considers anathema to society. The final book, 'Horoscope', is an apocalyptic plea for putting things to rights. *Past and Present* is notable for Carlyle's compassionate reaction to the sufferings caused by industrial-

ism and for his concept of the hero, embodied in the shrewd Samson.

Paston letters, The The correspondence and documents of the Paston family of Norfolk in 1425–95. Recording the daily lives of three generations, they provide an invaluable record for social and literary historians.

pastoral Literature about an idealized rural life, concentrating especially on the loves and laments of shepherds and shepherdesses. The kind is established by Theocritus' *Idylls* in the 3rd century BC. Virgil's *Eclogues* provide the major Roman example. A pastoral poem therefore can also be called an IDYLL or an ECLOGUE (or a bucolic). The GEORGIC also deals with rural life, but more realistically, concerning itself with farming and its labours rather than with the singing, dancing and loving of shepherds.

The chief example of pastoral romance in English is SIDNEY's *ARCADIA*, SPENSER's *SHEPHEARDES CALENDER* being the chief poetic example. There is little pastoral of merit after the Elizabethan period, though EMPSON's *Some Versions of Pastoral* seizes on the moral implication of pastoral – that rural life is simpler and more wholesome than court or city – and extends the definition to any such moral world, whether rural or not. Hence a Western and a gangster movie might count as pastoral.

Patchen, Kenneth 1911–72 American poet and novelist. His experimental verse, with its proletarian stance, influenced the work of the BEATS. It appeared in *Before the Brave* (1936), *First Will and Testament* (1939), *The Teeth of the Lion* (1942), *Cloth of the Tempest* (1943), *Pictures of Life and Death* (1946), *To Say If You Love Someone* (1948), *Hurrah for Anything* (1957), *Because It Is* (1960) and *Collected Poems* (1968). His fiction includes: *The Journal of Albion Moonlight* (1941), a surrealist ALLEGORY; *Memoirs of a Shy Pornographer* (1945), a SATIRE; *Sleepers Awake* (1946); and *See You in the Morning* (1948). *Panels for the Walls of Heaven* (1947) and *The Famous Boating Party* (1954) are prose poems.

Patent Theatres The Letters Patent issued by Charles II to KILLIGREW and D'AVENANT in 1662 gave them the sole right to arrange performances of plays in the City of Westminster. Killigrew established his company at DRURY LANE, while D'Avenant's patent was finally invested in COVENT GARDEN in 1732. Already challenged by the HAYMARKET THEATRE in the 18th century, the monopoly of Drury Lane and Covent Garden over the performance of legitimate drama in London was ended by Act of Parliament in 1843.

Pater, Walter (Horatio) 1839–94 Essayist, critic and novelist. A diffident Oxford don, he secured his reputation as leader of the AESTHETIC MOVEMENT with *STUDIES IN THE HISTORY OF THE RENAISSANCE* (1873). It was followed by a novel, *MARIUS THE EPICUREAN* (1885), *Imaginary Portraits* (1887), the unfinished *Gaston de Latour* (1888), *Appreciations with an Essay on Style* (1889), *Plato and Platonism* (1893), *The Child in the House* (1894) and several posthumous publications, *Miscellaneous Studies* (1895), *Greek Studies* (1895) and *Essays from 'The Guardian'* (1896). 'Appreciation' was a byword with Pater, whose criticism rarely took an opposing stance. To him an understanding and an apprehension of beauty were paramount, as was a melancholy recognition of the brevity of human life. Disciples often misrepresented him as a hedonistic voice of 'Art for Art's sake' but he never wholly relinquished the ethical implications of aestheticism. The morbid side to his work, most apparent in *Gaston de Latour*, was seized on by followers in the 1890s.

Paterson A long poem in free verse by WILLIAM CARLOS WILLIAMS, published in five books from 1946 to 1958. Fragments of a sixth book were published posthumously in 1963. The title refers both to a city near Williams's home town of Rutherford, New Jersey, and to a character in the poem who merges details of the poet's private life with public history. The dominant image is that of the Passaic River, which in its fluid, continual movement unites the particulars of human experience with time.

Paterson, A(ndrew) B(arton) 1864–1941 Australian poet, journalist and novelist. 'Banjo' Paterson is remembered less for his journalism and novels, which include *The Outback Marriage* (1906), than for the BALLADS he published in his best-selling *The Man from Snowy River* (1895). He also collected authentic bush ballads, gathered in an anthology, *Old Bush Songs* (1905). His *Collected Verse* appeared in 1921. Their slangy idiom and infectious rhythms make Paterson's own poems, and the ones he collected, immediately memorable; everyone in the English-speaking world knows 'Waltzing Matilda', which he adapted from a traditional source. *Happy Dispatches* (1934) is a volume of reminiscences.

pathetic fallacy A term coined by RUSKIN, in the third volume of *MODERN PAINTERS* (1856), for the practice of attributing human emotions to the inanimate or unintelligent world.

Pathfinder, The See LEATHERSTOCKING TALES, THE.

Patience A late 14th-century poem in ALLITERATIVE VERSE and the West Midlands dialect. Preserved in the same manuscript as *SIR GAWAIN AND THE GREEN KNIGHT*, *PEARL* and *CLEANNESS*, it is usually grouped with them as the work of the same, unidentified author, known for convenience as the *GAWAIN*-poet. It illustrates its theme, the virtue of patience, with the story of Jonah – humorously portrayed and skilfully transferred to a medieval setting.

Patient Grissel, The Pleasant Comedy of A play by DEKKER in collaboration with CHETTLE and William Haughton, first published in 1603. The story comes from CHAUCER's *The Clerk's Tale*, in THE CANTERBURY TALES, which derives from Boccaccio. The play contains Dekker's songs, 'Art Thou Poor Yet Hast Thou Golden Slumbers? O Sweet Content!' and 'Golden Slumbers Kiss Your Eyes'.

Patmore, Coventry (Kersey Dighton) 1823–96 Poet and critic. Soon after *Poems* (1844), he became associated with the PRE-RAPHAELITES. Millais took one of his early verses, 'The Woodman's Daughter', as the subject for a painting. *Tamerton Church-Tower and Other Poems* (1853) was followed by his most popular work, *THE ANGEL IN THE HOUSE* (1854–63), a celebration of married love based on his marriage to Emily Andrews. After her death in 1862 he went on to marry twice more, in 1864 and 1881. He became a Roman Catholic in the year of his second marriage, and the 42 odes of *The Unknown Eros* (1877) show him entering a new – and to contemporaries, less accessible – phase. Their theme once again is love, now harmonized with the transcendental. Afterwards he turned chiefly to prose, beginning with the study of METRE introducing his next volume of poems (1878) and continuing with such critical, philosophical and aphoristic studies as *Principle in Art* (1879), *Religio Poetae* (1893) and *The Rod, the Root and the Flower* (1895).

Paton, Alan (Stewart) 1903–88 South African novelist and short-story writer. The account of black living conditions in *Cry, the Beloved Country* (1948) alerted world opinion to South Africa's racial inequalities. It was followed by an altogether more accomplished novel about Afrikaner inflexibility, *Too Late the Phalarope* (1953), *Debbie Go Home: Stories* (1961; as *Tales from a Troubled Land* in USA, 1965), and *Ah, But Your Land is Beautiful* (1981), an uneasy combination of 'experimental' fiction and 1950s history. *Towards the Mountain* (1981) is an autobiography.

Paton Walsh, Jill [Gillian] 1937– Novelist and writer of CHILDREN'S LITERATURE. Most of her fiction uses a historical setting. Adult novels include *Farewell the Great King* (1972), *Lapsing* (1986), *A School for Lovers* (1989), *The Wyndham Case* (DETECTIVE FICTION; 1993) and *The Knowledge of Angels* (1994), retelling the fable of the wolf-child. Children's novels include *The Emperor's Winding-Sheet* (1974), *A Parcel of Patterns* (1983), *The Dolphin Crossing* (1967), *Fireweed* (1969) and *A Chance Child* (1978), mixing history with fantasy. *Goldengrove* (1972) and its sequel *Unleaving* (1976) deal with the problems of adolescence.

Patten, Brian See LIVERPOOL POETS.

Pattison, Mark 1813–84 Scholar. A Fellow and, from 1861, Rector of Lincoln College, Oxford, he held liberal views on University affairs and theology, as his contribution to *ESSAYS AND REVIEWS* (1860) demonstrated. His chief interest was in the Renaissance scholars Isaac Casaubon and Joseph Scaliger; his biography of Casaubon appeared in 1875 but his work on Scaliger was never finished. His wife, the art historian Emilia Francis Strong, was many years younger than himself; she later married the politician Sir Charles Dilke. These facts have prompted the suggestion that Pattison was the model for Casaubon in GEORGE ELIOT's *MIDDLEMARCH*. His memoirs were published by his widow in 1885.

Paulding, James Kirke 1778–1860 American man of letters. With WASHINGTON IRVING and Irving's brother William he founded and contributed to *SALMAGUNDI* (1807–8), producing a second series of *Salmagundi* single-handedly in 1819–20. A staunch defender of his native country in the Anglo-American literary dispute, he wrote *The Diverting History of John Bull and Brother Jonathan* (1812), *The Lay of the Scottish Fiddle* (1813; a PARODY of SIR WALTER SCOTT) and *The United States and England* (1815). He also produced *The Backwoodsman* (1818), a poem celebrating the frontier spirit, over 70 tales and five novels.

Paulin, Tom 1949– Poet and critic. Bleaker and more urban than that of other contemporary Ulster poets, his poetry is charged with a brooding political awareness of the Irish predicament and, in particular, the matter of Protestant identity. Volumes include *A Sense of Justice* (1977), *The Strange Museum* (1980), *The Liberty Tree* (1983) and *Fivemiletown* (1987). Similar concerns, as well as resonances of the Ulster dialect verse first explored by JOHN HEWITT, inform his versions of Sophocles' *Antigone*, *The Riot Act* (1985), and of Aeschylus' *Prometheus Bound*, *Seize the Fire* (1990). Paulin has also published a critical study of HARDY's poetry (1975) and *Ireland and the English Crisis* (1984), a collection of critical essays, as well as editing two anthologies, *The Faber Book of Political Verse* (1986) and *The Faber Book of Vernacular Verse* (1990).

Payne, John Howard 1791–1852 American playwright and actor. His first play, *Julia: or, The Wanderer* (1806), staged when he was only 14, was followed by a successful adaptation of Kotzebue's *Lover's Vows* (1809). In 1813 he went to England; his work there included: *Brutus: or, The Fall of Tarquin* (1818), a clever compilation; *Thérèse: The Orphan of Geneva* (1821), which restored his fortunes after he had failed as manager of Sadler's Wells Theatre; *Clari: or, The Maid of Milan* (1823), which contained 'Home Sweet Home', set to music by Henry Bishop; and *Charles the Second* (1824), in collaboration with WASHINGTON IRVING. After his return to New York in 1832 he collected notes on the Cherokee Indians, unpublished during his lifetime. Grant Foreman edited *Indian Justice: A Cherokee Murder Trial* (1934).

p'Bitek, Okot 1931–82 Ugandan poet. His writings were seminal to the East African search for cultural identity in the 1970s. *Song of Lawino* (1966) and *Song of Ocul* (1970) are in the manner of Acoli oral verse. *Two Songs* (1971) laments post-Independence penury, though he argued in *African Religions in Western Scholarship* (1971) and *Africa's Cultural Revolution* (1973) that neo-colonialism was cultural rather than economic.

Peabody, Elizabeth 1804–94 American educator. The bookshop she opened in Boston in 1839 made her a leading figure in TRANSCENDENTALISM. Its printing press issued works by HAWTHORNE (her brother-in-law) and MARGARET FULLER, and, in 1842–3, *THE DIAL*. Most of her writings were textbooks of grammar and history. She opened the first American kindergarten in 1860, published the *Kindergarten Messenger* in 1873–7, and lectured at BRONSON ALCOTT's Concord School of Philosophy in 1879–94, having earlier assisted at his experimental Temple School. Her final days were spent supporting Indian education and compiling *A Last Evening with Allston* (1886), which combines memoirs with early articles for *The Dial*.

Peacham, Henry *c.* 1576–*c.* 1643 Author of essays and 'characters'. He is best remembered for *The Complete Gentleman* (1622), advice to young men about to enter the world. Other works were *Graphice* (1606), a treatise on art frequently republished as *The Gentleman's Exercise, Coach and Sedan* (1636), *The Truth of Our Times* (1638) and *The Art of Living in London* (1642).

Peacock, Thomas Love 1785–1866 Novelist, poet and essayist. A modest inheritance enabled him to live as private scholar and man of letters, and he was not obliged to seek regular employment until he was in his thirties, when he obtained a senior post at the East India Company. He remained at India House until his retirement in 1856, succeeding JAMES MILL as Examiner in 1837.

His development as a writer was inseparable from his friendship with SHELLEY, who gave him confidence in his powers and drew him into a wider literary circle. By the time he made his debut as a novelist his manner was already that of the informed insider. *HEADLONG HALL* (1816), *MELINCOURT* (1817) and *NIGHTMARE ABBEY* (1818) all presuppose a reader versed in contemporary intellectual controversy. Although some characters are meant to be identified with real-life counterparts, the primary target of Peacock's urbane SATIRE is the philosophical, social and political attitudes they typify. His most characteristic formal device is the suspension of narrative for a kind of wickedly parodied Socratic dialogue or Platonic symposium, in which the characters argue each other under the well-laden tables of their hosts. Discussion is leavened by FARCE, witty songs and love-plots ending in incongruous marital alliances. *MAID MARIAN* (1822) and *THE MISFORTUNES OF ELPHIN*

(1829) combine topical satire with historical romance, but *CROTCHET CASTLE* (1831) returns to his earlier, and perhaps more congenial, form. Many readers regard *GRYLL GRANGE* (1860–1), a satire on the mid-Victorian age, as his masterpiece.

Peacock's poetry includes *Rhododaphne* (1818), which anticipates KEATS's *LAMIA*; lyrical pieces such as 'Long Night Succeeds the Little Day' (1826) and 'Newark Abbey' (1842); and *The Paper Money Lyrics* (1837), a satire on political economy and the banking fraternity. His most systematic critical writings are the fragmentary *Essay on Fashionable Literature* (1818) and *The Four Ages of Poetry* (1820), which provoked Shelley to write *A DEFENCE OF POETRY*. The two-part *Memoirs of Shelley* appeared in 1858–60.

Peake, Mervyn (Laurence) 1911–68 Novelist, artist and poet. He showed himself a master of the grotesque with his first novel, *Titus Groan* (1946), a minutely detailed Gothic fantasy set in an ancient castle peopled by monumental and bizarre figures. *Gormenghast* (1950) and *Titus Alone* (1959) followed; all were reissued as a trilogy in 1967. Peake's verse includes *Rhymes without Reason* (1944), *The Glassblowers* (1950) and *The Rime of the Flying Bomb* (1962), a BALLAD of the blitz. He illustrated most of his work himself, as well as providing drawings for editions of COLERIDGE's *THE RIME OF THE ANCIENT MARINER* in 1943, and STEVENSON's *TREASURE ISLAND* in 1949. *A Book of Nonsense* was published posthumously in 1972.

Pearce, (Ann) Philippa 1920– Writer of CHILDREN's LITERATURE. *Tom's Midnight Garden* (1958) describes the lonely Tom's visit to an old house, where each night he travels into the past, always meeting an equally lonely Edwardian little girl whom he eventually recognizes as the present owner of the house, now a crabbed old lady. Another minor classic is *A Dog So Small* (1962), about the clash in a child's mind between fantasy and reality. Stories for younger readers include *The Tooth Ball* (1987) and *Freddy* (1988).

Pearl A late-14th-century poem in ALLITERATIVE VERSE and the West Midlands dialect. Preserved in the same manuscript as *SIR GAWAIN AND THE GREEN KNIGHT*, *PATIENCE* and *CLEANNESS*, it is usually grouped with them as the work of the same, unidentified author, known for convenience as the *GAWAIN*-poet. It is an allegorical DREAM-VISION and an ELEGY on the death of a young child, probably the poet's daughter. She appears to the dreaming narrator as the Pearl-maiden, teaching him points of doctrine and rebuking his outraged grief. He is shown the Heavenly City, the procession of the 144,000 virgin brides of Christ and the Lamb of God bleeding. Overcome by longing, he attempts to cross the stream separating him from his daughter and wakes with a better understanding of how to cope with his grief.

A powerful allegory of personal loss and spiritual crisis, the poem contrasts the emotional dryness of rational argument and doctrine with the overwhelming love and pity the Dreamer feels for the Lamb, to show that both reason and love are necessary to faith. The central symbol is subtly developed: the pearl the narrator has lost in the grass, a metaphor for the dead daughter he mourns, becomes identified with the biblical pearl of great price (Matthew 13: 45–6), spiritual purity and perfection, the state of salvation and divine grace, and the Kingdom of Heaven.

Pearse, Patrick [Padraig] 1879–1916 Irish poet. His main work was as a publicist for DOUGLAS HYDE's Gaelic

League. His execution for his part in the Easter Rising, mourned by YEATS in 'Easter 1916', drew greater attention to his poems and plays of patriotic dedication, chiefly in Gaelic but including some poems in English, such as 'The Fool', 'The Rebel' and 'The Mother'. His *Plays, Stories and Poems* were collected and published (in English) in 1917.

Pearson, John 1613–86 Divine. His academic and ecclesiastical preferments after the Restoration culminated in the mastership of Trinity College, Cambridge and the see of Chester. Acknowledged as the most learned divine of an age rich in contenders, he produced a standard work in his *Exposition of the Creed* (1659). He also collected HALES's sermons and tracts as *Golden Remains* (1659).

Pecock, Reginald *c.* 1395–*c.* 1460 Religious writer. A controversial figure who provoked all sections of theological opinion, he was noted for his anti-Lollard views. His most important work, *Repressor of Over Much Blaming of the Clergy*, was finished in 1455, when he was Bishop of Chichester. It anticipates HOOKER by arguing in favour of moral law based on natural reason. The *Book of Faith* (1456) analyses the roles of reason and Scriptural authority. He was expelled from the Privy Council in 1457 for denying the authority of the patristic writers, setting natural law above the Scriptures and writing in the vernacular. Besides *Repressor* and the *Book of Faith*, his surviving works are *The Book of Christian Religion*, *The Donet* and *The Follower to the Donet*, the last two in the form of dialogues, all written before 1454.

Peele, George 1558–96 Playwright. One of the UNIVERSITY WITS, he earned what he could from plays, poems and pageants, spending his last years in sickness and poverty. Peele's best play is THE OLD WIVES' TALE (published 1595), whose mockery of romantic drama anticipates THE KNIGHT OF THE BURNING PESTLE. Other pieces are often memorable chiefly for their songs. *The Arraignment of Paris* (published 1584), is a combination of debate and PASTORAL written for court performance. *The Battle of Alcazar* (*c.* 1589) owes its style to MARLOWE's *TAMBURLAINE*. *King Edward the First* (published 1593) is more romance than history play. *The Love of King David and Fair Bathsheba* (*c.* 1594, published 1599) is better constructed. Poems like *Polyhymnia* (1590), *The Honour of the Garter* (1593) and *Anglorum Feriae* (1595) were apparently written for recitation at court.

Pelham: or, The Adventures of a Gentleman A SILVER-FORK NOVEL by EDWARD BULWER LYTTON, published in 1828. The hero is a fashionable dandy, whose habit of wearing black for dinner started a trend which has lasted to the present day. He succeeds in clearing a friend from suspicion of a vicious murder (based on the Thurtell case of 1824).

Pendennis, The History of A novel by THACKERAY, published in monthly parts in 1848–50. A leisurely *BILDUNGSROMAN*, often compared to DICKENS's *DAVID COPPERFIELD*, it has strongly autobiographical elements.

Arthur Pendennis is brought up by his widowed mother, who lives with her adopted daughter Laura Bell. His worldly uncle, Major Pendennis, saves him from an imprudent marriage to an actress, Miss Fotheringay, daughter of the tipsy Captain Costigan. Pen goes to Oxbridge, where he becomes idle and extravagant. Back at home he flirts with the shallow Blanche Amory, daughter of the second wife of Sir Francis Clavering, and dutifully proposes to Laura, who rejects him. In London, where he lodges with George Warrington, he starts to write for the *Pall Mall Gazette* and publishes a successful novel. He meets Blanche again and becomes attracted to a porter's daughter, Fanny Bolton. She nurses him when he is ill and his mother wrongly suspects her of being his mistress. Mother and son are reconciled before her sudden death. Major Pendennis uses his knowledge of family scandal to try to arrange a worldly marriage between Pen and Blanche. When Pen discovers the scandal, that Blanche's father is alive and a criminal, he repudiates the arrangement but decides to honour his engagement. She, however, has transferred her affections to his friend Harry Foker. Pen proposes to Laura, whom he has come to love, and she accepts him.

Penguin New Writing See LEHMANN, JOHN.

Penn, William 1644–1718 Quaker and founder of Pennsylvania. The son of Admiral Sir William Penn, he was converted to Quakerism and defended his new faith in *The Sandy Foundation Shaken* (1668). It resulted in his imprisonment in the Tower, where he wrote *No Cross, No Crown* (1669), a classic of Quaker literature. His inheritance and a grant of land in the New World enabled him to found Pennsylvania, where he hoped to establish liberty of conscience for all settlers. Penn's support of James II after his return to England in 1684, and his continuing friendship with the monarch after the Revolution of 1688, lost him the governorship. He spent his remaining years in England preaching and writing, except for his spell of retirement to the Colonies in 1699–1701. *Some Fruits of Solitude* (1692), a collection of aphorisms, has some literary interest.

Pennant, Thomas 1726–98 Naturalist and travel-writer. He was in touch with Linnaeus, Sir Joseph Banks, Buffon and GILBERT WHITE, who addressed some of the letters which make up *The Natural History of Selborne* to him. His most important works of natural history were *The British Zoology* (1766; revised 1768–70) and a *History of Quadrupeds* (1781). The most influential of his learned and detailed travel books were *A Tour in Scotland* (1771), revised as *A Tour in Scotland and Voyage to the Hebrides* (1774–6), and *A Tour in Wales* (1778–81). SAMUEL JOHNSON defended Pennant's account of Scotland against THOMAS PERCY's criticisms: 'He's a Whig, sir; a sad dog. But he's the best traveller I ever read.'

pentameter See METRE.

Pepys, Samuel 1633–1703 Diarist. The famous *Diary* covers barely more than eight years (1 January 1660 to 31 May 1669) in the busy life of a man who started his career as a secretary in the household of his relative, Sir Edward Montagu (later the 1st Earl of Sandwich), and rose steadily in the Navy Office, becoming Secretary to the Admiralty in 1672. In an age when the efficient official was still a rarity, Pepys was a first-rate civil servant and bureaucrat to whose reforms in supply and administration the Navy was long indebted. He was also a JP, an MP, and a Fellow of the Royal Society, as well as being a man about town and a figure in court circles. In 1679 he was imprisoned in the Tower of London on the charge of involvement in the 'Popish Plot' and deprived of office. He was reinstated in 1684 but had to resign with the ousting of James II in 1688. He was imprisoned by the new government but released, and in 1700 retired to his house in Clapham, which he shared with his faithful confidant and factotum, William Hewer, who features strongly in the *Diary*.

Pepys was a personal friend of EVELYN, like him an early fellow of the newly established Royal Society, and a man of lively and enquiring intelligence. It was the publication of Evelyn's *Memoirs* (1818) which led to the rediscovery of the encoded diary which Pepys had left to his *alma mater*, Magdalene College, Cambridge, along with a sizeable bequest of contemporary pamphlets, broadsides, ballads and manuscripts. It first appeared in 1815, though this edition has now been superseded by the full annotated edition by R. Latham and W. Matthews (11 volumes, completed in 1983). As the private, first-hand record of a historical personality the *Diary* can scarcely be rivalled, and the decade which it so evocatively chronicles could hardly have been a more colourful one into which an ambitious, self-interested and passionately enthusiastic young man could have launched himself. More neatly perhaps than any other individual contemporary (bar the monarch himself), Pepys seems to embody the more youthful attributes of the Restoration era; indeed, much of the colourful detail which has reached us has filtered through the very medium of his clandestine document. His record catches exactly that balance of civility and coarseness, *laissez-faire* and rationalism which typified his age. Apart from its historical interest, the *Diary* is a fine achievement in the literature of privacy: quirky, self-conscious, voyeuristic and intimate. The whole document is wonderfully enlivened by the comedy of the diarist's own frank descriptions of himself and his constantly shifting attention, a mind 'with child to see any strange thing'.

Percy, Thomas 1729–1811 Antiquarian. A clergyman, he rose to become Dean of Carlisle (1778) and Bishop of Dromore in Ireland (1782). The great success of MACPHERSON's Ossianic poetry stimulated him to publish *Five Pieces of Runic Poetry Translated from the Islandic Language* (1763) and to begin his collection of early and traditional poetry. His most important acquisition was the Percy Folio (as it became known), a 17th-century manuscript of BALLADS and other material, including a 14th-century allegorical poem, 'Death and Life'. The Folio was the main source for the ballads in his *Reliques of Ancient English Poetry* (1765; expanded in 1767, 1775 and 1794). Though Percy followed the custom of his age in adapting the original texts freely, *The Reliques* was an important step in reviving the ballad tradition and an acknowledged influence on the Romantic poets. The Percy Folio, now in the British Library, was edited by FURNIVALL and J. W. Hales (1867–8).

Percy, Walker 1916–90 American novelist. Most of his novels are about Southerners, usually alienated people in search of fulfilment. They include: *The Moviegoer* (1961), about a New Orleans stockbroker; *The Last Gentleman* (1966) and its sequel *Second Coming* (1980); *Love in the Ruins* (1971), a satire about a scientist; *Lancelot* (1977); and *The Thanatos Syndrome* (1987). Percy's essays on language were collected in *The Message in the Bottle* (1975).

Percy Folio, The See PERCY, THOMAS.

Peregrine Pickle, The Adventures of The second novel by SMOLLETT, published in 1751. The story is farcical and violent, and its reception was mixed enough to make Smollett issue an expurgated version (1758). Peregrine is an ungovernable youth who goes from bad to worse before being tamed by disillusion and imprisonment. He is released by the good offices of those to whom he has formerly been generous and is rewarded by the hand of Emilia, whom he has treated badly, despite their mutual love. The novel has two unusual

features. One is the interpolated story of the widowed Lady Vane's remarriage and subsequent adulteries, which she is believed to have paid Smollett to publish. The other (chapter 95) is Peregrine's purchase of a beggar girl, whom he tries to make a fine lady. The parallels with SHAW's *PYGMALION* have been noted.

Perelman, S(idney) J(oseph) 1904–79 American humorist. A sharp observer of American society, he published some 20 books, mostly collections of pieces which had appeared in THE NEW YORKER, beginning with *Dawn Ginsbergh's Revenge* (1929). In Hollywood he wrote scripts for the Marx brothers and the screenplays for *Ambush* (1939) and *The Golden Fleecing* (1940), both with his wife Laura Weinstein, the sister of NATHANAEL WEST. He also wrote travel books, including *Westward Ha! or Around the World in Eighty Clichés* (1948) and *Eastward Ha!* (1977).

Pericles, Prince of Tyre A play of which SHAKESPEARE wrote a substantial part; the first two acts have been often ascribed to George Wilkins. It was first performed *c.* 1608, published in Quarto (Q1) in 1609 but not included in the First Folio of 1623. Based on GOWER's *CONFESSIO AMANTIS* and using Gower himself as Chorus, it followed the contemporary fashion for extravagant adventure and pictorial staging. Critics often group it with *CYMBELINE*, *THE WINTER'S TALE* and *THE TEMPEST*.

After guessing King Antiochus' incestuous relationship with his daughter, Pericles leaves Tyre for Pentapolis, where he marries the king's daughter, Thaisa. On the return voyage Thaisa gives birth to a daughter, Marina, and then apparently dies, her body being cast adrift in a chest. Pericles entrusts Marina to the care of Cleon, governor of Tarsus. When she grows up her beauty arouses the jealousy of Cleon's wife Dionyza. A plan to kill her fails but she is kidnapped by pirates and sold to a brothel in Mytilene, where she attracts the love of Lysimachus, the governor. He accidentally brings about Marina's reunion with Pericles, who had been led to think her dead. Impelled by a dream, Pericles sets sail for Ephesus and is there united with his long-lost wife, who has become a priestess of Diana.

Perkin Warbeck A tragedy by JOHN FORD, published in 1634. There is no record of its first production. It closely follows the historical facts of Warbeck's claim to be Richard, younger son of Edward IV and true heir to the throne occupied by Henry VII. Warbeck marries Lady Katherine Gordon at the court of James IV of Scotland, who leads an unsuccessful expedition to England. Warbeck lands in Cornwall, fails to gain support, and is captured and executed. The love and loyalty of Lady Katherine are movingly portrayed.

Persuasion JANE AUSTEN's last completed novel, published in 1818. Though written when her health was rapidly failing, it shows no loss of power: the social comedy is deftly handled and the overriding tone is one of serious and profound reflection.

The snobbish Sir Walter Elliot of Kellynch Hall has three daughters: the haughty, unmarried Elizabeth; Mary, married to Charles Musgrove, the local squire's son; and the admirable but neglected Anne. When Sir Walter is forced to let Kellynch to Admiral and Mrs Croft, Anne again meets Captain Frederick Wentworth, Mrs Croft's brother, whose proposal she had refused eight years before on the advice of her godmother, Lady Russell. Anne, who still loves Wentworth, is at once disappointed and relieved when he appears to care for her no longer. Wentworth soon becomes a favourite with the Musgrove family, particularly Charles's two high-spirited sisters, Louisa and Henrietta. Anne's suspicion that he is attracted to Louisa seems to be confirmed by his concern when she suffers an accident during a jaunt to Lyme Regis. In Bath, where her father and sister have settled, Anne is courted by William Elliot, her cousin and father's heir, but discovers his scheming nature. Unexpected news arrives of Louisa Musgrove's engagement to Captain Benwick, and soon afterward Wentworth appears, anxious to renew his addresses to Anne but uncertain of his reception. He is finally emboldened to make a declaration and the couple are at last united.

Peter Grimes See BOROUGH, THE.

Peter Pan: or, The Boy Who Would Not Grow Up A play for children by BARRIE, first produced in 1904. Part PANTOMIME, it is now established as an annual Christmas favourite. Peter Pan returns to the Darlings' Bloomsbury flat to fetch his shadow, which he lost when the dog scared him away on a previous visit. After Wendy Darling has sewn the shadow back on, he teaches the three Darling children to fly. They accompany him to the Never Land, where he lives with all the lost boys, protected by a tribe of Red Indians. A pirate gang led by Captain Hook overcomes the Red Indians while Peter is away, and Wendy, who has become mother to the lost boys, is captured along with all her 'family'. Peter arrives just in time to prevent Hook from making them walk the plank, defeats the pirate in a duel and sees him eaten by the crocodile which has stalked him for years. He takes Wendy and her brothers home and declines Mrs Darling's offer to adopt him. She promises to let Wendy return to the Never Land each year to do the spring cleaning.

Peters, Lenrie 1932– Gambian poet and novelist. One of the calmest and least doctrinal voices in contemporary African literature, he has urged the need for a pan-African outlook. His verse, seldom reliant on oral tradition and easily accessible to non-African readers, has appeared in *Poems* (1964), *Satellites* (1967), *Katchikali* (1971) and *Selected Poetry* (1981). His novel, *The Second Round* (1965), portrays the predicament of a young doctor returning to Sierra Leone.

Petrarchan After Petrarch, the anglicization of the surname of Francesco Petrarca (1304–74), a scholar and poet of the Italian Renaissance chiefly remembered for his collection of lyric poems and sonnets, *Rime sparse* (or *Canzoniere*). The term is sometimes used for the style of his poetry, particularly its use of antithesis, paradox, OXYMORON and the CONCEIT. More usually it distinguishes what might be regarded as the standard form of the SONNET from the Shakespearean sonnet.

Petrie, George 1790–1866 Irish antiquarian, musicologist and scholar. A pioneering contributor to the scholarly aspect of the CELTIC REVIVAL, he is best remembered for his continuation of EDWARD BUNTING's work preserving traditional music in *The Petrie Collection of the Ancient Music of Ireland* (1855–82).

Pettie, George 1548–89 Influenced by both the popularity and the name of PAINTER's *Palace of Pleasure* (1566), he issued *A Petite Palace of Pettie His Pleasure*, licensed in 1576 and published soon after, although the first edition is not dated. It consists of 12 stories, including those of Alcestis, Tereus and Pygmalion. Pettie also translated Guazzo from a French version as *Civil*

Conversation (1581). His prose style anticipates EUPHUISM.

Peveril of the Peak A novel by SIR WALTER SCOTT, first published in 1823. Its background is religious strife in the reign of Charles II. The Royalist Sir Geoffrey Peveril and the Puritan Major Bridgenorth, two neighbouring Derbyshire gentlemen who have managed to live through the Civil War as friends, quarrel when their children, Julian Peveril and Alice Bridgenorth, fall in love.

Peyton [née Herald], **K(athleen) M.** [Wendy], 1929– Writer of CHILDREN'S LITERATURE. Pony or adventure books were followed by *Windfall* (1963), a tale of danger at sea reminiscent of ARTHUR RANSOME. Other successes culminated in *Flambards* (1967), the first of a trilogy about a decayed Edwardian landed family, and another trilogy about a brilliant but disturbed school-boy musician first encountered in *Pennington's Seventeenth Summer* (1970). She has also produced a ghost story, *A Pattern of Roses* (1973), and stories about humanized animals, including *Plain Jack* (1988).

Phalaris controversy See TEMPLE, SIR WILLIAM.

Philaster: or, Love Lies A-Bleeding A tragicomedy by BEAUMONT and FLETCHER, performed c. 1609 and published in 1620. It has often been compared with SHAKESPEARE's *CYMBELINE*. Philaster, dispossessed heir to the throne of Sicily, lives at the court of the usurping King of Calabria. To further his love-affair with Arethusa, the King's daughter, he places his page, Bellario, in her service. A marriage is arranged between Arethusa and the Spanish prince, Pharamond, but she prevents it by revealing that he has been amusing himself with Megra. Pharamond accuses Arethusa of misconduct with Bellario. Philaster believes the story and becomes distracted, but is saved by the loyalty of Arethusa and Bellario, who is finally revealed as a nobleman's daughter who had disguised herself out of love for him. The usurper is overthrown and Philaster restored to his inheritance.

Philip, The Adventures of A novel by THACKERAY, serialized in THE CORNHILL MAGAZINE in 1861–2 and published in book form in 1862. Narrated by Arthur Pendennis, it completes the trio of interconnected and semi-autobiographical novels begun with THE HISTORY OF PENDENNIS and THE NEWCOMES.

Philip Firmin is the son of Dr Brand Firmin, the 'Brandon' of *A SHABBY GENTEEL STORY*, who has since married a wealthy woman, Lord Ringwood's niece. Her death leaves Philip rich and his independent spirit wins Lord Ringwood's approval. He suspects his father's shady past and discovers that he is being blackmailed by Tufton Hunt, the dissolute clergyman who officiated at the sham wedding between Brandon and Caroline Gann in the earlier story. Dr Firmin loses Philip's fortune by speculation and flees to America. The rest of the novel deals with Philip's rejection by his cousin Agnes Twysden in favour of a wealthy suitor, his marriage to Charlotte Baynes, his early career as a journalist, and the kindness shown him by Arthur and Laura Pendennis, as well as Caroline. The discovery of Lord Ringwood's will restores him to prosperity.

Philips, Ambrose c. 1675–1749 Poet. His chief claim to fame is the contempt he earned after his *Pastorals* appeared in TONSON's *Miscellany* of 1709 beside the undoubtedly superior examples by POPE. Pope elegantly demolished Philips's poetic reputation in THE GUARDIAN and a 'pastoral war' in print ensued, with

GAY parodying Philips in *THE SHEPHERD'S WEEK*. Philips's verses for children were praised by SAMUEL JOHNSON but earned him the nickname 'Namby-Pamby' from HENRY CAREY.

Philips, John 1676–1709 Poet. He is remembered for writing BLANK VERSE when the couplet was fashionable. *The Splendid Shilling* (1701), in BURLESQUE Miltonic verse, contrasts the well-being of the man who possesses a shilling with the privation of being a poet. A Tory, Philips was persuaded by ROBERT HARLEY and BOLINGBROKE to write *Blenheim* (1705) in answer to ADDISON's *The Campaign* (1704). It was not a success but *Cider: A Poem in Two Books* (1708) is a notable performance in the manner of Virgil's *Georgics*.

Philips, Katherine See FOWLER, KATHERINE.

Phillips, John 1631–1706 Poet, journalist and translator. Although educated by his uncle, MILTON, he produced one of the most extreme anti-Puritan poems of any literary quality, *The Satire against Hypocrites* (1655). He also wrote BURLESQUES, edited a periodical and translated *Pharamond* (by La Calprenède) and *Almahide* (by Madeleine de Scudéry).

Phillips, Stephen 1864–1915 Playwright and poet. The success of *Poems* (1898) created a short-lived vogue for his sonorous poetic dramas, *Herod* (1900), *Ulysses* (1902), *Nero* (1906), *Faust* (1908) and *Paolo and Francesca* (1902). *Iole* (1913) and *The Sin of David* (1914) failed and he died destitute.

Phillpotts, Eden 1862–1960 Novelist and playwright. He wrote well over 200 books, the best of them novels about Dartmoor like *Children in the Mist* (1898), *The Secret Woman* (1905), *The Thief of Virtue* (1910) and *Widecombe Fair* (1913). He collaborated with his daughter Adelaide on two successful comedies, *The Farmer's Wife* (1924) and *Yellow Sands* (1926), as well as on several shorter pieces.

Philotus An anonymous play written *c.* 1600 and printed at Edinburgh in 1603, the only complete survival of early Scottish drama apart from LYNDSAY's *SATIRE OF THE THREE ESTATES*. It deals with the failed attempt by two old men, Philotus and Alberto, to marry the young Emilie and Brisilla.

Phineas Finn: The Irish Member A novel by TROLLOPE, serialized in 1867–9 and published in volume form in 1869. The second of his PALLISER NOVELS, and the first to deal with Parliament itself, it follows the fortunes of the charming Irish barrister and MP, Phineas Finn. Despite his commitment to Mary Jones, he wins the love of Lady Laura Standish, who continues to help his career after marrying Robert Kennedy. Phineas's interest in Violet Effingham provokes a duel with Lord Chiltern, though the two men are reconciled and Violet marries Chiltern. The background to these intrigues is the new reform bill which the Liberals are trying to steer through Parliament. Phineas is forced to resign his post as junior minister when he supports Irish tenant rights. He refuses the hand and fortune of the widowed Madame Max Goesler, the Duke of Omnium's companion, and returns to Ireland, where he marries Mary Jones and becomes Inspector of the Cork Poor Houses. The novel is thought to portray aspects of DISRAELI in Mr Daubeny and of Gladstone in Mr Gresham.

Phineas Redux The fourth of TROLLOPE's PALLISER NOVELS, serialized in 1873–4 and published in volume form in 1873. Now widowed, Phineas Finn re-enters Parliament. His attempt to mediate between Lady Laura Kennedy and her increasingly insane husband aggravates matters and is publicized in its worst light by his old enemy Quintus Slide, a radical journalist. More scandal ensues when Phineas quarrels publicly with a cabinet minister, Mr Bonteen, who is afterwards murdered. Phineas is arrested and brought to trial but acquitted with the help of his lawyer, Chaffanbrass, and Madame Max Goesler. Suspicion falls on Mr Emilius, Lady Eustace's estranged husband, who escapes prosecution through lack of evidence. Disillusioned with public life, Phineas refuses a government post and finally marries Madame Max. The death of the old Duke of Omnium enables Plantagenet Palliser's cousin Adelaide to marry her penniless suitor Gerard Maule. The novel's pessimism is balanced by the rise of Plantagenet Palliser, the new Duke of Omnium, as Trollope's ideal statesman.

Phiz See BROWNE, HABLOT K.

Phoenix, The An Old English poem preserved in the EXETER BOOK. Its account of the phoenix myth is loosely based on Pliny and *De Ave Phoenice*, a poem attributed to Lactantius, but it goes beyond these sources in making the bird a symbol of Christ and the Christian life.

Phoenix and the Turtle, The A 67-line poem by SHAKESPEARE which appeared, with verse by JONSON, CHAPMAN and MARSTON, as an occasional poem appended to Robert Chester's *Love's Martyr* (1601). Chester's poem tells ramblingly of the love of the phoenix and the turtledove. Shakespeare's enigmatic contribution is an ELEGY for the birds.

Phoenix Nest, The A poetic miscellany published in 1593. The contributors include LODGE, PEELE, BRETON, THOMAS WATSON and, perhaps, SIR WALTER RALEIGH. The phoenix of the title is clearly SIR PHILIP SIDNEY, whose death (1586) is lamented in several poems.

Physician's Tale, The See CANTERBURY TALES.

Piazza Tales, The A volume of six stories by HERMAN MELVILLE, published in 1856. It is introduced by 'The Piazza', Melville's descriptive recollection of his Massachusetts farmhouse, to which he added a piazza. The two most important stories are 'Benito Cereno' and 'Bartleby the Scrivener'. In the former, set in 1799, Amasa Delano encounters a Spanish ship apparently commanded by the enfeebled Benito Cereno but in fact controlled by his Senegalese valet Babo, who has led his fellow slaves in a mutiny. 'Bartleby the Scrivener' is about an enigmatic copyist whose response to any unwelcome request is 'I would prefer not to'. Other stories in the collection are: 'The Bell Tower', about an over-reaching artist named Bannadonna; 'The Lightning-Rod Man', about a man who refuses an insistent lightning-rod salesman because he believes that man should not fear acts of God; and 'The Encantadas: or, Enchanted Isles', about the Galapagos Islands.

picaresque A term derived from the Spanish *pícaro*, originally a low-life character who lived dishonestly by his wits but later anyone at odds with, or outside, society. The picaresque novel, an episodic narrative describing the progress of the *pícaro*, began with the anonymous *Lazarillo de Tormes* (1554) and Mateo Alemán's *Guzmán de Alfarache* (1559), translated into English by JAMES MABBE. In English literature the tradition begins with NASHE's *THE UNFORTUNATE TRAVELLER* (1594) and continues in the work of DEFOE (*MOLL FLANDERS*), FIELDING, SMOLLETT and DICKENS, forgetting its origin in the literature of roguery and usually becoming just an episodic story involving a journey. In America, the picaresque novel influenced TWAIN's *HUCKLEBERRY FINN* and many later works chronicling the adventures of the open road.

Pickwick Papers, The DICKENS's first novel, formally titled *The Posthumous Papers of the Pickwick Club*, published in monthly parts in 1836–7. It takes its loose, easy structure from the travels to Ipswich, Rochester, Bath and elsewhere of Samuel Pickwick and his fellow members of the Pickwick Club, Tracy Tupman, Augustus Snodgrass and Nathaniel Winkle. Mr Pickwick's innocent and trusting nature repeatedly makes him the butt of comic adventures. In the book's most prolonged episode he gives his landlady Mrs Bardell the impression that he wishes to marry her, and so provokes a suit for breach of promise. Interspersed among these adventures are moral and melodramatic stories – 'The Bagman's Story', 'The Convict's Return', 'The Stroller's Tale' and others – which counterbalance the prevailing comedy of the book. Most memorable among the wide variety of characters are: Sam Weller, Pickwick's sharp-witted Cockney servant, and his coachman father Tony; the glib strolling player Alfred Jingle and his rascally servant Job Trotter; the medical student Bob Sawyer; and the good-natured Wardles. The rapacious Dodson and Fogg, the pompous Serjeant Buzfuz and others connected with Mrs Bardell's lawsuit hint – like Pickwick's own experiences in prison near the end of the novel – at the darker vision Dickens's later work would explore.

Picture of Dorian Gray, The A novel by OSCAR WILDE, published in 1890. Once regarded as daringly modern in its portrayal of *fin-de-siècle* decadence, it draws on traditional motifs to create a powerful GOTHIC NOVEL. Dorian sells his soul to keep his youth and beauty. His tempter is the amoral Lord Henry Wotton and his good angel, or conscience, is the portrait painter Basil Hallward, whom he murders. The story highlights the tension between the polished surface and the secret vices of high life.

Pictures from Italy A book by DICKENS, published in 1845. It is based on his travels in 1844–5, when he had stayed in Genoa and visited Rome, Pisa, Ferrara, Parma, Florence, Bologna and Venice, getting as far south as Pompeii, Paestum and Naples. His experience with AMERICAN NOTES may have taught him to deal discreetly with national customs and habits, but *Pictures from Italy* also shows a genuine warmth and friendliness toward its subject absent from the earlier book. Local fiestas, gambling, bowls, puppetry, shops, food and wine-drinking are described in compelling detail. Little is remarked about art or religion, although the activities of Holy Week are drily observed.

picturesque The term for an ideal of beauty which flourished during the 18th and early 19th centuries, principally in relation to landscape and gardens and the depiction of these scenes in painting and literature. It departed from NEOCLASSICISM in cultivating the irregular, disordered or decayed but stopped short of ROMANTICISM by admiring these effects in a spirit of judicious connoisseurship (or taste) rather than exalted feeling. Its chief manifestations were a tradition of landscape gardening which stretched from William Kent (1685–1748) to Humphry Repton (1752–1818) and beyond; an increased interest by travellers in the scenery of Wales, the Wye Valley and the Lake District and in Gothic ruins; and the popularity of paintings by Gaspard Poussin (1615–75), Claude (Claude Lorrain, 1600–82) and Salvator Rosa (1615–73). Writers on the picturesque include: WILLIAM MASON in his poem *The English Garden* (1771–81); THOMAS GRAY in his travel journal (published 1775); Richard Payne Knight (1750–1824)

in *The Landscape: A Didactic Poem* (1794) and his *Analytical Enquiry into the Principles of Taste* (1805); Sir Uvedale Price (1747–1829) in his *Essay on the Picturesque* (1794); and GILPIN, probably the most influential theorist, in his *Three Essays* and various travel books. Picturesque feeling imbues landscape description in novels by RADCLIFFE and SIR WALTER SCOTT, though JANE AUSTEN and PEACOCK adopted a sceptical attitude and the cult was satirized by WILLIAM COMBE.

Pied Piper of Hamelin, The A poem for children by ROBERT BROWNING, published in *Dramatic Lyrics* (1842). The story of the piper whose music lures away first the rats and then the children of Hamelin is based on what was apparently a common legend of the Middle Ages, though Browning encountered it in NATHANIEL WANLEY's *The Wonders of the Little World* (1678).

Pierce Penniless His Supplication to the Devil A pamphlet by NASHE, printed in 1592. Prevented by society from using his talents, Pierce asks the Devil for a loan. The SATIRE attacks foreigners, Nashe's enemy Richard Harvey, and the Puritans for the MARPRELATE tracts and their criticism of the theatre.

Pierce the Ploughman's Crede A poem (*c.* 1394) imitating LANGLAND's *PIERS PLOWMAN*. The narrator questions friars of various orders but finds only corruption and abuse of other orders. Eventually he meets the poor ploughman Pierce, who offers him comfort, exposes the sins of the friars and teaches him his Creed.

Piercy, Marge 1937– American novelist and poet. Most of her work deals with women's assigned place in a male-dominated society. *Woman on the Edge of Time* (1976) is a dystopian feminist fantasy. Other novels include *Going Down Fast* (1969), *Dance the Eagle to Sleep* (1970), *Small Changes* (1973), *Vida* (1979), *Braided Lives* (1982), *Fly Away Home* (1984), *Gone to Soldiers* (1987) and *Body of Glass* (1992). Her poetry includes *Breaking Camp* (1968), *Hard Loving* (1969), *4-Telling* (1971), *To be of Use* (1973), *Living in the Open* (1976), *The Twelve-Spoked Wheel Flashing* (1978), *The Moon is Always Female* (1980), *Circles on the Water: Selected Poems* (1982) and *Stone, Paper, Knife* (1983).

Pierre: or, The Ambiguities A novel by HERMAN MELVILLE, published in 1852. Pierre Glendinning, the son of a wealthy widow in upstate New York, abandons his fiancée, Lucy Tartan, for Isabel, who claims to be his illegitimate half-sister. At first he believes his motive is merely protective, though he allows the world to think he has married her. Later he is forced to realize his true feelings. Pierre kills his cousin, Glen, in a violent confrontation and is arrested. Lucy and his mother die of grief. Torn by conflicting emotions about their forbidden love, Pierre and Isabel commit suicide in his prison cell.

Piers Plowman A religious poem in ALLITERATIVE VERSE by WILLIAM LANGLAND, written during the second half of the 14th century. It survives in three versions, known as the A-, B- and C-texts, representing different stages of revision almost certainly carried out by Langland himself. The A-text, 2500 lines long, dates from the 1360s and was probably complete by 1369–70. The B-text, referring to events of 1376–9, trebles the poem's length. The C-text was complete in time for USK (d. 1388) to borrow from it in his *Testament of Love*. The same length as the B-text, it seems intended to elucidate the earlier version and incorporate subsequent events; the result is not always superior. The B-text is the version most commonly read.

Although basically a DREAM-VISION, *Piers Plowman* moves in and out of dream-experience, just as it makes a complex, shifting and unconventional use of ALLEGORY. Its concern with religious and theological abstractions does not prevent it rendering details of contemporary life. The *Visio*, the first of its two parts, reveals the corrupt state of government and the established Church, and attempts to remedy it by creating an ideal society. When this fails, the *Visio* initiates a search for Truth – Charity and the means to salvation – which provides the impetus for the rest of the poem. The *Vita*, the poem's second part, explores the reasons for the failure in the *Visio* by intellectual enquiry. Allegorical narrative is largely replaced by interviews with personified abstractions: Wit, Thought, Conscience, Study, Clergy and Reason. The Dreamer's search for Dowel, Dobet and Dobest, the stages of Christian life and understanding, is beset with problems. At one stage he disappears, to be replaced by Rechelesnesse, representing his temporary abandonment of the quest in favour of worldliness. The Dreamer returns to continue his search through more interviews and a vision of the history of Christianity, the progress of which must be echoed in the individual's spiritual growth. The Devil's undermining of man's attempts is revealed and the consequent need for divine grace stressed. After a vision of the Crucifixion and the Harrowing of Hell the Dreamer sees the establishment of the Church and returns to its state of decay in the 14th century with an ultimate realization that the search must begin again.

The figure of Piers Plowman is part of the shifting allegorical fabric of the poem. He first appears as a humble servant of God who organizes an ideal society in the episode of the Ploughing of the Half Acre. He then leads his followers in the search for Truth, but disappears after the reading of an enigmatic pardon from Truth (which states only that those who live well shall be saved) and is absent from the first stages of the Dreamer's search for the meaning of living well. He reappears towards the end of the *Vita* as the Good Samaritan and as the incarnated form of Christ.

Pilgrim's Progress, The: *From this World to That Which is to Come* A religious ALLEGORY by BUNYAN, in two parts (1678 and 1684).

Presented as the author's dream, Part I recounts Bunyan's own experience of conversion in figurative terms. He sees Christian with a book in his hand and a burden on his back, in great distress because the book tells him he lives in the City of Destruction and will suffer death and judgement. Leaving behind his wife and children, Christian follows Evangelist's advice to flee towards a Wicket Gate. His pilgrimage takes him through the Slough of Despond, past the Burning Mount, thence to the Wicket Gate, the Interpreter's House, the Cross (where his burden rolls away), the Hill Difficulty, the House Beautiful, the Valley of Humiliation, the Valley of the Shadow of Death, Vanity Fair, Lucre Hill, the River of the Water of Life, By-Path Meadow, Doubting Castle, the Delectable Mountains, the Enchanted Ground and the country of Beulah, until he finally passes over the River into the Celestial City. On the way he is helped by Faithful, who is put to death in Vanity Fair, and then Hopeful, who accompanies him into the Celestial City. They encounter enemies (the fiend Apollyon, Lord Hategood and Giant Despair) and unreliable friends (Mr Worldly Wise-man, Ignorance, Talkative and By-ends).

The greater number and variety of pilgrims in Part II make it more like a social novel. Christian's wife Christiana follows him, with her children and their neighbour Mercy. Great-heart, who joins them at the Interpreter's House, slays Giant Despair and various other giants and monsters. Fellow pilgrims include Mr Feeble-mind, Mr Ready-to-halt, Mr Honest, Valiant-for-truth, Mr Stand-fast, Mr Despondency and his daughter Much-afraid. At the end they pass over the River.

From the moment of its publication Bunyan's allegory has appealed to an extraordinarily wide readership. It has appeared in innumerable editions and been translated into well over 100 languages. The book's popularity owes much to the beauty and simplicity of Bunyan's prose, the vividness of his allegorical characters, and the deftness with which he renders colloquial speech. Though allegorical in form, the work is also profoundly realistic, particularly in its portrayal of the pilgrims striving to hold to their beliefs in a hostile and uncomprehending world.

Pindar, Peter [Wolcot, John] 1738–1819 Satirist. *Lyric Odes to the Royal Academicians* (1782–5) attacked the established painters of the day. *The Lousiad* (1785–95), a MOCK-HEROIC poem, took the Royal Family as its target and *Ode upon Ode* (1787) the yearly official ODES to the king. *Bozzy and Piozzi* (1786) satirized SAMUEL JOHNSON's friends BOSWELL and Mrs Thrale. Pindar elsewhere turned his attention to JAMES BRUCE, William Pitt and EDMUND BURKE. His verse was collected in 1812.

Pindaric ode See ODE.

Pinero, Sir Arthur Wing 1855–1934 Playwright. He led his age in two distinct fields, FARCE and the PROBLEM PLAY. *The Magistrate* (1885), *The Schoolmistress* (1886) and *Dandy Dick* (1887) are among the finest of English farces. *Sweet Lavender* (1888) is a comedy, while *The Profligate* (1889) and *The Cabinet Minister* (1890) paved the way for social dramas highlighting the plight of women in an unforgiving world. They include THE SECOND MRS TANQUERAY (1893), *The Notorious Mrs Ebbsmith* (1895), *The Benefit of the Doubt* (1895), *Iris* (1901), *Letty* (1903), *His House in Order* (1906), *The Thunderbolt* (1908) and *Mid-Channel* (1909). A readiness to examine, if not quite to challenge, convention also distinguishes two effective comedies, *The Princess and the Butterfly* (1897) and *The Gay Lord Quex* (1899). Pinero's best comedy, TRELAWNY OF THE 'WELLS' (1898), is a nostalgic celebration of the mid-Victorian theatre.

Pinter, Harold 1930– Playwright. Although influenced by BECKETT and associated with him in the THEATRE OF THE ABSURD, he is better appreciated as the inventor of a new kind of comedy, sometimes called the 'comedy of menace'. His plays include *The Room* (1957), THE BIRTHDAY PARTY (1957), *The Dumb Waiter* (1960), THE CARETAKER (1960), *A Slight Ache* (1961), *The Collection* (1962), *The Dwarfs* (1963), *The Lover* (1963) and THE HOMECOMING (1965), perhaps his most enigmatic play, which began a long association with Sir Peter Hall, continued in *No Man's Land* (1975), *Betrayal* (1978) and *A Kind of Alaska* (1982). *One for the Road* (1984), *Mountain Language* (1988) and *Party Time* (1991) mark a renewed political urgency.

Pioneers, The See LEATHERSTOCKING TALES, THE.

Pippa Passes A dramatic poem by ROBERT BROWNING, published in 1841. Pippa is a silk winder who spends her holiday wandering through Asolo, singing songs and thinking of the local people she considers the most blessed: Ottima, Phene, Luigi and the Bishop. In reality, they are entirely different from her innocent imaginings.

Pirate, The A novel by SIR WALTER SCOTT, published in 1822. It is set in the 17th century in a remote part of Zetland (Shetland), where the shipwreck of the buccaneer, Cleveland, disrupts the life of Mordaunt and his relations with Minna and Brenda, daughters of the wealthy Magnus Troil. Mordaunt finally foils Cleveland's attempt to capture Magnus and his daughters, and marries Brenda.

Pistil of Swete Susan, The See SUSANNA: OR, THE PISTIL OF SWETE SUSAN.

Pit, The: A Story of Chicago The second volume of FRANK NORRIS's uncompleted trilogy The Epic of the Wheat, posthumously published in 1903. The first volume is THE OCTOPUS (1901); the third volume was never written.

The pit is the Chicago stock exchange, where Curtis Jadwin speculates successfully in the wheat market and is driven almost to madness by his obsession with money. His material success is paralleled by the decline of his marriage to Laura Dearborn, who resumes an old relationship with the aesthete Sheldon Corthell. She returns to Jadwin at the end, after a glut in the market has destroyed his fortune.

Plaatje, Solomon Tshekisho 1877–1932 South African politician and writer. Newspaper editor and first Secretary of the African National Congress (1912), he attacked the 1913 Natives Land Act for turning blacks into pariahs in Native Life in South Africa (1916). Mhudi, written about 1917 but published in 1930, was the first novel to present pre-colonial African society sympathetically. Plaatje's Boer War Diary was discovered and published in 1972.

Plain Dealer, The A RESTORATION COMEDY by WYCHERLEY, derived from Molière's Le Misanthrope, produced in 1676 and published in 1677. The most mordant of his plays, it is also often regarded as his finest. The plain dealer is the misanthropic Manly, a sea-captain who believes that only his betrothed Olivia and his friend Vernish are sincere. He returns from the Dutch wars to find that Olivia has married another and will not return the money he left with her. In his scheme to revenge himself and dishonour her, he uses his page Fidelia as go-between, unaware that Fidelia is really a girl who follows him in disguise out of love. Olivia makes an assignation with Fidelia. Manly attends as well, and Olivia's husband, none other than Vernish, arrives unexpectedly. Fidelia is wounded in the resulting scuffle and her identity revealed. Touched by her devotion, Manly abandons his obsession with Olivia.

Planché, James Robinson 1796–1880 Playwright, musician, historian of costume, herald and antiquarian. He wrote well over 150 plays and libretti, the best known being The Vampyre: or, The Bride of the Isles (1820). His crucial role in the development of the English PANTOMIME is widely recognized.

Plater, Alan (Frederick) 1935– Playwright. He is best known for his long career of writing for television, which has ranged from scripts for Z Cars and Softly, Softly to adaptations of TROLLOPE and of MANNING's Balkan Trilogy and Levant Trilogy (as Fortunes of War). He has also adapted several of his own TV plays for the stage, though his true vitality emerges best in regional 'epics', like Close the Coalhouse Door (1968), combining songs, music-hall sketches and gags with serious social themes.

Plath, Sylvia 1932–63 American poet. Her short life and early death by suicide continue to fascinate biographers and generate controversy. Born in Boston, and educated at Smith College and Cambridge, she married TED HUGHES in 1957. The Colossus and Other Poems (Britain, 1960; USA, 1962) was the only volume of poetry published during her lifetime. Posthumous volumes include Ariel (1965), Crossing the Water (Britain, 1971; USA, 1972) and Winter Trees (Britain, 1971; USA, 1972). Though her work has clear affinities with CONFESSIONAL POETRY, she often distances herself from her personal subject matter by IRONY. The Bell Jar (Britain, 1963; USA, 1971) is a partly autobiographical novel. Her prose is collected in Johnny Panic and the Bible of Dreams: Short Stories, Prose, and Diary Excerpts (1979). The Journals of Sylvia Plath appeared in 1982.

Playboy of the Western World, The A comedy by SYNGE, produced at the ABBEY THEATRE, Dublin, in 1907, when it prompted a riot. Christy Mahon arrives at a village near the coast of County Mayo, confessing himself a fugitive because he has killed his tyrannical father. Overwhelmed by his boldness, the villagers lionize him. He wins a mule race and is rewarded with a promise of marriage to Pegeen Mike, daughter of the owner of the local shebeen. His triumph is cut short when his father arrives, bandaged but not dead, to reclaim him. For the second time Christy 'kills' his father and for the second time old Mahon rises from the dead. Christy eventually goes with him, but no longer into servitude. Pegeen grieves over his departure.

Plomer, William (Charles Franklyn) 1903–73 Poet and novelist. Born in South Africa, he founded the magazine Voorslag with ROY CAMPBELL in 1926. His first novel, Turbott Wolfe (1926), treats racism. After travelling widely, Plomer settled in England. The poems in Notes for Poems (1927), The Family Tree (1929), The Fivefold Screen (1932), Visiting the Caves (1936), The Dorking Thigh (1945), Collected Poems (1960) and Celebrations (1972) are divided between serious work ('The Taste of the Fruit') and SATIRE. Besides editing KILVERT's diaries (1938–40) and HERMAN MELVILLE's poems, Plomer collaborated with Benjamin Britten as librettist for Gloriana (1953) and his three 'church operas'.

Plough and the Stars, The A play by O'CASEY, produced at Dublin's ABBEY THEATRE in 1926, when its blunt treatment of the Easter Rising of 1916 caused a riot. The occupants of a Dublin tenement make up a cross-section of Irish social and political attitudes. Jack Clitheroe belongs to the Irish Citizen Army. His wife Nora is concerned only for his safety. Her uncle, Peter Flynn, supports independence from a safe distance. Jack's cousin, Covey, merely hopes for social revolution and Fluther Good merely talks a lot. Mrs Gogan is ghoulishly fascinated by death. Bessie Burgess, finest of them all, is a fruit-vendor with a son in the British army. Jack is killed in the Rising and Bessie is shot by a sniper. Fluther, Covey and others become looters.

Plowman's Tale, The: or, The Complaint of the Plowman An early 15th-century poem in ALLITERATIVE VERSE, probably written by one, or perhaps two, LOLLARD sympathizers. A prologue added in the 16th century claimed it as an addition to THE CANTERBURY TALES, assuring its inclusion in the CHAUCERIAN APOCRYPHA. A debate between a pelican and a griffin, it supports Lollard ideals against the Church.

Plumed Serpent, The A novel by D. H. LAWRENCE, published in 1926. Kate Leslie, an Irish widow, visits Mexico in search of some quality that will renew her life. She meets General Don Cipriano Viedma, a pure-bred Indian, and Don Ramón Carrasco, scholar and political leader, whose mission is to revive the old cult of Quetzalcoatl, the plumed serpent. Attracted by Don Cipriano's sexual energy and the cult's violent, elemental power, she takes on the role of Malintzi, a fertility goddess and bride of Cipriano, now elevated by Don Ramón to the status of war god, Huitzilopochtli.

Plumptre, Anne 1760–1818 Translator, novelist and traveller. Her novels were largely unnoticed and her most ambitious translations, from the German playwright Kotzebue in the 1790s, overshadowed by the work of INCHBALD and SHERIDAN. She attracted more attention with two travel books: *Narrative of Three Years' Residence in France* (1810), based on a trip begun in the company of AMELIA OPIE, and *Narrative of a Residence in Ireland* (1817). The former is remembered for its defence of Napoleon, though it also contains sharp and independent-minded comments on fellow radicals. *Tales of Wonder, of Honour and of Sentiment* (1818) is a moralistic work for children written jointly with her sister Annabella. JAMES PLUMPTRE was her brother.

Plumptre, James 1771–1832 Playwright, critic, editor and traveller. Of several plays he wrote in youth the most notable are two comedies, *The Coventry Act* (produced and published in 1793) and *The Lakers* (unproduced but published in 1798), a genial SATIRE of PICTURESQUE tourism. His Evangelical bias in later years prompted him to produced censored editions, in the manner of BOWDLER, of popular airs in a *Collection of Songs* (1805) and English stage classics in *The English Drama Purified* (1812). Unlike many Evangelicals, he still believed that the drama could be purified, a case he argued in a steady stream of pamphlets and attempted to illustrate in *Original Dramas* (1816). None of these achievements was as significant as the journals in which he recorded his tours, usually walking tours, round England, Wales and Scotland between 1790 and 1800. A selection has been published as *James Plumptre's Britain: The Journals of a Tourist in the 1790s* (1992). ANNE PLUMPTRE was his sister.

Poe, Edgar Allan 1809–49 American poet, short-story writer, writer of DETECTIVE FICTION and critic. Born in Boston, he spent an apparently unhappy childhood with the foster-father from whom he took his middle name. Several years in England (1815–20) were followed by unsuccessful spells at university and in the army. His career in journalism shuttled him backwards and forwards between Richmond in Virginia, Philadelphia and New York, though he never ceased to regard himself as a Southerner. His child-bride, Virginia Clemm, whom he married in 1836, died an early death in 1847. Poe himself died at Baltimore in squalid and partly unexplained circumstances.

In the course of this makeshift and itinerant life, increasingly complicated by poverty, nervous disorder and alcoholism, he still managed to produce a steady stream of writing. The title work of *The Raven and Other Poems* (1845), his chief popular success as a poet, prompted him to write 'The Philosophy of Composition' (1846), which – together with his lecture, 'The Poetic Principle' (posthumously published, 1850) – constitutes his chief aesthetic statement. The emphasis on calculated craftsmanship and intensity of effect is reflected in the stories partly collected in *Tales of the Grotesque and Arabesque* (1840) and *Tales* (1845). Leading titles include

'Ligeia', 'The Fall of the House of Usher', 'William Wilson', 'The Masque of the Red Death', 'The Pit and the Pendulum', 'The Tell-Tale Heart', 'The Black Cat', and 'The Cask of Amontillado'. Three stories, 'The Murders in the Rue Morgue', 'The Purloined Letter' and 'The Mystery of Marie Roget', had a decisive influence on the development of the detective story. All his work begins by borrowing the conventions, and usually the European settings, of GOTHIC FICTION but creates its own distinctive milieu of private horror, psychological rather than physical, observed with clinical, even grimly humorous detachment. His only novel, *The Narrative of Arthur Gordon Pym* (1838), belongs to the same world as the stories, while an ambitious treatise, *Eureka* (1848), attempts to explore its philosophical implications.

Poems of the Past and Present A volume by HARDY, published in 1902. 'War Poems', about the Boer War, includes the finely wrought 'Drummer Hodge'. 'Poems of Pilgrimage' evokes literary and historical memories of SHELLEY and GIBBON, Rome, Genoa and Fiesole. 'Miscellaneous Poems' includes 'To an Unborn Pauper Child', 'Lizbie Brown', 'The Darkling Thrush', 'The Ruined Maid', 'In Tenebris' (I–III) and 'The Lost Pyx'.

Poet Laureate Originally a title given generally to British poets in recognition of their achievement, it became in later times an official post awarded to a poet who received a stipend as an officer of the Royal Household. The formal duty of writing occasional verses and appropriate odes for public occasions is no longer demanded, and the title is largely honorific. The stipend, similarly, is nominal. JONSON and D'AVENANT first performed the duties of Poet Laureate, though the post was first bestowed officially on DRYDEN, who was followed by SHADWELL, TATE, ROWE, EUSDEN, CIBBER, WHITEHEAD, THOMAS WARTON THE YOUNGER, PYE, SOUTHEY, WORDSWORTH, TENNYSON, AUSTIN, BRIDGES, MASEFIELD, DAY-LEWIS, BETJEMAN and TED HUGHES.

In 1915 California became the first of many states in the US to appoint writers of local reputation as poets laureate. The post of national laureate (formally Poet Laureate Consultant to the Library of Congress), created in 1986, has been held by ROBERT PENN WARREN, RICHARD WILBUR, HOWARD NEMEROV, MARK STRAND, JOSEPH BRODSKY, Rita Dove and Mona Van Duyn.

Poetaster, The: *or, The Arraignment* A comedy by JONSON, produced in 1601 and published in 1602. The thin storyline, set at the court of the Emperor Augustus, concerns the efforts of Crispinus (MARSTON) and Demetrius (DEKKER) to defame Horace (Jonson). Dekker, perhaps helped by Marston, replied with SATIROMASTIX.

Poetical Rhapsody, A A collection of Elizabethan verse (1602), including 'The Lie', attributed to RALEIGH, and poems by SIR PHILIP SIDNEY, SPENSER, DONNE, GREENE, WOTTON and THOMAS WATSON.

Poetry: *A Magazine of Verse* An American monthly journal, founded in 1912 by HARRIET MONROE, who edited it until her death in 1936. Since the days when she published early work by EZRA POUND and T. S. ELIOT, most major American 20th-century poets and many foreign poets have appeared in its pages.

Poetry Bookshop See MONRO, HAROLD.

Pohl, Frederik 1919– American writer of SCIENCE FICTION. *The Space Merchants* (1953), one of several novels he wrote with C. M. Kornbluth, is a prophetic SATIRE about advertising agencies. *The Singers of Time* (with Jack Williamson; 1991) is one of the few science-fiction novels to dramatize modern cosmological theories. His many solo novels include: *Man Plus* (1976), the 'Heechee' series begun with *Gateway* (1977), and *Chernobyl* (1987), a drama-documentary account. Notable collections of stories include *The Case against Tomorrow* (1957), *The Man Who Ate the World* (1960), *Day Million* (1970), *In the Problem Pit* (1976), *The Years of the City* (1984) and *The Day the Martians Came* (1988).

Pollock, Sharon 1936– Canadian playwright. *A Compulsory Option* (1972), a black comedy, was followed by a series of works which focus on political and social issues in both present and past: *Walsh* (1974), *Out You Go* (1975), *The Komagata Maru Incident* (1978) and *One Tiger to a Hill* (1980). Her best-known play, *Blood Relations* (1980), is about Lizzie Borden, the New England spinster charged with and acquitted of the axe murder of her parents in 1892. A tightly constructed family drama, it leaves the central question of the protagonist's guilt open while suggesting a revisionist feminist perspective. Pollock has also written *Generations* (1979), *Whiskey Six* (1983), *Doc* (1984) and a number of children's plays.

Polly A BALLAD OPERA by GAY, a sequel to *THE BEGGAR'S OPERA*. Walpole's government refused it a performing license in 1729 and it was eventually produced, in an adaptation by GEORGE COLMAN THE ELDER, in 1777. The plot follows Polly Peachum to the West Indies in search of the transported Macheath, where she unintentionally delivers him to justice on the scaffold.

Poly-Olbion An enormous poem by DRAYTON, running to some 30,000 lines, planned as early as 1598 and published as two parts in 1612 and 1622. Its 'Chorographical Description' (a description of a country or locality) embraces the landscapes, notable sights, ancient history and beliefs of England and Wales. The result is both a versified map and a vast storehouse of antiquarian information. Drayton's chief source was CAMDEN's *Britannia*.

Pomfret, John 1667–1702 Poet. He owed his immense contemporary popularity to *The Choice* (1700), a civilized and elegant account of a life at once genteel and epicurean. Its appeal later eluded JOHNSON and SOUTHEY, who asked in 1807: 'Why is Pomfret the most popular of the English Poets? The fact is certain, and the solution would be useful.' Pomfret's other works include moral reflections, Pindaric essays and the disappointingly unexciting *Cruelty and Lust*.

Poole, John 1786–1872 Playwright. *Hamlet Travestie* (1811) set a fashion for BURLESQUE versions of SHAKESPEARE. Only with *Paul Pry* (1825) did Poole again rise above the journeyman level.

Poor Richard's Almanac An almanac published and written by BENJAMIN FRANKLIN under the pseudonym of Richard Saunders from 1732 to 1758. From 1747 onwards it was entitled *Poor Richard Improved*. As well as calendars and astronomical data, it contains maxims recommending homely wisdom, virtue and frugality. Its fictional author, Richard, and his wife Bridget became popular literary characters. Franklin sold the almanac in 1758, but it continued publication until 1796.

Poor White A novel by SHERWOOD ANDERSON, published in 1920. It tells how late-19th-century technology changes the lives of the inhabitants of Bidwell, Ohio, and particularly that of Hugh McVey, a telegraph operator who begins as a shy, inhibited 'poor white' but becomes rich and famous, as well as isolated, through the success of his inventions. Disillusioned, he finally realizes the negative effects of industrial progress.

Pope, Alexander 1688–1744 Poet and satirist. His health was damaged from childhood by tuberculosis and asthma; he would later half-jokingly refer to 'this long disease, my life'. Precociously bright but barred by his Catholicism from attending university, he had an uneven education and was largely self-taught. His poetic apprenticeship included paraphrase and IMITATION of classical poets, the Psalms, CHAUCER and COWLEY. He claimed to have written his first significant work, *The Pastorals*, at the age of 16. They appeared in 1709.

The accomplished tone of his *ESSAY ON CRITICISM* (1711) caught the attention of ADDISON, and Pope acquired powerful friends in WYCHERLEY and CONGREVE. His religious ECLOGUE, *Messiah*, published in *THE SPECTATOR* in 1712, was followed by the first version of *THE RAPE OF THE LOCK* (expanded in 1714), the wittily feminized EPIC which established his reputation. By 1713 he had drifted away from Whig circles towards SWIFT and the Tory coterie embodied in the SCRIBLERUS CLUB. He collaborated with two fellow members, ARBUTHNOT and GAY, on his one play, *THREE HOURS AFTER MARRIAGE*, a comedy unsuccessfully staged in 1717. *Windsor Forest*, a Royalist PASTORAL begun in 1704 and published in 1713, confirmed his Tory allegiance.

At this time Pope was also working on an ambitious translation of Homer into HEROIC COUPLETS. The first volume of the *Iliad* appeared in 1715 and the project was completed in 1720. With its less fortunate successor, *The Odyssey* (completed with the help of Elizabeth Fenton and William Broome, 1725–6), it made Pope financially independent. The appearance of his collected works in 1717 established him as the leading contemporary man of letters. It included an adaptation of Chaucer's *THE HOUSE OF FAME*, the 'Ode for Music on St Cecilia's Day' and two melancholy love poems, *Eloisa to Abelard* and the *Elegy to the Memory of an Unfortunate Lady*. Their mood may well have been influenced by his affectionate relationships with LADY MARY WORTLEY MONTAGU, from whom he eventually became bitterly estranged, and Martha Blount, a lifelong friend to whom he addressed epistles which are among his most attractive works. In 1719 he moved to the villa at Twickenham which remained his home for the rest of his life. Lady Mary was a neighbour and his many visitors included Swift, whom he helped with the publication of *GULLIVER'S TRAVELS*.

The completion of his *Odyssey* followed one of his less distinguished projects, an edition of SHAKESPEARE (1725) commissioned by TONSON. THEOBALD's pamphlet *Shakespeare Restored* (1726) pointed out Pope's scholarly deficiencies. The three-volume *Miscellany* of pieces by the Scriblerian group (1727–8) contained an early version of the masterful *An Epistle to Dr Arbuthnot* and a prose piece, *Martinus Scriblerus peri Bathous: or, The Art of Sinking in Poetry*, inverting Longinus' treatise on the sublime and ridiculing his former collaborator Broome, together with Theobald, AMBROSE PHILIPS (with whom Pope had disagreed over the *Pastorals*) and JOHN DENNIS, the opinionated critic.

Pope had for some time planned an elaborate 'Opus Magnum' which would comprise four parts. The first was his *ESSAY ON MAN* (1733–4), four epistles mapping out the intellectual plan for the larger work. The second part was to be *THE DUNCIAD*, his all-embracing satire of Dullness in contemporary culture. Its first version (1728), consisting of three books, was enlarged in 1729 and a fourth book added in 1742; these appeared in a revised version in 1743. In the process Pope transferred his malignant displeasure from Theobald, the original anti-hero of the piece, to CIBBER, the POET LAUREATE. The epic conceived as the third part of his 'Opus Magnum' was never finished but its final part appeared as his four *MORAL ESSAYS* (1731–5). Though their philosophical content is hardly original, the poems epitomize the highly developed intellectual concerns with which he was preoccupied.

In 1733 he began to produce his miscellaneous *Imitations of Horace*, 11 translations and adaptations of Horace's odes, satires and epistles. They are probably his easiest verses to enjoy, demonstrating the fundamental affinity between his genius and the poets of the classical age. *An Epistle from Mr Pope to Dr Arbuthnot* (1735), effectively a 'Prologue' to these satires, was his most brilliantly sustained rhetorical performance. Addressed to his dying friend, it embodies the ideals of civilized friendship, good sense and honesty, as well as offering blistering verse-portraits of, among others, Addison and Lady Mary Wortley Montagu. *One Thousand Seven Hundred and Thirty Eight*, named for the year of its publication, consists of two satirical dialogues modelled on Horace. Pope also prepared an edition of his correspondence, doctored to his own advantage, and had it published by Edmund Curll in 1735, though he subsequently pretended the edition was piratical.

Pope's reputation did not long outlive the AUGUSTAN AGE. Drastic changes of taste later in the 18th century made his sophistication appear unfeeling and his satire malicious. He did not appeal to writers or readers again until this century, when he has come once more to be highly regarded. Pope is perhaps our foremost poet of culture; his audience is urban, urbane and civilized. His sense of proportion and awareness of contrasting effects within the 'correctness' of a design do not make his poetry impersonal or unemotional.

Porson, Richard 1759–1808 Classical scholar. He became a Fellow of Trinity College, Cambridge, in 1782 and Regius Professor of Greek in the university in 1792. Expert in Greek metres and idiomatic usage, he produced notable editions of Euripides and Aeschylus, among much other work. His contributions to THE GENTLEMAN'S MAGAZINE included three letters on Sir John Hawkins's biography of SAMUEL JOHNSON. Contemporaries considered he wasted his brilliant talents on journalism, as well as the heavy drinking and habit of procrastination which grew on him with age. The Greek typeface called 'Porson' is supposedly based on his hand.

Porter, Anne Maria 1780–1832 Novelist and younger sister of the more successful JANE PORTER. The most popular of her many novels was *The Hungarian Brothers* (1807), about the French Revolutionary war.

Porter, Hal 1911–84 Australian short-story writer, novelist, poet and playwright. Although he worked in many genres, he is best known for his three volumes of autobiography, *The Watcher on the Cast-Iron Balcony* (1963), *The Paper Chase* (1966) and *The Extra* (1975), and his precise, carefully crafted stories. They are collected in *Short Stories* (1942), *A Bachelor's Children* (1962), *The Cats of Venice* (1965), *Mr Butterfry and Other Tales of New Japan* (1970), *Fredo Fuss Love Life* (1974) and *The Clairvoyant Goat* (1981). He was both one of Australia's finest prose stylists and a chronicler of uncelebrated aspects of the country's social life. His novels – *A Handful of Pennies* (1958), *The*

Tilted Cross (1961) and *The Right Thing* (1971) – are sympathetic towards loners and eccentrics. Other works include three plays, *The Tower* (1963), *The Professor* (1966) and *Eden House* (1969), and several volumes of poetry, *The Hexagon* (1956), *Elijah's Ravens* (1968) and *In an Australian Country Graveyard* (1974).

Porter, Jane 1776–1850 Novelist and sister of ANNE MARIA PORTER. Highly successful in their day, her historical romances were among the earliest examples of the form. *The Scottish Chiefs* (1810), about William Wallace and Robert Bruce, and ending with the Battle of Bannockburn, appeared before SIR WALTER SCOTT began his Waverley novels.

Porter, Katherine Anne 1890–1980 American short-story writer and novelist. She is best remembered for *Ship of Fools* (1962), an ambitious, allegorical novel set on a German passenger ship sailing from Mexico in 1931. Her shorter fiction was gathered in *The Collected Stories of Katherine Anne Porter* (1965). Her other publications include *Collected Essays and Occasional Writings* (1970) and *The Never-Ending Wrong* (1977), an account of the infamous Sacco-Vanzetti trial and execution.

Porter, Peter (Neville Frederick) 1929– Poet. Born in Australia, he emigrated to Britain in 1951. Early collections, beginning with *Once Bitten, Twice Bitten* (1961), are characterized by the SATIRE of poems such as 'Annotations of Auschwitz' and 'Your Attention Please'. The matter-of-fact tone, erudite WIT and wry detachment of subsequent work gave way to the moving ELEGIES for his wife in *The Cost of Seriousness* (1978), widely acclaimed as his finest poems. Later work has included *English Subtitles* (1981), *Fast Forward* (1984), *Automatic Oracle* (1987), *Chair of Babel* (1992). *Complete Poems* appeared in 1988 and *Porter Selected* in 1989. *After Martial* (1972) is a volume of translations.

Portnoy's Complaint A novel by PHILIP ROTH, published in 1969. It takes the form of an account by Alexander Portnoy to his analyst of his relationship with his suburban Jewish family. Portnoy's guilty responses to his family's needs alternate with self-conscious rebellion: he masturbates, refuses to get married and has affairs with gentile women. In Israel he finds himself impotent with an Israeli girl, who confronts him with the contradictions of his existence and embodies for him a noble, self-sacrificing model of Jewishness.

Portrait of a Lady, The A novel by HENRY JAMES, serialized in 1880–1 and published in volume form in 1881. Isabel Archer, a young American girl, arrives in England to stay with her aunt and uncle, Mr and Mrs Touchett, and their tubercular son, Ralph. Ralph persuades Mr Touchett to include her in his will, so his death makes her rich. To preserve her freedom, Isabel has turned down proposals of marriage from Casper Goodwood, an American, and Lord Warburton. In Florence with Mrs Touchett and her friend, Madame Merle, she meets and marries the American expatriate Gilbert Osmond, only to discover him to be a selfish and sterile dilettante interested in her money. He forbids her to visit the dying Ralph in England; she goes, after learning that Madame Merle is the mother of his daughter Pansy. Casper Goodwood makes a last attempt to gain Isabel but she returns to Osmond and Pansy in Italy.

Portrait of the Artist as a Young Man, A An autobiographical novel by JOYCE, serialized by THE EGOIST in 1914–15 and published in volume form in 1916. It was developed from *Stephen Hero*, begun in 1904. Part of the earlier work survived and was edited by T. Spencer in 1944.

Stephen Dedalus, an intelligent but frail child, struggles towards maturity in Ireland. The novel traces his intellectual, moral, and artistic development from babyhood to the completion of his education at University College, Dublin. His individuality is stifled by many levels of convention, dictated by the family, Catholicism and Irish nationalism. He finally embraces the wider and more rewarding world of literature, philosophy and aesthetics, and frees himself from the claims of family, church and state. He resolves to leave Ireland for Paris to forge 'the uncreated conscience' of his race. He reappears in ULYSSES.

Positivism A creed deriving from Auguste Comte (1798–1857), who believed that humanity, both the individual and the race, progressed by three stages: the theological, the metaphysical and the positive. Theology and philosophy were treated as illegitimate. Cultural maturity was evinced by confining intellectual enquiry to observable facts. FREDERIC HARRISON was a leading English advocate of positivism, GEORGE ELIOT briefly embraced it and HARRIET MARTINEAU produced a condensed version of Comte's *Cours de philosophie positive*. Positivism led to the 20th-century school of 'Logical Positivists' which denies the existence of metaphysics.

post-modernism An international movement, affecting all the contemporary arts, which has succeeded MODERNISM. In literature, and particularly the novel, it rejects traditional REALISM in favour of a heightened sense of artifice, a delight in games and verbal pyrotechnics, a suspicion of absolute truth and a resulting inclination to stress the fictionality of fiction. All these traits were already present in modernist works such as JOYCE's *FINNEGANS WAKE* but they re-emerged with special force in early American examples of post-modernism such as NABOKOV's *Pale Fire* (1962), PYNCHON's *V* (1963) and VONNEGUT's *Slaughterhouse 5* (1969).

Its distrust of traditional mimetic genres, allied to the philosophical climate of STRUCTURALISM and DECONSTRUCTION, has also encouraged post-modernism to embrace popular forms, such as DETECTIVE FICTION (Umberto Eco's *The Name of the Rose*, 1983), SCIENCE FICTION (DORIS LESSING's *Canopus in Argos* sequence) and fairy tale (a recurrent source in the work of ANGELA CARTER). Equally post-modernist is the blurring of boundaries between the novel and journalism in TRUMAN CAPOTE's *In Cold Blood* (1966), the New Journalism of Tom Wolfe and others, and Robert Pirsig's *Zen and the Art of Motorcycle Maintenance* (1974). The fiction of SALMAN RUSHDIE, probably the most striking British practitioner, would seem to confirm the link between post-modernism and the post-colonial experience already suggested by the MAGIC REALISM of Gabriel García Márquez.

post-structuralism A modern critical theory which begins by asserting the unstable relationship between signifier and signified (see SEMIOTICS). The signifier refuses to be tied to a single signified, as is evident in jokes, dreams and poetry. This theory is expressed in a number of characteristic positions: (1) the author should not be regarded as the origin of his text or the authority for its meaning; (2) there are no objective 'scientific' discourses; (3) literature cannot be isolated as a separate discourse but is always contaminated with the entire universe of discourses. Roland Barthes (1915–80) attacked STRUCTURALISM for attempting to find the

structure of narrative, arguing that narrative draws upon the 'codes' which form a grid of possible meanings permitting no ultimate 'closure'. Under the influence of Nietzsche's belief that all knowledge is the 'will to power', Michel Foucault (1926–84) examined the historical construction of knowledge. Edward Said (1935–) has taken up Foucault's historical kind of post-structuralism to emphasize the pressures of reality which constrain the possibilities of knowledge; literary critics, he argues, can grasp a past text only within the discursive 'archive' of the present.

Potter, (Helen) Beatrix 1866–1943 Writer and illustrator of CHILDREN'S LITERATURE. To enliven her otherwise dull life with well-to-do parents in Kensington, she kept a journal in code (edited by Leslie Linder; 1966) and painted, often using specimens from the nearby Natural History and Victoria & Albert museums. A letter to a young friend illustrated with drawings of animals grew into *The Tale of Peter Rabbit* (privately printed, 1901), followed by *The Tailor of Gloucester* (1902). Subsequent picture-books, issued during a long and profitable association with the publisher Frederick Warne, include: *The Tale of Squirrel Nutkin* (1903), *The Tale of Benjamin Bunny* (1904), *The Tale of Two Bad Mice* (1904), *The Tale of Mrs Tiggy-Winkle* (1905), *The Tale of Jeremy Fisher* (1906), *The Story of a Fierce Bad Rabbit* (1906), *The Story of Miss Moppet* (1906), *The Tale of Tom Kitten* (1907), *The Tale of Jemima Puddle-Duck* (1908), *The Tale of the Flopsy Bunnies* (1909), *The Tale of Mrs Tittlemouse* (1910), *The Tale of Timmy Tiptoes* (1911) and *The Tale of Pigling Bland* (1913). They range from adventure stories to charming, eventless catalogues of animal domesticity, illustrated with a minute eye for detail. After her marriage in 1913 she lived in the Lake District, the setting for many of her books. There she put most of her energies into sheep farming and conservation, leaving 4000 acres of land to the National Trust. *The Tale of Little Pig Robinson* (1930) was the only story of note to appear in her declining years.

Potter, Dennis (Christopher George) 1935–93 Playwright. His work for television began with two plays about politics, *Vote Vote Vote for Nigel Barton* (1965; staged in 1968) and *Stand Up, Nigel Barton* (1965), and *Son of Man* (staged and screened in 1969), about a human and self-doubting Christ. Later TV series, rich in their feeling for popular culture and the music which expresses it, included *Pennies from Heaven* (1978), *Blue Remembered Hills* (1979), *The Singing Detective* (1986), the poorly received *Blackeyes* (1989) and, a return to form, *Lipstick on Your Collar* (1993).

Pound, Ezra (Weston Loomis) 1885–1972 American poet. After a brief academic career he left the USA for Europe in 1908, living in London, Paris and Rapallo and becoming a crucial influence on his contemporaries (notably T. S. ELIOT). During World War II he made radio broadcasts for the Axis in Rome expressing his pro-Fascist and anti-semitic views. In 1945 he was arrested by partisans and handed over to the American authorities, who judged him unfit to stand trial for treason on grounds of insanity. He was confined to St Elizabeth's Hospital in Washington D.C. until 1958, when he returned to Italy.

His early volumes include *A Lume Spento* (1908), *Personae* (1909), *Exultations* (1909), *Provença* (1910) and *Canzoni* (1911), showing the influence of medieval literature, Provençal poetry, troubadour ballads and ROBERT BROWNING. His translation of *The Sonnets and Ballate of Guido Cavalcanti* and the volume entitled *Ripostes* (both

1912) marked the beginning of his association with IMAGISM, which encouraged experimentation with verse forms, the economic use of language, brevity of treatment, and concreteness of detail. Pound promoted the work of fellow imagists, as well as that of T. S. Eliot and ROBERT FROST, in HARRIET MONROE's magazine POETRY and published an anthology, Des Imagistes (1914), which included contributions by HILDA DOOLITTLE, RICHARD ALDINGTON, JOYCE, AMY LOWELL, and WILLIAM CARLOS WILLIAMS. He was also involved in VORTICISM, which opposed representational art in favour of abstract forms and structures. His next volumes of poetry were Lustra (1916), Quia Pauper Amavi (1919) and Hugh Selwyn Mauberly (1920), the clearest expression of his disillusionment with what he saw as a decayed civilization. A Draft of XVI Cantos (1925) announced the begining of THE CANTOS, the epic work which would occupy him for the rest of his life, appearing as A Draft of Cantos XVII to XXVII (1928), A Draft of XXX Cantos (1933), Eleven New Cantos, XXXI–XLI (1934), The Fifth Decad of Cantos (1937), Cantos LII–LXXI (1940), The Pisan Cantos (1948), Section: Rock-Drill: 85–95 de los Cantares (1956) and Thrones: 96–109 de los Cantares (1959). The Cantos of Ezra Pound appeared in 1970. Personae: The Collected Poems of Ezra Pound was published in 1926; Selected Poems, edited by T. S. Eliot, appeared in 1928. Collected Early Poems was published posthumously in 1976.

His volumes of criticism include The Spirit of Romance (1910), Pavannes and Division (1918), Instigations (1920), Indiscretions (1923), How to Read (1931), ABC of Reading (1934), Polite Essays (1937), and A Guide to Kulchur (1938). He also published Gaudier-Brzeska: A Memoir (1916), an adaptation from the Chinese, The Classic Anthology Defined by Confucius (1954), and a translation of Sophocles' The Women of Trachis (1956).

Powell, Anthony (Dymoke) 1905– Novelist. His early novels – Afternoon Men (1931), Venusberg (1932), From a View to a Death (1933), Agents and Patients (1936), and What's Become of Waring? (1939) – are polished, elliptical SATIRES which made critics link his name with that of EVELYN WAUGH. His main achievement is A DANCE TO THE MUSIC OF TIME, a 12-volume ROMAN FLEUVE beginning with A Question of Upbringing (1951) and ending with Hearing Secret Harmonies (1975), which amounts to a leisurely survey of English society as Powell has experienced it. Later, more eccentric novels are O, How the Wheel Becomes It! (1983) and The Fisher King (1986). He has also published a biographical study of JOHN AUBREY (1948) and a selection from Brief Lives (1949), as well as two collections of book reviews, Miscellaneous Verdicts (1990) and Under Review (1992). To Keep the Ball Rolling (1976–82) is a four-volume autobiography.

Power and the Glory, The A novel by GRAHAM GREENE, published in 1940. It is set in Mexico, where the new revolutionary republic has outlawed the Church. A lapsed priest, drunk and lecherous, rediscovers his original commitment despite (or perhaps because of) being banned. His life is contrasted with that of a fellow priest, Padre Jose, who has capitulated to the regime, and a 'gringo' thief and murderer, hunted by the police. His opponent, a good and honourable police lieutenant, finally corners the priest at the bedside of the dying 'gringo'. The priest's execution is imbued with Christlike implications, and the novel closes on a subdued note of triumph.

Power of Sympathy, The An EPISTOLARY NOVEL by WILLIAM HILL BROWN, published anonymously in 1789

and generally considered to be the first American novel. It warns young women of the danger from would-be seducers by telling a tragic tale based in part on an actual scandal in Boston society. Harrington is determined to win Harriot Fawcet, unaware that she is his half-sister. When the truth of her parentage is revealed, she collapses and dies soon afterwards, while the grief-stricken Harrington eventually commits suicide.

Powys, John Cowper 1872–1963 Novelist. He was the brother of LLEWELYN POWYS and T. F. POWYS. Although he worked for much of his life as a lecturer in the USA, his writings are imbued with the atmosphere of the West Country, where he spent his boyhood, and Wales, where he lived on his return to Britain. He published poetry, essays on literature, religion and philosophy, and an early group of romances (Wood and Stone, 1915; Rodmoor; 1916; and Ducdame, 1925). However, his reputation – still controversial – depends on ambitious, esoteric novels which combine folklore and the supernatural with elements of the EPIC: Wolf Solent (1929); A Glastonbury Romance (1932); Weymouth Sands (1934; revised as Jobber Skald in 1935 but restored to its original form in 1963), about the intense relationship between Jobber, his lover Perdita and his enemy Dog Cattistock; Maiden Castle (1936), set among the excavations of the Dorchester fort; and Morwy: or, The Vengeance of God (1937), about man's inhumanity to man. Later novels include: Owen Glendower (1940) and Porius: A Romance of the Dark Ages (1951), historical romances; The Inmates (1952), about madness; Atlantis (1954), a fantastic tale about Odysseus; and The Brazen Head (1956), about ROGER BACON.

Powys, Llewelyn 1884-1939 Essayist, journalist and novelist. He was the brother of JOHN COWPER POWYS and T. F. POWYS. His many books include: Ebony and Ivory (1923), based on his experiences in Kenya; Skin for Skin (1925), about the tuberculosis which eventually killed him; and other loosely autobiographical works such as Love and Death: An Imaginary Autobiography (1939). Earth Memories (1934) and Dorset Essays (1935) were his best-known volumes. Confessions of Two Brothers (with John Cowper Powys; 1916) and Damnable Opinions (1935) show the independent-mindedness that characterized all three brothers. Black Laughter (1924) and Apples be Ripe (1930) are novels.

Powys, T(heodore) F(rancis) 1875-1953 Novelist and short-story writer. The brother of JOHN COWPER POWYS and LLEWELYN POWYS, he is best known for two allegorical fantasies which explore paradoxes about good and evil: Mr Weston's Good Wine (1927), in which God and the archangel Michael visit the village of Folly Down in the person of Mr Weston, wine merchant, and his junior partner; and Unclay (1931), in which John Death visits the village of Dodder with orders from God to kill various inhabitants. Other works include An Interpretation of Genesis (1907) and Soliloquies of a Hermit (1916), showing his preoccupation with religion, and many volumes of short stories, among them The Left Leg (1923), Black Bryony (1923), Mr Tasker's Gods (1924) and Bottle's Path (1946), one of his very few books after 1940.

practical criticism See RICHARDS, I. A.

Praed, Mrs Campbell 1851–1935 Australian novelist. My Australian Girlhood (1902) is the story of her early years in Queensland. After settling in England in 1876 she produced some 40 novels, frequently drawing on her experience of Australia and contrasting refined English gentlemen with crude, spiky Australians whose qualities prove more enduring. Titles include *An Australian Heroine* (1880), *Policy and Passion* (1881), *Miss Jacobsen's Chance* (1886), *The Romance of a Station* (1889), *Mrs Tregaskiss* (1895), *Nulma* (1897), *The Maid of the River* (1905), *Opal Fire* (1910) and *Sister Sorrow* (1916).

Praed, William Mackworth 1802–39 Poet. At its best his verse is humorous, light, unforced and of a social inclination redolent of the order to which he belonged. He also wrote some romantic poetry, a mode he often touched with mockery. He had a turn for the grotesquely amusing, as well as a taste for SATIRE, frequently expressed in 'squibs' against prominent figures like BROUGHAM and Palmerston. His *Poems* appeared in 1864.

Praeterita The unfinished autobiography of RUSKIN, serialized in 1885–9. Although written between bouts of madness, it contains some of his most lucid and carefully formulated prose. Selective in detail and concentrating on the first half of his long life, it is at its most engaging in its loving yet merciless portrait of his parents, particularly his father, a Victorian middle-class merchant on his way up.

Pragmatism: A New Name for Some Old Ways of Thinking A book by WILLIAM JAMES, published in 1907. As he describes it, pragmatism is not so much a theory as a method of choosing among theories, a means of mediating between rationalist absolutism and empiricist materialism. While distrusting the abstract manipulation of words (rationalism), James accepts abstractions insofar as they redirect one profitably into experience. Ideals are 'real' because they have results. Truth, an abstraction, does not reside innately within any proposition; rather, one can call a proposition truthful if it has practical consequences. For the pragmatist, therefore, truth is relative.

Prairie, The See LEATHERSTOCKING TALES, THE.

Pratchett, Terry [Terence] **(David John)** 1948– Novelist. His comic fantasies set on Discworld, cleverly subverting the clichés of genre fantasy and other kinds of imaginative fiction, began with *The Colour of Magic* (1983), achieved bestseller status with *Mort* (1987) and rapidly extended to more than a dozen volumes. They are enormously popular with teenagers, and much of Pratchett's other work is aimed specifically at a younger audience. *Truckers* (1989) began a trilogy about tiny extraterrestrials marooned on Earth. *Only You Can Save Mankind* (1992) and *Johnny and the Dead* (1993) are moral fables.

Pratt, E(dwin) J(ohn) 1882–1964 Canadian poet. His work embodies central Victorian themes such as the conflict between man and nature and within nature itself. *The Witches' Brew* (1925) is a comic ALLEGORY about Prohibition. *The Iron Door* (1927), about his mother's death, concludes with an ambivalent affirmation of faith. *The Titanic* (1935) places the ship and the iceberg which destroyed it in contrast as an ironic commentary on man's belief in technological progress. Pratt's best-known works are two long poems which raise subjects from Canadian history to epic status: *Brébeuf and His Brethren* (1940) is about a group of missionaries massacred by the Iroquois in the 17th century, and *Towards the Last Spike* (1952) deals with the building of the transcontinental railroad. Other volumes include *Newfoundland Verse* (1923), *Titans* (1926), *The Roosevelt and the Antinoe* (1930), *Verses of the Sea* (1930), *Many Moods* (1932), *The Fable of the Goats* (1937), *Still Life* (1943), *Behind the Log* (1947) and *Collected Poems* (1958).

Prayer Book, The See BOOK OF COMMON PRAYER.

Pre-Raphaelites A mid-19th-century school of painters and poets. Its nucleus was the Pre-Raphaelite Brotherhood, founded in 1848 by Holman Hunt, John Everett Millais, DANTE GABRIEL ROSSETTI, WILLIAM MICHAEL ROSSETTI, F. G. Stephens, James Collinson and Thomas Woolner. The PRB rebelled against the Royal Academy and, under RUSKIN's influence, tried to recapture the purity art had before Raphael and the Renaissance. Its principles found later recruits in WILLIAM MORRIS and Edward Burne-Jones, and Pre-Raphaelitism became an influential tendency in Victorian art. In painting it cultivated bright colours, vividly naturalistic details and subjects drawn from religion or literature. The poetry of Rossetti, CHRISTINA ROSSETTI, COVENTRY PATMORE and Morris used medieval subjects and medieval forms (like the BALLAD) to express a dreamy melancholy. Turning its back on REALISM, and the realities of 19th-century industrial society, Pre-Raphaelitism occasionally anticipated SYMBOLISM.

Prelude, The: or, Growth of a Poet's Mind An autobiographical poem in BLANK VERSE by WILLIAM WORDSWORTH. Unpublished during his lifetime, it is available to modern readers in three versions: a two-part text written in 1798–9, published in 1973; the earliest full-length *Prelude* of 1805, in 13 books, edited by Ernest de Selincourt in 1926; and the poet's own definitive version in 14 books, put aside in 1839, and published after his death in 1850. Its present title, suggested by his widow, reflects the fact that it began as a 'sort of portico' to *The Recluse*, an ambitious philosophical poem which Wordsworth attempted but never completed (see THE EXCURSION). The poem is his greatest work, and it is astonishing that his fame as the architect of conservative ROMANTICISM was achieved without it.

His chosen confessional form does not announce an intention to write literal autobiography. Although the fact does not become fully evident until the final books, *The Prelude* is a reflection on poetry itself, derived from his own personal experience and the exemplary significance of his own development. The fortunes of Wordsworth and the fate of poetry are thus essentially one. His encompassing claims for his craft are grounded in a comprehensive critique of the negativity of modern civilization. The deadening equation of knowledge with books; the debased conception of human community in London (Book VIII); the bloodless abstractions of the rationalistic philosophy of WILLIAM GODWIN; and, above all, the degeneration of the French Revolution into 'domestic carnage' and wars of foreign conquest (IX, X, XI) are all, in the final analysis, both causes and symptoms of man's estrangement from his true purpose and being. Only the poetic imagination can restore him to wholeness. The poet's own privileged purchase upon truth is the reward of his intuitive intimacies with Nature. Yet Wordsworth is not a nature mystic. Enhanced by vision though it may be, the model for his lost totality is a recognizable social order, which he finds in the world of his Cumberland childhood and youth.

Prescott, William Hickling 1796–1859 American historian. He made his reputation with *History of the Reign of Ferdinand and Isabella, the Catholic* (1838), *History of the Conquest of Mexico* (1843), *History of the Conquest of Peru* (1847) and *History of the Reign of Philip the Second* (1855–8). His careful use of sources and adventurous narrative method provided a model for a younger generation of historians.

Preston, Thomas See CAMBISES, KING OF PERSIA.

Price, Richard 1723–91 Unitarian minister and writer on philosophy and politics. He opposed the 'moral sense' view of ethics taken by SHAFTESBURY and Francis Hutcheson, and argued in *A Review of the Principal Questions in Morals* (1756) that the rightness and wrongness of any action belonged to that action intrinsically. He supported both American independence in *Observations on the Nature of Civil Liberty, the Principles of Government and the Justice and Policy of the War with America* (1776; supplemented in 1777 and 1778) and the French Revolution in a famous sermon and *A Discourse on the Love of our Country* (1789), which prompted BURKE to write his REFLECTIONS ON THE REVOLUTION IN FRANCE.

Price, Sir Uvedale See PICTURESQUE.

Prichard, Katherine Susannah 1883–1969 Novelist and poet. Born in Fiji, she published her first novel, *The Pioneers* (1915), while working as a journalist in London. In Australia she took pains to familiarize herself with the background of novels such as *Working Bullocks* (1926), about teamsters, *Coonardo* (1929) – her best novel – about a cattle station, and *Haxby's Circus* (1930). A trilogy, *The Roaring Nineties* (1946), *Golden Miles* (1948), and *Winged Seeds* (1950), is set in the goldfields of Western Australia. Her poetry includes *Clovelly Verses* (1913) and *The Earth Lover and Other Verses* (1932).

Prick of Conscience, The An early-14th-century poem, drawn from many Latin and English sources, and surviving in many versions. The title expresses the author's hope that the poem will stir men to repentance. It deals with man's miserable state, the world and worldly life, death, Purgatory, the signs of Doomsday, the torments of Hell and the joys of Heaven.

Pride and Prejudice A novel by JANE AUSTEN, written in 1796–7 under the title 'First Impressions', revised and finally published in 1813. Mr and Mrs Bennet of Longbourn are an ill-matched couple, he detached and ironic, she gossipy and absorbed in finding husbands for their five daughters. Jane, the eldest, falls in love with the wealthy Charles Bingley but her sister, the witty and high-spirited Elizabeth, dislikes Bingley's still wealthier friend, FitzWilliam Darcy, for his coldness and arrogance. Her prejudice is confirmed by George Wickham, an engaging militia officer who describes the injustices he has suffered from Darcy. Finding the Bennets vulgar, Darcy and Bingley's sisters persuade him to abandon Jane. Elizabeth is briefly wooed by William Collins, a clergyman who will inherit Mr Bennet's property. He marries her friend, Charlotte Lucas, instead. On a visit to the couple Elizabeth again meets Darcy, staying with his aunt and Collins's patron, Lady Catherine de Bourgh. He falls in love with her but proposes so condescendingly that she refuses. In a letter he defends himself and exposes Wickham as an adventurer. The couple meet again when she visits his seat, Pemberley, during a tour of Derbyshire. His charm and grace begin to impress her. When her sister Lydia elopes with Wickham, Darcy helps to trace them and ensure that they marry. Bingley renews his courtship of Jane and, despite interference from Lady Catherine, Darcy persists in his courtship of Elizabeth. Both couples are finally united.

Priestley, J(ohn) B(oynton) 1894–1984 Novelist, playwright, critic and broadcaster. He wrote over 60 books and more than 40 plays. His wide-ranging interest in England and the English character, and his appeal to 'the man in the street', made him one of the most popular 'middlebrow' authors of his day. His first success was *The Good Companions* (1929), about three people who join a concert party. *Angel Pavement* (1930) is a more sombre tale of London. His best-known works for the stage are *Dangerous Corner* (1932), *I Have been Here Before* (1937) and *Time and the Conways* (1937), known collectively as the 'Time' plays because of the use they made of theories from J. W. Dunne's *An Experiment with Time* (1927). *Postscripts* (1940), *Britain Speaks* (1940) and *All England Listened* (1968) are selections from wartime broadcasts. Post-war publications include novels (*Festival at Farbridge*, 1951; *Saturn over the Water*, 1961; *It's an Old Country*, 1967) and criticism, including *The Art of the Dramatist* (1957) and *Literature and Western Man* (1960), influenced by Jung. *Martin Released* (1962) and *Instead of the Trees* (1977) are autobiographical.

Priestley, Joseph 1733–1804 Writer on science, religion and politics. He is remembered in the history of science for his ground-breaking experiments with electricity in the 1760s and, after he turned his attention to chemistry, his discovery of oxygen (1774). Trained as a Presbyterian minister, he developed increasingly unorthodox views – made notorious by *A History of the Corruptions of Christianity* (1782) and *A History of Early Opinions concerning Jesus Christ* (1786) – and became a founder of the Unitarian Society in 1791. His politics were as radical as his theology. *An Essay of the First Principles of Government* (1768) first stated the idea, later developed by BENTHAM and the UTILITARIANS, that the happiness of the majority is 'the great standard by which everything relating to that state must finally be determined'. His support for the French Revolution, expressed in his *Letters to Edmund Burke* (1791), earned him the nickname 'Gunpowder' Priestley and provoked a Church and King mob to wreck his house in Birmingham. He went to America in 1794 and spent his remaining years in Northumberland, Pennsylvania.

Prime Minister, The The fifth of TROLLOPE'S PALLISER NOVELS, serialized in 1875–6 and published in volume form in 1876. Emily Wharton defies her father to marry Ferdinand Lopez but discovers his dishonesty. Plantagenet Palliser, Duke of Omnium, becomes Prime Minister of an insecure coalition government, which Lady Glencora helps to sustain with lavish entertaining at Gatherum Castle. Her foolish encouragement of Lopez associates the duke with his affairs until Phineas Finn silences the gossip with an effective speech in the Commons. Meanwhile the financial affairs of Lopez and his partner deteriorate, and he commits suicide. In due course Emily marries Arthur Fletcher, her father's first choice for her, and the duke's coalition government falls. Too thin-skinned for party politics, the duke is a model of integrity, Trollope's 'perfect gentleman'.

Prime of Miss Jean Brodie, The A novel by MURIEL SPARK, published in 1961. Miss Jean Brodie, a schoolmistress in Edinburgh during the 1930s, fascinates her pupils at the Marcia Blaines School for Girls with her vigorously eccentric approach to teaching. Her 16-year-old charges, the 'Brodie set', are increasingly drawn into Miss Brodie's emotional life and her relationships with the two fellow masters, Teddy Lloyd and Gordon Lowther. Sandy Stranger has an affair with Lloyd during the summer of 1938 and betrays Miss Brodie to the headmistress, Miss Mackay, who dismisses her for teaching Fascism. The 'Brodie set' leave school to meet different and in some cases tragic fates but the colourful, morally ambiguous influence of 'Miss Jean Brodie in her prime' endures long after her death.

Prince, F(rank) T(empleton) 1912– Poet and scholar. He established his reputation with the widely anthologized 'Soldiers Bathing', which became the title poem of a later collection (1954). Subsequent volumes include *The Doors of Stone* (1963), *Collected Poems* (1979), *Later On* (1983) and *Walls in Rome: Poems* (1987). Many poems derive from imaginary confrontations with past events and people, including Michelangelo, BYRON, SHELLEY and RUPERT BROOKE. Scholarly works include the Arden edition of SHAKESPEARE's *Poems* (1960).

Prince's Progress, The An allegorical poem by CHRISTINA ROSSETTI, published in 1866. A prince sets out on a journey to claim his bride but is distracted by pleasures on the way. He arrives to find that she has died of despair.

Princess, The: *A Medley* A poem by TENNYSON, first published in 1847. Set in the typically English estate of Sir Walter Vivian, it tells the story of a Prince whose betrothed, Princess Ida, daughter of King Gama, rejects marriage and founds a centre of learning for feminists. The Prince and his friends Florian and Cyril gain admittance disguised as women but their identities are soon revealed. Further complications involve the adventures in love of Cyril and Florian and the quarrel between the kingly fathers of the Prince and Princess. Eventually the Princess modifies her feminism and all parties are happily reconciled. The poem is notable for such lyrics as 'Sweet and Low, Sweet and Low' and 'The Splendour Falls on Castle Walls' (added to the 1850 edition), 'Tears, Idle Tears' and 'Now Sleeps the Crimson Petal'.

Princess Casamassima, The A novel by HENRY JAMES, serialized in 1885–6 and published in volume form in 1886. Set in London in the 1880s, it portrays characters from all classes. The hero is Hyacinth Robinson, an orphan brought up by a poor dressmaker, Miss Pynsent. He meets Paul Muniment, a proletarian revolutionary, and joins a secret society, through which he also comes into contact with Christina, the Princess Casamassima (see *RODERICK HUDSON*), separated from her Italian husband. European travels alter his views, but he is ordered to assassinate a duke. The Princess Casamassima visits his apartment to offer to take his place, but Hyacinth has already killed himself.

Principles of Moral and Political Philosophy, The A theological treatise by PALEY, published in 1785. Its argument is heavily indebted to TUCKER's *The Light of Nature Pursued* (1768–78) but presented with greater system and clarity. Paley's version of theological utilitarianism is firmly grounded in Christianity, and his ethical system requires the acknowledgement of rewards and penalties after death. Paley's skill as an expositor kept his book widely read for many years.

Principles of Psychology, The A book by WILLIAM JAMES, published in 1890. His observations in his psychological laboratory at Harvard indicated that the mind operates as a part of the body and that an individual's mental adjustments are in fact environmental responses. *Principles* defines the mind as an instrument which, by controlling choice, effort, and will, makes adjustments which are modified by factors such as heredity and biology. The book is also notable for coining the term STREAM OF CONSCIOUSNESS.

Pringle, Thomas 1789–1834 Poet. After publishing *The Institute: A Heroic Poem* (1811) and *The Autumnal Excursion* (1819), he went to South Africa, where his hopes of bringing the country's various cultural groups together caused controversy. After his return in 1826 he devoted his energies to the Anti-Slavery Society and brought the first authentic breath of South Africa to English literature. His poems were published in *Ephemerides* (1828) and *African Sketches* (1834). *The History of Mary Prince, a West Indian Slave* (1831) and *Narrative of a Residence in South Africa* (1835) reinforce the humanitarian tone of his poems, admired by COLERIDGE and TENNYSON.

Prior, Matthew 1664–1721 Poet and diplomat. Of a humble but respectable family, he completed his education at Westminster School and St John's College, Cambridge, thanks partly to the generosity of CHARLES SACKVILLE, a debt warmly acknowledged in the dedication to Prior's first collection of poems (1709). He began his career in public service as secretary to the British ambassador at The Hague, became a trusted itinerant representative of William III and, in the next reign, handled public and private negotiations for peace with France on behalf of ROBERT HARLEY's Tory ministry. The controversial Treaty of Utrecht (1713) was popularly known as 'Matt's Peace'. With the accession of George I he suffered arrest and imprisonment for more than a year. Prior retired into private life, occupying himself with the great subscription edition of his works (1718) and his country house.

As a poet, Prior first achieved fame with SATIRES on DRYDEN, particularly the lively, good-humoured BURLESQUE of *The Hind and the Panther* as *The Hind and the Panther Transversed to the Story of the Country Mouse and the City Mouse* (1687), written with Charles Montague. The bulk of his work consists of occasional pieces: burlesques, epistles, lyrics, patriotic ODES, BALLADS and imitations of CHAUCER and SPENSER. His comic writing is made particularly vivid by his wry self-characterization. Serious works include *Carmen Seculare* (1700), eulogizing William III, and the weighty *Solomon on the Vanity of the World* (1718). *Alma: or, The Progress of the Mind* (1718), written in prison, is a witty mock-scholastic conversation between Matt and a friend, a burlesque counterpart to *Solomon*. These were the two works Prior himself most valued. In his last years he began work on the superlative *Dialogues of the Dead*, a sequence of imaginary conversations; that between Montaigne and JOHN LOCKE is the most brilliant.

Prioress's Tale, The See *CANTERBURY TALES*.

Prisoner of Zenda, The A novel by ANTHONY HOPE, published in 1894. It follows the swashbuckling adventures of Rudolf Rassendyll, an Englishman whose striking resemblance to the King of Ruritania helps thwart a plot to usurp the throne by Black Michael and Rupert of Hentzau. *Rupert of Hentzau* (1898) is a sequel.

Pritchett, Sir V(ictor) S(awdon) 1900– Man of letters. Although he has also published travel books, journalism and biographies, he is best known for the short stories collected in such volumes as *The Spanish Virgin and Other Stories* (1932), *You Make Your Own Life* (1938), *It May Never Happen* (1945), *When My Girl Comes Home* (1961) and *The Camberwell Beauty* (1974). *Dead Man Leading* (1937) and *Mr Beluncle* (1951) are novels. His criticism includes studies of GEORGE MEREDITH (1970), Balzac (1973) and Turgenev (1977). *A Cab at the Door* (1968) is a notable autobiography.

Private Lives A comedy by NOËL COWARD, produced in 1930. A divorced couple, Elyot and Amanda, meet while honeymooning at Deauville after their marriage to new partners. They run off to Paris together, only to rediscover why they originally separated, but sneak off again when their deserted spouses catch up with them. For all their differences, Elyot and Amanda always prefer each other's company.

Private Memoirs and Confessions of a Justified Sinner, The A novel by JAMES HOGG, published in 1824. It is the most ambitious, and now the most widely read, of his prose works. Set in late 17th-century Scotland, the story is divided into two main parts. The first contains the 'editor's narrative' of the strife-torn marriage of the Lord of Dalcastle and the murder of his son and heir, George Colwan, in circumstances pointing to the complicity of his half-brother Robert Wringhim, a Calvinist bigot. The second part consists of Wringhim's own memoir, discovered in his grave a century after his presumed suicide. It reveals how, with the aid of a malign *alter ego*, or *doppelgänger*, who persuaded him he was doing God's work, he murdered first a preacher, then his brother, and then apparently his mother. Wringhim gradually realizes that the companion is really the Devil, who appears to have claimed him in the end.

Private Papers of Henry Ryecroft, The A semi-autobiographical novel by GISSING, published in 1903. It takes the form of a journal kept by a recluse who has been helped by a legacy from a friend to withdraw from the London literary world where he had failed as a writer.

private theatres The indoor playhouses of Elizabethan, Jacobean and Caroline London were, and still are, sometimes called 'private theatres' to distinguish them from the open-air PUBLIC THEATRES. They were, in fact, open to the public on payment of an admission charge but the fiction that they were private helped to defend them against interference from the civic authorities. The first actors to use private playhouses were choristers (see BOYS' COMPANIES). The main private theatres were: the unknown home of the Boys of St Paul's (c. 1575); the first Blackfriars (1576) and the second Blackfriars (1600), used by RICHARD BURBAGE and the KING'S MEN from 1608; the Whitefriars (1605–8); the Cockpit or Phoenix (1616); and the Salisbury Court (1629). More genuinely private were the COURT THEATRES.

problem play A term used at the end of the 19th century for plays which followed Ibsen in dealing with contemporary social and moral issues. They include work by PINERO, HENRY ARTHUR JONES, GALSWORTHY and GRANVILLE-BARKER, as well as the more openly subversive early plays of SHAW.

Critics also use the term for SHAKESPEARE's three tragicomedies, *ALL'S WELL THAT ENDS WELL*, *MEASURE FOR MEASURE* and *TROILUS AND CRESSIDA*, which address the interrelationship of private and public morality with a harshness untypical of the comedies. Some would add *JULIUS CAESAR* and even *HAMLET* to the group.

Procter, Adelaide Anne 1825–64 Poet. The daughter of BARRY CORNWALL, she published several volumes of sentimental verse: *Legends and Lyrics* (two series, 1858 and 1861), *A Chaplet of Verses* (1862) and *The Message* (1892). Admirers included DICKENS.

Professor, The CHARLOTTE BRONTË's first completed novel, written in 1846 but not published until 1857. It draws on the same experiences that she later used more successfully in *VILLETTE*. An Englishman, William Crimsworth, goes to Brussels as a schoolmaster and falls in love with Frances Henri, a fellow teacher and Anglo-Swiss girl.

Prometheus Unbound A CLOSET DRAMA by SHELLEY, published in 1820. It is drawn from Aeschylus' *Prometheus Bound* and what is known of its lost sequel *Prometheus Unbound*, though Shelley departed from the

Greek dramatist's 'feeble' idea of 'reconciling the Champion with the Oppressor of mankind'. A second, more positive, source of inspiration was MILTON's Satan, whom Shelley considered to be the real hero of *PARADISE LOST*. Combining and updating these two myths, he creates a Prometheus of beauty, energy and moral perfection, whose liberation by the personified forces of Hope, Love and 'Necessity' brings about the triumph of mankind over tyranny.

Act I opens with Prometheus chained to a precipice in the Indian Caucasus, his heart daily consumed by Jupiter's eagle. Aided by his mother, the Earth, he recalls his curse of Jupiter and his hatred turns to pity. Mercury arrives with a vast chorus of Furies who tempt him to despair with visions of the failure of the French Revolution and the corruption of Christianity. Panthea (Hope) reminds him of her sister Asia (Love). In Act II Panthea and Asia visit the dark underworld realm of Demogorgon ('people-monster'), an inscrutable ultimate source of revolutionary power, whom Asia rouses into action with her declaration of love for suffering humanity. Jupiter is overthrown by Demogorgon at the beginning of Act III, and the unchained Prometheus is reunited with Asia. The Spirit of the Hour describes the universal liberation consequent upon the fall of kings, and the end of social classes, nations and racial distinctions. Act IV, added as an afterthought, is sung by Spirits of the Hour and Spirits of the Human Mind, then by the Spirit of the Earth and the Spirit of the Moon.

Proposal for the Universal Use of Irish Manufacture The first of SWIFT's pamphlets about Ireland (1720). It protests against English exploitation of the Irish economy, proposing that home-produced Irish cloth should be promoted as an industry and imported fabrics from England should be boycotted.

Prothalamion SPENSER invented the word for his poem (1596) celebrating the double betrothal of Katherine and Elizabeth, daughters of the Earl of Worcester, by analogy with 'epithalamion' (marriage-song). His own *EPITHALAMION* had appeared in 1595. The poem offers a description by a discontented courtier of sights along the Thames, the most important being 'two swans of goodly hue' (Katherine and Elizabeth Somerset). Its famous refrain 'Sweet Thames run softly, till I end my song' is echoed by T. S. ELIOT in *THE WASTE LAND*.

Prout, Father See MAHONY, FRANCIS SYLVESTER.

Proverbial Philosophy See TUPPER, MARTIN.

Provoked Wife, The A comedy by VANBRUGH, produced and published in 1697. The title character is Lady Brute, whose husband Sir John is a coward and bully disillusioned with marriage. She is tempted into dalliance with her admirer, Constant, partly by her niece Bellinda, who is being successfully wooed by Constant's friend Heartfree. Sir John returns home unexpectedly from his drunken adventures to discover Constant and Heartfree hiding in a closet. He is outfaced, though sure in his own mind that he has been cuckolded. The jealous Lady Fancyfull attempts to make mischief but fails when her fellow conspirator Rasor, Sir John's valet, baulks at the extent of her spite. The play ends with Bellinda's marriage to Heartfree.

CIBBER later completed and staged Vanbrugh's unfinished *A Journey to London* as *The Provoked Husband* (1728). It does not involve the same characters.

Provost, The See GALT, JOHN.

Prynne, J(eremy) H(alward) 1936– Poet. As the leading British exponent of a post-modernist, experimental poetry which has its origins in the later work of EZRA POUND and in the 'projective verse' of CHARLES OLSON, he has attracted a considerable following. His volumes include *Kitchen Poems* (1968), *Brass* (1971), *Into the Day* (1972), *High Pink on Chrome* (1975), *Down Where Change* (1979), *Poems* (1982) and *The Oval Window* (1983).

Prynne, William 1600–69 Pamphleteer. Though he wrote 200 miscellaneous works, he is remembered for his Puritan attack on the theatre in *Histrio-Mastix* (1632), a 'pamphlet' of over 1000 pages. Its alleged criticism of Charles I and Henrietta Maria earned him life imprisonment, a huge fine, loss of his law and university degrees, loss of his ears in the pillory and branding for sedition. Freed in 1640, he played an independent-minded role in politics, opposing the trial and execution of Charles I, the Commonwealth Army and the Rump Parliament until in 1660 he introduced the bill dissolving Parliament for the restoration of the monarchy. Charles II made him Keeper of the Tower Records.

Psalters The book of 150 psalms in the Old Testament, traditionally ascribed to King David, was the basis for the liturgy of the medieval church. There is a long tradition of Old and Middle English Psalters. The version in the BOOK OF COMMON PRAYER is largely based on COVERDALE's translation in his first complete Bible of 1535 (see BIBLE IN ENGLISH). Coverdale's metrical version of 13 psalms, *Ghostly Psalms and Spiritual Songs*, with words and tunes mainly adapted from Lutheran sources, was printed *c*. 1539. Frequently reprinted – even annually after 1549 – was the *Whole Books of Psalms Collected into English Metre*, by T. Sternhold and J. Hopkins, a version with tunes adapted from the Genevan Psalter. This was the Old Version (hence 'Old Hundredth' as the name of the hymn tune for 'All People That on Earth Do Dwell'). *The Bay Psalm Book* (1640), a translation by RICHARD MATHER, JOHN ELIOT and Thomas Weld which replaced the Sternhold and Hopkins version in the Massachusetts Bay Colony, was the first book printed in America; revised by Henry Dunster and Richard Lyon as *The Psalms, Hymns and Scriptural Songs of the Old and New Testament* (1651), it was reissued several times in the following century. In England there were many publications of metrical psalms in various arrangements between the Old Version and the New Version by Nicholas Brady and NAHUM TATE (1696). The whole Psalter was translated by PARKER, SIR PHILIP SIDNEY and JAMES I, and parts by MILTON, FRANCIS BACON, GEORGE HERBERT, CRASHAW, HENRY VAUGHAN and others. For over a thousand years the Psalter has been one of the greatest influences on English lyric poetry.

Pseudodoxia Epidemica*: or, Enquiries into Very Many Received Tenents and Commonly Presumed Truths.* Often known as *Vulgar Errors*. SIR THOMAS BROWNE's second work (1646), revised and expanded in 1650, 1658 and 1672. It investigates credulity and popular hearsay, analysing the reasons for mistaken beliefs and tracing their origins in the susceptibility of humans to the dictates of others, as well as the agency of Satan.

psychoanalytic criticism A loose label for the various methods or theories of criticism ultimately derived from Freud's therapeutic technique for uncovering the unconscious repressions of childhood emotions. His analytic methods have sometimes been applied to literary texts on the assumption that the author's repressed emotions were at work in the text's affective patterns – that texts are shaped by unconscious desire. Roman Jakobson showed that two Freudian concepts, displace-

ment (of an emotional focus from one object to another) and condensation (of several ideas into one), correspond to two figures of speech, METAPHOR and METONYMY. Norman Holland's 'ego-psychology' concentrates on the relations between reader and text, arguing that readers use texts in order to satisfy unconscious wishes. Most influential in recent years has been Jacques Lacan's reinterpretation of Freud in the light of STRUCTURALISM and POST-STRUCTURALISM, which inserts a structural linguistics into Freud's theory of unconscious processes. His theories have encouraged a criticism which focuses not on the author but on the linguistic processes of the text.

Jung's theory of a collective unconscious manifested in certain recurring images, stories and forms, which he called 'archetypes', has also left its imprint on criticism. BODKIN, FRYE, Leslie Fiedler and others have traced in literary texts the presence of the archetypal patterns which express the most profound and universal experiences of human existence.

Public Advertiser, The A newspaper founded in 1752 as *The London Daily Post and General Advertiser*. It was amalgamated with NEWBERY's *Public Ledger* in 1798. The paper carried home and foreign news as well as political correspondence, including a dispute between WILKES and TOOKE. The letters of JUNIUS were published in its pages by Henry Sampson Woodfall, editor in 1758–93.

public theatres The open-air playhouses of Elizabethan, Jacobean and Caroline London were, and still are, sometimes called 'public' to distinguish them from the equally public but more exclusive indoor PRIVATE THEATRES. They were, in approximate order of their foundation: the Theatre in Shoreditch (1576), home of the company to which SHAKESPEARE belonged, later known as the KING's MEN; the Curtain (1577); a theatre of unknown name in Newington Butts (*c*. 1580); the Rose (*c*. 1587), where ALLEYN acted with the Admiral's Men; the Swan (1595); the GLOBE (1599), second home of Shakespeare's company; the Boar's Head (*c*. 1599); the Fortune (1600); the Red Bull (1605); the second Globe (1614), built on the same site after the first was burned; the Hope (1614); and the second Fortune (1623). A sketch by the Dutchman De Witt of the Swan is the only reliable evidence of what the auditoria of these theatres looked like. Philip Henslowe (d. 1616), a speculator involved in building and managing several theatres, left a valuable record of income and expenditure for the Rose in his *Diary*.

Puck of Pook's Hill A collection of 10 stories and accompanying poems by KIPLING, published in 1906. It was intended for both adults and children. The meeting of two children, Dan and Una (loosely modelled on Kipling's own children), with the nature spirit Puck provides the framework for tales reaching back in English history, past the Normans and Saxons to the Roman invaders. Most show individuals who are able to illuminate their historical predicaments, and point to the capacity of civilization to renew itself. A sequel, *Rewards and Fairies* (1910), followed a similar format. Both volumes contain some of Kipling's best-known verse. 'A St Helena's Lullaby', 'The Way through the Woods' and 'If', in the latter volume, have been much admired.

Puckering, Sir John 1544–96 He is identified as the 'John Pickering' who wrote *Horestes*, a play which is itself identified as the *Orestes* acted at court in 1567 or 1568 and published just before it was produced. Though personifications of Vice, Revenge and Nature survive from the MORALITY PLAY, *Horestes* was a distinct advance on the bombastic clumsiness of works such as *CAMBISES*. Puckering was a lawyer who became Lord Keeper of the Seal.

Pudd'nhead Wilson, The Tragedy of A novel by MARK TWAIN, published in 1894. The title character is a lawyer, David Wilson, called 'Pudd'nhead' by a community – Dawson's Landing in the 1830s – which ridicules his eccentric ideas. The story of confused identities chiefly concerns Tom and Chambers, sons of the slave-owner Percy Driscoll, and Chambers's mother, the slave Roxana. Wilson establishes their true identities and becomes a town celebrity. The disgraced Chambers is sold down the river as a slave and Roxy is supported by her surrogate son, Tom.

Pulitzer Prizes A group of American literary prizes awarded annually to works in the following categories: fiction, drama, poetry, history, biography and general non-fiction (or journalism). They were founded in 1917 as part of the bequest with which the newspaper proprietor Joseph Pulitzer (1847–1911) established the Columbia University School of Journalism. The prizes for poetry and for journalism were added to the original categories in 1921 and 1962 respectively. The original terms of the fiction prize were relaxed in 1932 to allow novels without a specifically American setting to be considered and in 1947 to embrace collections of short stories as well as novels.

Major novelists, playwrights and poets among the prize-winners have included EUGENE O'NEILL (1920, 1922, 1928 and posthumously in 1957), EDITH WHARTON (1921), EDWIN ARLINGTON ROBINSON (1922, 1925 and 1928), WILLA CATHER (1923), ROBERT FROST (1924, 1931, 1937 and 1943), THORNTON WILDER (1928, 1938 and 1943) and JOHN STEINBECK (1940). Any list of prescient choices would mention the awards to ROBERT PENN WARREN for *All the King's Men* in 1947, TENNESSEE WILLIAMS for *A STREETCAR NAMED DESIRE* in 1948 and *CAT ON A HOT TIN ROOF* in 1955, and ARTHUR MILLER for *DEATH OF A SALESMAN* in 1949. Yet several major writers have been acknowledged only belatedly: HEMINGWAY had to wait until 1953, FAULKNER until 1955, WALLACE STEVENS and WILLIAM CARLOS WILLIAMS until the year of their deaths. The fiction category, in particular, has often been criticized for conservative attitudes which created a preference for safe best-sellers, such as Margaret Mitchell's *GONE WITH THE WIND*, and excluded SCOTT FITZGERALD.

Punch: *or, The London Charivari* A weekly comic magazine founded in 1841, partly through the efforts of HENRY MAYHEW, with MARK LEMON and Joseph Stirling Coyne (1803–68), his joint editors, and a circle of contributors which included GILBERT À BECKETT, THOMAS HOOD, DOUGLAS JERROLD and THACKERAY. JOHN LEECH was the chief artist and RICHARD DOYLE drew the famous cover. Originally noted for its radical abrasiveness, *Punch* soon settled for a more comfortable style of humour that came to be seen as typically English. Shirley Brooks (1816–74) and TOM TAYLOR were among later editors; its artists included SIR JOHN TENNIEL (1820–1914), Charles Keene (1823–91), GEORGE DU MAURIER and Linley Sambourne (1845–1910). It ceased publication in 1992.

Punch's Prize Novelists PARODIES of contemporary novelists by THACKERAY, published in *PUNCH* in 1847 and later retitled *Novels by Eminent Hands*. The targets include BULWER LYTTON, FENIMORE COOPER, G. P. R. JAMES, CHARLES LEVER and DISRAELI, whose *CONINGSBY* is mocked in 'Codlingsby'. Thackeray's playful critique

throws light on his intentions and achievements in *VANITY FAIR*, written at the same time.

Purchas, Samuel *c.* 1575–1626 Historian and travel-writer. He published *Purchas His Pilgrimage: or, Relations of the World and the Religions Observed in All Ages* (1613), *Purchas His Pilgrim: Microcosmus: or, the Histories of Man* (1619) and a continuation of the work of HAKLUYT, whom he had assisted, in *Hakluyt Posthumous: or, Purchas His Pilgrims: Containing a History of the World, in Sea Voyages and Land Travels by Englishmen and Others* (1625). Though generally inferior to Hakluyt's *Voyages*, it contains some notable accounts, particularly William Adams's description of his journey to Japan and his residence there.

Purdy, Al(fred) (Wellington) 1918– Canadian poet. His verse is firmly rooted in the landscapes and idioms of Eastern Ontario, whose people he presents against a vivid background of allusion and imagery drawn from mythological and historical sources. It is gathered in *Being Alive* (1978) and *The Collected Poems of Al Purdy* (1986), since which he has published another volume, *The Woman on the Shore* (1990), and a novel, *A Splinter in the Heart* (1990).

Purdy, James 1923– American novelist. Much of his fiction focuses on small-town provincial America. It includes: *Malcolm* (1959); *The Nephew* (1960); *Cabot Wright Begins* (1964); *Eustace Chisholm and the Works* (1967); *I am Elijah Thrush* (1972); a trilogy, *Sleepers in Moon-Crowned Valleys*, comprising *Jeremy's Version* (1970), *The House of the Solitary Maggot* (1974) and *Mourners Below* (1981); *In the Hollow of His Hand* (1986); and *Garments the Living Wear* (1989). He has also published poetry, plays and short stories, collected as *The Candle of Your Eyes* (1987).

Purity See CLEANNESS.

Pusey, Edward Bouverie 1800–82 Theologian. A close associate of NEWMAN and KEBLE in the OXFORD MOVEMENT, he contributed essays on the holy eucharist and baptism to *TRACTS FOR THE TIMES*. He defended Newman's analysis of the Thirty-Nine Articles in the controversial 'Tract 90' and was suspended from the office of university preacher in 1843, but remained firm in his allegiance to High Church Anglicanism after Newman's conversion to Catholicism. His *Doctrine of the Real Presence* was published in 1856.

Puttenham, George 1529–90 It was probably George rather than his brother Richard (?1520–?1601) who wrote of *The Art of English Poesy* (1589), although each has, at various times, seemed the likelier candidate. Both were nephews of SIR THOMAS ELYOT. The work is a critical discussion of poetry, mainly from the formal aspect. Book I defines poetry, defends it in terms similar to PHILIP SIDNEY's *APOLOGY FOR POETRY*, and gives major divisions of fiction (e.g. epic, tragedy, comedy) and minor divisions of poems (e.g. of praise, lamentation, marriage). Book II is concerned with METRE, and Book III with figures of speech, giving English equivalents for the Greek terms of rhetoric.

Pye, Henry James 1745–1813 POET LAUREATE from the death of THOMAS WARTON THE YOUNGER in 1790 until his own death, when SOUTHEY was appointed to the office. Pye's work – which includes plays, translations from the classics and critical essays as well as poetry – was not highly regarded during his lifetime and has not been reprinted since 1822.

Pygmalion A comedy by SHAW, produced in German at Vienna in 1913 and in England in 1914. It turns on the claim made by Professor Higgins (a character based on the scholar HENRY SWEET) that he could pass off Eliza, a Cockney flower girl, as a duchess by teaching her to speak properly. In the course of her education she emerges not merely as a presentable lady but as a beautiful woman of increasing sensitivity. To Higgins, however, she is just a successful experiment and the play ends with Eliza rejecting him. The film adaptation (1938), which Shaw approved, brought them together at the end. This version was made into the musical comedy, *My Fair Lady* (1956).

Pyle, Howard 1853–1911 American author and illustrator of CHILDREN'S LITERATURE. After some success contributing to children's magazines, he became famous with *The Merry Adventures of Robin Hood of Great Renown in Nottinghamshire* (1883), followed by a succession of historical romances before he turned to fairy-stories. His outstanding work, *King Arthur and His Knights* (1903), continued into three more volumes, ending with *The Story of the Grail and the Passing of Arthur* (1910). Perfectionist in detail, Pyle's picture-books also abound in inventive good humour.

Pym, Barbara (Mary Crampton) 1913–80 Novelist. After success with novels such as *Excellent Women* (1952) and *A Glass of Blessings* (1958) she fell out of favour until, with the publication of *Quartet in Autumn* (1977), her work was championed by LARKIN. *The Sweet Dove Died* (1979) was followed by four posthumous novels, *A Few Green Leaves* (1980), *An Unsuitable Attachment* (1982), *Crampton Hodnet* (1985) and *An Academic Question* (1986). Her books are wistful, delicate comedies with an unsparingly sad undertow; frustration in love is their common theme and the intrigue-ridden world of middle-class churchgoing a distinctive milieu.

Pynchon, Thomas 1937– American novelist. Though not prolific, his work is inventive and highly regarded. It includes: *V.* (1963), a long, dark-toned fantasy; *The Crying of Lot 49* (1966), about the attempts of the modern mind to organize an apparently chaotic universe; *GRAVITY'S RAINBOW* (1973); and *Vineland* (1990), a shorter and more conventional narrative. *Slow Learner* (1984) is a collection of stories.

pyrrhic See METRE.

Q See QUILLER-COUCH, SIR ARTHUR.

Quality Street A comedy by BARRIE, first produced in 1902. Two sisters, Susan and Phoebe Throssel, pin their hopes on a young doctor, Valentine Brown, proposing to Phoebe. However, he enlists in the army and poverty forces the sisters to start a school. When Brown returns ten years later, having lost a hand in battle, he is shocked by Phoebe's drabness. She masquerades as her own niece, first captivating him and finally driving him to prefer 'the schoolmistress in her old-maid's cap'.

quantitative metre See METRE.

Quarles, Francis 1592–1644 Poet. He found favour at court, wrote pamphlets in defence of Charles I and suffered for his Royalist sympathies when the Parliamentary party came to power. Although he published a mass of work, he is remembered only for *Emblems* (1635), the most popular 17th-century EMBLEM BOOK and perhaps the most popular verse of its age. *Enchiridion* (1640–1), a book of aphorisms, was also highly regarded.

Quarterly Review, The A Tory rival of the Whig *EDINBURGH REVIEW*, founded in 1809 by JOHN MURRAY. Its guiding principles were suggested by SIR WALTER SCOTT, and its early editors were WILLIAM GIFFORD, COLERIDGE's nephew Sir J. T. Coleridge, and J. G. LOCKHART. Scott himself contributed reviews of JANE AUSTEN's *Emma* and his own *Tales of My Landlord*, while JOHN WILSON CROKER wrote the notorious attack on KEATS's *ENDYMION* in 1818. Other contributions came from SOUTHEY, GEORGE CANNING, JOHN HOOKHAM FRERE, SAMUEL ROGERS and MATTHEW ARNOLD. *The Quarterly* survived until 1967.

quatrain A four-line STANZA, usually but not necessarily rhymed. The heroic (or elegiac) quatrain is in iambic pentameter (see METRE). For the ballad quatrain, see BALLAD.

Queen Mab A visionary philosophical and political poem in nine CANTOS, with prose notes, by SHELLEY, published in 1813. The spirit of the sleeping maiden Ianthe is transported by a spectral chariot to the Fairy Queen's 'etherial palace' in deep space. Here Mab rewards her for her personal virtue with a synoptic vision of history, the present and the new moral, social and economic order which will inevitably ensue. The Queen's speeches, which occupy most of the poem, attack conditions in contemporary England: the monarchy (canto III), law (III), warfare (IV), marriage and commerce (V), and established religion (VI and VII). Canto VIII evokes the state of perpetual peace which will follow the work of 'Necessity'. Of equal if not greater interest are the 17 prose notes, almost as long as the poem itself and clearly intended to be read as part of it. Six are fully developed essays, dealing with the labour theory of value (note 7); free love (9); necessity in the moral and material universe (12); atheism (13); Christianity (15); and vegetarianism (17).

Queen's Wake, The A poem by JAMES HOGG, published in 1813. The 'Introduction' describes Queen Mary's return from France to assume the Scottish throne and the announcement of her Christmas 'wake' at Holyrood Palace, during which 13 bards, including Rizzio, compete in song. The story of 'Kilmeny', the rasping 'Witch of Fife' and 'The Fate of Macgregor' are particularly effective.

Quennell, Peter 1905–93 Man of letters. An early reputation as a poet launched him on a career chiefly memorable for biographical studies of BYRON (1934–5), RUSKIN (1949), HOGARTH (1955) and, in *Four Portraits* (1945), BOSWELL, GIBBON, STERNE and JOHN WILKES. *The Marble Foot* (1976) is autobiographical.

Quentin Durward A novel by SIR WALTER SCOTT, published in 1823. Its background is the rivalry between Louis XI and Charles the Bold, Duke of Burgundy, in 15th-century France. Quentin Durward, a young Scot in the king's guard, conducts the Burgundian heiress, Isabelle de Croye, to the protection of the Bishop of Liège. Their journey is beset by dangers from the duke and also from the villainy of the king's servant, William de la Marck, the Wild Boar of the Ardennes. Quentin kills de la Marck and wins Isabelle's hand, and Louis outwits the duke.

Quiet American, The A novel by GRAHAM GREENE, published in 1955. The narrator is Thomas Fowler, a cynical, middle-aged English journalist in Vietnam during the French war against the Vietminh. His story concerns the murder of Alden Pyle (the Quiet American), a naïve and high-minded idealist. It alternates between the aftermath of Pyle's death and the events leading up to it. Pyle has stolen Fowler's mistress, Phuong, and become involved in subversive politics. When Fowler learns of his part in a bomb explosion in a local café, he lays information which prompts Pyle's murder. At the end, Fowler finds himself in a position to marry Phuong, but is left wishing that 'there existed someone to whom I could say that I was sorry'.

Quiller-Couch, Sir Arthur 1863–1944 Critic, novelist and poet, better known by his pseudonym, Q. After working in journalism he returned to his native Cornwall in 1892 and used it as background for novels which include *Dead Man's Rock* (1887), *Troy Town* (1888), *The Splendid Spur* (1889) and *The Ship of Stars* (1899). Volumes of poetry include *Verses and Parodies* (1893), *Poems and Ballads* (1896) and *The Vigil of Venus* (1912). *The Oxford Book of English Verse* (1900) was the first of several famous anthologies he compiled for Oxford University Press. He was knighted for political services in 1910 and appointed the first King Edward VII Professor of English Literature at Cambridge in 1912. Two volumes of lectures, *On the Art of Writing* (1916) and *On the Art of Reading* (1920), enjoyed great popularity.

Raban, Jonathan 1942– Travel writer and critic. His drily ruminative travel books include: *Arabia* (1979), about the Arab Middle East states; *Old Glory* (1981), about his journey down the Mississippi; *Coasting* (1986), about his circumnavigation of the British Isles; and *Hunting Mr Heartbreak* (1990), an exploration of the American sensibility. *The Technique of Modern Fiction* (1969) and *The Society of the Poem* (1971) are early works of literary criticism; *For Love and Money* (1987) collects his later book reviews. He has also written a novel, *Foreign Land* (1985).

Rabe, David (William) 1940– American playwright. His experience in Vietnam prompted his best-known work, the trilogy consisting of *The Basic Training of Pavlo Hummel* (1971), *Sticks and Bones* (1971) and *Streamers* (1976). Other plays include *Goose and Tomtom* (1982, 1986), about a bizarre robbery, and *Hurlyburly* (1984) and its prequel *These the River Keeps* (1991), about Hollywood. His work combines grotesque comedy, surreal fantasy and SATIRE. Screenplays include *I'm Dancing As Fast As I Can* (1982), *Streamers* (1983) and *Casualties of War* (1990).

Rackham, Arthur 1867–1939 Artist and illustrator of CHILDREN'S LITERATURE. His illustrations for BARHAM's *Ingoldsby Legends* (1898) first showed his talent for the grotesque, also apparent in *Fairy Tales by the Brothers Grimm* (1900), BARRIE's *Peter Pan in Kensington Gardens* (1906) and *Mother Goose: The Old Nursery Rhymes* (1913). His illustrations for a new edition of THE WIND IN THE WILLOWS (1940), left incomplete at his death, are in a more mellow style.

Radcliffe, Ann 1764–1823 Novelist. Although she did not originate the GOTHIC NOVEL, she established herself as its best-known and most popular exponent with six works: *The Castles of Athlin and Dunbayne* (1789), *A Sicilian Romance* (1790), *The Romance of the Forest* (1791), THE MYSTERIES OF UDOLPHO (1794), *The Italian* (1797) and the posthumously published *Gaston de Blondeville* (1826). Her persecuted heroines, wild and lonely settings, cliffhanging chapter endings and apparently supernatural events became widely imitated conventions. Mrs Radcliffe also wrote verse, included in her novels and collected in two volumes (1834). *A Journey Made in the Summer of 1794 through Holland and the Western Frontier of Germany* (1795) shows the same mastery of landscape description as her novels.

Railway Children, The See NESBIT, E.

Rainbow, The A novel by D. H. LAWRENCE, published in 1915. It chronicles the lives of three generations of the Brangwen family in Nottinghamshire during a period which spans the transition from rural to urban culture. Tom Brangwen inherits Marsh Farm in the Erewash Valley and marries a Polish widow, Lydia, who already has a daughter, Anna. Tom becomes devoted to Anna but estranged from his wife, even after the birth of two sons, Tom and Fred. Anna marries Will Brangwen, Tom's nephew, but after a rapturous honeymoon the couple grow apart and Anna devotes herself to her children. The narrative concentrates increasingly on the growth of the oldest child, Ursula. She goes to university and becomes a teacher, and has an unsatisfactory affair with Anton Skrebensky, an army officer. They have separated by the end of the novel and Ursula is left, alone and recovering from illness, to contemplate a

rainbow: 'the earth's new architecture' symbolically sweeping away 'the old, brittle corruption of houses and factories'. Ursula and her younger sister Gudrun reappear in WOMEN IN LOVE.

Although Lawrence's publisher had forced him to make changes to his original text, *The Rainbow* was prosecuted and banned for obscenity; unsold copies were destroyed. A scene involving the pregnant Anna gave particular offence. The novel was reissued in 1926 from an American edition which had been further censored.

Raine, Craig 1944– Poet. His work celebrates the ordinary by presenting domestic objects in unfamiliar ways. JAMES FENTON has dubbed him and his followers the MARTIAN POETS, from the title of Raine's second collection, *A Martian Sends a Postcard Home* (1979). Other volumes are *The Onion, Memory* (1978) and *Rich* (1984). His libretto for Nigel Osborne's opera, *The Electrification of the Soviet Union* (1986), commissioned by Glyndebourne, is adapted from Pasternak's novella *The Last Summer*.

Raine, Kathleen (Jessie) 1908– Poet and critic. Influenced by YEATS and EDWIN MUIR, her poetry is contemplative and lyrical, concerned mainly with the relationship between man and nature, with dreams, and with an inner spiritual quest. It includes *Collected Poems* (1981), *To the Sun: Three Poems* (1988), *The Presence: Poems 1984–7* (1988) and *Living with Mystery: Poems 1987–91* (1992). She has also published criticism, in *Defending Ancient Springs* (1967) and studies of BLAKE (1969) and YEATS (1986), and an autobiography, *Farewell Happy Fields* (1973), *The Land Unknown* (1975) and *The Lion's Mouth* (1977).

Raleigh [Ralegh], Sir **Walter** 1554–1618 Courtier, adventurer, poet and historian. He was established as Elizabeth I's favourite by 1582, rewarded with monopolies, estates in Ireland and England, a knighthood, the Captaincy of her Guard and the Vice-Admiralship of Devon and Cornwall. Unpopular with the court for his pride and extravagance, and suspected of unorthodox thought, he was briefly committed to the Tower after his secret marriage to Elizabeth Throckmorton, one of the queen's attendants. In 1595 he led an expedition up the Orinoco and in 1596 he took part in Essex's raid on Cadiz. He was arrested again in 1603, on suspicion of conspiracy to dethrone James I, and, after an unfair trial, committed to the Tower until 1616. He was released to undertake an expedition to the Orinoco in search of gold, but again arrested after its failure. Raleigh was executed at Westminster in 1618.

Very little of his verse appeared in print during his lifetime and some works are only doubtfully attributed to him. Even the authenticity of the famous 'Passionate Man's Pilgrimage' ('Give me my scallop shell of quiet') is in doubt. Other anthology pieces attributed to Raleigh are the reply to MARLOWE's *PASSIONATE SHEPHERD TO HIS LOVE* and the poignant 'What is our life?', which appeared in a madrigal setting by Orlando Gibbons in 1612. Some poems in THE PHOENIX NEST may also be his. Undoubtedly in Raleigh's hand are 'The Eleventh and Twelfth Books of the Ocean to Cynthia', a formalized courtship devoted to Elizabeth, though it is not certain whether this formed part of a longer work.

Raleigh published *A Report of the Truth of the Fight about* the Isles of the Azores (1591), about Sir Richard Grenville's encounter with the Spanish fleet, and A Discovery of the Empire of Guyana (1596), describing his 1595 expedition. The History of the World (1614), written during his imprisonment, started with the creation and proceeded as far as the 2nd century BC. It was published unfinished.

Raleigh, Sir **Walter Alexander** 1861–1922 Critic. Having been professor of English at Aligarh (India), Liverpool and Glasgow, he became the first professor in the subject at Oxford in 1904. His books include The English Novel: From the Earliest Times to the Appearance of Waverley (1891) and studies of ROBERT LOUIS STEVENSON (1895), MILTON (1900), WORDSWORTH (1903), SHAKESPEARE (1907), and SAMUEL JOHNSON (1910).

Ralph Roister Doister A comedy by NICHOLAS UDALL, who probably intended it for performance by schoolboys. Some scholars date it before 1541, when Udall was dismissed from Eton, and others as late as 1553. What is certain is that Udall drew the contrasting characters of braggart lover (Ralph Roister Doister) and flattering parasite (Matthew Merrygreek) from Terence, particularly Eunuchus and Miles gloriosus, adding to his classical model such homely English figures as the servants, Meg Mumblecrust and Tib Talkapace, and combining them all in lively rhyming doggerel. The action takes place outside the house of Christian Custance, a widow betrothed to the absent merchant, Gawyn Goodluck.

Ramanujan, **A(ttipat)** **K(rishnaswami)** 1929– Indian poet. A poet of delicate, thoughtful sensibility who always aims at purity and translucence of expression, he has published The Striders (1966), Relations (1971), Second Sight (1986) and Selected Poems (1976). He also writes in Kannada and translates from classical Tamil.

Rambler, *The* A twice-weekly periodical edited by SAMUEL JOHNSON, for 208 issues published between 20 March 1750 and 14 March 1752. All but four were written by Johnson himself: No. 30 was by Catherine Talbot, No. 97 by SAMUEL RICHARDSON, and Nos. 44 and 100 by ELIZABETH CARTER, while parts of three others, notably the second letter in No. 15 by GARRICK, were also from outside contributors. Consisting of essays on many topics, it is a highly moral work and, with RASSELAS (1759), has been regarded as a prose companion to and explication of THE VANITY OF HUMAN WISHES (1749). Reprinted nine times in Johnson's lifetime, it did more than any other work, except his DICTIONARY, to establish his reputation.

Ramsay, Allan 1686–1758 Scottish poet and anthologist. A vigorous member of Edinburgh's literary society, he contributed to the revival of Scots secular poetry with an edition (1718) of Christis Kirk on the Grene, a poem attributed to JAMES I OF SCOTLAND, and several anthologies. The Tea Table Miscellany (1724–32) was a collection of songs and BALLADS which gave ROBERT BURNS and other later Scottish writers the impetus for their work. The Ever Green, being a Collection of Scots Poems, Wrote by the Ingenious before 1600 (1724) presented the work of such poets as ROBERT HENRYSON and WILLIAM DUNBAR from the Bannatyne Manuscript (see GEORGE BANNATYNE). Always ready to 'improve' original texts, Ramsay modified the originally coarse and vital expressions in his Collection of Scots Proverbs (1736). His own poems were gathered in a volume of 1728. A pastoral drama, The Gentle Shepherd (1725), was staged as a BALLAD OPERA with Scots airs.

Rand, Ayn 1905–82 American novelist and social critic. Born in St Petersburg, she emigrated to the USA in 1926

and first attracted a popular audience with a novel, The Fountainhead (1943). Her credo that humans are rational, self-interested and pledged to individualism was advocated in Atlas Shrugged (1957), a novel about the dangers of altruism, The Objectivist, a journal she founded in 1962 and The Ayn Rand Letter (1971–82). Critical works include For the New Intellectual (1961), The Virtue of Selfishness (1965) and The New Left: The Anti-Industrial Revolution (1971).

Randolph, Thomas 1605–35 Playwright. He owed his contemporary reputation to the work he produced at Cambridge. His pastoral play, Amyntas (1630), is enlivened by its comic scenes but his other full-length piece, The Jealous Lovers (1632), is dramatically insipid. Aristippus: or, The Jovial Philosopher (c. 1626) proposes that study of the philosophy of drinking should be added to the university syllabus, a theme pursued with variations in The Drinking Academy (c. 1626). The Conceited Pedlar (1627) is an ephemerally witty monologue. The Muses' Looking-Glass (1630), in which an actor out-argues Puritan opposition to the theatre, is his most interesting work, reflecting the influence of JONSON, of whom Randolph was a favoured 'son'.

Ransom, John Crowe 1888–1974 American poet and critic. His first collections of verse were Poems about God (1919), Chills and Fever (1924), Grace after Meat (1924) and Two Gentlemen in Bonds (1927). A leading member of the FUGITIVES, he also edited I'll Take My Stand: The South and the Agrarian Tradition (1930). In 1939 he founded THE KENYON REVIEW and in 1941 he gave currency to the principles of the NEW CRITICISM in a book of that title. His other critical writings include God without Thunder: An Orthodox Defense of Orthodoxy (1930), The World's Body (1938) and Poems and Essays (1955).

Ransome, Arthur (Michell) 1884–1967 Journalist and writer of CHILDREN'S LITERATURE. His work in Russia produced Old Peter's Russian Tales (1916) and an account of the Bolshevik Revolution, Six Weeks in Russia (1919). Swallows and Amazons (1931) was the first in a series of children's adventure stories reflecting his enthusiasm for sailing, the outdoor life and those parts of England (the Lake District, the Norfolk Broads) which favour such activities. Other titles in this vein included Pigeon Post (1936), We Didn't Mean to Go to Sea (1938), The Big Six (1940), and Great Northern? (1947). Ransome also wrote Racundra's First Cruise (1923) and Mainly about Fishing (1959). Rupert Hart-Davis edited The Autobiography of Arthur Ransome (1976).

Rao, Raja 1908– Indian novelist. His early stories were in Kannada and English, the latter published as The Cow of the Barricades (1947) and The Policeman and the Rose (1978). His expansive novels include Kanthapura (1938), The Serpent and the Rope (1960), The Cat and Shakespeare (1965) and Comrade Kirillov (1976; in French translation, 1965). Later works, such as The Chessmaker and His Moves (1988) and On the Ganga Ghat (1989), a collection of stories, require stamina and patience.

Rape of Lucrece, *The* A narrative poem by SHAKESPEARE, first published in 1594. It tells the story, which Shakespeare could have read in Livy, Ovid and CHAUCER's THE LEGEND OF GOOD WOMEN, of the rape of Lucretia (Lucrece) by Tarquinius ('lust-breathed Tarquin'), son of the King of Rome. The first section describes his furious ride to Collatium, his entertainment there by an unsuspecting Lucrece, his restlessness and night journey by torchlight through the house to her chamber, in the course of which he has an internal debate between 'frozen conscience and hot-burning will'. After Lucrece has been described in bed, she awakens to hear Tarquin's threats and pleads unavailingly with him. In the second section, after the rape, Lucrece rails at length against night, opportunity and 'misshapen time', all of which conspired in her violation. When day comes she summons her husband Collatinus (who had extolled her chastity), identifies Tarquin as her attacker and stabs herself. Although Shakespeare turned in *The Rape of Lucrece* from the mythic world of *VENUS AND ADONIS* to a grim Roman tragedy, his verse remained packed with ornamented language and CONCEITS, an obviously self-conscious delight in verbal artifice.

Rape of the Lock, The A poem by POPE, published in a two-CANTO version in 1712 and expanded to five cantos in 1714. One of his most glittering performances, it was prompted by Lord Petre's forceful cutting of a lock of hair from Lady Arabella Fermor's head. This apparently trivial event caused dissension between their two families, and Pope's intention was 'a jest to laugh them together again'. His extended MOCK-HEROIC treatment plays on the war between the sexes, feminizes EPIC conventions and satirizes the superficiality of society women while still celebrating their beauty. The poem traces the course of the fateful day when Belinda wakes up, glorifies her appearance at a ritualistic dressing table, plays cards, flirts, drinks coffee and has her hair ravaged. The enlarged version of the poem includes some elaborate 'machinery', or accompanying details of supernatural elements surrounding the mortal events, partly modelled on Boileau's *Le Lutrin*.

Rasselas, Prince of Abyssinia, The History of A philosophical romance by SAMUEL JOHNSON, published in 1759. It is said to have been written in the evenings of a single week to pay for his mother's funeral. The exotic setting ensured it instant success.

The book tackles Johnson's habitual theme of the 'choice of life'. Rasselas, son of the Abyssinian Emperor, determines to seek the world outside the luxurious 'happy valley' to which he has been confined, setting out full of theoretical hopes and fruitless meditations with his sister Nekayah and the elderly philosopher Imlac. His romantic notions are contradicted by the miseries, hardships and disappointments of the real world. The plot itself is slender, but the whole work is invigorated by Johnson's robust common sense and occasional glints of humour. Idealism and innocence, the pastoral values, are gently deflated. 'The Conclusion, in which Nothing is concluded' illustrates the book's deliberate structure, and affirms Johnson's conviction that action is superior to introspection.

Rattigan, Sir Terence 1911–77 Playwright. *French without Tears* (1936), a light comedy, established him as a West End favourite. He is best remembered for carefully crafted plays and screenplays in which character and plot take precedence over social comment. *The Winslow Boy* (1946), *Ross* (a study of T. E. LAWRENCE; 1960) and *A Bequest to the Nation* (1970) are all based on historical incidents and characters. Rattigan's compassion for the humiliated also distinguishes *Flare Path* (1942), *The Browning Version* (1948), *The Deep Blue Sea* (1952) and *Separate Tables* (1954).

Rattlin the Reefer A novel by Edward Howard (?1791–1841), published in 1836. He was a shipmate of MARRYAT and his story resembles Marryat's own more famous novels of the sea. Marryat himself thought

enough of the work to prepare it for publication, describing it as 'Edited by the author of *Peter Simple*'.

Rauf Coilyear, The Tale of A late-15th-century Scottish poem in ALLITERATIVE VERSE. Rauf, a charcoal-burner, entertains Charlemagne (Charles) in his hut without realizing who he is. The Emperor invites him to court and knights him. Rauf fights a Saracen, Magog, and becomes a Marshal of France.

Raven, Simon 1927– Novelist. A prolific writer, whose rakish wit quickly earned him a name as an *enfant terrible*, he has consolidated his reputation with two ROMANS FLEUVES: the 10-volume *Alms for Oblivion*, beginning with *Fielding Gray* (1967) and ending with *The Survivors* (1976); and the 7-volume *The First-born of Egypt*, beginning with *Morning Star* (1984) and ending with *The Troubadour* (1992).

Raverat, Gwen(dolen) (Mary) 1885–1957 Wood engraver and autobiographer. The granddaughter of CHARLES DARWIN, she married the French artist Jacques Raverat. *Period Piece: A Cambridge Childhood* (1952) is a charmingly illustrated portrait of her extended family, which included many people of academic or scientific consequence.

Raworth, Tom 1938– Poet. An important figure in the 'underground' poetry of the 1960s, he used the techniques of CHARLES OLSON's 'projectivist verse', often to comic and surreal effect, in *The Relation Ship* (1966), *The Big Green Day* (1968), *Lion, Lion* (1970) and *Moving* (1971). Later work includes *Ace* (1977), *Writing* (1982), *Tottering State: Selected and New Poems 1963–83* (1984), *Lazy Left Hand: Notes from 1970–1975* (1986) and *From External Sections* (1990).

Read, Sir Herbert (Edward) 1893–1968 Critic and poet. His poetry, much influenced by IMAGISM, included *Songs of Chaos* (1915), *Naked Warriors* (1919), *The End of a War* (1933) and several *Collected Poems*, the last published in 1966. His critical work included *Reason and Romanticism* (1926), *English Prose Style* (1928), *Form in Modern Poetry* (1932), *Art and Industry* (1934), *The True Voice of Feeling* (1953) and *The Literature of Sincerity* (1968). Read also produced editions of T. E. HULME, Kropotkin, Orage and Jung, several volumes of autobiography and one novel, *The Green Child* (1945), an allegorical fantasy.

Reade, Charles 1814–84 Novelist, playwright and journalist. The various offices he held at Magdalen College, Oxford, did not distract him from a vigorous career in literature. His interest in theatre management led to collaboration with TOM TAYLOR in several plays, beginning with *Masks and Faces* (1852), which he turned into a novel, *Peg Woffington* (1853). His first success as a novelist came with *It is Never Too Late to Mend* (1856), intended to reform prisons. Other 'novels with a purpose' included: *Hard Cash* (1863), attacking abuses in private lunatic asylums; *Foul Play* (1868), about abuses at sea; *Put Yourself in His Place* (1870), attacking Trade Union closed shops; *A Terrible Temptation* (1871), returning to the attack on private asylums; and *A Woman-Hater* (1877), about the disadvantages of village life. Still involved in the theatre, he dramatized several of his novels, including *Griffith Gaunt* (1866), which he considered his best work, and collaborated with BOUCICAULT. Ill-health made him turn to short stories but did not prevent him writing *Hang in Haste, Repent at Leisure* (1877), a series of letters which led to the reprieve of four people condemned to death for murder, and adapting Zola's *L'Assommoir* for the English stage as *Drink*. Unflaggingly energetic, fiercely polemical and cannily commercial, he was ranked with DICKENS and GEORGE ELIOT in his day. Now he is remembered, if at all, for THE CLOISTER AND THE HEARTH (1861), his most carefully researched historical novel.

Reade, (William) Winwood 1838–75 Historian, novelist and travel-writer. His travel books deal with his experiences in Africa, where he studied the habits of the gorilla, and his novels imitate the work of his uncle, CHARLES READE. He made his name with *The Martyrdom of Man* (1872), a history of civilization frankly hostile to religion. It remained popular for some years after his early death.

realism A term first used in France in the 1850s for literature concerned with representing the world as it is rather than as it ought to be. Realism observes and documents contemporary life and everyday scenes as objectively as possible in low-key, unrhetorical prose and reproduces the flavour of colloquial speech in its dialogue. Though realist writers may portray characters from all social levels, they often look to the lowest social classes and take cruelty or suffering as their subject.

Realism became the dominant mode of the 19th-century European novel and, from the late 1880s, the theatre as well. The great works of European realist fiction include Flaubert's *Sentimental Education*, Tolstoy's *Anna Karenina* and Dostoevsky's *Crime and Punishment*. Accurate observation and attention to the structures of society make GEORGE ELIOT's *MIDDLEMARCH* a notable English example. The chief American realists are HOWELLS and SINCLAIR LEWIS, while the line of English realist writing continues in the 20th century via ARNOLD BENNETT to the post-World War II evocations of English middle-class life by ANGUS WILSON and the Northern working-class fiction of the 1950s. Realism played an important part in reviving the English theatre in the first decade of this century (GRANVILLE-BARKER, GALSWORTHY) and again in the 1950s (OSBORNE and his generation). In Ireland O'CASEY and in America O'NEILL and ARTHUR MILLER developed native versions of the dramatic realism of Ibsen and Strindberg. See also NATURALISM.

Reaney, James (Crerar) 1926– Canadian poet and playwright. He has been seen as a 'mythopoeic' poet under the influence of NORTHROP FRYE but both *The Red Heart* (1949), his first volume, and *Twelve Letters to a Small Town* (1962), his finest volume, are strongly regional, rooted in his native Ontario. Other poetry includes *A Suit of Nettles* (1958), *The Dance of Death at London, Ontario* (1963) and *Performance Poems* (1990). He has turned to plays which, like his poetry, reveal a world of fantasy and the macabre lurking beneath the surface. They use the conventions of MELODRAMA but later work displays greater theatrical artifice. Mime is joined by music, dance, puppets and magic lanterns in his masterpiece, the trilogy consisting of *Sticks and Stones* (1975), *The St Nicholas Hotel* (1976) and *Handcuffs* (1977). Other plays include *Colours in the Dark* (1969), *Listen to the Wind* (1972), *The Dismissal* (1978) and *The Canadian Brothers* (1984). He has also written opera libretti.

Rebecca of Sunnybrook Farm See WIGGIN, KATE DOUGLAS.

Rechy, John (Francisco) 1934– American novelist. His work generally portrays the homosexual communities of major cities such as New York and Los Angeles. It includes *City of Night* (1963), *Numbers* (1967), *This Day's Death* (1969), *The Vampires* (1971), *The Fourth Angel* (1973), *Rushes* (1979), *Bodies and Souls* (1983), *Marilyn's Daughter*

(1988) and *The Miraculous Day of Amalia Gómez* (1991). He has also published a study of urban homosexual lifestyles, *The Sexual Outlaw* (1977).

Recollections of the Lakes and the Lake Poets A series of autobiographical reflections and literary portraits by DE QUINCEY, first published in *Tait's Magazine* in 1834–9. Written some 20 years after the period of his association and intimacy with them, his reminiscences of his friends and former neighbours, WORDSWORTH, COLERIDGE, SOUTHEY and DOROTHY WORDSWORTH, are a revealing blend of fulsome praise for their literary achievements, and mischievous – occasionally malicious – gossip, unflattering personal description, and the carefully placed negative inference.

Recruiting Officer, The A comedy by FARQUHAR, first performed in 1706. His experience as a recruiting officer in Lichfield and Shrewsbury inspired not only the plot but also the decision to set it in Shrewsbury, against the prevailing view that comedy required a London setting. Captain Plume recruits men by courting their sweethearts, his sergeant, Kite, by posing as an astrologer. Sylvia, daughter of Justice Ballance, falls in love with Plume and disguises herself as a man to be near him. A secondary plot concerns the failure of a rival recruiting officer, Captain Brazen, to win a rich wife.

Red Badge of Courage, The A novel by STEPHEN CRANE, published in 1895. Set during the American Civil War, it contrasts the frightening realities of battle with conventional war narratives. Eager for glory, Henry Fleming enlists in the Union army but flees from his second encounter with the enemy into the forest. There he attempts to find solace in Nature, but fails to justify his desertion in his own eyes. A meeting with a dying soldier sparks his anger at the injustices of war. He returns, marked by the 'red badge' of a soldier who has fought, and behaves heroically but without pride in his heroics. He remains haunted by the memory of the 'tattered' soldier, a wounded man deserted on the field.

Redburn: His First Voyage A novel by HERMAN MELVILLE, published in 1849. It draws on his own first voyage as an apprentice seaman. Wellingborough Redburn ships from New York on the *Highlander*, a trader bound for Liverpool. He is treated with indifference and cruelty by Captain Riga and his fellow seamen, particularly Jackson. After finding appalling poverty in Liverpool, Redburn goes to London with Harry Bolton, a spendthrift aristocrat. The pair join the *Highlander* for its return voyage to America. Jackson's treacheries continue, though he dies as they near New York. Captain Riga cheats Harry and Redburn out of their wages.

Redeemed Captive, Returning to Zion, The An account by John Williams (1664–1729), published in 1707, of his two-year captivity among the Mohawk Indians and French Jesuits in Quebec. A minister at Deerfield, Massachusetts, he was taken prisoner in a raid in 1704 during the French and Indian Wars. Williams stresses that the afflictions of Indian raids and captivities have been visited on the colony for its sins.

Redgauntlet An EPISTOLARY NOVEL by SIR WALTER SCOTT, published in 1824. The background to the story is the supposed return to Scotland of the Young Pretender after the defeat of the 1745 rebellion. Herries of Birrenswork (Sir Edward Redgauntlet), a fanatical Jacobite, kidnaps Sir Arthur Darsie Redgauntlet, his nephew and the head of the family, but Alan Fairford sets out to rescue his friend. The novel includes 'Wandering Willie's Tale', a classic ghost story.

Redgrove, Peter (William) 1932– Poet and novelist. He was a founder member of the GROUP. Packed with visual imagery, and developing a strongly mystical vein, his poetry has appeared in *The Collector and Other Poems* (1960), *At the White Monument* (1963), *Sons of My Skin: Selected Poems* (edited by Marie Peel; 1975), *The Weddings at Nether Powers* (1979) and *The Moon Disposes: Poems 1954–87* (1987). Muscular power and rich language also marks his novels, which include *In the Country of the Skin* (1973) and *The Beekeepers* (1980). Collaborative work with his wife, Penelope Shuttle, includes a documentary on the human fertility cycle, *The Wise Wound* (1978).

Reed, Henry 1914–86 Poet and radio playwright. *A Map of Verona* (1946) includes 'Lessons of the War', three poems dealing with army training; the precise and poignant 'Naming of Parts' is often anthologized. *Collected Poems* appeared in 1991. His radio drama includes the verse plays collected in *The Streets of Pompeii* (1971) and the satirical prose plays in *Hilda Tablet and Others* (1971).

Reed, Ishmael (Scott) 1938– Black American novelist and poet. Combining surrealism and angry satire, his novels aspire to break the cycle of oppression of American minorities. They include *The Free-Lance Pall-Bearers* (1967), *Yellow Back Radio Broke-Down* (1969), *Mumbo-Jumbo* (1972), *The Last Days of Louisiana Red* (1974), *Flight to Canada* (1976), *The Terrible Twos* (1982), *Reckless Eyeballing* (1986) and *The Terrible Threes* (1989). His poetry includes *Catechism of D Neo-American HooDoo Church* (1970), *Chattanooga* (1973) and *A Secretary to the Spirits* (1978). *Shrovetide in New Orleans* (1978) and *God Made Alaska for the Indians* (1982) are collections of essays.

Reed, Talbot Baines 1852–93 Writer of CHILDREN'S LITERATURE. *The Fifth Form at St Dominic's* (1887), *Cock House at Fellsgarth* (1891) and *The Master of the Shell* (1894) are boys' stories glamorizing public-school life.

Reeve, Clara 1729–1807 Novelist. She earned herself an important place in the development of the GOTHIC NOVEL with *The Champion of Virtue* (1777; republished as *The Old English Baron*, 1778). Other novels were *The Two Mentors* (1783), *The Exiles* (1788), *The School for Widows* (1791), *Memoirs of Sir Roger de Clarendon* (1793) and *Destination* (1799).

Reeve's Tale, The See CANTERBURY TALES.

Reeves, James 1909–78 Poet. His 12 volumes for adults include *Collected Poems 1927–74* (1974). His first collection for children, *The Wandering Moon* (1950), was followed by volumes illustrated by EDWARD ARDIZZONE. In later life be took to retelling classics to a child audience, notably in *The Exploits of Don Quixote* (1959) and *Fables from Aesop* (1961). In 1973 he published his *Complete Poems for Children*. The irreverent humour, lively imagination and occasional melancholy of his poetry made him a favourite with readers of all ages.

Reflections on the Revolution in France A treatise by EDMUND BURKE, published in 1790, the year after the outbreak of the French Revolution. Burke attacked the idea that people have the right to destroy the state and its institutions in the hope of some contingent improvement. Liberty is dismissed as an abstraction, equality as impossible because contrary to nature and fraternity as 'cant and gibberish'. A memorable passage laments that with the destruction of the *ancien régime* 'the age of chivalry is gone ... and the glory of Europe is extinguished forever'.

Prompted by RICHARD PRICE's sermon and *Discourse* in praise of the Revolution, Burke's treatise in turn provoked replies from PAINE in *THE RIGHTS OF MAN*, James Mackintosh in *Vindiciae Gallicae* and WOLLSTONECRAFT in her two *Vindications*.

Rehearsal, The A BURLESQUE play by BUCKINGHAM, perhaps with the help of SAMUEL BUTLER and others, first performed in 1671. The pompous Bayes attends a rehearsal of his heroic tragedy, constantly providing ludicrous annotation to his overblown verse and his account of the attempted usurpation of the kingdom of Brentford. Buckingham's original target was probably D'AVENANT, but the revised version was aimed at DRYDEN, who retaliated in *ABSALOM AND ACHITOPHEL*.

Reid, Christopher (John) 1949– Poet. *Arcadia* (1979) and *Pea Soup* (1982), concentrating on unusual perceptions of everyday reality and using a technique built on the deliberate misrecognition of signs, identified him with the MARTIAN POETS and made comparisons with CRAIG RAINE inevitable. Subsequent volumes are *Katerina Brac* (1985) and *In the Echoey Tunnel* (1991).

Reid, Forrest 1875–1947 Irish novelist. Most of his 16 novels are centred on childhood and set their values against those of the decaying commercial society of north-east Ulster. *Peter Waring* (1937) is widely regarded as his best work, although the Tom Barber trilogy, *Uncle Stephen* (1931), *The Retreat* (1936) and *Young Tom* (1944), is almost as well known. His autobiographies, *Apostate* (1926) and *Private Road* (1940), are steeped in the nostalgia which characterizes the best of his fiction.

Reid, Captain (Thomas) Mayne 1818–83 Anglo-American writer of CHILDREN'S LITERATURE. Born in County Down, he drew on his American adventures in popular novels for boys, notably *The Rifle Rangers: or, Adventures in Southern Mexico* (1850), *The Scalp Hunters: or, Romantic Adventures in Northern Mexico* (1851), *The Boy Hunters* (1853), *The Maroon* (1862), *The Cliff-Climbers* (1864), *Afloat in the Forest* (1865), *The Headless Horseman* (1866), *The Castaways* (1870) and *Gwen-Wynne* (1877). *The Quadroon: or, A Lover's Adventure in Louisiana* (1856) was adapted for the stage by BOUCICAULT as *THE OCTOROON* (1859). He also wrote travel books, poetry, plays and a book on croquet (1863).

Reid, Thomas 1710–96 Scottish philosopher. He succeeded ADAM SMITH as professor of moral philosophy at Glasgow University and made his mark with *An Inquiry into the Human Mind on the Principles of Common Sense* (1764). *Essays on the Intellectual Powers of Man* (1785) and *Essays on the Active Powers of Man* (1788) confirmed him as founder of the 'common-sense' school of philosophy, ranging the principles common to the understanding of all rational men against the scepticism generated by philosophers such as LOCKE, BERKELEY, and HUME.

Reid, V(ictor) S(tafford) 1913–87 Jamaican novelist. With ROGER MAIS and the sculptress Edna Manley, he was a member of the Focus group which helped to promote a sense of cultural nationalism in Jamaica in the 1940s. His first novel, *New Day* (1949), was seminal in the development of Caribbean fiction. The first work to use Creole as its narrative medium, it describes changes in Jamaican society between 1865, the date of the Morant Bay rebellion, and 1944, when a new constitution was introduced. Reid's other novels include: *The Leopard* (1958), set in Kenya at the time of the Mau Mau freedom fighters' struggle; *Sixty-Five* (1960), a children's novel about the Morant Bay rebellion; *Peter of Mount Ephraim* (1971); and *The Jamaicans* (1976).

Relapse, The: or, Virtue in Danger VANBRUGH's first play (1696), written in riposte to CIBBER's LOVE's LAST SHIFT . Cibber had shown the reform of the rakish Loveless. Vanbrugh shows his immediate relapse when he becomes involved with the witty widow, Berinthia. A more substantial sub-plot involves the vain efforts of Lord Foppington to marry Miss Hoyden, a spirited girl brought up in rustic seclusion by her father, Sir Tunbelly Clumsy. Ironically, Cibber himself scored a major success as Lord Foppington in the first production at DRURY LANE.

Religio Medici SIR THOMAS BROWNE's first book, originally written for his 'private exercise and satisfaction', published without his permission in 1642 and reissued in an authorized edition in 1643. It affirms his Christian faith but refers to such a wide diversity of topical thought as to transcend the normal barriers of devotional literature, becoming a fascinating and allusive investigation of the richness of God's creation. Browne is both sceptical and celebratory, erudite and fantastical in his attitudes. The book includes two fine prayers in verse, and discussion of subjects ranging from the occult to the nature of sleep.

Reliques of Ancient English Poetry See PERCY, THOMAS.

Renaissance, The See STUDIES IN THE HISTORY OF THE RENAISSANCE.

Renault, Mary [Challans, Mary] 1905–83 Novelist. Her reputation rests mainly on her lively but learned historical novels about the ancient world: *The Last of the Wine* (1956), *The King Must Die* (1958) and *The Bull from the Sea* (1962), about Theseus; *The Lion in the Gateway* (1964), for young people; *The Mask of Apollo* (1966), *Fire from Heaven* (1970), *The Persian Boy* (1972) and *Funeral Games* (1981), about Alexander; and *The Praise Singer* (1978). *The Charioteer* (1953) is about servicemen and homosexuality during World War II.

Rendell, Ruth 1930– Writer of DETECTIVE FICTION. She has established a reputation with talented and prolific work which falls into several categories. *From Doon with Death* (1965) started a popular series about Detective Chief Inspector Reginald Wexford of the Kingsmarkham police. In contrast to its solid and conventional reliance on police procedure, other novels have treated crime in deliberately unsettling ways. Notable titles have included *To Fear a Painted Devil* (1965), *One Across, Two Down* (1971), *The Face of Trespass* (1974), *A Demon in My View* (1976), *Make Death Love Me* (1979), *Master of the Moor* (1982) and *The Bridesmaid* (1989). Similar preoccupations have been yet more freely treated in the novels she has published under the pseudonym of Barbara Vine: *The Dark-Adapted Eye* (1986), *A Fatal Inversion* (1987), *The House of Stairs* (1989) and *Gallowglass* (1990).

Representative Men A book by EMERSON, published in 1850. It consists of seven essays based on lectures. The first proposes that truly great men are representative of their time and place: the genius is not aloof from society but is the earliest and finest manifestation of its possibilities. The six representative men are Plato, Swedenborg, Montaigne, SHAKESPEARE, Napoleon and Goethe.

Restoration comedy With the reopening of the theatres after the Restoration of Charles II, a competitive comedy of wit and repartee, concluding in marriage only after extensive foreplay with adultery, was pioneered by such gentleman-writers as ETHEREGE and SEDLEY. The masterpieces of the genre are Etherege's

SHE WOULD IF SHE COULD (1668) and THE MAN OF MODE (1676), WYCHERLEY's THE COUNTRY WIFE (1675) and THE PLAIN DEALER (1676), CONGREVE's THE DOUBLE DEALER (1693), LOVE FOR LOVE (1695) and THE WAY OF THE WORLD (1700) and VANBRUGH's THE RELAPSE (1696) and THE PROVOKED WIFE (1697). Plots are characteristically based on the deception of the witless and the would-be wits by the truly witty. Opposition to the immorality of Restoration comedy came to a head with JEREMY COLLIER's *Short View* (1698), in the wake of which Congreve abandoned the theatre. A new comedy of conscience and reformation was signalled by the success of CIBBER's LOVE's LAST SHIFT (1696) and immediately challenged by Vanbrugh's sequel, *The Relapse*. FARQUHAR's plays mark a transition from the Restoration comedy of manners to 18th-century SENTIMENTAL COMEDY.

Return of the Native, The A novel by HARDY, published in 1878. It is set on Egdon Heath.

Damon Wildeve, an engineer turned landlord of 'The Quiet Woman', carries on an affair with Eustacia Vye but marries the gentle Thomasin Yeobright. Clym Yeobright, Thomasin's cousin, wearies of life in Paris and returns to the heath intending to become a schoolmaster. He marries Eustacia, but his sight fails and he is reduced to furze-cutting for a livelihood. In despair she renews her association with Wildeve and becomes partially responsible for the death of Clym's mother. She leaves home and drowns herself in Shadwater Weir; Wildeve dies trying to save her. The remorseful Clym becomes an open-air preacher and Thomasin marries Diggory Venn, the 'isolated and weird' reddleman who moves in and out of the narrative.

Revelation of Divine Love, A See JULIAN OF NORWICH.

Revenge of Bussy D'Ambois, The A REVENGE TRAGEDY by CHAPMAN, first performed c. 1610 and published in 1613. It is a sequel to BUSSY D'AMBOIS. Bussy's ghost urges his brother Clermont D'Ambois to avenge his murder. Clermont sends a challenge to Bussy's murderer, Montsurry, who proves himself a coward. When the ghost renews his plea, Clermont forces Montsurry to fight and kills him. He then learns that his friend, the Duc de Guise, has been assassinated and, despairing of the vicious time in which he lives, kills himself.

revenge tragedy A type of TRAGEDY derived from Seneca and made fashionable on the Elizabethan and Jacobean stage by KYD's THE SPANISH TRAGEDY (c. 1589). Revenge tragedies usually begin with the ghost of a wronged and/or murdered man appearing to a descendant or friend and demanding vengeance. In carrying it out, the avenger sometimes feigns madness and uses the device of the play-within-the-play. Playwrights usually incorporated those features that best suited their purpose whilst adapting or ignoring others. SHAKESPEARE's two revenge tragedies, TITUS ANDRONICUS (c. 1592) and HAMLET (c. 1601), exhibit almost the full range of their kind. Other notable examples include MARSTON's ANTONIO's REVENGE (1600), THE REVENGER'S TRAGEDY (1607), WEBSTER's THE WHITE DEVIL (c. 1612) and THE DUCHESS OF MALFI (?before 1614), and THOMAS MIDDLETON's THE CHANGELING (1622) and WOMEN BEWARE WOMEN (c. 1625).

Revenger's Tragedy, The A REVENGE TRAGEDY published in 1607 and generally, though not confidently, ascribed to TOURNEUR. He was not named as its author until 1656, and the manifest inferiority of his other surviving play, THE ATHEIST'S TRAGEDY, has strengthened the critical case that THOMAS MIDDLETON is the author.

The revenger is Vindice, whose mistress was poisoned by the corrupt Duke when she would not yield to his lust. With his brother Hippolito, he plots the downfall of the Duke's family, aided its member's own rivalries. The Duke meets a startlingly apt death when Vindice tricks him into kissing the poisoned skull of his dead mistress. The climax comes at the inauguration of Lussurioso as the new duke. Disguised as masquers, Vindice and Hippolito assassinate Lussurioso and his corrupt noblemen; his half-brothers Spurio, Ambitioso and Supervacuo turn on each other in a paroxysm of mutual murder. The restoration of the shattered dukedom rests with the virtuous Antonio, whose first act is to order the execution of Vindice and Hippolito.

Review, The A periodical founded in 1704 by DEFOE with the help of ROBERT HARLEY, Earl of Oxford. Originally a weekly, it soon began to appear twice a week and then, from 1705 until it ceased publication in 1713, three times a week. Written almost entirely by Defoe himself, it offered well-informed comment on European affairs during the war with France, dealt with the social life of the day, and kept its readers informed on commerce and trade. Defoe's essays on politics made him the first leader writer of the English press.

Revolt of Islam, The A poem by SHELLEY, in SPENSERIAN STANZAS, published in 1818. It was originally called 'Laon and Cythna' and the principal characters, who become lovers, were brother and sister. Cythna, dedicated to the freedom of her sex from harsh laws, joins forces with Laon, another revolutionary. They unite the people in revolt and briefly succeed, but the ruling tyrants crush their revolt and lay waste the land. Laon and Cythna are burned alive.

Rexroth, Kenneth 1905–82 American poet. Often surreal and experimental, his work includes elegiac, erotic and political verse. Early volumes are *In What Hour* (1940), *The Phoenix and the Tortoise* (1944), *The Art of Worldly Wisdom* (1949) and *The Signature of All Things* (1949). He was briefly associated with the BEATS but later distanced himself from them. Other volumes are *Poems* (1955), *Natural Numbers* (1963), *The Collected Shorter Poems* (1967), *The Collected Longer Poems* (1968), *New Poems* (1974), *The Silver Swan* (1976) and *The Morning Star: Poems and Translations* (1979). He also published a collection of four verse plays entitled *Beyond the Mountains* (1951), many translations, critical essays and *An Autobiographical Novel* (1966).

Reynard the Fox A prose translation by WILLIAM CAXTON, published in 1481, of the Dutch *Hystorie van Reynaert die Vos*, a version of the Renard Cycle. This probably originated in Latin but is best known in the French verse *Roman de Renart*, CHAUCER's source for *The Nun's Priest's Tale* in THE CANTERBURY TALES. It is dominated by the deceitful character of the fox and by satiric attacks on the Church and nobility. The episode given by Caxton tells how Reynard, summoned to court to answer for his misdeeds, uses trickery to escape death and to defeat the wolf Isengrim in single combat.

Reynolds, John Hamilton 1796–1852 Poet. He is now chiefly remembered for his friendship with KEATS, though LEIGH HUNT's 'Young Poets' issue of THE EXAMINER (November 1816) ranked him with Keats and SHELLEY as one of the most promising writers of the day. His most craftsmanly work is *The Garden of Florence* (1821), but he never found his own voice as a poet. A witty and mercurial figure, his real genius lay in imitation and PARODY. *Peter Bell: A Lyrical Ballad* (1819), his

wickedly effective skit on WORDSWORTH's *Peter Bell*, inspired Shelley to try his own hand in *Peter Bell the Third*. Reynolds collaborated with THOMAS HOOD in *Odes and Addresses to Great People* (1825).

Reynolds, Sir Joshua 1723–92 Painter and writer on art. As President of the Royal Academy he delivered the lectures (1769–90) published as *Discourses on Art*. Based on the theories of Aristotle and Plato, they regard truth and beauty as generalizations resulting from particular examples and as inextricably linked with moral qualities. Reynolds also recommended copying the masters as a key element in the education of the student. In keeping with the doctrines of NEOCLASSICISM, creation was thus presented as an entirely rational process. Reynolds also contributed three papers on art to THE IDLER (Nos. 76, 79 and 82) and annotated WILLIAM MASON's verse translation of Du Fresnoy's *Art of Painting*. Some of his notes on SHAKESPEARE were printed in the final volume of Johnson's edition and others in MALONE's supplement of 1780.

Reynolds also encouraged SAMUEL JOHNSON to found the literary gathering known as the Club in the winter of 1763–4. Its other original members were Beauclerk, BURKE, Chamier, GOLDSMITH, Hawkins, Langton and Nugent. Others, including GARRICK, Banks and Malone, were later elected. BOSWELL dedicated THE LIFE OF JOHNSON (1791) to him, as Goldsmith did THE DESERTED VILLAGE (1770). In his long and highly successful career as a portraitist he painted many literary and theatrical figures, including: Boswell, Burke, FOOTE, Garrick (seven times), Johnson (five times), SHERIDAN, STERNE and HORACE WALPOLE. His short descriptions of Garrick, Goldsmith and Johnson were published posthumously.

Reznikoff, Charles 1894–1976 American poet. Generally identified with OBJECTIVISM, his work emphasized the role of Judaism in his life. His publications include *Rhythms* (1918), *Poems* (1920), *Uriel Acosta: A Play and a Fourth Group of Verse* (1921), *Chatterton, The Black Death, and Meriwether Lewis: Three Plays* (1922), *Coral and Captive Israel: Two Plays* (1923), *Five Groups of Verse* (1927), *Nine Plays* (1927), *Jerusalem the Golden* (1934) and *Inscriptions: 1944–1956* (1959). *Testimony: The United States, 1885–1890* (1965) and *Testimony: The United States, 1891–1900* (1968) are poetic meditations on history. *The Lionhearted* (1944) is a historical novel.

rhyme royal Stanza form of seven decasyllabic lines rhyming ababbcc. Its name probably derives from its use in THE KINGIS QUAIR, attributed to JAMES I OF SCOTLAND. An alternative name, the Chaucerian stanza, pays tribute to CHAUCER's fondness for it (*TROILUS AND CRISEYDE*, THE PARLEMENT OF FOULES, some of THE CANTERBURY TALES). Later poets who wrote in rhyme royal include WYATT, SPENSER, SHAKESPEARE (*THE RAPE OF LUCRECE*), DRAYTON and WILLIAM MORRIS.

Rhymers' Club, The A group of poets who met at the Cheshire Cheese in Fleet Street between 1891 and 1894. It included its founders, Ernest Rhys and YEATS, RICHARD LE GALLIENNE, ERNEST DOWSON, LIONEL JOHNSON, ARTHUR SYMONS and JOHN DAVIDSON. The group published two collections of verse, in 1892 and 1894. See also AESTHETIC MOVEMENT.

Rhys, Jean 1894–1979 Novelist and short-story writer. Born in Dominica, she came to England in 1909 and spent most of the inter-war years in Paris. Appearing after a long period of silence and artistic oblivion, her finest novel, *Wide Sargasso Sea* (1966), invents the tragic story of Rochester's mad wife in JANE EYRE. The same painful clarity in portraying personal, sexual and social exploitation marks her other writing. Earlier work includes the stories in *The Left Bank* (1927) and the novels *Postures* (1928; as *Quartet* in USA, 1929 and subsequently), *After Leaving Mr Mackenzie* (1930), *Voyage in the Dark* (1934) and *Good Morning, Midnight* (1939). Later work includes *Tigers are Better-looking* (1968) and a finely designed collection of stories, *Sleep It Off Lady* (1976). *Smile Please: An Unfinished Autobiography* appeared in 1979, *Letters 1931–1966* in 1984.

rhythm See METRE.

Ricardo, David 1772–1823 Political economist. A stockbroker and MP, he began by studying monetary economics, particularly the high price of gold and the depreciation of paper money, the role of the Bank of England and monetary theory. His writing, never brilliant, is at its clearest in *The High Price of Bullion* (1810) and the *Reply to Mr Bosanquet's Practical Observations on the Report of the Bullion Committee* (1811). *Proposals for an Economical and Secure Currency* (1816) demonstrates that inflation is caused by too much money in circulation. Ricardo's pamphlets brought him into contact with MALTHUS and JAMES MILL, who encouraged him to develop the ideas in the *Essay on the Low Price of Corn on the Profits of Stock* (1815) into his major work, *On the Principles of Political Economy and Taxation* (1817; twice revised by 1821). It develops a theory of value to explain how the proportions of the wages of labour and the profits of capital are determined, as well as the effects of taxes.

Rice, Elmer 1892–1967 American playwright. He wrote over 50 plays, of which the best known are *THE ADDING MACHINE* (1923), an early example of EXPRESSIONISM in the American theatre, and *Street Scene* (1929), about a day in the life of a New York tenement. His first play, *On Trial* (1914), is often credited with introducing the technique later called flashback. Though it experiments with various theatrical modes, his work consistently displays a devotion to social justice and liberal causes. *The Home of the Free* (1917) and *The Iron Cross* (1917) took up pacifist themes at an unpopular time; *The Subway* (1929) tells the story of a young working girl victimized by lecherous men; *We, the People* (1933) attacks conditions during the Depression; *Judgement Day* (1934) is a fictionalized account of the trial which followed the Reichstag fire; and *Between Two Worlds* (1934) debates the merits of the American and Soviet systems. Other plays include *See Naples and Die* (1929), *The Left Bank* (1931), *Dream Girl* (1945); *Love among the Ruins* (1963); and *Close Harmony* (1929; also called *The Lady Next Door*) written in collaboration with DOROTHY PARKER. Rice wrote several novels, Hollywood screenplays, an autobiography (*Minority Report*, 1963), and a history of the theatre. He was a founding member of the American Civil Liberties Union and the FEDERAL THEATRE PROJECT.

Riceyman Steps A novel by ARNOLD BENNETT, published in 1923. It concentrates on the life of Henry Earlforward in and around the antiquarian bookshop he has inherited in Clerkenwell. In middle age he courts and marries Violet Arb but she fails to bring warmth into a household dominated by his miserliness. Only when he is near death can he acknowledge the effects of his life-denying passion. A contrast is offered by the life of the maidservant Elsie, who nurses and marries the shell-shocked Joe.

Rich, Adrienne (Cecile) 1929– American poet. Her early work, gathered in *Collected Early Poems, 1950–1970*

(1993), turned increasingly innovative forms and a startlingly frank idiom to explore feminist themes. Volumes representing her later career include *Diving Into the Wreck: Poems 1971–72* (1973), *The Dream of a Common Language: Poems 1974–1977* (1978), *A Wild Patience Has Taken Me This Far: Poems 1978–1981* (1981), *Your Native Land, Your Life* (1986), *Time's Power: Poems 1985–1988* (1989) and *An Atlas of the Difficult World: Poems 1988–1991* (1991). *Of Woman Born: Motherhood as Experience and Institution* (1976) established her as an influential radical feminist critic. She has also published *On Lies, Secrets, and Silence: Selected Prose 1966–1978* (1979), *Compulsory Heterosexuality and Lesbian Existence* (1981), *Blood, Bread, and Poetry: Selected Prose 1979–1985* (1986) and *Women and Honor: Some Notes on Lying* (1990).

Rich, Barnabe 1542–1617 Miscellaneous writer. He published some 25 books, of which the most important were a series of romances in the popular style of EUPHUISM: notably *Rich his Farewell to the Military Profession* (1581), where SHAKESPEARE found his source for the plot of *TWELFTH NIGHT* in the story 'Apolonius and Silla'. He also wrote tracts and pamphlets on military affairs and the state of government in Ireland, reflecting his career as a soldier and his service in Ireland for most of the decade 1572–82. His later works were mainly satirical.

Richard II, The Life and Death of A play by SHAKESPEARE, first performed *c.* 1595 and published in two good Quartos in 1597 (Q1) and 1608 (Q4) before the First Folio of 1623. Although it stands as the first of a sequence of English history plays (derived largely from HOLINSHED's *Chronicles*), to be completed by the two parts of *HENRY IV* and by *HENRY V*, it was written as a single tragedy. Its subject, the deposition of an anointed king, made it controversial: Shakespeare's company earned the queen's displeasure by performing *Richard II* on the eve of Essex's rebellion in 1601.

Richard orders Henry Bolingbroke, John of Gaunt's son, and Thomas Mowbray, Duke of Norfolk, to settle their differences in a duel but then intervenes and banishes them both. He takes advantage of John of Gaunt's death to confiscate Bolingbroke's inheritance, giving the calculating Bolingbroke a pretext for bringing an invading force to England. The support of the overtaxed English lords encourages Bolingbroke to claim the throne. In a famous scene, the histrionic Richard stages his own deposition. Confined to Pomfret Castle, he reflects on the divine right of kings before being killed by Sir Pierce of Exton. Bolingbroke, now firmly enthroned as Henry IV, repudiates the deed even though he had wished it, and expresses his intention of making a pilgrimage of expiation to the Holy Land.

Richard III, The Life and Death of A historical tragedy by SHAKESPEARE, first performed *c.* 1594 and published in Quarto (Q1) in 1597 as well as in the First Folio of 1623. Although continuing the story told in the *HENRY VI* trilogy, it is entirely self-sufficient, concentrating on the deformed, ambitious and maliciously intelligent Richard, Duke of Gloucester, his pursuit of the throne and his final downfall. Richard woos Anne, widow and daughter-in-law of his previous victims, and arranges the death of his brother, George, Duke of Clarence. With the connivance of the Duke of Buckingham, he eliminates Hastings, Rivers and Grey, further rivals. Once on the throne he makes his position secure by ordering the deaths of his young nephews, the sons of the dead Edward IV, and insisting on marrying their sister. Opposition to his tyrannies hardens, and Richard is troubled by the prophecy that the Earl of Richmond will become king. Buckingham, now alienated by Richard's ingratitude, raises an army but is captured and executed. Richard's isolation increases when Richmond invades. Disquieted by dreams on the eve of the Battle of Bosworth, Richard rallies his strength in a desperate fight, but is eventually killed in single combat by the Earl of Richmond, who, as Henry VII, establishes the Tudor dynasty on the throne of England.

Richard Coeur de Lyon A VERSE ROMANCE written soon after 1300, telling the story of Richard the Lionheart. The central episode of the Crusade, during which he dines on Saracens' heads, includes detailed accounts of the military campaigns leading to the capture of Babylon and Jaffa.

Richard Mahony, The Fortunes of A trilogy of novels by HENRY HANDEL RICHARDSON, consisting of *Australia Felix* (1917), *The Way Home* (1925) and *Ultima Thule* (1929), first published together in 1930. Richard Townshend Mahony gives up his medical practice and emigrates to join the Australian gold rush in the 1850s. When prospecting proves fruitless, he opens a 'Diggers' Emporium', which prospers until he refuses to support the diggers in militant action against the authorities. His wife, Mary, persuades him to return to medicine, but he fails and retreats into himself, turning first to religion and then to spiritualism. When things seem at their lowest ebb some shares in a dubious mine soar in value and Mahony can return to Europe with Mary. Back in Australia, he learns that he is ruined because his agent has absconded. Hiding the full truth from Mary, he is eventually driven to mental and physical collapse. Mary, resolute and uncomplaining, works as a postmistress in a remote settlement, nursing her husband in the last weeks of his life.

Richard the Redeless See MUM AND THE SOTHSEGGER.

Richards, David Adams 1950– Canadian novelist. He has written about his native Maritime Canada and the tightly knit, often intense lives of its inhabitants in *The Coming of Winter* (1974), *Blood Ties* (1976), the more ambitious *Lives of Short Duration* (1981), *Nights below Station Street* (1988) and *Evening Snow* (1990). *Dancers at Night* (1978) is a volume of short stories.

Richards, Frank See HAMILTON, CHARLES.

Richards, (Franklin Thomas) Grant 1872–1948 Publisher. Despite habitual irresponsibility with money (he twice went bankrupt), Richards developed a strong literary list for the firm he established in 1897. It included BUTLER'S THE WAY OF ALL FLESH, JOYCE'S *DUBLINERS* and the work of A. E. HOUSMAN. His lighthearted autobiography, *Author Hunting* (1934), owes much to his correspondence with SHAW. He also wrote well on Housman (1941).

Richards, I(vor) A(rmstrong) 1893–1979 Critic. His most influential works were *Principles of Literary Criticism* (1924), *Science and Poetry* (1926) and *Practical Criticism* (1929). The last work, based on an experiment in which he gave his Cambridge students unsigned poems for comment, catalogued the various kinds of misreading to which poetry can be subjected. It prompted a new practice of 'close reading' for verbal ambiguities, ironies and other complexities in the work of his pupil WILLIAM EMPSON, F. R. LEAVIS and the *SCRUTINY* group, and the proponents of NEW CRITICISM. 'Practical criticism' became a standard classroom exercise throughout the English-speaking world. Always

concerned with clarity of communication, Richards also worked with C. K. Ogden to formulate Basic English, a simplified system for learners of the language, with a vocabulary of only 850 words. As well as other works on language and literature, he published four volumes of poetry (1938).

Richardson, Dorothy M(iller) 1873–1957 Novelist. She is remembered for *Pilgrimage*, a 12-novel sequence which made an early use of STREAM OF CONSCIOUSNESS. The individual volumes are: *Pointed Roofs* (1915), *Backwater* (1916), *Honeycomb* (1917), *Interim* (1919), *The Tunnel* (1919), *Deadlock* (1921), *Revolving Lights* (1923), *The Trap* (1925), *Oberland* (1927), *Dawn's Left Hand* (1931), *Clear Horizon* (1935) and *Dimple Hill* (1938).

Richardson, Henry Handel [Richardson, Ethel Florence] 1870–1946 Australian novelist. Born in Melbourne, she studied music in Germany and finally settled with her husband in London. Music supplies the background for *Maurice Guest* (1908) and *The Young Cosima* (1939). *The Getting of Wisdom* (1910) draws on her adolesence in Australia. She revisited the country only once, to ensure the authenticity of *Australia Felix* (1917), the first part of a trilogy completed in *The Way Home* (1925) and *Ultima Thule* (1929) and published as THE FORTUNES OF RICHARD MAHONY (1930). An autobiography, *Myself When Young* (1948), appeared after her death.

Richardson, Samuel 1689–1761 Novelist and printer. Although he was born in Derbyshire, his father was a London joiner and the family had returned to the capital by 1700. His father could not afford the classical education needed to make Richardson a clergyman, and he was bound apprentice to a printer in 1706. He proved diligent, marrying his master's daughter and setting up in business by himself as a master printer in 1721, and continued to prosper throughout his life. In 1754 he was elected Master of the Stationers' Company and in 1760 he purchased a share of the patent of the printer to the king. In later years he suffered from ill health which he considered nervous in origin. His virtues were those of the industrious apprentice; his weakness was agreed to be his vanity.

The Apprentice's Vade Mecum (1733), urging the ambitious youth to diligence, sobriety and self-denial, was followed by a didactic version of *Aesop's Fables*, an edition of *The Negotiations of Sir Thomas Roe in his Embassy to the Ottoman Port for the years 1621 to 1628 Inclusive* and an anonymous continuation of DEFOE'S *A Tour through the Whole Island of Great Britain*. His three works of fiction are all EPISTOLARY NOVELS, a form he did not invent but brought to a new height of sophistication, as he did the novel of common life, avoiding 'the improbable and the marvellous'. *PAMELA* (first part 1740; second part 1741) made him famous and *CLARISSA* (1747–8), his masterpiece, consolidated his reputation as both a celebrant of female virtue and a subtle psychologist. THE HISTORY OF *SIR CHARLES GRANDISON* (1753–4), a portrait of male virtue, was influential in its day but is now less well remembered. Taking up a hint from his friend SAMUEL JOHNSON, he also published *A Collection of the Moral and Instructive Sentiments, Maxims, Cautions and Reflections, Contained in the Histories of Pamela, Clarissa and Sir Charles Grandison, Digested under Proper Heads* (1755).

HENRY FIELDING'S mockery was expressed in *An Apology for the Life of Mrs Shamela Andrews* (1741) and *JOSEPH ANDREWS* (1742), but otherwise Richardson's reputation stood high during his lifetime. He attracted a wide circle of admirers, typically female, which included two sisters, LADY BRADSHAIGH and Lady Echlin, whose correspondence with him survives. Johnson, though admitting that 'if you were to read Richardson for the story your impatience would be so much fretted that you would hang yourself', also affirmed that 'there is more knowledge of the human heart in one letter of Richardson's than in all of TOM JONES'. During the 19th century, Richardson's supposedly effeminate preoccupations were denigrated by comparison with Fielding's manliness, but his greatness has now been once more acknowledged.

Richler, Mordecai 1931– Canadian novelist. His early work – notably *The Apprenticeship of Duddy Kravitz* (1959) – is broadly comic, satirizing Canadian sacred cows and showing an ambivalent attitude to his Jewish heritage. *St Urbain's Horseman* (1971), a product of his years in England, is centred on the experience of a Jewish-Canadian in London. His finest work to date, *Solomon Gursky was Here* (1989), is peopled by a rich gallery of comic characters and moves between 19th-century London, Franklin's Arctic expedition, the Prairie during the years of Prohibition and contemporary Quebec to provide an unconventional view of Canadian history. He has also written screenplays, essays, sketches and CHILDREN'S LITERATURE, including *Jacob Two-Two Meets the Hooded Fang* (1975) and *Jacob Two-Two and the Dinosaur* (1988).

Rickword, (John) Edgell 1898–1982 Critic. He edited the short-lived *CALENDAR OF MODERN LETTERS* in 1925–7 before adopting Marxism and working as associate editor and then editor of *Left Review* in the 1930s. He published six volumes of poetry and a short study of Rimbaud, but his most important work is collected in *Essays and Opinions 1921–1931* (1974) and *Literature and Society: Essays and Opinions 1931–1978* (1978).

Riders to the Sea A one-act tragedy by SYNGE, produced at the ABBEY THEATRE, Dublin, in 1904. The single scene is the kitchen of a cottage on one of the Aran Islands. When the play opens Maurya has already lost four sons and a husband to the sea; a fifth son is missing. Only the youngest, Bartley, remains to help his mother and his two sisters. By the end, the missing son's death has been confirmed and Bartley is also dead, drowned on his way to the horse fair in Connemara.

Ridge, Lola 1871–1941 American poet. Born in Dublin, she spent her childhood in Australia and New Zealand before emigrating to the USA in 1907. *The Ghetto and Other Poems* (1918), *Sun-Up* (1920), *Red Flag* (1927), *Firehead* (1929) and *Dance of Fire* (1935) all reflect her lifelong concern with the exploitation and martyrdom of the working class.

Riding, Laura 1901–95 American poet, novelist, short-story writer and critic. Born Laura Reichenthal, she published her work as Laura Riding Gottschalk until she adopted the surname of Riding in 1926. During a stay in Europe (1926–39) she lived with ROBERT GRAVES on Mallorca; together they founded the Seizin Press and edited the influential *A Survey of Modernist Poetry* (1927). Her own early poetry associated her with the FUGITIVES. *The Close Chaplet* (1926), her first volume, was followed by a steady stream of work throughout the late 1920s and the 1930s, culminating in *Collected Poems* (1938; reprinted with a new introduction in 1980). She wrote less and less verse after 1938, and her early work, expressing private feeling in strikingly concrete imagery, is usually considered her best. Other works of

criticism include *Contemporaries and Snobs* (1928) and *Anarchism is Not Enough* (1928). She also wrote novels, including *Description of Life* (1980), and three volumes of short stories.

Ridler, Anne (Barbara) 1912– Poet. Her output has been relatively small: among her collections are *The Nine Bright Shiners* (1943), *The Golden Bird and Other Poems* (1951), *A Matter of Life and Death* (1959), *Selected Poems* (1961) and *Some Time After and Other Poems* (1972). She has also written verse dramas such as *Cain* (1943). A devotional poet, she brings a traditional craft to religious experience, married love, children, the sense of mortality, and the feelings aroused by places and paintings.

Ridley, James 1736–65 Novelist. He is remembered for *The Tales of the Genii: or, the Delightful Lessons of Horan, the Son of Asmar* (1764), originally presented as a translation from the Persian but in fact a lively exercise in Orientalism modelled on *The Arabian Nights*. It proved immensely popular and was many times reprinted, sometimes in censored versions for children.

Rienzi: The Last of the Tribunes A novel by EDWARD BULWER LYTTON, published in 1835. The hero is Cola di Rienzi, a visionary idealist who briefly succeeded in subduing the warring factions of 14th-century Rome and in establishing a republic with himself as tribune. He was eventually torn to pieces in the streets. The story thus had a message about the dangers of liberty in post-Reform Bill England.

Rights of Man, The A tract by THOMAS PAINE, published in 1791–2. Written to defend the French Revolution against BURKE's attack in *REFLECTIONS ON THE REVOLUTION IN FRANCE* (1790), it prompted Pitt's government to introduce a law against seditious publication. Paine fled to France but was convicted of sedition in his absence and outlawed.

The first part advocates a social contract, embodied in a formal constitution, to protect the freedom and security of the individual. The second compares British institutions, to their disadvantage, with the constitutions of the United States and revolutionary France. The work is most interesting in the radical social policy which it outlines. Paine proposed, among other measures, a tax on income above a certain level, old-age pensions, free education for the poor, family allowances and the limitation of armaments by treaty.

Riley, James Whitcomb 1849–1916 American poet. He achieved great popularity as a regional writer of light and sentimental verse, particularly of dialect poems such as 'Little Orphant Annie', 'The Raggedy Man' and 'When the Frost is on the Punkin'. His most famous collection was *The Old Swimmin'-Hole and 'Leven More Poems* (1883).

Riley, John 1937–78 Poet. Founder of the Grosseteste Press and *The Grosseteste Review*, he was also a leading experimental poet. His work owed little to any native tradition but was influenced instead by POUND, OLSON and OPPEN, and by Hölderlin and Mandelstam, whom he translated. Volumes include *Ancient and Modern* (1967), *What Reason Was* (1970), *Ways of Approaching* (1973) and *That is Today* (1978), gathered with other work in *Collected Poems* (1981), which contains the important long poem 'Czargrad'.

Rime of the Ancient Mariner, The A BALLAD by SAMUEL TAYLOR COLERIDGE, published in *LYRICAL BALLADS* (1798). Coleridge added the elaborate prose gloss accompanying it when he included it in *Sybilline Leaves* (1817).

The 'ancient mariner' tells his story to one of three gallants on their way to a wedding feast. He shot an albatross which appeared as a bird of good omen when his ship escaped from the ice of the South Pole. When they are becalmed and run short of water, his shipmates hang the dead albatross around his neck. They begin to die after a ghost ship passes them. The mariner's redemption starts with a vision of the creatures of God and the beauty of His world, seen by moonlight. When he is at last able to pray, the dead bird falls from his neck and the Virgin Mary sends rain. Eventually rescued, the mariner confesses to a hermit but knows his penance will continue throughout his life: he must go on relating his story.

Ring and the Book, The A poem by ROBERT BROWNING, serialized in 1868–9. Divided into 12 books and running to 21,000 lines of BLANK VERSE, it is his most ambitious and complex work. The 'Roman murder-story' was based on a 17th-century *cause célèbre* he found summarized in an 'Old Yellow Book' he had bought in Florence. The unscrupulous Count Guido Franceschini arranged a marriage with Pompilia and then mistreated her. A young canon, Giuseppe Caponsacchi, took her back to her adopted parents, the Comparinis, in Rome but Franceschini arranged the family's murder. Brought to trial with his accomplices, Franceschini took advantage of a technicality and appealed to Pope Innocent XII for special privilege as a cleric. His plea was rejected and he was executed in 1698.

The poem begins with Browning's account of his sources and an invocation to the Muse, in tribute to ELIZABETH BARRETT BROWNING, who had died in 1861. Succeeding books narrate the story from different points of view: gossips in Rome favourable to Count Guido, those favourable to the hapless Pompilia, an impartial observer (Tertium Quid), Guido himself, Giuseppe Caponsacchi, and Pompilia on her deathbed. These are followed by statements for the defence and for the prosecution, and Pope Innocent's soliloquy on the nature of evil and the fallibility of human judgement, and his decision to let the sentence stand. The closing books are occupied by Guido's expression of abject cowardice when he realizes he is doomed, and the Pope's declaration of Pompilia's innocence.

Ringwood, Gwen Pharis 1910–84 Canadian playwright, born in the USA. Her plays became more socially conscious as they moved away from their local concerns. They include: *Still Stands the House* (1938), a classic one-act folk drama; *Dark Harvest* (1945), a prairie tragedy based on local history; *The Rainmaker* (1945); *Widger's Way* (1952); *Mirage* (1979); and *Garage Sale* (1981). She also wrote short stories and a novel, *Younger Brother* (1959).

Ripley, George 1802–80 American philosopher and man of letters. A leading figure in TRANSCENDENTALISM, whose doctrines he advanced in his sermon *Jesus Christ, the Same Yesterday, Today, and Forever* (1834), he founded the Transcendental Club (1836), handled the business affairs of THE DIAL (1840–4), established the communal experiment at BROOK FARM (1841–7) and edited the weekly *Harbinger* (1845–9). He helped to found HARPER'S NEW MONTHLY MAGAZINE in 1850, as well as publishing *Specimens of Foreign Standard Literature* (1838–42), translations of European idealistic philosophy, and *The New American Cyclopedia* (with Charles A. Dana; 1858–63).

Rippingale, C(uthbert) E(dward) 1825–97 Novelist. Born into a Nonconformist manufacturing family, he rejected both aspects of his background in his early

work. *Robert Higden: or, The Sweat Shop* (1851) attacks conditions in the clothing trade and *The Lion Yard Meeting* (1852) the hypocrisies of evangelical religion. *Can These Bones Live?* (1859), his only other novel of the 1850s, suggests a spiritual crisis. Later novels, such as *The Testing of Sir Richard Fortescue* (1865) and *The Trials of Sir Clarence* (1872), combined High Anglican fervour with a love of medieval chivalry.

Rise of Silas Lapham, The A novel by WILLIAM DEAN HOWELLS, serialized in 1884–5 and published in volume form in 1885. Colonel Silas Lapham, makes a fortune manufacturing paint, moves his family from Vermont to Boston and urges his wife and daughters to enter fashionable society. The family does not fit in and Lapham gets drunk at the Coreys' dinner party. His business speculations fail but he resists his partners' suggestion that he sell some property to a British firm despite knowing it to be worthless. Bankrupt, disgraced but morally restored, he returns to Vermont. His older daughter Penelope and Tom Corey run away together to Mexico to escape the social barriers that made them unhappy in New England.

Ritchie, Anne (Isabella) Thackeray, Lady 1837–1919 Novelist, biographer and elder daughter of THACKERAY. Of her eight novels, *Old Kensington* (1873) and *Mrs Dymond* (1885) are still remembered. Although VIRGINIA WOOLF and others have paid tribute to their impressionistic charm, Lady Ritchie's most enduring work was as a memorialist of the Victorian writers she had known, notably in *Records of Tennyson, Ruskin and Robert and Elizabeth Browning* (1892), *Chapters from Some Memoirs* (1894), and her introductions to the 13-volume 'Biographical Edition' of her father's works (1894–8). She is portrayed as Mrs Hilbery in Woolf's *Night and Day*.

Ritson, Joseph 1753–1803 Antiquary. His excessively punctilious scholarship is best seen in his two-volume accumulation of allusions to ROBIN HOOD in popular literature, which appeared in 1795 with woodcuts by BEWICK. He issued numerous similar anthologies of popular literature. Most of his literary productions were vitriolic attacks on what he saw as the shortcomings of other editions: THOMAS WARTON's *History of English Poetry*, THOMAS PERCY's *Reliques of Ancient English Poetry* and the SHAKESPEARE edition by JOHNSON and STEEVENS.

Rivals, The A comedy by RICHARD BRINSLEY SHERIDAN, produced in 1775. Captain Jack Absolute comes to Bath disguised as Ensign Beverley to suit the romantic yearnings for love and poverty of his beloved Lydia Languish. Lydia's more robust friend Julia is loved by the self-tormenting man of feeling, Faulkland. The play brings the lovers to a happy agreement, despite the obstacles erected by Lydia's aunt, Mrs Malaprop, and the impecunious Irish knight, Sir Lucius O'Trigger. Mrs Malaprop's uncertain grasp of long words ('No caparisons, miss, if you please') gave the term 'malapropism' to the language.

Road to Ruin, The A comedy by HOLCROFT, produced and published in 1792. When Harry Dornton's extravagance brings his father's bank close to ruin he resolves to court the wealthy and unpleasant Mrs Warren, though he is in love with her daughter. In the end the bank is saved by its chief clerk, the grim Mr Sulky, and Harry, a reformed character, can marry Miss Warren.

Road to Wigan Pier, The A work by GEORGE ORWELL, commissioned and published by the LEFT BOOK CLUB in 1937. It is an account of unemployment in the north of

England, written as a modern, urban equivalent of COBBETT's *RURAL RIDES*. The first part contains a damning record of poverty, apathy, malnutrition, and overcrowding; the second leads Orwell to confront his own class prejudices. Fashionable 'bourgeois socialism' provokes his scorn, and there are excellent analyses of middle-class prejudices about 'the lower classes'.

Roaring Girl, The: or, *Moll Cutpurse* A comedy by THOMAS MIDDLETON and DEKKER, produced in 1610 and published in 1611. It gives a fictional role to the notorious thief and forger Moll Cutpurse, who was not arrested until 1612. In the play she helps the young lovers Sebastian Wentgrave and Mary Fitzallard to overcome the objections of his mean and mean-spirited father Sir Alexander, who is tricked into giving his consent by their pretence that Sebastian has fallen in love with Moll.

Rob Roy A novel by SIR WALTER SCOTT, published in 1817. Set in the early 18th century, it follows the adventures of Frank Osbaldistone. At the home of his uncle, Sir Hildebrand, in the north of England he falls in love with Diana Vernon and meets the malicious Rashleigh, Sir Hildebrand's youngest son, who is plotting to ruin Frank and his father. Frank goes to the Highlands with Bailie Nicol Jarvie and is helped by the outlaw Rob Roy MacGregor in thwarting Rashleigh, who eventually dies at Rob Roy's hand.

The historical Rob Roy (1671–1734), a drover, became a powerful and dangerous outlaw when he and his clan were proscribed as Jacobite sympathizers. A ruthless opponent of the government, he was famous for disinterested kindness and sympathy with the oppressed.

Robert Elsmere A novel by MRS HUMPHRY WARD, published in 1888. It describes the hero's spiritual pilgrimage. He begins as a young Anglican clergyman of untroubled faith but is exposed to the unsettling influences of modern thought, particularly in the library of the local squire, Roger Wendover. Elsmere's studies gradually lead him to abandon his faith in miracles and in Christ as anything more than a symbol of the divine spirit at work in humanity, a position which estranges him from his orthodox wife. Eventually he founds the New Brotherhood of Christianity, an educational settlement in the London slums. The fact that the novel was commonly supposed to offer portraits of T. H. GREEN, PATER and MARK PATTISON ensured its topical success. Gladstone's lengthy review boosted its sales yet further.

Robert of Gloucester *fl.* 1250–1300 A monk at Gloucester and principal author of a Middle English verse CHRONICLE (12,000 lines long in its earliest version), to which two other writers apparently contributed. It covers the history of England from the beginning of Stephen's reign to Henry III's death. The accounts of the town and gown riots in Oxford (1263), the Battle of Evesham and the death of Simon de Montfort (1265) toward the end are probably first-hand. Elsewhere, the chronicle culls sources from GEOFFREY OF MONMOUTH to the Annals of Winchester, mixes fact with legend and devotes generous space to King Arthur (see ARTHURIAN LITERATURE).

Roberts, Sir Charles G(eorge) D(ouglas) 1860–1943 Canadian poet, short-story writer and novelist. Called 'the father of Canadian literature', he was a prolific writer, producing ten books of poetry, several romances and 18 collections of short stories, including *Earth's Enigmas* (1896), *The Kindred of the Wild* (1902), *The Watchers of the Trails* (1904) and *Kings in Exile* (1909). His earlier

poetry, found in volumes such as *In Divers Tones* (1886) and *Songs of the Common Day* (1893), is generally thought his best. *Selected Poems* appeared in 1936.

Roberts, Michael (William Edward) 1902–48 Anthologist, poet and critic. His Marxist anthologies *New Signatures* (1932) and *New Country* (1933) featured the work of AUDEN and his generation. The influential *Faber Book of Modern Verse* (1936) introduced GEORGE BARKER, DAVID GASCOYNE and DYLAN THOMAS. Roberts's own poetry is now neglected, despite the appearance of a *Selected Poems and Prose* (1980). His diverse prose writings include a fine study of T. E. HULME (1938), *The Recovery of the West* (1941), and the unfinished *The Estate of Man* (1951), a pioneering ecological work.

Robertson, Thomas William 1829–71 Playwright. Only a few of the 50 or so plays and adaptations for which he was responsible are of lasting value, but these have enormous significance. Six comedies – *Society* (1865), *Ours* (1866), *CASTE* (1867) and *School* (1869), with the less successful *Play* (1868) and *M. P.* (1870) – set a standard for realistic attention to domestic detail that prepared the way for a revival of serious drama. The term 'cup-and-saucer drama' was applied to Robertson and his imitators.

Robertson, William 1721–93 Historian. He was a major force in the Scottish Enlightenment. His *History of Scotland* (1759), *History of Charles V* (1769) and *History of America* (1777) were all widely praised. The success of the first led to his election as principal of Edinburgh University (1762) and Moderator of the General Assembly of the Church of Scotland (1763), in which capacity he established the independence of the Church from government interference.

Robin Hood An outlaw hero of English folktale. There is little evidence in favour of the several historical figures identified as the 'real' Robin Hood or, indeed, to show he was ever anything but legendary. The first reference suggests that he was already famous by the last quarter of the 14th century. Five poems and a fragment of a play preserve the medieval legend. Robin Hood's struggle against the sheriff of Nottingham and his poaching of the king's deer are the only constant features in the stories attached to his name over the centuries. His practice of robbing from the rich to give to the poor is a post-medieval addition. Little John and Will Scarlet (or Scarlok) appear in medieval versions but Maid Marian was not introduced until the 16th century. Her character and that of Friar Tuck owe something to PEACOCK's *MAID MARIAN* (1822) which, with SCOTT's *IVANHOE* (1819), assured the survival of the legend in the Romantic period and its continuing popularity in the age of film and TV.

Robinson, Edwin Arlington 1869–1935 American poet. Influenced by ROBERT BROWNING and HARDY, he began his poetic career with character sketches of, or DRAMATIC MONOLOGUES by, the inhabitants of the fictional Tilbury Town in *The Torrent and the Night Before* (1896; expanded as *The Children of the Night*, 1897), which contained 'Richard Cory', *Captain Craig* (1902) and *The Town down the River* (1910), which contained 'Miniver Cheevy'. His mature style – direct, ironic but still traditional – emerged in *The Man against the Sky* (1916) and *Collected Poems* (1921), which contained two favourite anthology pieces, 'The Tree in Pamela's Garden' and 'Rembrandt to Rembrandt'. Later volumes enjoyed a mixed reception which never completely reduced him to the margins of 20th-century poetry. They include a trilogy based on ARTHURIAN LITERATURE, *Merlin* (1917), *Lancelot* (1920) and *Tristram* (1927), and *The Man Who Died Twice* (1924), about a musician's betrayal of his talent. *Collected Poems, Tristram* and *The Man Who Died Twice* all won the PULITZER PRIZE.

Robinson, Henry Crabb 1775–1867 Lawyer, journalist and diarist. He is now chiefly remembered for his voluminous diaries and letters, first published in 1869, which are a valuable source for the early Romantic period. His friends included BLAKE (of whose last years he gave the only first-hand account), WORDSWORTH, LAMB, HAZLITT and COLERIDGE, of whose public lectures he made careful notes. A renowned conversationalist, Robinson was noted for breakfast parties which brought together poets and men of affairs.

Robinson, (Esmé Stuart) Lennox 1886–1958 Irish playwright, actor, director and critic. He was associated with the ABBEY THEATRE from the production of his first play, *The Clancy Name* (1908) until his death. His work includes serious plays about Irish politics like *Patriots* (1912), *The Dreamers* (1913), *The Lost Leader* (1918) and *The Big House* (1926), comedies like *The White-Headed Boy* (1916), *Crabbed Youth and Age* (1922), *The Far-Off Hills* (1928), and the more experimental *Church Street* (1934). He wrote *A History of the Abbey Theatre* (1951) and edited *The Oxford Book of Irish Verse* (1958) with DONAGH MACDONAGH.

Robinson, 'Perdita' (Mary) 1758–1800 Novelist, poet and playwright. She achieved fame as an actress and notoriety as the mistress of the future George IV, who addressed his amorous letters to 'Perdita'. Her reputation helped the popularity of her writing, which included: poems, notably a collection of SONNETS, *Sappho and Phaon* (1796); several insignificant plays; and a succession of romances beginning with a GOTHIC NOVEL, *Vancenza* (1792). She was a friend of WILLIAM GODWIN and MARY WOLLSTONECRAFT, who encouraged her to write *Thoughts on the Condition of Women* (1798).

Robinson Crusoe *(The Life and Strange Surprising Adventures of Robinson Crusoe, of York, Mariner. Written by himself)* A novel by DEFOE, published in 1719. Although it subsequently assumed a near-mythological status, the story is based squarely on the true account published by Alexander Selkirk, a fugitive sailor who went to sea in 1704 and was put ashore at his own request on an uninhabited Pacific island, where he survived until his rescue in 1709.

In Defoe's imaginative reworking, Crusoe is a mariner who takes to the sea despite parental warnings, suffers misfortunes at the hands of Barbary pirates and the elements, and is shipwrecked off South America. A combination of systematic salvaging, resourcefulness and good fortune enables him to survive on his island for some 28 years, two months and 19 days, according to the painstaking journal in which the adventures are recorded. During this time he needs to adapt to his alien environment, demonstrate the self-sufficiency so admired by Defoe himself, and come to terms with his own spiritual listlessness. If *Robinson Crusoe* now seems inconsistent and even unconvincing as a psychological study, it should be remembered that it owes more to Puritan spiritual autobiographies and allegories than to the novel, then still in its infancy. It is at any rate a deliberate amalgam of the specific and the general, combining typical characteristics of the adventure story with the exotic fables of travel literature.

Robinson Crusoe enjoyed instant and permanent suc-

cess, and has become one of those classics of English literature which (like GULLIVER'S TRAVELS, perhaps, or PILGRIM'S PROGRESS) appeal at various levels to adults and children alike. It draws its strength from a combination of disparate echoes and shapes: Jonah, Job, Everyman, the Prodigal Son, the colonial explorer and the proto-industrialist are all elements in Crusoe's character. Defoe continued the story in *The Farther Adventures of Robinson Crusoe* (1719), in which he revisits the island and loses Friday in an attack by savages, and *The Serious Reflections ... of Robinson Crusoe* (1720), neither of which has achieved wide recognition.

Rochester, 2nd Earl of [Wilmot, John] 1647–80 Poet and wit. One of the most dashing and notorious personalities of the Restoration, a peculiar combination of libertine and intellectual, he distinguished himself in the second Dutch War (1665) and was involved in a number of subsequent civil 'imbroglios' for which he was banished from court. Alcohol and venereal disease having taken their toll, he died a reformed character after the religious instruction of GILBERT BURNET persuaded him to renounce HOBBES and scepticism. Little of Rochester's poetic output was published during his lifetime, much of it evidently designed for clandestine circulation in manuscript, being scurrilous or pornographic ('Signior Dildo', 'The Imperfect Enjoyment', 'A Ramble in St James's Park' and 'The Maim'd Debauchee'). As a satirical poet he was more accomplished than his status now suggests. 'A Satire against Reason and Mankind' (1675), his best-known poem, ranges the sensualist against the rationalist attitude towards the capabilities of the human mind. His other two substantial achievements are the 'Letter from Artemisia in the Town to Chloe in the Country', a pungent social satire on dissembling and gullibility, and the superbly contemptuous 'Allusion to Horace: The 10th Satire of the First Book'.

rocking feet See METRE.

Roderick Hudson A novel by HENRY JAMES, serialized in 1875, published in volume form in 1876 and revised in 1879. Roderick Hudson, an amateur sculptor, is taken to Europe by the wealthy connoisseur Rowland Mallet. In Rome his work suffers when he becomes fascinated by the American expatriate Christina Light. Rowland brings Roderick's mother and fiancée, Mary Garland, from New England and their presence has the desired effect until Christina marries Prince Casamassima (see THE PRINCESS CASAMASSIMA). Rowland attempts to rekindle Roderick's work by taking him, Mrs Hudson and Mary to Switzerland but he borrows money to follow Christina. After a quarrel in which Rowland calls him an ungrateful egoist, Roderick dies in the mountains, perhaps by suicide.

Roderick Random, The Adventures of The first novel by SMOLLETT, published in 1748. Modelled on Le Sage's *Gil Blas*, it has the savage energy of true PICARESQUE. The hero describes a violent, adventurous life which includes a spell as surgeon's mate in the navy, shipwreck, service as a footman, fortune-hunting for an heiress with his friend and companion in roguery Hugh Strap, and time in debtors' prison. He finally encounters his long-lost, but now wealthy, father and marries his true love, Narcissa. Strap marries her maid. Episodes frequently draw on the author's own youthful experience of life at sea and in the theatrical world of London.

Unlike later novelists in the English tradition – including those whom he strongly influenced, such as

DICKENS – Smollett saw no need to soften the roguery of his villains or temper the coarseness of their adventures. *Roderick Random* does not seek to engage the reader's sympathy or moral approval, but commands attention by the unabashed vitality of the writing.

Roethke, Theodore (Huebner) 1908–63 American poet. His early work – which appeared in *Open House* (1941), *The Lost Son and Other Poems* (1948), *The Waking: Poems, 1933–1953* (1953) and *Words for the Wind: The Collected Verse of Theodore Roethke* (1957) – often returns to the landscapes of his childhood as a means of reconstructing transcendent moments of 'waking'. Later volumes, which include a good deal of love poetry, are *I am! Says the Lamb* (1961), *Sequence, Sometimes Metaphysical, Poems* (1963) and *The Far Field* (1964). *The Contemporary Poet as Artist and Critic* (1964) and *On the Poet and His Craft: Selected Prose* (1965) are posthumous collections of prose pieces.

Rogers, Samuel 1763–1855 Poet. A man of private fortune and a generous patron, he commissioned Turner to illustrate his popular poem *Italy* (1822–8), which paid tribute to BYRON by following Childe Harold's footsteps. Rogers declined the office of POET LAUREATE on WORDSWORTH's death. Other volumes include *Ode to Superstition* (1786), *The Pleasures of Memory* (1792), *Columbus* (1810) and *Jacqueline* (1814), though his most enduring monuments are *Recollections of the Table-Talk of Samuel Rogers* (1856; edited by Alexander Dyce) and *Recollections* (1859; edited by William Sharpe).

Rogers, Will(iam) (Penn Adair) 1879–1935 American actor and humorist. Of Cherokee ancestry, he began his career as a rodeo cowboy in vaudeville shows, going on to perform in the *Ziegfield Follies* and to appear in silent films and 'talkies'. In 1926 he began an immensely successful newspaper column which commented humorously on American politics and society. His books include *The Cowboy Philosopher on Prohibition* (1919), *The Illiterate Digest* (1924), *Letters of a Self-Made Diplomat to His President* (1927) and *There's Not a Bathing Suit in Russia* (1927).*The Autobiography of Will Rogers* appeared in 1949, and a collection of his newspaper pieces, *Sanity is Where You Find It*, in 1955.

Roget's Thesaurus A reference book originated by Peter Mark Roget (1779–1869), a doctor who spent most of his life in medical and scientific research, and first published as *Thesaurus of English Words and Phrases, Classified and Arranged So As to Facilitate the Expression of Ideas and Assist in Literary Composition* (1852). After going through 28 editions in his lifetime, it was edited by his son and grandson, being many times revised, abridged and modernized. Despite its elaborate taxonomic arrangement of vocabulary into six major classes of 'Ideas' and about 1000 subdivisions, 'Roget' is more often than not viewed as a collection of synonyms. Users generally consult the alphabetically arranged index of common words at the back as a way of finding their way to a topic appropriate to their needs.

Roland and Vernagu A VERSE ROMANCE (*c.* 1330–40) based on the Old French prose *Estoire de Charlemagne* (1206). It forms the first part of the composite *Charlemagne and Roland*, of which the second fragment is OTUEL AND ROLAND. The episodic story describes Charlemagne's journey to Constantinople and his conquest of Spain, together with the duel in which Roland defeats the Saracen giant Vernagu.

Rolfe, Frederick William 1860–1913 Novelist and short-story writer, who also styled himself Baron Corvo

and Fr. (i.e. Father) Rolfe. His paranoid sensibility and ornate prose style are best displayed in *Hadrian the Seventh* (1904), the story of how George Arthur Rose, a failed priest, is elected Pope. Rose is clearly modelled on the author, a Catholic convert and rejected candidate for the priesthood. Other works include *Stories Toto Told Me* (1898) and *In His Own Image* (1901), collections of stories. *Chronicles of the House of Borgia* (1901) is a collection of essays showing the fascination with late medieval and Renaissance Italy which also informs two romances, *Don Tarquinio* (1905) and *Don Renato* (1909). Two posthumously published works are extravagantly fictionalized autobiography. *The Desire and Pursuit of the Whole* (1934) takes savage revenge on his friends and patrons, and *Nicholas Crabbe* (1958) is based on the unhappy years at the start of his writing career. A. J. A. Symons's *The Quest for Corvo* (1934) gives a classic account of the difficulty in separating the reality of Rolfe's life from the lies and fantasy in which he shrouded it.

Rolle of Hampole, Richard *c.* 1300–49 Religious writer and poet, in English and Latin. He lived as a hermit in various parts of Yorkshire, finally near a Cistercian convent in Hampole, where he died. He taught that the contemplative must renounce the world and the self in total love of God; knowledge would come in Heaven but love must be exercised on earth. *De incendio amoris*, his chief mystical work, was a product of his youth. His best writing is found in his lyrics on God's love and the crucified Christ.

Rolliad, Criticism on The A series of political SATIRES published in *The Morning Herald* and *The Daily Advertiser* after William Pitt's election victory in 1784. The authors – members of a Whig club, the Esto Perpetua – included General Richard Fitzpatrick, Lord John Townshend, George Ellis, and French Laurence. The satires were reviews of *The Rolliad*, an imaginary epic about the Norman Duke Rollo, ancestor of Pitt's supporter John Rolle. They were followed by *Political Eclogues* and *Probationary Odes* for the post of POET LAUREATE when it fell vacant at the death of WILLIAM WHITEHEAD in 1785.

roman à clef A 'novel with a key', in which real people appear under fictitious names, lightly disguised but still recognizable. The purpose is often satiric, if only mildly so, as the novels of PEACOCK and ALDOUS HUXLEY's *Crome Yellow* demonstrate.

roman à thèse A 'thesis novel', intended to popularize or propagate an idea or cause. The political novels of DISRAELI and KINGSLEY's *ALTON LOCKE* are examples.

Roman Actor, The A tragedy by MASSINGER, produced in 1626 and published in 1629. Although it has not been revived, Massinger considered it his best work and it was highly regarded in its time. The plot comes from Suetonius, whom Massinger could have read in PHILEMON HOLLAND's translation. The Emperor Domitian takes Domitia Longina, wife of the senator Aelius Lamia, from her husband and makes her his empress. She falls in love with an actor, Paris, whom Domitian kills. Domitia heaps contempt and abuse on him until he adds her name to a list of those marked for death. Domitia discovers the proscription and conspires with Domitian's niece Julia, his cousin Domitilla, Parthenius and others on the list to kill him.

roman fleuve A sequence of novels, in which the individual books are linked by recurrent characters. It may describe a family (as in GALSWORTHY's *FORSYTE SAGA*) or a social milieu (as in TROLLOPE's BARSETSHIRE NOVELS and POWELL's *DANCE TO THE MUSIC OF TIME*).

romance See VERSE ROMANCE.

Romans of Partenay, The (Lusignan) A lengthy VERSE ROMANCE (*c.* 1500) translated from the French of La Coudrette (*c.* 1400). The first half deals with Raymond and Melusine, condemned by her mother to change periodically into a serpent; she leaves him when he discovers her secret. The second half follows the stories of her sisters Melior and Palestine, also victims of the mother's punishment, and Melior's ten deformed sons. Geoffrey of the Great Tooth becomes something of a central figure in a tale otherwise lacking a focal point.

Romanticism A comprehensive term for all the various tendencies towards change observable in European literature, art and culture in the later 18th and early 19th centuries. Although it manifested itself everywhere in the form of a pronounced shift in sensibility, Romanticism was not a unified movement with a clearly agreed agenda, and its emphases varied widely according to time, place and individual author. The English Romantic poets – BLAKE, COLERIDGE, WORDSWORTH, KEATS, SHELLEY and BYRON – belonged to two distinct generations, came from disparate backgrounds, differed sharply in theory and practice, held conflicting political views, and in some cases cordially disliked each other.

What the English Romantics did share was a belief in the poet's mission. Perhaps the most lasting achievement of Romanticism, in England and Germany, and later in France (where writers such as Chateaubriand, Hugo, and De Vigny were strongly influenced by the English poets), was what might be called the institutionalization of the Imagination: the emergence of the poet as a person possessing a special kind of faculty which sets him apart from his fellows. Intellectually, it pulled away from the philosophical rationalism and NEOCLASSICISM of the Enlightenment, developing an alternative aesthetic of freedom from the 'dead' letter of formal rules and conventions, and of uninhibited self-expression, of which the German *Sturm und Drang* movement of the 1770s was an important precursor. A corresponding sense of strong feeling, but also of original, fresh and, above all, authentic feeling was also important, and the development of natural, unforced poetic diction became an essential qualification for the standing of the poet (as in the *LYRICAL BALLADS*). The most typical Romantic attitude is individualism. Underlying the Romantic epoch as a whole is a pervasive sense of the collapse within the individual subject of those intricate systems which were being shaken apart at the public or institutional level by the American and French Revolutions. The Romantic hero is either a solitary dreamer, or an egocentric plagued by guilt and remorse but, in either case, a figure who has kicked the world away from beneath his feet.

A similar derangement of the official political economy of the emotions seems to have been the effect, if not the conscious intention, of the GOTHIC NOVEL, which anticipates and to some extent overlaps with Romanticism proper. Other important harbingers were introspective 18th-century poets such as COWPER and the GRAVEYARD POETS, as well as the cult of the primitive in the Celtic bardic verse of MACPHERSON's Ossianic poetry, and the folk ballads collected by PERCY. The Romantic valorization of personal experience was accompanied by a deepening sense of history, memorably expressed in SIR WALTER SCOTT's novels.

Romany Rye, The GEORGE BORROW's sequel to *LAVENGRO*, published in 1857. It continues the story of the author's life after 1825 in the same unchronological, episodic, open-ended way. The book contains some of Borrow's best writing, not least the enigmatic conclusion to the Isopel Berners episode, a tale which soon established itself as a classic of prose romance. Instead of giving the book a conventional structure, Borrow abruptly broke off the account of his life in mid-career and added the 'Appendix', one of the most powerfully written pieces of invective in the English language, attacking 'gentility nonsense' and critics of *Lavengro*.

Romaunt of the Rose, The A fragmentary translation of the French *Roman de la rose* (begun *c.* 1327 by Guillaume de Lorris and continued some 40 years later by Jean de Meun), a DREAM-VISION and ALLEGORY which played an important role in developing the medieval ideal of COURTLY LOVE. The first of the three English fragments has been attributed to CHAUCER, who seems to claim the translation as his own in *THE LEGEND OF GOOD WOMEN*.

Romeo and Juliet A tragedy by SHAKESPEARE, first performed *c.* 1595 and published in a corrupt Quarto (Q1) in 1597 and an authentic one (Q2) in 1599 as well as in the First Folio of 1623. Theatrical popularity has been assured by its clear plotting and the lyrical heights of its love poetry, together with the vivid creation of its minor characters, particularly Mercutio and the Nurse. The source was a poem by Arthur Brooke (1562) but the main outlines of the story were well known.

The Prince of Verona orders the warring families of Capulet and Montague to keep the peace. Romeo, son of Montague, attends Capulet's masqued ball and falls in love with his daughter Juliet. He waits under her balcony and they arrange a secret marriage, with the collusion of their confessor, Friar Lawrence, and Juliet's Nurse. It is immediately followed by disaster, when Romeo tries to prevent a duel between his mercurial friend Mercutio and the angry Tybalt. Mercutio is fatally wounded and Romeo kills Tybalt in reprisal. He is banished from Verona. Capulet decides that Juliet must marry Count Paris immediately. Friar Lawrence advises Juliet to acquiesce, but gives her a potion which creates the appearance of death for 42 hours. She will be taken to the family vault, where he will arrange for Romeo to greet her when she wakes. The friar's message fails to reach Romeo in Mantua. Desperate at the news of Juliet's death, he buys poison, goes to the Capulet vault, and, encountering Paris, kills him before drinking the fatal draught. Juliet wakes, finds Romeo dead and stabs herself. The tragedy, related by Friar Lawrence, reconciles the two families.

Romola A novel by GEORGE ELIOT, published in *THE CORNHILL MAGAZINE* in 1862–3 and in book form in 1863. It is set in Florence during the 1490s.

Tito Melema, an unscrupulous young Greek, ingratiates himself with the blind scholar Bardo de' Bardi and marries his high-minded daughter Romola. When her love is replaced by contempt, Romola turns for spiritual guidance to the fundamentalist friar Savonarola. Tito is eventually killed by his adoptive father, Baldassare. Romola finds fulfilment in caring for the sick during an outbreak of plague and in looking after her children and Tessa, a peasant girl Tito had betrayed. The fanatical Savonarola is burned at the stake for heresy. Other characters include Machiavelli, Piero di Cosimo and 50 or more lesser figures of the time. George Eliot spent months researching the historical background, which abounds with details of almost every aspect of life in Renaissance Florence.

rondeau Strictly, a poem of 13 lines in iambic pentameter or tetrameter (see METRE), divided into two unequal STANZAS, using only two rhymes throughout and repeating the opening phrase as a refrain at the end of each stanza. It is sometimes distinguished from and sometimes taken to be synonymous with the rondel (which may be 14 lines long and occasionally has a third rhyme). The English 'roundel' is used for either or both. However, poetic practice – in England mostly confined to the late 19th century – varies enough to justify a looser definition: a short poem in which the idea of 'rounding' is prominent, using only two rhymes and repeating some part of the beginning at the end and also, normally, at the end of each stanza.

Room with a View, A A novel by E. M. FORSTER, published in 1908. Lucy Honeychurch and her chaperone, the genteel Miss Bartlett, are frustrated in their hopes of obtaining a room with a view at the Pensione Bertolini in Florence. Miss Bartlett accepts the offer of an exchange with Mr Emerson and his son, George, after being reassured by a respectable acquaintance, the Rev. Mr Beebe. But George, after rescuing Lucy when she has witnessed a street murder, impulsively embraces her during a visit to Fiesole. Affronted, she and Miss Bartlett take themselves off to Rome and then return to Surrey. Here she becomes engaged to the cultured but shallow Cecil Vyse but breaks off the engagement when she realizes that she loves George, who has come to live nearby. The novel ends with George and Lucy on their honeymoon at the Pensione Bertolini.

Rosalynde A prose romance by LODGE, published in 1590. Based on the 14th-century *TALE OF GAMELYN*, it offered a popular blend of PASTORAL, EUPHUISM and Arcadian romance. The story of the usurping brothers Torismond and Saladyne, and the banished lovers Rosalynde and Rosader in the forest, gave SHAKESPEARE his main source for *AS YOU LIKE IT*.

Roscommon, 4th Earl of See DILLON, WENTWORTH.

Rosenberg, Isaac 1890–1918 Poet and artist. He studied at the Slade School and published at his own expense two collections of poems, *Night and Day* (1912) and *Youth* (1915), and *Moses: A Play* (1916). He joined the army in 1915 and was killed in battle near Arras. Many of his best poems, including 'Break of Day in the Trenches' and 'Louse Hunting', were written at the front, where he also began a second play, *The Unicorn*, which survives only in fragments. GORDON BOTTOMLEY edited a selection of his poems and letters in 1922. *Collected Works* (1937), edited by Bottomley and D. W. Harding, gained him a wider recognition. A new *Collected Works* (1979) edited by Ian Parsons includes paintings, drawings and letters.

Rosencrantz and Guildenstern are Dead A play by STOPPARD, performed in 1966 and revised in 1967. It is a wittily resourceful footnote to SHAKESPEARE's *HAMLET*, in which the two minor characters, now 'heroes', puzzle over their own identities, their relationship to the great events at Elsinore, the possibility of making decisions and the extent to which their roles have already been determined.

Ross, (James) Sinclair 1908– Canadian novelist and short-story writer. He achieved wide recognition with his first novel, *As for Me and My House* (1941), a classic of Western Canadian fiction which portrays the repressive nature of prairie life from the point of view of a small-

town minister's wife. It was followed by *The Well* (1957), *The Lamp at Noon and Other Stories* (1968), *Whir of Gold* (1970), *Sawbones Memorial* (1974) and *The Race and Other Stories* (1982).

Rossetti, Christina (Georgina) 1830–94 Poet. The sister of DANTE GABRIEL ROSSETTI and WILLIAM MICHAEL ROSSETTI, she showed early promise as a poet in small privately printed collections and the lyrics 'An End' and 'Dream Lane', contributed to the first number of *THE GERM* (1850) under the pseudonym of Ellen Alleyne. The High Anglicanism which moulded much of her finest verse – expressed in delicate, frank meditations on death and Heaven – did not impede her love of verbal experiment or the imaginative vigour of *GOBLIN MARKET*, title-poem of her first major collection (1862). It was followed by *THE PRINCE'S PROGRESS and Other Poems* (1866), and *Sing Song: A Nursery Rhyme Book* (illustrated by Arthur Hughes; 1872). *A Pageant and Other Poems* (1881) contained the SONNET sequence 'Monna Innominata', celebrating the superiority of divine love over human passion, while *Time Flies: A Reading Diary* (1885) consisted of 130 poems and thoughts for each day. The last original work published in her lifetime was *The Face of the Deep: A Devotional Commentary on the Apocalypse* (1892). William Michael Rossetti edited her complete works (1904).

Rossetti, Dante Gabriel 1828–82 Poet, painter and translator. Born in London into a family of Italian exiles and christened Gabriel Charles Dante, he studied at Cary's Art Academy (1843–6) before spending unfruitful periods at the Antique School of the Royal Academy and with the painter Ford Madox Brown. His friendship with Holman Hunt and John Everett Millais led in 1848 to the formation of the Pre-Raphaelite Brotherhood, the first generation of PRE-RAPHAELITES, whose other members were Thomas Woolner, Frederick George Stephens, WILLIAM MICHAEL ROSSETTI and James Collinson. A dominant figure in the early stages of the Pre-Raphaelite attempt to revolutionize Victorian art, he worked with unusual consistency in the late 1840s and throughout the 1850s both as painter and poet. In the former capacity he produced 'The Girlhood of Mary Virgin', 'How They Met Themselves', 'Ecce Ancilla Domini' and other works inspired by the Bible, Dante and ARTHURIAN LITERATURE. Except for 'Found', a study of modern city life, his paintings are highly symbolic, spiritually charged and redolent of remote worlds. His poetry included an early draft of *JENNY*, a DRAMATIC MONOLOGUE about a London prostitute, and a second version of his best-known poem, *THE BLESSED DAMOZEL*, which appeared in *THE GERM*, as well as early studies of 'Dante at Verona', 'The Bride's Prelude' and the pseudo-medieval *SISTER HELEN*. Rossetti's poetry, like his painting, is detailed, symbolic, concerned with the remote and sometimes erotic. It is often cast in BALLAD form and sometimes archaic in language.

During the 1850s he also joined Millais and Holman Hunt in illustrating an edition of TENNYSON (1857) and encountered the second generation of Pre-Raphaelite artists, notably Burne-Jones and WILLIAM MORRIS, during a project to decorate the walls of the Oxford Union. He would later produce designs for work in stained glass, furniture and tiles for Morris's firm. In 1860 he finally married Elizabeth Siddal, a shopgirl and then Pre-Raphaelite model whom he had met and fallen in love with in 1850. She died from an overdose of laudanum in 1862 and, although he had not been a faithful lover or husband, the loss encouraged an increasing morbidity in his work. However, *The Early Italian Poets* (1861; revised as *Dante and His Circle*, 1874) showed his gift in translating Dante, Guido Cavalcanti, Fazio degli Uberti and others. *Poems* (1870) drew on the manuscripts he had first remorsefully interred with Lizzie Siddal but later exhumed. He was attacked by ROBERT BUCHANAN in a scurrilous pamphlet, 'The Fleshly School of Poetry' (1872), to which he replied with 'The Stealthy School of Criticism'. Illness and paranoia increasingly beset him and he attempted suicide in 1872. *Ballads and Sonnets* (1881), which included a SONNET sequence, THE HOUSE OF LIFE, as well as THE KING'S TRAGEDY and 'The White Ship', appeared shortly before he died, a near-recluse.

Rossetti, William Michael 1829–1919 Man of letters. He was the brother of DANTE GABRIEL ROSSETTI and CHRISTINA ROSSETTI. One of the founders of the PRE-RAPHAELITES, he edited THE GERM and wrote about the movement in *Ruskin, Rossetti, Praeraphaelitism [sic]* (1899) and *Praeraphaelite Diaries and Letters* (1900). He also contributed countless articles on literature and art to journals, translated Dante's *Inferno*, wrote a life of KEATS (1887), edited SHELLEY, BLAKE and WHITMAN as well as the work of his brother and sister, and published *Some Reminiscences* (1906).

Roth, Henry 1906– American novelist. His reputation is largely based on *Call It Sleep* (1934), about a Jewish boy, David Schearl, growing up in New York. *A Star Shines Over Mount Morris Park* (1994) and *A Diving Rock in the Hudson* (1995) initiated a six-volume ROMAN FLEUVE entitled *Mercy of a Rude Stream*. *Nature's First Green* (1979) is a volume of memoirs and *Shifting Landscapes* (1987) a collection of shorter writings.

Roth, Philip 1933– American novelist. Jewish-American life in particular, and modern American society in general, are the subjects of his comedies of manners, which include *Goodbye, Columbus* (a novella and stories; 1959), *Letting Go* (1962), *When She was Good* (1967), PORTNOY'S COMPLAINT (1969), *The Breast* (1972), *The Great American Novel* (1973), *My Life as a Man* (1974) and *The Professor of Desire* (1977). *Our Gang* (1971) is a satire on the Nixon administration. Later work has elided the boundaries between fiction and autobiography. *The Ghost Writer* (1979), *Zuckerman Unbound* (1981), *The Anatomy Lesson* (1983) and *The Counterlife* (1986) form a semi-autobiographical sequence about the education, sudden fame, and subsequent disillusion of a writer. Recent work includes: two volumes of memoirs, *The Facts* (1988) and *Patrimony: A True Story* (1991), an essay about his father; and *Deception* (1990), combining fiction and self-revelation.

roundel See RONDEAU.

Rowe, Nicholas 1674–1718 Playwright, poet and editor. His best plays held a prominent place in the English repertoire well into the 19th century. *Tamerlane* (1701) transforms the hero of MARLOWE'S TAMBURLAINE to represent the values of William III in contrast to those of a villainous Bajazet (Louis XIV). It was less popular than Rowe's three 'she-tragedies', *The Fair Penitent* (1703), JANE SHORE (1714) and *Lady Jane Grey* (1715), the first two of which provided Sarah Siddons with famous roles. *The Fair Penitent* is derived from MASSINGER and FIELD'S THE FATAL DOWRY, from which it deviates into pathos. *Lady Jane Gray* portrays its heroine as a Protestant martyr, who rejects a pardon from the Catholic Queen Mary. Rowe's competent handling of blank verse was extrava-

gantly admired by some contemporaries – he was POET LAUREATE from 1715 until his death – and temperately praised by JOHNSON. His edition of SHAKESPEARE (1709) is rightly seen as innovatory.

Rowlands, Samuel *c.* 1570–*c.* 1630 Satirist. He is remembered for the spirited *The Letting of Humours Blood in the Head-vein* (1600), '*Tis Merry when Gossips Meet* (1602), *Democritus: or, Doctor Merry-Man His Medicines against Melancholy Humours* (1607) and *The Melancholy Knight* (1615), a verse monologue which ridicules nostalgia for a romantic past. He also wrote religious poetry.

Rowlandson, Mary White *c.* 1635–*c.* 1678 American Puritan writer. During King Philip's War (1674–6) she was held captive by the Narragansett Indians for three months. Her account of her experiences, *The Sovereignty and Goodness of God, Together with the Faithfulness of His Promises Displayed; being a Narrative of the Captivity and Restoration of Mrs Mary Rowlandson* (1682), went through many editions and became a classic of its genre.

Rowley, Samuel *c.* 1575–1624 Actor and playwright. His only known surviving play, *When You See Me, You Know Me* (1603), is a rambling chronicle about Henry VIII. His name is associated with the lost *The Taming of a Shrew* (*c.* 1589), which SHAKESPEARE knew, and Henslowe records paying him for 'additions' to MARLOWE'S DOCTOR FAUSTUS in 1602.

Rowley, William *c.* 1585–1626 Actor and playwright. Nothing is known of his acting career except that he played fat clowns. He collaborated with THOMAS MIDDLETON on *A Fair Quarrel* (published in 1617) and THE CHANGELING (1622), with DEKKER and JOHN FORD on THE WITCH OF EDMONTON (*c.* 1621), and probably with WEBSTER and FLETCHER as well. *The Birth of Merlin* (published in 1662) found its way into the SHAKESPEARE APOCRYPHA. His unaided plays include a muddled tragedy, *All's Lost by Lust* (*c.* 1620), and two CITIZEN COMEDIES, *A New Wonder: A Woman Never Vexed* (published in 1632) and *A Match at Midnight* (published in 1633).

Rowson, Susanna Haswell *c.* 1768–1824 American novelist, poet and playwright. Born in England, she went to America with her family as a child and began to write after her return to England in 1777, producing several books of verse and SENTIMENTAL NOVELS. The most famous was CHARLOTTE TEMPLE (1791, US publication 1794), the first American best-seller. After she and her husband returned to the USA in 1793 to pursue stage careers, she turned her hand to comedies and romances: *Slaves in Algiers* (1794), *The Female Patriot* (1794), *The Volunteers* (1795), *A Kick for a Bite* (1795), *Trials of the Human Heart* (1795), and *Americans in England* (1796). Latterly she devoted herself to didactic works for youth, including *Charlotte's Daughter: or, The Three Orphans* (1828), a sequel to *Charlotte Temple*.

Roxana: or, the Fortunate Mistress A novel by DEFOE, published in 1724. It is presented as the autobiography of the beautiful Mlle Beleau, daughter of Huguenot refugees in England. Ambitious for a more exciting life, she deserts her husband after squandering his fortune and producing five children. Nicknamed Roxana, she becomes a high-class kept woman moving between 'protectors' across England, Holland and France. Her faithful maid Amy accompanies her progress. After amassing a considerable fortune, Roxana marries a wealthy Dutch merchant but he discovers her deviousness. She receives only a pittance from his will and is left in penury and penitence. Despite its sometimes unconvincing psychology and anticlimactic ending, the book has unmistakable energy and narrative strength.

Royal Court Theatre A theatre in London's Sloane Square, opened in 1888. It has twice made a major contribution to English drama. In 1904-7, under the management of J. E. Vedrenne and GRANVILLE-BARKER, it established SHAW as a force in the British theatre. After 1956, as home of the English Stage Company, it spearheaded a revival of serious drama, staging OSBORNE's *LOOK BACK IN ANGER* and giving ARDEN, JELLICOE, BOND, BRENTON and HARE, among others, their first significant opportunities.

Royal National Theatre Britain's National Theatre, established only after long struggle, opened under the direction of Sir Laurence (later Lord) Olivier at the OLD VIC in 1962. In 1976-7, when Olivier had been succeeded by Sir Peter Hall, the company moved to a new complex, designed by Denys Lasdun, on the South Bank. It consists of three theatres: the open-stage Olivier, the proscenium arch Lyttelton and the experimental Cottesloe. Despite a decline in public subsidy and some loss of its original idealism, the National Theatre has kept its foremost place among British companies, rivalled only by the ROYAL SHAKESPEARE COMPANY.

Royal Shakespeare Company The title adopted in 1961 by the Shakespeare Theatre Company, which had run a seasonal festival of SHAKESPEARE's plays at Stratford-upon-Avon since 1879. Under Sir Peter Hall's directorship, the RSC supplemented its work at Stratford's Shakespeare Memorial Theatre with productions, modern as well as Shakespearean, at London's Aldwych Theatre. Under the artistic directorship of Trevor Nunn (1968-86) two further theatres were opened in Stratford: The Other Place (1974) and the Swan (1986). In 1982 the RSC moved its London headquarters to the Barbican Arts Centre, where it has a smaller studio theatre, the Pit, as well as a main auditorium.

Rubáiyát of Omar Khayyám of Naishápúr, The A free translation by EDWARD FITZGERALD from the Persian, first published as an anonymous pamphlet in 1859. Omar Khayyám was a 12th-century astronomer and poet; *Rubáiyát* is the plural of the Persian for 'a poem of four lines'. FitzGerald's version distils the spirit rather than extracting the specific meaning from its original. The *Rubáiyát* crept on to the market but, thanks to praise from DANTE GABRIEL ROSSETTI, MONCKTON MILNES, SWINBURNE, RUSKIN and MORRIS among others, slowly achieved a recognition it has never forfeited. In its own time its colourful, exotic and remote imagery appealed greatly to the Victorian interest in the Oriental, its Epicurean motifs linked it with the AESTHETIC MOVEMENT and its romantic melancholy anticipated the pessimistic poetry of MATTHEW ARNOLD, JAMES THOMSON and HARDY,

Rudd, Steele [Davis, Arthur Hoey] 1868-1935 Australian humorist. His broad comic sketches about the hapless Rudd family, set in the Darling Downs, were gathered in several collections: *On Our Selection* (1899), *Sandy's Selection* (1904), *Back at Our Selection* (1906), *Dad in Politics* (1908), *On an Australian Farm* (1910), *We Kaytons* (1921) and *Me an' th' Son* (1924).

Rudkin, (James) David 1936- Playwright. *Afore Night Come* (1960), about the murder of an Irish tramp, revealed an instinct for high tragedy and myth. The relationship between Ireland and England is the subject of *Cries from Casement as his Bones are Brought to Dublin* (1973)

and *Ashes* (1974), about a Belfast couple whose infertility is mysteriously linked to the struggle in Northern Ireland. Later work includes *Sons of Light* (1976), *The Triumph of Death* (1981), *Space Invaders* (1983), *Will's Way* (1984) and *The Saxon Shore* (1986). An accomplished linguist and musician, he has translated the libretto to Schoenberg's *Moses and Aaron* (1965) and adapted Euripides' *Hippolytus* (1978).

Ruin, The A 45-line fragment of an Old English poem preserved in the EXETER BOOK. Following the classical tradition of the *encomium urbis* (or poem praising a city), it describes a decaying Roman town, probably Bath, evoking its past splendour and present ruin.

Rukeyser, Muriel 1913-80 American poet. Her many volumes of verse, which include *Theory of Flight* (1935), *U.S.1.* (1938), *The Turning Wind* (1939), *The Green Wave* (1948), *Body of Waking* (1958) and *The Gates* (1976), reflect her concern with the Spanish Civil War, women's rights and the Vietnam War. She also wrote a novel, *The Orgy* (1965), and biographies of Willard Gibbs (1942) and Wendell Wilkie (1957).

Rule, Jane 1931- Canadian novelist and short-story writer, born in the USA. Canada's best-known lesbian writer, she has written several novels: *Desert of the Heart* (1964), *This is not for You* (1970), *Against the Season* (1971), *The Young in One Another's Arms* (1977), *Contract with the World* (1980) and *After the Fire* (1989). Her short stories include *Theme for Divers Instruments* (1975) and *Inland Passage* (1985). She has also written *Lesbian Images* (1975), a study of GERTRUDE STEIN, Colette and V. SACKVILLE-WEST among others, and *Outlander* (1980), a collection of essays.

Rule a Wife and Have a Wife A comedy by JOHN FLETCHER, first performed in 1624 and published in 1640. It is one of several works by Fletcher to influence RESTORATION COMEDY. Margarita, a rich heiress, wishes to marry only to give a cover to her amorous intrigues. Her companion Altea persuades her brother Leon to court her in the guise of a simpleton. Once married, Leon wins her admiration and fidelity.

Rumens, Carol 1944- Poet. *Strange Girl in Bright Colours* (1973), *A Necklace of Mirrors* (1979) and *Unplayed Music* (1981) are characterized by detailed observation of domesticity and female experience. Later work – *Star Whisper* (1983), *Direct Dialling* (1985), *The Greening of Snow Beach* (1989) and *From Berlin to Heaven* (1989) – has developed her preoccupation with suffering, persecution and the sense of loss or exile. *Selected Poems* appeared in 1987. She has also published a novel, *Plato Park* (1988), and edited *Making for the Open: The Chatto Book of Post-Feminist Poetry 1964-1984* (1985).

Runyon, (Alfred) Damon 1884-1946 American short-story writer and humorist. The New York scene provided the material for his unique vernacular humour: athletes, show people, gamblers, hustlers, crooks and their women are transformed into recognizable types. His volumes of stories include *Guys and Dolls* (1931), *Blue Plate Special* (1934), *Take It Easy* (1938), *Furthermore* (Britain 1938, USA 1941), *Runyon à la Carte* (1944), *Short Takes* (1946) and *Runyon on Broadway* (1950). He also wrote a successful FARCE, *A Slight Case of Murder* (1940), in collaboration with Howard Lindsay.

Rural Rides An anthology of essays by WILLIAM COBBETT, selected from pieces written for his newspaper, *The Political Register*, in 1822-6, and published together in 1830 as *Rural Rides in the Counties of Surrey, Kent, Sussex, Hampshire, Wiltshire, Gloucestershire,*

Herefordshire, Worcestershire, Somersetshire, Oxfordshire, Berkshire, Essex, Suffolk, Norfolk, and Hertfordshire: With Economical and Political Observations Relative to Matters Applicable to, and Illustrated by, the State of those Counties Respectively. In 1853 his son James Paul added further material dealing with his father's eastern and northern tours of 1830 and 1832 to make the version of *Rural Rides* that has been most frequently read in the 20th century.

Cobbett wished his campaign for Parliamentary reform to be based on up-to-date, first-hand observation of living conditions in rural England. The power of his writing comes from its immediacy. Through page after page of detailed description spiced with indignation and acerbity, the social concerns of the convinced democrat are expressed in witty, energetic prose that soon established *Rural Rides* as a classic.

Rushdie, (Ahmed) Salman 1947– Novelist. Born in Bombay, he emigrated to Britain in 1965. An important example of MAGIC REALISM, his fiction attempts to reshape the history of his time to make it congruent with identities fractured by imperialism and questions how fiction dare undertake so colossal a task. *Grimus* (1975), an extravagant fable, was followed by *Midnight's Children* (1981), a winner of the BOOKER PRIZE, about India, and *Shame* (1983), about Pakistan. Nothing in his previous success prepared Rushdie or his publishers for the reception of *THE SATANIC VERSES* (1988), whose oblique but energetic consideration of religion – particularly Islam – provoked an *affaire* raising questions of censorship and freedom of expression. Islamic protest against the novel's 'blasphemy' culminated in the *fatwa*, or death sentence, pronounced against the author by the Ayatollah Khomeini of Iran in February 1989. Rushdie was forced into hiding, from which he has given occasional interviews and published: a children's story, *Haroun and the Sea of Stories* (1990); a volume of essays, *Imaginary Homelands* (1991); a monograph on the film version of *The Wizard of Oz* (1992); and *East, West* (1994), short stories. *The Jaguar Smile* (1987) is a pertinent travel book about Nicaragua under the Sandinistas.

Ruskin, John 1819–1900 Critic of art, architecture and society. He was born in London, the only child of a prosperous wine merchant, John James Ruskin, and his wife Margaret. His overly protective parents educated him at home and at small private schools, and his mother accompanied him when he went to Christ Church, Oxford. In 1848 he married Euphemia (Effie) Chalmers Gray. The marriage was annulled on the grounds of non-consummation in 1854 and she married the painter John Everett Millais in 1855.

Ruskin became famous with the first volume of *MODERN PAINTERS* in 1843. Originally a defence of Turner, it had outgrown its original purpose long before its digressive course ended with the fifth volume in 1860. *THE SEVEN LAMPS OF ARCHITECTURE* (1849) was followed by *THE STONES OF VENICE* (1851–3), an epic of detailed research which includes the famous essay on 'The Nature of Gothic'. These works established him as England's most prominent if also most controversial art critic: the eloquent champion of Turner, Gothic architecture, medieval Italian painting and the controversial attempt by the PRE-RAPHAELITES to revive its principles.

Yet Ruskin could never be contained by a single discipline or resist the attempt to synthesize his varied interests. In particular, his public lectures and work for the Working Men's College in the 1850s showed his interest in social and economic problems. Its most trenchant result was *UNTO THIS LAST* (serialized in *THE CORNHILL MAGAZINE* in 1860 and published as a book in 1862) and the 'Essays on Political Economy' which appeared in *FRASER'S MAGAZINE* in 1862–3, subsequently revised and republished as *MUNERA PULVERIS* (1872). His lectures were collected under such arresting titles as *Sesame and Lilies* (1865) and *The Crown of Wild Olive* (1866). *The Ethics of the Dust* (1866) consists of moral dialogues, *Time and Tide, by Weare and Tyne* (1867) is a series of letters on social problems and *The Queen of the Air* (1869) a study of Greek myths. His proliferating interests found their most remarkable expression in *FORS CLAVIGERA*, a miscellany published monthly in 1871–8 and then continued irregularly. His Utopian ideals were embodied in the Guild of St George, founded in 1871.

In 1870 Ruskin had been appointed the first Slade Professor of Fine Arts at Oxford. His lectures were published as *Aratra Pentelici* (on sculpture; 1872), *The Eagle's Nest* (on science and art; 1872), *Love's Meinie* (on ornithology; 1873–81), *Val d'Arno* (on Tuscan art; 1876) and *Ariadne Florentina* (on wood and metal engraving; 1876). Further writings on drawing, Venice, Florence, botany, geology and fiction cascaded forth. But by now his mind was seriously disturbed, not least because of the death in 1875 of Rose La Touche, the young Irish girl he had despairingly loved since the 1860s. He suffered severe breakdowns in the late 1870s and 1880s; one of them prevented his testifying at the libel suit brought by the artist Whistler in 1878. Nevertheless, he managed to deliver a prophetic masterpiece, 'The Storm Cloud of the Nineteenth Century' (1884), and to begin his last enduring work, the autobiographical *PRAETERITA*, serialized in 1885–9. His tragically disturbed last years were spent at his Lake District home, Brantwood.

Ruskin remains one of the most vital of the great Victorians. As an art critic his importance goes far beyond his decisive impact on the reputations of Turner, the Pre-Raphaelites and the Italian painters. Works like *Modern Painters* are key documents in the development of the aesthetics of ROMANTICISM. As a critic of architecture he did far more than praise the Gothic style and so confirm the fashion for medievalism. His discovery in the medieval churches and cathedrals of moral and social values paved the way for WILLIAM MORRIS and the Arts and Crafts Movement. His vision of society powerfully influenced later thinkers who have sought to resist the dehumanizing effects of industrial culture.

Russell, Bertrand (Arthur William), 3rd Earl 1872–1970 Philosopher and mathematician. His chief philosophical works are *The Principles of Mathematics* (1903) and *Principia Mathematica* (with A. N. Whitehead; 1910–13); others include *The Analysis of Mind* (1921), *An Inquiry into Meaning and Truth* (1940) and *Human Knowledge: Its Scope and Limits* (1948). Always ready to apply mathematical reasoning to ethical and political questions, and known throughout his life as a champion of progressive causes, Russell also wrote many controversial books aimed at a wider audience, including *The Practice and Theory of Bolshevism* (1920), *Power, A New Social Analysis* (1938), *Human Society in Ethics and Politics* (1954) and *Why I am Not a Christian* (1957). He also wrote two collections of short stories, *Satan in the Suburbs* (1953) and *Nightmares of Eminent Persons* (1954), and a significant autobiography (1967–9). He was awarded the Nobel Prize for Literature in 1950.

Russell, George William 1867–1935 Irish poet, play-wright and painter. His pseudonym, AE (or A. E.), started as a printer's error for AEON (an eternal being in gnostic belief) on the title-page of his first book, *Homeward: Songs by the Way* (1894). He was a poet, as well as painter, of mystical landscapes, incidents and figures owing much to Theosophy. *Selected Poems* (1935) gives a sample. In 1902 his poetic drama *Deirdre* was presented with YEATS's CATHLEEN NÍ HOULIHAN by the Irish National Theatre Society (see the ABBEY THEATRE), which he helped to form. Russell also edited *The Irish Homestead* (1905–23) and *The Irish Statesman* (1923–30) and organized dairy co-operatives for the Department of Agriculture. His friend JOHN EGLINTON published a memoir (1937).

Russell, Willy 1947– Playwright. Born near Liverpool, he writes straightforward and usually very funny chronicles of ordinary life. They include *John, Paul, Ringo and ... Bert* (1974), a musical about the Beatles, *Breezeblock Park* (1975), *One for the Road* (1976), *Stags and Hens* (1978) and an adaptation of BOUCICAULT, *Blood Brothers* (1981; musical version, 1983). He is best known for two works, successful on film as well as the stage: *Educating Rita* (1979), about a working-class girl and her male mentor, and *Shirley Valentine* (1986), about a middle-aged woman breaking away from her humdrum life.

Ruth A novel by ELIZABETH GASKELL, published in 1853. Ruth Hilton, an innocent seamstress, is seduced and abandoned in Wales during her pregnancy by Henry Bellingham, a country gentleman. Thurstan Benson, a dissenting parson, and his sister Faith take her to his northern parish of Eccleston, where she lives as their widowed relative, Mrs Denbigh, gives birth to a son, Leonard, and works as governess to the Bradshaws. When Bellingham (now calling himself Donne) reap-pears as the local parliamentary candidate, he proposes marriages but Ruth refuses. When her secret becomes public, she, Leonard and the Bensons are treated as pari-ahs. She rehabilitates herself by brave deeds during a cholera epidemic and, in a last gesture, nurses Bellingham back to health before falling ill and dying herself. A sub-plot deals with the attachment between Bradshaw's daughter Jemima and his partner Walter Farquhar.

Rutherford, Mark See WHITE, WILLIAM HALE.

Ryga, George 1932– Canadian playwright. Much of his work has pleaded the case of oppressed minorities. It includes *The Ecstasy of Rita Joe* (1967), about an Indian torn between the traditional ways of her people and the contemporary urban world, and *Grass and Wild Strawberries* (1969), about the conflict between the hip-pie movement and middle-class society. His technique aspires to the quality of the BALLAD, incorporating ele-ments such as film projection, recorded sound, dance and song. He has also written for radio and television, as well as publishing novels, poetry and *The Athabasca Ryga* (1990), a selection from his early writing.

Rymer, Thomas 1641–1713 Critic and historian. An extreme advocate of NEOCLASSICISM, he is remembered for his attack on SHAKESPEARE – particularly *OTHELLO* – in *A Short View of Tragedy* (1693). Rymer was appointed Historiographer Royal in 1692 and undertook the task of collecting English treaties, covenants and similar documents in the 20-volume *Foedera* (1704–35).

Sackville, Charles, 6th Earl of Dorset 1638–1706 Poet and courtier. A dissolute roisterer like his fellow wits, ROCHESTER and SEDLEY, he later led a more responsible life, leaving England during James II's reign and playing a role in the Glorious Revolution of 1688. He was a patron to DRYDEN and PRIOR, who admired his work in return, and POPE regarded him as one of the wittiest poets of the day. His reputation now rests on a handful of lyrics, like 'To All You Ladies Now at Land', a song composed in 1665. Rochester rated him highly as a satirist ('The best good man, with the worst-natured muse') and verses such as 'On Mr Howard' are certainly lively. Four poems to Katherine Sedley (later James II's mistress) are remarkable for their expression of contemporary attitudes to women and the city.

Sackville, Thomas, 1st Earl of Dorset 1536–1608 Playwright and poet. With THOMAS NORTON he wrote *Gorboduc*, which has some claim to be the first proper English tragedy (acted in 1561 and printed in 1565). He also contributed the 'Induction' and the 'Complaint of Buckingham' to the 1563 edition of *A MIRROR FOR MAGISTRATES*. During the course of his long and successful career as a statesman, he had the task of announcing her death sentence to Mary Queen of Scots. James I confirmed him for life in the office of Lord High Treasurer and made him Earl of Dorset.

Sackville-West, Vita [Victoria] **(Mary)** 1892–1962 Novelist, poet, biographer and gardener. The wife of HAROLD NICOLSON, she produced some 50 books. *Knole and the Sackvilles* (1922; revised 1958) is an account of her family and the family home in Kent. She first achieved recognition with her long poem *The Land* (1926), a realistic PASTORAL set in the Weald of Kent. *The Eagle and the Dove: A Study in Contrasts* (1943) examines Teresa of Avila, the Spanish mystic, and Thérèse of Lisieux, the 'Little Flower' of France. *Daughter of France* (1959) is a biography of 'La Grande Mademoiselle'. Of her novels, *The Edwardians* (1930) and *All Passion Spent* (1931) have been rated most highly. Known for her creation of the gardens at Sissinghurst, her home with Harold Nicolson, she also published several collections of the weekly gardening columns she contributed to *The Observer*. VIRGINIA WOOLF used her as the model for the androgynous hero of *ORLANDO*.

Sacred Fount, The A short novel by HENRY JAMES, published in 1901. During a weekend party at the country house of Newmarch the narrator observes that his hostess, Grace Brissenden, though much older than her husband, Guy, seems the more youthful and energetic of the two. He speculates that Guy is the 'sacred fount' from which his wife draws her new vitality, leaving him correspondingly devitalized. He then applies this theory to another pair of guests, Gilbert Long and May Server. He further decides that Gilbert and Grace, the dominant partners of their respective marriages, and Mary and Guy, the weaker partners, are drawing closer together. But Grace, whom he takes into his confidence, tells him that he has imagined the whole thing. The reader is left uncertain.

Sad Fortunes of the Reverend Amos Barton, The See SCENES OF CLERICAL LIFE.

Sahgal, Nayantara 1927– Indian novelist and jour-

nalist. As Nehru's niece she was close to Gandhian idealism before Independence and political in-fighting thereafter, experiences reflected in elegantly written novels such a *A Time to be Happy* (1958), *This Time of Morning* (1965), *Storm in Chandigarh* (1969), *The Day in Shadow* (1971), *A Situation in New Delhi* (1977), *Rich Like Us* (1985), *Plans for Departure* (1986) and *Mistaken Identity* (1988). *Prison and Chocolate Cake* (1954) and *From Fear Set Free* (1962) are autobiographical. Her biography of her cousin Indira Gandhi (1982) is highly critical.

Saint Joan A play by SHAW, produced in New York in 1923 and in London in 1924, when it was also published. The action follows Joan of Arc's career from her meetings with Robert de Baudricourt and the Dauphin and her relief of the siege of Orleans. Her claim to divine inspiration raises the suspicion of heresy. The Bishop of Beauvais and John de Stogumber believe her soul can be saved, but the Earl of Warwick sees her merely as a dangerous enemy. He hands her over to the Church after she has been captured by the Burgundians and sold to the English. At her trial the threat of burning at first makes her recant, but she destroys her recantation and is taken to the stake. The witty Epilogue deals with the nullification of the Church's verdict of 1431 and Joan's canonization.

St Ronan's Well A novel by SIR WALTER SCOTT, published in 1824. It abandons his usual historical settings for a fashionable Scottish spa in the early 19th century. The enmity of two half-brothers, sons of the late Earl of Etherington, is inflamed by their vexed and tragic relationship with Clara Mowbray, daughter of the laird of St Ronan's. Scott's portrait of Meg Dods, a down-to-earth landlady, has been praised.

saint's life Prose and verse accounts of saints' lives flourished during the Middle Ages. They are preserved both independently and in collections such as THE GOLDEN LEGEND and THE SOUTH ENGLISH LEGENDARY. Usually taken from Latin *Vitae*, the stories often include fanciful as well as miraculous episodes, adding entertainment to their didactic function.

Saintsbury, George (Edward Bateman) 1845–1933 Critic and literary historian. A busy reviewer for the contemporary journals, he ended his career as professor of rhetoric and English literature at the University of Edinburgh. Much of his work testifies to his interest in French literature. Other books include *A Short History of English Literature* (1898), *A History of Criticism* (1900–4), *A History of English Prosody* (1906–10) and *The English Novel* (1913), as well as studies of individual periods and writers, and the Oxford edition of the works of THACKERAY (1907). He was also a wine connoisseur: *Notes on a Cellar Book* (1920) is an acknowledged classic.

Saki [Munro, Hector Hugh] 1870–1916 Short-story writer and novelist. His first book, *The Rise of the Russian Empire* (1899), was his only serious work. Thereafter he adopted the name of the cup-bearer in THE RUBÁIYÁT OF OMAR KHAYYÁM and published collections of short stories: *Reginald* (1904), *Reginald in Russia and Other Sketches* (1910), *The Chronicles of Clovis* (1912) and *Beasts and Superbeasts* (1914). Whimsical in their plots and light-heartedly cynical in their tone, they are also given a darker side by memories of his unhappy childhood with his maiden aunts in Devon. He also wrote two novels, *The Unbearable Bassington* (1912) and *When William Came* (1913), the latter a satirical fantasy subtitled 'A Story of London under the Hohenzollerns'. Two further collections appeared after Munro's death in World War I, *The Toys of Peace and Other Papers* (1919) and *The Square Egg and Other Sketches* (1924).

Sala, G(eorge) A(ugustus) 1828–96 Journalist and travel-writer. He contributed to DICKENS's HOUSEHOLD WORDS and ALL THE YEAR ROUND, in which *A Journey Due North* (1858), about Russia, first appeared. *My Diary in the Midst of the War* (1865) was based on his work as a *Daily Telegraph* correspondent during the American Civil War. His most successful book was *Twice Around the Clock: or, The Hours of the Day and Night in London* (1859), a series of social sketches. He also wrote *Things I Have Seen and People I Have Known* (1894).

Salinger, J(erome) D(avid) 1919– American novelist and short-story writer. His only novel has been the highly successful THE CATCHER IN THE RYE (1951), narrated by a teenager in rebellion against the adult world. *Nine Stories* (as *For Esmé – With Love and Squalor* in Britain; 1953) introduces the Glass family, who reappear in *Franny and Zooey* (1961), *Raise High the Roofbeam, Carpenters* (1963) and *Seymour: An Introduction* (1963). Further brief instalments in their history have appeared in magazines but Salinger has since announced that he now writes only for personal diversion.

Salkey, (Felix) Andrew (Alexander) 1928–95 Jamaican novelist, poet and writer of CHILDREN's LITERATURE. His children's novels include *Hurricane* (1964), *Earthquake* (1965), *Drought* (1966) and *Riot* (1967). Adult novels like *A Quality of Violence* (1959) and *The Late Emancipation of Jerry Stover* (1968) stress the aridity of Caribbean experience. English society proves no less bleak and inhospitable in *Escape to an Autumn Pavement* (1960), *The Adventures of Catullus Kelly* (1969) and *Come Home, Michael Heartland* (1976). *Havana Journal* (1971) and *Georgetown Journal* (1972) are travel books. Salkey also published volumes of poetry and edited anthologies of Caribbean writing.

Salmagundi: or, The Whim-Whams of Opinions of Launcelot Langstaff Esq. and Others A series of satirical essays and poems by WASHINGTON IRVING, his brother William, and JAMES KIRKE PAULDING, issued in periodical pamphlets and then in book form in 1807–8. It covers aspects of life in New York, the authors' political stance favouring aristocratic federalism in opposition to Jeffersonian democracy. Paulding was the sole author of a further series of *Salmagundi* papers (1819–20).

Salome A play by OSCAR WILDE, written in French. An English translation by LORD ALFRED DOUGLAS, with illustrations by AUBREY BEARDSLEY, appeared in 1894. Its depiction of Salome's destructive love for John the Baptist was banned by the Lord Chamberlain in 1893. The first production, with Sarah Bernhardt, took place in Paris in 1896 and the play was not performed in Britain until 1931. It inspired Richard Strauss's opera (1905).

Samson Agonistes: A Dramatic Poem A CLOSET DRAMA by MILTON, published in 1671. Its subject is the biblical Samson, blind (like the poet himself) and a prisoner of the Philistines. 'Agonistes' refers to Samson as athlete or wrestler. The poem is cast in the form of a Greek tragedy, using a Chorus, confining the action to one place and compressing its narrative into the last hours

of the hero's life. Although Milton never intended it for the stage, it has been successfully performed and Handel used it as the basis for an oratorio.

On a festival day Samson is brought into the open air, where he reflects on his blindness. A succession of visitors arrives: the men of Dan, his tribe, trying to comfort him; his father Manoa, eager to ransom him from the Philistines; a repentant Dalila, whom he spurns; and Harapha the Philistine, a taunting bully whom Samson defies. The Chorus praises his unquenchable spirit. A Philistine officer brings news that the Philistines want a demonstration of his strength at the festival to their god Dagon. Samson dismisses him but then, realizing that he has regained his old strength now that his hair has regrown, agrees to go. After he leaves, Manoa arrives with the news that the Philistines will accept a ransom. He is interrupted by the shouting in the streets as the Philistines see their enemy in chains. The poem ends with the Messenger's description of Samson's destruction of the temple and his death.

Sandburg, Carl 1878–1967 American poet. His reputation as a poet of the Midwest was established by *Chicago Poems* (1916), a volume of free verse on 20th-century urban themes, and consolidated by *Cornhuskers* (1918; PULITZER PRIZE), *Smoke and Steel* (1920), *Slabs of the Sunburnt West* (1922), *Good Morning, America* (1928), *The People, Yes* (1936) and *Complete Poems* (1950; Pulitzer Prize). Though Sandburg kept his belief in ordinary working people, his later verse reveals a darker vision, tempered by the Depression. He also wrote a two-part biography of Abraham Lincoln (1926–39); a novel, *Remembrance Rock* (1948), CHILDREN's LITERATURE; and an autobiography, *Always the Young Strangers* (1952).

Sanditon An unfinished novel which JANE AUSTEN worked on during the early months of 1817, the year of her death. It was first published in 1925. Charlotte Heywood is a guest of the Parker family at Sanditon, a seaside village rapidly developing into a fashionable resort. There she meets Lady Denham and her nephew and niece, Sir Edward and Miss Denham.

Sandys, George 1578–1644 Translator, poet and travel-writer. He published a widely read account (1615) of his travels in Italy and the Levant. In 1621 he went to America as treasurer of the Virginia Company for five years and began the translations for which he was best known. His version of Ovid's *Metamorphoses* (1626) was widely admired. A later edition (1632) added the first book of *The Aeneid. Christ's Passion: A Tragedy*, from the Latin of Hugo Grotius, was published in 1640. Sandys also undertook verse translations from the Psalms (1636) and the Song of Solomon (1641).

Sansom, William 1912–76 Short-story writer and novelist. His first collection of stories, *Fireman Flower* (1944), drawing on his experiences in wartime London, was followed by *South* (1948), *Something Terrible, Something Lovely* (1948), *The Passionate North* (1950), *A Touch of the Sun* (1952), *Lord Love Us* (1954), *A Contest of Ladies* (1956), and *Among the Dahlias* (1957). Sansom also wrote novels, travel books, film scripts, television plays and lyrics.

Santayana, George 1863–1952 American philosopher. Born Jorge Ruiz de Santayana y Borras in Madrid, he was professor of philosophy at Harvard from 1889 until 1912, when he returned to Europe. He is best remembered for his only novel, *The Last Puritan* (1935), about Oliver Alden's youth in New England and Europe. *The Life of Reason* (1905–6) and *The Realms of Being* (1927–40) argue that matter itself is the only reality.

Santayana also wrote three studies of American life: *Philosophical Opinion in America* (1918), *Character and Opinion in the United States* (1920), on the conflict of idealism and materialism, and *The Genteel Tradition at Bay* (1931), a criticism of the 'new humanism'. His memoirs, *Persons and Places*, appeared as *The Backgrounds of My Life* (1944), *The Middle Span* (1945) and *My Host the World* (1953).

Sapphics A verse form named after Sappho, Greek poetess of 7th–6th century BC. It consists of four-line STAN-ZAS, the first three lines being long ($-\smile/--/-\smile\smile/-\smile/-\smile$), the fourth short ($-\smile\smile/-\smile$). Attempts to reproduce classical quantities in English inevitably seem unnatural, but Victorian poets often tried their hand at Sapphics. See also METRE.

Sardanapalus A tragedy by BYRON, published in 1821 and produced in 1834. The action is set about 640 BC and is based on the history of Diodorus Siculus. Beleses, a Chaldean soothsayer, and Arbaces, a governor of Medea, organize a revolt against Sardanapalus, the extravagantly spendthrift king of Assyria, who finally dies on a funeral pyre with his beloved Myrrha.

Sargeson, Frank 1903–82 New Zealand short-story writer and novelist. His first collection, *Conversations with My Uncle* (1936), showed his skill at using the language of the ill-educated and semi-literate. *Collected Stories* was published in 1965. He is also the author of *I Saw in My Dream* (1949), *I for One* (1956) and *Joy of the Worm* (1969).

Saroyan, William 1908–81 American playwright, novelist and short-story writer. His first collection of short stories, *The Daring Young Man on the Flying Trapeze* (1934), typifies his genial vision. Other collections include *Inhale and Exhale* (1936), *Three Times Three* (1936), *The Trouble with Tigers* (1938), *My Name is Aram* (1940) and *Dear Baby* (1944). *The Human Comedy* (1943), *The Adventures of Wesley Jackson* (1946), *Rock Wagram* (1951), *Mama, I Love You* (1956), *Papa, You're Crazy* (1957) and *One Day in the Afternoon of the World* (1964) are novels. Saroyan perhaps achieved greatest fame with his plays, which include *My Heart's in the Highlands* (1939), *The Time of Your Life* (1939), *Love's Old Sweet Song* (1941), *The Beautiful People* (1942), *Across the Board on Tomorrow Morning* (1942), *Hello Out There* (1943), *Don't Go Away Mad* (1949) and *The Cave Dwellers* (1957). *The Bicycle Rider in Beverly Hills* (1952), *Here Comes, There Goes, You Know Who* (1961) and *Obituaries* (1979) are autobiographical.

Sarton, May 1912–95 American novelist and poet. Her work addresses moral and political issues in a distinct and localized idiom. Her novels include *The Single Hound* (1938), *The Birth of Grandfather* (1957), *The Small Room* (1961), *Mrs Stevens Hears the Mermaids Singing* (1965), *Kinds of Love* (1970), *As We are Now* (1973), *Anger* (1982) and *The Education of Harriet Hatfield* (1990). Her verse is gathered in *Collected Poems* (1974). Autobiographical writings include *I Knew a Phoenix* (1959), *Plant Dreaming Deep* (1968), *Journal of Solitude* (1973), *Recovering* (1980) and *Honey in the Hive* (1988).

Sartor Resartus A prose work by CARLYLE, serialized in *FRASER'S MAGAZINE* in 1833–4 and published in book form in the USA in 1836 and in Britain in 1838. Written under the influence of German Romantic thought, *Sartor Resartus* ('The Tailor Re-patched') is rich in SYMBOL and ALLEGORY, frequently rough in humour and bizarre in style. The first part satirically examines the philosophy of clothes, their importance as symbols and as coverings of an inner reality. The enquiry is made through

the papers and memoranda of the idealistic Professor Diogenes Teufelsdröckh ('God sent Devil's-dung'). The second movement is largely Carlyle's spiritual autobiography in the guise of Teufelsdröckh's romantic wanderings. These come to a spiritual climax in the chapters 'The Everlasting Nay', 'The Centre of Indifference' and 'The Everlasting Yea'. The final part is a poetic hymn to the romantic aspirant towards a nobler universe.

Sassoon, Siegfried (Louvain) 1886–1967 Poet and autobiographer. During World War I he served in France, where he met ROBERT GRAVES and was awarded the MC, which he later threw away. As a result of his protest, 'A Soldier's Declaration' (July 1917), he was sent to W. H. R. Rivers, the neurologist at Craiglockhart Hospital, Edinburgh, where he met WILFRED OWEN, whose poems he edited in 1920. His own savagely ironic anti-war poems appeared in *The Old Huntsman* (1917) and *Counter-Attack* (1918). Later volumes included *Satirical Poems* (1926), *Vigils* (1935), *Sequences* (1956) and *Collected Poems* (1961). He also wrote a semi-autobiographical trilogy, *Complete Memoirs of George Sherston* (1937), consisting of *Memoirs of a Fox-Hunting Man* (1928), *Memoirs of an Infantry Officer* (1930) and *Sherston's Progress* (1936), and three volumes of autobiography, *The Old Century and Seven More Years* (1938), *The Weald of Youth* (1942) and *Siegfried's Journey* (1945).

Satanic Verses, The A novel by SALMAN RUSHDIE, published in 1988. It announces its assault on certainty in the opening image of Gibreel Farishta and Saladin Chamcha plummeting earthwards after their airliner has been blown apart. The byzantine plot follows their fortunes on landing, often transmuting them into other identities, notably the exiled Imam waiting to return to his decadent homeland of Sodom and the prophet-figure Mahound. Islamic outrage was also provoked by an imaginary brothel scene in which the girls are named after the prophet's 12 wives and another dream sequence dramatizing the question of whether disputed verses in *The Koran* may have been written by the Devil rather than God. Such criticism ignores Rushdie's deliberately combative IRONY and the ostentatious fictiveness of his whole project. Energetic, comic and self-questioning, *The Satanic Verses* is anything but polemical or categorical.

Satchell, William 1860–1942 New Zealand novelist. Born in London, he studied at Heidelberg and emigrated to New Zealand in the 1880s. His first novel of New Zealand life, *The Land of the Lost*, appeared in 1902. Others were *The Toll of the Bush* (1905), *The Elixir of Life* (1907) and the highly praised *The Greenstone Door* (1914), about Anglo-Maori relations.

satire Defined by SAMUEL JOHNSON as 'a poem in which wickedness or folly is censured'. Provided we amend 'a poem' to 'literature' the definition is adequate, for though the main weapons of European satire are IRONY and WIT, it is not necessarily a form of COMEDY. ORWELL's *ANIMAL FARM* is certainly a comic satire, but *NINETEEN EIGHTY-FOUR* is a horrific one.

It usually assumes some moral or social norms by which degrees of wickedness or folly can be measured. Attacks which are descended from the curse intended to wreak effective harm on the victim would now be styled 'lampoon'. On the other hand, when stylistic caricature and farcical content so predominate that malice and morality melt away in the mockery, BURLESQUE or MOCK HEROIC would be preferred. Satire is usually designated as either Juvenalian or Horatian, the former indignantly attacking wickedness, the latter suavely attacking folly. Elizabethan satire is almost entirely Juvenalian, partly because it inherits a morality tradition and partly because of a belief that satire should be rough (the result of an etymological mistake deriving the word from the shaggy satyr of mythology). The satire of the AUGUSTAN AGE, on the other hand, as befits a 'polite' society, more often follows Horace; its major exemplar is POPE.

Satire of the Three Estates, Ane Pleasant A MORALITY PLAY by SIR DAVID LYNDSAY performed before James V of Scotland in 1540. His intention was to denounce corruption wherever he found it. Its attack on the Lords Spiritual made the play a favourite source for the advocates of reform in the Scottish Church. Part I dramatizes the temptations of Rex Humanitas, beset by evil counsellors and falling prey to Sensuality; moral order returns to his court only with the arrival of Divine Correction. An interlude details the misfortunes of an impoverished farmer and the chicanery of a pardoner. Part II brings the Three Estates before the King, to be denounced by John the Commonweill. Lords and Commons confess their faults and promise reform, but the Lords Spiritual defy the complainants and are forcibly dispossessed. The play ends with a stringent sermon from Folly.

Satires of Circumstance, Lyrics and Reveries Poems by HARDY, published in 1914. Foremost are the deeply felt 'Poems of 1912–13', written after the death of his first wife, Emma, and among the great achievements of English elegiac verse. The 1912–13 verses idealize her youthful beauty ('Beeny Cliff'), lament her sudden death ('The Going'), recall visiting her at Tintagel ('I Found Her Out There') and reply to her dead spirit ('The Voice'). The volume also contains 'Channel Firing', 'Wessex Heights', 'When I Set Out for Lyonnesse', 'Ah, are You Digging on My Grave' and 'Under the Waterfall'.

Satiromastix A play by DEKKER, perhaps with contributions by MARSTON, first produced in 1601. A rejoinder to JONSON's POETASTER, it mixes an archaic plot (virgin takes poison rather than lose her honour to a lustful king) with abuse of Jonson in the character of Horace.

Saturday Review, The A periodical founded in 1855 by A. J. B. Beresford Hope (1820–87) with John Douglas Cook as its first editor. Under the editorship of FRANK HARRIS (1894–8) its literary interests broadened with contributions from HARDY, WELLS, BEERBOHM and SHAW, its drama critic. It survived until 1938.

Saunders, James 1925– Playwright. He was influenced by poetic drama and the THEATRE OF THE ABSURD in Next Time I'll Sing to You (1963), suggested by the life of an Essex hermit, and A Scent of Flowers (1964), also about loneliness. Later work includes Bodies (1978) and Making It Better (1992).

Savage, Marmion 1803–72 Anglo-Irish novelist. Editor of THE EXAMINER, he published six novels, including Falcon Family (1845), a SATIRE on the Young Ireland party.

Savage, Richard c. 1696–1743 Poet and playwright. His claim to be the illegitimate son of the 4th Earl Rivers and the Countess of Macclesfield is no longer accepted, though The Bastard (1728), his poem censuring his supposed mother, convinced his friend SAMUEL JOHNSON, who wrote a sympathetic biography in LIVES OF THE POETS. Savage's first poem, The Convocation (1717), was followed by a comedy, Love in a Veil (1718), and The Tragedy

of Sir Thomas Overbury (1723). His work is forgotten except for The Wanderer (1729), a rambling philosophical poem. Savage died in a debtors' prison.

Savile, George, Marquess of Halifax 1633–95 Politician and writer on politics. A man of independent politics, he sucessfully led the opposition to Shaftesbury and the Exclusion Bill in the Lords (see ABSALOM AND ACHITOPHEL). As chairman of the committee of peers it was later his task to offer the throne to William and Mary. The last office he held was Lord Privy Seal. His political tracts and essays include The Character of a Trimmer (1688), a bold and seminal pamphlet which contains a famous passage in praise of truth. The main body of his work appeared in two posthumous publications, Miscellanies (1700) and A Character of King Charles the Second: And Political, Moral and Miscellaneous Thoughts and Reflections (1750).

Savile, Sir Henry 1549–1622 Scholar and translator. He served Elizabeth I as both Greek tutor and Latin secretary, and was rewarded with the provostship of Eton. One of those commissioned by JAMES I to produce the Authorized Version of the Bible (see BIBLE IN ENGLISH), he also translated part of Tacitus' Histories (1619) and edited St John Chrysostom (1610–13) and Xenophon's Cyropaedia (1613). He assisted BODLEY in founding his great library and endowed Oxford with professorships in geometry and astronomy.

Savoy Operas, The A group of 13 comic operas, excluding the early Thespis (1871), by W. S. GILBERT (librettist) and Arthur Sullivan (composer): Trial by Jury (1875), The Sorcerer (1877), H.M.S. Pinafore (1878), The Pirates of Penzance (1879), Patience (1881), Iolanthe (1882), Princess Ida (1884), The Mikado (1885), Ruddigore (1887), The Yeomen of the Guard (1888), The Gondoliers (1889), Utopia Limited (1893) and The Grand Duke (1896). Although the first five were originally produced elsewhere, the series is always called after the Savoy Theatre, London, built for their performance by the impresario Richard D'Oyly Carte. They established new standards of writing and presentation for the English musical theatre, proved immensely popular throughout the English-speaking world, and have been widely performed ever since. Gilbert's libretti are characterized by a strong satirical streak allied to a personal vein of fantasy. Sullivan's scores add the warmth which Gilbert's work lacked and heighten his wit and satire by their vivacity.

Sawles Warde A homiletic prose ALLEGORY freely translated in the late 12th century from part of the De anima attributed to Hugh of St Victor. The body, the house of the soul, is helped by Wit and the Four Daughters of God (Righteousness, Prudence, Temperance and Ghostly or Spiritual Strength) to withstand the assaults of the Devil. Descriptions of Hell by Fear, the messenger of Death, and of Heaven by Mirth are vivid pieces of writing.

Sayers, Dorothy L(eigh) 1893–1957 Writer of DETECTIVE FICTION, playwright and translator. Her reputation rests on the series of novels about her elegant and apparently light-hearted amateur detective, Lord Peter Wimsey: Whose Body? (1923), Clouds of Witness (1926), Unnatural Death (1927), The Unpleasantness at the Bellona Club (1928), Strong Poison (1930), which also introduced Harriet Vane, The Five Red Herrings (1931), Have His Carcase (1932), Murder Must Advertise (1932), set in an advertising agency, The Nine Tailors (1934), set in the Fens, Gaudy Night (1935), with Wimsey and Vane in Oxford, and Busman's Honeymoon (1937), in which Wimsey and Vane are married. The later novels in the series determinedly introduce a new note of seriousness. Her only detective novel without Wimsey is *The Documents in the Case* (with Robert Eustace; 1930). Other work includes a sequence of radio plays about the life of Christ, *The Man Born to be King* (1941–2) and translations of Dante's *Inferno* (1949), *Purgatorio* (1955) and *Paradiso* (completed by Barbara Reynolds; 1962) and of *The Song of Roland* (1957).

Scannell, Vernon 1922– Poet. His work, formally traditional but rooted in recognizable 20th-century experience, has appeared in many volumes from *Graves and Resurrections* (1948) onwards. They include *Selected Poems* (1971), *New and Collected Poems 1950–1980* (1980), *Winterlude* (1982), *Funeral Games* (1987), *Dangerous Ones* (1991) and *A Time for Fire* (1991). His novels include *The Fight* (1953), *The Wound and the Scar* (1953) and *Ring of Truth* (1983). *The Tiger and the Rose* (1971) and *Drums of Morning: Growing Up in the 1930s* (1992) are autobiographical.

Scarlet Letter, The A novel by HAWTHORNE, published in 1850. An introductory section describes his work in the Salem Custom House. The novel itself is set in 17th-century Boston. Charged with adultery, Hester Prynne refuses to reveal the identity of her lover and the father of her illegitimate baby. She is condemned to wear a scarlet 'A' on her breast but, as the years pass, finds a place in society by helping other outcasts and unfortunates. Her daughter, Pearl, develops into a mischievous 'elfin' child. Meanwhile her husband, who arrived in time to witness her public humiliation, adopts the name Roger Chillingworth and swears her to secrecy about his identity. He guesses correctly that her lover was the young minister, Arthur Dimmesdale, and under the guise of giving medical help torments Dimmesdale with veiled allusions to his guilt. Hester begs Dimmesdale to escape with her to Europe. He briefly yields to the temptation, and Hester even removes the letter from her breast, before the moment passes. Having delivered a powerful Election Day Sermon, Dimmesdale bids Hester and Pearl to join him on the pillory, publicly confesses his sin and dies in her arms. Hester and Pearl leave Boston. Pearl settles in Europe but Hester voluntarily returns, resumes her scarlet 'A' and continues her life of penance.

scène à faire The scene of crucial confrontation between two adversaries whose meeting or recognition has been delayed. In the WELL-MADE PLAY it is the prelude to the DÉNOUEMENT.

Scenes of Clerical Life Three tales by GEORGE ELIOT, serialized in 1857 and published in volume form in 1858. 'The Sad Fortunes of the Reverend Amos Barton' concerns the well-meaning but maladroit curate of Shepperton, who acquires the sympathy and understanding of his parishioners only after the death of his wife, Milly. 'Mr Gilfil's Love-Story' centres on the tragic life of an earlier clergyman of the same parish, Shepperton. Maynard Gilfil falls in love with a talented singer, Caterina Sarti (Tina), but she loves the feckless Captain Anthony Wybrow and becomes dangerously unbalanced when he dies. Gilfil seeks her out, restores her to health and marries her, but her spirit is so broken that she dies soon afterwards, leaving him to a lonely old age. 'Janet's Repentance' tells the tragic story of the hostility of the drunken, braggard lawyer, Robert Dempster, towards the conscientious Reverend Edgar Tryan of Milby. Dempster is joined in the hostility by his wife, Janet, also addicted to drink. But Tryan helps her

when she is forced to flee her home and, now able to resist the temptation of alcohol, she is at his bedside when he dies, exhausted by his work for the parish.

Scholar-Gipsy, The A poem by MATTHEW ARNOLD, published in *Poems: A New Edition* (1853). It derives from a legend, told by JOSEPH GLANVILL in *The Vanity of Dogmatizing* (1661), about an Oxford student who left the university to live with gipsies. In Arnold's poem the speaker envies the scholar-gipsy's escape into the countryside around Oxford whilst acknowledging that no such escape is possible for himself and his generation.

School for Scandal, The A comedy by RICHARD BRINSLEY SHERIDAN, produced in 1777. Lady Teazle, the young and ingenuous wife of the ageing Sir Peter, meets the brothers, Charles and Joseph Surface. Charles is dissolute but good-hearted; Joseph is decorous but hypocritical. Each would like to marry Sir Peter's ward, Maria, who is also being courted by Sir Benjamin Backbite, a member of Lady Sneerwell's malicious circle. The plot is complex and ingeniously handled. It hinges on the return of Sir Oliver Surface from Bengal, his discovery of the true characters of his nephews, and the eventual unmasking of Joseph Surface in a justly famous 'screen scene'. Charles Surface is united with Maria and the much-tried Teazles are reconciled.

Schreiner, Olive 1855–1920 South African novelist. She moved to Britain in 1881 and achieved success with *The Story of an African Farm* (1883), originally published under the pseudonym of Ralph Iron, attacking the heroic image of the frontier and presenting a heroine who makes the novel an important feminist document. *Trooper Peter Halket of Mashonaland* (1897) attacks Cecil Rhodes and his Chartered Company's treatment of blacks in 'Rhodesia'. Two novels she often re-worked appeared posthumously as *From Man to Man* (1926) and *Undine* (1929). She saw herself less as a novelist than a writer trying to transform an uncaring society – hence such works as *Dreams* (1891) and *Dream Life and Real Life* (1893). Her polemical writings championed the victims of injustice: the Boer republics in *A South African's View of the Situation* (1898), unfranchised South African blacks in *A Letter on the South African Union and the Principles of Government* (1909) and women in *Woman and Labour* (1911).

Schwartz, Delmore 1913–66 American poet, short-story writer and critic. An influential Jewish writer who emerged after World War II, he served on the editorial board of *PARTISAN REVIEW* in 1943–55. His principal concern was with the complex relationship between the private self and the outside world. *In Dreams Begin Responsibilities* (1938), *Genesis, Book One* (1943) and *Vaudeville for a Princess, and Other Poems* (1950) combine poetry and prose. *Shenandoah* (1941) is a verse play and *The Imitation of Life* (1941) a collection of essays. *The World is a Wedding* (1948) consists of stories dealing with the problems of Jewish life in America. *Summer Knowledge: New and Selected Poems 1938–58* appeared in 1959 and *Successful Love, and Other Stories* in 1961.

science fiction Stories set in the future, or in a contemporary setting disrupted by an imaginary device such as a new invention or the introduction of an alien being. They differ from other kinds of fantastic narrative in claiming that they respect the limits of scientific possibility, and that their innovations are plausible extrapolations from present knowledge, though relatively few examples are genuinely conscientious in this respect.

Although elements of science fiction appear in many

stories of imaginary voyages, it was not until the 19th century that the advancement of science inspired a good deal of work in this vein. MARY SHELLEY's *FRANKENSTEIN* (1818) is an early example, and science-fictional themes appear in the work of POE and HAWTHORNE. George Chesney's account of an imaginary invasion, 'The Battle of Dorking' (1871), helped a spate of future war stories, and Jules Verne popularized tales of flying machines, submarines and spaceships. Movements for political reform and the theory of evolution encouraged speculation about the future. These various threads were drawn together by H. G. WELLS in *THE TIME MACHINE* (1895), *The Island of Dr Moreau* (1896), *The Invisible Man* (1897), *THE WAR OF THE WORLDS* (1898), *When the Sleeper Wakes* (1899), *The First Men in the Moon* (1901) and *The War in the Air* (1908). Other important works before World War I were M. P. SHIEL's *The Purple Cloud* (1901), WILLIAM HOPE HODGSON's *The House on the Borderland* (1908), J. D. Beresford's *The Hampdenshire Wonder* (1912), DOYLE's *The Lost World* (1912) and, in the USA, JACK LONDON's *THE IRON HEEL* (1907).

After World War I British futuristic fiction was dominated by the idea that a new war could and probably would obliterate civilization. It appears in Edward Shanks's *People of the Ruins* (1920) and Cicely Hamilton's *Theodore Savage* (1922) as well as the work of prolific new writers like STAPLEDON, S. Fowler Wright, Neil Bell and John Gloag. Wells's *The Shape of Things to Come* (1933) reaches an optimistic conclusion, but only after describing devastation by war and plague. A frequent corollary was that man must ultimately be replaced by a new species, an idea at its most extravagant in Stapledon's *Last and First Men* (1930) and *Odd John* (1935) but also informing E. V. Odle's *The Clockwork Man* (1923), Gloag's *Tomorrow's Yesterday* (1930), Shiel's *The Young Men are Coming!* (1937) and Beresford's 'What Dreams May Come ...' (1941). Utopian speculation was not entirely stifled but undermined and opposed by a cynicism most comprehensively expressed in Muriel Jaeger's *The Question Mark* (1923) and HUXLEY's *BRAVE NEW WORLD* (1932).

The USA, by contrast, was relatively untouched by World War I and its futuristic fictions were haunted by no such anxieties. Space adventure stories, contemptuously dubbed 'space operas' by their critics, were encouraged by the gaudy fantasies of EDGAR RICE BURROUGHS and the magazines introduced by Hugo Gernsback, who first popularized the term 'science fiction'. But with the anxieties bred by the Depression in the 1930s the magazine editor John W. Campbell Jr encouraged a more sober and realistic approach. The new generation of writers he recruited – ASIMOV, HEINLEIN, Clifford D. Simak, Theodore Sturgeon, VAN VOGT and Fritz Leiber – brought a measure of intellectual sophistication to science fiction while retaining its imaginative fertility and adventurousness. Many notable American works of the 1940s were magazine series subsequently assembled into book form: these include Asimov's robot stories (*I, Robot*, 1950) and *Foundation* trilogy (1951–3), Heinlein's 'Future History' series and the series collected in Simak's *City* (1952).

The British tradition of scientific romance petered out after World War II, its last notable practitioners being C. S. LEWIS and Gerald Heard. Its pessimistic tone (further encouraged by Hiroshima) culminated in ORWELL's *NINETEEN EIGHTY-FOUR* (1949) and Aldous Huxley's *Ape and Essence* (1949). The best of the British writers of futuristic fiction who came to prominence after the war combined serious and anxious concerns with the greater imaginative scope and ideative playfulness of science fiction. They included JOHN WYNDHAM, BRIAN ALDISS, John Brunner and J. G. BALLARD, all of whom retained a strong interest in the catastrophist tradition in their best works. The most successful of the British post-war writers of science fiction, ARTHUR C. CLARKE, is more strongly affiliated to the American optimistic tradition, but shows marked Stapledonian influences in *Childhood's End* (1953) and *The City and the Stars* (1956).

In the USA the popularity of science fiction increased dramatically with the advent of paperbacks, shifting the form towards novels and, eventually, novel series. Most of the best writers of the 1950s, though, made their names with clever short stories, and some of the apologists for the genre who helped it to gain respectability – notably KINGSLEY AMIS – argued that science fiction works best in short-story form because its strengths lie with the ingenious development of ideas rather than with elaborate characterization. Significant American works of the 1950s and 1960s include RAY BRADBURY's *The Martian Chronicles* (1950) and *Fahrenheit 451* (1953), FREDERICK POHL and Cyril M. Kornbluth's *The Space Merchants* (1953), Alfred Bester's *The Demolished Man* (1953) and *The Stars My Destination* (1956), James Blish's *A Case of Conscience* (1958) and Walter M. Miller's *A Canticle for Leibowitz* (1960). The last two show a preoccupation with religion which has –rather paradoxically and perhaps surprisingly – become noticeable in modern science fiction. Even where religion is not explicitly evoked, a fascination with the relationship between moral and metaphysical issues still survives.

The mid-1960s saw a modishly experimental phase in both Britain and the USA. In Britain a 'new wave' was promoted by MICHAEL MOORCOCK, who converted the magazine *New Worlds* into an Arts Council-supported *avant-garde* periodical. In America Harlan Ellison promoted a series of anthologies begun with *Dangerous Visions* (1967). Moorcock's tetralogy of novels featuring Jerry Cornelius (1968–77) exemplified his new approach, while Ellison's graphic short fictions are best displayed in *I Have No Mouth and Must Scream* (1967). The best of the experimental new writers were Roger Zelazny, SAMUEL R. DELANY, Barry Malzberg, John Sladek and THOMAS M. DISCH – all American, though the last two were first received more enthusiastically in Britain. Their most impressive works include Delany's *Dhalgren* (1975) and Disch's *Camp Concentration* (1968). Alongside this *avant-garde*, however, great commercial success was achieved by many more conventional science-fiction writers. Writers like Pohl and ROBERT SILVERBERG found new success as novelists. Asimov, Clarke and Heinlein all attained best-seller status, as did FRANK HERBERT with *Dune* (1965) and VONNEGUT with *Slaughterhouse-Five* (1969). Following Vonnegut's success the American academic establishment began to pay serious attention to science fiction, helping to boost the reputations of PHILIP K. DICK and URSULA LE GUIN. The former attracted attention because of his ingenuity in presenting images of artificial and hallucinatory worlds which dissolve into confusion, the latter because of her moral earnestness and purity of style.

The feminist movement in America helped several new female writers to emerge in the 1970s, including

Joanna Russ and the pseudonymous James Tiptree Jr (Alice Sheldon). In recent years science fiction has been partly displaced in the marketplace by 'sword and sorcery' fantasies, following the extraordinary success of US paperback editions of TOLKIEN's The Lord of the Rings. The two genres overlap in the work of best-selling writers like Anne McCaffrey and Piers Anthony, while the situation has been further complicated by a resurgence of interest in horror fiction, with writers such as Stephen King frequently borrowing science-fictional ideas to mingle with traditional supernatural motifs.

The boundaries of the genre are now more difficult to outline than ever before. Its imagery has diffused throughout contemporary culture to become familiar in some measure to everyone. This familiarity has enabled some writers and individual works to escape stigmatization, and has helped make the products of the scientific imagination available to reputable writers. PYNCHON's GRAVITY'S RAINBOW (1973), VIDAL's Kalki (1978) and Jeremy Leven's Creator (1980) are examples of American 'mainstream' novels which use science-fictional elements. The difficulty of achieving elaborate characterization and density of environmental detail in futuristic and hypothetical settings still prevents even the best science-fiction novels from living up to the expectations of traditionally minded literary critics, but the excellence of fabulists like Vonnegut and Disch is helping to change hidebound expectations of what novels can and ought to be.

Scot [Scott], **Reginald** ?1538–99 Writer on witchcraft. The Discovery of Witchcraft (1584), which numbered SHAKESPEARE and THOMAS MIDDLETON among its readers, was so sceptical of the supposed activities of witches and spirits that it laid Scot open to the charge of sadducism (or disbelief in the existence of spirits). There is a tradition that the Discovery was burned by the public hangman at the order of JAMES I, who attacks it in the preface to his Demonology. Scot's earlier book, A Perfect Platform of a Hop Garden (1574), was the first practical treatise on the subject in English.

Scott, Dennis 1939– Jamaican poet and playwright. He commanded international attention with Uncle Time (1973), confirming his technical assurance and ability to mix Caribbean subject matter with wider concerns in a second collection, Dreadwalk (1982). His plays include: An Echo in the Bone (1974), Terminus (1966) and Dog (1981). His work for the stage seeks to make fundamental statements about man's historical behaviour. His poetry is at times more intimate and personal.

Scott, Duncan Campbell 1862–1947 Canadian poet and short-story writer. Encouraged by his friend LAMPMAN, he published his first book of verse, The Magic House, in 1893. Later volumes include New World Lyrics and Ballads (1905), Beauty and Life (1921), The Green Cloister (1935) and The Circle of Affection (1947). In the Village of Viger (1896) and The Witching of Elspie (1923) are collections of short stories.

Scott, F(rancis) R(eginald) 1899–1985 Canadian poet and lawyer. His poetry, beginning with Overture (1945), demonstrates the same sense of social responsibility that made him a champion of civil rights and a leading authority on constitutional law. Later volumes include Selected Poems (1966), Trouvailles (1967), The Dance is One (1973) and Collected Poems (1981).

Scott, Paul (Mark) 1920–78 Novelist. His principal achievement is the Raj Quartet, consisting of The Jewel in the Crown (1966), The Day of the Scorpion (1968), The Towers of Silence (1972) and A Division of the Spoils (1974). It covers the final years of British India (1942–7), as the British are progressively shown to be governing an alien, often violently antagonistic land. Staying On (1977), a coda which won the BOOKER PRIZE, is a sanguine comedy about Tusker and Lucy Smalley, minor characters from the Quartet, living out a bleak retirement in India. Like the Quartet, Scott's earlier novels show a dense, painstaking realism and are set in either India or Malaya, except for The Bender (1963), which takes place in London. The best is generally thought to be The Birds of Paradise (1962), which illustrates his preoccupation with the process of history and the shifting perspectives of the past.

Scott, Sir **Walter** 1771–1832 Novelist, poet, editor and critic. Born and educated in Edinburgh, he was admitted to the Scottish Bar in 1792 and married Margaret Charlotte Carpenter (Charpentier) in 1795. Absorbed in folklore and the supernatural, he entered literature through poetry, most notably with Minstrelsy of the Scottish Border (1802–3), an edition of old and new BALLADS. He made his name with THE LAY OF THE LAST MINSTREL (1805), a poem based on an old border narrative, which launched a series of verse romances taking history or legend as their subject: MARMION (1808), THE LADY OF THE LAKE (1810), The Vision of Don Roderick (1811), Rokeby and THE BRIDAL OF TRIERMAIN (both 1813), The Lord of the Isles and The Field of Waterloo (both 1815), and Harold the Dauntless (1817). During these years Scott was also involved in editorial work with Original Memoirs Written during the Great Civil War (1806), an edition of DRYDEN (1808), Memoirs of Captain George Carleton (1808), The State Papers of Sir Ralph Sadler (1809) and The Secret History of James I (1811). After writing reviews for the Whig EDINBURGH REVIEW, he took an active part in establishing the Tory QUARTERLY REVIEW in 1809.

By 1811 Scott's always muddled business interests, which included printing and publishing agreements with John and James Ballantyne, brought him near bankruptcy. He was rescued by Archibald Constable, who published WAVERLEY in 1814. One reason for attempting fiction was the astonishing success in 1810 of the first two CANTOS of BYRON's CHILDE HAROLD'S PILGRIMAGE, whose sophistication quite eclipsed the once successful romance narratives in which he excelled. The fact that Scott issued Waverley anonymously implies caution, but its immediate and enormous popularity decisively turned his career from poetry to fiction. A torrent of novels, merely identified as being by 'the author of Waverley', poured forth: GUY MANNERING (1815), THE ANTIQUARY (1816), The Black Dwarf and OLD MORTALITY (both 1816 and constituting the first series of Tales of My Landlord), ROB ROY (1817), THE HEART OF MIDLOTHIAN (1818; second series of Tales of My Landlord), THE BRIDE OF LAMMERMOOR and A LEGEND OF MONTROSE (1819; third series of Tales of My Landlord), IVANHOE (1819), THE MONASTERY and The Abbot (both 1820), KENILWORTH and THE PIRATE (both 1821), THE FORTUNES OF NIGEL (1822), PEVERIL OF THE PEAK, QUENTIN DURWARD and ST RONAN'S WELL (all 1823), REDGAUNTLET (1824), The Betrothed and THE TALISMAN (as Tales of the Crusaders, 1825) and WOODSTOCK (1826).

Scott was still busy with editions, antiquarian studies and literary criticism, including an edition of SWIFT (1814), Memories of the Somervilles (1815), The Border Antiquities of England and Scotland (1814–17), and Lives of the Novelists, contributed to Ballantyne's Novelists'

Library (1821–4). He was also entertaining on a baronial scale at his country house, Abbotsford, enjoying the role of laird, and working at the law as well as letters. It is not surprising that his health was considerably undermined. In 1825–6 a financial crisis involving Ballantyne and Co. and Archibald Constable left him with a debt of £130,000. Honourably disdaining bankruptcy, he set to work at an even more furious pace to produce CHRONICLES OF THE CANONGATE, with *The Two Drovers*, *The Highland Widow* and *The Surgeon's Daughter* in its first series (1827) and *St Valentine's Day: or, The Fair Maid of Perth* in the second (1828), *Anne of Geierstein* (1829), and *Count Robert of Paris* and *Castle Dangerous* (1832) in the fourth series of *Tales of My Landlord*. The merciless toil finally overwhelmed him while he was recuperating in Italy and he returned to die at Abbotsford.

Few authors have enjoyed a higher reputation than Scott once did. In his lifetime and for nearly a century after his death he was not merely an immensely popular writer but a major cultural force. His Scottish novels, particularly *Waverley* and *Rob Roy*, did much to rescue that country from the low esteem it had acquired after the 1745 rebellion and to make it at once respectable and romantic. The descriptions of landscape and ruins with which his books abound helped to shape ROMANTICISM. Above all, his use of history confirmed the taste for medievalism which lasted throughout the 19th century, and the conduct of his historical figures served as the model of the chivalric code by which Victorian gentlemen attempted to live. Yet today Scott is forgotten as a poet and neglected as a novelist. The immense bulk of his writing and the sheer length of his individual works intimidate. Current neglect overlooks his humour, his gift for memorably eccentric characters, his erudite and down-to-earth mastery of folklore and, most important, the underlying seriousness of his preoccupation with history and the processes of social and political change.

Scottish Chaucerians, The The name given to the 15th- and 16th-century Scottish poets influenced by CHAUCER, principally HENRYSON, GAVIN DOUGLAS, DUNBAR and the author of the KINGIS QUAIR.

Scottish renaissance A movement in Scottish literature which flourished between 1920 and 1940. It was originally applied to the work of several minor poets (Marion Angus, Violet Jacob, Sir Alexander Gray and Lewis Spence) dedicated to reviving Scots as a literary language, through regional dialects or the language of 15th- and 16th-century Scottish poetry. The term acquired new meaning with HUGH MACDIARMID's poems in revived or synthetic Scots, especially *A Drunk Man Looks at the Thistle* (1926). MacDiarmid's literary-political programme embraced the recreation of Scots as a national language, the revival of Gaelic and the re-establishment of separate Scottish social and political institutions. Some of his aims were shared by LEWIS GRASSIC GIBBON, WILLIAM SOUTAR and SORLEY MACLEAN. In the 1940s and 1950s younger poets writing in Lallans (as they now called Scots) attempted a second phase of the renaissance, though MacDiarmid himself was by then writing mostly in English.

Scovell, E(dith) J(oy) 1907– Poet. Although she has written since the 1920s, she did not publish collections until *Shadows of Chrysanthemums* (1944), *The Midsummer Meadow* (1946), *The River Steamer* (1956) and *The Space Between* (1982). *Collected Poems* (1988) introduced her quiet, meditative work, with its exact perceptions of nature, childhood and old age, to a wider readership.

Scriblerus Club, The A group of Tory intellectuals and writers, flourishing in about 1713. Its purpose was to discuss topics of contemporary interest and ridicule 'all the false tastes in learning'. The members were SWIFT, POPE, ARBUTHNOT, GAY, PARNELL, ATTERBURY, CONGREVE and ROBERT HARLEY. Collectively they invented a character named Martinus Scriblerus, a pedantic hack whose intellectual shortcomings they recorded in the *Memoirs of Martinus Scriblerus* (published in the second volume of Pope's *Works*, 1741). Gay, Pope and Arbuthnot also collaborated on the comedy, THREE HOURS AFTER MARRIAGE, unsuccessfully performed in 1717.

Scrutiny The most influential English critical journal of its time, founded in Cambridge by L. C. KNIGHTS and Donald Culver in 1932 and mainly edited until its closure in 1953 by F. R. LEAVIS and Q. D. LEAVIS. Serving largely as a forum for the approach and judgements of the Leavises, it depended heavily on contributions from their pupils, colleagues and followers. As well as advancing the Leavisite view of literary and cultural history it questioned current reputations (AUDEN, EDITH SITWELL, DYLAN THOMAS) in a challenging and abrasive fashion. *Scrutiny* was reprinted as a bound set in 1963; F. R. Leavis edited a selection in 1968.

Scupham, (John) Peter 1933– Poet. A formalist interested in regular METRE and strict rhyme, he often writes an essentially domestic poetry, examining places, objects and heirlooms and filtering them through his deepening sense of history, geology and geography. Collections are *The Snowing Globe* (1972), *The Gift* (1973), *Prehistories* (1975), *The Hinterland* (1977), *Summer Palaces* (1980), *Winter Quarters* (1983), *Out Late* (1986), *Selected Poems* (1991) and *Watching the Perseids* (1991).

Sea-Wolf, The A novel by JACK LONDON, published in 1904. Humphrey Van Weyden is thrown overboard when two ferry boats collide in San Francisco Bay. A sealing schooner, the *Ghost*, saves him but its brutal captain, Wolf Larsen, presses him into service. In the sealing grounds off Japan they pick up Maude Brewster, who joins him in the struggle against Larsen. The pair flee the ship and reach a deserted island, where the *Ghost* is driven ashore. Deserted by his crew and suffering from cerebral cancer, Larsen dies, still defiant. Van Weyden and Maude make the *Ghost* seaworthy and set out for civilization.

Seafarer, The An Old English poem in the EXETER BOOK. It falls into two unconnected halves. The first is a seafarer's monologue about the hardships of his life and his love of the sea; the second is a homiletic discourse, perhaps intended to draw a general moral.

Seasons, The A poem in BLANK VERSE by JAMES THOMSON, consisting of one book for each season and a final 'Hymn to Nature'. *Winter* first appeared in 1726, *Summer* in 1727, *Spring* in 1728 and *Autumn* in the first collective edition of *The Seasons* in 1730. Helped perhaps by POPE and LYTTELTON, Thomson produced a greatly enlarged edition in 1744.

The poem presents a vision of the world progressing amid change. *Winter* describes the bitterness of the elements, the death of a wayfarer in a snowdrift, the comfort of life indoors and the Arctic circle. *Summer* presents outdoor scenes of pastoral industry, and the mythical stories of Celadon and Amelia, and Damon and Musidora. *Spring* gives glowing descriptions of the season's effect on the whole of Nature, including man, who appears in the charmingly idealized image of the contented angler. *Autumn* contains a vigorous denunciation of shooting and hunting, and an episode narrating the love affair of Palemon and Lavinia. The poem as a whole is distinguished by fine, evocative descriptions of rural life.

Though it combines several genres, *The Seasons* has its roots in Virgil's *Georgics* and in MILTON. At the same time it marks a shift in taste and sensibility, anticipating elements of the PICTURESQUE and of ROMANTICISM. COWPER and WORDSWORTH, in particular, owe a debt to Thomson.

Second Jungle Book, The See *JUNGLE BOOK, THE*.

Second Mrs Tanqueray, The A play by PINERO, first performed in 1893. Paula Tanqueray has concealed her past from her respectable husband, Aubrey, but it catches up with her when her step-daughter becomes engaged to her seducer. She ends by committing suicide.

Second Nun's Tale, The See *CANTERBURY TALES*.

Secret Agent, The: *A Simple Tale* A novel by CONRAD, published in 1907. The ironic sub-title establishes the tone of this novel about revolutionary politics in contemporary London. Mr Verloc works as a double agent, infiltrating the anarchist underworld to supply information to Inspector Heat of Scotland Yard and the Russian *agent provocateur*, Vladimir. Frustrated by English complacency, Vladimir orders Verloc to blow up the Greenwich Observatory. Verloc equips himself with explosives from the sinister 'Professor' and recruits his weak-witted stepson Stevie as his innocent accomplice. Stevie's horrifying death in Greenwich Park drives Verloc's wife Winnie to kill him. She plans to leave the country with the anarchist Ossipon, but he deserts her on learning of the murder. Driven to madness, she jumps overboard from a Channel ferry.

Secret Garden, The See BURNETT, FRANCES HODGSON.

Secret Service A MELODRAMA by WILLIAM GILLETTE, produced in 1895. A series of fast-moving scenes follow the ruses and eventual unmasking of a gallant Union spy, Captain Thorne, in the Confederate city of Richmond, Virginia.

Sedgwick, Catharine Maria 1789–1867 American novelist. Her first novel, *A New England Tale* (1822), which traces the growth of the orphaned Jane Elton, became one of America's first best-sellers. *Redwood* (1824), about another orphan, Ellen Bruce, brought its author a popularity equal to that of JAMES FENIMORE COOPER and WASHINGTON IRVING. *Hope Leslie* (1827) is about relations between whites and Indians in 17th-century New England. Other works include *Clarence* (1830), *The Linwoods* (1835) and a trilogy consisting of *Home* (1835), *The Poor Man and the Rich Man* (1836), and *Live and Let Live* (1837). Her last novel, *Married or Single?* (1857), reflects her awareness of the social difficulties faced by unmarried women.

Sedley, Sir Charles c. 1639–1701 Playwright and poet. In youth he led a dissolute life like that of his friend ROCHESTER. Later, as MP for Romney, he was an active parliamentary speaker and became something of a patron to men of letters. He wrote some lyrics, two forgotten tragedies and three comedies, of which the best are *The Mulberry Garden* (1668), influenced by Molière and ETHEREGE, and the ribald *Bellamira: or, The Mistress* (1687), based on Terence's *Eunuchus*.

Seeger, Alan 1888–1916 American poet. He lived in France for most of his short adult life, joining the Foreign Legion at the outbreak of World War I and dying in the Battle of the Somme. *Poems* (1916) contained the famous 'I Have a Rendezvous with Death', originally published in THE NORTH AMERICAN REVIEW. Seeger's *Letters and Diary* appeared in 1917.

Seeley, Sir J(ohn) R(obert) 1803–95 Historian and essayist. He succeeded CHARLES KINGSLEY as professor of modern history at Cambridge in 1869. His most famous book, *Ecce Homo* (1865), was an account of the life and work of Christ made controversial by its failure to acknowledge Christ's divinity. Other works include *The Life and Times of Stein: or, Germany and Prussia in the Napoleonic Age* (1878) and two books justifying British imperialism, *The Expansion of England in the Eighteenth Century* (1883) and *The Growth of British Policy* (1895).

Selborne, The Natural History of See WHITE, GILBERT.

Selby, Hubert Jr 1928– American novelist and short-story writer. His best-known work, the collection of stories entitled *Last Exit to Brooklyn* (1964), was the subject of a much-publicized obscenity trial in Britain. It deals with homosexuality, prostitution and brutality, while exploring human isolation in the city. Selby has also published three novels – *The Room* (1971), *The Demon* (1976) and *Requiem for a Dream* (1978) – and a volume of short stories, *Song of the Silent Snow* (1986).

Selden, John 1584–1654 Lawyer and scholar. A man of independent and often controversial views, as his *History of Tithes* (1618) and his record as an MP demonstrate, he withdrew from public affairs before the trial of Charles I. His most notable work is the posthumous *Table Talk* (1689), collected by his amanuensis Richard Milward, in which he pronounces upon matters of law, personal freedom, and the motives of authority. He contributed notes ('illustrations') to the first 18 cantos of DRAYTON's *POLY-OLBION* and wrote books on antiquities and law. Selden was a friend of JONSON and admired by MILTON.

Selvon, Samuel (Dickson) 1923– Trinidadian novelist, short-story writer and playwright, of Indian and Scottish descent. He pioneered the use of Caribbean Creole dialect for other than merely comic effects in *A Brighter Sun* (1952), *Turn Again, Tiger* (1958), *An Island Is A World* (1955), *I Hear Thunder* (1963), *The Plains of Caroni* (1970) and *Those Who Eat the Cascadura* (1973). His sharp-edged accounts of West Indian settlement in Britain include *The Lonely Londoners* (1956) and *The Housing Lark* (1965). British racism and its concomitant Black Power protests are satirical targets in the more pungent *Moses Ascending* (1975) and *Moses Migrating* (1983). He has also written short stories, collected in *Ways of Sunlight* (1958), and many radio plays, from *Lost Property* (1965) to *Zeppi's Machine* (1977). *Eldorado West One* (1988) is a collection of seven one-act plays about characters who first appeared in *The Lonely Londoners*. *Highway in the Sun* (1988) brings together four of his longer plays. *Foreday Morning* (1989) is a selection of his prose.

semiotics [semiology] The science of 'signs', pioneered by C. S. Peirce (1839–1914) and Ferdinand de Saussure (1857–1913) and used by Claude Lévi-Strauss (1908–), Roland Barthes (1915–80) and others to examine social forms (kinship systems, myths, fashions, etc.) as if they were languages. Peirce showed that a sign never arrives at a definite meaning; any definition is subject to a further definition. He also distinguished between three types of sign: the 'iconic' (where sign resembles referent, as in a road-sign for falling rocks), the 'indexical' (where sign is associated with referent, as in smoke and fire), and the 'symbolic' (where sign and referent bear an arbitrary relationship, as in language). Saussure made the primary distinction between language as a system (*langue*) and language as individual utterance (*parole*). He went on to reject the view of language as a system of symbols corresponding to referents (things in the world). Words are 'signs' which have two sides: a mark, either written or spoken, called a 'signifier', and a concept, called a 'signified'. In this model of language, 'things' have no place; words acquire meaning only in so far as they enter a system of relations. Saussure's theory of the divided nature of the sign is fundamental to developments not only in semiology but in STRUCTURALISM, POST-STRUCTURALISM and Lacanian PSYCHOANALYTIC CRITICISM.

Sendak, Maurice (Bernard) 1928– American writer and illustrator of CHILDREN'S LITERATURE. After illustrating other authors' books he began supplying his own texts, in *Kenny's Window* (1956), *The Sign on Rosie's Door* (1958) and *Where the Wild Things Are* (1963), his most famous work, which divided critics between those who thought it too frightening and those who championed its imaginative brilliance. Subsequent books include *In the Night Kitchen* (1970) and *Outside Over There* (1981), both illustrated with Sendak's characteristic blend of pastel colours, stunted, tough children and dream-like imagery.

Senior, Olive 1941– Jamaican short-story writer and poet. The stories in *Summer Lightning* (1986) draw on her own broad experience of Jamaican social life, examining issues of race, class, colour and gender in a variety of styles that span the full range of the Jamaican linguistic continuum. A second collection, *Arrival of the Snake Woman* (1989), again contains stories written from a child's perspective, as well as pieces which reflect the discontent of adults who look nostalgically back to their childhood. She has also published: *The Message is Change* (1972), about the 1972 Jamaican General Elections; *A–Z of Jamaican Heritage* (1983), a valuable source of information about folk customs and traditions; *Talking of Trees* (1985), a collection of verse; and *Working Miracles: Women's Lives in the English-Speaking Caribbean* (1991), a sociological study.

sensation novel A type of Victorian novel which took mystery and crime as its subject and suspense as its narrative method. Like the earlier GOTHIC NOVEL, it appealed directly to the reader's sensations by seeking to induce fear, excitement and curiosity, but it preferred a modern setting and sometimes included criticism of current social abuses. The sensation novel enjoyed its heyday in the 1860s, with the work of WILKIE COLLINS, particularly his hugely successful *THE WOMAN IN WHITE* (1860), and with MARY ELIZABETH BRADDON'S *LADY AUDLEY'S SECRET* (1862). DICKENS was influenced by the form, most obviously in *THE MYSTERY OF EDWIN DROOD* (1870).

Sense and Sensibility JANE AUSTEN's first published novel (1811). It originated in a story, 'Elinor and Marianne' (1795), which she began to rewrite in 1797. When Henry Dashwood dies the estate of Norland Park in Sussex passes to John, his son by his first marriage, with the recommendation that he take care of the second Mrs Dashwood and her daughters. But John and his wife, encouraged by her mother, Mrs Ferrars, selfishly ignore the obligation. The second Mrs Dashwood and her daughters retire to a cottage in Devonshire. Marianne, the embodiment of 'sensibility', falls in love with the charming and penniless John Willoughby, who abandons her for an heiress. Elinor, the embodiment of 'sense', loves Mrs John Dashwood's brother Edward Ferrars. Her self-control enables her to conceal her distress at learning that he has for some time been secretly engaged to Lucy Steele. News of the engagement causes Mrs Ferrars to disinherit him in favour of his brother Robert. Lucy transfers her attention to Robert, freeing Edward from a commitment he regretted and allowing him to marry Elinor instead. The staunch and generous Colonel Brandon wins Marianne.

sentimental comedy Often loosely applied to the plays by writers like FARQUHAR and CIBBER who replaced RESTORATION COMEDY on the English stage, the term properly refers to works of a slightly later date, when mere variety of emotion had become an object of fascination. Plots rewarded benevolence and relied on a timely change of heart to bring about a happy ending. The arrival of sentimental comedy as a popular form was announced by the success of HUGH KELLY's *False Delicacy* at DRURY LANE in 1768, eclipsing GOLDSMITH's less bland *THE GOOD-NATURED MAN*. The most consistently successful purveyor was CUMBERLAND, particularly with *The Brothers* (1769) and *The West Indian* (1771). It was against sentimental comedy in general and Cumberland in particular that RICHARD BRINSLEY SHERIDAN sought to revive a more astringent comedy of manners. See also the SENTIMENTAL NOVEL.

Sentimental Journey through France and Italy, by Mr Yorick, A A novel by STERNE, published in 1768. He had travelled through France and Italy from 1765–6 to help his tuberculosis. For the resulting fiction he adopted the character of Yorick from *TRISTRAM SHANDY*. Hastily undertaken, Yorick's journey whisks the reader across the Channel on the first page but never reaches Italy: the narrative breaks off with memorable suddenness when he is still short of Lyons. Indifferent to tourist sights, Yorick is a virtuoso of emotion, continually finding experiences that affect his delicate sensibilities, stimulate his benevolence, arouse his libido or cause comic confusion. SMOLLETT, whom Sterne met in Italy, is caricatured as the learned Smelfungus.

sentimental novel [novel of sensibility] A style of fiction, fashionable from the mid-18th century onwards, reflecting a belief that the natural emotions were good, kindly and innocent, and that society, law and civilization were to blame for corrupting man. The highly charged emotional world of RICHARDSON's *PAMELA* (1740), *CLARISSA* (1747–8) and *SIR CHARLES GRANDISON* (1753–4) contributed to its rise, though the sentimental novel reached full expression in works such as BROOKE's *THE FOOL OF QUALITY* (1766–72), STERNE's *A SENTIMENTAL JOURNEY THROUGH FRANCE AND ITALY* (1768) and MACKENZIE's *THE MAN OF FEELING* (1771), in all of which effusive emotion is celebrated as evidence of a good heart. GOLDSMITH's *THE VICAR OF WAKEFIELD* (1766) is frequently included among the hundreds of sentimental novels produced in the period, though it is arguably an early PARODY. In a later generation, writers as diverse as MARY WOLLSTONECRAFT, HANNAH MORE and JANE AUSTEN all react against the uncontrolled excesses of sentimentalism.

Sepamla, Sipho 1932– South African poet and novelist. *Hurry Up to It* (1975), *The Blues is You in Me* (1976), *The Soweto I Love* (1977) and *Children of the Earth* (1983) belong to the creative outburst of black 'township' poetry which broke a decade of post-Sharpeville silence and found voice in the work of MTSHALI, SEROTE and the other poets in the anthology, *Black Poets in South Africa* (1974). *The Root is One* (1979) and *A Ride on the Whirlwind* (1981) are novels.

Serjeant Musgrave's Dance: *An Unhistorical Parable* A play (1959) by ARDEN. It is as deliberately enigmatic as its title character, who arrives with his soldiers in a northern town, either as recruiter or strike-breaker. After one of his men dies in an encounter with a barmaid, Musgrave goes ahead with a public meeting, dancing his macabre dance of vengeance as a Gatling gun is unveiled and pointed at the crowd – and the audience.

Serote, Mongane Wally 1944– South African poet and novelist. Volumes such as *Yakhal'inkomo* (1972), *Tsetlo* (1974), *No Baby Must Weep* (1975), *Behold Mama, Flowers* (1978) and *The Night Keeps Winking* (1983) belong to the creative outburst of black 'township' poetry which broke a decade of post-Sharpeville silence and found voice in the work of MTSHALI, SEPAMLA and the other poets in the anthology, *Black Poets in South Africa* (1974). *To Every Birth Its Blood* (1981) is a novel.

Service, Robert W(illiam) 1876–1958 Canadian poet and novelist. Born in Lancashire and brought up in Scotland, he emigrated to Canada in 1897. The Klondike gold rush provided the impetus for melodramatic, witty BALLADS such as 'The Shooting of Dan McGrew', 'The Cremation of Sam McGee' and 'The Law of the Yukon', published in *Songs of a Sourdough* (1907), *The Spell of the Yukon* (1907) and *Ballads of a Cheechako* (1909). His success as 'the Canadian KIPLING' enabled him to write his first novel, *The Trail of '98* (1910). Of later volumes, *Rhymes of a Red-Cross Man* (1916) came from his experience as a stretcher-bearer with the Canadian army between 1912 and 1916. He settled in France after World War I. Other books include *Rhymes of a Rolling Stone* (1912), *Ballads of a Bohemian* (1921), *Bar-Room Ballads* (1940), the novels *The Pretender* (1914) and *The Roughneck* (1923), and two volumes of autobiography, *Ploughman of the Moon* (1945) and *Harper of Heaven* (1948).

Seth, Vikram 1952– Poet, novelist and travel-writer. He was born in Calcutta. His collections are: *The Humble Administrator's Garden* (1985), quiet, graceful pieces influenced by HARDY and LARKIN; *The Golden Gate* (1986), a novel in verse about Californian life; and *All You Who Sleep Tonight* (1990). *From Heaven Lake* (1983) is an account of his journey through Sinkiang and Tibet to Nepal. *A Suitable Boy* (1993), which claims to be the longest serious 20th-century novel in English, examines the lives of four families against the background of a turbulent post-Independence India.

Seton, Ernest Thompson 1860–1946 Canadian naturalist. Government Naturalist in Manitoba, and founder of the Boy Scouts of America and the Woodcraft League, he wrote and illustrated many popular books on wildlife, including *Wild Animals I Have Known* (1898), *Biography of a Grizzly* (1900), *Lives of the Hunted* (1901), *Biography of a Silver Fox* (1909), *The Arctic Prairies* (1911), *Wild Animals at Home* (1913) and *Woodland Tales* (1921). *The Trail of an Artist-Naturalist* (1940) is his autobiography.

Settle, Elkanah 1648–1724 Playwright. *Cambyses, King of Persia* (1667) was a grandiloquent heroic tragedy whose success encouraged him to keep writing in the same style. *The Empress of Morocco* (c. 1671) is his best-known work. *The Female Prelate, Pope Joan* (1680) was con-

sidered offensive by some. Settle later achieved some success with musical pieces, particularly his adaptation of *A MIDSUMMER NIGHT'S DREAM* as *The Fairy Queen* (1692), for which Purcell wrote the music. When he fell out of favour, he wrote drolls (short comic pieces often based on scenes from well-known plays) for Bartholomew Fair. One, *The Siege of Troy* (1707), survives. His poem *Absalom Senior* (1682) answered DRYDEN's *ABSALOM AND ACHITOPHEL*. Dryden retaliated with the wicked portrait of him as Doeg in the second part of *Absalom and Achitophel*. which, more than his own work, has given him a place in literary history.

Seuss, Dr [Giesel, Theodor Seuss] 1904–91 American writer and illustrator of CHILDREN'S LITERATURE. *And To Think That I Saw It on Mulberry Street* (1937) established his distinctive style, marrying catchy, doggerel verse to energetic, sometimes outlandish illustrations. *The Cat in the Hat* (1957), achieving wonders of surreal humour with only a limited vocabulary, was followed by over 50 such 'Beginner' books, many written and designed by Seuss himself and the rest produced by a company of which he was president.

Seven Lamps of Architecture, The A treatise on architecture by RUSKIN, published in 1849. Its purpose was 'to show that certain right states of temper and moral feeling were the powers by which all good architecture, without exception, had been produced'. To that end he argues that architecture should be informed by seven lamps (or spirits): Sacrifice, Truth, Power, Memory, Beauty, Obedience and Life. Into his discourse Ruskin weaves problems involving the exertion of the worker, the bearing of labour upon architecture, the matter of ornamentation (its truth or falsity), the significance of colour and the contemporary habit of building houses for only one generation.

Seven Sages of Rome, The A collection of 15 tales based on the French *Les Sept Sages de Rome* (before 1150). It survives in several versions, of which the earliest is *c.* 1300–25. The wife of Diocletian, Emperor of Rome, tells him seven tales, one each night, to convince him that his son tried to rape her. The seven sages, the boy's tutors, tell a tale each morning to persuade him of the queen's duplicity. Each day Diocletian condemns and frees his son, until the eighth day when the boy himself tells a tale which makes the queen confess. The narrative framework linking the stories is a common medieval device, used in CHAUCER's *CANTERBURY TALES* and GOWER's *CONFESSIO AMANTIS*.

Sewall, Samuel 1652–1730 American Puritan writer. He was a humane and liberal jurist, most notably while he was chief justice of the Superior Judicature in Massachusetts (1718–28). His writings include: *The Revolution in New-England Justified* (1691), written with Edward Rawson, defending the uprising of 1689 which deposed Royal Governor Andros; *The Selling of Joseph* (1700), one of the earliest published arguments against slavery; *A Memorial Relating to the Kennebeck Indians* (1721), arguing for the humane treatment of the Indians; and *'Talitha Cumi'* (1873), rebutting the theological position which denied the resurrection to women. His greatest contribution to colonial literature is his diary (1878–82) covering the years 1674–7 and 1685–1729.

Sewanee Review, The An American literary journal, affiliated with the University of the South (Sewanee, Tennessee) and published since 1892. It played a leading role in advocating the NEW CRITICISM, particularly under the editorship of ALLEN TATE (1944–6).

Seward, Anna 1747–1809 Poet. She spent most of her life in Lichfield, Staffordshire, where she was the centre of a literary circle and known as the Swan of Lichfield. SIR WALTER SCOTT edited her poems, with a memoir, in 1810. Her letters, carefully written with an eye to publication, appeared in 1811.

Sewell, Anna 1820–78 Writer of CHILDREN'S LITERATURE. Born into a family of Norfolk Quakers, she sometimes assisted her mother, who wrote verses and stories for children. Not until she was 50, when she had become invalid, did she begin writing her only novel, *BLACK BEAUTY*. This enduringly popular story of a horse appeared in 1877, a few months before her death.

Sexton, Anne 1928–74 American poet. Her work is CONFESSIONAL POETRY, dealing with the loneliness and depression which finally led to her suicide, her experiences as a daughter, wife, and mother, and the landscape of the Massachusetts coastline and Maine. Volumes include *To Bedlam and Part Way Back* (1960), *All My Pretty Ones* (1962), *Selected Poems* (1964), *Live or Die* (1966; PULITZER PRIZE), *Love Poems* (1969), *Transformations* (1971), *The Book of Folly* (1972), *The Death Notebooks* (1974) and *The Awful Rowing towards God* (1975). *45 Mercy Street* (1976) and *Words for Dr Y: Uncollected Poems with Three Stories* (1978) were edited by Linda Gray Sexton. MAXINE KUMIN, who wrote two childrens' books with Anne Sexton, contributed a sensitive preface to her *Collected Poems* (1981).

Seymour, Alan 1927– Australian playwright. He first attracted attention with *Swamp Creatures* (1957), a surrealist ALLEGORY set in a Gothic house, more typical of his work than the comparatively naturalistic *The One Day of the Year* (1960), which has come to be regarded as an Australian classic. Other plays include *The Gaiety of Nations* (1965), *A Break in the Music* (1966), *The Pope and the Pill* (1968), *The Shattering* (1973), *Structures* (1973) and *The Float* (1980). He has also published *The Coming Self-Destruction of the United States of America* (1980), a novel, and turned *The One Day of the Year* into a novel. His television adaptations of L. P. HARTLEY's *Eustace and Hilda*, JOHN MASEFIELD's *The Box of Delights* and Antonia Fraser's *Frost in May* have won acclaim.

Shabby Genteel Story, A A story by THACKERAY, serialized in 1840 and published in book form in 1852. 'George Brandon', a fashionable young gentleman fleeing his creditors, lodges with the shabby genteel Gann family at Margate and seduces the youngest daughter, Caroline, into a mock marriage. The unfinished story is developed in *THE ADVENTURES OF PHILIP*, where 'Brandon' reappears under his real name, Firmin.

Shadbolt, Maurice 1932– New Zealand novelist and short-story writer. Prolific but uneven, he has often tackled large public themes. Collections of short stories include *The New Zealanders* (1959), *Summer Fires and Winter Country* (1963) and *Figures in Light* (1978). Novels include: *Among the Cinders* (1965); *Strangers and Journeys* (1972), a solidly realistic work taking in events such as the Depression and the 1951 waterfront strike; *A Touch of Clay* (1974); *Danger Zone* (1976), about French nuclear testing in the Pacific; *The Lovelock Version* (1980), which breaks with realistic narrative conventions; *Season of the Jew* (1986), about the rebellion of the 19th-century Maori leader Te Kooti; and *Monday's Warriors* (1990).

Shadow of a Gunman, The A play by O'CASEY, produced in 1923 at the ABBEY THEATRE, Dublin. His fellows lodgers in a Dublin tenement mistakenly believe the poet Donal Davoren to be on the run from the British.

The bitter conclusion sees the admiring and admirable Minnie Powell killed in an ambush as a result of her attempts to shield him.

Shadwell, Thomas *c.* 1642–92 Playwright and poet. He began with *The Sullen Lovers* (1668), a comedy indebted to JONSON, and never wholly abandoned the mode. His best work, *Epsom Wells* (1672), *The Virtuoso* (1676), *The Squire of Alsatia* (1688) and *Bury Fair* (1689), blended the Jonsonian urge to instruct through SATIRE with the witty style pioneered by ETHEREGE. His adaptation of *THE TEMPEST* (1674) owed more to the fashion for spectacular opera than to SHAKESPEARE; a second opera, *Psyche* (1675), tamely exploited the popularity of the first. *The Libertine* (1675) and an adaptation of *TIMON OF ATHENS* (1678) are weak examples of the heroic tragedy brought into vogue by DRYDEN.

Even so, the punishment inflicted on Shadwell's reputation by the magnificent satire of Dryden's *MAC FLECKNOE* (1678) is excessive. That he should have succeeded Dryden as POET LAUREATE in 1689 is an irony that has done Shadwell no posthumous favours. His best verse is contained either in his plays or in the satirical prologues and epilogues that accompanied them. The Juvenalian satire of *The Medal of John Bayes* (1682) and the version of Juvenal's *Tenth Satire* (1687) has lost its bite and the panegyric of his 'Laureate' poems is predictably empty.

Shaffer, Peter 1926– Playwright. Although *Five Finger Exercise* (1958), his first stage success, showed his command of drawing-room drama he is best known for tackling large themes in such plays as: *The Royal Hunt of the Sun* (1964), about the Spanish destruction of the Inca civilization of Peru; *Equus* (1973), in which a psychoanalyst grapples with the mysterious Dionysiac faiths of a delinquent youth; and *Amadeus* (1979), about the rivalry between Salieri and Mozart. Other work includes: *Black Comedy* (1965), later matched in a double bill with *White Lies* (1968), *Lettice and Lovage* (1987) and *The Gift of the Gorgon* (1992).

Shaftesbury, 3rd Earl of [Cooper, Anthony Ashley] 1671–1713 Philosopher. His grandfather was the 1st Earl of Shaftesbury, politician, champion of the Duke of Monmouth's cause and the Achitophel of DRYDEN's *ABSALOM AND ACHITOPHEL*. The CAMBRIDGE PLATONISTS were his intellectual ancestors. He rejected the bleakness of HOBBES and LOCKE, while at the same time questioning religious dogma and despising religious controversy. His uncomplicated prose and reliance on 'moral sense' – the innate capacity to distinguish right and wrong – had strong appeal in an age of stridently conflicting dogmatists and philosophers. Shaftesbury collected his writings in *Characteristics of Men, Manners, Opinions, Times* (1711, revised edition 1714); his unfinished *Second Characters: or, The Language of Forms* was published in 1914.

Shakespeare, William 1564–1616 In a flamboyant age and a notoriously flamboyant profession – he was an active member of a theatre company for at least 20 years – Shakespeare was notably reticent. As a result, scholars have had painstakingly to piece together the story of his life from surviving scraps of evidence, and there remains ample room for speculation.

He was born in Stratford-upon-Avon, where his father was a prosperous glover and one of the town's 14 principal burgesses. In 1565 John Shakespeare was promoted to the rank of alderman and in 1571 was appointed Chief Alderman. It is a reasonable assumption that such a man would send his son to the grammar school in Stratford. The evident decline in John Shakespeare's fortunes after 1576 has allowed speculation that his son did not complete his education. He is known to have married Anne Hathaway in 1582. A daughter was born to the couple within six months. She was the Susanna who later married the physician John Hall and lived prosperously in Stratford. The family was completed with the birth of the twins, Judith and Hamnet, in 1585: Hamnet died in 1596 and Judith lived until 1662.

Virtually nothing is known of Shakespeare's life from 1585 to 1592. Tradition and conjecture have filled these 'seven lost years' with various activities – schoolmastering, soldiering or working in the law – designed to explain the expert knowledge of these branches of life which some readers have detected in the plays. One of the many possibilities is that Shakespeare left Stratford with a group of London actors. Certainly his name was sufficiently well known in the London theatre by 1592 to invite GREENE's jibe at him as an 'upstart Crow'. Greene had in mind Shakespeare's part in writing HENRY VI. This early collaboration suggests that his apprenticeship as a playwright was served alongside the growing number of aspiring writers, seeking to benefit from the demand for plays in the emergent professional theatre. The texts that survive from the 1590s imply that Shakespeare preferred to work alone, though there is no means of telling what may have been lost. Only in SIR THOMAS MORE (c. 1593–5) of works outside the early canon has his hand been confidently detected. By 1594, when he found the money and professional commitment to purchase a share in the newly formed Lord Chamberlain's Men, Shakespeare had probably written his three early comedies, THE COMEDY OF ERRORS, THE TWO GENTLEMEN OF VERONA and THE TAMING OF THE SHREW, and two corpse-laden tragedies, TITUS ANDRONICUS and RICHARD III, the latter bringing the three Henry VI plays to a brilliantly original conclusion. He had also reached a fashionable audience with the two narrative poems, VENUS AND ADONIS (1593) and THE RAPE OF LUCRECE (1594). It was enough to encourage the mature actors who formed the Lord Chamberlain's Men to accept him, not merely as an actor, but also as a potential resident writer for their proposed London home, the Theatre in Shoreditch.

Living in the region of Bishopsgate, not far from the Theatre, Shakespeare continued to write plays at the rate of approximately two a year. The period 1594–8 may have seen the first productions of KING JOHN (sometimes dated as early as 1589), the middle comedies LOVE'S LABOUR'S LOST (scholars continue to argue about the Love's Labour's Won mentioned by MERES), A MIDSUMMER NIGHT'S DREAM and THE MERCHANT OF VENICE, the outstandingly popular tragedy ROMEO AND JULIET and the cycle of English history plays, RICHARD II, the two parts of HENRY IV and HENRY V. That he also had aspirations as a gentleman, and the means to support them, is apparent in the application, on his father's behalf, for a coat of arms in 1596; it was granted. The following year Shakespeare bought one of Stratford's finest houses, New Place. Early in 1598 he made a small investment in malt (malting was Stratford's principal industry). The London theatres were experiencing hardship at this time, and it is possible that he was contemplating the life of a country gentleman with his wife and daughters in Stratford. If so, he changed his mind. With other shareholders of the Lord Chamberlain's Men, he met the landlord's threat of eviction from the Theatre by moving its timbers to the south bank of the Thames and re-erecting them as the GLOBE.

Shakespeare wrote his greatest plays during the first decade of his company's occupation of the Globe. They include the mature comedies, MUCH ADO ABOUT NOTHING (more probably dating from 1598), AS YOU LIKE IT and TWELFTH NIGHT; the darker comedies, sometimes called PROBLEM PLAYS, ALL'S WELL THAT ENDS WELL, MEASURE FOR MEASURE and TROILUS AND CRESSIDA; a pot-boiler, THE MERRY WIVES OF WINDSOR, bringing Falstaff back to life from Henry IV; and the succession of great tragedies, JULIUS CAESAR, HAMLET, OTHELLO, KING LEAR, MACBETH, ANTONY AND CLEOPATRA, CORIOLANUS and TIMON OF ATHENS. It was a period that saw the Lord Chamberlain's Men honoured by the new monarch with the title of the KING's MEN and confirmed in their ascendancy at court. Shakespeare had moved his London lodgings to Southwark, but maintained his financial interests in Stratford. A small investment in land in 1602 was followed by a larger one in 1605. But theatrical fashions were changing. The faddish interest in BOYS' COMPANIES, playing in indoor theatres, had attracted the interest of some of the best playwrights of the age. As the interest in the boys waned, these playwrights began to write for the adult companies. BEAUMONT and FLETCHER were particularly adept at suiting the new fashions almost before they declared themselves. Shakespeare was probably feeling the need to look to his well-established laurels. When the King's Men decided to invest in an indoor playhouse of their own, at the BLACKFRIARS, he joined them, perhaps recognizing the greater scenic scope offered by indoor playing. His last plays, PERICLES, PRINCE OF TYRE (written in collaboration, probably with George Wilkins), CYMBELINE, THE WINTER'S TALE and THE TEMPEST, are romances, which acknowledge even as they transcend the growing interest in spectacle, magic and improbable resolutions. The collaborations with Fletcher on HENRY VIII, THE TWO NOBLE KINSMEN and the lost Cardenio (see also SHAKESPEARE APOCRYPHA) suggest a dulling of his own creativity. It was at a performance of HENRY VIII in 1613 that the Globe was burned down. Shakespeare had just bought the upper floor of one of the Blackfriars gatehouses and may not have wished to pay out more money for the rebuilding of the Globe. The probability is that he spent his last years in Stratford, dying there in 1616.

It was as a poet as well as a playwright that Shakespeare was honoured by his contemporaries. THE PHOENIX AND THE TURTLE had appeared in Robert Chester's Love's Martyr (1601). SONNETS (1609), written probably many years before they were published with an enigmatic dedication to Mr 'W. H.', confirmed his genius, if confirmation were needed. Two fellow actors, John Heminges and Henry Condell, produced the posthumous collection of his plays known as the First Folio in 1623. It was a vast undertaking, without which 20 of Shakespeare's plays may have been lost to posterity. Plays were not highly prized as literature. SIR THOMAS BODLEY had classed most of them among the 'idle books, and riff-raffs' he did not wish to have catalogued in his library in 1612, so that the decision to publish so many by one man, and in the exalted folio form, is evidence of the esteem in which Shakespeare was held, not only by the public, but also by his fellow professionals. The Folio was republished three times in the course of the seventeenth century, and the first scholarly edition of his work followed in 1709, edited by the playwright NICHOLAS ROWE.

Shakespeare apocrypha Plays attributed to SHAKESPEARE at one time or another, but not appearing in the First Folio of 1623 and not accepted by modern scholarship. They include six originally printed with his name, or the initials 'W.S.', on the title-page: *Locrine* (1595), a tragedy, possibly by CHAPMAN; Part I of *Sir John Oldcastle* (1600), by MUNDAY and others; *Thomas, Lord Cromwell* (1602), a chronicle play; *The London Prodigal* (1605), a comedy; *The Puritan* (1607) and *A YORKSHIRE TRAGEDY* (1608), both possibly by THOMAS MIDDLETON. These appeared in a supplement added to the Third Folio of 1663. The rest of the apocrypha is an anthology of popular drama associated with Shakespeare on various and tenuous grounds: *ARDEN OF FEVERSHAM* (1592); *Fair Em, the Miller's Daughter of Manchester* (1593); *Mucedorus* (1598); *The Merry Devil of Edmonton* (1608); and *The Birth of Merlin*, attributed to Shakespeare and WILLIAM ROWLEY when it was first printed in 1662.

Scholars now admit *PERICLES* (1609) to the canon despite its absence from the First Folio. *THE TWO NOBLE KINSMEN* (1634) continues to provoke debate, but is probably by Shakespeare in collaboration with JOHN FLETCHER. Three pages of the late Elizabethan manuscript of *SIR THOMAS MORE* (?1593–5) are widely accepted as Shakespeare's own revision of a rejected scene. Many scholars have believed that Shakespeare wrote *EDWARD III* (1596) wholly or in part. Some would add *The Double Falsehood: or, The Distressed Lovers* (1728) to the core of plays whose attribution is more than fanciful. THEOBALD presented it as his own reworking for the 18th-century theatre of a play by Shakespeare and Fletcher known to us only by its title, *Cardenio*. Attempts are still occasionally made to attach Shakespeare's name to further unassigned plays of his period.

Shakespeare: performance and criticism After the Restoration in 1660 Shakespeare's plays were altered to suit new tastes and performance methods. Actresses superseded young men and boys in female roles, perspective scenery was used on stage. Some plays were radically revised, while in others, adaptation was achieved by omission rather than alteration. Critical response valued Shakespeare's energy in language and character but censured his breaches of decorum in plot, imagery and characterization. DRYDEN, in *AN ESSAY OF DRAMATIC POESY* (1668) and elsewhere, expressed this mingled dispraise and celebration, crediting Shakespeare with the 'largest and most comprehensive soul' among the moderns. Less willing to admit celebration was RYMER, who found the 'tragical part' of *Othello* 'plainly none other than a bloody farce without salt or savour'. The theatre still offered compromise. TATE rewrote *King Lear*, omitting the Fool and supplying a happy ending which reprieves Lear and Gloucester and unites Cordelia with Edgar. His version survived in stage practice until the early 19th century.

The notion of Shakespeare as a natural genius with more or less pardonable faults was developed in the next century. The works were presented to readers in a succession of handsome and scholarly editions by POPE (1725), Hanmer (1743–4), Warburton (1747), JOHNSON (1765), CAPELL (1767–8), STEEVENS (1773, etc.), MALONE (1790; augmented by James Boswell the younger in 1821). These encouraged attention to Shakespeare's own (rather than his adapters') words. Pope, in the preface to his edition of the *Works*, describes him as 'not so much an imitator as an instrument of Nature'. In Johnson's preface he is the 'poet of nature' whose artistic failings should be forgiven if not imitated.

This confidence in Shakespeare's mimetic powers was reflected in a renewed emphasis on his characters. In the 1740s GARRICK and Charles Macklin broke with an oppressively 'formal' manner of playing the tragic roles. At the same time the language and structure of the plays gradually returned to the stage. Explorations of psychology resulted in performances which impressed audiences as startlingly 'real', for example Macklin's new, serious (and villainous) Shylock and the jarred sensibilities of Garrick's Hamlet. Maurice Morgann, defending his subject against charges of cowardice in an *Essay on the Dramatick Character of Falstaff* (1777), established a precedent for elaborate reconstructions of a dramatic character's personality.

Romantic criticism confirmed Shakespeare's pre-eminence. In various lectures between 1808 and 1819, in *BIOGRAPHIA LITERARIA* (1817) and elsewhere, COLERIDGE proclaimed his discovery of the characters as vividly individualized examples of human types. The 'organic regularity' of Shakespeare's characters and plots, distinguished from the 'mechanic regularity' of neoclassical drama, corresponded to the order of nature. Obscurities and compression in poetic language were beginning to be valued rather than condemned or merely condoned. HAZLITT's *Characters of Shakespeare's Plays* (1817), informed by experience of stage performances, described forcefully the aesthetic impact of dramatic characters. *Tales from Shakespeare* (1807) by LAMB and his sister Mary and BOWDLER's expurgated *Family Shakespeare* (1807 in 4 vols., 1818 in 10 vols.) helped to make the plays current in education and in middle-class family reading.

In the theatre of the early 1800s Sarah Siddons and her brother John Philip Kemble imbued tragic roles with neoclassical grace and dignity, inspiring sensations of awe rather than intimacy. In contrast, Edmund Kean's acting startled by its carefully prepared effects of sudden and intense emotion. Coleridge compared the audience's experience to that of reading Shakespeare 'by flashes of lightning'. Hazlitt described the 'fresh shocks of delight and surprise' afforded by the rapid transitions in his Shylock (1814). The more measured emotionalism of Kean's contemporary and successor William Charles Macready marked a transition to a recognizably Victorian cultivation of private, domestic feelings. Kemble's acting versions were closer than Garrick's to the original texts, although still cut to remove indecencies and suit pictorial staging. Public taste now required costumes and settings that rendered the historical milieu of each play as accurately as possible. Satisfying the taste for historical pageantry was an expensive business, and the actor-managers who presented these shows were expected to dominate them with personal performances of great vigour. In the 1840s to 1860s Shakespearean production in London was led by Charles Kean's management at the Princess's Theatre in Oxford Street and the more modest but energetic and idealistic enterprise of Samuel Phelps at Sadler's Wells in Islington. In the 1880s and up to World War I the providers of such 'traditional' Shakespeare were Henry Irving and Herbert Beerbohm Tree, both famous for their ability to make characters part of a striking stage-picture.

In the 19th century editions began to cater for a variety of tastes and pockets: Charles Knight issued a *Pictorial Shakespeare* in parts between 1839 and 1842, providing a wealth of historical material and illustrations at a popular price; one-volume editions of the works were edited by Clark and Wright (the Globe, 1864), FURNIVALL (the Leopold, 1877) and Craig, whose 1891 Oxford edition remained in print well into the 1980s. More august scholarly enterprises were the edition by HALLIWELL, or Halliwell-Phillipps, (1853–65) and the New Variorum, begun by Furness in 1874. Cheap reprints of the plays proliferated, and the introduction of Shakespeare into the curriculum of the Board Schools created a market for editions annotated (and expurgated) for the use of pupils.

Victorian criticism focused mainly on character and dramatic effect. JAMESON's *Shakespeare's Heroines* (originally called *Characteristics of Women*, 1832) and the writings of the actress Helen Faucit offered sentimental accounts of the female characters. CARLYLE's *HEROES, HERO-WORSHIP AND THE HEROIC IN HISTORY* (1841) included a eulogy of Shakespeare as a type of the 'poet as hero', confirming him in the Romantic tradition of poets-as-legislators. Against this sentiment and celebration should be set a growth of interest in matters of chronology and attempts to find the dramatist's life in his art. Furnivall's energetic work as an editor and as founder of the New Shakspere [sic] Society was the basis of much scholarly and critical thinking in the later decades of the century. DOWDEN, in *Shakspere: A Critical Study of his Mind and Art* (1875), traced the playwright's career as a struggle for self-mastery. His *Primer* (1877) made this construction of the biography current at all levels of education. The reverential manner that prevailed in Victorian writing on Shakespeare was challenged by SHAW.

BRADLEY's *Shakespearean Tragedy* (1904), in some respects a culmination of Romantic preoccupations, centres the tragic ethos on individual characters. But it also proposes a world-view bleaker and less sentimental than any offered in earlier criticism: the plays are treated as dramas in the manner of later 19th-century naturalism. Theatrical interpretation was moving away from what had come to seem cluttered scenic realism. William Poel's experiments with Elizabethan staging conventions, and the growth of scholarly interest in theatrical history, joined the generally felt impulse to discover non-naturalistic modes of theatre. In GRANVILLE-BARKER's productions of *Winter's Tale, Twelfth Night* and *A Midsummer Night's Dream* (1912–14) open staging, simplified stylized settings and full texts rapidly delivered revealed Shakespeare as a dramatist whose techniques had little in common with the quasi-operatic spectacle of most Victorian and Edwardian productions. Granville-Barker's example and the principles enunciated in his subsequent series of *Prefaces to Shakespeare* (1927–47) set standards for a new generation of interpreters working in the brisker schedules, tighter budgets and integrated ensembles of the repertory theatres. The new, non-commercial companies in the provincial cities and at the OLD VIC in London offered a greater variety of plays in simpler stagings and quicker succession than had been possible in the commercial actor-managers' theatre.

Criticism in the decades after Bradley extended awareness of Elizabethan literary as well as theatrical conventions. L. L. Schücking's *Character Problems in*

Shakespeare's Plays (1919; translated, 1922) and E. E. Stoll's *Art and Artifice in Shakespeare* (1933) were influential in displacing Romantic notions of characterization and dramatic method. Bernard Spivack's *Shakespeare and the Allegory of Evil* (1958) reached back into earlier dramatic and literary works to establish a non-naturalistic system of significance underlying such characters as Iago and Richard III. Bradley's mode of speculation on character had been challenged on other grounds by LEAVIS and by KNIGHTS, whose 'How Many Children Had Lady Macbeth?' (1933; reprinted in *Explorations*, 1946) provided a catch-phrase for anti-Bradleyans. The discipline of editorial experience informed JOHN DOVER WILSON's teasing out of plot and characterization in *What Happens in Hamlet* (1935). The poetic texture of the plays was investigated by Caroline Spurgeon (*Shakespeare's Imagery*, 1935) and, more subtly, Wolfgang Clemen (*The Development of Shakespeare's Imagery*, 1936; revised and translated, 1951). Studies by KNIGHT (notably *The Wheel of Fire*, 1930, on the tragedies) focused on verbal imagery and patterning. This important shift of emphasis, together with the example of the NEW CRITICISM and EMPSON's explorations of ambiguity and wordplay, helped to establish a way of reading the plays as poems that characterized much post-1945 criticism. A parallel development was the historical study of 'background', exemplified in Hardin Craig's *The Enchanted Glass* (1936) and TILLYARD's construction of a 'world picture' which the plays (especially the histories) were held to set forth. A. P. Rossiter's essays, collected in *Angel With Horns* (1961), challenge the notion that the plays endorse the 'Tudor myth'.

Criticism of the comedies was given a new impetus by FRYE's formulation of an archetypal comic structure in *An Anatomy of Criticism* (1957) and the complementary thesis of C. L. Barber's *Shakespeare's Festive Comedy* (1959). The bleak outlook in Jan Kott's *Shakespeare Our Contemporary* (1967) has influenced theatrical directors as well as readers; less abrasive, reflecting the more optimistic liberalism of the humanities in the 1960s, was Norman Rabkin's *Shakespeare and the Common Understanding* (1967). A dominant feature of criticism in the 1970s – working alongside MARXIST CRITICISM and STRUCTURALISM – has been a renewed feminist interrogation of the texts, of which the work of Marilyn French, Coppelia Kahn and Irene Dash is representative.

Research into the conditions of Shakespeare's theatre, consolidated by CHAMBERS's documentary labours, has resulted in work on the theatrical language of the plays by J. L. Styan, Nevill Coghill, Bernard Beckerman and others. The use of the play metaphor in Shakespeare, set out concisely in Anne Barton's *Shakespeare and the Idea of the Play* (1969), has been pursued by many critics and directors. Another kind of stage-centred scholarship concentrates on the plays' stage-life in the centuries since Shakespeare: A. C. Sprague's *Shakespeare and the Actors* (1944) described points of interpretation using prompt-books and reports of performances in a manner that set the standard for many later studies. Investigations of the biographical evidence, although no longer widely accepted as a route into the interpretation of the plays, were set in order by Chambers's magisterial *William Shakespeare: A Study of the Facts and Problems* (1930) and have been brought up to date by Samuel Schoenbaum, in *William Shakespeare: A Documentary Life* (1975). The same author's *Shakespeare's Lives* (1971) provides an amusing and comprehensive account of the history of Shakespeare biography.

Editions of the plays published since the turn of the century have reflected changes in bibliographical theory and the development of English studies in higher education. The Arden edition (1899–1924) was superseded by the New Arden (1951–) and a Cambridge edition known as the New Shakespeare (1921–62) is being replaced by a New Cambridge (1984–). Paperback editions have included the original Penguin series (1937–59), a breakthrough in popular publishing followed by the Pelican (1956–67), the American Signet (1963–) and the New Penguin (1967–). Oxford University Press's editions of individual plays (1982–), the New Cambridge Shakespeare and the New Arden editions have also appeared in paperback. Important one-volume editions of the complete *Works* are Peter Alexander's (1951), and the American Riverside (1974). A new Oxford edition (1986) offers two versions (rather than a conflated text) of *Lear*.

After Granville-Barker, Shakespearean production in Britain has been characterized by diversity of style: it would be hard to identify a 'tradition'. Directorial practice ranged from the scholarly but enterprising Elizabethanism of Robert Atkins to the cheery, trenchant iconoclasm of Tyrone Guthrie. Between the wars a number of leading Shakespearean actors and actresses established themselves, but their personal styles were diverse: John Gielgud, Laurence Olivier, Ralph Richardson and Peggy Ashcroft worked on occasion with each other, with various directors and in a number of different companies. In the 1940s an actor-manager of the old kind emerged in Donald Wolfit. The parallel institutions of the Old Vic in London and the Memorial Theatre in Stratford were developed (with the advent of state subsidy) into the ROYAL NATIONAL THEATRE and the ROYAL SHAKESPEARE COMPANY. Laurence Olivier's management of the National (Old Vic, 1964–74) achieved critical acclaim with an all-male *As You Like It* and Franco Zeffirelli's *Romeo and Juliet*. Olivier himself appeared in *Othello* and in Jonathan Miller's production of *The Merchant of Venice*. Neither company can be said currently to offer a 'house style' for Shakespeare, although the RSC's cycle *The Wars of the Roses* (1963–4) set new standards in the presentation of the history plays. The scale and breadth of main-stage Stratford productions has been challenged lately by more intimate stagings by other companies. The RSC's own studio work has contributed to this movement: a powerful impression was made by Trevor Nunn's *Macbeth* (1974) and Buzz Goodbody's *Hamlet* (1975). Peter Brook, a *Wunderkind* in the late 1940s and 1950s and now more of a guru, achieved world-wide success with his *Titus Andronicus* (with Olivier, 1956) and *A Midsummer Night's Dream* (RSC, 1970). Mention should also be made of the 'offshoots' in which modern dramatists have reworked Shakespearean material, either in direct confrontation with the originals (e. g. Charles Marowitz's *Hamlet* and other plays) or in order to capitalize on received ideas about characters and circumstances (WESKER's *The Merchant*; BOND's *Lear*). Some stage versions have hovered between interpreting and revising the plays: Brecht's *Coriolanus* is a famous example.

Shakespeare's plays attracted film-makers from the earliest days of commercial cinema. The first 'talkie' based on Shakespeare was *The Taming of the Shrew* with

Douglas Fairbanks and Mary Pickford (1929). In 1936 Max Reinhardt, who had staged the play many times in Europe and America, directed a Hollywood film version of *A Midsummer Night's Dream* with a cast including James Cagney as Bottom and Mickey Rooney as Puck. Olivier, as actor and director, made popular movies of *Henry V* (1944), *Hamlet* (1947) and *Richard III* (1955); Orson Welles filmed idiosyncratic versions of *Macbeth* (1948) and *Othello* (1950) and an epic compilation of Falstaffian episodes, *The Chimes at Midnight* (1965). Franco Zeffirelli's *The Taming of the Shrew* (1966), *Romeo and Juliet* (1968) and *Hamlet* (1990), Roman Polanski's *Macbeth* (1971) and Kenneth Branagh's *Henry V* (1989) have enjoyed great popularity. *Hamlet* (1964) and *King Lear* (1971) by the Russian director Grigori Kozintsev and Akira Kurosawa's Japanese versions of *Macbeth* (as *Throne of Blood*, 1957) and *Lear* (as *Ran*, 1984) have been widely acclaimed. Shakespeare's plays have been a regular feature of British radio broadcasting since the 1920s, although these productions have never enjoyed the attention lavished on such television adaptations as those included in the BBC's series covering the whole canon (1978–84).

A full survey of the transpositions of Shakespeare's work into the other arts would have to include graphic representations (especially the Shakespearean paintings so popular in the 19th century), music and writings inspired by the plays and poems. It seems prudent to restrict the present account to works offering to perform the plays in a new medium. Shakespearean operas may be said to date from the Restoration versions of *The Tempest* and, particularly, *A Midsummer Night's Dream* (as *The Fairy Queen*, 1692, with music by Purcell and a libretto by SETTLE). Incidental music – by, for example, Berlioz, Liszt, Tchaikovsky and Elgar – has sometimes been provided on such a scale as to turn the plays into semi-operatic entertainments, while Mendelssohn's *Dream* music was for long almost inseparable from the play. Verdi's *Macbeth* (1847 and 1865) and *Otello* (1887) are vigorous, perceptive readings of the plays, and his last opera, *Falstaff* (1893), has a poetic quality not usually found in *The Merry Wives of Windsor*. A popular and likeable adaptation of the same work is Otto Nicolai's *Die lustigen Weiber von Windsor* (1849). Benjamin Britten's *A Midsummer Night's Dream* (1960) is considered by many to be the best Shakespeare opera since Verdi. Shakespeare has also been put to good account in musical comedy: Rodgers and Hart made *Comedy of Errors* into *The Boys from Syracuse* (1938); Cole Porter's *Kiss Me, Kate* (1948) is about the tribulations of actors touring with *The Taming of the Shrew*; and in *West Side Story* (1957) Leonard Bernstein and Jerome Robbins transposed the story of *Romeo and Juliet* to New York. Choreographers as well as composers have found inspiration in the plays, with results that range from the brief psychodramas of Robert Helpmann's *Hamlet* (1948) and Jose Limon's *The Moor's Pavane* (1949) to the lavish full-length *Romeo and Juliet* ballets using Sergei Prokofiev's score (1938). *The Taming of the Shrew* was made into a ballet by John Cranko (1969).

Shakespeare's Sonnets Printed in 1609, though it seems likely that most were written during the vogue for the SONNET in the 1590s. MERES's *Palladis Tamia* (1598) spoke of Shakespeare's 'sugared sonnets' circulating among his friends, while versions of 138 and 144 appeared in THE PASSIONATE PILGRIM (?1599). The sonnets are dedicated to Mr 'W. H.', their 'only begetter'. His identity and whether he is to be identified with the apparenty arisocratic youth addressed in the poems is still a matter for debate: Henry Wriothesley, Earl of Southampton, and William Herbert, Earl of Pembroke, have long been popular candidates. Attempts to identify the so-called 'Dark Lady', the troublesome and unfaithful mistress of the later sonnets, and the 'Rival Poet' of such poems as sonnet 86 have been even less successful.

The order of the sonnets in the 1609 quarto remains the usual one, though there is no means of telling whether it is authorial. It lacks even the barely suggested narrative lines of SIDNEY's ASTROPHIL AND STELLA and SPENSER's AMORETTI, but it is just possible to glimpse the poet's love for a young man, whom he initially persuades to marry and beget children, and promises to immortalize, and who is then seduced by the poet's mistress. The sequence falls into two sections: 1–126 are concerned mainly with the youth and 127–154 mainly with the mistress. Smaller groups of poems can be identified within the larger divisions. Sonnets 1–7 urge the youth to marry as a means of immortality. The poet also offers his poetry as a means of immortality for both the youth and himself (see, for example, the end of sonnet 18, the famous 'Shall I Compare Thee to a Summer's Day'). The sonnets up to 126 record the oscillations in the relationship between poet and youth: 33–42 tell of a temporary estrangement and then reconciliation. The promises of immortality have to contend with the threat of change and time, and 65 is one of the many poems dwelling on 'sad mortality'. Others speak of the discrepancy between the poet's age and the friend's youth. In some poems from 97 onwards we hear of the poet's absence from the youth. Sonnet 116, 'Let Me Not to the Marriage of True Minds', is untypical in its unshaken faith in the permanence of affection. Sonnet 126, a truncated sonnet of only 12 lines, may be intended as a conclusion to the first group. The rest of the sonnets are mainly about the poet's relationship with the mistress. Sonnet 130, 'My Mistress' Eyes are Nothing Like the Sun', parodies the excessive hyperbole of sonneteering conventions. Many poems are bitter about her infidelity, and some express sexual disgust with bawdy quibbles (135 puns relentlessly on 'will' and 129 describes lust as 'Th'expense of spirit in a waste of shame').

Shamela Andrews, An Apology for the Life of Mrs
See PAMELA and FIELDING, HENRY.

Shapcott, Thomas (William) 1935– Australian poet, novelist and critic. *Selected Poems 1956–1988* (1989) is the best introduction to the range of a poet who has shown his commitment to both traditional and experimental forms in many volumes, beginning with *Time on Fire* (1961). He also turned to fiction in the 1980s, producing novels (*Flood Children*, 1981; *The Birthday Gift*, 1982), experimental narratives (*The White Stag of Exile*, 1984; *The Search for Galina*, 1989), stories (*Limestone and Lemon Wine*, 1988) and CHILDREN'S LITERATURE (*Holiday of the Icon*, 1984; *Mr Edmund*, 1990; *His Master's Ghost*, 1990). He has tried to define the direction of Australian verse in a succession of influential anthologies. He has also published *Biting the Bullet: A Literary Memoir* (1990).

Shapiro, Karl 1913– American poet and critic. He first gained widespread attention with *Person, Place, and Thing* (1942) and *V-Letter and Other Poems* (1944; PULITZER PRIZE), about his war-time experiences. Volumes such as *Poems 1940–1953* (1953), *The House* (1957) and *Poems of a Jew*

(1958) are often caustic and iconoclastic. After the Whitmanesque prose paragraphs of *The Bourgeois Poet* (1964) he returned to more traditional forms in *White-Haired Lover* (1968) and *Adult Bookstore* (1976). Shapiro's criticism includes *English Prosody and Modern Poetry* (1947), *Beyond Criticism* (1953; reissued in 1965 as *A Primer for Poets*), *In Defense of Ignorance* (1960), *The Writer's Experience* (with RALPH ELLISON; 1964), a study of RANDALL JARRELL (1967), *To Abolish Children and Other Essays* (1968) and *The Poetry Wreck: Selected Essays 1950–1970* (1975). He has embarked on a projected three-volume autobiography with *The Younger Son* (1988) and *Reports of My Death* (1990).

Sharp, Cecil J. See FOLK REVIVAL.

Sharp, William 1855–1905 Scottish poet, novelist and author of works as Fiona Macleod. Under his own name he produced novels, including *The Sport of Chance* (1888) and *The Children of Tomorrow* (1889) and several volumes of poetry: *The Human Inheritance, The New Hope, Motherhood and Other Poems* (1882), *Earth's Voices* (1884), *Romantic Ballads and Poems of Phantasy* (1888) and *Sospiri di Roma* (1891). This work is less interesting than the rhapsodic verse and prose romances on Celtic themes which he represented as being by Fiona Macleod, less a pseudonym then a second literary personality whose identity he kept a closely guarded secret. They include *Pharais* (1894), *The Mountain Lovers* (1895), *The Sin-Eater and Other Tales* (1895), *The Washer of the Ford* (1895) and a collection of articles, *The Winged Destiny* (1904). See also CELTIC REVIVAL.

Shaughraun, The A MELODRAMA by BOUCICAULT, first performed in New York in 1874. The feckless but charming Conn the Shaughraun helps Robert Ffolliott, a convicted Fenian, escape from Australia and return to Ireland to visit his sweetheart Arte O'Neal. Robert is arrested by Captain Molyneux and Conn apparently killed in helping him to escape. The happy ending sees Robert pardoned and three couples united: Robert with Arte, Molyneux with Robert's sister Claire, and Conn with his sweetheart Moya.

Shaw, George Bernard 1856–1950 Playwright, critic and novelist. Born in Dublin, he left school at 15 and migrated to London with his mother in 1876. There he undertook a programme of reading and became a socialist, joining the Fabian Society in 1884. WILLIAM ARCHER helped him find work in journalism. He made his mark reviewing music for *The Star* (1888–90) as 'Corno di Bassetto' and drama for THE SATURDAY REVIEW (1895–8). *Cashel Byron's Profession* (1886) and *An Unsocial Socialist* (1887) are fiction, a form he returned to several times, most notably in the socio-political parable, *The Adventures of the Black Girl in Her Search for God* (1932).

The Quintessence of Ibsenism (1891) is as much a manifesto for Shaw's own future work in the theatre as it is an advocacy of Ibsen's genius. WIDOWERS' HOUSES (1892) made a vigorous attack on slum landlordism. Like MRS WARREN'S PROFESSION (written 1893, produced 1902) and *The Philanderer* (written 1893, produced 1905), it was considered too strong to pass the censor and confined to private performance. *Arms and the Man* (1894), wittily subverting the conventions of male gallantry, was his first play to be presented publicly. It was followed by *Candida* (1897), *The Devil's Disciple* (1897), *The Man of Destiny* (1897), *You Never Can Tell* (1899) and *Captain Brassbound's Conversion* (1900). Shaw owed his fame to HARLEY GRANVILLE-BARKER and J. E. Vedrenne at the ROYAL COURT THEATRE. They presented *John Bull's Other*

Island (1904), a provocative thrust at the Irish question, *How He Lied to Her Husband* (1904), *MAN AND SUPERMAN* (1905), *MAJOR BARBARA* (1905) and *Doctor's Dilemma* (1906). *Caesar and Cleopatra* (1907) maintained his growing reputation for mischief and iconoclasm, as did *Getting Married* (1908), *The Shewing Up of Blanco Posnet* (1909), censured for blasphemy, *Misalliance* (1910), *Fanny's First Play* (1911), *Androcles and the Lion* (1913) and *PYGMALION* (1913). Shaw contributed four of his most serious plays to the new theatre of the 1920s: *HEARTBREAK HOUSE* (1920), *BACK TO METHUSELAH* (1922), *SAINT JOAN* (1923) and *The Apple Cart* (1929). Of his later plays, the best include *Too True to be Good* (1932), *The Millionairess* (1936) and *In Good King Charles's Golden Days* (1939).

His social, political and ethical opinions are aired in lively *Prefaces* to his plays (collected in a single volume in 1934, revised and expanded in 1938 and 1965), as well as in such works as *Common Sense about the War* (1914), *How to Settle the Irish Question* (1917), *The Intelligent Woman's Guide to Socialism and Capitalism* (1928, revised 1937) and *Everybody's Political What's What* (1944). His voluminous correspondence includes exchanges with Ellen Terry (edited by C. St John, 1931), Mrs Patrick Campbell (edited by A. Dent, 1952) and Granville-Barker (edited by C. B. Purdom, 1957). Michael Holroyd has written the authorized biography (1988–91).

She: *A History of Adventure* A novel by HAGGARD, published in 1887. The scholar Horace Holly, who narrates the story, goes to Africa with his ward, Leo Vincey, on a quest to avenge Leo's first ancestor, Kallikrates, murdered by an unknown woman. They discover the underground tombs of Kôr, ruled over by a mysterious queen who has the secret of eternal life: She-Who-Must-Be-Obeyed, or Ayesha. She recognizes Leo as the reincarnation of Kallikrates, whom she murdered because he would not accept her love. Leo and Holly are taken to the Place of Life, an underground cavern where they may step into the Fire of Life and be made immortal. When Ayesha herself enters the Fire she becomes immeasurably old and then monkey-like before dying. Shattered and transformed by their experience, the heroes set out for Tibet, where they hope to encounter Ayesha again. Haggard wrote two sequels, *Ayesha* (1905) and *Wisdom's Daughter* (1923), both lacking the haunting power of the original.

She Stoops to Conquer: *or, The Mistakes of a Night* A comedy by GOLDSMITH, produced and published in 1773. Mr and Mrs Hardcastle have a daughter, Kate, and Mrs Hardcastle has a son by a previous marriage, the oafish and dissolute Tony Lumpkin. Sir Charles Marlow has proposed a match between his son and Kate Hardcastle. Young Marlow and his friend Hastings accordingly make the journey to the Hardcastles' home in the country but, thanks to Tony Lumpkin's misdirections, arrive there believing it to be an inn. The scene is thus expertly laid for the comedy that follows. Young Marlow takes Kate to be a servant and falls in love with her. Kate's friend Constance Neville falls in love with Hastings; Mrs Hardcastle, who dotes on her son Tony and had intended him to marry Constance, is thoroughly displeased. Sir Charles Marlow's arrival puts everything to rights.

She Would If She Could The second of ETHEREGE's three comedies, staged in 1668. Unlike *THE COMICAL REVENGE* (1664), it has no heroic plot to contrast with the comedy of sexual misadventure and is thus a clearer

model of RESTORATION COMEDY. Sir Oliver Cockwood, his wife and Sir Joslin Jolley come to London, bringing Sir Joslin's two nieces, Ariana and Gatty, whose charms attract the attention of Courtall and Freeman, two young men-about-town. Assignations lead to the comic crises of the final act, resolved by the pairing of the young lovers but no more than partially resolved for their elders, who return, not much wiser, to the country.

Sheffield, John, 3rd Earl of Mulgrave and 1st Duke of Buckingham and Normanby 1648–1721 Politician and poet. He spent most of his flamboyant life at court. Literary works include the *Essay on Satire* (?1680) and *Essay on Poetry* (1682), some love lyrics, and several prose pieces. His reworking of SHAKESPEARE's *JULIUS CAESAR* as *Julius Caesar* and *Marcus Brutus* appeared in the edition of his *Works* (1723) prepared by his friend POPE. He was a generous patron to DRYDEN, whose monument in Westminster Abbey he financed.

Shelley, Mary (Wollstonecraft) 1797–1851 Novelist and editor. She was the only daughter of WILLIAM GODWIN and MARY WOLLSTONECRAFT, who died a few days after her birth. At 16 she ran away to France and Switzerland with SHELLEY, marrying him in 1816 on the death of his wife Harriet. Her most famous work, *FRANKENSTEIN: or, The Modern Prometheus* (1818), was begun on Lake Geneva in the summer of 1816 as her contribution to a ghost-story competition devised by BYRON, Shelley and Byron's friend Polidori. She returned to England after Shelley's death and devoted herself to the welfare of their only surviving child, Percy Florence, and to her career as a writer. None of her later novels matched the power, originality, and mythical sweep of her legendary first work. Of more abiding interest, however, are: *Mathilde*, an unfinished novel begun in 1819 (published in 1959), which draws strongly on her relations with Godwin and Shelley; *Valperga* (1823), a romance set in 14th-century Italy which portrays the lovelessness and destructiveness of personal political ambition; and *The Last Man* (1826), a vision of the end of human civilization, set in the 21st century. She also edited the first authoritative edition of Shelley's poems (1839). *Rambles in Germany and Italy, in 1840, 1842 and 1843* (1844), was well received.

Shelley, Percy Bysshe 1792–1822 Poet. The elder son of Timothy (later Sir Timothy) Shelley, he was born at Field Place in Sussex. At Eton, where he was nicknamed 'Mad Shelley' and 'Eton Atheist', he privately published a GOTHIC NOVEL, *Zastrozzi* (1810). It was followed by the anonymous *Original Poetry by Victor and Cazire* (1810), written with his sister Elizabeth, and another Gothic tale, *St Irvine: or, The Rosicrucian* (1811). At University College, Oxford, he and his friend Thomas Jefferson Hogg circulated an anonymous pamphlet, *The Necessity of Atheism* (1811); their refusal to answer questions from the college authorities resulted in summary expulsion. This affair, and his elopement later in 1811 with the 16-year-old Harriet Westbrook, whom he married in Edinburgh, caused a permanent break with his family.

Shelley then embarked on nomadic living and political pamphleteering. At Lynmouth he launched copies of his broadsheet, *A Declaration of Rights*, to sea in open bottles, and at Tremadoc in Wales he observed the labourers' living conditions during the harsh winter of 1812. *QUEEN MAB* (1813) brought him no immediate recognition. In London the Shelleys became friends with PEACOCK and GODWIN, who became his philosophical mentor and received in return 'the amount of a considerable fortune'. After the failure in 1813 of his marriage to Harriet, who drowned herself three years later, Shelley eloped to the Continent with Mary (MARY SHELLEY), Godwin's 16-year-old daughter by MARY WOLLSTONECRAFT, accompanied by Jane 'Claire' Clairmont, who was 15. The triangular relationship lasted until his death. Their journey produced an unfinished novella, *The Assassins* (1814), and a combined journal, later reworked by Mary Shelley and published as *History of a Six Weeks' Tour* (1817). Back in England, Shelley wrote ALASTOR (1816) during a calmer period which coincided with the birth of his favourite son, William ('Willmouse'). Two philosophical poems, the 'Hymn to Intellectual Beauty' and 'Mont Blanc' belong to the same stay with BYRON on Lake Geneva which prompted Mary to begin *FRANKENSTEIN*. LEIGH HUNT, the first to praise Shelley's work in print, introduced him to KEATS, HAZLITT and other members of their circle. At Marlow, where the family settled near Peacock in 1817, he wrote *An Address to the People on the Death of Princess Charlotte*, perhaps his finest political pamphlet, and worked on 'Laon and Cythna', published as *REVOLT OF ISLAM* (1818).

Shelley left England in spring 1818 and spent the rest of his life in Italy. He stayed first at Lucca, Venice and Este, where he wrote *JULIAN AND MADDALO*, exploring his relations with Byron. The 'Stanzas Written in Dejection' belong to the winter at Naples, while the 'Roman spring' of 1819 saw completion of the major part of *PROMETHEUS UNBOUND*. The death in Rome of 'Willmouse' was a devastating blow. The now childless household settled in Tuscany, first near Livorno, then Florence and finally Pisa, which became more or less their permanent base until 1822. Despite these difficulties the year from summer 1819 to summer 1820 was Shelley's most creative period. He completed the fourth act of *Prometheus Unbound* and wrote: another drama, *THE CENCI*; his great political poem, *The Mask of Anarchy*; 'Ode to the West Wind'; his SATIRE on WORDSWORTH, *Peter Bell the Third*; his political ODES 'To Liberty' and 'To Naples'; his *Letter to Maria Gisborne* and *The Witch of Atlas*; smaller-scale propaganda poems, 'Young Parson Richards', 'Song to the Men of England' and 'Sonnet: England 1819', and such lyrics as 'To a Skylark' and 'The Cloud'. During the Pisan period (1820–1) he completed his remarkable political document, *A Philosophical View of Reform* (1820), the entertaining *Essay on the Devil*, *THE DEFENCE OF POETRY* and a sequence of exquisite short poems: 'To the Moon', 'The Two Spirits', 'The Aziola' and 'Evening: Ponte Al Mare, Pisa'. His BURLESQUE, *Swellfoot the Tyrant*, was published in 1820. In 1821 the news of Keats's death prompted *ADONAIS*, and a platonic affair with Teresa Viviani produced *Epipsychidion*. Joined by Byron in the winter of 1821, he formed the centre of a circle which included Jane and Edward Williams, EDWARD TRELAWNY and a colourful assortment of exiles, expatriates and adventurers. He translated scenes from Goethe's *Faust* and wrote his last completed verse drama, *Hellas*, to raise money in England for the Greek war of independence. It appeared in 1822, though his drama of the Civil War, *Charles I*, was abandoned.

After the breakup of the Pisan group in 1822 the Shelleys moved to the village of Lerici on the Bay of Spezia, where he began his last major poem, *The Triumph of Life*, and composed a sequence of short lyrics: 'The Keen Stars are Twinkling', 'When the Lamp is Shattered' and the sad 'Lines Written in the Bay of Lerici'. Leigh Hunt reached Livorno in July to assume editorship of a new journal, *THE LIBERAL*. On the way back from the meeting Shelley, Edward Williams and their boatboy were drowned in the Bay of Spezia. Shelley's body was cremated on the beach at Viareggio in the presence of Byron, Trelawny and Hunt.

Until recently Shelley's colourful life and his achievements as a lyric poet have obscured the central aspects of his art. He drew no essential distinction between poetry and politics. His work continues and revitalizes the radical tendencies of earlier Romantic writing, expanding its critique of social injustice into an attack on specific institutions of oppression. The revolutionary optimism of his great visionary poems is wrung from a painful consciousness of the moral, psychological and historical dimensions of social and political bondage.

Shenstone, William 1714–63 Landscape gardener and poet. Much of his verse has been properly forgotten. His best-known work was *The Schoolmistress* (1742). His major achievement was in landscaping the gardens of the Leasowes, the estate near Birmingham he acquired in 1754. They became a famous showpiece of the PICTURESQUE style, though SAMUEL JOHNSON described them disdainfully in his *LIVES OF THE POETS* and HORACE WALPOLE summed Shenstone up as a man who 'had much more fame than his talents entitled him to'. His friend RICHARD GRAVES edited a volume of *Recollections* (1788).

Shepard, E(rnest) H(oward) 1879–1976 Illustrator. He started contributing cartoons to *PUNCH* in 1907 and maintained the association for the next 50 years. His illustrations for MILNE's quartet of Christopher Robin and Winnie-the-Pooh books (1924–8) established his fame in CHILDREN'S LITERATURE. Even more successful were his illustrations for a new edition of GRAHAME's *WIND IN THE WILLOWS* (1931).

Shepard, Sam 1943– American playwright, screenwriter and film actor. More than 40 plays, beginning with *Cowboys* (1964), have established him as a leader of the *avant-garde* theatre as well as perhaps the most critically acclaimed contemporary American playwright. Eclectic and volatile, his work has dealt with the myth of the West, the American dream, the travail of the family and the search for roots. Major works include: *La Turista* (1966); *The Tooth of Crime* (1972), a rock-drama; *Curse of the Starving Class* (1976), *Buried Child* (1979; PULITZER PRIZE) and *True West* (1980), a trilogy exploring the relationship of Americans to their land, their family and their history; *Fool for Love* (1979); *A Lie of the Mind* (1985); and *The States of Shock* (1991), an ambiguous look at post-Vietnam America. He has appeared as a film actor in his own *Fool for Love* and written the award-winning screenplay for *Paris, Texas* (1985).

Shepard, Thomas 1605–49 American Puritan minister. Though he did not emigrate from England until 1635, and thus lived only 14 years in Massachusetts Bay, he exerted a powerful influence on the Puritan experiment. His exploration of the stages leading to conversion, *The Sincere Convert* (1641), soon became the most widely read formulation of the theory of preparation. Two other tracts, *Theses Sabbaticae* (1649) and *Church Membership of Children and Their Right to Baptism* (1663), demonstrate his contribution to the central ecclesiastical debates of American Congregationalism. Shepard's autobiography (not published until 1747) and his sermons, notably those collected in *The Parable of the Ten Virgins Opened and Applied* (1660), show that he tempered his religious conviction with empathy for the common Puritan's struggle with spiritual truths.

Shepheardes Calender, The SPENSER's first important poem, published under the pseudonym Immerito (unworthy) in 1579. It consists of twelve poems, one for each month of the year, beginning and ending in winter, with Colin Clout's complaints in January and December. The other months contain dialogues between shepherds concerning love, poetry and religious affairs; April contains a panegyric of Eliza, queen of shepherds (Elizabeth I), November is an elegy on Dido ('some maiden of great blood'), and October contemplates the profession and responsibilities of the poet. In October Piers encourages Cuddie to turn from pastoral poetry to sing of wars, jousts and knights. *The Shepheardes Calender* is typical of PASTORAL in its constant regret for lost golden ages – of purity in love, poetry, morality and religion – and a consequent 'satirical bitterness' about contemporary failings.

Shepherd's Calendar, The A cycle of poems by CLARE, published in 1827. It develops his own PASTORAL idiom, adopting rural 'realism' in the use of dialect words, in the proliferating detail and extraordinary concreteness of his observation of seasonal changes, in his eye for the unromantic harshness of agricultural labour, and in his criticism of enclosing farmers and 'tyrant justice'. The poem did not please his London publisher, who pruned the text to half its original length, corrected Clare's idiosyncratic grammar, and introduced punctuation. A modern edition by E. Robinson and G. Summerfield (1964) returns to the original manuscript.

Shepherd's Life, A: *Impressions of the South Wiltshire Downs* W. H. HUDSON's account of life around Salisbury Plain before the automobile age, published in 1910. Hudson's observations of the wildlife of the country, both flora and fauna, together with his arresting stories about dogs, in themselves make the book worth reading; but the recollections of a shepherd, Caleb Bawcombe, in addition make it a classic of country life from about 1840 to the first years of the 20th century.

Shepherd's Week, The Six poems by GAY, published in 1714. Partly designed to parody the work of AMBROSE PHILIPS, these witty pieces are at once mock-classical and realistic. In Gay's version of PASTORAL, rustic conditions are grubby, superstitious, fractious and exhausting as well as endearing and amorous.

Sheridan, Frances 1724–66 Novelist and playwright. The mother of RICHARD BRINSLEY SHERIDAN, she moved from Dublin to London in 1754 with her husband, the actor-manager Thomas Sheridan. She launched her career as a novelist with the popular *Memoirs of Miss Sidney Biddulph: Extracted from Her Own Journal* (1761), heavily influenced by RICHARDSON's *PAMELA*, and followed her heroine's further tribulations in a *Continuation of the Memoirs* (1767). Her other novels were *The History of Nourjahad* (1767) and *Eugenia Adelaide*, her first effort, not published until 1791. Three plays, *The Discovery* (1763), *The Dupe* (1764) and *A Trip to Bath* (1765), were produced at DRURY LANE.

Sheridan, Richard Brinsley 1751–1816 Playwright. He was the son of FRANCES SHERIDAN and the actor-manager Thomas Sheridan. His gallant and romantic courtship of his future wife, the singer Elizabeth Linley, at Bath provided him with the setting and some sugges-

tions for his first play, *THE RIVALS* (1775). Its success prompted two other pieces in the same year: *St Patrick's Day: or, The Scheming Lieutenant*, a farce, and *THE DUENNA*, a comic opera with music by his father-in-law Thomas Linley. In 1776 he bought a share in DRURY LANE, for which all his remaining work was written. The best of it appeared before the end of 1779: *A Trip to Scarborough* (1777), a softening of VANBRUGH's *THE RELAPSE*; *THE SCHOOL FOR SCANDAL* (1777), perhaps the finest of all 18th-century comedies; and *THE CRITIC* (1779), modelled on BUCKINGHAM's *THE REHEARSAL*. Of his later work only *Pizarro* (1799), a bombastic version of a German play by Kotzebue, matched his earlier success. Although he maintained a major share in the management of Drury Lane until it burned down in 1809, he devoted most of his energy to politics after he became an MP in 1780, rivalling EDMUND BURKE as a parliamentary speaker and taking a famous part in the impeachment of Warren Hastings in 1788–94.

Sherlock Holmes stories Four novels and 56 short stories by SIR ARTHUR CONAN DOYLE. They are not just the most famous and enduring contribution to DETECTIVE FICTION but also probably the most imitated, parodied and adapted literary works in the language.

Holmes and his colleague Dr Watson first appear in two novels, *A Study in Scarlet* (published in *Beeton's Christmas Annual* for 1887) and *The Sign of Four* (1890), but did not reach a wide readership until Doyle began the short stories for *THE STRAND MAGAZINE* collected as *The Adventures of Sherlock Holmes* (1892) and *The Memoirs of Sherlock Holmes* (1894). To free himself from his creation Doyle killed Holmes off in the last story, 'The Final Problem', but the resulting outcry forced him to return to a subject which he increasingly saw as a distraction from his serious work. *The Hound of the Baskervilles* (1902) narrates an early case of the dead detective's, but 'The Adventure of the Empty House', in *The Return of Sherlock Holmes* (1905), reveals how Holmes had in fact survived apparent death at Moriarty's hands. Holmes appeared in a further novel, *The Valley of Fear* (1915), and two more collections, *His Last Bow* (1917) and *The Case-Book of Sherlock Holmes* (1927).

Doyle's literary model was POE's stories about Dupin, from which he elaborated the brilliant but eccentric detective, the admiring friend who narrates the story, the cases which are puzzling and fantastic as much as sensationally criminal, and the dramatically revealed solution. To them he added a strong feeling for late Victorian and Edwardian London, witty dialogue and a chivalric concern for the unjustly oppressed. Such qualities are perhaps best displayed in the early short stories, particularly 'A Scandal in Bohemia', 'The Red-Headed League' and 'The Adventure of the Speckled Band'. Of the novels, *The Hound of the Baskervilles*, mainly set on Dartmoor, is the most firmly constructed. The first of many actors to play Holmes was GILLETTE, who toured for over 30 years in his MELODRAMA, *Sherlock Holmes* (1899).

Sherlock, Thomas 1678–1761 Churchman and theologian. Son of WILLIAM SHERLOCK, he became Bishop of London in 1748. He made a reputation as a preacher and opposed HOADLY in the 'Bangorian controversy'. His exercise in Christian apologetics, *The Trial of the Witnesses of the Resurrection of Jesus* (1729), is his most notable published work.

Sherlock, William 1641–1707 Churchman and theologian. He became Master of the Temple, a post in which he was succeeded by his son, THOMAS SHERLOCK, and later Dean of St Paul's. His best-known book was *A Practical Discourse concerning Death* (1689). His change of mind over the Oath of Allegiance to William and Mary and his *Vindication of the Doctrine of the Trinity and of the Incarnation* (1690) made him a target of criticism, particularly the witty attacks of SOUTH.

Sherriff, R(obert) C(harles) 1896–1975 Playwright and screenwriter. *Journey's End* (1928), about bravery and cowardice in World War I, is the best-known work. Of his other plays, only *Badger's Green* (1930) and the radio drama *The Long Sunset* (1955) earned critical attention. His film credits include *The Invisible Man* (1933), *Goodbye Mr Chips* (1939), *Odd Man Out* (1947) and *The Dam Busters* (1955).

Sherwood, Mary Martha 1775–1851 Writer of CHILDREN'S LITERATURE. The best remembered of her many pious stories and tracts is *The History of the Fairchild Family* (1818), about the misadventures of Lucy, Emily and Henry Fairchild. In a notorious passage Mr Fairchild shows them a rotting corpse hanging on a gibbet as a warning against family disputes.

Sherwood, Robert E(mmet) 1896–1955 American playwright. His experiences in World War I led him to adopt an outspoken pacifism, evident in his first play, *The Road to Rome* (1927), a comedy about Hannibal's deferred march to Rome. The advocacy of participation in a virtuous war in *There Shall be No Night* (1940) marked a change of heart in a man who was by then serving as special assistant to the Secretary of War as well as writing many of President Roosevelt's speeches. Other plays include *The Queen's Husband* (1928), *Reunion in Vienna* (1931), *The Petrified Forest* (1935), *Idiot's Delight* (1936), *Abe Lincoln in Illinois* (1938), *The Rugged Path* (1945) and *Small War on Murray Hill* (1957). He also wrote screenplays, including *The Best Years of Our Lives* (1946). *Roosevelt and Hopkins: An Intimate History* (1948) is a political memoir.

Shiel, M(atthew) P(hipps) 1865–1947 Writer of DETECTIVE FICTION, fantasy and SCIENCE FICTION. He wrote grotesque detective and horror stories in *Prince Zaleski* (1895) and *Shapes in the Fire* (1896) before cashing in on the boom in future war stories with *The Yellow Danger* (1898). A fervent believer in social and evolutionary progress, he combined a quasi-Nietzschean interest in 'overmen' with insistence on the necessity of altruism. His masterpiece is *The Purple Cloud* (1901), which visits catastrophe on the earth to test the faith of a modern Job. His philosophy is most comprehensively displayed in later novels such as *How the Old Woman Got Home* (1928) and *Dr Krasinski's Secret* (1929) and a last scientific romance, *The Young Men are Coming!* (1937).

Shiels, George 1881–1949 Irish playwright. He began writing for the ABBEY THEATRE with *Bedmates* and *Insurance Money* (1921), achieved his first major success with a characteristically sardonic comedy, *Paul Twyning* (1922), and became the most consistently effective Abbey dramatist in the years following O'CASEY's departure. His best work, unrelentingly realistic in its presentation of unscrupulous 'decent' people, includes *Cartney and Kevney* (1927), *Mountain Dew* (1929), the challenging comedy *The New Gossoon* (1930), *The Passing Day* (1936), *Give Him a House* (1939), *The Rugged Path* (1940) and its sequel *The Summit* (1941), *The Fort Field* (1942) and *The Caretakers* (1948).

Shipman's Tale, The See CANTERBURY TALES..

Shirley A novel by CHARLOTTE BRONTË, published in 1849. A CONDITION OF ENGLAND NOVEL, it is set in Yorkshire during the Luddite riots. Robert Gérard Moore, a millowner, falls into conflict with his workers in trying to install new machinery. His brother, Louis, is tutor to the wealthy Keeldar family and, even though he loves the rector's niece, Caroline Helstone, Robert proposes to Shirley Keeldar. She rejects him with contempt. The end of the Napoleonic war frees him from his difficulties and the devoted Caroline accepts him. Shirley, meanwhile, is drawn to Louis. The character of Shirley, which made the Christian name popular, is believed to have been modelled on EMILY BRONTË.

Shirley, James 1596–1666 Playwright. He turned to the stage after converting to Catholicism and losing his job as headmaster at St Albans. The 36 plays he wrote between 1625 and the closing of the theatres in 1642 made him the leading dramatist of the Caroline theatre. Shirley's avowed admiration for the work of BEAUMONT and FLETCHER is evident in the cleverly contrived multiple plots of his comedies and tragicomedies. These include his first play, *The School of Compliment* (1625; later renamed *Love Tricks*), *Hyde Park* (1632), THE GAMESTER (1633), *The Young Admiral* (1633), *The Lady of Pleasure* (1635), *The Imposture* (1640) and THE SISTERS (1642). His tragedies, also reflecting the influence of Beaumont and Fletcher in their vivid opposition of good and evil, include THE TRAITOR (1631), *Love's Cruelty* (1631), *The Politician* (c. 1639) and THE CARDINAL (1641). Several MASQUES and a modest volume of poems (1646) survive. Shirley's famous dirge, 'The Glories of Our Blood and State', concludes a dramatization from Ovid of *The Contention of Ajax and Ulysses for the Armour of Achilles* (published 1658).

Shoemaker's Holiday, The: *or, The Gentle Craft* A comedy by DEKKER, first performed in 1599. The subtitle apparently acknowledges its source in DELONEY's prose fiction, *The Gentle Craft*. One of the finest CITIZEN COMEDIES, the play is less remarkable for its various interrelated plots than for the gallery of characters it creates. Simon Eyre, a high-spirited shoemaker, and his bustling household of workmen are barely controlled by his wife, Margery. One employee is a nobleman, Rowland Lacy, disguised in order to pursue his love for Simon's daughter, Rose. Another is Ralph, loving husband of Jane, whose departure for the wars leaves her threatened by the attentions of the wealthy Hamond. The ending sees Simon appointed Lord Mayor.

Shorthouse, Joseph Henry 1834–1903 Novelist. He is remembered for *John Inglesant* (privately printed, 1880; published, 1881), a historical novel set in the reign of Charles I which offers glimpses of FERRAR's religious community at Little Gidding. The book also reflects Shorthouse's preoccupaion with Victorian tensions between Anglicans and Roman Catholics in the aftermath of the OXFORD MOVEMENT. Apart from other novels, he also wrote *The Platonism of Wordsworth* (1882) and edited GEORGE HERBERT's *The Temple* in 1882.

Shropshire Lad, A See Housman, A. E.

Shute, Nevil [Norway, Nevil Shute] 1899–1960 Novelist. He often worked his expertise as an aircraft engineer into his novels: *No Highway* (1948) makes metal fatigue into the stuff of mystery and suspense. Other novels include *Marazan* (1926), *So Disdained* (1928), *Lonely Road* (1932), *Ruined City* (1938), *What Happened to the Corbetts* (1939), *Pied Piper* (1942), *Pastoral* (1944), *The Far Country* (1952), *In the Wet* (1953), *The Breaking Wave* (1955), *On the Beach* (1957) and *The Trustee from the Toolroom* (1960). *A Town Like Alice* (1949), his best-known nov invests its bleak Australian setting with romance and adventure.

Sidgwick, Henry 1838–1900 Philosopher. A follower of JOHN STUART MILL, he made ethics his special study, most notably in *The Methods of Ethics* (1874). Knightbridge Professor of Moral Philosophy at Cambridge, Sidgwick was a leading advocate of reform in the university, opposing the religious test and supporting women's education.

Sidney, Sir **Philip** 1554–86 Courtier, poet, critic and author of prose romance. Born at Penshurst in Kent, he attended Shrewsbury School and Christ Church, Oxford, before touring France, Italy, Germany and the Low Countries in 1572–5. His ardent Protestantism prevented the cautious Elizabeth I entrusting him with important diplomatic missions. After a visit to German princes in 1577 to sound out the possibilities for a Protestant league, he was left chafing at the lack of employment and made, unsuccessfully, a clandestine attempt to join Drake's expedition to the Spanish coast in 1585. He finally had to settle for a minor appointment as governor of Flushing in the same year. He died there, before reaching his 32nd birthday, from wounds suffered during an unimportant skirmish at Zutphen. The grief felt in England and in Europe was as profound as the long funeral progress from the Low Countries to St Paul's Cathedral was spectacular. The London crowds are said to have cried out 'Farewell, the worthiest knight that lived' as the funeral passed. In life Sidney had easily commanded admiration: 'wheresoever he went he was beloved and obeyed', according to SIR FULKE GREVILLE, his lifelong friend and biographer. In death he was celebrated as the embodiment of all the graces that distinguish the perfect courtier, and mourned in particular by his fellow writers. ARTHUR GOLDING remembered him as a Protestant knight, NASHE as a 'Maecenas of learning' and patron of virtue and wit, and SPENSER in *Astrophel* (1595) as 'a gentle shepherd' and poet. For later generations he would become the idealized hero of an idealized Elizabethan age. SHELLEY, in *ADONAIS*, called him 'Sublimely mild, a spirit without spot', and YEATS a 'perfect man'.

Sidney's references to his literary works are the self-deprecating remarks of a Renaissance courtier. He speaks in the *APOLOGY FOR POETRY* of 'having slipped into the title of a poet'. His massive prose romance, *ARCADIA*, is this 'idle work of mine' and 'but a trifle'. Yet the debt of English literature to Sidney is enormous. *ASTROPHIL AND STELLA* is the first English SONNET sequence, the *Apology* is the most important and best-written critical work of its period in English, and the *Arcadia*, as well as being the finest work of English prose fiction of the period, has also been seen as the ancestor of the English novel. His minor works include: the playlet *The Lady of May*, composed in 1578 for the entertainment of Elizabeth; a translation of a work on the truth of the Christian religion by de Mornay, which was completed by Arthur Golding; and a metaphrase of the first 43 Psalms. Sidney was interested in metrical experimentation and his poems display an astonishing variety of stanzaic and metrical forms, some used for the first time in English. None of his works was published in his lifetime (the folio containing his major works appeared in 1598) but were circulated in manuscript.

Sidney, Sir **Robert** 1563-1626 Poet, courtier and younger brother of SIR PHILIP SIDNEY. His poetry, never printed in his lifetime, was rediscovered and edited by Peter Croft (1983). Consisting of a planned sequence of songs, sonnets and pastorals, it shows the influence of his elder brother's verse at every turn, and is chiefly remarkable as the largest body of original verse to have descended to us from the Elizabethan period in a text entirely set down by the poet himself. A patron as well as a poet, Robert Sidney is paid noble tribute as the lord of the manor to whom JONSON's *To Penshurst* is addressed.

Siege of Jerusalem, The A poem in ALLITERATIVE VERSE, *c.* 1390–1400, derived from several sources. Although the subject is mainly religious, it is given the courtly and chivalric setting of VERSE ROMANCE. The Roman Titus is cured of cancer by his belief in Christ, while his leprous father Vespasian is healed by touching the veil of St Veronica. Titus and Vespasian attack Jerusalem, defeating the Jews, and Vespasian becomes Emperor of Rome. An inferior version in couplets (*c.* 1400) is known as *Titus and Vespasian*.

Sigurd the Volsung and the Fall of the Niblungs, The Story of An epic poem by WILLIAM MORRIS, published in 1876. Based on the Niblung legend and written at the same time as Wagner was completing *Der Ring des Nibelungen*, it draws its material from the Icelandic *Volsunga Saga* rather than the German version of the story. The first book tells the story of Sigmund and the other three of his son Sigurd. Morris eliminates Latin and Romance language words as far as possible and uses the long anapaestic line he had developed for his *Aeneid of Virgil* (1875).

Silas Marner: The Weaver of Raveloe A novel by GEORGE ELIOT, first published in 1861. Falsely judged guilty of theft, Silas Marner leaves his dissenting community and, as the novel opens, has been living for 15 years as a linen-weaver in Raveloe, lonely but increasingly wealthy. Squire Cass has two sons: Godfrey, attracted to Nancy Lammeter but secretly married to the opium-ridden Molly Farren, and the good-for-nothing Dunstan (Dunsey). Dunstan steals Marner's gold and disappears. Molly dies in the snow-covered fields trying to reach the squire's residence to disclose her marriage. Their little girl, Eppie, toddles away from her dying mother to the threshold of Marner's cottage, where she is cared for by the lonely weaver. In his eyes she becomes more precious than his lost gold. The narrative moves forward 16 years to the discovery of the skeleton of Dunstan Cass with Silas's gold in a newly drained stone-pit. This revelation prompts Godfrey Cass to admit to Nancy, now his wife but childless, that Eppie is his daughter. They try to adopt the young girl, but neither Eppie nor Silas wish to be separated, and the novel concludes with her marriage to the worthy Aaron Winthrop. The story is spiced with rustic humour and forceful village characters.

Silkin, Jon 1930– Poet and editor. A poet of commitment, he writes of persecuted minorities; his main theme is growth through the experience of pain, and the parallel existence of joy. Volumes since *The Peaceable Kingdom* (1954) have included *The Re-ordering of the Stones* (1961), *Nature with Man* (1965) and *Selected Poems* (1988). He is also well-known for his work as editor of the literary magazine *Stand* from 1952 to 1957 and again from 1960, and for several anthologies, *Poetry of the Committed Individual: A Stand Anthology* (1973), *Out of Battle: Poetry of the Great War* (1972) and *The Penguin Anthology of First World War Poetry* (1979).

Silko, Leslie Marmon 1948– American poet, novelist and short-story writer. She is partly of Laguna Pueblo ancestry and her work draws on traditional Laguna sources to explore contemporary issues. *Ceremony* (1977), a novel about a half-breed Laguna haunted by his experiences in the Pacific during World War II, remains her best-known work. *Laguna Woman* (1974) is a collection of poems and *Storyteller* (1981) a collection of poetry and short fiction.

Sillitoe, Alan 1928– Novelist. He remains best known for *Saturday Night and Sunday Morning* (1958) and the title story of *The Loneliness of the Long-Distance Runner* (1959), working-class fiction which linked his name with that of other provincial realists of the late 1950s and early 1960s such as JOHN BRAINE and STAN BARSTOW.

Silver King, The A MELODRAMA by HENRY ARTHUR JONES, first performed in 1882. Persuaded that he has committed a murder, Wilfred Denver flees to America, where he makes a fortune and becomes the Silver King. He returns to England to save his starving family, but first needs to discover both his own innocence and the identity of the real murderer.

Silver Tassie, The A play by O'CASEY, staged in London in 1929. The first act shows Harry Heegan, on leave from World War I, leading his Dublin football team to victory and the trophy of the silver tassie. The second act, whose EXPRESSIONISM caused the play's rejection by Dublin's ABBEY THEATRE, is a macabre theatrical poem enacted in a battle-scarred landscape. The remaining two acts return Harry to Ireland where, maimed and bitter, he cannot reconcile himself to his changed circumstances.

silver-fork novel A mocking name for early-19th-century novels of fashionable life and manners. Authors included Lady Charlotte Bury (1775–1861), THEODORE HOOK, LADY BLESSINGTON, Lady Caroline Lamb (1785–1828), EDWARD BULWER LYTTON, BENJAMIN DISRAELI, FRANCES TROLLOPE, Thomas Henry Lister (1800–42), Robert Plumer Ward (1765–1846), CATHERINE GORE and SUSAN FERRIER.

Silverberg, Robert 1935– American novelist and short-story writer. He has produced more than 100 works of SCIENCE FICTION, more than 60 non-fiction books and various works in other genres. His finest achievement is a series, including *Thorns* (1967), *The Man in the Maze* (1969), *A Time of Changes* (1971), *Dying Inside* (1972) and *Shadrach in the Furnace* (1976), using the science-fictional vocabulary of ideas to model situations of extreme psychological alienation. Other novels include *Downward to the Earth* (1970), *Son of Man* (1971), *Gilgamesh the King* (1984) and *Lord of Darkness* (1985). *The Reality Trip and Other Implausibilities* (1972), *Born with the Dead* (1974) and *The Conglomeroid Cocktail Party* (1984) are among his many collections of short stories.

simile Where METAPHOR asserts the identity of unlike things, simile asserts their similarity: 'My love is like a red, red rose' (BURNS). The concrete element of a simile, therefore, has to be taken figuratively not literally. Burns's love is not to be envisaged as suffering from some skin disease that renders her prickly and bright red, but as sweet, natural and voluptuous. Cognition, in fact, plays at least as large a part as visualization in the appreciation of simile.

Simile naturally lends itself to expansion – a process reaching its peak in the EPIC SIMILE – while metaphor tends to condensation. The parallelism of simile has led some critics to see it as a paradigm of ALLEGORY, metaphor being more akin to a symbolic work, particularly one based on a central SYMBOL.

Simms, William Gilmore 1806–70 American novelist, short-story writer and poet. His 30 novels, immensely successful in their day, depicted the Old South and helped to propagate the Southern myth of perfectibility. The best-known is *The Yemassee: A Romance of Carolina* (1835), about the 1715 uprising by the Yemassee Indians against the English colonists. Others include: *Martin Faber* (1833), a study of a murderer; *Guy Rivers: A Tale of Georgia* (1834), a romance of the Southern frontier; *The Partisan: A Tale of the Revolution* (1835); *Mellichampe: A Legend of the Santee* (1836), also about the Revolutionary War; and *Woodcraft: or, Hawks about the Dovecote* (1854; originally published as *The Sword and the Distaff: or, 'Fair, Fat, and Forty'*, 1852). As well as short stories, many books of verse and much ephemeral journalism, he also published several works of non-fiction: the essay 'Slavery in America' (1837), *The History of South Carolina* (1840), *The Geography of South Carolina* (1843) and *The Life of Francis Marion* (1844).

Simon, (Marvin) Neil 1927– American playwright. Since *Come Blow Your Horn* (1961) he has enjoyed more Broadway hits than any other American playwright, though critical acclaim has been tempered by his reputation for writing gags which appease rather than challenge audiences. His major successes are *Barefoot in the Park* (1963), *The Odd Couple* (1965), *The Star Spangled Girl* (1966), *Plaza Suite* (1968), *The Last of the Red Hot Lovers* (1969), *The Prisoner of Second Avenue* (1971), *The Sunshine Boys* (1972), *California Suite* (1976), *Chapter Two* (1977), *Brighton Beach Memoirs* (1983), *Biloxi Blues* (1984), *Broadway Bound* (1986) and *Lost in Yonkers* (1991; PULITZER PRIZE).

Simple Story, A A novel by INCHBALD, published in 1791. Dorriforth, a priest, and his ward, Miss Milner, fall in love but cannot marry until he inherits a peerage and is released from his vows. When she resumes an affair with a former suitor, Dorriforth (now Lord Elmwood) banishes her and their daughter Matilda. Lady Elmwood dies of remorse and Elmwood's feelings are revived when Matilda is abducted by a libertine. He restores her to her home and position. The character of Dorriforth/Elmwood was apparently based on the actor John Philip Kemble.

Simpson, Louis 1923– American poet and critic. His poetry combines a mythical, dream-like quality with a colloquial, often ironic tone. His first volume, *The Arrivistes: Poems 1940–1949*, appeared in Paris in 1949 and *Collected Poems* in 1988. *At the End of the Open Road* (1963) received a PULITZER PRIZE. Simpson's criticism includes: *An Introduction to Poetry* (1967, revised edition 1973); *Three on the Tower* (1975), essays on EZRA POUND, T. S. ELIOT and WILLIAM CARLOS WILLIAMS; *A Revolution in Taste* (1978), studies of DYLAN THOMAS, ALLEN GINSBERG, SYLVIA PLATH and ROBERT LOWELL; and *A Company of Poets* (1981).

Simpson, N(orman) F(rederick) 1919– Playwright. He came to prominence with *A Resounding Tinkle* (1957), a zany disruption of middle-class normality, like his other successful piece, *One-Way Pendulum* (1959). Written during the brief popularity of the THEATRE OF THE ABSURD in Britain, Simpson's work also belongs to a comic tradition that links Will Hay to *The Goon Show* and *Monty Python*.

Sinclair, May [Mary] **(Amelia St Clair)** 1863–1946 Novelist. *The Three Sisters* (1914), about middle-class women in the repressive society of Victorian and Edwardian Britain, was the first of her 'psychological' novels, showing the influence of Freud, Jung and HAVELOCK ELLIS. She was also an admirer of DOROTHY RICHARDSON's *Pilgrimage* and became a leading exponent of STREAM OF CONSCIOUSNESS. *The Three Sisters* was followed by *Mary Oliver* (1919), an intense study of a mother–daughter relationship, and *The Life and Death of Harriet Frean* (1922). In all, she wrote 24 novels as well as short stories and literary criticism.

Sinclair, Upton 1878–1968 American novelist. *The Jungle* (1906), an exposé of the meat-packing industry in Chicago, remains his best-known work and perhaps the most famous of all 'muckraking novels'. Sinclair went on to publish more than 100 books, including a series of pamphlets on American life: *The Profits of Religion* (1918); *The Brass Check* (1919), on journalism; *The Goslings* (1924), on education; *Money Writes!* (1927), on art and literature; and *The Flivver King* (1937) on the motor industry. *World's End* is an 11-volume ROMAN FLEUVE following the life of Lanny Budd, the illegitimate son of a munitions tycoon, from the eve of World War I through the turbulence of inter-war politics to World War II and the anti-Communist climate in the USA after the war. Its individual volumes are *World's End* (1940), *Between Two Worlds* (1941), *Dragon's Teeth* (1942), *Wide is the Gate* (1943), *The Presidential Agent* (1944), *Dragon Harvest* (1945), *A World to Win* (1946), *A Presidential Mission* (1947), *One Clear Call* (1948), *O Shepherd, Speak!* (1949) and *The Return of Lanny Budd* (1953). Sinclair published a selection from his correspondence, *My Lifetime in Letters* (1960), and an autobiography (1962).

Singer, Burns (James Hyman) 1928–64 Poet. Only one volume of poems, *Still and All* (1957), appeared in his lifetime. An inadequate *Collected Poems* (1970) left much of his work unpublished and he remains largely unread. Influenced by W. S. GRAHAM, MACDIARMID and Wittgenstein, his poetry explores personal and public language and identity, and humanity's place in the complex and beautiful processes revealed by science.

Sir Charles Grandison, The History of An EPISTOLARY novel by SAMUEL RICHARDSON, published in 1753–4. Harriet Byron arrives in London society and excites the desires of the wealthy, dishonourable Sir Hargrave Pollexfen. When she repeatedly refuses him, he has her abducted and packed off to his country estate in a carriage. She is saved by the intervention of the wealthy and gallant Sir Charles Grandison, and the pair fall in love. While in Italy, though, Sir Charles had become attached to Clementina della Porretta, daughter of a noble family. Clementina suffers a mental breakdown and her parents beg Sir Charles to return urgently to Italy, to save her at any price. The lady recovers when he arrives, but the hero's honour is saved from a difficult dilemma by Clementina's decision that their different religions constitute too great an impediment. With a clear conscience Sir Charles returns to England and marries Harriet.

Sir Cleges A late-14th-century VERSE ROMANCE, from an unknown source. Sir Cleges's generosity makes him poor but his fortunes revive when he goes to court, making his way past corrupt officials, with a gift of cherries for the king.

Sir Degare A VERSE ROMANCE, written before 1325, set in Brittany and displaying features associated with the BRETON LAY. Abandoned at birth, Degare becomes a proficient knight in searching for his parents, a fairy knight and the woman he raped. He unwittingly marries his mother, and fights with his father until the lat-

ter reveals himself. Degare's parents marry and he marries the lady he has also won in the course of his adventures.

Sir Degrevant A late-14th-century VERSE ROMANCE notable for its portrayal of feudal society. Degrevant falls in love with Melidor, daughter of a neighbouring earl who has become his enemy, defeats a suitor for her hand and escapes an ambush laid when he goes to visit her secretly. The earl finally relents and the couple are allowed to marry.

Sir Eglamour of Artois A mid-14th-century VERSE ROMANCE. Christabelle and her new-born son Degrebelle are set adrift. Her lover Eglamour finds them, though not before Degrebelle has been stolen by a griffin and unwittingly married his mother. The wife set adrift and the child stolen by animals are common motifs in romance and folk literature.

Sir Firumbras [*Sir Ferumbras*] A late-14th-century VERSE ROMANCE. Its plot is substantially the same as the second half of *THE SOWDON OF BABYLON*. Charlemagne comes to aid Rome after its capture by the Sultan and Oliver defeats Firumbras, the Sultan's son, who is baptized. Roland, Oliver and Guy fall prisoner but the Sultan's daughter Floripas arranges their escape and her father's defeat. She marries Guy, and Charlemagne rewards Guy and Firumbras.

Sir Gawain and the Carle of Carlisle A VERSE ROMANCE (*c.* 1400). It centres on the traditional courtesy of Gawain and rudeness of Kay who, with Bishop Baldwin, seek shelter with the giant Carle of Carlisle. Gawain politely obeys the Carle's extraordinary requests, even agreeing to behead his host, who then regains the shape of a normal knight and joins the Round Table. Gawain marries his daughter.

Sir Gawain and the Green Knight A late-14th-century VERSE ROMANCE preserved in the same manuscript as *PEARL*, *PATIENCE* and *CLEANNESS*. Although these are explicitly religious and *Sir Gawain* is not, all four are linked by similarities of dialect (west Midlands), diction and style. They are usually taken to be the work of the same, unidentified author, known for convenience as the GAWAIN-POET.

Sir Gawain is written in ALLITERATIVE VERSE and divided into four fitts (or sections) of roughly equal length. A huge, bright green knight appears at Arthur's court one Christmas and challenges any knight to borrow his axe and deal him a blow, to be returned the following year at his own home, the Green Chapel. Gawain accepts the challenge and beheads the knight, who promptly recovers, reminding him of the bargain before leaving. The second fitt describes Gawain's preparations and his winter journey to the north of England. The poet deals at length with the pentangle blazoned on Gawain's shield, an emblem of the interlocking virtues to which he is dedicated. Gawain arrives at a castle near the Green Chapel and is persuaded to stay there until his appointment on New Year's Day. The third fitt describes the last three days of his stay, when he and his host, Sir Bertilak de Hautdesert, agree to exchange at dinner whatever they have gained during the day. While Bertilak hunts (first deer, then a boar, and on the third day a fox), his beautiful wife tries vainly to seduce Gawain. She gives a kiss to him on the first day, two kisses on the second and three on the third, all of which he duly gives to his host. But he conceals the gift the lady persuades him to accept on the third day, a green girdle which protects its wearer from violent death. In the fourth fitt Gawain rides to the Green Chapel. The Green Knight swings three times with his axe, twice stopping short but nicking Gawain's neck with the third blow. Then he reveals that he is in fact Sir Bertilak and knows all about his wife's actions; the wound is punishment for Gawain's failure to keep his bargain by concealing the girdle on the third day. Apparently, the Green Knight's appearance at Arthur's court was a plot by Morgan le Fay meant to frighten Guinevere to death. Gawain returns wearing the girdle as a badge of shame, but the other knights adopt it as a badge of honour.

The poem has no single known source, though it shares several motifs with French and Celtic traditions. The skill with which they are woven into a story combining sensuous description, gentle humour and a profound portrait of the tension between Gawain's idealism and his urge for self-preservation makes *Sir Gawain* the finest surviving Middle English romance and one of the great contributions to ARTHURIAN LITERATURE.

Sir Gowther A VERSE ROMANCE and BRETON LAY (c. 1400), taking the popular story of *Robert the Devil* from a 12th-century French version. Gowther grows up unremittingly evil until he learns that his father was a devil who raped his mother. He then goes to Rome to confess, and submits himself to penances which make people think him foolish. Eventually he marries the Emperor's daughter, works miracles and is revered as a saint.

Sir Harry Hotspur of Humblethwaite A novel by TROLLOPE, serialized in 1870 and published in volume form in 1871. A study in ancestral pride and the stubbornness born of high breeding and noble feelings, it has a tragic power and concentration unique in Trollope's work. Sir Harry Hotspur, a wealthy Cumberland squire, prefers to leave his property to his daughter Emily rather than George Hotspur, a distant cousin. The rakish George wins Emily's heart and her father refuses his consent. Pressed by creditors and the threat of legal action, George undertakes never to see Emily again in return for payment of his debts and an annuity. Emily is taken to Italy by her parents, where she learns of George's marriage to his mistress and dies broken-hearted.

Sir Launcelot Greaves, The Life and Adventures of A novel by SMOLLETT, published in volume form in 1762. His fourth novel, it is generally regarded as one of his weakest. Sir Launcelot Greaves is an 18th-century Don Quixote, riding about England in armour with his ludicrous squire, Timothy Crabshaw. The humour is harsh and the main interest of the book lies in its picture of England before the Industrial Revolution and in a few of its characters: the rogue Ferret, Mrs Gobble, a justice's wife and Captain Crowe, a naval knight-errant.

Sir Launfal [*Launfalus Miles*] A late-14th-century VERSE ROMANCE, the only work certainly attributed to Thomas Chestre, who might also have written *LIBEAUS DESCONUS*. It is the most inventive Middle English version of MARIE DE FRANCE's *Lanval*. Quitting Arthur's court because of a feud with Guinevere, the hero encounters Tryamour, daughter of a faery king, who becomes his mistress, gives him riches and appears at his command as long as their love remains secret. Launfal boasts of her beauty to Guinevere, who challenges him to produce her within a year. She arrives at the last moment, blinds Guinevere, and takes Launfal to Olyroun where they still live.

Sir Orfeo An early-14th-century VERSE ROMANCE, perhaps by the same poet who wrote *LAI LE FREINE*. The best English BRETON LAY, it is based loosely on the story of Orpheus and Eurydice from Ovid and Virgil; no medieval source has been identified, though Celtic and French features can be discerned. Orfeo's wife Herodis is abducted by the king of faery, and he wanders in the forest for years before gaining access to the faery otherworld and winning back his wife as a reward for his harp-playing. The tragic ending of the legend is omitted, Orfeo and his queen regaining their own kingdom.

Sir Thomas More A play dated *c*. 1593–5 but apparently not produced, following the main events of MORE's life from his rise to favour to his death on the scaffold. It was printed in 1844. The incomplete manuscript, preserved in the British Museum, is in five different hands of which one has been identified as SHAKESPEARE's; his collaborators were apparently MUNDAY, CHETTLE, THOMAS HEYWOOD and DEKKER. The scene attributed to Shakespeare shows More confronting the rebellious London apprentices.

Sir Thopas, The Tale of See *CANTERBURY TALES*.

Sir Torrent of Portyngale A VERSE ROMANCE, late 14th or early 15th century, constructed from familiar motifs (compare *OCTAVIAN* and *SIR EGLAMOUR OF ARTOIS*). Torrent wants to marry Desonell but her father, the cruel king of Portugal, gives him apparently impossible tasks, promises his daughter to a rival and then sets her and her twin sons adrift. Torrent punishes the king with the same fate and spends 15 years in battles before being reunited with Desonell and his sons.

Sir Triamour A late-14th-century VERSE ROMANCE notable for the conventional motifs it includes. The false steward Marrok persuades King Ardus of Aragon to banish his wife Margaret, accompanied by the old knight Roger and a dog. Marrok kills Roger but Margaret escapes and bears a son, Triamour. After guarding Roger's grave for 12 years (seven in one version), the dog returns to court, kills Marrok and leads the courtiers to the grave. Ardus goes in search of Margaret and encounters Triamour, at first as enemy and then as ally in battle.

Sir Tristrem A late-13th-century VERSE ROMANCE, the only Middle English treatment of the Tristan and Iseult story apart from MALORY's prose *LE MORTE DARTHUR*. Though based on the same Anglo-Norman source used by Gottfried von Strassburg, it offers only an incomplete, condensed and disappointing version of one of the great stories associated with COURTLY LOVE, and is less interested in the hero's relationship with his beloved than in his other adventures. The orphaned son of the sister of King Mark of Cornwall, Tristrem is brought up in Parmenie and abducted by pirates before making his way to Mark's court. In Ireland he claims the queen's daughter, Ysonde, as Mark's bride but they accidentally drink a love-potion intended for Mark and Ysonde. Their love affair eventally causes Mark to banish Tristrem. In Brittany he marries Ysonde of the White Hands on account of her name, without consummating the union. The narrative breaks off shortly after Tristrem has been wounded on his return to England, but other versions of the story supply the ending. Tristrem sends for Ysonde to heal him in Brittany, demanding that the ship bear white sails if she is aboard and black if she is not. When it returns, his jealous wife tells him it has black sails and he dies of grief before Ysonde arrives. She dies beside him.

Sisson, C(harles) H(ubert) 1914– Poet, novelist, translator and essayist. An Anglican and a conservative, he is also a classicist, both in his pessimism and rejection of Romantic possibilities, and in the influence of Latin literature. Volumes of verse have included *In the Trojan Ditch: Collected Poems and Selected Translations* (1974), *Anchises* (1976), *Exactions* (1980), *Collected Poems 1943–1983* (1984) and *God Bless Karl Marx!* (1987). His large *oeuvre* extends to: translations from German, French and Italian as well as Latin literature; *An Asiatic Romance* (1953) and *Christopher Homm* (1965), novels; and *English Poetry 1900–1950: An Assessment* (1971) and *The Avoidance of Literature: Collected Essays* (1978), vigorously debunking critical works.

Sister Carrie A novel by DREISER, published in 1900. Carrie Meeber, a Midwestern country girl, moves to Chicago and becomes the mistress of Charles Drouet, a salesman, before taking up with his friend George Hurstwood, a middle-aged, married restaurant manager. He embezzles money and elopes with Carrie to New York, where he opens a saloon. It fails and Carrie begins a successful career when she is forced to work as a chorus girl to support them. She deserts Hurstwood, who ends up a drunken beggar on Skid Row, eventually committing suicide.

Sister Helen A BALLAD by DANTE GABRIEL ROSSETTI, first published in 1870. It derives from the medieval superstition that revenge may be obtained by melting a waxen image of one's enemy. The carefully wrought exchanges between Sister Helen and her younger brother reveal that Keith of Ewern has violated his troth and is to die in pain and fear, despite successive pleas from his relations.

Sisters, The A comedy by SHIRLEY, produced in 1642 and published in 1652. The bandit Frapolo disguises himself as a fortune teller and persuades the haughty Paulina she will marry a prince; he is easily accepted when he returns as the Prince of Parma. The real Prince arrives and falls in love with Paulina's sister, the unassuming Angellina. Frapolo is exposed and Paulina discovered to be a changeling, the daughter of a peasant.

Sitwell, Dame Edith (Louisa) 1887–1964 Poet and critic. With her brothers, OSBERT SITWELL and SACHEVERELL SITWELL, she played a highly publicized role in literary life from the 1920s onwards. Her poetry included: *Façade* (1922), a suite of 'abstract poems' or 'patterns in sound' performed to musical accompaniment by William Walton; *Troy Park* (1925), which contained 'Colonel Fantock' and other poems about her family background; and *Gold Coast Customs* (1929). A preoccupation with war and suffering marked her later poetry, notably *Street Songs* (1942), which included the famous 'Still Falls the Rain', and *The Shadow of Cain* (1947), provoked by the nuclear attack on Hiroshima. *Collected Poems* appeared in the USA in 1954 and in an enlarged edition in Britain in 1957. Prose work includes: a study of POPE (1930); *English Eccentrics* (1933); a biography of Queen Victoria (1936); *Aspects of Modern Poetry* (1934), examining HOPKINS, YEATS, ELIOT, POUND, JOYCE and STEIN; *I Live under a Black Sun* (1937), her only novel, about SWIFT; two books on Elizabeth I, *Fanfare for Elizabeth* (1946) and *The Queens and the Hive* (1962); an appreciation of American poetry, *The American Genius* (1951); and a volume of autobiography, *Taken Care Of* (1965). Her popularity was increased by lecture tours in America during the 1950s, and the eccentricities of her dress and appearance were made famous by Cecil Beaton's photographs.

Sitwell, Sir (Francis) Osbert (Sacheverell) 1892–1969 Novelist and poet. The brother of EDITH SITWELL and SACHEVERELL SITWELL, he wrote variously and prolifically. His poetry includes political and pacifist satires in *The Winstonburg Line* (1919), the text for William Walton's choral work, *Belshazzar's Feast* (1931), and *Demos the Emperor* (1949), a 'Secular Oratorio'. *Before the Bombardment* (1926) is the best-known of several novels. He is most likely to be remembered for his autobiography: *Left Hand, Right Hand* (1945), *The Scarlet Tree* (1946), *Great Morning!* (1948), *Laughter in the Next Room* (1949) and *Noble Essences* (1950). A later volume was *Tales My Father Taught Me* (1962).

Sitwell, Sacheverell 1897–1988 Poet and art historian. Brother of EDITH SITWELL and OSBERT SITWELL, he published over 40 books on a wide variety of subjects. His poetry, more traditional than his sister's, includes *The People's Palace* (1918) and the lengthy *Dr Donne and Gargantua* (1930). *The Dance of the Quick and the Dead* (1936) is 'An Entertainment of the Imagination', consisting of interrelated prose reflections and fantasias on art, literature, life and death. *Journey to the End of Time* (1959) is similar but more despairing. *Southern Baroque Art* (1924) and *German Baroque Art* (1927) appeared when these subjects had been little studied.

Sizwe Bansi is Dead A play satirizing the South African 'pass laws', by ATHOL FUGARD with Kani and Ntshona, the black actors who first performed in it in 1972. It was published in 1974. A migratory worker lacking an identity card steals one from the corpse of Sizwe Bansi and thus loses his dignity and sense of identity.

Skeat, W(alter) W(illiam) 1835–1912 Literary scholar and philologist. A lecturer in mathematics at Cambridge from 1864, he was appointed professor of Anglo-Saxon in 1878. He made his reputation largely as an editor of Old and Middle English texts. Skeat's editions of PIERS PLOWMAN (1867–85) and CHAUCER (1894–7) remained standard authorities for many years. He also edited CHATTERTON (1871). As a philologist he founded the English Dialect Society in 1873 and produced, among other works, *An Etymological Dictionary of the English Language* (1882).

Skeffington, Sir Lumley St George 1771–1850 Playwright. A fashionable dandy who later sank into chronic poverty, he wrote several slight pieces which BYRON called 'skeletons of plays'. They include two comedies, *The Word of Honour* (1802) and *The High Road to Marriage* (1803), and a MELODRAMA, *The Sleeping Beauty* (1805).

Skelton, John ?1460–1529 Poet and satirist. Appointed court poet to Henry VII in 1489, he was tutor to the future Henry VIII, who awarded him the title of 'Orator Regius' in 1512. He also held the living of Diss, Norfolk, from *c.* 1503 until his death. *The Bowge [rations] of Court*, written in 1498 and printed the following year by WYNKYN DE WORDE, is a satirical dream-allegory about Henry VII's court. *Philip Sparrow*, probably written in 1505, is a lament by Jane Scroupe for her sparrow which was killed by Gib the cat. *A Ballad of the Scottish King*, printed in 1513, celebrates the English victory at Flodden. *Magnyficence*, probably performed *c.* 1516, is a huge secular MORALITY PLAY which owes something to Skelton's experience as tutor to the future Henry VIII and more to his perception of himself as Orator Regius: the central character must learn from Adversity, Poverty and Despair to trust in the advice of Sad Circumspection and Perseverance. *The Tunning of Elinor*

Rumming, probably written in 1517 and printed in 1521, is far more vigorous, though its portrait of a drunken woman and her customers at an alehouse was largely responsible for POPE's description of Skelton's subject matter as 'beastly'. *Speak Parrot, Colin Clout* and *Why Came Ye Not to Court* (1521–2) are satiric attacks on Wolsey, though *How the Doughty Duke of Albany* (1523) was written at the Cardinal's suggestion. In *The Garland of Laurel* (1523) Skelton presents himself among the great poets. He was certainly held in high regard by most contemporaries: ERASMUS called him 'the light and glory of English letters', while CAXTON praised him for his classical learning and his 'polished and ornate terms'. Later readers have often been deterred by his 'Skeltonics': headlong, irregular lines with no apparent metre or rhyme scheme.

Sketch Book of Geoffrey Crayon, Gent., The A book of essays and tales by WASHINGTON IRVING, serialized in 1819–20. Most pieces are descriptive and thoughtful essays on England, though two of the most famous tales, 'The Legend of Sleepy Hollow' and 'Rip Van Winkle', are set in America. *The Sketch Book* made Irving the first American author to receive international recognition.

Sketches by Boz: *Illustrative of Every-Day Life and Every-Day People* Essays, stories and sketches by DICKENS, contributed mainly to periodicals in 1833–6 and collected in 1836–7, with illustrations by GEORGE CRUIKSHANK. Dickens's first published book, it shows a vivid eye for the pertinent detail, whether driving home the moral lesson of 'The Drunkard's Death', parodying the pretensions of 'The Tuggses at Ramsgate' or visiting Astley's Circus. He gives kindly accounts of the schoolmaster, beadle, curate and other inhabitants of the parish, and records a rural election and a dispossession. For grimmer subjects, he turns to Seven Dials, the gin shop, the criminal court and Newgate.

Slessor, Kenneth 1901–71 Australian poet. His earliest work, *The Thief of the Moon* (1924), was reprinted with illustrations by NORMAN LINDSAY as *Earth-Visitors* (1926). Other works were 'Five Visions of Captain Cook' (in *Trio: A Book of Poems*, 1931), *Darlinghurst Nights and Morning Glories* (including verse by Virgil Gavan Reilly; 1933), *Five Bells: XX Poems* (a moving ELEGY for a drowned friend; 1939) and *One Hundred Poems: 1919–1939* (1944). While controlled and formal, Slessor's verse is elaborately decorative and highly visual.

Small House at Allington, The The fifth of TROLLOPE's BARSETSHIRE NOVELS, serialized in 1862–4 and published in book form in 1864. The widowed Mrs Dale lives with her daughters Lily and Bell at the Small House at Allington as tenant of her brother-in-law Squire Dale. Lily falls in love with a civil servant, Adolphus Crosbie, but he jilts her for an unhappy and unsuccessful marriage to Lady Alexandrina De Courcy. Lily's love for him prevents her marrying the devoted Johnny Eames. A related plot deals with Eames's romantic and financial entanglements in London; the public thrashing he gives Crosbie makes him a local hero. Lily's sister resists an advantageous match with her cousin Bernard and instead marries a local physician, Dr Crofts. The saddest of the Barsetshire novels, it established Lily Dale as a favourite heroine with the public. Plantagenet Palliser, a central character in the PALLISER NOVELS, first appears in *A Small House at Allington*.

Smart, Christopher 1722–71 Poet. He was first an undergraduate and then, from 1745, a Fellow of Pembroke College, Cambridge, where he fell into debt and began to display signs of erratic and obsessive behaviour which intensified with age. In 1749 he went to London and worked as a journalist for the publisher NEWBERY, whose stepdaughter he married in 1752.

Poems on Several Occasions (1752) was followed by *The Hilliad* (1753), a rather weak SATIRE on the quack doctor John Hill. *Hymn to the Supreme Being* (1756) gave thanks for his recovery from illness, but he was already teetering on the brink of a religious mania which gave rise to sudden, impassioned bouts of prayer and extravagant incantation. During the next seven years he was forcibly confined in St Luke's Hospital for intermittent periods, busying himself with his gardening, his cat Jeffrey and his writing. He produced two exceptional poems. The first, *A Song to David* (1763), was largely disregarded by his contemporaries but has become his best-known work. It is a hymn of praise to the author of the Psalms, an alliterative ecstasy which combines the compression of lyric with the splendour of religious language. Less conventional, *Jubilate Agno* (not published until 1939) is unique in 18th-century verse: an extended incantation on the divinely designed patterns in the natural world with catalogues of rousing, irregular stanzas in praise of the significative variety of Creation. A blend of biblical and Renaissance archaisms and exotic vocabulary, it appears to anticipate some of the verbal effects of more recent verse – though its obscurity seems at points to shade off into absurdity.

For a writer with such an idiosyncratic concept of the effects of language, Smart was notably precise in his classical scholarship. He was much influenced by Horace's *Ars poetica*, and translated the poet's work into prose (1756) and verse (1767), including the notoriously difficult SAPPHICS in the complex variety of metrical schemes he imitated. Among his other work was *A Translation of the Psalms of David* (1765), *The Parables ... Done into Familiar verse* (1768) and *Hymns for the Amusement of Children*, written in 1770 during his final imprisonment for debt.

Smart, Elizabeth 1913–86 Canadian novelist and poet. She spent most of her adult life in England. Her long liaison with GEORGE BARKER prompted *By Grand Central Station I Sat Down and Wept* (1945), a passionate love-poem in prose. She also published a second short novel, *The Assumption of the Rogues and Rascals* (1978), as well as two collections of poems, *A Bonus* (1977) and *Eleven Poems* (1982), and a collection of poetry and prose, *In the Mean Time* (1984). As an expatriate writer, her closest affinities were with English poetry.

Smectymnuus The name adopted by five Presbyterian writers (Stephen Marshall, Edward Calamy, Thomas Young, Matthew Newcomen and William Spurstow) for a pamphlet against episcopacy in 1641. It was attacked by bishops JOSEPH HALL and USSHER and defended by MILTON.

Smedley, Francis Edward 1818–64 Novelist. He was known for novels blending romance with sport and adventure. The most popular was *Frank Fairleigh: or, Scenes from the Life of a Private Pupil* (1850); others were *Lewis Arundel* (1852) and *Harry Coverdale's Courtship* (1855).

Smiles, Samuel 1812–1904 Biographer and essayist. His belief in work and self-improvement emerges clearly from his biographies of successful men of the industrial age: *George Stephenson* (1857), *The Lives of the Engineers* (1867, expanded 1874) and *Josiah Wedgwood*

(1894). *Self-Help: With Illustrations of Character and Conduct* (1859) sold in enormous numbers. *Character* (1871), *Thrift* (1875) and *Duty* (1880) continued his work as a popular moralist.

Smith, A(rthur) J(ames) M(arshall) 1902–80 Canadian poet. *News of the Phoenix and Other Poems* (1943), *A Sort of Ecstasy* (1954), *Collected Poems* (1962), *Poems: New and Collected* (1967) and *The Classic Shade* (1978) demonstrate his sharp and finely controlled style. He published a number of anthologies of Canadian verse as well as works of criticism: *Towards a View of Canadian Letters: Selected Essays 1928–72* (1973) and *On Poetry and Poets* (1977).

Smith, Adam 1723–90 Philosopher and political economist. While professor of logic and of moral philosophy at Glasgow University he delivered the lectures which became THE THEORY OF MORAL SENTIMENTS (1759). The book made his reputation, leading to his election as a Fellow of the Royal Society in 1766 and allowing him to leave Glasgow for a Continental tour, as tutor to the young Duke of Buccleuch, during which he met Voltaire in Geneva and the Physiocrats in Paris. His major work, THE WEALTH OF NATIONS (1776), was begun during the tour and was continued in his native Kirkcaldy as well as Edinburgh and London. In London he spent time at 'the Club' with GIBBON, BURKE, JOSHUA REYNOLDS, JOHNSON (with whom he was not on good terms), BOSWELL and GARRICK. He read a draft of parts of *The Wealth of Nations* to BENJAMIN FRANKLIN. He was also intimate with the major figures of the Scottish Enlightenment, notably John Millar, WILLIAM ROBERTSON, ADAM FERGUSON, Joseph Black, James Hutton, Hugh Blair and DUGALD STEWART. After DAVID HUME's death Smith showed his loyalty by publishing a controversial edition of his friend's autobiography (1777).

He moved to Edinburgh in 1778 as Commissioner of Customs for Scotland and of Salt Duties, taking an active part in the intellectual life of the city and becoming a founder-member of the Royal Society of Edinburgh in 1783. He was elected Lord Rector of Glasgow University in 1787, serving until 1789. He also edited the poems of the Jacobite William Hamilton of Bangour (1748) and wrote *On the First Formation of Languages* (1761). Some essays, including the 'History of Astronomy', appeared posthumously in 1795 as *Essays on Philosophical Subjects*, and *Lectures on Jurisprudence* in 1896.

Smith, Alexander 1830–67 Poet. *Poems* (1853) contained 'A Life Drama' praised by reviewers but ridiculed by AYTOUN as part of the SPASMODIC SCHOOL OF POETRY. *Sonnets on the War*, with DOBELL, appeared during the Crimean War in 1855. *City Poems* (1857) contained what is usually regarded as his best poem, 'Glasgow'. *Edwin of Deira* (1861) helped him live down his reputation but provoked the accusation that he had plagiarized from TENNYSON's IDYLLS OF THE KING. He turned to prose.

Smith, Charlotte 1749–1806 Novelist and poet. Her first published work was a translation of Prévost's *Manon Lescaut* (1785), though she became known as a poet and, chiefly, as a novelist. *Emmeline: or, The Orphan of the Castle* (1788) and *The Old Manor House* (1793) were widely admired.

Smith, George (Murray) 1824–1901 Publisher. He took charge of his father's firm, Smith Elder, in 1843. The BRONTË sisters were his most famous discovery, but he added many great Victorians to his list: RUSKIN, THACKERAY, HARRIET MARTINEAU, ELIZABETH GASKELL,

ROSSETTI, WILKIE COLLINS, CHARLES READE, ROBERT BROWNING, DARWIN, MEREDITH and MRS HUMPHRY WARD. He founded THE CORNHILL MAGAZINE in 1860 and, with Frederick Greenwood, THE PALL MALL GAZETTE in 1865. In 1882 he started to publish *The Dictionary of National Biography*, edited by LESLIE STEPHEN.

Smith, Goldwin 1823–1910 Historian, literary critic and reformer. Appointed Regius Professor of Modern History at Oxford in 1859, he identified himself with the cause of liberal reform, taking a sceptical position about religion in a disagreement with Bishop Wilberforce, attacking imperialism in *The Empire* (1863), supporting the North in the American Civil War, and joining JOHN STUART MILL to urge the impeachment of Governor Eyre of Jamaica in 1867. He became the first professor of English and constitutional history at Cornell University in 1868 and finally settled in Canada. Later works include political histories of the United States (1893) and the United Kingdom (1899), a volume on COWPER (1880) and a life of JANE AUSTEN (1892).

Smith, Iain Crichton 1928– Scottish poet, translator, playwright, novelist and short-story writer. He writes in English and Gaelic and translates his own work and that of other Scottish Gaelic poets, such as SORLEY MACLEAN. The Gaelic language and the landscape and people of the Scottish islands and Highlands figure prominently in his writing. Fiction includes *Consider the Lilies* (1968), *The Dream* (1990), *Selected Stories* (1990) and *An Honourable Death* (1992). Verse, gathered in *Collected Poems* (1992), includes the sequence 'Shall Gaelic Die?' and the much-anthologized 'Old Woman'.

Smith, John Thomas 1766–1833 Miscellaneous writer. As well as many antiquarian and topographical books, he published a maliciously candid biography of the sculptor Joseph Nollekens (1828), his father's employer and his own teacher. *A Book for a Rainy Day: or, Recollections of the Events of the Years 1766–1833* (1845) is a mine of information on literary and artistic life.

Smith, Ken(neth) (John) 1938– Poet. His work is populist, humorous and subversive. Early volumes are featured in *The Poet Reclining: Selected Poems 1962–1980* (1982). Other works are: *Abel Baker* (1981); *Burned Books* (1981); *Terra* (1985); *A Book of Chinese Whispers* (1987), in prose; *Inside Time* (1989), prompted by his work as writer-in-residence in Wormwood Scrubs; and *Berlin: Coming in from the Cold* (1990).

Smith, Michael 1954–83 Jamaican poet. He was associated with the Rastafarian movement and radically influenced by the writings of Marcus Garvey and the teachings of the Guyanese political theorist Walter Rodney. Although some of his work is available in anthologies, he never brought out a printed collection and relied almost entirely on public performance. As a result his poems are now best heard on records such as *Word* (1978), *Me Cyaan Believe It* (1980) and *Roots* (1980). Among the new generation of poets in the Caribbean and 'black' Britain he has been, with Bob Marley and LINTON KWESI JOHNSON, much the most influential.

Smith, Pauline (Janet) 1882–1959 South African short-story writer and novelist. Though she lived mostly in Britain, the austere, rigorously crafted short stories in *The Little Karoo* (1925), and her novel about late 19th-century Boer peasant life, *The Beadle* (1926), show a sensitive grasp of Afrikaner culture. *A.B.* (1933) is a tribute to ARNOLD BENNETT, who first encouraged her.

Smith, Stevie [Florence Margaret] 1902–71 Poet and novelist. She published three novels, *Novel on Yellow*

Paper (1936), *Over the Frontier* (1938) and *The Holiday* (1949), and eight collections of poetry, including *Not Waving But Drowning* (1957). Her wittily barbed verse found a wide and enthusiastic audience, promoted by her distinctive public readings and recordings. It was often illustrated with naive line drawings in the manner of EDWARD LEAR, with whom she shared an often sad but irrepressible love of life. *Collected Poems* appeared in 1975.

Smith, Sydney 1771–1845 Essayist, parson and wit. 'The wisest of witty men, and the wittiest of wise men', he was educated at Winchester and New College, Oxford, and pursued a career in the Church which culminated in his appointment as Canon Residentiary at St Paul's in 1831. During his years in Edinburgh he joined the circle of SIR WALTER SCOTT, DUGALD STEWART and FRANCIS HORNER and helped to found THE *EDINBURGH REVIEW* in 1802. In London he became a popular preacher, a lecturer in moral philosophy and a familiar among the Whigs of Holland House. Charming, witty and blessed with common sense, Sydney Smith is rare among divines of any age. He published sermons as well as pamphlets, reviews and essays on matters as varied as Dissent, Catholic Emancipation, alehouse licensing and female education.

Smith, Sydney Goodsir 1915–75 Scottish poet. Several minor books of verse appeared before *Under the Eildon Tree* (1948), 24 elegies on the unhappy loves of poets, with a wide range of literary reference reinforcing the autobiographical element. For all its background in earlier texts, his fluent and effective Scots has the suppleness of spoken language. His other major works are a play, *The Wallace* (1960), and a novel, *Carotid Cornucopius* (1947, revised 1964). Smith was in many ways the principal successor to HUGH MACDIARMID, with whom his linguistic affinities are strong.

Smith, William Robertson 1846–94 Biblical scholar. His contributions to the ninth edition of the *Encyclopaedia Britannica*, which began publication in 1875, were influenced by the HIGHER CRITICISM and angered the General Assembly of the Free Church of Scotland by their failure to present the Bible as the authoritative word of God. He was dismissed from his professorship at Aberdeen in 1881. After working as joint editor of the *Encyclopaedia Britannica*, he became professor of Arabic at Cambridge in 1883.

Smithyman, Kendrick 1922– New Zealand poet and critic. Although associated with ALLEN CURNOW, he has always been less interested in a poetry of national identity, drawing adroitly and innovatively on MODERNISM. Early work in *The Blind Mountain* (1950) and other volumes is tortuously difficult. *Earthquake Weather* (1972) and *The Seal in the Dolphin Pool* (1974) continue earlier preoccupations with place, history and language in a more relaxed style and more open forms. *Dwarf with a Billiard Cue* (1978) and *Stories about Wooden Keyboards* (1985) have pronounced social and comic elements. *A Way of Saying* (1965) remains the only full-length critical study of New Zealand poetry.

Smollett, Tobias (George) 1721–71 Novelist, travel-writer, critic, political controversialist, unsuccessful playwright and poet. Born at Leven, near Loch Lomond, he studied at Glasgow and Edinburgh universities and became a surgeon's mate in the navy, serving under Admiral Vernon at the siege of Cartagena in 1741. His youthful writing included poetry – *The Tears of Scotland* (1746), about the Duke of Cumberland's reprisals after

the 1745 rebellion, and the satirical *Advice* (1746) and *Reproof* (1747) – and a stubbornly unperformed play about James I of Scotland, *The Regicide*, which he published in 1749. His first novel, THE *ADVENTURES OF RODERICK RANDOM* (1748), drew on his naval experience and theatrical disappointments. THE *ADVENTURES OF PEREGRINE PICKLE* (1751) continued the vein of violent, hard-bitten PICARESQUE for which his novels are known. Though he obtained the degree of Doctor of Physic in 1752, he soon abandoned his practice in Bath for London, where he earned an insecure living from literary hack work. THE *ADVENTURES OF FERDINAND COUNT FATHOM* appeared in 1753 and his translation of *Don Quixote* in 1755. A comedy, *The Reprisal: or, The Tars of Old England*, was staged in 1757 at DRURY LANE by GARRICK, whom he had caricatured as Marmoset in *Roderick Random*. As editor of the *Critical Review or Annals of Literature* in 1756–63 he was relentlessly quarrelsome with other authors and spent three months in prison for libel. While there, he wrote THE *LIFE AND ADVENTURES OF SIR LAUNCELOT GREAVES*, printed in *The British Magazine* (which he edited 1760–1) and in volume form in 1762. His *Complete History of England Deduced from the Defeat of Julius Caesar to the Treaty of Aix-la-Chapelle, 1748* (1758) brought him some financial success. *The Briton*, the journal he started in 1762 to defend the Earl of Bute, the Prime Minister, prompted WILKES to reply with THE *NORTH BRITON*. The controversy dissolved their friendship, without preventing Bute's resignation or earning Smollett his gratitude.

Smollett went to France and Italy for his health in 1764. *TRAVELS THROUGH FRANCE AND ITALY* (1766) confirmed his reputation for ill-temper and prompted STERNE to caricature him in *A SENTIMENTAL JOURNEY* as 'the learned Smelfungus'. *Adventures of an Atom* (1769) is a political SATIRE. A journey, again in search of health, to Edinburgh and Inverary in 1770 contributed impressions to his last and arguably most accomplished novel, THE *EXPEDITION OF HUMPHRY CLINKER* (1771). He died at Leghorn.

Snodgrass, W(illiam) D(eWitt) 1926– American poet. Usually autobiographical, his poetry uses traditional forms and a sensitive, often delicate tone. His first volume, *Heart's Needle* (1959; PULITZER PRIZE), centred on his divorce from his first wife and the resulting separation from his daughter. Later volumes include *Selected Poems 1957–1987* (1987). He has also published translations and *Radical Pursuit: Critical Essays and Lectures* (1975).

Snow, C(harles) P(ercy), 1st Baron Snow of Leicester 1905–80 Novelist. His career as scientist and eventually politician is mirrored in his ROMAN FLEUVE, *Strangers and Brothers* (1940–70). *Strangers and Brothers* (1940; later retitled *George Passant*), *The Light and the Dark* (1947), *Time of Hope* (1949), *The Masters* (1951), *The New Men* (1954), *Homecomings* (1956), *The Conscience of the Rich* (1958), *The Affair* (1959), *Corridors of Power* (1963), *The Sleep of Reason* (1968) and *Last Things* (1970) follow the career of Lewis Eliot in a leisurely manner permitting a wide survey of contemporary life. His influential *The Two Cultures and the Scientific Revolution* (1959), arguing that literary intellectuals and scientists had ceased to communicate, was savagely attacked by F. R. LEAVIS for its utilitarian approach to the study of the humanities. *Science and Government* (1961) examined the power factor in government-sponsored research. *Public Affairs* (1971) deals with the dangers as well as the benefits of technology. A

Variety of Men (1967) presents biographical studies. Snow married PAMELA HANSFORD JOHNSON in 1950.

Snyder, Gary 1930– American poet. He shares with JACK KEROUAC, ALLEN GINSBERG and other members of the BEATS an interest in experimental forms, a rejection of mainstream American values and a preoccupation with Buddhism, which he studied in Japan. The many volumes which have followed his first, *Riprap* (1959), include *Turtle Island* (1974; PULITZER PRIZE), *Left Out in the Rain: Poems 1947–1984* (1986) and *No Nature: New and Selected Poems* (1992). *Earth House Hold* (1969), *The Old Ways: Six Essays* (1977) and *The Real Work: Interviews and Talks 1964–1979* (edited by Scott McLean; 1980) are among his prose collections.

Sohrab and Rustum: *An Episode* A poem by MATTHEW ARNOLD, published in *Poems: A New Edition* (1853). The story comes from Firdousi's *Shah Nameh*, a Persian epic. The Persian hero Rustum encounters Sohrab, the son he never knew he had, in single combat when the Tartar armies attack Persia. When he realizes that he is fighting his father, Sohrab recoils and is struck down. He dies at his father's feet. With its heroic subject and frequent use of the EPIC SIMILE, the poem deliberately sets out to avoid the melancholy subjectivity which the preface to the volume diagnosed as one of the ills of contemporary poetry.

Soldiers Three A collection of 13 stories by KIPLING, published in 1888 alongside the booklets entitled *Under the Deodars*, *The Phantom Rickshaw* and *Wee Willie Winkie* and reprinted with them in a two-volume collection (1892). The stories depict the soldierly virtues necessary to sustain the Empire and the daily life of the British fighting man on the alert against potential invaders from Afghanistan. Elements of FARCE and MELODRAMA are most evident in the short episodes of battle and skirmish. But the strongest ingredients are the atmosphere of the brooding landscape and the men's stoicism, companionship and ability to survive a tedious, emotionally cheerless routine.

soliloquy The convention permitting an actor, alone on the stage, to address the audience directly. Although it dates from the earliest years of English drama, the use of the soliloquy to allow an actor to talk revealingly to himself was largely an invention of the Elizabethan playwrights. The opening speech of MARLOWE'S *DOCTOR FAUSTUS* is a flamboyant early example.

Soliloquy of the Spanish Cloister A poem by ROBERT BROWNING, published in *Dramatic Lyrics* (1842). It is a DRAMATIC MONOLOGUE by a spiteful monk who envies the innocent happiness of his fellow, Brother Lawrence.

Somerville, Edith See SOMERVILLE AND ROSS.

Somerville, William 1675–1742 Poet. His slender reputation depends on *The Chace* (1735), a poem in four books of Miltonic BLANK VERSE, describing the pleasures of hunting and the variety of dogs, hounds, terrain and quarry. The work enjoyed a certain circulation, though it prompted a scathing treatment of its author in JOHNSON's *LIVES OF THE POETS*. *Field Sports* (1742) deals with hawking and *Hobbinol* (1740) is a MOCK-HEROIC PASTORAL.

Somerville and Ross [Somerville, Edith Anna Oenone (1858–1949) and Martin, Violet Florence (1862–1915)] Novelists, short-story writers and travel-writers. The most popular of the cousins' work represents the Anglo-Irish tradition of exploiting the humours of the true Irish in relation to the owners of the big houses and estates. It includes: *An Irish Cousin* (1889), their first book; *The Real Charlotte* (1894), their most ambitious novel; *In the Vine Country* (1893); *The Silver Fox* (1898), a novel about hunting; and the enormously popular *Some Experiences of an Irish RM* (1899), stories about a resident magistrate in Ireland, continued in *Further Experiences of an Irish RM* (1908). Edith Somerville continued to use the pseudonym after Violet Martin's death, in *The Big House of Inver* (1925) among other works.

Songs of Innocence and of Experience *Shewing the Two Contrary States of the Human Soul* A collection of poems and etchings by BLAKE, issued in 1794 but incorporating his *Songs of Innocence* (1789).

Some of the *Songs of Innocence* appear to issue directly from the mouths of children; others view infancy through the eyes of mothers and nurses. Poems such as 'The Divine Image', 'Night' and 'On Another's Sorrow', on the other hand, quietly suggest an opposite world of sorrow and violence of which the child is necessarily unaware. The *Songs of Experience* – including 'The Tyger' and 'The Sick Rose', Blake's most frequently quoted and interpreted works – contain a number of poems whose titles echo the *Songs of Innocence*, showing how the experiences of adult life corrupt and finally destroy innocence. The two Nurse's songs are a striking instance of Blake's antithetical procedure. Similarly, the innocent anarchy of 'The Echoing Green' contrasts with the religious prohibitions of 'The Garden of Love'. Blake's attack on institutionalized coercion and enslavement embraces the creation of poverty in the midst of plenty ('Holy Thursday', 'Infant Sorrow') and the moral and psychological devastations of early capitalism ('London').

sonnet COLERIDGE defined the sonnet as 'a small poem, in which some lonely [i.e. single and coherent] feeling is developed'. Traditionally it is a short single-stanza lyric in iambic pentameters (see METRE), usually consisting of 14 lines, rhyming in various patterns. The PETRARCHAN sonnet has an octave (8 lines) rhyming abba abba and a sestet (6 lines) rhyming cde cde (or some variation such as ccd ccd). WYATT was an early imitator of Petrarchan sonnets in England. The English or Shakespearean sonnet, developed by SURREY and others in the 16th century, consisted of three quatrains and a concluding couplet. The late 16th century saw a vogue for sonnet sequences, such as SHAKESPEARE'S *Sonnets*, SIDNEY's *ASTROPHIL AND STELLA* and SPENSER's *AMORETTI*. In the 17th century DONNE and MILTON expanded the sonnet's range from love poetry to include religious feelings and serious contemplation. Most of the Romantic poets wrote sonnets, and the form is still used by practising poets.

Sonnets from the Portuguese A sequence of SONNETS by ELIZABETH BARRETT BROWNING, published in *Poems* (1850). The deliberately misleading title – there are no Portuguese originals – veils the intensely personal nature of these love poems, written before her marriage to ROBERT BROWNING in 1846.

Sonnets of Shakespeare See SHAKESPEARE'S *SONNETS*.

Sons and Lovers A novel by D. H. LAWRENCE, published in 1913. Largely autobiographical, it is based on his childhood and youth. Gertrude Coppard, a schoolteacher, marries Walter Morel, a miner, but he drinks heavily and resists her efforts to change him. She concentrates her energies on her children and, after the death of her oldest son, William, makes Paul Morel the focus of her emotions and aspirations. Walter Morel is scorned and excluded by his family. Paul works as a junior clerk in Nottingham and paints in his spare time. He falls in love with Miriam Leivers, an intense, reserved and 'spiritual' girl. Mrs Morel is jealous. Later Paul has an affair with Clara Dawes, a married woman, and is also powerfully drawn to her husband, Baxter. Mrs Morel suffers a long and painful illness, which Paul relieves by administering morphia. After her death he determines to set out and make his own life.

Sontag, Susan 1933–   American critic. She is best known for her essays on *avant-garde* film and for her literary criticism, collected in *Against Interpretation* (1966), *Styles of Radical Will* (1969) and *Under the Sign of Saturn* (1980). Influential longer studies are: *On Photography* (1977); *Illness as Metaphor* (1977), written after she contracted cancer; and *AIDS and its Metaphors* (1989). Her novels are *The Benefactor* (1963), *Death Kit* (1967) and *The Volcano Lover* (1992), about Nelson. *I, etcetera* (1978) is a collection of short fiction. She has also written two filmscripts, *Duet for Cannibals* (1969) and *Brother Carl* (1971).

Sordello A poem by ROBERT BROWNING, published in 1840. Set in the early 13th century against the background of the struggles between Guelphs and Ghibellines, it concerns the troubadour Sordello, torn between his vocation as a poet and the duties of his birthright. It remains the most challenging and impenetrable of Browning's works.

Sorley, Charles (Hamilton) 1895–1915 Poet. He served with the Suffolk Regiment in World War I and was killed at the Battle of Loos. *Marlborough and Other Poems* (1916) contained several SONNETS which anticipate the anti-romanticism of later war poets, notably those beginning 'When you see millions of the mouthless dead' and 'Such, such is death; no triumph: no defeat.' *The Letters of Charles Sorley* (1919) contain some of his best writing, including acute criticism of RUPERT BROOKE. *Collected Poems* was edited by Jean Moorcroft Wilson (1985).

Sound and the Fury, The A novel by WILLIAM FAULKNER, published in 1929. The decline of the Compson family, and the crucial role played by the daughter, Caddy, who ran away, is evoked in four separate sections, largely reliant on STREAM OF CONSCIOUSNESS. The first three are narrated by Caddy's brothers: Benjy, an 'idiot'; Quentin, who kills himself while a freshman at Harvard; and the embittered Jason. The final section concentrates on the Compsons' black servant, Dilsey, and her grandson, Luster. An appendix which Faulkner added in 1946 reviews the history of the Compson family from 1699 to 1945 and ends with this assessment of the blacks who served the Compsons: 'They endured.'

Souster, Raymond 1921–   Canadian poet. Above all a poet of Toronto, he is a prolific writer of short lyrics describing ordinary aspects of the urban experience in an economical, understated manner. The colloquialism of his style stands in marked contrast to the academicism of much modern Canadian verse. His many volumes include the four-volume *Collected Poems, 1940–80* (1980–3), *Going the Distance* (1983) and *Asking for More* (1988). Throughout his career he has been active in promoting the work of other poets through editions, anthologies and Contact Press, which he founded with LOUIS DUDEK and IRVING LAYTON. He has also published two novels.

Soutar, William 1898–1943 Scottish poet. He worked in the same vein as HUGH MACDIARMID to establish a distinctively contemporary Scots poetry (see SCOTTISH RENAISSANCE). His first publication was *Gleanings by an Undergraduate* (1923), his last the posthumous *The Expectant Silence* (1944). Most of his work is brought together in *Collected Poems* (1948), edited with an introductory essay by MacDiarmid, and *Poems in Scots and English* (1961), edited by W. R. Aitken. The autobiographical *Diaries of a Dying Man* (1954) was edited by A. Scott.

South, Robert 1634–1716 Preacher and theologian. He was chaplain to CLARENDON, Public Orator to the University of Oxford and rector of Islip in Oxfordshire. His sermons (eventually collected and published in 1823) were known for their clarity and wit, qualities also displayed in his attack on the unfortunate WILLIAM SHERLOCK in *Animadversions on Mr Sherlock's Book* (1693) and *Tritheism Charged* (1695).

South English Legendary, The A collection of narrative EXEMPLA incorporating biblical history and SAINTS' LIVES, developed by accretion through the 13th to 15th centuries. A successor to the *Legenda aurea* (*THE GOLDEN LEGEND*), it was apparently written by friars for a secular audience. Over 50 manuscripts survive, each in effect a different version.

Southall, Ivan (Francis) 1921–   Australian writer of CHILDREN'S LITERATURE. After producing orthodox adventure stories, he found his true talents in tough, realistic stories, often involving disasters: *Hills End* (1962), *Ash Road* (1965), *To the Wild Sky* (1967) and its sequel, *A City out of Sight* (1985), and *Finn's Folly* (1969). *Let the Balloon Go* (1968) and *Josh* (1971) concentrate more on inner conflict than external threat.

Southern Literary Messenger, The The longest-lived of American antebellum Southern literary magazines, published in Richmond, Virginia, in 1834–64. It printed fiction, poetry, travel accounts, and sketches of Southern life and manners by such writers as JOHN ESTEN COOKE, WILLIAM GILMORE SIMMS, JOSEPH G. BALDWIN and AUGUSTUS BALDWIN LONGSTREET, as well as tales, poems and reviews by POE, editor in 1835–7.

Southerne, Thomas 1660–1746 Playwright. Of his ten plays, the best are *Sir Anthony Love* (1690) and *The Maid's Last Prayer* (1693), both comedies, and two sentimental tragedies adapted from stories by BEHN, *The Fatal Marriage* (1694) and *OROONOKO* (1695). *The Wives' Excuse* (1691) is of interest as a transitional piece between the work of ETHEREGE and WYCHERLEY and the more elegant plays of CONGREVE and VANBRUGH.

Southey, Robert 1774–1843 Poet, historian and man of letters. In his rebellious youth he was expelled from Westminster School for criticizing corporal punishment. While at Oxford he wrote *Joan of Arc* (1792, published 1796), a poem in support of the French Revolution, and *Wat Tyler* (published 1817), a republican play. In 1794 he met COLERIDGE, with whom he collaborated on another play, *The Fall of Robespierre*, and abortive plans for a 'Pantisocratic' community in America. In 1795 he married Elizabeth Fricker, whose sister, Sara, married Coleridge. During this period Southey wrote many of his best-remembered lyrics and BALLADS: 'My Days among the Dead are Past', 'The Inchcape Rock', 'The Battle of Blenheim' and 'The Holly Tree'.

Visits to Portugal in 1795 and to Portugal and Spain in 1800–1 confirmed the change from radical to Tory which would make him the *bête noire* of the next generation of Romantics. Settled at Greta Hall in Keswick, he was misleadingly classed with WORDSWORTH and Coleridge as one of the LAKE POETS. *Thalaba the Destroyer* (1801), an oriental epic which gave SHELLEY the irregular verse form for *QUEEN MAB*, was followed by another exotic narrative, *Madoc* (1805). A growing family and the additional responsibility of caring for Coleridge's family during his erstwhile friend's absence in Malta obliged Southey to write virtually without pause. His abridgement of *Amadis of Gaul* (1803) was followed by a translation of *Palmerin of England* (1807), *Letters from England by Don Manuel Alvarez Espriella* (observations on English manners and society; 1807), a translation of the *Chronicle of the Cid* (1808), and *The Curse of Kehama* (1810), another tale in the oriental mode. Between 1809 and 1838 he contributed more than 100 political articles to the Tory *QUARTERLY REVIEW*. Other works include a very readable *Life of Nelson* (1813), a Christian romance entitled *Roderick the Last of the Goths* (1814), a three-volume *History of Brazil* (1810–19) and a *Life of Wesley* (1820).

His appointment as POET LAUREATE in 1813 led to various public poems, including 'The Poet's Pilgrimage to Waterloo' (1816), 'Princess Charlotte's Epithalamium and her Elegy' (1817) and several ODES. Such work set the seal on his reputation as a radical who had prostituted himself to the Establishment. In 1817 he failed to stop the publication of *Wat Tyler* by his liberal enemies. Other attacks included PEACOCK's caricature of him as Mr Feathernest in *MELINCOURT* (1817). Southey responded with provocations of his own, most disastrously *A VISION OF JUDGEMENT* (1821), an apotheosis of George III prefaced by a violent attack on BYRON, who replied devastatingly with *THE VISION OF JUDGEMENT*. Until his mind became clouded in his last years, Southey's prolific output continued with: *The Book of the Church* (1824); *A Tale of Paraguay* (1825), a poem; *Sir Thomas More* (1829), a conversation between the author and More's ghost; the long ballads *All for Love* and *The Pilgrim to Compostella* (1829); *Essays Moral and Political* (1832); a *History of the Peninsular War* (1823–32); *Lives of the British Admirals* (1833); and, most interesting of all his late works, *The Doctor* (1834–7), a miscellany of anecdote, quotation and comment.

Southwell, Robert ?1561–95 Poet and Catholic martyr. Trained at the Jesuit School in Douai and ordained in Rome, he returned to England as part of the Jesuit mission in 1586. He was captured in 1592 and finally executed in 1595. Some early Latin poems and meditations survive from the period of his novitiate, but the bulk of his poetry is in English. His best-known poem, 'The Burning Babe' (published in the collection *Maeoniae*, 1595), uses PETRARCHAN language to meditate on Christ's Passion. *St Peter's Complaint* (1595) is a lengthy narrative about the life of Christ, put into the mouth of the repentant saint. A prose work, *An Epistle of Comfort*, was secretly printed in 1587 and his letters were circulated in manuscript. His *Fourfold Meditation on the Four Last Things* appeared in 1606. Southwell was beatified in 1929.

Sowdon of Babylon, The A VERSE ROMANCE (c. 1400). The Sowdon (Sultan) captures Rome before the arrival of Charlemagne's army. The Sowdon's son, Ferumbras, is taken and submits to baptism (see *SIR FIRUMBRAS*) but Roland, Oliver and other knights are captured. The Sowdon's daughter, Floripas, falls in love with one of them and releases them. The Sowdon is defeated by Charlemagne and is executed.

Soyinka, Wole 1934– Nigerian playwright, novelist and poet. His basic dramatic mode is comedy, ranging from geniality to angry FARCE and SATIRE in such works as *The Trials of Brother Jero* (*Three Plays*, 1963), *The Lion and the Jewel* (1963), *A Dance of the Forests* (1963), *Kongi's Harvest* (1967), *Madmen and Specialists* (1971), *Jero's Metamorphosis* (1973), *A Play of Giants* (1984) and *Requiem for a Futurologist* (1985). Yoruba cosmography and culture, explicated in *Myth, Literature and the African World* (1976), are used persistently but questioningly as dramatic themes in *The Swamp Dwellers* and *The Strong Breed* (*Three Plays*, 1963), *The Road* (1965) and *Death and the King's Horseman* (1975). The relation of Yoruba belief to modern life is also examined in the title-poem of *Idanre and Other Poems* (1968) and novels such as *The Interpreters* (1965) and the powerful *Season of Anomy* (1973). He writes about his imprisonment during the Nigerian Civil War in a prose journal, *The Man Died* (1973), and verse collections, *Poems from Prison* (1969) and *A Shuttle in the Crypt* (1972). His long poem *Ogun Abibiman* (1976) and some poems in *Mandela's Earth* (1988) call for the liberation of South Africa. *Aké: The Years of Childhood* (1981) and *Isara: A Voyage around 'Essay'* (1990) are memoirs. Other works include *Art, Dialogue and Outrage: Essays on Literature and Culture* (1988). He received the Nobel Prize for Literature in 1986.

Spanish Tragedy, The: or, *Hieronimo is Mad Again* A play by THOMAS KYD, produced c. 1589 and published in 1592. It made the REVENGE TRAGEDY, derived from Seneca, popular on the Renaissance stage. Hieronimo is a marshal of Spain at the time of his country's victory over Portugal in 1580. His son Horatio loves Bel-imperia but her brother Lorenzo and the King want her to marry Balthazar, son of the Viceroy of Portugal. Lorenzo and Balthazar surprise the lovers and kill Horatio. Beside himself with grief, Hieronimo persuades them to join him and Bel-imperia in a play acted before the court, and carries out his revenge in the play within the play. Hieronimo and Bel-imperia then take their own lives.

Spark, Muriel (Sarah) 1918– Novelist, short-story writer and poet. She established her talent for IRONY and black humour in *The Comforters* (1957), *Memento Mori* (1959) and *The Ballad of Peckham Rye* (1960). She is perhaps best known for *THE PRIME OF MISS JEAN BRODIE* (1961), successfully filmed, and *Girls of Slender Means* (1963), set in Kensington. Other novels include *The Mandelbaum Gate* (1965), *The Public Image* (1968), *The Driver's Seat* (1970), *The Take-Over* (1976), *Loitering with Intent* (1981), *A Far Cry from Kensington* (1988) and *Symposium* (1990). *Collected Stories* and *Collected Poems* both appeared in 1967. *Curriculum Vitae* (1992) is an autobiography.

Spasmodic School of Poetry, The A term coined by WILLIAM AYTOUN to ridicule the extravagance of feeling and language in the work of PHILIP JAMES BAILEY, SYDNEY DOBELL and ALEXANDER SMITH.

Spectator, The A journal founded and jointly conducted by STEELE and ADDISON, appearing daily from 1 March 1711 to 6 December 1712 (a total of 555 issues). Addison revived it for a further 80 issues in 1714. Other contributors included POPE, AMBROSE PHILIPS, LADY MARY WORTLEY MONTAGU, TICKELL, EUSDEN and PARNELL. *The Spectator* was presented as the work of a small club of representative gentlemen: Sir Andrew Freeport (commerce), Captain Sentry (the army), Will Honeycombe (the townsman), and an anonymous lawyer and anonymous clergyman. The periodical's most enduringly famous creation, Sir Roger de Coverley, was the country gentleman. Mr Spectator himself was a detached observer.

Speed, John ?1552–1629 Map-maker and historian. His pioneering series of 44 maps of England and Wales was collected in 1611 as *The Theatre of the Empire of Great Britain*, the same year as his *History of Great Britain*, a project in which he had been encouraged by CAMDEN and SIR ROBERT BRUCE COTTON.

Speed the Plough A melodramatic comedy by THOMAS MORTON, produced in 1800. The main plot is a mawkish story of quarrelling brothers eventually reconciled. Much better is a sub-plot displaying Farmer Ashfield's simple goodness. The play earned a place in cultural history by its author's invention of Mrs Grundy, who never appears but is constantly referred to by Ashfield's wife as an arbiter of acceptable behaviour.

Speke, John Hanning 1827–64 Explorer. He was SIR RICHARD BURTON's companion on two East African expeditions, to Somaliland (1854) and to the interior (1857–9), where they discovered Lake Tanganyika. Speke continued alone to discover Lake Victoria, which he took, correctly but without evidence, to be the source of the Nile. His *Journal of the Discovery of the Source of the Nile* appeared in 1863.

Spencer, Elizabeth 1921– American novelist and short-story writer. Her Southern experience is evident in many of her short stories and in her first three novels, *Fire in the Morning* (1948), *This Crooked Way* (1952) and *The Voice at the Back Door* (1956). Other novels include: *The Light in the Piazza* (1960), *Knights and Dragons* (1965), *No Place for an Angel* (1968), *The Snare* (1972), *The Salt Lines* (1984) and *The Night Travellers* (1991). Her stories have been collected as *Ship Island and Other Stories* (1968), *The Stories of Elizabeth Spencer* (1981), *Jack of Diamonds and Other Stories* (1988) and *On the Gulf* (1991).

Spencer, Herbert 1820–1903 Philosopher and social scientist. He left school at 16, worked as a railway engineer and became sub-editor of *The Economist* in 1848. His speculative and synthesizing bent of mind began to declare itself in powerful writing in the 1850s, which includes *Social Statics: or, The Conditions Essential to Human Happiness Specified* (1851), later much admired, and 'Development Hypothesis' (1852), an essay setting forth a general theory of evolution before DARWIN. The determination to work from *First Principles* (1862) through to a 'synthetic philosophy' dominated his writing career. *Education* (1861), which stressed the importance of scientific study, and *The Principles of Sociology* (1876–96) in particular caused great interest and controversy among his contemporaries. Though his polymathism was uneven in depth, his stamina and range of enquiry are still remarkable, as can be seen from *The Principles of Psychology* (1855–72), *The Principles of Biology* (1864–7, enlarged 1898–9) and *The Principles of Sociology*. Spencer was an intimate early friend of GEORGE ELIOT, who may have used him as a model for Casaubon in *MIDDLEMARCH*. His work influenced both HARDY and H. G. WELLS.

Spender, Sir Stephen (Harold) 1909–95 Poet and man of letters. A member of AUDEN's circle at Oxford, he produced his best work in his first major collection, *Poems* (1933). 'I Think Continually of Those Who are Truly Great' displays a natural lyric gift unfulfilled in later writing but, under Auden's influence, muted by a sense of obligation to include the detritus of contemporary life (as in the often anthologized 'The Express' and 'The Pylons'). *Vienna* (1934) is an unsuccessful long poem. *The Still Centre* (1939) contains effective poems about Spain but generally marks a movement towards

more personal work. Although *Poems of Dedication* (1947), *The Edge of Being* (1949) and *The Generous Days* (1969) appeared, Spender seemingly wrote little verse since the war. Instead, he engaged in the busy life of a man of letters, holding many academic posts, editing *ENCOUNTER* (1953–66) and producing critical works which include *The Creative Element* (1953), *The Struggle of the Modern* (1963) and *Love-Hate Relations: A Study of Anglo-American Sensibilities* (1974). *World within World* (1951) is a revealing account of himself and his generation. *Journals 1939–1983* (1987) gives an engagingly frank self-portrait. His poetic career can be surveyed in *Collected Poems 1928–1985* (1985).

Spenser, Edmund ?1552–99 Poet. Born in London, he attended Merchant Taylors' School, where MULCASTER was headmaster and KYD, ANDREWES and THOMAS LODGE were fellow pupils, and Pembroke Hall, Cambridge, where he met GABRIEL HARVEY. In 1579, the year of his first marriage, he entered the Earl of Leicester's service and became familiar with SIR PHILIP SIDNEY and SIR EDWARD DYER. In 1580 he went to Ireland, as secretary to Lord Grey de Wilton, where he lived until 1598 apart from intermittent visits to England. He was buried in Westminster Abbey.

THE SHEPHEARDES CALENDER, his first exercise in PASTORAL, appeared in 1579, dedicated to Sidney. *AMORETTI* and *EPITHALAMION*, published together in one volume in 1595, are a SONNET sequence and marriage hymn which may record his courtship of and marriage to Elizabeth Boyle in 1594. *COLIN CLOUT'S COME HOME AGAIN* (1595) is an autobiographical pastoral. *FOUR HYMNS* (1596) are platonizing reflections on human and divine love, while *PROTHALAMION* (1596) celebrates the double betrothal of Katherine and Elizabeth, the Earl of Worcester's daughters. The first three books of Spenser's great poem, *THE FAERIE QUEENE*, appeared in 1590, with Books IV–VI added in 1596. The six completed books, with the addition of the 'Mutability Cantos', appeared in folio in 1609. Minor works include: the anonymous translations of sonnets by Petrarch and Du Bellay anthologized in *A Theatre Wherein be Represented As Well the Miseries and Calamities That Follow the Voluptuous Worldlings* (1569); the volume *Complaints* (1591); *Daphnaida* (1591), an ELEGY on the death of Lady Howard in imitation of CHAUCER'S *BOOK OF THE DUCHESS*; and the prose dialogue, *A View of the Present State of Ireland*, apparently written in 1598 but not published until 1633. A translation of the pseudo-Platonic *Axiochus* is also attributed, very doubtfully, to Spenser. His collected works were first published in 1611.

The Shepheardes Calender provided English literature with a series of pastorals that could stand comparison with European examples, *The Faerie Queene* with a heroic romance that could claim to outshine the work of Ariosto and Tasso. Sidney's complaints about Spenser's archaisms were repeated by JONSON, who claimed that he 'writ no language' while still commending his 'matter', thus agreeing with MILTON's admiration of the 'sage and serious' Spenser. The 18th century was a great period of Spenser scholarship, with THOMAS WARTON's *Observations on the Faerie Queene* (1754) and Upton's annotated edition of the poem. The AUGUSTAN AGE liked the pictorial quality of Spenser and saw *The Faerie Queene* as a poem of the imagination, although it found its allegory distasteful and its form disquieting. For the Romantics, Spenser was the poet's poet, a poet of dreams, beauty and sensuous appeal, but HAZLITT was not alone in not wishing to meddle with the allegory. In recent years, thanks partly to the championship of C. S. LEWIS, readers and scholars on both sides of the Atlantic have found that Milton's didactic Spenser and the Romantics' charmed dreamer are happily the same man, one whose speaking pictures both teach and delight.

Spenserian stanza A form of STANZA first used by SPENSER in THE FAERIE QUEENE, varying OTTAVA RIMA and adding a final alexandrine to eight iambic pentameters to produce a nine-line stanza rhyming ababbcbcc. BYRON used it in CHILDE HAROLD'S PILGRIMAGE, KEATS in THE EVE OF ST AGNES and SHELLEY in ADONAIS.

Spirit of the Age, The A volume of essays by HAZLITT, published in 1825. Widely regarded as his critical masterpiece, it attempts to synthesize the intellectual life of the Romantic age and the period preceding it. Incisive and authoritative essays deal with the work and personalities of many contemporaries, and contain some of his most mature and balanced criticism of GODWIN, COLERIDGE, WORDSWORTH, BYRON, LAMB and SIR WALTER SCOTT.

Spiritual Quixote, The See GRAVES, RICHARD.

Spoils of Poynton, The A short novel by HENRY JAMES, serialized in 1896 as The Old Things, and published in volume form in 1897. Poynton Park is the home of Owen Gereth and the 'spoils' are the antiques and objets d'art with which his mother has filled it. Mrs Gereth tries to prevent Owen from marrying the tasteless Mona Brigstock by interesting him instead in her kindred spirit, Fleda Vetch. He is increasingly attracted to Fleda, thus reassuring his mother's worries about the fate of the spoils, but Mona insists on the marriage. Owen writes to Fleda from abroad, asking her to choose from Poynton whatever object she would like. She arrives just as the house and its contents inexplicably go up in flames.

spondee See METRE.

Spoon River Anthology A collection of 245 epitaphs in free verse by EDGAR LEE MASTERS, published in 1915. The speakers, from a small town in rural Illinois, reveal their secret ambitions, transgressions and miseries, as well as the interconnectedness of their lives.

Spoonerism The popular name for metathesis, the transposition of the initial letters of two or more words, usually to comic effect. The name derives from the Rev. W. A. Spooner (1844-1930) of New College, Oxford, whose own accidental utterances are said to have included 'Kinquering congs their titles take'.

sprung rhythm See HOPKINS, GERARD MANLEY and METRE.

Squire, Sir **J(ohn) C(ollings)** 1884-1958 Critic and poet. As a journalist, he was a powerful influence in the literary world of the 1920s, leading a clique of Georgian writers (known to its enemies as the 'Squirearchy') in a campaign against MODERNISM. He published several volumes of PARODIES and edited anthologies of modern verse, as well as The Comic Muse (1925). Collected Poems, edited by BETJEMAN, appeared in 1959.

Squire of Low Degree, The A VERSE ROMANCE (c. 1500) made up of motifs familiar from other romances. A poor squire loves a princess, who imposes a seven-year period of trial during which he is betrayed by a dishonest steward and she supposes him dead. He returns as she is about to become an anchoress and they are married. Though the use of the romance form is largely nostalgic and artificial, the descriptions of courtly life are memorably extravagant and picturesque.

Squire's Tale, The See CANTERBURY TALES, THE.

Stacpoole, Henry de Vere 1863-1951 Novelist and short-story writer. He wrote well over 50 novels, of which the first commercial successes were The Crimson Azaleas (1907) and The Blue Lagoon (1908). The latter is a romantic story of a boy and girl shipwrecked on a Pacific island and has been compared to BARRIE's PETER PAN and Maeterlinck's The Blue Bird. It was later filmed. Stacpoole wrote four more 'Blue Lagoon' novels: The Beach of Dreams (1919), The Garden of God (1923), The Gates of Morning (1925) and The Girl of the Golden Reef (1929). He was also a poet and a translator of Sappho and Villon.

Stafford, Jean 1915-79 American novelist and short-story writer. She was part of the literary circle which included ROBERT LOWELL (her former husband), DELMORE SCHWARTZ and RANDALL JARRELL. Her novels are Boston Adventure (1944), The Mountain Lion (1947) and The Catherine Wheel (1952). Her highly crafted stories, originally published in volumes such as Children are Bored on Sunday (1953) and Bad Characters (1964), were gathered in The Collected Stories of Jean Stafford (1969).

Stalky & Co. A collection of nine stories by KIPLING, published in 1899. Five other tales, originally scattered in separate collections, were added to The Complete Stalky & Co. (1929). Kipling drew on his boyhood experiences at the United Services College at Westward Ho! in Devon. Stalky, M'Turk and Beetle (a loose self-portrait of Kipling) conduct a battle of wits with the masters and other boys. It is notable that the authority of the headmaster, 'Prooshian' Bates, is never seriously questioned and that the trio affirms the laws of social responsibility and self-discipline. In the final story the ex-schoolboys continue their exploits in India.

Standing Bear, Luther 1868-1939 American Indian writer. His works deal with Sioux customs and beliefs as well as the life of adjustment in white America, and often criticize government Indian policy. They include My People, My Sioux (an autobiography; 1928), My Indian Boyhood (for children; 1931), The Land of the Spotted Eagle (1933) and Stories of the Sioux (1934).

Stanihurst, Richard 1547-1604 Scholar and historian. One of the most important of the Roman Catholic 'Old English' writers in Ireland, he is best remembered for the Description of Ireland he contributed to the 1577 edition of HOLINSHED's Chronicles and for his friendship with SIR PHILIP SIDNEY. Most of his writings are in Latin.

Stanley, Arthur Penrhyn 1815-81 Churchman. A favourite pupil of THOMAS ARNOLD at Rugby, he became Dean of Westminster in 1864. His conciliatory, anti-dogmatic position won admiration well beyond the bounds of the Anglican Church but made enemies within it. The Life of Dr Arnold (1844) remained his most substantial work, whilst Essays, Chiefly on Questions of Church and State from 1850 to 1870 (1870) provides the best guide to his views on many topical controversies. His determination to celebrate uncontroversial absolutes such as Truth and Unity made the hymns he wrote blandly unremarkable.

Stanley, Sir **Henry Morton** 1841-1904 Journalist and explorer. Born John Rowlands, he emigrated to America at the age of 15 and turned to journalism after an adventurous youth. He became world famous in 1871, when he successfully carried out his assignment for The New York Daily Herald to find the Scottish missionary and explorer, David Livingstone, in Africa. His own career as an explorer included tracing the Congo (Zaire) river from its source to its mouth. How I Found Livingstone

(1872), *Through the Dark Continent* (1878), *In Darkest Africa* (1890) and the autobiography posthumously edited by his widow in 1909 record his experiences.

Stanley, Thomas 1625–78 A descendant of the Stanley family who rose to prominence with the accession of Henry VII, he published a *History of Philosophy* (1655–62), an early and commendable effort at popularization, an edition of Aeschylus (1663), translations from classical poets, and some poems of his own, collected in 1650.

stanza A group of lines of verse, making up a unit repeated throughout a poem. It is often referred to as a 'verse', but strictly speaking a verse (from Latin, 'furrow' or 'turning') is a single line. Since that strict sense accords with such uses as 'rhymed verse', 'free verse' and 'blank verse', stanza is to be preferred for a repeated group of lines.

Stapledon, W[illiam] Olaf 1886–1950 Writer of SCIENCE FICTION. His novels are painstaking exemplary fictions presenting ideas about ethics and evolution. The most famous are *Last and First Men* (1930), a history of man's descendants extending over billions of years, and *Star Maker* (1937), a spectacular vision of the whole universe and its creator. His more orthodox scientific romances – *Odd John* (1935), *Sirius* (1944), *The Flames* (1947) and *A Man Divided* (1950) – deal with exceptional individuals doomed to personal failure.

Stark, Dame Freya 1893–1993 Travel-writer. A long lifetime of courageous solitary expeditions in Arabia, Turkey, etc., has provided material for her many travel books from *Bagdad Sketches* (1933) onwards. Vividly written, with a strong sense both of history and topography, they owe much to their author's indomitable personality, which also suffuses her six-volume collected *Letters* (1974–81).

Stead, C(hristian) K(arlson) 1932– New Zealand critic, poet, short-story writer and novelist. He has published studies of MODERNISM, *The New Poetic* (1964) and *Pound, Yeats, Eliot and the Modernist Movement* (1986), as well as *In the Glass Case* (1981), about New Zealand literature, and *Answering to the Language* (1989), which includes essays on English and Australian writers. His poetry was influenced first by T. S. ELIOT and then by POUND and later American modernists. Collections include *Whether the Will is Free* (1962), *Crossing the Bar* (1972), *Walking Westward* (1979), *Poems of a Decade* (1983) and *Voices* (1990). His novels, often markedly political, include *Smith's Dream* (1971), *All Visitors Ashore* (1984), *The Death of the Body* (1986) and *Sister Hollywood* (1989). *Five for the Symbol* (1981) is a collection of stories.

Stead, Christina (Ellen) 1902–83 Australian novelist and short-story writer. She lived abroad between 1928 and 1974, in Britain, France and the USA, and set only one major work, *Seven Poor Men of Sydney* (1934), in Australia. As a result, though internationally recognized, she was at first not seen as an Australian writer and not properly acknowledged in her own country. Her gift for minute, objective observation of experience is perhaps seen at its best in three novels: *The Man Who Loved Children* (1940), set in America but about her early struggles against a domineering father; *For Love Alone* (1944), about her fight to get to Britain; and *The Dark Places of the Heart* (1966; retitled *Cotter's England* in UK, 1967), about Britain during the Cold War. Other works include: *The Salzburg Tales* (1934), a collection of stories; *The Beauties and Furies* (1936) and *The House of All Nations* (1938), set in Paris; *Letty Fox: Her Luck* (1946), *A Little Tea, A Little Chat* (1948) and *The People with the Dogs* (1952), set in

America; *The Little Hotel* (1973); *Miss Herbert (The Suburban Wife)* (1976); *The Puzzleheaded Girl* (1967), four novellas; *Ocean of Story* (1985), a posthumous collection of stories; and the unfinished *I'm Dying Laughing* (1986). Two collections of letters have appeared (1992).

Stead, W(illiam) T(homas) 1849–1912 Journalist. As editor of THE PALL MALL GAZETTE in 1883–90 he initiated the strident, courageous and influential 'new journalism' of the 1880s. 'The Maiden Tribute of Modern Babylon', articles on procuring a female child for sexual purposes, led to his imprisonment in 1889, but also to a change in the age of consent. He later edited *The Review of Reviews*, became a spiritualist and died in the *Titanic* disaster.

Steele, Sir Richard 1672–1729 Essayist and playwright. Born in Dublin, he was educated at Charterhouse (where he first met ADDISON) and Oxford, which he left without a degree in order to join the Life Guards. *The Christian Hero* (1701), a popular guide to conduct, announced his life-long campaign against duelling. A comedy, *The Funeral* (1701), was followed by two unsuccessful pieces derived from Corneille and Molière. In 1707 ROBERT HARLEY appointed him to write the government-sponsored *Gazette*, and in 1709 Steele founded THE TATLER, which he edited under the pseudonym of ISAAC BICKERSTAFF. Two months after it came to a sudden, unexplained end in January 1711 Addison, who had contributed to *The Tatler*, joined him in founding THE SPECTATOR. This was followed by THE GUARDIAN (March–October 1713) and the more political *Englishman* (1713–14). The most notable of his political pamphlets during this period were *The Importance of Dunkirk Considered* (1713), which provoked a strong reply from SWIFT, and *The Crisis* (1714), an ill-timed consideration of the Hanoverian succession which prompted a charge of seditious libel and lost him his seat as MP for Stockbridge.

With the accession of George I this expulsion was palliated by several official appointments, the most important being patentee of the Theatre Royal, DRURY LANE. The subsequent loss of the patent prompted him to publish *The Theatre* (January–April 1720), a periodical full of details of the contemporary stage. The patent was restored in 1721, enabling Steele to stage his only important dramatic piece, THE CONSCIOUS LOVERS (1722), derived from Terence's *Andria*. Its instant success was in part due to the publicity provoked by *The Theatre*, though its high moral tone also influenced the development of SENTIMENTAL COMEDY.

Steevens, George 1736–1800 Shakespearean scholar. JOHNSON, whom he helped with THE LIVES OF THE POETS, agreed to his plan for a more fully annotated version of his own edition of SHAKESPEARE. The 10-volume Johnson–Steevens edition appeared in 1773 and was several times revised, the last edition, edited by James Boswell the younger in 1821, being based largely on MALONE's work. Steevens had quarrelled with Malone, who had been an earlier collaborator, and tried to displace his edition of Shakespeare with his own 15-volume edition (1793), which took emendation to ridiculous lengths and bore witness to the spite for which he was known. A journalist as well as a scholar, he revelled in EPIGRAM and PARODY. His interest in forgery was shown by his role in the controversies about CHATTERTON and IRELAND. Steevens was also an expert on HOGARTH.

Stein, Gertrude 1874–1946 American woman of letters. From 1903 until her death she lived in France, remaining in Paris except for the period of Nazi occupation. With her companion, Alice B. Toklas, she became the hostess to a circle of painters and writers, including Picasso, Braque, Matisse, Juan Gris, HEMINGWAY, SHERWOOD ANDERSON and F. SCOTT FITZGERALD. Altogether she produced over 500 titles: novels, poems, plays, articles, portraits of famous people and memoirs. *Three Lives: Stories of the Good Anna, Melanctha, and the Gentle Lena* (1909), introduced her highly experimental style, with repeated phrases, sentences and paragraphs, and little punctuation. *The Autobiography of Alice B. Toklas* (1933), probably her best-known work, is a fictionalized account of her own life from her companion's point of view. Others include: *Composition as Explanation* (1926), a critical study; *Lucy Church Amiably* (1930), a novel; *Four Saints in Three Acts* (1929), a lyric drama staged as an opera (with music by Virgil Thompson) in 1934; *Lectures in America* (1935); *Everybody's Autobiography* (1937), which is her own autobiography; *Wars I Have Seen* (1945), a memoir; and *Brewsie and Willie* (1946), a novel about American soldiers in France during and immediately after World War II.

Steinbeck, John 1902–68 American novelist. He came to prominence with *Tortilla Flat* (1935), a vivid portrait of life among the *paisanos* in Monterey. The tone of his work changed with *In Dubious Battle* (1936), a novel about a strike among migratory workers in the California fruit orchards, *Of Mice and Men* (1937), the story of two itinerant farm workers who yearn for some sort of home, and *The Long Valley* (1938), 13 stories set in Salinas Valley. His best-known work is *THE GRAPES OF WRATH* (1939), about a family fleeing from the Oklahoma dust bowl to California. It was followed by *The Moon is Down* (1942), a short novel about Norwegian resistance to the Nazi occupation, *Cannery Row* (1945), in which he returned to the *paisanos* of Monterey, and *The Wayward Bus* (1947), in which passengers on a stranded bus in California become a microcosm of contemporary American frustrations. Among his other novels are *The Pearl* (1947), *East of Eden* (1952), *Sweet Thursday* (1954) and *The Winter of Our Discontent* (1961). His non-fiction includes *Bombs Away: The Story of a Bomber Team* (1942), *The Log of the Sea of Cortez* (1951), a selection of his dispatches as a war correspondent, *Once There was a War* (1958), and *Travels with Charley* (1962), about his personal rediscovery of America. He received the Nobel Prize for literature in 1962.

Steiner, (Francis) George 1929– Critic. His cosmopolitan life and academic career are appropriate to a *Kulturkritik* in the humanist traditions of Central European Jewry, showing a truly international range of learning. The shadow of the Holocaust falls over all his work, but especially *Language and Silence* (1967), *In Bluebeard's Castle* (1971), and the novel *The Portage to San Cristobal of A. H.* (1981). A later venture into fiction, *Proofs and Three Parables* (1992), takes the collapse of Marxism in Eastern Europe as its subject. Steiner's characteristic concern is with the status of language and the literary imagination in a century of barbarism and political terror. His other principal works are *Tolstoy or Dostoevsky* (1959), *The Death of Tragedy* (1961), *After Babel* (1975), *Antigones* (1984) and *Real Presences: Is There Anything in What We Say?* (1989), his most complete and eloquent statement of his critical stance.

Stephen, Sir Leslie 1832–1904 Critic and scholar. He was educated at Eton, King's College, London, and Trinity Hall, Cambridge, where he was ordained and

appointed a college tutor. He resigned his orders in 1870, adopting the agnosticism set forth in *Essays on Free Thinking and Plain Speaking* (1873) and the *Agnostic's Apology* (first published in 1876). By this time he was well established as a literary journalist, contributing to *THE SATURDAY REVIEW*, *FRASER'S MAGAZINE* and *THE FORTNIGHTLY REVIEW* and, in 1871–82, editing *THE CORNHILL MAGAZINE*. His lively essays were gathered in *Hours in a Library* (1874, 1876 and 1879). *A History of English Thought in the Eighteenth Century* (1876) is generally regarded as his most important work, though he also wrote studies of JOHNSON (1878), POPE (1880), SWIFT (1882), GEORGE ELIOT (1902) and HOBBES (1904). *The Playground of Europe* (1871) reflects his love of mountaineering. His best monument is his work as first editor of *The Dictionary of National Biography* in 1882–91.

Stephen was the model for Vernon Whitford in MEREDITH's *THE EGOIST*. His first wife was THACKERAY's daughter Harriet Marian ('Minny'), and his youngest daughter by his marriage to Julia Duckworth was VIRGINIA WOOLF, who used him as the model for Mr Ramsay in *TO THE LIGHTHOUSE*.

Stephen Hero See *PORTRAIT OF THE ARTIST AS A YOUNG MAN, A*.

Stephens, James 1882–1950 Irish poet and novelist. He became famous with *The Crock of Gold* (1912) a prose fantasy which weaves Irish folk traditions and ancient legends into a tale of whimsical charm. *The Demi-Gods* (1914) is in the same vein, while *Deirdre* (1923) again took Celtic legend for its subject. Stephens had begun his career with *Insurrections* (1909), the first of several volumes of verse later gathered in *Collected Poems* (1926, enlarged 1954). Collections of stories include *Here are Ladies* (with poems; 1913), *In the Land of Youth* (1924), *Etched in Moonlight* (1928) and *Irish Fairy Tales* (1920). An active Sinn Feiner, he also edited the poems of his friend and colleague THOMAS MACDONAGH, executed in the Easter Rising of 1916, and published *The Insurrection in Dublin* (1916).

Sterne, Laurence 1713–68 Novelist. The son of an army subaltern, he was born in Tipperary, brought up in garrison towns and educated for eight years in Halifax until his father's death in 1731 left the family penniless. A cousin helped him to enter Jesus College, Cambridge, as a 'sizar' (poor scholar). He received his degree in 1737 and then took orders, becoming vicar of Sutton-on-the-Forrest in Yorkshire in 1738 and later prebendary of York Minster. After marrying Elizabeth Lumley in 1741 he moved to Stillington, another Yorkshire parish. His wife suffered an emotional breakdown in 1758, when he was involved in a number of 'sentimental' dalliances with local ladies.

The first two volumes of his novel, *TRISTRAM SHANDY*, appeared in 1760, immediately catapulting him to literary fame; further volumes appeared in 1761, 1762, 1765 and 1767. In London Sterne was lionized by fashionable society, an experience he relished. Taking a flamboyant delight in playing the parts of his own characters in real life, he became a cult figure, the subject of outlandish anecdotes and, to some, the object of disapproval. His new recognition brought him the perpetual curacy of Coxwold, near his other Yorkshire parishes, where he named his home Shandy Hall. He adopted the persona of the parson in *Tristram Shandy* for *The Sermons of Mr Yorick*, of which successive volumes appeared in 1760, 1766 and 1769. They were extremely well subscribed, despite their lack of doctrinal content and infrequent attention to such devotional topics as faith. In 1762–4 Sterne lived abroad at Toulouse, with his depressed wife and his daughter Lydia, spending much of his remaining life in Continental travel intended to relieve his tuberculosis. A seven-month tour of France and Italy during 1765 resulted in *A Sentimental Journey* (1768), a second novel as arresting and fragmentary as his first. During 1767 Sterne formed an attachment to Eliza Draper, the wife of an East India Company officer for whose eyes he kept a journal published after his death as *Letters from Yorick to Eliza* (1775).

Despite the immense popularity of *Tristram Shandy*, in particular, during Sterne's lifetime, his full importance has been acknowledged only since his death. SAMUEL JOHNSON, SAMUEL RICHARDSON and GOLDSMITH were among contemporaries to denounce his whirling, anarchic method or take offence at his playful indecency. Yet Sterne's oddity is neither accidental nor perverse; it is the strategy of an inventive, thoughtful comic talent. His work points the way to later experiments (by JOYCE and his successors, for example), though not all of these would be conducted with the vein of good humour, delicate yet often dark, which runs so riddlingly through his work.

Steuart [Steuart-Denham], Sir **James** 1712–80 Political economist. *An Inquiry into the Principles of Political Economy* (1767) partly anticipated the work of ADAM SMITH, not least in its view of man as 'acting uniformly in all ages, in all countries, and in all climates, from the principles of self-interest, expediency, duty and passion'.

Stevens, Wallace 1879–1955 American poet. He worked for the legal staff of the Hartford Accident and Indemnity Company from 1916 until his death. Poetry for Stevens was 'a part of the structure of reality'. He worked with the joint awareness of his Romantic heritage and his distinctively modern sensibility, striving to reconcile the product of his imagination with fundamental reality while expressing disbelief in the possibility of any such reconciliation. His use of language is meticulous, though frequently exotic, as in 'Sunday Morning', a famous early poem which first appeared in HARRIET MONROE's magazine *Poetry* in 1915. 'Three Travelers Watch a Sunrise', a verse play produced in 1917, and his first volume, *Harmonium* (1923), were followed, after considerable period of silence, by the volumes which established his reputation: *Ideas of Order* (1935), *Owl's Clover* (1936), *The Man with the Blue Guitar and Other Poems* (1937), *Parts of a World* (1942), *Notes toward a Supreme Fiction* (1942), *Esthétique du Mal* (1945), *Transport to Summer* (1947) and *The Auroras of Autumn* (1950). *Collected Poems* (1954) won Stevens a belated PULITZER PRIZE. *The Necessary Angel: Essays on Reality and the Imagination* (1951) gathers essays and addresses on poetry and art; *Opus Posthumous* (1957) contains poems, essays and plays. *The Letters of Wallace Stevens* appeared in 1966.

Stevenson, Anne (Katherine) 1933– Poet. Her central themes are the limits of language and the continuing attempt to use it to express the infinite. The dilemma is often mirrored in a landscape: Sierra Nevada in *Reversals* (1969), the Fens and the Scottish coast in *Enough of Green* (1977). Other collections have been *Living in America* (1965), *Correspondences: A Family History in Letters* (1974), *Minute by Glass Minute* (1982), *The Fiction Makers* (1985), *Selected Poems 1965–1986* (1987) and *The Other House* (1990). She has also written a study of ELIZABETH BISHOP (1966) and a biography of SYLVIA PLATH (1990).

Stevenson, Robert Louis 1850–94 Novelist, poet, playwright, essayist, travel-writer and writer of CHILDREN'S LITERATURE. Born in Edinburgh, he was not prevented by poor health from being an enthusiastic traveller. *An Inland Voyage* (1878), describing a canoe tour of France and Belgium, was followed by the enduringly popular *Travels with a Donkey in the Cevennes* (1879). *The Amateur Emigrant* (posthumously published, 1895) described his journey to California in 1879. In America he married Mrs Fanny Osbourne, for whose son Lloyd he first devised *Treasure Island* (1883). Back in England determined to make his living by writing, he devoted much of his energy to carefully crafted essays and short stories, collected in *Virginibus Puerisque* (1881), *Familiar Studies of Men and Books* (1882), *New Arabian Nights* (1882), *The Merry Men* (1887), *Memories and Portraits* (1887), *Across the Plains* (1892) and *Island Nights' Entertainments* (1893). The list of his novels mixes popular romance with steadily developing psychological intensity. In addition to *Treasure Island*, it includes *Prince Otto* (1885), *THE STRANGE CASE OF DR JEKYLL AND MR HYDE* (1886), *KIDNAPPED* (1886) and its sequel, *Catriona* (1893), *THE BLACK ARROW* (1888), *THE MASTER OF BALLANTRAE* (1889), and *The Wrong Box* (1889) and *The Wrecker* (1892), both with Lloyd Osbourne. He left unfinished *WEIR OF HERMISTON* (1896) and *St Ives* (1897 and 1898), completed by QUILLER-COUCH. Other work includes books of poems, *A Child's Garden of Verses* (1885) and *Underwords* (1887), and several fustian dramas, *Deacon Brodie* (1880), *Admiral Guinea* (1884), *Beau Austin* (1885) and *Macaire* (1885), written with HENLEY. Stevenson left England in 1888 and finally settled in Samoa, where he enjoyed a period of comparative health and productivity before his early death. *In the South Seas* (1896) and *A Footnote to History* (1892) document his indignation at European exploitation of the Polynesian islands. Even more important are his two novellas: *The Beach of Falesá*, so inimical to his readers that, though a version was included in *The Island Nights' Entertainments*, its full text was not published until 1984, and *The Ebb-Tide* (1894), prefiguring CONRAD's *HEART OF DARKNESS*.

Long categorized merely as a belletrist and children's writer, Stevenson is now being widely revalued and his novels are beginning to take their rightful place in the adult tradition of early MODERNISM. 'Victor Hugo's Romances' (1874), 'A Gossip on Romance' (1883) and 'A Humble Remonstrance' (1884) – a reply to HENRY JAMES's 'The Art of Fiction' which led to a lifelong friendship between the two writers – show his search for a fiction which would avoid the trap of representationalism, his focus on 'incident' as a type of narrative epiphany, and his use of old forms for new purposes.

Stewart, Douglas 1913–85 Playwright and poet. Born in New Zealand, he crossed to Australia in 1938. His interest in the Australian bush BALLAD is evident in his own poem *Glencoe* (1947) and his editions with Nancy Keesing (1955, 1957, 1967 and 1968). Though experimenting with narrative forms, his other poetry remains memorable for shorter lyrics. *Collected Poems, 1936–1967* was published in 1967. His high reputation as a writer of verse plays rests on three written for radio – *The Fire on the Snow* (1941), about Captain Scott's expedition, *The Golden Lover* (1943), a Maori love story, and *The Earthquake Shakes the Land* (1944) – and three written for the stage – *Ned Kelly* (1944), *Shipwreck* (1948) and *Fisher's Ghost* (1961).

Stewart, Dugald 1753–1828 Philosopher. A disciple of THOMAS REID, he did much to encourage a distinguished generation of Scottish writers and philosophers. Among his pupils were JAMES MILL, SIR WALTER SCOTT, HENRY BROUGHAM and SYDNEY SMITH. His philosophical works include *The Elements of the Philosophy of the Human Mind* (1792–1827), *Outlines of Moral Philosophy* (1794), and *The Philosophy of the Active and Moral Powers* (1828).

Stewart, J(ohn) I(nnes) M(ackintosh) 1906–94 Critic, novelist and author of DETECTIVE FICTION. Under his own name he wrote novels and critical studies, notably *Eight Modern Writers* (1963). But he is better known for his long career as Michael Innes, beginning with *Death at the President's Lodging* (1936; as *Seven Suspects* in USA), *Hamlet, Revenge!* (1937), *Lament for a Maker* (1938) and *Stop Press* (1939). Ingenious, urbane and playful, they remain classics. Their policeman hero, John (later Sir John) Appleby, later featured in chase novels – notably *The Secret Vanguard* (1940), *From London Far* (1946), *The Journeying Boy* (1949) and *Operation Pax* (1951; as *The Paper Thunderbolt* in USA) – as well as fantastic adventures, such as *The Daffodil Affair* (1942) and *Appleby's End* (1945).

stichomythia Dialogue in alternating lines of verse, usually signifying conflict or quarrel. It is a common device in classical drama. The exchange between Richard and Elizabeth in SHAKESPEARE'S *RICHARD III* (Act 4, Scene iv) provides a famous example from the English theatre.

Stoddard, Solomon 1643–1729 American Puritan minister. At Northampton, Massachusetts, he practised 'Stoddardeanism', which abolished the distinction between full and Half-Way church members and made the sacraments available to all seeking salvation. Though the policy was widely accepted in western Massachusetts and laid the theological groundwork for the Great Awakening, it also earned him the wrath of the orthodox Ministry. At the synod in 1679 he explained himself in 'Nine Arguments against Examinations Concerning a Work of Grace before Admission to the Lord's Supper', a paper attacked by INCREASE MATHER. The exchange started a pamphlet war in which Stoddard defended himself with *The Doctrine of Instituted Churches* (1700), *The Inexcusableness of Neglecting the Worship of God, under the Pretence of Being in an Unconverted Condition* (1708) and *An Appeal to the Learned* (1709). JONATHAN EDWARDS was Stoddard's grandson.

Stoker, Bram [Abraham] 1847–1912 Novelist. He worked as a civil servant and drama critic in Dublin before becoming personal manager to Sir Henry Irving. *DRACULA* (1897) is the most famous of his 15 works of fiction. He also wrote the two-volume *Personal Reminiscences of Henry Irving* (1906).

Stone, Louis 1871–1935 Australian novelist. Born in Leicester, he was taken to Australia by his parents in 1884. *Jonah* (1911), a realistic account of the life of a working-class larrikin ('street rowdy' or 'Jack the lad'), is now highly regarded as the first classic novel of Sydney life, though it failed to win recognition when it first appeared. He produced only one further novel, *Betty Wayside* (1915), which describes the fortunes of a woman pianist in Sydney.

Stones of Venice, The A study of architecture, history and society by RUSKIN, published in 1851–3. The first volume is an architectural essay of authoritative dryness and stylistic restraint whose initial chapter, 'The

Quarry', is a panoramic anticipation of the entire work. In the second volume, most notably in the chapter on 'The Nature of Gothic', it assumes epic scope in its praise of Venetian Gothic architecture as an expression of the feelings and aspirations of those who laboured to form it, in contrast to the debased productions of 19th-century industrial society. The last volume records the fall of Venice in the Renaissance through Pride, Luxury, Self-Adulation and Infidelity.

Stonor letters, The The correspondence and papers of the Stonor family, from Stonor in Oxfordshire, dating from *c.* 1290 to 1483 and written in English, Latin and Anglo-Norman. The letters give a valuable insight into everyday life during the Middle Ages.

Stoppard [Straussler], **Tom** 1937– Playwright. He was born in Czechoslovakia. The modest success of some early radio and television pieces preceded the startling popularity of *ROSENCRANTZ AND GUILDENSTERN ARE DEAD* (1966). Its quizzical investigation of artistic conventions and cultural assumptions is also characteristic of *The Real Inspector Hound* (1968), the short farce *After Magritte* (1970), *Jumpers* (1972) and *Travesties* (1974). *Every Good Boy Deserves Favour* (1977), the short *Cahoot's Macbeth* (1979) and *Night and Day* (1979) show greater engagement with social and political realities. A preoccupation with the farcical side of espionage enlivens *Neutral Ground* (TV, 1968), *Professional Foul* (TV, 1977), *The Dog It Was that Died* (radio, 1982) and *Hapgood* (1988). *The Real Thing* (1982) is a neat boulevard play, and *Artist Descending a Staircase* (1988) pays comic homage to the surrealists. *Arcadia* (1993) and *Indian Ink* (1995) use double time-schemes to consider, respectively, English country-house life and the days of the British Raj.

Storey, David 1933– Novelist and playwright. The grim, rawly realistic portrait of a Rugby League footballer in *This Sporting Life* (1960) prefigures the more extreme depictions of isolated men in crisis in *Radcliffe* (1963) and *Pasmore* (1972). *Saville* (1976), which won the BOOKER PRIZE, *A Prodigal Child* (1982) and *Present Times* (1985), continue Storey's two major themes: the loss of working-class roots and the crises of marriage and career arising out of mid-life stasis. His realistically set but tangentially plotted plays include: *The Contractor* (1970), about the putting-up of a marquee at a wedding; *Home* (1970), set in a mental home; and *The Changing Room* (1972), about football. *Collected Poems* appeared in 1992.

Stow, John 1525–1605 Historian and antiquary. A tailor for many years, he was collecting and transcribing manuscripts and writing histories from 1560 onwards. His annotated edition of CHAUCER (1561) was followed by a summary of English CHRONICLES (1565), and then, with the encouragement of MATTHEW PARKER, editions of Matthew of Westminster's *Flores Historiarum* (1567), Matthew Paris's *Chronicle* (1571), Thomas of Walsingham's *Chronicle* (1574), and *Chronicles of England* (1580), known as *Annals* in later editions. Stow's most famous work is *A Survey of London* (1598); it was revised and enlarged in 1603, and then again by STRYPE.

Stow, Randolph 1935– Australian novelist, poet and writer of CHILDREN'S LITERATURE. He established his reputation with five novels: *A Haunted Land* (1956) and *The Bystander* (1957), linking poetic feeling for landscape with an account of turbulent, emotional lives; *To the Islands* (1958, revised edition 1982), a symbolic fable reminiscent of PATRICK WHITE'S *Voss*; the densely symbolic *Tourmaline* (1963); and the more realistic *The Merry-Go-Round in the Sea* (1965). He then wrote a popular children's book, *Midnite: Stories of a Wild Colonial Boy* (1967), and continued with the poetry collected in *A Counterfeit Silence* (1969). From 1971 to 1981 he wrote for musical theatre with the composer Peter Maxwell Davies. He returned to the novel with one of his finest books, *Visitants* (1979), followed by *Girl Green as Elderflower* (1980) and *The Suburbs of Hell* (1984), both set in East Anglia, where he has lived for some years.

Stowe, Harriet Beecher 1811–96 American novelist. She was the daughter of Lyman Beecher, rector of the First Church in Litchfield, Connecticut, and later president of the Lane Theological Seminary in Cincinnati, Ohio. Her brother, HENRY WARD BEECHER, became an influential preacher and her sister Catharine a prominent writer and ideologue of domesticity, female education and woman's separate sphere. Her husband, Calvin E. Stowe, whom she married in 1836, was a professor at Lane and then at Bowdoin College, Maine.

Here she wrote her first novel, UNCLE TOM'S CABIN (1851–2). Its attack on slavery made it an immediate and controversial best-seller both in the USA and abroad. Triumphal tours of Europe in 1853, 1856 and 1859 forged friendships with GEORGE ELIOT and ELIZABETH BARRETT BROWNING, and provided material for *Sunny Memories of Foreign Lands* (1854). *The Key to Uncle Tom's Cabin* (1853) defended the accuracy of her portrait of the South. A second anti-slavery novel, *Dred: A Tale of the Great Dismal Swamp* (1856), told the story of a dramatic attempt at a slave rebellion, attacking ministers who failed to oppose slavery and again demonstrating the redemptive powers of Christian womanhood, white and black. She turned away from political controversy in: *The Minister's Wooing* (1859), about love and marriage in the shadow of Calvinist uncertainty; *Agnes of Sorrento* (1862), set in the Catholic Italy of Savonarola; *The Pearl of Orr's Island* (1862), exploiting the local colour of the New England shore; and three novels of New York society, *Pink and White Tyranny* (1871), *My Wife and I* (1871) and its sequel, *We and Our Neighbours* (1875). *Oldtown Folks* (1869) and *Oldtown Fireside Stories* (1871), drew on her husband's childhood memories, and *Poganuc People* (1878), her last novel, on her own. She also wrote CHILDREN'S LITERATURE, travelogues, theological works, temperance tracts and practical articles about housekeeping, decoration and the 'servant problem', including the highly influential *The American Woman's Home* (1869), co-written with her sister Catharine.

Strachey, (Giles) Lytton 1880–1932 Biographer and essayist. He was a prominent member of the BLOOMSBURY GROUP. *Eminent Victorians* (1918) consisted of iconoclastic revaluations of Florence Nightingale, Cardinal Manning, THOMAS ARNOLD, and General Gordon. With *Queen Victoria* (1921), *Books and Characters, French and English* (1922), *Elizabeth and Essex: A Tragic History* (1928), *Portraits in Miniature* (1931) and *Characters and Commentaries* (1933), it has been cited as originating the art of modern biography. Strachey was, perhaps, the first biographer to use Freudian insights, accompanied by sharp but affectionate satire and fine narrative skill. Strachey himself is the subject of a widely admired biography (1967–8) by MICHAEL HOLROYD. *Spectatorial Essays*, a collection of reviews published in *The Spectator* (1904–14), appeared in 1964.

Strand Magazine, The A periodical founded by George Newnes in 1891, it survived until 1950. Perhaps best known for publishing SIR ARTHUR CONAN DOYLE'S SHERLOCK HOLMES STORIES, it also included fiction by KIPLING, WELLS, W. W. JACOBS, SOMERSET MAUGHAM, ARTHUR MORRISON, STANLEY WEYMAN, ANTHONY HOPE, JEROME K. JEROME and WODEHOUSE, among others.

Strand, Mark 1934– American poet. He was US POET LAUREATE in 1990–1. His volumes of verse include *Reasons for Moving* (1968), *Darker* (1970), *The Story of Our Lives* (1973), *The Late Hour* (1978), *Selected Poems* (1980), *Rembrandt Takes a Walk* (1987) and *Dark Harbor: A Poem* (1993). An active advocate of the work of other poets, he has edited *The Contemporary American Poets: American Poetry since 1940* (1969) and, with Charles Simic, *Another Republic: 17 European and South American Writers* (1976); other translations include *Owl's Insomnia: Selected Poems of Rafael Alberti* (1973) and *Souvenir of the Ancient World: Carlos Drummond de Andrade* (1976).

stream of consciousness A technique used by novelists to represent a character's thoughts and sense impressions without syntax or logical sequence. The term was first used by WILLIAM JAMES in his *PRINCIPLES OF PSYCHOLOGY* (1890) to describe the random flux of conscious and sub-conscious thoughts and impressions in the mind. A parallel description can be found in Bergson's account (1889) of the *élan vital*, popularized in England by SHAW. Literature can show many examples before both James and Bergson, notably STERNE'S *TRISTRAM SHANDY* (1767), but stream of consciousness becomes important with the rise of MODERNISM in the 20th century. It can be seen in the works of JOYCE (who preferred the term *monologue intérieur* and claimed to have discovered the technique in Edouard Dujardin's *Les Lauriers sont coupés*, 1888), DOROTHY RICHARDSON, VIRGINIA WOOLF and FAULKNER.

Streatfeild, Noel 1895–1986 Writer of CHILDREN'S LITERATURE. *Ballet Shoes* (1936), her first and best book for children, describes a family of orphans who eventually make good in the ballet and theatre world. Other 'career' novels include *Tennis Shoes* (1937) and *White Boots* (1951), about skating. *The Bell Family* (1954) chronicles the domestic adventures of a gently idealized middle-class family which first featured in plays for BBC radio's *Children's Hour*.

Streetcar Named Desire, A A play by TENNESSEE WILLIAMS, produced in 1947 and awarded a PULITZER PRIZE. Blanche Du Bois is a failed and lonely alcoholic who lives by the illusion that she is still a Southern belle. On a visit to her sister Stella, who lives in New Orleans near the stop of the streetcar named Desire, Blanche becomes locked in antagonism with Stella's brutish husband Stanley Kowalski. Stanley destroys her relationship with his friend Mitch and rapes her. Blanche tells Stella, who does not believe her, and is taken into psychiatric care.

Strickland, Agnes 1796–1874 Writer of miscellaneous works. The sister of SUSANNA MOODIE and CATHARINE PARR TRAILL, she wrote poetry and CHILDREN'S LITERATURE before turning eventually to the short popular biographies for which she is remembered: *The Lives of the Queens of England from the Norman Conquest* (1840–8) and *The Lives of the Queens of Scotland, and English Princesses* (1850–9).

Strong, L(eonard) A(lfred) G(eorge) 1896–1958 Novelist, playwright and man of letters. *Dewer Rides* (1929), set on Dartmoor, launched his career as a novelist. *Travellers* (1945) won the James Tait Black Prize. Versatile and fluent, Strong wrote plays and radio scripts, compiled anthologies, and produced several biographies and autobiographies. *The Body's Imperfection* (1957), a collection of verse, shows him pausing more reflectively than his vast output usually allowed.

structuralism A movement of thought affecting a number of intellectual disciplines, including anthropology, philosophy, history and literary criticism. The common element derives from linguistics and especially the writings of Ferdinand de Saussure (see SEMIOTICS). He argued that linguistics should study the 'synchronic' dimension of language (the system of relations within language operating at a given moment) rather than its 'diachrony' (temporal dimension). Speakers are able to use the system by registering the differences between possible elements within it. For example, at the level of the phoneme (minimum unit of sound) we distinguish between 'bus' and 'buzz' on the basis of a difference between a voiced (s) and an unvoiced (z) sibilant.

Structuralists applied the patterns of 'binary oppositions' derived from phonemics, syntax or grammar to human sign-systems of various kinds. Claude Lévi-Strauss (1908–) developed 'phonemic' analyses of kinship relations, myths, rites, and so on. Roland Barthes (1915–80) examined *haute cuisine*, narrative discourse, garments and all kinds of social artefacts. Structuralist narratology, aimed at identifying the underlying 'grammar' of narrative form, is represented by the work of Tzvetan Todorov, Gérard Genette and A. J. Greimas.

Strutt, Joseph 1749–1802 Antiquary. Among his illustrated works, often the first in their field, were *The Regal and Ecclesiastical Antiquities of England* (1773), *Manners, Customs, Arms, Habits, &c. of the People of England* (1774–6), and his *Biographical Dictionary of Engravers* (1785–6), upon which all subsequent such dictionaries have been based. His best-known work is the curiously titled *Glig Gamena Angel Deod* (1801), a history of popular sports and pastimes.

Strype, John 1643–1737 Church historian. His magnum opus, *Annals of the Reformation and Establishment of Religion, and other Occurrences in the Church of England, during the First Twelve Years of Queen Elizabeth's Reign* (1709–31), was accompanied by biographies of figures from the Tudor period and his *Ecclesiastical Memorials relating Chiefly to Religion and the Reformation of It under Henry VIII, Edward VI and Mary* (1721). Strype's remarkable collection of Tudor documents is now in the British Library. He also edited and extended STOW's *Survey* adding a life of Stow (1720, enlarged 1754).

Stuart, Francis 1902– Irish novelist. A lifelong Republican, he married Iseult, daughter of Maud Gonne, the Irish nationalist loved by YEATS. His experience in Germany during World War II is reflected in *The Pillar of Cloud* (1948), *Redemption* (1949) and *The Flowering Cross* (1950), a trilogy balanced by three novels dealing variously with the Irish political crisis, *Memorial* (1973), *A Hole in the Head* (1977) and *The High Consistory* (1981). *Black List, Section H* (1971), an autobiographical novel, brought him wider acclaim.

Stubbes, Philip ?1555–1610 Puritan pamphleteer. He is best known for *The Anatomy of Abuses* (1583), a denunciation of sinful customs and fashions which includes a section on stage plays. He also wrote BROADSIDE ballads, usually demonstrating God's vengeance on sin, and *A Christal Glass for Christian Women* (1591), a biographical account of his wife Katherine.

Stubbs, William 1825–1901 Historian. A follower of the

OXFORD MOVEMENT, he was Regius Professor of Modern History at Oxford and later Bishop of Oxford. He is remembered for contributions to the medieval Rolls Series and for *Select Charters and Other Illustrations of English Constitutional History from the Earliest Times to the Reign of Edward I* (1870) and *The Constitutional History of England* (1873–8), which takes its subject up to the accession of the Tudors.

Studies in the History of the Renaissance Essays by WALTER PATER, published in 1873 and later retitled *The Renaissance: Studies in Art and Poetry*. Although he includes an early essay on Winckelmann (the 'last fruit of the Renaissance'), one on Du Bellay and an opening essay on 'Two Early French Stories', Pater is mainly concerned with Italy. With grace and simplicity, he advances his own aesthetic theories in discussions of Pico della Mirandola, Botticelli, Leonardo, della Robbia and others. The 'Conclusion', excised from the second edition for fear it might 'mislead' young men, became the manifesto of the AESTHETIC MOVEMENT. It stresses that the intensity of the moment and the profundity of experience are central to self-realization: 'To burn always with this hard, gemlike flame, to maintain this ecstasy, is success in life.'

Stukeley, William 1687–1765 Antiquary. A Fellow of the Royal Society and first secretary of the Society of Antiquaries, which he helped to found, he was interested in astronomy and Gothic architecture as well as prehistoric monuments. Though indebted to previous scholars such as AUBREY, his early work on Stonehenge and Avebury was remarkable. After 1729 an obsession with the Druids as builders of the stone circles took hold of him: he produced *Stonehenge: A Temple Restored to the British Druids* (1740) and *Abury: A Temple of the British Druids* (1743). Eccentric as this Druidism may now appear, poets such as WILLIAM COLLINS, WILLIAM MASON, THOMAS GRAY and BLAKE stand clearly in his debt.

Sturt, George 1863–1927 Essayist and historian of rural society. Books published under the pseudonym of George Bourne include *The Bettesworth Book* (1901) and its sequel, *Memoirs of a Surrey Labourer* (1907), *Change in the Village* (1912) and *A Farmer's Life* (1922). *The Wheelwright's Shop* (1923), published under his own name, sensitively chronicles the family business in Farnham, Surrey, which he had inherited and run on lines suggested by his reading of RUSKIN.

Styron, William 1925– American novelist. His work, preoccupied with all the various forms of oppression, includes *Lie Down in Darkness* (1951), *The Long March* (1952), *Set This House on Fire* (1960), *The Confessions of Nat Turner* (1967; PULITZER PRIZE), about a black slave rebellion, and *Sophie's Choice* (1979), about the consequences of the Holocaust. *This Quiet Dust* (1982) is a collection of essays and *Darkness Visible* (1990) an account of his battle with depression.

Subjection of Women, The An essay by JOHN STUART MILL, published in 1869. Designed 'to maintain the claim of women, whether in marriage or out of it, to perfect equality in all rights with the male sex', it draws together the political, moral and social ideas diffused throughout the rest of his work in pungent rhetorical form. It remains an important document in the history of feminism.

Suckling, Sir John 1609–41 CAVALIER POET and playwright. After military and ambassadorial adventures on the Continent, he returned to England in 1632 to dissipate his patrimony, quickly establishing a reputation for both wit and extravagance. His SATIRE, *The Wits* (or *Sessions of the Poets*), was sung before the king in 1637, and his tragedy *Aglaura* was staged and magnificently published in 1638. After taking part in the 'Army Plot' to free the imprisoned Earl of Strafford, he fled to France, where he died, possibly by suicide. *The Goblins*, a musical comedy-romance indebted to THE TEMPEST, and *Brennoralt* (or *The Discontented Colonel*), a tragedy whose protagonist has often been considered a self-portrait, were both in the repertoire of the KING's MEN by the year of his death. They were published in *Fragmenta Aurea* (1646), the collection which also includes Suckling's most famous poems, 'Ballade. Upon a Wedding' and 'Why So Pale and Wan, Fond Lover?' His 'easy pen', as ROCHESTER called it, makes him one of the most attractive Cavalier poets.

Summer of the Seventeenth Doll A play by RAY LAWLER, performed in Melbourne in 1955. It was the first Australian play to win an international audience. Roo and Barney are sugarcane cutters who work for half the year and return each summer to their waiting women, bringing always a kewpie doll among their gifts. They are unprepared for the discovery that the 17th summer cannot be the same as its predecessors.

Summoner's Tale, The See CANTERBURY TALES.

Sun Also Rises, The A novel by ERNEST HEMINGWAY, published in 1926. The English edition (1927) was entitled *Fiesta*. It deals with the 'lost generation' of American and British expatriates in Paris. The narrator is Jake Barnes, an American journalist rendered impotent by a wound in World War I and hence unable to consummate his relationship with Lady Brett Ashley. Jake's self-taught emotional pragmatism is contrasted with the self-pitying sentimentalism of his acquaintance Robert Cohn.

Surfacing A novel by MARGARET ATWOOD, published in 1972. The unnamed narrator-protagonist journeys with her lover Joe and two friends to northern Quebec in search of her missing father. It becomes clear that the novel is more centrally about a quest for her own past, particularly its repressed aspects, which she comes to terms with when she dives into a lake and discovers her father's drowned body. 'Surfacing' with a new-found awareness, she regresses into an animal-like state of existence that enables her to free herself from the negative cultural influences of her past. The end sees her emerging from this state, possibly about to go back to the city with Joe.

Surrey, Earl of [Howard, Henry] ?1517–47 Poet and translator. His brief career at court and in public life, already interrupted by confinement at Windsor on suspicion of sympathizing with the Pilgrimage of Grace, was cut short when Henry VIII's failing health prompted him to ill-advised remarks about the claims of his father, the Duke of Norfolk, to assume the Protectorship of the young Prince Edward. He was arrested on a technicality, imprisoned in the Tower and executed on Tower Hill.

With WYATT, Surrey is one of the early imitators of Petrarch and the Italian SONNET in English. Instrumental in developing the English or Shakespearean sonnet, his work represents one of the first flowerings of 16th-century poetry. Most of it (some 40 poems) was published for the first time in TOTTEL'S MISCELLANY (1557). SIR PHILIP SIDNEY found in his lyrics 'many things tasting of a noble birth, and worthy of a noble mind'. Surrey's translation of Books II and IV of the *Aeneid* introduced BLANK VERSE in English poetry.

Surtees, R(obert) S(mith) 1805–64 Sporting novelist and journalist. He came of a long line of country gentlemen in County Durham. After qualifying in the law, he started writing for the *Sporting Magazine* and founded the *New Sporting Magazine* with Rudolph Ackermann in 1831, editing it until 1836, when he retired to the family property. His major works were: his trilogy about John Jorrocks, the sporting grocer, JORROCKS'S JAUNTS AND JOLLITIES (1838; enlarged, posthumous version, 1869), HANDLEY CROSS (1843; enlarged version, 1854) and HILLINGDON HALL (1845); *Mr Sponge's Sporting Tour* (1853); *Ask Mamma* (1858); *Plain or Ringlets?* (1860); and *Mr Facey Romford's Hounds*, a sequel to *Mr Sponge's Sporting Tour* which was being serialized when he died and appeared in book form in 1865. They are loosely, sometimes carelessly, constructed. What gives them life are the hard-bitten, talkative, closely observed characters taken from the whole spectrum of country life. The foxhunting episodes ring true and the notation of speech, especially North Country dialect, is masterly.

Susanna: or, The Pistil of Swete Susan A poem in ALLITERATIVE VERSE written 1350–80. It tells the story of Susanna and the Elders from an apocryphal addition to the Book of Daniel, augmented by a description of a garden drawn from the *Roman de la rose*. The poem has been dubiously identified with the *Pistil of Swete Susan* mentioned by ANDREW OF WYNTOUN as the work of HUCHOWN OF THE AWLE RYALE.

Sutcliff, Rosemary 1920– Children's historical novelist. *The Chronicles of Robin Hood* (1950) was the first of more than 30 novels, showing a strong and sophisticated grasp of history. Classics include: *The Eagle of the Ninth* (1954), about the Roman occupation of Britain; *Songs for a Dark Queen* (1978), a savage novel about Boadicea; and *The Light Beyond the Forest* (1979), beginning a cycle about King Arthur. *Blue Remembered Hills* (1983) tells the story of her own early life.

Sutherland, Efua (Theodora Morguel) 1924– Ghanaian playwright and writer of CHILDREN's LITERATURE. The leading figure in the Ghanaian theatre, she has made a career of promoting traditional dramatic forms, particularly in her work for the Ghana Drama Studio, which she founded. She dramatizes the conflict between traditional Ghanaian and contemporary Western values tragically in *Edufa* (1969) and comically in *The Marriage of Anansewa* (1975). Other published plays include *You Swore an Oath* (1964), *Foriwa* (1967), *Odasini* (1967) and *The Original Bob* (1969). *Vulture! Vulture!* (1968) is among the most frequently performed of her many children's plays in both Akan and English. *Playtime in Africa* (photographs by Willis Bell; 1962) is a pictorial essay for older children.

Sweet, Henry 1845–1912 Scholar. He had invented his own system of phonetics and published an edition of ALFRED's version of the *Cura pastoralis* before leaving Oxford in 1873. His *History of English Sounds* (1874) became a standard textbook, as did the *Anglo-Saxon Reader* (1876). These were followed by his *Handbook of Phonetics* in 1877, the year in which Sweet persuaded the Oxford University Press to consider publishing the Philological Society's new dictionary, which became the OXFORD ENGLISH DICTIONARY. He was not rewarded by the University until he was appointed to a readership in 1901. SHAW used him as the model for Professor Higgins in *PYGMALION*.

Swift, Graham 1949– Novelist and short-story writer. The preoccupation with history and memory announced by *The Sweet-Shop Owner* (1980) and *Shuttlecock* (1981) has continued in subsequent work: *Waterland* (1983), an ambitious Fenland saga which has much in common with MAGIC REALISM and the early fiction of Günter Grass, *Out of This World* (1987), and *Ever After* (1992), again exploring inheritance and family history. *Learning to Swim* (1982) is a collection of short stories.

Swift, Jonathan 1667–1745 Satirist and poet. Born in Dublin, the posthumous child of an English lawyer, he went to Kilkenny School, where CONGREVE was a fellow pupil, and Trinity College, Dublin, where his academic record was undistinguished. Arriving in England in 1689, he became secretary to SIR WILLIAM TEMPLE at Moor Park in Surrey. Apart from a period in Ireland after his ordination in 1694, he remained in Temple's service until the latter's death in 1699 – writing his largely unsuccessful Pindaric ODES, acting as tutor to the eight-year-old Esther Johnson (Stella), editing Temple's correspondence and writing *THE BATTLE OF THE BOOKS* (1704), which further identified him with his patron. Yet his service never brought Swift the advancement for which he had hoped and Temple's death left him 'unprovided both of friend and living'.

He returned to Dublin as chaplain to Lord Berkeley, the new Lord Justice, obtained the living of Laracor, and was granted a prebend in St Patrick's, Dublin, where Stella and her companion Rebecca Dingley joined him. Visits to London in the following years yielded his *Discourse of the Contests and Dissensions in Athens and Rome* (1701), a pamphlet about the impeachment of several Whig lords, and introduced him to ADDISON and STEELE. *A TALE OF A TUB* (1704), a vehement and comprehensive SATIRE on contemporary intellectual abuses, brought him notoriety and a certain popularity in Whig literary circles. His writings on religious matters, notably the ironic *ARGUMENT AGAINST ABOLISHING CHRISTIANITY* (written 1708, published 1711), show him a staunch Anglican intolerant of Dissent, especially those factions associated with 'enthusiasm'. This attitude was one reason for his abandoning his Whig associates and inclining towards the Tories. In 1708 he invented the character of ISAAC BICKERSTAFF for *Predictions for the Ensuing Year*, a spoof at the expense of the astrologer John Partridge, and in 1709 he published two of his more famous short poems in *THE TATLER*.

In 1710 he sealed his allegiance to the Tory ministry of ROBERT HARLEY by becoming editor of *THE EXAMINER*, a post he relinquished the following year to concentrate on *THE CONDUCT OF THE ALLIES*, supporting proposals for peace in the Continental campaign. He was by now on terms of close familiarity with Harley and enjoyed an increasingly bright reputation in London, where he befriended POPE, ARBUTHNOT and GAY. Their association was formalized in the SCRIBLERUS CLUB. The intimate, playful letters Swift addressed to Stella in Dublin, posthumously published as the *JOURNAL TO STELLA* (selection, 1766; edition, 1768), tell us much about his movements during these years. Meanwhile, he was also seeing Esther Vanhomrigh (whom he nicknamed Vanessa), a young London lady whose love he first encouraged but then rebuffed. His poem, *CADENUS AND VANESSA* (written 1713, published 1726), represents the equivocal nature of the affair. Indeed, his exact relationship with Stella has also been the cause of much speculation, one theory holding that they were secretly

married in 1716, another that they were already related illegitimately by blood. The extent of his involvement with any of the women in his life remains unclear, but his reputation as a misogynist is patently unfounded.

Swift's official appointments reached a peak when he became Dean of St Patrick's, Dublin, in 1713, though his literary reputation in London continued to grow until the collapse of the Tory ministry with which he was socially and intellectually identified. The death of Queen Anne in 1714 began a period of self-imposed exile in Ireland, where despite his persistent claims to loathe the country, he championed Irish rights. He defended the cause of the Irish economy, in particular, with his *PROPOSAL FOR THE UNIVERSAL USE OF IRISH MANUFACTURE* (1720) and the *DRAPIER'S LETTERS* (1724), which effectively prevented the exploitation of Ireland through the issuing of debased coinage. Ironically, Swift succeeded in establishing himself as one of the leading Irish patriots of his century.

Despite his many protests to the contrary, Swift seemed reasonably content in Dublin. He exchanged bantering correspondence with DELANY and SHERIDAN, and maintained contact with those friends in England whom he missed. As well as writing a good deal of satirical verse, he began his best-known book, *GULLIVER'S TRAVELS*, published in 1726 to great acclaim and the only piece of writing for which he was ever paid. He saw his old Scriblerian friends for the last time in England the following year. Stella's death in 1728 committed him to an intermittently lonely existence, though there is certainly no evidence that his mental powers were fading until much later in life. His writings prove the contrary. As well as maintaining a vigorous correspondence with his many friends and founding a short-lived weekly paper, *THE INTELLIGENCER*, in 1728, he produced a diverse and talented body of work, including his notoriously powerful *A MODEST PROPOSAL* (1729), poems such as 'The Grand Question Debated' (1729), 'On Poetry: A Rhapsody' (1733) and *VERSES ON THE DEATH OF DR SWIFT* (1739), and the delightful dialogues of his *Polite and Ingenious Conversation* (1738).

Swift was both a prolific and a versatile writer, the originality of his imagination never in doubt despite all the many fluctuations in his reputation. The close and constant proximity of his complex personality and his writings has often caused Swift to be severely misrepresented. The myth that he went mad from misanthropy persists, though in fact the senility of his last years was largely the result of physical causes such as Ménière's syndrome. The tenacity with which he held his views, his fierce dislike of injustice and his intolerance of folly, which combine to make the satirist's *saeva indignatio* (fierce indignation), were tempered by his charitable concern for the ordinary people of Ireland, his love of pranks and spoofs and his devotion to common sense.

Swinburne, Algernon Charles 1837–1909 Poet, playwright, novelist and critic. The son of an admiral, he was educated in France and at Eton but left Balliol College, Oxford, without a degree. From the start his eclectic interests ensured that his vast literary output would reflect a wide variety of influences. Mastery of Greek and Latin, as well as French and Italian, gave him a strong classical bias and an abiding fascination with the intricacies of poetic form. Admiration for LANDOR, Mazzini, Victor Hugo and later WHITMAN encouraged his own defiant individualism, political and literary. Of English contemporaries, he had most in common with

DANTE GABRIEL ROSSETTI, whom he met in Oxford and later lodged with in London.

Two early plays, *The Queen-Mother* and *Rosamund* (both 1860), were followed by *Chastelard* (1865), beginning a trilogy about Mary Queen of Scots continued in *Bothwell* (1874) and *Mary Stuart* (1881). ATALANTA IN CALYDON (1865) is a verse drama containing lyrics which later became favourite anthology pieces. But Swinburne first became notorious for *Poems and Ballads* (1866), which included THE GARDEN OF PROSERPINE, HYMN TO PROSERPINE and LAUS VENERIS. Their themes of moral and political rebellion, and their sometimes blasphemous or sadistic subjects, created a literary furore. The volume announced a radical break with High Victorian taste and pointed to the *fin-de-siècle*. *Poems and Ballads* was followed by the lyrically and politically charged *A Song of Italy* (1867) and *Songs before Sunrise* (1871). *Under the Microscope* (1872) defended Rossetti against ROBERT BUCHANAN's 'The Fleshly School of Poetry'. Returning to his Greek models, Swinburne published another drama, *Erechtheus* (1876), and *Poems and Ballads: Second Series* (1876), still touched by paganism. It included 'The Forsaken Garden' and a tribute to Baudelaire, AVE ATQUE VALE. One novel, *Love's Cross-Currents: A Year's Letters* (1877), belongs to this period; another, *Lesbia Brandon*, was not published until 1952.

By the 1870s Swinburne had sunk into alcoholism. With his family's consent THEODORE WATTS-DUNTON carried him off in 1879 to The Pines, Putney, where he spent the rest of his life in a passive, suburban existence under his friend's solicitous eye. Tamed but not extinguished, he continued to write prodigiously. A venture into PARODY, *The Heptalogia: or, The Seven against Sense*, appeared in 1880, with *Songs of the Springtides* and *Studies in Song*. They were followed by *Tristram of Lyonnesse* (1882), *A Century of Roundels* (1883), *A Midsummer Holiday* (1884), *Poems and Ballads: Third Series* (1889), *Astrophel* (1894), *The Tale of Balen* (1896) and *A Channel Passage* (1904). Among his verse dramas were *Marino Faliero* (in rivalry with BYRON's MARINO FALIERO; 1885), *Locrine* (1887), *The Sisters* (1892), *Rosamund Queen of the Lombards* (1899) and *The Duke of Gandia* (1908). He was also a discerning if impetuous critic of Baudelaire, BLAKE (whose genius he was early to note), Hugo, WEBSTER, SHAKESPEARE, BYRON, Rossetti, DICKENS and others.

A child of both the romantic and classical traditions, Swinburne used old forms imaginatively and experimented boldly with new ones. His poetry is chiefly notable for its verbal cascades, luxurious imagery and metrical pyrotechnics. He deserves to be remembered as one of the more courageous spirits to survive Victorian England, taking arms against the prudery of the age and reinvigorating its poetic language.

Swinnerton, Frank (Arthur) 1884–1982 Novelist and critic. His novel *Nocturne* (1917) was a critical and commercial success which he felt overshadowed subsequent work. This consisted of nearly 40 novels and 20 critical books. To his work as publisher (responsible for 'discovering' DAISY ASHFORD's *The Young Visiters*) and critic for *The Evening News* and *The Observer*, he added the dimension of close personal contact. Living to the age of 98, he became an important link between the Georgian literary scene and later writing.

Sword of Honour A trilogy by EVELYN WAUGH, comprising *Men at Arms* (1952), *Officers and Gentlemen* (1955) and *Unconditional Surrender* (1961), published as a single work in 1965. It follows the experiences of Guy Crouchback, a Catholic and man of honour, in World War II. The comedy of *Men at Arms*, much concerned with an eccentric fellow officer, Apthorpe, gives way to the disillusioning accounts of action in Alexandria and Crete in *Officers and Gentlemen* and Italy and Yugoslavia in *Unconditional Surrender*. The portraits of Virginia Troy, Guy's ex-wife, her second husband, Tommy Blackhouse, and the extraordinary Brigadier Ritchie-Hook blend nostalgia with SATIRE.

Sybil: or, The Two Nations A novel by BENJAMIN DISRAELI, published in 1845. About Chartist agitation, it was the earliest and in some ways the best CONDITION OF ENGLAND NOVEL, famous for its description of the miserable living and working conditions of the poor. The story contrasts the lives of a spurious aristocracy, ennobled by monastic plunder and commercial greed, with the noble aspirations of the journalist, Stephen Morley, and his friend, Walter Gerard, thoughtful representatives of the working class. Walter's daughter, Sybil, is a Catholic who wishes to take the veil but eventually marries a member of the 'aristocracy' and herself turns out to be the heir to an ancient title.

Sydney Opera House Designed by Jorn Utzon and opened in 1973, this remarkable building houses four separate auditoria, of which one is specifically for drama. Since 1979 it has been the home of the Sydney Theatre Company.

syllabic metre See METRE.

syllepsis The application of one word to two semantically different parts of a sentence: 'Here, thou, great Anna! whom three realms obey,/ Dost sometimes counsel take – and sometimes tea' (POPE, THE RAPE OF THE LOCK). Zeugma is the same, except that one of the applications is, strictly, incorrect: 'Kill the boys and the luggage', says Fluellen in SHAKESPEARE's HENRY V.

Sylvester, Joshua ?1562–1618 Poet and translator. A member of Prince Henry's circle, he was also friendly with JOSEPH HALL. Among voluminous translations from French and Latin, his version of Du Bartas (*The Divine Weeks and Works*, 1592–1608) brought him fame but little fortune. Original poems include the entertaining *Tobacco Battered; and the Pipes Shattered* (1617) and the allegorically autobiographical *The Wood-man's Bear*, written in 1587 but published posthumously in 1620. Folio editions of Sylvester's works appeared in 1621, 1633 and 1641.

Sylvia's Lovers A novel by ELIZABETH GASKELL, published in 1863. Set in Monkshaven (Whitby) during the late 18th century, it combines a realistic portrait of whaling and the cruelties of the press gangs with an increasingly melodramatic plot. Sylvia Robson loves Charley Kinraid, a 'spectioneer' (harpooner), and is loved by her earnest cousin Philip. When Kinraid is taken by the press gang Philip fails to deliver his parting message of constancy to Sylvia and allows her to suppose him dead. Her father Daniel is hanged for his part in a riot against the press gangs. She contracts a loveless marriage with Philip. When Kinraid returns three years later, she refuses to go away with him but disdains her husband for his dishonesty. Philip leaves in disgrace, enlists in the navy and encounters Kinraid, whose life he saves. Eventually Philip returns to Monkshaven, sick and friendless, and is reconciled with Sylvia before his death.

symbol For literary purposes, as opposed to those of the mathematician, grammarian, or computer programmer, it may profitably be distinguished from sign and

SIMILE to give an imprecise but usable meaning. Signs are purely conventional: green stands for Go, red for Stop, by agreement not by nature. In a simile some natural affinity between the two parts is presupposed but the difference is equally important, and the figurative part is not meant to be 'really' like its referent. The symbol, however, draws together different worlds, usually tangible and intangible, into a unity that purports to be more real than either. It may be thought of as a METAPHOR that becomes more than 'merely metaphorical'. In practice, this means that metaphors with many referents and an indefinite reverberation of suggestions (like BLAKE's 'Sick Rose') tend to be distinguished as symbols.

Symbolism A term applied to the work of late-19th-century French writers who reacted against the descriptive precision and objectivity of REALISM and the scientific determinism of NATURALISM. They include the poets Verlaine, Mallarmé, Rimbaud and Laforgue, the novelists Joris-Karl Huysmans and Edouard Dujardin, and the playwrights Maurice Maeterlinck and Villiers de l'Isle Adam. Symbolism emphasized the primary importance of suggestion and evocation in expressing a private mood or reverie. The symbol was held to evoke subtle relations and affinities, especially between sound, sense and colour, and between the material and spiritual worlds (although in the works themselves these were often antagonistic). The notion of affinities led to an interest in esoteric and occult writings, and to ideas about the 'musicality' of poetry which, combined with the Wagner cult, stressed the possibility of orchestrating the theme of a poem through the evocative power of words. Outside France T. S. ELIOT, YEATS, POUND, JOYCE, VIRGINIA WOOLF and WALLACE STEVENS were all variously interested in Symbolism. SYMONS's The Symbolist Movement in Literature (1899), which characterized it as an 'attempt to spiritualise literature', was dedicated to Yeats.

Symonds, John Addington 1840–93 Poet, translator and art historian. A student of JOWETT at Balliol College, Oxford, and a friend of EDWARD LEAR, SWINBURNE, LESLIE STEPHEN and ROBERT LOUIS STEVENSON, he spent much of his life in Italy and Switzerland. His most ambitious work The Renaissance in Italy (1875–86) arose from his admiration for the Hellenism of the Renaissance. Other works include studies of Dante (1872), the Greek poets (1873), Cellini (1888), WHITMAN (1893) and Michelangelo (1892), translations and collections of essays, Essays Speculative and Suggestive (1890) and In the Key of Blue (1892). He published two privately printed pamphlets in a discreet campaign for legal reforms and recognition of 'inversion' (homosexuality), A Problem in Greek Ethics (1883) and A Problem in Modern Ethics (1891), and anonymously contributed his own case history to HAVELOCK ELLIS's Sexual Inversion (1897). Among his poetry are two SONNET sequences dealing obliquely with 'l'amour de l'impossible', Anima Figura (1882) and Vagabundulis Libellus (1884).

Symons, Arthur (William) 1865–1945 Critic and poet. A leading light of the Decadence in the 1890s, Symons contributed to THE YELLOW BOOK and in 1896 became editor of The Savoy. His friends included ERNEST DOWSON, LIONEL JOHNSON, WILDE and YEATS. His own poetry, published in Days and Nights (1889), Silhouettes (1892), London Nights (1895) and Images of Good and Evil (1899), is forgotten but he is still remembered for The Symbolist Movement in Literature (1899), which introduced French SYMBOLISM to English readers. He also wrote studies of ROBERT BROWNING (1886), BLAKE (1907), Baudelaire (1920), and Elizabethan drama (1920), and translated Baudelaire's Les Fleurs du mal and Zola's L'Assommoir.

synecdoche A figure of speech which replaces the whole by the part, or vice versa. Thus a newly arrived person becomes a 'new face' and in the phrase 'Chelsea beat Liverpool' the proper nouns refer to football teams. See also METONYMY.

Synge, J(ohn) M(illington) 1871–1909 Irish playwright. Born into a moderately affluent Protestant family near Dublin, he attended Trinity College before studying music at the Royal Irish Academy and on the Continent. YEATS advised him to develop his growing interest in the Irish language and traditions. Five summers in the Aran Islands between 1898 and 1902 filled the notebooks from which he culled his commentary, The Aran Islands (1907). The posthumously published In Wicklow, West Kerry and Connemara (1911) is equally relevant. The two books are the authentic background material for the plays arising from his involvement with Yeats and LADY GREGORY in the movement which culminated in the opening of the ABBEY THEATRE in 1904. He was one of its directors until his death.

His first play, the one-act In the Shadow of the Glen (1903), is a conscious celebration of the independent spirit of the Irish. Its view of Ireland offended the prudish section of the Dublin audience, whose hostility to Synge's work continued throughout his brief dramatic career. The tragedy RIDERS TO THE SEA (1904) is both a threnody and a song of praise to the indomitable spirit of the Aran islanders. The Well of the Saints (1905) is a bitter comedy. After the riots that greeted his masterpiece, THE PLAYBOY OF THE WESTERN WORLD (1907) at the Abbey Theatre, it was thought prudent to stage his comedy, The Tinker's Wedding (1909) in London rather than Dublin. DEIRDRE OF THE SORROWS (1910), his only dramatization of Irish mythology, was written during the late stages of Hodgkin's disease and was never subjected to the rigorous revision that was his habit. Poems and Translations (1909) gives some indication of Synge's range, from the spiritual delicacy of Petrarch to the earthiness of Villon, from nature mysticism to acute observation of Irish people in an Irish landscape.

System of Logic, The A treatise by JOHN STUART MILL, published in 1843. It lays the groundwork for his re-evaluation of UTILITARIANISM. His attack on all forms in which an assumption of a priori knowledge of the external world manifested itself led him first to an analysis of meaning and then to a discussion of inferential knowledge derived from the data of experience. He drew his proofs first from mathematics and then, by extension, from the moral sciences of psychology and sociology. In this latter part Mill's tolerant liberalism is justified by asserting that human behaviour is both causally explicable and still free, and that society can never be greater than the sum of its constituent parts. The book's socio-political implications ensured a wide readership.

Tagore, Rabindranath 1861–1941 Bengali mystic, poet and novelist. He helped to inspire the Bengali literary revival with the poems, short stories and popular songs he began to publish at the age of 20. To the wider world his appeal came through his own English translations of his work. *Gitanjali* ('song offerings'), 103 short poems on the love of God clothed in simple English dress, was published with an enthusiastic introduction by YEATS for the India Society in 1912 and for the general public in 1913. Further translations included: poems such as *Fruit Gathering* (1916) and *The Crescent Moon* (1918); philosophical plays such as *Chitra* (1913) and *The King of the Dark Chamber* (1914); and *The Home and the World* (1919) and *Gora* (1924), both novels. In 1913 he became the first Asian to receive the Nobel Prize for Literature. He renounced his knighthood (1915) after a massacre by British troops in Amritsar in 1919.

tail-rhyme A verse form, common in medieval VERSE ROMANCE, which uses a short line followed by two or more long lines and then another short line rhyming with the first.

Tale of a Tub, A A prose SATIRE by SWIFT, his first major work, written *c.* 1696 and published in 1704. The principal narrative is the 'fable of the coats', an ALLEGORY following the fortunes of three brothers each left a coat by their father with strict instructions never to alter it. Peter (the Catholic Church), Martin (the Anglican) and Jack (the Calvinist) all exercise ingenuity in treating what they have inherited as they please and the fable traces the resulting squabble. More interesting are the many digressions – on, for example, critics, madness and digressions – designed to carry the main satiric force of the book. The title itself (as well as meaning 'flim-flam') refers to the practice of throwing tubs off the back of ships to distract the attention of whales; the digressions act in similar fashion. The chief targets of this most complex and accomplished of Swift's early works include religious fanaticism, pedantry, scientific credulity, quackery and self-delusion.

Tale of Two Cities, A A novel by DICKENS, serialized in *ALL THE YEAR ROUND* and published in volume form 1859. Set in London and Paris at the time of the French Revolution, it is most alive in its descriptions of mob violence.

After being imprisoned for 18 years in the Bastille, Dr Manette is released and comes to England. His daughter Lucy loves Charles Darnay, an honourable man cursed by his descent from the Evrémondes, and is hopelessly loved by the wastrel Sydney Carton. After his marriage to Lucy, Darnay returns to France and is arrested by the revolutionaries but released through Manette's intercession. When he is arrested again the evidence against him is a denunciation of the Evrémondes written by Manette during his imprisonment. Darnay is condemned to death but saved by the heroic self-sacrifice of Carton, who exploits his physical resemblance to Darnay and takes his place at the guillotine. Minor characters include the fanatical Madame Defarge, the upright Miss Pross and Jerry Cruncher, part-time grave robber.

Tales from Shakespeare See LAMB, CHARLES.

Talfourd, Sir **Thomas Noon** 1785–1854 Judge, play-wright and literary critic. He knew most leading writers of his day, including LAMB, whom he remembered in a reverent edition of his letters (1834 and 1848). His vapid blank-verse tragedies, *Ion* (1836), *The Athenian Captive* (1838) and *Glencoe* (1840), are forgotten. His journalism included articles on SCOTT, GODWIN and MATURIN and an influential essay on WORDSWORTH. He is also remembered for introducing the Copyright Bill, eventually passed in 1842.

Talisman, The A novel by SIR WALTER SCOTT, the second of his *Tales of the Crusades*, published in 1825. The talisman of the title has a historical basis in the amulet, known as the Lee-penny, brought back from the Crusades by Sir Simon Lockhart and kept in the possession of his heirs, the Lockharts of the Lee. In Scott's novel the talisman is given to the hero, Sir Kenneth, the Knight of the Leopard, during his adventures in the Holy Land at the time of Richard I. The book once rivalled *IVANHOE* in popularity.

Tam O'Shanter A narrative poem by BURNS, published in 1791. After a satirical prologue, the drunken Tam is found in a tavern with his crony, Souter Johnnie. He lurches out, mounts his mare and starts for home. Passing Alloway Kirk, he sees a witches' celebration in progress and watches in fascination. The witches pour out of the kirk with Auld Nick himself and pursue Tam. He is barely able to make it across the bridge over the Doon. Once on the other side he is safe, since witches will not cross water.

Tamburlaine the Great A tragedy by MARLOWE, written in two parts and probably first performed in 1587. *Part I* shows Tamburlaine's irresistible rise through conquest of the Persian king Mycetes and the Turkish Emperor Bajazet, who dies with his Empress Zabina in the cage in which Tamburlaine exhibits them. Tamburlaine's only tenderness is his love for Zenocrate, at whose pleading he spares the life of the Soldan of Egypt, her father, when he captures Damascus. *Part II* continues the story of Tamburlaine's conquests, which reach their peak when he has his carriage drawn to Babylon by the captured kings of Trebizond and Soria in relay with the kings of Anatolia and Jerusalem. Zenocrate's death precipitates his raging against mortality, whose victory over Tamburlaine himself ends the play.

Taming of the Shrew, The An early comedy by SHAKESPEARE, first performed *c.* 1594. The First Folio of 1623 provides the accepted, though still defective, text; a quarto, *The Taming of a Shrew* (1594), is usually taken to be a corrupt or pirated version. The source for the main plot is GASCOIGNE's *Supposes*, a translation from Ariosto.

In the Induction a lord plays a practical joke on the drunken tinker Christopher Sly, treating him as a lord and inviting him to the performance of a comedy, *The Taming of the Shrew*, in his honour. In the Folio text Sly then disappears from the action, which continues with the play within the play. Baptista, a rich Paduan, has two daughters but will not allow the younger, Bianca, to marry until a husband has been found for the notoriously ill-tempered Katharina. Petruchio, a visitor from Verona in search of a rich wife, decides to take her on: oblivious of her rudeness and evidently delighting in what others find offensive, he succeeds in getting a marriage arranged, behaves eccentrically at the wedding and then systematically humiliates her. Finally he can present her as the most docile wife in the whole company.

Tancred: or, The New Crusade A novel by BENJAMIN DISRAELI, published in 1847. The third in the trilogy begun by CONINGSBY and SYBIL, it draws together characters from the earlier books and reintroduces the enigmatic Sidonia, who is revealed as an international negotiator. Tancred, Lord Montacute, retraces the journey made by his Crusader ancestors to Jerusalem to find the roots of Christianity. There he becomes an unwitting pawn in political machinations, is kidnapped, discovers a community worshipping the old Greek gods, and falls in love with Eva, an acute theologian who lectures him on the history of Mediterranean civilization. She refuses his proposal of marriage and swoons at the moment his parents come from England to claim him. The book is a piece of special pleading for Jewish culture by and about a 19th-century Christian who cannot revert to Judaism, however deep his nostalgia.

Tancred and Gismund A tragedy by Robert Wilmot, Christopher Hatton, Henry Noel and others, based on a story by Boccaccio. The version presented before Elizabeth I, probably in 1568, as *Gismond of Salerne* was in rhyming verse. The published version of 1591 changes the title and is in blank verse.

Tannahill, Robert 1774–1810 Poet. A weaver from Paisley, he achieved brief success with lyrics such as 'Jessie the Flower of Dunblane' (set to music by R. A. Smith). *Poems and Songs* appeared in 1807, but Tannahill burned his manuscripts and drowned himself after a publisher rejected a new collection.

Tarkington, (Newton) Booth 1869–1946 American novelist, writer of CHILDREN'S LITERATURE and playwright. His first novel, *The Gentleman from Indiana* (1899), was a realist study in the manner of HOWELLS and his second, *Monsieur Beaucaire* (1900), a historical romance. Subsequent works include *The Turmoil* (1915), *The Magnificent Ambersons* (1918; PULITZER PRIZE) and *The Midlander* (1924), published together as *Growth* (1927), about the effects on society of the rise of the *nouveau riche* businessman; and *Alice Adams* (1921; Pulitzer Prize), an ironic novel of manners about a girl who seeks but fails to marry a rich man. Among his nostalgic novels of boyhood and adolescence for children are *Penrod* (1914), *Seventeen* (1916), *Penrod and Sam* (1916) and *Penrod Jashber* (1929). Plays include an adaptation of *Monsieur Beaucaire* (1901), *The Man from Home* (1908), *The Country Cousin* (1921), *The Intimate Strangers* (1921), *The Wren* (1922) and *Bimbo, the Pirate* (1926).

Task, The A poem in BLANK VERSE by COWPER, published in 1785. The 'task' set by his friend Lady Austen was to write a poem about his sofa, which provides the title for the first of its six books. Their purpose, Cowper stated, was 'to recommend rural ease and leisure as friendly to the cause of piety and virtue', though his delight in country life is interspersed with anger at the failings of the clergy and the cruelty of blood sports. Generally acknowledged as Cowper's masterpiece, *The Task* earned praise from BURNS and COLERIDGE.

Tate, (John Orley) Allen 1899–1979 American poet and critic. A leading member of the FUGITIVES, he contributed a famous piece, 'Ode to the Confederate Dead', to *Fugitives: An Anthology of Verse* (1928), and an essay to RANSOM's *I'll Take My Stand* (1930). Volumes of poetry include *Mr Pope and Other Poems* (1928), *Poems: 1928–1931*

(1932), *The Mediterranean and Other Poems* (1936), *Selected Poems* (1937), *Poems: 1922–1947* (1948), *Poems* (1960) and *Collected Poems* (1977). Their concern for the history of the South is also apparent in his biographies of Stonewall Jackson (1928) and Jefferson Davis (1929) and in his only novel, *The Fathers* (1938). Critical works include *Reactionary Essays on Poetry and Ideas* (1936), *Reason in Madness, Critical Essays* (1941), *On the Limits of Poetry, Selected Essays 1928-1948* (1948), *The Forlorn Demon: Didactic and Critical Essays* (1953), *Collected Essays* (1959) and *Essays of Four Decades* (1968). A leading proponent of the NEW CRITICISM, he edited *The KENYON REVIEW* (1938) and *THE SEWANEE REVIEW* (1944–6).

Tate, Nahum 1652–1715 Poet, translator and playwright. A busy career in literature was rewarded by his appointment as POET LAUREATE in 1692. His reputation as a poet is sustained by his collaboration with DRYDEN in the second part of *ABSALOM AND ACHITOPHEL* and by the carol 'While Shepherds Watched Their Flocks by Night', as a translator by his *New Version of the Psalms of David* (1696) with Nicholas Brady (see PSALTERS) and his version from Fracastoro of *Syphilus: A Poetical History of the French Disease* (1686). He is best remembered for his libretto for Purcell's *Dido and Aeneas* (1689) and his popular version of *KING LEAR* (1681), which gives the tragedy a happy ending.

Tatler, The A periodical founded by STEELE and edited by him under the pseudonym of ISAAC BICKERSTAFF, appearing three times a week from April 1709 until January 1711. It presented its reports as coming from different coffee and chocolate houses: on entertainment from White's, politics and foreign news from St James's, poetry from Will's. As it grew successful, *The Tatler* developed into an arbiter of conduct and taste. Of 271 numbers Steele wrote the entire contents of nearly 190, ADDISON wrote 42 and 36 were produced in collaboration. It was succeeded by *THE SPECTATOR*.

Taylor, Bayard 1825–78 American travel-writer, poet and novelist. *Views A-Foot* (1846), about Europe, and *Eldorado: or, Adventures in the Path of Empire* (1850), about the California Gold Rush of 1849, were followed by a succession of books reflecting his travels and adventures: *A Journey to Central Africa* (1854), *The Lands of the Saracen* (1855), *A Visit to India, China and Japan in the Year 1853* (1855), *Northern Travel* (1857), *Travels in Greece and Russia* (1859) and *At Home and Abroad* (1860). His international experience and varied tastes also inform his many volumes of verse, which include *Rhymes of Travel, Ballads and Poems* (1849), *Lars: A Pastoral of Norway* (1873) and *The Echo Club and Other Literary Diversions* (1876). He wrote several novels, all set in America, including *Hannah Thurston* (1863), *John Godfrey's Fortunes* (1864), *Joseph and His Friend* (1870) and *Beauty and the Beast and Tales of Home* (1872).

Taylor, Cecil P(hilip) 1928–81 Playwright. Without losing the socialism of his Glasgow Jewish childhood, he moved from the revolutionary tone of early plays such as *Aa Went to Blaydon Races* (1962) to the warm humour of such works as *The Black and White Minstrels* (1972). In *Good* (1981), his most successful play, moral cowardice finally leads a liberal German professor to work in Auschwitz.

Taylor, Edward *c.* 1645?–1729 American poet. The minister of Westfield, Massachusetts, he was a friend of SEWALL, and a correspondent of STODDARD. Today he is considered the pre-eminent poet of early New England, but his work was not published until 1939. In addition to a few occasional poems, it includes the devotional *Meditations* and a long series treating Puritan dogma,

God's Determinations Touching His Elect; and the Elects' Combat in Their Conversion, and Coming Up to God in Christ: Together with the Comfortable Effects Thereof.

Taylor, Elizabeth 1912–75 Novelist and short-story writer. Her novels, written with simplicity and precision, include: *At Mrs Lippincote's* (1946), a gentle study of bourgeois life; *Palladian* (1947); *A Wreath of Roses* (1950), about a middle-aged woman and a younger man; *The Soul of Kindness* (1963); *Mrs Palfrey at the Claremont* (1972), about old age; and *Blaming* (1976), about a young woman's turmoil after her husband's death. *Hester Lilly* (1954), *The Blush* (1958), *A Dedicated Man* (1965) and *The Devastating Boys* (1962) contain short stories. *Mossy Trotter* (1967) is for children.

Taylor, Sir Henry 1800–86 Playwright. His verse dramas were never produced but one, *Philip van Artevelde* (1834), was much admired as a study of character. He also wrote *The Statesman* (1836), a satirical essay on the art of succeeding as a civil servant, and an autobiography (1885).

Taylor, Jeremy 1613–67 Devotional writer. A chaplain to both Charles I and Archbishop Laud, he produced much of his best work whilst in retirement at Golden Grove in Carmarthenshire following the defeat of the Royalist cause. At the Restoration he was given the see of Down and Connor, and later of Dromore, where he is buried. His writings did much to shape the Church of England. In clear, unadorned prose he set forth a plea for tolerance: men should be allowed to differ in opinion when they plainly agreed on Christian fundamentals. His principal works are *A Discourse on the Liberty of Prophesying* (1647), *The Golden Grove* (1655), *Discourse of the Nature, Offices and Measures of Friendship* (1657), *The Worthy Communicant* (1660) and, best known of all, *The Rule and Exercises of Holy Living* (1650) and *The Rule and Exercises of Holy Dying* (1651). The last was written following the deaths of his wife and his patroness at Golden Grove, Lady Carbery.

Taylor, John 1580–1653 The 'Water Poet'. A Thames waterman, he hit on the expedient of collecting sponsors for whimsical journeys, on foot or by water, and writing up his experiences in lively prose and doggerel. In this fashion he travelled to the Continent and Bohemia, and made water journeys from London to York, Salisbury and Queenborough. *The Penniless Pilgrimage* (1618) describes a walk from London to Edinburgh and Braemar without money; when some of his sponsors complained that he had cheated, Taylor upbraided them in *A Kicksey Winsey* (1619). He eventually became an innkeeper in Oxford and then London.

Taylor, Tom 1817–80 Playwright, editor and critic. His energetic career embraced university teaching, the law and public service as well as literature. He contributed to the newspapers on a wide range of subjects, edited *PUNCH* from 1874 until his death and wrote 80 plays. Usually derivative, they follow almost all the current styles: FARCE in *A Trip to Kissingen* (1844), PANTOMIME in popular favourites like *Cinderella* (1845) and *Little Red Riding Hood* (1851), historical verse drama in *The Fool's Revenge* (adapted from Victor Hugo; 1859), MELODRAMA in *Plot and Passion* (with John Lang; 1853) and *THE TICKET-OF-LEAVE MAN* (1863), and comedy in *Masks and Faces* (with CHARLES READE; 1852), *To Oblige Benson* (1854), *Still Waters Run Deep* (1855), *Contested Election* (1859), *Victims* (1857), *The Overland Route* (1860) and *New Men and Old Acres* (with A. W. Dubourg; 1869). Abraham Lincoln was assassinated at a performance of *Our American Cousin* (1858) in Washington DC.

telestich See ACROSTIC.

Tempest, The A play by SHAKESPEARE, first performed *c.* 1611 and published in the First Folio of 1623. Formally a comedy, *The Tempest* is more aptly associated with the tragicomic romances which mark Shakespeare's last period: *PERICLES*, *CYMBELINE* and *THE WINTER'S TALE*. It draws on accounts of a shipwreck off the Bermudas in 1609 and Montaigne's essay 'Of the Cannibals' (as translated by FLORIO), but no single main source has been identified.

Prospero, the exiled Duke of Milan, has lived with his daughter Miranda for 12 years on a remote island, previously inhabited only by the airy spirit, Ariel, and the earthy Caliban, deformed son of the dead witch, Sycorax. His skill in magic enables him to bring about a storm that shipwrecks on the island a group of figures from his past. From Milan come his usurping brother Antonio and the loyal counsellor Gonzalo; from Naples come King Alonso, his son Ferdinand and Sebastian, the king's scheming brother. The play recounts their various adventures, overseen by Prospero and organized by Ariel. The outcome is that Miranda, who could recall no man save Caliban and her father, falls in love with Ferdinand, that Sebastian's malice is exposed to Alonso, and that Antonio restores the dukedom of Milan to Prospero. At the end Prospero releases Ariel from his service, returns the island to a chastened Caliban, breaks his staff and buries his books.

Temple, Sir William 1628–99 Diplomat and essayist. In 1655 he married Dorothy Osborne (1627–95), despite the opposition of her severely Royalist father. Her letters to him in 1652–4 were first published in 1888. He retired after serving Charles II on diplomatic missions on the Continent and arranging the marriage between William of Orange and Princess Mary, the future King and Queen. SWIFT worked as his secretary at Moor Park, Surrey. An informed and opinionated amateur, Temple is remembered for his *Memoirs* (1692), his letters (edited by Swift; 1701) and his essays, mostly gathered in *Miscellanea* (1680, 1690 and 1701). Its second volume contains his *Essay upon the Ancient and Modern Learning*, which compared modern writers and philosophers unfavourably with their classical counterparts and lavishly praised the epistles of Phalaris, the tyrant of Agrigentum in the 6th century BC. RICHARD BENTLEY showed the epistles to be forgeries, and the result was a controversy which produced Swift's *THE BATTLE OF THE BOOKS*.

Tenant of Wildfell Hall, The ANNE BRONTË's second novel, published in 1848. Helen Graham, the tenant of Wildfell Hall, is young, beautiful and said to be a widow. Markham, a neighbouring farmer who narrates the story, falls in love with her and defends her reputation against local gossip until he overhears her in affectionate conversation with her landlord, Frederick Lawrence. Helen's diary shows that she loves Markham but also reveals her secret. She is married to Arthur Huntingdon, a drunkard who made her life so miserable that her brother, Lawrence, offered her Wildfell Hall as a refuge. She tells Markham the truth, and then has to return to her husband, now dangerously ill. His death frees Helen to marry Markham.

Although the novel was a popular success, its frank portrait of Huntingdon's alcoholism and of Helen's struggle to free herself from such a husband struck some contemporaries as offensive. Anne Brontë was unrepentant.

Tender is the Night The last complete novel by F. Scott Fitzgerald, published in 1934. A revised edition (1948) reorganized the action into chronological order but most modern editions follow the original version, which begins on the Riviera. It is about the decline of Dick Diver, a promising young American psychiatrist studying in Zurich. He marries a beautiful American patient, Nicole Warren, but grows frustrated by their leisurely, sociable life on the Riviera. He becomes infatuated with Rosemary Hoyt, an American actress much younger than himself, and starts to drink heavily. Nicole falls in love with Tommy Barban, a French mercenary and member of their Riviera circle, and eventually divorces Dick. His failure is complete when he returns to a small-town medical practice in America.

Tennant, Emma 1937– Novelist. Her most original work, such as *The Bad Sister* (1978), *Wild Nights* (1980) and *Faustine* (1992), explores extreme psychological states and alternative notions of reality through fantasy, dreams and STREAM OF CONSCIOUSNESS. *Queen of Stories* (1982), *Woman Beware Woman* (1983), *The House of Hospitalities* (1987) and *A Wedding of Curiosity* (1988), the last two beginning a projected sequence called *Cycle of the Sun*, are more conventional.

Tennant, Kylie 1912–88 Australian novelist and writer of CHILDREN'S LITERATURE. IRONY, a talent for the swift evocation of atmosphere and an inclination to value the country more than the city characterize her novels: *Tiburon* (1935), *Foveaux* (1939), *The Battlers* (1941), *Ride on Stranger* (1943), *Time Enough Later* (1945), *Lost Haven* (1946), *The Joyful Condemned* (1953), *The Honey Flow* (1956), *Tell Morning This* (1967) and *Tantavallon* (1983). Other work includes: a children's book, *All the Proud Tribesmen* (1959); a study of Aborigines, *Speak You So Gently* (1959); and an autobiography, *The Missing Heir* (1986).

Tennant, William 1784–1848 Poet. *Anster Fair* (1812) is a MOCK-HEROIC description of a rural fair in the reign of James V of Scotland.

Tenniel, Sir John 1820–1914 Cartoonist and illustrator. After the success of his illustrations for *Aesop's Fables* (1848) he joined PUNCH as leading cartoonist with JOHN LEECH, serving the magazine for more than 50 years. He is now better remembered for his illustrations to CARROLL'S *ALICE'S ADVENTURES IN WONDERLAND* (1865) and *THROUGH THE LOOKING-GLASS* (1871). In all, he submitted over 90 drawings, of which only one was accepted without reservation by the author.

Tennyson, Alfred Lord 1809–92 Poet. One of eight children born to the vicar of Somersby, Lincolnshire, he was educated at Louth grammar school, at home and at Trinity College, Cambridge, where he was elected to the APOSTLES and formed a close friendship with ARTHUR HENRY HALLAM before his undergraduate career was cut short by his father's death in 1831. As early as 1823–4 he had written *The Devil and the Lady*, a precocious fragment in the Elizabethan manner, unprinted until 1930. The misnamed *Poems by Two Brothers* (1827), unobtrusively published in Louth and including work by his brothers Frederick and CHARLES TENNYSON TURNER, marked his debut. It was followed by *Poems, Chiefly Lyrical* (1830) and *Poems* (published in December 1832 but dated 1833), to which JOHN WILSON CROKER gave a savage mauling in *THE QUARTERLY REVIEW*. There followed 'Ten Years' Silence', when his life lacked direction and his emotional instability seemed unusually apparent. He suffered the shock of Hallam's early death in 1833, fell briefly in love with Rosa Baring and began his long,

interrupted engagement to Emily Sellwood. He ended his silence with the masterly *Poems* (1842), its first volume composed of earlier, revised work (*THE LADY OF SHALOTT*, *THE LOTOS-EATERS*) and the second containing new poems (*LOCKSLEY HALL*, *ULYSSES*). It was followed by *THE PRINCESS* (1847), an amorous polemic on the rights of women. 1850 was Tennyson's *annus mirabilis*. He published his most enduring work, *IN MEMORIAM A. H. H.*, an ELEGY for Hallam begun as early as 1834, succeeded WORDSWORTH as POET LAUREATE and finally married Emily Sellwood.

Henceforth Tennyson trod the leonine, bardic path, though his abnormal shyness still made him unclubbable and wary of public honours. He took his seat in the Lords in 1883 only after several times refusing a baronetcy. The poetry continued to pour forth. *MAUD and Other Poems* (1855) included 'The Charge of the Light Brigade' and the magnificent 'Ode on the Death of the Duke of Wellington'. In 1859 'Enid' (already privately printed in 1857), 'Vivien', 'Elaine' and 'Guinevere' began *THE IDYLLS OF THE KING*, his magisterial contribution to ARTHURIAN LITERATURE, gathered together in 1872–3 but not complete until the appearance of *Balin and Balan* in 1885. In 1864 he published *ENOCH ARDEN* in a volume which also contained *TITHONUS*. His plays included *Queen Mary* (1875), *Harold* (1876), *Becket* (1884) and *The Cup* (1881), though not even the combined talents of Henry Irving and Ellen Terry could save the last from oblivion. Later volumes of verse included *Ballads and Other Poems* (1880), *Tiresias and Other Poems* (1885), *Locksley Hall Sixty Years After* (1886) and *Demeter and Other Poems* (1889), which contained *CROSSING THE BAR*. *The Death of Oenone, Akbar's Dream, and Other Poems* appeared posthumously in 1892.

Perhaps no poet's reputation has received – and withstood – so severe a buffeting since his death. A poet of twilight and half-shadows marked by his delicate poignancy and controlled sadness, yet also the trumpeter of Empire and exponent of a higher morality, Tennyson remained a supreme technician torn between the bardic voice and the solitary lyric.

Tennyson Turner, Charles 1808–79 Poet. After joining his brothers Frederick and ALFRED TENNYSON in the misnamed *Poems by Two Brothers* (1827), he went on to produce four volumes of restrained but distinguished SONNETS (1830, 1864, 1868, 1874).

tercet See TRIPLET.

Terson, Peter [Patterson, Peter] 1932– Playwright. An amusing observer of life in the Midlands and the North, able to seize on an idea which raises naturalism toward myth, he is known for *A Night to Make the Angels Weep* (1964), *The Mighty Reservoy* (1964), *Mooney and His Caravans* (TV, 1966; stage, 1968), *Zigger Zagger* (1967), *The Apprentices* (1968), *Spring-Heeled Jack* (1970), *Good Lads at Heart* (1971) and *Strippers* (1984).

terza rima A series of three-line STANZAS interlocked by rhyme, as follows: aba bcb cdc ded ... The form was originally Italian, used by Dante in *The Divine Comedy*. The relative difficulty of rhyming in English has not prevented poets from CHAUCER to AUDEN attempting it. SHELLEY'S 'Ode to the West Wind' is a famous example.

Tess of the d'Urbervilles: *A Pure Woman Faithfully Presented* A novel by HARDY, published in 1891. It provoked a controversy, continued by *JUDE THE OBSCURE*, which encouraged him to abandon fiction for poetry.

Learning of his descent from the ancient Norman family of d'Urbervilles, poor John Durbeyfield of

Marlott joins his wife Joan in encouraging their daughter Tess to seek the kinship of the parvenu Stoke d'Urbervilles. She is seduced by the vulgar Alec d'Urberville and bears a child who dies. To make a fresh start, she goes to work in southern Wessex at the fertile Talbothays farm. There she meets Angel Clare, younger son of a parson, and accepts his offer of marriage. On their wedding night Tess confesses her unhappy past to Angel, who recoils in puritanical horror. He goes off to Brazil and she works at the grim upland farm of Flintcomb Ash. There she is again approached by Alec, now an itinerant preacher. Angel returns to England, weakened but wiser, and traces Tess to Sandbourne, where she is living as Alec's wife. In her despair she kills Alec and, after a brief idyllic period with Angel, is arrested at Stonehenge, tried, and hanged in Wintoncester (Winchester) jail.

Testament of Cresseid, The A continuation of CHAUCER'S *TROILUS AND CRISEYDE* by ROBERT HENRYSON. Full of Chaucerian echoes, it introduces an elaborate astrological machinery and gives Cresseid a fine complaint on the transitoriness of beauty and security in this world. Abandoned by Diomede, she is punished by Saturn and the Moon with leprosy, which Henryson's readers would have identified with syphilis. Troilus (whom Diomede had killed in Chaucer's version) takes pity on the lepers, though without recognizing Cresseid. When she learns that her benefactor is Troilus, she makes her 'testament' (will), leaving her wealth to the lepers and returning a ring given her by Troilus.

tetrameter See METRE.

Tey, Josephine See MACKINTOSH, ELIZABETH.

Thackeray, William Makepeace 1811–63 Novelist. Born in Calcutta of Anglo-Indian parents, he came to England in 1817 to be educated at private schools and, in 1822–8, at Charterhouse. In 1830 he left Trinity College, Cambridge, after two spendthrift years. He travelled on the Continent, dabbled in journalism, studied law in a desultory manner and, when most of his patrimony was swallowed up in the Indian bank failures of 1833, studied painting in London and Paris. In 1836 he published his first book, lithograph caricatures of the ballet 'La Sylphide' entitled *Flore et Zéphyr*, and, on the strength of his post as Paris correspondent of *The Constitutional*, married Isabella Shawe. By 1840 the signs of her insanity were unmistakable and she was confined, leaving him to care for his daughters: Anne, born in 1837, later ANNE THACKERAY RITCHIE, and Harriet Marian ('Minny'), born in 1840, future wife of LESLIE STEPHEN.

Three early travel books – *The Paris Sketch Book* (1840), *The Irish Sketch Book* (1843) and *Notes of a Journey from Cornhill to Grand Cairo* (1846) – anticipate his later manner less clearly than the stream of reviews, comic sketches, PARODIES and SATIRES he contributed to periodicals, often with his own illustrations and under colourful pseudonyms. For *FRASER'S MAGAZINE* he wrote *THE YELLOWPLUSH PAPERS* (1837–8), *CATHERINE* (1839–40), *A SHABBY GENTEEL STORY* (1840), *THE GREAT HOGGARTY DIAMOND* (1841) and *The Fitz-Boodle Papers* (1842–3). George Savage Fitz-Boodle reappears as the editor of Thackeray's first real novel, *BARRY LYNDON*, serialized in *Fraser's* in 1844. His growing reputation was consolidated by his work for *PUNCH* from 1842 onwards, particularly *The Book of Snobs* (1846–7). His social awareness, and the discontent with contempo-

rary fiction evident in his masterly parody, *PUNCH'S PRIZE NOVELISTS* (1847), inform the satirical, anti-heroic vision of his first major novel, *VANITY FAIR* (1847–8).

An immediate popular and critical success, *Vanity Fair* was followed by a semi-autobiographical *BILDUNGSROMAN*, *THE HISTORY OF PENDENNIS* (1848–50), and *THE HISTORY OF HENRY ESMOND* (1852), a carefully planned historical novel whose melancholy tone reflects his pain at the end of his platonic relationship with Jane Brookfield the previous year. His growing interest in the reign of Queen Anne and the 18th-century is reflected in *The English Humorists of the Eighteenth Century*, casual, anecdotal lectures delivered in 1851, published in 1853, and made the basis of his first American lecture tour in 1852–3. *THE NEWCOMES* (1853–5), a panoramic novel of English social life, was followed by *The Rose and the Ring* (1855), the last and best of his six Christmas Books. On a second visit to the United States in 1855–6 he lectured on *The Four Georges* (1860), treating the Hanoverian kings in the same gossipy manner he had used to discuss the writers of the period. *THE VIRGINIANS*, a historical novel continuing the Esmond family saga, appeared in 1857–9. Thackeray became the founding editor of *THE CORNHILL MAGAZINE*, a monthly journal launched by the publisher GEORGE SMITH in 1860. His last works were published in the *Cornhill*: a short novel, *LOVEL THE WIDOWER* (1860), the discursive essays gathered as *The Roundabout Papers* (1860–3), and his last complete novel, *THE ADVENTURES OF PHILIP* (1861–2). *DENIS DUVAL* (1864) was unfinished.

Thackeray's reputation rests on *Vanity Fair*, *Henry Esmond*, and, less securely, *Pendennis* and *The Newcomes*. The authorial garrulity of his later fiction and essays has not always been fashionable, but recent critics have rediscovered the keen satirical eye and comic irreverence of his early works, which have the energy of the 18th-century writers he admired. His sceptical, ironic but compassionate vision of a society dominated by the power of money and class gives his best work the authority of major art.

Theatre of Cruelty See CRUELTY, THEATRE OF.

Theatre of the Absurd See ABSURD, THEATRE OF THE.

Theobald, Lewis 1688–1744 Scholar of SHAKESPEARE, playwright and hack. He turned his hand to translation, tragedy, prose romance, opera, MASQUE, biography, adaptation from Shakespeare and PANTOMIME. POPE'S 1725 edition of Shakespeare provoked him to publish *Shakespeare Restored* (1726), which contains some fine emendations adopted by Pope in his second edition of 1728. The debt did not prevent Pope from satirizing Theobald in *Peri Bathous* and making him hero of the first *DUNCIAD*. One of the works satirized in *Peri Bathous* was *The Double Falsehood* (produced 1727, published 1728), which Theobald claimed derived from an old manuscript of Shakespeare's lost comedy *Cardenio*; it may belong to the tradition of Shakespearean forgery which became so strong later in the 18th century (see also SHAKESPEARE APOCRYPHA). Theobald produced editions of Shakespeare (1734) as well as WYCHERLEY (1728) and BEAUMONT and FLETCHER (posthumously completed, 1750). Lack of money kept him writing for the stage; STEEVENS suggested that Theobald is the subject of HOGARTH'S *The Distressed Poet* (1737).

Theory of Moral Sentiments, The A treatise on ethics by ADAM SMITH, published in 1759. It investigates the forms and objects of moral consciousness and identifies sympathy as a source of moral sentiments.

Sympathy can have real value only when it comes from an 'impartial and well-informed spectator' and such a spectator is an ideal, not an actual person. In ordinary life self-interest or imperfect understanding frequently affects our attitudes.

Theron Ware, The Damnation of A novel by HAROLD FREDERIC, published in 1896. Its British title was *Illumination*. It tells the story of a talented young Methodist minister's growing disillusionment with conservative, small-town life in upstate New York, and his interest in exotic, sophisticated ideas. He becomes increasingly detached from his wife and congregation, and increasingly drawn to the beautiful and free-spirited Celia, a Catholic church organist, whom he follows to New York. Humiliated by their encounter, he falls ill. When he recovers, he and his wife go west to Seattle, where he will try to go into business and perhaps into politics.

Theroux, Paul 1941– Novelist, short-story writer and travel writer. Born in Massachusetts, he now lives in Britain. *The Great Railway Bazaar* (1975), *The Old Patagonian Express* (1978) and *Riding the Iron Rooster* (1988) are travel books about train journeys. *The Kingdom by the Sea* (1983) tours the coast of the British Isles, while *The Happy Isles of Oceania* (1992) explores the South Pacific. His witty, stylish fiction essays many genres. *Girls at Play* (1969) and *Jungle Lovers* (1971) are tales of naive Westerners in Africa; *The Family Arsenal* (1976) is an atmospheric thriller; *The Consul's File* (1977) and *The London Embassy* (1982) are collections of stories about expatriates in Malaya and London. *The Mosquito Coast* (1981) is a graphic parable set in the Honduran jungle and *My Secret History* (1989) an ambitious BILDUNGSROMAN. Other fiction includes *Saint Jack* (1973), *Doctor Slaughter* (1985), *O-Zone* (1986) and *Chicago Loop* (1990).

Thersites A comedy sometimes attributed to NICHOLAS UDALL, acted in 1537 and printed *c.* 1562. It was adapted from the Latin of Ravisins Textor, a French scholar whose text was acted at Queens' College, Cambridge, in 1543. The setting is the siege of Troy. The English version introduces allusions to ROBIN HOOD into the story of Thersites, who persuades Mulciber (Vulcan) to make him a suit of armour to render him invulnerable but still cannot overcome his own fear.

Things Fall Apart CHINUA ACHEBE's first novel, published in 1958. It tells the story of Nigeria from the inside by depicting the arrival of British missionaries and colonial administrators at Umuofia, an Igbo village, at the end of the 19th century. Okonkwo, originally a wealthy elder, becomes progressively discredited until he is imprisoned for his role in burning the new church. He kills a messenger sent by the District Commissioner and commits suicide. Achebe's depiction of an intricate, finely balanced social structure and his ironic portrayal of the colonial encounter set an influential new pattern for African writing. It has been translated into more than 50 languages.

Thirlwall, Connop 1797–1875 Historian. With J. C. Hare he translated Barthold Niebuhr's *History of Rome* (1828–42). His principal work was *A History of Greece* (1835–44), overshadowed by the work of his former schoolfellow, GEORGE GROTE.

Thomas, Audrey 1935– Canadian novelist and short-story writer. Born in the USA, she moved to England before emigrating to Canada in 1959. Her fiction is eclectic, influenced by POST-MODERNISM and strongly feminist in its exploration of women's ambitions and self-contradictions. Collections of short stories include *Ten Green Bottles* (1967), *Real Mothers* (1981), *Goodbye Harold, Good Luck* (1986) and *The Wide Blue Yonder* (1990). Her novels include *Mrs Blood* (1970), *Songs My Mother Taught Me* (1973) and *Blown Figures* (1975), a trilogy centred on one female protagonist, and *Latakia* (1979) and *Intertidal Life* (1985).

Thomas, Augustus 1857–1934 American playwright. Much of his work depends on a specific locality for its effect: *Alabama* (1891), *In Mizzoura* (1893), *Arizona* (1899), *Colorado* (1901) and *Rio Grande* (1916). His greatest success, *The Copperhead* (1918), is about an Illinois farmer who helps President Lincoln by pretending to be a supporter of the Confederacy. *The Witching Hour* (1907) and *The Harvest Moon* (1909) reflect his interest in mindreading and hypnotism.

Thomas, (Walter) Brandon 1856–1914 Actor and playwright. Of the many plays he wrote, mainly in collaboration, only the immensely popular FARCE *CHARLEY'S AUNT* (1892) is remembered.

Thomas, D(onald) M(ichael) 1935– Novelist, poet and translator. He remains best known for a controversial novel, *The White Hotel* (1981), a pastiche of a Freudian case history in which the protagonist's neuroses are shown to have been premonitory of her eventual mutilation and death in the Babi Yar massacre. Other fiction includes *The Flute Player* (1979), *Birthstone* (1980), a *Russian Quartet* consisting of *Ararat* (1983), *Swallow* (1984), *Sphinx* (1986) and *Summit* (1987), *Lying Together* (1990) and *Flying into Love* (1992), about the Kennedy assassination. A poet before he became a novelist, Thomas has published several volumes of verse, including *Selected Poems* (1983), and translations from the Russian of Anna Akhmatova, Yevtushenko and Pushkin. *Memories and Hallucinations* (1988) is a sexually candid autobiography.

Thomas, Dylan (Marlais) 1914–53 Poet. Born in Swansea, he worked there as a reporter before moving to London in 1934. *18 Poems*, published the same year, was followed by *Twenty-five Poems* (1936), which attracted the attention of EDITH SITWELL among others. During World War II he worked as a scriptwriter and broadcaster for the BBC, publishing two volumes of stories, *The Map of Love* (1939) and *Portrait of the Artist as a Young Dog* (1940) as well as *New Poems* (1943), which together established his reputation. *Deaths and Entrances* (1946) and *In Country Sleep* (1952), were followed by *Collected Poems* (1953), rapturously received by both critics and the public. In 1950, 1952 and 1953 he made reading tours of the USA which confirmed his reputation as a charismatic reader of poetry and a hard-drinking Bohemian. He died of alcoholic poisoning in New York.

His elaborate and frequently obscure style, influenced centrally by HOPKINS and more marginally by psychoanalysis and surrealism, deploys religious, archetypal and biological imagery in rhetorical patterns to evoke an exuberant, pantheistic mysticism. Overpraised during his lifetime, his poetry has since suffered critical disparagement. Nevertheless, at least some poems – 'The Force that through the Green Fuse Drives the Flower', 'And Death Shall Have No Dominion', 'Do Not Go Gentle into That Good Night' and 'Fern Hill' – seem likely to remain popular, as does his 'play for voices', *UNDER MILK WOOD* (1953).

Thomas, Edward (Philip) 1878–1917 Poet, critic, biographer and writer on nature. A prodigiously active full-time author, he produced more than 40 books before his early death in World War I. They include literary biographies, editions, critical studies and nature writings, such as *The Woodland Life* (1897), *The Heart of England* (1906), *The South Country* (1909), *The Icknield Way* (1913) and *In Pursuit of Spring* (1914), which place him in the tradition of RICHARD JEFFERIES and GEORGE BORROW, of whom he wrote studies (1909 and 1912 respectively). His poetry, written with encouragement from ROBERT FROST, belongs to the last two and a half years of his life. Two prose experiments, *The Happy-Go-Lucky Morgans* (1913) and *The Childhood of Edward Thomas* (1938), preceded his discovery of a poetic form without 'the exaggerations of rhetoric'. His verse is subtle and quizzical, plain in diction and irregular in rhythm, drawing both on material from his nature writings and on his response to World War I. Thomas had much difficulty in finding a publisher for it. Twenty-seven poems appeared under the pseudonym of Edward Eastaway in *An Anthology of New Verse* in early 1917. *Poems* 'by E. E.' appeared posthumously in October 1917, followed by *Last Poems* (1918). The definitive *Collected Poems of Edward Thomas* (1978), edited by R. George Thomas, is the fullest of several collections which progressively established his reputation. His wife Helen Thomas wrote two memoirs, *As It Was* (1926) and *World without End* (1931).

Thomas, R(onald) S(tuart) 1913– Poet. Reflecting his work as a Church of Wales clergyman, his poetry renders the grimness of people's lives with granitic honesty and occasional anger while still evoking a created world 'stubborn with beauty'. The volumes gathered in *Song at the Year's Turning: Poems 1942–54* (1955) and sampled in *Selected Poems 1946–1968* (1973; reissued 1986) display his rich early style. *H'm* (1972) is the major flowering of his later, more economical style. Subsequent work, represented by *Later Poems: A Selection* (1983) and *Counterpoint* (1990), has confirmed a development from rootedness in a particular landscape towards ALLEGORY and prophecy which has disappointed some previous admirers. Nevertheless, he remains the leading Anglo-Welsh poet since DAVID JONES. *Selected Prose* appeared in 1986.

Thompson, Flora (Jane) 1876-1947 Writer on rural life. She is famous for the subtle and unsentimentally precise evocation of the culture of her childhood in *Lark Rise to Candleford* (1945), a trilogy originally issued as *Lark Rise* (1939), *Over to Candleford* (1941) and *Candleford Green* (1943). *Still Glides the Stream*, posthumously published in 1948, weaves memories again drawn from childhood into a fictional story. She also published a volume of verse, *Bog Myrtle and Peat* (1921).

Thompson, Francis 1859-1907 Poet. He abandoned his first ambition of entering the Catholic priesthood, spent six years at Owens College (now the University of Manchester) failing to become a doctor and sank into poverty and opium addiction after arriving in London in 1885. ALICE MEYNELL and her husband Wilfred, the editor of *Merry England*, rescued him, publishing his poetry and taking charge of his life. Despite their care, he never fully recovered, though he did publish three volumes, *Poems* (1893), *Sister Songs* (1895) and *New Poems* (1897). The best-known example of his ornate, densely metaphorical style is 'The Hound of Heaven', in the first volume, describing his flight from and recapture by God. Thompson's prose writings include 'Health and Holiness' (1905) and an essay on SHELLEY (1909). Wilfred Meynell edited a three-volume *Works* (1913).

Thomson, James 1700–48 Poet and playwright. Born at Ednam in the Borders, he attended Edinburgh University and arrived in London in 1725, becoming friendly with POPE, GAY, ARBUTHNOT and DAVID MALLET. He made his reputation with *THE SEASONS*, still the poem for which he is best remembered. It originally appeared in separate parts: *Winter* in 1726, *Summer* in 1727 and *Spring* in 1728. *Autumn* was published in the first collective edition of *The Seasons* in 1730. Thomson may have been aided in the corrected and greatly enlarged edition of 1744 by Pope and LYTTELTON, one of the patrons and influential friends he was always fortunate in acquiring.

He did not repeat the success with *Liberty* (1734–6), a lengthy patriotic poem remarkable for its HYPERBOLE and its failure to sell. His work for the stage included: *Sophonisba* (1730), a tragedy famous for the line, 'Oh! Sophonisba, Sophonisba, Oh!'; *Agamemnon* (1738); the unacted *Edward and Eleanora*; *Tancred and Sigismunda* (1745); and *Coriolanus*, posthumously produced in 1749. *Alfred* (1740), the MASQUE on which he collaborated with Mallet, is remembered only for containing 'Rule Britannia'; Mallet later laid claim to the ODE but it was in fact by Thomson. *THE CASTLE OF INDOLENCE*, an ALLEGORY in SPENSERIAN STANZAS which had occupied him for 15 unhurried years, appeared in 1748. WILLIAM COLLINS commemorated Thomson in his ode 'In Yonder Grave a Druid Lies'.

Thomson, James 1834–82 Poet and essayist. In the course of a varied life whose most consistent thread was its melancholy and apparent failure, he worked as teacher, solicitor's clerk, contributor to the rationalist Charles Bradlaugh's *National Reformer*, secretary to a gold and silvermine company in the USA and journalist in Spain. His masterpiece, *THE CITY OF DREADFUL NIGHT*, appeared in the *National Reformer* in 1874 and in volume form in 1880, followed by *Vane's Story, Weddah and Om-el-Bonain and Other Poems* (also 1880), *Essays and Phantasies* (1881) and two posthumous volumes, *A Voice from the Nile and Other Poems* and *Satires and Profanities* (both 1884). Though poems such as 'Sunday at Hampstead' and 'Sunday up the River' show a vein of realistic humour, and others express romantic yearnings or a bent for SATIRE, Thomson is above all a poet of despair. His vision of life as futile and man as trapped in loneliness and desolation makes him an expressive voice of late Victorian pessimism.

Thoreau, Henry David 1817–62 American man of letters. Born in Concord, Massachusetts, and educated at Harvard, he spent most of his life in the vicinity of his native town, working as a writer, teacher, essayist and orator and earning extra income as a gardener, pencilmaker and surveyor. Though an individualist, often scornful of authority, he was deeply influenced by TRANSCENDENTALISM and particularly by his friendship with EMERSON. He contributed to *THE DIAL*; but his mature writing dates from 1845-7, when he lived at Walden Pond. There he put into final form *A Week on the Concord and Merrimack Rivers* (1849), based on a trip with his brother John in 1839. His experience at Walden itself became the source of *WALDEN* (1854), a lengthy autobiographical essay which sets forth many of his ideas on how the individual should live life to the best advantage of his nature and principles. *ON THE DUTY OF CIVIL DISOBEDIENCE* (1849), deriving from his arrest and brief imprisonment for refusing to pay his poll tax in 1846, expresses similar values. Selections from his travel journals were edited and posthumously published as *The Maine Woods* (1864), *Cape Cod* (1865) and *A Yankee in Canada* (1866). *Excursions* (1863) is a collection of magazine pieces. Emerson edited his letters in 1865 (enlarged 1894). *Poems of Nature* appeared in 1895, *Collected Poems* in 1943. The immense collection of journals which form the basis of most of his major writing was published in 1906.

Three Clerks, The A novel by TROLLOPE, published in 1858. It offers a lively picture of the Victorian Civil Service and also a self-portrait of the young Trollope in Charley Tudor, of the widowed Mrs Woodward and her three daughters. Harry Norman and Alaric Tudor, of the prestigious Weights and Measures office, and Alaric's cousin Charley Tudor are regular visitors at the home of the widowed Mrs Woodward and her three daughters. Alaric marries the eldest, Gertrude, but is tried and imprisoned for embezzlement. Harry marries the second Woodward girl, Linda, and settles down as a country squire. Charley, an honest scapegrace, extricates himself from debt and an imprudent entanglement with an Irish barmaid, Norah Geraghty, marries Katie Woodward and wins promotion to the Weights and Measures office.

Three Hours after Marriage A comedy written collectively by GAY, POPE and ARBUTHNOT and unsuccessfully performed in 1717. Partly a FARCE and partly a dramatized Varronian SATIRE, it takes as targets for its humour the characteristic concerns of the SCRIBLERUS CLUB: pedantry, credulity and intellectual pretension. It is densely written and the plot turns on elaborate metamorphoses and disguises. The satire being no longer topical, the chief interest of the play is that it contains the only formal dramatic writing by Pope, and that its production prompted backstage fisticuffs between Gay and CIBBER, who had realized that his part of Plotwell was a lampoon on himself.

Through the Looking-Glass and What Alice Found There A fantasy (1871) by LEWIS CARROLL. Like its predecessor, ALICE'S ADVENTURES IN WONDERLAND, it was illustrated by TENNIEL. Alice enters the back-to-front land behind the mirror, where she meets characters caught up like herself in a cosmic chess game. Favourites among them include the Red Queen, the White Queen, Tweedledum and Tweedledee, the White Knight, the Walrus and the Carpenter and Humpty Dumpty. Poems include the memorable, slightly sinister 'Jabberwocky'.

Thurber, James (Grover) 1894–1961 American humorist and cartoonist. Gently satirical, his work expresses the dilemma of the moral innocent in a complex modern world. Many of his most famous drawings and writings first appeared in THE NEW YORKER, including his short story, 'The Secret Life of Walter Mitty' (1932). Collections of stories and sketches include *The Owl in the Attic, and Other Perplexities* (1931), *The Seal in My Bedroom, and Other Predicaments* (1932), *Let Your Mind Alone* (1937), *My World – And Welcome to It!* (1942) and *The Beast in Me, and Other Animals* (1948). Thurber wrote *Is Sex Necessary?* (1929) with E. B. WHITE and a successful comedy, *The Male Animal* (1940), with Elliot Nugent. *My Life and Hard Times* (1933) is autobiographical, and *The Years with Ross* (1959) a memoir of his years on the staff of *The New Yorker*. *The Thirteen Clocks* (1950) is one of several books for children.

Thwaite, Anthony (Simon) 1930– Poet. *Poems 1953–1983* (1984) sums up a poetic career which has embraced the impersonal, aphoristic mode of *Home Truths* (1957), the desolate, resigned evocation of everyday life in *The Owl in the Trees* (1963), and the interest in the DRAMATIC MONOLOGUE, which culminates in later work such as *Victorian Voices* (1980). Thwaite has edited the collected poems (1988) and letters (1992) of PHILIP LARKIN, an important influence on his own writing. He has also worked as co-editor of ENCOUNTER.

Thyrsis A poem by MATTHEW ARNOLD, published in *New Poems* (1867). It commemorates his friend CLOUGH, who had died in 1861, in a PASTORAL lament recalling the Oxford countryside they both knew as undergraduates – territory Arnold had earlier described in THE SCHOLAR-GIPSY.

Tickell, Thomas 1686–1740 Poet. A protégé of ADDISON, he wrote *On the Prospect of Peace* (1712), a poem widely read in the period leading to the Treaty of Utrecht, contributed to THE GUARDIAN and THE SPECTATOR and translated the first book of the *Iliad* at the same time as POPE, to the latter's annoyance. Tickell's elegy on Addison (1721) is sometimes remembered.

Ticket-of-Leave Man, The A MELODRAMA by TOM TAYLOR, first performed in 1863. It is notable for introducing a stage detective, Hawkshaw, adept at disguise and more than a match for the London underworld. His persistence exonerates the hero, Bob Brierly, a convict released on ticket-of-leave.

Till Eulenspiegel Eulenspiegel (Owlglass) was a German prankster, supposedly born *c.* 1300 in Brunswick, who features as the cunning peasant outwitting his social superiors in farcical and bawdy stories. The first collection was probably printed in German *c.* 1500. An English translation of some stories appeared at Antwerp *c.* 1510 and William Copland published *Here Beginneth a Merry Jest of a Man that was Called Owlglass* (*c.* 1528).

Tillotson, John 1630–94 Archbishop of Canterbury. His importance lies in his sermons, frequently reprinted during the 18th century and influencing theological thought and English prose style not only in their own right but through borrowings by other sermon writers. Rather than deliver their own work, some clergymen would simply read one of Tillotson's sermons, which in 1742–4 were published weekly, presumably with this trade in mind.

Tillyard, E(ustace) M(andeville) W(etenhall) 1889–1962 Critic. A Cambridge man by birth and lifelong residence, he helped to establish the new school of English at the University. He published five books on MILTON, including *Milton* (1930) and *The Miltonic Setting* (1938), and three on SHAKESPEARE: *Shakespeare's Last Plays* (1938), *Shakespeare's History Plays* (1944) and *Shakespeare's Problem Plays* (1950). His best-known work, *The Elizabethan World-Picture* (1943), is a brief explanation of the late medieval concept of a 'chain of being' as the harmonious design of the universe.

Timber: or, Discoveries Made upon Men and Matter JONSON's commonplace book, posthumously published in 1640, a fascinating collection of notes, mordant observations, aphorisms, short essays, and adaptations from Latin originals. It demonstrates the learning and wisdom of England's first great neoclassical critic and poet.

Time Machine, The A short novel by H. G. WELLS, developed from a series of speculative articles and twice serialized before book publication in 1895. The Time Traveller invents a machine for travelling through time to investigate the destiny of the human species. In the year 802,701 the meek and beautiful Eloi are living in apparently idyllic circumstances, but they are prey to the degenerate Morlocks, descendants of labourers who have lived underground for centuries. In later eras the Time Traveller sees the life-forms which survive the extinction of man, and 30 million years hence he is witness to the world's final decline as the sun cools.

Time's Laughingstocks and Other Verses Poems by HARDY, published in 1909. Divided into four parts – 'Time's Laughingstocks', 'More Love Lyrics', 'A Set of Country Songs' and 'Pieces Occasional and Various' – it is stamped with personal associations and recollections of rural and family life. Short poems about his parents and grandparents are set beside love lyrics written during his youth, country songs celebrating Casterbridge Fair and a small handful of Dorset dialect poems. Several are BALLADS, including Hardy's own favourite, the powerful 'Tramp-woman's Tragedy'.

Times Literary Supplement, The Originally a weekly section of *The Times*, begun in 1902, it became a separate paper in 1914. The *TLS* publishes poems by established writers, but is devoted chiefly to reviewing books across a wide range from fiction to science, politics, music and the other arts. Reviews were anonymous until John Gross abolished the practice on assuming the editorship in 1974.

Timon of Athens A tragedy by SHAKESPEARE, first performed *c.* 1607 and published in the First Folio of 1623. Shakespeare probably found the story in NORTH's Plutarch, though he may also have known Lucian's satiric dialogue, *Timon misanthropus*. Stark in structure and unrelentingly stringent in tone, the play has always been the least loved of Shakespeare's great tragedies. Timon is a rich Athenian whose generosity leaves him penniless and shunned by his friends. He invites them all to a banquet, where he serves them with dishes of water, which he throws in their faces. He leaves Athens and lives in a cave, committed to misanthropy. He accidentally uncovers a hoard of gold and gives some of it to support the exiled Athenian general, Alcibiades, on his way to Athens with an avenging army. The rest of the treasure goes to Timon's faithful servant, Flavius. When the bitter philosopher Apemantus spreads news of Timon's sudden riches, the Athenian senators come in vain to seek his help against Alcibiades. The victorious Alcibiades promises to destroy only those who are his own or Timon's enemies, but a soldier brings him news that Timon is dead, and Alcibiades decides to offer peace with mercy.

Timrod, Henry 1828–67 American poet. He was best known for his verse during the Civil War, which earned him the title of the 'Laureate of the Confederacy'. It was collected by his friend Paul Hamilton Hayne in 1872. *Katie*, a love poem addressed to his wife, was published in 1884. With Hayne, Basil Gildersleeve and WILLIAM GILMORE SIMMS, Timrod founded *Russell's Magazine* in Charleston in 1867, modelling it on *BLACKWOOD'S Edinburgh Magazine*.

Tindal, Matthew 1655–1733 Religious writer. *Christianity as Old as the Creation: or, The Gospel a Republication of the Religion of Nature* (1730) established him as leading proponent of DEISM by arguing that the Gospels neither added to nor detracted from the perfect and unchanging law of reason, but freed man from superstition. Other writings include *The Rights of the Christian Church Asserted against the Romish and All Other Priests Who Claim an Independent Power over It* (1706) and *A Defence of the Rights of the Christian Church* (1709).

'Tis Pity She's a Whore A tragedy by JOHN FORD, first performed between 1625 and its publication in 1633. Its central theme is the incestuous love of Giovanni and Annabella, a pure thing in the enveloping context of corruption. Finding that she is pregnant, she agrees to marry and chooses Soranzo from a trio of unsatisfactory suitors. Soranzo breaks off his adulterous affair with Hippolita, adding her jealousy to that of her husband Richardetto. Soranzo's servant Vasques foils Hippolita's attempt to kill his master (contriving to make her drink the poison instead) and also reveals the secret of Annabella's incest. The climax is the banquet at which Soranzo intends to expose his wife and Giovanni. Forewarned, Giovanni kills Annabella and arrives carrying her heart. After defiantly proclaiming their love, he kills Soranzo and is, in turn, killed by Vasques.

Tithonus A DRAMATIC MONOLOGUE in BLANK VERSE by TENNYSON, originally drafted as a companion piece to *ULYSSES* in 1833 but not published until it appeared in *THE CORNHILL MAGAZINE* (1860) and again in a volume with *ENOCH ARDEN* (1864). In Greek myth Zeus acted on his daughter Aurora's request and granted Tithonus eternal life. But she neglected to ask for eternal youth as well and so Tithonus grew ever older without dying.

Titus Andronicus A tragedy by SHAKESPEARE, perhaps written collaboratively. It was one of the first works with which his name was associated and some critics have argued that it was first staged as early as 1590. It was published in Quarto (Q1) in 1594 and in the First Folio of 1623. Although the influence of Seneca is manifest, no specific source has been found in literature or Roman history. When Titus sacrifices the eldest son of the defeated Gothic queen Tamora he starts a chain of revenge. The horrors which follow in relentless succession include the kidnapping of Titus's daughter Lavinia, the death of his son Mutius, the murder of the late emperor's son Bassianus, the rape and mutilation of Lavinia, the self-mutilation of Titus, the beheading of two more of his sons, the murder of Tamora's remaining sons and the use of their blood to make pies containing their severed heads, Titus's mercy-killing of Lavinia, his murder of Tamora after she has eaten the pies containing her sons' heads, the killing of Titus by the Emperor Saturninus and of Saturninus by Titus's remaining son, Lucius. Elected emperor, Lucius decrees honourable burial for Saturninus, Titus and Lavinia and execution for Tamora's Moorish lover Aaron.

To Kill a Mockingbird See LEE, HARPER.

To the Lighthouse A novel by VIRGINIA WOOLF, published in 1927. It works through STREAM OF CONSCIOUSNESS and imagery to create an atmospheric record of the characters' moment-by-moment experiences. Mr Ramsay is a tragic and self-pitying philosopher. Mrs Ramsay is warm, creative and intuitive, the centre of the household. The first section, 'The Window', describes a day during their summer holiday on the west coast of Scotland, where their guests include: a painter, Lily Briscoe; an ageing poet, Augustus Carmichael; a scientist, William Bankes; and a priggish young academic, Charles Tansley. The action focuses on the conflict arising from young James Ramsay's desire to visit the lighthouse, and his father's quenching of this hope. In the second section, 'Time Passes', Mrs Ramsay has died, her eldest son, Andrew, has been killed in World War I, and the daughter, Prue, has died in childbirth. The Ramsays' seaside house lies deserted and desolate, but at the end of the section Lily Briscoe and Augustus Carmichael arrive to reawaken life. Lily Briscoe assumes the 'visionary' mantle left by Mrs Ramsay, and during the final section ('The Lighthouse') Mr Ramsay and his son, James, at last make the long-delayed voyage to the lighthouse. Lily completes a painting which had been inspired by Mrs Ramsay.

Toccata of Galuppi's, A A poem by ROBERT BROWNING in *Men and Women* (1855). Its rhythms are designed to capture the spirit of the composer Baldassare Galuppi (1706–85), whose music epitomizes the decadent gaiety of Venice in the 18th century.

Tocqueville, Comte Alexis de See *DEMOCRACY IN AMERICA*.

Toland, John 1670–1722 Religious controversialist. *Christianity Not Mysterious* (1696) made a vital contribution to DEISM by dismissing the 'mysteries' of Christianity as pagan intrusions maintained by the priesthood. Toland moved further away from orthodoxy in his biography of MILTON (1698), *Amyntor: or, A Defence of Milton's Life* (1699), *Nazarenus: or, Jewish, Gentile and Mahometan Christianity* (1718; about the apocryphal literature of the early church) and *Tetradymus* (1720; on biblical miracles). He coined the term 'pantheism', expressing the creed in *Pantheisticon* (1720).

Tolkien, J(ohn) R(onald) R(euel) 1892–1973 Scholar and writer of fantasy. He ended his long association with Oxford as Merton Professor of English (1945–59). His expertise in Anglo-Saxon literature, particularly EPIC and folklore, and his fluency in medieval languages formed a natural background to his imaginative writing. *The Hobbit* (1937) is a children's story about Bilbo Baggins, an amiable type of gnome required to destroy a menacing dragon. The same characters and a similar quest to destroy evil – this time reluctantly undertaken by the hobbit Frodo – appear in *The Lord of the Rings* (3 vols., 1954–5), a longer and more ambitious work which seeks to create a history and mythology for an unspecified period of the past which Tolkien calls 'Middle Earth'. Tolkien's underlying pessimism about the destruction of rural England struck a chord with new generations of readers concerned about conservation and the threat of nuclear extinction, helping his novel to achieve cult status. A posthumous sequel, *The Silmarillion* (1977), did not enjoy the same popularity.

Tom Brown's Schooldays A novel by THOMAS HUGHES, published in 1857. Written when its author was still young enough to remember his own days at Rugby, it describes the experiences of an upper middle-class boy progressing from shyness to self-confidence. His two best friends are the gentle, idealistic Arthur and the mischievous, irreverent East. When younger boys are bullied by Flashman, it is East and Tom who stand up to him. The story ends with Tom as Head Boy under the kindly tutelage of THOMAS ARNOLD himself. The first great school story, Hughes's novel helped to found a long tradition of uncritical acceptance for public-school values and practices in CHILDREN'S LITERATURE.

Tom Jones, A Foundling, The History of A novel by HENRY FIELDING, published in 1749. A foundling brought up by the rich and benevolent Mr Allworthy, Tom is torn between his love for Sophia Western, a neighbouring squire's daughter, and the more available charms of Molly Seagrim, the gamekeeper's daughter. His enemies include his tutor Thwackum, the philosopher Square, and the mean-spirited Blifil, Allworthy's nephew and heir. Blifil uses Tom's affair with Molly to discredit him in Allworthy's eyes. Banned from his home, Tom takes to the road with Partridge, the schoolmaster. He encounters Sophia, who has run away from her father because he insists that she marry Blifil, and follows her to London. His adventures on the way allow Fielding to portray a rich gallery of characters. In London Tom drifts into an affair with Lady Bellaston, thus further offending Sophia. When he apparently kills his opponent in a duel, Lady Bellaston and her friend Lord Fellamar arrange his arrest and imprisonment. Fortunately, Tom's opponent does not die, and it is revealed that Blifil knows the secret of Tom's birth. He is the son of Allworthy's sister Bridget and hence Allworthy's proper heir. Sophia forgives him his infidelities, and they are married.

The novel is Fielding's masterpiece. The introductory chapters that preface each of the novel's 18 books cultivate the reader in a way then unprecedented in English fiction, establishing a narrative voice satisfying contemporary fondness for moral commentary. The tangled comedies of coincidence are offset by the neat, architectonic structure of this most shapely novel. The portrait of the virtuous Sophia is triumphantly free from stereotypes while Tom Jones himself is both a vital and a fallible hero.

Tom Sawyer, The Adventures of A novel by MARK TWAIN, published in 1876. Tom lives with his respectable Aunt Polly in the Mississippi River town of St Petersburg, Missouri. An intelligent and imaginative boy who is nevertheless careless and mischievous, he prefers the outdoor and parentless life of his friend Huck Finn, with whom he enjoys various comic adventures. They culminate in exposing Injun Joe for murdering the town doctor and in finding his buried treasure. THE ADVENTURES OF HUCKLEBERRY FINN (1884) continues the boys' story in a different vein.

Tomlinson, (Alfred) Charles 1927– Poet, translator and painter. A career beginning with *The Necklace* (1955) is summed up in *Collected Poems* (1985), to which *The Return* (1987), *Annunciations* (1989) and *Boot in the Wall* (1992) have been added. In attempting to accord 'objects their own existence', his poems are often imagistic, visual responses to landscapes, experiences and events which bear an obvious relation to his work as an artist. *In Black and White* (1975) is a collection of his graphic work. *Some Americans: A Personal Record* (1981), casts light on his debts to POUND, ELIOT, WILLIAM CARLOS WILLIAMS, WALLACE STEVENS and LOUIS ZUKOFSKY. His interest in Spanish-American literature, another influence, has prompted a collaboration with Octavio Paz on a SONNET sequence, *Airborn/Hijos del Aire* (1981), and the work gathered in *Translations* (1983). He has also edited *The Oxford Book of Verse in Translation* (1980).

Tomlinson, H(enry) M(ajor) 1873–1958 Novelist and journalist. He is chiefly remembered for *Gallions Reach* (1927) and a powerful anti-war novel, *All Our Yesterdays* (1930), containing descriptions of the trenches based on his experience as a correspondent in France during World War I. Other novels include *The Sea and the Jungle* (1912), a result of his visit to South America, *Old Junk* (1918), *London River* (1921), *Waiting for Daylight* (1922), *The Snows of Helicon* (1933), *All Hands* (1937) and *Morning Light* (1946). *South to Cadiz* (1934) and *Malay Waters* (1950) are travel books, and *A Mingled Yarn* (1953) brings together autobiographical essays.

Tono-Bungay A novel by H. G. WELLS, published in 1909. Often regarded as a latter-day CONDITION OF

ENGLAND NOVEL, it follows the narrator George Ponderevo's quest for moral and intellectual certainties. After a childhood at Bladesover, a country house where his mother is housekeeper, he becomes apprentice to the narrow-minded Evangelical baker, Nicodemus Frapp. His uncle, Edward Ponderevo, makes him salesman for 'Tono-Bungay', a quack medicine which makes the family a fortune. George's marriage to Marion Ramboat, like his experience of religion and commerce, is a failure. His real destiny is with science, and he becomes a student of aeronautics. Uncle Edward's fortunes decline and George's expedition to an island off Africa to collect 'quap', a radioactive material, fails. George's perpetual quest continues amid recurring disillusions. He flies his dying uncle to France to save him from imprisonment and has a love affair with the Hon. Beatrice Normandy. Eventually, he emerges as the harbinger of inexorable change with his latest invention, a destroyer.

Tonson, Jacob the elder 1655–1736 Publisher. He has a major claim to fame for publishing DRYDEN, who edited the sequence of poetic anthologies known as *Tonson's Miscellany* in 1684–90, CONGREVE and many other leading writers of his time. He acquired the copyright of *Paradise Lost* and took over publication of both THE TATLER and THE SPECTATOR. His business was continued, after 1720, by his nephew, Jacob the younger. Tonson was secretary of the KIT-CAT CLUB, a coterie of Whig writers.

Tooke, John Horne 1736–1812 Radical politician and philologist. A skilled and witty speaker and pugnacious campaigner for constitutional reform, he was involved in numerous legal battles and skirmishes: his support for the American colonists against the King led to conviction and one year's imprisonment for blasphemous libel in 1777–8, but he was acquitted (with HOLCROFT and Thelwall) in the treason trials of 1794. In 1801 he was elected to the House of Commons, but immediately afterwards an Act (which is still in force) excluding the Anglican clergy from membership was passed, and he was disqualified. His literary reputation was established by *Epea Pteroenta: or, the Diversions of Purley* (1786–1805, two volumes of a projected three), which launched the science of comparative philology. He was among the first to see languages as historical developments rather than fixed structures, and stressed the importance of the study of Gothic and Anglo-Saxon. The work was extremely popular and greatly admired by JAMES MILL and other exponents of Utilitarianism. Tooke's friends and acquaintances included BOSWELL, BENTHAM, COLERIDGE, GODWIN, PAINE and WILKES.

Toole, John Kennedy 1937–69 American novelist. *A Confederacy of Dunces* is a satirical comedy about his native New Orleans. Appearing in 1980, 11 years after Toole's suicide, it won a PULITZER PRIZE.

Toomer, Jean (Nathan Eugene) 1894–1967 Black American writer and central figure in the HARLEM RENAISSANCE. His most widely read work, *Cane* (1923), is a mixture of stories and poems partly based on his work at a black school in rural Georgia. The mystic Georges Gurdjieff influenced later work such as *Essentials* (1931), a collection of philosophical aphorisms. *The Wayward and the Seeking* (edited by Darwin T. Turner; 1980) gathers previously unpublished poems, stories, and autobiographical sketches.

Toplady, Augustus 1740–78 Hymn writer and theologian. He is remembered for his hymns ('Rock of Ages' is

the most famous) and his violent reaction to the teaching of JOHN WESLEY, whom he had once admired. Toplady regressed into Calvinism and wrote *The Historic Proof of the Doctrinal Calvinism of the Church of England* (1774).

Torrington, 5th Viscount See BYNG, THE HONOURABLE JOHN.

Tottel's Miscellany The first of the poetic miscellanies popular in the later 16th century, brought out in 1557 by the printer Richard Tottel in collaboration with GRIMALD. Its formal title was *Songs and Sonnets Written by the Right Honourable Lord Henry Howard Late Earl of Surrey and Other* (i.e. others). SURREY and WYATT are generously represented, the first time that the work of either poet had appeared in print. Other writers include Grimald himself, THOMAS NORTON and VAUX.

The Tour of Dr Syntax in Search of the Picturesque See COMBE, WILLIAM.

Tourgée, Albion W(inegar) 1838–1905 American novelist. A Northerner, he moved to North Carolina in 1864 and served as a judge of its Supreme Court in 1868–74. His commitment to Reconstruction and the reform of the South is reflected in novels such as *Toinette* (1874; republished as *A Royal Gentleman*, 1881) and *A Fool's Errand* (1879), which began an attack on the Ku Klux Klan continued in *Bricks without Straw* (1880), published the year after he left the South, and in *Our Continent*, the journal he edited in 1882–4. Of his later novels, *Hot Plowshares* (1882), *Black Ice* (1888) and *Eighty-Nine: or, The Grand Master's Story* (1891) return to the theme of Republican reform of the South. Tourgée served as US consul in Bordeaux from 1897 until his death.

Tourneur, Cyril c. 1575–1626 Playwright. Virtually nothing is known of Tourneur's life before 1613, when he was a government courier to Brussels. He was involved in the 1625 raid on Cadiz and put ashore in Ireland after its failure. He died there early the next year, perhaps from wounds suffered in the expedition. His literary reputation rests on a magnificent play, THE REVENGER'S TRAGEDY (1607), which he may not have written. It was not ascribed to him until 1656 and is so superior to THE ATHEIST'S TRAGEDY, published under his name in 1611, that the attribution has often been doubted. THOMAS MIDDLETON is the most favoured of rival candidates. Tourneur's first published work was an obscure poetic SATIRE, *The Transformed Metamorphosis* (1600). He is known to have written a play called *The Nobleman* (1612–13) and been asked to contribute one act to *The Arraignment of London* (1613), but neither play has survived.

Tourtel, Mary 1874–1948 Writer and illustrator of CHILDREN'S LITERATURE. In 1920 she created her comic-strip hero Rupert Bear, unfailingly turned out in check trousers, jumper and scarf. By the time she handed over her strip, published in *The Daily Express*, to ALFRED BESTALL in 1935 Rupert's adventures were enjoying equal success in book form.

Towneley cycle See MIRACLE PLAYS.

Townsend, Sue [Susan] **(Lilian)** 1946– Novelist and playwright. She is best known for the solemn, bookish hero whose accidentally comic adventures are chronicled in *The Secret Diary of Adrian Mole Aged $13\frac{3}{4}$* (1982) and its several sequels. *The Queen and I* (1992) follows the fortunes of a dethroned royal family in a republican Britain. Her work for the stage includes adaptations of *The Secret Diary of Adrian Mole Aged $13\frac{3}{4}$* (1985) and *The Queen and I* (1994).

Townshend, Aurelian ?1583–?1643 Poet. He supplanted JONSON in 1632 as collaborator with Inigo Jones on two court MASQUES, *Albion's Triumph* and *Tempe Restored*. These, and a handful of lyrics and occasional poems, uncollected in his lifetime, constitute his literary work. His letters to his patron, Sir Robert Cecil, show a proficiency in French and Italian, but little else is known of Townshend's life.

Toynbee, Arnold (Joseph) 1889–1975 Historian. His 12-volume *A Study of History* (1934–61; two-volume condensation by D. C. Somervell, 1946–57) views the history of mankind as a recurring cycle of growth, breakdown and eventual dissolution, arguing that a new universal church would provide the chrysalis from which a new civilization could emerge. Other works include *The World and the West* (1952), *Hellenism: The History of a Civilization* (1959) and *Hannibal's Legacy* (1965). An enthusiastic traveller, Toynbee also wrote *Between Oxus and Jumna* (1961), *Between Niger and Nile* (1965) and *Between Maule and Amazon* (1967). *Comparing Notes: A Dialogue across a Generation* (1963) was written with his son, the critic and novelist Philip Toynbee (1916–81).

Tracts for the Times A series of religious pamphlets and treatises, published between 1833 and 1841 by members of the OXFORD MOVEMENT, including NEWMAN, KEBLE, PUSEY and ISAAC WILLIAMS, earning them an alternative label: the Tractarians. Newman's *Tract XC* (1841), arguing that the 39 Articles of the Anglican Church were compatible with Catholic theology, caused an outcry which ended the series.

Traffics and Discoveries A collection of 11 stories and 11 poems by RUDYARD KIPLING, first published in 1904. The stories range in subject matter from mystery and the supernatural ('Mrs Bathurst', 'They', 'Below the Mill Dam' and 'Wireless') to the Boer War ('A Sahib's War').

tragedy Nobody has explained how the Greeks came to apply a word meaning 'goat song' to poetic dramas in which kings and heroes confronted their gods. Aristotle's *Poetics*, analysing tragedy in 5th-century BC Athens, established its responsibility to deal with the fall of the great, a requirement enforced with increasing exactness by his neoclassical interpreters, particularly in Renaissance France.

In England it was the Roman poet Seneca (*c.* 4 BC–AD 65), rather than Aeschylus, Sophocles or Euripides, who influenced the earliest tragedies. His work encouraged, for example, the corpse-strewn plot of SHAKESPEARE'S *TITUS ANDRONICUS* and the flourishing sub-genre of REVENGE TRAGEDY. But Shakespeare, though obedient to the expectation that rulers or noblemen were proper protagonists, is typical of Renaissance dramatists in his readiness to throw off classical models, using prose as well as verse and introducing comic characters and episodes to create a unique emotional breadth. Beside the colour of Shakespeare and MARLOWE, JONSON'S severe Roman tragedies look almost impoverished.

The subsequent elevation of tragedy into the rhymed bombast of heroic tragedy was not helpful. The best work of LEE, OTWAY, DRYDEN and ROWE derives from its ability, however sporadically, to recall Shakespeare, while the great actors of the 18th and 19th centuries made their names in Shakespearean revivals. Domestic or bourgeois tragedy, already present on the Elizabethan and Jacobean stage in works such as *ARDEN OF FEVERSHAM* and THOMAS HEYWOOD'S *A WOMAN KILLED WITH KINDNESS*, was made fashionable in the 18th century by Lillo with *THE LONDON MERCHANT*. But his moral directives about thrift and industry were soon absorbed into MELODRAMA and the full development of bourgeois tragedy had to await Ibsen. The conviction that tragedy was the proper preserve of poets continued to tempt most of the greatest from Dryden to T. S. ELIOT. Some, like COLERIDGE, BYRON, BROWNING and TENNYSON, had fleeting success but few of their plays have lasted well and most now look like reproduction antiques. Those who argue that the 20th-century English-speaking theatre has revived tragedy usually cite domestic and social dramas by O'NEILL and MILLER in the USA and O'CASEY in Ireland. Their determined emphasis on the world of everyman removes these works from Aristotelian high tragedy.

Traherne, Thomas 1637–74 Religious poet and essayist. He was rector of Credenhill near Hereford in 1657 and chaplain to Sir Orlando Bridgeman, the Lord Keeper of the Great Seal, from 1667. He remained an unregarded writer until early this century when the discovery of his poems and the *Centuries of Meditations* revealed him as a man of outstanding religious sensibility. The *Centuries* transmit Traherne's childhood sense of living in an earthly paradise, surrounded by the beauty of the creation. Written in lucid metrical prose and possessing a psalm-like quality of praise and thanksgiving, they express a kind of luminous spirituality that is quite exceptional. His poems complement the experience of the *Centuries*.

Traill, Catharine Parr 1802–99 Canadian writer. The sister of AGNES STRICKLAND and SUSANNA MOODIE, she emigrated to Canada in 1832. Though she also wrote CHILDREN'S LITERATURE, her most enduring works grew out of her pioneering days: *The Backwoods of Canada* (subtitled 'Letters from the Wife of an Emigrant Officer, Illustrative of the Domestic Economy of North America', 1836) and *The Female Emigrant's Guide* (1854). An accomplished naturalist, she published several books on Canadian wildlife.

Traitor, The A tragedy by SHIRLEY, first produced in 1631 and published in 1635. The play has some basis in the history of the Medici family of Florence. Plotting to seize power, Lorenzo plays a double game with his kinsman, the Duke, helping him try to seduce Amidea whilst also warning her brother, Sciarrha. Sciarrha kills Amidea to save her honour and Lorenzo seizes the opportunity to kill the Duke. Sciarrha kills Lorenzo before dying of his own wounds.

Transcendentalism A literary and philosophical movement which flourished in New England in the early and middle part of the 19th century. Critical of formalized religion, it opposed the idea that man needs an intercessor for reaching the divine. Its most notable voices were those of EMERSON, THOREAU, MARGARET FULLER and BRONSON ALCOTT. GEORGE RIPLEY founded the BROOK FARM community in practical application of its ideals.

Tranter, John (Ernest) 1943– Australian poet. At the head of a group of young writers credited with bringing MODERNISM into Australian poetry in the 1970s, he has experimented with different linguistic approaches to perception and the poetic process in successive volumes: *Parallax* (1970), *Red Movie* (1972), *The Blast Area* (1974), *The Alphabet Murders* (1976), *Crying in Early Infancy* (1977), *Dazed in the Ladies Lounge* (1979), *Gloria* (1986) and *Under Berlin: New Poems* (1988). *Selected Poems* appeared in 1982. He has also advanced his view of Australian poetry through influential anthologies, including *The Penguin Book of Modern Australian Poetry* (with Philip Mead; 1991).

Traveller, The: *or, A Prospect of Society* A poem by GOLDSMITH, published in 1764, the first work to appear under his own name. The traveller – or compulsive wanderer – is the poet himself. From a peak in the Alps he ponders the lessons of his travels and notes the faults and virtues of the countries he has visited. Happiness, he realizes, may be found in any place, as well as discontent.

Travers, Ben 1886–1980 Playwright. Between 1922 and 1933 he wrote custom-made FARCES for the Aldwych company under the supervision of Tom Walls. The best include *A Cuckoo in the Nest* (1925), *Rookery Nook* (1926), *Thark* (1927) and *Plunder* (1928). His last play, *The Bed before Yesterday* (1975), is a touching retrospect on the younger world of 1930.

Travers, P(amela) L(yndon) 1906– Writer of CHILDREN'S LITERATURE. Born in Australia, she came to England in 1923. The mixture of strong nursery discipline with exciting magic in *Mary Poppins* (1934) made it an immediate success, leading to four sequels as well as a Walt Disney musical (1964). Her other children's novels include *The Fox at the Manger* (1963) and *Friend Monkey* (1971). She is also a talented poet.

Trease, (Robert) Geoffrey 1909– Writer of CHILDREN'S LITERATURE. *Bows against the Barons* (1934), about ROBIN HOOD, and *Comrades of the Charter* (1934) are historical novels from a left-wing viewpoint. His many subsequent books, less politically motivated but still ahead of their time in the determination to write for and about ordinary children, include *No Boats on Bannermere* (1949), *Follow My Black Plume* (1963) and *Song for a Tattered Flag* (1992).

Treasure Island An adventure novel for children by ROBERT LOUIS STEVENSON, serialized as *The Sea Cook: or, Treasure Island* by 'Captain George North' in 1881–2 and published in book form in 1883. Stevenson himself did not take it seriously, but it has always been his most popular work. Jim Hawkins, the landlady's son at the Admiral Benbow inn, acquires a map showing where Captain Flint's treasure is buried from Billy Bones, an old pirate hunted by his former confederates. Squire Trelawney and Dr Livesey charter a schooner and set sail for Treasure Island with Jim. He discovers that the crew includes the pirates, led by the ship's one-legged cook, Long John Silver. The rest of the story, telling how the pirates are defeated and the treasure found, takes second place to the interest Stevenson finds in Silver, embodying every young boy's image of what a pirate should be. The character is said to have been modelled on W. E. HENLEY.

Treatise of Human Nature, A An essay by DAVID HUME, published in three volumes in 1739–40. It marks his first and most comprehensive attempt to formulate a philosophical position. Separate aspects are developed in *AN ENQUIRY CONCERNING HUMAN UNDERSTANDING* (1748), *An Enquiry concerning the Principles of Morals* (1751) and the discussion of the passions in *Four Dissertations* (1757). Book I, on understanding, examines the origin of man's ideas – of space, time, causality, and so forth – in experience and the data of the senses. Book II, on the 'passions', provides an elaborate psychological machinery and assigns a subordinate role to reason. Book III, on morals, describes 'moral goodness' in terms of 'feelings' of approval or disapproval generated by the agreeable or disagreeable consequences of behaviour.

Treece, Henry 1911–66 Poet and writer of CHILDREN'S LITERATURE. A founder of the NEW APOCALYPSE movement, he published several volumes of poetry, including *The Black Seasons* (1945) and *The Exiles* (1952). Critical works include *How I See Apocalypse* (1946) and the first book on DYLAN THOMAS (1949). *The Legion of the Eagle* (1954) was the first of many historical novels for children, dealing mostly with the Vikings and Romans. *The Children's Crusade* (1958), widely translated and probably his best book, deals with one of the most baffling episodes of medieval history. Treece also wrote a series of thrillers for children.

Trelawny, Edward (John) 1792–1881 Author and adventurer. The son of an army officer from an old Cornish family, he entered the Royal Navy at the age of 13 and received his discharge in 1812. His experiences as a midshipman form the basis of his autobiographical novel, *Adventures of a Younger Son* (1831), in which he claims to have deserted in India and assumed command of a French privateer. In 1822 he surfaced in Pisa where he became a member of the circle round BYRON and SHELLEY. He supervised the cremation of Shelley's body on the beach at Viareggio and accompanied Byron to Greece, where he was married, for the second time, to a Greek girl in 1824. *Recollections of the Last Days of Byron and Shelley* (1858; republished as *Records of Byron, Shelley and the Author*, 1878) gives an extremely lively and readable account of this period, though it is none too scrupulous with the facts. Trelawny sustained his reputation as an adventurer by his elopement in 1841 with the married Lady Augusta Goring, which caused a major social scandal and led to his third unsuccessful marriage. A larger-than-life figure of striking appearance and enormous social charm, he had become the monument of the Byronic age by the end of his long life.

Trelawny of the 'Wells' A comedy by PINERO, first performed in 1898. It is a nostalgic recollection of theatrical conditions in 1860. Rose Trelawny is to quit the stage and marry. Her theatrical friends give her a farewell party, but she finds her fiancé's respectable family unattractive, and returns to the theatre. All ends happily when her fiancé turns up as her leading man.

Trench, Richard Chenevix 1807–86 Philologist, theologian and poet. He first made his name as a poet with *The Story of Justin Martyr, and Other Poems* (1835), but achieved real fame with *Notes on the Parables of Our Lord* (1841) and *Notes on the Miracles of Our Lord* (1846), written while he was a country clergyman. His most popular book, *On the Study of Words* (1851) was followed by *English Past and Present* (1855). Trench played a crucial part in launching THE OXFORD ENGLISH DICTIONARY. Dean of Westminster from 1856, he returned to his birthplace as Archbishop of Dublin in 1864.

Trevelyan, G(eorge) M(acaulay) 1876–1962 Historian. The son of SIR GEORGE OTTO TREVELYAN, he became Regius Professor of Modern History at Cambridge in 1927. *England in the Age of Wycliffe* (1899) and *England under the Stuarts* (1904) made his reputation as a scholarly but popular writer, but his academic stature was established with *Garibaldi's Defence of the Roman Republic* (1907), *Garibaldi and the Thousand* (1909) and *Garibaldi and the Making of Italy* (1911), published as a single work in 1933. *British History in the Nineteenth Century* (1922) and *History of England* (1926) were both popular successes and his nostalgic *English Social History* (1944) became his most widely read book, though it was not considered his best. Other publications include *England under Queen Anne* (1930–4), *Grey of Falloden* (1937), *Autobiography and Other Essays* (1949) and *A Layman's Love of Letters* (1954), based on his Clark lectures.

Trevelyan, George Otto 1838-1928 Historian. His first major historical writing was the *Life and Letters* of his uncle, MACAULAY (1876). It was followed by *The Early History of Charles James Fox* (1880), a vivid presentation of social and political life in the late 18th century, intended as the first part of an exhaustive biography. However, he went on to write *The American Revolution* (1899-1907) and its sequel, *George III and Charles Fox* (1912-14).

Trevisa, John de 1326-1412 An early prose writer on secular topics, he translated and augmented a CHRONICLE, Higden's *Polychronicon*, in 1387 and an encyclopedia, *De proprietatibus rerum* by Bartholomew de Glanville (or Bartholomaeus Anglicus), in 1398. CAXTON credited him with translating the Bible. An Oxford Fellow in 1362-79, he became chaplain to Lord Berkeley, vicar of Berkeley and a canon of Westbury-on-Severn.

Trevor, William [Cox, William Trevor] 1928- Novelist and short-story writer. Much of it set in Ireland, his fiction shows a penchant for settings of faded gentility and often deals with the corruption or destruction of innocence, represented by childhood and old age. Novels include *The Old Boys* (1964), *Mrs Eckdorf in O'Neill's Hotel* (1969), *Elizabeth Alone* (1973), *The Children of Dynmouth* (1976), about a psychopathic teenager menacing a retirement resort, *Fools of Fortune* (1983) and *The Silence in the Garden* (1988). His prolific output of shorter fiction includes a collected volume (1983), *The News from Ireland* (1986), *Family Sins* (1989) and a pair of novellas, *Two Lives* (1991).

Trick to Catch the Old One, A A comedy by THOMAS MIDDLETON, performed by a BOYS' COMPANY *c.* 1605 and published in 1608. The plot gave MASSINGER the basis for *A NEW WAY TO PAY OLD DEBTS*. It concerns Theophilus Witgood, a young ne'er-do-well, and his attempts to get money from his miserly uncle, Pecunius Lucre. His former mistress, a courtesan known as the Widow Medler, agrees to pose as his wealthy 'intended' but marries Lucre's sworn enemy, the usurer Walkadine Hoard. Lucre is so pleased to hear of Hoard's fate that he helps his nephew, who has secretly married Hoard's niece Joyce.

Trilby A novel by GEORGE DU MAURIER, published in 1894 with his own illustrations. Trilby is an artist's model who, manipulated by Svengali, becomes a famous singer. Svengali has given his name to the language; Trilby's name survives as that of a man's felt hat, dented across the crown.

Trilling, Lionel 1905-75 American critic. He taught at Columbia University for most of his life. His publications include studies of MATTHEW ARNOLD (1939) and E. M. FORSTER (1943) and essays collected in *The Liberal Imagination* (1950), *The Opposing Self* (1955), *A Gathering of Fugitives* (1956), *Beyond Culture: Essays on Literature and Learning* (1965) and *Sincerity and Authenticity* (1972). Trilling addressed the broadest cultural questions: the relation of morality to politics, and the aesthetic as well as the political meaning of liberalism. His single novel, *The Middle of the Journey* (1947), reflects these concerns. *Of This Time, of That Place and Other Stories* appeared posthumously in 1979.

trimeter See METRE.

triolet A verse form, derived from French poetry, which consists of eight lines and two RHYMES. The first, fourth and seventh lines, and the second and eighth lines, are the same or very similar. The few English poets who have attempted it include AUSTIN DOBSON and FRANCES CORNFORD (in 'To a Fat Lady Seen from a Train').

triplet A three-line STANZA, usually on a single RHYME, or a variation of three rhyming lines in a poem of HEROIC COUPLETS. As a stanza, it is also referred to as a tercet.

Tristram and Iseult A poem by MATTHEW ARNOLD, published in *Empedocles on Etna and Other Poems* (1852). In Brittany the dying Tristram remembers his happiness with Iseult of Ireland while her rival, Iseult of Brittany, watches over him. Iseult of Ireland arrives and there is one last passionate exchange between the lovers before he dies.

Tristram Shandy, Gentleman, The Life and Opinions of A novel by STERNE, published in instalments: Volumes I and II in 1760, III and IV in 1761, V and VI in 1762, VII and VIII in 1765 and Volume IX in 1767. Its immediate popularity was surprising for a novel which defies convention at every turn. *Tristram Shandy* distributes its narrative content across a bafflingly idiosyncratic time-scheme interrupted by digressions, authorial comments and interferences with the printed fabric of the book.

The story does manage to start *ab ovo*, with the narrator-hero describing his own conception, but he is not actually born for several volumes and disappears from the book in Volume VI. His father is Walter Shandy, the science-smitten but benevolent head of Shandy Hall, where he lives in continuous exasperation with his wife. 'My uncle Toby' is an old soldier wounded in the groin at the siege of Namur, who passes his time recreating military sieges, helped by the devoted Corporal Trim. These are some of the characters whose behaviour can be understood in terms of their personal 'hobby-horses'. Dr Slop is the man-midwife delayed in delivering the infant Tristram, the Widow Wadman is the neighbour with amorous designs on Uncle Toby, and Yorick is the amiable local parson. After Tristram is born, Volume IV opens with the story of Slawkenbergius (a mock-ENCOMIUM on noses) and an account of how the baby mistakenly came to be christened 'Tristram'. After Trim's discourse on morality in Volume V there is a fine dialogue between Tristram's parents in Volume VI, about the 'breeching' (or dressing) of their child, and the sentimental story of Le Fevre. The novel then follows the author's adult travels to France, returning to an account of the Widow Wadman's designs on Uncle Toby in Volume IX.

With its black pages, wiggly lines, misplaced chapters and other surprises, *Tristram Shandy* stands in part against the idea of literature as finished product, its surfaces capable of reflecting the conditions of life. That is one reason why it has proved so fertile an influence on 20th-century fiction. Yet it was also very much in keeping with the mood of an age caught up in the cults of 'sensibility' (see SENTIMENTAL NOVEL) and the PICTURESQUE. And, aside from his debt to LOCKE's theory of the association of ideas, Sterne was working in a long tradition of intellectual SATIRE embracing Montaigne, Rabelais, ERASMUS and SWIFT, as well as drawing on PICARESQUE and travel literature.

Trivia: or, The Art of Walking the Streets of London A poem in three parts by GAY, published in 1716. An ambitious and popular work, it subjects the topography of the capital to a Juvenalian treatment, surveying its dangers and delights in a splendid combination of the heroic and realistic styles. There is advice on reading the weather signs, escaping the filth, taking one's bearings, recognizing the street cries, avoiding criminals and so forth.

trochee See METRE.

Troilus and Cressida A play by SHAKESPEARE, first performed c. 1602 and published in Quarto (Q1) in 1609 as well as in the First Folio of 1623. Often grouped with the PROBLEM PLAYS, ALL'S WELL THAT ENDS WELL and MEASURE FOR MEASURE, it is more accurately a tragicomedy than either of these pieces. Translations of Homer as well as LYDGATE, CHAUCER and many other sources would have given Shakespeare the main outline of his story. Troilus confesses his love for Cressida to her uncle, Pandarus, who contrives their meeting and oversees their love-making. Cressida's father Calchas, a seer who has deserted to the Greeks, persuades them to offer a captured Trojan general in exchange for her. Having promised eternal love to Troilus, Cressida finds herself admired and flattered by the Greeks and becomes Diomedes' mistress. Pandarus leaves Troy, rejected by Troilus, whose abuse of him is an attack also on the concupiscent Cressida. This story of doomed love is interwoven with events in the Trojan war, particularly the death of Hector, the play's only consistently high-principled character, at the hands of a reluctant and deceitful Achilles. It is not the least dispiriting feature of the play that the cynical invective of the scabrous Greek soldier Thersites should come closer to typifying its mood than the nobility of Hector.

Troilus and Criseyde A poem by CHAUCER, probably a late work and perhaps written c. 1385-90. The story, which he found in Boccaccio's Il Filostrato, takes place during the Trojan War. Criseyde and the Trojan warrior Troilus fall in love and begin a secret affair with the help of her uncle and guardian, Pandarus. From fear of public scorn the lovers comply when the Greeks and her father Calchas, who has defected after foreseeing the fall of Troy, demand Criseyde in exchange for a prisoner of war. At first reluctantly, Criseyde takes the Greek Diomede as a lover. Warned of his betrayal in a dream, Troilus spies on them. In despair he devotes himself to the battle, dies in glory and looks down on earth to recognize the vanity of worldly concerns.

The poem's concern with love is central and has been variously interpreted as in praise or bitter criticism of COURTLY LOVE. More than a pair of courtly lovers, Troilus and Criseyde are fully developed individuals, sufficiently complex to make some modern critics liken the poem to a novel. Its subtle comedy is maintained by the articulate dialogue and the self-effacing narrator reluctant to speak ill of Criseyde. The poet's interest in Boethius' philosophy (witness his translation Boece) is shown in Criseyde's discussion of false felicity and in Troilus' eventual vision of the insignificance of worldly things. Dante also contributes to the philosophical fabric of the poem, and the influence of Machaut, Petrarch, Ovid and Joseph of Exeter may be found in its content.

Trollope, Anthony 1815-82 Novelist. He was educated at Harrow and Winchester, where his family's poverty's exposed him to humiliation and unhappiness vividly remembered in his Autobiography (1883). The Trollopes' fortunes improved when his mother, FRANCES TROLLOPE, embarked on a successful literary career with Domestic Manners of the Americans (1832). Trollope himself worked in the Post Office from the age of 19, making an inauspicious start reflected in his novel, THE THREE CLERKS (1858). He later travelled widely, worked in Ireland and invented the pillar box, though he felt that his services were not sufficiently recognized by his superiors.

By the time he resigned in 1867 he was already a successful and respected novelist. Recognition came with his fourth novel, THE WARDEN (1855), which inaugurated the BARSETSHIRE NOVELS, about clergymen and their families in a fictional western county: BARCHESTER TOWERS (1857), DOCTOR THORNE (1858), FRAMLEY PARSONAGE (1860), THE SMALL HOUSE AT ALLINGTON (1862-4), and THE LAST CHRONICLE OF BARSET (1866-7), Trollope's favourite in the series. With their recurrent characters in a familiar, unfolding community, these books marked a new departure for the English regional novel; their realistic presentation of middle-class domestic relationships proved highly congenial to the reading public. His other great sequence was the political or PALLISER NOVELS. Political interests are peripheral in the first, CAN YOU FORGIVE HER? (1864-5), and the third, THE EUSTACE DIAMONDS (1871-3), but PHINEAS FINN (1867-9), PHINEAS REDUX (1873-4), THE PRIME MINISTER (1875-6) and THE DUKE'S CHILDREN (1879-80) paint an unrivalled portrait of parliamentary political society in the high Victorian period. The series owes much to the steadily deepening presentation of Plantagenet Palliser and his wife Glencora, the characters on whom, with Mr Crawley of The Last Chronicle, Trollope believed his reputation with posterity would rest. The pessimistic vision of Phineas Redux reflects his own experience as unsuccessful Liberal candidate for Beverley in 1868, also treated in a separate novel, Ralph the Heir (1870-1). A broader pessimism informs THE WAY WE LIVE NOW (1874-5), a wide-ranging social satire which many consider his masterpiece.

His best-known works – the Barsetshire Novels, the Palliser Novels and The Way We Live Now – make up less than a quarter of his fictional output. It also includes: THE BERTRAMS (1859), Castle Richmond (1860), ORLEY FARM (1861-2), THE BELTON ESTATE (1865-6), THE CLAVERINGS (1866-7), HE KNEW HE WAS RIGHT (1868-9), THE VICAR OF BULLHAMPTON (1869-70), SIR HARRY HOTSPUR OF HUMBLETHWAITE (1870), Lady Anna (1873-4), The American Senator (1876-7), DR WORTLE'S SCHOOL (1880), Ayala's Angel (1881), and MR SCARBOROUGH'S FAMILY (1882-3). The indifferent reception of Nina Balatka (1866-7) and Linda Tressel (1867-8) which he published anonymously, confirmed his suspicion that 'a name once earned carried with it too much favour'. Trollope also produced travel books on The West Indies and the Spanish Main (1859), North America (1862), Australia and New Zealand (1873) and South Africa (1878); wrote biographies of Cicero (1880) and Lord Palmerston (1882), a politician congenial to his own position as an 'advanced conservative liberal'; and a study of THACKERAY (1879), the novelist he considered his master.

Few of Trollope's works are without interest. His productivity meant that he relied unduly on the entanglements of romantic plot-making (for which he professed indifference) and cultivated an even professionalism of style which can lull the reader into ignoring the subtle and varied understanding of human nature on which his best work is based. To this strength should be added his understanding of the institutions of mid-Victorian England and the unobtrusive irony which informs his sympathetic vision of human fallibility.

Trollope, Mrs Frances 1780-1863 Novelist and travel-writer. She married Thomas Anthony Trollope in 1809. Two of their six children, ANTHONY TROLLOPE and THOMAS ADOLPHUS TROLLOPE, became novelists. Her husband's scheme to set up a fancy goods emporium in

Cincinnati failed but a book about her American experiences, *Domestic Manners of the Americans* (1832), made her a best-selling author at the age of 52. Driven by family debts, she published 40 more volumes in the next 25 years, mainly novels but also several travel books. Two novels have a place in the history of Victorian fiction: the anti-evangelical novel *Vicar of Wrexhill* (1837), an early contribution to the novel of religious controversy, and *The Life and Adventures of Michael Armstrong, the Factory Boy* (1840), one of the first Victorian 'industrial' novels.

Trollope, Joanna 1943– Novelist. She is a descendant of ANTHONY TROLLOPE. Set in the upper middle-class Home Counties or Cotswolds, *The Choir* (1988), *A Village Affair* (1989), *The Rector's Wife* (1991), *The Men and the Girls* (1992) and *The Best of Friends* (1995) examine the crises of vocation and self-respect that afflict outwardly comfortable lives. Trollope has also written *Britannia's Daughters* (1983), a study of women in the British Empire, and published historical romances under the pseudonym of Caroline Harvey.

Trollope, Thomas Adolphus 1810–92 Novelist and historian. Eldest son of FRANCES TROLLOPE and older brother of ANTHONY TROLLOPE, he settled in Florence in 1843 and Rome in 1873. His 60 volumes of history, fiction and travel are all now forgotten, although his autobiography, *What I Remember* (1887–9), is valuable for its picture of expatriate life in Italy in mid-Victorian times, and for its reminiscences of DICKENS, ELIZABETH BARRETT BROWNING, ROBERT BROWNING, GEORGE ELIOT and G. H. LEWES.

Trumbull, John 1750–1831 American poet. One of the CONNECTICUT WITS, he contributed to *The Anarchiad* (1786–7) and *The Echo* (1791–1805) and joined the campaign to include the study of contemporary American literature in Yale's curriculum and to defend Federalist politics. His work includes: *An Essay on the Uses and Advantages of the Fine Arts* (1770), a poem condemning neoclassical aesthetics; *The Progress of Dullness: or, The Adventures of Tom Brainless* (1772), a SATIRE on college education; *An Elegy on the Times* (1774), a patriotic poem; and *M'Fingal* (1775, 1776 and 1782), a mock EPIC satirizing British conduct during the American Revolution.

Trumpet-Major, The A novel by HARDY, published in 1880. It is set during the Napoleonic wars. Anne Garland and her mother live in one part of Overcombe Mill. The other part is occupied by Miller Loveday, who has two sons: Robert, a sailor, and John, trumpet-major of a regiment of Dragoons. Anne is loved by John but does not return his affection, and does not welcome the attentions of the buffoonish Festus Derriman. John rescues his brother from the clutches of Matilda Johnson. Robert eventually marries Anne. Mrs Garland succumbs to the charms of Miller Loveday. John leaves 'to blow his trumpet till silenced for ever upon one of the bloody battle-fields of Spain'.

Tucker, Abraham 1705–74 Amateur philosopher. His principal work was *The Light of Nature Pursued* (1768–78), so long and diffuse that its ideas were not recognized until systematized by PALEY in *THE PRINCIPLES OF MORAL AND POLITICAL PHILOSOPHY*. Tucker asserted that the principle of moral conduct was to be found in general happiness, while the motive of the individual could be found in his own content. The two do not always agree. Moral conduct demands self-sacrifice, which is justified by religion with its hope of a future life.

Tuckerman, Frederick Goddard 1821–73 American poet. His only volume, *Poems* (1860), notable for its personal, often melancholy SONNETS, was praised by HAWTHORNE, EMERSON and LONGFELLOW. Tuckerman was generally forgotten until the poet Witter Bynner published a selection from *Poems* in 1931 along with three previously unpublished sonnets. His work was collected and edited by N. SCOTT MOMADAY in 1965.

Tupper, Martin (Farquhar) 1810–89 Poet. He became famous with *Proverbial Philosophy: A Book of Thoughts and Arguments, Originally Treated* (1838), a collection of loosely versified commonplaces which ran to over 50 editions in England and was extremely popular in America. Tupper continued to write prolifically – publishing three more series of *Proverbial Philosophy* (1842, 1867, 1869) as well as novels, plays and occasional verse – but his work, never well received by critics, had lost popularity before his death.

Turn of the Screw, The A short novel by HENRY JAMES, published in 1898. A governess takes charge of two children, Miles and Flora, at the lonely country house of Bly. She sees the ghosts of the former steward, Peter Quint, and governess, Miss Jessel. Her suspicion that the children are in touch with the ghosts is confirmed by their evasiveness when questioned. In a final confrontation, she is determined to free Miles from Quint's malign influence, but the boy dies in her arms. The fact that, after a brief introductory section, the story is told from the point of view of the governess raises doubts about whether the ghosts are 'real' or merely her hallucinations.

Turner, Ethel 1872–1958 Australian writer of CHILDREN'S LITERATURE. Born in Yorkshire, she emigrated to Australia with her family in 1880. She scored an immediate success with her first novel, *Seven Little Australians* (1894), about the unruly children of Captain Woolcott. They reappear in a sequel, *The Family at Misrule* (1895), while many of the stories that followed pit good-hearted if mischievous children against insensitive or negligent parents. Often very funny, Ethel Turner is comparable to NESBIT in her depiction of family life and anticipates CROMPTON in her relish for children's ability to discomfort adults.

Turner, Frederick Jackson 1861–1932 American historian. He taught at the University of Wisconsin and at Harvard. 'The Significance of the Frontier in American History', delivered to the American Historical Association in 1893, argued that the continual challenge presented by the frontier was the primary factor in American development, more important than European influences of ancestry and culture. It was collected with other essays as *The Frontier in American History* (1920). His earlier publications include *The Character and Influence of the Indian Trade in Wisconsin* (1891) and *Rise of the New West, 1819–1829* (1906). *The Significance of Sections in American History* (1932) and *The United States, 1830–1850, The Nation and Its Sections* (1935), a continuation of *Rise of the New West*, were both awarded PULITZER PRIZES.

Turner, Sharon 1768–1847 Historian. Primarily an antiquarian, he nevertheless produced, after 16 years' work, *A History of England from the Earliest Period to the Norman Conquest* (1799–1805), which encouraged serious study of England's ancient past. Other books were *The History of England from the Norman Conquest to 1500* (1814–23), *The History of the Reign of Henry VIII* (1826) and *The Reigns of Edward VI, Mary and Elizabeth* (1829).

Tusser, Thomas ?1524–80 Agricultural writer and poet. *A Hundred Points of Good Husbandry* (1557) is a manual in verse about farming and gardening, adorned with aphorisms on behaviour which make it a rich source of proverbs and maxims. *A Hundred Good Points of Housewifery* was added in the 1570 edition; by 1573 the 100 good points had grown to 500.

Tutuola, Amos 1920– Nigerian writer. He inaugurated West African literature in English with *The Palm-Wine Drinkard* (1952), a sequence of 30 episodes of quest, endurance and the achievement of wisdom, adapted mainly from Yoruba folk-tales and written in the best English his scanty schooling permits. His other books are: *My Life in the Bush of Ghosts* (1954), *Simbi and the Satyr of the Dark Jungle* (1955), *The Brave African Huntress* (1958), *Feather Woman of the Jungle* (1962), *Ajaiyi and His Inherited Poverty* (1967),*The Witch-Herbalist of the Remote Town* (1981) and *The Wild Hunter in the Bush of Ghosts* (1989).

Tuwhare, Hone 1922– New Zealand poet. His first collection, *No Ordinary Sun* (1964), was one of the best-selling poetry books ever published in New Zealand. *Mihi: Collected Poems* (1987) offers an overview of his work. Influenced by the rhythms and cadences of the oral Maori tradition and the Bible, by the English lyric, and by contemporary Maori and Pakeha (European) working-class vernacular, Tuwhare writes lyrics, ELEGIES, conversation poems and political poems. Like WITI IHIMAERA and PATRICIA GRACE, he is preoccupied with the Maori land issue. He has also written stories and plays.

Twain, Mark [Clemens, Samuel Langhorne] 1835–1910 American novelist, short-story writer and humorist. Born in Florida, Missouri, and brought up in the Mississippi River town of Hannibal, he spent his youth as a river pilot, journeyman printer, soldier in the Confederate Army and silver prospector in Nevada. In San Francisco he worked as a journalist with BRET HARTE. He adopted the name of Mark Twain in 1863 and made it famous with *The Celebrated Jumping Frog of Calaveras County*, a short story which gave its name to a collection published in 1867. A trip to Europe and the Holy Land prompted his first major work, *The Innocents Abroad* (1869). After he settled in the East and married in 1870, he confirmed his popularity with: *Roughing It* (1872), a humorous narrative of his early travels out West; *The Gilded Age* (1873), a satirical novel of the post-Civil War era co-written with CHARLES DUDLEY WARNER; THE *ADVENTURES OF TOM SAWYER* (1876); and *A Tramp Abroad* (1880). The last works of what might be called Twain's optimistic period were *The Prince and the Pauper* (1882), a romance set in the time of Henry VIII, and *LIFE ON THE MISSISSIPPI* (1883). After unwise investment made him bankrupt he published THE *ADVENTURES OF HUCKLEBERRY FINN* (1884), which has a moral dimension lacking in *Tom Sawyer*, followed by *A CONNECTICUT YANKEE IN KING ARTHUR'S COURT* (1889) and *THE TRAGEDY OF PUDD'NHEAD WILSON* (1894), both deeply pessimistic. *The American Claimant* (1892), *Tom Sawyer Abroad* (1894), and *Tom Sawyer, Detective* (1896) sought to recapture the innocent fun of his early works, but *The Man That Corrupted Hadleyburg* (1900) and *What is Man?* (1906) furthered the journey into pessimism. Recovered from bankruptcy but afflicted by family sorrows, Twain continued to lecture widely in the USA and abroad. At his death he left a wealth of unpublished material, including *The Mysterious Stranger* (1916) and *Letters from the Earth* (1962). His *Autobiography* was published in 1924.

Twelfth Night: or, What You Will A comedy by SHAKESPEARE, performed *c*. 1600 and published in the First Folio of 1623. The most direct source was probably RICH's *Apolonius and Silla*. A shipwreck brings Viola to the coast of Illyria, saddened by the loss of her 'identical' twin brother, Sebastian. Disguised as a boy (Cesario), she becomes page to Orsino, Duke of Illyria; he uses her to press his hopeless suit with Olivia, who lives in seclusion mourning her dead brother. Viola, secretly falling in love with Orsino, is so persuasive an emissary that Olivia falls in love with her. Sebastian arrives in Illyria with his faithful friend Antonio. Accidents of mistaken identity lead to Antonio's belief that Sebastian has betrayed him, to the astonished Sebastian's marriage to Olivia, and to a near-crisis when Orsino believes that Viola has stolen Olivia from him and threatens dire punishment. Only when Sebastian and Viola are allowed on stage together does confusion turn to clarity. Orsino is free to marry the loving Viola and Olivia to keep faith with her new husband, Sebastian. In a busy sub-plot, Olivia's drunken kinsman Sir Toby Belch takes advantage of the gullible Sir Andrew Aguecheek, plays an enthusiastic part in humiliating Olivia's presumptuous steward Malvolio, and marries the plot's inventor, Olivia's lady-in-waiting Maria. Feste, the fool, ends a play uncommonly confident in its use of music with a song.

Two Foscari, The A tragedy by BYRON, published in 1821, the same year as his other Venetian tragedy, *MARINO FALIERO*, and produced in 1837. In the 15th century the twice-exiled Jacopo Foscari is interrogated on the rack for his alleged crimes and his father, the aged Doge Francesco, has to sign the decree for his perpetual exile. The sentence is too much for Jacopo, who dies when he hears the news. The council then demands the abdication of Francesco, who dies as he leaves the palace, while the bells of St Mark's toll for the election of a new Doge. Verdi used the play as the basis for an opera (1844).

Two Gentlemen of Verona, The An early comedy by SHAKESPEARE, first performed *c*. 1593 and published in the First Folio of 1623. The romantic plot derives from Jorge de Montemayor's *Diana enamorada*, but Shakespeare may have come upon it by way of a lost play performed in 1585. The two gentlemen are the friends Valentine and Proteus, who both fall in love with the Duke of Milan's daughter Silvia, though Proteus was originally contracted to Julia in Verona. Proteus betrays Valentine to the Duke, who wants his daughter to marry Thurio, and Valentine becomes the leader of an outlaw band. Julia disguises herself as a boy and becomes page to Proteus. Silvia is captured by robbers and rescued by Proteus, still pressing his unwelcome suit. Eventually the confusions and identities are resolved; the Duke withdraws his objections to Valentine, allowing him to marry Silvia and Proteus to marry Julia. Some of the best theatrical opportunities are given to Proteus's comic servant Launce, much troubled by his dog.

Two Noble Kinsmen, The A play first published in 1634, with a title-page attributing it to SHAKESPEARE and JOHN FLETCHER. Most critics agree that, whatever Shakespeare's contribution may have been, it was not sufficient to make a good play of it. It is based on CHAUCER's *The Knight's Tale* (see *THE CANTERBURY TALES*) with the addition of the character of the jailer's daughter, who plays an active part in Palamon's escape and then goes mad with love for him.

Two on a Tower A novel by HARDY, published in 1882. Swithin St Cleeve, a young astronomer, meets Lady Viviette Constantine, some ten years his senior, and secretly marries her when news comes of Sir Blount Constantine's death in Africa. Then they learn that Sir Blount, although now dead, was alive when they married, thus rendering the union void. Under pressure from Viviette, Swithin claims an inheritance which is contingent on his remaining single until he is 25. He travels abroad. Discovering that she is pregnant, Viviette marries the Bishop of Melchester, who dies soon afterwards. When Swithin returns and proposes again, she dies of the shock.

Two Years Before the Mast See DANA, RICHARD HENRY.

Tyler, Anne 1941– American novelist. *The Accidental Tourist* (1985), about a lonely writer of guide books for business travellers, typifies her work in its oddball characters, whimsical tone and emphasis on family life. Other novels include *If Morning Ever Comes* (1965), *A Slipping-Down Life* (1970), *Celestial Navigation* (1975), *Searching for Caleb* (1976), *Morgan's Passing* (1980), *Dinner at the Homesick Restaurant* (1982), *Breathing Lessons* (1989; PULITZER PRIZE), *Saint Maybe* (1991) and *Ladder of Years* (1995).

Tyler, Royall 1757–1826 American playwright and novelist. He combined writing with a distinguished legal career. His reputation rests largely on *THE CONTRAST* (1787), the first comedy by a native American writer to be professionally produced. It was followed, less successfully, by several lost plays – including a comic opera, *Mad Day in Town: or, New York in an Uproar* (1787) – and four unproduced works. *The Island of Barrataria* is a FARCE based on an episode from Cervantes; *The Judgment of Solomon*, *The Origin of the Feast of Purim* and *Joseph and his Brethren* are sacred verse dramas. *THE ALGERINE CAPTIVE* (1797) was his only novel. *The Yankey in London* (1809) is a collection of essays and sketches.

Tynan, Katharine 1861–1931 Irish poet, novelist and journalist. A prolific writer, she produced 105 novels, 18 volumes of poetry and 38 other miscellaneous volumes as well as journalistic pieces that were not collected. *Collected Poems* appeared in 1930. Much of her work is strongly Roman Catholic in its preoccupations. She is widely regarded as one of the most promising but blighted poets of the Irish revival.

Tynan, Kenneth (Peacock) 1927–80 Drama critic. He made a vital contribution to the revival of post-war British theatre with his reviews for *The Observer* (1954–8 and 1960–3) and *THE NEW YORKER* (1958–60). Collections of his criticism include *He That Plays the King* (1950), *Curtains* (1961), *Tynan Right and Left* (1968) and *A View of the English Stage* (1975). He was literary manager of the ROYAL NATIONAL THEATRE in 1963–9. *Oh! Calcutta!*, the erotic revue which he produced in 1968–9, was in part a celebration of the abolition of the Lord Chamberlain's powers.

Tyndale, William ?1494–1536 Protestant martyr, humanist and translator of the Bible. Thwarted in his project for an English translation of the Bible, he left England for good in 1524. Printing of his English New Testament (from ERASMUS' Greek text) was begun at Cologne and completed at Worms in 1525–6. Such copies as found their way to England were ordered to be burned. Tyndale spent most of the rest of his life in Antwerp, revising his New Testament and completing the Pentateuch (1530) and Jonah (1531). COVERDALE continued the work: see also BIBLE IN ENGLISH. Tyndale's view of the king as sole authority in the state was expressed in his *The Obedience of a Christian Man* (1528), which won Henry VIII's approval – though Tyndale nonetheless later opposed the king's divorce. He entered into controversy with THOMAS MORE, notably in *An Answer unto Sir Thomas More's Dialogue* (1530). A translation of Erasmus' *Enchiridion militis christiani* as *The Manual of the Christian Knight* is also attributed to him. Tyndale was arrested for heresy at Antwerp, imprisoned at Vilvorde near Brussels, and strangled and burned at the stake.

Tyndall, John 1820–93 Scientist. He made his reputation with work on magnetic force and radiant heat, but reached a wider audience with a graphic and graceful expository style that made him perhaps the greatest popularizer of 19th-century physical science. His essays were gathered in the multi-volume *Fragments of Science for Unscientific People* (1871–89). With his friends LESLIE STEPHEN and THOMAS HENRY HUXLEY, he was a leader of agnostic opinion.

Typee: A Peep at Polynesian Life. During a Four Months' Residence in a Valley of the Marquesas HERMAN MELVILLE's first novel, published in 1846. It is based on his own experiences in the South Seas. Tommo and Toby jump ship in the Marquesas Islands, where they meet the Typees. Left alone with the tribe, Tommo finds it friendly and criticizes the destructive effects of white missionary efforts – an aspect of the book which provoked controversy. However, he becomes increasingly homesick for the Western world and, seeing evidence of ritual cannibalism, begins to fear that he will be the next victim. He decides to flee the valley and is rescued by the boat of an Australian whaler. *OMOO* is a sequel.

Tyrwhitt, Thomas 1730–86 Scholar. His edition of CHAUCER's *CANTERBURY TALES* (1775–8) helped establish the canon but was most important for explaining the principles of Chaucer's heroic line, which had gone undiscerned for four centuries. Tyrwhitt also edited CHATTERTON's Rowley poems in 1777, a time when they were still the object of great curiosity and dispute as to their authenticity. He himself became persuaded that they were forgeries, as he argued in an appendix added to his edition in the following year.

U

USA A trilogy of novels by DOS PASSOS, consisting of *The 42nd Parallel* (1930), *1919* (1932) and *The Big Money* (1936). One of the most ambitious as well as saddest and most angry works the USA has yet produced, it aims to chronicle the essential experience of the first 30 years of the 20th century. Only its immense length has prevented it finding a permanent readership. The most conventional, and least satisfactory, of its several approaches follows the lives of various 'typical' fictional characters, ending in disaster or disappointment. Their individual stories are supplemented by: 'Camera Eye' sections, written in STREAM OF CONSCIOUSNESS, which present the experiences of a young boy growing to manhood; 'Newsreels', or montages, of slogans, newspaper headlines, popular songs and political speeches; and, most fruitful of all, incisive miniature biographies of historical figures, who include Eugene V. Debs, RANDOLPH BOURNE, THORSTEIN VEBLEN, Thomas Edison, Frank Lloyd Wright, Theodore Roosevelt, Woodrow Wilson, Henry Ford, Isadora Duncan and Rudolph Valentino.

Udall [Uvedale], **Nicholas** 1505–56 Playwright. It is known that he was commissioned by Queen Mary to present masques and plays. Only *RALPH ROISTER DOISTER*, which vies with *GAMMER GURTON'S NEEDLE* for the title of the earliest English comedy, can be called his with any certainty, though several other works (e.g. *JACK JUGGLER* and *THERSITES*) have been attributed to him. His academic career took him from Winchester to Oxford and was not permanently checked by his dismissal from the headmastership of Eton in 1541 for violence, buggery and stealing the candlesticks. Translations from ERASMUS and *Ezechias*, a lost play celebrating the king's triumph over the Pope, helped his rehabilitation and announced his support of the Reformation. He became canon of Windsor in 1551 and headmaster of Westminster School in 1555.

Ulster Literary Theatre An amateur theatre company founded in 1902 by Bulmer Hobson and David Parkhill (Lewis Purcell) to assert a regional identity in a fashion comparable to the ABBEY THEATRE. RUTHERFORD MAYNE, as well as Hobson and Parkhill, contributed plays to its repertoire. It changed its name to the Ulster Theatre in 1915 and survived until 1934.

Ulysses A DRAMATIC MONOLOGUE by TENNYSON, published in 1842 but written in 1833. Its sources are Book IX of *The Odyssey* and Canto XXVI of Dante's *Inferno*. In old age Ulysses looks back on his past travels and forward to his last voyage, summoning the values of endurance, determination and hope to his aid.

Ulysses A novel by JOYCE, serialized in *THE LITTLE REVIEW* from 1918 until a prosecution for obscenity in 1920, and first published in volume form in Paris by Harriet Shaw Weaver's Egoist Press in 1922. It was banned in the USA until 1933 and in Britain until 1937.

The action takes place in Dublin on a single day, 16 June 1904. Its main protagonists are: Leopold Bloom, a Jewish advertisement canvasser; his unfaithful wife Molly, a concert singer; and Stephen Dedalus, from *A PORTRAIT OF THE ARTIST AS A YOUNG MAN*. Bloom and Stephen wander separately around Dublin until they meet at the end of the day, an event which may or may not alter the sense of futility, frustration and loneliness which possesses them. The minutely detailed account of the mundane, and occasionally sordid, episodes of the day, and of the topography of Dublin, would seem to place *Ulysses* at the extreme edge of REALISM. A different purpose is implied by the systematic allusion to Homer's *Odyssey* which dominates the book's manifold references to literature, music, philosophy, history and myth and gave the original titles to its 18 chapters. According to this scheme Bloom represents Odysseus (Ulysses), Molly is Penelope and Stephen is Telemachus. The Homeric parallel has a double and deliberately contradictory purpose: making SATIRE, or at least MOCK-HEROIC, of the contrast between ancient grandeur and pitiful modernity but also asserting that the present can provide valid material for EPIC. Joyce's relentlessly experimental method answers this complex challenge. He uses STREAM OF CONSCIOUSNESS (notably in 'Penelope') without relying on it to sustain a book which also embraces PARODY (of the whole history of English prose style in 'Oxen of the Sun') and EXPRESSIONISM in 'Circe'.

Uncle Remus See HARRIS, JOEL CHANDLER.

Uncle Silas: *A Tale of Bartram-Haugh* A suspense novel by LE FANU, published in 1864. Maud Ruthyn becomes the ward of her sinister uncle Silas at his remote house, Bartram-Haugh, Derbyshire. He tries to force her into marrying his unpleasant son, Dudley, and then plots her murder. The web of intrigue tightens with the introduction of the grotesque French governess, Madame de la Rougierre. In the event, Dudley kills the governess by mistake and Maud makes her escape.

Uncle Tom's Cabin: *or, Life among the Lowly* A bestselling anti-slavery novel by HARRIET BEECHER STOWE, serialized in 1851–2 and published in book form in 1852. Uncle Tom, a saintly and faithful slave, is separated from his family and sold to a slave trader when his owners, the Shelbys, fall into financial difficulties. Young George Shelby vows to redeem him one day. On his voyage down the Mississippi Tom saves the life of Eva St Clare ('little Eva'), whose father buys him out of gratitude. In New Orleans he grows close to Eva and her black friend Topsy, but little Eva dies, her father is killed in an accident and Tom is sold to the villainous Simon Legree. He is finally whipped to death for refusing to betray two escaped slaves. George Shelby arrives as Tom is dying, and vows to fight for the Abolitionist cause.

Unconditional Surrender See *SWORD OF HONOUR*.

Under Milk Wood A 'play for voices' by DYLAN THOMAS, written in 1952, revised for performance in the USA in 1953 and broadcast as a radio play in 1954. In liltingly poetic prose it describes a day in the life of some of the inhabitants of a small fishing town in South Wales called Llareggub (a jesting reversal of 'buggerall').

Under the Greenwood Tree: *or, The Mellstock Quire* A novel by HARDY, published in 1872. Termed 'a rural painting of the Dutch school', it is set in and about Mellstock (Stinsford) and concerns the love of Dick Dewey, a tranter, for the flighty but charming Fancy Day, whom he finally marries against the rivalry of Farmer Shiner and Parson Maybold. The sunny tone is touched with regret at the changing of the old rural order as the village band is replaced by a 'cabinet-organ'.

Under the Volcano A novel by MALCOLM LOWRY, published in 1947. A year after the event Jacques Laruelle recalls the last day in the life of Geoffrey Firmin, the British Consul in Cuernavaca, Mexico, in 1938. The alcoholic Firmin, his estranged wife Yvonne (who has had an affair with Laruelle) and Firmin's brother Hugh visit the festival of the Day of the Dead: Yvonne is killed by a runaway horse which the Consul has unleashed, and he is murdered by fascist thugs. Dense with SYMBOL and allusion, the narrative can be read as an unparalleled evocation of extreme alcoholism, a synthesis of arcane myth systems or an unforced ALLEGORY of a world on the brink of war.

Under Western Eyes A novel by CONRAD, published in 1911. The narrator, an elderly English teacher of languages in Geneva, tells the story of the Russian student Razumov, using Razumov's diary as well as his own observation. Razumov's quiet life in St Petersburg is disrupted when Victor Haldin, a revolutionary idealist who has just assassinated a minister of state, seeks shelter with him. He betrays Haldin, only to find that the autocracy now regards him as a suspect. Dispatched to Geneva as a secret agent, he is repelled by revolutionaries like the grotesque Peter Ivanovitch and made more guilty by the admiration of Haldin's mother and sister, Natalia, who think him a revolutionary hero. When he confesses to Natalia (whom he loves) and to the revolutionaries, they burst his eardrums. He is struck down and crippled by a tram he cannot hear.

Underwoods A collection by JONSON of what he called 'lesser poems', published in 1640. It includes the poem on SHAKESPEARE from the First Folio of 1623, 'An Ode: To Himself', 'A Celebration of Charis' and the 'Hymn on the Nativity'.

Unfortunate Traveller, The A prose tale (1594) by NASHE, sometimes claimed as the first PICARESQUE novel in English. It follows the Continental adventures of Jack Wilton, a young English page in the reign of Henry VIII, from his tricks at the English camp during the siege of Tournai to his hair-raising experiences in Italy, where he is involved in rapes, murders, revenges and schemings. Nashe is nowhere more brutal or sensational in his writing, perhaps in an attempt to burlesque the stock situations and tone of popular Elizabethan journalism.

University Wits The group of playwrights, among whom MARLOWE, GREENE, NASHE and PEELE were prominent, who received their education at Oxford or Cambridge and wrote for the London stage in the 1580s and 1590s. Most were hostile to the rising generation of playwrights, including JONSON and SHAKESPEARE, who lacked their educational advantages.

Unto this Last Essays on political economy by RUSKIN, published in THE CORNHILL MAGAZINE in 1860 and in book form in 1862. His most important and succinct social pronouncement, it rejects the *laissez-faire* doctrines of the 'Manchester School' and argues that 'that country is the richest which nourishes the greatest number of noble and happy human beings'. Like his mentor, CARLYLE, Ruskin calls for a benevolent paternalism in which enlightened 'Captains of Industry' work with their employees towards a way of life that will yield true wealth. The book's idealistic message was respected by both Tolstoy and Gandhi.

Updike, John (Hoyer) 1932– American novelist, short-story writer and poet. He established a reputation as a keen observer of modern American life with the novel *Rabbit Run* (1960), whose central character, Harry Angstrom, also appears in *Rabbit Redux* (1971), *Rabbit is Rich* (1981; PULITZER PRIZE) and *Rabbit at Rest* (1990; Pulitzer Prize). Assured, urbane and ironic, his fiction is as versatile as it is prolific. It includes *The Centaur* (1963), *Bech: A Book* (1970) and its sequel *Bech is Back* (1982), *Couples* (1968), *The Coup* (1978), *The Witches of Eastwick* (1982), *Roger's Version* (1986), *S* (1988), *Memories of the Ford Administration* (1993) and *Brazil* (1994). His collections of short stories include *A Month of Sundays* (1975), *Marry Me* (1976), *Trust Me* (1987) and *The Afterlife* (1995). He has also published: poetry in, for example, *Tossing and Turning* (1977); CHILDREN'S LITERATURE; art criticism in *Just Looking* (1989); and autobiography in *Self-Consciousness* (1989). His reviews and essays are gathered in *Assorted Prose* (1965), *Picked-Up Pieces* (1978), *Hugging the Shore* (1983) and *Odd Jobs* (1991).

Upward, Edward (Falaise) 1903– Novelist. A lifelong friend of ISHERWOOD, he joined the Communist Party in the 1930s. *Journey to the Border* (1938) is a Kafkaesque political allegory about a private tutor's progress towards radicalism and the Workers' Movement. Like many radicals of his generation, Upward was caught in the trap of Party dogmatism during the Stalin era. *The Spiral Ascent* – a trilogy consisting of *In the Thirties* (1962), *Rotten Elements* (1969) and *No Home but the Struggle* (1977) – chart his political soul-searching and personal struggles during the years of silence.

Urn Burial See HYDRIOTAPHIA.

Urquhart [Urchard], Sir **Thomas** c. 1611–c. 1660 Translator of Rabelais. The first two books of his spirited version of *Gargantua and Pantagruel* appeared in 1653; the work was completed by MOTTEUX after his death. Urquhart was also the author of curious treatises on mathematics and language to which he gave elaborate Greek titles.

Usk, Thomas d. 1388 *The Testament of Love*, his only surviving work, was written shortly before his execution. Usk had formerly been confidential clerk to John of Northampton, whom he betrayed in 1384. *The Testament* is a prose ALLEGORY describing how Love (meaning divine love) consoles him, finally showing how Grace may be attained. Though poorly written, it was sufficiently influenced by CHAUCER's *Boece* and THE HOUSE OF FAME to assure its inclusion in the CHAUCERIAN APOCRYPHA.

Ussher, James 1581–1656 Irish churchman and scholar. A tireless preacher, controversialist and antagonist of Rome, he ended his career as Archbishop of Armagh, Primate of the Anglican Church in Ireland. He was famed for his skill in languages and his unrivalled knowledge of patristic literature and the history of the primitive church. Frequent visits to England brought him in touch with CAMDEN, SIR ROBERT COTTON and SELDEN. Most of his many scholarly works are in Latin. They include *Britannicarum ecclesiarum antiquitates* (1639), a lengthy study of the early church in the British Isles, and *Annales Veteris et Novi Testamenti* (1650), long accepted as providing a definitive chronology of the world up to the dispersion of the Jews. It determined that the Creation had taken place on 23 October 4004 BC and the Flood in 1656 BC.

Utilitarianism An ethical doctrine which judges an act to be right or wrong according to its tendency to promote the happiness of the majority affected by it. BENTHAM is usually named as its founding father, although he acknowledged his debt to other 18th-century philosophers, including HUME. Bentham's Utilitarianism formed the ideological basis for a programme of moral and legal reforms which he and followers such as JAMES MILL and RICARDO wished to introduce. JOHN STUART MILL widened the doctrine's scope, notably in 'Utilitarianism' (1861), to include private as well as public moral sanctions and to refine the concept of 'pleasure'. Later in the 19th century HENRY SIDGWICK suggested that the method involved in determining the right course of action could frequently be more complex than early Utilitarian theory had allowed for, and in the early 20th century G. E. MOORE argued for the recognition of non-hedonistic values, independent of the pain-pleasure principle.

Utopia A prose work by THOMAS MORE, written in Latin and printed at Louvain in 1516 as *Libellus vere aureus, nec minus salutaris quam festivus, de optimo reipublicae statu deque nova insula Utopia* ('A truly golden little book, no less beneficial than entertaining, about the best state of a commonwealth and the new island of Utopia'). Ralph Robinson's English version appeared in 1551 and GILBERT BURNET's translation in 1684. In Book I More meets the traveller Raphael Hythlodaeus at Antwerp and discusses the state of European society with him. Book II (which was written first) contains Raphael's description of the happy island state of Utopia, where all things are held in common, gold is despised and the people live communally. Interpretations of *Utopia* (the name plays on two Greek words *eutopos*, 'a good place', and *outopos*, 'no place') are many and diverse. It has been seen as a programme for an ideal state, a vision of the ideal to be contemplated (like Plato's *Republic*), a SATIRE

of contemporary European society, and a humanist *jeu d'esprit*.

Models for More's island state can be found in earlier literature and its influence can be felt in BACON's *NEW ATLANTIS* (1627), one of many such works in the 17th century, when 'Utopian' became current as an adjective. The ambiguities of More's island, whether it is ideal, possible or even desirable, continue in subsequent Utopian literature, as does the use of imagined strange lands for satirical purposes (SWIFT's *GULLIVER'S TRAVELS*, BUTLER's *EREWHON*). 'Dystopian' was first used as an adjective in the late 19th century by J. S. MILL, to suggest an imagined state which was not desirable. But the desirability of Utopia is deliberately open to question even in More's work. ALDOUS HUXLEY's *BRAVE NEW WORLD* and ORWELL's *NINETEEN EIGHTY-FOUR* describe apparent Utopias that reveal themselves to be dystopian.

Uttley, Alison 1884–1976 Writer of CHILDREN'S LITERATURE. *The Little Grey Rabbit* (1929) was followed by over 30 titles in the same series, all illustrated by Margaret Tempest and appearing in the same small format. *Tales of Four Pigs and Brock the Badger* (1939) introduced Sam Pig, who went on to feature in 35 separate adventures. Sometimes reaching back into ancient legend and history, Uttley's imaginary world is gentle, much taken up with the domestic details of humanized squirrels, hares and moles. Her autobiography, *The Country Child* (1931), brilliantly records a harsher side of rural life. In her finest story for older children, *A Traveller in Time* (1939), a modern child is transported back into plots involving the imprisoned Mary, Queen of Scots.

Valentinian A tragedy by JOHN FLETCHER, performed *c.* 1612 and published in 1647. The sensational plot has some basis in late Roman history. Maximus takes revenge against Valentinian III for dishonouring his wife Lucina and driving her to suicide, and succeeds in replacing him as Emperor. He takes Valentinian's widow, Eudoxia, as consort but makes the mistake of confiding in her. She poisons him before he can be crowned. The play contains some fine lyrics.

van der Post, Sir **Laurens (Jan)** 1906– South African man of letters. *In a Province* (1934), his first and most convincing novel, is an early indictment of white South African racism. Elsewhere his narrative skills are most successful in non-fictional works expressing his openness to other cultures, the intuitive and the mythopoeic, derived from childhood exposure to San (Bushman) and other African societies, and reinforced by his friendship with Jung. These include *Venture to the Interior* (1952), about exploration in Malawi, and *The Lost World of the Kalahari* (1958), *The Heart of the Hunter* (1961), *A Mantis Carol* (1975) and *Testament to the Bushman* (with Jane Taylor; 1984), records of surviving San culture.

Van Vechten, Carl 1880–1966 American novelist. He is best known for novels such as *Peter Whiffle* (1922), *The Blind Bow-Boy* (1923), *Firecrackers* (1925) and *Parties* (1930), which deal with the cultural life of New York in the 1920s. *Nigger Heaven* (1926), his most highly acclaimed work, is set in Harlem. Other novels include a SATIRE of Hollywood, *Spider Boy* (1928), and *The Tattooed Countess* (1924), set in his home state of Iowa. He was also a music and drama critic and wrote several memoirs, including *Sacred and Profane Memoirs* (1932) and an account of GERTRUDE STEIN, published as an introduction to her *Three Lives* (1909).

van Vogt, A(lfred) E(lton) 1912– Canadian-born writer of SCIENCE FICTION. A colourful pulp writer, he has produced many stories whose harassed heroes gradually achieve control of awesome superhuman powers, including *Slan* (1940; in book form, 1948), *The World of Null-A* (1945; in book form, 1946; revised, 1965) and the two stories in *Masters of Time* (1950). His intellectual substance is perhaps best displayed in his non-fantasy novel about brainwashing, *The Violent Man* (1962). His writing career was interrupted when he became a follower of L. Ron Hubbard's Scientology.

Vanbrugh, Sir **John** 1664–1726 Architect and playwright. He was honoured more for his buildings than his plays. His most famous designs include Castle Howard (begun 1701), Blenheim Palace (begun 1705) and Seaton Delaval (begun 1720). He is said to have drafted a comedy while imprisoned in the Bastille for espionage (1688–92), but his first performed play was THE RELAPSE (1696), a cynical sequel to CIBBER's *LOVE'S LAST SHIFT*. With his other major work, THE PROVOKED WIFE (1697), it was singled out for attack by JEREMY COLLIER in his *Short View of the Immorality and Profaneness of the English Stage* (1698). Vanbrugh was stung into replying with *A Short Vindication* (1698). His remaining plays are mostly adaptations, the two-part *Aesop* (1697) from Boursault, *The Country House* (1698) from Dancourt, *The Pilgrim* (1700) from JOHN FLETCHER, *The False Friend* (1702) from Le Sage, *The Confederacy* (1705) from Dancourt and *The Mistake* (1705) from Molière. He collaborated with CONGREVE and William Walsh in *Squire Trelooby* (1704), another version of Molière, wrote the unsuccessful *The Cuckold in Conceit* (1707) and left unfinished *A Journey to London*, which Cibber completed and staged as *The Provoked Husband* (1728).

Vanderhaeghe, Guy 1951– Canadian novelist and short-story writer. The stories in his first collection, *Man Descending* (1982), chronicle the disillusionment and pain of daily life in the contemporary world. Earlier stories were gathered in *The Trouble with Heroes and Other Stories* (1983). His novel, *My Present Age* (1984), further explores isolation while *Homesick* (1989), like many recent Canadian novels, deals with a female protagonist's need to return to and connect with her origins.

***Vanity Fair:** A Novel without a Hero* A novel by THACKERAY, published in monthly parts in 1847–8 and in volume form in 1848.

A vast satirical panorama of a materialistic society and a landmark in the history of REALISM, it is set during the period of Waterloo. The plot traces the destinies of two contrasted heroines: the poor but resourceful Becky Sharp and her affectionate, trusting friend Amelia Sedley. Thwarted in her attempt to trap Amelia's brother Jos into marriage, Becky becomes governess to the Crawley family. Sir Pitt Crawley proposes to her, only to find that she has already married his soldier son, Rawdon. The news alienates the wealthy aunt on whom Rawdon depends, and the couple live by their wits. Amelia's fortunes decline: her stockbroker father is ruined and her love affair with the vain George Osborne is opposed by his purse-proud father. Although in love with Amelia himself, George's friend William Dobbin persuades him to marry her. The principal characters move with the army to Brussels and George is killed at Waterloo. The grieving Amelia dotes on her son, Georgy, and the memory of George.

Becky neglects her son, Rawdon, in favour of a life of fashion, abruptly ended when her husband finds her in a compromising situation with Lord Steyne. She flees to the Continent, where she is discovered by Amelia, whose fortunes have revived with the return of Dobbin and Jos from India and Georgy's adoption by his wealthy grandfather. The meeting leads to the revelation that George had proposed to elope with Becky on the eve of Waterloo, thus destroying the sentimental memories which prevented Amelia marrying the faithful Dobbin. Becky regains her hold over Jos, who dies in suspicious circumstances. Rawdon dies abroad and his son inherits the Crawley estate. Becky ends in the guise of a pious widow.

Vanity Fair An American magazine, published since 1859, though with interruptions and changes of character. Under its first editors, C. G. Leland and ARTEMUS WARD, it offered humorous commentary on contemporary affairs. From 1913, when it was bought by Condé Nast, until 1939, when it was absorbed by *Vogue*, it became a sophisticated review of literature, art and fashion. It reappeared in 1983, chiefly as a magazine of high fashion and living, though it has also printed work by Márquez, Calvino, Brodsky and MAILER.

Vanity of Human Wishes, The A poem by SAMUEL JOHNSON in IMITATION of Juvenal's Tenth Satire, published in 1749. The poet surveys the aspirations and delusions of mankind through the ages and across the busy geography of human ambition, selecting (as in the Latin original on which it is skilfully modelled) representative figures for examination. The section on the fearsomeness of old age and the treatment of physical beauty are especially effective. The atmosphere of weary inevitability and the tragic irony of the human examples are enhanced by the poem's intensely regular movement.

Vansittart, Peter 1920– Novelist. A distinctive though often neglected writer, preoccupied with language at the expense of narrative, he has frequently made imaginative use of historical settings. His many titles include *I am the World* (1942), *Broken Canes* (1950), *A Little Madness* (1953), *Carolina* (1961), *Quintet* (1976), *Aspects of Feeling* (1986) and *Parsifal* (1988). *Paths from the White Horse* (1985) is his autobiography.

Varieties of Religious Experience, The A book by WILLIAM JAMES, published in 1902. Concentrating on personal instead of organized religion, and particularly on the process of conversion, he argues that the particulars of religious faith are true insofar as they provide the believer with emotional fulfilment. The book stimulated study of the psychology of religion.

Vathek: *An Arabian Tale* A novel by BECKFORD, written in French and first published in English in 1786. The translation, probably by Samuel Henley, may have been undertaken at Beckford's request and with his help, but was presented as Henley's own version from the Arabic. Corrupted by power and his thirst for forbidden knowledge, Caliph Vathek becomes a servant of Eblis, the devil. He finally realizes the vanity of earthly treasures and wonders but not before he and his companions are condemned to eternal torment: their bodies will remain intact but their hearts will burn for ever inside them. Although Beckford's fantasy owes much to the fashion for the GOTHIC NOVEL, its setting allies it with the Orientalism already apparent in JOHNSON's *RASSELAS* and later to reach its full flowering in the work of BYRON and THOMAS MOORE.

Vaughan, Henry 1621/2–95 Poet. The twin brother of THOMAS VAUGHAN, he returned to his native Newton-upon-Usk in Wales as a physician after fighting as a Royalist in the Civil War. *Poems, with the Tenth Satire of Juvenal Englished* (1646) is, apart from its translation of Juvenal, a slender offering of courtly Cavalier verse. *Olor iscanus* ('The Swan of Usk'), complete by 1647 but not published until 1651, tried to create a poetry of rural retreat in a Welsh setting. *Silex scintillans* (1650), one of the outstanding volumes of meditative verse of the century, marked a complete change. 'The Flashing Flint' of the title announces the theme of the hardened heart struck by affliction until it yields a holy fire. Stylistically the poems are deeply influenced by GEORGE HERBERT. An enlarged edition (1655) was followed by *Thalia rediviva* (1678), a dry miscellany. Prose works include a meditative treatise *The Mount of Olives: or, Solitary Devotions* (1652), and several translations of religious and medical writings. He liked to style himself 'Henry Vaughan, Silurist', a reference to his homeland in the border country of Wales once occupied by the ancient British tribe of the Silures.

Vaughan, Thomas 1621/2–66 Hermetic philosopher. Twin brother of the poet HENRY VAUGHAN, he engaged in chemical research at Oxford and London, and died, according to ANTHONY À WOOD, as a result of an experiment with mercury, 'which getting up into his nose,

marched him off'. Under the name Eugenius Philalethes ('The well-born lover of Truth') he published in the 1650s a number of treatises of hermetic philosophy, and was regarded as one of the most notable alchemists of his time. His works explore the occult influences that operate throughout the creation and justify the pursuit of alchemy as the supreme philosophic quest. His prose is learned, allusive and cryptic; it may however be admired for its aggressive ebullience. Vaughan was lampooned by SAMUEL BUTLER in *HUDIBRAS*, and by SWIFT in *A TALE OF A TUB*. Some of his poems were printed in Henry Vaughan's collection *Thalia rediviva* (1678).

Vaux, Thomas, 2nd Baron Vaux of Harrowden 1510–56 Poet. He contributed two poems to *TOTTEL'S MISCELLANY* (1557), one of them 'The Aged Lover Renounceth Love', and 13 to *THE PARADISE OF DAINTY DEVICES* (1576).

Veblen, Thorstein (Bunde) 1857–1929 American economist and social critic. His first and most famous book, *The Theory of the Leisure Class: An Economic Study in the Evolution of Institutions* (1899), was popular among radicals for its attack on the caste system which grew out of the pursuit of wealth. Veblen's abiding interest in the economic determinants of modern society – in particular, his concern with the disjunction between those who produce goods and those who control the production process and the distribution of products – is evident in several of his other works: *The Theory of Business Enterprise* (1904), *The Instinct of Workmanship* (1914), *The Vested Interests and the State of the Industrial Arts* (1919), *The Engineers and the Price System* (1921) and *Absentee Ownership* (1923).

Venice Preserved A tragedy by OTWAY, first performed in 1682. Persuaded by his brave friend, Pierre, to join a conspiracy against the Venetian republic, Jaffeir entrusts his wife Belvidera to Renault, leader of the conspiracy, as proof of his loyalty. Renault forces his attentions on Belvidera, and she persuades Jaffeir to warn her father Priuli, a senator. When the senators break their promise to spare the conspirators' lives, Jaffeir kills Pierre to save him from being broken on the wheel. He then kills himself, and Belvidera, her mind unbalanced, dies. A sub-plot of surprising comic potential matches a courtesan, Aquilina, with a masochistic senator, Antonio. Some contemporaries recognized Antonio and Renault as a composite caricature of the EARL OF SHAFTESBURY.

Venus and Adonis A narrative poem by SHAKESPEARE, first printed in 1593 and popular enough to go through many editions in his lifetime. A sensuous and witty EPYLLION, it retells a favourite Renaissance myth which Shakespeare took mainly from Ovid's *Metamorphoses*: Venus' repeated attempts to woo the chaste Adonis and his death while boar-hunting. The poem is like many of Shakespeare's comedies in its alternately sympathetic and ironic scrutiny of the pains, humour and pathos of wooing. Like *THE RAPE OF LUCRECE*, it is full of rhetorical display, ornamented language, verbal display, elaborate CONCEITS and witty play. In addition there are fine descriptions of the countryside and its animals.

Vercelli Book A 10th-century manuscript of Old English verse and prose preserved in the cathedral library at Vercelli. It contains two poems by CYNEWULF (*ELENE* and *The Fates of the Apostles*), *The Address of the Soul to the Body*, *ANDREAS* and *THE DREAM OF THE ROOD*, together with a prose life of ST GUTHLAC and prose HOMILIES.

verse romance A form originating in 12th-century France, where the greatest exponent was Chrétien de Troyes, and flourishing in England during the 13th and 14th centuries. Early romances like ATHELSTON, KING HORN and THE TALE OF GAMELYN tell old English stories but most derive from the French. Characteristically, they tell the story of a knight, sometimes a character from ARTHURIAN LITERATURE, who leaves the court and undergoes adventures, often involving the supernatural, before returning in triumph; his rewards frequently include marriage. Occasionally there are two central figures, either a couple (FLORES AND BLANCHEFLOUR) or close companions (AMIS AND AMILOUN). The chief concern is with courtly life and the chivalric code, though few romances match the sophistication of their French counterparts or achieve the subtlety of SIR GAWAIN AND THE GREEN KNIGHT. Some works usually called verse romances (such as THE SOWDON OF BABYLON) are concerned with military campaigns and the opposition of Christianity to pagan religions. The romance declined towards the end of the 15th century and those later examples which are not translations use a stock of familiar motifs. The most common verse forms are TAIL-RHYME, ALLITERATIVE VERSE and the octosyllabic couplet.

Verses on the Death of Dr Swift A poem by SWIFT himself, published in 1739. It imagines the circumstances of his own death, the reaction of those who had known him and his subsequent misrepresentation for posterity. The poet's IRONY and raillery about contemporary values, and his good-natured gibes at the expense of his friends, do not conceal his views on the ingratitude and fickleness of human nature.

Vertue, George 1684–1756 Engraver and antiquary. Official engraver to the Royal Society of Antiquaries and a man constantly employed on major projects, he also collected materials for a history of the arts in England. After his death HORACE WALPOLE bought the working papers from his widow and incorporated much of the material in his *Anecdotes of Painting*. The notebooks have also been published separately (Walpole Society, 1929–52).

Very, Jones 1813–80 American poet. A mystic who believed in the absolute surrender of the will to God, he wrote devotional verse in the vein of the METAPHYSICAL POETS. His work was highly praised by WILLIAM CULLEN BRYANT and WILLIAM ELLERY CHANNING, as well as EMERSON, who edited and published Very's first book, *Essays and Poems* (1839). *Poems* (1883) and *Poems and Essays* (1886) appeared posthumously.

Vicar of Bullhampton, The A novel by TROLLOPE, serialized in 1869–70 and published in volume form in 1870. Frank Fenwick's vigorous, practical Christianity shows in his concern for the children of the local miller Jacob Brattle. When Sam Brattle is accused of complicity in the murder of a local farmer, Fenwick helps to bring the real murderers to trial. He also rescues Sam's fallen sister Carry, restoring her to her father's home and forgiveness. Love-interest is provided by the hopeless passion of the local squire, Harry Gilmore, for Mary Lowther and her eventual marriage to her cousin Walter Marrable.

Vicar of Wakefield, The The only novel by GOLDSMITH, written in 1761 or 1762 but not published until 1766. The Vicar, Dr Primrose, tells the story of his family's fall from contentment. Their hardships begin when he loses his personal fortune in the bankruptcy of a merchant company. He finds a new living through the patronage of Squire Thornhill but the Squire persuades the eldest daughter, Olivia, into a false marriage ceremony and then deserts her. She is found by her father and brought back home. When his vicarage burns down and his debts are called in, Dr Primrose is thrown into prison. He is joined by George, his son, who has challenged Thornhill to a duel. The younger daughter, Sophia, is abducted and the deserted Olivia, so the Vicar is told, has died of grief. Dr Primrose endures all these blows with stoicism. A kind-hearted but apparently seedy gentleman, calling himself Mr Burchell but in fact the Squire's uncle Sir William, rescues Sophia, and proves that Olivia's marriage was after all a true one and that she is not dead. George is able to marry his love, Arabella Wilmot, and Dr Primrose's fortune is restored to him by the reformation of the swindler, Ephraim Jenkinson. The story has the perennial charm of a fairy-tale: the rural setting is cosy, the characters are divided into stereotypes of good and evil, and their sufferings can be magically relieved by a happy ending. It incorporates three notable short poems: 'The Hermit: or, Edwin and Angelina', 'When Lovely Woman Stoops to Folly' and 'Elegy on the Death of a Mad Dog'.

Vices and Virtues The earliest surviving dialogue in Middle English, written *c*. 1200. The beginning is lost. A Soul confesses in detail its sins to Reason and the latter explains the nature and value of the Christian virtues in a dignified and carefully ordered series of expositions. There is an interesting allegorical representation of the meeting between Mercy, Truth, Pity, Peace and Patience.

Victory A novel by CONRAD, published in 1915. The story is set in Indonesia. On a rare impulse the cynical Axel Heyst helps Morrison, the captain of a trading brig, by paying his fines. He is offered a share in the Tropical Belt Coal Company and becomes its owner when Morrison dies. The Company fails but Heyst remains on the island of Samburan, alone except for his servant Wang. Schomberg, the hotel keeper in Sourabaya, circulates rumours that Heyst murdered Morrison and has secreted a fortune on the island. His malignancy increases when Heyst, on a rare visit, rescues an English girl, Lena, from his unwanted attentions. Schomberg invites a trio of desperadoes to raid Heyst's island: 'plain Mr Jones', Ricardo, and Pedro. Lena is mortally wounded trying to baffle their plans. She dies in Heyst's arms with the smile of private 'victory' on her lips. Heyst commits suicide in despair.

Vidal, Gore 1925– American novelist, playwright and essayist. He made use of his experiences in World War II in *Williwaw* (1946) and *In a Yellow Wood* (1947). *The City and the Pillar* (1948, revised 1965), a best-seller, deals frankly with homosexuality. Since then a series of long, exhaustively researched novels has scrutinized famous times and epochs from American history: *Burr* (1973), *1876* (1976), *Lincoln* (1984), *Empire* (1987) and *Hollywood* (1989). *Creation* (1982) tackles ancient history. Other novels are jaundiced, often apocalyptic comedies: *Myra Breckenridge* (1968), *Kalki* (1978), *Live from Golgotha* (1992) and *Duluth* (1983). The evils of popular culture, American right-wing politics and fundamentalist religion are also favourite targets of the essays collected in *Homage to Daniel Shays* (as *Collected Essays 1952–72* in Britain, 1972), *Matters of Fact and Fiction* (1977), *The Second American Revolution* (as *Pink Triangle and Yellow Star* in Britain, 1982) and *At Home* (as *Armageddon?* in Britain, 1988). *Screening History* (1992) is a series of essays on film.

Village, The A poem in two books by CRABBE, published in 1783. It opposes descriptions of pain, want and deprivation to the idyllic sentimentalism of conventional PASTORAL. Crabbe fails to sustain this kind of attack in the second book, and the poem ends with a rather lame homily on misery and distress as the general human condition, though both are earlier seen as the special preserve of the rural poor. Warmly approved by JOHNSON and BURKE, it established Crabbe's reputation.

Villette A novel by CHARLOTTE BRONTË, published in 1853. It develops material already used in her first novel, THE PROFESSOR. Lucy Snowe goes to teach at a girls' school in Villette, a Belgian town based on the author's experience of Brussels, and proves her worth to Madame Beck, the headmistress. She is condescendingly befriended by a pupil, Ginevra Fanshawe, whose admirers include Dr John Bretton, the son of Lucy's godmother. Lucy represses her own feelings for him and Bretton, realizing Ginevra's vanity, falls in love with Paulina Home. Lucy buries herself in her work but gradually awakens to the fascination of the professor, Paul Emmanuel, a waspish man who finds in her a response that mellows and softens him. When he is obliged to go to the West Indies he leaves Lucy in charge of his school, promising to return in three years.

Vindication of the Rights of Woman, A See WOLLSTONECRAFT, MARY.

Virgin Martyr, The A tragedy by MASSINGER and DEKKER, first produced c. 1620 and published c. 1622. The martyr of the title is Dorothea (St Dorothy). She is tortured and executed for her Christian faith after she has provoked the anger of the Emperor Diocletian's daughter Artemia, jealous of Antoninus' love for her. He dies at her side. The last part of the play deals with the struggle for the soul of her persecutor Theophilus between his evil secretary Harpax and the good Angelo. Angelo prevails and Theophilus is in turn martyred as a Christian.

Virginian, The See WISTER, OWEN.

Virginians, The A novel by THACKERAY, published in parts in 1857–9 and in book form in 1858–9. A stately and rather static historical romance, it continues the story of the Esmond family from THE HISTORY OF HENRY ESMOND by following the fortunes of Esmond's twin grandsons, George and Harry Warrington.

George, the elder, is reported killed in action against the French. Harry visits England, becomes a favourite of his aunt (the Beatrix of Esmond, now the Baroness Bernstein) and falls in love with his middle-aged cousin, Lady Maria Esmond. He falls into debt but is rescued by George, escaped from French imprisonment. Now that Harry is no longer the heir, Maria releases him from his engagement. George settles in London, turns to writing plays and, to his mother's disapproval, marries the middle-class Theo Lambert. On the death of his English uncle, Sir Miles Warrington, he succeeds to the title and the Warrington estates in England. Meanwhile Harry serves with General Wolfe at the capture of Quebec, buys an estate in Virginia and marries the daughter of his mother's companion. The brothers find themselves on opposing sides during the Revolution and George, who has fought for the King, resigns his Virginian estate to Harry and retires to England.

Vision of Judgement, A A poem by SOUTHEY, published in 1821. An apotheosis of George III, who had died the previous year, it describes the king's shade triumphing over critics and enemies and being admitted to Paradise. An ill-judged performance from a POET LAUREATE despised by the younger generation of poets as an ex-radical turned apologist for the Establishment, it was made even more provocative by a savage attack on BYRON in the preface. Byron replied with THE VISION OF JUDGEMENT, taunting Southey again in the preface to DON JUAN.

Vision of Judgement, The A satirical poem by BYRON, prompted by SOUTHEY's eulogy of George III, A VISION OF JUDGEMENT. It was published in 1822 by LEIGH HUNT in THE LIBERAL. Hunt incurred a £100 fine and would probably have suffered a heavier penalty if he had included Byron's preface, which further attacked both Southey and George III.

Byron transforms Southey's solemn heroics into comedy. His PARODY has a bored St Peter disputing with the archangel Michael and Satan over George III's entry into Heaven. The king's critics are cut short, and Washington and BENJAMIN FRANKLIN prevented from speaking, by the entry of a devil carrying Southey. St Peter implores him to speak in prose but Southey insists on reading his Vision of Judgement. In the ensuing uproar St Peter fells Southey with his keys and George III slips unnoticed into Paradise, where Byron leaves him 'practising the hundredth psalm'.

Vivian Grey The first novel by BENJAMIN DISRAELI, published in 1826. The scrappily plotted narrative follows the fortunes of Vivian, a clever and manipulative young man much like his creator. The most interesting character is Essper George, a conjuror who becomes Vivian's servant and entertains him with tall stories. The book may owe something to the tradition of TOM JONES and PEREGRINE PICKLE, with their scapegrace heroes accompanied by faithful servants.

Vizenor, Gerald 1934– Native American poet and novelist. His volumes of English haiku poetry include Raising the Moon (1964), Seventeen Chirps (1964), Two Wings the Butterfly (1967) and Matsushima: Haiku (1984). Recent works include The Trickster of Liberty (1988), Griever: An American Monkey in China (1990), Bearheart (1990), Landfill Meditation: Wise Blood Stories (1991) and Dead Voices: Natural Agonies in the New World (1992). A novel, Darkness in Saint Louis Bearheart (1978), is a self-reflexive exercise in POST-MODERNISM. He has also published several collections of Native American writing and Narrative Chance: Postmodern Discourses of Native American Indian Literature (1989).

Volpone: or, The Fox A comedy by BEN JONSON, performed in 1605–6 and published in 1607, the most frequently revived of his plays. Although formally set in Venice, it directs its moral scrutiny on the customs and values of the rising merchant classes of Jacobean London. The wealthy Volpone lets it be known that he is near death and avaricious legacy-hunters flock to his bedside, there to be duped by himself and his quick-witted servant, Mosca (fly). Voltore (vulture), Corbaccio (crow) and Corvino (raven) all reveal their true corruption. Volpone overreaches himself when, having willed his property to Mosca, he pretends to be dead. The infuriated Voltore takes the matter to court, where Mosca recognizes and exploits the personal advantage of his master's 'death'. To thwart Mosca, Volpone has to come alive and reveal the whole plot, on the strength of which revelation he, along with everyone else, is appropriately punished. Only the virtuous – Corvino's wife and Corbaccio's son – are rewarded.

Vonnegut, Kurt, Jr 1922– American novelist, short-story writer, playwright and writer of SCIENCE FICTION.

His novels are ironic jeremiads combining dark humour with unashamed sentimentality. *Player Piano* (1952) is a dystopian novel about automation. *The Sirens of Titan* (1959) is satirical science fiction, introducing the Tralfamadorian aliens who reappear in his most substantial work, *Slaughterhouse-Five: or, The Children's Crusade* (1969), which draws upon his experiences as a prisoner of war during the firestorming of Dresden. *Cat's Cradle* (1963) and *Galapagos* (1985) are sarcastic apocalyptic fantasies. Vonnegut's non-fantastic novels, including *Mother Night* (1961), *God Bless You, Mr Rosewater* (1965), *Jailbird* (1979), *Deadeye Dick* (1985) and *Hocus Pocus* (1991), are character studies with innocent, unlucky protagonists. His short fiction is collected in *Welcome to the Monkey House* (1968). Plays include *Happy Birthday, Wanda June* (1960) and *Timesteps* (1979). His non-fiction is collected in *Wampeters, Foma and Granfalloons* (1974) and two volumes of 'autobiographical collage', *Palm Sunday* (1981) and *Fates Worse Than Death* (1991).

vorticism A movement in British art which flourished in 1913–15 under the leadership of WYNDHAM LEWIS. He adopted POUND's term, 'vortex', to signify his version of the concentrated energy of the new arts of MODERNISM. He was largely responsible for the vorticist magazine *BLAST* (1914–15) and, with followers who included the painters Frederick Etchells, Cuthbert Hamilton and Edward Wadsworth, founded the Rebel Art Centre in 1914. It attracted more artists – the sculptor Jacob Epstein and several poets of IMAGISM – in rebellion against the prevailing orthodoxy of post-impressionism. They preferred German aesthetics, EXPRESSIONISM, cubism and futurism to the decorative art of Matisse. Vorticist paintings and drawings tended towards sharp-lined and angular abstraction, though they often celebrated modern machinery and industrial landscapes.

Voss A novel by PATRICK WHITE, published in 1957. It was inspired by White's reading of the journals of the Australian explorers Leichhardt and Eyre. The first part, set in Sydney in the 1840s, describes preparations for an expedition into the Australian interior. The long central section, which employs a dense, metaphorical style, is the story of the journey itself and of how the megalomaniac explorer Voss gradually comes to acknowledge humility. The final section returns to Sydney and deals ironically with the making of the myth of Voss, who has perished, along with all the members of the expedition except one. Voss's actual journey is complemented by the metaphorical journey of Laura Trevelyan, who remains in Sydney but functions as his anima and 'spiritual wife'.

Voyage Out, The VIRGINIA WOOLF's first novel, written in 1912–13 but not published until 1915. Unlike her later works, it is realistic in form, though it contains passages of lyrical intensity. Rachel Vinrace, an innocent young woman, sails to South America on her father's ship, accompanied by her aunt, Helen Ambrose, and uncle Ridley. At Lisbon she meets Richard and Clarissa Dalloway, who reappear in *MRS DALLOWAY*. In South America she falls in love with Terence Hewet, an aspiring writer interested in women's experiences and concerned about their position in society. They determine to establish their future marriage on a new basis of equality, but Rachel is taken ill and dies. The novel ends with the English party at the hotel retiring to bed.

Vulgar Errors See *PSEUDODOXIA EPIDEMICA*.

Waddell, Helen (Jane) 1889–1965 Scholar, translator and novelist. The sister of RUTHERFORD MAYNE, she is remembered for *The Wandering Scholars* (1927), a pioneering study of European learning in the 12th century and the sometimes ribald goliardic verse associated with it, the verse translations in *Medieval Latin Lyrics* (1933) and her moving novel, *Peter Abelard* (1933).

Waddington [*née* Dworkin]**, Miriam** 1917– Canadian poet. Meticulously crafted, her poems are lyric celebrations of the baffling richness within common things. Collections include *Green World* (1945), *The Second Silence* (1955), *The Glass Trumpet* (1966), *Say Yes* (1969), *Driving Home* (1972), *The Price of Gold* (1976) and *The Visitants* (1981). Her short stories are collected in *Summer at Lonely Beach* (1982). She is also a distinguished critic and translator of prose and poetry from the Yiddish.

Wade, Thomas 1805–75 Poet and playwright. He succeeded with *Woman's Love: or The Trial of Patience* (1829), a play in verse and prose, and *The Phrenologists* (1830), a FARCE, before the failure of his tragedy *The Jew of Arragon* (1830). His verse includes *Tasso and the Sisters* (1825) and *Mundi et cordis: de rebus sempiternis et temporariis: carmina* (1835), a volume of remarkable SONNETS.

Wain, John 1925–94 Novelist, poet and critic. His most famous novel is still his first, *Hurry On Down* (1953), a PICARESQUE comedy recognized as a leading example of the fiction produced by the ANGRY YOUNG MEN. Later novels include *The Contenders* (1958), *Strike the Father Dead* (1962), *The Smaller Sky* (1968), *A Winter in the Hills* (1971), *Young Shoulders* (1982) and two BILDUNGSROMANEN, *Where the River Meets* (1988) and *Comedies* (1990). *Nuncle* (1960) and *Death of the Hind Legs* (1966) contain short stories. His cerebral, witty verse is collected in *Poems 1949–79* (1981). He also wrote a biography of SAMUEL JOHNSON (1974), literary criticism and radio plays.

Wainwright, Jeffrey 1944– Poet. Although riven with IRONY and self-questioning, his poetry is a poetry of political commitment, written in terse and humane language. It includes: *Heart's Desire* (1978), which contains 'Thomas Muntzer'; a stage adaptation of Péguy's *Le Mystère de la charité de Jeanne d'Arc* (1984); and *Selected Poems* (1985).

Waiting for Godot A play by BECKETT, written and performed in French (*En attendant Godot*, 1953) before being performed in Beckett's English translation in 1955. Its cryptic allusiveness was first derided and then admired to a degree that has made it one of the most influential works of the post-war European theatre. Two tramps, Vladimir and Estragon, wait beside a leafless tree for Godot, passing the time in verbal games reminiscent of music-hall comedians' cross-talk. Pozzo arrives with his slave Lucky but denies all knowledge of Godot. He makes Lucky 'dance' and 'think' in an incoherent tirade. After they go, a boy arrives to promise that Godot will come tomorrow. In Act Two the tree has leaves, but there is apparently no other change. The tramps continue waiting. Pozzo enters again, blind and dependent on Lucky, who is now dumb. After they go, a boy (claiming to be the previous messenger's brother) arrives with the same message. Still determining to leave, the tramps do not move.

Waiting for Lefty A play by CLIFFORD ODETS, produced in New York in 1935 and published in Britain by the LEFT BOOK CLUB in 1937. In this urgently polemical piece the theatre audience is addressed as if it were at a meeting held by a corrupt union. Short naturalistic scenes involving the characters and issues are acted out. The play ends with the exposure of the union bosses and a call for strike action.

Wake, William 1657–1737 Divine. He became Archbishop of Canterbury in 1716. His ambition to achieve a union between the Church of England and the Gallican Church came to nothing but he is remembered for his translation, *The Genuine Epistles of the Apostolic Fathers* (1693), and for *The State of the Church and Clergy of England* (1703).

Wakefield cycle See MIRACLE PLAYS.

Wakoski, Diane 1937– American poet. *Coins and Coffins* (1962) is the first of more than 30 volumes, sampled in *Emerald Ice: Selected Poems 1962–1987* (1989). Much of her work resembles CONFESSIONAL POETRY, focusing in particular on her unhappy childhood and painful experiences with men. Wakoski has also published several volumes of prose, including *Form is an Extension of Content* (1972), *Creating a Personal Mythology* (1975) and *Toward a New Poetry* (1980).

Walcott, Derek (Alton) 1930– Caribbean poet and playwright. Widespread recognition came with *In a Green Night* (1962), *The Castaway* (1965), *The Gulf* (1970), and *Another Life* (1973) – ironic, antithetical poetry of personal and artistic discovery. Detached and sceptical poetry, simultaneously 'religious' in drift, has followed in *Sea Grapes* (1976), *The Star-Apple Kingdom* (1980), *The Fortunate Traveller* (1981) and *Midsummer* (1983). A volume of selected poetry appeared in 1981, *Collected Poems* in 1986 and *The Arkansas Testament* in 1987. Walcott's plays include *Henri Christophe* (1950), *Henri Dernier* (1951), *Ione* (1954), *Drums and Colours* (1961), *Dream on Monkey Mountain* with *Ti-Jean and His Brothers*, *Malcochon*, and *The Sea at Dauphin* (1971), *The Joker of Seville* with *O Babylon* (1978), *Remembrance* with *Pantomime* (1980), *Three Plays* (1982) – *The Last Carnival*, *Beef, No Chicken* and *A Branch of the Blue Nile* – and *Viva Detroit* (1992). His fascination with parallels between Homer's Aegean and the Caribbean is most fully expressed in his poem *Omeros* (1989) and a play, *The Odyssey* (1992). 'What the Twilight Says', which introduces the *Monkey Mountain* volume, and 'The Muse of History' are illuminating essays on the Caribbean creative imagination and New World history respectively. He was awarded the Nobel Prize for Literature in 1992.

Walden: or, Life in the Woods An autobiographical narrative by THOREAU, published in 1854. It describes the period in 1845–7 when he lived alone at Walden Pond, putting into action a programme of self-reliance which allowed the individual spirit to thrive in detachment from mass society. The book consists of 18 essays which effectively create a sense of the multiple dimensions of the author's self. His prose can be complex and poetically evocative, but also lucid, even scientifically direct; at times he engages in ALLEGORY and parable. Other passages catalogue the various animals and plants in the area. The narrative often digresses into lengthy discussions of philosophy and poetry. Famous sections describe visits to a Canadian woodcutter and an Irish family, a trip to Concord and his bean field.

Waldhere An Old English poem, surviving in two brief fragments which suggest it told a well-known story recorded in a Latin poem by Ekkehard of St Gall (d. 973). Hagen, Walter and Hildegund escape from Attila the Hun. Hagen joins Gunther, king of the Franks, in attacking Walter and Hildegund for their treasure. Walter kills all but Hagen and Gunther. The fragments are from speeches by Hildegund, Gunther and Walter.

Waley, Arthur (David) 1889–1966 Poet and Sinologist. He is best known for his translations: *A Hundred and Seventy Chinese Poems* (1918); *The Tale of Genji* (1925–33), an 11th-century Japanese novel; *The Pillow-Book of Sei Shonagon* (1928); *The Analects of Confucius* (1938); and *Monkey* (1942), a 16th-century Chinese novel. His work, which contributed greatly to interest in the East during the 1920s, was related to IMAGISM.

Walker, Alice 1944– Black American novelist, short-story writer and poet. She is best known for her novels: *The Third Life of Grange Copeland* (1970); *The Color Purple* (1982; PULITZER PRIZE), an EPISTOLARY NOVEL about a black woman raped by the man she believed to be her father; *Meridian* (1977); *The Temple of My Familiar* (1989); and *Possessing the Secret of Joy* (1992), a harsh exploration of female circumcision. *Once: Poems* (1968), *Revolutionary Petunias and Other Poems* (1973), *Good Night, Willie Lee, I'll See You in the Morning* (1979) and *Horses Make a Landscape Look More Beautiful: Poems* (1984) are collections of verse.

Walker, George (Frederick) 1947– Canadian playwright. An urban writer, influenced by the THEATRE OF THE ABSURD as well as television and films, he has written *The Prince of Naples* (1971), *Beyond Mozambique* (1974), *Ramona and the White Slaves* (1976), *Gossip* (1977), *Zastrozzi* (1977), *Filthy Rich* (1979), *Theatre of the Film Noir* (1981), *The Art of War* (1982), *Criminals in Love* (1985) and *Nothing Sacred* (1988), a reworking of Turgenev's *Fathers and Sons*.

Walker, Kath See OODGEROO.

Wallace A poem written *c.* 1477 by the Scottish poet Blind Harry (*c.* 1440–*c.* 1492), of whom little is known. The 12 books into which the poem is divided narrate the life of Sir William Wallace and his struggle against the English, developing him into a figure of mythic proportions. Wallace's final betrayal to the English and execution by Edward I in 1305 are glossed over in favour of celebrating him as a saintly national hero. Enduringly popular, *Wallace* influenced BURNS and WORDSWORTH among others.

Wallace, (Richard Horatio) Edgar 1875–1932 Thriller writer. He combined newspaper work with a prodigious writing career which began with *The Four Just Men* (1906) and extended to nearly 100 more thrillers, over 50 volumes of short stories, nearly 30 plays and screenplays, four volumes of verse and many miscellaneous books. The 11 books featuring 'Sanders of the River' were among his most popular works. Of his DETECTIVE FICTION, the stories about J. G. Reeder were particularly successful: *Room 13* (1924), *The Mind of Mr J. G. Reeder* (1925), *Terror Keep* (1927), *Red Aces* (1929) and *The Guv'nor* (1932).

Wallace, Lew(is) 1827–1905 American novelist. As well as the enormously successful BEN-HUR (1880), he wrote: *The Fair God* (1873), a novel about the Spanish conquest of Mexico; *The Boyhood of Christ* (1888); *The Wooing of Malkatoon* (1897), a tragic poem; and an autobiography. After fighting with distinction in the Mexican War and

the Civil War, he practised law and served as governor of New Mexico and US minister to Turkey.

Wallace-Crabbe, Chris(topher) (Keith) 1934– Australian poet and critic. Frequently concerned with the shaping of beliefs, his early poetry quickly attempted to move beyond a personal vision to a more objective consideration of social and political issues. Australian themes loom larger in later work, though the voice which handles them is generally ironic. His books include *Selected Poems* (1973), *Act in the Noon* (1974), *Foundations of Joy* (1976), *The Emotions Are Not Skilled Workers* (1980), *The Amorous Cannibal* (1985), *I'm Deadly Serious* (1988) and *For Crying Out Loud* (1990). *Splinters* (1981) is a novel about contemporary Melbourne. Critical writing includes *Melbourne or the Bush* (1974), *Toil and Spin* (1980), *Three Absences in Australian Writing* (1983) and *Falling into Language* (1990).

Wallant, Edward (Lewis) 1926–62 American novelist. *The Pawnbroker* (1961), his most acclaimed work, is about Sol Nazerman, a Polish Jew who owns a pawnshop in Harlem, where he relives the horrors of a Nazi concentration camp in nightmares and flashbacks. Wallant's first novel, *The Human Season* (1960), is the story of a middle-aged immigrant Jew after his wife's death. *The Tenants of Moonbloom* (1963) and *The Children at the Gate* (1965) appeared posthumously.

Waller, Edmund 1606–87 Poet. A member of FALKLAND's circle at Great Tew, he sought to steer a politically moderate course between the king and his opponents in the 1640s. In 1643, however, he was discovered in a plot to oust the Parliamentary rebels from London and saved himself only by confessing and by pleading for clemency before Parliament. He spent part of his Continental exile in EVELYN's company, returned to England in 1652, enjoyed royal favour after the Restoration and died in his bed, aged 81.

Waller was a famous wit and poet, renowned for both his panegyrics (on Cromwell as well as Charles II) and his lyrics (particularly those addressed to 'Sacharissa', Lady Dorothy Sidney). His reputation fast declined and today his eulogy of the Dutch Wars, *Instructions to a Painter* (1666), is unread, survived by its PARODY, MARVELL's *Last Instructions*. Only two of his short pieces are well known: 'On a Girdle' and the exquisite song 'Go, Lovely Rose'. Yet Waller deserves recognition for the refinement he brought to the HEROIC COUPLET and to standards of poetic eloquence and linguistic purity. He proved a significant model for 18th-century ideals of literature.

Wallis, John 1616–1703 Mathematician. He became Savilian Professor of Geometry at Oxford (1649–1703) and was one of the founders of the Royal Society. His *Arithmetica infinitorum* (1655) contains the first evaluation of π as a method of measurement, the first use of ∞ as the symbol for infinity, and the germ of the differential calculus. A moderate Puritan, he used his mathematical skill to decipher Royalist coded messages during the Civil War.

Walmsley, Leo 1892–1966 Novelist and playwright. His novels portray the austere and often dangerous lives of Yorkshire fishermen. They include *Three Fevers* (1932), *Foreigners* (1935) and *Sally Lunn* (1937) later dramatized.

Walpole, Horace, 4th Earl of Orford 1717–97 Letter-writer and aesthetician. The youngest son of the Whig politician Sir Robert Walpole, he was educated at Eton and King's College, Cambridge. A Continental tour (1739–41) with his schoolfellow THOMAS GRAY was marred by a quarrel which did not, however, prevent their lifelong friendship. Walpole's *Aedes Walpolianae* (1747), an annotated catalogue of the extensive family collection of paintings, was his first contribution to art studies.

In the same year he moved to Twickenham and started to Gothicize his house, Strawberry Hill, an activity which absorbed him for nearly 25 years. The fame of Strawberry Hill, aided by his *Description of the Villa of Horace Walpole* (1774), was a major factor in the Gothic Revival. The *Description* was printed on his own press, which he also used to issue an edition of *Odes by Mr Gray* (1757) and his own *Catalogue of the Royal and Noble Authors of England* (1758), a combination of bibliography, antiquarianism and criticism which was typical of his interests and abilities. Other books were his reworking of GEORGE VERTUE's manuscripts as *Anecdotes of Painting in England* (1762–71), his own *Catalogue of Engravers Who Have Been Born or Resided in England* (1763), *Historic Doubts of the Life and Reign of Richard III* (1768), *Essay on Modern Gardening* (1785) and an edition of Lucan's *Pharsalia* with BENTLEY's notes (1760). Walpole's political connections and his own career as an MP led to several posthumous works: *Memoirs of the Last Ten Years of the Reign of George the Second* (1822), *Memoirs of the Reign of George the Third* (1845) and *Journal of the Reign of King George the Third from the Year 1771 to 1783* (1859).

Walpole also wrote *THE CASTLE OF OTRANTO* (1764), a *jeu d'esprit* which began the taste for the GOTHIC NOVEL. His blank-verse tragedy, *The Mysterious Mother* (1768), takes as its central theme the protagonist's remorse for an act of incest and so was not thought suitable for presentation on stage. But all his other work is insignificant in comparison with his letters. Over 4000 survive, now gathered in the monumental 48-volume Yale edition (1937–83). Addressed to many correspondents and clearly written with an eye to publication, they discuss antiquarian matters, politics, literature, architecture, painting and the gossip of the day with *brio* and playful but unflagging intelligence.

Walpole, Sir Hugh (Seymour) 1884–1941 Novelist. In all, he wrote over 40 popular novels. They include: *Mr Perrin and Mr Traill* (1911), based on his own brief experiences as a teacher; *Fortitude* (1913); *The Duchess of Wrexe* (1914); *The Dark Forest* (1916) and *The Secret City* (1919), based on his experiences with the Russian Red Cross in World War I; and *The Herries Chronicle*, a family saga set in Cumberland, consisting of *Rogue Herries* (1930), *Judith Paris* (1931), *The Fortress* (1932) and *Vanessa* (1933).

Walsh, Jill [Gillian] **Paton** See PATON WALSH, JILL [GILLIAN].

Walsh, William 1663–1708 Critic and poet. His PASTORALS and amorous verses were fashionable but his enduring claim to attention rests on his encouragement of the young POPE in praising his *Pastorals* and suggesting improvements to them. Pope published their letters in 1735. Walsh's *Works in Prose and Verse* appeared in 1736, and JOHNSON included a biography of him in *LIVES OF THE POETS*.

Walton, Izaak 1593–1683 Author of *THE COMPLEAT ANGLER* (1653). Apart from this classic work, which has assured him a unique place in English letters and an international reputation, Walton also wrote sympathetic biographical sketches of his contemporaries, beginning with the life of his friend DONNE which he took over from WOTTON and published in the 1640 edition of the poet's sermons. It was followed by further

'Lives', each of which he scrupulously updated, of Wotton himself (1651), RICHARD HOOKER (1665), GEORGE HERBERT (1670) and Bishop Sanderson (1678). After the Restoration Walton became Steward to the Bishop of Worcester and died in his 90th year at Winchester, where he was buried in the Cathedral.

Wanderer, The An Old English poem in the EXETER BOOK. It may represent a monologue containing two reported speeches or, alternatively, speeches by different characters. The first says that the solitary wanderer often experiences the grace of God despite the hardships he endures. The second gives a personal account of exile, concluding that the world's wealth is transitory and faith in God is the only source of security.

Wanley, Nathaniel 1634–80 Poet and cleric. His religious verse declares its debt to HENRY VAUGHAN in its title, *Scintillulae sacrae*. With his narratives, *The Witch of Endor* and *Lazarus*, it was first collected in 1928. His prose compilation, *The Wonders of the Little World* (1678), was a source for ROBERT BROWNING's *THE PIED PIPER OF HAMELIN*.

War of the Worlds, The A novel by H. G. WELLS, serialized in 1897 and published in book form in 1898. A classic story of alien invasion, it provided a model for countless cruder imitations; Orson Welles's famous radio adaptation in the USA in 1938 was realistic enough to cause panic. In the first part missiles from Mars land in England, arousing only mild interest until they disgorge fearful war machines. Panic spreads as resistance fails and London is destroyed. In the second part survivors of the catastrophe live in hiding. Finally, the Martians prove unprotected against earthly bacteria, which succeed where men's best efforts failed in destroying them.

Ward, Artemus [Browne, Charles Farrar] 1834–67 American humorist. He wrote mock letters to the editor of *The Cleveland Plain Dealer* in 1857–9 and pioneered the comic lecture (a form TWAIN would later adopt), attacking Abolitionists, Mormons, Shakers, feminists, temperance advocates and anyone else he considered hypocritical or ineffectual. As staff member and then editor of *VANITY FAIR*, he became known as the 'unofficial dean of American humour'. His publications include *Artemus Ward, His Book* (1862), *Artemus Ward, His Travels* (1865) and, after his death during a lecture tour of England, the posthumous *Artemus Ward in London and Other Papers* (1867).

Ward, Mrs Humphry (Mary Augusta) 1851–1920 Novelist. The niece of MATTHEW ARNOLD, she married Thomas Humphry Ward, Oxford don and later art critic of *The Times*. Acquaintance with Oxford figures such as J. R. GREEN, T. H. GREEN, JOWETT, PATER and MARK PATTISON encouraged her academic interests and her adoption of an unorthodox religious position, close to that of Matthew Arnold, which abandoned belief in the historical truth of the Gospels and concentrated on applying the spiritual truths of Christianity to humanitarian work. Her novel *ROBERT ELSMERE* (1888) records the intellectual and emotional implications of such a pilgrimage. The next phase of her life showed its practical results, particularly in her work for the Passmore Edwards Settlement, opened in Bloomsbury in 1897. Despite her support for higher education for women, she became president of the Women's Anti-Suffrage League in 1908.

Apart from *Robert Elsmere*, the most notable of her 25 novels are *The History of David Grieve* (1892) and *Helbeck of*

Bannisdale (1898) for their treatment of religious issues, and *Marcella* (1894) and *Delia Blanchflower* (1915) for their debate of social and political issues. *England's Effort* (1916), *Towards the Goal* (1917) and *Fields of Victory* (1919) describe the Allied effort during World War I. *A Writer's Recollections* (1918) provides interesting accounts of the many major literary figures she had met and a record of the social and intellectual life of Oxford in her early years. Her translation of the *Journal Intime* of the Swiss mystic Henri Amiel (1885) long remained the standard English edition.

Ward, Nathaniel 1578–1652 American Puritan writer. Born in Essex, he emigrated to Massachusetts in 1634 and became influential in the colony's politics. His literary reputation rests on *The Simple Cobbler of Aggawam*, published in 1647, after his return to England. An ebullient SATIRE in the Elizabethan rather than the Puritan manner, it takes the side of the Presbyterians in the English Civil War but appeals for an end to hostilities.

Ward, Ned [Edward] 1667–1731 London tavern keeper and writer of doggerel verse. *The London Spy*, a series of sketches begun in 1698 and collected in 1703, gives a lively account of life in the capital. Ward's verse, racy and scurrilous in the manner of SAMUEL BUTLER, was notoriously indiscreet: he was sentenced to the pillory for passages in *Hudibras redivivus* (1705).

Warden, The The first of TROLLOPE'S BARSETSHIRE NOVELS, published in 1855. The Bishop of Barchester appoints Septimus Harding, a gentle and unworldly clergyman, warden of the almshouse of Hiram's Hospital. A local reformer, John Bold, and the *Jupiter* newspaper (*The Times*) attack the discrepancy between Harding's comfortable annual salary and the small weekly allowance given to the old men. Bold abandons the campaign at the request of Harding's youngest daughter, Eleanor, whom he marries. But the battle continues between reformers and conservatives, led by Archdeacon Grantly, and the warden resigns. One of Trollope's finest and most characteristic works, the novel contains an implicit defence of his own art and moral vision in portraits of CARLYLE as Dr Pessimist Anticant and DICKENS as Mr Popular Sentiment.

Ware, Sir James 1594–1666 Irish antiquarian and historian. He succeeded his father as Attorney-General of Ireland, an office which exposed him to the political hazards of the English Civil War. His great work was the *Antiquities of Ireland* (1626–54) and his most popular work the *Writers of Ireland* (1639). His reputation suffered grievously from interpolations and forgeries introduced into his writings by his son Robert and not exposed until 1917.

Warner, Charles Dudley 1829–1900 American novelist and essayist. He is best remembered for *The Gilded Age* (1873), his first published novel, written in collaboration with TWAIN. He also produced several collections of essays, including *Summer in a Garden* (1870), *Being a Boy* (1878) and *The Relation of Literature to Life* (1896), and a trilogy of novels: *A Little Journey in the World* (1889), *The Golden House* (1894) and *That Fortune* (1899).

Warner, Rex 1905–86 Poet, novelist and translator. *Poems* (1937) was inspired by the same anti-totalitarian fervour which animated AUDEN, ISHERWOOD and other writers of his generation during the 1930s. *The Wild Goose Chase* (1937) and *The Professor* (1938) are bleak novels showing the influence of Kafka. *The Aerodrome* (1941), his best-known novel, depicts the conflict between the aerodrome, whose personnel believe in cleanliness,

health and discipline, and an unnamed but quintessentially English village. Warner's many translations include: Euripides' *Medea* (1944), *Hippolytus* (1950) and *Helen* (1951); Aeschylus' *Prometheus Bound* (1947); Xenophon's *Anabasis* (1949); Thucydides (1954); Plutarch (1958); and George Seferis (1960). His studies of classical subjects include *The Young Caesar* (1958) and *Pericles the Athenian* (1963).

Warner, Sylvia Townsend 1893–1978 Novelist, poet and short-story writer. Her poetry, influenced by HARDY, includes *The Espalier* (1925), *Time Importuned* (1928), *Opus 7* (1931) and *Rainbow* (1932). Her novels include: *Lolly Willowes* (1926), a supernatural story; *Mr Fortune's Maggot* (1927), about a missionary; and *The True Heart* (1929), a story of love set in the Essex Marshes, which shows her at her imaginative and lyrical best. *A Garland of Straw* (1943) and *Museum of Cheats* (1947) are volumes of short stories.

Warner, William ?1558–1609 Poet and translator. *Pan His Syrinx* (1584) is a collection of seven prose tales. It is unlikely that SHAKESPEARE had seen the unpublished manuscript of Warner's translation of Plautus' *Menaechmi* (1595) when he wrote THE COMEDY OF ERRORS. Warner's major work is *Albion's England*, a verse history of Britain which enjoyed a high reputation in its own time. The first edition (1586) tells the story from Noah to the Norman Conquest; later editions (1589, 1592, 1612) carried the history to the reign of JAMES I.

Warren, Mercy Otis 1728–1814 American playwright. The sister of a colonial political leader and the wife of James Warren, president of the Provincial Congress of Massachusetts, she was at the centre of Revolutionary politics. She is best known for her anti-Loyalist political dramas, *The Adulateur* (1773) and *The Group* (1775). Other plays have been attributed to her, most notably *The Blockheads* (1776) and *The Motley Assembly* (1779). She also published *Poems Dramatic and Miscellaneous* (1790) and the *History of the Rise, Progress and Termination of the American Revolution* (1805).

Warren, Robert Penn 1905–89 American poet, novelist and critic. A member of the FUGITIVES, he helped to found and edit the group's magazine, *The Fugitive* (1922–5), contributed to the Southern Agrarian manifesto, *I'll Take My Stand: The South and the Agrarian Tradition* (1930), and became editor of *The Southern Review* with CLEANTH BROOKS in 1935. His poetry and fiction are marked by a brooding, philosophical intelligence, and he wrote perceptively on writers with a similar cast of mind, notably CONRAD and FAULKNER. His many volumes of verse include *Selected Poems 1923–1943* (1944), *Selected Poems: New and Old 1923–1966* (1966) and *New and Selected Poems 1923–1985* (1985). *A Robert Penn Warren Reader* (1988) is a useful anthology of his poetry and prose. As a novelist he remains best known for *All the King's Men* (1946; PULITZER PRIZE), the story of a corrupt Southern politician, Willie Stark, apparently modelled on Governor Huey Long of Louisiana. Other works include *New and Selected Essays* (1989) and several volumes of criticism and creative writing edited in collaboration with Cleanth Brooks, notably *Understanding Poetry: An Anthology for College Students* (1938; revised editions 1950, 1960 and 1976) and *Understanding Fiction* (1943; revised editions 1959 and 1979). He became the first POET LAUREATE of the USA in 1986.

Warren, Samuel 1807–77 Novelist. His melodramatic *Passages from the Diary of a Late Physician* appeared in *BLACKWOOD'S EDINBURGH MAGAZINE* in 1830–7. Ten

Thousand a Year (1841) led some reviewers to compare him favourably with DICKENS. Packed with sensational incident and portraits of the legal profession and high society, it describes the rise and fall of Mr Tittlebat Titmouse. *Now and Then* (1847) was less successful and Warren, a qualified barrister who later became a Conservative MP, turned to writing legal textbooks.

Warton, Joseph 1722–1800 Critic. The son of THOMAS WARTON THE ELDER and brother of THOMAS WARTON THE YOUNGER, he became headmaster of Winchester College. He is remembered for his literary criticism, particularly his essays on POPE (1756, 1782), rather than his own verse and his translations of Virgil's *Eclogues* and *Georgics*.

Warton, Thomas, the elder 1688–1745 Scholar, poet, and father of JOSEPH WARTON and THOMAS WARTON THE YOUNGER. He was professor of poetry at Oxford in 1718–28. His *Poems on Several Occasions* (1748), edited by his son Joseph, included two 'Runic Odes' which influenced THOMAS GRAY.

Warton, Thomas, the younger 1728–90 Poet and literary historian. The younger son of THOMAS WARTON THE ELDER and younger brother of JOSEPH WARTON, he spent his entire life at Oxford, following his father in serving as professor of poetry (1757–67). He was appointed POET LAUREATE in 1785. His poetry, collected in a volume of 1777, frequently imitated SPENSER and MILTON, and revived interest in the SONNET. His most important scholarly work was the *History of English Poetry from the Close of the Eleventh to the Commencement of the Eighteenth Century* (1774–81, expanded 1824). The interest it shows in medieval literature is also apparent in his contribution to the CHATTERTON controversy, *An Enquiry into the Authenticity of the Poems Attributed to Rowley* (1782), and in the high regard for Gothic architecture he shared with his contemporary FRANCIS GROSE, manifest in the posthumous *Essays on Gothic Architecture by the Rev. T. Warton, Rev. J. Bentham, Captain Grose, and the Rev. J. Milner* (1800). Warton contributed three papers (Nos. 33, 93 and 96) to THE IDLER.

Washington, Booker T(aliaferro) 1856–1915 Black American leader. He was the son of a slave mother and a white father. His advocacy of gradual development for blacks brought him into conflict with other black leaders, including W. E. B. DU BOIS. His publications include *The Future of the American Negro* (1899), *Sowing and Reaping* (1900), *Character Building* (1902), *Working with the Hands* (1904), *The Story of the Negro* (1909), *My Larger Education* (1911), *The Man Farthest Down* (1912) and a biography of FREDERICK DOUGLASS (1906). His autobiography, *Up from Slavery*, appeared in 1901.

Washington Square A short novel by HENRY JAMES, serialized in 1880 and published in volume form in 1881. Catherine Sloper, the daughter of a wealthy New York physician, leads a bleak existence until she is courted by Morris Townsend. Believing Morris to be a fortune-hunter, Dr Sloper opposes their engagement and takes Catherine to Europe for a year. Morris returns seventeen years later, after Dr Sloper has died, and proposes again. She rejects him and settles down to the life of a spinster in the family house in Washington Square.

Waste Land, The A poem by T. S. ELIOT, published in THE CRITERION and, with footnotes, in book form in 1922. It became his most influential poem and hence one of the most influential texts of MODERNISM.

The title – suggested by *From Ritual to Romance* (1920), Jessie L. Weston's study of the Grail legend (see ARTHURIAN LITERATURE) – refers to a dry and desolate country which can be revived by a fertility ritual. Eliot uses the SYMBOL to explore the sterility of modern life in five sections: 'The Burial of the Dead', 'A Game of Chess', 'The Fire Sermon', 'Death by Water' and 'What the Thunder Said'. The method is deliberately fragmentary, abandoning traditional verse forms for FREE VERSE and juxtaposing monologues or overheard snatches of conversation with allusions to previous literature, religious teaching and myth. The resulting 'heap of broken images' both intensifies the portrait of spiritual decay and hints at the possibility of redemption. Much critical interpretation of *The Waste Land* has concentrated on gauging the extent of its pessimism.

The original manuscript, published in facsimile in 1971, is considerably longer than the published version and shows the revisions proposed by POUND, to whom the poem is dedicated.

Water-Babies, The: *A Fairy Tale for a Land Baby* A fantasy for children by CHARLES KINGSLEY, serialized in 1862–3 and published in volume form in 1863. Tom, a young chimney-sweep, runs away from his brutal employer, Grimes. In his flight he falls into a river and is transformed into a water baby. Thereafter, in the river and the seas, he meets all sorts of creatures and learns a series of moral lessons.

Waterhouse, Keith (Spencer) 1929– Novelist, playwright and journalist. He made his name as a novelist with *Billy Liar* (1959), which mixed whimsy with the provincial realism of contemporaries such as JOHN BRAINE and STAN BARSTOW. Its successors include a sequel, *Billy Liar on the Moon* (1976), *Maggie Muggins* (1981) and *Unsweet Charity* (1992). His collaborative work for stage, screen and television with Willis Hall includes an adaptation of *Billy Liar* (1960), *Celebration* (1961), *All Things Bright and Beautiful* (1963) and *Say Who You Are* (1965). *Jeffrey Bernard is Unwell* (1989) is a stage adaptation of Jeffrey Bernard's *Spectator* columns.

Waterman, Andrew (John) 1940– Poet. His subject is often his own life and the South London suburbia where he grew up, and his style is deliberately ordinary, sometimes conversational and demotic. Works include *Living Room* (1974), *From the Other Country* (1977), *Over the Wall* (1980), *Out for the Elements* (1981), *Selected Poems* (1986) and *In the Planetarium* (1990).

Watkins, Vernon (Phillips) 1906–67 Poet. Volumes include *The Ballad of the Mari Lwyd and Other Poems* (1941), *The Lady with the Unicorn: Poems* (1948), *The Death Bell: Poems and Ballads* (1954), and the posthumous *Fidelities* (1968) and *Collected Poems* (1986). Throughout his career Watkins pursued one theme: the time-annulling revelation of the transcendent. His admiration for YEATS helped to offset the influence of the NEW APOCALYPSE poets and DYLAN THOMAS, his long-standing friend.

Watson, Richard 1737–1816 Polymath. Without training in either subject, he succeeded in becoming professor of chemistry and Regius Professor of Divinity at Cambridge. He was appointed to the see of Llandaff in 1782 and went to live on Lake Windermere. He answered GIBBON's DECLINE AND FALL OF THE ROMAN EMPIRE with an *Apology for Christianity* (1776), courteously acknowledged by the historian, and PAINE with an *Apology for the Bible* (1796).

Watson, Sheila 1919– Canadian novelist and short-story writer. Her novel, *The Double Hook* (1959), received much critical and popular attention. An attack on the rural NATURALISM of much Canadian literature, it draws on native myths to create one of the few masterpieces of MODERNISM in Canada. *Four Stories* was published in 1980.

Watson, Thomas ?1557–92 Translator and poet. He produced Latin verse and Latin translations from the Greek, including Sophocles' *Antigone* (1581). He is notable as an English poet largely for his SONNETS. *The Hekatompathia: or, Passionate Century of Love* (1582) is a collection of 18-line poems which he calls 'sonnets', mainly imitations or paraphrases of classical, Italian and French models. *The Tears of Fancy* (1593) contains 60 sonnets, largely inspired by Petrarch and Ronsard. *The First Set of Italian Madrigals Englished* (1590) contains English versions of Marenzio. His verse appeared in poetical miscellanies: THE PHOENIX NEST, ENGLAND'S HELICON and *A POETICAL RHAPSODY*.

Watson, Sir William 1858–1935 Poet. He published several volumes heavily indebted to TENNYSON, among them *Wordsworth's Grave* (1890), *Lachrymae Musarum* (1892), which included poems on the death of Tennyson, *The Year of Shame* (1896) and *The Heralds of Dawn* (1912). *Collected Poems* appeared in 1899 and 1906.

Watts, Isaac 1674–1748 Hymn-writer. A Nonconformist, he promoted the practice of hymn-singing in congregations where only the Metrical Psalms had previously been used. His chief collections were *Hymns and Spiritual Songs* (1707) and *The Psalms of David* (1719). *Divine Songs* (1715) was the first hymn book for children and *Horae Lyricae* (1706) a book of verse. His most popular hymns include 'Our God, Our Help in Ages Past' (JOHN WESLEY changed its opening to 'O God, our help in ages past'), 'Jesus Shall Reign Where'er the Sun' and 'When I Survey the Wondrous Cross'. LEWIS CARROLL parodied Watts in ALICE'S ADVENTURES IN WONDERLAND ('How Doth the Little Busy Bee').

Watts-Dunton, (Walter) Theodore 1832–1914 Novelist and critic. Born Theodore Watts, he published contributions to THE ATHENAEUM, some Shakespearean criticism, a volume of poetry and *Aylwin* (1898), a novel which includes a thinly disguised portrait of DANTE GABRIEL ROSSETTI. Also a student of gypsy-life, he edited BORROW'S *LAVENGRO* (1893) and THE *ROMANY RYE* (1900). His literary aspirations outpaced his abilities and Watts-Dunton is usually remembered for taking care of SWINBURNE during the last 30 years of the poet's life.

Waugh, Alec [Alexander] **(Raban)** 1898–1981 Novelist. He was the elder brother of EVELYN WAUGH. Successes in the course of his long career as a middlebrow novelist include *The Loom of Youth* (1917), a precocious first novel about public-school homosexuality, and *Island in the Sun* (1956).

Waugh, Evelyn (Arthur St John) 1902–66 Novelist. Son of the publisher Arthur Waugh and younger brother of ALEC WAUGH, he was educated at Lancing and Hertford College, Oxford. In 1928 he married Evelyn Gardner (whom he divorced in 1930) and was received into the Catholic Church. *DECLINE AND FALL* (1928), *Vile Bodies* (1930), *Black Mischief* (1932), *A HANDFUL OF DUST* (1934), *Scoop* (1938) and *Put Out More Flags* (1942) caught the witty and cynical mood of his generation and established him as its leading satirical novelist. His wide travels also produced several books: *Labels: A Mediterranean Journal* (1930), *Remote People* (about Africa; 1931), *Ninety-Two Days* (about South America; 1934), *Waugh in Abyssinia* (about Mussolini's invasion; 1936), and *Robbery under Law: The Mexican Object Lesson* (1939). His last travel book was *A Tourist in Africa* (1960).

In 1937 Waugh married Laura Herbert and settled in the West Country. *Work Suspended* (1942), two chapters of an unfinished novel, was followed by *BRIDESHEAD REVISITED* (1945), marking a change from his earlier satirical mode. *Men at Arms* (1952), *Officers and Gentlemen* (1955) and *Unconditional Surrender* (1961) make up a trilogy, *SWORD OF HONOUR*, published together in 1965. Its account of World War II echoes Waugh's own disillusioning experiences, particularly with the British Military Mission to Yugoslavia in 1944. *The Loved One* (1948) is a black little fable about Hollywood and the California funeral industry. *Helena* (1950), a historical novel set in the Rome of the Emperor Constantine, was Waugh's favourite work, but not his readers'. *The Ordeal of Gilbert Pinfold* (1957) is a frankly autobiographical account of a middle-aged writer who suffers a nervous breakdown. *A Little Learning* (1964) began an autobiography which he did not live to complete. It has been supplemented by editions of his *Diaries* (1976) and *Letters* (1980).

Waverley SIR WALTER SCOTT's first novel, published anonymously in 1814. It is set during the 1745 rebellion. When young Edward Waverley goes to join his regiment in Scotland he finds himself attracted both to the gentle Rose Bradwardine and the beautiful Flora, who, like her brother Fergus Mac-Ivor, is an ardent Jacobite. Waverley's romantic vacillation corresponds to a political vacillation between loyalty to the Crown and interest in the Jacobite cause. Unfairly blamed for an incipient mutiny, cashiered from his regiment and saved from prison only by Rose's intervention, he is driven to join the Jacobites. After the rebels are defeated Fergus Mac-Ivor is executed but Waverley, who has saved the life of Colonel Talbot, is pardoned. Rejected by Flora, who enters a convent, he eventually marries Rose. The novel's success, which confirmed Scott in changing from poetry to fiction, did much foster a romantic interest in Scotland and Scottish history among English readers.

Waves, The A novel by VIRGINIA WOOLF, published in 1931. Her most experimental novel, it uses STREAM OF CONSCIOUSNESS to trace the lives of six characters – Bernard, Susan, Rhoda, Neville, Jinny and Louis – from childhood, when they share a house together, to their reunions in later life and finally to their old age. Each character's life story is revealed incidentally and, although there is no differentiation in their speech, their individual personalities are revealed by recurring phrases and images. Italicized passages record the ascent and descent of the sun, the rise and fall of the waves, and the passing of the seasons. The novel is often considered Woolf's masterpiece.

Way of All Flesh, The A semi-autobiographical novel by SAMUEL BUTLER, posthumously published in 1903. The narrator, Overton, follows four generations of the Pontifex family and particularly the career of Ernest Pontifex. After an unhappy childhood with his tyrannical and strictly religious father, Ernest becomes a clergyman, lands up in prison and makes a disastrous marriage, from which he is freed when his drunken wife turns out to be already married. Anxious to avoid repeating the Pontifex paternal tyranny, he farms out the children of his union. Having inherited an income from his aunt Alethea, he embarks upon a solitary life, literary vocation and eclectic interests much resembling Butler's own adult career.

The fortunes of the Pontifex family are designed to

show that personal happiness stems from the liberating effect of acting on inherited and largely unconscious stores of vitality. The play between the conscious and unconscious also fuels the thrust of the novel's attack upon the conventions and hypocrisies of Victorian family life.

Way of the World, The A comedy by CONGREVE, first performed in 1700, when its comparative failure encouraged his decision to abandon the theatre. It is a complex play, whose elegant, witty dialogue polishes a plot that gradually reveals how far self-interest may go to make money and mar marriages. To marry Millamant, Mirabell must win the consent of her aunt, Lady Wishfort, and overcome the spite of Mrs Marwood, who conspires with Lady Wishfort's avaricious son-in-law Fainall. Nor is Millamant herself easily won: in the famous 'proviso' scene (Act IV) she lays down her conditions for marrying Mirabell. Lady Wishfort, gullible and constantly being gulled, is finally shaken into consent when the villainies of Fainall and Mrs Marwood are exposed.

Way We Live Now, The A novel by TROLLOPE, serialized in 1874–5 and published in volume form in 1875. Undervalued in his own day, it is now seen as one of his finest works, a SATIRE comparable in scope to VANITY FAIR and LITTLE DORRIT. At its centre is the fitfully heroic figure of Augustus Melmotte, a wealthy financier of obscure origins. Courted by impecunious aristocrats eager to get on the boards of his companies, he quickly rises to social prominence and enters the House of Commons. The bubble bursts with the discovery of fraud and he commits suicide. A related plot involves Lady Carbury's efforts to arrange a marriage between her son, Sir Felix, and Melmotte's daughter Marie, which collapse when Felix gambles away the money Marie has obtained for their elopement. The only character to denounce the widespread corruption is Lady Carbury's cousin Roger Carbury, a middle-aged country squire in love with her daughter Hetta. Another plot concerns Roger and his friend Paul Montague, the erstwhile lover of Winifred Hurtle, a passionate American. Although the marriage of Paul and Hetta provides the conventional happy ending, the loneliness and disappointment of Mrs Hurtle and Roger Carbury ensure that the mood of Trollope's most sombre novel is sustained to the end.

Wealth of Nations, The A treatise on political economy by ADAM SMITH, fully titled *An Inquiry into the Nature and Causes of the Wealth of Nations* and published in 1776. It analyses the effects of the pursuit of self-interest and recommends that market forces be left to ensure the accumulation of wealth, though inside a framework of law and with some government intervention. Book I argues that the division of labour increases productivity. Book II analyses capital (fixed and circulating), its accumulation and different uses. Book III attempts to explain, partly historically, different rates of growth in different countries. Book IV attacks mercantilism for regarding wealth as money and not the goods it can buy, and argues for free trade among nations. Book V turns to domestic political economy and outlines the case for some government intervention.

The Wealth of Nations has exerted a profound influence over generations of economists; indeed, it virtually defined the content of the subject for over 150 years. Marx was influenced by its sociological underpinning, and Smith's economics provided a manifesto for British

politicians seeking to reduce state intervention in economic life.

Webb [*née* Potter]**, (Martha) Beatrice** 1858–1943 and **Webb, Sidney**, 1st Baron Passfield 1859–1947 Social historians. They were married in 1892. Committed Socialists and members of the Fabian Society, they played a leading role in founding the London School of Economics in 1895 and *The New Statesman* in 1913. *The History of Trade Unionism* (1894) and *Industrial Democracy* (1897) established labour history as a separate study. Their minority report of the Poor Law Commission (1905–9) laid the foundations for the Welfare State. Other collaborative works included the seven-volume *History of English Local Government* (1903–30). Beatrice Webb also wrote two autobiographical works, *My Apprenticeship* (1926) and *Our Partnership* (posthumously published, 1948), which reveal an unsuspected gift for psychological perception. Norman and Jeanne Mackenzie have edited her diary (1982–5).

Webb [*née* Meredith]**, (Gladys) Mary** 1881–1927 Novelist. *Precious Bane* (1924) became a best-seller after it had been praised by the Prime Minister, Stanley Baldwin, who wrote an introduction to the 1928 edition. Its stark descriptions of the Shropshire countryside, infused with a romantic and often naive passion, were brilliantly parodied by Stella Gibbons in *COLD COMFORT FARM* (1932). Mary Webb's other novels include *The Golden Arrow* (1916), *Gone to Earth* (1917), *The House in Dormer Forest* (1920) and *Seven for a Secret* (1922).

Webster, John c. 1580–c. 1634 Playwright. Almost nothing is known of him until his collaboration with DEKKER on *WESTWARD HO* in 1604. Another work with Dekker, *THE FAMOUS HISTORY OF SIR THOMAS WYATT*, may belong to the same year, and another, *NORTHWARD HO*, to 1605. *Appius and Virginia* (c. 1608), based on Roman history, was probably written with THOMAS HEYWOOD. The three plays that followed are supposed to be Webster's alone. *The Devil's Law Case* (c. 1610) is a sensational but careless tragicomedy. *THE WHITE DEVIL* (c. 1612) and *THE DUCHESS OF MALFI* (? before 1614) are among the finest – and darkest – of all Jacobean tragedies. The last 20 years of Webster's life are as obscure as the first 20. A pageant survives and two collaborations, with THOMAS MIDDLETON on *Any Thing for a Quiet Life* (c. 1621) and WILLIAM ROWLEY on *A Cure for a Cuckold* (c. 1624). Other plays may have been lost.

Webster's Dictionary The popular name for the works derived from *An American Dictionary of the English Language* (1828) by Noah Webster (1758–1843). Webster's *American Spelling Book* (1806) was to a great extent responsible for those spellings now considered American. The word 'American' remained in subsequent editions of his dictionary until replaced by 'International'. The current *Webster's Third New International Dictionary*, much the size of the *Shorter Oxford English Dictionary*, was, when first published in 1961, greatly criticized for its relative lack of editorial prescriptivism. See also ENGLISH DICTIONARIES.

Wedde, Ian 1946– New Zealand poet, novelist, short-story writer and editor. A leading exponent of open forms, informal language and verbal collage, he was strongly influenced by modern American poets, particularly WILLIAM CARLOS WILLIAMS and A. R. AMMONS. Collections include: *Homage to Matisse* (1971); *Earthly: Sonnets for Carlos* (1975); *Castalay* (1980), which includes *Pathway to the Sea*; *Tales of Gotham City* (1984) and *Tendering* (1988). His introduction to *The Penguin Book of New*

Zealand Verse (1985), which he co-edited, is an important sequel to ALLEN CURNOW's introduction to the previous Penguin anthology (1960). Wedde argues that New Zealand poetry has now moved beyond nationalism and cultural alienation, developing a language fully acclimatized to its setting. His novels include *Dick Seddon's Great Dive* (1976), the richly allusive *Symmes Hole* (1986) and *Survival Arts* (1988). *The Shirt Factory* (1981) is a volume of short stories.

Wedding of Sir Gawen and Dame Ragnell, The A VERSE ROMANCE (*c.* 1450) telling the same story as *The Wife of Bath's Tale* in CHAUCER's *CANTERBURY TALES*. On condition that she marry Gawen, the hideous Dame Ragnell answers the question – what do women most desire? – which her brother, Sir Gromer Somer Joure, has posed to King Arthur. In bed she becomes young and beautiful and, when Gawen lets her choose whether to be fair by day or night, promises to be beautiful always.

Wedgwood, Dame **C(icely) V(eronica)** 1910– Historian. *Strafford* (1935) and *The Thirty Years' War* (1938) established her as a successful popular historian of 17th-century Europe. Among the most notable of many subsequent books which confirmed her reputation are *Oliver Cromwell* (1939), *William the Silent* (1944) and a major history of the English Civil War, comprising *The King's Peace* (1955), *The King's War* (1958) and *The Trial of Charles I* (1964; as *A Coffin for King Charles* in USA).

Weever, John 1576–1632 Poet and antiquary. His early SATIRE, in *Epigrams* (1599) and *Faunus and Melliflora* (1600), is an important source of literary gossip. His later antiquarian studies culminated in *Ancient Funeral Monuments within the United Monarchy of Great Britain* (1631).

Weir of Hermiston An unfinished novel by ROBERT LOUIS STEVENSON. Although the fragment published posthumously in 1896 does little more than set the scene and introduce the chief characters, it is generally acknowledged as a potential masterpiece. The formidable hanging judge, Adam Weir, Lord Hermiston, banishes his son Archie to the remote and uncivilized village of Hermiston, where he lives as a recluse with his devoted housekeeper, Kirstie. Her four nephews, the 'Black Elliotts', are notorious for their ruthless hunting-down of their father's murderer. Archie falls in love with their sister Christina. The couple's meetings become known to Kirstie and Frank Innes, Archie's treacherous friend. Archie tells Christina that their relationship must end. The fragment ends here, but Stevenson's plans show that Archie would kill Innes in a quarrel and be tried by his father before being rescued by the 'Black Elliotts'. He would escape to America with Christina, while Lord Hermiston would die from the shock of having sentenced his own son to death.

Welch, Denton (Maurice) 1915–48 Novelist, short-story writer and artist. He published many poems, 60 short stories and three largely autobiographical novels: *Maiden Voyage* (1943), introduced by EDITH SITWELL, *In Youth is Pleasure* (1945) and *A Voice through a Cloud* (1950). His *Journals* (1952) give a vivid account of a life increasingly restricted by a severe spinal injury.

Weldon, Fay 1933– Novelist and television playwright. Her prolific output has alternated between television plays and vigorous, resourceful novels articulating a contemporary feminist consciousness. These include: *Female Friends* (1975); *Praxis* (1978); *Puffball* (1980), an extended evocation of the process of conception; *The President's Child* (1982) and *The Life and*

Loves of a She-Devil (1983), caustic SATIRES of male-dominated society; *The Rules of Life* (1987), a novella; *The Hearts and Lives of Men* (1987); *Darcy's Utopia* (1990); *Growing Rich* (1992); and *Life Force* (1992). *Sacred Cows* (1989) is a trenchant pamphlet prompted by her opposition to the *fatwa* pronounced against SALMAN RUSHDIE.

Well at the World's End, The A prose romance by WILLIAM MORRIS, published in 1896. Ralph, youngest son of King Peter of Upmeads, sets out on a quest for the 'Well at the World's End', whose waters give the drinker long life and an ever-youthful 'lucky' appearance. He falls in love with the Lady of Abundance who has drunk from the Well, but she is killed before she can lead him to it. After a period of despair Ralph's quest finds a parallel in his search for Ursula, his first love. Together they reach the Well, drink from it and eventually return to rule Upmeads and live in peace.

Well-Beloved, The: *A Sketch of a Temperament* A novel by HARDY, serialized as *The Pursuit of the Well-Beloved* in 1892 and substantially revised for book publication in 1897. It is set on the Isle of Slingers (Portland), where the sculptor Jocelyn Pierston pursues his ideal Well-Beloved by courting, successively, a mother, daughter and granddaughter all named Avice. With illness and encroaching age the ideal recedes and he marries another old flame, Marcia Bencomb.

well-made play Strictly, the term applies to English imitations (by, for example, HENRY ARTHUR JONES and PINERO) of the *pièce bien faite* whose formula was devised by the prolific French playwright Eugène Scribe (1791–1861). Its aim is less to create a finely paced structure than to pace effects and revelations so as to keep the audience in suspense. Particularly suited to MELODRAMA, the formula was also used in FARCE. See also DÉNOUEMENT and SCÈNE À FAIRE.

Wells, H(erbert) G(eorge) 1866–1946 Novelist, writer of SCIENCE FICTION and student of politics, history and society. The son of an unsuccessful Bromley tradesman, he won a scholarship to the Normal School of Science (now Imperial College), London, in 1884. The teaching of T. H. HUXLEY was a profound influence. His literary career began with science fiction fables: *THE TIME MACHINE* (1895), *The Wonderful Visit* (1895), *The Island of Dr Moreau* (1896), a grim parable of the blind and bestial forces underlying civilization, *The Invisible Man* (1897), *THE WAR OF THE WORLDS* (1898), *When the Sleeper Wakes* (1899), *The First Men in the Moon* (1901) and *The War in the Air* (1908). Their implicit note of warning about the impact of alien races or advanced science on established society prefigures his later concern with social and political realities. His interest in the changing social order reappears in *A Modern Utopia* (1905), which, with other works such as the later 'discussion' novel, *The New Machiavelli* (1911), displays his didactic tendency. A quarrelsome member of the Fabian Society, he frequently engaged in public controversy with leading thinkers of the day, notably SHAW.

Wells's major novels with a bias towards social realism drew heavily on his own youthful experiences. *LOVE AND MR LEWISHAM* (1900) and *KIPPS* (1905) were followed by *TONO-BUNGAY* (1909), his most ambitious novel, and *THE HISTORY OF MR POLLY* (1910). *Ann Veronica* (1909) was considered scandalous for its portrayal of an emancipated woman. Later works, less distinguished though still popular, were *MR BRITLING SEES IT THROUGH* (1916), *Mr Blettsworthy on Rampole Island* (1928) and *The Bulpington of Blup* (1932). Wells's public reputation survived the disgrace which attached to his views on sexual freedom and his widely reported liaison with REBECCA WEST during his second marriage. He continued to see himself as a popular educator, in works like *The Outline of History* (1920), and resisted despair in the face of the Great War and the rise of fascism, though World War II prompted a pessimistic last work, *Mind at the End of Its Tether* (1945). *Experiment in Autobiography* (1934) is a lively and engaging self-portrait.

Wells, Robert 1947– Poet and translator. He is a classicist, both literally in his translations from Virgil (1982) and Theocritus (1988) and in the precision and muscular clarity of his style, which is joined to an intense physical awareness of the natural world. His poetry appeared in *Shade Mariners* (with DICK DAVIS and Clive Wilmer; 1970), *The Winter's Task* (1977), *Selected Poems* (1986) and *Place by Pieces* (1992).

Welty, Eudora 1909– American short-story writer and novelist. She established herself as a major Southern writer with *A Curtain of Green, and Other Stories* (1941), *The Wide Net, and Other Stories* (1943), *The Golden Apples* (1949) and *The Bride of the Innisfallen, and Other Stories* (1955). She has also written novels in the Southern Gothic tradition, among them *The Robber Bridegroom* (1942), *Delta Wedding* (1946), *The Ponder Heart* (1954), *Losing Battles* (1970) and *The Optimist's Daughter* (1972; PULITZER PRIZE). Her literary autobiography, *One Writer's Beginnings*, appeared in 1984.

Wendt, Albert 1939– Western Samoan novelist, short-story writer, critic and poet. The one writer from the South Pacific with an international reputation, he is best known for his novel, *Leaves of the Banyan Tree* (1979), a three-generation saga of Western Samoan life which corrects sentimentalized Western versions of the 'South Seas'. His earlier novels were *Sons for the Return Home* (1973) and *Pouliuli* (1977). *Ola* (1991) moves for first time outside the South Pacific. *Flying-Fox in a Freedom Tree* (1974) and *The Birth and Death of the Miracle Man* (1986) are collections of short stories. *Inside Us the Dead* (1976) and *Shaman of Visions* (1984) are volumes of poetry. Wendt also founded the first literary journal in the South Pacific, *Mana*, and edited the first anthology of Pacific writing, *Lali* (1980).

Wesker, Arnold 1932– Playwright. He made a national reputation with plays drawing on his background and expressing his utopian socialism: the trilogy consisting of *Chicken Soup with Barley* (1958), *Roots* (1959) and *I'm Talking about Jerusalem* (1960); *The Kitchen* (1959); and *Chips with Everything* (1962). *Their Very Own and Golden City* (1965) and *The Friends* (1970) reflect some of his frustration in running Centre 42, of which he was founder-director in 1961–70. Other work moves towards a more lyrical, disillusioned and introverted theatre: *The Four Seasons* (1965), *The Wedding Feast* (1974), *The Journalists* (1975), *Love Letters on Blue Paper* (1976), *The Merchant* (1977), *Caritas* (1981) and a one-woman trilogy, *Annie Wobbler* (1984). *As Much As I Dare* (1994) is an autobiography.

Wesley, John 1703–91 and **Wesley, Charles** 1707–88 Founders of Methodism. Born at Epworth in Lincolnshire, the brothers were both undergraduates at Christ Church, Oxford. In 1729 John, then a Fellow of Lincoln College, joined Charles in a group nicknamed the 'Holy Club' or 'Methodists' and quickly became its leader. Members, who later included JAMES HERVEY and George Whitefield, met for study and religious discussion, visited the poor, sick and imprisoned and prac-

tised strict self-discipline. Their self-examinations, frequently recorded in coded diaries, became the quarry for their *Journals*. John's was published periodically between 1739 and 1790 and Charles's posthumously in 1849.

Having first tried to work through Church of England pulpits, both brothers resorted to open-air preaching in 1739, using Bristol, London and Newcastle as their chief centres. In 1743 John drew up *Rules* for the societies they had established and in 1744 held the first conference for lay preachers. The implicit incompatibility of Methodism's evolving structure with the Anglican Church was never admitted by John, but caused Charles to retire from itinerant work in 1756. John continued, covering some 250,000 miles of the British Isles by foot, horse and post-chaise and preaching three or four times a day.

John Wesley's *Journal*, a textbook of experiential religion, served to maintain contact between far-flung societies. He also engaged in polemical debate with the Moravians and Calvinists, wrote religious tracts and treatises, produced practical handbooks on medicine and translated, edited or abridged the work of others for more popular consumption. John and Charles both recognized the value of hymns in worship. Of the thousands composed by Charles, and often edited by John, many are still in use well beyond the confines of Methodism. Such favourites include 'Love Divine, All Loves Excelling', 'Hark, the Herald-Angels Sing' and 'Jesu, Lover of My Soul'.

Wessex The name borrowed by HARDY from Anglo-Saxon history for the West Country setting of most of his novels and many of his poems. It was first used in *FAR FROM THE MADDING CROWD*. It is centred on Dorset and particularly Dorchester, whose fictional name is Casterbridge. The slight transposition is typical of Hardy's use of real placenames to create a 'partly real, partly dream' landscape.

Wessex Poems and Other Verses The first collection of poetry by HARDY, published in 1898. These 51 poems (some dating from the 1860s) range from the speculative 'Hap' to the embittered 'Neutral Tones', from the mildly Chaucerian 'The Bride-Night Fire' to the poignant 'Thoughts of Phena', and from the gravity of 'Nature's Questioning' to the hearty 'Sergeant's Song'. *Wessex Poems* is the prelude to 30 years of sustained poetic writing.

West, Nathanael [Weinstein, Nathan Wallenstein] 1903–40 American novelist. His preoccupation with the barrenness of contemporary life dominates his best-known work. *Miss Lonelyhearts* (1933) is the story of a newspaperman who writes an advice-to-the-lovelorn column, *A Cool Million: The Dismantling of Lemuel Pitkin* (1934) is a SATIRE of the American Dream and *The Day of the Locust* (1939) exposes the squalid hidden world of Hollywood, where West worked as a scriptwriter for a minor studio from 1935.

West, Dame Rebecca 1892–1983 Novelist and journalist. Born Cicily Isobel Fairfield, she had a brief career as an actress (her role in Ibsen's *Rosmersholm* suggesting the name she was to adopt). She then became a journalist and outspoken advocate of women's rights. Her relationship with H. G. WELLS resulted in the birth of a son, Anthony West, in 1914. Her first novel, *The Return of the Soldier* (1918), was about a shell-shock victim. Others include *The Judge* (1922), *The Strange Necessity* (1928), *Harriet Hume* (1929), *The Thinking Reed* (1936), *The Fountain*

Overflows (1957), *The Birds Fall Down* (1966), *This Real Night* (1984), a sequel to *The Fountain Overflows*, and *Sunflower* (1986). Recent studies have applauded the strong characterization of her heroines. Her other works include a study of Yugoslavia, *Black Lamb and Grey Falcon* (1941–2), and *The Meaning of Treason* (1949, revised 1952 and 1965), an account of the treason trials following World War II, revised to include later espionage trials.

Westminster Review, The A quarterly journal published between 1824 and 1914. It was conceived by BENTHAM as the organ of 'philosophical radicalism' and drew heavily on contributions from JAMES MILL and JOHN STUART MILL, though they began an alternative periodical, *The London Review*, in 1835. It was amalgamated with the *Westminster* under the effective but undeclared editorship of J. S. Mill in 1836–40. When John Chapman bought the *Westminster* in 1851, he appointed GEORGE ELIOT as assistant editor (1851–3) and accepted contributions from J. A. FROUDE, T. H. HUXLEY, G. H. LEWES and JOHN TYNDALL. With a further change of ownership and its conversion to a monthly in 1887, the review lost its high seriousness and eventually dropped its literary coverage.

Westward Ho A comedy by DEKKER and WEBSTER, produced in 1604 and published in 1607. Three wives enjoy an innocent escapade with their admirers but are forgiven by their husbands. In the sub-plot an Italian merchant, Justiniano, believes his wife unfaithful and goes off to enjoy the comedy of London life. Though she nearly becomes involved with a dubious nobleman, the couple are finally reconciled.

Westward Ho! A historical novel by CHARLES KINGSLEY, published in 1855. Now remembered chiefly as CHILDREN'S LITERATURE, it was Kingsley's most ambitious novel, an epic of England's heroic victory over Spain and the fear of Catholic domination in the 16th century. The story is packed with incident and clotted with pedantry and preaching: Drake, SIR WALTER RALEIGH, SPENSER and other real-life heroes crowd the pages, as do references to HAKLUYT and Plato. Its heady mixture of patriotism, sentiment and romance set the attitudes of English children for several generations.

Wetherell, Elizabeth [Warner, Susan Bogert] 1819–85 American writer of CHILDREN'S LITERATURE. Two bestsellers, *The Wide Wide World* (1850) and *Queechy* (1852), launched her career producing moral and sentimental novels, some written with her sister Anna.

Weyman, Stanley (John) 1855–1928 Novelist. He began his highly successful historical romances with *The House of the Wolf* (serialized in 1888–90; published in book form, 1890). *A Gentleman of France* (1893), set in the period of Henry of Navarre, was praised by R. L. STEVENSON. It was followed by *Under the Red Robe* (1894; successfully dramatized in 1896), *The Red Cockade* (1895), *The Castle Inn* (1898), *Count Hannibal* (1901), about the Massacre of St Bartholomew, *Chippinge* (1906), set at the time of the Reform Bill, and many others.

Whale, The An Old English poem in the EXETER BOOK. Borrowing from a version of the *Physiologus*, it describes how the whale encourages sailors to believe it is an island but then dives and drowns them. This is interpreted as an ALLEGORY of the devil's use of deception to trap the unwary.

Wharton, Edith (Newbold) 1862–1937 American novelist and short-story writer. Born into a wealthy New York family, she moved to France with her husband in 1907, remaining there after her divorce in 1913. Her close friendship with HENRY JAMES was a major influence on her work, acknowledged in *The Writing of Fiction* (1925). *THE HOUSE OF MIRTH* (1905) was her first popular success. *Madame de Treymes* (1907) tackled a characteristic theme, the difference between American and European social customs, though her range extended to the study of rural New England which made *ETHAN FROME* (1911) enduringly popular. *The Reef* (1912) and *The Custom of the Country* (1913) attacked the hypocrisies of New York society. *The Marne* (1918) and *A Son at the Front* (1923) are about World War I. *THE AGE OF INNOCENCE* (1920) made her the first woman to receive a PULITZER PRIZE. *The Mother's Recompense* (1925), *Twilight Sleep* (1927) and *The Children* (1928) deal with inter-generational differences in families. *Hudson River Bracketed* (1929) and *The Gods Arrive* (1932) examine the artistic temperament through the character of Vance Western, a struggling novelist. At her death she was working on *The Buccaneers* (1938), set in Saratoga in the 1860s. The best-known of her 11 collections of short stories is probably *Xingu and Other Stories* (1916). *A Backward Glance* (1934) is autobiographical.

What Every Woman Knows A comedy by BARRIE, first produced in 1908. Determined to find her a husband, Maggie Wylie's father and brother trap a burglar in their house. He is John Shand, forced by poverty to abandon his studies. The Wylies agree to help him if, after five years, he gives Maggie the right to marry him. The marriage takes place after he has become a successful MP. When he falls for Lady Sybil Tenterden, Maggie arranges for them to meet at a country cottage, knowing they will bore each other. Shand at last realizes 'what every woman knows': that he owes his success to Maggie, who has added brilliance to his dull speeches.

What Maisie Knew A novel by HENRY JAMES, published in 1897. Though written in the third person, it is told from the point of view of the perceptive but somewhat naive Maisie. Her parents, Beale and Ida Farange, divorce when she is six and it is arranged that she spend half the year with her father and half with her mother. Beale marries Miss Overmore, who had been Maisie's governess; Ida marries Sir Claude but still has a succession of lovers. Her two new step-parents become attracted to one another and eventually marry. Maisie is abandoned by Beale and Ida to the care of her new governess, Mrs Wix. Sir Claude invites her to live with him and the former Miss Overmore, but she cannot abide Mrs Wix, the one 'safe' adult whom Maisie absolutely trusts. The novel ends with Maisie refusing to live with Sir Claude and his new wife in Boulogne and departing for England with Mrs Wix.

Wheatley, Phillis 1753–84 Black American poet. Born in Africa and sold as a slave in Boston at the age of eight, she was educated with her master's family. Whilst in London she published *Poems on Various Subjects, Religious and Moral* (1773). Her work contains frequent allusions to classical mythology and mixes topical or contemporary matter with religious and moral concerns. Subjects include tributes to friends and famous people; discourses on Imagination, Recollection and Friendship; and occasionally incidents in her own life. *Memoirs and Poems of Phillis Wheatley* appeared in 1834 and a volume of her letters in 1864.

Wheelwright, John Brooks 1897–1940 American poet. His poetry, about Boston and its environs, is often accompanied by prose 'arguments' which serve as interpretations. It appeared in several privately printed volumes: *Rock and Shell* (1933), *Mirrors of Venus* (1938) and *Political Self-Portrait* (1940). *Dusk to Dusk*, on which he was working at his death, appeared in *The Collected Poems of John Wheelwright* (1972).

Where Angels Fear to Tread The first novel by E. M. FORSTER, published in 1905. The widowed Lilia Herriton visits Italy with her friend Caroline Abbott and falls in love with Gino Carella, a dentist's son. Mrs Herriton, her mother-in-law, dispatches Philip, her brother-in-law, but he arrives to find that Lilia has married Gino. The marriage fails and Lilia dies in childbirth. Philip is again dispatched, with his sister Harriet, to join Caroline in rescuing the baby. Philip and Caroline begin to succumb to the charm of Italy but Harriet, refusing to admit defeat, steals the baby. It dies in a carriage accident. Gino assaults Philip and the three English characters return home. On the journey, Philip discovers that he has fallen in love with Caroline, she with Gino.

Whetstone, George ?1544–?1587 Miscellaneous writer. *The Rock of Regard* (1576) is mainly a collection of prose and verse tales, largely drawn from Italian sources. His unacted play *Promos and Cassandra* (1578) takes a story from Cinthio's *Hecatommithi* which reappears, with other work by Cinthio, in his collection of prose romances, *An Heptameron of Civil Discourses* (1582). One or other version, or perhaps both, served as the main source for SHAKESPEARE'S *MEASURE FOR MEASURE*. Whetstone's other works are a verse eulogy commemorating GASCOIGNE (1577) and a series of biographical elegies of distinguished contemporaries, including SIR PHILIP SIDNEY (with whom he had fought at Zutphen).

White, Antonia 1899–1980 Novelist. Her first novel, *Frost in May* (1933), is a largely autobiographical account of Nanda Grey's convent education. Clara Batchelor, the heroine of *The Lost Traveller* (1950), *The Sugar House* (1952) and *Beyond the Glass* (1954), suffers in her relationships with men, is confined in an asylum, and eventually returns to the faith which she had rejected early in life. The conclusion echoes *The Hound and the Falcon* (1965), Antonia White's account of her own reconversion to Catholicism. She also translated works by Colette.

White, E(lwyn) B(rooks) 1899–1985 American essayist, journalist and critic. He became a writer and contributing editor for THE NEW YORKER in 1926. His long-term friendship with JAMES THURBER included a collaboration, *Is Sex Necessary?* (1929). Other works include *Alice through the Cellophane* (1933), *Quo Vadimus? Or the Case for the Bicycle* (1938), *One Man's Meat* (1942), *The Second Tree from the Corner* (1954) and *The Points of My Compass* (1962). His contribution to CHILDREN'S LITERATURE includes two notable books, *Stuart Little* (1945) and *Charlotte's Web* (1952).

White, Edmund 1940– American novelist. A leading homosexual author, he has published: *Forgetting Elena* (1973); *Nocturnes for the King of Naples* (1978); *A Boy's Own Story* (1982), his best-known work; *Caracole* (1985); and *The Beautiful Room is Empty* (1988). *States of Desire: Travels in Gay America* (1980) investigates gay communities. David Bergman has edited *The Burning Library: Writings on Art, Politics and Sexuality 1969–93* (1994).

White, Gilbert 1720–93 Naturalist. He was born in Selborne, Hampshire, and spent most of his life in the village, holding several local curacies. A keen observer of wildlife and the changing seasons, with a gift for painstaking fieldwork and an eye for luminous detail, he published his observations as *The Natural History and Antiquities of Selborne* (1789), a volume of letters

addressed to PENNANT among others. *The Natural History of Selborne*, as it is usually called, is a scientific classic as well as a book of lasting charm. *A Naturalist's Calendar*, edited by JOHN AIKIN after White's death, appeared in 1795.

White, Henry Kirke 1785–1806 Poet. Articled to a solicitor in Nottingham, he published *Clifton Grove* (1803), a volume in the style of GOLDSMITH'S *DESERTED VILLAGE*, which attracted the attention of SOUTHEY. He entered St John's College, Cambridge, to prepare for ordination but died while still an undergraduate. Southey compiled *The Remains of Henry Kirke White* (1807); its evangelical tone ensured its brief popularity.

White, Patrick 1912–90 Australian novelist, short-story writer and playwright. He came from a wealthy Australian family but was born and educated in Britain. He returned to live in Australia after World War II. The rediscovery of his Australianness ultimately led to three of his finest novels: *The Tree of Man* (1955), covering a period from pioneer settlement to suburbanization, *Voss* (1957) and *Riders in the Chariot* (1961), which contains a powerful indictment of Australian suburban life. Other novels include *The Happy Valley* (1939), *The Living and the Dead* (1941), *The Aunt's Story* (1948), *The Solid Mandala* (1966), *The Vivisector* (1970), *The Eye of the Storm* (1973), *A Fringe of Leaves* (1976) and *The Twyborn Affair* (1979), which he declared would be his last. He broke his resolution in 1986 with *Memoirs of Many in One* 'by Alex Xenophon Demirjian Gray, edited by Patrick White'. *The Burnt Ones* (1964) and *The Cockatoos* (1974) are collections of short stories. Plays such as *The Season at Sarsaparilla* (1961), *Night on Bald Mountain* (1962) and *Signal Driver* (1983) established him as one of Australia's finest non-naturalistic dramatists. His autobiography, *Flaws in the Glass* (1981), openly acknowledged his homosexuality. *Patrick White Speaks* (1990) is a collection of essays and speeches, often campaigning, from 1958 to 1988. He was awarded the Nobel Prize for Literature in 1973.

White, T(erence) H(anbury) 1906–64 Writer of CHILDREN'S LITERATURE. His early work was hardly successful, though *England Have My Bones* (1937), in praise of the English countryside, had its admirers. Profoundly affected by MALORY'S *LE MORTE DARTHUR*, which, as a pacifist, he considered 'a quest for an antidote to war', he made a major contribution to ARTHURIAN LITERATURE with his quirky, humorous retelling of the legend in *The Sword in the Stone* (1939), *The Witch in the Wood* (1940), *The Ill-Made Knight* (1941) and *The Candle in the Wind* (1958). The series was revised as *The Once and Future King* (1958). A fifth volume, *The Book of Merlyn*, was posthumously discovered and published in 1977. Other works included *Mistress Masham's Repose* (1946), about descendants of the Lilliputians from *GULLIVER'S TRAVELS*; *The Goshawk* (1951), about training a pet hawk; *The Book of Beasts* (1954), a translation from a medieval bestiary; and *The Master* (1957), part parable and part SCIENCE FICTION.

White, William Hale 1831–1913 Novelist and essayist under the pseudonym of Mark Rutherford. He was born into a Dissenting family in Bedford and began to train as an Independent minister but was expelled for raising issues of biblical criticism. He worked as a journalist and civil servant. In his fifties White began to publish in two distinct, but for him related, fields: fiction and philosophy. *The Autobiography of Mark Rutherford, Dissenting Minister* (1881) relates, in thinly veiled form, his own spiritual pilgrimage from orthodoxy through Unitarianism, theism and agnosticism to stoic resignation. What distinguishes his account both here and in the sequel, *Mark Rutherford's Deliverance* (1885), is the narrator's air of absolute fidelity to the truth, however drab, sombre or inconvenient to the demands of fictional structure. These two novels, together with *The Revolution in Tanner's Lane* (1887), provide a portrait of 19th-century dissent where nostalgia for the past glories of Puritanism informs the astringent analysis of its present decay. Under his own name White published studies of BUNYAN, WORDSWORTH and Spinoza. His other writings, the novels *Catherine Furze* (1893), *Miriam's Schooling and Other Papers* (1893) and *Clara Hopgood* (1896), and the essays and stories published in *Pages from a Journal* (1900), *More Pages from a Journal* (1910) and *Last Pages from a Journal* (1915) confirm the picture of a deeply self-critical moral earnestness schooling an innately depressive temperament for survival in an often uncongenial world.

White Devil, The A tragedy by WEBSTER, published in 1612 and probably first produced the same year. The Duke of Brachiano tires of his wife Isabella and falls in love with Vittoria Corombona. Her evil brother Flamineo helps him dispose of both Isabella and Vittoria's husband, Camillo. Flamineo also quarrels with his brother, Marcello, and murders him in sight of their mother, Cornelia. Despite vigorous pleading in her own defence, Vittoria is convicted of murder and adultery. Brachiano rescues her and they flee to Padua. Isabella's brother Francisco is determined to avenge her death, and his men Gasparo and Lodovico kill Brachiano. Vittoria confronts Flamineo, who feels unrewarded for his services. Gasparo and Lodovico intervene to complete Francisco's vengeance on them both.

White-Jacket: *or, The World in a Man-of-War* A novel by HERMAN MELVILLE, published in 1850. It describes the homeward voyage of the frigate *Neversink* from Peru eastward round the Horn to Virginia, emphasizing the degrading conditions the men live in and the tyrannies practised by the captain and officers. The criticism of flogging was timely, and copies of the book were sent to Congress during its debate of the issue. The title refers to the nickname which the narrator earns by making himself a white jacket from scraps of cloth.

Whitehead, Charles 1804–62 Novelist, poet and playwright. He wrote several popular works: a poem, *The Solitary* (1831), two romantic novels, *Jack Ketch* (1834) and *Richard Savage* (1842), and a verse drama, *The Cavalier* (1836). His career was blighted by drunkenness and he ceased writing about 1850, dying in Australia.

Whitehead, William 1715–85 Poet and playwright. His plays include: two well-received tragedies, *The Roman Father* (1750) and *Creusa, Queen of Athens* (1754); a successful comedy, *The School for Lovers* (1762); and a FARCE, *The Trip to Scotland* (1770). *Elegies, with an Ode to the Tiber, Written Abroad*, inspired by his experiences as tutor on the Grand Tour, appeared in 1757, the year he became POET LAUREATE on the death of CIBBER. Critics of the ODES he wrote in performance of his duties included SAMUEL JOHNSON and CHARLES CHURCHILL in *The Ghost* (1762–3). Whitehead made a dignified reply in *A Charge to the Poets* (1762) and *A Pathetic Apology for All Laureates, Past, Present, and to Come*, privately circulated and posthumously published. His later poems include *Variety: A Tale for Married People* (1776) and *The Goat's Beard* (1777). His collected works appeared in two volumes in 1774. WILLIAM MASON added a third volume with a memoir for the collected edition of 1788.

Whiteing, Richard 1840–1928 Novelist and journalist. *The Island* (1888) and its sequel, *Number 5 John Street* (1889), depict social unrest in late Victorian Britain and criticize accepted values. A series of satirical articles dating from Whiteing's time in Paris appeared in *The Evening Star* from 1866.

Whitfield, James M. 1823–78 Black American poet and Abolitionist. He began to write while working as a barber in Buffalo, publishing *Poems* (1846) and *America, and Other Poems* (1853). In 1858 he founded a journal, *African-American Repository*. His later poetry appeared primarily in magazines such as the *Liberator* and *Frederick Douglass' Paper* (see FREDERICK DOUGLASS). He died in California, en route to Central America to examine the possibility of establishing a colony of free blacks.

Whiting, John 1917–63 Playwright. An unfashionable figure in a period when the theatre was dominated by social commitment, he wrote a whimsical comedy, *A Penny for a Song* (1951), and several plays dramatizing spiritual struggles: *Saint's Day* (1951), *Marching Song* (1954), *The Gates of Summer* (1956) and *The Devils* (1961), derived from ALDOUS HUXLEY's *The Devils of Loudun*. His perceptive criticism is collected in *Whiting on Theatre* (1966).

Whitman, Walt(er) 1819–92 American poet. Born on Long Island and brought up in Brooklyn, he had little formal education before working as a printer's apprentice, itinerant teacher and, for much of his life, journalist in the New York area. His early writings include *Franklin Evans* (1842), a temperance tract in the form of a novel, and the stories recollected in *The Half-Breed and Other Stories* (1927). In 1848 he travelled to New Orleans, his experience of the vastness of the American landscape and the variety of its people making a decisive impact on *LEAVES OF GRASS*, the volume of poems which became his masterwork. Consisting of just 12 untitled poems when he first printed it himself in 1855, it grew steadily but without critical encouragement until the 'Deathbed' edition of 1891–2. Whitman's verse, with its use of colloquial language and its reference to everyday events, marks a turning-point in the history of American poetry: a poetic form fashioned out of specifically American experience in a distinctively American idiom. Some of the finest poems grew out of the horrors of the Civil War, during which he served as a volunteer nurse in army hospitals and as a correspondent for *The New York Times*, and out of an attempt to reconcile the war with a visionary concept of America. *Democratic Vistas* (1871), written while he was working in Washington, reaffirmed democratic principles in the face of the widespread corruption of the Reconstruction era. Other prose works are *Specimen Days and Collect* (1882) and *November Boughs* (1888), a collection of his newspaper pieces.

Whittier, John Greenleaf c. 1807–92 American poet. *Poems Written During the Progress of the Abolition Question* (1838), *Voices of Freedom* (1846), his first collected *Poems* (1849), *Songs of Labor* (1850) and his prolific work as a journalist testify to his ardent Abolitionism and his active Quaker conscience. Other volumes – beginning with his first, *Legends of New-England in Prose and Verse* (1831) – turn for inspiration to the history, folklore and countryside of New England; they include *Snowbound* (1866), *The Tent on the Beach* (1867), *Among the Hills* (1869), *Miriam and Other Poems* (1871), *Hazel-Blossoms* (1875), *The Vision of Echard* (1878), *Saint Gregory's Guest* (1886) and *At Sundown* (1890).

Who's Afraid of Virginia Woolf? A play by ALBEE, first performed in 1962. George, a history professor at a small New England college, and his wife Martha bring Nick and Honey, a young colleague and his nervous wife, back home from a party and involve them in the verbal abuse that seems to be their nightly ritual. Honey drinks too much and becomes ill. Martha tries to seduce Nick. Albee calls this second act 'Walpurgisnacht'. Act Three, in which Martha declares the death of the imaginary son she and George have created, is called 'Exorcism'.

Whyte-Melville, G(eorge) J(ohn) 1821–78 Novelist. He published some 23 novels on historical, romantic and sporting subjects. His sporting novels, such as *Market Harborough* (1861), have survived best, being perceptive, vivid and curiously undated. He was killed, characteristically, in a hunting accident.

Widowers' Houses SHAW's first play, produced in 1892. The aristocratic Dr Henry Trench falls in love with Blanche Sartorius. Her father will consent to the match only if Trench can guarantee his family's acceptance of Blanche. Trench is horrified to learn that Sartorius's wealth comes from slum landlordism, but Sartorius points out that Trench's income, however little he may concern himself with it, comes from the same sources. Trench capitulates and agrees to marry Blanche, who is not much more admirable than her father and Trench himself.

Widsith A 7th-century Old English poem in the EXETER BOOK, one of the oldest vernacular works to survive. The minstrel Widsith visits various courts and catalogues the heroes of the European tribes. The chronological span, from Eormanric (d. 375) to Aelfwine's invasion of Italy in 568, is too broad for it to derive from the reminiscences of a real minstrel.

Wiebe, Rudy (Henry) 1934– Canadian novelist and short-story writer. His first novel, *Peace Shall Destroy Many* (1962), has been followed by works notable for revisionist accounts of the history of Canadian minorites: Mennonites in *The Blue Mountains of China* (1970), Cree Indians in *The Temptations of Big Bear* (1973) and the Métis population of Manitoba in *The Scorched-Wood People* (1977). *Playing Dead* (1989) is 'a contemplation concerning the Arctic'. *Where is the Voice Coming From?* (1974) is a collection of stories.

Wieland: or, The Transformation A GOTHIC NOVEL by CHARLES BROCKDEN BROWN, published in 1798 and generally recognized as one of America's first major novels. In a letter Clara, only surviving member of the Wieland family, tells how the mystical Wieland senior died of spontaneous combustion. Following his wife's death, their children, Clara and Wieland Jr, are cared for by Catherine Pleyel, whom Wieland eventually marries. When Catherine's brother Henry arrives, Clara falls in love with him and the four enjoy each other's company insulated from the outside world. The arrival of the mysterious Carwin destroys their peace. Disembodied voices tell of the death of Henry's fiancée, encouraging him to fall in love with Clara, but then suggest that Clara and Carwin are having an affair. Henry finds his fiancée alive and marries her. The voices eventually drive Wieland to murder his wife and children. He is confined in an asylum but escapes on the very evening when Carwin confesses to Clara that he himself has created the voices by ventriloquism. When the voices order him not to kill his sister, Wieland commits suicide instead. Carwin disappears. After his wife's death Henry finally marries Clara.

Wife of Bath's Tale, The See CANTERBURY TALES.

Wife's Lament, The An Old English poem in the EXETER BOOK, recording the poignant lament of a wife whose husband has been exiled. Apparently an alien in his homeland, she is now friendless and reduced to living in an earth-barrow in the forest. The poem may be connected with THE HUSBAND'S MESSAGE, in the same collection.

Wiggin [*née* Smith], **Kate Douglas** 1856–1923 American writer of CHILDREN'S LITERATURE. Her first novels were written to raise money for her free nursery school in San Francisco, but her great bestseller, *Rebecca of Sunnybrook Farm* (1903), came many years later. It describes the conflict between the lively heroine and her spinster aunt, Matilda Sawyer, in small-town Maine. Other works include the autobiographical *My Garden of Memory* (1923).

Wigglesworth, Michael 1631–1705 American Puritan minister and poet. His most widely read poems were written either to present the articles of faith in a form which allowed them to be easily memorized, or to prescribe behaviour fitting for a Christian. *The Day of Doom* (1662), dealing with salvation and damnation, was used as a supplement to the catechism in educating young Puritans. *Meat out of the Eater* (1670) expounds the uses the virtuous can find in the experience of ill health. A posthumously published verse jeremiad, 'God's Controversy with New England', interprets the drought of 1662 as a providential warning to reform. Wigglesworth's *Diary* records the psychological struggle inherent in spiritual growth.

Wilbur, Richard (Purdy) 1921– American poet. *The Beautiful Changes* (1947) and *Ceremony and Other Poems* (1950) in part respond to the personal and public dislocation he perceived in the war and its immediate aftermath. *Things of This World* (1956) won both a PULITZER PRIZE and the National Book Award for poetry. Subsequent volumes culminate in *New and Collected Poems* (1988; Pulitzer Prize). His verse is oblique, witty and formally strict, qualities which ideally equipped him for translating Molière and Racine's *Andromaque* (1982). He has also published children's verse, as well as *Responses: Prose Pieces 1953–1976* (1976) and *On My Own Work* (1983), an exercise in self-criticism.

Wild Wales A travel book by GEORGE BORROW, published in 1862. Based on holiday visits and solitary walking tours, it is notable for the immediacy of its narrative, the high colouring given to simple episodes and the raciness of the dialogue. Borrow's affectionate account draws on a lifelong interest in the Welsh language and its literature, some of which he had translated.

Wild-Goose Chase, The A comedy by JOHN FLETCHER, first performed *c.* 1621 and published in 1652. The wild goose is Mirabell, whose aversion to marriage forces Oriana, his betrothed, to desperate measures. FARQUHAR revised it as *The Inconstant* (1702).

Wilde, Jane Francesca, Lady 1820–96 Irish poet and journalist. The wife of SIR WILLIAM WILDE and mother of OSCAR WILDE, she was more famous as a personality than as a writer, making her home one of the best-known social centres in Dublin. She contributed nationalistic poems and prose pieces under the pseudonym of Speranza to *The Nation*, the newspaper of the Young Ireland movement, and achieved something of a reputation with *Ancient Legends, Mystic Charms, and Superstitions of Ireland* (1887).

Wilde, Oscar (Fingal O'Flahertie Wills) 1854–1900 Playwright, novelist, essayist, poet and wit. The son of

SIR WILLIAM WILDE and JANE FRANCESCA WILDE, he studied at Trinity College, Dublin, and later at Magdalen College, Oxford, where he declared himself a disciple of PATER and the AESTHETIC MOVEMENT as well as distinguishing himself in classical studies. His first volume of poetry appeared in 1878. In 1882 he toured the USA as a lecturer, though his play *Vera* flopped in New York in 1883. *The Happy Prince and Other Tales* (1888) are fairy-stories written for the two sons by his marriage in 1884. A similar collection, *A House of Pomegranates*, followed in 1891, together with *Lord Arthur Savile's Crime and Other Stories* and *The Duchess of Padua*, an uninspired verse tragedy. Altogether more important was the insolently epigrammatic WIT, and the fascination with the relations between serene art and decadent life, expressed in *THE PICTURE OF DORIAN GRAY* (1890). Wilde found his true theatrical voice with *LADY WINDER-MERE'S FAN* (1892), *A WOMAN OF NO IMPORTANCE* (1893), *AN IDEAL HUSBAND* (1895) and his masterpiece, *THE IMPORTANCE OF BEING EARNEST* (1895). *SALOME*, written in French, was published in 1894 in an English translation by LORD ALFRED DOUGLAS.

Wilde's homosexuality was an open secret. When the Marquess of Queensberry, Lord Alfred's father, publicly insulted him, Wilde sued for libel but lost his case. He was prosecuted and imprisoned for homosexual acts in 1895. His bitter letter of reproach to Lord Alfred was published incomplete as *DE PROFUNDIS* (1905), though his poem, *THE BALLAD OF READING GAOL* (1898), is a more characteristic, because more generous, reaction to his imprisonment. On his release in 1897 he went to France, calling himself 'Sebastian Melmoth', and died in Paris after, it is said, being received into the Catholic church. ROBERT HICHENS's *The Green Carnation* (1894) remains the best attempt at PARODY of a literary style which invited imitation while remaining confident of its inimitability.

Wilde, Sir William 1815–76 Irish antiquarian. The husband of JANE FRANCESCA WILDE and father of OSCAR WILDE, he was a specialist in diseases of the eye and ear. Also a gifted writer, he won a reputation in the field of antiquarian and archaeological history. *Irish Popular Superstitions* (1852) helped to preserve a vanishing culture.

Wilder, Laura Ingalls 1867–1957 American writer of CHILDREN'S LITERATURE. She was over 60 before she began to write stories remembered from her pioneering childhood. *Little House in the Big Woods* (1932) describes life in a log cabin, with Laura herself appearing in the third person. *Little House on the Prairie* (1935) tells how Laura's father takes his family out West. In *The Long Winter* (1940) the family finally settles in a small town, where their hardships are again described with compassionate realism. Subsequent novels take Laura to marriage and a teaching career.

Wilder, Thornton (Niven) 1897–1975 American playwright and novelist. His best-known novel is *The Bridge of San Luis Rey* (1927; PULITZER PRIZE), a study of the role of destiny, or providence, in the death of five travellers when the bridge near Lima collapses in 1714. Other novels are: *The Cabala* (1926); *The Woman of Andros* (1930), set in ancient Greece; *Heaven's My Destination* (1934), about the fortunes of a good and simple man during the Depression; *The Ides of March* (1948), about the last days of Julius Caesar; and two late works, *The Eighth Day* (1967) and *Theophilus North* (1973). The six one-act sketches in *The Long Christmas Dinner and Other Plays* (1931) mingle REALISM and experimental modes, notably EXPRESSIONISM, designed to 'shake up' the American theatre. His reputation as a playwright rests primarily on three works: *OUR TOWN* (1938; Pulitzer Prize); *The Skin of Our Teeth* (1942; Pulitzer Prize), about mankind's precarious survival; and *The Matchmaker* (1955), revised from an earlier play called *The Merchant of Yonkers* (1939) and later the basis for the musical comedy *Hello Dolly!* (1963). Several of Wilder's essays on the theatre are included in *American Characteristics and Other Essays* (1979).

Wilding, Michael 1942– Australian short-story writer, novelist, critic and editor. He was born and educated in England. An energetic champion of *avant-garde* fiction, he founded the magazine *Tabloid Story* with FRANK MOORHOUSE and the publishing imprint of Wild and Woolley. His short-story collections are *Aspects of the Dying Process* (1972), *The West Midland Underground* (1975), *Scenic Drive* (1976), *The Phallic Forest* (1978), *Reading the Signs* (1985) and *A Man of Slow Feelings* (1985), selected from the previous volumes, and *Great Climate* (1991). *Under Saturn* (1988) is a collection of four novellas. His novels are *Living Together* (1974), *The Short Story Embassy* (1975), *Pacific Highway* (1982) and *The Paraguayan Experiment* (1985). Critical works include studies of *PARADISE LOST* (1969) and MARCUS CLARKE (1977) and *Political Fictions* (1980).

Wilkes, John 1727–97 Politician and journalist. A lively rake and member of the Hellfire Club, he was elected MP for Aylesbury in 1755 and turned to journalism when the Earl of Bute came to power, attacking the new prime minister's incompetence. In June 1762, with the help of CHARLES CHURCHILL, he launched *THE NORTH BRITON* as a rival to *The Briton*, which Bute had established with SMOLLETT as its editor. No. 45, impugning the truth of statements made in the speech from the throne, and the 'obscene' *Essay on Woman* led to the suppression of *The North Briton* in April 1763. Wilkes was expelled from the House of Commons and banished, though he escaped prosecution by claiming parliamentary privilege. Changes in the administration allowed him to return to England in 1768. He became MP for Middlesex but was expelled again the following year. Re-elected three times, he was three times denied his seat in the Commons. His persistence in the face of authority made him a popular hero and in 1774, when he became first Sheriff and then Lord Mayor of London, he took his seat without further opposition.

Wilkinson, Anne 1910–61 Canadian poet. She published two volumes, *Counterpoint to Sleep* (1951) and *The Hangman Ties the Holly* (1955). *Collected Poems* (1968), edited by A. J. M. SMITH, celebrates the elemental organic principles of life in lyrics comparable to the work of the METAPHYSICAL POETS. Her last poems, about death, stand with the best in Canadian literature.

Will to Believe, The, *and Other Essays in Popular Psychology* A treatise by WILLIAM JAMES, published in 1897. It sets out his philosophy of 'radical empiricism', emphasizing the importance of instinct and finding a belief in absolute truth philosophically untenable.

William of Palerne A VERSE ROMANCE in ALLITERATIVE VERSE (*c.* 1350–61), also known as *William and the Werewolf*, adapted from the French by an unknown 'William' whose patron was Humphrey de Bohun (d. 1361). The beginning of this enchanting, well-told story is missing but can be deduced from its source. The werewolf, the bewitched heir to the Spanish throne, saves the infant prince William of Sicily from his wicked uncle and helps him in later adventures. William regains his kingdom and marries Melior, daughter of the Emperor of Rome. Released from enchantment, the werewolf marries William's sister. The poem is unusual among English romances in preserving a detailed description of the symptoms of COURTLY LOVE from its source.

William of Shoreham 14th-century poet. He lived in Kent, probably at Shoreham near Sevenoaks, and is reported to have been vicar of Chart. Of his seven surviving poems, four are didactic explanations of Christian doctrine and three are in praise of the Virgin: one translates 'Patris sapientia, veritas divina' from the *Horae canonicae salvatoris* and another a work by GROSSETESTE.

Williams, Charles (Walter Stansby) 1886–1945 Poet, novelist, theologian and critic. Imbued with his Christian faith, his writings deal with man's relation to God and the problem of good and evil. *Thomas Cranmer of Canterbury* and *The House of the Octopus* are among the verse dramas written in 1936–41 and collected in JOHN HEATH-STUBBS's edition (1963). Equally characteristic is the intense, sometimes obscure contribution to ARTHURIAN LITERATURE in two volumes, *Taliessin through Logres* (1938) and *The Region of the Summer Stars* (1944), admired by C. S. LEWIS. Williams's novels, or 'metaphysical thrillers', include *War in Heaven* (1930), *Many Dimensions* (1931), *Descent into Hell* (1937) and *All Hallows' Eve* (1945). *He Came down from Heaven* (1937) and *The Descent of the Dove* (1939) are works of theology. His literary criticism includes a study of Dante (1943).

Williams, Helen Maria ?1762–1827 Poet, novelist and essayist on politics. She mixed in London's literary and BLUESTOCKING circles in the 1780s. *Poems* (1786) contained the 'Sonnet to Twilight' which prompted WORDSWORTH to his first published poem, 'Sonnet, On Seeing Miss Helen Maria Williams Weep at a Tale of Distress'. In 1788 she went to France, where she spent most of her remaining life, her liberalism growing into support of the Revolution. Her various *Letters from France* covering the years 1790–95 made English conservatives regard her as the embodiment of dangerous extremism. She also published SENTIMENTAL NOVELS, *A Tour of Switzerland* (1798) and translations of Saint-Pierre's *Paul et Virginie* and Humboldt's travels.

Williams, Isaac 1802–65 Poet and follower of the OXFORD MOVEMENT. A Fellow and then Dean of Trinity College, Oxford, he also acted as NEWMAN's curate at St Mary's church. He contributed Tracts 80, 86 and 87 to *TRACTS FOR THE TIMES*. His verse includes *Lyra Apostolica* (with Newman and KEBLE; 1836), *The Cathedral* (1838), *Thoughts in Past Years* (1838), *The Baptistery* (1842), *The Altar* (1847) and *The Christian Seasons* (1854).

Williams, John See REDEEMED CAPTIVE, RETURNING TO ZION, THE.

Williams, Nigel 1948– Novelist, playwright and television scriptwriter. A prolific author, he is best known for his fiction, which began with accomplished and witty examples of the *BILDUNGSROMAN*, such as *My Life Closed Twice* (1977), and has continued with energetically plotted black comedies in an implacably suburban setting: *The Wimbledon Poisoner* (1990), *They Came from SW19* (1992), *East of Wimbledon* (1993) and *Scenes from a Poisoner's Life* (1994).

Williams, Raymond (Henry) 1921–88 Critic. *Culture and Society 1780–1950* (1958), *The Long Revolution* (1961) and *Keywords* (1976) revised the concept of culture, turning away from the élitism of the Cambridge school towards the socially responsible ideal of a 'common cul-

ture'. *Communications* (1962) and *Television: Technology and Cultural Form* (1974) broadened the analysis by considering other media as well as literature. Always an active socialist, Williams moved closer to Marxism in his later work, including *Orwell* (1971), *The English Novel from Dickens to Lawrence* (1971), *The Country and the City* (1973), *Marxism and Literature* (1977) and *Culture* (1981). He ended his career at Cambridge as professor of drama (1974–83), a subject on which he wrote influentially in *Drama from Ibsen to Eliot* (1952; revised as *Drama from Ibsen to Brecht*, 1968) and *Modern Tragedy* (1966). Other lectures and essays were collected in *Problems in Materialism and Culture* (1980) and *Writings in Society* (1983).

Williams, Roger 1603–83 American Puritan minister. Born in London, he emigrated to Massachusetts Bay in 1631 but did not easily find a home for his separatist views. He eventually founded the first Rhode Island settlement, at Providence among the Narragansett Indians, whom he described in *A Key into the Language of America* (1643). The book was published during a visit to England to secure a charter for the Providence Plantations. The same stay also produced his most important work, *The Bloody Tenet of Persecution* (1644), a defence of freedom of conscience and the separation of church and state against the arguments of JOHN COTTON and others. He also wrote *Christenings Make Not Christians* (1645) and, though tolerant of both Jews and Quakers, a critique of Quaker reliance on the 'inner light' in *George Fox Digged Out of his Burrows* (1672).

Williams, Tennessee (Thomas Lanier) 1911–83 American playwright. He made his reputation with *THE GLASS MENAGERIE* (1944) and confirmed it with *A STREETCAR NAMED DESIRE* (1947; PULITZER PRIZE). Both plays show a sympathy for the lost and self-punishing individual which reappears in subsequent dramas, such as *Summer and Smoke* (1947; revised as *The Eccentricities of a Nightingale*, 1964). His gift for comedy is evident in *The Rose Tattoo* (1951). After the experimental *Camino Real* (1953) he returned to his familiar themes of the intricacies of Southern families and Southern culture in *CAT ON A HOT TIN ROOF* (1955; Pulitzer Prize), *Sweet Bird of Youth* (1956) and *The Night of the Iguana* (1959, revised 1961). Other plays include *Suddenly Last Summer* (1958), *The Milk Train Doesn't Stop Here Anymore* (1962), *In the Bar of a Tokyo Hotel* (1969), *Small Craft Warnings* (1974), *Vieux Carré* (1977) and *Clothes for a Summer Hotel* (1980). Williams also published two volumes of poetry, *In the Winter of Cities* (1956) and *Androgyne, Mon Amour* (1977), several collections of prose and a novel, *The Roman Spring of Mrs Stone* (1950). His *Memoirs* (1975) portray a life consumed with guilt, anger and a sense of failure. *Collected Stories* appeared in 1985.

Williams, William Carlos 1883–1963 American poet. His work, among the most original and influential achievements of the 20th century, is deceptively simple. 'No ideas but in things', he declared, finding his subjects in such homely items as refrigerated plums and wheelbarrows. His early verse was influenced by IMAGISM in its objective, precise manner of description; later poems went well beyond imagism and became more personal. They are also notable for using the 'variable foot', which he felt approximated to colloquial American speech. *PATERSON*, his most ambitious work, is an epic treatment of his home town in New Jersey; five books appeared between 1946 and 1958 and fragments of a sixth in 1963. Other volumes include *Poems* (privately printed; 1900), *The Tempers* (1913), *Al Que Quiere!* (1917),

Kora in Hell: Improvisations (1920), *Sour Grapes* (1921), *Spring and All* (1923), *The Desert Music and Other Poems* (1954), *Journey to Love* (1955) and *Pictures from Brueghel and Other Poems* (1962), which brought him a belated PULITZER PRIZE. A posthumously edited two-volume *Collected Poems* appeared in 1986-8.

Williams also published: *The Great American Novel* (1923) and *In the American Grain* (1925), two collections of essays supplemented by *Selected Essays of William Carlos Williams* (1954); short stories, gathered in *The Farmer's Daughter: The Collected Stories* (1961); novels such as *A Voyage to Pagany* (1928), *White Mule* (1937), *In the Money* (1940) and *The Build-Up* (1952); *Many Lives and Other Plays* (1961); and an autobiography (1951).

Williamson, David (Keith) 1942– Australian playwright. *The Coming of Stork* (1970), *The Removalists* (1971), *Don's Party* (1971) and *The Club* (1977) established his reputation in Australia's 'New Wave' as a naturalistic writer with a witty, satirical style and an interest in personal confrontations and institutional power struggles. Later plays continue the anatomy of Australian society, but the satirical dimension is less prominent. They include *Travelling North* (1979), *The Perfectionist* (1982), *Son of Cain* (1985) and *Emerald City* (1987). His work for the cinema includes versions of *Don's Party* (1976) and *The Club* (1980), and screenplays for *Gallipoli* (1981), *Phar Lap* (1983) and *The Year of Living Dangerously* (1985), the last written in collaboration with Peter Weir and CHRISTOPHER KOCH, author of the novel on which it is based.

Williamson, Henry 1895-1977 Novelist and naturalist. He is best remembered for *Tarka the Otter* (1927), a minutely observed and moving tale of animal life which became a popular classic. Like *The Peregrine's Saga* (1923), *The Old Stag* (1926), *Salar the Salmon* (1935), *The Phasian Bird* (1948) and *Tales of Moorland and Estuary* (1953), it reflects his debt to RICHARD JEFFERIES. His other pre-war writings include *The Wet Flanders Plain* (1929) and *A Patriot's Progress* (1930), about World War I, and *The Flax of Dreams*, a sequence of novels comprising *The Beautiful Years* (1921), *Dandelion Days* (1922), *The Dream of Fair Women* (1924) and *The Pathway* (1928). After World War II, during which he was briefly interned because of his Fascist sympathies, he published *A Chronicle of Ancient Sunlight*, a partly autobiographical 15-novel sequence beginning with *The Dark Lantern* (1951) and concluding with *The Gale of the World* (1969).

Willobie, Henry ?1574-?1596 Poet. His reputation rests on a complex, riddling poem, *Willobie His Avisa* (1594), the most comprehensive account of which explains it as a veiled history of the courtships of Queen Elizabeth. References to 'W. S.', characterized as 'the old player', have tantalized Shakespearean myth-makers.

Wills, William Gorman 1828-91 Anglo-Irish playwright and portrait painter. His verse dramas provided Henry Irving with many of his successes, including *Charles I* (1872), *Eugene Aram* (1873), *Vanderdecken* (1878) and *Faust* (1885), though his most enduring work was *Olivia* (1878), an adaptation of GOLDSMITH's *THE VICAR OF WAKEFIELD*.

Wilmot, John, Earl of Rochester See ROCHESTER, JOHN WILMOT, EARL OF.

Wilson, A(ndrew) N(orman) 1950– Novelist, biographer and critic. His prolific output of fiction began with baleful comedies, such as *The Sweets of Pimlico* (1977) and *Unguarded Hours* (1978), but his reputation rests mainly on *The Healing Art* (1980), *Who was Oswald*

Fish? (1981) and *Wise Virgin* (1982), intricately plotted tragicomedies which confront perplexing moral dilemmas. Subsequent novels include *Scandal* (1983), *Gentlemen in England* (1985), *Incline Our Hearts* (1988) and *A Bottle in the Smoke* (1990). He has also published acclaimed biographies of SIR WALTER SCOTT (1980), MILTON (1983), BELLOC (1984), Tolstoy (1988) and C. S. LEWIS (1990). His stringent literary criticism is collected in *Penfriends from Porlock* (1988).

Wilson, Sir Angus (Frank Johnstone) 1913-91 Novelist, short-story writer and critic. The realistic surface of his work and its determined if sceptical engagement with moral values made comparison with E. M. FORSTER inevitable, though in fact he challenged the tradition of liberal humanism. Novels include: *Hemlock and After* (1952), about a writer's attempt to establish a literary colony; *Anglo-Saxon Attitudes* (1956), about middle age; *The Middle Age of Mrs Eliot* (1958), about widowhood; *Late Call* (1964), about the spiritual desolation of a new town in the Midlands; *No Laughing Matter* (1967), about the Matthews family from 1912 to 1967; *As If by Magic* (1973), about a world-ranging quest for meaning; and *Setting the World on Fire* (1980), contrasting the lives of two brothers. *The Old Men at the Zoo* (1961) is a bizarre and violent fable about the near future. Equally important are the short stories in *The Wrong Set* (1949), *Such Darling Dodos* (1950) and *A Bit off the Map* (1957). Other work included studies of Zola (1950), DICKENS (1970) and KIPLING (1977), and *Diversity and Depth in Fiction: Selected Critical Writings* (1983). As professor of English literature at the University of East Anglia from 1966, he presided with MALCOLM BRADBURY over Britain's only notable university course in creative writing. MARGARET DRABBLE has written his biography (1995).

Wilson, August 1945– Black American playwright. Drawing on his experience of growing up in a slum district of Pittsburgh, he has written a series of plays, each set in a different decade, which he terms his 'view of the black experience of the 20th century'. They include *Ma Rainey's Black Bottom* (1984) *Joe Turner's Come and Gone* (1986), *Fences* (1987; PULITZER PRIZE), *The Piano Lesson* (1988; Pulitzer Prize), *Two Trains Running* (1990) and *The Piano Lesson* (1990).

Wilson, Colin (Henry) 1931– Critic, novelist and miscellaneous writer. He shot to fame with *The Outsider* (1956), an enthusiastic, disorganized study of alienation hailed by some as a manifesto of the ANGRY YOUNG MEN generation. Wilson survived his subsequent abrupt rejection by critics and has, by his prolific output, to some extent succeeded in removing himself from their influence. The first of his 'psychological thrillers' was *Ritual in the Dark* (1960), based on the Jack the Ripper case. Other novels include *The Mind Parasites* (1967), *The Killer* (1970), *The Black Room* (1975) and *The Janus Murder Case* (1984). Numerous works of non-fiction deal with literature, philosophy (particularly existentialism), psychology, the occult and the paranormal, and crime.

Wilson, Edmund 1895-1972 American man of letters. He combined a distinguished career in journalism, as associate editor of *THE NEW REPUBLIC* in 1926-31 and regular book reviewer for *THE NEW YORKER* in 1944-8, with a wider reputation as literary critic and political commentator. His books include: *Axel's Castle: A Study in the Imaginative Literature of 1870-1930* (1931), a standard work on SYMBOLISM; *Travels in Two Democracies* (1936), a Marxist critique of life in the USA and Russia; *To the*

Finland Station: A Study in the Writing and Acting of History (1940), about the origins of the Russian Revolution; *The Boys in the Back Room: Notes on California Novelists* (1941); *The Wound and the Bow: Seven Studies in Literature* (1941), which contains an influential reassessment of DICKENS; and *Patriotic Gore: Studies in the Literature of the American Civil War* (1962). His fiction consists of two novels, *I Thought of Daisy* (1929) and *Galahad* (1957), and a collection of short stories, *Memoirs of Hecate County* (1946, revised 1958). *A Piece of My Mind: Reflections at Sixty* (1956), *A Prelude: Landscapes, Characters and Conversations from the Earlier Years of My Life* (1967), *The Twenties* (1975), *The Thirties* (1980) and *The Forties* (1983) are memoirs. Wilson's third wife was MARY MCCARTHY.

Wilson, Ethel 1890–1980 Canadian novelist and short-story writer. She was born in South Africa and spent part of her childhood in England. Her first novel, *Hetty Dorval* (1947), was followed by *The Innocent Traveller* (1949), *Swamp Angel* (1954) and *Love and Salt Water* (1956), developing her gift for poised studies of human relationships, their modest surface and apparently traditional structure belying a keen ironic intelligence. *The Equations of Love* (1952) brings together two novellas, and *Mrs Golightly and Other Stories* (1961) most of her important short stories.

Wilson, J(ohn) Dover 1881–1969 Scholar and critic. His major work on SHAKESPEARE was as co-editor of the New Cambridge edition in 1919–66, during which time he also published *The Essential Shakespeare* (1932), *What Happens in Hamlet* (1935), *The Fortunes of Falstaff* (1943) and *Shakespeare's Happy Comedies* (1962). During his days as a school inspector Wilson contributed to the Newbolt Report on the teaching of English (1921) an impassioned appeal for literature to be taught to working-class children. He also edited ARNOLD'S *CULTURE AND ANARCHY* in 1932 and wrote a graceful autobiography, *Milestones on the Dover Road* (1969).

Wilson, John 1626–c. 1695 Playwright. *The Cheats* (1664) and *The Projectors* (1665) are comedies in the manner of JONSON. *Belphegor: or, The Marriage of the Devil* (1690) is a tragicomedy based on Machiavelli's story, and *Andronicus Comnenius* (1664) a tragedy about the Byzantine emperor. He also wrote occasional verse.

Wilson, John 1785–1854 Critic. Though he published poetry and fiction he is chiefly remembered for his connection with *BLACKWOOD'S EDINBURGH MAGAZINE*. With JAMES HOGG and JOHN GIBSON LOCKHART he wrote the satirical *Chaldee MS* (October 1817) and under the pseudonym of Christopher North he wrote the greatest number of the *Noctes Ambrosianae* papers (1822–35). In 1820 he was elected to the chair of moral philosophy at Edinburgh University on the strength of his firm Tory principles.

Wilson, Lanford (Eugene) 1937– American playwright. He is best known for *The Hot l Baltimore* (1973), about social outcasts living in a condemned hotel, whose broken sign gives the play its title. Other works, which have prompted comparison with TENNESSEE WILLIAMS, include: *Balm in Gilead* (1965), about an all-night coffee shop in New York; *Rimers of Eldritch* (1966), about small-town spite and hypocrisy; *The Mound Builders* (1975); *5th of July* (1978); *Talley's Folly* (1979; PULITZER PRIZE); *Angel's Fall* (1983); and *Burn This* (1988).

Wilson, Robert d. 1600 Actor and playwright. *The Ladies of London* (c. 1581), *The Three Lords and Three Ladies of London* (c. 1589) and *The Cobbler's Prophecy* (c. 1594), the three surviving plays which he wrote or helped to write,

show his ability to adapt the MORALITY PLAY to the changing taste of the early public theatres.

Wilson, Thomas ?1528–81 Humanist and diplomat. He served Elizabeth I on embassies to Portugal and the Netherlands, becoming a Privy Councillor *c.* 1572 and Secretary of State in 1578. *The Rule of Reason* (1551) is an introduction to logic and the conduct of argument. *The Art of Rhetoric* (1553) urges the use of plain English and discourages the affectation of foreign phrases and 'inkhorn terms'. Wilson's translation of some of Demosthenes' orations was printed in 1570 and his treatise on usury in 1572.

Winchilsea, Countess of [Finch, Anne] 1661–1721 Poet. Born Anne Kingsmill, she married Heneage Finch, later 6th Earl of Winchilsea, in 1684. Her first poems appeared in 1701 and a collection, *Miscellany Poems*, in 1713. Her nature poetry, particularly the 'Nocturnal Reverie', was praised by WORDSWORTH and her small output is thought to have influenced POPE's *ESSAY ON MAN* and SHELLEY's *Epipsychidion*.

Wind in the Willows, The A novel for children by KENNETH GRAHAME, published in 1908. Three bachelor animals live easy lives on the banks of the Thames: the timid but friendly Mole, the forceful Water Rat and the irresponsible Toad, owner of Toad Hall. When Toad is imprisoned for enthusiastically dangerous driving, Toad Hall is invaded by the stoats and weasels who normally live in the Wild Wood beyond. Escaping from prison dressed as a washerwoman, Toad recaptures his ancestral home with his two friends and the curmudgeonly Badger. The book's strength lies in its animal characterizations and the charming descriptions of the countryside, which include a meeting with the god Pan. Helped in its popularity by the illustrations of E. H. SHEPARD and ARTHUR RACKHAM, it has enjoyed a second, equally enduring life on the stage, usually in MILNE's adaptation as *Toad of Toad Hall* (1929).

Winesburg, Ohio A collection of 23 stories by SHERWOOD ANDERSON, published in 1919. Partly based on the author's hometown in Ohio, they explore American small-town life and are given further unity by the character of George Willard, a reporter for the local newspaper who has literary ambitions and to whom all the other characters gravitate in the course of the book.

Wings of the Dove, The A novel by HENRY JAMES, published in 1902. Kate Croy and Merton Densher are secretly engaged. She becomes friends with the wealthy Milly Theale, whose death from a mysterious illness can be postponed only by happiness. Kate encourages Merton to take an interest in Milly, hoping that they will get married and that he will soon be a rich widower. Milly learns of the true relationship between Kate and Merton from the fortune-hunting Lord Mark and dies soon afterwards. When Merton learns that Milly has made him rich enough to marry Kate he offers to marry her only if she agrees not to accept the money. Kate declines and they separate.

Winner and Waster A political ALLEGORY in ALLITERATIVE VERSE (c.1352). In a DREAM-VISION the narrator witnesses a debate between the leaders of two armies arrayed for battle: Wynnere (Winner), representing those who produce and gain wealth through labour, and Wastoure (Waster), who spends freely and wastes resources. The king sends Wynnere to live with the Pope in Rome and Wastoure to Cheapside. The anonymous author may also have written *THE PARLIAMENT OF THE THREE AGES*.

Winnie-the-Pooh See MILNE, A. A.

Winter Words in Various Moods and Metres A collection of verse by HARDY, posthumously published in 1928. Written mostly after 1925, the poems stem from incidents and feelings of many decades before, some reaching back to the 1860s. The final poem is appropriately and movingly entitled 'He Resolves to Say No More'.

Winter's Tale, The A play by SHAKESPEARE, first performed c. 1611 and published in the First Folio of 1623. The main source is GREENE's *Pandosto* (1588). Like Shakespeare's other late plays, *PERICLES*, *CYMBELINE* and *THE TEMPEST*, it is a multi-faceted romance. The first part forms a rounded tragedy. Leontes, King of Sicilia, is driven to insane jealousy by the friendship between his queen Hermione and his friend Polixenes, King of Bohemia. Instead of obeying Leontes' order to poison Polixenes, Camillo warns him and they escape to Bohemia together. Leontes charges the pregnant Hermione with adultery but the news first of his son's death and then of Hermione's death shames him to his senses. He vows to spend the rest of his life in penance. His new-born daughter has already been carried off by Antigonus to the Bohemian shore, where he is eaten by a bear, leaving the infant Perdita to be found by an old shepherd. Sixteen years pass before the second part of the play, a comedy of rebirth and renewal. Brought up in the shepherd's home, Perdita is loved by Polixenes' son, Prince Florizel. But Polixenes comes in disguise to shatter the joy of the sheep-shearing feast by demanding the end of the match. With Camillo's help, Perdita and Florizel escape to Sicilia, where Leontes welcomes them. Polixenes, on learning the secret of Perdita's birth, greets the forthcoming marriage as a guarantee of his reconciliation with Leontes. Antigonus' wife, Paulina, gathers the leading characters to see the newly completed statue of Hermione. It comes to life and Hermione is 'reborn' into her marriage with Leontes.

Winters, (Arthur) Yvor 1900–68 American poet and critic. His verse, severely restrained and meticulously patterned, is among the first notable poetry of the American West. It appeared in *Poetry: The Immobile Wind* (1921), *The Magpie's Shadow* (1922), *The Bare Hills* (1927), *The Proof* (1930) and *To the Holy Spirit* (1947). His critical writings, which allied him with the NEW CRITICISM, include *In Defense of Reason* (1947), *The Function of Criticism* (1957) and *Forms of Discovery* (1967).

Winthrop, John 1588–1649 American Puritan leader. He was elected governor of the Massachusetts Bay Colony in 1629 for his services in negotiating its charter and arrived there from England the following year. *A Defence of an Order of Court Made in the Year 1637* supports the legislation denying citizenship to 'dissenters' which arose from the case of Anne Hutchinson. His account of the Hutchinson trial was incorporated into Thomas Welde's *A Short History of the Rise, Reign and Ruin of the Antinomians* (1644). His many comments on the political affairs of New England are collected in his journal, *The History of New England 1630–1649*, published in part in 1790 and complete in 1826.

Winthrop, Theodore 1826–61 American novelist and travel-writer. None of his books was published before his death in the Civil War. His novels include *Cecil Dreeme* (1861), *Edwin Brothertoft* (1862) and *John Brent* (1862), his best-known work, which exploits its Western setting to produce a melodramatic plot involving kidnappings and unscrupulous Mormons. *Life in the Open Air* (1863) and *The Canoe and the Saddle* (1863) are travel books.

Winton, Tim(othy) (John) 1960– Australian novelist, short-story writer and writer of CHILDREN'S LITERATURE. His fiction lovingly records the land and seascape of Western Australia and the communities of its small towns, concentrating with particular compassion on the lives of the inarticulate. His novels are *An Open Swimmer* (1982), *Shallows* (1984), *That Eye, The Sky* (1986), *In the Winter Dark* (1988) and the ambitious *Cloudstreet* (1991). *Scission* (1985) and *Minimum of Two* (1987) are collections of short stories. *Jesse* (1989), *Lockie Leonard, Human Torpedo* (1990) and *The Bugalugs Bum Thief* (1991) are children's books.

Wise, John c. 1652–1725 American Puritan minister. *The Churches' Quarrel Espoused* (1710) and *A Vindication of the Government of New England Churches* (1717) advocate autonomous congregations and oppose the arguments for ecclesiastical centralization put forward by COTTON MATHER and INCREASE MATHER. Both works advance egalitarian principles which appealed to American revolutionaries and Abolitionists in the 18th and 19th centuries. *A Word of Comfort to a Melancholy Country* (1721) is a defence of paper money.

Wise, T(homas) J(ames) 1859–1937 Book collector, bibliographer and forger. A successful businessman, he gathered many honours by collecting and cataloguing a valuable library. In 1934 John Carter and Graham Pollard showed that he had also been forging first editions of major authors. At the present count it is known that Wise forged or pirated more than 50 works by, among others, MATTHEW ARNOLD, CHARLOTTE BRONTË, ELIZABETH BARRETT BROWNING, ROBERT BROWNING, DICKENS, GEORGE ELIOT, WILLIAM MORRIS, DANTE GABRIEL ROSSETTI, SHELLEY, SWINBURNE, TENNYSON, THACKERAY and WORDSWORTH. The forgeries took a variety of forms: type facsimiles of genuine pamphlets; genuine works to which bogus title-pages with false dates were added; and works to which bogus cancels were added. In 1959 David Foxon demonstrated that Wise had torn out leaves from perfect copies of Jacobean plays in the British Library in order to make up his own imperfect copies, which he then sold.

Wiseman, Adele 1928– Canadian novelist. *The Sacrifice* (1956), a modern version of the Abraham and Isaac story, and the more experimental *Crackpot* (1974) deal with the Jewish experience on the Canadian Prairies. She has also written two plays, a children's book and *Old Woman at Play* (1978), a fragmentary memoir of her mother.

Wister, Owen 1860–1938 American novelist and short-story writer. *Red Man and White* (1896), *Lin McLean* (1896) and *The Jimmyjohn Boss* (1900) are collections of stories set in the Western cattle country which he had first visited for reasons of health. His best-known novel, *The Virginian* (1902), was an enormous popular success. Its heroic cowpuncher, unassumingly masterful, crude but innately gentle, set the mould for the Western hero in countless novels and movies. Wister then turned to the East for his subjects. *Philosophy Four* (1903) is about undergraduate life at Harvard; *Lady Baltimore* (1906) is set in Charleston. He also wrote a biography of Ulysses S. Grant (1900) and reminiscences of Theodore Roosevelt (1930), the boyhood friend to whom he had dedicated *The Virginian*.

wit A concept, like humour, which has varied not only from period to period but also within each period. Yet in both cases all the variations share the common property of being in some way in touch with, or derivable from, their etymological origins. Wit (Old English 'witan', to know) in all its manifestations remains within hailing distance of the idea of intelligence, cleverness or judgement. Humour (Latin *humor*, moisture) can always be seen to have some relationship – though eventually a rather distant one – with its early medical meaning: a bodily fluid. Wit, that is to say, is associated with qualities of mind and manners, humour with qualities of body and mood.

In Elizabethan medical theory man was governed by four humours: black bile, yellow bile (or choler), phlegm and blood. Properly mixed they rendered him a balanced, equable, 'good-humoured' person. An excess of any one, however, rendered him melancholic, choleric, phlegmatic or sanguine, respectively: unbalanced, obsessive and therefore absurd. JONSON turned the medical theory into one for COMEDY (in the Prologue to EVERY MAN IN HIS HUMOUR, 1598) by generalizing it to include any kind of obsession or unbalancing folly. Physical imbalance becomes associated with temperamental oddity. Taken along with the gradual disappearance of humours from medical theory, this makes understandable the transition to the modern idea of humour as geniality about others or good-natured deprecation of oneself; it is in fact a modulation of what 'good-humoured' originally implied. So humorous comedy now implies something less moralistic than it used to: it is amusement without judgement, attack without malice. However, it still tends to be associated with situation and type-characters, with clever plotting that manoeuvres people into situations exposing their one-sided unadaptability.

In Jonson and SHAKESPEARE wit is usually close to good sense, intelligence, inventiveness. DONNE and the METAPHYSICAL POETS begin the shift towards ingenuity which seems to be the source of the Restoration distinction between true wit and false wit: wit that illuminates and wit that merely dazzles. HOBBES's definition of wit as a combination of Fancy (imagination) and Judgement never quite drops out of sight, though for the AUGUSTAN AGE wit was predominantly good sense, or propriety of idea and diction, or the natural made civilized, or inventiveness, or perceptive cleverness. ROMANTICISM tended to deprecate wit as frivolity, introducing the modern meaning of witticism or joke. Freud's *Jokes and their Relation to the Unconscious* (translated by James Strachey, 1960) brilliantly analyses and codifies this kind of wit. The essential perception is that wit – as distinct from amusing cleverness of a fully conscious kind, like IRONY – has its roots in the subconscious, but only its roots. It combines cognitive cleverness with emotional release or aggression. But this does not exhaust the meaning of wit in the post-Romantic period. Though there is a difference of emphasis today, earlier meanings of wit have not come to seem foreign, as is the case with humour. In literature, witty comedy still tends to be characterized by dialogue rather than situation, verbal cleverness rather than type-characters, surprising congruities rather than incongruities, in contrast to humour.

Witch of Edmonton, The A tragicomedy performed *c.* 1621 but not published until 1658, when the leading collaborators were named as WILLIAM ROWLEY, DEKKER and JOHN FORD. Dekker's sympathy for the ill-used is apparent in the story of Elizabeth Sawyer, driven by her neighbour's persecution into a pact with the Devil which gives her the powers of a witch. The other part of the play, chiefly by Ford, is a domestic tragedy in which Frank Thorney, secretly married to the servant Winifred, bigamously marries Susan Carter to obey his father's wishes and murders her, trying to throw the guilt on her two rejected suitors.

Wither, George 1588–1667 Poet. A convinced Puritan, he attained the rank of major-general in the Civil War. His main claim to be remembered is the PASTORAL poetry he contributed to WILLIAM BROWNE's *The Shepherd's Pipe* (1614) and published in his own *The Shepherd's Hunting* (1615), *Fidelia* (1617), *Fair Virtue* (1622) and *Juvenilia* (1622). The merit of these verses has been obscured by the notoriety of Wither's satire – *Abuses Stripped and Whipped: or, Satirical Essays* (1613) sent him to the Marshalsea, *Wither's Motto* (1621) to Newgate – and by the leaden didactic poetry of his later years.

Wives and Daughters The last novel by ELIZABETH GASKELL, almost complete at her untimely death in 1865. It was serialized in 1864–6 and published in book form in 1866. At the centre of its various skilfully interwoven plots is Molly Gibson's development from a confused, insecure girl to a poised young woman. The daughter of the local doctor in Hollingford, she extricates her step-sister Cynthia Kirkpatrick from an unwise commitment to the land agent Preston, is a ministering angel at the home of the old-fashioned Squire Hamley and finally marries Hamley's younger son Roger, a respected scientist who had been briefly engaged to the magnetic Cynthia. Socially, the novel ranges from the Lord and Lady Cumnor, the Hamleys and the Gibsons down to mob-capped spinsters, tenant farmers and ordinary labourers to register a lively, informative picture of early 19th-century England. A host of lesser characters contribute a leavening humour, a dramatic moment or a small turn to the plot. *Wives and Daughters* is an enduring work as narrative, social history and psychological study.

Wodehouse, Sir P(elham) G(renville) 1881–1975 Novelist and short-story writer. Beginning in 1902, he published well over 100 books, as well as contributing lyrics to a number of successful musical comedies with Cole Porter, Irving Berlin and George Gershwin. Set in leisured upper-class society, his comic novels and short stories are sustained by romantic, gently farcical plots and a carefully wrought prose style which combines literary allusion, the slang of the day and the occasional audacious SIMILE. Jeeves and Bertie Wooster, the omnicompetent manservant and his amiably incompetent master, have proved his most enduring creations. Introduced in *The Man with Two Left Feet* (1917), they appear in a long series of novels and collections of short stories bearing such expressive titles as *The Inimitable Jeeves* (1923), *Carry On, Jeeves!* (1925) and *Right Ho, Jeeves* (1934). *Blandings Castle* (1935) began a similar series centred on the eccentric Lord Emsworth.

Wolcot, John See PINDAR, PETER.

Wolfe, Thomas (Clayton) 1900–38 American novelist. *Look Homeward, Angel* (1929), his strongly autobiographical first novel, follows the early life of Eugene Gant. His story is continued in *Of Time and the River* (1935), in which he attends Harvard and leaves for Europe after a disappointing love affair. Wolfe also wrote a collection of stories, *From Death to Morning* (1935), several plays and *The Story of a Novel* (1936), a critical examination of his own work. The sprawling manuscripts he left at his death were edited by Edward C. Aswell as *The Web and the Rock* (1939) and *You Can't Go Home Again* (1940). Another volume of short stories, *The Lost Boy*, was published in 1965.

Wolfe, Tom [Thomas] **(Kennerly)** 1930– American journalist and novelist. He has been a major proponent of the New Journalism in *The Kandy-Kolored Tangerine Flake Streamline Baby* (1966), *The Pump House Gang* (1968), *Radical Chic and Mau-Mauing the Flak-Catchers* (1971), *Mauve Gloves and Madmen, Clutter and Vine and Other Stories* (1976), *In Our Time* (1980), *The Right Stuff* (1979), *The Painted Word* (1975) and *From Bauhaus to Our House* (1982). *The Electric Kool-Aid Acid Test* (1968) describes the wild lifestyle of KEN KESEY and his friends. Despite his earlier strictures against fiction, he scored a major success with *The Bonfire of the Vanities* (1988), a novel combining SATIRE and indignant reportage of Reagan's America.

Wollstonecraft, Mary 1759–97 Novelist, essayist and educational writer. The daughter of an unsuccessful gentleman farmer, she was largely self-taught. In youth she served as companion to a wealthy widow in Bath, and took care of her sick mother and the younger children of the family. With her sisters and her close friend Fanny Blood, she opened a school at Newington Green, where she met RICHARD PRICE and other Dissenting ministers and intellectuals. Following the collapse of the school and the death of Fanny Blood, she began *Thoughts on the Education of Daughters*. It appeared in 1787, the same year she went to Ireland as governess to the daughters of Lord Kingsborough, where she wrote the self-pitying *Mary: A Fiction* (1788). After being dismissed she worked as translator, reader, reviewer and editorial assistant, meeting Henry Fuseli, PAINE, BLAKE and GODWIN.

Between 1787 and 1790 she wrote two books for children, *Original Stories from Real Life; with Conversations Calculated to Regulate the Affections, and Form the Mind to Truth and Goodness* and *The Female Reader*, a selection of texts for girls. Her *Vindication of the Rights of Men* (1790) replied to BURKE'S *REFLECTIONS ON THE REVOLUTION IN FRANCE*. In it she identifies herself with the democratic programmes of the European Enlightenment and deplores both the complacency of British society and its trivialization of women. The latter theme is taken up at greater length in her most famous work, *A Vindication of the Rights of Woman* (1792), a sometimes chaotically written but rhetorically powerful plea for fundamental change in society's perception of the function, place and potential of women.

Following an obsessive, though unrewarding, relationship with Fuseli, she travelled alone to Revolutionary France in 1792. While condemning many of the events there, her *History and Moral View of the Origin and Progress of the French Revolution* (1794) still supports the basic principles of the revolutionary experiment. In Paris she met HELEN MARIA WILLIAMS and GILBERT IMLAY, with whom she fell in love. Their daughter, Fanny, was born in 1794, though Imlay rapidly lost interest in the relationship. An unlikely solo journey to Scandinavia as his business representative is described in *Letters Written during a Short Residence in Sweden, Norway and Denmark* (1796). Slowly recovering from the affair, which had prompted two suicide attempts, she formed an attachment with Godwin, who encouraged her to begin her last novel, *The Wrongs of Woman*. They married after she became pregnant, but she died eleven days after the birth of their daughter, the future MARY SHELLEY. In 1798 Godwin published his *Memoirs* of his

wife and edited her *Posthumous Works*, which included letters to Imlay, an autobiographical fictional fragment, *The Cave of Fancy*, and the unfinished *Wrongs of Woman*. She is also portrayed in his novel *St Leon* (1799). By this time, conservative reaction had set in in England, and she was much attacked as an unsexed woman, 'a hyena in petticoats' and a 'philosophizing serpent'.

Woman in White, The A novel by WILKIE COLLINS, serialized in 1859–60 and published in volume form in 1860. One of the most popular SENSATION NOVELS of its day, it shows Collins at the height of his powers.

The story is told through eyewitness accounts by the main characters. At Limmeridge House in Cumberland the new drawing master, Walter Hartright, meets the pretty Laura Fairlie and her ugly, intelligent half-sister Marian Halcombe. He falls in love with Laura but she insists on marrying Sir Percival Glyde despite the warnings of Anne Catherick, the mysterious woman in white who has escaped from the mental asylum to which Sir Percival has committed her. Marian continues the investigation. Sir Perceval enlists the help of the charming but sinister Count Fosco to gain control of Laura's fortune. They exploit the resemblance between Laura and Anne Catherick, now dead, to bury Anne under Laura's name and commit Laura to an asylum as Anne. Marian helps her escape and is joined by Walter. They discover that Sir Percival is illegitimate; he dies attempting to destroy the parish register revealing his secret. Fosco admits his part in the conspiracy before being killed by the Italian secret societies he has betrayed. Laura and Walter marry.

Woman Killed with Kindness, A A domestic tragedy by THOMAS HEYWOOD, first performed in 1603. When Frankford, a country gentleman, discovers his wife Anne in the arms of their guest Wendoll, he kills her with kindness by banishing her to live remote from the family but in comfort. He finally forgives her on her death-bed.

Woman of No Importance, A A play by OSCAR WILDE, produced in 1893. The illegitimate Gerald is torn between his father, Lord Illingworth, and his long-suffering mother, Mrs Arbuthnot. She refuses Lord Illingworth's proposal of marriage, which has come 20 years too late. Lord Illingworth betrays his baseness by attempting to kiss a young American heiress, in love with Gerald. Gerald is able to secure his future by marrying her.

Women Beware Women A tragedy by THOMAS MIDDLETON, perhaps dating from as late as 1625. Bianca, daughter of a noble house, marries Leantio, a merchant's clerk, but becomes the Duke of Florence's mistress. Livia, who plays cynical bawd to the adulterers, also takes Leantio as her lover and furthers the incestuous lust of her brother Hippolito for their niece Isabella. When the Duke's brother, the Cardinal, denounces the adultery, the Duke decides to be rid of Leantio. The outraged Hippolito kills him and Livia takes her revenge by denouncing Hippolito's incest. The various revenges reach a climax of black farce in the final act: lethal incense, poisoned arrows, fatal trapdoors and tainted gold are used to kill off the victims of their own depravity.

Women in Love A novel by D. H. LAWRENCE, first published in 1920. Ursula and Gudrun Brangwen, from *THE RAINBOW*, are central characters in what is not strictly a sequel but rather a continuation of Lawrence's inquiry into the possibilities that human relationships hold amid the unpromising circumstances of modern industrial culture. Ursula falls in love with Rupert Birkin, a school inspector. Gudrun is drawn into a tense relationship with Gerald Crich, son of the local mineowner. Birkin and Gerald are close friends, though Gerald rejects Birkin's attempt to establish a closer intimacy between them. Ursula and Birkin marry. Gudrun's destructive relationship with Gerald reaches its climax when the four go to Innsbruck together. Gudrun flirts with a decadent German sculptor, Loerke. Gerald attacks them before wandering off to die alone in the snow. Birkin grieves for Gerald and attempts to explain to a sceptical Ursula his vision of a male love to complement his love for her. The minor characters include a portrait of LADY OTTOLINE MORRELL as the neurotic Hermione Roddice.

Wood, Anthony à 1632–95 Antiquary and diarist. Anthony Wood (he archaized his name in later life) lived in Oxford, though he never became a fellow of his college, dying in the same house where he had been born. His researches into the history of Oxfordshire were largely unpublished in his lifetime, though sections dealing with the University were printed as *Historia et antiquitates universitatis oxoniensis* (1674). Wood made an English version, *The History and Antiquities of the University of Oxford*, which appeared in 1791–6. In the biographical sections of his *History* and his lives of distinguished Oxonians, *Athenae oxonienses* (1691–2), he was helped by AUBREY, whom he later treated ungratefully. In 1693 the *Athenae* was judged to contain a libel against CLARENDON: the relevant pages were publicly burned and Wood was expelled from the university. Besides his antiquarian collections, he left an autobiography and a remarkable diary for 1657–95, edited as *The Life and Times of Anthony Wood ... As Described by Himself* (1891–1900).

Wood, Mrs Henry (Ellen) 1814–87 Novelist. Although her mixture of sentiment, MELODRAMA and piety did not command universal admiration, she achieved world-wide fame with her second novel, *EAST LYNNE* (1861). Its many successors included *Mrs Halliburton's Troubles* (1862), *The Channings* (1862), *Verner's Pride* (1862–3) and *Roland Yorke* (1869). She considered *The Shadow of Ashlydat* (1863) her best novel. Much of her work was serialized in *The Argosy*, a journal she bought in 1867 and edited thereafter. A memoir by her son appeared in 1894.

Woodforde, James 1740–1803 Diarist. His diary begins in 1758, when he was an undergraduate at New College, Oxford, and continues for 45 years, covering the period when he held several Somerset curacies and became, in 1776, rector of Weston Longville in Norfolk. Mentioning public events only in passing and revealing no intellectual interests, Woodforde concentrates on the daily minutiae of domestic and parish life: meals, cricket matches, charities, hare-coursing, card games, bastard children and household remedies. Eccentricities of grammar and spelling add piquancy to the record.

Woodlanders, The A novel by HARDY, published in 1887. Socially ambitious for his daughter Grace, the timber merchant George Melbury regrets committing her to the rustic Giles Winterbourne, and uses Winterbourne's financial and legal misfortunes as an excuse to end their relationship. Melbury insists that Grace marry Dr Edred Fitzpiers though she, knowing about Fitzpiers' dalliance with Suke Damson, is not enthusiastic. Fitzpiers forms a liaison with Felice Charmond of Hintock Manor House and goes with her to the Continent, where they quarrel and part. The shadowy figure of the 'gentleman from South Carolina' kills Mrs Charmond in a jealous rage. Supported by her father's vain hope that she can obtain a divorce, Grace encourages Giles and is forced to seek shelter at his cottage in bad weather. Out of propriety he takes to a hopelessly inadequate outdoor retreat and dies of exposure. Grace is reunited with Fitzpiers, and the ever-faithful Marty South is left to mourn Giles.

Woodstock: or, The Cavalier. A Tale of the Year 1651 A novel by SIR WALTER SCOTT, published in 1826. The story concerns the escape of the future Charles II after the Battle of Worcester to Woodstock, where an old Cavalier, Sir Henry Lee, is ranger. His daughter Alice loves her cousin Everard, but Lee disdains him because Everard serves Cromwell and has earned his favour. Charles falls in love with Alice, Everard behaves honourably and Cromwell appears in the story. On his escape Charles leaves a parting message reconciling Sir Henry and Everard, who is now able to marry Alice.

Woodworth, Samuel 1785–1842 American poet and playwright. Much of his poetry appeared in *Melodies, Duets, Songs, and Ballads* (1826). He published one novel, *The Champions of Freedom* (1816), a romance set during the war of 1812. His plays include a MELODRAMA, *Lafayette* (1824), a domestic tragedy of the Revolutionary period entitled *The Widow's Son* (1825) and a comedy, *The Forest Rose: or, American Farmers*, which presents the typical Yankee character, Jonathan Ploughboy.

Woolf, Leonard (Sidney) 1880–1969 Writer, social reformer and husband of VIRGINIA WOOLF, whom he married in 1912. After Cambridge, where he became a member of the APOSTLES and was profoundly influenced by G. E. MOORE, he entered the Ceylon Civil Service. On his return to England he became an active member of the Fabian Society and a focal member of the BLOOMSBURY GROUP, wrote for various political journals, and published two novels, *The Village in the Jungle* (about Ceylon; 1913) and *The Wise Virgins* (1914). Other works are about politics and international affairs. *Sowing* (1960), *Growing* (1961), *Beginning Again* (1964), *Downhill All the Way* (1967) and *The Journey Not the Arrival Matters* (1969) are highly regarded volumes of autobiography.

Woolf, (Adeline) Virginia 1882–1941 Novelist. She was born Virginia Stephen, the daughter of SIR LESLIE STEPHEN by his second wife. The Bloomsbury house she shared with her sister Vanessa (later the wife of CLIVE BELL) and her brothers Thoby and Adrian after their father's death in 1904 became the original meeting-place of the BLOOMSBURY GROUP. She married one of the Group's members, LEONARD WOOLF, in 1912. Together they founded the Hogarth Press, which published *Two Stories* in 1917 ('The Mark on the Wall' by Virginia, and 'Three Jews' by Leonard), KATHERINE MANSFIELD's *Prelude* (1918), T. S. ELIOT's *Poems* (1919) and *THE WASTE LAND* (1923).

By this time she was herself a published novelist, though the appearance of her first work, *THE VOYAGE OUT*, completed in 1913, was delayed until 1915 by one of the mental breakdowns from which she suffered throughout her life. *Night and Day* (1919) is a realistic novel set in London, contrasting the lives of two friends, Katherine and Mary. *JACOB'S ROOM* (1922), based on the life and death of Thoby, broke away from traditional

REALISM. Like *Mrs Dalloway* (1925) it fulfilled the purpose laid down in her essay 'Modern Fiction' (1919), to capture as faithfully as possible the reality which she described as 'a luminous halo, a semi-transparent envelope surrounding us from the beginning of consciousness to the end.' With *To the Lighthouse* (1927) and *The Waves* (1931) she fully established herself as a leading exponent of MODERNISM. Her greatest commercial success was *Orlando* (1928), a fantastic biography tracing its androgynous protagonist through four centuries. It was dedicated to her intimate friend VITA SACKVILLE-WEST. Another 'biography', *Flush* (1933), revolves around the life of ELIZABETH BARRETT BROWNING's pet spaniel. *The Years* (1937) was more conventional, but her last novel, *Between the Acts*, posthumously published in 1941, returned to the experimental. It was completed just before the final attack of mental illness which drove her to suicide.

Virginia Woolf is now generally acknowledged as one of the major innovative novelists of the 20th century, best known, perhaps, for her use of STREAM OF CONSCIOUSNESS. Her contribution to FEMINIST CRITICISM has been widely recognized: *A Room of One's Own* (1929) and its still more radical sequel, *Three Guineas* (1938), are now established classics. Her critical essays, notably those in *The Common Reader* (1925) and *The Second Common Reader* (1932), were reprinted in *Collected Essays of Virginia Woolf* (1966-7). Her letters, edited by Nigel Nicolson and J. Trautmann (1975-80), include correspondence with nearly everyone associated with the Bloomsbury Group. Her diaries, edited by Anne Olivier Bell and A. McNeillie (1977-84), give an invaluable picture of her creative method.

Woolson, Constance (Fenimore) 1840-94 American novelist. Her wide knowledge of the USA is reflected in *Castle Nowhere: Lake-Country Sketches* (1875), *Rodman the Keeper: Southern Sketches* (1880), *Anna* (about a girl from Mackinac Island, Michigan, in New York; 1882), *For the Major* (set in North Carolina; 1883), *East Angels* (set in Florida; 1886) and *Jupiter Lights* (about the conflict between North and South; 1889). *Horace Chase* (1894) is about a woman who discovers, almost too late, the sterling character of her self-made husband. *Dorothy, and Other Italian Stories* (1896), her last book, concerns Americans in Europe.

Worde, Wynkyn de d. ?1534 Printer. 'Wynkyn from Worth' (in Alsace) assisted WILLIAM CAXTON and inherited his press and materials in 1491. Unlike Caxton, he did not make forays into translation and editing but contented himself with printing. The works he issued include MALORY's *Morte Darthur* (1498), CHAUCER's *Canterbury Tales* (1498) and, for the popular market, many small service books (e.g. the *Sarum Hours*), grammar books and romances. He was the first English printer to use italic type, in 1524.

Wordsworth, Dorothy 1771-1855 Sister of WILLIAM WORDSWORTH and author of journals. Born a year and a half after William at Cockermouth, Cumberland, she spent her later childhood, after her parents' death, with relatives in Halifax, Penrith and Norfolk. The strong bond between her and William was renewed in 1795, when they were able to realize a long-cherished plan of setting up house together, settling first at Racedown in Dorset, and then in the Quantocks at Alfoxden, Somerset, in order to be close to COLERIDGE at Nether Stowey. They were to remain inseparable through William's marriage until his death in 1850.

Dorothy's *Alfoxden Journal* was written, like all her work, without thought of publication. Although only the entries for January–April 1798 have survived, they are remarkable not only for the light they shed on William and his friendship with Coleridge in the *annus mirabilis* of the LYRICAL BALLADS, but also for their powerfully poetic quality as descriptive prose. It is clear that the imaginative economy of her writing was an important source of stimulation to Wordsworth and Coleridge in the composition of individual poems. This is equally true of the *Grasmere Journals* for 1800-3, upon which William frequently drew for themes, motifs and images, most famously in the poem 'I Wandered Lonely As a Cloud'. Her lively accounts of *An Excursion on the Banks of Ullswater 1805* and *An Excursion to Scawfell Pike 1818* were used by Wordsworth in his *Guide to the Lakes* (1825). Longer journeys are captured in her *Visit to Hamburgh and a Journey to … Goslar 1798-99*, *Recollections of a Tour made in Scotland 1803* (finished in 1805), *The Journal of a Tour on the Continent 1820*, *Journal of a Second Tour in Scotland* (1822) and *Journal of a Tour in the Isle of Man* (1828).

Wordsworth, William 1770-1850 Poet. He was born at Cockermouth in Cumberland, son of the attorney to Sir James Lowther (later Earl of Lonsdale). His mother's death in 1778 and his father's in 1783 left him and his siblings only modestly provided for. He attended schools in Cockermouth, Penrith and Hawkshead, leaving the last in 1787, the same year he published his first poem ('On Seeing Miss HELEN MARIA WILLIAMS Weep at a Tale of Distress') and entered St John's College, Cambridge. He never felt entirely at ease there and read widely outside the curriculum. A Continental walking tour in 1790 provided the impressions for *Descriptive Sketches*, written in 1792. After leaving Cambridge in 1791 he spent a year in Revolutionary France, cut short by lack of money but still one of the most important periods of his life. He became a supporter of the Girondists and fell in love with Annette Vallon, by whom he had a daughter, Caroline, born in December 1792. Their affair is the basis of the poem *Vaudracour and Julia*, first published in 1820. Back in England, he made his debut as an author in 1793 with 'An Evening Walk' and *Descriptive Sketches*.

The period 1793-5 was one of great personal unhappiness, professional uncertainty, and moral and intellectual confusion. He held fast to his belief in the French experiment, despite dismay at the Jacobin dictatorship, and England's declaration of war against France in February 1793 left him grievously divided in his loyalties, and well as effectively separating him from Annette and his child for good. He did not finally become disenchanted with France until her occupation of Switzerland in 1798. A legacy from a friend in 1795 allowed him to follow his vocation as a poet. He and his sister, DOROTHY WORDSWORTH, settled first at Racedown in Dorset, where Wordsworth wrote the first version of 'The Ruined Cottage' and his only play, the BLANK-VERSE tragedy *The Borderers*, and then at the manor house at Alfoxden, Somerset, to be near to their exciting new friend COLERIDGE, then living at Nether Stowey. Both poets entered a period of intense creativity which produced the LYRICAL BALLADS (1798), a collection which virtually inaugurated ROMANTICISM in English poetry. During the course of a tour in Germany in 1798-9 Wordsworth wrote the enigmatic 'Lucy' poems.

On their return to England the Wordsworths moved

in December 1799 to Dove Cottage at Grasmere in their native Lake District. In the next year Wordsworth completed Book I of 'The Recluse' (later THE EXCURSION) and wrote many of the poems included in the second edition of *Lyrical Ballads* (1800), as well as the controversial new Preface which became the aesthetic manifesto of conservative ROMANTICISM. In 1802 the payment of the money long owed to his father improved his finances further and he married a childhood friend, Mary Hutchinson, who was to bear him five children. Dorothy remained a member of the household. 'Resolution and Independence' and parts of his ODE 'Intimations of Immortality from Recollections of Early Childhood' were also written in 1802; they appeared in *Poems in Two Volumes* (1807), along with other later work such as the 'Ode to Duty', 'Miscellaneous Sonnets' and 'Sonnets Dedicated to Liberty'.

Wordsworth's life was now relatively uneventful, though the completion of the second, 13-book version of *THE PRELUDE*, his poetic autobiography, in 1805 showed him at the height of his creative powers. He had begun the poem in Germany in 1798 and completed a two-book version the following year. He would return again to it in later years, putting aside a 14-book version in 1839. It appeared posthumously in 1850. In 1813 he was appointed to the sinecure of Distributor of Stamps for Westmorland, which carried a substantial salary, and moved from Allan Bank (where he had lived since 1808) to Rydal Mount, Ambleside, remaining there for the rest of his life. *The Excursion* was published in 1814, *The White Doe of Rylstone* in 1815, and *Poems, Including Lyrical Ballads* in 1815 – the first of many collected editions of old and new poetical work, frequently revised and reclassified, to appear over the next 35 years. *Peter Bell: A Tale in Verse* (composed 1798) and *The Waggoner* (composed 1805) were both published in 1819.

Wordsworth had by now moved a long way from the cosmopolitan radicalism of his youth. Though a point of contention between him and the second generation of Romantic poets, his conservatism encouraged public honours to flow in. He was appointed POET LAUREATE on the death of his old associate SOUTHEY in 1843. Yet his poetic powers had markedly declined. Much of the best of his late work commemorates his travels: *The River Duddon: A Series of Sonnets* (1820), and *Yarrow Revisited and Other Poems* (1835). His prose works include: *The Convention of Cintra* (1809); an 'Essay on Epitaphs' (1810); a guidebook to the Lake District, originally designed as an introduction to Joseph Wilkinson's *Select Views of Cumberland* (1810) but later expanded and published separately, notably in an edition of 1835; and two famous public letters opposing the Kendal and Windermere railway (1845).

Workers in the Dawn The first novel by GISSING, published in 1880. It is about rich and poor, degradation, drink, destitution and the effects of heredity. Two solutions are proposed: revolution, which the author rejects, and education, which he endorses. But to educate the masses is seen as a hard struggle. The noble Helen, who has embraced the doctrines of 'Schopenhauer, Comte and SHELLEY', wears herself out giving free lessons in adult literacy and dies of inherited consumption. Arthur, in love with Helen, carelessly marries Carrie, a woman of low morals, and is defeated by misfortune.

Wotton, Sir Henry 1568–1639 Poet and diplomat. The only work published during his lifetime was *The*

Elements of Architecture (1624). The poems and miscellaneous writings collected in *Reliquiae Wottonianae* (1651) included three favourite anthology pieces: 'Elizabeth of Bohemia', 'The Character of a Happy Life' and 'Upon the Sudden Restraint of the Earl of Somerset'. Wotton planned a life of his friend DONNE but the task devolved on their mutual friend WALTON, who contributed a memoir of Wotton to the *Reliquiae*. Wotton's definition of an ambassador is famous: 'An Ambassador is an honest man, sent to lie abroad for the good of his country.'

Wren, P(ercival) C(hristopher) 1885–1941 Novelist. The most famous of his many popular novels of romance and adventure is *Beau Geste* (1924), about the Foreign Legion. It was followed by more stories about the three Geste brothers, *Beau Sabreur* (1926), *Beau Ideal* (1928) and *Good Gestes* (1929). Other titles include *Dew and Mildew* (1912), *The Wages of Virtue* (1916), *Valiant Dust* (1932), *Sinbad the Sailor* (1935), *Rough Shooting* (1938) and *The Uniform of Glory* (1941).

Wright, David (Murray) 1920– Poet and anthologist. With the painter Patrick Swift he edited the brilliant but short-lived quarterly *X* in 1959–62. His anthologies include *The Faber Book of Twentieth-Century Verse* (with JOHN HEATH-STUBBS; 1953), *Mid-Century: English Poetry 1940–60* (1965), *The Penguin Book of English Romantic Verse* (1968) and *The Penguin Book of Everyday Verse* (1976). His poetry, which includes *Moral Stories* (1954), *To the Gods the Shades: New and Selected Poems* (1976) and *Metrical Observations* (1980), is distinguished by the rhythm of ordinary speech, a vivid rendering of appearances and a power to celebrate. He has also produced a version of *THE CANTERBURY TALES* (1985) and an autobiography, *Deafness* (1969).

Wright, James 1927–80 American poet. Whether writing about nature, politics, social outcasts or his home town in Ohio, he emphasized the common human element in his subjects. His language is colloquial and his tone compassionate. Volumes are *The Green Wall* (1957), *Saint Judas* (1959), *The Lion's Tail and Eyes* (1962), *This Branch Will Not Break* (1963), *Shall We Gather at the River?* (1968), *Collected Poems* (1971; PULITZER PRIZE), *Two Citizens* (1973), *Moments of the Italian Summer* (1976) and *To a Blossoming Pear Tree* (1977).

Wright, Judith (Arundell) 1915– Australian poet, critic and essayist. Although concerned for the environment and the Aboriginal community, she helped to ease the 'aggressive regionalism' of earlier Australian poetry. Her many volumes are best represented by *The Double Tree: Selected Poems 1942–1976* (1978) and *The Human Pattern: Selected Poems* (1990). *The Generations of Men* (1959) traces her family history, while *The Cry for the Dead* (1981) deals with the destruction of the Aborigines – also a prominent topic of the essays selected in *Born of the Conquerors* (1991). Her criticism includes the seminal *Preoccupations in Australian Poetry* (1965).

Wright, Richard 1908–60 Black American novelist and social critic. *NATIVE SON*, the novel which won him recognition, appeared in 1940, the year he left the USA, first for Mexico and then for Paris. His other novels are *The Outsider* (1953), chronicling a black intellectual's search for identity, *Savage Holiday* (1954) and *The Long Dream* (1958). *Eight Men* (1961) gathers short stories, radio plays, a novella, and an autobiography. Wright's non-fictional work includes an illustrated folk history of American blacks, *Twelve Million Black Voices* (1941), an acclaimed autobiography, *Black Boy* (1945), and its sequel, *American Hunger* (1977). He also published three books of social criticism inspired by his travels: *Black Power* (1954), about Africa; *The Color Curtain* (1956), about Asia; and *Pagan Spain* (1957). *White Man, Listen!* (1957) is a collection of lectures on racial injustice.

Wright, Thomas 1810–77 Antiquary. A founding member of the Camden Society (1838) and the Percy Society (1841), he edited many volumes of medieval texts. Only two volumes of his ambitious biography of literary characters, *Biographia Britannica Literaria*, were completed (1842 and 1846).

Wrightson, (Alice) Patricia 1921– Australian writer of CHILDREN'S LITERATURE. Her best-known novel, *I Own the Racecourse!* (1968), deals sympathetically with the tragicomic delusions of a backward Australian adolescent. Later works, notably *The Nargun and the Stars* (1973), link her talent for realistic description to an exploration of Aboriginal folk-tales.

Wulf and Eadwacer An Old English poem in the EXETER BOOK. Short and enigmatic, it poignantly expresses the sorrow of a woman separated from her lover Wulf by the enmity of their clans and her fear that their child will be persecuted.

Wulfstan d. 1023 Author of tracts, HOMILIES, and law codes. Successively Bishop of London (996–1002) and Worcester (1002–16) and Archbishop of York (1002–23), he wrote about political problems and church reform. His distinctive style helps to identify his work. *Sermo Lupi ad Anglos* (1014) calls for repentance and reformation after Aethelred's defeat. Wulfstan also wrote *The Canons of Edgar* and the *Institutes of Polity*, as well as contributing to a vernacular version of the Benedictine office and a northern redaction of the *ANGLO-SAXON CHRONICLE*.

Wuthering Heights The only novel by EMILY BRONTË, published in 1847. Its complex plot centres on the remote farmhouse of Wuthering Heights on the Yorkshire moors, and on two generations of the Earnshaw family. It is narrated by Lockwood, a visiting gentleman, and Mrs Dean, servant to the Earnshaws. Heathcliff, a foundling from Liverpool, is brought to the Heights by Mr Earnshaw to be treated like his own children, Catherine and Hindley. But after Earnshaw's death Hindley bullies and degrades Heathcliff. He leaves because Catherine, despite returning his love, would find it humiliating to marry him. She chooses the genteel Edgar Linton of neighbouring Thrushcross Grange instead. Heathcliff returns to wreak vengeance on his tormentors. Weakened by his accusations of betrayal, Catherine dies after giving birth to a girl, another Catherine. Heathcliff marries Edgar's sister Isabella and mistreats her until she runs away. He destroys Hindley, a drunkard and gambler, and gains control of the Heights. To secure the Linton family property he forces a marriage between young Catherine and Linton, his sickly son by Isabella. When Linton dies the young widow develops an interest in Hareton, Hindley's son, whom Heathcliff has brought up in brutish ignorance. By now, all passion spent, Heathcliff longs only for union with Catherine. He dies, leaving young Catherine and Hareton with hopes of a richer life.

The novel's stern power, which shocked contemporaries but impressed later generations, owes much to the enigmatic portrait of Heathcliff. Hardly less remarkable is the way that the tortuous, violent plot is given solidity by the precisely realized Yorkshire locations and subtlety by the shifting narrative viewpoints.

Wyatt, Sir Thomas ?1503–42 Poet. A courtier and diplo-

mat, he twice lost Henry VIII's favour: in 1536, when he was imprisoned in the Tower on suspicion of being one of Anne Boleyn's lovers, and in 1541, when Bishop Bonner accused him of misconduct as ambassador to Charles V. He survived both episodes but died suddenly at Sherborne, Dorset, on his way abroad on another diplomatic mission. His son and namesake was executed for his rebellion against Mary I in 1554.

None of Wyatt's poems appeared in print in his lifetime. His first published work was *Certain Psalms ... Drawn into English Metre* (1549), a version of the penitential psalms from a prose paraphrase by Aretino. More of his poetry, lyrics and satires appeared in TOTTEL'S MISCELLANY (1557); the rest remained in manuscript until the 19th and 20th centuries. With SURREY, he was the first to domesticate the SONNET into English, providing it with its characteristic final rhyming couplet. His versions of Petrarch show an extraordinary facility in the difficult task of imitation in another language: 'I Find No Peace' is a remarkably close rendering of Petrarch's 'Pace non trovo', while 'Whoso List to Hunt' imitates and transforms Petrarch's 'Una candida cerva' to produce a radically different poem. Wyatt was also successful in his handling of such new forms in English as the RONDEAU and the TERZA RIMA. With their song-like refrains, his poems also continued native traditions of the English lyric. Some, especially those referring to the poet's lute (e.g. 'My Lute Awake' and 'Blame Not My Lute'), may have been sung to a courtly audience. One of Wyatt's best and most famous poems, 'They Flee from Me', shows his ability to combine native traditions and classical influence.

Wycherley, William 1640–1716 Playwright. After living in France, then briefly studying at Oxford and the Inner Temple, he pursued fashion in the company of ROCHESTER, ETHEREGE and SEDLEY. *Hero and Leander* (1669), a verse BURLESQUE, made a bid for membership of the cleverly dismissive literary elite. He may have been an actor and dabbler in theatrical management before writing his first play, *Love in a Wood: or, St James's Park* (1671), a mordant SATIRE of a sexually and financially rapacious society. *The Gentleman Dancing-Master* (1672), derived from Calderón, is more generous to its characters than either of his greatest comedies, THE COUNTRY WIFE (1675) and THE PLAIN DEALER (1676). In these plays, Wycherley describes a world he knew: unpleasant and, although the comic contrivance is masterly, portrayed without affection.

Wycherley turned his back on the theatre after 1676 and lived almost like a character in one of his plays. He forfeited Charles II's patronage by his marriage to a wealthy widow in 1679, was imprisoned for debt after her death, received a pension from James II and grew increasingly cantankerous. From the family estate near Shrewsbury, he tried to guard his literary reputation and wrote unimpressive, sometimes obscene verse, published as *Miscellany Poems* (1704). His second marriage, shortly before his death, was apparently intended to disinherit his nephew. His strange friendship with the young POPE resulted in Pope and THEOBALD's edition of Wycherley's *Posthumous Works* (1729).

Wyclif [Wycliffe], John c. 1320–84 Theologian and Church reformer. Born near Richmond, Yorkshire, he studied at Oxford and became Master of Balliol College. From 1374 he was rector of Lutterworth. Renowned as a lecturer in theology and philosophy, he took an increasingly anti-papal stance which, with his challenge to the doctrine of transubstantiation, prompted condemnation and threats of excommunicaton. The following he amassed, particularly in Oxford, developed into the LOLLARD movement. The majority of his writings are in Latin, but he made a crucial contribution to English literature in his project for a vernacular translation of the Bible, though his part in its execution was probably restricted to an unfinished version of the New Testament. (See BIBLE IN ENGLISH.) Of the many sermons, commentaries, glosses and tracts attributed to Wyclif, some are undoubtedly the work of his followers, though most draw on his own Latin works.

Wyndham, John [Harris, John Wyndham Parkes Lucas Beynon] 1903–69 Novelist who used various combinations of his names in different phases of his career. He is best known for his post-war SCIENCE FICTION novels: *The Day of the Triffids* (1951), *The Kraken Wakes* (1953), *The Chrysalids* (1955), *The Midwich Cuckoos* (1957) and *The Trouble with Lichen* (1960). The best of his short fiction is in *Consider Her Ways and Others* (1961). Concentrating on the reactions of ordinary people to terrible circumstances which plunge them into a struggle for survival, his work bridged traditional British scientific romance and the more varied science fiction which has replaced it.

Wynnere and Wastoure See *WINNER AND WASTER*.

Yates, Dornford [Mercer, Cecil William] 1885–1960
Novelist. His novels, almost invariably sustained by gently farcical plots and centred on an elegant leisured society, found a huge popular readership in the 1920s and 1930s. Books about Berry Pleydell and his circle include *Berry and Co.* (1921), *Jonah and Co.* (1922) and *Maiden Stakes* (1929). His 'Chandos' thrillers include *Blind Corner* (1927) and *Perishable Goods* (1928).

Years, The A novel by VIRGINIA WOOLF, published in 1937. Unlike her other late works, it is a conventional family saga, chronicling the lives of the Pargiters from 1880 to the 1930s. At the beginning, Colonel Pargiter's wife, Rose, is dying and their seven children live under the oppressive weight of her illness. Subsequent chapters trace the lives of each of the children in a series of separate but connected episodes, which include some vivid descriptions of London life.

Yeast: *A Problem* A novel by CHARLES KINGSLEY, serialized in 1848 and published in book form in 1850. It is unashamedly a novel of ideas, in which Lancelot Smith, a gentleman and heedless atheist, learns about life from Paul Tregarva, one of the 'Dissenting poor'. The picture of rural degradation is vivid and the descriptions of the poor memorable. Kingsley deplores the waste of sewage, which fouls rivers when it should be fertilizing fields, attacks the game laws and defends the 'true idea of Protestantism' against the lure of Roman Catholicism. Though claiming to avoid taking sides, he preaches that art is a mere self-indulgence when political action (reformist, not revolutionary) is needed.

Yeats, William Butler 1865–1939 Irish poet and playwright. Born in Dublin, the son of the painter John B. Yeats, he moved between Ireland and England from his earliest years and eventually spent two-thirds of his life outside his native country. By the age of 30 he was acquainted with the Irish aspect of the CELTIC REVIVAL and its political implications in Irish nationalism, the PRE-RAPHAELITES as embodied by WILLIAM MORRIS, and various esoteric cults encountered through his friendship with GEORGE WILLIAM RUSSELL (A.E.). ARTHUR SYMONS had also introduced him to French SYMBOLISM. These various influences are apparent in the early poetry published in *The Wanderings of Oisin and Other Poems* (1889), *The Countess Kathleen and Other Legends and Lyrics* (1892; the poetry from this volume subsequently organized into two sections, 'Crossways' and 'The Rose'), *The Wind among the Reeds* (1899) and *In the Seven Woods* (1903). These volumes also testify to his fruitless love for Maud Gonne, whom he met in 1889. He also edited several volumes of Irish writing and folklore as well as the poetry of BLAKE (in collaboration with Edwin Ellis; 1893) and SPENSER (1906).

In 1890 he joined Ernest Rhys in founding the RHYMERS' CLUB in London. Many of the following years were taken up with 'theatre business' in Dublin. With GEORGE MOORE and EDWARD MARTYN he formed the Irish Literary Theatre, inaugurated in 1899 with a production of *The Countess Kathleen*, a dramatized Irish folktale. He collaborated with the Fay brothers in a production of his most successful play, *Cathleen Ni Houlihan* (1902), a propaganda piece with Maud Gonne in the title-role. The team evolved into the Irish National Theatre, which opened the ABBEY THEATRE in 1904 with Yeats, SYNGE and LADY GREGORY as its joint directors. Later plays, starting with *At the Hawk's Well* (1916), show the influence of Japanese Noh drama, to which POUND introduced him.

The Green Helmet and Other Poems (1910) and *Responsibilities* (1914) showed him simplifying his poetry by turning to dramatic speech and public occasions, contrasting Greek mythology and Renaissance Italy with contemporary Dublin, the dispute over funding for the Municipal Gallery and the General Strike of 1913. *The Wild Swans at Coole* (1919) significantly extended his range, notably in the ELEGY 'In Memory of Major Robert Gregory'. It also introduced several key symbols – the Phases of the Moon, the Great Wheel and the Gyres – expounded in his mystical prose treatise, *A Vision* (1925, revised 1937) and elaborated in much of his mature poetry. *Michael Robartes and the Dancer* (1921) included 'The Second Coming' and 'Easter, 1916', his elegy for those who died in the Easter Rising, among them THOMAS MACDONAGH and PATRICK PEARSE. *The Tower* (1928) included 'Sailing to Byzantium', 'Leda and the Swan', 'Among School Children' and two sequences on the Civil War. In these he achieved a rich lyricism that encompassed the apparent contradictions between art and politics. *The Winding Stair* (1933) is a powerfully pessimistic collection which included 'Byzantium', 'Coole Park, 1929' and 'Coole Park and Ballylee'. It also included the sequence 'Words for Music Perhaps', 25 songs written for the puppet-characters Crazy Jane, Jack the Journeyman, the Bishop, Old Tom and God, set in a world of dreams, rhymes, madness songs and riddling refrains. *Parnell's Funeral and Other Poems* (1935) began the theme of 'lust and rage' which dominated *New Poems* (1938) and the posthumous *Last Poems and Two Plays* (1939); these include 'The Municipal Gallery Revisited' and 'The Circus Animals' Desertion', both retrospective judgements on the vision of Ireland in his work. 'Lapis Lazuli' drew on the ideas of Spengler, whose *The Decline of the West* had many similarities with *A Vision*.

Other works included *Collected Poems* (1933), *Collected Plays* (1934), several volumes of autobiography (*Reveries over Childhood and Youth*, 1914; *The Trembling of the Veil*, 1922; *Dramatis Personae*, 1935), several volumes of essays and a controversial edition of *The Oxford Book of Modern Verse* (1936). Posthumous publications include *Collected Plays* (1953), *The Letters of W. B. Yeats* (1954), *Auto-biographies* (1955), *Mythologies* (1959), *Essays and Introductions* (1961), *Explorations* (1962), *Uncollected Prose* (1970, 1975), *Memoirs* (1972) and *The Poems: A New Edition* (1984) edited by R. Finneran. Variorum editions of the *Poems* (1957) and *Plays* (1966) were edited by R. Alspach and P. Allt. Yeats became an Irish Senator in 1922 and was awarded the Nobel Prize for Literature in 1923. He died at Roquebrune in France. His coffin was disinterred in 1948 and taken to Sligo, the home of his mother's family.

Yellow Book, The A literary and art periodical which ran from 1894 to 1897, published by John Lane and edited by HENRY HARLAND. Considered decadent and shocking by many readers, it had a distinctive yellow cover by AUBREY BEARDSLEY, the art editor. The first issue included BEERBOHM's controversial essay 'A Defence of Cosmetics'. Contributors included HENRY JAMES, EDMUND GOSSE, ARNOLD BENNETT, WELLS and YEATS. Walter Sickert and Wilson Steer were among the many artists who also contributed.

Yellowplush Papers, The Comic sketches by THACKERAY, serialized as *The Yellowplush Correspondence* in 1837–40 and reprinted under its present title in *Comic Tales and Sketches* (1841). Charles James Yellowplush, a footman, writes his memoirs in cockney idiom. His first master is a respectable gentleman who turns out to be a crossing-sweeper; his second is a card-sharping aristocrat, the Hon. Algernon Deuceace.

Yezierska, Anzia c. 1885–1970 Russian-American novelist and short-story writer. Born in Russian Poland, she emigrated with her family to the USA in the 1890s. She dealt realistically with the lives of ghetto immigrants in collections of stories such as *Hungry Hearts* (1920) and *Children of Loneliness* (1923) and in novels such as *Salome of the Tenements* (1922), *Bread Givers* (1925), *Arrogant Beggar* (1927) and *All I Could Never Be* (1932). *Red Ribbon on a White Horse* (1950) is her autobiography.

Yonge, Charlotte M(ary) 1823–1901 Novelist and writer of CHILDREN'S LITERATURE. She lived all her life in Otterbourne, Hampshire, deeply influenced by KEBLE, vicar of neighbouring Hursley. Tirelessly energetic, she edited a girls' magazine, *The Monthly Packet*, for nearly 50 years and produced 160 books, including biographies of Bishop Patterson (1874) and HANNAH MORE (1888), histories and textbooks as well as fiction aimed at young female readers. Success first came with *The Heir of Redclyffe* (1853), about the blameless Sir Guy Morville. *The Daisy Chain* (1856) deals with the widowed Dr May's large family, whose fortunes are followed in several later volumes. The authentic home and family background makes these books an excellent source of information about Victorian middle-class life. Historical romances include *The Little Duke* (1854), *The Lances of Lynwood* (1855), *The Prince and the Page* (1865) and *The Caged Lion* (1870).

York cycle See MIRACLE PLAYS.

Yorkshire Tragedy, A A domestic tragedy, probably first performed in 1606 and implausibly attributed to SHAKESPEARE on its publication in 1608. THOMAS MIDDLETON has been suggested as a possible author. Based on the story of Walter Calverley, executed in 1605, it describes with grim haste his passage from gambling debts to the attempted murder of his family, arrest and final repentance.

Young, Andrew (John) 1885–1971 Poet. His long poetic career began with *Songs of Night* (1910). After the short nature lyrics of *The Green Man* (1947), he wrote two long visionary poems, *Into Hades* (1952) and *A Traveller in Time*, published together as *Out of the World and Back* (1958). Young also published prose pieces, including *A Prospect of Flowers* (1945), *A Retrospect of Flowers* (1950), *A Prospect of Britain* (1950) and *The Poet and the Landscape* (1962).

Young, Arthur 1741–1820 Writer on agriculture and travel. He became known as an agricultural theorist with *A Farmer's Letters to the People of England* (1768), *A Six Weeks Tour through the Southern Counties of England and Wales* (1768), *A Six Months Tour through the North of England* (1771), *The Farmer's Tour through the East of England* (1771), *Political Arithmetic* (1774) and *A Tour in Ireland* (1780), works which also show him to be a shrewd observer of architecture, landscape and politics. The same qualities inform his most important work, *Travels during the Years 1787, 1788, 1789 and 1790, Undertaken with a View of Ascertaining the Cultivation, Wealth, Resources and National Prosperity of the Kingdom of France* (1792), usually known simply as *Travels in France*, a damning indictment of conditions immediately before the Revolution. *The Example of France a Warning to England* (1793) appeared in the year he became Secretary to the Board of Agriculture. Young also founded and edited a periodical, *The Annals of Agriculture* (1784–1809).

Young, Edward 1683–1765 Poet and playwright. His early poems met with little success but his tragedies, *Busiris, King of Egypt* (1719) and *The Revenge* (1721), proved popular. A series of seven SATIRES, *The Universal Passion* (1725–8; later called *The Love of Fame*), enjoyed a considerable vogue until eclipsed by POPE's satires. His only published poem in the next decade was a patriotic ODE, *The Foreign Address* (1735). The death of his stepdaughter in 1736 and his wife, Lady Elizabeth Lee, in 1740 prompted him to begin the work which made him famous: *The Complaint: or, Night-Thoughts on Life, Death and Immortality* (1742–6). *NIGHT THOUGHTS*, as it is usually known, allied him with both an older tradition of moral writing and the contemporary GRAVEYARD POETS. Latterly, he published a play he had written earlier,*The Brothers* (1753), *The Centaur Not Fabulous* (1755), *Conjectures on Original Composition* (1759) and a final long poem, *Resignation* (1762).

Young, Francis Brett 1884–1954 Novelist, short-story writer and poet. He is best remembered for *Portrait of Clare* (1927) and *My Brother Jonathan* (1928), set in the west Midlands. Later novels with a South African setting included *Jim Redlake* (1930), *They Seek a Country* (1937), about the Great Trek, and *The City of Gold* (1939). *The Island* (1944) is a verse history of England, using verse forms appropriate to each period.

Ywain and Gawain A VERSE ROMANCE probably written in the first half of the 14th century. The only Middle English translation of Chrétien de Troyes, it condenses and simplifies *Yvain*. Gawain persuades Ywain to live for a year as a knight. When he forgets to return to his wife, she rejects him, and the couple are reconciled, with the help of the go-between Lunet, only after he has suffered madness and undergone several adventures. Ywain is known as the Knight of the Lion because he is accompanied by a lion he saved.

Zangwill, Israel 1864–1926 Novelist, playwright and translator. Of Russian-Jewish descent, he captured the stark reality of immigrant life in London in *Children of the Ghetto* (1892), *Ghetto Tragedies* (1893), *The Kings of Shnorrers* (1894) and *The Mantle of Elijah* (1900), which established him as a leading figure and powerful spokesman in the struggle for Jewish rights. *The Melting Pot* (1909), the best known of his plays, dealt with a similar theme, as did various non-fictional works, including *The War for the World* (1916) and *The Voice of Jerusalem* (1920). *The Big Bow Mystery* (1892) is a canny venture into DETECTIVE FICTION.

Zaturenska, Marya 1902–82 Russian-American poet. Born in Kiev, she emigrated to the USA in 1910 and married HORACE GREGORY in 1925. They edited many anthologies and wrote *A History of American Poetry 1900–1940* (1946). Her own volumes include *Threshold and Hearth* (1934), *Cold Morning Sky* (1937), *The Listening Landscape* (1941), *Golden Mirror* (1943), *Terraces of Light* (1960) and *The Hidden Waterfalls* (1974).

zeugma See SYLLEPSIS.

Zukofsky, Louis 1904–78 American poet. Associated with OBJECTIVISM, he published his first poetry in *An 'Objectivists' Anthology* (1932), which he edited. *First Half of 'A'* (1940) began a long poem, finally complete in 1978, exploring the interrelationship of poetry and music and treating aesthetics, philosophy and history. Other works include *55 Poems* (1941), *Anew* (1946), *Some Time* (1956), *Barely and Widely* (1958), *I's* (1963), *After I's* (1964) and *I Sent Thee Late* (1965). *All: The Collected Shorter Poems, 1923–1964* appeared in 1966. *A Test of Poetry* (1948) and *Prepositions* (1967) are collections of essays, *Arise, Arise* (1965) is a play and *Little: A Fragment for Careenagers* (1970) is a novel.

Zuleika Dobson: *or, An Oxford Love Story* A novel by MAX BEERBOHM, published in 1911. He preferred to call it a 'fantasy' rather than a SATIRE. When Zuleika visits her grandfather, the Warden of Judas College, during Eights Week her beauty devastates the undergraduates, even the splendid Duke of Dorset. She remains disappointed in her quest for a man 'who would not bow down to her'. The Duke drowns himself, followed by the entire undergraduate population except the pedestrian Noaks. At the end of the novel Zuleika consults the train timetable to Cambridge.